AF830670

West's Law School Advisory Board

JESSE H. CHOPER
Professor of Law,
University of California, Berkeley

YALE KAMISAR
Professor of Law, University of San Diego
Professor of Law, University of Michigan

MARY KAY KANE
Professor of Law, Chancellor and Dean Emeritus,
University of California,
Hastings College of the Law

LARRY D. KRAMER
Dean and Professor of Law, Stanford Law School

WAYNE R. LaFAVE
Professor of Law, University of Illinois

JONATHAN R. MACEY
Professor of Law, Yale Law School

ARTHUR R. MILLER
University Professor, New York University
Professor of Law Emeritus, Harvard University

GRANT S. NELSON
Professor of Law, Pepperdine University
Professor of Law Emeritus, University of California, Los Angeles

JAMES J. WHITE
Professor of Law, University of Michigan

CASES AND MATERIALS ON

LAND USE AND COMMUNITY DEVELOPMENT

Seventh Edition

By

John R. Nolon

Professor of Law
Pace University School of Law
Visiting Professor of Environmental Law
Yale University School of Forestry and Environmental Studies

Patricia E. Salkin

Associate Dean and Professor of Law
Director, Government Law Center
Albany Law School

Morton Gitelman

Emeritus Distinguished Professor of Law
University of Arkansas

AMERICAN CASEBOOK SERIES®

THOMSON
WEST™

Mat # 40658533

Thomson/West have created this publication to provide you with accurate and authoritative information concerning the subject matter covered. However, this publication was not necessarily prepared by persons licensed to practice law in a particular jurisdiction. Thomson/West are not engaged in rendering legal or other professional advice, and this publication is not a substitute for the advice of an attorney. If you require legal or other expert advice, you should seek the services of a competent attorney or other professional.

American Casebook Series and West Group are trademarks registered in the U.S. Patent and Trademark Office.

COPYRIGHT © 1969, 1976, 1982, 1991 WEST PUBLISHING CO.
© West, a Thomson business, 1997, 2004
© 2008 Thomson/West
610 Opperman Drive
St. Paul, MN 55123
1–800–313–9378

Printed in the United States of America

ISBN: 978–0–314–18498–6

TEXT IS PRINTED ON 10% POST CONSUMER RECYCLED PAPER

To the memory of Robert R. Wright
1931–2006

*

Preface

The predecessor of this casebook was first produced on a mimeograph machine in 1954 by Professor Jacob H. Beuscher at the University Wisconsin School of Law. The book was revised in the late 1950s, again in 1964 and 1966, and then, in 1969, it became the first book on the subject of land use in West's American Casebook Series. That book was adapted from its mimeographed origins by Professor Robert R. Wright. Subsequent editions appeared in 1976 (co-authored by Professor Morton Gitelman), 1982, 1990, 1997, and 2003 (when Professors Nolon and Salkin joined in). With this book, the authors complete the eleventh revision of Professor Beuscher's foundational work in 57 years. What is happening to land use—and the law that governs it—that requires a new edition nearly twice a decade?

Many of the parents of today's graduate students were born in the 1950s. If they were alive in 1954, they might have been the first children to watch color TV, which became available commercially that year. They would have been the first to enjoy the Interstate Highway system, authorized by the Highway Act of 1954 or to witness the demolition and redevelopment of inner-city slums under the Urban Renewal Program authorized by the Housing Act adopted by Congress that same year. If they grew up in Minneapolis, they might have been the last to ride on the city's streetcar system, which ceased operating in 1954. They were also among the last students to study materials produced on a mimeograph machine.

The population of the 48 American states topped 150 million in 1950. On October 16, 2006, our 50 states reached the 300 million population mark. New York was the most populous state in 1950; today it ranks third, trailing California and Texas. In 1950 only three states had over 10 million residents; today there are seven. The fastest growing states between 1950 and 1990 were those on the west coast, plus Florida and Texas. In 1950, just over half of the population resided in metropolitan areas; today that percentage exceeds 80%. The number of people 65 years of age or older has doubled in that time. The percentage of single-person households has increased by a factor of 2.5. In 1900, 1 out of 8 Americans was of a race other than white. A hundred years later, the ratio was 1 out of 4.

Between 1950 and 1960, when Professor Beuscher's students were first learning land use law, 20 million Americans moved to the suburbs, dwarfing in scale the western migration of the 1880s. The amount of land converted to urban uses increased steadily from 15 million acres per year in 1945 to 60 million acres in 2000, mostly in areas dedicated to farming, ranching, or forestry. In the years after 1950, nearly 2,250 of the 3,000 counties in the coterminous U.S. lost 10% or more of their farmland. This vast movement of people on the landscape was fueled by low cost mortgages, highway construction, and improvements in building technology. These influences lowered per acre population densities on average and caused development to sprawl as it grew, using land at much higher percentages of growth than the increase in population itself. Between 1950 and 1990, for example, St. Louis experienced a 355% increase in developed land while its population grew by only 35%. From 1950 to 1980, the population in the vast Chesapeake Bay watershed area increased by 50%, while the land developed to serve that population increased by 180%. As the population shifted, cities lost their affluent residents and businesses to nearby suburbs and became more and more deteriorated and impoverished: "tight knots of despair from which men turn," to quote the U.S. Supreme Court in Berman v. Parker.

Each of these changes implicates land use law. In just two generations the American landscape has been transformed and land use law has adapted in response. This casebook has changed accordingly. Professor Beuscher composed an ingenious exposition of the law of nuisance. He organized that body of law and explained its changing rules by context, following land use conflicts from open country, to the rural/urban interface, to older settled areas, and into districts governed by zoning: a public law that governs land use within defined districts. Professors Wright and Gitelman continued that approach and in subsequent editions 10% of the casebook was dedicated to these common law notions, including the doctrine of waste and the use of restrictive covenants to control private land uses. That material has been greatly reduced in this edition, but their good sense in tracking the change in law and practice with the changing landscape has been retained. Chapter 8 in this new edition, for example, starts at the urban core and traces legal attempts to stem neighborhood decay, induce urban redevelopment, overcome the competition for jobs and affluent households occurring in outlying suburbs, and prevent those suburbs from excluding low- and moderate-income households. That chapter also puts the controversial and largely misunderstood Kelo v. New London case in its proper historical and geographical context so that it can be studied objectively.

It seems to us that the legacy of the earlier editions was to teach graduate students to think about the law as a method of ordering community development in cities, suburbs, developing exurban areas, and rural places. Accordingly we have renamed the book *Cases and Materials on Land Use and Community Development*. Chapter 1 covers the history, relevance, and practice of land use law, starting students on familiar ground including the law of nuisance and servitudes which serve as predicates for public land use regulation and protect community residents from the excesses of their neighbors. The failure of nuisance rules—the product of binary lawsuits usually between neighbors—to resolve emerging land use and environmental issues helps explain the proliferation of governmental land use regulation in recent times. Chapter 2 discusses land use plans and planning and discloses the breadth of topics covered by land use regulation, from restoring urban neighborhoods and preserving historic buildings to protecting the environment in developing areas and stemming the loss of agricultural land in rural communities. Chapter 3 covers zoning—America's unique adaptation—the principal technique employed to implement the goals and objectives of comprehensive land use planning. Cities and urban villages adopted the zoning technique with breakneck speed in the 1920s as their strategy for ordering urban growth in a booming economy. It was our first attempt to use land use law to achieve safe and livable communities and landscapes. Chronologically, subdivision regulations were next on the scene. That topic follows in Chapter 4. It demonstrates how such regulations are used to build communities that are properly organized, carefully engineered, and environmentally sound, and how responsibility for paying the costs of growth is allocated among taxpayers, developers, and new residents.

Chapter 5 discusses constitutional constraints found in the Fifth Amendment of the U.S. Constitution that limit land use regulators and protect property rights. We follow the twisted path of case law interpretations of property rights as a clutch on excessive government regulation. The recently decided Lingle v. Chevron case greatly clarified some aspects of this murky field of jurisprudence by drawing a clear line between due process challenges and those claiming that a land use regulation constitutes a regulatory taking. In the process, students are exposed to regulatory strategies that protect fragile coastlines, promote alternative modes of transportation, regulate mining to prevent surface subsidence, maintain viewsheds, protect historic buildings and tidal wetlands, and deal with the consequences of flooding. These are interests that have arisen as our population has grown, shifted, and expanded causing coastal erosion, traffic congestion, environmental dangers, aesthetic losses, threats to our patrimony, and the ravaging consequences of climate change, including flooding and coastal inundation. In learning about the process of resolving the tension between protected property rights and these critical social issues, students probe deeply into the role of the courts and the deferential standards judges use when asked to second guess the judgments of the legislative branch of government.

Chapter 6 continues this theme, looking at First Amendment constitutional constraints on land use law and federal and state statutes that promote superseding state and national interests by limiting the reach of local land use laws. Many of these deal with and address our nation's changing demographics and the grievances of emerging cohorts who request equal and fair treatment under land use standards. The First Amendment protects against discrimination based on race and religion, and these protections provide needed constraints on the occasional biases that can pop up in parochial local legislation. Persons with disabilities, families with children, racial minorities, and religious groups can be prejudiced by local land use laws and have been protected by federal statutes such as the Americans with Disabilities Act, the Religious Land Use and Institutionalized Persons Act, and the Fair Housing Act. The advent of cellular telephony and the interest of the federal government in promoting interstate commerce by providing an efficient communication system are advanced by the Telecommunication Act of 1996, which prevents local governments from limiting cellular service on the basis of public health considerations. In some states, special populations such as group home residents and important economic interests such as mining and agriculture are protected by statute from overreaching local land use laws. In reflecting on these constitutional provisions and statutes as checks on local power, students learn the context of the federal system and the various interests, authorities, and roles of federal, state, and local governments.

Chapter 7, Smart Growth and Growth Management follows the efforts of local and state governments to tease some balance out of intense development pressures in metropolitan areas and the developing fringe. The cases involve critical strategies such as timed-growth laws, moratoria on development, growth caps, infrastructure planning as a growth control device, urban growth boundaries, and the protection of fertile agricultural land within metropolitan areas. They also describe and discuss a panoply of innovative land use techniques such as floating zoning, clustered subdivisions, environmental impact review, performance zoning, planned unit developments, traditional neighborhood districts, the transfer of development rights, and overlay and incentive zoning. As communities address the challenges presented by the growing population and market pressures, they continue to invent new land use techniques and reshape older tools to control market forces and accomplish the objectives of their comprehensive plans. How localities get such flexible authority and what the courts think about it is explored in this chapter.

Housing and urban development are the subjects of Chapter 8. The chapter contemplates early strategies for stemming urban decay and newer efforts for redeveloping ailing cities. It examines the efforts of cities and older suburbs to stem the flight of capital and human resources to outlying communities. The chapter ends with a look at the legal limitations that apply to community efforts to exclude lower cost housing, nontraditional families, mobile homes, and manufactured housing, as well as positive efforts of localities to meet their housing needs through inclusionary zoning programs.

Chapter 9 examines the surprising trend toward the adoption of local environmental law, a 40-year phenomenon that has picked up speed in the last 15 years as local planners, citizens, and regulators confront the disappearance of open space and the critical environmental features it contains. Traditionally thought of as the domain of federal law, environmental law has grown a useful local appendage as communities move to protect habitat, watersheds, wetlands, viewsheds, and floodplains and to protect themselves from erosion, sedimentation, flooding, and the loss of their natural character.

This theme is continued in Chapter 10: Aesthetic, Historic, and Cultural Interest Preservation. Cases and statutes look at local sign and billboard regulation in the interest of protecting aesthetics and prevent traffic accidents. They reveal the tension between such laws and the First Amendment's protection of the freedom of expression. Local laws also protect against a variety of visual interruptions and aim to improve the visual environment. The role of the federal, state, and local government in the protection of historical landmarks and cultural assets is probed, with a close look taken at the adoption of historic district and landmark preservation legislation at the local level.

Chapter 11 returns to the issue of judicial review of contested land use regulations and examines the rules that the judiciary adopts when confronted with challenges to land use laws. The types of remedies available to litigants, the burdens of proof they must bear, and the barriers to court access such as standing, ripeness, and finality are studied. The casebook is unique in that it presents an extensive section on the mediation of land use disputes including a description of how mediation works, when it is effective, how it can affect lawyering, and how it has been used to resolve conflicts ranging from disputes between neighbors to conflicts between developers of huge projects and their multiple opponents. The chapter also includes an examination of how the people through initiatives and referendums can adopt land use regulations directly and review and reverse local and state land use laws in some states.

Chapter 12 presages the future of land use law. It examines emerging issues, focusing heavily on climate change, the natural disasters that come with it, and the conservation practices that can mitigate it, ending with a brief look at an emerging technology: Geographic Information Systems.

In the Preface to the first national edition of this casebook in 1969, Professor Wright wrote that what was new at that time was not land use regulation itself, but the heightened emphasis on it as the law responds "to the needs of an increasingly urban, increasingly complex, increasingly frustrating society in which the use of our natural resources affects the lives of all of us. In the final analysis, this is why the subject is so important." These words couldn't be more apt today.

During the lifetimes of today's graduate students, unprecedented challenges to the land and its resources will be confronted. In the introduction to Chapter 8 we note that by 2043 the population of the U.S. will have grown by an additional 100 million, calling on the private sector to add up to 70 million new homes and 100 billion square feet of non-residential buildings. Where these 100 million live and work and the nature of the spaces they occupy will greatly affect global climate change.

The seventh edition of this casebook follows on the heels of the reports of the Intergovernmental Panel on Climate Change which express the consensus of the scientific community that climate change is with us to stay, is caused in substantial part by human activity, and carries serious consequences if we fail to reduce our use of fossil fuel and to check our production of greenhouse gases. Where people live and work, how they travel, and the amount of energy their buildings consume are governed by land use law: our blueprint for the human settlements of the future. Land use law provides society with a critical tool for reshaping these settlements and demonstrates, yet again, why the topic of this casebook is "so important" as the world continues to turn.

John R. Nolon
Patricia E. Salkin
Morton Gitelman

November, 2007

Summary of Contents

Table of Contents

*

Table of Cases

The principal cases are in bold type. Cases cited or discussed in the text are roman type. References are to pages. Cases cited in principal cases and within other quoted materials are not included.

CASES AND MATERIALS ON

LAND USE AND COMMUNITY DEVELOPMENT

Seventh Edition

*

Chapter I

THE HISTORY, RELEVANCE, AND PRACTICE OF LAND USE AND COMMUNITY DEVELOPMENT LAW

SECTION 1. THE PRACTICE OF LAND USE AND COMMUNITY DEVELOPMENT LAW

Land use plans create the long term context for community development and, together with land use regulations, provide for jobs, housing, infrastructure, recreation, and the preservation of a sound environment. Many types of professionals are engaged in the practice of land use law and community development, but two stand out: planners and lawyers. Lawyers and planners are employed by local governments that adopt land use plans. They also serve the local zoning and planning boards that adopt the standards governing development and that approve or deny developers' proposals to build. These professionals also represent landowners whose investments are affected by land use regulations and developers who seek local approval for their projects. Environmentalists and neighbors employ lawyers and planners, on occasion, to help them oppose development proposals that affect their interests adversely. Architects and civil engineers also play key roles in advising public agencies and private owners and a host of other professionals may be involved in the process of local regulation of private land use.

When lawyers represent individuals and companies who sell or purchase land and existing buildings they must know intimately the local land use provisions that affect the use and development of the subject property. In the contract for sale there is usually a provision that states that the buyer "takes title subject to all land use laws and regulations in effect at the time of the closing." Lawyers are retained to advise sellers and purchasers of real property regarding these matters. If the purchaser wishes to build a supermarket, to add an addition to a single-family home, or to create a large condominium project, it is critical that the land use laws and regulations of the locality in which the property is located allow the intended development. In putting a property on the market, the seller needs to know the highest and best use of the land and hires an attorney to discover and interpret the land use laws that define the full development potential of the land. Lawyers perform what is known as "due diligence" in the buying and selling of property, assisted by other professionals as needed. Their job is to discover and explain to their clients all of the risks and circumstances that can affect the investment in real estate. Land use law is of critical importance in this process.

Planners interpret land use rules and regulations by applying them in particular contexts. Whether the soils, topography, slopes, environmental constraints, roads, and water, sewer, and utility systems will support development that is allowed by land use law is their domain. The legal rules dictate how much development is allowed, while the natural condition of the land dictates the rest. Landowners, developers, and local land use boards need planners, along with architects, engineers, environmental scientists, and other professionals, to determine whether a developer's proposal is appropriate to the site and its neighborhood.

This book is designed to provide upper division education to law and planning students in these matters. It covers the history, common law antecedents, and traditional techniques of local public land use regulation. Students are exposed to the adoption of the comprehensive land use plan, the adoption and amendment of zoning regulations that conform to the plan, and the application of regulations that govern the division of property into lots for sale and the development of individual sites. Innovative smart growth regulations that create economical and environmentally friendly land use patterns are explored along with techniques used to revitalize urban neighborhoods and promote affordable housing. Constitutional and statutory limitations on local land use laws and decisions are discussed along with the role of the people, parties, and courts in reviewing land use law and decisions. The casebook ends with a chapter that reviews a number of contemporary issues that are addressed by lawyers and planners and the important public and private interests they represent.

SECTION 2. THE APPLICATION OF LAND USE AND COMMUNITY DEVELOPMENT LAW TO A TYPICAL DEVELOPMENT PROJECT

In order to grasp the subtleties and complexities of land use and community development practice, a description of a typical land development project is discussed to provide some insights as to how such a project intersects with the material covered in this book. We use as our example a forty-acre parcel of land located near the western edge of a growing small city and follow the conversion of this piece of land into a residential subdivision containing a number of dwelling units. We assume that the land is owned by an individual who lives in an old farmhouse on the land and that many years ago it was a farm and more recently it has been used to grow hay and graze livestock. Once the land was outside the city limits, but it was annexed into the city several years ago along with several other parcels to the north, south and east. Most of those other parcels now contain single-family dwellings at a density of three houses per acre. One of the other pieces of this annexed land has a small shopping center and some low-rise apartment buildings as well as some single-family houses. We will meet the participants in the land use process as we follow the course of development and encounter many of the typical problems that occur during the development process.

STEP 1. The Farmer and the Developer.

Ms. Developer is in the business of developing and building residential subdivisions. Having noticed that the city is experiencing significant growth in a westerly direction, she undertakes a market analysis of the potential for developing a subdivision of fifty or sixty houses. Concluding that the market for homes in the $300,000—$400,000 range is pretty good, she looks for land. Ms. Developer locates the forty-acre farm and makes a decision that this parcel would be worth developing. Her research indicates that current residential development is getting near to this farm and that city infrastructure (streets, water, sewer) is not too remote. Also, the local school district has planned a new elementary school somewhere in the western part of the city. A visit to City Hall indicates that the land in question is currently zoned A–1, a designation that allows agricultural uses and very low density residential development, and has been zoned for such use ever since it was annexed. The City has a policy of zoning all newly annexed land as A–1. The long-range comprehensive land use plan shows that residential uses are planned for that part of the City.

The Farmer is unhappy with the growth of new residential subdivisions in the vicinity of his property. In the past few years, his real estate tax assessments have risen because of nearby development. Also, some of the new residents in up-scale houses a quarter mile from the farm have been complaining to the City about strong smells coming from the farm when the wind is coming from the west. Maybe the time has come to think about selling and retiring.

Our Developer and Farmer are about to meet.

STEP 2. What sort of transaction?

When Ms. Developer first contacts Farmer, the parties verbally agree on a price of $10,000 per acre, or a total price of $400,000. Sometimes a developer might offer a price based on the number of buildable lots that a city will allow in a development proposal. At this point, several possibilities emerge. If the Developer has sufficient capital, she may buy the farm outright. Another type of deal could be an offer of an option to pay $25,000 for each housing unit allowed by the City, at the time the development is approved. This could mean more money for Farmer, but a longer wait for a payout. Another possibility is an offer to enter into an arrangement with Farmer to set up a separate entity to develop the land, such as a limited liability company (L.L.C.), a limited liability partnership (L.L.P.) or a traditional corporation. Farmer would convey the farm to the entity and participate in the profits of the development. This sort of deal, to make Farmer a partner or participant, means lower costs at the front end of the development, as the land constitutes Farmer's contribution to the entity. This can be significant because Developer knows that she (or the entity) will have to borrow considerable funds to prepare the land for development. On the other hand, once the subdivision is built out, if Farmer is to receive a portion of the profits, Developer's profits will be limited. This sort of analysis might dictate the percentage of profits for both sides. Farmer must look at this deal from the perspective of how long he must wait to realize any real money from the development (the approval and build-out of the subdivision may take six or more years), whether he assumes any of the risk of failure beyond the land, and whether he wants to become a financial risk taker in the development.

Whichever option is selected, Ms. Developer must look ahead to the process of local government approval of the development. If Developer is not very well known in the community, or is an "outsider," she will probably want Farmer to be around to offer enhanced credibility to her proposal. If Farmer is not part of the development entity, Developer's purchase of the land might proceed with an option to purchase, contingent upon Farmer securing a zoning change and other local approvals. Communities are often friendlier to local residents than to outsiders in making land use decisions. Farmer can play the part of a long-term community resident who wants to sell the farm and retire, and who has a buyer, if he can get the land rezoned and the project approved.

After working through the nature of the transaction, we can proceed on the assumption that Farmer has no desire to become a partner in the development and the farm is now in the hands of Developer. She borrowed most of the money from a lending institution, putting as little of her money into the venture purchase as possible. Also, Developer has consulted Attorney to set up a limited liability company, called Sunrise Woods, L.L.C., to develop the property. Developer is now ready to begin the land use approval process.

STEP 3. What kind of development?

Developer must make an initial determination of what kind of development to pursue. Should the forty acres be devoted to single-family homes only? The public street that will provide access to the land is a collector street that will carry more traffic in the future. If the local school district locates the new elementary school along that same street, perhaps even across from her development, that street will carry a great deal of traffic. Developer might consider that the portion of the farm along that street would be less desirable for up-scale homes. Maybe a mixed-use development would be better, locating some low-rise, lower cost attached townhouses along the street, and reserving the interior acres for single lot detached homes with the parking in the rear so that the owners would have some insulation from noise.

Mixing attached and detached homes requires a zone change, which is a discretionary act of the city council. Proposing attached housing risks opposition from neighboring single-family homeowners who might fear that the development will lower their property value. In addition, building attached housing on the street might turn away some potential buyers of single-family homes in the subdivision. Should Developer perhaps build toward the back of the farm and postpone any decisions about the area along the street? Is there a danger that putting off the decision may harden opposition to the construction of attached homes at a later time from the residents now within the subdivision?

Developer contacts the school board to find out what sites it is considering for the new school and she discovers that the board is thinking about three locations, one of which is right across the street from the farm. A final decision will not be made for a year or so. This information prompts Developer to try for a mixed-use development. She could build the attached townhouses first, and use the profits to help finance the upscale homes, thereby reducing her interest load with the bank. A quick market analysis indicates that some townhouses and amenities like a pool and tennis court could attract young couples and affluent singles, so Developer pursues this plan.

Fortunately for Developer the City has a zoning category that seems just right for Sunrise Woods: Planned Residential Development District, or PRD. The PRD provisions allow for mixed types of housing and seem to provide for a great deal of development flexibility. However, Developer sees a few drawbacks. She must present a very detailed plan and if it is approved she cannot deviate from the plan without approval by the planning commission. Also, the PRD provisions specify a greater setback of the proposed development from adjacent properties, 200 feet on the north, east and west sides of her land. Those setbacks would consume several acres. Developer sees more benefits than burdens and decides to seek approval for a PRD rather than asking the city council to zone part of her land for single family and part for attached homes.

STEP 4. Securing a zone change.

Developer retains a land use attorney at this point who explains that the city's PRD zoning district operates like a floating zone. It exists already in the zoning law to be applied to specific parcels of eligible land upon the application of the land owner to the council itself. The PRD provisions stipulate that the development be set back from neighboring parcels and subject to design restrictions intended to preserve surrounding property value. Lawyer prepares an application to the city council requesting that Developer's parcel be included in the PRD zone.

The rezoning process under state law and local requirements involves several formalities that the attorney made sure were met. The neighboring property owners were served with personal notice of the request for PRD designation. A public hearing of the city council is scheduled and notice of the hearing published in the official newspaper designated by the city council. The public hearing must be held within sixty-five days of the Developer's application for rezoning and the council's decision made within sixty-five days of the close of the public hearing. These requirements vary from jurisdiction to jurisdiction. Because of the protections built into the PRD provisions and the relatively few neighbors who will be directly affected by the development, few citizens attended the public hearing and the city council approves the application and the land now conforms to local zoning.

STEP 5. Laying out the subdivision.

Now Developer is ready to get the land subdivided into building lots, which requires that the local planning commission approve a subdivision application. As part of the zone change process, Developer hired a local planner and engineering firm to prepare a very preliminary layout of the development, including the location of lots and the streets and utilities needed to service them. In this city, like most, the subdivision approval process allows a developer to present a "concept plat" that depicts the general idea of the subdivision to the local officials. This saves much expense because if the concept is not acceptable, then money is saved by not surveying lots, streets, and other features of the subdivision.

In our case, the first meeting with local planning officials, an informal work session offers an opportunity to see if the city is amenable to a mixed-use subdivision with townhouses and single-family houses. To make her concept look better, Developer hires an architect to do a rendering of the concept showing some nice looking townhouses clustered around a large pool, with some attractive single-family houses nearby. The architect may also have access to previously built similar developments and can provide photographs or slides of upscale mixed-use projects like that planned by Developer.

The concept is accepted informally and Developer proceeds now to the next step, preparation of a preliminary plat, and initiation of the subdivision approval process. Also, Developer at this time may take her concept and plan to the lending institution to obtain approval of a line of credit for construction loans and other necessary subdivision costs, especially installation of infrastructure—streets, sidewalks, water and sewers.

STEP 6. Preparation of preliminary plat.

Now Developer must invest a significant amount of money in the preparation of a preliminary plat of her proposed subdivision. The Engineer will work on the plat. The land must be surveyed and proposed lots must be shown precisely. Also, this plat must show land contours, streets within the subdivision, utility easements, and many other details that will be important to the city planning commission. In the course of this process Developer may be confronted with problems related to the physical nature of the property. For example, Engineer discovers while reviewing the contours that a portion of the land is located in a previously mapped flood plain and may be classified as a "wetland." Even if no standing water is visible on that part of the farm, any change in the elevation of that area would require a wetland permit. Likewise, a stand of mature trees covering eight acres along the north side of the farm might be covered by a city "tree ordinance" that requires a special permit for cutting and removing trees. The PRD zoning provisions allow up to four dwelling units per acre. Developer learns early in the platting process that the potential maximum of 160 dwelling units on the forty-acre farm is illusory. Some of the land—especially the stand of trees and the possible wetland—must be subtracted from the density calculation. These problems will also dictate how the internal streets within the subdivision must be laid out to provide proper access to all lots and to avoid or minimize disturbing the woods and wetlands.

Developer will ask the planner, architect, and engineer to design a layout that will be attractive to potential home buyers, maximize the natural features of the land, make the proposed townhouses fit in nicely with the single-family homes, and make other suggestions for the subdivision. Lawyer is also contacted to be sure all government regulations are considered in the design. The professionals work together and come up with a plan that places an entrance to the subdivision close to the center of the south frontage along the collector street with an attractive fence (brick pillars and wood) along the street. The entrance will be "gated" and landscaped, following current national trends in up-scale subdivisions. Past the entrance, the plat shows a curvilinear street circling through the subdivision with several cul-de-sacs each serving six lots. Just opposite the entrance the plat shows a recreation area with a large swimming pool and clubhouse and several tennis courts. Four low-rise buildings each containing four townhouses are located between the street frontage and the curving street. Open space is preserved around the cul-de-sacs and a nature trail connects the open space and the stand of trees. This plan allows for thirty-six single-family houses and sixteen townhouses, a total of fifty-two dwelling units. Developer knows, however, that the approval process for a subdivision plat involves extensive negotiation with the city planning office and the planning commission. She asks her team to develop "Plan B" showing more units on slightly smaller lots, so she will have something to concede to meet the demands of the commission.

Developer must now sharpen her focus on the profitability of the development, predicting the total development costs and the selling price of the proposed units. Obviously, many unknowns enter into this calculation. How long will it take to obtain all the approvals and permits? Will the cost of building materials and labor rise in the near future? Will interest rates go up or down (for both future buyers and for Developer)? Will the market stay hot in this part of town? Where will that new school be located? Will property taxes go up or down? The considerations are many.

As the preliminary plat takes shape, Developer consults again with the lending institution to confirm its commitment to the plan. At the same time, Developer prepares for her request to have the subdivision approved. Engineer might take the lead in this process, or Developer might ask Attorney to shepherd the subdivision approval through the planning commission. The commission is an administrative agency and must follow administrative procedures that are well understood by land use attorneys. Sensing that opposition is growing because of the townhouses, Developer carefully directs her strategy.

STEP 7. Subdivision approval.

Developer visits City Hall and files an application for subdivision approval. She pays the required fee and is given a set of instructions that include the duty to notify all adjacent property owners of the request by certified mail. Also, the City will post a sign on the property that is clearly visible from the street. The sign will include a copy of the request and the time and date for a public hearing before the planning commission. Developer is also required to place a legal notice in the local newspaper containing the same information.

This provides some time for the public to take notice of the petition and for members of the planning commission to visit the property and the neighborhood. The planning commissioners are local citizens who are volunteers appointed by the city council. The commission is empowered by state statute and local ordinance to conduct hearings on requests for subdivision approval and to approve, deny, or approve with conditions all subdivision applications.

After making the application, Developer goes to the city planning office to ask whether there have been many inquiries from the public. She wants to get a feel for potential opposition regarding the townhouses, now that the details of their number, design, and location have been made public. She learns that a citizens group committed to open space preservation and growth restrictions will oppose Sunrise Woods. She also learns that a dozen telephone calls came into the office.

At this point, a number of technical, legal, and political matters converge. The neighbors' opposition is fueled by a hardened no-growth advocate who found out that the so-called "town homes" were going to be placed in condominium ownership. By pointing out that these will be the first commonly owned "condos" in this changing rural environment and questioning the exclusive nature of the "gated community," this advocate has raised concerns arising a number of neighbors and interest groups. They complain to the city council—who are the elected leaders—about the rezoning and threaten to oppose their reelection if something isn't done to stop this project. The planning commission, called a planning board in some jurisdictions, is required to make independent decisions and must follow defined legal rules for approving the project; these rules include the process that must be followed and the standards that can be used to approve, approve on conditions, or deny the subdivision application. While the rezoning decision was a discretionary one on the part of the council, a legislative body, the subdivision approval decision is an administrative one. If Developer can show that her development meets all of the standards of the zoning law and subdivision regulations, the board will be unable to deny her application.

Developer now sharpens the focus of her development team and asks her technical advisers to do the very best job they can of designing and explaining the high quality of her development. Her planner and lawyer also meet with her to discuss both the political and administrative strategy. They review all of the substantive regulatory standards they must meet and gauge the basis, if any, for the commission to deny the project or subject it to onerous conditions. They also look at the required time periods the commission must respect in conducting its review and approval: a public hearing must be held within sixty-five days of the subdivision application, the hearing must be preceded by public notice in the official paper and by certified mail notices to nearby property owners, and the decision of the commission must be made within sixty-five days of the public hearing.

While Developer's architect, engineer, and planner meet with the city's planner, engineer, street superintendent, and fire chief to be sure they are satisfied with all design elements, the Developer considers how to defuse the opposition. She finds out from her lawyer that the time periods may be waived by her and that a public hearing can be conducted that allows all interested parties to speak and engage in a meaningful exchange. She makes a decision to extend the approval process by a couple of months, to slow the project down, and to visit all of the stakeholders who have any interest in the project. In addition to opponents, this group includes the local labor unions, builders, material suppliers, the chamber of commerce, and affordable housing advocates who favor the townhomes because they would be a source of housing for young families and singles who have no other place to live. Since all of these parties have an interest in the development proceeding, Developer meets with each group.

With the "opponents" she is calm, moves slowly, asks them to explain their opposition, and provides answers over a course of several weeks. They learn that she can be trusted to be open and direct and they also learn that condominium ownership, by itself, does not lower surrounding property values and is simply a legal structure for private ownership that provides ample motivation for the condo owners to maintain and improve their properties. She explains that a townhome is an architectural concept, while the condominium is a legal one. By focusing on the townhome design and architectural quality, she gradually changes the terminology of the discussion and persuades most of the concerned neighbors that they do not need to fear her development. At the same time, she succeeds in getting teachers' groups, union leaders, builders, and the chamber of commerce to send representatives to the public hearing to speak in favor of the development.

The day of the planning commission hearing arrives and Developer and her team present the plan. Planning commissioners have several questions for Developer. One concern for some of the commissioners is that there is only one entrance to Sunrise Woods and that could present traffic flow problems. Developer answers by saying that Sunrise Woods would only have fifty to sixty dwelling units when completed, far less than a "maximum" development of 160 units, and that planning another entrance would mean that residents of Sunrise Woods would drive through other adjacent subdivisions on the east and west to the detriment of those residents, and they, in turn, would be driving through Sunrise Woods. The planning commission then opens the floor to the public and a lively interchange ensues among members of the audience, Developer, her team, and commissioners. The presence of condos in the neighborhood still concerns many people. Developer's reassurances that the four condominium structures would be only two stories, well designed, and limited to sixteen condos, does not calm the fears. Some speakers state that owners of the condos could rent them out to strangers and neighborhood stability would decline. Developer answers by pointing out that owners of single-family houses often rent their houses and that people are willing to purchase the single-family homes in Sunrise Woods even though condos are part of the development. Developer also notes that under the PRD designation she must provide a set of covenants protecting the open space and housing densities in Sunrise Woods and that the City has enforcement powers under the restrictions.

The commissioners are impressed that six individuals ask to speak in favor of the project who support having somewhat more affordable homes and who will benefit economically from the development. The commissioners inform the public and Developer that they will study the proposal, consider the comments made at the public hearing and vote on the proposal at their next regularly scheduled meeting. The public hearing is adjourned after all who wished to speak were heard.

STEP 8. Subdivision plat approval.

Prior to the next meeting, the development team meets with the technicians representing the City and learn that a number of conditions will be imposed on the application, but that the application would likely be approved, subject to them. Among these conditions is that Plan B be downsized to fifty-two dwelling units, comprising thirty-six single-family homes and sixteen townhomes, to be owned as condominiums. They want Developer to "stub out" a road from the curvilinear street to the western edge of the property, so that when a future subdivision is developed to the west of Sunrise Woods, a future street can be built providing for better traffic management.

Also, the commissioners insist upon a storm drain running along the western edge of the property from the stubbed street to the nearby collector street. Developer protests the expense and points out that when the property to the west is developed, that subdivider will reap the benefit of the drain without having to pay for it. The commissioners agree that the City will pay half the cost of the drain and Developer will pay the other half. When the property to the west is platted, the City will collect half the cost from the new subdivider.

Another demand is that Developer create and record a conservation easement to protect the wetland and wooded areas in perpetuity in favor of the City. Finally, the commissioners ask for a twenty foot wide strip of land to be dedicated to the City across the entire southern frontage of the land for the purpose of future street widening (the commissioners are concerned that if the new school is built across from Sunrise Woods the collector street will have to be widened, and it would be wise to secure land for the widening at no cost to the City through dedication on the plat).

Developer objects to these conditions. Attorney informs her that there is no appeal to the city council from such administrative decisions. Any challenge would go directly to the courts and an appeal is costly and time consuming. Developer decides the costs of challenging these demands are too high and she needs to start building her fifty-two homes as soon as possible. Developer agrees to accept the conditions as negotiated and the fifty-two unit preliminary subdivision application is approved by the commission at its next meeting.

State and local law require that once a preliminary subdivision is approved, the developer applicant must submit a final plat for approval. The final plat must conform to the approved preliminary subdivision and to all conditions required by the commission. It is prepared at a greater level of design detail and on special material, in a prescribed size, and contains notes regarding all conditions to which it is subject. This final plat is approved by the commission, signed by its chair, and filed with the city clerk and in the land records office in the jurisdiction, making it and its restrictions part of the title to the forty-acre parcel.

From the date of the land purchase until recordation of the final plat of Sunrise Woods, fourteen months have gone by and Developer has paid out a large amount of money, but has not seen any income. From this moment on, her expenses will escalate very rapidly.

STEP 9. The development begins.

Developer decides to begin Sunrise Woods by building one of the condominium structures and one model home on the cul-de-sac nearest the entrance to the subdivision. At the same time a marketing program must begin. Developer decides to work through a local realtor in advertising the condos and homes. The realtor can help work up a feature story in the Sunday newspaper about the homes and also try to get the model home in the next "Parade of Homes" run by the newspaper. By starting at the front part of the subdivision, Developer can put off the cost of paving the entire curvilinear street and the other cul-de-sacs. Also, the sewer and water connections will not have to run as far from the collector street. Once sales begin, money will become available to complete installation of the rest of the infrastructure. The City, like most, requires developers to post a bond for completion of the streets and sidewalks, and water and sewer connections, recognizing that an entire subdivision is rarely built all at once.

Developer has Architect design the condos and the model home and then, since she has no building crew of her own, arranges with a building contractor to construct the condominium building and the home for her to sell to individual purchasers. Some developers contract with a group of different builders, giving them the exclusive right to buy the lots, build and sell homes in the subdivision. The contract may pass some of the risk to the builders by providing that the builders agree to purchase lots on a fixed time schedule; in an expanding market builders like this arrangement because it protects them from lower quality houses nearby. Another similar arrangement is to form a list of preferred builders and give homebuyers freedom to choose from those on the list.

Developer also consults with Attorney about creating and recording the restrictive covenants that govern the use and occupancy of the homes. One decision to be made is whether to have a separate set of covenants for the condos and for the single-family homes along with two separate owner associations. Most developers currently use the community or homeowners' association form of governance and a declaration of covenants and restrictions that protect the common interest community from undesirable alterations of structures, unsightly fences and other activities detrimental to the integrity of the community. The community association is a "governing body" for the development, empowered to prevent violations of the restrictions and to collect funds to maintain areas such as the swimming pool, tennis courts, nature trails, and other open space. Developer decides to have one association and treat all of Sunrise Woods as one common interest community. She also wants Attorney to write the covenants in such a manner that she—as owner of all unsold lots and condos—can have a controlling interest in governing the community, at least until the majority of units are sold.

Aggressive marketing during the first phase of construction, which will take four to six months, is essential to Developer so that sales will run ahead of construction and a positive cash flow will occur.

STEP 10. Sunrise Woods waxes and wanes.

A development of fifty-two housing units takes a long time. After two years, Sunrise Woods has six completed houses, one condominium structure fully sold, and another of the condominium buildings under construction. Many things can slow or stop the momentum. Suppose a major employer in the city closes down and the housing market suffers; sales in Sunrise Woods may also slow down. Maybe a few "For Sale" signs appear in Sunrise Woods and Developer is now competing with her own former buyers. On the other hand, suppose the local school board finally decides to build the new elementary school right across the road from Sunrise Woods. Developer advertise that children living in the subdivision can walk to and from school; that might spur sales or it might discourage families without young children from buying.

If sales slow down too much, Developer may try to raise money by selling a few lots to other builders, even though she will lose control of the design of the houses. Another risk in the early years is that a buyer might want a house on a lot near the back of the subdivision, close to the wooded area, thus forcing Developer to do a lot of paving and run sewer and water to that area prematurely. Development does not usually proceed in a neat and orderly manner.

After a few more years, more people in the City are speaking out against "urban sprawl," and are joining a loose coalition of citizen groups that want the planning commission to curb growth toward the west; they are lobbying for a moratorium on the issuance of any new building permits until a "slow growth" plan can be adopted and implemented. Developer joins with a number of other developers to condemn such ideas. After all, the new school is a magnet for residential development and the State is planning to improve a road about a mile west of the current city limits; which will also spur growth. Even though Sunrise Woods is not threatened by the movement to slow or stop westward growth, Developer feels that any interference with natural market forces for development is bad for developers. She is insulated from these threats, personally, because she has vested rights by now in her approved subdivision.

Although the City does not change its development ordinances to restrain growth, the pressure of increased population results in the need to upgrade the sewage treatment facilities. The cost of a new treatment plant is beyond the current budget. The planning commission recommends the imposition of an "impact fee" on all new residential construction to go toward a new sewage treatment plant. This fee will be scaled to the square footage of new dwelling units and will be collected at the same time building permits are issued. Developer's new units will be subject to this fee. She is worried that she will have to raise the prices of her units and does not like the idea of becoming a "tax collector" for the City. She asks Attorney whether she would be covered by the new impact fee or would be "grandfathered" in because Sunrise Woods was previously approved. Attorney informs Developer that the only way to avoid the fee would be to secure building permits for undeveloped lots prior to the effective date of the impact fee ordinance. Developer feels that she is being put in a difficult situation. Securing building permits so far in advance of actual construction is costly and unrealistic, so her only option is to either pass the entire cost of the impact fee on to new buyers, or absorb some of the fee herself. She joins a group of developers and lobbies against the new impact fee, arguing that it is really a hidden tax on new homebuyers. The City, however, passes the impact fee ordinance. Council members state publicly that new residents are the cause of the problem of sewage treatment and they should pay for the new plant.

Sunrise Woods is now five years old. Thirty-three single-family homes and twelve condominiums are built. The development will probably take a few more years to complete, but Developer is now in a position to look for another property to develop. After counting up all her expenses for Sunrise Woods and the sales figures, she has not made a great deal of profit. Her return on investment is at the low end of the national average which ranges from 5–10% according to the National Association of Homebuilders. However, she feels that she has made an important contribution to the City by providing good quality residential living to a number of people, and considers herself a "community builder" as well as a developer. By setting up a separate company for each development she insulates her personal funds from failure of any one subdivision and obtains maximum leverage to engage in the risky business of subdivision development. Meanwhile the political climate in the City has changed. There are now three organized no-growth groups dedicated to preventing any similar rezonings and high density subdivisions. The groups are lobbying for the city council to pass a number of local laws to protect the environment, prevent open space disappearance, and reduce traffic congestion. Developers of the remaining undeveloped parcels are contacting neighbors and concerned stakeholders much earlier in the development process and using mediation to identify affected interests early and to accommodate them in the proposals taken to local land use boards in the first instance.

* * *

The Sunrise Woods scenario is fairly typical. Of course, many subdivisions are much smaller in scope and some much larger, but the problems and process of converting raw land into residential developments are well represented by this hypothetical. As we progress through the materials in this book you will encounter in much greater detail all of the issues raised in the Sunrise Woods story. Some of the questions that might have come to mind as you were reading the scenario are mentioned here, so that you will recognize them later in this course:

1. Where does the City get legal authority to adopt a master plan and zoning ordinance?
2. Under what circumstances can property be rezoned?
3. Should neighbors have some right to settled expectations about land uses in areas where they have bought homes?
4. What are the legal differences between the local board that amends the zoning ordinance and the one that approves development proposals such as Developer's subdivision request? Is there any significance in these differences?
5. Where are the rules found that the City followed in rezoning and approving the subdivision of Sunrise Woods?
6. What is the role of the land use lawyer in this development process? At what point should Developer consult with her land use attorney? What about other professionals?

7. Were the rezoning and the subdivision approval in conformance with the master plan?
8. Were all the required procedural steps followed by the city council and the commission?
9. Once Sunrise Woods is approved, do the neighbors have standing to challenge the approval in court?
10. Would a no-growth citizens' association have standing?
11. What could a municipality do to preserve agricultural land and open space if it wanted to?
12. What strategies could municipalities employ to manage growth and development?
13. What standards do the courts use to evaluate challenges of rezoning decisions made by legislative bodies?
14. Are those standards the same as those used to evaluate administrative approvals of subdivision applications?
15. If the rezoning was not awarded or the subdivision not approved, would the developer have any viable legal challenge to bring? What property and due process rights do developers have and how can they be violated in the land use approval process?
16. What do you make of Developer's negotiating process and strategy? Did she involve the neighbors soon enough and give them a meaningful enough role? Note how she responded to some of their concerns: What are the dangers in involving them too much? Not enough? What is the lawyer's role in counseling developer clients regarding these matters?
17. If the covenants recorded with the subdivision and distributed to every purchaser set up an association to enforce the covenants, along with the power to pass rules governing life in the subdivision, what do you think about this sort of "private government"?

SECTION 3. THE HISTORY OF LAND USE REGULATION

A. THE ORIGINS OF OUR LAND USE SYSTEM

The United States is not alone in having a governmental system for controlling land use, nor is the notion of regulating land use a new idea. In the early Roman period, around 450 B.C., a commission was formed to draft legislation regulating private behavior and public affairs. The result was the Twelve Tables, which included the following site planning provisions: "Whoever sets a hedge around his land shall not exceed the boundary; in the case of a wall, he shall leave one foot; in the case of a house, two feet.... If a well, a path, an olive or fig tree, nine feet." Treasury of Law 71, Nice ed., 1964.

Many of the great Latin American cities founded in the 16th century were developed following distinctly Spanish urban planning concepts. Under the Law of the Indies, decreed in 1572 by King Philip II, cities were laid out according to various guidelines that varied depending on the climate, geography, and characteristics of the place. Viceroys completed surveys akin to today's environmental impact assessments and sent them to Spain, where planners determined which guidelines were to be followed in each location. The Spanish founded new towns—villas—based on models in Spain, with space for homes, public buildings, and croplands.

In London, the great fire of 1666 led to the adoption of municipal building construction laws that required brick exteriors, wider streets, and open space along the Thames River for access to water for firefighting. Land use was regulated to a minor degree, as well, with activities such as breweries and tanneries prohibited in the central city. The law provided for compensation to be paid to any individual lot owner who was prohibited from building. These early land use rules were articulated first in a proclamation by King Charles II, supported by a report from an investigative committee established by the King, and formalized by the Act for the Rebuilding of London adopted by Parliament in 1667. The Act gave the municipality the power to regulate the construction of buildings: their size, height, and placement on the lot, and the materials used.

Other countries provide interesting examples of early land use regulation. Sweden enacted an early comprehensive town planning law in 1874 which made provisions for some land use planning in all of its towns and cities. In Germany, there is a strong tradition of comprehensive planning, directed from the top down, with plans at the state, regional, and local level, and with a tradition of self-government where local authorities adopted plans and zoning to control growth around preserved historic centers, with open space retained at the periphery. Early French city planning, which emphasized infrastructure development, particularly transportation planning, was conducted primarily at the national level until 1982, when the French Parliament adopted a law that transferred significant land use planning and project approval authority to the country's more than 35,000 municipalities.

B. THE AMERICAN APPROACH

(1) The Colonial Era

By the time that the American colonies were settled, individuals were thought to hold powerful control over their land—a concept that limited the power of the state to regulate that land. In this early period, land uses were regulated more by conditions imposed on the land titles conveyed by colonial authorities than by governmental regulation. Colonial settlements evolved into cities, townships, and counties, which eventually achieved governmental status and the power to legislate. These municipalities were regarded not as sovereign entities but as creatures of the state, authorized by state law to exercise a wide variety of powers affecting the health, safety, and welfare of their citizens. Most were deemed to have only those express powers delegated by their state legislatures, and those additional powers fairly implied in that delegation.

(2) The Federal Republic

The U.S. Constitution was drafted by state-selected delegates and was signed by them in 1787. It created a national government—one of delegated powers, limited to those specifically included in the Constitution. Notably, the full police powers of the states were not delegated to the federal government. The principal power given to the federal government that affects private land use is the authority to regulate interstate commerce, under Article I, § 8 of the U.S. Constitution. Article VI of the Constitution grants the federal government the power to enter into international treaties that legally bind federal, state, and local governments in the United States. Under this authority, the United States has entered into many bilateral, regional, and international agreements that promote resource conservation and prevent environmental pollution.

The Tenth Amendment of the U.S. Constitution reserves to the states all powers not delegated by the Constitution to the federal government; this power protects states against encroachments by Congress that are not within its delegated authority. The weight of legal and political opinion holds that this allocation of power in the federal republic leaves the states in charge of regulating how private land is used, subject to additional federal regulation protecting interstate commerce or enforcing an international treaty. The concept of dual sovereignty is dynamic and leaves room for flexibility in responding to challenges at the state and federal level, with tensions resolved by the U.S. Supreme Court.

C. THE MODERN ERA OF ZONING

(1) Comprehensive Zoning

The nation's first comprehensive zoning ordinance was adopted by New York City in 1916. As happened in England after the great fire of 1666, the march of unwanted land uses uptown precipitated a crisis leading to the creation of a commission which recommended stricter land use controls to protect the city's economy, private property values, and public health and safety. The resulting zoning law divided the city into multiple land use districts, or zones. These districts allowed private landowners to use their land only for the purposes permitted in the applicable district. This protected Fifth Avenue retailers, for example, from the incursion of garment factories—an industrial use—in that retail zone.

A few years after the adoption of this first comprehensive zoning ordinance, a federal commission formulated a model act—known as the Zoning Enabling Act—to be adopted by state legislatures to make it clear that their localities had the power to zone. In the United States, virtually all fifty states adopted some version of this model act; their legislatures have passed relatively similar zoning enabling laws giving municipalities the authority to regulate private land uses.

(2) Authority

Local governments are regarded as legal instrumentalities of their states. The legislative authority of municipalities is limited to that delegated by the state and extends only to their geographical boundaries, with modest exceptions. Planning and zoning enabling laws specifically authorize municipal governments to control the use of the land by adopting land use plans and creating zoning districts, within which specified land uses are allowed and various construction standards enforced. In most states, zoning regulations must conform to the locality's land use plan. State enabling laws also authorize localities to create administrative and quasi-judicial agencies to review and adjudicate proposals for land development and to hear petitions for relief from zoning regulations.

Municipalities adopt comprehensive plans that lay the foundation for the adoption of local land use laws. In a few states, these local plans must be consistent with regional or statewide land use plans. Municipalities also adopt traditional land use laws such as zoning ordinances and standards that regulate land subdivision and site plan development.

In most states, home rule authority is also delegated to local governments, giving them broad power to adopt laws that affect local property, affairs, and government so long as those laws do not conflict with general or preemptive state laws. States utilize a variety of methods to grant home rule powers to their localities. At a minimum, local home rule power authorizes localities to legislate regarding their own property, affairs, and government, except where general or preemptive state laws operate. In nearly all states, home rule authority is not deemed to prevent the state from legislating regarding legitimate state interests by guiding, directing, or preempting local land use control.

Local governments today are empowered to adopt innovative local land use laws that promote smart growth and that create more balanced land use patterns. More particularly, municipalities in many states have used their land use authority to develop a new body of local regulations designed to protect natural resources and prevent environmental pollution. Environmental objectives can now be found in local comprehensive plans, the boundaries of conservation zoning districts can be drawn to correspond to and protect watershed areas, environmental standards can now be found in subdivision and site plan regulations, and localities can adopt stand-alone environmental laws to protect particular unique and threatened natural resources. The clear purposes of these laws are to control nonpoint source pollution and preserve natural resources from the adverse impacts of land development. Although the majority of U.S. communities have not adopted numerous and sophisticated local environmental laws, the increasing number of these laws, in the aggregate, constitutes a significant body of land use practice.

Some land use projects are subject to permitting standards by multiple agencies and levels of government. According to the U.S. Census Bureau, there are about 39,000 governments that have or can be given authority to regulate private land use. In some areas, land developers must receive a permit to build near wetlands from the U.S. Army Corps of Engineers, the state department of environmental protection, and a local wetlands commission or planning board. Other examples of overlapping regulations that protect watersheds, habitats, surface waters, and other resources abound. As a result, the contemporary challenge is to integrate some of the various governmental influences on private land use to limit waste and redundancy while preserving the need for flexibility in addressing diverse regional, state, and federal interests.

(3) Zoning Procedure and Judicial Review

Local administrative agencies are established to review and approve individual development proposals. These agencies are required to hold public hearings on most proposals, to provide notice to affected parties of the hearings, to hold meetings open to the public, and to ensure that their voting members have no conflicts of interests that prevent their decisions from being objective. Procedures for adopting land use plans and laws provide for citizen participation in the process with varying degrees of input and effectiveness.

The two consistent standards that all land use laws must meet are that they accomplish a legitimate public objective and that they allow the landowner some economically viable use of the land. The U.S. Constitution also protects individual freedom of speech, and the right to assemble and worship. Land use regulations that affect these individual freedoms do not enjoy the usual presumption of constitutionality that courts otherwise afford local laws.

The judicial branch of government settles disputes among landowners, affected citizens, environmental organizations, and governmental regulators. Courts tend to defer to the judgment of land use regulators and impose a heavy burden on those who challenge land use regulations to prove that such regulations are arbitrary, capricious, not within the scope of local authority, deny owners an economical use of the land, or violate other constitutional protections such as equal protection of the law.

SECTION 4. THE NATURE OF PROPERTY RIGHTS

A. THE RIGHTS OF LANDOWNERS

The subject of land use law explores the extent of the authority of public entities to regulate private property rights by limiting the use, occupancy, and sale of land and natural resources. This requires that we think a bit about property rights. What rights does a private landowner have and to what extent are they protected from governmental interference? In Property Law, students study how rights to property arise, what estates and interests can be created, and common law limitations on those rights. They learn that with the fee simple absolute title to land comes a number of fundamental rights that are protected by common law doctrines and modern constitutional law, such as the Fifth Amendment.

Landowners are said, for example, to own the exclusive right to possess their property; they may exclude others from their domains. The right to exclude others from the land is protected by trespass actions in common law courts. Any intentional incursion onto the land of another, whether actual damage occurred or not, is actionable. Liability for intentional trespass is absolute, regardless of motive or harm effected. Damages are assessed in proportion to actual injury caused to the property. Even when no actual damage resulted from a trespass, courts award nominal damages as a means of settling property disputes. The right to possess is often said to be exclusive in nature, limited to the owner, and that every entry without the owner's permission is a trespass.

This right to exclusive possession is akin to the right that landowners have to use their property as they see fit. Similarly, title to land is tenaciously protected by the law; it may not be taken by the government except in very circumscribed situations. Finally, property owners can alienate their land: sell their complete title, or any lesser estate or interest, to third parties. The right to sell includes the right to create lesser estates and interests such as determinable fees, future interests, leases, easements, and covenants.

B. THE LIMITS OF LAND OWNERSHIP

Although they are described as "fundamental," the rights to possess, use, exclude, and alienate have never been absolute. Property theorists are fond of debating how tenacious private ownership is and to what degree it is limited by collective rights and the public interest. Our legal history is not kind to absolutist interpretations of property rights. At the beginning of our common law era, for example, all property was held either by or "of" the King. Those holding under the King were only possessors—always subject to his vast sovereign prerogatives. Beginning with the Magna Carta, the rights of English lords to control their land and insulate themselves from sovereign interference evolved, but slowly. The Statute of Quia Emptores, adopted in 1290, gave those who held land the power to transfer it to the private ownership of others, subject to the state's right to tax, take, and control the land.

Over the centuries, landowners obtained further rights. It took until 1540 for the owners of real property to secure the right to transfer their property at death by will to individuals of their own choice. The right to exclude had fully matured by 1782 when William Blackstone, one of the earliest commentators on the common law, referred to the right of property as "that sole and despotic dominion which one man claims over the external things of the world, in total exclusion of the right of any other individual in the universe." Although few land use regulations existed by this time, Blackstone noted, even then, that property rights were to be enjoyed "without any control or diminution, save only by the laws of the land."

Blackstone could have added that property rights are limited by common law duties and public law entitlements. Under nuisance law, for example, the right to use is limited by the private owner's duty not to injure the property of others. Commonwealth v. Tewksbury, 52 Mass. 55 (1846). The owner of land crossed by a navigable river may not obstruct the public's right to travel on the river or use it for commercial transportation. Owners of riparian lands adjacent to the sea or other tidal waters cannot exclude those who wish to enter upon their tidal wetlands and even to fish there. In Shelley v. Kraemer, 334 U.S. 1, 68 S.Ct. 836, 92 L.Ed. 1161 (1948), the conveyance of a racially restrictive covenant was held to be unenforceable under the Fourteenth Amendment of the U.S. Constitution. The entry of federal employees on a farmer's land to talk with migrant workers about their rights was held not to be a trespass. See also, State v. Shack, 58 N.J. 297, 277 A.2d 369 (1971). Limitations on the right to exclude have been created in the event of emergencies, necessities, the wrongful taking of a chattel, and to permit the continuance of minor encroachments.

C. PUBLIC CONTROL OF LAND USE

The seminal land use case is Village of Euclid v. Ambler Realty Co., 272 U.S. 365, 47 S.Ct. 114, 71 L.Ed. 303 (1926), a U.S. Supreme Court case. In Euclid, the legal issue before the Supreme Court was whether a zoning ordinance adopted by the village that divided the plaintiff's land into three separate use districts was constitutional. The village adopted its ordinance under the police power delegated to it by the State of Ohio. The state legislature had the power under the state constitution to enact laws to protect the public health, safety, morals, and welfare. In the land use area, it chose to protect the public by delegating the power to adopt zoning ordinances to its municipalities, including the Village of Euclid.

The plaintiff landowner objected. How does it accomplish a legitimate public interest, which a police power regulation must do, to limit the types of uses to which privately-owned land can be put? The Court instructed the plaintiff that, in deciding this issue, the "law of nuisances may be consulted, not for the purpose of controlling, but for the helpful aid of its analogies in the process of ascertaining the scope of the [police] power. Thus the question whether the power exists to forbid the erection of a building of a particular kind or for a particular use, like the question whether a particular thing is a nuisance, is to be determined, not by an abstract consideration of the building or the thing considered apart, but by considering it in connection with the circumstances and the locality."

Because the village had shown that certain dangers to the public lurked in the random mixing of industrial, commercial, and residential land uses, the Court upheld local zoning as a valid exercise of the police power.

SECTION 5. THE LAW OF NUISANCE

A. BACKGROUND

Euclid, Ohio, is a suburb of Cleveland. At the time that it adopted zoning, it was in the path of development moving outward from the metropolitan area. The Supreme Court in Euclid understood that there was a certain similarity between judicial policies observable in the common law of nuisance and land use law, or zoning. The context surrounding a particular land use matters in determining whether the use is a nuisance or is reasonably restricted by land use laws. This is a matter of reasonableness. We do not want pigs in parlors, but can abide them on the farm.

CLARK v. WAMBOLD

Supreme Court of Wisconsin, 1917.
165 Wis. 70, 160 N.W. 1039.

This is an action in equity to enjoin the defendant from maintaining a nuisance consisting of pig pens and pig yards immediately adjacent to plaintiff's premises on the east shore of Eagle Lake, in Waukesha county, Wis. The plaintiff owns two acres of land on the shore of the lake, which he purchased in 1905, part of it being purchased from the defendant, and all of which he uses for summer residence purposes. The defendant owns a farm immediately east of the plaintiff's premises, and also operates a feedmill thereon. For years before the commencement of this action he has made a business of raising pigs and selling them when about six weeks old, sometimes having eight or nine brood sows at a time. The yards or inclosures in which the pigs are bred are close to the feedmill, and also near the plaintiff's property. The brood sows are fed largely with sweepings from the feed mill. There was much evidence to the effect that the pig pens and inclosures were kept in a filthy condition, and that the odors arising therefrom and drifting over the plaintiff's premises were very offensive and continuous during the summer months. There was also considerable testimony to the effect that the pens and yards were kept in as clean and sanitary condition as reasonably possible, and better than most farmers are accustomed to keep such places. The pig pens and inclosures existed and were in use in 1905, when the plaintiff purchased his property along the lake shore, and at that time the plaintiff bought of the defendant two small parcels along the east side of his property, on which pig pens were situated, in order to remove the pens and keep the defendant's hogs further away from his summer house. The defendant raised more pigs during the years beginning with 1911 or 1912 than before.

The court found in substance that the pens and yards were kept in as clean and sanitary condition as can be expected, that there were no odors, except such as necessarily exist around well-kept pens and yards, and that the effect of such odors is not such as to materially interfere with the enjoyment of plaintiff's premises, or materially impair their use by people of ordinary sensibilities. Judgment was entered dismissing the complaint, without costs, except clerk's fees, and the plaintiff appeals.

WINSLOW, C.J. The raising of pigs is a perfectly lawful and respectable business. Doubtless it will remain so as long as the human palate craves the thin cut of juicy ham and the crisp slice of breakfast bacon. With all the marvelous advance in the science of animal husbandry which has taken place in recent years, we have not yet produced the odorless pig. He may come at some future time, in company with the voiceless cat and the fleasless dog; but he is not yet in sight. Whenever he comes he will be welcome; but in the meantime pigs will be pigs, and we must put up as best we may with the odorous pig and his still more odorous pen.

Manifestly pigs cannot be raised in the city; hence they must be raised on the farm. If they are raised there under conditions as clean and sanitary as can reasonably be attained, considering the characteristics of the animal and the necessity for confinement in close quarters, the fact that odors from those quarters are carried abroad on the summer breeze will not make an actionable nuisance.

It becomes one of those minor discomforts of life, which must be borne in deference to the principle that one man's enjoyment of property cannot always be the controlling factor, but must be considered in connection with the reasonable and lawful use of other property by his neighbors.

The trial court in the present case has found upon sufficient evidence that the pens are kept with reasonable cleanliness, and we do not find ourselves able to say that the clear preponderance of the evidence is against the finding. It follows that the judgment must be affirmed. Notwithstanding this result, it is not deemed improper to suggest to the respondent that insistence on extreme legal rights is not always good policy, to say nothing of good neighborliness. It is far better to make a friend of one's neighbor by foregoing, at his request, the exercise of some minor right which causes him discomfort than to make an enemy of him by insisting upon the right simply because the law gives it. It does not appear that it would be difficult, or even inconvenient, to remove the pig yards which are nearest to the plaintiff's property to some other spot upon the farm. Good neighborliness strongly suggests that he ought to do so. A good neighbor is a great treasure. We can generally have such treasures if we are neighborly ourselves. The golden rule is just as good a rule of conduct now as it was nineteen hundred years ago. We are confident that, if the defendant acts upon it in the present case, he will in the end experience greater satisfaction from that action than he now experiences in the affirmance of this judgment.

Judgment affirmed.

Notes

1. Contrast the principal case with the holding of Mitchell v. Hines, 305 Mich. 296, 9 N.W.2d 547 (1943), in which the court enjoined a large scale piggery where dead animals and municipal refuse were brought to and dumped on the fields to feed the animals. In Mitchell, there were numerous nearby residential owners, the intensity of the noxious uses had increased since they moved in, and the degree of nuisance was extensive, leading the court to comment on the "revolting odors" emanating from the fields.

2. Historically, the powerful right of individuals to use their land under the common law was balanced to a degree by the doctrine of nuisance, which established that private landowners may not use their property in a way that is injurious to property held by others. Private nuisance actions originated in the twelfth century, in the assize of nuisance which was replaced in the fifteenth century by an action on the case for nuisance. Nuisance remedies were limited, by and large, to injunctions and damages awarded to owners or occupants of adjacent land who could prove substantial injuries. Offensive intrusions included the effects of smoke, dust, noise, odors, heat, or other discernable effects that interfered with or diminished the normal uses of nearby property. Nuisance rules limiting injurious land uses evolved slowly and only in response to one private party's dispute against another.

B. PUBLIC AND PRIVATE NUISANCE

The Restatement of Torts defines a private nuisance as a nontrespassory invasion of another's interest in the private use and enjoyment of land. When one property owner brings a nuisance action against another, she is attempting to control land use through a civil action. Only those parties significantly affected by the nuisance have standing to bring the action, and the court is interested only in balancing and ordering the equities between the plaintiff and defendant. The Restatement's general rule of nuisance law indicates that a landowner is subject to a nuisance action for a land use—such as operating a pig farm—if that land use is "unreasonable." Whether a use is unreasonable or not depends. To help courts determine reasonableness, the Restatement uses a number of tests including the suitability of the activity on the land to the character of the place, the value to society of the alleged nuisance, and the hardship on the defendant of an injunction or damage award. The social value of the plaintiff's use of her land is also considered along with the extent to which that use is harmed. Courts weigh the gravity of harm to the plaintiff against the utility of the defendant's use.

Land uses that significantly interfere with public health, safety, comfort, or convenience are designated public nuisances: unreasonable interferences with a "right common to the general public," according to the Restatement of Torts. Such land uses are deemed "unreasonable" when significant interference is proved by evidence produced by the plaintiffs or when the conduct is proscribed by a duly enacted law, ordinance, or administrative regulation. Zoning laws constitute such ordinances; the violation of land use standards found in zoning laws subjects violators to civil penalties, such as fines, or to criminal penalties, including imprisonment. In most cases involving land use that interfere with the public interest generally, zoning enforcement has replaced the public nuisance suit as the tool of choice.

C. ZONING AND THE LAW OF NUISANCE

In Euclid, the plaintiff landowner alleged that the village's zoning ordinance would "confiscate and destroy a great part of its value..., constitute[s] a cloud upon the land, [and] reduce[s] and destroy[s] its value...." In Restatement terms, this focuses on the financial hardship of the owner of the land creating the nuisance. The Court, in response, centered its attention on the reasonableness of the zoning ordinance, particularly the creation of separate zoning districts for different land uses. It referenced "comprehensive reports" prepared by "commissions and experts" bearing evidence of "painstaking consideration"—reports that recommended the creation of land use districts that separated residential, business, and industrial buildings. Before police power legislation of this type can be declared unconstitutional, said the Court, it must be found that it is "clearly arbitrary and unreasonable, having no substantial relationship to the public health, safety, morals, or general welfare." In this critical and deferential judicial test for measuring the constitutionality of land use laws, the echoes of nuisance law and the Restatement of Torts reverberate. The question is one of reasonableness.

Comprehensive zoning, of the type adopted by Euclid, was new in the early 1920s when it was adopted, but the concept of adopting local laws to proscribe land uses in the U.S. was not. Prior to the widespread adoption of zoning ordinances in the 1920s such ordinances were challenged as "takings" of property without just compensation prohibited by the Fifth Amendment: "Nor shall private property be taken for public use without just compensation." Regulatory takings will be considered at length further in Chapter V, but some of the early Supreme Court cases relied heavily on nuisance theory to resolve the issue. Consider the following case and notes.

HADACHECK v. SEBASTIAN

Supreme Court of the United States, 1915.
239 U.S. 394, 36 S.Ct. 143, 60 L.Ed. 348.

MR. JUSTICE MCKENNA delivered the opinion of the court.

Habeas corpus prosecuted in the Supreme Court of the State of California for the discharge of plaintiff in error from the custody of defendant in error, Chief of Police of the City of Los Angeles.

Plaintiff in error, to whom we shall refer as petitioner, was convicted of a misdemeanor for the violation of an ordinance of the City of Los

Angeles which makes it unlawful for any person to establish or operate a brickyard or brick kiln, or any establishment, factory or place for the manufacture or burning of brick within described limits in the city. Sentence was pronounced against him and he was committed to the custody of defendant in error as Chief of Police of the City of Los Angeles.

Being so in custody he filed a petition in the Supreme Court of the State for a writ of habeas corpus. The writ was issued. Subsequently defendant in error made a return thereto supported by affidavits, to which petitioner made sworn reply. The court rendered judgment discharging the writ and remanding petitioner to custody. The Chief Justice of the court then granted this writ of error.

* * *

How the Supreme Court dealt with the allegations, denials and affidavits we can gather from its opinion. The court said, through Mr. Justice Sloss, 165 California, p. 416:

> "The district to which the prohibition was applied contains about three square miles. The petitioner is the owner of a tract of land containing eight acres, more or less, within the district described in the ordinance. He acquired his land in 1902, before the territory to which the ordinance was directed had been annexed to the city of Los Angeles. His land contains valuable deposits of clay suitable for the manufacture of brick, and he has, during the entire period of his ownership, used the land for brickmaking, and has erected thereon kilns, machinery and buildings necessary for such manufacture. The land, as he alleges, is far more valuable for brickmaking than for any other purpose."

The court considered the business one which could be regulated and that regulation was not precluded by the fact "that the value of investments made in the business prior to any legislative action will be greatly diminished," and that no complaint could be based upon the fact that petitioner had been carrying on the trade in that locality for a long period.

And, considering the allegations of the petition, the denials of the return and the evidence of the affidavits, the court said that the latter tended to show that the district created had become primarily a residential section and that the occupants of the neighboring dwellings are seriously incommoded by the operations of petitioner; and that such evidence, "when taken in connection with the presumptions in favor of the propriety of the legislative determination, overcame the contention that the prohibition of the ordinance was a mere arbitrary invasion of private right, not supported by any tenable belief that the continuance of the business was so detrimental to the interests of others as to require suppression."

The court, on the evidence, rejected the contention that the ordinance was not in good faith enacted as a police measure and that it was intended to discriminate against petitioner or that it was actuated by any motive of injuring him as an individual.

The charge of discrimination between localities was not sustained. The court expressed the view that the determination of prohibition was for the legislature and that the court, without regard to the fact shown in the return that there was not another district in which brickmaking was prohibited, could not sustain the claim that the ordinance was not enacted in good faith but was designed to discriminate against petitioner and the other brick yard in the district. "The facts before us," the court finally said "would certainly not justify the conclusion that the ordinance here in question was designed, in either its adoption or its enforcement, to be anything but what it purported to be, viz., a legitimate regulation, operating alike upon all who came within its terms."

We think the conclusion of the court is justified by the evidence and makes it unnecessary to review the many cases cited by petitioner in which it is decided that the police power of a state cannot be arbitrarily exercised. The principle is familiar, but in any given case it must plainly appear to apply. It is to be remembered that we are dealing with one of the most essential powers of government, one that is the least limitable. It may, indeed, seem harsh in its exercise, usually is on some individual, but the imperative necessity for its existence precludes any limitation upon it when not exerted arbitrarily. A vested interest cannot be asserted against it because of conditions once obtaining. *Chicago & Alton R.R. v. Tranbarger*, 238 U.S. 67, 78, 35 S.Ct. 678, 59 L.Ed. 1204. To so hold would preclude development and fix a city forever in its primitive conditions. There must be progress, and if in its march private interests are in the way they must yield to the good of the community. The logical result of petitioner's contention would seem to be that a city could not be formed or enlarged against the resistance of an occupant of the ground and that if it grows at all it can only grow as the environment of the occupations that are usually banished to the purlieus.

The police power and to what extent it may be exerted we have recently illustrated in *Reinman v. Little Rock*, 237 U.S. 171, 35 S.Ct. 511, 59 L.Ed. 900. The circumstances of the case were very much like those of the case at bar and give reply to the contentions of petitioner, especially that which asserts that a necessary and lawful occupation that is not a nuisance per se cannot be made so by legislative declaration. There was a like investment in property, encouraged by the then conditions; a like reduction of value and deprivation of property was asserted against the validity of the ordinance there considered; a like assertion of an arbitrary exercise of the power of prohibition. Against all of these contentions, and causing the rejection of them all, was adduced the police power. There was a prohibition of a business, lawful in itself, there as here. It was a livery stable there, a brick yard here. They differ in particulars, but they are alike in that which cause and justify prohibition in defined localities—that is, the effect upon the health and comfort of the community.

The ordinance passed upon prohibited the conduct of the business within a certain defined area in Little Rock, Arkansas. This court said of it: granting that the business was not a nuisance per se, it was clearly within the police power of the State to regulate it, "and to that end to declare that in particular circumstances and in particular localities a livery stable shall be deemed a nuisance in fact and in law." And the only limitation upon the power was stated to be that the power could not be exerted arbitrarily or with unjust discrimination. There was a citation of cases. We think the present case is within the ruling thus declared.

There is a distinction between *Reinman v. Little Rock* and the case at bar. There, a particular business was prohibited which was not affixed to or dependent upon its locality; it could be conducted elsewhere. Here, it is contended, the latter condition does not exist, and it is alleged that the manufacture of brick must necessarily be carried on where suitable clay is found and that the clay on petitioner's property cannot be transported to some other locality. This is not urged as a physical impossibility but only, counsel say, that such transportation and the transportation of the bricks to places where they could be used in construction work would be prohibitive "from a financial standpoint." But upon the evidence the Supreme Court considered the case, as we understand its opinion, from the standpoint of the offensive effects of the operation of a brick yard, and not from the deprivation of the deposits of clay, and distinguished *Ex parte Kelso*, 147 Cal. 609, 2 L.R.A. (N.S.) 796, 109 Am.St.Rep. 178, 82 Pac. 241, wherein the court declared invalid an ordinance absolutely prohibiting the maintenance or operation of a rock or stone quarry within a certain portion of the city and county of San Francisco. The court there said that the effect of the ordinance was "to absolutely deprive the owners of real property within such limits of a valuable right incident to their ownership,—viz., the right to extract therefrom such rock and stone as they might find it to their advantage to dispose of." The court expressed the view that the removal could be regulated but that "an absolute prohibition of such removal under the circumstances," could not be upheld.

In the present case, there is no prohibition of the removal of the brick clay; only a prohibition within the designated locality of its manufacture into bricks. And to this feature of the ordinance our opinion is addressed. Whether other questions would arise if the ordinance were broader, and opinion on such questions, we reserve.

* * *

Judgment affirmed.

Notes

1. Today, a brick factory in a residential neighborhood would be considered a *per se* nuisance. In other words, the balancing factors used in private nuisance cases do not pertain, and no weighing of the gravity of the harm to the plaintiff against the utility of the defendant's operation is required. Courts recognize that some uses (junkyards, cemeteries, ammuni-

tion factories, and brick manufacturing) are always nuisances in urbanized places, particularly in residential zones. Prior to the advent of extensive land use controls, courts effectively created judicial zoning in making such determinations. It was well established in American law that certain land uses should be prohibited in certain districts, or zones. In Powell v. Taylor, 222 Ark. 896, 263 S.W.2d 906 (1954), for example, the state found a neighborhood to be so residential in character that the conversion of a home into a funeral parlor would constitute a nuisance.

2. Notice how courts in nuisance cases directly, although imprecisely and unpredictably, affected a form of zoning, prescribing and proscribing land uses in certain "districts." We have seen that in agricultural or rural areas, farm uses are favored and those who move into farming areas are unable to proscribe such uses in most cases—they moved to the nuisance. In areas dedicated to industrial uses, we see the same result. In Bove v. Donner–Hanna Coke Corp., 236 App.Div. 37, 258 N.Y.S. 229 (4 Dept.1932), the court held that the nuisance doctrine does not apply where plaintiff intentionally locates within a known industrial area, regardless of whether the particular source of the nuisance existed at the time the plaintiff located there. Because courts look to the reasonableness of the land use that is the alleged nuisance, location counts. Different circumstances pertain in urban, suburban, fringe, and rural areas and the courts are cognizant of these differences. This results in a fair degree of consistency in judicial decisions with certain uses being zoned out—enjoined—in certain areas because they are not consistent, appropriate, or reasonable there.

3. Hadacheck v. Sebastian refers to and was decided in the same year as Reinman v. City of Little Rock, 237 U.S. 171, 35 S.Ct. 511, 59 L.Ed. 900 (1915). In Reinman, a livery stable was eliminated from the downtown area as a result of the ordinance. Other police power ordinances which predated comprehensive zoning were predicated upon nuisance-like situations and drew upon that analogy. Ordinances were upheld which regulated prostitution (L'Hote v. City of New Orleans, 177 U.S. 587, 20 S.Ct. 788, 44 L.Ed. 899 (1900)), laundries (Soon Hing v. Crowley, 113 U.S. 703, 5 S.Ct. 730, 28 L.Ed. 1145 (1885)), heavy industrial smoke emissions (Northwestern Laundry v. City of Des Moines, 239 U.S. 486, 36 S.Ct. 206, 60 L.Ed. 396 (1916)), gasoline storage facilities (Pierce Oil Corp. v. City of Hope, 248 U.S. 498, 39 S.Ct. 172, 63 L.Ed. 381 (1919)) and fertilizer operations (Northwestern Fertilizing Co. v. Hyde Park, 97 U.S. (7 Otto) 659, 24 L.Ed. 1036 (1878)).

D. THE EFFECT OF ZONING ON THE LAW OF NUISANCE

What is left of nuisance law now that land uses are so heavily regulated by local zoning? Does zoning trump nuisance claims? Again, it depends. In Maykut v. Plasko, 170 Conn. 310, 365 A.2d 1114 (1976), the plaintiff homeowner brought an action to enjoin their neighbor's use of a noise cannon to frighten birds away from their garden. The defendant had a valid permit for use of the cannon under both a state statute and the local zoning law. In awarding an injunction against further use of the cannon, the state court held that although the action was permitted by zoning law, that fact does not justify an activity that otherwise interferes with the use and enjoyment of a particular neighbor's property.

Zoning creates standards for land uses that are generally harmonious, in the legislature's opinion, with the character of the zoning district, while private nuisance actions allow individual lot owners to prove to the court that a permitted use affects a nuisance in the particular circumstances of the plaintiff's land. For example, consider the following case.

PRAH v. MARETTI

Supreme Court of Wisconsin, 1982.
108 Wis.2d 223, 321 N.W.2d 182.

ABRAHAMSON, JUSTICE.

This appeal [presents] an issue of first impression, namely, whether an owner of a solar-heated residence states a claim upon which relief can be granted when he asserts that his neighbor's proposed construction of a residence (which conforms to existing deed restrictions and local ordinances) interferes with his access to an unobstructed path for sunlight across the neighbor's property. This case thus involves a conflict between one landowner (Glenn Prah, the plaintiff) interested in unobstructed access to sunlight across adjoining property as a natural source of energy and an adjoining landowner (Richard D. Maretti, the defendant) interested in the development of his land.

The circuit court concluded that the plaintiff presented no claim upon which relief could be granted and granted summary judgment for the defendant. We reverse the judgment of the circuit court and remand the cause to the circuit court for further proceedings.

According to the complaint, the plaintiff is the owner of a residence which was constructed during the years 1978–1979. The complaint alleges that the residence has a solar system which includes collectors on the roof to supply energy for heat and hot water and that after the plaintiff built his solar-heated house, the defendant purchased the lot adjacent to and immediately to the south of the plaintiff's lot and commenced planning construction of a home. The complaint further states that when the plaintiff learned of defendant's plans to build the house he advised the defendant that if the house were built at the proposed location, defendant's house would substantially and adversely affect the integrity of plaintiff's solar system and could cause plaintiff other damage. Nevertheless, the defendant began construction. The complaint further alleges that the plaintiff is entitled to "unrestricted use of the sun and its solar power" and demands judgment for injunctive relief and damages.

After filing his complaint, the plaintiff moved for a temporary injunction to restrain and enjoin construction by the defendant. In ruling on that motion the circuit court heard testimony, received affidavits and viewed the site.

The record made on the motion reveals the following additional facts: Plaintiff's home was the first residence built in the subdivision, and although plaintiff did not build his house in the center of the lot it was built in accordance with applicable restrictions. Plaintiff advised defendant that if the defendant's home were built at the proposed site it would cause a shadowing effect on the solar collectors which would reduce the efficiency of the system and possibly damage the system. To avoid these adverse effects, plaintiff requested defendant to locate his home an additional several feet away from the plaintiff's lot line, the exact number being disputed. Plaintiff and defendant failed to reach an agreement on the location of defendant's home before defendant started construction. The Architectural Control Committee of the subdivision and the Planning Commission of the City of Muskego approved the defendant's plans for his home, including its location on the lot. After such approval, the defendant apparently changed the grade of the property without prior notice to the Architectural Control Committee. The problem with defendant's proposed construction, as far as the plaintiff's interests are concerned, arises from a combination of the grade and the distance of defendant's home from the defendant's lot line.

The circuit court denied plaintiff's motion for injunctive relief, declared it would entertain a motion for summary judgment and thereafter entered judgment in favor of the defendant.

* * *

We consider first whether the complaint states a claim for relief based on common law private nuisance. This state has long recognized that an owner of land does not have an absolute or unlimited right to use the land in a way which injures the rights of others. * * *

* * *

Although the defendant's obstruction of the plaintiff's access to sunlight appears to fall within the Restatement's broad concept of a private nuisance as a nontrespassory invasion of another's interest in the private use and enjoyment of land, the defendant asserts that he has a right to develop his property in compliance with statutes, ordinances and private covenants without regard to the effect of such development upon the plaintiff's access to sunlight. In essence, the defendant is asking this court to hold that the private nuisance doctrine is not applicable in the instant case and that his right to develop his land is a right which is *per se* superior to his neighbor's interest in access to sunlight. This position is expressed in the maxim "cujus est solum, ejus est usque ad coelum et ad infernos," that is, the owner of land owns up to the sky and down to the center of the earth. The rights of the surface owner are, however, not unlimited. *U.S. v. Causby*, 328 U.S. 256, 260–1, 66 S.Ct. 1062, 1065, 90 L.Ed. 1206 (1946). See also 114.03, Stats.1979–80.

The defendant is not completely correct in asserting that the common law did not protect a landowner's access to sunlight across adjoining property. At English common law a landowner could acquire a right to receive sunlight across adjoining land by both express agreement and under the judge-made doctrine of "ancient lights." Under the doctrine of ancient lights if the landowner had received sunlight across adjoining property for a specified period of time, the landowner was entitled to continue to receive unobstructed access to sunlight across the adjoining property. Under the doctrine the landowner acquired a negative prescriptive easement and could prevent the adjoining landowner from obstructing access to light.

Although American courts have not been as receptive to protecting a landowner's access to sunlight as the English courts, American courts have afforded some protection to a landowner's interest in access to sunlight. American courts honor express easements to sunlight. American courts initially enforced the English common law doctrine of ancient lights, but later every state which considered the doctrine repudiated it as inconsistent with the needs of a developing country. Indeed, for just that reason this court concluded that an easement to light and air over adjacent property could not be created or acquired by prescription and has been unwilling to recognize such an easement by implication. *Depner v. United States National Bank*, 202 Wis. 405, 408, 232 N.W. 851 (1930); *Miller v. Hoeschler*, 126 Wis. 263, 268–69, 105 N.W. 790 (1905).

Many jurisdictions in this country have protected a landowner from malicious obstruction of access to light (the spite fence cases) under the common law private nuisance doctrine. If an activity is motivated by malice it lacks utility and the harm it causes others outweighs any social values. VI–A Law of Property sec. 28.28, p. 79 (1954) This court was reluctant to protect a landowner's interest in sunlight even against a spite fence, only to be overruled by the legislature. Shortly after this court upheld a landowner's right to erect a useless and unsightly sixteen-foot spite fence four feet from his neighbor's windows, *Metzger v. Hochrein*, 107 Wis. 267, 83 N.W. 308 (1900), the legislature enacted a law specifically defining a spite fence as an actionable private nuisance. Thus a landowner's interest in sunlight has been protected in this country by common law private nuisance law at least in the narrow context of the modern American rule invalidating spite fences. See, *e.g., Sundowner, Inc. v. King*, 95 Idaho 367, 509 P.2d 785 (1973); Restatement (Second) of Torts, sec. 829 (1977).

This court's reluctance in the nineteenth and early part of the twentieth century to provide broader protection for a landowner's access to sunlight was premised on three policy considerations. First, the right of landowners to use their property as they wished, as long as they did not cause physical damage to a neighbor, was jealously guarded. *Metzger v. Hochrein*, 107 Wis. 267, 272, 83 N.W. 308 (1900).

Second, sunlight was valued only for aesthetic enjoyment or as illumination. Since artificial light could be used for illumination, loss of sunlight was at most a personal annoyance which was given little, if any, weight by society.

Third, society had a significant interest in not restricting or impeding land development. *Dillman v. Hoffman*, 38 Wis. 559, 574 (1875). This court repeatedly emphasized that in the growth period of the nineteenth and early twentieth centuries change is to be expected and is essential to property and that recognition of a right to sunlight would hinder property development.

* * *

Considering these three policies, this court concluded that in the absence of an express agreement granting access to sunlight, a landowner's obstruction of another's access to sunlight was not actionable. *Miller v. Hoeschler, supra*, 126 Wis. at 271, 105 N.W. 790; *Depner v. United States National Bank, supra*, 202 Wis. at 410, 232 N.W. 851. These three policies are no longer fully accepted or applicable. They reflect factual circumstances and social priorities that are now obsolete.

First, society has increasingly regulated the use of land by the landowner for the general welfare. *Euclid v. Ambler Realty Co.*, 272 U.S. 365, 47 S.Ct. 114, 71 L.Ed. 303 (1926); *Just v. Marinette*, 56 Wis.2d 7, 201 N.W.2d 761 (1972).

Second, access to sunlight has taken on a new significance in recent years. In this case the plaintiff seeks to protect access to sunlight, not for aesthetic reasons or as a source of illumination but as a source of energy. Access to sunlight as an energy source is of significance both to the landowner who invests in solar collectors and to a society which has an interest in developing alternative sources of energy.

Third, the policy of favoring unhindered private development in an expanding economy is no longer in harmony with the realities of our society. *State v. Deetz*, 66 Wis.2d 1, 224 N.W.2d 407 (1974). The need for easy and rapid development is not as great today as it once was, while our perception of the value of sunlight as a source of energy has increased significantly.

Courts should not implement obsolete policies that have lost their vigor over the course of the years. The law of private nuisance is better suited to resolve landowners' disputes about property development in the 1980's than is a rigid rule which does not recognize a landowner's interest in access to sunlight. As we said in *Ballstadt v. Pagel*, 202 Wis. 484, 489, 232 N.W. 862 (1930), "What is regarded in law as constituting a nuisance in modern times would no doubt have been tolerated without question in former times." We read *State v. Deetz*, 66 Wis.2d 1, 224 N.W.2d 407 (1974), as an endorsement of the application of common law nuisance to situations involving the conflicting interests of landowners and as rejecting *per se* exclusions to the nuisance law reasonable use doctrine.

* * *

We therefore hold that private nuisance law, that is, the reasonable use doctrine as set forth in the Restatement, is applicable to the instant case. Recognition of a nuisance claim for unreasonable obstruction of access to sunlight will not prevent land development or unduly hinder the use of adjoining land. It will promote the reasonable use and enjoyment of land in a manner suitable to the 1980's. That obstruction of access to light might be found to constitute a nuisance in certain circumstances does not mean that it will be or must be found to constitute a nuisance under all circumstances. The result in each case depends on whether the conduct complained of is unreasonable.

Accordingly we hold that the plaintiff in this case has stated a claim under which relief can be granted. Nonetheless we do not determine whether the plaintiff in this case is entitled to relief. In order to be entitled to relief the plaintiff must prove the elements required to establish actionable nuisance, and the conduct of the defendant herein must be judged by the reasonable use doctrine.

The defendant asserts that even if we hold that the private nuisance doctrine applies to obstruction of access to sunlight across adjoining land, the circuit court's granting of summary judgment should be affirmed.

Although the memorandum decision of the circuit court in the instant case is unclear, it appears that the circuit court recognized that the common law private nuisance doctrine was applicable but concluded that defendant's conduct was not unreasonable. The circuit court apparently attempted to balance the utility of the defendant's conduct with the gravity of the harm. Sec. 826, Restatement (Second) of Torts (1977). The defendant urges us to accept the circuit court's balance as adequate. We decline to do so.

The circuit court concluded that because the defendant's proposed house was in conformity with zoning regulations, building codes and deed restrictions, the defendant's use of the land was reasonable. This court has concluded that a landowner's compliance with zoning laws does not automatically bar a nuisance claim. Compliance with the law "is not the controlling factor, though it is, of course, entitled to some weight." *Bie v. Ingersoll*, 27 Wis.2d 490, 495, 135 N.W.2d 250 (1965). The circuit court also concluded that the plaintiff could have avoided any harm by locating his own house in a better place. Again, plaintiff's ability to avoid the harm is a relevant but not a conclusive factor. See secs. 826, 827, 828, Restatement (Second) of Torts (1977).

* * *

The judgment of the circuit court is reversed and the cause remanded for proceedings not inconsistent with this opinion.

CECI, J., not participating.

CALLOW, J. dissents.

Notes

1. In Maykut and Prah, the zoning laws applied generally to stipulate what land uses are appropriate in each district. The legislators adopting the

zoning did not intend to preempt individual nuisance actions where land uses authorized under the law had extreme effects on nearby properties. This might not always be the situation, especially where the zoning legislation appears to create an exclusive remedy for the matter regulated, but this is not normally the case.

2. Green v. Castle Concrete Co., 181 Colo. 309, 509 P.2d 588 (1973) held that where the zoning laws permit an activity, that activity cannot then be considered a public nuisance. A judicial finding that a land use constituted a public nuisance would be tantamount to overruling the clear intentions of the legislature that, as a general matter, the use is in the public interest, not inimical to it.

3. The influence of nuisance law in land use regulation is ubiquitous. In Lucas v. South Carolina Coastal Council, 505 U.S. 1003, 112 S.Ct. 2886, 120 L.Ed.2d 798 (1992), for example, the U.S. Supreme Court held that a land use regulation that prevents all economically beneficial uses of the land is a *per se* regulatory taking and requires the payment of just compensation by the regulator under the Fifth Amendment takings clause. The Court added, however, that the regulation is not a taking if the land use proscribed by the regulation can be enjoined under nuisance law or other background principles of state property law.

4. Zoning ordinances typically allow land uses that are in place at the time of the law's adoption to continue as legal nonconforming uses. Zoning laws state, however, that some uses, such as junkyards, unsightly billboards, and particularly noxious activities, must be terminated immediately or within a relatively short period. In this, the difference between a nuisance *per se* and nuisance *per accidens* is observable. *Per se* activities are judicially declared to be immoral or extra-hazardous, as are land uses that must be terminated by zoning. Nuisances *per accidens* must be proved by the plaintiff to be nuisances in fact. Such land uses are more likely to be called nonconforming uses under zoning law and allowed to continue, because of the injustice that would be done to the owner who had invested in the building before it was proscribed by the zoning ordinance.

5. Judicial policies that are evident in decisions regarding nuisances *per accidens*—nuisances in fact—are mirrored in variance provisions of zoning ordinances. Variances may be awarded by local zoning boards to property owners when they can show that the application of the zoning to their individual lot will create a hardship. A variance might be given, for example, to allow a property owner to build closer to a side yard lot line, in violation of a requirement found in the zoning ordinance, upon a showing that a stream or rock outcropping on the other side of the yard would prevent the owner from building a normal sized home on the property. Under many zoning laws, the zoning board is required to balance the hardship the zoning creates for the regulated owner against the adverse impact of the proposed building on the neighborhood, mimicking the balancing test in nuisance law used by the judiciary.

6. Nuisance law has had to adapt to changing times. Large-scale development and intense industrial uses have caused courts to rethink basic principles. When an entire subdivision moved to the nuisance (a stockyard), the court adjusted nuisance doctrine by allowing the subdivision to continue

and grow, but granting substantial damages to the stockyard to cover the cost of relocation. See Spur Industries, Inc. v. Del E. Webb Development Co., 108 Ariz. 178, 494 P.2d 700 (1972). The limitations of private nuisance actions as a solution to societal problems are apparent in Spur Industries. A comprehensive land use plan and zoning law for the jurisdiction would have prevented the costs of relocation, loss of business, and inflated subdivision home prices.

7. These limitations are equally evident in Boomer v. Atlantic Cement Co., Inc., 26 N.Y.2d 219, 309 N.Y.S.2d 312, 257 N.E.2d 870 (1970). In Boomer, the New York Court of Appeals refused to enjoin the operations of a large cement plant, because of its social utility and the economic hardship to its investors and employees, awarding damages instead to the individual plaintiffs who were adjacent landowners. Previous caselaw had held that an injunction was the proper remedy for protecting the adjacent owners. See Hulbert v. California Portland Cement Co., 161 Cal. 239, 118 P. 928 (1911), where local farmers brought a nuisance action against a cement factory and the court awarded an injunction, permanently closing the facility.

The Boomer case was a particularly complex matter for the court. The cement company had unilaterally appropriated an affirmative easement on the neighbors' property for the purpose of depositing cement dust. In effect, its operations imposed a "servitude" on the plaintiffs' land. By awarding damages for the imposed servitude, the court was placed in the awkward position of awarding damages for the involuntary taking of a property interest of the plaintiffs for a private purpose. The Fifth Amendment of the U.S. Constitution allows private property interests to be taken, but only for a public purpose by a public entity accompanied by an award of just compensation. Despite this awkwardness, the court could find no other way of balancing the equities between the parties in the absence of comprehensive zoning in the jurisdiction or other public regulations. Coincidentally, the Clean Air Act, based on the power of Congress to regulate interstate commerce, was adopted at the same time that Boomer was decided.

SECTION 6. SERVITUDES: EASEMENTS AND COVENANTS

A. INTRODUCTION

Nuisance law is intertwined with the law of servitudes. In a nuisance case, the aggrieved plaintiff claims that the offending land use imposes a burden on the plaintiff's property, adversely affecting its use and enjoyment. In Boomer, the burden was physical: discrete contaminants deposited on the land. In Clark and Mitchell, the burden was physical in a sense, since the odors of pig farming physically invaded the property. Under the law of servitudes (easements and covenants), we learn that burdens can be placed on private property but that normally those benefiting from these burdens have to purchase such rights from the burdened owners. O can convey to A an affirmative easement to cross O's land to gain access to a public road. Similarly, O can sell a restrictive covenant to A that limits the use of O's property to single-family housing.

Notice how this happens. A approaches O and asks to purchase an access easement or restrictive covenant from O. Lawyers are consulted. The seller's attorney, acting for O, draws up a deed conveying a property right to A. A's lawyer reviews the document and, if all goes well, a deed conveying the servitude is executed by O and filed in the land records, usually in the county where the land is located. All subsequent purchasers of O's land are then on record notice that O's land is burdened by an obligation to A, who is benefited by the limitation on O's parcel.

If this transaction is done correctly, the burden and benefit of the servitude "run with the land." This means that the agreement is not simply a personal covenant between O and A (which of course it is), but also a real covenant affixed to the parcels, the consequences of which "run" to subsequent owners of the benefited and burdened lands.

For the purposes of land use law as it is currently practiced, it is sufficient to understand the concepts and techniques that explain how servitudes gave rise to certain land use regulations and how servitudes function together with public regulations to control land uses in certain places. Land use regulations are public rules that limit private land use for the benefit of the community. Servitudes are private rules that limit the use of privately held land for the benefit of the owners of designated parcels of land, and only those owners. Where land use laws stop, servitudes can pick up to meet the needs of modern landowners, most frequently parcel owners in residential subdivisions.

Does zoning trump servitudes? What happens when a neighbor is carefully protected by restrictive covenants but the neighborhood is drastically altered because of zoning changes?

WEST ALAMEDA HEIGHTS HOMEOWNERS ASS'N v. BOARD OF COUNTY COMMISSIONERS OF JEFFERSON COUNTY

Supreme Court of Colorado, 1969.
169 Colo. 491, 458 P.2d 253.

[This was a class action by the homeowners association and certain individuals to enjoin the construction of two large shopping facilities on the property in question by Woolworth and Safeway. The covenants restricted the use of the land to residential, and the trial court declared the covenants null and void. The subdivision was a large one of over 350 lots, only 80 to 85 of which were undeveloped. The only commercial uses were a service station and a garden center located on land originally reserved in the plat for commercial use. Apartments were on other land set aside for commercial purposes. The proposed shopping facilities would be on residential land as restricted by the covenants. The action was precipitated by an application by George Newton, the original developer, to re-zone part of the blocks retained by him which front on a four-lane highway. Outside of the subdivision and close by, there had been extensive commercial development. The trial court invalidated the covenants on the basis that the character of the area had changed and that the subject land was not suitable for residential use and thus enforcement of the covenants would not be equitable.]

DAY, JUSTICE

* * *

The pertinent rule of law applicable to this case is most recently set out in *Zavislak v. Shipman*, 147 Colo. 184, 362 P.2d 1053, wherein this court adopted the language of *McArthur v. Hood Rubber Co.*, 221 Mass. 372, 109 N.E. 162, as follows:

> " ' * * * When the purpose for which the restriction was imposed has come to an end, and where the use of the tract of land for whose benefit it was established has so utterly changed that no party to the bill could be heard to enforce it in equity or would suffer any damage by its violation, * * * a proper case is made out for equitable relief. * * * ' "

Parties plaintiffs and defendants all rely on our pronouncement in *Zavislak*. The court, in striking down the covenants, attempted to apply the same rule of law. We hold, however, that the court misconceived and misapplied the rule to changes and developments outside of and beyond the subdivision itself. This is made evident by the court's reference to the changed traffic patterns on Wadsworth and Alameda and the development of Villa Italia Shopping Center and other developments east of the Alameda and Wadsworth intersection.

The true test here, however, as to whether the purpose of the restrictions has come to an end, is the development of the subdivision which is the subject of the covenants subsequent to their creation. Thus the courts look to whether the original purposes of insuring maintenance of residential character for the subdivision has been abandoned or changed by acquiescence or passiveness of the subdivision residents.

Newton, in planning the property with the restrictions which he imposed, intended to insure the maintenance of the residential character for the subdivision. That purpose has continued to the present time, and the effect of it is demonstrated by what has happened to land outside of its perimeter over which the West Alameda Heights residents had no control. It is undisputed that in the subdivision wherein the covenants did control no change of the use contemplated when the plat was filed has occurred. Only the property originally platted for use of commercial enterprises thereon has been occupied as such.

Another test announced in the *Zavislak* case is whether the parties would suffer any damage by the removal of the covenant. Touching on this phase the testimony of the individual plaintiffs was that their property would be subject to substantial decrease in value. One of plaintiffs' witnesses—a professional land planner—depicted the foreseeable increase in traffic to and from the proposed shopping facility with concomitant increase in noise, fumes, and hazard to children. The Traffic and Safety Engineer for Jefferson County stated that although he probably could control increased traffic through the residential area by the use of traffic signals and one-way streets, he candidly admitted that such a traffic pattern would inconvenience the homeowners as much as it might deter shoppers from driving through the area. There was testimony as to the present pleasant aspects of the neighborhood, undisturbed by the commercial activity beyond the borders.

Contrariwise, the defendants did not prove that the purpose of the protective covenants had come to an end; that the land use within the tract had changed from what it was intended to be at the time the plat was filed; and that no person would suffer any damage by its violation. The evidence therefore is contrary to the court's finding that plaintiffs will suffer no damage from commercial use of the subject property.

Cases are numerous from other jurisdictions wherein covenants have been sought to be removed because subject lands would be more valuable for commercial than for residential purposes, and wherein there were conditions such as the presence of commercial uses nearby, heavy street traffic on the perimeter of the tract, and some commercial property within a primarily residential subdivision. But the weight of authority supports the view that *changes outside* of the tract will not warrant the lifting of restrictive covenants affecting property within the subdivision if the covenants are still a benefit to the owners of the property under the restrictions. *Robertson v. Nichols*, 92 Cal.App.2d 201, 206 P.2d 898; *Batman v. Creighton*, 101 So.2d 587 (Fla.App.); *Cawthon v. Anderson*, 211 Ga. 77, 84 S.E.2d 66; *Redfern Lawns Civic Ass'n, et al. v. Currie Pontiac Co.*, 328 Mich. 463, 44 N.W.2d 8; *Weinstein v. Swartz*, 3 N.J. 80, 68 A.2d 865; *Chuba v. Glasgow*, 61 N.M. 302, 299 P.2d 774; *Frey v. Poynor*, 369 P.2d 168 (Okla.); *Pitts v. Brown*, 215 S.C. 122, 54 S.E.2d 538; *Bullock v. Steinmil Realty, Inc.*, 1 Misc.2d 46, 145 N.Y.S.2d 331, aff'd 3 A.D.2d 806, 161 N.Y.S.2d 602.

Normal growth and change and the possibility of encroachment of commercial uses, we can infer, were contemplated when the covenants and the master plan of development were created by the original owner and platter. There would be no need for the covenants to protect the subdivisions from inroads of commercial expansion if it were not expected that such might take place. As long as the original purpose of the covenants can still be accomplished and substantial benefit will inure to the restricted area by their enforcement, the covenants stand even though the subject property has a greater value if used for other purposes. See 4 A.L.R.2d 1111.

A comment in *Cowling v. Colligan*, 158 Tex. 458, 312 S.W.2d 943, appeals to us:

> "The reasoning of the courts is that if because of changed conditions outside the restricted area one lot or tract were permitted to drop from under the protective cover of residential-only restrictions, the owner of the adjoining lot would then have an equal claim on the conscience of the court, and, in due course, all other lots would fall

like tenpins, thus circumventing and nullifying the restriction and destroying the essentially residential character of the entire area."

In the case of protective covenants, it has sometimes been held that changes within the affected area may result in modification or removal of the covenant because the changes were within the control of those entitled to enforce the covenant. In other words, the doctrines of abandonment, estoppel and waiver are applicable. *See Thodos v. Shirk*, 248 Iowa 172, 79 N.W.2d 733; *Mechling v. Dawson*, 234 Ky. 318, 28 S.W.2d 18; *Greer v. Bornstein*, 246 Ky. 286, 54 S.W.2d 927; *Tull v. Doctors Bldg. Inc.*, 255 N.C. 23, 120 S.E.2d 817. However, as to changes in conditions occurring outside the area restricted, the parties affected have no control whatever, and the doctrines of waiver, abandonment and estoppel are not applicable. Here, the problem presents itself as to whether the outside conditions affect the entire subdivision in a way that the restrictive purposes of the protective covenants would be defeated. As stated in *Thodos v. Shirk*, *supra*:

> "In both cases the factual situation largely governs as to whether or not equity will refuse to enforce the restrictions for the reason that by so doing the result would be oppressive and inequitable without any appreciable value to other property in the restricted area. It has been said that in order for this equitable defense of change of conditions to arise, there must be a change in the character of the surrounding neighborhood sufficient to make it impossible any longer to secure in substantial degree the benefits sought to be realized through the performance of the building restriction."

The construction of Villa Italia Shopping Center and of other commercial properties outside of West Alameda Heights, but in close proximity to it, have not changed the residential character of the subdivision. If the changed conditions outside the tract have made the particular property held by the owner since the original platting less desirable for residential use than it previously was, this is not to say that the whole tract has been made unfit for residential use. On the contrary, the evidence shows that the subdivision is a residential area of high quality, with expensive homes and quiet streets. The construction of commercial facilities nearby are all the more reason why the covenants for West Alameda Heights must be strictly enforced. The covenants have no meaning if external forces and pressures result in their removal.

The judgment is reversed and the cause remanded to the trial court with directions to enter a permanent injunction as prayed for in the complaint.

Notes

1. In Redfern Lawns Civic Ass'n v. Currie Pontiac Co., 328 Mich. 463, 44 N.W.2d 8 (1950), cited in the principal case, the Michigan court said: "The only equitable consideration in the case at bar appears to be the undesirability of using the lots in question for resident purposes. On this point it may be observed that there must of necessity be a dividing line

somewhere. The original subdividers made no provision for possible business lots along Grand River avenue. It is inevitable that all lots on the fringe of a residential district may, with the changes of the surrounding neighborhood, become a buffer between the residential area and a business or commercial area. It is one of the factors inherent in considering the nature and value of such property. To lift the restriction under consideration here on the lots in question would only cut down this desirable residential area and create another buffer area. To permit the dividing line to be moved in the case at bar thereby creating another buffer district, now composed of both residences and vacant property, does not present sufficiently strong equitable considerations."

2. There have been a good many of these change of character cases over the years, and the problem usually comes from the effect of the commercialization of nearby property on border or buffer lots (as illustrated by the principal case). What if reasonable minds might differ on whether a change in character has occurred? In Semachko v. Hopko, 35 Ohio App.2d 205, 301 N.E.2d 560 (1973), the court stated that "reasonable minds can come to different conclusions whether there was a substantial change in the character of the neighborhood * * * so as to nullify the deed restrictions * * *. Under such circumstances, a court of equity will not enforce such restriction." Do you agree? In Albino v. Pacific First Fed. Sav. and Loan Ass'n, 257 Or. 473, 479 P.2d 760 (1971), the Oregon court said that in order to refuse to enforce the restrictions "the effect of the change upon the restricted area" must be "such as to 'clearly neutralize the benefits of the restrictions to the point of defeating the object and purpose of the covenant' "and that it is not enough that because of external changes the restricted residential area may now be more valuable for commercial purposes. See also Realvest Corp. v. Lane County, 196 Or.App. 109, 100 P.3d 1109 (2004). In Inabinet v. Booe, 262 S.C. 81, 202 S.E.2d 643 (1974), it was stated that the changes must be "so radical as to practically destroy the essential objectives and purposes of the agreement." See similarly, Murphey v. Gray, 84 Ariz. 299, 327 P.2d 751 (1958); Eilers v. Alewel, 393 S.W.2d 584 (Mo.1965); and Paschen v. Pashkow, 63 Ill.App.2d 56, 211 N.E.2d 576 (1965).

3. Equitable defenses can be employed in modification or termination cases, such as acquiescence, waiver and laches. In Underwood v. Webb, 544 S.W.2d 187 (Tex.Civ.App.1976), a violation on two lots in a 493 lot development was considered insufficient to eliminate the restriction. In Hargroder v. City of Eunice, 341 So.2d 463 (La.App.1976), there was no waiver of the limitation to residential use by the erection of numerous storage sheds in violation of the restriction. On the other hand, if landowners stand by for an unreasonable length of time while erection of the violating structure takes place, laches may preclude them from suing. Weinstein v. Tariff, 356 Mass. 738, 255 N.E.2d 595 (1970). One may also lose claim to title in property by laches when "unjustifiably" delaying prosecution of claim to title. Hovey v. Geraigery, 2004 WL 2782555 (Mass.Land Ct.). Estoppel may also apply, as it did in Kelly v. Lovejoy, 172 Mont. 516, 565 P.2d 321 (1977), where the landowners purchased their land knowing that their neighbors were keeping horses in violation of the restrictions. (It was also deemed that they acquiesced in the horses being there.)

B. COMMON INTEREST COMMUNITIES

A reference to common interest communities explains further how zoning has replaced servitudes and how, at the same time, servitudes supplement land use rules. Common interest communities are extremely popular in today's market and much of the country's new housing falls into this category. The terms for such communities include cooperatives, condominiums, townhouse communities, planned communities, new-towns, traditional neighborhood developments, or homeowner associations.

Prior to the advent of zoning in the 1920s, servitudes provided developers an effective method for creating high quality residential neighborhoods. The developer would buy a large parcel of land, subdivide it into lots, and sell those lots to individuals for the purpose of building homes. To control the quality of the subdivision, each deed would contain a set of covenants prescribing certain land use practices (each house is to be set back from the street by twenty feet, for example) and proscribing certain land uses (the lot is restricted to the construction of a single-family house and a garage).

Under zoning, this type of private land use restriction was no longer as necessary. Single-family zoning districts prevent the use of the land for any other purpose and require that houses be set back from the street a certain distance. Notwithstanding these public restrictions, a developer might want to develop a more exclusive community, one with deeper setbacks or larger lots, for example, or one that is governed by design standards to create a certain look or feel that is not achieved by the typical zoning ordinance. These more restrictive standards can be imposed by servitudes: covenants placed in the original deeds restricting homebuilding within thirty-five feet of the street, mandating larger lots than required by zoning, and requiring the use of a certain style of architecture.

As important, developers may want to build common facilities, such as a clubhouse, swimming pool, and tennis courts, and make them available to all homeowners in the subdivision. This will require revenue for operations and upkeep which can be secured by requiring the purchasers of individual lots to join an association created by the developer and to pay annual dues established by the association's board of directors. Many modern subdivisions are created in which lot owners own a common property interest in such facilities, enjoy easements to access them, and are required to pay dues to sustain them. All of these obligations are secured by covenants and affirmative easements included in their deeds, rather than through zoning or supplemental land use laws.

In common interest communities, the deeds contain or refer to a declaration of covenants and restrictions that burden and benefit each lot or unit owner reciprocally. If A purchases a lot from O, the developer, A's lot or unit is both a servient and dominant parcel, limited and enhanced by the declaration. A parallel expression exists in zoning law;

the Supreme Court found zoning constitutional, in part, because it exhibits "reciprocity of advantage." The zoning laws of a community burden and benefit all landowners. Land use restrictions limit what can be done by individual owners so that a secure, attractive, equitable, economically sound, and environmentally livable community can be created.

The early common law of servitudes created several obstacles to the creation of common interest communities governed by declarations of covenants and restrictions. Often the declaration was not contained in a particular purchaser's deed but recorded in the land records regarding the subdivision or evident by observing a common development scheme as the community was built out. In these cases, are the parcel owners in privity of estate? When lot owners are required to pay a monthly fee to the homeowners association to cover operations and capital costs, how does that burden touch and concern the land? Are affirmative burdens like this—the duty to pay—enforceable at all under the common law?

In the following case the issue was whether an early homeowners association could enforce the requirement that lot owners pay dues.

NEPONSIT PROPERTY OWNERS' ASS'N v. EMIGRANT INDUSTRIAL SAV. BANK

Court of Appeals of New York, 1938.
278 N.Y. 248, 15 N.E.2d 793, 118 A.L.R. 973.

LEHMAN, J.

* * *

It appears that in January, 1911, Neponsit Realty Company, as owner of a tract of land in Queens County, caused to be filed in the office of the clerk of the county a map of the land. The tract was developed for a strictly residential community, and Neponsit Realty Company conveyed lots in the tract to purchasers, describing such lots by reference to the filed map and to roads and streets shown thereon. In 1917, Neponsit Realty Company conveyed the land now owned by the defendant to Robert Oldner Deyer and his wife by deed which contained the covenant upon which the plaintiff's cause of action is based.

That covenant provides:

> "And the party of the second part for the party of the second part and the heirs, successors and assigns of the party of the second part further covenants that the property conveyed by this deed shall be subject to an annual charge in such an amount as will be fixed by the party of the first part, its successors and assigns, not, however exceeding in any year the sum of four ($4.00) Dollars per lot 20 X 100 feet. The assigns of the party of the first part may include a Property Owners' Association which may hereafter be organized for the purposes referred to in this paragraph, and in case such association is organized the sums in this paragraph provided for shall be

> payable to such association. The party of the second part for the party of the second part and the heirs, successors and assigns of the party of the second part covenants that they will pay this charge to the party of the first part, its successors and assigns on the first day of May in each and every year, and further covenants that said charge shall on said date in each year become a lien on the land and shall continue to be such lien until fully paid. Such charge shall be payable to the party of the first part or its successors or assigns, and shall be devoted to the maintenance of the roads, paths, parks, beach, sewers and such other public purposes as shall from time to time be determined by the party of the first part, its successors or assigns. And the party of the second part by the acceptance of this deed hereby expressly vests in the party of the first part, its successors and assigns, the right and power to bring all actions against the owner of the premises hereby conveyed or any part thereof for the collection of such charge and to enforce the aforesaid lien therefor.
>
> These covenants shall run with the land and shall be construed as real covenants running with the land until January 31st, 1940, when they shall cease and determine."

Every subsequent deed of conveyance of the property in the defendant's chain of title, including the deed from the referee to the defendant, contained, as we have said, a provision that they were made subject to covenants and restrictions of former deeds of record.

There can be no doubt that Neponsit Realty Company intended that the covenant should run with the land and should be enforceable by a property owners association against every owner of property in the residential tract which the realty company was then developing. The language of the covenant admits of no other construction. Regardless of the intention of the parties, a covenant will run with the land and will be enforceable against a subsequent purchaser of the land at the suit of one who claims the benefit of the covenant, only if the covenant complies with certain legal requirements. These requirements rest upon ancient rules and precedents. The age-old essentials of a real covenant, aside from the form of the covenant, may be summarily formulated as follows: (1) it must appear that grantor and grantee intended that the covenant should run with the land; (2) it must appear that the covenant is one "touching" or "concerning" the land with which it runs; (3) it must appear that there is "privity of estate" between the promisee or party claiming the benefit of the covenant and the right to enforce it, and the promisor or party who rests under the burden of the covenant. Clark on Covenants and Interests Running with Land, p. 74. Although the deeds "contained a provision to the effect that the covenants ran with the land, such provision in the absence of the other legal requirements is insufficient to accomplish such a purpose." *Morgan Lake Co. v. New York, N.H. & H.R.R. Co.*, 262 N.Y. 234, 238, 186 N.E. 685, 686. In his opinion in that case, Judge Crane posed but found it unnecessary to decide many of the questions which the court must consider in this case.

The covenant in this case is * * * an affirmative covenant to pay money for use in connection with, but not upon, the land which it is said is subject to the burden of the covenant. Does such a covenant "touch" or "concern" the land? These terms are not part of a statutory definition, a limitation placed by the State upon the power of the courts to enforce covenants *intended* to run with the land by the parties who entered into the covenants. Rather they are words used by courts in England in old cases to describe a limitation which the courts themselves created or to formulate a test which the courts have devised and which the courts voluntarily apply. Cf. Spencer's Case, Coke, vol. 3, part 5, 16a; *Mayor of Congleton v. Pattison*, 10 East 130. In truth such a description or test so formulated is too vague to be of much assistance and judges and academic scholars alike have struggled, not with entire success, to formulate a test at once more satisfactory and more accurate. * * *

* * * It has been often said that a covenant to pay a sum of money is a personal affirmative covenant which usually does not concern or touch the land. Such statements are based upon English decisions which hold in effect that only covenants, which compel the covenanter to submit to some *restriction on the use* of his property, touch or concern the land, and that the burden of a covenant which requires the covenanter to do an affirmative act, even on his own land, for the benefit of the owner of a "dominant" estate, does not run with his land. *Miller v. Clary*, 210 N.Y. 127, 103 N.E. 1114, L.R.A.1918E, 222, Ann.Cas.1915B, 872. In that case the court pointed out that in many jurisdictions of this country the narrow English rule has been criticized and a more liberal and flexible rule has been substituted. In this State the courts have not gone so far. We have not abandoned the historic distinction drawn by the English courts. * * * *Guaranty Trust Co. of New York v. New York & Queens County Ry. Co.*, 253 N.Y. 190, 204, 170 N.E. 887, 892, opinion by Cardozo, Ch. J.

Both in that case and in the case of Miller v. Clary, *supra*, the court pointed out that there were some exceptions or limitations in the application of the general rule. Some promises to pay money have been enforced, as covenants running with the land, against subsequent holders of the land who took with notice of the covenant. Cf. *Greenfarb v. R.S.K. Realty Corp.*, 256 N.Y. 130, 175 N.E. 649; *Morgan Lake Co. v. New York, N.H. & H.R.R. Co.*, *supra*. It may be difficult to classify these exceptions or to formulate a test of whether a particular covenant to pay money or to perform some other act falls within the general rule that ordinarily an affirmative covenant is a personal and not a real covenant, or falls outside the limitations placed upon the general rule. At least it must "touch" or "concern" the land in a substantial degree, and though it may be inexpedient and perhaps impossible to formulate a rigid test or definition which will be entirely satisfactory or which can be applied mechanically in all cases, we should at least be able to state the problem and find a reasonable method of approach to it. It has been suggested that a covenant which runs with the land must affect the legal relations—the advantages and the burdens—of the parties to the covenant, as owners of particular parcels of land and not merely as members of the community in general, such as taxpayers or owners of other land. Clark, op. cit. p. 76, Cf. Professor Bigelow's article on The Contents of Covenants in Leases, 12 Mich.L.Rev. 639; 30 Law Quarterly Review, 319. That method of approach has the merit of realism. The test is based on the effect of the covenant rather than on technical distinctions. Does the covenant impose, on the one hand, a burden upon an interest in land, which on the other hand increases the value of a different interest in the same or related land?

Even though we accept that approach and test, it still remains true that whether a particular covenant is sufficiently connected with the use of land to run with the land, must be in many cases a question of degree. A promise to pay for something to be done in connection with the promisor's land does not differ essentially from a promise by the promisor to do the thing himself, and both promises constitute, in a substantial sense, a restriction upon the owner's right to use the land, and a burden upon the legal interest of the owner. On the other hand, a covenant to perform or pay for the performance of an affirmative act disconnected with the use of the land cannot ordinarily touch or concern the land in any substantial degree. Thus, unless we exalt technical form over substance, the distinction between covenants which run with land and covenants which are personal, must depend upon the effect of the covenant on the legal rights which otherwise would flow from ownership of land and which are connected with the land. The problem then is: Does the covenant in purpose and effect substantially alter these rights?

* * *

Looking at the problem presented in this case from the same point of view and stressing the intent and substantial effect of the covenant rather than its form, it seems clear that the covenant may properly be said to touch and concern the land of the defendant and its burden should run with the land. True, it calls for payment of a sum of money to be expended for "public purposes" upon land other than the land conveyed by Neponsit Realty Company to plaintiff's predecessor in title. By that conveyance the grantee, however, obtained not only title to particular lots, but an easement or right of common enjoyment with other property owners in roads, beaches, public parks or spaces and improvements in the same tract. For full enjoyment in common by the defendant and other property owners of these easements or rights, the roads and public places must be maintained. In order that the burden of maintaining public improvements should rest upon the land benefitted by the improvements, the grantor exacted from the grantee of the land with its appurtenant easement or right of enjoyment a covenant that the burden of paying the cost should be inseparably attached to the land which enjoys the benefit. It is plain that any distinction or definition which would exclude such a covenant from the classification of covenants which "touch" or "concern" the land would be based on form and not on substance.

Another difficulty remains. Though between the grantor and the grantee there was privity of estate, the covenant provides that its benefit shall run to the assigns of the grantor who "may include a Property Owners' Association which may hereafter be organized for the purposes referred to in this paragraph." The plaintiff has been organized to receive the sums payable by the property owners and to expend them for the benefit of such owners. Various definitions have been formulated of "privity of estate" in connection with covenants that run with the land, but none of such definitions seems to cover the relationship between the plaintiff and the defendant in this case. The plaintiff has not succeeded to the ownership of any property of the grantor. It does not appear that it ever had title to the streets or public places upon which charges which are payable to it must be expended. It does not appear that it owns any other property in the residential tract to which any easement or right of enjoyment in such property is appurtenant. It is created solely to act as the assignee of the benefit of the covenant, and it has no interest of its own in the enforcement of the covenant.

* * *

The corporate plaintiff has been formed as a convenient instrument by which the property owners may advance their common interests. We do not ignore the corporate form when we recognize that the Neponsit Property Owners Association, Inc., is acting as the agent or representative of the Neponsit property owners. * * * Only blind adherence to an ancient formula devised to meet entirely different conditions could constrain the court to hold that a corporation formed as a medium for the enjoyment of common rights of property owners owns no property which would benefit by enforcement of common rights and has no cause of action in equity to enforce the covenant upon which such common rights depend. Every reason which in other circumstances may justify the ancient formula should not be applied in this case. In substance if not in form the covenant is a restrictive covenant which touches and concerns the defendant's land, and in substance, if not in form, there is privity of estate between the plaintiff and the defendant.

* * *

The order should be affirmed, with costs, and the certified questions answered in the affirmative. * * *

Notes

1. Compare the principal case with Phillips v. Smith, 240 Iowa 863, 38 N.W.2d 87 (1949), where a covenant in deeds to summer resort lots to pay $6.00 a year to the owner of Bluff Park Resort was said to run with the land. But the covenant was held to be "dependent" upon the carrying out of the duty of the owner to maintain the resort area. The owner of Bluff Park Resort allowed his horses and pigs to roam at will through the development and did little to maintain it. The action to establish and foreclose liens for the annual assessment failed. In Tentindo v. Locke Lake Colony Ass'n, 120 N.H. 593, 419 A.2d 1097 (1980) the court held assessments could not be

imposed on lot owners whose membership in the owner's association was involuntary; the association was created by the developer to take over management of common areas, and the deeds of the plaintiff lot owners provided only that an annual $15 premium was to be paid to the developer for benefits provided. Also see Holiday Pines Prop. Owners Ass'n, Inc. v. Wetherington, 596 So.2d 84 (Fla.App.1992).

2. Covenants to pay money can arise in contexts other than a common interest community. For example, where a developer created a seasonal subdivision involving a few lots and required the lot owners to pay an annual charge for water supplied by the developer, the court held that a successor in interest to a lot owner is not obligated to pay the charge. The original purchaser of the lot, of course, would be bound by her personal covenant to pay the charge, but, since the covenant did not run with the land, her successor was not. See Eagle Enterprises, Inc. v. Gross, 39 N.Y.2d 505, 384 N.Y.S.2d 717, 349 N.E.2d 816 (1976) (developer's successor did not show that the covenant to pay was integral to the operation or success of the small subdivision).

3. Sometimes the dispute over liability for monetary assessments is between a lot owner and the developer of a sizeable community. Can the development company write the covenants so as to result in lower annual assessments for the lots it retains while purchasers must pay a higher assessment? On this question, see Kell v. Bella Vista Village Property Owners Ass'n, 258 Ark. 757, 528 S.W.2d 651 (1975). One technique that large-scale developers often use is to have two (or more) classes of lot owners with different fees for each class. In large scale retirement communities the problem of inflationary costs of maintenance is especially critical because there may be large numbers of non-resident lot owners scattered around the country who are years away from building their retirement dream homes and who will vote against any increase in maintenance assessments; this group usually outnumbers the current residents who have an interest in raising the assessments to keep the community pleasant and well-maintained.

4. Note the language of Restatement (Third) § 7.12, Modification and Termination of Certain Affirmative Covenants:

> (1) A covenant to pay money or provide services terminates after a reasonable time if the instrument that created the covenant does not specify the total sum due or a definite termination point. This subsection does not apply to an obligation to pay for services of facilities concurrently provided to the burdened estate.
>
> (2) A covenant to pay money or provide services in exchange for services or facilities provided to the burdened estate may be modified or terminated if the obligation becomes excessive in relation to the cost of providing the services or facilities or to the value received by the burdened estate; provided, however, that modification based on a decrease in value to the burdened estate should take account of any investment made by the covenantee in reasonable reliance on continued validity of the covenant obligation. This subsection does not apply if the servient owner is obliged to pay only for services or facilities actually

used and the servient owner may practicably obtain the services or facilities from other sources.

(3) The rules stated in (1) and (2) above do not apply to obligations to a common interest community or to obligations imposed pursuant to a conservation servitude.

5. Servitudes play a major role in protecting natural resources and historic features of communities. This subject is covered in Chapter IX.

C. PRIVATE DESIGN CONTROLS

Public and private land use controls intersect with regard to restrictions on architectural design of individual structures. In many states, local governments are authorized to create architectural review boards and impose design restrictions on building construction to achieve design consistency or design compatibility in the community. Similarly, private developers may impose design standards on their residential subdivisions that require individual owners to conform to standards contained in the subdivision's declaration of covenants and restrictions. These private covenants are servitudes, imposed to enhance the marketability of the homes and to maintain house values over time. The validity of such private constraints is addressed in the following case.

RHUE v. CHEYENNE HOMES, INC.

Supreme Court of Colorado, En Banc, 1969.
168 Colo. 6, 449 P.2d 361.

PRINGLE, JUSTICE.

In the trial court, Cheyenne Homes, Inc., obtained an injunction prohibiting Leonard Rhue and Family Homes, Inc., hereinafter referred to as plaintiffs in error, from moving a thirty year old Spanish style house into a new subdivision which was about 80% Improved and which contained only modern ranch style or split level homes.

At the time that the subdivision in which the plaintiffs in error seek to locate this house was platted, the owner placed upon the entire area certain restrictive covenants contained in a 'Declaration of Protective Covenants,' which was duly recorded. As recited in the document, these protective covenants were for the purpose of 'protecting the present and future values of the properties located' in the subdivision. Admittedly, the house which the plaintiffs in error wish to put in the subdivision does not violate any of the few specific restrictions contained in the protective covenants. However, paragraph C–2 of the recorded protective covenants contains the following declaration:

'C–2 No building shall be erected, placed or altered on any lot until the construction plans and specifications and a plan showing the location of the structure shall have been approved by the architectural control committee * * * '

Plaintiffs in error failed to submit their plans to the architectural control committee, and the trial court, in entering its injunction, held (1) that such failure constituted a breach of the restrictive covenants, and (2) that the placing of the house would not be in harmony with the existing neighborhood and would depreciate property values in the area.

Plaintiffs in error contend that restriction C–2 is not enforceable because no specific standards are contained therein to guide the committee in determining the approval or disapproval of plans when submitted. We disagree.

It is no secret that housing today is developed by subdividers who, through the use of restrictive covenants, guarantee to the purchaser that his house will be protected against adjacent construction which will impair its value, and that a general plan of construction will be followed. Modern legal authority recognizes this reality and recognizes also that the approval of plans by an architectural control committee is one method by which guarantees of value and general plan of construction can be accomplished and maintained.

So long as the intention of the covenant is clear (and in the present case it is clearly to protect present and future property values in the subdivision), covenants such as the one before us have been up-held against the contention that they lacked specific restrictions providing a framework within which the architectural committee must act. *Winslette v. Keeler*, 220 Ga. 100, 137 S.E.2d 288; Kirkley v. Seipelt, 212 Md. 127, 128 A.2d 430; *Fairfax Community Assoc. v. Boughton*, 127 N.E.2d 641 (Ohio Com.Pl.); *Hannula v. Hacienda Homes*, 34 Cal.2d 442, 211 P.2d 302, 19 A.L.R.2d 1268. In *Kirkley v. Seipelt*, supra, the plaintiff in error argued unsuccessfully that a covenant requiring approval of plans failed in the test of reasonableness because there were no standards to guide the approving party.

* * *

We have recognized in Colorado that restrictive covenants placed on land for the benefit of purchasers within a subdivision are valid and not against public policy, and are enforceable in equity against all purchasers. *Pagel v. Gisi*, 132 Colo. 181, 286 P.2d 636; *Seeger v. Puckett*, 115 Colo. 185, 171 P.2d 415. While we have here enunciated the proposition that the covenant requiring approval of the architectural committee before erection of a house in the subdivision is enforceable, we point out that there is a corollary to that proposition which affords protection and due process of law to a purchaser of a lot in the subdivision, namely, that a refusal to approve plans must be reasonable and made in good faith and must not be arbitrary or capricious. *Kirkley v. Seipelt, supra*; *Winslette v. Keeler, supra*; *Hannula v. Hacienda Homes, supra.*

Since two of the three committee members testified that they would disapprove the plans if they were presented to them, we examine the evidence to determine if such refusal is warranted under the rules we have laid down. There was testimony that the house was about thirty years old, and that the other houses were no older than two years. The house of plaintiffs in error has a stucco exterior and a red tile roof. The other houses are commonly known as ranch style or split level, and are predominantly of brick construction with asphalt shingle roofs. There was further testimony that the style of the house would devalue the surrounding properties because it was 'not compatible' with the houses already in place.

One member of the committee expressed concern that the house of plaintiffs in error would devalue surrounding property. The other added that he thought the covenant gave the architectural committee the authority to refuse approval to plans for property which would seriously affect the market value of other homes in the area. Clearly, a judgment of disapproval of the plans by the committee is reasonable and in good faith and in harmony with the purposes declared in the covenant.

The judgment is affirmed.

Notes

1. When municipalities adopt architectural standards, they must be specific enough to guide the discretion of an architectural review board to avoid the claim that the standards are overly broad, constituting an invalid delegation of legislative prerogatives. In Rhue, the issue was similar: did the recorded declaration of protective covenants contain sufficient standards to guide the decisions of the architectural control committee of the common interest community that governs the subdivision?

2. How specific are the design guidelines contained in the declaration of protective covenants in the Rhue case? Do they provide real guidance to the subdivision's architectural control committee? The courts in some states would find that the general provisions contained in these covenants are not sufficiently specific. See, e.g., Prestwick Landowners' Ass'n v. Underhill, 69 Ohio App.2d 45, 429 N.E.2d 1191 (1980). In Prestwick the court declared a covenant requiring pre-construction consent invalid, because the homeowners "had no guidelines at all in submitting their plans, and the Architectural Committee had no guidelines at all as to accepting or rejecting them. In other words, there is too great a possibility here that the consent restriction can be exercised in an arbitrary, capricious, and unreasonable manner." Id. at 49. Students will find that courts differ as well in their views of how specific local land use legislation must be when it comes to design restrictions imposed on private property owners and enforced by local administrative bodies. In Waterfront Estates Development, Inc. v. City of Palos Hills, 232 Ill.App.3d 367, 173 Ill.Dec. 667, 597 N.E.2d 641 (1992), the court found that a city ordinance creating an appearance commission was an overbroad delegation of authority and that its standards were unconstitutionally vague.

Chapter II

LAND USE PLANS AND THE PLANNING PROCESS

This chapter introduces legal and policy debates that are central to the ability and power of local governments to regulate land uses. A brief discussion of the importance of economics in land use controls may explain the historical interests of the federal and state governments in regulating and attempting to regulate land use decisionmaking. The focus then shifts to an examination of the players in the land use game, exploring who these people are, how they are regulated and what basic powers and duties they possess. The historical development of planning and the comprehensive plan are then discussed to set the stage for the next chapter describing the legal techniques to implement the plan. The chapter concludes with consideration of the intergovernmental dynamics of planning.

SECTION 1. PUBLIC POLICY AND THE ECONOMICS OF LAND USE REGULATION

A recurring tension in the regulation of land use is the economic impact of the decisions regarding how a particular parcel of land may or may not be used. Understanding the economic dilemma and the demands of the market forces is key to appreciating the political realities that challenge the government's use of the police power to decide how private citizens can use their private property in an appropriate manner to benefit collectively the community as a whole.

Consider the following scenario:

> John Jones has recently sold his home in the big city and purchased approximately ten acres of land in a suburban community where he is semi-retired. On the land is an old farmhouse that he has started to renovate while he resides in the dwelling. Renovation plans include remodeling the kitchen, replacing the wrap-around porch and adding a new master bedroom off of the back of the

house. John decided that in addition to renovating the house, he would construct a barn wherein he would make and sell wooden toy cars, trains and planes, thereby turning his hobby into a part-time business venture. He also purchased a large satellite dish to get better television reception. He placed the dish in front of his house, and painted on it the following message: "Welcome to J.J.'s World of Wooden Toys."

Due in large part to growing development pressures in the community, about a year ago the community adopted a comprehensive land use plan and implemented a series of land use laws designed to protect the character of the community. Among the regulations that apply to Jones's land are restrictions on the siting of satellite dishes, home occupations and commercial/business use of residentially zoned property, and sign laws. Building permit applications, with the accompanying required fee, must also be submitted to the community's planning department for approval prior to any renovations and new construction taking place.

Jones knew nothing about the land use laws in the community and he is outraged when visited by the local zoning enforcement officer who issues a "stop work" order for the renovations. She ordered that the newly constructed barn be torn down since it fails to comply with set-back restrictions in the zoning ordinance, and she cited Jones for placing the satellite dish in the front of his house, rather than in the back, as also required by the zoning ordinance.

Questions:

1. Should government control the way in which Jones desires to use his ten acres of private property? What are the arguments in support and opposition to regulating the use of private property?
2. Should government restrict Jones from turning his "home hobby" into a small business on his property? What types of legitimate considerations should government apply when determining the allowed level of intensity of home occupations? Can government adopt home occupation laws that apply just to Jones' business or must they be broad enough to capture all imaginable home occupations? Why?
3. Should government regulate the placement of a satellite dish on private property?
4. Do land use regulations such as those described in the scenario above have a positive or a negative effect on the value of privately owned property?
5. Does government regulation of land use impact the market value of land? If so, at what points? If some regulations enhance the value of some property while at the same time decreasing the value of other property, is government responsible for compensating private property owners for a market loss? Would the property owners who

obtained an increase in value be responsible for paying the government or other landowners as a result of their windfall?

The following excerpt is from William A. Fischel's 1985 book, The Economics of Zoning Laws: A Property Rights Approach to American Land Use Controls (reprinted with permission):

> It is a truism in zoning law that no individual property owner or resident has a legal right to a particular zoning ordinance. Zoning is not a personal property right; it is a community property right. * * * It is not the same as owning one's car or home or personal effects, but there are enough similarities to draw some analogies.
>
> No zoning law says that the community has a legal right to control undeveloped land or to prevent redevelopment. The very broad, vague, and difficult-to-monitor purposes of zoning nonetheless provide an effective arsenal to accomplish as much. No law allows the community to sell this property right in the way one might sell his house. It is clear, though, that zoning can be changed at the discretion of community authorities. Zoning laws nominally vest authority in elected officials and hope that they will pay attention to planners, but every zoning procedure guarantees a great deal of public participation, especially by neighbors. Thus even though resident homeowners have no vested right to zoning, they appear to have a reliable political entitlement to the status quo in land use.
>
> The major difference between these public rights (zoning) and their closest private analog, private homeowners' associations, is that the latter do not include any property owners who have not agreed to the rules in advance (Ellickson 1982). Zoning is enacted by a local government, which usually has some involuntary members. The one-resident, one-vote rule and majority voting procedures open the possibility that public property rights might be expanded at the expense of politically effete members of the community. * * *

An excerpt from Fischel's chapter in the Encyclopedia of Law and Economics (see: http://encyclo.findlaw.com/2200book.pdf) appears below:

"ZONING AND LAND USE REGULATION" IN BOUDEWIJN, BOUCKAERT AND GERRIT DE GEEST (EDS). ENCYCLOPEDIA OF LAW AND ECONOMICS, VOL. II. CIVIL LAW AND ECONOMICS, CHELTENHAM, EDWARD, ZELGAR

2000.

6. THE TIEBOUT MODEL WITH ZONING MAKES LOCAL TAXES MORE EFFICIENT

> Land use controls in the US are regarded as a necessary condition for the model of local government embraced by the economics profession. Tiebout (1956) suggested that the free-rider

problem could be overcome for public goods that are confined to small geographic areas. For local public goods, Tiebout argued that preferences could be truly revealed if households could select among many geographically contiguous communities assumed to provide a wide range of public services. Because most large US metropolitan areas—in which most Americans live—have scores if not hundreds of municipalities, and because most people move several times during their lives, American cities approximate the necessary conditions for Tiebout's model.

Hamilton (1975, 1976) added the local property tax and 'fiscal' zoning to Tiebout's model. A criticism of Tiebout holds that the property tax system—the mainstay of American local government—encourages developers to build low-value housing in communities with high levels of public services. This creates two kinds of deadweight loss. The property tax itself discourages housing consumption, since a larger house increases one's tax bill but usually not one's benefits from public services. Second, willingness to pay for local services is not accurately revealed, since some low-demand immigrants can receive higher levels of local services than they are willing to pay for in property taxes. As a result, the Tiebout model's efficiency advantages are undermined.

Hamilton showed that both of these inefficiencies could be overcome if the original residents (or developers) of the community established a zoning regime that required subsequent development to generate property tax revenues that covered each household's expected cost of local public services. Such zoning is called 'fiscal zoning', though it is empirically indistinguishable from any other brand (Bogart, 1993). In the Tiebout–Hamilton system, the property tax has no deadweight loss, and the level of public services is efficient because mobility by households among communities allows them to choose a known level of public services for which they must pay. Mobility allows households to choose the mix of services and housing they prefer and also encourages communities to keep costs down (Martinez–Vazquez and Sjoquist, 1988).

In proposing this model, Hamilton implicitly embraced the view of zoning as a municipal property right. Economists often view the local government fisc in the same terms as the national fisc. Levels of spending and taxes are, in the conventional view, determined by an entirely political process. But in the Tiebout–Hamilton world, local governments are much different; they must respond as purveyors of public services to the regional property market. As Oates (1969) first showed, if local governments provide high-quality local services at a lower level of property taxes—that is, if they operate like efficient firms—they reward their established residents with higher owner-occupied housing values. (Oates's study has been replicated many times; a survey and additional evidence on capitalization of local fiscal variables in home values is Yinger et al., 1988).

The same incentive that homeowner-voters have for supporting efficient levels of taxes and spending—maximizing the value of their own homes—also influences their support for local zoning. Zoning laws (and changes in zoning) that increase resident homeowners' net worth will be favored, assuming residents control the local political process, and policies that decrease it will be opposed. Zoning is also a means of controlling other municipal costs by limiting the types of development that may raise taxes or require public expenditures (Oates, 1977).

There is ample evidence that owner-occupied housing in well-planned communities is more valuable than similar units in poorly controlled areas. For example, Lafferty and Frech (1978) found that suburban communities in the Boston area that kept their commercial areas within closely contiguous zones rather than letting them scatter about had higher single-family home values (see also Burnell, 1985). Speyrer (1989) found that houses protected either by covenants or by zoning in the Houston, Texas, area were more valuable than houses in sections of Houston that were both unzoned and uncovenanted. (Sprawling Houston, which is unzoned and has areas in which covenants have lapsed or were never established, surrounds two small cities that do have zoning.)

The fact that more stringent zoning restrictions can increase housing values raises the question of why all communities do not zone to the most restrictive degree possible. One reason is that zoning may be sufficiently fungible that homeowners can be compensated for devaluations of their property. Suppose a proposed office building is opposed by nearby homeowners, who credibly complain that their property will be devalued by the traffic, the building's shadow and other spillovers (Thibodeau, 1990). If the developer can compensate them with cash or in-kind payments, the existing residents may 'take the money and run', leaving behind houses that are devalued but neighborhoods whose aggregate property values (for both housing and office buildings) are higher. Thus the finding that spillovers devalue nearby housing is consistent with efficient land use.

The implication of the foregoing is that the efficiency of land-use controls is best evaluated by looking at aggregate land values, not simply owner-occupied houses (Lind, 1973; Sonstelie and Portney, 1978; Brueckner, 1990). But even this standard must be qualified. If the municipality possesses some monopoly power (vis-à-vis other communities) in its provision of developable land, maximization of aggregate land value may be inconsistent with Pareto efficiency (M. White, 1975; Pines and Weiss, 1976). While there is empirical evidence in support of the 'monopoly zoning' hypothesis (L. Rose, 1989; Thorson, 1996; Bates, 1993), it is nonetheless impressive how many local jurisdictions there are in US metropolitan areas (Fischel, 1981). At any rate, Congress in 1984 specifically exempted local governments from financial liability under the Sherman Act, thus staunching anti-monopoly litigation against municipalities (Deutsch and Butler, 1987).

* * *

Notes

1. Should zoning and local land use controls be used to regulate the housing market to the extent that it protects the value of investments in homeownership? For a discussion of this issue, see Edward C. Glaeser and Joseph Gyourko, "The Impact of Zoning on Housing Affordability," Harvard Institute of Economic Research, Discussion Paper Number 1948 (March 2002). This paper can be accessed at the following website: http://post.economics.harvard.edu/hier/2002papers/HIER1948.pdf. See also, William A. Fischel, "An Economic History of Zoning and a Cure for its Exclusionary Effects," (2001) available at http://www.dartmouth.edu/w̃fischel/Papers/02–03.pdf; Andrew G. Dieterich, "An Egalitarian's Market: The Economics of Inclusionary Zoning Reclaimed," 24 Ford. Urb. L.J. 231 (1996) and Allan Mallach, "The Tortured Reality of Suburban Exclusion: Zoning, Economics and the Future of the Berenson Doctrine," 4 Pace Envtl. L. Rev. 37 (1986).

2. What considerations, if any, should be given to economic impacts of local land use controls on property values when laws are designed to protect and preserve environmental interests? Is protection of the environment a significant community property interest? See, Nancy E. Bockstael and Elena G. Irwin, "Economics and the Land Use–Environment Link," The International Yearbook of Environmental and Resource Economics, Edward Elgar Publishing, H. Folmer and T. Tietenberg, ed. (2000). What are the economic impacts of land use controls on agriculture and farming? Can and should local governments impact the economic value of land used for agricultural purposes? Is this a local, state or federal government issue?

3. Should land use controls be used to protect investments in commercial businesses? In Superior Outdoor Signs, Inc. v. Eller Media Co., 150 Md.App. 479, 822 A.2d 478 (2003), the Maryland Court held that an owner of an outdoor advertising business did not have standing to challenge variances granted to a competitor. It noted that:

> It is not the function of county zoning ordinances to provide economic protection for existing businesses. Neither the fact that the parties may suffer reduced incomes or be put out of business by more vigorous or appealing competition, nor the fact that properties on which such businesses are operated would thus depreciate in value, give rise to a standing to sue.

See also Johnsson v. Planning & Zoning Commission of Monroe, 2001 WL 357634 (Conn.Super.). However, while courts are reluctant to entertain challenges to variances granted to competitors, courts are more likely to uphold the protectionist purposes of land use controls when commercial businesses challenge zoning ordinances that seek to protect other businesses from competition. For example, in Wal–Mart Stores, Inc. v. City of Turlock, 483 F.Supp.2d 987 (E.D. Cal. 2006), a federal court upheld an ordinance that prohibited the construction of "discount superstores." Although the ordinance was based in part on protecting local grocery stores from competition, the court held it nevertheless passed rational basis review because it did not discriminate on the basis of a suspect classification or infringe any fundamental rights.

SECTION 2. HISTORICAL DEVELOPMENT OF LAND USE PLANNING

Planning may be described as "an attempt to coordinate the development of all the interrelated aspects of the physical environment, and all the closely related aspects of the social and economic environment." See, Norman Williams. Jr. and John M. Taylor, American Land Planning Law, Vol. 1 (Thomson West 2003). The First National Conference on City Planning and the Problems of Congestion was convened in Washington, D.C. in 1909. Frederick Law Olmstead, the famous landscape architect and planning consultant described the city plan as "a compendium of all regulations on building, physical development, 'districting' of land, health ordinances, and 'police rules' for the use and development of land." Almost twenty years later, Alfred Bettman described the city plan as "a master design for the physical development of the territory of the city. It constitutes the division of land between public and private uses, specifying the general location and extent of new public improvements, grounds and structures . . . and, in the case of private developments, the general distribution [of land areas] amongst various classes of uses, such as residential, business and industrial uses."

The legal underpinnings of the current land use system were set nearly eighty years ago. They were designed in a different era to meet different challenges. In those days, "comprehensive planning" referred to "city-wide" planning because developing communities were separated by open spaces and land development impacts were local in character. At that time, conformance with a comprehensive plan was defined very loosely. Localities were not required to adopt discrete land use plans. It was enough that zoning ordinances contained some evidence of comprehensive planning.

Today, a comprehensive land use plan commonly refers to a written document that is formally adopted by a local legislative body that contains goals, objectives and strategies for the future development and conservation of the community. Further, zoning and other land use controls are typically required to be consistent with the comprehensive land use plan. Depending upon local definition, in general, comprehensive land use plan, master plan and general plan may be used interchangeably. The power possessed by local governments to plan is derived from a variety of federal, state and regional sources. What constitutes comprehensive planning and how planning is done is determined by state legislatures. Given the importance of land use and the central legal role of comprehensive planning, one would expect state statutes to carefully define a comprehensive land use plan and to provide a predictable, reliable, and effective method of land use planning. This is not the case in the majority of states.

A. STANDARD CITY PLANNING ENABLING ACT

The Standard City Planning Enabling Act ("Standard Act"), published by the U.S. Department of Commerce in 1928 covered six main subjects: the organization and power of the planning commission, which was directed to prepare and adopt a master plan; the content of the master plan for the physical development of the territory; provision for adoption of a master street plan by the governing body; provision for approval of all public improvements by the planning commission; control of private subdivision of land; and provision for the establishment of a regional planning commission and a regional plan. (A copy of the Standard Act can be viewed at: http://www.planning.org/growingsmart/pdf/CPEnablingAct1928.pdf). The function of local planning was designed to be dominated by non-elected officials, who arguably would be better able to take a hard look at challenging planning issues from a non-partisan perspective. The influence of the Standard Act continues to resonate today with many of the state planning enabling acts still based on this model. Although the Standard Act provided for optional rather than mandatory planning, which led to the controversial belief that planning was not necessarily a prerequisite to the adoption of zoning laws, Alfred Bettman, a member of the Advisory Committee, explained that "The zoning ordinance is, of course, execution and the planning precedes it..."

Today, the majority view in the state courts is that the adoption of a comprehensive plan is not a statutory prerequisite to the adoption and administration of zoning. A recent survey by the American Planning Association revealed that ten states make local planning optional (state law merely authorizes local governments to plan); twenty-five states make planning conditionally mandatory (local governments are only required to develop a plan if they choose to first create a planning commission); and fifteen states make planning a mandate (local governments must plan). See, Rodney L. Cobb, "Toward Modern Statutes: A Survey of State Laws on Local Land–Use Planning," in Modernizing State Planning Statutes: The Growing Smart Working Papers, vol. 2 (The American Planning Association, 1998). Some states, such as Oregon, require that local land use plans be consistent with the State adopted plan and policies. See, Or. Rev. Stat. § 197.250.

Many states adopted the Standard City Planning Enabling Act, but after they had first created the legal framework for zoning (after all, the federal government published the Standard State Zoning Enabling Act six years earlier). Most states failed in any meaningful way to prescribe how zoning and planning were to be integrated. This fissure remains today, narrowed by provisions in most states that require zoning to be in accordance with the comprehensive land use plan and by reforms in others that require a plan to be adopted before land use is regulated. Language in the Standard City Planning Enabling Act that defines the content and role of the comprehensive plan throws further light on the legal effect of the plan. The Standard City Planning Enabling Act defined the purpose of the master plan as:

> Guiding and accomplishing a coordinated, adjusted, and harmonious development of the municipality and its environs which will, in accordance with present and future needs, best promote health, safety, order, morals, convenience, prosperity, and general welfare as well as efficiency and economy in the process of development, including, among other things, adequate provision for traffic, the provision of safety from fire and other dangers, adequate provisions for light and air, the promotion of good civic design, wise and efficient expenditure of public funds, and the adequate provision of public utilities and other public requirements. Richard P. Fishman, ed., Housing for All Under Law, 329 (1978) (quoting SPEA § 7).

The Preface to the American Planning Association's 2002 Growing Smart Legislative Guidebook, provides the following reflection on the early model acts:

> The planning approaches of the 1920s are incapable of meeting the challenges of the twenty-first century. There are at least four reasons for this deficiency:
>
> **(1) A more significant governmental dimension for planning**. In the 1920s, government was simpler, and there were fewer governmental units. Planning was a local activity, not something that was expected of all levels of government. Indeed, the role of the federal and state governments in shaping our urban and rural areas ranged from minimal to nonexistent. Beginning in the 1950s, the federal government created programs addressing transportation, environment, and other functional areas that had statewide or regional significance. Increasingly, the federal government devolved or placed greater responsibility on the state and local governments for making transportation, environmental, and public facilities planning decisions when federal monies were involved. Moreover, the repercussions of decisions on development whose impacts spill over jurisdictional boundaries are no longer ignored. States recognized this concern and state legislatures responded. In some parts of the country, states now take an active role in managing this intergovernmental dimension to ensure uniformity, fairness, and the advancement of state interests.
>
> **(2) A marked shift in society's view of land**. People no longer believe, as they did in the nineteenth century, that land is something merely to be bought and sold. We now regard land as a resource. Where we once encouraged the filling in and development of swamps, we now regard those same wetlands as a vital part of nature's system of flood control and important for wildlife and their habitats that should be protected for the benefit of future generations. Where we once built without concern for scenic protection, we now value scenic beauty as an irreplaceable regional asset. We see vacant, developable land as having competing social values—it can be used for the construc-

tion of affordable housing or for the continuation of agriculture. We recognize that how we develop our land—at what density or intensity—will have consequences for the form and relative compactness of metropolitan areas, which in turn will affect how much we have to travel to conduct our lives and what consequences that has for the air we breathe.

(3) A more active citizenry. In the 1920s, community plans tended to be prepared by consultants working for business elites who sought little broad-based public support or involvement. What opportunities there were for citizen participation were rudimentary and perfunctory—a single public hearing after the major planning decisions had already been made. As a consequence, such plans were not often implemented. Although many planning statutes are silent on the tools and techniques of participation, citizens now expect to be engaged in the community planning processes, and, when they participate, they expect to see results from their efforts. The existence of the Internet, on which plans and information about development can be placed as part of a government's home page, also opens up new options for citizen involvement.

(4) A more challenging legal environment. Land-use controls are being employed to solve or prevent environmental problems, maintain open space, exact public improvements for schools and roads, and preserve agricultural land. The line between protecting the public from nuisances—the focus of the 1920s—and securing public benefits has blurred over the past 70 years. In response, courts have begun to require government to compensate land owners for regulations that result in either a permanent or temporary taking of private property, that go "too far" in pushing the envelope in protecting the public health, safety, and welfare—the traditional police power objectives of land use controls. Thus, the planning basis for our development decisions becomes even more significant as the justification for the regulatory and public expenditure systems it underpins.

B. ALI MODEL LAND DEVELOPMENT CODE

In 1975, after many years of effort and many drafts reviewed, debated and re-written, the American Law Institute published a Model Land Development Code. Much more sophisticated than its predecessor models, the Model Land Development Code was organized into the following twelve sections: General Provisions, Local Land Development Regulation, Local Land Development Planning, Discontinuance of Existing Land Use, Acquisition and Disposition of Land, Land Banking, State Land Development Regulation, State Land Development Planning, Judicial Review of Orders, Rules and Ordinances, Enforcement of Local Land Development Regulations, Public Records of Development Regulations, and Financial Coordination of Governmental Development.

By all accounts, the Model Land Development Code was a failure. With the exception of the State of Florida, which based its development of regional impacts law on the relevant provisions of this Code, no other state used the document in any meaningful way to make reforms to its state enabling statutes. This left a void for reformers who needed fresh ideas and perspectives to assist in modernizing individual state planning and zoning statutes, creating the need for the American Planning Association's contribution, discussed next.

C. GROWING SMART LEGISLATIVE GUIDEBOOK

The most recent chapter in the history of the evolution of land use planning and zoning is the 2002 American Planning Association *Growing Smart Legislative Guidebook* which offers the following view on the 1920s standard acts:

> Most states' planning statutes are the offspring of the two model statutes drafted by an advisory committee of the U.S. Department of Commerce in the 1920s. For many states, the *Standard City Planning and Zoning Enabling Acts* still supply the institutional structure for planning (such as the establishment of planning commissions and boards of adjustment or appeals), although some procedural and substantive components have changed over time.
>
> These acts regarded planning and zoning as matters of purely *local* and, more particularly, *urban* concern. The acts were intended to provide clear delegation of the state's police power authority to local government, which is the fundamental reason enabling legislation exists. They were also intended to preserve private property rights and to protect cities against slums, blight, congestion, and loss of amenities.
>
> Their drafters also wanted to ensure that private investments and the value they produce could be protected from nuisances and other incompatibilities from neighboring properties. They also wanted to establish a uniform national framework of planning and zoning that could survive challenges in state and federal courts.

Notes

1. Were the economic considerations of land use controls, based upon the early enabling acts designed to protect the property interests of the community as a whole? How can local governments ensure that local land use controls protect private investments in property? Should this be a leading consideration in adopting new plans and zoning laws? Can this be accomplished equitably?

2. For further explanations and critiques of the *Growing Smart Legislative Guidebook* see, Patricia E. Salkin, "The Next Generation of Planning & Zoning Enabling Acts Is on the Horizon: 2002 Growing Smart Legislative Guidebook Is a Must–Read for Land Use Practitioners," 30 Real Estate L.J. 353 (2002), and Edward J. Sullivan, "Out of the Chaos: Towards a National System of Land–Use Procedures," 34 The Urban Lawyer 449 (2002). Not all

stakeholders believe that the most recent effort offers effective guidance on all issues. See, for example, John J. Delaney, Esq. "APA's Growing Smart Legislative Guidebook: Will it Promote "Smart Process?" " and Robert Liberty, "Heart and Teeth to Go with the Brains of Smart Growth: Comments on the American Planning Association's Growing Smart Legislative Guidebook." Stuart Meck, AICP, editor of the Guidebook, provides a response in "Growing Smart: Drafting the Next Generation of Model Planning and Zoning Enabling Legislation for the United States (and Responding to Its Critics)."

3. The federal government has also played a role in influencing the way in which state and local governments control the use of land. For example, The National Commission on Urban Problems recommended that state governments enact legislation enabling appropriate governmental agencies to acquire land in advance of development for the following purposes: (a) assuring the continuing availability of sites needed for development; (b) controlling the timing, location, type and scale of development; (c) preventing urban sprawl; and (d) reserving to the public gains in land values resulting from the action of government in promoting and servicing development. National Commission on Urban Problems, Building the American City 251 (1968).

Congress responded by providing specific legislative authority in the Community Development Act of 1974 for the allocation of funds under the special revenue sharing program for "community development" grants to local governments for "the acquisition of real property * * * which is (a) blighted, deteriorated, deteriorating, undeveloped or inappropriately developed from the standpoint of sound community development and growth; (b) appropriate for rehabilitation or conservation activities; (c) appropriate for the preservation or restoration of historic sites, the beautification of urban land, the conservation of open spaces, natural resources, and scenic areas, the provision of recreational opportunities, or the guidance of urban development; (d) to be used for the provision of public works, facilities, and improvements eligible for assistance under this title; or (e) to be used for other public purposes." 42 U.S.C. 5305(a)(1) (1974).

For an historical examination of the extent of federal influence on state and local planning, See, Patricia E. Salkin, "Smart Growth and Sustainable Development: Threads of a National Land Use Policy," 36 Valparaiso U. L. Rev. 381 (2002); Robert I. McMurry, "Using Federal Laws and Regulations to Control Local Land Use," SG ALI–ABA 357 (2001); Shelby D. Green, "The Search for a National Land Use Policy: For the Cities' Sake," 26 Fordham Urb. L. J. 69 (1998); and John R. Nolon, "The National Land Use Policy Act," 13 Pace Envtl. L. Rev. 519 (1996). Professor Kayden argues that the U.S. does not have a national land use policy per se, and that it is unlikely that Congress will produce such legislation. See, Jerold S. Kayden, "National Land–Use Planning in America: Something Whose Time Has Never Come," 3 Wash. U.J.L. & Pol'y 445 (2000).

SECTION 3. THE PLAYERS IN THE LAND USE GAME

In his book, The Zoning Game: Municipal Practices and Policies, Richard F. Babcock identifies the following "players" in the zoning game: local decisionmakers (*e.g.*, members of local legislative bodies, planning boards and zoning boards), planners, lawyers and judges. Code enforcement officers, engineers, architects and members of the public may also participate in the process. This section offers insights into the legal status of planners who are key participants in the process, and it focuses on ethical considerations of parties involved.

A. PLANNERS

The following definition appears in the Bureau of Labor Statistics, U.S. Department of Labor, *Occupational Outlook Handbook, 2002–03 Edition*, Urban and Regional Planners, http://www.bls.gov/oco/ocos057.htm:

> Planners develop long- and short-term land use plans to provide for growth and revitalization of urban, suburban, and rural communities, while helping local officials make decisions concerning social, economic, and environmental problems. Because local governments employ the majority of urban and regional planners, they often are referred to as community, regional, or city planners.
>
> Planners promote the best use of a community's land and resources for residential, commercial, institutional, and recreational purposes. Planners may be involved in various other activities, including decisions on alternative public transportation system plans, resource development, and protection of ecologically sensitive regions. They address issues such as traffic congestion, air pollution, and the effect of growth and change on a community. They may formulate plans relating to the construction of new school buildings, public housing, or other infrastructure. Some planners are involved in environmental issues ranging from pollution control to wetland preservation, forest conservation, or the location of new landfills. Planners also may be involved with drafting legislation on environmental, social, and economic issues, such as sheltering the homeless, planning a new park, or meeting the demand for new correctional facilities.
>
> Planners examine proposed community facilities such as schools to be sure these facilities will meet the changing demands placed upon them over time. They keep abreast of economic and legal issues involved in zoning codes, building codes, and environmental regulations. They ensure that builders and developers follow these codes and regulations. Planners also deal with land use issues created by population movements. For example, as suburban growth and economic development create more new jobs outside cities, the

need for public transportation that enables workers to get to these jobs increases. In response, planners develop transportation models for possible implementation and explain their details to planning boards and the general public.

Before preparing plans for community development, planners report on the current use of land for residential, business, and community purposes. These reports include information on the location and capacity of streets, highways, airports, water and sewer lines, schools, libraries, and cultural and recreational sites. They also provide data on the types of industries in the community, characteristics of the population, and employment and economic trends. With this information, along with input from citizens' advisory committees, planners design the layout of land uses for buildings and other facilities such as subway lines and stations.

* * *

Planners prepare reports showing how their programs can be carried out and what they will cost. Urban and regional planners often confer with land developers, civic leaders, and public officials. They may function as mediators in community disputes and present alternatives acceptable to opposing parties. Planners may prepare material for community relations programs, speak at civic meetings, and appear before legislative committees and elected officials to explain and defend their proposals. In large organizations, planners usually specialize in a single area such as transportation, demography, housing, historic preservation, urban design, environmental and regulatory issues, or economic development. In small organizations, planners must be able to do various kinds of planning.

B. THE LEGAL STATUS OF PLANNERS

NEW JERSEY CHAPTER, AMERICAN INSTITUTE OF PLANNERS v. NEW JERSEY STATE BD. OF PROFESSIONAL PLANNERS

Supreme Court of New Jersey, 1967.
48 N.J. 581, 227 A.2d 313, appeal dismissed, certiorari denied
389 U.S. 8, 88 S.Ct. 70, 19 L.Ed.2d 8 (1967).

Francis, J. In this declaratory judgment proceeding the Chancery Division of the Superior Court declared unconstitutional a portion of section 11 of the professional planners licensing act, L.1962, c. 109; N.J.S.A. 45:14A–11. The condemned portion exempted duly licensed professional engineers, licensed land surveyors and registered architects of this State from the requirement, imposed by the statute on all other persons, to take and pass an examination for a planner's license, and it directed the State Board of Professional Planners (which was created by the same statute) to issue such a license on application therefor and payment of fee by any such exempted person. The trial court also held that the invalid portion of section 11 was severable, and not so intimately connected with the statute as to indicate that the Legislature would not have adopted the remainder without it. The Board was restrained from issuing licenses to persons who sought to qualify under the offending exemption. An appeal was taken to the Appellate Division, where the restraint was continued until final judgment. Thereafter, before the matter was reached for argument there, all parties moved for certification pursuant to R.R. 1:10–3, and we granted the motion.

The action was instituted by the New Jersey Chapter, American Institute of Planners, an unincorporated association of the State of New Jersey. The association is a professional society created to study and advance the art and science of city, regional, state and national planning.

* * *

Prior to 1962 unsuccessful attempts were made under the sponsorship of the American Institute of Planners to obtain passage by the Legislature of a so-called professional planners licensing act. The proposal encountered opposition from other established professional groups, principally engineers, land surveyors and architects, who were already subject to separate licensing statutes and who had qualified for licenses by meeting the conditions imposed thereby. Finally in 1962 the act in question, obviously a compromise measure (more of this later) was adopted with the acquiescence of the competing interests, as chapter 109 of the Laws of 1962.

The act provided that after July 10, 1962 no person could practice or offer to practice professional planning in this State unless he were licensed to do so under its provisions. The practice of professional planning is defined in most general terms in section 2 as "the administration, advising, consultation or performance of professional work in the development of master plans in accordance with the provisions of chapters 27 and 55 of Title 40 of the Revised Statutes, as amended and supplemented; and other professional planning services related thereto intended primarily to guide governmental policy for the assurance of the orderly and co-ordinated development of municipal, county, regional and metropolitan land areas, and the State or portions thereof." N.J.S.A. 45:14A–2.

Chapters 27 and 55 of Title 40 provide for the creation of county, regional and municipal planning boards to make and adopt master plans for the physical development of the political unit involved. * * *

In order to become licensed as a professional planner, a candidate must file an application under oath showing that he has the minimum educational qualifications. They are:

> (a) A graduate degree in professional planning from an accredited college or university in a curriculum in recognized planning subjects as shall be approved by the State Board of Professional Planners, plus a minimum of three years experience in the full-time practice of professional planning; or (b) an undergraduate degree

> from an accredited college or university in a curriculum offering a major or option comprising a minimum of 21 credit hours in such recognized planning subjects as shall be approved by the board, with a minimum of four years experience in the full-time practice of professional planning; or (c) graduation from a secondary school and at least 12 years of professional planning experience acceptable to the board; or, (d) for a period of eight years only subsequent to July 1, 1963, a degree in a *closely related course of study such as architecture, landscape architecture, engineering,* law, sociology, geography, public administration, political science or economics, with a minimum of 18 credit hours in recognized planning subjects included as part of or in addition to such courses of study in an accredited college or university, plus a minimum of five years experience in the full-time practice of professional planning. (Emphasis ours) In addition the applicant must obtain a passing grade as determined by the board upon a qualifying examination to be prepared by the board or by experts chosen by it, and given annually.

* * *

When the statute was adopted by the Legislature it contained section 11 consisting of five paragraphs dealing generally with the license-qualifying examinations. The fourth paragraph provides:

> The board upon application therefor and the payment of the application and license fees fixed by this act shall issue a certificate of license as a professional planner to any duly licensed professional engineer, licensed land surveyor or registered architect of New Jersey.

This paragraph was not included in the bill, A 546, as introduced in 1961 under the sponsorship of the New Jersey Chapter of the American Institute of Planners. It was inserted however, (along with section 3, N.J.S.A. 45:14A–3, and part of section 17, N.J.S.A. 45:14A–17, to be more specifically referred to hereafter in connection with the discussion of severability of section 11), in order to exempt the described engineers, land surveyors and architects from the obligation of satisfying the qualifications required of other aspiring planners and from the burden of taking and passing the licensing examination.

Plaintiffs challenge the validity of the fourth paragraph, saying it denies them equal protection of the law contrary to the guaranties of the Federal Constitution and the New Jersey Constitution. More specifically they say that by requiring all persons except licensed professional engineers, licensed land surveyors and registered architects of this State to possess certain educational qualifications and experience in the field of planning, and to take and pass an examination on subjects related to that field in order to be licensed as a practitioner of planning, the legislation violates the cited constitutional strictures against discrimination.

* * *

In this instance we are satisfied from the legislative history and from an examination of the statute as a whole that the Legislature would not have adopted it without the exemption provision contained in the fourth paragraph of section 11.

The first proposed planners' licensing act * * * did not contain an exemption for engineers, land surveyors and architects. There is no doubt it encountered opposition from those groups, particularly from the New Jersey Society of Professional Engineers. It was not adopted. Thereafter futile attempts were made in 1959 and 1960 to procure passage of such legislation. Then in 1961 two bills were introduced, one sponsored by the Society of Professional Engineers (A 483), and the other by the Institute of Planners. (A 546). The bills continued the conflict between the professions. The engineers' bill provided for the registration and licensing of professional planners, and created an administrative and examining board to carry out its provisions. The board was to consist of five engineers, one of whom would also be a licensed land surveyor, and one a licensed professional planner. The planners' bill called for establishment of a separate board of licensed professional planners. The statement originally attached said among other things:

> "Planning is a distinct, separate profession, which requires specialized training. It is not a branch of engineering, architecture, or any other profession. Thirty leading colleges and universities award degrees in planning, and more than 400 New Jersey municipalities and 15 counties have planning boards."

As we were advised at oral argument, it became apparent that neither bill could pass to the exclusion of the other. The engineers, land surveyors and architects seemed to feel there was no need at all to regard planning as a distinct profession and to require licenses for planners as such. But if the Legislature disagreed and found justification for such regulation, then they felt that persons in their professions who took and passed the examinations for licenses to practice in their respective fields, as already required by separate statutes, ought to receive automatic licensure under the planners' act. In 1962 an obvious compromise in the form of the present statute was submitted and adopted. It became chapter 109, L.1962.

* * *

The history of the act and its evolution into the form which made it acceptable legislatively demonstrate plainly that the establishment of prerequisites for licensing planners, and the provisions for exemption therefrom of licensed engineers, land surveyors and registered architects were intended to be interdependent and to exist as a whole or not at all. * * * We are satisfied that if the exemption provision were invalid, it would be usurpation of the legislative province for a court to allow the remainder of the enactment to stand without it. *Washington National Ins. Co. v. Board of Review*, 1 N.J. 545, 556, 64 A.2d 443 (1949). Therefore whether the entire act here shall stand or fall depends upon our determination of the constitutionality of the fourth paragraph of section 11, to which we now turn.

* * *

The more specific issue vigorously argued by plaintiffs is that by exempting licensed professional engineers, land surveyors and registered architects from the educational requirements and examination for a planner's license, while requiring all other persons, particularly those educated for and trained in planning to satisfy the requirements, the statute transgresses the constitutional mandate for equal protection of the law. They urge that all persons have a common right to aspire to and qualify for the practice of a profession or occupation, and are entitled to be treated equally with respect to State-imposed tests for license to do so. And they contend that creation of the exempt separate class of engineers, land surveyors and architects, and authorizing automatic licensure for such persons violates the basic charter right of all other persons not to be treated in discriminatory fashion.

* * *

There is no substantial dispute in the testimony of the expert witnesses who appeared on both sides of the case that there is a definite interrelationship among the disciplines of engineering, architecture, landscape architecture, land surveying and planning. * * *

Plaintiffs' experts concede that historically city planning had its origin and its early development "with architects, engineers and landscape architects. That is where we got our original planners"; "they were really planners"; they "came out of" architecture, engineering and landscape architecture. * * *

The text writers support the view that city planning had and has its roots in the three professions recognized by our Legislature. For example, McQuillin, in 1 Municipal Corporations 432 (1949) says:

> "The first instance of a comprehensive city plan was that of Christopher Wren for London following the destructive fire of 1666, but it was never adopted. In 1682 a plan for Philadelphia was drafted by civil engineers and surveyors appointed by William Penn. The plan adopted for the national capital was prepared by Major Pierre Charles L'Enfant, a French army engineer employed by Washington, who presented a scheme at once comprehensive and attractive, and the observance of which in the main has enabled the national capital to develop as one among the beautiful cities of the world."

Further:

> "As knowing how to do a thing before it is attempted is needed, it is plain that satisfactory city planning and zoning must be the result of the united efforts of the applied talents working in harmony of the various professions, arts and sciences, particularly that of the civil engineer, the architect, the landscape architect, or designer, the economist and the lawyer." Id., at pp. 434–435.

See also, James, Land Planning in the United States for the City, State and Nation (1926), where it is pointed out in chapter 3 that the concept of city planning in the modern sense was first introduced at the Chicago World's Fair in 1893, and that the exposition was the joint effort of architects, landscape architects and engineers.

Plaintiffs' witnesses assert that the modern "new breed" planner is one step removed from the engineers, architects and land surveyors. His claimed separate expertise in the preparation of master plans, they say, comes from knowledge of and training in community studies, which include preparation of base maps, land use surveys, housing conditions, review of business uses, environmental studies in neighborhoods, community facilities, population and economic surveys. This expertise is applied to the conditions and circumstances of a particular community, and a master plan for its physical development is evolved. Thus, plaintiffs say, planners operate on the top-most echelon of the process which in the ultimate produces the comprehensive master plan; at that level they apply their understanding of the operation of socio-economic forces to the component data prepared or compiled by the other professional groups such as engineers, architects and land surveyors, as well as lawyers, financial experts, and experienced men of public affairs, in order to fashion what they believe is the appropriate master plan.

There is no doubt that in more recent years community planning has drawn into its creative work social and economic considerations to a greater extent than in its formative period. And it may be that in the course of time the Legislature will conclude that such a high degree of specialized expertise has come into being in planning that the practice ought to be treated as uniquely separate from and independent of all other professional disciplines. * * * In this connection, however, the evidence is uncontradicted that at present there is a shortage of persons engaging in planning, whatever may be their professional, educational or experiential background. According to the Executive Director of the American Society of Planning Officials, the Society advertised about 1300 professional planning jobs during 1965, and at the end of the year about 400 of them were open and unfilled. That number was higher than at the end of 1964, which in turn was higher than in 1963. It may well be that the Legislature felt the need could be alleviated by admitting to the practice of planning without examination those persons who had already qualified for licenses in the related professional fields of engineering, land surveying and architecture. Under all of the circumstances it cannot be said reasonably that planning did not have its gestative stirrings and its early and continued practice in the three exempted disciplines, particularly in engineering and architecture. Nor can it be said on the record before us that it was wholly arbitrary and without reasonable basis for the Legislature to regard licensed members of the three professions as possessing sufficient minimal qualifications for planning to warrant treatment as a distinct class and to grant them exemption from the licensing requirements of the professional planners act, if they wish to practice in that field.

The notion that the lawmakers felt the desirability of some control of the developing practice of community planning must be accepted. It is reasonable also to conclude from the record that an awareness existed of the present shortage of persons engaged in the practice. Further, the evidence submitted warrants the inference that the legislators were aware of the historical part played by the engineers, land surveyors and architects in the development of community planning, and the continuing practice of such planning as an incident of their professional work. All of these circumstances suggest the view that the Legislature felt the current need in the field of community planning was for regulation of those persons who wished to engage in the practice but who had not demonstrated to any public agency that they had sufficient qualifications to do so. The circumstances suggest also satisfaction on the part of the lawmakers that achievement of licensure in one of the three named professions demonstrates possession of sufficient minimal competence to engage in planning to warrant treating such license holders as a separate class and exempting them from the requirements imposed upon those who have no license of any kind to practice planning. Under the principles of law laid down for the control of judicial review, we cannot say that the exempt class created by the fourth paragraph of section 11 is purely arbitrary and without any rational relation to the statutory objective of regulation of the planning profession.

Accordingly the challenged portions of the professional planners act cannot be declared violative of the constitutional mandate for equal protection of the laws. The judgment of the trial court is reversed, and the restraint imposed upon the New Jersey State Board of Professional Planners respecting the issuance of planners' licenses to those licensed in the exempt professions is vacated.

[A partial dissent is omitted.]

Notes

1. Michigan statutes define "community planner" as "a person qualified to prepare comprehensive community plans * * *" MI ST. 339.2301, and further provide that "[a] community planner shall not engage in the practice of architecture, engineering, or land surveying * * * unless licensed * * * as an architect, professional engineer, or land surveyor." MI ST 339.2304. In New Jersey, the "practice of professional planning" is defined to include "the administration, advising, consultation or performance of professional work in the development of master plans * * * and other professional planning services related thereto intended primarily to guide governmental policy for the assurance of the orderly and coordinated development of municipal, county, regional, and metropolitan land areas, and the State or portions thereof. The work of the professional planner shall not include or supercede any of the duties of an attorney at law, a licensed professional engineer, land surveyor or registered architect * * *" N.J.S.A. 45:14A–2(c).

2. In addition to the problem of the principal case, defining the "planner," the type of work done by the planner, whoever she may be, can

raise serious questions. Planners frequently participate in the drafting of land use ordinances, and may also appear before some governmental agency as an advocate. Do these activities constitute the unauthorized practice of law? Consider the following excerpts from an article, Care, The City Planner and the Unauthorized Practice of Law, 2 Land Use Controls Q. No. 4, pp. 23–30 (1968):

> A zoning ordinance is a complicated, highly technical, legal instrument which is, or should be, related in some way to a comprehensive plan. Few attorneys are capable of preparing a zoning ordinance. Probably even fewer members of the planning profession have the experience and legal knowledge for such work despite the fact that many planners do prepare zoning ordinances as well as amendments to ordinances. In the past, planners have tended to utilize a "cut and paste" technique, with the almost verbatim transfer of language or standards from other zoning ordinances to their own. As a result, many communities are now saddled with zoning ordinances that are outmoded and inappropriate and which, in general, reflect the concepts and personal prejudices of the person or persons who prepared the original text. * * *
>
> Although it is sometimes difficult to establish a line of demarcation between the functions of the planner and those of the municipal attorney during the preparation of a zoning ordinance, guidelines have been established by the professional legal and planning organizations. The American Institute of Planners has adopted a statement of principles of responsibility relating to the preparation of land-use control and other planning regulations which attempts to delineate the area of responsibility of both the planner and the attorney. This statement acknowledges the contribution of the legal profession to the planning process in these words:
>
>> Attorneys contribute significantly to the substantive portion of planning and to the application of planning concepts. They assist in developing and clarifying the relationship of planning to government, and to the means of applying planning processes and proposals to public policy and private activity * * *.
>
> This statement of principles also admits that "a planner, unless he is also an attorney and member of the Bar, *does not have the professional competence to put the technical provisions of an ordinance into suitable final legal form.*" (Emphasis added.) There are perhaps no more than a dozen planners in this country who can satisfy this requirement. There are a great many more practicing attorneys with some expertise in zoning enactments and litigation, but few of them have any practical experience in the technical phases of plan preparation. (There is a need for individuals with such dual competence within both professions.) It is apparent that the planners' professional organization is aware of the need for coordination of the activities of both the planner and the municipal attorney during the preparation of a zoning enactment. It is clear, also, that this organization realizes that the professional planner is not competent to relate the concepts of due process, private property rights, and other constitutional guarantees to planning proposals and land-use control regulations. It is unfortunate that many practicing

planners recognize neither this limitation on their part nor the importance of preserving the constitutional guarantees with respect to the rights of individual property owners.

* * *

There is literally no case law relating to this subject, although in 1964 the Illinois State Bar filed suit against Evert Kinkaid and Associates, Inc., a planning consulting firm located in Chicago, alleging that the firm was in the business of drafting zoning ordinances for various municipalities in Illinois and that such activity constituted the unauthorized practice of law. The Circuit Court of Madison County, Illinois, entered a consent decree which enjoined the defendant from drafting zoning ordinances and which read in part as follows:

> "That the Defendant shall not prepare or purport to prepare any legal documents in a form which may be adopted as an ordinance or resolution by the legislative body of the County of Madison. That the Defendant and its agents and employees shall in connection with providing professional planning consultant services to the County of Madison restrict themselves solely and completely to the preparation and recommendation of technical planning standards which may be embodied in a subsequent draft of a zoning ordinance, it being understood that the preparation of the draft of such zoning ordinance shall be the responsibility of a member of the Bar of the State of Illinois to be designated by the Board of Supervisors of Madison County."

It has been well established in the majority of states that representation before state agencies conducting adversary administrative proceedings constitutes the practice of law and that laymen may not appear in such proceedings in a representative capacity nor may they do the necessary preparatory work. The practice of law has been broadly defined as including not only proceedings where trial work is involved but also "the preparation of legal documents, their interpretation, the giving of legal advice, or the *application of legal principles to problems of any complexity* * * *."

* * *

In Liebtag v. Dilworth [25 Pa. D. & C. 2d 221, Ct. of Common Pleas, 1st Dist., Philadelphia (1961)] the Philadelphia Zoning Board of Adjustment had adopted a rule which prohibited non-lawyers from practicing before that body. The plaintiff, a planner, filed a mandamus suit, complaining that he had been unlawfully and improperly deprived of his right to earn a livelihood. The court not only held the rule to be valid and enforceable, but that such practice constituted the practice of law and that those sections of the city's zoning ordinance which related to the operation of the Zoning Board of Adjustment were invalid, null, and void to the extent that they purported to authorize any lay person to engage in the practice of law before that body. Thus the court indicated in no uncertain terms that the representation of an applicant before an administrative body of this nature by a non-lawyer—even a planner who may have specialized training in a related field—constitutes the unauthorized practice of law.

Liebtag relates only to lay practice before a board of appeals, at least that was the only body directly involved in the case. It is suggested here that because of differences between the nature of the activities of a planning commission and a board of appeals, representation before a commission is not necessarily the practice of law although practice before a board may well be so.

* * *

It would appear, then, that whereas practice before a board of appeals may very well constitute the practice of law as defined by the court in Liebtag v. Dilworth, practice before a planning commission may not necessarily be considered as such. The legal elements of a proceeding before a board of appeals are obvious and inescapable, while proceedings before a planning commission may be entirely without legal significance. A final determination as to whether the practice of law is involved depends to a large extent upon the nature of the proceedings before the planning commission and the type of presentation made by the individual involved. If the proceedings before a planning commission require the application of case law and legal principles, or an understanding of the rules of evidence and the historical development of property rights, the practice of law is involved, and it would be improper for a planner to appear in any capacity other than as an expert witness.

Thus far we have considered only the status of the planning consultant or privately employed planner practicing before a board of appeals and, under certain conditions, before a planning commission. A more complex, and perhaps more important, problem is raised by planners employed by public agencies. * * *

It is customary for planners employed by a planning commission or board of appeals to prepare a written analysis of each application considered by that agency. Such reports are frequently legally oriented and may recommend denial of a specific application because it constitutes a "spot zone" or a "strip zone," both of which are terms that require legal interpretation, or because the applicant is unable to satisfy certain legal criteria established by the courts or by enabling statutes. These comments may then be reiterated or even amplified during a verbal presentation of the staff recommendation, so that the planner is, in effect, using conclusions of law to influence the decision of an administrative agency. Such a situation is particularly unfair and inappropriate in view of the fact that, once a request for an ordinance amendment or a variance has been denied, there is a presumption that the legislative or administrative body involved has acted properly, and the courts will generally be loath to overturn such a decision.

The question, then, appears to be whether the public, and, more particularly, an applicant appearing before a planning commission or board of appeals, is being deprived of the proper determination of substantial rights in an instance where a publicly employed planner, acting in an advisory capacity, is able to convince such body that the applicant cannot legally substantiate his request. Is such an individual qualified to interpret the law, to quote legal precedent, and to relate precedent to the application under consideration? Under the circumstances, it is logical to conclude that this individual is performing much the same type of service that the court considered the practice of law in Liebtag v. Dilworth, the only distinction being that he is a public employee and his "client" is the administrative body rather than an individual appearing before the body.

Even more significant is the fact that many city planners, dissatisfied with "Euclidean" zoning because it does not provide either the amount of flexibility or the control felt necessary to achieve certain planning goals, are experimenting with new methods of land-use control—frequently without professional counsel and sometimes without the actual knowledge of the administrative agency involved. This is often accomplished by establishing requirements for the submission of so-called development plans, which may or may not contain restrictive covenants or be required to be filed of record. This is, however, only one of the methods being used to overcome the shortcomings of "Euclidean" zoning. Another method is to prepare and recommend the adoption of bylaws or rules of procedure that substantially affect the rights of the public, or suggest the use of restrictive methods of processing applications.

The most unfortunate aspect of this effort on the part of the planner is that, in most cases, he has little or no appreciation of the legal significance of some of the procedures and requirements that he has helped to establish. His concern is not with the property rights of individuals but with how to overcome such rights—rights he sometimes considers to be an impediment to the public welfare—in order to achieve the above-mentioned "goals." This is not to say that there is no need for an improvement in the existing land-use control system, but only that we should move in that direction only with the advice and assistance of legal counsel and only after the administrative body involved and the general public have been apprised of the rights they may be surrendering in the process.

C. SHOULD PLANNERS BE LICENSED?

This article by Joseph A. Pobiner, AICP is excerpted from the April/May 1994 issue of Texas Planning Review, the newsletter of the Texas Chapter of the American Planning Association. Copyright by Joseph A. Pobiner.

At present, only Michigan and New Jersey regulate the practice of planning at the state level through a process of certification and licensure. Hawaii has considered similar legislation, and other states are likely to follow. Licensing probably won't solve any problems related to the practice of planning, but it might give planners a way to improve the quality of such practice. Many associated disciplines—engineers, landscape architects, architects, lawyers—offer professional planning consulting services. The discipline of planning sprang from these (and other) professions. Yet all of these professions are strictly regulated. By law, a certified planner cannot legally call him/herself an engineer, architect, and so on. With planning becoming increasingly specialized, would licensing ensure the quality of work from those calling themselves "planners"?

How would such a system work? Probably planning would copy the certification processes of other professions. An overall national exam with sections of state-specific questions could be administered. The exam used by the American Institute of Certified Planners (an institute of the American Planning Association) seems to be the logical vehicle for such a test. But since APA is composed of professional and citizen planners, would/should the "lay planners" be allowed to take the exam or not? Would such a distinction alienate a large segment of APA's membership? Grandfathering all existing practicing planners, regardless of certification or education, would also undoubtedly be required. That means, in effect, that it would take quite some time to ensure that all "licensed" practicing planners had gone through the certification process. One solution might be the introduction of a system for naming AICP "fellows," similar to the system used by the American Society of Landscape Architects and the American Institute of Architects. If planners were certified, perhaps there would be a provision in the state procurement code that would exempt planning proposals from competitive bids. That would assure public clients that planning services were selected based on merit and experience, not merely price.

Note

1. To be licensed in Michigan, planners must meet the following statutory requirements:

(a) Has passed an examination approved by the department and the board.

(b) Is of good moral character.

(c) Has had not less than 6 years of planning experience in the type of work necessary to the preparation or implementation of comprehensive community plans, not less than 2 years of which shall have been in the United States. However, only 2 years of planning experience is mandatory. A maximum waiver of 4 years may be allowed for 1 degree only as follows:

i. Doctorate or master's degree in planning, 4 years' credit.

ii. Bachelor's degree in planning, 3 years' credit

iii. Doctorate or master's degree in a related field including architecture, landscape architecture, civil engineering, sociology, economics, geography, political science, or public administration, 3 years' credit.

iv. Any other degree in a related field, 2 years' credit.

MI St. 339.2306.

New Jersey's licensure requirements provide in part that it " ... shall be unlawful for any person to practice or to offer to practice professional planning in this State, or to use the title 'professional planner' or any other title, sign, card or device in such manner as to tend to convey the impression that such person is practicing professional planning or is a professional planner, unless such person is duly licensed ..." N.J.S.A. 45:14A–1. Similar to the qualifications for licensure in Michigan, New Jersey requires at a minimum that applicants for a professional planner license:

(1) Be of good moral character;

(2) Be a citizen of the United States or have declared his intention to become a citizen of the United States;

(3) Pass the required examinations.

* * *

The applicant for license as a professional planner shall submit the following minimum educational and experience qualifications:

(1) A graduate degree in professional planning from an accredited college or university in a curriculum offering instruction in such recognized planning subjects as principles of land use planning, history of city planning, planning project design, and planning law and administration * * * with a minimum of two years' experience in the full-time practice of professional planning * * *; or

A graduate degree in a field other than professional planning from an accredited college or university with a minimum of four years' experience in the full-time practice or professional planning * * *; or

(2) An undergraduate degree in professional planning from an accredited college or university; or curriculum offering a major or option comprising a minimum of 21 credits in such recognized planning subjects * * * with a minimum of three years' experience in the full-time practice of professional planning * * *; or

An undergraduate degree in a field other than professional planning from an accredited college or university with a minimum of four years' experience * * *

(3) Graduation from a secondary school and at least 8 years of professional planning experience * * *;

N.J.S.A. 45:14A–9.

D. TRAINING REQUIREMENTS FOR PLAYERS IN THE LAND USE GAME

Unlike other players in the land use decision making process, such as professional planners, code enforcement officers and engineers, members of local legislative bodies and land use boards often have no specific education or training in land use matters prior to their election or appointment. In fact, in most jurisdictions, the only legal requirements to be satisfied prior to running for office or seeking an appointment to a planning or zoning board is that the individuals be of voting age (18 years old) and that they reside in the jurisdiction where they seek to serve. Board members are required, however, to follow procedural and substantive requirements contained in the law. With limited exceptions, once seated on these boards, individuals are not required to participate in formal training programs specifically focused on land use planning and zoning law, putting them in the position to learn solely from "on the job training." Over the past few years, however, states have begun to recognize the need for mandatory training and continuing education of members of planning and zoning boards. Currently, six states (Kentucky, Louisiana, New Jersey, New York, South Carolina, and Tennessee), have enacted training requirements for members of planning and zoning boards (see, Ky. Rev. Stat. Ann. § 147A.027 (2001), La. Rev. Stat. Ann. § 33:103.1 (2004), N.J. Stat. Ann. § 40:55D–23.4 (2005), N.Y. Gen. City Law § 27 (2006), S.C. Code Ann. §§ 6–29–1340, 6–29–1350 (2003), and Tenn. Code Ann. § 13–4–101 (2002)).

Many of the state mandated training programs require board members to attend preliminary training sessions either before or shortly after taking their positions. Following this orientation training, which may be from four to six hours long, continuing education requirements are mandated. Some states have provided a laundry list of potential topics appropriate to satisfy these requirements. In Kentucky, for example, training programs may cover land use planning, zoning, floodplains, transportation, community facilities, ethics, public utilities, wireless telecom facilities, parliamentary procedure, public hearing procedure, administrative law, economic development, housing, public buildings, building construction, land subdivision, powers and duties of boards of adjustment, and additional topics approved by the planning commission. In the other states it has been left to the local governments to determine the content of the training based upon locally assessed educational needs. See, Patricia E. Salkin, "States Beginning to Recognize that Training is Essential for Members of Planning and Zoning Boards and Local Legislative Bodies," 35 Real Estate L.J. 315 (Fall 2006).

In the spring of 2007, the American Institute of Certified Planners adopted mandatory continuing education requirements for their members called "Certification Maintenance." The requirements mandate a minimum of thirty-two credits every two years, with a minimum of 1.5 credits in ethics and 1.5 credits in planning law. Details concerning the AICP's continuing education requirements can be found at http://www.planning.org/certification/maintenance.htm.

E. ETHICAL CONDUCT OF PARTIES IN THE LAND USE ARENA

Ethical dilemmas in the land use arena can be categorized into (1) conflicts of interest; (2) compatibility of dual office holding; and (3) bias and prejudgment. By far, the overwhelming amount of litigation centers on alleged conflicts of interest on the part of planners, attorneys, members of planning and zoning boards, and other participants in the planning and land use regulation process. This section examines relevant regulations and explores, through cases and notes, a variety of ethics issues that have captured the public's attention. Attorneys must be conversant with ethical challenges facing all of the parties in the land use game to best provide guidance to their government clients and to ensure that there is integrity in the land use planning and decisionmaking processes.

(1) Planners

Professional planners who are members of the American Institute of Certified Planners [AICP] are required to adhere to a written code of ethics. AICP is a voluntary membership organization that requires successful completion of a written examination as a condition of membership. Excerpts from the AICP Code of Ethics are reprinted below:

AICP CODE OF ETHICS AND PROFESSIONAL CONDUCT

(Adopted March 19, 2005).

* * * The principles to which we subscribe in * * * the Code derive from the special responsibility of our profession to serve the public interest with compassion for the welfare of all people and, as professionals, to our obligation to act with high integrity.

As the basic values of society can come into competition with each other, so can the aspirational principles we espouse under this Code. An ethical judgment often requires a conscientious balancing, based on the facts and context of a particular situation and on the precepts of the entire Code.

As Certified Planners, all of us are also members of the American Planning Association and share in the goal of building better, more inclusive communities. We want the public to be aware of the principles by which we practice our profession in the quest of that goal. We sincerely hope that the public will respect the commitments we make to our employers and clients, our fellow professionals, and all other persons whose interests we affect.

A. Principles to Which We Aspire

1. *Our Overall Responsibility to the Public*

Our primary obligation is to serve the public interest and we, therefore, owe our allegiance to a conscientiously attained concept of the public interest that is formulated through continuous and open debate. We shall achieve high standards of professional integrity, proficiency, and knowledge. To comply with our obligation to the public, we aspire to the following principles:

a) We shall always be conscious of the rights of others.

b) We shall have special concern for the long-range consequences of present actions.

c) We shall pay special attention to the interrelatedness of decisions.

d) We shall provide timely, adequate, clear, and accurate information on planning issues to all affected persons and to governmental decision makers.

e) We shall give people the opportunity to have a meaningful impact on the development of plans and programs that may affect them. Participation should be broad enough to include those who lack formal organization or influence.

f) We shall seek social justice by working to expand choice and opportunity for all persons, recognizing a special responsibility to plan for the needs of the disadvantaged and to promote racial and economic integration. We shall urge the alteration of policies, institutions, and decisions that oppose such needs.

g) We shall promote excellence of design and endeavor to conserve and preserve the integrity and heritage of the natural and built environment.

h) We shall deal fairly with all participants in the planning process. Those of us who are public officials or employees shall also deal evenhandedly with all planning process participants.

2. Our Responsibility to Our Clients and Employers

We owe diligent, creative, and competent performance of the work we do in pursuit of our client or employer's interest. Such performance, however, shall always be consistent with our faithful service to the public interest.

a) We shall exercise independent professional judgment on behalf of our clients and employers.

b) We shall accept the decisions of our client or employer concerning the objectives and nature of the professional services we perform unless the course of action is illegal or plainly inconsistent with our primary obligation to the public interest.

c) We shall avoid a conflict of interest or even the appearance of a conflict of interest in accepting assignments from clients or employers.

3. Our Responsibility to Our Profession and Colleagues

We shall contribute to the development of, and respect for, our profession by improving knowledge and techniques, making work relevant to solutions of community problems, and increasing public understanding of planning activities.

a) We shall protect and enhance the integrity of our profession.

b) We shall educate the public about planning issues and their relevance to our everyday lives.

c) We shall describe and comment on the work and views of other professionals in a fair and professional manner.

d) We shall share the results of experience and research that contribute to the body of planning knowledge.

e) We shall examine the applicability of planning theories, methods, research and practice and standards to the facts and analysis of each particular situation and shall not accept the applicability of a customary solution without first establishing its appropriateness to the situation.

f) We shall contribute time and resources to the professional development of students, interns, beginning professionals, and other colleagues.

g) We shall increase the opportunities for members of underrepresented groups to become professional planners and help them advance in the profession.

h) We shall continue to enhance our professional education and training.

i) We shall systematically and critically analyze ethical issues in the practice of planning.

j) We shall contribute time and effort to groups lacking in adequate planning resources and to voluntary professional activities.

B. Our Rules of Conduct

We adhere to the following Rules of Conduct, and we understand that our Institute will enforce compliance with them. If we fail to adhere to these Rules, we could receive sanctions, the ultimate being the loss of our certification:

1. We shall not deliberately or with reckless indifference fail to provide adequate, timely, clear and accurate information on planning issues.

2. We shall not accept an assignment from a client or employer when the services to be performed involve conduct that we know to be illegal or in violation of these rules.

3. We shall not accept an assignment from a client or employer to publicly advocate a position on a planning issue that is indistinguishably adverse to a position we publicly advocated for a previous client or employer within the past three years unless (1) we determine in good faith after consultation with other qualified professionals that our change of position will not cause present detriment to our previous client or employer, and (2) we make full written disclosure of the conflict to our current client or employer and receive written permission to proceed with the assignment.

4. We shall not, as salaried employees, undertake other employment in planning or a related profession, whether or not for pay,

without having made full written disclosure to the employer who furnishes our salary and having received subsequent written permission to undertake additional employment, unless our employer has a written policy which expressly dispenses with a need to obtain such consent.

5. We shall not, as public officials or employees; accept from anyone other than our public employer any compensation, commission, rebate, or other advantage that may be perceived as related to our public office or employment.

6. We shall not perform work on a project for a client or employer if, in addition to the agreed upon compensation from our client or employer, there is a possibility for direct personal or financial gain to us, our family members, or persons living in our household, unless our client or employer, after full written disclosure from us, consents in writing to the arrangement.

7. We shall not use to our personal advantage, nor that of a subsequent client or employer, information gained in a professional relationship that the client or employer has requested be held inviolate or that we should recognize as confidential because its disclosure could result in embarrassment or other detriment to the client or employer. Nor shall we disclose such confidential information except when (1) required by process of law, or (2) required to prevent a clear violation of law, or (3) required to prevent a substantial injury to the public. Disclosure pursuant to (2) and (3) shall not be made until after we have verified the facts and issues involved and, when practicable, exhausted efforts to obtain reconsideration of the matter and have sought separate opinions on the issue from other qualified professionals employed by our client or employer.

8. We shall not, as public officials or employees, engage in private communications with planning process participants if the discussions relate to a matter over which we have authority to make a binding, final determination if such private communications are prohibited by law or by agency rules, procedures, or custom.

9. We shall not engage in private discussions with decision makers in the planning process in any manner prohibited by law or by agency rules, procedures, or custom.

10. We shall neither deliberately, nor with reckless indifference, misrepresent the qualifications, views and findings of other professionals.

11. We shall not solicit prospective clients or employment through use of false or misleading claims, harassment, or duress.

12. We shall not misstate our education, experience, training, or any other facts which are relevant to our professional qualifications.

13. We shall not sell, or offer to sell, services by stating or implying an ability to influence decisions by improper means.

14. We shall not use the power of any office to seek or obtain a special advantage that is not a matter of public knowledge or is not in the public interest.

15. We shall not accept work beyond our professional competence unless the client or employer understands and agrees that such work will be performed by another professional competent to perform the work and acceptable to the client or employer.

16. We shall not accept work for a fee, or pro bono, that we know cannot be performed with the promptness required by the prospective client, or that is required by the circumstances of the assignment.

17. We shall not use the product of others' efforts to seek professional recognition or acclaim intended for producers of original work.

18. We shall not direct or coerce other professionals to make analyses or reach findings not supported by available evidence.

19. We shall not fail to disclose the interests of our client or employer when participating in the planning process. Nor shall we participate in an effort to conceal the true interests of our client or employer.

20. We shall not unlawfully discriminate against another person.

21. We shall not withhold cooperation or information from the AICP Ethics Officer or the AICP Ethics Committee if a charge of ethical misconduct has been filed against us.

22. We shall not retaliate or threaten retaliation against a person who has filed a charge of ethical misconduct against us or another planner, or who is cooperating in the Ethics Officer's investigation of an ethics charge.

23. We shall not use the threat of filing an ethics charge in order to gain, or attempt to gain, an advantage in dealings with another planner.

24. We shall not file a frivolous charge of ethical misconduct against another planner.

25. We shall neither deliberately, nor with reckless indifference, commit any wrongful act, whether or not specified in the Rules of Conduct, that reflects adversely on our professional fitness.

Notes

1. Planners are members of the community too, and occasionally their personal needs and interests could present a potential for conflicts of interest. Should planners live in the community where they work? What should planners do when confronted with "investment" opportunities in

their community to participate in a small development project? Should they be able to invest in real estate development in the same municipality where they work? Can their spouse? Is disclosure enough? In a case decided on procedural grounds (reversal of a summary judgment order) one court found that more information was needed to determine whether a conflict of interest existed where the property-owner applicant was the director of the county planning and zoning department and he submitted an application for a conditional use permit (needed in order to lease his property for the installation of a telecommunications tower) to his own office for review. Crozer v. Reichert, 275 Ga. 118, 561 S.E.2d 120 (2002).

2. The new AICP Code of Ethics was adopted following an independent critique of the 1991 AICP Code of Ethics for Planners. Among the purposes of the critique was an assessment of whether the language of the Code was clear and enforceable and whether the Code provided for appropriate due process. The assessment is available at http://www.planning.org/ethics/salkin.htm. A complete version of the current AICP Code of Ethics, including procedural requirements, is available at: http://www.planning.org/ethics/conduct.html. See also, Patricia E. Salkin, "Examining Land Use Planning and Zoning Ethics from a Planner's Perspective: Lessons for All Stakeholders in the Real Estate Game," 34 Real Estate L.J. 508 (Spring 2006).

(2) Attorneys

Although lawyers do have a professional code of ethics to follow, there is no code of ethics or professional conduct that specifically covers lawyers who participate in land use matters. Consider the following ethics questions:

1. A lawyer sits as a member if the planning board. May she step down to represent a client before the board and then return to her seat after the matter is presented and/or resolved?

2. A lawyer in private practice who advised the zoning board for five years was recently replaced with another attorney when the new mayor took office. Can he now represent an applicant before that same board?

3. When a full-time city attorney is assigned to review a matter pending before the planning and zoning boards and to advise them on appropriate action(s), who is the client of the city attorney? Does it make a difference if the various offices and divisions within the government have different ideas on how to proceed?

4. May an attorney who serves as counsel to the municipal water supply board represent a developer in applications for subdivision approval before the city planning and zoning commission?

5. What is the appropriate conduct for a lawyer-member of the planning commission when a partner or associate in her law firm appears before the commission? Who should be disqualified—the attorney-commission member or the law firm? Why?

6. What is the appropriate ethical conduct where the planning commissioner's daughter is a member of a law firm appearing before the

board? Does it make a difference whether her daughter is the attorney of record in the matter?

NICHOLAS v. WILTON ZONING BOARD OF APPEALS

Superior Court of Connecticut, 2001.
2001 WL 1200339, 30 Conn. L. Rptr. 386.

MEMORANDUM OF DECISION RE MOTION TO DISQUALIFY #109

HICKEY, J.

The defendant, the Zoning Board of Appeals of the town of Wilton, has moved to disqualify Robert A. Fuller (Fuller) from representing the plaintiff in this case on the grounds that: (1) the representation violates Rule 1.9 of the Rules of Professional Conduct because Fuller formerly represented the town of Wilton, as town counsel, in connection with the same property and same issue involved in this case, and the town of Wilton has not consented to Fuller's representation of the plaintiff in this case; and (2) the documents and/or testimony arising from Fuller's prior representation may be presented in the trial of this case, in violation of Rules 1.6 and 3.7 of the Rules of Professional Conduct. On September 11, 2001, during a hearing held by this court, the parties were provided with an opportunity to present oral arguments and evidence in support of their respective positions.

A brief summary of the background of this case is useful to an understanding of the issues raised by the motion presently before this court. The plaintiff, Nick P. Nicholas, is the owner of a parcel of land located at 92 Hulda Hill Road in Wilton, Connecticut. The subject property contains 2.104 acres located in a two-acre residential zone, and is shown as Lot No. 1 on the subdivision map #2829, approved by Planning and Zoning Commission for the town of Wilton in 1969. On September 20, 1999, the plaintiff applied for a zoning permit to build a single-family residence on the subject property. On September 23, 1999, the zoning enforcement officer, relying on a legal opinion provided by the town's land use counsel, denied the application on the ground that the parcel was not a valid building lot.

Prior to the plaintiff's purchase of Lot No. 1, however, in an opinion letter drafted in 1975, the plaintiff's present attorney, Robert A. Fuller, then town counsel, advised the town planner that a permit could be issued on the lot in accordance with various sections of the zoning regulations in effect at that time, and furthermore, advised the town planner that if it was impossible for the property owner to comply with certain regulations, the town could not validly deny the owner use of the property. In July of 1986, Fuller resigned from his position as town counsel for the town of Wilton and has not since represented the town of Wilton in any capacity.

On October 21, 1999, the plaintiff filed an appeal of the zoning enforcement officer's decision with the Zoning Board of Appeals of the town of Wilton. A public hearing was held on December 20, 1999. Fuller was present at the hearing and provided testimony in relation to the 1975 opinion letter he rendered while serving as town counsel. On January 19, 2000, the board denied the appeal on the ground that the subdivision lot was not a valid lot. The plaintiff now appeals the decision of the board, the defendant herein, and asserts that it acted illegally, arbitrarily, and in abuse of its discretion. Fuller is the plaintiff's counsel in this case, the appeal of the board's decision.

In its memorandum, the defendant argues that the plaintiff's interests are adverse to Fuller's former client's interests. Moreover, the defendant argues that the present matter is the same or at least substantially related to Fuller's prior representation, inasmuch as this case and Fuller's 1975 opinion letter both deal with the same piece of property and the same issue of whether or not that property is a buildable lot. Furthermore, the defendant argues that the scope of Rule 1.9 of the Rules of Professional Conduct is not limited to situations where the lawyer might disclose privileged information received from the former client. Rather, the defendant contends that unless the former client consents, Rule 1.9 is a blanket prohibition that applies regardless of whether the lawyer now states that he relied on public records or documents. Consequently, the defendant requests that Fuller be disqualified from serving as the plaintiff's counsel in this case.

In response, Fuller argues that the similarity in the subject matter of the present litigation and the 1975 opinion letter is insufficient, by itself, to provide a basis for his disqualification. Fuller contends that the 1975 opinion letter was not a confidential document and has been part of the public record since it was rendered, and was not based on any confidential information obtained by him while serving as town counsel. Fuller also maintains that Rule 1.9 is not as sweeping as the defendant contends and requires the court to make its determination based on the facts of each case. Thus, Fuller concludes that the facts of this case do not warrant his disqualification.

"The trial court has the authority to regulate the conduct of attorneys and has a duty to enforce the standards of conduct regarding attorneys * * * Since October 1986, the conduct of attorneys has been regulated also by the Rules of Professional Conduct, which were approved by the judges of the Superior Court and which superseded the Code of Professional Responsibility * * * The trial court has broad discretion to determine whether there exists a conflict of interest that would warrant disqualification of an attorney." Bergeron v. Mackler, 225 Conn. 391, 397, 623 A.2d 489 (1993). "Disqualification of counsel is a remedy that serves to enforce the lawyer's duty of absolute fidelity and to guard against the danger of inadvertent use of confidential information * * * In disqualification matters, however, we must be solicitous of a client's right freely to choose his counsel, * * * mindful of the fact that a client whose attorney is disqualified may suffer the loss of time and money in finding new counsel and may lose the benefit of its longtime counsel's specialized knowledge of its operations * * * The competing interests at stake in the motion to disqualify, therefore, are: (1) the defendant's interest in protecting confidential information; (2) the plaintiffs' interest in freely selecting counsel of their choice; and (3) the public's interest in the scrupulous administration of justice." The mere appearance of impropriety, however, "will not stand alone to disqualify an attorney in the absence of any indication that the attorney's representation risks violating the Rules of Professional Conduct."

Rule 1.9 of the Rules of Professional Conduct governs disqualification of counsel for a conflict of interest relating to a former client. The rule states, in relevant part, that: "A lawyer who has formerly represented a client in a matter shall not thereafter: (1) Represent another person in the same or a substantially related matter in which that person's interests are materially adverse to the interests of the former client unless the former client consents after consultation * * *" Furthermore, the Commentary to Rule 1.9 states, in relevant part, "The scope of a 'matter' for purposes of subdivision (1) may depend on the facts of a particular situation or transaction. The lawyer's involvement in a matter can also be a question of degree * * * The underlying question is whether the lawyer was so involved in the matter that the subsequent representation can be justly regarded as a changing of sides in the matter in question * * * Information acquired by the lawyer in the course of representing a client may not subsequently be used by the lawyer to the disadvantage of the client. However, the fact that a lawyer has once served a client does not preclude the lawyer from using generally known information about that client when later representing another client."

In the present case, this court has considered the relationship between Fuller's representation of the defendant as town counsel for the town of Wilton several years ago, and his representation of the plaintiff against the defendant, the Zoning Board of Appeals of the town of Wilton, in this appeal. In balancing the competing interests at stake in this case, this court notes that the defendant does not allege that it divulged any confidential information to Fuller. This court finds that twenty-six years have passed since Fuller authored the opinion letter for the town of Wilton, at a time when the town was not in an adversarial position with respect to the subject property. This court finds that fifteen years have gone by since Fuller severed his relationship with the defendant. Furthermore, this court finds that the public's interest in the scrupulous administration of justice will not be compromised by Fuller's continued representation of the plaintiff in this case. Consequently, this court finds that in this case, the plaintiff's interest in the free selection of the counsel of his choice outweighs the defendant's interest in protecting confidential information. * * * Accordingly, this court finds that Fuller's prior representation of the defendant does not provide a sufficient relationship to the facts surrounding this present matter to warrant his disqualification pursuant to Rule 1.9.

Next, the defendant asserts that Rule 3.7 prohibits a lawyer from acting as an advocate at trial where the lawyer is likely to be a necessary witness, except under limited circumstances not applicable here. The defendant asserts that Fuller has already provided testimony in relation to this matter in the past, on December 20, 1999, at the public hearing held by the Zoning Board of Appeals of the town of Wilton. The defendant argues that Fuller's continued representation of the plaintiff may result in a violation of Rule 3.7 of the Rules of Professional Conduct.

In response, Fuller argues that speculation as to a possible future violation of Rule 3.7 is not a valid ground for his disqualification. Fuller maintains that Rule 3.7 is not applicable in this case, as he does not intend to testify on any issue in this case. Rule 3.7 provides the framework for disqualification where counsel is likely to be called as a necessary witness in the present litigation. * * * Nevertheless, "[t]estimony may be relevant and even highly useful but still not strictly necessary * * * A finding of necessity takes into account such factors as the significance of the matters, weight of the testimony and availability of other evidence * * * [T]he mere statement that the attorney will be a necessary party witness [would] not support [the] motion." (Brackets in original; citations omitted; internal quotation marks omitted.) Somers & Associates v. Kendall, supra, Superior Court, Docket No. 064478; Bopko v. Bopko, supra, 28 Conn. L. Rptr. 557. A strong showing that the testimony of the opposing attorney is truly necessary is required before the court may grant a motion to disqualify opposing counsel. Somers & Associates v. Kendall, supra, Docket No. 064478; DeMarco v. Fire Command, Inc., Superior Court, judicial district of New Haven at New Haven, Docket No. 297381 (July 27, 1990) (Downey, J.) (2 Conn. L. Rptr. 101). In this case, the defendant simply fails to persuade this court that Fuller's testimony will truly be necessary, in violation of Rule 3.7.

Accordingly, for the foregoing reasons, the defendant's motion to disqualify is denied without prejudice.

Notes

1. A case somewhat contrary to the Wilton case is Walden Federal Sav. and Loan Ass'n v. Village of Walden, 212 A.D.2d 718, 622 N.Y.S.2d 796 (2d Dept. 1995), leave to appeal dismissed, 86 N.Y.2d 777, 631 N.Y.S.2d 603, 655 N.E.2d 700 (1995), where a law firm represented a municipality at various times for approximately thirty years, and during the scope of that representation the law firm, among other things, worked on the drafting of a local site plan law. The New York appellate court held that six years after the last representation, the law firm was prohibited under the applicable Code of Professional Responsibility from appearing before the municipality on behalf of another client requesting site plan review. This case has chilling implications for land use attorneys who represent municipal clients as part of their private practice. But see, Kay F. Sterrett v. Loundon County Board of Supervisors, 22 Va. Cir. 148 (1990) where the Virginia Court held that a law firm would not be disqualified where the firm employs a former county attorney who was involved in land-use matters during her employ as a county attorney.

2. For a review of legal ethical dilemmas in land-use planning and zoning see, Eric Dyas, "Conflicts of Interest in Planning and Zoning Cases," 17 J. Legal Prof. 219 (1992); Mark W. Cordes, "Policing Bias and Conflicts of Interest in Zoning Decisionmaking," 65 N.D.L.Rev. 161 (1989); Patricia E. Salkin, "Legal Ethics and Land–Use Planning," 30 The Urban Lawyer 383 (Spring 1998); Salkin, "1998 Survey of Ethics in Land Use Law," 26 Fordham Urb. L.J. 1393 (1999); and Salkin, "Ethics Allegations in Land Use Continue to Fill the Court Dockets," Zoning and Planning Law Report (April 2003); Salkin, "Ethics in Land Use: Using Ethical Allegations as a Sword Rather Than a Shield," 33 Real Estate L.J. 100 (Summer 2004); Salkin, "A Woody Allen Movie, Show Me the Money, and Other Ethical Considerations in Land Use Planning," Zoning and Planning Law Report (March 2004); Salkin, "Conflicts of Interest and Other Legal Ethical Considerations for Planners and Lawyers," Planning and Environmental Law vol. 57 no. 8 at 3 (American Planning Association) (August 2005); Salkin, "Land Use Ethics Update 2005: Conflicts of Interest, Improper Conduct and Other Ethical Considerations," Zoning and Planning Law Report (March 2005); Salkin, "Tips for Ethical Considerations in Land–Use Decision Making: No Gobbly Goop in the 2006 Annual Review of Cases and Opinions," Zoning and Planning Law Report (May 2006).

3. In addition to planners and lawyers, there are other professionals who are involved in the land use arena. For example, the American Association of Engineering Societies represents over 500,000 engineers and in 1984 they issued a Model Guide for Professional Conduct. The National Society for Professional Engineers represents over 75,000 engineers and in 1993 they issued a revised Code of Ethics for Engineers. The National Association of Realtors represents more than 750,000 realtors and in 1994 they issued a revised Code of Ethics and Standard of Practice. In a recent opinion, the New York Attorney General found that a member of a village design review board who is a professional architect need not resign from the board although he is a partner in a firm that about once a year accepts projects over which the board has jurisdiction. However, the Attorney General advised that the board member should "unquestionably" recuse himself from any consideration of a project or matter involving his firm. While noting that "to maintain public confidence in the integrity of government, public officials must avoid even the appearance of impropriety," the opinion concludes that, "* * * if resignation and not recusal was the appropriate remedy in every instance where a local official's private endeavors raised a potential conflict of interest * * * local units of government would have difficulty finding qualified individuals to serve the public interest." See, Op. N.Y. Atty. Gen. 2002–8 (March 4, 2002).

(3) Members of Planning and Zoning Boards

Individuals who serve on planning boards and zoning boards are typically community volunteers who receive little or no financial remuneration for their service. Membership on these boards is most often left to the discretion of the appointing authority, which may be the chief elected official or the local legislative body. With sparse limitations on membership qualifications, board members are usually only required to reside within the community they serve. This very fact raises ethics questions with some degree of frequency. Consider the following:

1. Can or should a member of a planning board discuss and vote on an application involving her neighbor's property? What if it is an application of a landowner within her development? Can a board member leave her seat on the board during a public hearing to speak in favor or in opposition to the application before the board where the board member has a personal interest in the matter? If it is permissible for the board member to do this, must she recuse herself from voting? How about her ability to discuss and debate the matter with her colleagues on the board? May she question the applicant or the applicant's representative(s)?

2. Can or should individuals in the following professions serve on planning board and zoning boards: engineers, architects, lawyers, planners, realtors, land surveyors, bankers, developers? Does their potential expertise in land use planning and zoning matters make them more suitable candidates for membership on the boards? When might they be confronted with ethical dilemmas?

3. Can or should board members vote on matters that could impact members of their immediate family? How significant would the impact need to be? Must it be financial?

Few states provide statutory guidance for members of planning and zoning boards who may find themselves in a conflict of interest situation. For example, Connecticut General Statutes provides in part: "No member of any zoning commission or board and no member of any zoning board of appeals shall participate in the hearing or decision of the board or commission of which he is a member upon any matter in which he is directly or indirectly interested in a personal or financial sense." Conn. Gen. Stat. § 8–11, see also § 8021 for similar language for members of planning commissions.

A number of states provide authorization for the appointment of alternate members of planning and zoning boards in cases of conflicts of interest. See, Salkin, "Planning for Conflicts of Interest in Land Use Decisionmaking: The Use of Alternate Members of Planning and Zoning Boards," 31 Real Estate L. J. 375 (Spring 2003).

SECTION 4. THE CONTENT AND EFFECT OF THE MASTER PLAN

The early Standard Act provided some guidance as to the general purpose of the plan and what information should be included in the land use plan.

UNITED STATES DEPARTMENT OF COMMERCE, A STANDARD CITY PLANNING ENABLING ACT

(1928).

Sec. 6. General Powers and Duties—It shall be the function and duty of the commission to make and adopt a master plan for the physical development of the municipality, including any areas outside of its boundaries which, in the commission's judgment, bear relation to the planning of such municipality. Such plan, with the accompanying maps, plats, charts, and descriptive matter, shall show the commission's recommendations for the development of said territory, including, among other things, the general location, character, and extent of streets, viaducts, subways, bridges, waterways, water fronts, boulevards, parkways, playgrounds, squares, parks, aviation fields, and other public ways, grounds and open spaces, the general location of public buildings and other public property, and the general location and extent of public utilities and terminals, whether publicly or privately owned or operated, for water, light, sanitation, transportation, communication, power, and other purposes; also the removal, relocation, widening, narrowing, vacating, abandonment, change of use or extension of any of the foregoing ways, grounds, open spaces, buildings, property, utilities, or terminals; as well as a zoning plan for the control of the height, area, bulk, location, and use of buildings and premises. As the work of making the whole master plan progresses, the commission may from time to time adopt and publish a part or parts thereof, any such part to cover one or more major sections or divisions of the municipality or one or more of the aforesaid or other functional matters to be included in the plan. The commission may from time to time amend, extend, or add to the plan.

Sec. 7. Purposes in View—In the preparation of such plan the commission shall make careful and comprehensive surveys and studies of present conditions and future growth of the municipality and with due regard to its relation to neighboring territory. The plan shall be made with the general purpose of guiding and accomplishing a coordinated, adjusted, and harmonious development of the municipality and its environs which will, in accordance with present and future needs, best promote health, safety, morals, order, convenience, prosperity, and general welfare, as well as efficiency and economy in the process of development; including, among other things, adequate provision for traffic, the promotion of safety from fire and other dangers, adequate provision for light and air, the promotion of the healthful and convenient distribution of population, the promotion of good civic design and arrangement, wise and efficient expenditure of public funds, and the adequate provision of public utilities and other public requirements.

See Knack, Meck and Stollman, The Real Story Behind the Standard Planning and Zoning Acts of the 1920's, Land Use Law (Feb. 1996) p. 3.

The Model Land Development Code provides model enabling legislation for planning that differs considerably from the Standard Act.

The content of the comprehensive plan and the level of detail at which the subjects are addressed, vary from jurisdiction to jurisdiction. As previously discussed, some state statutes merely authorize local governments to adopt land use plans, providing no further guidance or mandates. Other states, such as New York, provide suggested elements that might be included in a local comprehensive land use plan. For example, the New York law provides that a comprehensive plan may include the following topics at the level of detail adapted to the special requirements of the town:

(a) General statements of goals, objectives, principles, policies, and standards upon which proposals for the immediate and long-range enhancement, growth and development of the town are based.

(b) Consideration of regional needs and the official plans of other government units and agencies within the region.

(c) The existing and proposed location and intensity of land uses.

(d) Consideration of agricultural uses, historic and cultural resources, coastal and natural resources and sensitive environmental areas.

(e) Consideration of population, demographic and socio-economic trends and future projections.

(f) The location and types of transportation facilities.

(g) Existing and proposed general location of public and private utilities and infrastructure.

(h) Existing housing resources and future housing needs, including affordable housing.

(i) The present and future general location of educational and cultural facilities, historic sites, health facilities and facilities for emergency services.

(j) Existing and proposed recreation facilities and parkland.

(k) The present and potential future general location of commercial and industrial facilities.

(*l*) Specific policies and strategies for improving the local economy in coordination with other plan topics.

(m) Proposed measures, programs, devices, and instruments to implement the goals and objectives of the various topics within the comprehensive plan.

(n) All or part of the plan of another public agency.

(*o*) Any and all other items which are consistent with the orderly growth and development of the town.

See, N.Y. Town Law § 272–a.

The American Planning Association's Growing Smart Legislative Guidebook recommends that state planning enabling statutes reflect a three tiered approach to local comprehensive plan elements: mandatory (issues and opportunities, land use, transportation, community facilities, housing, and program implementation); mandatory with an opt-out alternative (economic development, critical and sensitive areas, and natural hazards); and optional (agriculture, forest, and scenic preservation, human services, community design, historic preservation, and sub-plans as needed). The Guidebook also calls for consideration of issues, opportunities and needs of the larger region when preparing the local plan. See, Stuart Meck, FAICP, ed., "Growing Smart Legislative Guidebook: Model Statutes for Planning and the Management of Change," 7–62 (American Planning Association, 2002).

The relationship between planning and regulation has been the subject of discussion for many years. Two articles debating the subject are Sullivan and Kressel, Twenty Years After—Renewed Significance of the Comprehensive Plan Requirement, 9 Urban Law Ann. 33 (1975) and Tarlock, Consistency with Adopted Land Use Plans as a Standard of Review: The Case Against, 9 Urban Law Ann. 69 (1975). For a more recent updates on the evolving role of the comprehensive plan, see, Sullivan and Pelham, "The Evolving Role of the Comprehensive Plan," 29 The Urban Lawyer 363 (1997) and Sullivan, "The Role of the Comprehensive Plan," 31 The Urban Lawyer 915 (1999). In this last article, Sullivan discusses the organization of caselaw into three major categories: 1) the traditional approach which gives no significance to the plan; 2) the "planning factor" approach, which gives the plan a role in such determinations; and 3) the "planning mandate" approach which treats the plan as a dispositive standard for land-use regulations and standards.

CREATIVE DISPLAYS, INC. v. CITY OF FLORENCE

Supreme Court of Kentucky, 1980.
602 S.W.2d 682.

STEPHENS, JUSTICE.

The issue before the court is whether Boone County and Florence, Kentucky, have properly enacted planning and zoning ordinances, pursuant to KRS chapter 100 (1966).

* * *

Until 1966, the City of Florence and Boone County fiscal court were separate planning bodies. The record shows that Florence adopted its zoning ordinance in December of 1962, and Boone County adopted its in February of 1966. In September of 1966, a county-wide planning unit was formed, encompassing Florence, Walton, Hopeful Heights, and Boone County, and known as the Boone County Planning and Zoning Commission. This entity was created in response to House Bill 390, which passed the Kentucky Legislature and became effective on June 16, 1966, and is presently contained in KRS chapter 100.

In October, 1966, the Boone County Planning and Zoning Commission adopted its "comprehensive plan," pursuant to KRS 100.183. This plan consisted solely of the already existing plans of Florence and Boone County. The statute provides that the minimum requirements for the plan include a statement of goals and objectives, a land use plan, a transportation plan, and a community facilities plan. KRS 100.187. It is not argued that the comprehensive plan adopted by the Commission did not contain these elements. On the contrary, it is admitted that the individual plans of Florence and Boone County comply in every respect with the substantive requirements of chapter 100. Yet, Creative Designs still challenges the plan adopted by the Commission as invalid under the statute, and we agree.

* * *

The actions of the Boone County Planning and Zoning Commission in *pro forma* adopting the pre-existing plans of Florence and Boone County do not constitute the "preparation" of a comprehensive plan for the newly created unit.

Further, although the plan adopted by the Commission contains all the elements listed in KRS 100.187, that section requires "a statement of goals and objectives, principles, policies, and standards, which shall serve as a guide for the physical development and economic and social well-being *of the planning unit.*" (emphasis added). In this instance the planning unit includes Florence, Walton, Hopeful Heights, and Boone County. The goals and objectives expressed by Florence and Boone County in their individual plans in no way address the question of the proper goals for the new, county-wide planning unit. The same is true of the specialized research, analysis, and projections which are required to support the elements of the comprehensive plan. KRS 100.191. Research into population distribution, economic and business activity, and transportation and community facility needs, done in advance of the local plans, will not suffice as the basis for the county-wide plan.

Finally, and probably most significantly, the statutory scheme set out in KRS 100.197 requires the planning commission to hold a public hearing before adoption of the comprehensive plan. Florence and Boone County admit that no hearing was held to consider the county-wide plan. They argue that the prior hearings held with regard to the individual plans of Florence and Boone County are sufficient to satisfy the mandates of the statute. We disagree. The citizens of Florence, the largest population center in the county, have never had the opportunity to express their opinions about the future planning and zoning of the rest of Boone County. Residents of Hopeful Heights, Walton, and rural areas of the county have not been able to voice their concerns about the same issues in Florence. And none of the people of Boone County have been allowed to speak their minds with regard to the comprehensive plan for the county-wide planning unit in which they now live. For this reason, we hold that the comprehensive plan adopted by the Boone County Planning and Zoning Commission does not comply with the requirements of KRS 100.183, et seq.

KRS 100.367 provides that all plans in existence on the effective date of KRS chapter 100 (June 16, 1966), may continue in effect until they are superseded by new plans or until five years have passed. Thus, all plans which did not conform to the new law on June 16, 1971, ceased to exist on that date. Regrettably, the comprehensive plan in the case at bar falls into that category. The comprehensive plan of the Boone County Planning and Zoning Commission, and any zoning ordinances adopted pursuant thereto, are void.

* * *

The decision of the Court of Appeals is reversed and the case is remanded to the trial court for entry of a judgment consistent with this opinion.

* * *

Notes

1. Compare with the principal case Lazy Mountain Land Club v. Matanuska–Susitna Borough Bd. of Adjustment and Appeals, 904 P.2d 373 (Alaska 1995) where the court rejected a developer's argument that piecemeal adoption of various planning documents and incorporation by reference of a previous document evidenced the lack of a comprehensive plan.

2. Courts have had very little concern with the question of adequacy of the plan. The enabling legislation for planning rarely makes provision for judicial (or any other) review of the finished product. One notable exception to this state of affairs is found in the State of Oregon. In 1973, Oregon amended its planning enabling statute to make land use planning mandatory for local government units, and created a state level administrative agency, the Land Conservation and Development Commission (LCDC), which has power to establish statewide planning "goals" and to review local plans for consistency with the established "goals." Since 1975, when the 14 statewide "goals" were promulgated, several hundred contested disputes concerning the consistency of local land use decisions with the "goals" have been adjudicated by LCDC. For three divergent views on the efficacy of this approach, see Comprehensive Plans and the Law: The Oregon Experience, 32 Land Use Law & Zoning Digest 6 (Sept. 1980). Also see Rajneesh Medical Corp. v. Wasco County, 300 Or. 107, 706 P.2d 948 (1985).

3. The Creative Displays case is one of the few that looks at the process of adopting and evaluating the comprehensive plan. In many states the enabling legislation for zoning, subdivision regulations and other land use regulations specifies that these regulations may be adopted or enacted only after the adoption of a comprehensive plan. In a later chapter the question of the validity of regulations where the comprehensive planning process is insufficient will be taken up in greater detail. In Wolf v. City of Ely, 493 N.W.2d 846 (Iowa 1992) the court held a zoning ordinance invalid because the town had not adopted a comprehensive plan; the court acknowledged

that "[a] majority of courts in states where zoning must be 'in accordance with a comprehensive plan' hold a plan external to the zoning ordinance is not required." However, the court stated that the trend of decisions is in the other direction and aligned Iowa with the trend.

ELYSIAN HEIGHTS RESIDENTS ASSOCIATION, INC. v. CITY OF LOS ANGELES

California Court of Appeal, Second District, 1986.
182 Cal.App.3d 21, 227 Cal.Rptr. 226.

COMPTON, ACTING PRESIDING JUSTICE.

Elysian Heights Residents Association, Inc., et al., hereinafter appellants, appeal from a judgment of the superior court denying their petition for administrative mandamus. (See Code Civ.Proc., § 1094.5.) By way of this petition, appellants sought the revocation of a building permit issued by respondents City of Los Angeles, et al. to Morton Park Associates [Morton] for the construction of a three story, 45–unit apartment complex. Pursuant to appellants' request, and in order to preserve the status quo, we stayed further development of the project pending the outcome of this appeal. We now affirm the judgment and vacate the stay order.

* * *

In December 1984, while the administrative appeal was still pending, the Department of Building and Safety, pursuant to the terms of an ordinance imposing a moratorium on all projects which exceeded the zoning and height requirements of the District Plan, ordered Morton to immediately cease all construction work. At approximately the same time various homeowner associations filed an action in superior court, entitled *Federation of Hillside Canyon Associations, Inc. et al. v. City of Los Angeles* (Los Angeles Sup.Ct. No. 526,616), to prevent the City from issuing building permits for development of property inconsistent with the general plan. * * *

[The court found that the existing plan would have permitted a 12–unit apartment building.]

In January 1985, the superior court, in ruling on the *Federation* case, issued a writ of mandate requiring the City to bring its zoning ordinances into conformity with the General Plan, but denied the petitioners' request for an injunction against the issuance of building permits for inconsistent development. * * *

We first consider appellants' contention that the disputed building permit was issued in violation of state statute and was thus void *ab initio* and must be revoked. The major thrust of appellants' argument in this regard is that building permits, to be validly issued, must be consistent with a municipality's general plan. It is, therefore, necessary to determine whether Government Code section 65860 mandates such conformity.

* * *

[W]e first note that in recent years the Legislature has enacted a number of statutes as part of the State Planning & Zoning Law (Gov. Code, § 65000, et seq.), the combined effect of which is to require that cities and counties adopt a general plan for the future development, configuration, and character of a city and county and require that future land use decisions be made in harmony with that general plan. (*City of Los Angeles v. State of California* (1982) 138 Cal.App.3d 526, 530, 187 Cal.Rptr. 893; *Bownds v. City of Glendale* (1980) 113 Cal.App.3d 875, 880, 170 Cal.Rptr. 342.) These requirements, forming what is generally referred to as the consistency doctrine, promote a particular nexus between land-use plans and government regulation of land use, such as zoning and subdivision map approval.

The doctrine has its roots in the language of the Standard Zoning Enabling Act (U.S. Dept. of Commerce, The Standard State Zoning Enabling Act, 1922 [rev. ed., 1926.]), which provides that zoning shall be done "in accordance with" a comprehensive plan. (See DiMento, *Improving Development Control through Planning: The Consistency Doctrine* (1978) 5 Colum.J.Envt'l L. 1.) Under this historical antecedent of the consistency doctrine, violations of the "in accordance with" language were found when (1) only selected areas within a municipality were regulated by zoning; (2) zoning was done by means of an interim ordinance that was enacted by legally questionable government practices; or (3) the zoning ordinance failed to control one or more of the factors it was intended to regulate. (See DiMento, *Developing the Consistency Doctrine: The Contribution of the California Courts* (1980) 20 Santa Clara L.Rev. 285, 286.)

California's state planning laws took what some may consider a giant step forward when the Legislature, in 1973, mandated that zoning changes and subdivision approvals be consistent with the local general plan, and that the plan itself be internally consistent. (Lefcoe, *California's Land Planning Requirements: The Case for Deregulation* (1981) 54 So.Cal.L.Rev. 447, 488.) Although the Planning and Zoning Law establishes the authority of most local government entities to regulate the use of land (*Topanga Assn. for a Scenic Community v. County of Los Angeles* (1974) 11 Cal.3d 506, 518–519, fn. 18, 113 Cal.Rptr. 836, 522 P.2d 12), it commands municipalities to adopt "a comprehensive, long-term general plan for the physical development of the county or city. . . ." (Gov.Code, § 65300.) The plan itself must include, inter alia, a statement of policies, and nine specified elements: land use, circulation, housing, conservation, open-space, seismic safety, noise, scenic highway, and safety. (Gov.Code, § 65302.) Section 65566 requires that acquisition, regulation, and any other actions of the local government related to open space conform to the local open-space plan. Under section 65567, building permits, subdivision maps, and zoning ordinances affecting *open space* must be consistent with the *open space* plan. Section 65803 exempts charter cities from the consistency statutes unless they adopt these requirements or fall within the provisions of section 65860. And, sections 66473 and 66474 set forth various requirements for attaining subdivision consistency with general and specific plans.

Most relevant here, of course, is section 65860, which generally requires that county or city zoning ordinances be consistent with the general plan of the county or city, and allows private citizens to bring suit to enforce consistency of zoning with the general plan. Subdivision (d) specifically makes the statute applicable to Los Angeles and establishes a time table for bringing the City's zoning ordinances into conformity with the general plan.

As can be seen, neither the language of section 65860 nor the statutory scheme in general mandates that building permits be scrutinized for plan consistency. Indeed, had the Legislature intended to fashion such a requirement, it clearly had the power to do so. In this regard, the State Planning and Zoning Law specifically prohibits the adoption or issuance of permits, subdivision maps, or zoning ordinances that are inconsistent with *open space* plans; requires that tentative subdivision tract maps be drawn in conformity with the general plan (Gov.Code, § 66474.61, subd. (a)); and allows a court to enjoin issuance of all permits where a *general plan* is found to be inadequate. (Gov.Code, § 65755.) There is, however, nothing in the legislative history of section 65860 to suggest that the Legislature intended to prohibit the issuance of building permits for projects consistent with the zoning of a particular community but not the general plan. Moreover, there is no mention of any remedies available to halt construction of projects which are not in conformity with the general plan, and no sanctions are provided for noncompliance with section 65860, subdivision (d).

* * *

Generally, the enumeration of acts or things as coming within the operation of a statute precludes the inclusion by implication of other acts or things not listed. (*Western Pioneer Insurance Co. v. Estate of Taira* (1982) 136 Cal.App.3d 174, 181, 185 Cal.Rptr. 887.) Applying this rule to the instant case, we think it clear that the Legislature has purposefully failed to prohibit the issuance of building permits while the consistency process is being implemented. In the absence of any such provision it would ill-behoove any court to indirectly mandate the withholding of permits that are not in conformity with a municipality's general plan. If the Legislature desires such consistency, it should specifically say so.

Recognizing that amending zoning ordinances to make them consistent with a general plan would take time, the Legislature added subdivision (c) to section 65860 which states: "In the event that a zoning ordinance becomes inconsistent with a general plan by reason of amendment to such plan, or to any element of such plan, such zoning ordinance *shall be amended within a reasonable time* so that it is consistent with the general plan as amended." (Emphasis added.) The trial court had before it evidence that in 1982 the City had approximately 200,000 lots which had zoning inconsistent with the applicable General Plan. If appellants' contentions were correct, no new building permits could be issued until all inconsistently-zoned lots were made to conform to the provisions of the General Plan. This would bring new construction in the City to a grinding halt and cause economic havoc. As one commentator has aptly observed, "Halting construction for the years it takes to adopt a general plan [or amend zoning ordinances] works great hardship. During those years of delay, some projects that were once economically feasible will become impracticable. Even those projects that survive the de facto moratorium will be costly to consumers if developers are able to recoup their increased land holding, construction, and borrowing costs through higher prices. For buyers priced out of the market by these delays, the loss may be irretrievable; anyone who doubts it should talk to a renter who could have afforded a house some years ago, but who had been left behind by rising prices. Neither the courts nor the Legislature seem to have understood who really pays the price when zone changes, building permits, and subdivision approvals are withheld pending the adoption of a general plan." (Lefcoe, *California's Land Planning Requirements: The Case for Deregulation, supra,* 54 So.Cal.L.Rev. 447, 489.)

* * *

The City's Interim Ordinance, which does require permit/plan consistency, was given only prospective application and thus did not affect the validity of Morton's permit. After balancing competing interests, the City Council properly determined that projects which had been approved prior to the ordinance's effective date, and did not vary from their originally approved plans, were entitled to go forward. As found by the trial court in the *Federation* case, the enactment of the Interim Ordinance represented a good faith effort by the City to bring its regulations into substantial compliance with state law. Zoning ordinances are, of course, presumed to be a valid exercise of the police power with every intendment in favor of their validity. "The wisdom of the prohibitions and restrictions is a matter for legislative determination, and even though a court may not agree with that determination it will not substitute its judgment for that of the zoning authorities if there is any reasonable justification for their action." (*Lockard v. City of Los Angeles* (1949) 33 Cal.2d 453, 461, 202 P.2d 38.) We agree with respondents that for this court to now say that the issuance of Morton's building permit constituted an abuse of discretion would seriously undermine the City Council's authority to enact land-use regulations and invite a further, unending spiral of litigation. It must be remembered that the Plan which appellants view as sacrosanct was itself a creature of the City and presumptively can be changed by the City.

Having concluded that the State Planning and Zoning Law does not preclude issuance of permits which may be inconsistent with a community's general plan, and that Morton's building permit was issued in compliance with City ordinances, we need not discuss appellants' remaining contentions.

The judgment is affirmed and the stay order is vacated.

[Dissenting opinion omitted.]

Notes

1. Assuming that the plan is valid, how should a court view a land use regulation that is not consistent with the plan? See DiMento, The Consistency Doctrine: Continuing Controversy, 4 Zoning and Planning Law Report No. 1 (Jan. 1981). The author points out that only a few states have accepted the principle that a regulation must either be consistent with the plan or valid despite the plan because of changed circumstances. The majority of jurisdictions still view the plan as advisory to local officials. See, e.g., Barrie v. Kitsap County, 93 Wash.2d 843, 613 P.2d 1148 (1980), holding that a land use decision was not invalid because of inconsistency with the plan, and City of Sanibel v. Goode, 372 So.2d 181 (Fla.App.1979), holding a decision invalid despite its consistency with the plan.

2. In Haines v. City of Phoenix, 151 Ariz. 286, 727 P.2d 339 (1986), the appellate court held that the city council could rationally have found consistency with the general plan in allowing a 500 foot building to be constructed, despite the plan's 250 foot height limit!

3. Some other California cases that explore the consistency doctrine at length are Lesher Communications, Inc. v. City of Walnut Creek, 262 Cal.Rptr. 337 (Cal.App.1989), reversed 52 Cal.3d 531, 277 Cal.Rptr. 1, 802 P.2d 317 (1990), and Mira Development Corp. v. City of San Diego, 205 Cal.App.3d 1201, 252 Cal.Rptr. 825 (1988).

4. In his recent article, 3 Wash. U.J.L. & Pol'y 295 (2000), addressing the legislative requirement that zoning and local land use controls be consistent with an independently adopted local comprehensive plan, Stuart Meck, AICP offers the following model statute:

CONSISTENCY OF LAND DEVELOPMENT REGULATIONS AND LAND USE ACTIONS WITH A LOCAL COMPREHENSIVE PLAN: A MODEL ACT

(1) Land development regulations and amendments thereto, including amendments to the zoning map, and any land use actions shall be consistent with the local comprehensive plan that has been adopted by the legislative body of a local government, provided that in the event the land development regulations, as amended, become inconsistent with the local comprehensive plan by reason of amendment to the plan or adoption of a new plan, the regulations shall be amended within [6] months of the date of amendment or adoption so they are consistent with the local comprehensive plan, as amended.

(a) Except as provided in paragraph (1) above, any land development regulations and amendments thereto and any land use actions that are not consistent with the local comprehensive plan shall be voidable.

(b) Any land development regulations and amendments thereto shall be void [6] months from the date on which a local comprehensive plan is required to be adopted, if a comprehensive plan must be adopted pursuant to [cite to section in statute] but no comprehensive plan has been adopted.

(c) As used in this Section, "land use action" means: preliminary or final approval of a subdivision plat; approval of a planned unit development [or similar site-specific development plan]; approval of a conditional use; granting of a variance; or a decision by the local government to construct a capital improvement and/or acquire land for community facilities, including transportation facilities.

(2) A local government shall determine, in the manner prescribed in this Section, whether such land development regulations, amendments thereto, and land use actions are consistent with the local comprehensive plan. Before the legislative body of a local government may enact or amend land development regulations and before the legislative body, the local planning commission, the hearing examiner, the Land Use Board of Review, any other body with administrative authority may take any land use action, the local planning agency shall prepare a written report to the legislative or administrative body regarding the consistency with the local comprehensive plan of: the proposed land development regulations; a proposed amendment to existing land development regulations; or a proposed land use action. The written report shall be advisory to the legislative or administrative body. Pursuant to paragraph (3) below, the written report shall state whether or not, in the opinion of the local planning agency, the regulations, amendment, or action is consistent with the local comprehensive plan. The written report shall also contain recommendations pursuant to paragraph (4) below as to whether or not to approve, deny, substantially change, or revise the regulations, amendment, or action. The local planning agency shall make the written report available to the public at least [7] days prior to any public hearing or meeting on the regulations, amendment, or action that is the subject of the report.

(3) The local planning agency shall find that proposed land development regulations, a proposed amendment to existing land development regulations, or a proposed land use action is consistent with the local comprehensive plan when the regulations, amendment, or action:

(a) furthers, or at least does not interfere with, the goals and policies contained in the local comprehensive plan;

(b) is compatible with the proposed future land uses and densities and/or intensities contained in the local comprehensive plan; and

(c) carries out, as applicable, any specific proposals for community facilities, including transportation facilities, other specific public actions, or actions proposed by nonprofit and for-profit organizations that are contained in the local comprehensive plan.

In determining whether the regulations, amendment, or action satisfies the requirements of subparagraph (a) above, the local planning agency may take into account any relevant guidelines contained in the local comprehensive plan.

(4) If the local planning agency determines that the regulations, amendment, or action is not consistent with the local comprehensive plan, it:

(a) shall state in the written report what changes or revisions in the regulations, amendment, or action are necessary to make it consistent; and

(b) may state in the written report what amendments to the local comprehensive plan are necessary to eliminate any inconsistency between the plan and the regulations, amendment, or action.

(5) The legislative or administrative body shall, upon receipt of the written report of the local planning agency, review it and, giving the report due regard, shall in the written minutes of its deliberations:

(a) adopt the report;

(b) reject the report; or

(c) adopt the report in part and reject it in part.

(6) If the legislative or administrative body rejects the report in part or in whole, in the written minutes of its deliberations:

(a) it shall state whether the proposed land development regulations, a proposed amendment to existing land development regulations, or a proposed land use action is consistent with the local comprehensive plan pursuant to paragraph (3) above; and/or

(b) if the legislative or administrative body determines that the regulations, amendment, or action is not consistent with the local comprehensive plan:

1. it shall state what changes or revisions in the regulations, amendment, or action are necessary to make it consistent; and/or

2. it may state what amendments to the local comprehensive plan may be necessary to eliminate any inconsistency between the plan and the regulations, amendment, or action.

5. If regulatory decisions are not readily subject to attack by way of the consistency doctrine, can citizens attack the plan itself prior to the issuance of building permits or the rendering of zoning decisions? Consider the following materials.

COCHRAN v. PLANNING BD. OF CITY OF SUMMIT

Superior Court of New Jersey, Law Division, 1965.
87 N.J.Super. 526, 210 A.2d 99.

FELLER, J.S.C.

This is an action * * * challenging the adoption of a master plan by the Planning Board of the City of Summit and seeking to enjoin the city and its agencies, boards, and officials from implementing the master plan in any way. In particular, plaintiffs object to that part of the plan which would permit an expansion of the Ciba Corporation's parking area and research and office space into the residential area which adjoins the rear of plaintiffs' property.

Plaintiffs are citizens, taxpayers and owners of lands located at 249 Kent Place Boulevard in Summit. Their property is adjacent and contiguous to property owned by the Ciba Corporation (hereinafter Ciba). Plaintiffs' premises and that portion of the Ciba tract in question are presently in the A–15 zoning district, which is limited to one-family residences with a minimum lot area of 15,000 square feet. Prior to 1958 the Ciba tract was in an A–10 zone, which was limited to one-family residences with a minimum lot area of 10,000 square feet. The tract is bordered on three sides by one-family residences and is presently subject to enforceable deed restrictions which limit the use of the tract to the erection of one-family residences until 1975.

On December 9, 1963 defendant planning board adopted a master plan for the city, which provided in part that the Ciba tract, namely, 63½ acres in the A–15 zone, should be rezoned for parking areas and research and office building use. This rezoning is for the purpose of providing for the eventual expansion therein of Ciba's existing operations. The plan requires a 125–foot buffer zone, which would separate the rear line of plaintiffs' property from the proposed Ciba construction. This zone would contain trees, shrubs and a screen, all of them calculated to preserve the existing residential atmosphere of the area.

Plaintiffs claim that the adoption of the master plan is arbitrary, discriminatory, capricious, unreasonable and an abuse of the planning board's discretion; * * * that it was procedurally defective because it was adopted on improper notice, ten days' notice not having been given of the December 9, 1963 hearing at which the plan was adopted, as required by the act, and that the planning board was illegally constituted. Plaintiffs further contend that the master plan was an abuse of discretion in that it was contrary to the expressed wishes of the citizens of the city made known at the hearings thereon and prior thereto; was contrary to the purpose of the plan to preserve the already established pattern of the better single-family areas of Summit; was contrary to the general welfare and health of the citizens; was *ultra vires* the planning board's power, and did not conform to the character of the neighborhood.

Plaintiffs also contend that the * * * action of the board was allegedly based on insufficient and incompetent facts and findings and on insufficient surveys and studies, in violation of N.J.S.A. 40:55–1.12.

* * *

Defendants contend that the master plan was properly adopted at a meeting held on December 9, 1963; insist there was proper notice of the meeting, and that the meeting was a continuance of a previous one held on November 26, 1963.

* * *

Defendants further contend that the plan was the result of a comprehensive study by the planning board which commenced in January 1962 and terminated on December 9, 1963, after an average of a meeting every two weeks with interested persons and citizens. They say that all the work and the final plan are in accordance with the requirements of N.J.S.A. 40:55–1.1 et seq.

A review of the evidence indicates that the following questions should be resolved: whether the planning board had the authority or power to adopt a master plan under the ordinance setting up the board; whether the plaintiffs' property has been harmed or damaged by the adoption of the plan or whether their suit is premature; whether the plan is arbitrary, capricious, unreasonable, or an abuse of discretion * * *.

I

Initially, plaintiffs contend that the ordinance of March 16, 1954, which created the Planning Board of the City of Summit, did not give the board the power to prepare and adopt a master plan; furthermore, they contend that since no other ordinance granted this power to the board, the provisions of N.J.S.A. 40:55–1.3 have been violated by such preparation and adoption, and that the master plan should be set aside as *ultra vires* the power of the planning board. N.J.S.A. 40:55–1.3 provides in relevant part that:

> "The governing body may by ordinance grant any of the powers exercisable by a planning board to a planning board continued by section twenty-seven of this act or to be created under section four of this act, *but no particular power may be exercised until expressly granted by ordinance* and until compliance is made with the conditions, standards, procedures and regulations enumerated in the sections describing such power." (Emphasis added).

The defendants rely in part on the passage of an ordinance by the Summit governing body on December 19, 1961, which made an appropriation for the engagement of special consultants for the preparation of a master plan. It is argued that this ordinance is sufficient to satisfy the demands of N.J.S.A. 40:55–1.3. The ordinance provided:

Section 1. That pursuant to Chapter 48, P.L.1956, the sum of $24,000 is hereby appropriated for the engagement of special consultants for the preparation and the preparation, of a master plan or plans, when required in order to conform to the planning laws of the State, and shall be deemed an emergency appropriation as defined and provide [sic] for in R.S. 40:50–12.

Such appropriation and/or the 'special emergency notes' authorized to finance the appropriation shall be provided for in succeeding annual budgets by the inclusion of at least ⅕ of the amount authorized pursuant to this act.

Section 2. This ordinance shall take effect immediately after final passage and publication as provided by law.

If the above ordinance does not by implication grant the planning board power to prepare and adopt a master plan, then the other sections of the Planning Act do. * * *

For the above reasons, and specifically because of the legislative expression in N.J.S.A. 40:55–1.10, this court is of the opinion that the Summit Planning Board had the power to enact a master plan and that such action by the board was not *ultra vires*.

II

The second question is whether plaintiffs' property has been harmed or damaged by the adoption of the master plan and whether their suit is premature. If the action is premature, they have sustained no damage or harm to their property, and a determination of the procedural inadequacies and conflicts of interest alleged by plaintiffs would be unnecessary.

Plaintiffs request the court to declare the master plan null and void because it represents a taking of private property for public use without just compensation. * * *

Defendants contend that plaintiffs' failure to allege and prove injury to their property rights results in the presentation of legal questions which are premature and which do not present justiciable controversies. This court agrees that such allegations and proof of injury to private property rights are necessary before the requested relief may be considered and granted by this court. Plaintiffs have not demonstrated that degree of injury which would entitle them to relief.

* * *

If plaintiffs cannot demonstrate injury, then they may not obtain relief; if their claims are based upon assumed potential invasions of rights, then these are not enough to warrant judicial intervention. See Ashwander v. T.V.A., 297 U.S. 288, 56 S.Ct. 466, 80 L.Ed. 688 (1936).

The crux of this problem is clear when it is remembered that a master plan is of no force and effect until it is adopted by the governing body of the municipality. Thus, the master plan under consideration in the City of Summit is of no effect until it is adopted by the municipal governing body.

The master plan represents at a given time the best judgment of the planning agency as to the proper course of action to be followed. In this stage the plan for community development remains flexible and is not binding, either on government or individual. See Webster, Urban Planning & Municipal Policy 265 (1958). A master plan is not a straitjacket delimiting the discretion of the legislative body, but only a guide for the city, Rhyne, Municipal Law, sec. 32–59, p. 977 (1957); furthermore, a master plan is nothing more than the easily changed instrumentality which will show a commission from day to day the progress it has made. Haar, Land Use Planning 693 (1959).

The mere adoption and recording of a master plan has no legal consequence. The plan is merely a declaration of policy and a disclosure of an intention which must thereafter be implemented by the adoption of various ordinances. Horack & Nolan, Land Use Controls 36 (1955).

In New Jersey the fact that a master plan adopted by a planning board has no legal consequences is substantiated, not only by the absence of statutory language to that effect, but also by the necessity of a municipality's adoption of the master plan by the governing body before the plan takes effect. See N.J.S.A. 40:55–1.13; Wollen v. Fort Lee, 27

N.J. 408, 424, 142 A.2d 881, 890 (1958), where the court said that "the master plan is not conclusive on the governing body." Moreover, it is not mandatory for a township to create a planning board, and a governing body could assume directly the duties of a planning board. Jones v. Zoning Bd. of Adjustment of Long Beach Tp., 32 N.J.Super. 397, 406, 108 A.2d 498 (App.Div.1954).

* * *

It is clear that a master plan is only a plan, and that it requires legislative implementation before its proposals have binding effect and legal consequences. If the necessary legislative implementation is taken—and, of course, such implementation must be taken according to the applicable statutes—then a zoning ordinance and not a master plan would be before the court. Until appropriate municipal legislative action is taken, however, the municipality has only a dormant plan which differs from proposals that may be under consideration by any municipal board or citizen of the municipality in that it is comprehensive and has been reduced to printed form. Indeed, a master plan is not even a statutory prerequisite to zoning action. Kozesnik v. Montgomery Township, 24 N.J. 154, 165, 131 A.2d 1 (1957).

The issue here is whether a plan for municipal development, not yet implemented by the necessary legislative action, may be legally considered to deprive one of the enjoyment of his property, contrary to the United States and New Jersey Constitutions. The statutes providing for the adoption of a master plan were upheld as constitutional in Mansfield & Swett, Inc. v. West Orange, 120 N.J.L. 145, 198 A. 225 (Sup.Ct.1938). The court, in the course of its opinion, said that the State possesses the inherent authority to resort, in the building and expansion of its community life, to such measures as may be necessary to secure the essential common material and moral needs. The public welfare is of prime importance, and the correlative restrictions upon individual rights, either of person or of property, are considered a negligible loss compared with the resultant advantages to the community as a whole. Municipal planning confined to the common need is inherent in the authority to create the municipality itself. It is as old as government itself; it is of the very essence of civilized society. A comprehensive scheme of physical development is requisite to community efficiency and progress.

* * * The principle is firmly established in our federal jurisprudence that injury to private property ensuing from governmental action in a proper sphere, reasonably taken for the public good, and for no other purpose, is not necessarily classable as a "taking" of such property within the intendment of the constitutional guaranties against the deprivation of property without due process of law, or the taking of private property for public use without compensation.

* * *

Attention is also called to the following cases: Headley v. City of Rochester, 272 N.Y. 197, 5 N.E.2d 198 (Ct.App.1936); Reopening of

Philadelphia Parkway Between Twentieth and Twenty–Second Street, 295 Pa. 538, 145 A. 600, 64 A.L.R. 542 (Sup.Ct.1929); Windsor v. Whitney, 95 Conn. 357, 111 A. 354, 12 A.L.R. 669 (Sup.Ct.Err.1920); Harrison v. City of Philadelphia, 217 F. 107 (E.D.Pa.1914); Bauman v. Ross, 167 U.S. 548, 17 S.Ct. 966, 42 L.Ed. 270, 64 A.L.R. 542 (1897). These authorities indicate that the power of a municipality to plan for the future is part of the police power. The adoption of maps and/or reports, commonly called a "master plan," does not result in a "taking" of property in violation of our Federal and State Constitutions.

The plaintiffs have alleged that the adoption of the master plan destroys property values. To support this thesis they called as witnesses George Goldstein, who is a real estate appraiser and a consultant for the Federal Government and many public agencies, as well as for many of the largest industrial companies in the country, and Norman Lemcke, who is a retired vice-president of the Prudential Mortgage Loan Department. Goldstein testified that the adoption of the master plan had diminished adjacent property values up to 25%, as in the case of plaintiffs' home. Lemcke testified that before the plan he would have granted a 66% mortgage on the plaintiffs' house, but after its adoption he would only grant a 50% mortgage. He further testified that for financing purposes lending institutions take into account whether there is a master plan affecting the property, and the manner in which it is affected. Plaintiffs also rely upon N.J.S.A. 40:55–1.12, which requires, among other things, that a master plan be made with the general purpose of the maintenance of property values previously established. * * *

The contentions of plaintiffs' two experts are disputed by several witnesses for the defense; but without considering the relative merits of the contentions raised by the conflicting views, this court feels that the testimony, taken in the light most favorable to plaintiffs, is at best mere conjecture. There has been no attempted sale by plaintiffs of their property, and the damages which they claim they will sustain if and when they do try to sell their property, is at this point a matter of speculation. * * *

It is the opinion of this court that plaintiffs' suit is premature. Not until their property is actually taken or damaged will they be in a position to establish that its value will be destroyed or diminished.

III

Plaintiffs question the soundness of the master plan on the ground that it is arbitrary, capricious and unreasonable. In view of the position taken by this court that plaintiffs are premature in their suit, it is not necessary to discuss this issue. However, the court feels that even if the reasonableness of the master plan were properly before it, the result would be the same. The action of a planning board is only an initial step; it is not even required by law, Kozesnik v. Montgomery Township, supra; it is only the manifestation of an advisory step in connection with *quasi*-judicial action the board may take in the future. As stated by Horack and Nolan, Land Use Controls 36 (1955):

> [The master plan] is merely a declaration of policy and a disclosure of an intention which must thereafter be implemented.

Since this master plan may never be adopted by the governing body of Summit, there is at present no justiciable controversy before the court. There may be such a controversy if and when the proposed plan is adopted by the governing body. Until implementation of the proposal is attempted, there can be no purpose in an adjudication by this court at this time.

If the court, for example, declared the master plan or any portion thereof arbitrary, capricious, and/or unreasonable, would a property owner be permitted to make use of his property other than in a manner now permitted or other than in a manner that would be permitted if the plan were sustained? Would the governing body be limited in the adoption of land use ordinances other than as they are at the moment if the plan were stricken by this court? The answers to these questions appear obvious.

This suit to test the reasonableness of the master plan is premature, and the issues involved are clearly not ready for judicial determination. Furthermore, should the plaintiffs follow the normal administrative pattern of going first to the planning board and then, if necessary, to the governing body, they may very well be able to persuade these bodies to compromise their differences in connection with the master plan, in which case they would be able to avoid further litigation.

* * *

Complaint dismissed and judgment for defendants.

BONE v. CITY OF LEWISTON

Supreme Court of Idaho, 1984.
107 Idaho 844, 693 P.2d 1046.

BISTLINE, JUSTICE.

On February 9, 1982, Mr. John Bone filed an application with the City of Lewiston Planning and Zoning Commission requesting that his land be rezoned from a low-density residential use to a limited commercial use. The City's land use plan map shows Mr. Bone's land as being zoned for commercial use.

The Commission recommended to the City Council that Mr. Bone's request be denied for the following reasons: (1) The uses allowed in the zoning classification Mr. Bone seeks would not be compatible with the established low-density residential uses of the various properties bordering Mr. Bone's land; and (2) Lewiston has an over-abundance of unused commercial properties. No need presently exists for further classification of property for commercial use. The City Council, without adopting any findings of fact and conclusions of law, agreed with the Commission's recommendation and denied Mr. Bone's application.

Mr. Bone subsequently filed suit in district court against the City, requesting declaratory relief and a writ of mandamus forcing the City to enact a zoning ordinance in conformity with its comprehensive plan pursuant to I.C. § 67–6511. * * *

[The Court first disposes of a procedural issue and then moves to discuss the question of conformity with the comprehensive plan.]

Mr. Bone argues that he is entitled to have his property zoned in conformance with the City's land use map. He cites I.C. § 67–6511 as support for his position. That section states that zoning ordinances shall be "in accordance with" a comprehensive plan. For Mr. Bone, § 67–6511's terminology "in accordance with" means as a matter of law that a zoning applicant is entitled to have his or her property zoned exactly as the City's land use map shows it to be zoned. We do not agree with such a proposition for two reasons.

First, construing § 67–6511 as Mr. Bone would have us read it results in an interpretation of the section that contradicts itself. Subsections 67–6511(a) and (b) discuss the amendment process of zoning districts. In subsection (b) it states that if a rezone request is in accordance with the applicable comprehensive plan, the planning and zoning commission "*may* recommend and the governing board *may* adopt or reject the [zoning] amendment [request]" as proposed. (Emphasis added.)

Requiring all rezone applications to be granted when they agree with the land use map's designation of the property ignores the permissive language used in subsection (b). Had the legislature intended the result Mr. Bone proposes, they would have used the word "shall" instead of "may" and not used the words "or reject."

* * *

Second, adopting Mr. Bone's interpretation would elevate the comprehensive plan and land use map to the status of a zoning ordinance. This result finds no basis in law or reason, for the three—the comprehensive plan, the land use map, and the zoning ordinances—serve different purposes. The City of Lewiston's land use map, as § 67–6508(c) indicates, is a map displaying "*suitable projected* land uses for the jurisdiction." (Emphasis added.) It is not a map of how the City should presently be zoned, but a map of projected uses in the year 2000. In fact, the City's comprehensive plan describes the City's land use map as depicting "the projected structure and land use interrelationships for the City in the year 2000." It goes on further to say, "This map is not an attempt to show precise boundaries or locations, but is a general representation of the relative extent and patterns of *projected land uses.*" (Emphasis added.) Thus, the land use map, in essence, is a goal or forecast of future development in the City. This is contrasted with zoning ordinances, which represent the present uses allowable for the various pieces of property in the City.

It is illogical to say that what has been projected as a pattern of projected land use is what a property owner is entitled to have zoned today. The land use map is not intended to be a map of present zoning uses, nor even a map which indicates what uses are presently appropriate. Its only purpose is that which I.C. § 67–6508(c) mandates—to indicate "suitable projected land uses." Therefore, we hold that a city's land use map does not require a particular piece of property, as a matter of law, to be zoned exactly as it appears on the land use map.

Our holding is supported by a large body of case law which states that comprehensive plans do not themselves operate as legally controlling zoning law, but rather serve to guide and advise the various governing bodies responsible for making zoning decisions. *See Theobald v. Board of County Commissioners, Summit County,* 644 P.2d 942, 949 (Colo.1982); *Barrie v. Kitsap County,* 613 P.2d 1148, 1152 (Wash.1980); *Holmgren v. City of Lincoln,* 199 Neb. 178, 256 N.W.2d 686, 690 (1977); 82 Am.Jur.2d, Zoning and Planning, § 69; 3 Anderson, *American Law of Zoning* 609.

Our holding that "in accordance with" does not require that governing bodies, as a matter of law, zone their land as it appears on their land use maps does not mean that such bodies can ignore their comprehensive plans when adopting or amending zoning ordinances. Section 67–6511 requires governing bodies to zone in accordance with their comprehensive plan. We hold that "in accordance with" is a question of fact. What a governing body charged to zone "in accordance with" under § 67–6511 must do is make a factual inquiry into whether the requested zoning ordinance or amendment reflects the goals of, and takes into account those factors in, the comprehensive plan in light of the present factual circumstances surrounding the request.

Here, the district court found that Mr. Bone's rezone application was in accordance with the City's comprehensive plan without having before it the record of either the planning and zoning commission or the City Council. The district court furthermore refused to allow the City to submit evidence of whether Mr. Bone's rezone application was factually in accordance with its comprehensive plan and the present circumstances surrounding the application. Thus, the district court erred in reaching its conclusion by failing to have before it the necessary information upon which to decide the case.

For the foregoing reasons we reverse and remand this case to the district court with directions for that court to remand to the City Council for the adoption of findings of fact and conclusions of law.

* * *

DONALDSON, C.J., and SHEPARD, BAKES AND HUNTLEY, JJ., concur.

Notes

1. In Selby Realty Co. v. City of San Buenaventura, 10 Cal.3d 110, 109 Cal.Rptr. 799, 514 P.2d 111 (1973), the court held that adoption of a comprehensive plan that showed proposed streets crossing the landowner's property did not amount to a taking of the property. The court said: "The fact that some of the proposed streets, if ultimately constructed, will cross plaintiff's property gives this plaintiff no greater right to secure a declaration as to the validity of the plan or its effect upon his land than that available to any other citizen whose property is included within the plan. The plan is by its very nature merely tentative and subject to change. Whether eventually any part of plaintiff's land will be taken for a street depends upon unpredictable future events." In CACO Three, Inc. v. Board of Supervisors, 845 A.2d 991 (Pa.Cmwlth.2004) the Court noted that "[a]lthough a comprehensive plan is a useful tool for properly guiding growth and development of the community, it is only intermediate and inconclusive step in land use planning.... Unlike a specific and regulatory zoning ordinance, a comprehensive plan is, by its nature, an abstract recommendation as to desirable approaches to land utilization and development of the community....Consequently, any inconsistence with the comprehensive plan, standing alone, cannot justify disapproving the land development plan." In Fifth Ave. Corp. v. Washington County, 282 Or. 591, 581 P.2d 50 (1978) the court reiterated the generally accepted rule that "*mere* plotting or planning in anticipation of a public improvement does not constitute a taking or damaging of property affected."

2. Standing requirements may provide one way for a court to avoid resolving the issue of inconsistency between an ordinance and a comprehensive plan. For example, in Citizens Growth Management Coalition of West Palm Beach, Inc. v. City of West Palm Beach, 450 So.2d 204 (Fla.1984), the court relied on standing grounds in declining to consider a community group's claim that zoning ordinances authorizing a downtown large-scale redevelopment were inconsistent with the comprehensive plan.

3. It has sometimes been argued that a zoning ordinance should be invalidated on the basis that a municipality has not enacted a required comprehensive plan at all. However, most courts in these cases hold that the requirement of a general plan may be satisfied by means other than a separate and distinct comprehensive plan. For example, in State ex rel. Chiavola v. Village of Oakwood, 886 S.W.2d 74 (Mo.App.1994), the court held that a zoning ordinance satisfied the statutory requirement despite the lack of a separate comprehensive plan given the comprehensive scope of the ordinance and the nature of the village as a small suburb of a large city. Accord: State ex rel. Westside Development Co., Inc. v. Weatherby Lake, 935 S.W.2d 634 (Mo.App.1996).

4. The most acute everyday problem in assessing the legal effect of the plan is the usual lack of public interest or participation in the adoption of the plan, especially in the undeveloped parts of the community. Some years after the adoption of the plan a developer may seek a zoning change or development approval on a vacant parcel which is designated as, say, multifamily. Nearby neighbors living in recently developed single-family subdivisions will be vociferous objectors to the implementation of the plan. Of

course they were not participants in the adoption of the plan and probably never knew of its existence. Is there a solution to this problem? One possibility is suggested by the case of Dennis v. Mayor and City Council of Rockville, 286 Md. 184, 406 A.2d 284 (1979), where the city had enacted an ordinance requiring all sellers of property to either provide purchasers with a copy of the master plan or to escort them to a place where the plan could be inspected. Violation of the duty imposed on sellers gives the purchaser a right to terminate the sales agreement prior to conveyance. The Court of Appeals of Maryland upheld the ordinance against arguments that it works a forfeiture of property and interferes with contractual rights. Do you think the Rockville ordinance is a more effective means of promulgating the plan than the typical public hearings held by a planning commission attended by a handful of developers and real estate brokers?

Also see Nev. Rev. Stat. § 113.070, which requires sellers of residences to provide the buyer with a written document disclosing "the zoning designations and the designations in the master plan regarding land use * * * for the adjoining parcels of land."

Somewhat related is the problem of whether purchasers of homes in subdivisions must be given notice of off-site environmental hazards. See, in this regard, Strawn v. Canuso, 140 N.J. 43, 657 A.2d 420 (1995) where the court stated that a broker-developer of residential real estate may be liable for nondisclosure of off-site physical conditions known to it and unknown and not readily observable by the purchaser, if those conditions may affect the habitability, use, or enjoyment of the property; in this case the off-site condition was a closed toxic landfill near a residential development. Just five months after *Strawn* was decided, state-wide legislation was enacted to define the disclosure duties of sellers of newly constructed residential real estate. See N. J. Stat. § 46:3C–1 et seq.

5. See McClanahan v. Richland County Council, 350 S.C. 433, 567 S.E.2d 240 (2002) where the Court found no due process violation where the plan was ignored, stating "the Plan is only a guideline and that there had not been an impairment of the appellant's rights." For a discussion of this case and its implications for community planning and smart growth, see David J. Harmon, Comment: Problems and Opportunities for Progressive Comprehensive Land Use Planning in Richland County, South Carolina After McClanahan v. Richland City Council, 54 S.C.L.Rev. 837 (2003).

6. Legislation has also been used to clarify the approach that should be taken when zoning ordinances conflict with comprehensive plans. A Minnesota statute, for example, specifies that when a zoning ordinance is in conflict with the comprehensive plan, either the ordinance must be brought into line with the plan, or the plan must be amended. Minn. Stat. § 473.858 (1). See also Mendota Golf v. City of Mendota Heights, 708 N.W.2d 162 (Minn. 2006) (explaining that a city's comprehensive plan controls over conflicting ordinances).

SECTION 5. STATE AND REGIONAL PLANNING

A. FEDERAL LAND USE LEGISLATION

The history of land use controls in the United States has primarily been one of delegation of the power to plan to local governments along with the power to implement the plans at that level of government. One major effect of localizing land use controls has been the fostering of parochialism and the avoidance of a rational basis for dealing with regional problems. Beginning in the late 1960's and accelerating in the 1970's, states and to some degree the federal government began to demonstrate greater interest in intervening in the local planning process. This was likely spurred in part by the increasing emphasis on environmental controls, in part by federal transportation, housing and urban redevelopment programs, and in part by a concern over the problems created by "urban sprawl" and the proliferation of local, largely uncoordinated controls over a widespread metropolitan area encompassing a multiplicity of municipalities. The energy crisis of the late 1970's has also been a factor. The movement toward state and regional planning has been in four directions:

(1) Federal land use legislation that would spur state level planning;

(2) Removal of some planning decisions from local to regional or state political jurisdiction;

(3) Efforts to modernize or reform state planning and zoning enabling acts; and

(4) Interstate compacts.

Federal impact on land use planning has been evident for several years. The millions of acres still in the public domain have required, in addition to management, some thought devoted to planning for the future. Also, some of the massive federal spending programs that have land use impacts have led to requirements of planning by state agencies charged with operations. In addition to urban redevelopment, typical in this respect is the federal highway program (see, e.g., the Highway Act of 1962, 76 Stat. 1145). Much federal money has gone into education about planning as well as research and public dissemination of planning materials. In other words, there has been and continues to be pervasive federal influence on land use planning, albeit in a non-coordinated fashion. The influences just described, however, have been of low visibility.

However, when considering the influence of federal environmental regulations on state and local land use planning, a more noticeable pattern emerges. This is particularly evident in the efforts of the Environmental Protection Agency ("EPA") to control air and water pollution.

Early attempts by EPA to reduce air pollution by intervening in local development matters were recognized as a threat to the power of the states to control land use, secured by the Tenth Amendment: "The powers not delegated to the United States by the Constitution, nor prohibited by it to the States, are reserved to the States respectively, or to the people." These attempts were met with amendments to the Clean Air Act in 1977 that expressly prohibited federal requirements aimed directly at land use control. 42 U.S.C. § 7431 (1994) (stating that "[n]othing in this chapter constitutes an infringement on the existing authority of counties and cities to plan or control land use, and nothing in this chapter provides or transfers authority over such land use").

The 1977 Clean Air Act Amendments were not an isolated example of the reluctance of the federal government to interfere with the plenary land use authority of the states. More recently, the efforts of the Army Corps of Engineers to prevent the construction of a landfill by a consortium of municipalities in the Chicago area were struck down by the U.S. Supreme Court. In Solid Waste Agency of Northern Cook County v. United States Army Corps of Engineers, 531 U.S. 159, 121 S.Ct. 675, 148 L.Ed.2d 576 (2001) the Court held that the Corps lacked jurisdiction under the Clean Water Act to regulate development in intrastate, non-navigable waters solely on the basis of the presence of migratory birds. The jurisdictional limits of federal agencies to protect the environment, resting in part on the Interstate Commerce Clause of the federal Constitution, were at issue in this case. Such jurisdictional limits, of course, do not constrain state governments or their localities in regulating wetland disturbances or other private land uses.

These jurisdictional, constitutional, and political obstacles have redirected federal energies from regulating land use to influencing state land use regulation. The Clean Water Act provides states with federal funds to encourage land use planning to prevent nonpoint source pollution. 33 U.S.C. § 1281(g)(1) (1994). State and local governments are encouraged under the federal Coastal Zone Management Act to adopt plans to preserve coastal areas. The Act provides grants to coastal states to develop management programs for their coastal zones. 16 U.S.C. §§ 1451–1465 (1994). State programs must meet several requirements, including providing for management of land uses having a significant impact on coastal waters and making a clear statement of which agencies and officials are to take action to implement the program. See Linda A. Malone, The Coastal Zone Management Act and the Takings Clause in the 1990's: Making the Case for Federal Land Use to Preserve Coastal Areas, 62 U. Colo. L. Rev. 711, 727 (1991) (stating that "[if] the requirements for state programs were more specific, the CZMA could come close to the most controversial form of land control—federal land control. The passage of the CZMA was possible because the Act required state programs to implement federal policy rather than federal regulations."). Federal financial aid is denied for developments in sensitive coastal areas under the Coastal Barrier Resources Act. 16 U.S.C. § 3501 (1994 & Supp. V 1999).

The modification of habitats that may harm endangered species is prohibited under the Endangered Species Act ("ESA") unless the modification is allowed by a permit issued pursuant to an approved habitat conservation plan. 16 U.S.C. § 1539 (1994). The ESA is an example of a federal environmental law that pursues objectives other than the prevention of nonpoint source pollution and illustrates how federally prescribed standards and procedures may interfere with the prerogatives of local governments to control land use. Under the ESA, landowners and developers may prepare Habitat Conservation Plans ("HCPs") that fully describe proposed land development activities and demonstrate measures that will mitigate their adverse impact on endangered or threatened species. § 1539(a)(2)(A). An approved HCP is a prerequisite for the issuance of a permit for land development activities that result in an incidental taking of a protected species. § 1539(a). This regulatory regime is based on the ESA's ban on taking of endangered species by any person subject to the jurisdiction of the United States. § 1538(a)(1). "Persons" subject to the Act include private citizens and entities such as local governments and officials. § 1532(13). The process of preparing and reviewing an HCP is somewhat redundant of local requirements contained in site plan or subdivision regulations that require developers to prepare detailed development plans and submit them to local administrative agencies for review and approval.

Similar efforts to influence state and local action are evident in federal transportation policies. Regional transportation planning must conform to State Implementation Plans that meet national ambient air quality standards under the Clean Air Act. 42 U.S.C. § 7506(i) (1994). Federal funding can be denied to any development project that does not conform to the State Implementation Plan. Environmental Def. Fund v. EPA, 167 F.3d 641, 644 (D.C.Cir.1999). A tepid attempt is made under this scheme to conform federal transportation planning to local land use planning, recognizing that land use planning is done, in most states, at the local rather than the regional level. Under the Intermodal Surface Transportation Efficiency Act, regional transportation planning agencies known as Metropolitan Planning Organizations ("MPOs") must develop long-and short-term transportation plans that consider "the likely effect of transportation policy decisions on land use and development and the consistency of transportation plans and programs with the provisions of all applicable short and long-term land use and development plans." 23 U.S.C. § 134(f)(4) (1994). The enigma embodied in this requirement is easily described: it requires regional transportation agencies to achieve consistency with land use plans that are predominantly local in nature and not consistent with one another at the regional level. The federal Transportation Equity Act for the 21st Century provides regional transportation planning agencies with the authority to fund projects that reduce traffic congestion and to acquire scenic easements and create bicycle trails. Transportation Equity Act for the 21st Century, Pub. L. No. 105–178, 112 Stat. 107 (1998). It also provides tax breaks for employers who subsidize employees' use of mass transit.

These are but a few of many federal actions that are aimed at stemming air and water pollution, but that recognize that the direct power to regulate land use for such purposes is not within the legal authority of federal agencies. These efforts are nonetheless a heroic effort on the part of the federal government to reach down to the local level and directly influence the effects that land use has on air and water quality and on natural resources.

A manifestation of this struggle is seen in the EPA proposal to delay a Clean Water Act rule that revises the federal impaired waters program. Susan Bruninga, "EPA Moves to Delay Action on TMDL Rule; Rule Changes May Be Proposed in Spring," 32 Env't Rep. (BNA) 1415 (2001). The Total Maximum Daily Load ("TMDL") program established under section 303(d) of the Clean Water Act requires states to identify and list waters not meeting federally established water quality standards. States are required to allocate the quantities of particular pollutants among the sources that discharge into impaired waters, to ensure that pollutants do not exceed federal standards, and to provide reasonable assurances to EPA that their allocations will be enforced. On July 16, 2001, EPA filed its proposal in the U.S. Court of Appeals for the District of Columbia to delay by eighteen months the effective date of its final rule under the TMDL program. Id. at 1415.

The acronyms and technical vocabulary should not mask the simple reality of the TMDL program: the pollutants it regulates emanate largely from development projects and land uses that are regulated by local and state agencies. The type of nonpoint source pollution of water affected by the TMDL program includes the runoff from impervious surfaces such as roofs, driveways, parking lots, and roads; erosion and sedimentation caused by development activities, including the removal of vegetation and site disturbance; and the movement into water bodies of fertilizer, pesticides, and herbicides from lawns, golf courses, and farms. While federal authority to regulate point source discharges from air stacks, effluent pipes, and other discernable, discrete conveyances has been established, federal power to regulate nonpoint source pollution is far from clear, in part because of the independent authority of state governments to regulate the land uses that cause such pollution. The Tenth Circuit Court of Appeals held that the Clean Water Act does not give EPA the authority to regulate nonpoint source pollution. American Wildlands v. Browner, 260 F.3d 1192, 1198 (10th Cir. 2001); see also Appalachian Power Co. v. Train, 545 F.2d 1351, 1373 (4th Cir. 1976) (stating that "Congress consciously distinguished between point source and nonpoint source discharges, giving EPA authority under the [Clean Water] Act to regulate only the former"). The American Wildlands case made it clear, however, that the TMDL Program established under 33 U.S.C. § 1313 requires states to "assure that there shall be achieved * * * cost-effective and reasonable best management practices for nonpoint source control." American Wildlands, 260 F.3d at 1198 (quoting 40 C.F.R. § 131.112(a)(2)); see also Kentucky Waterways Alliance v. Johnson, 426 F.Supp.2d 612, 630 (W.D.Ky.2006) (stating that nonpoint source pollution is not subject to federal regulation).

It is interesting to ask what recourse EPA has, assuming its authority to enforce TMDL standards, if a state refuses to cooperate or fails to do an adequate job of preventing the nonpoint source pollution of waters that are designated as impaired under the TMDL program. The circuitous route traveled by EPA to influence local land use regulation under the TMDL program is being tracked by the National Marine Fisheries Service ("NMFS") in its attempt to protect seasonal species of Pacific Northwest Salmon listed as threatened under the ESA. Under Section 4(d) of the Act, NMFS has issued regulations requiring states and municipalities to adopt protective regulations. NMFS issued these regulations under authority of 16 U.S.C. § 1533 (1994). Since local governments in northwest states regulate and permit land use activities in watersheds that contain salmon habitat, localities that fail to adopt protective standards can be said to have neglected their duties under the ESA.

An emerging legal theory posits that local governments are liable for third party developer and landowner actions that endanger protected species. This is implicit in the NMFS rules that grant immunity from such liability for local governments that adopt regulations to protect salmon and for third parties acting under approved local regulations. In Loggerhead Turtle v. County Council, 148 F.3d 1231 (11th Cir.1998), the Eleventh Circuit held that an environmental plaintiff had standing to challenge a Florida county for failing to regulate beachfront lighting when that lighting was shown to be the proximate cause of the disorientation and death of turtle hatchlings in their attempt to return to the sea. This injury to a protected species was found to be "fairly traceable" to the actions of the county. Id. at 1249. On remand, it was found that the county's regulations did not cause the taking of an ESA-protected species. Loggerhead Turtle v. County Council, 92 F.Supp.2d 1296 (M.D.Fla.2000). This specific holding, however, did not negate the general principle of the circuit court's decision that local governments may be liable for third party actions taken under their regulations. See, Seattle Audubon Society v. Sutherland, 2007 WL 1300964 (W.D.Wash.2007). Hypothetically, EPA could assume the state's role, classify its waters, and issue, condition, or deny permits for proposed land uses under a pollution prevention system of federal design. Because of the cost and controversy involved in making EPA responsible for the regulation of nonpoint source pollution, this threat may be illusory. There are, however, precedents for this type of EPA preemptive strike and penalties within EPA's control for state noncompliance, such as withholding discretionary funding or denying point source permit applications that would further degrade impaired waters.

Assuming that states wish to comply with the TMDL program, classify their waters as required, and establish allocation systems for the loading of pollutants within each water source, how is the program to be implemented? To act effectively, the states inevitably must require their local governments to amend their land use controls to meet TMDL standards or preempt local authority to the extent necessary to meet those standards through more direct state action. Simply stating this proposition reveals the depth of the problem.

Since 1972 an intense public debate has emerged, centered around a bill passed by the Senate (S. 632, 92d Cong.), known colloquially as the Jackson bill, and officially as the Land–Use Policy and Planning Assistance Act of 1972. That bill never passed the House, nor did any of the similar bills introduced in the House. A federal land use bill has, however, been an idea still raised in congressional sessions since. Strong forces have been aligned on both sides of the debate about the propriety and wisdom of a federal land use bill. So far, the forces of opposition to such legislation have prevailed. See John R. Nolon, National Land Use Planning: Revisiting Senator Jackson's 1970 Policy Act, Land Use Law, May, 1996, p. 3. The House and the Senate again revisited federal assistance for state and local planning with the introduction and subsequent Senate Hearings on the Community Character Act. See Patricia E. Salkin, Congress Misses Twice with the Community Character Act: Will Three Times Be a Charm?, 31 Real Estate L.J. 167 (Fall 2002).

The proponents of federal intervention into the land use planning process base their case mainly on the failure of widespread planning on the state and regional levels, which is blamed for much of the preventable environmental damage occurring daily; also, leaving planning to local initiative is seen as no solution to regional problems. The opponents see federal support of state land use planning as the first step in a process that would lead next to federal demands for such planning and eventually to federal takeover of planning and even worse, federal implementation of plans through controls administered by a federal agency.

B. STATE PLANNING

Even apart from any handwriting on the federal wall, some states have already taken steps to provide for state agencies not only to engage in land use planning, but to regulate the development of land under the auspices of a state plan. The two leading states are Vermont and Hawaii. Consider the utility of these models in states with greater geographical area than Hawaii or Vermont.

In Vermont, Act 250 removed from local control certain large-scale developments. A state level agency was created to issue permits for developments within the definitions of the Act. A good description of Act 250 can be found in a federal case brought by a developer who was denied a permit to develop near a ski resort because the state agency found that a large part of the proposed development contained a deeryard (winter habitat for white-tailed deer). In Southview Associates, Ltd. v. Bongartz, 980 F.2d 84 (2d Cir.1992) Chief Judge Oakes wrote:

> Act 250 has been a major feature of the Vermont legal landscape for over twenty years. Its enactment represented the culmination of an effort to create a process that would subject subdivisions and

other large developments in Vermont to administrative review so as to ensure economic growth without environmental catastrophe. See Governor's Commission on Environmental Control, Reports to Governor 2 (January 1970; May 1970). A brief discussion of the backdrop to the statute's enactment underscores its purpose.

Beginning in the mid–1960s, Vermont experienced a massive increase in second-home construction and other recreational development, particularly in the southern portion of the state and around ski areas. Robert K. Reis, *Vermont's Act 250: Reflections on the First Decade and Recommendations for the Second* 9 (1980); David G. Heeter, *Almost Getting it Together in Vermont, in Environmental and Land Controls Legislation* 323, 326 (David R. Mandelker ed. 1976); Fred Bosselman & David Callies, *The Quiet Revolution in Land Use Control* 54 (1971) (prepared for the Executive Office of the President, Council on Environmental Quality); Erickson, *The Vermont Environmental Protection Act of 1970, in Environmental Protection* 678, 679 (Louis L. Jaffe & Laurence H. Tribe, eds. 1971). These developments shifted economic activity away from agriculture and forestry—the traditional mainstays of the region. Erickson, supra, at 679. The Town of Dover, located in Southern Vermont, provides an example. As one writer explained, in Dover, in 1969, developers were completing, building or planning 19 vacation home subdivisions. According to a regional planner, if all the planned lots had been improved and occupied, the town's population would have increased from 370 to 16,000 within a few years. Id.

This spate of development was fueled by several factors, including the construction of interstate highways, the increased popularity of skiing and other outdoor activities, and what might be termed America's fascination with "the country life." See Reis, supra, at 9. Although the development yielded considerable tax revenue and increased property values, at times it threatened to destroy the very base of its existence: Vermont's relatively unspoiled environment. Poorly planned vacation home subdivisions in mountainous areas—typified by steep slopes and thin soil cover—caused soil erosion, water pollution from sewage systems, and a decline in the aesthetic quality of the land. Erickson, supra, at 680; Bosselman & Callies, supra, at 54–55; Heeter, supra, at 327. Public concern over the side-effects of this new and rapid growth reached the high water mark when, in the summer of 1968, the International Paper Company proposed to construct a huge recreational and vacation home development on 20,000 acres of wilderness in the towns of Stratton and Winhall. Governor's Commission on Environmental Control, supra, at 3; Bosselman & Callies, supra, at 54; Heeter, supra, at 328.

In May of 1969, then Governor Deane C. Davis responded by creating the Governor's Commission on Environmental Control. Governor Davis charged the Commission with determining how economic growth could be attained without environmental destruction. Heeter, supra, at 329 (quoting opening remarks by Governor

Deane C. Davis, *Proceedings of the Governor's Conference on Natural Resources* 1 (May 14, 1969)). The Commission's recommendations included the enactment of a land use law that would require large developments, including subdivisions, to undergo administrative review prior to construction. Governor's Commission on Environmental Control, supra, at 3–4. This proposal formed the basis of Act 250, enacted by the Legislature in 1970.

Not all development projects are subject to Act 250 review. Essentially, an Act 250 permit is required if a person wishes to construct (1) improvements on a parcel or parcels involving more than ten acres located within a radius of five miles; (2) housing projects with 10 or more units located on land owned or controlled by that person within a radius of 5 miles; (3) a subdivision partitioned for resale into ten or more lots within a radius of 5 miles; and (4) improvements above the elevation of 2500 feet. No permit is necessary for construction required for farming, logging or forestry purposes below the elevation of 2500 feet. 10 V.S.A. §§ 6001, 6081(a) (1984 & Supp.1991).

A person whose project is subject to Act 250 jurisdiction must file an application with the regional three-person district commission. 10 V.S.A. §§ 6026, 6083 (1984 & Supp.1991). The district commission evaluates the project according to ten criteria relating to: (1) water and air pollution that will result; (2) availability of water to meet the project's needs; (3) the project's burden on the existing water supply; (4) soil erosion that will result; (5) the project's effect on congestion and safety of transportation routes; (6) the burden the project will place on municipal and local government provision of educational and other services; (7) whether the project will have an undue adverse effect on "the scenic or natural beauty of the area, aesthetics, historic sites or rare and irreplaceable natural areas"; and (8) whether the project conforms with various state, regional and local development plans. 10 V.S.A. § 6086 (1984 & Supp.1991). If the district commission grants the application for a permit, it may attach conditions to it to assure compliance with the criteria for permit issuance. 10 V.S.A. § 6086(c) (1984).

A permit applicant may appeal the decision of the district commission to the nine-member Vermont Environmental Board. 10 V.S.A. §§ 6021(a), 6089(a) (1984 & Supp.1991). The Board reviews challenged findings de novo. 10 V.S.A. § 6089(a) (Supp.1991). The permit applicant may, in turn, appeal the Board's decision to the Supreme Court of Vermont, 10 V.S.A. § 6089(b) (Supp.1991), which will uphold the Board's findings of fact "if supported by substantial evidence in the record as a whole." 10 V.S.A. § 6089(c) (Supp.1991); see In re Southview Associates, 153 Vt. 171, 177, 569 A.2d 501, 504 (1989).

The Vermont Legislature accompanied the enactment of Act 250 with a statement of legislative intent, which provides, in part:

> [T]he unplanned, uncoordinated and uncontrolled use of the lands and the environment of the state of Vermont has resulted in usages of the lands and the environment which may be destructive to the environment and which are not suitable to the demands and needs of the people of the state of Vermont * * *.
>
> * * *
>
> * * * [I]t is necessary to regulate and control the utilization and usages of lands and the environment to ensure that, hereafter, the only usages which will be permitted are not unduly detrimental to the environment, [and] will promote the general welfare through orderly growth and development * * *.
>
> Findings and declaration of intent, 1969, No. 250 (Adj.Sess.), § 1, in 10 V.S.A. annotations following § 6001 (1984).
>
> Subsequently, in 1973, the legislature further clarified the purpose of the act by adopting a "Capability and Development Plan" to guide the implementation of Act 250. 1973 Capability and development plan; statement of intent and findings, 1973 No. 85, § 7, in 10 V.S.A. annotations following § 6042 (1984). See Norman Williams & Tammara Van Ryn–Lincoln, *The Aesthetic Criterion in Vermont's Environmental Law*, 3 Hofstra Prop.L.J. 89, 94–95 (1990). The plan states, in relevant part:
>
> (2) Utilization of Natural Resources [C]onservation of the recreational opportunity afforded by the state's hills, forests, streams and lakes * * * are matters of public good. Uses which threaten or significantly inhibit these resources should be permitted only when the public interest is clearly benefited thereby.
>
> * * *
>
> (6) General Policies for Economic Development In order to achieve a strong economy * * * economic development should be pursued selectively so as to provide maximum economic development with minimal environmental impact.
>
> * * *
>
> (10) Recreational Resources The use and development of land and waters should occur in such a way as not to significantly diminish the value and availability of outdoor recreational activities to the people of Vermont, including hunting * * *.
>
> * * *
>
> (11) Special Areas Lands that include or are adjacent to sites or areas of historical, cultural, scientific, architectural, or archeological value * * * should only be developed in a manner that will not significantly reduce that value of the site or area.

Thus, the Legislature intended Act 250 to protect Vermont's environmental resources with an eye towards maintaining, among other things, existing recreational uses of the land—such as hunting, for example—and preserving lands, when possible, that have special values to the public. In recognition of the importance of economic growth, however, the focus of the Act is not on barring development but on molding it to minimize its environmental impact. And in practice, one commentator has stated that "[t]he statute has * * * been administered not as a 'no-growth' law, but as a law designed to improve the quality of growth." Williams & Van Ryn–Lincoln, supra, at 94.

IN RE JUSTER ASSOCIATES

Supreme Court of Vermont, 1978.
136 Vt. 577, 396 A.2d 1382.

[Juster Associates had previously received a permit from the Vermont Environmental Conservation Board for a 31 acre shopping center in the Town of Rutland. After construction was completed and the center was in operation, the septic tank sewage disposal system failed. Several alternatives also failed and Juster Associates returned to the Board seeking an amendment of its original permit to allow installation of a new system on a 4 acre site near, but not abutting the shopping center. The Board granted the new permit and an appeal was taken by the city and downstream riparian owners.]

DALEY, JUSTICE.

* * *

No one questions the applicability of our so-called Act 250, found in 10 V.S.A. chapter 151. The project in question is to be located on more than one acre of land within a municipality which has not adopted permanent zoning and subdivision bylaws * * * and therefore comes within the scope of the statute. The initial issue * * * is whether the Board had jurisdiction over Juster's application for a permit to develop the four acre tract as a sewage disposal facility. * * *

The purpose of Act 250 is to protect and conserve the environment of the state and to insure that lands slated for development are devoted to uses which are not detrimental to the public welfare and interest. 1969 No. 250 (Adj.Sess.), § 1; In re Great Eastern Building Co., 132 Vt. 610, 614, 326 A.2d 152, 154 (1974). These ends are served by a system of land use permits established by the Legislature. Where the Act applies, property may not be developed without a permit. 10 V.S.A. § 6081. An application for a permit must be made to a District Commissioner. 10 V.S.A. § 6083. The District Commission must provide general notice, by newspaper publication, and notice to certain persons designated by statute and by Board rule. 10 V.S.A. § 6084. After hearing, the District Commission may approve the application and issue a permit. 10 V.S.A. § 6086. Within this framework, the Board acts as a quasi-judicial appellate body, to hear appeals from commission decisions. Environmental Board Regulations, Rule 1(C)(1).

Notwithstanding the statutory procedure of hearings at the District Commission level with appeals to the Board, the Board seeks, by granting an amendment to an outstanding permit, to allow a four acre tract of land to be developed without proceedings before the District Commission. It contends that its power to do so lies in its jurisdiction to enforce the permits that it issues. The Board argues that it has jurisdiction because the land is to be used to fulfill a condition attached to an existing permit. We cannot agree.

We do not dispute the Board's authority to police its permits. It may, under the statute, revoke a permit if the conditions attached to the permit are violated. 10 V.S.A. § 6090. But we cannot allow it, under the guise of permit enforcement, to subvert the protective scheme ordained by the Legislature. The statute is intended, by a system of notice and hearings, to assure full consideration of land use proposals for all parcels of land. In bypassing the District Commission, the Board precluded a complete discussion of the issues involved in constructing a waste disposal facility on new acreage. This land was not considered in the previous hearings. When the original permit was issued, the matters now under discussion were not even contemplated. Development of the four acre plot may affect persons other than those who participated in the hearings that were conducted on the shopping center. However, the public was not notified that the land was to be developed, thus circumventing its participation.

* * * To accept the Board's rationale is to diminish the scrutiny given to land use under the statutory framework, because it allows for approval of a development without the discussion provided for by the statute.

Our review of the record convinces us that the Board lacked authority to entertain the application filed by Juster. Initial consideration of a land use proposal is a function assigned by the Legislature to the District Commission. The Board is not vested with concurrent jurisdiction to hear and decide the same matters.

* * *

Notes

1. This case gives some illustration of how the Vermont system operates. Also see In re Wildlife Wonderland, Inc., 133 Vt. 507, 346 A.2d 645 (1975), where the court upheld the environmental board's denial of a permit to construct and operate a game farm where some 300 wild and domestic animals could be viewed by the paying public.

The Juster case has been one long saga illustrating a dispute between developer and city. Another round in that dispute is Juster Associates v. City of Rutland, 901 F.2d 266 (2d Cir.1990), which involves an antitrust challenge against the city.

2. In 1988 the Vermont legislature adopted Act 200, which has been referred to as a growth control law. The statute is designed to encourage towns to adopt comprehensive growth control regulations by offering state

funds to pay for the planning; towns that do not elect to participate are disabled from participating in regional planning. Act 200 fostered a bitter fight in Vermont. At least fifty-one towns rejected the Act in 1990 town meeting elections. Also, some towns returned money to the state and backed out of the program. The opposition to Act 200 appeared to focus on the loss of local control of land use regulation and a perceived threat to property rights. The future of the program is in some doubt.

In Hawaii the state has preempted a sizeable amount of what would normally be considered local zoning authority. The Hawaii statutory framework is set forth here:

Hawaii Revised Statutes (1968):

§ 205–1 Establishment of the commission. There shall be a state land use commission, hereinafter called the commission. The commission shall consist of nine members who shall hold no other public office and shall be appointed in the manner and serve for the term set forth * * *

§ 205–2 Districting and classification of lands. (a) There shall be four major land use districts in which all lands in the State shall be placed: urban, rural, agricultural, and conservation. The land use commission shall group contiguous land areas suitable for inclusion in one of these four major districts. The commission shall set standards for determining the boundaries of each district, provided that:

(1) In the establishment of boundaries of urban districts those lands that are now in urban use and a sufficient reserve area for foreseeable urban growth shall be included;

(2) In the establishment of boundaries for rural districts, areas of land composed primarily of small farms mixed with very low density residential lots, which may be shown by a minimum density of not more than one house per one-half acre and a minimum lot size of not less than one-half acre shall be included, except as herein provided;

(3) In the establishment of the boundaries of agricultural districts the greatest possible protection shall be given to those lands with a high capacity for intensive cultivation; and

(4) In the establishment of the boundaries of conservation districts, the "forest and water reserve zones" provided in Act 234, section 2, Session Laws of Hawaii 1957, are renamed "conservation districts" and, effective as of July 11, 1961, the boundaries of the forest and water reserve zones theretofore established pursuant to Act 234, section 2, Session Laws of Hawaii 1957, shall constitute the boundaries of the conservation districts; provided that thereafter the power to determine the boundaries of the conservation districts shall be in the commission.

In establishing the boundaries of the districts in each county, the commission shall give consideration to the master plan or general plan of the county.

(b) Urban districts shall include activities or uses as provided by ordinances or regulations of the county within which the urban district is situated.

(c) Rural districts shall include activities or uses as characterized by low density residential lots of not more than one dwelling house per one-half acre, except as provided by county ordinance pursuant to section 46–4(c), in areas where "city-like" concentration of people, structures, streets, and urban level of services are absent, and where small farms are intermixed with low density residential lots except that within a subdivision, as defined in section 484–1, the commission for good cause may allow one lot of less than one-half acre, but not less than 18,500 square feet, or an equivalent residential density, within a rural subdivision and permit the construction of one dwelling on such lot, provided that all other dwellings in the subdivision shall have a minimum lot size of one-half acre or 21,780 square feet. Such petition for variance may be processed under the special permit procedure. These districts may include contiguous areas which are not suited to low density residential lots or small farms by reason of topography, soils, and other related characteristics.

(d) Agricultural districts shall include activities or uses as characterized by the cultivation of crops, orchards, forage, and forestry; farming activities or uses related to animal husbandry, aquaculture, game and fish propagation; aquaculture, which means the production of aquatic plant and animal life for food and fiber within ponds and other bodies of water; wind generated energy production for public, private and commercial use; bona fide agricultural services and uses which support the agricultural activities of the fee or leasehold owner of the property and accessory to any of the above activities, whether or not conducted on the same premises as the agricultural activities to which they are accessory, including but not limited to farm dwellings as defined in section 205–4.5(a)(4), employee housing, farm buildings, mills, storage facilities, processing facilities, vehicle and equipment storage areas, and roadside stands for the sale of products grown on the premises; wind machines and wind farms; small-scale meteorological, air quality, noise and other scientific and environmental data collection and monitoring facilities occupying less than one-half acre of land, provided that such facilities shall not be used as or equipped for use as living quarters or dwellings; agricultural parks; and open area recreational facilities, including golf courses and golf driving ranges, provided that they are not located within agricultural district lands with soil classified by the land study bureau's detailed land classification as overall (master) productivity rating class A or B.

These districts may include areas which are not used for, or which are not suited to, agricultural and ancillary activities by reason of topography, soils, and other related characteristics.

(e) Conservation districts shall include areas necessary for protecting watersheds and water sources; preserving scenic and historic areas; providing park lands, wilderness, and beach reserves; conserving indigenous or endemic plants, fish, and wildlife, including those which are threatened or endangered; preventing floods and soil erosion; forestry; open space areas whose existing openness, natural condition, or present state of use, if retained, would enhance the present or potential value of abutting or surrounding communities, or would maintain or enhance the conservation of natural or scenic resources; areas of value for recreational purposes; other related activities; and other permitted uses not detrimental to a multiple use conservation concept.

§ 205–3.1 Amendments to district boundaries. (a) District boundary amendments involving land areas greater than fifteen acres shall be processed by the land use commission pursuant to section 205–4.

(b) Any department or agency of the State, and department or agency of the county in which the land is situated, or any person with a property interest in the land sought to be reclassified may petition the appropriate county land use decision-making authority of the county in which the land is situated for a change in the boundary of a district involving lands less than fifteen acres presently in the agricultural, rural, and urban districts.

(c) District boundary amendments involving land areas of fifteen acres or less, except in conservation districts, shall be determined by the appropriate county land use decision-making authority for said district and shall not require consideration by the land use commission pursuant to section 205–4. District boundary amendments involving land areas of fifteen acres or less in conservation districts shall be processed by the land use commission pursuant to section 205–4. The appropriate county land use decision-making authority may consolidate proceedings to amend state land use district boundaries pursuant to this subsection, with county proceedings to amend the general plan, development plan, zoning of the affected land or such other proceedings. Appropriate ordinances and rules to allow consolidation of such proceedings may be developed by the county land use decision-making authority.

(d) The county land use decision-making authority shall serve a copy of the application for a district boundary amendment to the land use commission and the department of business, economic development and tourism and shall notify the commission and the department of the time and place of the hearing and the proposed amendments scheduled to be heard at the hearing. A change in the state land use district boundaries pursuant to this subsection shall become effective on the day designated by the county land use decision-making authority in its decision. Within sixty days of the effective date of any decision to amend state land use district boundaries by the county land use decision-making authority, the decision and the description and map of the affected property shall be transmitted to the land use commission and the department of planning and economic development, and tourism by the county planning director. [L 1985, c 230, § 3]

§ 205–4 Amendments to district boundaries involving land areas greater than fifteen acres. (a) Any department or agency of the State, any department or agency of the county in which the land is situated, or any person with a property interest in the land sought to be reclassified, may petition the land use commission for a change in the boundary of a district. This section applies to all petitions for changes in district boundaries of lands within conservation districts and all petitions for changes in district boundaries involving lands greater than fifteen acres in the agricultural, rural, and urban districts, except as provided in section 201E–210. * * *

* * *

(2) All departments and agencies of the State and of the county in which the land is situated shall be admitted as parties upon timely application for intervention.

(3) All persons who have some property interest in the land, who lawfully reside on the land, or who otherwise can demonstrate that they will be so directly and immediately affected by the proposed change that their interest in the proceeding is clearly distinguishable from that of the general public shall be admitted as parties upon timely application for intervention.

(4) All other persons may apply to the commission for leave to intervene as parties. Leave to intervene shall be freely granted, provided that the commission or its hearing officer if one is appointed may deny an application to intervene when in the commission's or hearing officer's sound discretion it appears that: (A) the position of the applicant for intervention concerning the proposed change is substantially the same as the position of a party already admitted to the proceeding; and (B) the admission of additional parties will render the proceedings inefficient and unmanageable. A person whose application to intervene is denied may appeal such denial to the circuit court pursuant to section 91–14.

* * *

§ 205–6 Special permit. The county planning commission may permit certain unusual and reasonable uses within agricultural and rural districts other than those for which the district is classified. Any person who desires to use his land within an agricultural or rural district other than for an agricultural or rural use, as the case may be, may petition the planning commission of the county within which his land is located for permission to use his land in the manner desired. Each county may establish the appropriate fee for processing the special permit petition.

The planning commission, upon consultation with the central coordinating agency, except in counties where the planning commission is advisory only in which case the central coordinating agency, shall establish by rule or regulation, the time within which the hearing and action on petition for special permit shall occur. The county planning commission shall notify the land use commission and such persons and agencies that may have an interest in the subject matter of the time and place of the hearing.

The county planning commission may under such protective restrictions as may be deemed necessary, permit the desired use, but only when the use would promote the effectiveness and objectives of this chapter. A decision in favor of the applicant shall require a majority vote of the total membership of the county planning commission.

Special permits for land the area of which is greater than fifteen acres shall be subject to approval by the land use commission. The land use commission may impose additional restrictions as may be necessary or appropriate in granting such approval, including the adherence to representations made by the applicant.

A copy of the decision together with the complete record of the proceeding before the county planning commission on all special permit requests involving a land area greater than fifteen acres shall be transmitted to the land use commission within sixty days after the decision is rendered. Within forty-five days after receipt of the complete record from the county planning commission, the land use commission shall act to approve, approve with modification, or deny the petition. A denial either by the county planning commission or by the land use commission, or a modification by the land use commission, as the case may be, of the desired use shall be appealable to the circuit court of the circuit in which the land is situated and shall be made pursuant to the Hawaii Rules of Civil Procedure.

* * *

§ 205–18 Periodic review of districts. The office of state planning shall undertake a review of the classification and districting of all lands in the State, within five years from December 31, 1985, and every fifth year thereafter. The office, in its five-year boundary review, shall focus its efforts on reviewing the Hawaii state plan, county general plans, and county development and community plans. Upon completion of the five-year boundary review, the office shall submit a report of the findings to the commission. The office may initiate state land use boundary amendments which it deems appropriate to conform to these plans. The office may seek assistance of appropriate state and county agencies and may employ consultants and undertake studies in making this review.

One notable feature of the Hawaii statute is the provision for a review of district boundaries and regulations each five years after the adoption of the first district boundaries (which occurred in 1964). The second review was completed in 1974, and published in February, 1975.

See Report to the People (Hawaii Land Use Commission, 1975). The report indicates that during the 1969–1974 period proposals were made to change the district classification of 133,438 acres of land. Approved changes in that period totaled 66,670 acres. Id., at p. 25. Out of the approved changes, a total of 5,438 acres were placed in the urban district while 4,056 acres were removed from the urban district. Ibid. See, generally, P. Myers, Zoning Hawaii: An Analysis of the Passage and Implementation of Hawaii's Land Classification Law (1975) and Mandelker & Kolis, Whither Hawaii: Land Use Management in an Island State, 1 U.Hawaii L.Rev. 48 (1979). In 1978, Hawaii adopted a new state planning act, Hawaii Rev.Stat. § 226–1 et seq. The reviews have been sporadic in recent years, with the latest in the early 1990's.

For a case interpreting the Hawaiian classifications in relation to the special permit procedures, see Neighborhood Bd. No. 24 (Waianae Coast) v. State Land Use Comm'n, 64 Hawaii 265, 639 P.2d 1097 (1982). A developer sought and received a special permit to construct an amusement park on a 103 acre parcel of land in the agricultural district. The court held that the special permit was improper and that the developer should have sought a district boundary amendment; use of the special permit procedure would, in this type of large-scale development, allow ad hoc infusion of major urban uses into agricultural districts. Compare Maha'ulepu v. Land Use Comm'n, 71 Hawaii 332, 790 P.2d 906 (1990) where the court held that the commission could issue special permits for golf courses on prime agricultural land. (In 1985 the legislature amended the definition of permitted uses in agricultural districts (Section 205–2, supra) to include golf courses.) See Comment, *Maha'ulepu v. Land Use Commission*: A Symbol of Change; Hawaii's Land Use Law Allows Golf Course Development on Prime Agricultural Land by Special Use Permit, 13 Haw. L. Rev. 205 (1991).

C. REGIONAL PLANNING

The first regional planning agency with authority to plan—the Boston Metropolitan Improvement Commission—was created by the Massachusetts Legislature in 1902. The federal and state governments have established regional planning agencies with limited authority to develop plans for the protection and preservation of certain natural or environmentally significant resources (*e.g.*, the Tahoe Regional Planning Agency, the Adirondack Park Agency and New Jersey Pinelands Commission), or for certain functional purposes (*e.g.*, Metropolitan Planning Organizations which are the federally recognized transportation planning entities). In other cases, regional planning agencies have been statutorily established or authorized for the purpose of providing greater than local perspectives on trends and resources in a multi-jurisdictional geographic area. Depending upon the legislation establishing these regional planning entities, they may or may not have authority to develop binding land use plans for their jurisdictional area.

With the growing recognition that the impacts of local land use decisions know no political boundaries, there has been significant movement in the direction of voluntary intermunicipal cooperation in land use planning and controls. Most states grant broad statutory authorization to local governments to cooperate that have led to, among other things, the development of joint comprehensive land use plans. It is increasingly common to find statements in local comprehensive plans that acknowledge that the municipality exists as part of a larger region and that there is a desire to consider the plans and actions of neighboring jurisdictions when making local land use decisions.

Although the political culture in most states rejects any notion of "regional" government, one state that has a history of regional approaches to problem solving is Minnesota. Statutes in that state seek to promote regional land use problem solving. Some excerpts from Minnesota Statutes Annotated (1963):

462.383

The legislature finds that problems of growth and development in urban and rural regions of the state so transcend the boundary lines of local government units that no single unit can plan for their solution without affecting other units in the region; that various multi-county planning activities conducted under various laws of the United States are presently being conducted in an uncoordinated manner; that intergovernmental cooperation on a regional basis is an effective means of pooling the resources of local government to approach common problems; and that the assistance of the state is needed to make the most effective use of local, state, federal, and private programs in serving the citizens of such urban and rural regions.

It is the purpose of sections 462.381 to 462.398 to facilitate intergovernmental cooperation and to insure the orderly and harmonious coordination of state, federal, and local comprehensive planning and development programs for the solution of economic, social, physical, and governmental problems of the state and its citizens by providing for the creation of regional development commissions.

Laws 1969, c. 1122, § 3, eff. June 1, 1969.

* * *

462.387

Any combination of counties or municipalities representing a majority of the population of the region for which a commission is proposed may petition the commissioner by formal resolution setting forth its desire to establish, and the need for, the establishment of a regional development commission. For purposes of this section the population of a county does not include the population of a municipality within the county.

462.39

The commission shall prepare and adopt, after appropriate study and such public hearings as may be necessary, a comprehensive development plan for the region. The plan shall consist of a compilation of policy statements, goals, standards, programs, and maps prescribing guides for an orderly and economic development, public and private, of the region. The comprehensive development plan shall recognize and encompass physical, social, or economic needs of the region, and those future developments which will have an impact on the entire region including but not limited to such matters as land use, parks and open space land needs, access to direct sunlight for solar energy systems, the necessity for and location of airports, highways, transit facilities, public hospitals, libraries, schools, public and private housing, and other public buildings. In preparing the development plan the commission shall use to the maximum extent feasible the resources, studies and data available from other planning agencies within the region, including counties, municipalities, special districts, and subregional planning agencies, and it shall utilize the resources of the director to the same purpose. No development plan or portion thereof for the region shall be adopted by the commission until it has been submitted to the director for review and comment and a period of 60 days has elapsed after such submission. When a development plan has been adopted, the commission shall distribute it to all local government units within the region.

* * *

462.391

The commission may participate as a party in any proceedings originating before the Minnesota municipal board under chapter 414, if the proceedings involve the change in a boundary of a governmental unit in the region.

Notes

1. What major differences do you see between the Vermont approach, the Hawaii approach, and the Minnesota approach? Which model do you think affords the best accommodation between regional concerns and the "rights" of local property owners? Are there practical considerations that commend one approach over the other?

2. The approaches described above were hailed in the early 1970's as the "wave of the future." See Bosselman and Callies, The Quiet Revolution in Land Use Control (Council on Environmental Quality 1971). Statewide planning control, as in Vermont and Hawaii, did not spread to other states and regional planning has been utilized only in special circumstances. See, e.g., Booth, Developing Institutions for Regional Land Use Planning and Control—The Adirondack Experience, 28 Buffalo L.Rev. 645 (1979). See generally, Callies, The Quiet Revolution Revisited, American Planning Association J. 135 (Apr. 1980). Also see Marie L. York, Regions: Blind Isolation or Shared Vision?, Land Use Law, April, 1995, p. 3.

3. Several states have adopted planning enabling legislation which is somewhere in between state level control and local autonomy. In Florida, for example, areas that have been designated as of "critical environmental concern" are subject to planning and regulation at the state level; this

approach can be viewed as a partial preemption of the traditional planning function. Some states have opted for mandatory local planning with the state (either by statute or administrative regulation), mandating particular elements of the plans. See, e.g., Cal.Govt.Code § 65101; Or.Rev.Stat. § 215.505 et seq.; Rev.Code Wash.Ann. § 36.70.010. Many states have preempted local planning and regulation of particular types of activities that have a widespread impact, such as power plant sitings. See, e.g., Town of Preston v. Connecticut Siting Council, 20 Conn.App. 474, 568 A.2d 799 (1990). Industrial pollution has also engendered preemption of local control. See, e.g., Niro, Illinois Environmental Law—State Preemption of Local Governmental Regulation of Pollution Related Activities, 67 Ill.Bar J. 118 (1978).

D. INTERSTATE COMPACTS

PEOPLE EX REL. YOUNGER v. COUNTY OF EL DORADO

Supreme Court of California, In Bank, 1971.
5 Cal.3d 480, 96 Cal.Rptr. 553, 487 P.2d 1193.

SULLIVAN, JUSTICE.

The Attorney General, on behalf of the People of the State of California, seeks a writ of mandate commanding the Counties of El Dorado and Placer to pay to the Tahoe Regional Planning Agency (Agency) the amounts of money respectively allotted to them by the Agency as being necessary to support its activities. We issued an alternative writ of mandate to which respondents have made return by answer. The issues thus presented to us are of great concern to California, to its neighbors and, indeed, to the entire country.

The controversy which we are required to review focuses upon the Lake Tahoe Basin—an area of unique and unsurpassed beauty situated high in the Sierras along the California–Nevada border. Mark Twain, an early visitor to the region, viewed the lake as "a noble sheet of blue water lifted six thousand three hundred feet above the level of the sea * * * with the shadows of the mountains brilliantly photographed upon its still surface * * * the fairest picture the whole earth affords." Year after year the lake and its surrounding mountains have attracted and captivated countless visitors from all over the world.

However, there is good reason to fear that the region's natural wealth contains the virus of its ultimate impoverishment. A staggering increase in population, a greater mobility of people, an affluent society and an incessant urge to invest, to develop, to acquire and merely to spend—all have combined to pose a severe threat to the Tahoe region. Only recently has the public become aware of the delicate balance of the ecology, and of the complex interrelated natural processes which keep the lake's waters clear and fresh, preserve the mountains from unsightly erosion, and maintain all forms of wildlife at appropriate levels. Today, and for the foreseeable future, the ecology of Lake Tahoe stands in grave danger before a mounting wave of population and development.

In an imaginative and commendable effort to avert this imminent threat, California and Nevada, with the approval of Congress (Pub.Law 91–148, 83 Stat. 360), entered into the Tahoe Regional Planning Compact (Compact) the provisions of which are found in Government Code section 66801. The basic concept of the Compact is a simple one—to provide for the region as a whole the planning, conservation and resource development essential to accommodate a growing population within the region's relatively small area without destroying the environment.

To achieve this purpose, the Compact establishes the Tahoe Regional Planning Agency with jurisdiction over the entire region. (§ 66801, art. III, subd. (a).) The Agency has been given broad powers to make and enforce a regional plan of an unusually comprehensive scope. This plan, to be adopted on or before September 1, 1971, must include, as correlated elements, plans for land-use, transportation, conservation, recreation, and public services and facilities. (§ 66801, art. V, subd. (b).) The Compact emphasizes that in formulating and maintaining this regional plan, the Agency "shall take account of and shall seek to harmonize the needs of the region as a whole * * *." (Id.)

The Agency is given the power to "adopt all necessary ordinances, rules, regulations and policies to effectuate the adopted regional * * *" plan. (§ 66801, art. VI, subd. (a).) While ordinances so enacted establish minimum standards applicable throughout the region, local political subdivisions may enact and enforce equal or higher standards. "The regulations shall contain general, regional standards including but not limited to the following: water purity and clarity; subdivision; zoning; tree removal; solid waste disposal; sewage disposal; land fills, excavations, cuts and grading; piers, harbors, breakwaters; or channels and other shoreline developments; waste disposal in shoreline areas; waste disposal from boats; mobile-home parks; house relocation; outdoor advertising; flood plain protection; soil and sedimentation control; air pollution; and watershed protection. Whenever possible without diminishing the effectiveness of the * * * general plan, the ordinances, rules, regulations and policies shall be confined to matters which are general and regional in application, leaving to the jurisdiction of the respective states, counties and cities the enactment of specific and local ordinances, rules, regulations and policies which conform to the * * * general plan." (Id.) The Compact also provides that "[v]iolation of any ordinance of the [A]gency is a misdemeanor." (§ 66801, art. VI, subd. (f).) Finally, it states that "all public works projects shall be reviewed prior to construction and [except for certain state public works projects] approved by the [A]gency as to the project's compliance with the adopted regional general plan." (§ 66801, art. VI, subd. (c).) * * *

The Compact permits the Agency to receive fees for its services, gifts, grants and other financial aids. It also provides for Agency financing as follows: "Except as provided in subdivision (e), on or before December 30 of each calendar year the agency shall establish the amount of money necessary to support its activities for the next succeeding fiscal year commencing July 1 of the following year. The agency shall apportion not more than $150,000 of this amount among the counties within the region on the same ratio to the total sum required as the full cash valuation of taxable property within the region in each county bears to the total full cash valuation of taxable property within the region. Each county in California shall pay the sum allotted to it by the agency from any funds available therefor and may levy a tax on any taxable property within its boundaries sufficient to pay the amount so allocated to it. Each county in Nevada shall pay such sum from its general fund or from any other moneys available therefor." (§ 66801, art. VII, subd. (a).)

After ratification of the Compact by Congress and upon proclamation of the Governors of California and Nevada, the Agency came into existence on March 19, 1970. It adopted a budget, pursuant to section 66801, article V, subdivisions (a) and (e), for the fourth quarter of the fiscal year 1969–1970—that is, for the months April through June 1970. Of the total budget of $81,770.85, $22,344.68 was allotted to El Dorado County, and $10,322.98 to Placer County. However, no specific demand was made upon the counties to pay the amounts apportioned to them, and they have consistently refused to do so.

The Agency has also adopted a budget of $180,000 for the fiscal year 1970–1971. Of this sum, the amount apportioned to El Dorado County is $60,150 and that allotted to Placer County is $33,600. No demand was made upon either county for such sums until December 29, 1970. The counties have refused to pay the above sums or any part of them.

For the fiscal year 1971–1972, the Agency has adopted a budget of $222,400, of which El Dorado County's share is $54,450, and Placer County's share is $40,350. The Attorney General asserts that, absent an order of this court, the counties will refuse to pay these sums.

The positions of the parties before us may be summarized as follows: the Attorney General contends that the respondent counties have a clear duty, imposed by the Compact, to pay their share of the funds necessary to support the activities of the Agency and that we should compel the performance of this duty by a writ of mandate. The counties contend first, that they are not required to make any payments to the Agency because the Compact is unconstitutional and void and, secondly, that the remedy here sought is inappropriate because the People have a plain, speedy and adequate remedy at law. * * *

We turn to the merits. The counties first contend that the Compact violates former sections 11, 12 and 13 of article XI of the California Constitution * * * Generally speaking, these sections confer upon specified local governmental bodies broad powers over purely local affairs. But, as we shall point out, the Compact is unaffected by any of the above provisions since its subject matter is of regional, rather than local, concern.

The regional nature of the Compact is manifest from the express language of the legislation. Article I of the Compact which sets forth legislative findings and declarations of policy, provides in relevant part:

"It is found and declared that the waters of Lake Tahoe and other resources of the Lake Tahoe region are threatened with deterioration or degeneration. [Par.] It is further declared that by virtue of the special conditions and circumstances of the natural ecology, developmental pattern, population distribution and human needs in the Lake Tahoe region, the region is experiencing problems of resources use and deficiencies of environmental control." The same article further declares the "need to maintain an equilibrium between the region's natural endowment and its manmade environment," and specifically recognizes "that for the purpose of enhancing the efficiency and governmental effectiveness of the region, it is imperative that there be established an areawide planning agency with power to adopt and enforce a regional plan of resource conservation and orderly development, to exercise effective environmental controls and to perform other essential functions * * *." Of course, such findings and declarations of policy are entitled to great weight. (Bishop v. City of San Jose (1969) 1 Cal.3d 56, 63, 81 Cal.Rptr. 465, 460 P.2d 137; Housing Authority v. Dockweiler (1939) 14 Cal.2d 437, 449–450, 94 P.2d 794; Wilson, Consideration of Facts in Constitutional Cases (1944) 17 So.Cal.L.Rev. 335.)

Even without such explicit findings we could hardly avoid a conclusion that the purpose of the Compact is to conserve the natural resources and control the environment of the Tahoe Basin as a whole through area-wide planning. Lake Tahoe itself is an interstate body of water; the surrounding region, defined by the Compact, is also interstate, since it includes not only the lake but the adjacent parts of three counties of Nevada and two counties of California. (§ 66801, art. III, subd. (a).) The water that the Agency is to purify cannot be confined within one county or state; it circulates freely throughout Lake Tahoe. The air which the Agency must preserve from pollution knows no political boundaries. The wildlife which the Agency should protect ranges freely from one local jurisdiction to another. Nor can the population and explosive development which threaten the region be contained by any of the local authorities which govern parts of the Tahoe Basin. Only an agency transcending local boundaries can devise, adopt and put into operation solutions for the problems besetting the region as a whole. Indeed, the fact that the Compact is the product of the cooperative efforts and mutual agreement of two states is impressive proof that its subject matter and objectives are of regional rather than local concern. * * *

Furthermore, problems which exhibit exclusively local characteristics at certain times in the life of a community, acquire larger dimensions and changed characteristics at others. "It is * * * settled that the constitutional concept of municipal affairs is not a fixed or static quantity. It changes with the changing conditions upon which it is to operate." (Pac. Tel. & Tel. Co. v. City & County of S.F. (1959) 51 Cal.2d 766, 771, 336 P.2d 514, 517.) When the effects of change are felt beyond the point of its immediate impact, it is fatuous to expect that controlling such change remains a local problem to be solved by local methods. Old attitudes confer no irrevocable license to continue looking with unseeing eyes. The Compact gives the Agency power to adopt regional planning and regional zoning ordinances to solve regional problems of resource management; it does not delegate to the Agency the same powers granted to the counties.

In short, since the powers conferred upon the Agency are for regional purposes, not local purposes, and since no power to enact penal legislation has been delegated to the Agency, former section 11 is not violated.

* * *

The Counties of El Dorado and Placer also contend that the Compact is void because it denies their residents equal protection of the laws in violation of sections 11 and 21 of article I of the California Constitution and of the Fourteenth Amendment to the United States Constitution. Such violation of equal protection is asserted on two separate grounds: (1) That the Compact by failing to provide therefor denies to the citizens of the Tahoe Basin their right of initiative, referendum and recall; and (2) that the method of selecting the governing body of the Agency violates the "one person, one vote" rule.

The counties' first argument is essentially this: Since the Legislature has provided for initiative, referendum and recall for counties but has made no such provision for the Agency, there is an unreasonable and arbitrary classification "[d]enying the citizens of the Tahoe Basin such basic rights * * *." The point seems to be that although the citizens of El Dorado and Placer Counties do have such rights in respect to their counties, they are constitutionally entitled to an additional bundle of similar rights in respect to the Agency. We can discern no merit in this line of argument.

As we recently said, the concept of equal protection of the laws means simply "that persons similarly situated with respect to the legitimate purpose of the law receive like treatment." (Purdy & Fitzpatrick v. State of California (1969) 71 Cal.2d 566, 578, 79 Cal.Rptr. 77, 85, 456 P.2d 645, 653.) So far as the procedures of the initiative, referendum and recall are concerned, the Agency is treated no differently than other districts in California. All districts, including regional agencies such as the present one, are excluded from the initiative, referendum and recall provisions of the Elections Code where, as here, the district has been "formed under a law which does not provide a procedure for elections * * *." (Elec.Code, § 5150.) Since the residents of the Tahoe Basin are thus treated in the same way as those of other districts created under similar laws, they have suffered no denial of equal protection.

Nor can we discern any constitutional infirmity in the appointment, rather than the election of the governing body of the Agency. (See § 66801, art. III, subd. (a).) Certainly such a scheme of organization is not without precedent. (See, for example, the San Francisco Bay Conservation and Development Commission; Gov.Code, § 66620; see also Gov.

Code, § 66400 et seq.; § 65063 et seq.; § 66500 et seq.) Indeed, in the instant case, the selection of the governing body by appointment would appear to be a necessary consequence of the interstate nature of the Agency. * * *

The counties' "one person, one vote" argument is also lacking in merit. They urge that the Agency exercises "general governmental powers" and that, therefore, under Avery v. Midland County (1968) 390 U.S. 474, 88 S.Ct. 1114, 20 L.Ed.2d 45 and its progeny, the governing board of the Agency must be apportioned in a manner which conforms with the "one person, one vote" requirement of the Fourteenth Amendment.

Clearly the members of the governing board of the Agency do not represent equal numbers of residents of the region. The United States census for 1970 gives the following populations for the counties here involved: Placer, 76,218; El Dorado, 41,704; Washoe, 119,965; Ormsby, 15,264; and Douglas, 6,046. Since one member of the Agency's governing board represents each of these counties some members of the board represent far more residents than do others. Furthermore, the 11,998 residents of the City of South Lake Tahoe are, in a sense, represented twice, since both that city and El Dorado County within which it is located have a member on the Agency. Finally, the *ex officio* members and the members appointed by the governors do not represent residents at all, but rather "the public at large." If the Agency's governing board must be selected on a "one person, one vote" basis, it obviously fails the test. (See Calderon v. City of Los Angeles (1971) 4 Cal.3d 251, 93 Cal.Rptr. 361, 481 P.2d 489.)

However, the members of the Agency's governing board are appointed, not elected. In Sailors v. Board of Education (1967) 387 U.S. 105, 87 S.Ct. 1549, 18 L.Ed.2d 650, the United States Supreme Court upheld a similar system of appointing members of a county school board over the objection that it violated the "one person, one vote" principle. There, the residents of each local school board district elected a local school board. Each of these boards, in turn, selected a delegate to a biennial meeting at which the delegates elected a five-member county board.

The court stated: "Viable local governments may need many innovations, numerous combinations of old and new devices, great flexibility in municipal arrangements to meet changing urban conditions. We see nothing in the Constitution to prevent experimentation. At least as respects nonlegislative officers, a State can appoint local officials or elect them or combine the elective and appointive systems as was done here. * * * Since the choice of members of the county school board did not involve an election and since none was required for these nonlegislative offices, the principle of 'one man, one vote' has no relevancy." (387 U.S. at pp. 110–111, 87 S.Ct. at p. 1553.)

* * *

The members of the Agency's governing board are appointed; consequently, the fact that they do not "represent" equal numbers of people does not deny those who are "underrepresented" equal protection of the laws.

Furthermore, we perceive significant state interests which justify the Compact's provisions for appointment of the Agency's governing board. In the first place, the Agency presents unique problems because of its interstate nature. If the board were apportioned on the basis of population within the region, Nevada would be accorded more votes than California, since the population of Washoe, Ormsby and Douglas Counties is 141,275 whereas the population of El Dorado and Placer Counties is 117,922. California, whose concurrence was essential to the formation of the Agency, would be less interested in the Agency if its vote were less than equal to Nevada's. Secondly, persons not residing within the Tahoe Basin have a very real and direct interest in the actions of the Agency. Aside from the general interest of the people of this state, including its vacationers, in the preservation of Lake Tahoe, it is common knowledge that many nonresidents own vacation homes and other property within the region. They will, of course, be directly affected by any planning or zoning by the Agency. Finally, the Compact represents an innovative attempt to deal with a problem directly affecting nonresidents of the Tahoe Basin, as well as residents. The Compact gives to the residents of the region a clear majority of the representation on the governing board, since such residents are the persons most intimately involved with the Agency. Yet, as we have seen, the general population of the state has a very substantial, if lesser, interest in the Agency. The public at large is represented by the two members sitting *ex officio* and by the two members appointed by the governors.

* * *

We, therefore, reach these final conclusions: Section 66801 of the Government Code, which constitutes the enactment by the California Legislature of the Tahoe Regional Planning Compact, is constitutional. The Compact imposes on respondent counties a clear and present duty to pay to the Tahoe Regional Planning Agency the sums heretofore and hereafter allotted to them by the Agency as representing their respective shares of the amount of money necessary to support the Agency's activities. Respondents have consistently failed and refused to perform their duty enjoined on them by said law. The performance of respondents' duty properly can and should be compelled by issuance of a peremptory writ of mandate.

* * *

Let a peremptory writ of mandate issue as prayed.

Notes

1. The Supreme Court of Nevada also ordered a county to pay its share of the expenses of the agency. State ex rel. List v. County of Douglas, 90

Nev. 272, 524 P.2d 1271 (1974). The exact governmental nature of the Tahoe agency has inspired a considerable amount of litigation. See, e.g., Lake Country Estates, Inc. v. Tahoe Regional Planning Agency, 440 U.S. 391, 99 S.Ct. 1171, 59 L.Ed.2d 401 (1979); California Tahoe Regional Planning Agency v. Jennings, 594 F.2d 181 (9th Cir.1979).

2. In the Lake Country Estates case, supra, the Supreme Court was asked to decide whether the Tahoe Agency was protected by sovereign immunity under the Eleventh Amendment. The agency argued that any agency that is so important that it could not even be created by the States without a special act of Congress should receive the same immunity that is accorded to the States themselves. The majority rejected the argument finding that the tenor of the interstate compact and the understanding of both states all indicated that the agency was a "political subdivision" like a county or municipality, and not an "arm of the State."

3. In People, California Dept. of Transportation v. City of South Lake Tahoe, 466 F.Supp. 527 (E.D.Cal.1978), the court held that the interstate agency could be held to the higher environmental standards of either state agency. The California Tahoe Regional Planning Agency had adopted a transportation plan which did not show a "loop road" extending from the City of South Lake Tahoe, California to an existing casino area in Nevada. The Tahoe Regional Planning Agency had adopted a plan showing such a road and authorized construction without submitting its plan or proposal to the California Tahoe Regional Planning Agency. Although the court held that both the city and the Tahoe Regional Planning Agency were bound to comply with the California requirements, an injunction against construction was denied because the project only involved a few thousand dollars and if it was ultimately disapproved by the California agency, the road could be blocked off.

Chapter III

THE BASICS OF ZONING

SECTION 1. HISTORY OF ZONING

A. BACKGROUND

Land use in this country is determined by zoning ordinances adopted by local governments. Their provisions dictate the types of uses to which land may be put, the density at which development may occur, the height, size, and shape of buildings, and the mix of commercial, residential, public, and other land uses in each locality. Zoning is a key method by which society marshals market forces to locate houses, manufacturing, and offices, protects local natural resources and the environment, and defines the character of its communities.

The law of most states stipulates that zoning is valid only if it is in accordance with a comprehensive land use plan. As the predicate for zoning, comprehensive planning is a critical public function. Since plans can be whatever localities want them to be, zoning is also malleable, since its purpose is to accomplish the objectives of the comprehensive plan. Judicial decisions make it clear that land use regulations will not be sustained if they are ad hoc, arbitrary, capricious, unjust, unfair or irrational—characteristics they risk assuming if not demonstrably in conformance with a discrete and well considered plan.

A vigorous debate over the wisdom of conforming market forces to a public plan for orderly development took place during the early part of this century. Zoning was "seen either as a protection of the suburban American home against the encroachment of urban blight and danger, or as the unrestrained caprice of village councils claiming unlimited control over private property in derogation of the Constitution." Arthur V. N. Brooks, *The Office File Box—Emanations from the Battlefield*, in Zoning and the American Dream 3, 7 (Charles M. Haar & Jerold S. Kayden eds.,1989). The acceptance of comprehensive zoning spread quickly as landowners began to realize that reasonable restrictions—public control of the landowner's and neighboring property for the public good—would tend to stabilize and preserve the value of all property. It culminated decisively in 1926 in favor of comprehensive control of development in the United States Supreme Court decision, Village of Euclid v. Ambler

Realty Co., 272 U.S. 365, 47 S.Ct. 114, 71 L.Ed. 303 (1926). Justice Sutherland's opinion reflected a gathering consensus among state supreme court judges that public guidance of private development was within the police power of the states.

During the first 25 years of the twentieth century, local officials came to realize that narrowly focused, nuisance preventing legislation was not sufficient to address the needs of the nation's increasingly complex urban areas. In 1916, New York City passed the first comprehensive zoning ordinance in the United States; other cities soon followed.

In 1922, the U.S. Department of Commerce published a model statute, the Standard State Zoning Enabling Act, to promote zoning. Standard State Zoning Enabling Act (U.S. Dep't of Commerce 1926) reprinted in 5 Edward H. Ziegler, Jr., Rathkopf's The Law of Zoning and Planning app. A. (2002). The model act, with certain variations, was adopted by most states as a method of encouraging and guiding their municipalities in adopting zoning ordinances. So great was the perceived need for the regulation of land development, that by the time the Euclid case was decided in 1926, forty-three states had passed enabling statutes and 500 municipalities had adopted local zoning ordinances. In this way, public control of market forces in land development was codified.

Zoning, according to one view, was intended to be an end in itself. The "unitary" view of zoning holds that the zoning ordinance itself contains comprehensive planning principles and can exist independently from a comprehensive plan without violating the legal requirement that zoning be "in accordance with" a comprehensive plan. The historical reason that zoning came before planning in the United States is said to be the urgent need for its adoption to protect single-family districts, the local tax-base, and property values. In part, the urgency for promoting zoning before planning resulted from Herbert Hoover's effort to relieve housing shortages through the adoption of zoning plans which would protect residential districts and provide assurance to home builders and buyers that their investments are secure. There is evidence that early proponents of zoning were also motivated by public health and safety matters, traffic congestion, and the like. Norman Williams, Jr. & John M. Taylor, American Planning Law 311 (1988).

However, the drafters of the enabling acts thought that more was needed. A second model act, the Standard City Planning Enabling Act, promulgated in 1928 by the U.S. Department of Commerce, promoted the adoption of a local comprehensive land use plan as a document separate and distinct from zoning (for a full discussion of this act see Chapter II). This act, and its adoption by the states, gave rise in some quarters to the notion that comprehensive land use planning should precede the zoning ordinance and serve as its predicate. Lewis wrote that: "The danger is that [zoning] may be considered a substitute for city planning and that, a zoning plan having been adopted, enthusiasm and interest may die out. Zoning is not a substitute for a city plan; it is an essential part of a comprehensive plan." 1 Harold M. Lewis, Planning The Modern City 261–262 (1949).

In the promulgation of the model acts and the progress of local land use regulation, however, zoning came first. Many states adopted the Standard City Planning Enabling Act, but only after they had created the legal framework for zoning. Many states have failed in any meaningful way to prescribe how zoning and planning are to be integrated. Because zoning preceded planning in both the Hoover Commission and in most state legislatures, the enigma of conforming zoning to planning is as old as comprehensive land use regulation itself.

B. LAND USE LAW AND PRACTICE

Land use law, broadly defined, encompasses the full range of laws and regulations that influence or affect the development and conservation of the land. This law is intensely intergovernmental and interdisciplinary. In land use law there are countless intersections among federal, state, regional, and local statutes. It is significantly influenced by other legal regimes such as environmental, administrative, and municipal law, to name a few.

By dividing their jurisdictions into zoning districts and prescribing the specifications for land development pertaining to each district, local governments create a blueprint for the future development of each community. The aggregate result of these blueprints, when aligned on an intermunicipal basis, is a plan for the future development of the region. These patterns evolve as local boards and agencies review, approve, and condition applications for site plans, subdivisions, and special permits; they change as the local legislature rezones discrete areas and as property owners are awarded variances from the strict application of the zoning law.

Many of the intersecting laws and regulations of higher levels of government are adopted, in the first instance, either to influence or remedy the consequences of local land use planning and regulation. This is true particularly in the area of environmental law where state and federal agencies shape and sometimes preempt local decision-making in the interest of protecting endangered natural resources such as rivers and aquifers. Nonetheless, it is the decisions made by boards and agencies at the municipal level that constitute the primary regulatory influence on the land.

(1) Balancing Property Rights and the Public Interest: Limiting Doctrines

The critical role given to local governments in regulating land use involves them in a delicate act of balancing private property rights with the greater public interest. Local land use decisions affect the right of landowners to use their land in the interest of protecting the health, safety, welfare, and morals of the public as a whole. Citizen groups of all kinds and landowners have a coequal interest in what local governments do in the land use area. Where it serves their interests, they are vigilant in employing the legal doctrines that limit the government's authority to regulate land use. These limitations are numerous:

- The first is the doctrine of substantive due process that requires land use regulations to serve a legitimate public purpose.
- Second, the administrative process by which regulations are adopted and enforced must follow the procedural requirements of state statutes and meet the fairness requirements of procedural due process.
- Third, localities must avoid improperly discriminating among similar parcels or against types of land users in violation of equal protection guarantees.
- Fourth, since local governments can exercise only those powers delegated to them by the state legislature, land use regulations cannot be *ultra vires*—beyond the scope of local authority. The action of the municipality must be undertaken pursuant to legislative power that has been delegated to it.
- Fifth, local land use regulations must not effect a taking of private property for a public purpose without just compensation in violation of the takings provisions of the state and federal constitutions.
- Sixth, the doctrine of vested rights limits the authority of municipalities in certain cases to impose significant new regulations on existing investments in land, such as completed structures, projects under construction, or projects already approved.
- Seventh, local land use regulations are not permitted to control matters whose regulation has been preempted by the state legislature.
- Finally, local regulations must not abridge freedoms of speech, expression and the exercise of religion protected by the state and federal constitutions.

Local land use authority is also limited by the power of state and federal legislatures and rights created by constitutional provisions. A number of these are based in equity. For example, a local zoning law that excludes all growth or types of housing affordable to lower income people is said to be unconstitutionally exclusionary. The police power is to be exercised in the interests of all the people of the state and cannot, by definition, be used for exclusionary purposes, an inherent constitutional principle. In some states, statutes provide that housing for groups of developmentally disabled individuals or substance abusers must be considered single-family housing and allowed in single-family zoning districts. The courts have found either an express or implied intention in these statutes to preempt local government's authority to exclude these types of group residences from single-family districts, the predominant residential zoning district in most communities.

Other types of preemptive effects are found in federal statutes that provide for the exclusive licensing of public utilities, which serve the public's interest in the utility's service district. Such statutes can preempt or partially preempt local governments' authority to regulate public utilities, which may not be excluded from the municipality or unduly constrained.

(2) Zoning Practice

Zoning practice varies from state to state. The configuration of local legislative and administrative bodies and the nomenclature may be different. No central standard-setting agency has drafted the model zoning law, named and labeled the types of permissible zoning districts, or dictated the terms used in local zoning practice. Despite this lack of central control, much about the practice is the same in many states. Under the typical local zoning law, private land use is governed by five basic techniques. Each triggers a different procedure and is governed by different substantive standards. These five categories are as follows:

As–of–Right Uses and Their Accessory Uses

In each zoning district, certain land uses are permitted as the principal and primary uses of land. Accessory uses that are customarily found in association with these principal uses, but which are incidental and subordinate to them, are also permitted as-of-right. In a single-family zoning district, a single-family home is the principal use and a garage or shed is allowed as an accessory use. In most cases, the owner of an individual lot who proposes an as-of-right use of that lot need only submit construction drawings and secure a permit from the building inspector or department. Typically, no administrative agency decisions are involved in such an application.

Nonconforming Uses

A use of land that was in existence when a zoning restriction was adopted and that is prohibited by that restriction is called a nonconforming use. Because of the landowner's investment in that use, most zoning laws permit nonconforming uses to continue but not to be expanded or enlarged. Typically, nonconforming uses may not be reestablished after they have been abandoned or reconstructed after serious damage. Where certain nonconforming uses are particularly inconsistent with the as-of-right uses permitted in a district, the zoning law can require the nonconforming uses to be terminated, or amortized, after a specified number of years. Nonconforming uses that are considered threats to public health or safety can be required to cease immediately. The local zoning administrator must decide questions raised as to whether a use is nonconforming or conforming, whether it has been abandoned, or whether proposed improvements constitute a prohibited expansion or enlargement. The administrator's decision on these matters can be appealed to a board of appeals that handles zoning matters.

Variances

If a proposed use of property does not conform to applicable zoning restrictions, it can be authorized by a use or area variance awarded by a board of appeals in certain circumstances. Use variances allow property owners to use their buildings and parcels for purposes otherwise prohibited by the zoning law. Since use separation is the fundamental characteristic of zoning, this is precariously close to a legislative determination, and boards of appeal are limited in their discretion to award use variances. Often they are limited to parcels of land which can not be used profitably under any of the use categories allowed in their zoning district. An area variance is given because of practical difficulties encountered by property owners in complying with the dimensional or physical requirements of the applicable zoning regulations, such as height or setback requirements. In most states, boards of appeal are allowed to impose limiting conditions on variances as corrective measures designed to protect neighboring properties against the possible adverse effects of the use of the property benefited by the variance.

Special Use Permits

In addition to permitting certain land uses as-of-right in zoning districts, the zoning law can authorize other uses to be made of the land, but only if they receive a special—or conditional—use permit issued by a local administrative agency such as the board of appeals or the planning board. Typical land uses that are permitted by special or conditional permits include religious institutions, nursing homes, and day care centers. In most states, when such uses are listed as specially permitted uses in the zoning law, they are declared by the local legislature to be uses that are harmonious with as-of-right uses, in general, with the recognition that, in a specific location, they can negatively impact adjacent properties and need to be limited or conditioned to mitigate such impacts. If an applicant for a special use permit can demonstrate conclusively that no such impacts will result, or that the proposal mitigates those impacts effectively, the special use permit will usually be granted.

Rezoning

Finally, where a proposed use is not permitted by one of the above devices, the property owner may request that the local government rezone the property, making the proposed activity an as-of-right use under that zoning amendment. Alternatively, the local legislature, at its initiative, can rezone a parcel or area in the public interest. In most cases, the local legislature is not required to entertain a single owner's rezoning petition.

What constitutes a valid zoning regulation has been the subject of much debate. The restrictive view is that zoning is a rigid, district bound technique and that the locality is constrained by a literal reading of the enabling statutes. This view asserts, additionally, that zoning can regulate only the "use," not the "user" of property. The breadth of the statutes delegating zoning authority to local governments and the presumption of validity accorded zoning regulations by the courts have made it possible, in most states, for localities to create a variety of zoning mechanisms not referred to in the statutes but upheld by the courts as within the locality's implied authority to legislate to achieve the most appropriate use of the land.

(3) Local Boards

Land use law is interesting, in part, because it involves practice before a variety of public bodies. These include legislatures, administrative bodies and their ministerial officers, quasi-judicial bodies such as boards of appeals, and courts to which final decisions of local land use boards may be appealed. In most municipalities, the most critical land use decisions are made by the legislative body, which adopts the zoning law and other land use regulations, and the planning board, board of appeals, and the zoning enforcement officer which are charged with reviewing development proposals and enforcing the zoning law's provisions. The procedures that must be followed by the legislature in adopting laws and by these administrative agencies in reviewing and approving project proposals are contained in specific enabling statutes adopted by the state legislature as supplemented by the provisions of local law.

In the typical community, when an application for a building permit is submitted to the local building inspector or zoning enforcement officer, the administrator must ascertain before issuing the permit that the proposed construction is in compliance with the zoning law and other land use regulations. If the proposed development is not in compliance with the use and dimensional requirements of the zoning law, then the permit must be denied. This denial can be appealed to the board of appeals, which can reverse the officer's interpretation of zoning provision if in error or issue a use or area variance in conformance with the standards of state law.

If, on the other hand, the proposed development complies with the zoning provisions, but requires subdivision, site plan, special permit, or other approval, the applicant will be referred to the appropriate administrative agency for its review and determination. The decision-making process must follow prescribed time periods, honor requirements to provide public notice of the matter and hold public hearings, maintain a record of the agency's deliberations, and file and circulate its final determination on the matter. Most states have laws requiring that local agency meetings be open to the public and that copies of local records be provided to the public upon request.

Only if the standards of local land use regulations are met and the proposal is approved by the administrative agency can a building permit be issued. In most communities, one may not commence construction without a building permit and may not occupy buildings without a certificate of occupancy. To qualify for a building permit and certificate of occupancy, the property owner must honor any conditions imposed by the approving agency and construction plans for the development must conform to the requirements of the applicable building codes.

C. EARLY CASES

Our unique land use system could have evolved differently. When local governments began adopting zoning regulations, it was by no means clear that the public sector had such extensive power. Private property owners were accustomed to doing what they wished with their land, so long as their activities were not injurious to the public. It was settled that local statutes could proscribe potentially injurious or dangerous activity on the land, but not that whole sections of a community could be limited to single-family residential use where two-family homes, shops, and multi-family buildings were prohibited. In the early days of reviewing challenges to comprehensive zoning, the state courts split. The majority deferred to the wisdom of comprehensive zoning while a significant number of courts believed that separating land uses in designated districts was not within the power of local governments to protect the health, safety, and welfare of the public.

GOLDMAN v. CROWTHER

Court of Appeals of Maryland, 1925.
147 Md. 282, 128 A. 50, 38 A.L.R. 1455.

[Only a small part of the lengthy opinion is given.]

OFFUTT, J.

Daniel Goldman and his wife, as tenants by the entireties, own the property known as 1513 Park Avenue in a part of Baltimore City, which, under Ordinance No. 922 of the Mayor and City Council of Baltimore City, known as the "zoning ordinance," is classified as a residence district. In May, 1923, Goldman undertook to use the basement of a four story dwelling on that property for repairing, by hand and an ordinary sewing machine, for hire, used clothing for such patrons as had occasions to require his services. The business which he thus carried on required no alteration or repair of the building, and in the opinion of Goldman no permit was necessary to use it for that purpose. He was however informed that by so using it without a permit he was violating certain ordinances of the Mayor and City Council of Baltimore and shortly thereafter he was arrested for such violation, and while that complaint against him was pending he applied to the inspector of buildings of Baltimore City for a permit to use the premises for the purposes referred to. The inspector of buildings refused to grant the permit, partly at least on the ground that he was compelled under the zoning law to disapprove applications for such a use of property in a residence district. Goldman then filed in the Superior Court of Baltimore City a petition in which he asked that a writ of mandamus be issued against the building inspector of Baltimore City and the mayor of said city, directing them to issue to him a permit for the use of his premises for the purposes referred to above. The defendants answered that petition, and in their answer they averred that the permit was refused not only upon the authority of the zoning ordinance, but as well, upon the authority of other ordinances of the City of Baltimore vesting a discretion in the building inspector as to the issuance of permits in such cases, and that in refusing the permit in this case the building inspector acted in the exercise of that discretion. In connection with such issues of fact as were presented by the petition and the answer thereto, an agreed statement of facts was filed, and from that statement and the admissions found in the pleadings it further appears that the real and substantial reason for refusing the permit was that Goldman's property is located in a residence district of Baltimore City, the outlines of which are fixed by the zoning ordinance referred to. The verdict of the trial court was in favor of the defendants and the writ of mandamus refused, and from the judgment on that verdict this appeal was taken.

The important and controlling, and indeed under the agreed statement of fact the only question presented by the appeal is whether the zoning ordinance of Baltimore City, known as Ordinance No. 922, in so far as it affects the right of the appellant to use his property in the manner we have described, is a valid and an enforceable enactment, and in dealing with that question it can be said that there is nothing in the record from which it can be inferred that such use is offensive to the eye, the ear, or the nose of a person of ordinary sensibilities, or that it imperils the public health, welfare or safety, any more than would the same character of work if done by Goldman for himself and his family, except that possibly more of it is done.

This question can be approached by either of two avenues: One legal; the other political and sociological. If approached by the former the validity of the restraints and prohibitions of the ordinance must depend upon whether they violate certain definite guaranties and assurances found in the Federal and State Constitutions and the law of the land. If approached by the latter, the question is to an extent freed from the embarrassment of harmonizing any apparently repugnant provisions of the act with those guaranties, since in such case the end to be accomplished and the benefit to be derived are the main factors to be considered, and the rights of mere individuals may be subordinated to the public convenience, upon the principle that such rights are always subject to the paramount authority of the State to subordinate them to what is conceived by those speaking for it to be for the benefit of the State, as representing all the citizens.

Which one of these two methods of approach should be used in this case is a question which goes to the root of our system of government, but without referring further to that, it is sufficient to say that in our opinion, we are not at liberty to examine the question from any other than a legal standpoint, and therefore we cannot be controlled in our consideration of the validity of this ordinance by its possible benefit to the public, if in point of fact that benefit is purchased by appropriating the rights and property of individuals to the public use without just compensation, and by the violation of the guaranties of the State and Federal Constitutions.

* * *

By this ordinance all the land in the city of Baltimore is subjected to restrictions which limit the number of families who may dwell on it, the use to which it may be put, the height of buildings which may be constructed on it, and the proportion of each lot of ground which a building may occupy, except that in the "industrial use district" the land or structures thereon may be used for any lawful purpose. Many of these restrictions relating to the use of property bear no apparent relation to the public health, safety or welfare, nor does the ordinance contain any definite or fixed standards by which the reasonableness or the necessity for the restrictions may be measured or determined, nor are they necessarily uniform or definite in their application. For after specifying with the most meticulous particularity the nature, extent and application of the restrictions, the board of zoning appeals is authorized in its discretion to disregard the "strict letter" of the ordinance, and to vary or modify any of the regulations or provisions contained in it relating to "the use, construction or alteration of buildings or structures or the use of land, so that the spirit of the ordinance shall be observed, public safety and welfare secured and substantial justice done." This sonorous but vague and cloudy formula is to say the least of it a poor and uncertain substitute for those guaranties of the State and Federal Constitutions which assure to every citizen the right to hold and enjoy and use his property in any manner he pleases so long as he does not thereby injuriously affect the health, security or welfare of his neighbor or the public, as the words health, security and welfare have hitherto been understood in this State. There may also be an appeal from the board of zoning appeals to the Baltimore City Court, but that remedy, if anything, increases rather than lessens the difficulty and hardship which the ordinance inflicts upon the landowner, for it only transfers the discretion from the board of zoning appeals, which would presumably have some special knowledge and training, to a jury which might have none and who, in the absence of any fixed or definite rules or standards to guide them, would naturally exercise that discretion varyingly in accordance with the views of different juries.

Before dealing with the constitutionality of the ordinance in whole or in part, we will refer briefly to the territory upon which it is to operate.

From a small village containing a few scattered houses on the shores of the Patapsco in 1729, Baltimore City has grown into a great maritime city, with a population currently estimated in round numbers at eight hundred thousand, occupying over eighty square miles. Within its confines are found an infinite variety of commercial and industrial enterprises and activities. Its commerce is borne over the world by great land and water transportation systems which serve its people. It includes within its boundaries property devoted to every variety of use, including residential, commercial, agricultural, industrial, maritime and recreational. It is constantly expanding and constantly with its growth and changing conditions the use of property in it changes, so that what was formerly residential property has become commercial property, and property which was at one time most useful for commercial or agricultural purposes is now most valuable for industrial purposes. Heretofore these changes have been in response to conditions created by the growth of the city, the increase of its population, the demands of new enterprises, changes in transportation facilities, changing markets, and various other factors which cannot be readily anticipated or controlled. This ordinance at a stroke arrests that process of natural evolution and growth, and substitutes for it an artificial and arbitrary plan of segregation, under which the landowner may only use his property for certain designated purposes, and under which he may be forbidden to use it for the only purpose for which it is adapted and most valuable.

* * *

There is a theory which has obtained some recognition, that the guaranties of written constitutions are not inflexible, and that the decisions construing them at one period of the state's history, under conditions existing then, ought not to bind the courts at some later period when conditions have changed, and when from economic, sociological or political considerations it is desirable that a different or more liberal construction be given. That theory is based upon the conception that any constitutional guaranty, no matter how plain and clear it may be, can be dissolved and avoided by the application of the police power of the state. That the police power is a real and essential element in the sovereignty of the state cannot be questioned or denied, and that written constitutions are presumed to have been made with conscious knowledge of that fact must be admitted. But it has never been supposed in this State that the police power is a universal solvent by which all constitutional guaranties and limitations can be loosed and set aside regardless of their clear and plain meaning, nor that it is a substitute for those guaranties, for far-reaching and powerful as it is, it has its limitations. Just what those limits are have not been, and in the nature of things, cannot be clearly and definitely marked, except that any exercise of the power which interferes with some right protected by the letter of the Constitution must bear some substantial relation to the public health, morals, safety, comfort or welfare. For while the existence of the police power may be invoked to determine what rights are guaranteed by the Constitution, it can never be invoked to justify an invasion of those rights once they have been ascertained. * * *

One of the most striking manifestations of this tendency [to encroach on individual rights] is the great volume of so-called zoning legislation which has in recent years been written into the laws of the several states, of which the ordinance before us is an apt illustration and which subject private property to an infinite variety and number of restrictions limiting its use, many of which rest for sanction upon no more definite or substantial foundation than that they are supposed to be in the interest of general prosperity or the public convenience. That the right to hold, enjoy and use property is not absolute but subject to the police power of the State is axiomatic (6 R.C.L. 194), and that that power may be affected by changing conditions is inevitable and unquestionable, for a use which at one time may be inoffensive and harmless may at another affect the security or the welfare of others with equal rights, and one of the sources of the police power is the maxim, "Sic utere tuo ut alienum non laedas." So, property in a populous urban community may be properly subjected to restrictions which would be unreasonable and arbitrary in a thinly settled rural community, so long as the restrictions bear some definite relation to the protection of the public health, morals, safety or comfort. These principles are self evident and are almost universally accepted. But the question before us goes much further than that. It is whether the power to hold, use and enjoy property can be restricted or taken away by the State under the guise of the police power for purely aesthetic reasons or for any such elastic and indeterminate object as the general prosperity without compensation.

* * *

From an examination of the maps which form a part of the ordinance, it appears that the residence zones or districts of Baltimore City comprise a number of separated areas varying in extent, irregular in outline, and located without apparent reference to any definite plan, but which nevertheless in the aggregate include a very large part of the total area of that city. And by reference to the ordinance it appears that in those districts no land or building can be used and no buildings erected except for one of fifteen specified uses, to which reference has already been made, unless specially authorized by the board of zoning appeals. These restrictions are wholly arbitrary and have no logical relation to the public welfare, but rest solely upon aesthetic grounds. Under the provisions of sections 3 and 7d and 7g of article 3 of the ordinance, a neighborhood drug store might be forbidden, and a crematory permitted, a bakery forbidden and a sewage disposal plant permitted, an office building prohibited and a refuse dump permitted, a grocery store forbidden and an amusement park allowed. Nor is there any rule or standard prescribed to guide the discretion of those entrusted with the administration of the ordinance in deciding what shall be allowed or what forbidden any more definite than that, in any departure from the letter of the law, the spirit of the ordinance shall be preserved, public safety and welfare secured, and substantial justice done. But as the ordinance itself is based upon the theory that its prescriptions are in the interest of the public welfare, it is not clear how any departure from them can be justified on that ground, for if the restrictions are not necessary to the public welfare, there can be no justification for them at all, and in fact there is none. Their only apparent purpose was to prevent the encroachment of business establishments of any kind upon residential territory, regardless of whether they affected in any degree the public health, morals, safety, or welfare. In effecting that purpose they take from the property owner the right to use his property for any purpose not sanctioned by the letter of the ordinance or allowed by the practically unfettered discretion of the board of zoning appeals, and deprive him of privileges guaranteed by the twenty-third article of the Maryland Bill of Rights.

We have reached the conclusion, therefore, that so much of the ordinance as attempts to regulate and restrict the use of property in Baltimore City is void: first, because it deprives property owners of rights and privileges protected by the Constitution of the State; second, because such deprivation is not justified by any consideration for the public welfare, security, health, or morals apparent in the ordinance itself; and third, because it does not require that the restrictions shall in fact be based upon any such consideration. But in reaching this conclusion we do not hold that the use of property in Baltimore City may not be regulated or restricted where such regulation or restriction is based upon such consideration. * * *

STATE EX REL. CARTER v. HARPER

Supreme Court of Wisconsin, 1923.
182 Wis. 148, 196 N.W. 451, 33 A.L.R. 269.

Mandamus to compel the issuance of a building permit. The relator is in the wholesale and retail milk and dairy products business in the city of Milwaukee. In September, 1919, he purchased a lot and erected thereon a building which he is using as a dairy and milk pasteurizing plant. During the summer of 1921 he found that his business had outgrown the capacity of his plant to such an extent that it became impossible for him to conduct his business in said building in accordance with city and state health regulations. He made application to the inspector of buildings of the city of Milwaukee for a permit to erect an addition to the present building. The application was denied for the reason that the proposed addition to the building was in violation of the terms of the so-called zoning ordinance of the city of Milwaukee, adopted pursuant to authority conferred by sec. 62.23, Stats.

An alternative writ of mandamus issued out of the circuit court for Milwaukee county in the usual form, addressed to the inspector of buildings of the city of Milwaukee, to compel the issuance of said permit. The respondent made return setting forth the so-called zoning ordinance, to which return the relator demurred. The demurrer was overruled, and judgment ordered quashing the alternative writ and dismissing the petition. From the judgment thus entered this appeal is taken.

OWEN, J. The so-called zoning ordinance of the city of Milwaukee established within said city four classes of use districts designated: residence districts, local business districts, commercial and light manufacturing districts, and industrial districts. Relator's property is within a residence district. The ordinance then prescribes the uses to which property within the districts so created may be devoted. The present use of relator's property does not conform to the use permitted by the ordinance in residence districts. The ordinance further provides that no building within a residence district devoted to a non-conforming use shall be enlarged unless the use is changed to a conforming use.

This is a brief statement of the provisions of the ordinance upon which the building inspector relies as a justification for the denial of the permit. That the terms of the ordinance do furnish such justification, if the ordinance is a valid regulation, is not denied by the appellant. He claims, however, that the ordinance is unreasonable and oppressive, that it deprives him of the equal protection of the laws, and takes his property without due process of law and without just compensation.

The constitution of this state, sec. 13, art. I, provides that the property of no person shall be taken for public use without just compensation therefor, and the Fourteenth amendment of the federal constitution provides that no person shall be deprived of his property without due process of law. These provisions are intended to secure the enjoyment of most substantial and fundamental rights, and the allegation that one is being deprived of his property without just compensation or without due process of law calls for most serious consideration. It has long been settled, however, that these constitutional provisions interpose no barrier to the exercise of the police power of the state. Thus it was said in *State ex rel. Kellogg v. Currans*, 111 Wis. 431, 87 N.W. 561, at page 435, speaking of constitutional limitations upon legislative power:

> "These limitations, however, according to all the authorities, state and federal, are to be read as not extending so far as to deprive the states of their power to so control the conduct of individuals as to protect the welfare of the community—a power commonly described as the 'police power.' "

Many declarations appear in our Reports, coming from the pen of Mr. Justice Marshall, tending to create the impression that there are constitutional limitations upon the exercise of this power. *State ex rel. Milwaukee Med. Coll. v. Chittenden*, 127 Wis. 468, 107 N.W. 500; *Bonnett v. Vallier*, 136 Wis. 193, 116 N.W. 885; *Mehlos v. Milwaukee*, 156 Wis. 591, 146 N.W. 882. A careful reading of these cases, however, will indicate that the constitutional limitations which were there in the mind of the court were either some express constitutional provision prohibiting certain specified legislation, or the line of reasonableness beyond which the legislature could not go. * * *

It is thoroughly established in this country that the rights preserved to the individual by these constitutional provisions are held in subordination to the rights of society. Although one owns property he may not do with it as he pleases, any more than he may act in accordance with his personal desires. As the interest of society justifies restraints upon individual conduct, so also does it justify restraints upon the use to which property may be devoted. It was not intended by these constitutional provisions to so far protect the individual in the use of his property as to enable him to use it to the detriment of society. By thus protecting individual rights, society did not part with the power to protect itself or to promote its general well-being. Where the interest of the individual conflicts with the interest of society, such individual interest is subordinated to the general welfare. If in the prosecution of governmental functions it becomes necessary to take private property, compensation must be made. But incidental damage to property resulting from governmental activities, or laws passed in the promotion of the public welfare, is not considered a taking of the property for which compensation must be made. * * *

The legislation authorizing so-called zoning ordinances is of comparatively recent origin, and it is not unnatural that those adversely affected shall regard them as an unjust and unwarranted interference with their property rights. The question of whether such ordinances fall legitimately within the realm of the police power has been considered by a few courts, presently to be noted, with conflicting results. The pioneer nature of the legislation requires that it have careful consideration, tested by the fundamental principles to which we have alluded. We are required to consider whether such ordinances have any reasonable tendency to promote the public morals, health, or safety or the public comfort, welfare, or prosperity.

The purpose of the law is to bring about an orderly development of our cities; to establish residence districts into which business, commercial, and industrial establishments shall not intrude; and to fix business districts and light industrial districts upon which heavy industrial concerns may not encroach. This is no new idea, although it has but recently taken the form of legislation. Everyone who has observed the haphazard development of cities, the deterioration in the desirability of certain residential sections by the encroachment of business and industrial establishments upon and into such sections, resulting in the consequent destruction of property values and in the ultimate abandonment of such sections for residential purposes, has appreciated the desirability of regulating the growth and development of our urban communities. The homeseeker shuns a section of a city devoted to industrialism and seeks a home at some distance from the business center. A common and natural instinct directs him to a section far removed from the commerce, trade, and industry of the community. He does this because the home instinct craves fresh air, sunshine, and well-kept lawns—home association beyond the noise of commercial marts and the dirt and smoke of industrial plants. Fresh air and sunshine add to the happiness of the home and have a direct effect upon the well-being of the occupants. It is not uncommon to witness efforts of promoters to preserve the residential character of their additions by placing covenants in their deeds restricting the use of the property to residential purposes and, in some instances, requiring the erection of a home according to specified standards. It cannot be denied that a city systematically developed offers greater attractiveness to the homeseeker than a city that is developed in a haphazard way. The one compares to the other about as a well-ordered department store compares to a junk-shop. If such regulations stabilize the value of property, promote the permanency of desirable home surroundings, and if they add to the happiness and comfort of the citizens, they thereby promote the general welfare.

When we reflect that one has always been required to so use his property as not to injure his neighbors, and that restrictions against the use of property in urban communities have increased with changing social standards, and that the luxuries of one decade become the necessities of another, can it be said that an effort to preserve various sections of a city from intrusion on the part of institutions that are offensive to and out of harmony with the use to which such sections are devoted is unreasonable? The present standards of society prompt a revolt against such unbecoming intrusions, and they constitute such a recognized interference with the rights of the residents of such sections as to justify regulation.

The benefits to be derived by cities adopting such regulations may be summarized as follows: They attract a desirable and assure a permanent citizenship; they foster pride in and attachment to the city; they promote happiness and contentment; they stabilize the use and value of property and promote the peace, tranquility, and good order of the city. We do not hesitate to say that the attainment of these objects affords a legitimate field for the exercise of the police power. He who owns property in such a district is not deprived of its use by such regulations. He may use it for the purposes to which the section in which it is located is dedicated. That he shall not be permitted to use it to the desecration of the community constitutes no unreasonable or permanent hardship and results in no unjust burden.

* * *

There remains a further question to be considered. Appellant claims that the ordinance is unreasonable in that it prohibits him from enlarging the business to which his property was devoted prior to the passage of the ordinance. The reasonableness of this feature of the ordinance, as well as its main purpose, is subject to judicial review. Where, however, a given situation is conceded to present a proper field for the exercise of the police power, the extent of the interference is a matter which lies very greatly in legislative discretion. *Mehlos v. Milwaukee*, 156 Wis. 591, 146 N.W. 882. If the appellant has acquired a vested right to enlarge his business, then every other person having an embryo business in a residential section must be accorded the same privilege, and an infant industry may grow to mammoth proportions, thereby to a very large extent defeating the purposes of the regulation.

In *Hadacheck v. Sebastian*, 239 U.S. 394, 36 S.Ct. 143, 60 L.Ed. 348, a brickyard of the value of $800,000, situated far outside the city limits when acquired, was suppressed after it had been included in the city limits. If property of that nature and of that value must yield to the supremacy of the police power, it is difficult to see how a regulation prohibiting appellant's enlargement of his business can be held unreasonable. Then, too, it may be remarked that an ordinance permitting those already engaged in business to enlarge the same while prohibiting all others from engaging therein, would not tend to make the ordinance less vulnerable. *See People ex rel. Roos v. Kaul*, 302 Ill. 317, 134 N.E. 740, and cases there cited.

It is further contended that the ordinance amounts to class legislation by reason of the provisions of sec. 26.46, Milwaukee Code, 1921 Supp., which provides that "A structure or premises may be erected or used in any location by a public-service corporation for any purpose which the railroad commission decides is reasonably necessary for the public convenience or welfare." When it is remembered that such buildings are erected to promote the comfort and convenience of the public and that it is within the power of the state to compel such erection, it would appear that this constitutes a reasonable and valid classification. It must be apparent that an ordinance enacted pursuant to state authority which prevents the erection of buildings or the conduct of business deemed inimical to public interest need not also prohibit the erection of buildings or the conduct of business which is essential to the comfort and convenience of the public and which the duly constituted authority of the state determines to be necessary for the public service which a public utility is required to render. A similar provision received the consideration of the court in *Opinion of the Justices*, 234 Mass. 597, 127 N.E. 525, concerning which it was said (p. 606) that the provision "is within settled principles touching legislative control over property devoted to that use."

It is our conclusion that the ordinance is, in the respects here considered, a reasonable, valid, and constitutional enactment. It is appreciated that there are other provisions of the ordinance the validity of which may be the subject of future challenge. It is to be understood that no opinion is expressed with reference to any features of the ordinance except such as are herein treated. So far as the ordinance affects the rights of appellant, it fully authorizes the denial of a building permit the issuance of which he seeks to coerce.

Judgment affirmed.

VILLAGE OF EUCLID v. AMBLER REALTY CO.

Supreme Court of the United States, 1926.
272 U.S. 365, 47 S.Ct. 114, 71 L.Ed. 303, 54 A.L.R. 1016.

MR. JUSTICE SUTHERLAND delivered the opinion of the court.

The village of Euclid is an Ohio municipal corporation. It adjoins and practically is a suburb of the city of Cleveland. Its estimated population is between 5,000 and 10,000, and its area from 12 to 14 square miles, the greater part of which is farm lands or unimproved acreage. It lies, roughly, in the form of a parallelogram measuring approximately 3 1/2 miles each way. East and west it is traversed by three principal highways: Euclid avenue, through the southerly border, St. Clair avenue, through the central portion, and Lake Shore boulevard, through the northerly border, in close proximity to the shore of Lake

Erie. The Nickel Plate Railroad lies from 1,500 to 1,800 feet north of Euclid avenue, and the Lake Shore Railroad 1,600 feet farther to the north. The three highways and the two railroads are substantially parallel.

Appellee is the owner of a tract of land containing 68 acres, situated in the westerly end of the village, abutting on Euclid avenue to the south and the Nickel Plate Railroad to the north. Adjoining this tract, both on the east and on the west, there have been laid out restricted residential plats upon which residences have been erected.

On November 13, 1922, an ordinance was adopted by the village council, establishing a comprehensive zoning plan for regulating and restricting the location of trades, industries, apartment houses, two-family houses, single family houses, etc., the lot area to be built upon, the size and height of buildings, etc.

The entire area of the village is divided by the ordinance into six classes of use districts, denominated U–1 to U–6, inclusive; three classes of height districts, denominated H–1 to H–3, inclusive; and four classes of area districts, denominated A–1 to A–4, inclusive. The use districts are classified in respect of the buildings which may be erected within their respective limits, as follows: U–1 is restricted to single family dwellings, public parks, water towers and reservoirs, suburban and interurban electric railway passenger stations and rights of way, and farming, noncommercial greenhouse nurseries and truck gardening; U–2 is extended to include two-family dwellings; U–3 is further extended to include apartment houses, hotels, churches, schools, public libraries, museums, private clubs, community center buildings, hospitals, sanitariums, public playgrounds and recreation buildings and a city hall and courthouse; U–4 is further extended to include banks, offices, studios, telephone exchanges, fire and police stations, restaurants, theaters, and moving picture shows, retail stores and shops, sales offices, sample rooms, wholesale stores for hardware, drugs and groceries, stations for gasoline and oil (not exceeding 1,000 gallons storage) and for ice delivery, skating rinks and dance halls, electric sub-stations, job and newspaper printing, public garages for motor vehicles, stables and wagon sheds (not exceeding five horses, wagons or motor trucks) and distributing stations for central store and commercial enterprises; U–5 is further extended to include billboards and advertising signs (if permitted), warehouses, ice and ice cream manufacturing and cold storage plants, bottling works, milk bottling and central distribution stations, laundries, carpet cleaning, dry cleaning and dyeing establishments, blacksmith, horseshoeing, wagon and motor vehicle repair shops, freight stations, streetcar barns, stables and wagon sheds (for more than five horses, wagons or motor trucks), and wholesale produce markets and salesrooms; U–6 is further extended to include plants for sewage disposal and for producing gas, garbage and refuse incineration, scrap iron, junk, scrap paper and rag storage, aviation fields, cemeteries, crematories, penal and correctional institutions, insane and feeble minded institutions, storage of oil and gasoline (not to exceed 25,000 gallons), and manufacturing and industrial operations of any kind other than, and any public utility not included in, a class U–1, U–2, U–3, U–4 or U–5 use. There is a seventh class of uses which is prohibited altogether.

Class U–1 is the only district in which buildings are restricted to those enumerated. In the other classes, the uses are cumulative; that is to say, uses in class U–2 include those enumerated in the preceding class, U–1; class U–3 includes uses enumerated in the preceding classes, U–2 and U–1; and so on. In addition to the enumerated uses, the ordinance provides for accessory uses, that is, for uses customarily incident to the principal use, such as private garages. Many regulations are provided in respect of such accessory uses.

The height districts are classified as follows: In class H–1, buildings are limited to a height of two and one-half stories or thirty-five feet; in class H–2, to four stories or fifty feet; in class H–3, to eighty feet. To all of these, certain exceptions are made, as in the case of church spires, water tanks, etc.

The classification of area districts is: In A–1 districts, dwellings or apartment houses to accommodate more than one family must have at least 5,000 square feet for interior lots and at least 4,000 square feet for corner lots; in A–2 districts, the area must be at least 2,500 square feet for interior lots, and 2,000 square feet for corner lots; in A–3 districts, the limits are 1,250 and 1,000 square feet, respectively; in A–4 districts, the limits are 900 and 700 square feet, respectively. The ordinance contains, in great variety and detail, provisions in respect of width of lots, front, side and rear yards, and other matters, including restrictions and regulations as to the use of billboards, sign boards and advertising signs.

A single family dwelling consists of a basement and not less than three rooms and a bathroom. A two-family dwelling consists of a basement and not less than four living rooms and a bathroom for each family; and is further described as a detached dwelling for the occupation of two families, one having its principal living rooms on the first floor and the other on the second floor.

Appellee's tract of land comes under U–2, U–3 and U–6. The first strip of 620 feet immediately north of Euclid avenue falls in class U–2, the next 130 feet to the north, in U–3, and the remainder in U–6. The uses of the first 620 feet, therefore, do not include apartment houses, hotels, churches, schools, or other public and semi-public buildings, or other uses enumerated in respect of U–3 to U–6, inclusive.

Annexed to the ordinance, and made a part of it, is a zone map, showing the location and limits of the various use, height and area districts, from which it appears that the three classes overlap one another; that is to say, for example, both U–5 and U–6 use districts are in A–4 area districts, but the former is in H–2 and the latter in H–3 height districts. The plan is a complicated one and can be better understood by an inspection of the map, though it does not seem necessary to reproduce it for present purposes.

The lands lying between the two railroads for the entire length of the village area and extending some distance on either side to the north and south, having an average width of about 1,600 feet, are left open, with slight exceptions, for industrial and all other uses. This includes the larger part of appellee's tract. Approximately one-sixth of the area of the entire village is included in U–5 and U–6 use districts. That part of the village lying south of Euclid avenue is principally in U–1 districts. The lands lying north of Euclid avenue and bordering on the long strip just described are included in U–1, U–2, U–3, and U–4 districts, principally in U–2.

The enforcement of the ordinance is entrusted to the inspector of buildings, under rules and regulations of the board of zoning appeals. Meetings of the board are public, and minutes of its proceedings are kept. It is authorized to adopt rules and regulations to carry into effect provisions of the ordinance. Decisions of the inspector of buildings may be appealed to the board by any person claiming to be adversely affected by any such decision. The board is given power in specific cases of practical difficulty or unnecessary hardship to interpret the ordinance in harmony with its general purpose and intent, so that the public health, safety and general welfare may be secure and substantial justice done. Penalties are prescribed for violations, and it is provided that the various provisions are to be regarded as independent and the holding of any provision to be unconstitutional, void or ineffective shall not affect any of the others.

The ordinance is assailed on the grounds that it is in derogation of Sec. 1 of the 14th Amendment to the Federal Constitution in that it deprives appellee of liberty and property without due process of law and denies it the equal protection of the law, and that it offends against certain provisions of the Constitution of the state of Ohio. The prayer of the bill is for an injunction restraining the enforcement of the ordinance and all attempts to impose or maintain as to appellee's property any of the restrictions, limitations or conditions. The court below held the ordinance to be unconstitutional and void, and enjoined its enforcement. 297 F. 307.

Before proceeding to a consideration of the case, it is necessary to determine the scope of the inquiry. The bill alleges that the tract of land in question is vacant and has been held for years for the purpose of selling and developing it for industrial uses, for which it is especially adapted, being immediately in the path of progressive industrial development; that for such uses it has a market value of about $10,000 per acre, but if the use be limited to residential purposes the market value is not in excess of $2,500 per acre; that the first 200 feet of the parcel back from Euclid avenue, if unrestricted in respect of use, has a value of $150 per front foot, but if limited to residential uses, and ordinary mercantile business be excluded therefrom, its value is not in excess of $50 per front foot.

It is specifically averred that the ordinance attempts to restrict and control the lawful uses of appellee's land so as to confiscate and destroy a great part of its value; that it is being enforced in accordance with its terms; that prospective buyers of land for industrial, commercial and residential uses in the metropolitan district of Cleveland are deterred from buying any part of this land because of the existence of the ordinance and the necessity thereby entailed of conducting burdensome and expensive litigation in order to vindicate the right to use the land for lawful and legitimate purposes; that the ordinance constitutes a cloud upon the land, reduces and destroys its value, and has the effect of diverting the normal industrial, commercial and residential development thereof to other and less favorable locations.

The record goes no farther than to show, as the lower court found, that the normal, and reasonably to be expected, use and development of that part of appellee's land adjoining Euclid avenue is for general trade and commercial purposes, particularly retail stores and like establishments, and that the normal, and reasonably to be expected, use and development of the residue of the land is for industrial and trade purposes. Whatever injury is inflicted by the mere existence and threatened enforcement of the ordinance is due to restrictions in respect of these and similar uses; to which perhaps should be added—if not included in the foregoing—restrictions in respect to apartment houses. Specifically, there is nothing in the record to suggest that any damage results from the presence in the ordinance of those restrictions relating to churches, schools, libraries and other public and semi-public buildings. It is neither alleged nor proved that there is or may be a demand for any part of appellee's land for any of the last named uses; and we cannot assume the existence of facts which would justify an injunction upon this record in respect of this class of restrictions. For present purposes the provisions of the ordinance in respect of these uses may therefore be put aside as unnecessary to be considered. It is also unnecessary to consider the effect of the restrictions in respect of U–1 districts, since none of the appellee's land falls within that class.

We proceed, then, to a consideration of those provisions of the ordinance to which the case as it is made relates, first disposing of a preliminary matter.

A motion was made in the court below to dismiss the bill on the ground that, because complainant (appellee) had made no effort to obtain a building permit or apply to the zoning board of appeals for relief, as it might have done under the terms of the ordinance, the suit was premature. The motion was properly overruled, the effect of the allegations of the bill is that the ordinance of its own force operates greatly to reduce the value of appellee's lands and destroy their marketability for industrial, commercial and residential uses, and the attack is directed, not against any specific provision or provisions, but against the ordinance as an entirety. Assuming the premises, the existence and maintenance of the ordinance in effect constitutes a present invasion of appellee's property rights and a threat to continue it. Under these circumstances, the equitable jurisdiction is clear. See *Terrace v. Thompson*, 263 U.S. 197, 215, 44 S.Ct. 15, 68 L.Ed. 255; *Pierce v. Society of Sisters*, 268 U.S. 510, 535, 45 S.Ct. 571, 69 L.Ed. 1070, 30 A.L.R. 468.

It is not necessary to set forth the provisions of the Ohio Constitution which are thought to be infringed. The question is the same under both Constitutions, namely, as stated by appellee: Is the ordinance invalid, in that it violates the constitutional protection 'to the right of property in the appellee by attempted regulations under the guise of the police power, which are unreasonable and confiscatory'?

Building zone laws are of modern origin. They began in this country about twenty-five years ago. Until recent years, urban life was comparatively simple; but with the great increase and concentration of population, problems have developed, and constantly are developing, which require, and will continue to require, additional restrictions in respect of the use and occupation of private lands in urban communities. Regulations, the wisdom, necessity and validity of which, as applied to existing conditions, are so apparent that they are now uniformly sustained, a century ago, or even half a century ago, probably would have been rejected as arbitrary and oppressive. Such regulations are sustained, under the complex conditions of our day, for reasons analogous to those which justify traffic regulations, which, before the advent of automobiles and rapid transit street railways, would have been condemned as fatally arbitrary and unreasonable. And in this there is no inconsistency, for while the meaning of constitutional guaranties never varies, the scope of their application must expand or contract to meet the new and different conditions which are constantly coming within the field of their operation. In a changing world, it is impossible that it should be otherwise. But although a degree of elasticity is thus imparted, not to the *meaning*, but to the *application* of constitutional principles, statutes and ordinances, which, after giving due weight to the new conditions, are found clearly not to conform to the Constitution, of course, must fall.

The ordinance now under review and all similar laws and regulations must find their justification in some aspect of the police power, asserted for the public welfare. The line which in this field separates the legitimate from the illegitimate assumption of power is not capable of precise delimitation. It varies with circumstances and conditions. A regulatory zoning ordinance, which would be clearly valid as applied to the great cities, might be clearly invalid as applied to rural communities. In solving doubts, the maxim "sic utere tuo ut alienum non laedas," which lies at the foundation of so much of the common law of nuisances, ordinarily will furnish a fairly helpful clew. And the law of nuisances, likewise, may be consulted, not for the purpose of controlling, but for the helpful aid of its analogies in the process of ascertaining the scope of, the power. Thus the question whether the power exists to forbid the erection of a building of a particular kind or for a particular use, like the question whether a particular thing is a nuisance, is to be determined, not by an abstract consideration of the building or of the thing considered apart, but by considering it in connection with the circumstances and the locality. * * *

There is no serious difference of opinion in respect of the validity of laws and regulations fixing the height of buildings within reasonable limits, the character of materials and methods of construction, and the adjoining area which must be left open, in order to minimize the danger of fire or collapse, the evils of overcrowding and the like, and excluding from residential sections offensive trades, industries and structures likely to create nuisances. See *Welch v. Swasey*, 214 U.S. 91, 29 S.Ct. 567, 53 L.Ed. 923; *Hadacheck v. Los Angeles*, 239 U.S. 394, 36 S.Ct. 143, 60 L.Ed. 348, Ann.Cas. 1917B, 927; *Reinman v. Little Rock*, 237 U.S. 171, 35 S.Ct. 511, 59 L.Ed. 900; *Cusack Co. v. City of Chicago*, 242 U.S. 526, 529, 530, 37 S.Ct. 190, 61 L.Ed. 472, L.R.A. 1918A, 136, App. Cas. 1917C, 594.

Here, however, the exclusion is in general terms of all industrial establishments, and it may thereby happen that not only offensive or dangerous industries will be excluded, but those which are neither offensive nor dangerous will share the same fate. But this is no more than happens in respect of many practice-forbidding laws which this court has upheld, although drawn in general terms so as to include individual cases that may turn out to be innocuous in themselves. *Hebe Co. v. Shaw*, 248 U.S. 297, 303, 39 S.Ct. 125, 63 L.Ed. 255; *Pierce Oil Corp. v. City of Hope*, 248 U.S. 498, 500, 39 S.Ct. 172, 63 L.Ed. 381. The inclusion of a reasonable margin, to insure effective enforcement, will not put upon a law, otherwise valid, the stamp of invalidity. Such laws may also find their justification in the fact that, in some fields, the bad fades into the good by such insensible degrees that the two are not capable of being readily distinguished and separated in terms of legislation. In the light of these considerations, we are not prepared to say that the end in view was not sufficient to justify the general rule of the ordinance, although some industries of an innocent character might fall within the proscribed class. It cannot be said that the ordinance in this respect 'passes the bounds of reason and assumes the character of a merely arbitrary fiat.' *Purity Extract Co. v. Lynch*, 226 U.S. 192, 204, 33 S.Ct. 44, 47 (57 L.Ed. 184). Moreover, the restrictive provisions of the ordinance in this particular may be sustained upon the principles applicable to the broader exclusion from residential districts of all business and trade structures, presently to be discussed.

It is said that the village of Euclid is a mere suburb of the city of Cleveland; that the industrial development of that city has now reached and in some degree extended into the village, and in the obvious course of things will soon absorb the entire area for industrial enterprises; that the effect of the ordinance is to divert this natural development elsewhere, with the consequent loss of increased values to the owners of the lands within the village borders. But the village, though physically a suburb of Cleveland, is politically a separate municipality, with powers of its own and authority to govern itself as it sees fit, within the limits of the organic law of its creation and the state and federal Constitutions.

Its governing authorities, presumably representing a majority of its inhabitants and voicing their will, have determined, not that industrial development shall cease at its boundaries, but that the course of such development shall proceed within definitely fixed lines. If it be a proper exercise of the police power to relegate industrial establishments to localities separated from residential sections, it is not easy to find a sufficient reason for denying the power because the effect of its exercise is to divert an industrial flow from the course which it would follow, to the injury of the residential public, if left alone, to another course where such injury will be obviated. It is not meant by this, however, to exclude the possibility of cases where the general public interest would so far outweigh the interest of the municipality that the municipality would not be allowed to stand in the way.

We find no difficulty in sustaining restrictions of the kind thus far reviewed. The serious question in the case arises over the provisions of the ordinance excluding from residential districts, apartment houses, business houses, retail stores and shops, and other like establishments. This question involves the validity of what is really the crux of the more recent zoning legislation, namely, the creation and maintenance of residential districts, from which business and trade of every sort, including hotels and apartment houses, are excluded. Upon that question this court has not thus far spoken. The decisions of the state courts are numerous and conflicting; but those which broadly sustain the power greatly outnumber those which deny it altogether or narrowly limit it; and it is very apparent that there is a constantly increasing tendency in the direction of the broader view. * * *

The matter of zoning has received much attention at the hands of commissions and experts, and the results of their investigations have been set forth in comprehensive reports. These reports, which bear every evidence of painstaking consideration, concur in the view that the segregation of residential, business and industrial buildings will make it easier to provide fire apparatus suitable for the character and intensity of the development in each section; that it will increase the safety and security of home life; greatly tend to prevent street accidents, especially to children, by reducing the traffic and resulting confusion in residential sections; decrease noise and other conditions which produce or intensify nervous disorders; preserve a more favorable environment in which to rear children, etc. With particular reference to apartment houses, it is pointed out that the development of detached house sections is greatly retarded by the coming of apartment houses, which has sometimes resulted in destroying the entire section for private house purposes; that in such sections very often the apartment house is a mere parasite, constructed in order to take advantage of the open spaces and attractive surroundings created by the residential character of the district. Moreover, the coming of one apartment house is followed by others, interfering by their height and bulk with the free circulation of air and monopolizing the rays of the sun which otherwise would fall upon the smaller homes, and bringing, as their necessary accompaniments, the disturbing noises incident to increased traffic and business, and the occupation, by means of moving and parked automobiles, of larger portions of the streets, thus detracting from their safety and depriving children of the privilege of quiet and open spaces for play, enjoyed by those in more favored localities,—until, finally, the residential character of the neighborhood and its desirability as a place of detached residences are utterly destroyed. Under these circumstances, apartment houses, which in a different environment would be not only entirely unobjectionable but highly desirable, come very near to being nuisances.

If these reasons, thus summarized, do not demonstrate the wisdom or sound policy in all respects of those restrictions which we have indicated as pertinent to the inquiry, at least, the reasons are sufficiently cogent to preclude us from saying, as it must be said before the ordinance can be declared unconstitutional, that such provisions are clearly arbitrary and unreasonable, having no substantial relation to the public health, safety, morals, or general welfare. * * *

It is true that when, if ever, the provisions set forth in the ordinance in tedious and minute detail, come to be concretely applied to particular premises, including those of the appellee, or to particular conditions, or to be considered in connection with specific complaints, some of them, or even many of them, may be found to be clearly arbitrary and unreasonable. But where the equitable remedy of injunction is sought, as it is here, not upon the ground of a present infringement or denial of a specific right, or of a particular injury in process of actual execution, but upon the broad ground that the mere existence and threatened enforcement of the ordinance, by materially and adversely affecting values and curtailing the opportunities of the market, constitute a present and irreparable injury, the court will not scrutinize its provisions, sentence by sentence, to ascertain by a process of piecemeal dissection whether there may be, here and there, provisions of a minor character, or relating to matters of administration, or not shown to contribute to the injury complained of, which, if attacked separately, might not withstand the test of constitutionality. In respect of such provisions, of which specific complaint is not made, it cannot be said that the landowner has suffered or is threatened with an injury which entitles him to challenge their constitutionality. *Turpin v. Lemon*, 187 U.S. 51, 60, 23 S.Ct. 20, 47 L.Ed. 70. In *Railroad Commission Cases*, 116 U.S. 307, 335–337, 6 S.Ct. 334, 388, 1191, 29 L.Ed. 636, this court dealt with an analogous situation. There an act of the Mississippi Legislature, regulating freight and passenger rates on intrastate railroads and creating a supervisory commission, was attacked as unconstitutional. The suit was brought to enjoin the commission from enforcing against the plaintiff railroad company any of its provisions. In an opinion delivered by Chief Justice Waite, this court held that the chief purpose of the statute was to fix a maximum of charges and to regulate in some matters of a police nature the use of railroads in the state. After sustaining the constitutionality of the statute 'in its general scope' this court said:

> 'Whether in some of its details the statute may be defective or invalid we do not deem it necessary to inquire, for this suit is brought to prevent the commissioners from giving it any effect whatever as against this company.'

Quoting with approval from the opinion of the Supreme Court of Mississippi, it was further said:

> 'Many questions may arise under it not necessary to be disposed of now, and we leave them for consideration when presented.'

And finally:

> 'When the commission has acted and proceedings are had to enforce what it has done, questions may arise as to the validity of some of the various provisions which will be worthy of consideration, but we are unable to say that, as a whole, the statute is invalid.'

The relief sought here is of the same character, namely, an injunction against the enforcement of any of the restrictions, limitations, or conditions of the ordinance. And the gravamen of the complaint is that a portion of the land of the appellee cannot be sold for certain enumerated uses because of the general and broad restraints of the ordinance. What would be the effect of a restraint imposed by one or more or the innumerable provisions of the ordinance, considered apart, upon the value or marketability of the lands, is neither disclosed by the bill nor by the evidence, and we are afforded no basis, apart from mere speculation, upon which to rest a conclusion that it or they would have any appreciable effect upon those matters. Under these circumstances, therefore, it is enough for us to determine, as we do, that the ordinance in its general scope and dominant features, so far as its provisions are here involved, is a valid exercise of authority, leaving other provisions to be dealt with as cases arise directly involving them.

And this is in accordance with the traditional policy of this court. In the realm of constitutional law, especially, this court has perceived the embarrassment which is likely to result from an attempt to formulate rules or decide questions beyond the necessities of the immediate issue. It has preferred to follow the method of a gradual approach to the general by a systematically guarded application and extension of constitutional principles to particular cases as they arise, rather than by out of hand attempts to establish general rules to which future cases must be fitted. This process applies with peculiar force to the solution of questions arising under the due process clause of the Constitution as applied to the exercise of the flexible powers of police, with which we are here concerned.

Decree reversed.

Notes

1. A year and a half after the Euclid decision, the U.S. Supreme Court, again speaking through Mr. Justice Sutherland, summarily declared a zoning

ordinance unreasonable and unconstitutional as applied to the plaintiff's particular tract of land. Nectow v. Cambridge, 277 U.S. 183, 48 S.Ct. 447, 72 L.Ed. 842 (1928). In Nectow, the property owner showed that the local zoning law permitted only residential uses and that there was no market for residential uses in the neighborhood. The owner's argument was that the zoning law, as applied to the parcel, did not accomplish a public purpose because of market conditions. In essence, the law allowed the owner no economical use of the land. Nectow won, and then the U.S. Supreme Court handed down no significant decisions implicating local land use matters for the next four decades. Nectow's claim is called an "as applied" challenge to local zoning authority, while Ambler Realty's is called a "facial" attack. Can you tell the difference? What exactly is being challenged in the Euclid case and what would the consequence have been if the court had found for the plaintiff? Which type of challenge do you think it is easier to win? Why?

2. Although the Euclid case was hailed as a great legal victory for the concept of zoning, in recent years a more critical re-analysis of Euclid has emerged. Today, there are many who question the wisdom of the strict segregation of uses with protection of single-family dwellings as the highest purpose of zoning. For example, Jane Jacobs, the urban economist, in her book, "The Death and Life of Great American Cities", points out that in an earlier era the mixture of apartments, stores, and small industrial uses promoted safety and vitality, as well as a sense of neighborhood and community, which is lacking in newer communities that comply with zoning's philosophy of separated uses. Some developers are harking back to that earlier era. See Maureen Milford, New Village with a 16th–Century Concept, N.Y. Times, Dec. 3, 1995, p. 31. The article describes a $30 million development in rural Pennsylvania, Stoudtburg Village, where the homeowners live over their shops. In Chapter VII, we explore a number of innovative zoning techniques that promote mixed-use and traditional neighborhood developments that are being used to add vitality to newly constructed neighborhoods.

3. Pay close attention to the substantive legal claims that are made by the plaintiffs in these and subsequent cases. What legal rights do the plaintiffs have that they claim have been violated? What remedies are they asking for? What standards do the courts use to review the municipal actions challenged? We explore these issues in depth in Chapter XI.

4. In Chapter I, we reviewed the principles of common law nuisance law. Consider the use of the Court in Euclid of these principles in determining that it is within the local police power to separate land uses, particularly to keep apartments out of single-family neighborhoods. How close is the analogy between what is accomplished by zoning and nuisance law?

5. What do you make of the following statement by the court in Euclid: "But the village, though physically a suburb of Cleveland, is politically a separate municipality, with powers of its own and authority to govern itself as it sees fit * * * "? Consider, for example, the problem of urban sprawl which is a contemporary manifestation of the suburban growth that was being experienced by the Cleveland suburbs in the 1920s. Is sprawl a local or a regional problem? Can the problem be solved if this judicial statement regarding local self-determination in land use matters remains true today? If

municipalities are creatures of state governments, is it theoretically within the power of state legislatures to address the problems of uncontrolled metropolitan growth? How?

6. From the beginning of the modern era, the work of competent and dedicated attorneys has shaped how American jurisdictions have decided to control the use of privately owned land. Consider the career of Alfred Bettman, a corporate lawyer in Cincinnati who submitted an amicus brief to the U.S. Supreme Court supporting the village of Euclid's position, arguing for the constitutionality of zoning. It is reported that Justice Sutherland had determined to write an opinion for the majority holding Euclid's ordinance unconstitutional when he read Bettman's brief and changed his mind. Bettman also drafted the first adopted planning enabling act in the nation for Ohio. He also served on the Hoover Commission and assisted in the creation of the Standard City Planning Enabling Act. See Amicus Curiae: The American Planning Association in the Courtroom, Lora A. Lucero, Zoning and Planning Law Report, vol. 26, no. 2, Feb. 2003.

SECTION 2. ZONING, REZONING, AND CONFORMANCE WITH THE COMPREHENSIVE PLAN

Local governments are municipal corporations that obtain their legal authority from their charters, home rule authority, and from state enabling acts. In the land use field, municipal authority comes primarily from discrete enabling acts adopted by the state legislatures modeled after the standard zoning and planning enabling acts described in Section One. If a local legislative body attempts to adopt or amend zoning laws in a manner that is inconsistent with the enabling laws, that attempt may be challenged successfully as *ultra vires*: beyond the corporate authority of the municipality. State statutes prescribe both the subject matter of local land use laws and their mode of adoption, for example, by requiring public notice of a zoning amendment and public hearing prior to its adoption. Attempts to adopt or amend zoning that do not follow prescribed procedures are described as being jurisdictionally defective or *ultra vires*.

Municipal attorneys examine closely the content of state enabling acts to confirm that zoning laws are within their client's municipal authority. Developers' attorneys need the same assurance so that their clients' approved projects are immunized from attack. Citizens and environmental groups that scrutinize local land use actions for validity employ attorneys who need to know if the local law their clients find objectionable was properly adopted and within the locality's power. Since the majority of state zoning enabling acts were patterned after the Standard Zoning Enabling Act promulgated by the Hoover Commission in the 1920s, it provides a proper place to begin our inquiry into the range of authority of local governments to adopt zoning and other land use laws. In its original form, the first three sections of the standard act read as follows:

A STANDARD STATE ZONING ENABLING ACT UNDER WHICH MUNICIPALITIES MAY ADOPT ZONING REGULATIONS

(Recommended by the U.S. Department of Commerce, 1926).

A STANDARD STATE ZONING ENABLING ACT

Section 1. Grant of Power. For the purpose of promoting health, safety, morals, or the general welfare of the community, the legislative body of cities and incorporated villages is hereby empowered to regulate and restrict the height, number of stories, and size of buildings and other structures, the percentage of lot that may be occupied, the size of yards, courts, and other open spaces, the density of population, and the location and use of buildings, structures, and land for trade, industry, residence or other purposes.

Section 2. Districts. For any or all of said purposes the local legislative body may divide the municipality into districts of such number, shape, and area as may be deemed best suited to carry out the purposes of this act; and within such districts it may regulate and restrict the erection, construction, reconstruction, alteration, repair, or use of buildings, structures, or land. All such regulations shall be uniform for each class or kind of buildings throughout each district, but the regulations in one district may differ from those in other districts.

Section 3. Purpose in View. Such regulations shall be made in accordance with a comprehensive plan and designed to lessen congestion in the streets; to secure safety from fire, panic, and other dangers; to promote health and the general welfare; to provide adequate light and air; to prevent the overcrowding of land; to avoid undue concentration of population; to facilitate the adequate provision of transportation, water, sewerage, schools, parks, and other public requirements. Such regulations shall be made with reasonable consideration, among other things, to the character of the district and its peculiar suitability for particular uses, and with a view to conserving the value of buildings and encouraging the most appropriate use of land throughout such municipality.

In Chapter IX, we explore the advent of local environmental law. That chapter explains how local legislatures have amended their zoning and other land use laws to protect natural resources such as ridgelines, watercourses, and habitats. Can you spot any possible authority in the standard act above that supports the adoption of such laws? Do such laws have anything to do with location and use of buildings, structures, and land; in other words, are they within the grant of power? If the local environmental law singles out just properties that contain ridges, streams and rivers, and habitats and subjects them to stricter standards, would the law violate the uniformity requirement: that all regulations shall be uniform for each kind or class of buildings throughout the zoning district? Are buildings that encroach on critical environmental areas themselves a separate class as to which standards must be uniform?

What if the local government has no formally adopted comprehensive plan and then adopts a zoning law or amendment? What if the comprehensive plan is fairly old and a zoning amendment itself contains findings that explain the planning rationale for the amendment? What if the local legislature wishing to add environmental standards to its zoning laws finds that its comprehensive plan has no findings, goals, or objectives that address themselves to environmental protection? In other words, what does it mean that zoning laws must be "made in conformance with the comprehensive plan?"

In the decades since the adoption of zoning enabling acts by the fifty states, many amendments have been made and new laws passed that enable local governments to meet modern land use challenges. In Chapter IV, we look at the delegation of the power to adopt regulations controlling the subdivision of land and development of individual sites; these laws contain standards that are more detailed than those of zoning laws. As times mature, state legislatures add provisions to their enabling laws, or pass new ones, that allow local governments to promote energy conservation, affordable housing, traditional neighborhood development, or the transfer of density from one district to another. These laws raise many issues for lawyers in the land use field to identify, analyze, and explain to their clients. In this section, we examine in some detail the issue of whether a zoning law is made in conformance with the comprehensive plan.

"Spot zoning" in many jurisdictions is a shorthand description of the legal flaw that exists when a zoning amendment does not conform to the comprehensive plan. In a broad sense, spot zoning is any change that departs from the comprehensive plan. More specifically, it is the singling out by a zoning amendment of a small parcel of land and permitting the owner to use it in a manner inconsistent with the permissible uses in the area. Some courts, in discussing it, apply the terms "arbitrary," "capricious," "unreasonable," and similar adjectives. See, e.g., Cassel v. Mayor and City Council of Baltimore, 195 Md. 348, 73 A.2d 486 (1950); and Pierce v. King County, 62 Wash.2d 324, 382 P.2d 628 (1963). In the oft-cited Cassel case, the court stated:

> Spot zoning, the arbitrary and unreasonable devotion of a small area within a zoning district to a use which is inconsistent with the use to which the rest of the district is restricted, has appeared in many cities in America as a result of pressure put upon councilmen to pass amendments to zoning ordinances solely for the benefit of private interest. * * * It is, therefore, universally held that a 'spot zoning' ordinance, which singles out a parcel of land within the limits of a use district and marks it off with a separate district for the benefit of the owner, thereby permitting a use of that parcel

> inconsistent with the use permitted in the rest of the district, is invalid if not in accordance with the comprehensive plan and is merely for private gain. (195 Md. at 355, 73 A.2d at 488–489.)

Another way of analyzing a zoning amendment that applies to a relatively small area is to ask whether it is *ultra vires*; if zoning must conform to the comprehensive plan, does this rezoning violate that statutory requirement? Or, the inquiry could be whether the amendment is a violation of substantive due process: if the only objective of a zoning amendment is to further private landowner interests, it is void, constitutionally, since it does not promote the public health, safety, or welfare. The state enabling acts delegate a portion of the state legislature's power to act in the public interest—its police power—to local governments; all such laws must promote the public interest in some demonstrable way.

To put the issue differently, imagine that you live in a quiet residential district, protected by the zoning district's proscription of all land uses save single-family residential. You learn that a neighbor has entered into a contract to sell her two acres to a developer, contingent on the ability of the purchaser to secure a zoning amendment allowing the land to be used for a small shopping center, offering many needed goods and services to the neighbors. Your sense of justice is offended! After all, you bought your home with the expectation that the zoning laws in the area would be enforced. You fear that your property values will be lowered. The customers of the businesses proposed will be parking, walking, talking, and carrying on unpredictably within earshot of your front door. Surely this cannot be legal. The developer makes a strong case to the zoning authorities. National studies decry the monotony of suburban neighborhoods. Health scholars tie the increasing obesity of Americans to urban sprawl—the car-dependent life induced by single-use zoning districts; they prescribe mixed land uses within neighborhoods: walkable communities. Certainly it makes sense to have a few places to shop within walking distance of the hundreds of homes in this zoning district? Would this zoning amendment be within the power of the local legislature to adopt? Do the nearby neighbors have a right to the investment-backed expectations in the zoning that existed when they bought?

Obviously, every departure from the plan that was originally instituted for a district does not constitute illicit spot zoning. Otherwise zoning would rigidify permissible land uses within the district to the point that no changes—not even variances or special permits—could be made without a general overhaul. In Penning v. Owens, 340 Mich. 355, 65 N.W.2d 831 (1954), the court said that the inconsistent zoning of a small area must be carefully scrutinized and can be sustained only when the circumstances are such as to warrant the action taken. In Little v. Winborn, 518 N.W.2d 384 (Iowa 1994), the court held that rezoning of agricultural property from "agricultural protection district" to "agricultural" in order to allow the owner to use his property for a shooting range was invalid spot zoning. Its purpose was to benefit the owner, not the public.

Whatever courts may purport to be doing in the spot zoning cases, much of it comes back to the adjectives previously mentioned: Is the action taken arbitrary and unreasonable? Did the zoning ordinance or amendment that singled out this parcel make good sense in the light of the facts involved? As the Iowa court said in Keller v. City of Council Bluffs, 246 Iowa 202, 209–210, 213–214, 66 N.W.2d 113, 117–118, 120, 51 A.L.R.2d 251 (1954):

> The spirit of a zoning ordinance is not violated nor is it inconsistent with a comprehensive zoning ordinance to grant a just and reasonable exception by amendment based upon the character and use of property not similar to other property in the district, but [which] is now and was distinguishable before the adoption of the comprehensive zoning ordinance. * * * "Spot zoning" when construed to mean reclassification of one or more *like tracts* or *similar lots* for a use prohibited by the original zoning ordinance and out of harmony therewith is illegal. When done under certain other conditions and circumstances in accordance with a comprehensive zoning plan, such action will not be declared void. It depends upon the circumstances of each case.

One of the objectives of the "in conformance with" requirement is to prevent the local legislature from using its power to benefit private property interests in ways that are counter to the public interest. Where the locality has a detailed, comprehensive, up-to-date, separately adopted comprehensive, or master, plan, it is easier to determine how, precisely, a zoning amendment advances the public interest. What happens where there is no adopted comprehensive plan at all, or where the plan is not specific or is out of date? The answer depends on what the modern planning and zoning enabling acts say in the state and the attitude of the state courts about the requirement that zoning must be consistent with the plan.

BARTRAM v. ZONING COMMISSION

Supreme Court of Errors of Connecticut, 1949.
136 Conn. 89, 68 A.2d 308.

MALTBIE, CHIEF JUSTICE.

This is an appeal by the defendants from a judgment sustaining an appeal from a decision of the zoning commission of the city of Bridgeport taken in accordance with the provisions of sec. 845 of the General Statutes. The commission changed the classification of a Sylvan Avenue lot, with a frontage of 125 feet and a depth of 133 feet, from a residence zone to a business No. 3 zone.

With some corrections to which the defendants are entitled, the controlling facts found by the court are these: Zoning regulations became effective in Bridgeport on June 1, 1926. They provided for three classes of residence zones, two classes of business zones, and two classes of industrial zones. In 1937 the regulations were amended to establish business zones No. 3 and special regulations were adopted as to them. These regulations, as further amended, contain provisions as to the type of construction of buildings and require open yards about them, a setback of thirty feet from the street and parking facilities for cars on private property; the sale of liquors was originally restricted but this provision was amended to forbid sales of liquor under any permit for a tavern, restaurant or all-liquor package store. The territory surrounding the lot in question is contiguous to the northern boundary of the city and quite a distance from its shopping and business center. Previous to 1936, both sides of Sylvan Avenue to a depth of 100 feet had for a considerable distance been in a business No. 1 zone, but in that year the classification was changed to residence A; and since that date, as before, a considerable territory in the neighborhood of the premises in question has been in residential zones. When zoning was originally adopted, the area was sparsely built up and contained much farm land. Beginning before 1936, people desiring to get away from the noise and congestion of the center of the city began to build homes there; at present it is quite generally built up with residences, at least 40 per cent of which have been constructed since 1936. Most of the houses in the immediate vicinity of the premises in question are comparatively new; they are neat, one-family homes, with well-kept lawns and attractive plantings; and they give every indication that a self-respecting community of people of moderate means have moved to this outlying section of the city. In the vicinity of the premises in question there exist as nonconforming uses four stores, three selling groceries or meat and one a liquor package store. One of the former is a small store in a building almost opposite the premises in question, the second floor of which is occupied as a residence. There is no drug store in the vicinity. There is also, near the premises in question, a small church. Sylvan Avenue is a street sixty feet wide and it is a principal traffic artery to and from the section surrounding it.

The application for the change of zone was made by the defendant Rome. He presented to the commission at the hearing plans for a building he proposes to erect, which in all respects would comply with the regulations for a business No. 3 zone, which would contain provision for five places of business—a drug, a hardware and a grocery store, a bakeshop and a beauty parlor—and which would provide for the parking of cars in the rear of the building, and between it and the street line. Aside from Rome, no one appeared to support his application, but ten residents and property owners in the neighborhood opposed it. They gave various reasons for the position they took, among them these: They desired to have the residential character of the section preserved from business development; in many instances they had purchased or developed their properties in reliance upon the residence zoning of the area and in the expectation that this zoning status would remain unchanged; they were fearful that the business zoning of any portion of the area would be destructive of the peace and quiet they desired to have preserved; they believed that the business zoning of any part of it, however small and wherever located, would have a tendency to break down the residence zoning of the area by making further business zoning in it more likely; and there was no present need for further and more adequate shopping facilities in the neighborhood. A remonstrance against granting the application signed by more than seventy residents in the neighborhood was also filed with the commission; but only some forty-six different addresses of the signers appear on it; in a number of instances the signers were husband and wife or two or more residing in the same house; and many of them lived at a considerable distance from the premises in question. Within a radius no longer than the distance to the addresses given by some of the signers are more than 200 residences.

The commission gave the following reasons for its decision: 1. The location is on Sylvan Avenue, a sixty-foot street, and there is no shopping center within a mile of it. To the north of this tract there is a very large development but only small nonconforming grocery stores to serve the people. 2. There is practically only one house, adjacent to this tract on the north, which will be directly affected by this change of zone. 3. Business No. 3 regulations, with their thirty-foot setback and liquor restrictions, were designed to meet conditions like this and help alleviate the great congestion in the centralized shopping districts. The court also found that a member of the commission testified that it was its policy to encourage decentralization of business in order to relieve traffic congestion and that, as part of that policy, it was considered desirable to permit neighborhood stores in outlying districts; and nowhere in the record is there any suggestion that this testimony is not true.

The trial court concluded that the change was an instance of "spot zoning." A limitation upon the powers of zoning authorities which has been in effect ever since zoning statutes were made applicable generally to municipalities in the state is that the regulations they adopt must be made "in accordance with a comprehensive plan." Public Acts, 1925, c. 242, sec. 3 (Rev.1949, sec. 837). "A 'comprehensive plan' means 'a general plan to control and direct the use and development of property in a municipality or a large part of it by dividing it into districts according to the present and potential use of the properties.' " *Bishop v. Board of Zoning Appeals*, 133 Conn. 614, 618, 53 A.2d 659; *State ex rel. Spiros v. Payne*, 131 Conn. 647, 652, 41 A.2d 908. Action by a zoning authority which gives to a single lot or a small area privileges which are not extended to other land in the vicinity is in general against sound public policy and obnoxious to the law. It can be justified only when it is done in furtherance of a general plan properly adopted for and designed to serve the best interests of the community as a whole.

The vice of spot zoning lies in the fact that it singles out for special treatment a lot or a small area in a way that does not further such a plan. Where, however, in pursuance of it, a zoning commission takes such action, its decision can be assailed only on the ground that it abused the discretion vested in it by the law. To permit business in a small area within a residence zone may fall within the scope of such a plan, and to do so, unless it amounts to unreasonable or arbitrary action, is not unlawful. *Bishop v. Board of Zoning Appeals*, supra; see *Parsons v. Wethersfield*, 135 Conn. 24, 29, 60 A.2d 771. The zoning regulations of Bridgeport were adopted under the provisions of the General Statutes which gave the commission power to divide the municipality into districts and in each district to regulate the construction and use of buildings and land, and to change the regulations from time to time. General Statutes, Rev.1930, secs. 424, 425, as amended (Rev.1949, secs. 837, 838); see *De Palma v. Town Plan Commission of Greenwich*, 123 Conn. 257, 265, 193 A. 868. The commission might be guilty of spot zoning either in the original regulations it made or in later amendments, but, if in one or the other it decides, on facts affording a sufficient basis and in the exercise of a proper discretion, that it would serve the best interests of the community as a whole to permit a use of a single lot or small area in a different way than was allowed in surrounding territory, it would not be guilty of spot zoning in any sense obnoxious to the law. That was the situation in this case, and we cannot sustain the conclusion of the trial court that the action of the commission was improper as an instance of spot zoning.

The trial court also concluded that the change in zoning was in violation of the declared objects of the zoning regulations of Bridgeport, as stated in their first section. That section states among the purposes to be served by them the promotion of the health, safety, morals and general welfare of the community and the lessening of congestion in streets. The reasons which led the commission to take the action it did, as we have stated them above, fall well within the scope of these purposes. The fact that the change was advocated only by Rome at the hearing and was opposed by numerous property owners and residents in the neighborhood did not, as the trial court concluded, deprive the commission of power to make it. It does not appear that there was anything like unanimous opposition to the change of property owners in the surrounding territory; but, even if there had been, it was the duty of the commission to look beyond the effect of the change upon them to the general welfare of the city. The reasons given before the commission by those who opposed the change were quite largely based on fear that other like changes might be made rather than upon the effect of the particular one in question. The property of no one was taken by the commission's decision; nor is there any finding or, indeed, evidence that property values would be affected; and no such situation is before us as was presented in *Strain v. Mims*, 123 Conn. 275, 193 A. 754, where, in speaking of a change in zoning from business to residence which practically affected only a single property, we said (p. 286): "However, where the value of property of an individual is seriously affected by a zoning regulation especially applicable to it, this fact imposes an obligation carefully to consider the question whether the regulation does in fact tend to serve the public welfare and the recognized purposes of zoning." Property owners in the neighborhood had no right to a continuation of the existing situation which could be effective against a decision by the commission reached legally and properly. The state, through the authority it vests in zoning authorities, "may regulate any business or the use of any property in the interest of the public health, safety or welfare, provided this be done reasonably. To that extent the public interest is supreme and the private interest must yield." *Windsor v. Whitney*, 95 Conn. 357, 366, 111 A. 354, 356, 12 A.L.R. 669; *Strain v. Mims*, supra. The commission could not properly be held, upon the record in this case, to have acted in violation of law in making the change it did.

How best the purposes of zoning can be accomplished in any municipality is primarily in the discretion of its zoning authority; that description [sic] is a broad one; and unless it transcends the limitations set by law its decisions are subject to review in the courts only to the extent of determining whether or not it has acted in abuse of that discretion. *First Nat. Bank & Trust Co. v. Zoning Board of Appeals*, 126 Conn. 228, 237, 10 A.2d 691. A court is without authority to substitute its own judgment for that vested by the statutes in a zoning authority. *Piccolo v. West Haven*, 120 Conn. 449, 455, 181 A. 615; *Mrowka v. Board of Zoning Appeals*, 134 Conn. 149, 155, 55 A.2d 909. In view of the facts presented in this case, the trial court could not properly find that the policy which determined the decision of the commission would so clearly fail to serve the proper purposes of zoning in the city that the court might set aside that decision; nor do the facts show that it was unreasonable to apply that policy in the situation before us. This is illustrated by the fact that, had this lot been placed in a business No. 3 zone as an incident to the adoption of an original plan for zoning the city as a whole, that action could not on this record be held an unreasonable exercise by the commission of its powers.

There is error, the judgment is set aside and the case is remanded with direction to enter judgment dismissing the appeal. * * *

[Dissenting opinion omitted.]

Notes

1. Although the Bartram case is rather old, the approach taken by the court in that case is still the prevailing approach in most jurisdictions. For another example, see Vella v. Town of Camden, 677 A.2d 1051 (Me.1996), where the owner of an inn sued to set aside zoning amendments that favored a competing innkeeper on grounds of spot zoning inconsistent with the comprehensive plan.

2. The court in Little v. Board of County Comm'rs of Flathead County, 193 Mont. 334, 631 P.2d 1282 (1981) declared illegal spot zoning where the municipality rezoned a parcel commercial within a residential district. The court identified three pertinent characteristics of illegal spot zoning:

> First, in spot zoning, the requested use is significantly different from the prevailing use in the area. Second, the area in which the requested use is to apply is rather small. This test, however, is concerned more with the number of separate landowners benefited by the requested change than it is with the actual size of the area benefited. Third, the requested change is more in the nature of special legislation.

In other words, it is designed to benefit only one or a few landowners at the expense of the surrounding landowners or the general public.

3. Is a decision refusing to rezone a parcel to a classification called for by the comprehensive plan presumptively invalid? See City of Gainesville v. Hope, 377 So.2d 736 (Fla.App.1979), where the court stated that a comprehensive plan is a "guide for future zoning," but it does "not affect existing zoning." Also see, Clinkscales v. City of Lake Oswego, 47 Or.App. 1117, 615 P.2d 1164 (1980), where the court stated that "the fact that a piece of property is zoned for a less intensive use than that contemplated by the comprehensive plan does not mean that a property owner has an immediate right to the more intensive use."

4. For an example of where a city's denial of plaintiff-landowner's requested rezoning is ruled illegal spot zoning, see Ross v. City of Yorba Linda, 1 Cal.App.4th 954, 2 Cal.Rptr.2d 638 (Ct.App. 4th Dist. 1991). The area surrounding plaintiff's parcel was zoned for one dwelling per acre, yet a majority of the surrounding houses sat on less than one acre lots. When the plaintiff requested a rezoning that would allow plaintiff to divide its 1.117–acre lot in two and build two houses, the neighbors complained and the city denied the rezoning. The court stated: "The city incorrectly denied the Rosses' request for rezoning. The plan amendment is nothing more than the city's attempt to tie its own hands so it supposedly cannot be ordered to do now what it should have done in the first place. We untie the city's hands by holding the plan amendment inapplicable to the Rosses' rezoning request."

5. In Rodgers v. Village of Tarrytown, 302 N.Y. 115, 96 N.E.2d 731 (1951), the New York Court of Appeals held that a village planning board had the authority to create a new, flexible zoning mechanism: a floating zoning district. The plaintiff argued that the floating zone that allowed multi-family buildings in a single-family zoning district on 15–acre or larger parcels violated the uniformity requirement of zoning districts or constituted illegal spot zoning. The court disagreed and sanctioned the novel concept of first creating a floating zoning district and later affixing it to a specific parcel upon the application of the landowner. In sustaining such techniques as within the locality's implied zoning power, the court noted that a "decision as to how a community shall be zoned or rezoned, as to how various properties shall be classified or reclassified, rests with the local legislative body; its judgment and determination will be conclusive, beyond interference from the courts, unless shown to be arbitrary."

ENTERPRISE PARTNERS v. COUNTY OF PERKINS

Supreme Court of Nebraska, 2000.
260 Neb. 650, 619 N.W.2d 464.

McCormack, J.

* * *

In April 1998, the Board became aware of proposals to build hog confinement facilities in Perkins County. At subsequent meetings of the Board, individuals and public groups expressed concerns about the effect these types of facilities would have on the environment, on the health of the citizens of Perkins County, and the need to prevent these facilities from being built. The Board sent a letter to the Nebraska Department of Environmental Quality (DEQ) voicing its concerns and going on record as opposing the approval of a permit to allow Enterprise to construct a hog confinement facility in Perkins County.

DEQ responded in a letter addressing the Board's concerns and explaining evaluation procedures and the requirements that needed to be met in order for a permit to be issued. DEQ also pointed out that two of the Board's concerns could not be addressed by DEQ as it did not have the authority to regulate those issues. These issues were the odor and insects and the impact on county roads. DEQ stated that "[t]he Legislature has given counties the authority to implement land use planning and adopt zoning regulations which could govern the location of livestock facilities. Odors, dust and insects are considered to be nuisances and are not regulated by the DEQ." With regard to the impact on county roads, DEQ stated that "[t]his is not an issue which DEQ can address, but as a local issue it may possibly be addressed through load limit restrictions."

Proposed ordinances were submitted to the Board, and discussion was held on December 21, 1998. Ordinance 98–1 attempts to locally regulate livestock confinement facilities by regulating odor emanating from the facility by requiring that certain parts of the facility be covered. By controlling odor, other problems with flies would be avoided. Ordinance 98–2 requires large-scale livestock operations to demonstrate that no livestock waste, liquid or solid, would be carried or washed onto or into county roads, ditches, or properties adjacent to the facility during or following a 25–year storm. This demonstration must also be updated on a yearly basis through inspections by the county. The Board passed both ordinances and increased the civil penalty contained in them from $200 to $5,000 per day for each violation.

Enterprise filed a petition for declaratory judgment arguing that the ordinances are zoning ordinances and were passed in violation of Neb. Rev.Stat. § 23–114.03 (Reissue 1997) which requires the Board to have a county comprehensive development plan before the adoption of zoning regulations. The Board stipulated that it had not adopted a comprehensive zoning plan pursuant to § 23–114.03. Enterprise also asserted that Ordinances 98–1 and 98–2 contain environmental requirements that are specifically reserved for the state. Enterprise also argued that these ordinances deprived it of property without due process of law and that the Board lacked the authority to impose civil penalties.

The trial court ruled that the ordinances were not zoning ordinances but fell within the exercise of police powers granted to the counties by the Legislature, that no preemption or conflict existed between the ordinances and state statutes, and that the ordinances were not arbitrary or unreasonable and did not violate the constitution. The trial court found generally for the Board and found that both ordinances were valid and enforceable.

* * *

Enterprise assigns that the trial court erred in not finding that Ordinances 98–1 and 98–2 were zoning ordinances. Enterprise asserts that the ordinances are zoning ordinances and were passed by the Board in violation of § 23–114.03. Section 23–114.03 provides that "[z]oning regulations shall be adopted or amended by the county board only after the adoption of the county comprehensive development plan by the county board * * *." Both Enterprise and the Board stipulated that "Perkins County, Nebraska, has not adopted a comprehensive zoning plan pursuant to Neb.Rev.Stat. § 23–114, et seq." Therefore, Enterprise concludes that Ordinances 98–1 and 98–2 are invalid because the Board does not have a comprehensive development plan. We agree.

A county is a political subdivision of the state having subordinate powers of sovereignty conferred by the Legislature. *Hoiengs v. County of Adams*, 245 Neb. 877, 516 N.W.2d 223 (1994). A political subdivision has only that power delegated to it by the Legislature; a grant of power to a political subdivision is to be strictly construed. *Metropolitan Utilities Dist. v. Twin Platte NRD*, 250 Neb. 442, 550 N.W.2d 907 (1996).

Counties have the statutory authority to regulate the use of lands within their jurisdiction to promote the public health, safety, and welfare pursuant to § 23–114.03 and Neb.Rev.Stat. § 23–174.10 (Reissue 1997). * * * Section 23–114.03 states:

> Zoning regulations shall be adopted or amended by the county board only after the adoption of the county comprehensive development plan by the county board and the receipt of the planning commission's specific recommendations. Such zoning regulations shall be consistent with the comprehensive development plan and designed for the purpose of promoting the health, safety, morals, convenience, order, prosperity, and welfare of the present and future inhabitants of Nebraska, including, among others, such specific purposes as:
>
> (1) Developing both urban and nonurban areas;
>
> (2) Lessening congestion in the streets or roads;
>
> (3) Reducing the waste of excessive amounts of roads;
>
> (4) Securing safety from fire and other dangers;
>
> (5) Lessening or avoiding the hazards to persons and damage to property resulting from the accumulation or runoff of storm or flood waters;
>
> (6) Providing adequate light and air;
>
> (7) Preventing excessive concentration of population and excessive and wasteful scattering of population or settlement;
>
> (8) Promoting such distribution of population, such classification of land uses, and such distribution of land development as will assure adequate provisions for transportation, water flowage, water supply, drainage, sanitation, recreation, soil fertility, food supply, and other public requirements;
>
> (9) Protecting the tax base;

(10) Protecting property against blight and depreciation;

(11) Securing economy in governmental expenditures;

(12) Fostering the state's agriculture, recreation, and other industries;

(13) Encouraging the most appropriate use of land in the county; and

(14) Preserving, protecting, and enhancing historic buildings, places, and districts.

Within the area of jurisdiction and powers established by section 23–114, the county board may divide the county into districts of such number, shape, and area as may be best suited to carry out the purposes of this section and regulate, restrict, or prohibit the erection, construction, reconstruction, alteration, or use of nonfarm buildings or structures and the use, conditions of use, or occupancy of land. All such regulations shall be uniform for each class or kind of land or buildings throughout each district, but the regulations in one district may differ from those in other districts. An official map or maps indicating the districts and regulations shall be adopted, and within fifteen days after adoption of such regulations or maps, they shall be published in book or pamphlet form or once in a legal newspaper published in and of general circulation in the county or, if none is published in the county, in a legal newspaper of general circulation in the county. Such regulations shall also be spread in the minutes of the proceedings of the county board and such map or maps filed with the county clerk. Nonfarm buildings are all buildings except those buildings utilized for agricultural purposes on a farmstead of twenty acres or more which produces one thousand dollars or more of farm products each year.

Section 23–174.10 states:

In any county which has adopted county zoning regulations, the county board, by resolution, may make regulations as may be necessary or expedient to promote the public health, safety, and welfare, including regulations to prevent the introduction or spread of contagious, infectious, or malignant diseases; to provide rules for the prevention, abatement, and removal of nuisances, including the pollution of air and water; and make and prescribe regulations for the construction, location, and keeping in order of all slaughterhouses, stockyards, warehouses, sheds, stables, barns, commercial feedlots, dairies, junk and salvage yards, or other places where offensive matter is kept, or is likely to accumulate. Such regulations shall be not inconsistent with the general laws of the state and shall apply to all of the county except within the limits of any incorporated city or village, and except within the unincorporated area where a city or village has been granted zoning jurisdiction and is exercising such jurisdiction.

The statutory language in these sections grants extensive powers to counties to regulate their lands. These powers, however, are rooted in zoning, and zoning regulations can be enacted only after adoption of a county comprehensive development plan by a county board. § 23–114.03.

Zoning is "the process that a community employs to legally control the use which may be made of property and the physical configuration of development upon the tracts of land located within its jurisdiction." *Ford v. Bd. of Cty. Com'rs of Converse*, 924 P.2d 91, 94 (Wyo.1996). According to this definition Ordinances 98–1 and 98–2 are zoning regulations.

* * *

Ordinance 98–1, regarding fly and odor control, states in pertinent part:

> The Commissioners of Perkins County find that large livestock confinement facilities use lagoons to store and treat waste produced by animals in confinement. These lagoons produce odor. The odor is made up of many different kinds of volatile compounds including ammonia, phenol, cresol, volatile fatty acids, aldehydes, bezene, xylene and hydrogen sulfide. The Commissioners find that there has [sic] been reports of adverse health effects to citizens of other jurisdictions from exposure to the odor. By controlling odors, other problems such as flies can also be avoided.
>
> * * *
>
> SECTION 2: COVERS REQUIRED
>
> 2.01 An owner or operator of a large livestock confinement facility shall not operate a facility in Perkins County unless the following are covered: livestock waste storage containment structures that receives [sic] livestock waste on a regular basis and permanent livestock waste containment structures in which an anaerobic pool is maintained. Facilities that have structures that receive livestock waste only on an [sic] sporadic baisis [sic] due to storm runoff are not required to have covers on their livestock waste containment structures.
>
> SECTION 3: INSPECTIONS
>
> 3.01 The County shall have the right to inspect the site to insure [sic] compliance with the provisions of this regulation.

Ordinance 98–1 attempts to legally control the use and development of property by requiring covers to be used for certain land uses and by restricting land use until inspection by the county. Ordinance 98–1 is therefore a zoning regulation.

The Board has been given the power by the Legislature to regulate through the use of zoning but, pursuant to § 23–114.03, zoning regulations shall be adopted only after the adoption by the Board of a comprehensive development plan. Why the Board has never adopted a comprehensive development plan is not apparent from the record. Because of the failure of the Board to adopt such a plan, these ordinances are not valid as to Enterprise's hog confinement facilities.

* * *

[Using similar logic, the court finds that Perkins County Ordinance 98–2 is also a zoning regulation.]

Counties in Nebraska have been delegated the power to regulate the use of lands within their jurisdiction to promote the public health, safety, and welfare pursuant to §§ 23–114.03 and 23–174.10 since 1967. A county board may by resolution make regulations as may be necessary to promote the health, safety, and welfare of its public if it has adopted a comprehensive development plan as required by § 23–114.03. Since the Board has failed to adopt a comprehensive development plan, the Board does not have the authority to pass Ordinances 98–1 and 98–2, as they are clearly zoning-related regulations. We therefore conclude that Ordinances 98–1 and 98–2 are invalid.

REVERSED.

Notes

1. The principal case involves an "evolved" enabling act, patterned after the standard enabling act but revised to meet the needs of a rural state and to comport with other legal norms held by the state legislature. Can you spot the similarities and differences between Section 23–114.03 and the standard act? What about the "in conformance with" language? Is it different? The Nebraska zoning enabling act contains this provision: "Zoning regulations shall be adopted or amended by the county board only after the adoption of the county comprehensive development plan * * *." Can you find that language in the standard act? Why was this language added by the Nebraska legislature? What does this addition mean? Given this language in the act, could the court have come to any other conclusion?

2. The Perkins County case raises a key question: when does a law constitute zoning? Note that the county did not adopt zoning wholesale, it simply passed a law regulating a uniquely modern phenomenon: the spread of concentrated animal feeding facilities across the rural landscape. If this is a zoning law, it is subject to the jurisdictional limitations of the zoning enabling act. If it is not, its authority must reside in another state enabling act. Some states have adopted municipal home rule statutes giving local governments the authority to adopt local laws to regulate municipal property, affairs, and government or, in some cases, to protect the physical environment. Would such an enabling law provide a separate source of authority for counties to regulate the environmental impacts of pig farms and feed lots? Or because the law controls the "use which may be made of property and the physical configuration of development," in the court's words, would it still be zoning and subject to the comprehensive plan requirement? How onerous is it to require a local government to adopt a comprehensive plan? How big is Perkins County? Why isn't it zoned? Does the county have a professional planner on staff or on retainer?

3. In a case where two property owners sought to declare a county zoning ordinance establishing agricultural zoning classification unconstitutional, the Appellate Court of Illinois ruled that the ordinance was constitutional and looked to the comprehensive plan for guidance. Wilson v. County of McHenry, 92 Ill.App.3d 997, 48 Ill.Dec. 395, 416 N.E.2d 426 (2d Dist. 1981). The county zoning ordinance was amended on November 1, 1979, to provide a 160–acre lot minimum in agricultural zones pursuant to the McHenry County Year 2000 plan. The plan attempted to channel development toward existing urban centers; particularly recognizing prime agricultural land as a primary, finite material resource. The Wilsons, the property owners, argued that by classifying their land as agricultural, they would lose substantial value in their property ($4,000 per acre if zoned agriculture versus $18,000 to $20,000 per lot if zoned one-acre residential). The Wilsons alleged that 37.4 percent of their land was not prime farm land and that the average yield was only 95 bushels of corn per acre. The court noted that "a significant aspect in the case is the county's adoption of a comprehensive plan for the area." The court stated that the adoption of a comprehensive plan which incorporates valid zoning goals increases the likelihood that the zoning of a particular parcel in conformity with the plan is not arbitrary or unrelated to the public interest. The Illinois courts have placed increasing importance on the existence of a comprehensive plan in reviewing zoning cases. The court also ruled that lower property values by themselves were insufficient to overcome the presumption of validity of the ordinance.

OSICEKI v. TOWN OF HUNTINGTON

New York Appellate Division, Second Department, 1991.
170 A.D.2d 490, 565 N.Y.S.2d 564.

MEMORANDUM BY THE COURT.

In an action for a judgment declaring, inter alia, that the one-acre residential zoning classification of the plaintiffs' property is invalid because it does not comply with a comprehensive plan, the plaintiffs appeal from a judgment of the Supreme Court, Suffolk County (Seidell, J.), dated December 20, 1988, which, after a nonjury trial, inter alia, declared the one-acre residential zoning classification valid.

ORDERED that the judgment is reversed, on the law, without costs or disbursements, and it is declared that the one-acre residential zoning classification of the plaintiffs' property is invalid because it does not comply with a comprehensive plan.

The plaintiffs own an approximately five and one-half acre parcel at the northwest corner of Old Country Road and Old New York Avenue in the Town of Huntington (hereinafter the Town). It is zoned for low density residential use (one-acre plots). Two other parcels to the west, on the north side of Old Country Road have been zoned for commercial office buildings and have been developed as such. The properties to the south and east of the subject property, across Old County Road and Old New York Avenue are zoned for one-acre residential use, but are respectively in current use as a farm and for water district purposes by the Town of Huntington. To the north of the subject property is the

Northern State Parkway. North of the Parkway is a Town Park also zoned one-acre residential.

The plaintiffs commenced this action for a judgment declaring the one-acre residential zoning of their property invalid as (1) inconsistent with the Town's comprehensive zoning plan, or (2) a violation of equal protection of the law in relation to the other commercially zoned property adjacent to it. After a nonjury trial, the court rejected the plaintiffs' assertions that the residential zoning of their property was invalid. We disagree.

Town Law § 263 provides that zoning ordinances must be made in accordance with a comprehensive plan. A comprehensive plan is a compilation of land use policies that may be found in any number of ordinances, resolutions, and policy statements of the town (*see, Curtiss–Wright Corp. v. Town of East Hampton*, 82 A.D.2d 551, 557, 442 N.Y.S.2d 125). As the Court of Appeals noted in *Udell v. Haas*, 21 N.Y.2d 463, 472, 288 N.Y.S.2d 888, 235 N.E.2d 897), "[t]hese policies may be garnered from any available source, most especially the master plan of the community, if any has been adopted, the zoning law itself and the zoning map".

Town Law § 272–a gives the planning board the authority to prepare a master plan for the development of the entire area of a town. The planning board of the Town adopted such a plan in 1965 and it was amended in 1966. The master plan designated the entire block, of which the subject parcel is a part, for commercial development and a large number of zoning changes and Town actions have been consistent with the master plan (see, *Tilles v. Town of Huntington*, 74 N.Y.2d 885, 547 N.Y.S.2d 835, 547 N.E.2d 90, *affg*. 137 A.D.2d 118, 528 N.Y.S.2d 386). In addition, as recently as 1986 the Town Planning Board and Planning Department recommended that the subject parcel be developed commercially. Unrefuted expert testimony indicated that the Town's action constituted comprehensive planning that the block be commercially developed. Indeed, the Town acknowledges that the numerous rezonings in the area show that it followed the master plan to a large extent.

Nevertheless, the Town maintains that it is not obliged to slavish servitude to the master plan and that it was free, in 1989, to determine that the master plan should not be followed with regard to this property (see, *Town of Bedford v. Village of Mount Kisco*, 33 N.Y.2d 178, at 188, 351 N.Y.S.2d 129, 306 N.E.2d 155; *Tilles v. Town of Huntington*, 137 A.D.2d 118, 528 N.Y.S.2d 386, *affd*. 74 N.Y.2d 885, 547 N.Y.S.2d 835, 547 N.E.2d 90, *supra*). However, the Town makes no attempt to justify its "determination" that disregarding the Town's specific master plan is not inconsistent with a comprehensive zoning plan for the area rather than an entirely ad hoc decision (cf., *Town of Bedford v. Village of Mount Kisco, supra*). To accept the Town's contention that it is free to determine that the master plan should no longer be followed, without articulating a reason for that determination, would invite the kind of ad hoc and arbitrary application of zoning power that the comprehensive planning requirement was designed to avoid (see, *Town of Bedford v. Village of Mount Kisco, supra,* 33 N.Y.2d at 187, 188, 351 N.Y.S.2d 129, 306 N.E.2d 155).

We find that the record establishes that the commercial development of the subject parcel was part of the Town's comprehensive development plan. The Town does not articulate any basis for changing that plan at the present time and we can find none. Thus, the residential zoning of the subject parcel is void as it fails to comport with the Town's comprehensive plan (see, *Udell v. Haas,* 21 N.Y.2d 463, 288 N.Y.S.2d 888, 235 N.E.2d 897, *supra*; *cf., Tilles v. Town of Huntington,* 74 N.Y.2d 885, 547 N.Y.S.2d 835, 547 N.E.2d 90, *supra*).

Notes

1. Separate provisions of the Town Law in New York authorize, but do not require, towns to adopt comprehensive plans and zoning laws. Parallel provisions are found in the Village Law and the General City Law so that all three types of municipalities in the state (towns, villages, and cities) have the same authority to control land use. These laws follow closely the pattern of the standard zoning enabling act. Section 263 of the Town Law states that "such regulations shall be made in accordance with a comprehensive plan." Section 272–a of the Town Law states that town boards "may" adopt a comprehensive plan, specifies fifteen subjects that a comprehensive plan "may" include, and ends by stating that "all town land use regulations must be in accordance with a comprehensive plan adopted pursuant to this section."

2. Dealing with slightly different language in these enabling acts at an earlier time, New York's highest court struck down a village zoning amendment because it failed to conform to the comprehensive plan requirement even though the village had not adopted a comprehensive plan. Udell v. Haas, 21 N.Y.2d 463, 235 N.E.2d 897, 288 N.Y.S.2d 888 (1968). In 1951, when the plaintiff bought the property, it was zoned Business A, allowing for retail, office, and laboratory uses. Nine years later, the plaintiff's representative presented building plans to the village for a business development. That same night, the planning board recommended that the area where the plaintiff's property was located be changed from business to residential. The local legislature rezoned the land shortly thereafter but failed to articulate the comprehensive planning objectives achieved by the rezoning. The court concluded that the "vague desires of a segment of the public were not a proper reason to interfere with the [plaintiff's] right to use his property in a manner which for some 20 odd years was considered perfectly proper. If there is to be any justification for this interference with [plaintiff's] use of his property, it must be found in the needs and goals of the community as articulated in a rational statement of land use control policies known as the comprehensive plan." In the absence of a formally adopted comprehensive plan, the court examined "all relevant evidence," including the zoning map and law, for evidence of comprehensive planning. The court also reviewed a 1958 zoning amendment entitled Development Policy for the Village. This amendment envisioned the village as a low-density, single-family community with commercial development limited to outlying areas. The court noted that

the plaintiff's land was located in that commercial area prior to the 1960 rezoning. The court reasoned that a "comprehensive plan requires that the rezoning should not conflict with the fundamental land use policies and development plans of the community" and invalidated the rezoning.

3. An interpretation of the Udell decision is found in McBride v. Town of Forestburgh, 54 A.D.2d 396, 388 N.Y.S.2d 940 (3d Dep't 1976). Here, the court wrote that "[i]t would appear that neither a master plan nor even a written plan is necessary." In the court's view, "the requirements of the enabling statute are met if implicit in the [zoning] law there is the element of planning which is both rational and consistent with the basic land use policies of the community." The court further held that there was a sufficient showing of a comprehensive plan based on the small size of the community and the planning done before the adoption of the law. See also State ex rel. Chiavola v. Village of Oakwood, 886 S.W.2d 74 (Mo.Ct.App. 1994), in which the court stated: "This court holds a comprehensive plan may be validly enacted in an ordinance itself without existing in some form separate from the ordinance."

4. Do New York communities have an obligation to formally adopt a comprehensive plan today, like Perkins County in Nebraska? The language quoted in note 1 above from § 272–a raises an untested issue in the state on this point. If not, how will a court find the comprehensive plan to which all land use regulations must conform? If a community adopts a new zoning regulation but does not have a comprehensive plan, how would it demonstrate that the regulation is in conformance with the comprehensive plan? Is Udell v. Haas still good law?

5. How difficult would it have been for the town board in Osieki to articulate a rationale for departing from the comprehensive plan in the adoption of the zoning amendment that is the subject of the plaintiff's suit? Depending on your answer, what kind of assurance does the comprehensive plan give to citizens that its provisions will be followed? Does a rationale articulated in adopting a rezoning amendment constitute an amendment of the comprehensive plan?

6. Also see Tilles Investment Co. v. Town of Huntington, 74 N.Y.2d 885, 547 N.Y.S.2d 835, 547 N.E.2d 90 (1989), where the owner of 52 acres zoned residential challenged the town's refusal to rezone his land for commercial (two other parcels had been rezoned). The court held that the decision was in accord with the comprehensive plan, stating that the statute mandated comprehensive planning, not slavish servitude to any particular comprehensive plan.

SECTION 3. ZONING ADMINISTRATION AND FLEXIBILITY

A. INTRODUCTION

How much flexibility do enabling acts provide local governments? What restrictions are there on localities that wish to change the rules by amending their zoning ordinances, or by giving their administrative boards discretionary authority to interpret the rules to effect desirable results in individual circumstances? The power to amend the zoning ordinance and change district lines and designations on the zoning map provides a degree of flexibility. In some states, localities are required to show that circumstances have changed which necessitate the amendment. When changing district lines or applying an existing zoning district to a new area, does the local government have the authority to impose conditions on development in the expanded or new area that do not apply in the other areas to which that district designation applies? Is this a violation of equal protection guarantees or at odds with the uniformity requirement in the zoning enabling act? How can the local government provide relief to single parcel owners who suffer practical difficulties or economic hardships when zoning standards are applied to their particular properties? Can local governments designate certain land uses, such as religious institutions or junkyards, as special uses and impose conditions on them to mitigate their adverse impacts on surrounding neighborhoods?

Let's begin with a review. The zoning ordinance establishes a number of zoning districts and contains a map indicating which parts of the community are within each district. Technical terms are defined, as-of-right uses permitted in each district, accessory uses are allowed, and a variety of dimensional requirements are applied to land development with the dimensions changing from district to district. Examples of area and bulk standards include maximum height of buildings, minimum width of lots, maximum area of lot that buildings can cover, minimum setback requirements from the lot lines, etc.

Zoning provisions are adopted in the first instance by the local legislative body after being drafted by a zoning commission or planning body and subjected to public scrutiny. Where local laws are codified, the zoning provisions become part of the municipal code. The code might be organized alphabetically by chapters and Zoning might be Chapter 40 of the code since it comes near the end of the alphabet. This Zoning Chapter is further subdivided into various articles. A typical chapter will have a variety of titles including, among others, the following:

Article I: General Provisions

A. Title—states the title.

B. Scope—establishes the breadth of issues to be covered by the chapter or law.

C. Statutory Authority—states the legal authority for enacting a zoning law.

D. Purposes—lists the reasons for adopting the zoning law.

Article II: Definitions

A. Definitions—defines words in the chapter that have substantive importance.

B. Word Usage—often explains that the normal dictionary definition of words shall be used where the words are not specifically defined.

Article III: Zoning Districts and Map

A. Districts Enumerated—sets forth the various use districts established by the chapter. Examples of district types include single-family residential, multi-family residential, commercial, light industrial, conservation, and agricultural. There are few limits on the types and number of districts that a community may establish.

B. Zoning Map—explains that the location and boundaries of the enumerated districts are shown on the zoning map and that the map, together with any amendments to it, if not appended to the chapter itself, is available in the municipal clerk's office.

Article IV: District Regulations

A. Application of Regulations—states that no building, structure, or land shall be used and no building, structure or part thereof shall be erected, moved, or altered unless for a use expressly permitted by and in conformance with the regulations for the district in which the building, structure, or land is located.

B. General Regulations—contains regulations that are applicable to all districts, including specifications regarding irregularly shaped lots, building height, minimum lot area, uses of yards, frontage, and driveways, roof structures, and easements.

C. Schedule of Permitted Uses (Schedule A)—lists the types of land uses permitted in particular districts. Where a use is not listed, it is prohibited.

D. Schedule of Area and Bulk Requirements (Schedule B)—defines the area and bulk requirements for each of the enumerated districts. Includes regulations governing minimum lot area, minimum lot width, minimum front and side yard setbacks, minimum rear yard, minimum road frontage, maximum lot coverage, maximum height, parking setback, and floor area ratio.

E. Off–Street Parking and Loading Regulations—sets forth the required number of parking spaces, and their dimensions, for a given use district and particular use.

Article V: Supplementary Regulations—Land Activities

A. Accessory Uses and Structures—establishes regulations governing land uses and structures incidental to the district's primary permitted uses, dwelling units, and structures.

B. Cemeteries—establishes minimum lot size and setback requirements from any street, right-of-way, or property line. May also require site plan approval.

C. Communications Antenna or Tower; Satellite Dishes—regulates the location, placement and appearance of communication facilities.

Under the Federal Telecommunications Act of 1996, municipalities are prohibited from excluding such facilities from their jurisdictions.

D. Home Occupations—provides for the regulation of home occupations such as professional offices, day-care facilities, and dance studios. May be included under the section on accessory uses.

E. Hotel or Motel—establishes requirements for the location of hotels and motels in particular districts. Sets forth a minimum lot size and required road frontage and side and rear yard setbacks.

F. Mobile Homes—establishes regulations controlling the location and appearance of individual mobile homes as well as mobile home developments within a community. Also establishes bulk and area requirements for such dwellings.

G. Places of Worship—in addition to regulating the placement of such facilities within particular zones and establishing minimum lot sizes and setbacks, many zoning laws also provide that places of worship are subject to a special permit and site plan approval. Some laws also require a design that is compatible with the existing neighborhood character.

H. Planned Unit Development—regulations designed to promote variety and flexibility in land development while stressing the efficient use of open space and public facilities. May provide for the type and number of residential and commercial uses allowed, as well as for bulk and area requirements and design of buildings.

I. Prohibitions—general categories of activities or uses that are prohibited in all districts.

Article VI: Special Use Permits

A. Purpose—sets forth the reasons for allowing special uses in a given district. Generally, because of their characteristics or the unique characteristics of the area in which they are to be located, special uses require careful consideration so that they may be properly located. Chapter will designate the planning board/commission or another administrative body to issue special use permits.

B. Submission of Application—may state that an application for a special use must be submitted to the zoning administrator along with the proper fee.

C. General Standards—establishes requirements applicable to all special uses. To grant a special use permit, the board must find:

1. that the proposed use is in harmony with the general purpose and intent of the land use chapter;

2. that there will be adequate access for fire and police protection;

3. that the streets serving the proposed use are adequate to carry prospective traffic and will not cause a traffic hazard or undue traffic congestion;

4. that the lot on which the use is to be located is of sufficient size and adequate dimension to permit the use in a manner not detrimental to surrounding property;

5. that the buildings, structures, facilities, and site layout will be adequately landscaped and maintained; and

6. that the proposed use, buildings and structures will not be detrimental to the public health, and safety, or to property values of the neighborhood.

Article VII: Planning Board/Commission

A. Establishment—authorizes the municipal legislature to create a planning board or commission. May also establish terms of office and eligibility for service.

B. Powers and Duties—sets forth the board's responsibilities, including the review of applications for certain land use approvals such as land subdivision, site plan approval, or special use permit applications.

C. Procedure—establishes the procedure for planning board review of various actions. May also provide procedure for referral of certain land use decisions to the county planning board.

D. Public Notice and Hearing—details the procedure utilized by the planning board to notify the public of hearings, meetings, and other actions.

Article VIII: Zoning Board of Appeals

A. Establishment—creates a zoning board of appeals, specifying the number of members who may serve. May also establish terms of office and eligibility for service.

B. Powers and Duties—sets forth the board's responsibilities, including hearing and reviewing appeals from any order, requirement, decision, or determination made by the zoning administrator. May provide that the board shall hear and decide applications for certain types of land use approvals and issue variances. Grants the board the authority to interpret the zoning law; many communities also provide the board with the authority to prescribe conditions in the granting of any special use permit or variance to preserve the general purpose and intent of the land use chapter.

C. Procedure—establishes the procedural requirements for actions before the board. Requires applications be in writing and to refer to the specific provisions of the law involved. Requires referral of applications to the local planning board and in certain instances to the county or regional planning board.

D. Public Notice and Hearing—requires that the zoning board of appeals to provide proper public notice. Fixes a reasonable time for a public hearing of any appeal or other matter referred to it.

Article IX: Administration and Enforcement

A. Zoning Administrator—establishes an administrative officer who has the authority and responsibility to administer and enforce the provisions of the zoning and land use chapter or law. Duties generally include the review and approval of all development permits (building permits, certificates of occupancy, wetland permits, etc.), the issuance of stop-work orders, and the maintenance of records and site inspection. Some communities charge the municipal building inspector with the administration of the zoning and land use chapter or law.

B. Building Permits—establishes that no building or structure in any district shall be erected, reconstructed or restored, structurally altered, or used without a building permit. Requires that the proposed construction conform to the provisions of the zoning and land use chapter before a building permit will be issued. Also establishes the information to be included in the application and application procedure.

C. Certificates of Occupancy—explains that a certificate of occupancy must be received before a structure is used or occupied. Attests to the fact that the actual construction is in conformance with the Uniform Fire Prevention and Building Code and is satisfactory for occupancy or use.

D. Penalties for Offenses—sets forth the penalties that may be levied for violations of the land use chapter or law, including fines and jail sentences.

E. Schedule of Fees—establishes that fees shall be paid on the filing of any application, in accordance with the fee schedule established by the municipal legislature.

Article X: Amendments

Amendment Procedure—sets forth the procedural requirements for amending the land use chapter or law. Generally states that the chapter or law may be amended, changed, modified, or repealed by the local legislature on its own initiative, on recommendation of the planning board, or on petition. Proposed amendments are subject to public notice and hearing requirements and must also be referred to the planning board for its recommendations.

By reference to the particular zoning chapter, the interested attorney can understand the standards and steps required for amending the zoning ordinance, the issuance of special or conditional permits, the award of use and area variances, the extent to which accessory uses or home occupations are permitted, whether and for how long uses that do not conform to new zoning standards can be continued, and other flexibility devices, such as the Planned Unit Development device, that can be employed to breathe flexibility into zoning administration. The attorney can also learn about the ministerial officers and administrative boards that play central roles in the execution of the zoning policies and procedures of the community. The zoning enforcement officer can interpret zoning provisions and issue rulings regarding the ordinance, these may be appealed to the board of appeals, and administrative agencies may be designated to decide on applications by landowners for variances, special or conditional permits, or approval to subdivide land or develop individual parcels.

In drafting and adopting zoning provisions, the local legislature must establish sufficient standards to guide the administrative review boards. In Hardin County v. Jost, 897 S.W.2d 592 (Ky.App.1995), the entire county was placed in one zone and every land use, except agriculture, was designated as a conditional use. To determine whether a conditional use permit would be issued, a point system under a "growth guidance assessment" scheme was utilized. The court found the entire ordinance invalid in that sufficient standards were not set forth, and the ordinance left land use "to the subjective whim and caprice of the zoning authority." In City of Virginia Beach v. Virginia Land Investment Ass'n No. 1, 239 Va. 412, 389 S.E.2d 312 (1990), the court held that the rezoning of some 400 acres of land from planned unit development to agricultural was invalid as piecemeal downzoning not justified by change in circumstances or prior mistake.

B. AMENDMENT OF ORDINANCE

CHURCH v. TOWN OF ISLIP

Court of Appeals of New York, 1960.
8 N.Y.2d 254, 203 N.Y.S.2d 866, 168 N.E.2d 680.

CHIEF JUDGE DESMOND.

Neighboring property owners brought this declaratory judgment suit against the Town of Islip in Suffolk County and against its Town Board and the owners of the involved property to have declared unconstitutional and void a 1954 zoning change (from Residence A to Business) of defendants Housler's corner lot in Islip, irregular in shape and about 210 feet on Bay Shore Road and 230 feet on Udall's Road. The complaint charged that the amendment was not in conformity with a comprehensive plan, that it was passed arbitrarily after a contrary recommendation by the Town Planning Board, that it arbitrarily singled out this one tract for business zoning, and that it was illegal as "contract zoning" because the Town Board's consent to the change of zone was subject to the condition that defendants owners Housler agree to the following:

1. The building shall not total more than 25% of the area.

2. An anchor post fence, or equal, six feet high, is to be erected five feet within the boundary line of the property.

3. Live Shrubbery, 3 feet high either within or outside of the fence is to be planted, and allowed to grow to the height of the fence and after that, to be maintained at the height of the fence.

4. The above must be performed or put in operation before carrying on any retail business on the property.

The trial was before an Official Referee who at the request of counsel inspected the properties of plaintiffs and defendants. He found for plaintiffs. He described the neighborhood as residential in use and zoning except for a substantial business zone on Bay Shore Road, one block east of the Housler property. He wrote that there were a number of unoccupied stores in that nearby business section, that there was not shown any need for rezoning the Housler lot for business, that the change was illegal "spot zoning", and that the imposition by the Town Board of conditions was illegal "contract zoning".

Defendants appealed to the Appellate Division which by a divided vote reversed on the law and facts and gave judgment declaring the amendment to be valid. The majority pointed out that this was a statutory change by the town's legislative body, that the Referee's finding of no public need or convenience was contrary to the evidence and that in any event the Town Board's legislative finding was conclusive since supported by a factual basis, that the evidence showed the Housler parcel to be located on a main traffic artery, that community growth pressures forcing zoning changes negatived the idea that the Town Board's action was arbitrary or without reason, and that there was nothing illegal about the Town Board's subjecting the new district to uses more restricted than customarily permitted in a business district. The court took notice of the recent enormous population increases in Nassau and Suffolk Counties and of the "consequent multiplication of practical problems presented to local legislative bodies by a deluge of applications for zoning district changes which are prompted by the necessities of such growth". Continuing, the Appellate Division said that "It is understandable that in the public interest and in the interest of practical expediency the practice of granting zoning changes and conditioning their uses by means of privately imposed restrictive covenants has seemingly become widespread [citing cases]." The majority denied that "such practice is contrary to the spirit of zoning ordinances" or "beyond the statutory powers of local legislative bodies".

The dissent, citing sections 262–265 of the Town Law, said that changes in zones by the Town Board could be made only according to a comprehensive plan, whereas this change was subject to special conditions imposed on this property only. The Presiding Justice thought this to be illegal and that it amounted to zoning by contract. He thought, further, that the owners had not complied with the conditions and that they are unenforcible [sic] anyhow since they were either invalidly agreed to in consideration of the zoning change or were not supported by any consideration. In this connection, see the reply brief where plaintiffs expressly concede that the owners Housler have complied with the conditions by recording an appropriate agreement.

We start with the proposition that this zoning being a legislative act (not a variance) is entitled to the strongest possible presumption of validity and must stand if there was any factual basis therefore (*Shepard v. Village of Skaneateles,* 300 N.Y. 115; *Wiggins v. Town of Somers,* 4 N.Y.2d 215). The Town Board's action in this instance was unanimous.

Appellants do not seem to question the Appellate Division's fact findings. It is undisputed that Bay Shore Road has become a busy arterial highway with a traffic light at this corner and that the very Town Planning Board which recommended against this zoning change recommended a shopping area (now established) only 600 feet from this parcel on Bay Shore Road. On the issue of arbitrariness, there was reliable testimony that all of Bay Shore Road would be eventually zoned for business and that this trend could not be stopped, that the subject property is more desirable for business use than for residential, and that there was nothing arbitrary, preferential or discriminatory about the Town Board action, unanimously voted after hearing and deliberation.

Appellants' arguments all revolve about the idea that this is illegal as "contract zoning" because the Town Board, as a condition for rezoning, required the owners to execute and record restrictive covenants as to maximum area to be occupied by buildings and as to a fence and shrubbery. Surely these conditions were intended to be and are for the benefit of the neighbors. Since the Town Board could have, presumably, zoned this Bay Shore Road corner for business without any restrictions, we fail to see how reasonable conditions invalidate the legislation. Since the owners have accepted them, there is no one in a position to contest them. Exactly what "contract zoning" means is unclear and there is really no New York law on the subject. All legislation "by contract" is invalid in the sense that a Legislature cannot bargain away or sell its powers. But we deal here with actualities, not phrases. To meet increasing needs of Suffolk County's own population explosion, and at the same time to make as gradual and as little of an annoyance as possible the change from residence to business on the main highways, the Town Board imposes conditions. There is nothing unconstitutional about it. Incidentally, the record does not show any agreement in the sense that the owners made an offer accepted by the board.

The judgment should be affirmed, without costs.

FROESSEL, J. (Dissenting).

I dissent and vote to reverse for the reasons stated in Presiding Justice Nolan's dissenting opinion below with respect to the Town Board's lack of power. The board is authorized by the Town Law to create districts subject to this condition: "All such regulations [within a district] shall be *uniform* for each class or kind of buildings, throughout such district" (§ 262), and "shall be made in accordance with a *comprehensive plan*" (§ 263: emphasis supplied). The purpose of a plan is to look ahead. Piecemeal, parcel by parcel, conditional zoning pending the adoption of a plan is unauthorized. Variances in appropriate situations may be granted by Zoning Boards of Appeal but only under prescribed safeguards (§§ 261, 267). The power exercised by the Town Board is without warrant in law.

JUDGES DYE, FULD, BURKE and FOSTER concur with CHIEF JUDGE DESMOND; JUDGE FROESSEL dissents in an opinion in which JUDGE VAN VOORHIS concurs.

Judgment affirmed.

Notes

1. Conditional zoning, in the sense that certain conditions are "unilaterally" imposed on the premises by the city in order for rezoning to become effective, or in the sense that the land is rezoned conditionally and subject to revocation of the action if the conditions are not met, has been upheld in Wisconsin, Kansas, Nebraska, Massachusetts, New York, North Carolina, and some other jurisdictions. But a number of jurisdictions, particularly in the South, have rejected conditional rezoning as being the same as contract rezoning or as amounting to spot zoning. A key issue is whether there is really a distinction and whether conditions are in fact imposed unilaterally by the city without there first having been a bargaining or negotiating process. A further question might be whether it should matter as to whether there is a discussion process which takes on the colorations of negotiation or bargaining.

2. Neither the Standard Zoning Enabling Act nor the enabling legislation of most states contemplated the problem of contract or conditional rezoning. Some state legislatures have sought to provide authority for this device in order to promote flexibility in rezoning. In 1973, for example, the Indiana legislature amended its enabling legislation (Public Law No. 185, April 23, 1973):

> Section 1 IC 1971, 18–7–2–20 is amended to read as follows: Sec. 20. To effectuate the purposes of this chapter, the metropolitan plan commission shall have the power and duty to:
>
> * * *
>
> 17. If deemed advisable by the commission, require or allow the owner of any parcel of property, in connection with any petition for amendment to the zoning ordinance changing the zoning classification of that parcel, to make written commitments relative to the use or development of that parcel of property. The commission shall have power to establish rules and regulations governing the creation, form, and recording of commitments and the designation of specially affected persons and categories of specially affected persons entitled to enforce commitments. Commitments shall be recorded in the office of the County Recorder and shall be effective upon adoption of the amendment to the zoning ordinance. Commitments, unless modified or terminated by the commission as hereinafter provided, shall be binding on the owner, subsequent owners of the parcel of property and other persons acquiring an interest therein. Commitments may be modified or terminated by the decision of the commission made at a public hearing after notice as provided by the rules and regulations. The requiring or allowing of such commitments shall not obligate the commission to take any official action nor shall it limit the power of the commission to take any official action regarding the parcel of property. The provisions of this subsection shall not affect the validity of any covenant, easement, equitable servitude or other land use restriction which is presently in effect or may be created in accordance with law.

3. Consider the following definitions of conditional zoning and contract zoning. Conditional zoning is a device employed to bring some flexibility of use to an otherwise rigid system of control. "Conditional Zoning" involves ordinances which provide either that rezoning becomes effective immediately with an automatic repealer if the specified conditions are not met, or that the zoning become effective only upon conditions being met within a certain time. This type of zoning seeks to minimize the potentially deleterious effect of a zone change on neighboring properties through reasonably conceived conditions which harmonize the landowner's need for rezoning with the public interest. 83 Am. Jur. 2d Zoning and Planning § 162. On the other hand, illegal contract zoning properly connotes a transaction wherein both the landowner who is seeking a certain zoning action and the zoning authority itself undertake reciprocal obligations in the context of a bilateral contract. See Hall v. City of Durham, 323 N.C. 293, 372 S.E.2d 564 (1988).

GIGER v. CITY OF OMAHA

Supreme Court of Nebraska, 1989.
232 Neb. 676, 442 N.W.2d 182.

WHITE, JUSTICE.

This appeal involves two lawsuits relating to a development known as One Pacific Place. The development is being constructed on an 84–acre tract of land formerly owned by Carl Renstrom located in southwest Omaha. The land, hereafter the Renstrom property, is approximately triangular in shape, bordered on the north by Pacific Street, on the east by the Happy Hollow and Sunset Hills residential developments, on the southwest by the Big Papillion Creek, and on the west by 105th Street.

In March 1983, appellee Midlands Development Company (Midlands) entered into a real estate purchase agreement with the Renstrom estate for the purchase of the property. Midlands then applied to the city to have the Renstrom property rezoned to permit the construction of a mixed-use development consisting of retail, office, and residential buildings. As part of the application process, Midlands submitted several development plans. A final plan was developed which indicated the following uses for 48 acres of the tract: 112,000 square feet of retail-space, 390,000 square feet of office space, 558,000 square feet of parking space, 300 residential units, a private lake, and a planned unit development (PUD). The plan also called for the construction of a public park on the remaining 36 acres to be deeded by Midlands to the city. In a "new procedure," Midlands and the city entered into four agreements incorporating the plan. The four agreements, collectively known as the development agreement, were submitted to the city for approval. In February 1985, the city passed an ordinance approving the development agreement, incorporating it as part of the ordinance, and passed five separate ordinances rezoning the Renstrom property. Building permits were then issued, including a permit allowing Midlands to fill in the flood plain of the Big Papillion Creek located on the land and to make modifications to the creek channel.

Construction on the site began approximately in September of 1985. Thereafter, two lawsuits were filed in the district court for Douglas County: *Giger et al. v. City of Omaha et al.,* filed by neighboring property owners, and *Witherspoon et al. v. City of Omaha et al.,* filed by downstream riparian property owners living along the Big Papillion Creek. The two petitions requested an order declaring the city's rezoning ordinance and accompanying building permits void, and an injunction to enjoin Midlands from developing the property in any manner inconsistent with prior zoning ordinances. The suits were ordered consolidated for trial. After a lengthy trial, the trial court denied the plaintiffs' requested relief.

Though the plaintiffs-appellants assign a total of 15 errors, these errors are consolidated into three issues for consideration on appeal. The first two issues relate to appellants' contention that the trial court erred in not finding that the Omaha City Council acted in an arbitrary, capricious, and unreasonable manner in adopting the rezoning ordinance. Specifically, the appellants allege that the city entered into a development agreement with Midlands, adopted a rezoning ordinance which incorporated that agreement, and rezoned the Renstrom property pursuant to that agreement and that the city adopted the rezoning ordinance without giving adequate consideration to the risk of flood created by the project. The last issue involves appellants' claim that the trial court erred in not granting a permanent injunction enjoining Midlands from filling the flood plain on the Renstrom property and altering the channel of the Big Papillion Creek.

* * *

The first argument raised by the appellants is that the city, by adopting a rezoning ordinance pursuant to an agreement between itself and Midlands, acted in an arbitrary, capricious, and unreasonable manner. In support of this argument, the appellants challenge the validity of the rezoning ordinance on two grounds. They assert, first, that rezoning by agreement is invalid per se and, second, that the rezoning ordinance violates the substantive standards set out in §§ 14–402 and 14–403.

Specifically, the appellants contend that because rezoning by agreement is illegal contract rezoning, it is invalid per se, is an ultra vires act, and fosters an "appearance of evil." They allege illegal contract rezoning occurred because the city bargained away and sold its police power. The appellants do not cite any Nebraska authority for this proposition and claim that this court has never faced a true contract zoning situation. However, we note that *Bucholz v. City of Omaha, supra,* a case where the city conditioned its granting of a rezoning ordinance on the developer's entering into a protective covenant, has been characterized as an example of contract rezoning. 2 R. Anderson, American Law of Zoning § 9.21 (3d ed. 1986); 1 N. Williams & J. Taylor, American Planning Law, Land Use and the Police Power § 29.03 (rev. 1988). Yet, *Bucholz* has also been labeled as an example of a conditional rezoning. Annot., 70 A.L.R.3d 125, 162 (1976); 2 A. Rathkopf & D. Rathkopf, Rathkopf's the

Law of Zoning and Planning § 27.05 (rev. 1989); Note, *The Validity of Conditional Zoning: a Florida Perspective,* 31 U.Fla.L.Rev. 968, 971 n. 21 (1979); Comment, *Land Use—Goffinet v. County of Christian: New Flexibility in Illinois Zoning Law,* 8 Loy.U.Chi.L.J. 642, 643 n. 15 (1977). This distinction is academic because our scope of review, as explained below, is limited to determining whether the conditions imposed by the city for rezoning are reasonably related to the interest of public health, safety, morals, and the general welfare.

This court realizes that in the development of a project such as One Pacific Place there are negotiations between the developer and the city. We are also aware that a city rezones property based on representations made and plans submitted by the developer. However, once a parcel of land has been rezoned, there is no guarantee the developer will follow through on the plans submitted to the city. Legally, the developer is entitled to use his or her land in any manner permitted by the zoning classification. Of course, the city would not be without a remedy if the land was used in a manner not contemplated in the original plans submitted by the developer. The city could rezone the property to another designation and then institute the appropriate proceedings to prevent the unwanted development. See Neb.Rev.Stat. § 14–415 (Reissue 1987).

However, as *Cummings Enterprises v. Shukert,* 231 Neb. 370, 436 N.W.2d 199 (1989), indicates, this is not always an effective remedy. In *Cummings Enterprises,* the developer's land was rezoned from second suburban district to first commercial. He applied for a building permit for a carwash, a permissible use under that classification, and his request was denied. Subsequently, the city rezoned the developer's property to a classification which excluded carwashes. The developer successfully sued for a writ of mandamus ordering the issuance of the building permit. The city issued the permit, and the developer built the carwash. We held that the city had waived its right to appeal the order, since it voluntarily complied with the order instead of obtaining a supersedeas.

In addition, this court gives great deference to the city's determination of which laws should be enacted for the welfare of the people. *Wolf v. City of Omaha, supra; City of Omaha v. Glissmann, supra.* When the city rezones a parcel of property, we presume the validity of that action absent clear and satisfactory evidence to the contrary. *Bucholz v. City of Omaha,* 174 Neb. 862, 120 N.W.2d 270 (1963); *Davis v. City of Omaha,* 153 Neb. 460, 45 N.W.2d 172 (1950). Therefore, when the city considers a request for rezoning based upon a plan or representation by the developer, it is presumed that the city grants the request after making the determination that the plan as represented is in the interest of public health, safety, morals, and the general welfare. We do not think a developer should be allowed to develop property in a manner inconsistent with the plan or representation on which the rezoning was based, despite the fact that the inconsistent use may be permissible under the new zoning classification. By developing the property in a manner not contemplated by the city in granting the rezoning classification, the developer contravenes a decision made by the city pursuant to its police power for the benefit of the community. If the city is limited to only enacting bare zoning ordinances and is not permitted to insist that developers construct buffer zones or make other changes in order to blend the development into the surrounding community, the city will be stripped of the power to act for the benefit of the general welfare. Accordingly, the city should be permitted to condition rezoning ordinances on the adoption of an agreement between the developer and the city, or any other means assuring the developer builds the project as represented. At the risk of confusion, but for the sake of convenience, we will refer to this zoning arrangement as conditional zoning. As Rathkopf notes:

> The purpose [of conditional rezoning] is to minimize the negative externalities caused by land development which otherwise benefits the community. The developer may agree to restrict development of its property, make certain improvements, dedicate a portion of land to the municipality, or make payments to the government. Conditional rezoning is valuable as a planning tool because it permits a municipality greater flexibility in balancing developmental demands against fiscal and environmental concerns. It also provides a municipality with flexibility to meet specific rezoning requests while preserving the integrity of adjacent property. For instance, the agreement can mitigate the harshness of commercial or industrial rezoning on neighboring residential property by requiring a buffer on the zone boundaries. Finally, conditional rezoning allows a municipality to maintain greater control over the development process.

2 A. Rathkopf & D. Rathkopf, Rathkopf's the Law of Zoning and Planning § 27.05 at 27–45 to 27–46 (rev. 1989). Thus, this device allows the city flexibility to extract improvements that bare zoning ordinances do not provide, grants a greater means of control over the development to the city, and gives the city a remedy to enforce the developer's plans and representations. Theoretically, if the rezoning ordinance adopts the plan, as in this case, the city could institute legal proceedings if the developer builds a project inconsistent with the plans without resorting to rezoning the property. For the foregoing reasons we hold conditional rezoning to be valid. Our holding today is a reflection of the trend started in this jurisdiction by *Bucholz* and the growing movement in this country permitting conditional rezonings. 2 A. Rathkopf & D. Rathkopf, *supra.*

However, our holding recognizing the validity of conditional rezoning is not without limitation. Conditional rezoning is a legislative function and therefore must be within the proper exercise of the police power. Accordingly, the conditions imposed by the city for the rezoning must be reasonably related to the interest of public health, safety, morals, and the general welfare. See, e.g., *Treme v. St. Louis County,* 609 S.W.2d 706 (Mo.App.1980) (where offer made or exaction demanded for rezoning bears no reasonable relationship to activities of developer, action of county or municipality in rezoning property in exchange for such offer or exaction is contracting away of police power, which is forbidden); *State ex rel. Myhre v. Spokane,* 70 Wash.2d 207, 422 P.2d 790 (1967) (amendment to zoning ordinance and concomitant agreement should be declared invalid only if it can be shown that there was no valid reason for change, that they are clearly arbitrary and unreasonable and have no substantial relation to public health, safety, morals, and general welfare, or that city is using concomitant agreement for bargaining and sale to highest bidder or solely for the benefit of private speculators). See 2 A. Rathkopf & D. Rathkopf, *supra.* Hence, to successfully challenge the validity of conditional rezoning, the appellants must prove that the conditions imposed by the city in adopting the rezoning ordinance were unreasonable, discriminatory, or arbitrary, and that the regulation bears no relationship to the purpose or purposes sought to be accomplished by the ordinance. This is the same test used for testing the validity of zoning ordinances in this jurisdiction. See, *Wolf v. City of Omaha,* 177 Neb. 545, 129 N.W.2d 501 (1964); *Bucholz v. City of Omaha,* 174 Neb. 862, 120 N.W.2d 270 (1963); *City of Omaha v. Cutchall,* 173 Neb. 452, 114 N.W.2d 6 (1962); *City of Omaha v. Glissmann,* 151 Neb. 895, 39 N.W.2d 828 (1949); *Cassel Realty Co. v. City of Omaha,* 144 Neb. 753, 14 N.W.2d 600 (1944). "The validity of a zoning ordinance will be presumed in the absence of clear and satisfactory evidence to the contrary." *Bucholz v. City of Omaha, supra* 174 Neb. at 865–66, 120 N.W.2d at 273, citing *Davis v. City of Omaha,* 153 Neb. 460, 45 N.W.2d 172 (1950).

The appellants argue that by entering into the development agreement the city has curtailed or bargained away its police powers because (1) the agreement prohibits amendment without the consent of the developer; (2) the city is committed to approve a PUD "without any present indication as to what such PUD's might contain"; (3) the city is obligated to issue building permits "without regard to compliance with other building codes, rules and regulations of the City"; (4) the city is required to spend $64,700 for offsite improvements; (5) the agreement mandates the manner in which the city is to levy special assessments for the payments of these improvements; and (6) "[t]hroughout the Subdivision Agreement [one of the agreements in the development agreement], the City obligates itself to deal in many ways involving its legislative and administrative authority with a *non-existent* Sanitary and Improvement District to be created in the future." Brief for appellants Witherspoon et al. at 18–19. However, the plain language in the provisions of the development agreement contradict appellants' contentions.

* * *

Simply stated, the agreement expressly provides that Midlands may vary the development only if the city does not find the variation deviates from the development plan and the variations do not violate any provision of the Omaha Municipal Code. Clearly, under this agreement, the powers of the city are unchanged. We fail to see how the development agreement can be construed as bargaining away the city's police power.

In fact, this agreement is in reality an enhancement of the city's police power. An examination of the development agreement and the evidence at trial establishes that the agreement provides more restrictive ceilings and development regulations than the current underlying zoning regulations. For example, a portion of the development, where the office buildings will be located, has been rezoned to ninth residence district (R–9). Absent the agreement, according to Omaha Mun.Code, ch. 55, art. XV, §§ 55–311 et seq. (1983), under the R–9 classification Midlands is free to erect any number of office buildings with no real limitations on the amount of square footage. Here, the agreement restricts Midlands to a maximum of three office buildings and a total of 390,000 square feet of office space.

In sum, we find that there is not clear and satisfactory evidence to support the appellants' contention that the city has bargained away its police power. The evidence clearly shows that the city's police powers are not abridged in any manner and that the agreement is expressly subject to the remedies available to the city under the Omaha Municipal Code. Further, we find that the agreement actually enhances the city's regulatory control over the development rather than limiting it.

The appellants' second contention is that the city engaged in an ultra vires act because there is no statutory enabling act permitting conditional rezoning. * * * In addition to having the power to enact zoning regulations, the city also has the power to amend, supplement, change, modify, or repeal those regulations. § 14–405. Further, § 14–403 in part provides:

> Whenever the City council shall determine that the use or contemplated use of any building, structure or land will cause congestion in the streets, increase danger from fire or panic, imperil public safety, cause undue concentration or congregation of people, or impede transportation, the council may include in such regulations requirements for alleviating or preventing such conditions when any change in use or zoning classification is requested by the owner.

It is axiomatic that zoning is a local concern. In light of this, plus the fact that the Legislature has used the general term "regulations" without explicitly delineating what regulations the city is permitted to use, coupled with a grant of power to the city to implement, amend, supplement, change, modify, or repeal those regulations, it is clear that the Legislature has given the city broad powers to regulate land uses within its jurisdiction as long as those regulations are within the police power. Thus, we find in chapter 14 of the Nebraska Revised Statutes an implied grant of power to the city to enact all necessary zoning regulations, including conditional rezoning, as long as those regulations are within the proper exercise of the police power.

The third contention by the appellants is that the city fostered an "appearance of evil" by engaging in conditional rezoning. They allege that conditional rezoning could result in corruption of officials and that if the practice is permitted, officials will concentrate more on what they can extract from the developer than on proper rezoning criteria. This argument lacks merit. The appellants admit there is no evidence of graft or corruption in the case at bar, and we believe our holding is more than adequate to protect against any alleged abuse of this type. We will not strike down a conditional zoning because it looks evil, but only if its application is evil. Accordingly, appellants' challenge to this conditional rezoning as invalid fails.

* * *

The appellants assert that the rezoning ordinance violates the uniformity provision in § 14–402 because the agreement results in concessions for both the city and Midlands which are not allowed to other developers. As an example, appellants state in their brief that " '[n]o other developers in the City' have 'been required to give a park for free to the City in exchange for rezoning.' " Brief for appellants Witherspoon et al. at 14. We note that the uniformity requirement in § 14–402 is derived from § 2 of the Standard State Zoning Enabling Act and that almost every jurisdiction has incorporated this limitation into its state zoning enabling legislation. 1 R. Anderson, American Law of Zoning § 5.25 (3d ed. 1986). In his treatise on zoning, Anderson states that there have been few cases interpreting the uniformity requirement and that attacks on conditional rezoning as being violative of the uniformity requirement have "not been notably successful." 2 R. Anderson, American Law of Zoning § 9.20 at 164 (3d ed. 1986); 1 R. Anderson, *supra,* § 5.25. The jurisdictions that have addressed the uniformity requirement have analyzed the challenged ordinances to see if they are reasonable and not discriminatory. 1 R. Anderson, *supra,* § 5.25. For instance, in *Mont. Co. v. Woodward & Lothrop,* 280 Md. 686, 719–20, 376 A.2d 483, 501 (1977), the court, construing a uniform provision comparable to Nebraska's, said:

> The uniformity provision contained in Art. 66D, § 8–102 was derived from § 2 of the Standard State Zoning Enabling Act, as to which it was said in 1 Anderson, *American Law of Zoning,* § 5.22 (2d ed. 1976), that the purpose of the provision was mainly a political rather than a legal one, *i.e.,* to give notice to property owners that there shall be no improper discriminations. [Citations omitted.] We have also recognized that invidious distinctions and discriminations in applying the uniformity requirement are impermissible. [Citations omitted.] The uniformity requirement does not prohibit classification within a district, so long as it is reasonable and based upon the public policy to be served.

See, *Oshtemo Twp v. Central Ad. Co.,* 125 Mich.App. 538, 336 N.W.2d 823 (1983) (township rural zoning act, providing that zoning ordinance provisions must be uniform for each class of land, buildings, dwellings, and structures throughout the district, is subject to "reasonableness" exception, allowing reasonable restrictions based upon different conditions within the zone); *Quinton v. Edison Park Development Corp.*, 59 N.J. 571, 285 A.2d 5 (1971) (statute which required that zoning regulations be uniform for each class or kind of buildings or other structures or uses of land throughout each district does not prohibit classifications within a district so long as they are reasonable).

We think allowing reasonable classifications within a district is a good rule, especially in view of the broad delegation of authority given by the Legislature to the city in making zoning regulations, as set forth above. Accordingly, the uniformity requirement in § 14–402 does not prohibit reasonable classifications within a district. To successfully challenge the rezoning ordinance on the grounds it violates the uniformity requirement of § 14–402, the appellants must prove that the actions of the city in adopting the rezoning ordinance were unreasonable, discriminatory, or arbitrary, and that the regulation bears no relationship to the purpose or purposes sought to be accomplished by the ordinance.

Other than pointing to the provisions of the agreement itself, the appellants cite no evidence in support of their claim that the rezoning action violates the uniformity requirement. Implicit in appellants' proposition is the assumption that no other developer will be able to take advantage of conditional rezoning. Today's holding clearly refutes that assumption. The appellants have failed to show by clear and satisfactory evidence, *Bucholz v. City of Omaha*, 174 Neb. 862, 120 N.W.2d 270 (1963), and *Davis v. City of Omaha*, 153 Neb. 460, 45 N.W.2d 172 (1950), that the city acted in an unreasonable, discriminatory, or arbitrary manner, and that the regulation bears no relationship to the purpose sought to be accomplished by the ordinance.

* * *

[Significant portions of the case dealing with whether the rezoning is invalid because it devalues nearby properties or fails to meet the "in conformance with the comprehensive plan" requirement are omitted. The court determined that it was not invalid for these reasons.]

Note

The issue of whether, and to what extent, struggling cities may use their delegated planning and zoning authority to negotiate with developers about the redevelopment of urban neighborhoods is taken up in Chapter VIII, Housing and Urban Development. This case involves a development agreement between a developer and the city that is incorporated by reference into the rezoning of the developer's land. The court holds that the provisions of the agreement, which impose stricter standards on the developer than the zoning itself, can be upheld as valid conditional zoning, even though the conditions are contained in a separate and extensive development agreement. The court sees in the development agreement an opportunity to further the general welfare by granting the city more control over development than is ordinarily available through the bare provisions of a zoning ordinance. It illustrates this by citing provisions of the agreement that restrict the developer to fewer office buildings and less square footage of office space than the zoning itself allows. This flexible technique, like conditional zoning itself, is found by the court to be within the implied authority of the city under the zoning enabling act.

MONTGOMERY COUNTY v. NATIONAL CAPITAL REALTY CORP.

Court of Appeals of Maryland, 1972.
267 Md. 364, 297 A.2d 675.

[The property owner sought rezoning from C–O, commercial office building, to C–2, general commercial. The planning staff recommended disapproval of the application, primarily on grounds of the height and ground coverage permissible in the C–2 zone. The Planning Board rejected the staff recommendation and approved the application after the applicant submitted a set of covenants, conditions and restrictions which would "become effective upon the approval" of the zoning application. The local legislative body reversed the Planning Board, relying on a memorandum from the County Attorney to the effect that conditional zoning was not allowed in Montgomery County. The trial court reversed and ordered approval of the application, and the county appealed.]

LEVINE, JUDGE.

* * *

Entirely apart from the "change" argument, we think resolution of the question whether the covenants constituted a form of impermissible conditional zoning is decisive of this case. For, as we have seen, by a determination of that point in appellant's favor, two of the main props to appellee's case would topple, i.e., the favorable recommendations of the Planning Board and Mr. Hussmann, respectively. This would then confront appellee with unfavorable positions of the staff and Hussmann and without any public agency support.

We think it clear that the covenants, coupled with the site plan attached thereto, if adopted as a basis for the requested reclassification, would have produced a form of conditional zoning. If recorded, the covenants would have bound appellee to compliance only on the condition that the C–2 classification first had been granted. Had the Council then granted the application on the strength of the covenants, as encouraged to do so by Mr. Hussmann and the Planning Board it would have committed what we believe would have been a classic illustration of conditional zoning. The invalidity of conditional zoning in Maryland is not seriously open to question. Citizens Ass'n v. Pr. Geo. County, 222 Md. 44, 158 A.2d 663 (1960); Rose v. Paape, 221 Md. 369, 376–377, 157 A.2d 618 (1960); Baylis v. City of Baltimore, 219 Md. 164, 169–170, 148 A.2d 429 (1959). It is interesting to note that in none of those cases was there cited a provision comparable to § 111–48(d) of the Montgomery County Zoning Ordinance also codified by that same designation in the Montgomery County Code, 1965, which provides:

"No application for a local or a sectional or District plan map amendment shall be approved conditionally for the erection on the land of a structure at a particular location, or within a particular time, or by a particular person, or of a particular type, or for the subdivision of the land in a particular manner, or on any other condition."

In 3 Rathkopf, Zoning and Planning 74–9, it is stated:

> "* * * The general rule in these jurisdictions in which the validity of such covenants has been litigated is that they are illegal. The basis of such rule is that the rezoning of a particular parcel of land upon conditions not imposed by the zoning ordinance generally in the particular district into which the land has been rezoned is prima facie evidence of 'spot zoning' in its most maleficent aspect, is not in accordance with a comprehensive plan and is beyond the power of the municipality."
>
> "Legislative bodies must rezone in accordance with a comprehensive plan, and in amending the ordinance so as to confer upon a particular parcel a particular district designation, it may not curtail or limit the uses and structures placed or to be placed upon the lands so rezoned differently from those permitted upon other lands in the same district. Consequently, where there has been a concatenated rezoning and filing of a 'declaration of restrictions' the general view (where the question has been litigated) is that both the zoning amendment and the restrictive covenant are invalid for the reasons expressed above."

Although the rule followed in Maryland has undergone erosion in some states we believe that it continues to be supported by the weight of authority.

Nor is appellee helped by our decisions in Funger v. Mayor of Somerset, 249 Md. 311, 328, 239 A.2d 748 (1968) and Greenbelt v. Bresler, 248 Md. 210, 215–216, 236 A.2d 1 (1967). What distinguishes those cases from those we have cited earlier is that in each, the municipality within which the subject land was located agreed to support the rezoning application before the respective county legislative body in exchange for certain commitments entered into by the applicant. Thus, since in both cases the legislative body was not a party to the agreement, neither the rezoning nor the agreement was invalidated. For the reasons we have stated, the Council was correct in refusing to grant the rezoning upon the conditions expressed in the Declaration of Covenants and the attached site plan.

Nothing we have said in distinguishing *Funger* and *Greenbelt* from the cases involving agreements entered into by legislative bodies supports enforceability of the covenants here by the Planning Board, since, as we have noted, the covenants were to become binding on appellee only if the Council granted the application. In short, we are concerned here merely with the fact that the Planning Board's favorable report was predicated solely on the existence of covenants which, in light of our holding, were worthless. Thus, they imparted the same value to the recommendation of the Board. What we have just said doubtlessly applies with greater force to Mr. Hussmann's recommendation, as he, being a county employee and in no respect a party to the covenants, gratuitously considered them in arriving at his favorable conclusion. Thus, we think the Council was correct in refusing to rely upon the covenants while deciding the zoning application, and the favorable recommendation of the Planning Board and Mr. Hussmann were entitled to no weight.

* * *

Order reversed.

Notes

1. Some state legislatures have sought to relax the prohibition of conditional zoning by providing statutory authority. Note that the principal case was superseded by statute as stated in Mayor and Council of Rockville v. Rylyns Enterprises, Inc., 372 Md. 514, 814 A.2d 469 (2002). In 1970, Maryland's state legislature amended the zoning enabling authority by enacting Section 4.01 of Article 66B which states:

> (B) The local legislative body of a county or municipal corporation, upon the zoning or rezoning or any land * * * may impose such additional restrictions, conditions, or limitations as may be deemed appropriate to preserve, improve, or protect the general character and design of the lands and improvements being zoned or rezoned, or of the surrounding or adjacent lands and improvements, and may, upon the zoning or rezoning or any land or lands, retain ore reserve the power and authority to approve or disapprove the design or buildings, construction, landscaping or other improvements, alterations, and changes made or to be made on the subject land or lands to assure conformity with the intent and purpose of this article and of the jurisdiction's zoning ordinance. The powers provided in 4.01(B) shall be applicable only if the local legislative body adopts an ordinance which shall include enforcement procedures and requirements for adequate notice of public hearing and conditions sought to be imposed.

This recodification "in effect authorized 'conditional zoning' in certain circumstances," so long as local governments meet the statutory requirements and adopt the proper ordinances. 814 A.2d at 498. Curiously, this statute was adopted before the Montgomery case was decided but was not called to the attention of the court, which relied on previous judicial interpretations of local authority to impose conditions on zoning.

2. In Y. Chung v. Sarasota County, 686 So.2d 1358 (1996), a rezoning petition was denied, litigated, and, in settlement, the Florida county agreed to rezone Chung's property subject to numerous stipulations and conditions. Based on the settlement, the trial court entered a stipulated final judgment, and retained jurisdiction over its enforcement. Adjacent neighbors intervened, claimed the settlement constituted illegal contract zoning, and the District Court agreed. The court noted:

> Contracts have no place in a zoning plan and a contract between a municipality and a property owner should not enter into the enactment

or enforcement of zoning regulations * * * One of the reasons contract zoning is generally rejected is because "[t]he legislative power to enact and amend zoning regulations requires due process, notice, and hearings." Terry Lewis et al., Spot Zoning, Contract Zoning, & Conditional Zoning, in 2 Florida Environmental & Land Use Law 9–1, 9–13 (James J. Brown, ed., 2d ed. 1994). Assuming that the developer and municipality bargain for a rezoning ordinance that is fairly debatable and nondiscriminatory, contract zoning is nevertheless illegal when they enter into a bilateral agreement involving reciprocal obligations. By binding itself to enact the requested ordinance (or not to amend the existing ordinance), the municipality bypasses the hearing phase of the legislative process. * * * If each parcel of property were zoned on the basis of variables that could enter into private contracts then the whole scheme and objective of community planning and zoning would collapse. The residential owner would never know when he was protected against commercial encroachment * * *. The adoption of an ordinance is the exercise of municipal legislative power. In the exercise of this governmental function a city cannot legislate by contract. If it could, then each citizen would be governed by an individual rule based upon the best deal that he could make with the governing body. We conclude that the County's settlement agreement here presents a case of improper contract zoning. Although the County Commission approved the settlement at its regular meetings, it bypassed the more stringent notice and hearing requirements for a rezoning. When it entered into the settlement agreement that obligated it to rezone Chung's property, the County contracted away the exercise of its police power, which constituted an ultra vires act.

3. What should happen if the city breaches its part of the agreement? In Sprenger, Grubb & Associates v. City of Hailey, 127 Idaho 576, 903 P.2d 741 (1995) a developer with a 654–acre parcel entered into a development agreement with the city that provided for a master residential-business plan and annexation into the city. After the annexation in 1973, the city zoned 12.6 acres of the land for business. From 1973 to 1993, the developer gradually built out the plan. The city, at the behest of the mayor and with a great deal of public support, pushed for rezonings to protect the core downtown business area that resulted in downzoning the developer's 12.6-acre parcel from business to "limited business." (The mayor had wanted downzoning to residential, but settled for the limited business designation.) The developer sued alleging that the downzoning devalued the property by $800,000, that the city was estopped from rezoning in breach of the development agreement, and that the downzoning was a taking. The Idaho Supreme Court held for the city, noting that under some circumstances a city might be estopped from breaching a development agreement, but that in this case the downzoning was not a breach because the limited business designation was in substantial compliance with the agreement. The court also found that the devaluation was not a taking because the developer still had residual economic value in the land.

4. Another case with a cautionary message for developers is Metropolitan Dade County v. Fontainebleau Gas & Wash, Inc., 570 So.2d 1006 (Fla.App.1990). In 1975, a developer sought rezoning of a parcel from

professional office to limited business and, in a letter accompanying the application, indicated that the company would offer a written covenant restricting use of the property to a bank. The county granted the rezoning, expressing in the resolution that the use would be limited to a bank, but the covenant was never recorded. The bank was never built and the property changed hands many times. Fifteen years after the rezoning, the present owner received a building permit and built a gas station. Just before the station was finished the county discovered the old restriction and issued a stop work order. In a suit by the developer, the court held for the county stating that owners are deemed to purchase property with constructive knowledge of applicable land use regulations, the county applies the zoning code by resolution, and the resolutions that are passed subsequent to public hearings can modify districts and restrict property use. "Anyone attempting to learn what, if any, use limitations apply to his property need only turn to the applicable resolution." The court went on to hold that the owner could not claim detrimental reliance on the permit inadvertently issued by the county.

5. However, in Santa Margarita Area Residents Together v. San Luis Obispo County Board of Supervisors, 84 Cal.App.4th 221, 100 Cal.Rptr.2d 740 (2000), the Second Appellate District upheld a development agreement that freezes zoning on the project property in return for the developer's commitment to submit a specific plan for construction in compliance with county land use requirements. Contingencies and further approvals remain, but the agreement commits the county and the builder to the project, including its public improvements and amenities. The court reasoned that a "[g]overnmental entity does not contract away its police power unless the contract amounts to the 'surrender' or 'abnegation' of a proper governmental function." The zoning freeze in the agreement was not a surrender or abnegation because it was not of unlimited duration. The county's action was described as a legitimate exercise of governmental police power in the public interest and not a surrender of police power to a special interest.

C. ADMINISTRATIVE TREATMENT

Lawyers are often engaged to secure or oppose variances from the local zoning board of appeals or a special use permit from a local administrative agency. Variances and special, or conditional, use permits provide flexibility in local zoning practice and provide relief for individual parcel owners while protecting the surrounding neighborhood. Municipal attorneys advise these boards and the local legislative bodies that design the local zoning apparatus. Local legislatures create the board of appeals and other administrative agencies, delegate authority to them, and prescribe the procedures that they must follow. Local legislatures are directed and limited by state statutes in establishing the local administrative regime and, as they adopt laws, their local boards and administrators are required to comply with the standards and procedural steps contained in them.

In most states, when a locality adopts a zoning ordinance, the state enabling statute requires that it establish a zoning board of appeals, which may be called a board of standards or board of adjustment.

Typically these boards serve in a review—or appellate—capacity. If an interpretation of the meaning and applicability of the zoning ordinance is rendered by the zoning administrative officer, that interpretation may be appealed to the board of appeals. If the administrative officer informs a property owner that her construction plans do not conform with the strict use or dimensional requirements of the zoning ordinance, she may appeal to the board for a variance.

A variance allows the owner of a particular parcel that is uniquely situated to prove that relief is needed but will not be detrimental to the integrity of the ordinance or the character of the surrounding neighborhood. Variances provide relief from unnecessary hardships that arise because of special conditions applicable to the affected parcel. They provide a safety valve that responds to unique circumstances, avoids as applied legal challenges by property owners, and preserves the spirit of the ordinance as drafted by the legislature.

It is said that the board of appeals, in this review capacity, serves as a quasi-judicial agency and operates as such. When the decisions of a board of appeals are appealed to a court, the court can certify the record of the quasi-judicial body and, in most states, does not conduct a de novo trial on the facts determined by the board. Boards of appeals conduct their proceedings in a formal fashion, allow evidence to be presented and confronted, create a record, and make fact-based decisions that are supported by that record. These decisions must be filed in a timely manner with the municipal clerk or in another office, and aggrieved parties are allowed to appeal them to the courts within a prescribed time after the date of the filing. Courts in most states defer to the discretion of boards of appeals and affirm their decisions unless the appellant can prove affirmatively that the decision is arbitrary or unreasonable, not based on facts on the record, or does not conform to applicable standards.

Section 7 of the Standard Zoning Enabling Act empowered the board of appeals:

* * *

> (b) to hear and decide special exceptions of the ordinance upon which such board is required to pass under such ordinance: and
>
> (c) to authorize upon appeal in specific cases such variance from the terms of the ordinance as will not be contrary to the public interest, where, owing to special conditions, a literal enforcement of the provisions of the ordinance will result in unnecessary hardship, and so that the spirit of the ordinance shall be observed and substantial justice done.

These or similar words are contained in most of the state zoning enabling laws today.

Boards of appeals may also be used for other functions. They may be assigned the task, for example, of issuing special use permits, known in some jurisdictions as conditional use permits or special exceptions. In hearing and determining applications for special use permits, the board is said to serve in an administrative capacity and to be exercising original jurisdiction. If an article of the zoning ordinance provides that a house of worship is permitted, subject to the issuance of a special use permit, the religious institution applies directly to the board of appeals for that permit. It is a matter of state law and local practice whether the board of appeals, planning board or commission, or other administrative agency is charged with the issuance of special permits.

Special land uses, such as gasoline stations, certain utilities, clubs, hospitals, sanatoria, junkyards, mobile home parks, and houses of worship are permitted in designated zoning districts, but are subject to the imposition of certain conditions that protect surrounding properties from adverse impacts. Conditional uses are different from the as-of-right uses permitted in each zoning district. They are declared to be harmonious with the zoning district in which they are allowed, by permit, but it is recognized that they are sufficiently different such that special conditions on construction and use may be needed to prevent adverse impacts on the district. This allows the administrative body to consider in detail the physical conditions in the area, the nature of the proposed conditional use, and to tailor the proposed use to its surroundings.

The essential difference, in most ordinances, is that a variance allows a property owner to use her land or buildings in a manner that is prohibited by the ordinance, while a special use permit authorizes uses that are allowed and encouraged by the ordinance and declared to be harmonious with the applicable zoning district. This distinction between these two forms of providing zoning fairness and flexibility is illustrated by judicial decisions. In most states, there is a brisk pace of litigation that results from the impact of board decisions regarding variances and special use permits on the property values and the daily lives of the affected parties.

(1) Variance Cases

LARSEN v. ZONING BOARD OF ADJUSTMENT OF CITY OF PITTSBURGH

Supreme Court of Pennsylvania, 1996.
543 Pa. 415, 672 A.2d 286.

[The owners of a house with a very steep back yard sloping toward the Ohio River sought and received a variance to add a 20–by–20–foot deck off the rear of the house to provide their two-year-old child with an outside play area. A neighbor residing in a multi-unit condominium next door appealed the grant of a variance. The trial court ruled that the house owners had failed to satisfy the criteria needed to support a variance, and the house owners appeal.]

CASTILLE, JUSTICE.

* * *

There are essentially four factors that appellants must prove to be entitled to a variance under the applicable statute and ordinance. The factors are:

> (1) that an unnecessary hardship exists which is not created by the party seeking the variance and which is caused by unique physical circumstances of the property for which the variance is sought;
>
> (2) that a variance is needed to enable the party's reasonable use of the property;
>
> (3) that the variance will not alter the essential character of the district or neighborhood, or substantially or permanently impair the use or development of the adjacent property such that it is detrimental to the public's welfare; and
>
> (4) that the variance will afford the least intrusive solution.

53 P.S. § 10910.2; § 909.05 of the Pittsburgh Code of Ordinance ("PCO"). * * * The failure of a zoning board to consider each requirement of a zoning ordinance prior to granting a variance is an error of law. * * * Here, the zoning board failed to consider each of these requirements. Furthermore, the record reveals that appellants failed to provide evidence that would satisfy even the first criteria. Accordingly, appellants' claim must fail.

1. Hardship Caused by Unique Physical Characteristics

(a) Unnecessary Hardship

In order to satisfy the first prong under both the statute and PCO, appellants must prove: (1) that the variance is needed to avoid an "unnecessary hardship;" (2) that the "unnecessary hardship" was not created by them; and (3) that the "unnecessary hardship" was caused by unique physical circumstances of the property for which the variance is sought. With respect to the first factor, in determining whether the denial of the variance would cause the level of hardship needed to warrant a variance, this Court held in *Richman v. Zoning Board of Adjustment*, 391 Pa. 254, 259–60, 137 A.2d 280, 283 (1958), that the hardship must truly be an "unnecessary" one, and not simply a " 'mere' hardship." Furthermore, the "unnecessary" hardship must be one that is "unique or peculiar" to the property. *Id.*

Here, the Board found that appellants would suffer an "unnecessary hardship" from a denial of the variance because they would be denied the reasonable use of their land if they could not provide a play area for their child. However, the mere desire to provide more room for a family member's enjoyment fails to constitute they type of "unnecessary hardship" required by the law of this Commonwealth.

In the matter of *In re Kline Zoning Case*, 395 Pa. 122, 124, 148 A.2d 915, 916 (1959), a property owner sought a variance from a thirty-foot setback requirement in order to enclose his front porch. The basis for his variance request was that his wife suffered from asthma and hay fever, and that his son suffered from a severe respiratory ailment as well as hay fever. The enclosure of the porch would have allowed his family to have additional room in which to habitate. This Court, applying the test set forth by Richman, supra, upheld the zoning board's denial of the variance finding that the owner's need for additional room for his family failed to establish an unnecessary hardship justifying the variance.

The circumstances of *In re Kline Zoning Case* are analogous to the circumstances at hand. In both cases, the property owners sought variances to modify their homes to add a greater area for the family members to play in or to use. Thus, under *In re Kline Zoning Case*, we find that the Zoning Board erred as a matter of law in granting the variance based simply upon appellants' need to provide a greater play area for their child. Variances are meant to avoid "unnecessary" hardships; the granting of relief cannot be done simply to accommodate the changing needs of a growing family.

(b) Creation of Hardship

Notwithstanding appellants' failure to establish an unnecessary hardship, appellants further failed to establish that the physical circumstances allegedly causing the unnecessary hardship were not created by them. * * * Section 909.05(a)(1)(A) of the Pittsburgh Code of Ordinances expressly provides that parties are not entitled to a variance for circumstances which are the result of "any act of the appellant or his predecessors in title subsequent to the adoption of this Zoning Ordinance, whether in violation of the provisions hereof or not." See also, 53 P.S. § 10910.2(a)(3). To the extent that the hardship found by the zoning board was the result of the fact that appellants' first addition to their residence covered 75% of the property, thereby precluding any additional building absent a variance, appellants themselves created the complained of hardship. When appellants purchased the property, the house had a seventy-six foot setback from the rear property line. It was appellants themselves who built the forty-four foot deep addition which left them with insufficient space to erect an outside deck that would have complied with the ordinance at issue without the need for a variance. Therefore, appellants failed to prove that the "unnecessary hardship" was not caused by their own making.

(c) Unique Physical Circumstances

Appellants also failed to demonstrate that the "unique physical circumstances" of their property caused the hardship. In order to prove that the physical circumstances of a property justify a variance, the party seeking the variance must demonstrate that the circumstances are unique or peculiar to the property in question and not a condition common to the neighborhood or zoning district. * * * Here, the record establishes that the physical circumstances were in fact not unique to appellants' property and that most of the properties along Grandview Avenue had similar precipitously steep backyards. This Court has held that a condition which affects only a small portion of a district is not sufficiently unique to warrant a variance, but rather should be remedied by re-zoning. *English v. Zoning Board of Adjustment of Norristown*, 395 Pa. 118, 120–21, 148 A.2d 912, 914 (1959) (where zoning board grants a variance where neighborhood changes affect a small group of properties on one street, it is "virtually enacting zoning legislation instead of merely performing its function of administering the zoning law prescribed by the governing body of the municipality"). See also, *Walter v. Zoning Board of Adjustment*, 437 Pa. 277, 280, 263 A.2d 123, 126 (1970) (party seeking variance cannot complain of hardship existing at time the land was purchased). Thus, the condition which gave rise to appellants' alleged "unnecessary hardship" was not unique or peculiar to their property.

2. Variance Needed to Enable Reasonable Use of Property

Even if appellants had established the existence of an unnecessary hardship, they would be entitled to a variance only if they could establish that the variance was necessary for the reasonable use of the land. * * * At the outset, the Zoning Board's failure to address this issue is an error of law. Furthermore, in order to meet this requirement, appellants would have to show that a denial of the requested variance would make the property practically useless. *Abe Oil Co. v. Zoning Hearing Board of Richmond Twp.*, 168 Pa.Commw. at 120, 125, 649 A.2d 182, 185 (1994) (variance for construction of gas station not justified where property was amenable to "any number" of uses) * * *. Because appellants' property can be used as a residential dwelling absent the 400–square foot deck, they have failed to meet this requirement for a grant of a variance.

3. Variance's Impact Upon Neighborhood

Appellants also had to establish that the variance would "not alter the essential character of the neighborhood or district in which the property is located" or be contrary to the public interest. Although the zoning board found that the variance would not be contrary to the public interest, the only factual finding on which that conclusion was based was that the objections to the variance were related to "precedence and aesthetics."

Appellee stated in his appeal that the variance would permit the construction of a deck further out over the hillside than any other property in the neighborhood, thereby obstructing the view of the Ohio River from other properties along the street and substantially altering the character of the neighborhood. Appellee's concerns that the variance will set a precedent for the granting of future variances which will result in an obstruction of the view of the Ohio River afforded from the properties along Grandview Avenue is a concern that the "essential character" of the neighborhood will be altered as a result of the variance. The zoning board's failure to consider appellee's concerns or otherwise address the effect of the variance on the neighborhood was a failure to address a requirement of the statute. * * *

4. Variance Must Be the Least Intrusive Solution

Finally, once the zoning board determines that a variance is justified, the variance granted must be the minimum variance necessary to afford relief, resulting in the least modification of the regulation at issue. No testimony was heard by the zoning board as to the possibility of less drastic alternatives. * * *

Because the zoning board committed both a manifest abuse of discretion in determining that appellants had established an unnecessary hardship and numerous errors of law in failing to address the majority of the requirements under both the state and local zoning laws, the Commonwealth Court did not exceed its standard of review in reversing the order. * * *

For the foregoing reasons, the order of the Commonwealth Court is affirmed.

[Concurring opinion omitted.]

Notes

1. The universal standard for granting a variance from the literal terms of the zoning ordinance is hardship. As you might expect, defining that term has been anything but simple for the courts. Consider the following examples:

(a) Sea View Realty Corp. v. Zoning Board of Review of Cranston, 1996 WL 936989 (R.I.Super.Ct.1996) illustrates the showing that one court required to be made by an applicant for a variance in order to demonstrate sufficient hardship. How "hard" should the "hardship" be? This case involved an application for a variance to allow the operation of an apartment complex in a commercially zoned district. The court, in affirming a denial of the variance, stated that, "In order to obtain a use variance an applicant must demonstrate to the board that literal application of the zoning ordinance would completely deprive the landowner of all beneficial use of his or her property. Furthermore, an applicant may not rely on bald assertions of economic hardship, but must present truly probative evidence to the zoning board, such as cost data or financial statements. A 'mere showing of a more profitable use that would result in a financial hardship if denied' does not satisfy the requirements for obtaining a use variance" (citations omitted). The court goes on further to state that, "The record shows that Sea View failed to meet its burden of proof before the Board." See similarly, Aloisio v. Zoning Board of Review of the City of Providence, 1999 WL 1276562 (R.I.Super.Ct.1999), in which a club owner was denied both a variance and a special use permit to construct an awning on a structure adjoining the building in which he operated his club. The court stated that, "The record reveals no evidence was introduced by the appellant at the hearing that would establish that he would be denied all beneficial use of the property if the requested relief were denied."

(b) Compare State ex rel. Tucker v. McDonald, 793 S.W.2d 616 (Mo.Ct. App.1990), in which petitioner was denied a variance to operate an auto body shop in a zoning district that did not permit such a use. Though obviously subject to economic hardship, the city denied petitioner a variance, stating that "[c]onditions causing an applicant's hardship must also be unique and peculiar to the property and not prevalent in the neighborhood." The court added that ". . . hardship [relied on as a ground for variance] must be due to conditions not personal to the owner, but rather to conditions affecting the land, thereby making the land unsuitable for the permitted use in the zone in which it lies." See Valley View Civic Association v. Zoning Board of Adjustment, 501 Pa. 550, 462 A.2d 637 (1983), in which applicant was granted a variance to operate a sandwich shop in a district zoned single family residential because ". . . the extensive commercial and industrial uses in the immediate vicinity rendered [applicant's] property virtually unusable and of scant value for traditional residential purposes." See also Allegheny West Civic Council v. Zoning Bd. of Adjustment, 547 Pa. 163, 689 A.2d 225 (1997).

(c) One consideration which arises is illustrated by Pollard v. Zoning Bd. of Appeals, 186 Conn. 32, 438 A.2d 1186 (1982), in which the court stated: "The hardship which justifies a board of zoning appeals in granting a variance must be one that originates in the zoning ordinance; and arises directly out of the application of the ordinance to circumstances or conditions beyond the control of the party involved." The court further stated: "Where the claimed hardship arises from the applicant's voluntary act, however, a zoning board lacks the power to grant a variance." In this case, a surveyor's error constituted the "self-inflicted" hardship, thus the court affirmed the Board's denial of front and side yard setback variances.

If anything, the foregoing cases seem to suggest that policies relative to variances differ from state to state even when the same general "unnecessary hardship" principle is expressly followed in one way or another. Yet facts and figures available suggest that a substantial majority of all applications for departures from zoning requirements are approved in locations that are widely separated geographically.

2. In most jurisdictions, the requirement for obtaining a variance also states that the problem causing the need comes from the property and not from any act of the owner. Not too many cases present this issue, but one interesting example can be found in Board of Zoning Appeals of Evansville and Vanderburgh County v. Kempf, 656 N.E.2d 1201 (Ind.App.1995). In this case, the property owner had his development plat approved on condition that he install a 10–foot wide greenspace across the front of his property. After the property was developed, the city discovered that the owner had paved over the 10–foot area where the green space was to have been installed. The owner then sought a variance on the ground that none of the other adjacent business had green space and that economic necessity established a hardship. The court held for the city, stating: "The Board concluded that Kempf was not entitled to the requested variance because he himself had created the need for the variance by paving over the area in question. We hold this requirement advances a legitimate governmental interest in preventing the type of 'end run' around the zoning ordinances and procedures employed in the present case."

SASSO v. OSGOOD

Court of Appeals of New York, 1995.
86 N.Y.2d 374, 633 N.Y.S.2d 259, 657 N.E.2d 254.

[The owner of a waterfront parcel of land containing a boathouse sought a variance to allow him to demolish the existing structure and build a larger boathouse. Neighbors objected to the application on the ground that the proposed boathouse would obstruct their access to light, air, and view, and that the foundations of their boathouses and septic systems would be damaged by construction and altered drainage patterns. The zoning board granted the variance and the neighbors appealed; the intermediate appellate court determined that the applicant had failed to show "practical difficulties sufficient to justify an area variance" primarily because he had not shown that strict enforcement of the ordinance would cause him a significant economic injury.]

SIMONS, JUDGE

* * *

Prior to July 1, 1992, the authority of town zoning boards of appeal to grant variances from local zoning ordinances was defined in former Town Law § 267. Zoning boards were authorized to grant variances "[w]here there are practical difficulties or unnecessary hardships in the way of carrying out the strict letter of [local] ordinances" provided that "the spirit of the ordinance shall be observed, public safety and welfare secured and substantial justice done" (former Town Law § 267[5]). Although the former statute did not distinguish between "use" and "area" variances or assign the specific tests to them, court decisions generally applied the "unnecessary hardship" test in use variance cases, while requiring a demonstration of "practical difficulties" in area variance cases (*see, Matter of Village of Bronxville v. Francis*, 1 A.D.2d 236, 238, *aff'd* 1 N.Y.2d 839; *see also, Matter of Hoffman v. Harris*, 17 N.Y.2d 138, 144; *Dauernheim, Inc. v. Town Bd. of Town of Hempstead*, 33 N.Y.2d 468, 471; *Matter of Off Shore Rest. Corp. v. Linden*, 30 N.Y.2d 160, 168).

A three-pronged test of "unnecessary hardship" was clearly articulated more than fifty years ago (*see, Matter of Otto v. Steinhilber*, 282 N.Y. 71, 76) and that test, now embodied in Town Law § 267–b(2), has been applied in use variance cases without substantial difficulty. * * * The definition and application of the "practical difficulties standard" has proven far more troublesome.

Lacking a statutory definition, we have recognized the existence of "practical difficulties" where the unusual topography of the subject parcel interfered with construction of a building (*see, Matter of Wilcox v. Zoning Bd. of Appeals of City of Yonkers*, 17 N.Y.2d 249, 255), and where area variances were required to build a house on an amply sized but oddly shaped parcel that did not meet frontage and side yard requirements (*Conley v. Town of Brookhaven Zoning Bd. of Appeals*, 40 N.Y.2d

309, 316). We have also suggested that an area variance could be granted upon a showing of "significant economic injury" (*Matter of Fulling v. Palumbo*, 21 N.Y.2d 30, 33; *see also, Matter of Cowan v. Kern*, 41 N.Y.2d 591, 596). In *Matter of National Merritt v. Weist* (41 N.Y.2d 438) we considered both unique topography and economic injury relevant to the application for an area variance. We have noted several times, however, that there is no precise definition of the term "practical difficulties" (*Matter of Doyle v. Amster*, 79 N.Y.2d 592, 595; *Matter of Fuhst v. Foley*, 45 N.Y.2d 441, 445), observing that "[t]he basic inquiry at all times is whether strict application of the ordinance in a given case will serve a valid public purpose which outweighs the injury to the property owner" (*Matter of De Sena v. Board of Zoning Appeals of Inc. Vil. of Hempstead*, 45 N.Y.2d 105, 108).

Without any legislative guidance defining the requirements for an area variance, the courts began to develop a list of criteria to be applied under former Town Law § 267 (*see, Matter of Wachsberger v. Michalis*, 19 Misc.2d 909, *aff'd* 18 A.D.2d 921; *see also, Matter of Friendly Ice Cream Corp. v. Barrett*, 106 A.D.2d 748; *Matter of Human Dev. Servs. of Port Chester v. Zoning Bd. of Appeals of Vil. of Port Chester*, 110 A.D.2d 135, *aff'd* 67 N.Y.2d 702). Although originally offered as guidance for determining whether "the spirit of the ordinance is observed, public safety and welfare secured and substantial justice done" (*see, Wachsberger v. Michalis, supra*, 19 Misc.2d, at 912 [Meyer, J.]), these criteria came to be known as the "practical difficulties" test (see, 2 Anderson, New York Zoning Law and Practice, § 23.34, at 208–209 [3d ed.]). These criteria notwithstanding, precise and concise definition of "practical difficulties" never emerged from the case law. In particular, it remained unclear whether a showing of "significant economic injury" was part of the "practical difficulties" test. * * *

Effective July 1, 1992, the Legislature repealed former Town Law § 267, and enacted comprehensive provisions governing zoning boards of appeals. Unlike former Town Law § 267, the new statute defines "use" and "area" variances, as well as the criteria to be evaluated in determining applications for each. Use variances may be granted upon an applicant's showing "that applicable zoning regulations and restrictions have caused unnecessary hardship," expressly incorporating that phrase as it existed in former Town Law § 267. The statute defines the elements of proof necessary to establish unnecessary hardship, essentially codifying the criteria originally set forth in *Matter of Otto v. Steinhilber* (282 N.Y. 71, 76, *supra*), with the added requirement that the applicant prove that "the alleged hardship has not been self-created" (Town Law § 267–b[2][b][4]).

The standard for area variances is governed by Town Law § 267–b(3) in a provision that does not expressly require the applicant to prove "practical difficulties". It states:

> In making its determination [whether to grant an area variance], the zoning board of appeals shall take into consideration *the benefit*

> *to the applicant if the variance is granted, as weighed against the detriment to the health, safety and welfare of the neighborhood or community by such grant.* In making such determination the board shall also consider: (1) whether an undesirable change will be produced in the character of the neighborhood or a detriment to nearby properties will be created by the granting of the area variance; (2) whether the benefit sought by the applicant can be achieved by some other method, feasible for the applicant to pursue, other than an area variance; (3) whether the requested area variance is substantial; (4) whether the proposed variance will have an adverse effect or impact on the physical or environmental conditions in the neighborhood or district; and (5) whether the alleged difficulty was self-created, which consideration shall be relevant to the decision of the board of appeals, but shall not necessarily preclude the granting of the area variance. (Town Law § 267–b[3][b] [emphasis added]).

The five factors listed parallel the criteria previously used by the lower courts and identified by Professor Anderson as the "practical difficulties" test. * * *

The precise question posed on this appeal is whether by failing to include the phrase "practical difficulties" in the new statute, the Legislature has eliminated the requirement that the applicant for an area variance make that showing.

* * *

Reference to the bill jacket for chapter 692 of the Laws of 1991 supports intervenor's contention that an applicant for an area variance need not show "practical difficulties" as required under former Town Law § 267 and prior case law. The Legislature enacted the statute to clarify existing law by setting forth readily understandable guidelines for both zoning boards of appeal and applicants for variances and to eliminate the confusion that then surrounded applications for area variances. As one memorandum in the bill jacket states:

> The rules governing the granting of area variances that have been established by the courts are not nearly as clear as those governing use variances, and the result has been a great deal of confusion by boards of appeals, with a high degree of potential exposure to litigation. The new Town Law, section 267–b(3) and Village Law, section 7–712–b(3) resolve this problem by establishing a statutory test for the issuance of area variances which is flexible and which incorporates what we believe are the best features of the court decisions in order to protect the community (Bill Jacket, L 1991, ch. 692, at 26, Memorandum of Executive Deputy Secretary of State James Baldwin).

The same intent may be found in several other memoranda and establish that the legislation was enacted to aid laypersons—both applicants and lay members of zoning boards of appeal—in understanding and implementing the existing case-law; it was intended to have "little impact on existing laws since the main thrust of the legislation is to clarify and establish, in statute, the powers of the Zoning Board as already defined by jurisprudence." * * *

We conclude Town Law § 267–b(3)(b) requires the Zoning Board to engage in a balancing test, weighing "the benefit to the applicant" against "the detriment to the health, safety and welfare of the neighborhood or community" if the area variance is granted, and that an applicant need not show "practical difficulties" as that test was formerly applied.

Applying the new statute we conclude that the action of the Henderson Zoning Board was rational and not arbitrary and capricious. * * * As required by Town Law § 267–b(3)(b), the Zoning Board addressed five specific criteria. First, it determined that no undesirable change would be produced in the character of the neighborhood, because Graham's Creek serves primarily as a site for boathouses and commercial marinas, and that the addition of intervenor's proposed three-slip boathouse will not result in a significant increase in boat traffic or noise. The Zoning Board's conclusion that the variance will have minimal impact on nearby properties is supported by evidence that intervenor's boathouse will comply with all setback and height restrictions imposed by local ordinances. In making this finding, the Board had before it and considered the conditions imposed on intervenor's construction by the Town Planning Board which mitigated concerns voiced by petitioners (see, Town Law § 267–b[3][b][1]).

Next, the Zoning Board concluded that no alternatives other than the grant of area variances existed, because intervenor's lot is of substandard size, and no improvement to the property could be made without the requested lot size and width variances. The Zoning Board then acknowledged that the variances sought were substantial, but that there was no available adjacent land for intervenor to purchase so that he could meet the zoning requirements, and granting the variances would merely permit intervenor to use his property for a permitted use equal to all other neighboring lots. The Zoning Board's conclusion under subdivision (4) that granting the variances would lead to no adverse effect or impact on the neighborhood other than the previously discussed effect on petitioners is also supported by the record.

The only determination of the Zoning Board not supported by the record is its conclusion that intervenor's difficulty was not self-created. The record reveals that the parcel was of substandard lot size when intervenor purchased it in 1989 and it is well established that, in such circumstances, the variance applicant's difficulty or hardship is self-created. Nevertheless, the statute expressly states that the fact that the applicant's difficulty was self-created does not necessarily preclude the granting of the area variance. Under all the circumstances presented, the Board did not act arbitrarily in granting a variance notwithstanding the applicant's self-created difficulty.

In sum, the Zoning Board weighed the benefit to intervenor—the opportunity to fully use his property for a permitted use—against any detriment to the health, safety and welfare of the neighborhood or community, and determined to grant the variance. Its conclusions find ample support from the photographs and other materials in the record, and its determination was not irrational, arbitrary or capricious. Thus, the Appellate Division erred in reversing the order of Supreme Court confirming the determination.

Accordingly, the order of the Appellate Division should be reversed, with costs to intervenor against petitioners, and the judgment of Supreme Court, Jefferson County reinstated.

Order reversed, with costs to intervenor against petitioners, and judgment of Supreme Court, Jefferson County, reinstated.

Notes

1. Other jurisdictions have recognized a different standard of hardship for area variances as opposed to use variances. See, e.g., Board of Adjustment v. Kwik–Check Realty, Inc., 389 A.2d 1289 (Del.1978); Arens v. City of St. Louis, 872 S.W.2d 631 (Mo.App.1994). But see Ouimette v. City of Somersworth, 119 N.H. 292, 402 A.2d 159 (1979), where the court held that the standard of proof is the same for both area and use variances.

2. In a jurisdiction applying the law of this case, would the result have differed if the facts were those of the Larsen case?

JANSSEN v. HOLLAND CHARTER TWP. ZONING BOARD OF APPEALS

Court of Appeals of Michigan, 2002.
252 Mich.App. 197, 651 N.W.2d 464.

PER CURIAM.

John W. Janssen and others appeal by leave granted from the March 22, 2000, order of the circuit court affirming the decision of defendant Holland Charter Township Zoning Board of Appeals (ZBA) granting a use variance permitting the construction of a 250–unit residential development in an area zoned agricultural. We affirm.

In September 1996, appellees Henry A. and Doris J. Pyle and Baker Brokerage & Development, Inc., filed an application with the Holland Charter Township Board requesting that certain parcels of property consisting of approximately 115 acres be rezoned from the A–Agricultural Zoning District to the R–1 Single Family Residential Zoning District. The township's planning commission voted to recommend that the board deny the rezoning application. Subsequently, these appellees amended their application by removing one fifteen-acre parcel, which left two contiguous parcels consisting of approximately one hundred acres. Again, the planning commission voted to deny the amended petition. Thereafter, the Pyles and Baker filed a use variance request with the ZBA. They sought to have the density requirements changed so as to allow them to build a 400–unit residential development on the property. After appellee Vistiana Properties, LLC, purchased the property, it and the Pyles filed an amended use variance petition, in which they reduced the number of residential units from 400 to 250. Eventually, after holding public hearings, the ZBA granted the use variance petition. Appellants then contested the ZBA's decision in the circuit court, and the court upheld the ZBA's decision.

Appellants first argue that the circuit court erred in concluding that defendant ZBA's decision to grant the use variance did not constitute impermissible rezoning because a one hundred-acre parcel is too large a parcel of land to be the subject of a use variance. Upon review de novo, we disagree. *Bennett v. Weitz*, 220 Mich.App. 295, 299, 559 N.W.2d 354 (1996).

The rules that determine when a zoning board of appeals may grant a use variance make no mention of the size of a parcel. A township zoning board of appeals is a municipal administrative body whose duties include, among other functions, the granting of variances. M.C.L. § 125.293; *Sun Communities v. Leroy Twp.*, 241 Mich.App. 665, 670, 617 N.W.2d 42 (2000). M.C.L. § 125.293 provides, in pertinent part, as follows:

> Where there are practical difficulties or unnecessary hardship in the way of carrying out the strict letter of the zoning ordinance, the board of appeals in passing upon appeals may vary or modify any of its rules or provisions so that the spirit of the ordinance is observed, public safety secured, and substantial justice done.

Likewise, Holland Charter Township's zoning ordinance provides as follows:

> Sec. 20.2 Jurisdiction and powers.
>
> The board of appeals shall have all powers and jurisdiction granted by the zoning act, all powers and jurisdiction prescribed in other articles of the ordinance and the following specific powers and jurisdiction. . . .

The jurisdiction and power to authorize, upon appeal, a variance or modification of this ordinance where there are practical difficulties or unnecessary hardship in the way of carrying out the strict letter of this ordinance so that the spirit of this ordinance shall be observed, public safety secured and substantial justice done.

The plain and ordinary language of both the statute and the ordinance do not set forth any limitations based on the size of the property owner's parcel of land. To conclude, as appellants urge, that the granting of a use variance to a large parcel of land constitutes de facto rezoning, we would have to, in effect, add an exclusion for such parcels to the above statute and ordinance. "This, however, is beyond our authority because courts may not legislate." *Brandon Charter Twp. v. Tippett*, 241 Mich.App. 417, 423, 616 N.W.2d 243 (2000).

Appellants next contend that the ZBA's decision to grant the use variance was not supported by competent, material, and substantial evidence on the record. We disagree. The decision of a zoning board of appeals should be affirmed unless it is contrary to law, based on improper procedure, not supported by competent, material, and substantial evidence on the record, or an abuse of discretion. *Reenders v. Parker*, 217 Mich.App. 373, 378, 551 N.W.2d 474 (1996).

A township zoning board of appeals has the authority to vary or modify any zoning ordinance to prevent unnecessary hardship if the spirit of the ordinance is observed, the public safety is secured, and substantial justice is done. M.C.L. § 125.293; *Dowerk v. Oxford Charter Twp.*, 233 Mich.App. 62, 70, 592 N.W.2d 724 (1998). To conclude that a property owner has established unnecessary hardship, a zoning board of appeals must find on the basis of substantial evidence that (1) the property cannot reasonably be used in a manner consistent with existing zoning, (2) the landowner's plight is due to unique circumstances and not to general conditions in the neighborhood that may reflect the unreasonableness of the zoning, (3) a use authorized by the variance will not alter the essential character of a locality, and (4) the hardship is not the result of the applicant's own actions. *Johnson v. Robinson Twp.*, 420 Mich. 115, 125–126, 359 N.W.2d 526 (1984); *Puritan-Greenfield Improvement Ass'n v. Leo*, 7 Mich.App. 659, 672–673, 677, 153 N.W.2d 162 (1967). We conclude that the Pyle appellees presented sufficient evidence to establish each of these criteria.

"Whether property used in trade or business or held for the production of income can reasonably be used for a purpose consistent with existing zoning will, no doubt, ordinarily turn on whether a reasonable return can be derived from the property as then zoned." Puritan-Greenfield at 673–674, 153 N.W.2d 162. Contrary to appellants' argument on appeal, the ZBA's conclusion that appellee Vistiana could not receive a reasonable economic return was not based on some "hypothetical value." Rather, the ZBA's finding was based on an analysis of the rental income received and the taxes assessed on the property as zoned. In concluding that the applicants established by substantial evidence that they could receive no reasonable economic return for the property as zoned, the ZBA noted that the annual rental income for the farm was $6,000, and the annual rental income for the two residences on the property yielded $12,900. The ZBA further pointed out that the 1998 taxes on the property amounted to $7,867.42. Thus, the ZBA concluded that the applicants could not realize a reasonable economic return, given the rental income from leasing the farm and the two houses. We hold that the ZBA's conclusion that the property cannot reasonably be used in a manner consistent with existing zoning was supported by competent, material, and substantial evidence on the record. *Reenders, supra at* 378, 551 N.W.2d 474.

We also believe this evidence supports the finding that the hardship is not the result of the applicants' own actions. The increasing taxable value of the property and the comparatively low rental income derived are not "self-created" burdens.

In addition, we hold that there was competent, material, and substantial evidence to support the ZBA's conclusion that the use authorized by the variance would not alter the essential character of the locality. In considering the essential character of this locality, one cannot, and should not, just look at the immediate neighboring properties. The character of the locality is defined in broader strokes than such a myopic viewpoint would provide.

The underlying situation presented in the case at bar involves the changing circumstances and character of this community. With the growing consolidation of farming operations throughout the country and the fewer children willing to follow their parents into farming, the family farm, once a mainstay of both the economic and cultural landscape in rural America, has begun to disappear. See Zeigler, *Who will teach our farmers: Learning the value of mentor programs from state and private programs*, 5 Drake J. Agric. L. 279, 280 (2000). Appellants and appellees have found themselves caught in the tide of this rural transformation. In other words, the essential character of this community is not immutable, and is, indeed, in a state of transition.

The use to be made of the subject property not only recognizes this unfolding change in circumstances, but it also takes measured steps to balance the pressures inherent in this course of development. In granting the variance, the ZBA explained that the proposed cluster housing development will provide "a large area of open space around the perimeter of the property, thereby maintaining a buffer area between the proposed residential uses and the surrounding agricultural property," and further concluded that this factor, as well as the other conditions imposed, will ensure that the variance will not alter the locality's essential character. Included in the list of conditions is a disclaimer to be included in all deeds conveying an interest in the subject property that informs purchasers of the neighboring farming activity and that further provides that, under certain circumstances, the Michigan Right to Farm Act protects a farm or farm operation from being considered a public or private nuisance.

This leaves the question whether Vistiana's plight was unique to the property. The requirement that the landowner's plight be due to unique circumstances does not mean that the circumstances must exclusively affect only the single landowner. Rather, "[t]he courts have repeatedly emphasized that the hardship to be unique is 'not shared by all others,' " *Beatrice Block Club Ass'n v. Facen*, 40 Mich.App. 372, 381, 198 N.W.2d 828 (1972), quoting *Tireman-Joy-Chicago Improvement Ass'n v. Chernick*, 361 Mich. 211, 216, 105 N.W.2d 57 (1960) (emphasis supplied by Facen Court).

While the subject property has no defining physical characteristics such as size or topographical peculiarities that make it unique, we do not believe this necessarily ends the inquiry. See, e.g., *Monaco v. Dist. of*

Columbia Bd. of Zoning Adjustment, 407 A.2d 1091, 1097 (D.C., 1979) (examining the actions of the zoning authorities and the zoning history of the case). The uniqueness inquiry should not in all cases be limited to an examination of whether there is a uniqueness that inheres in the land itself. See *Capitol Hill Restoration Society, Inc. v. Dist. of Columbia Bd. of Zoning Adjustment*, 534 A.2d 939, 942 (D.C., 1987).

Appellees' claim of "uniqueness" invites consideration of their plight in light of the situation of other landowners in the surrounding area. In making such a comparison, it quickly becomes evident that it is not the unreasonableness of the zoning ordinance that has led to appellees' plight. As the circuit court recognized, when the use variance was granted, the township's then current master plan envisioned that, although zoned agricultural, the subject land should eventually be used for residential purposes. Indeed, before appellees' request, the township had approved approximately fifty other instances of residential use of land in areas zoned agricultural. Thus, change in the character of the locality has not only been countenanced by the master plan, but the zoning history of the case reveals a steady, incremental movement in that direction. We believe that this shows that at the time the variance was sought, the hardship alleged was not due to the general conditions then existing in the area. In other words, the remedy does not necessarily lie in amendment of the zoning ordinance itself. Given the master plan's recognition of potential future growth specifically on lands zoned agricultural, we believe that restrained and managed development, in part through the issuance of use variances as the changing conditions create unique hardships for those remaining agricultural lands, is a reasoned approach. It satisfies the goals of upholding the spirit of the ordinance, protects public safety, and assures that substantial justice is done. *Dowerk, supra*. Further, when a "landowner has made the requisite showing of financial hardship and compatibility of the proposed use with the character of the neighborhood, the variance should be granted since to deny it [solely] on the ground that 'unique circumstances' have not been shown invites a potentially successful assault on the zoning ordinance as being confiscatory." *In re Family of Woodstock, Inc.*, 225 A.D.2d 854, 856, 638 N.Y.S.2d 825 (1996).

Affirmed.

Notes

1. Also see City of Ladue v. Zwick, 904 S.W.2d 470 (Mo.App.1995), where the property owner was denied a variance to build a tennis court. The property owner argued that a tennis court must be located on a north/south axis and that such orientation was precluded by the hilly topography and odd shape of his lot. The court said: "[N]ot every lot, even in Ladue, is a buildable lot. It is elementary that not every odd scrap of land in an unrestricted commercial district is suitable for a skyscraper, even though a skyscraper may be a 'permitted use.' Likewise, even though [the ordinance] permits tennis courts in residential districts, it is the proposed owner's burden to find a buildable lot. To take advantage of the City's permitted use,

a tennis enthusiast must find a lot with less hills, larger acreage, or a more conventional shape."

2. Many states, in their zoning enabling legislation, prohibit the granting of use variances. In these states, the distinction between unnecessary hardship for use variances and practical difficulties for area variances is meaningless. Should hardship be construed strictly in states that do not allow use variances? See International Funeral Services v. DeKalb County, 244 Ga. 707, 261 S.E.2d 625 (1979). Also see Nucholls v. Board of Adjustment of City of Tulsa, 560 P.2d 556 (Okl.1976), where the court held that the city zoning ordinance was unconstitutional insofar as it prohibited the granting of use variances.

3. An area variance was properly denied by the court in McMorrow v. Board of Adjustment for City of Town & Country, 765 S.W.2d 700 (Mo.App. E.D.1989). The McMorrow's applied for an area variance from set-back requirements to allow them to build a swimming pool on an irregularly shaped lot. The variance was denied because the board found no practical difficulties where the family was using the home reasonably for living purposes and because state law disfavors the award of variances.

4. Should a court be more or less ready to permit a variance where expansion of a non-conforming use is involved? Compare Johnny Cake, Inc. v. Zoning Bd. of Appeals of Burlington, 180 Conn. 296, 429 A.2d 883 (1980), with In re Kenney, 374 N.W.2d 271 (Minn.1985). In the Connecticut case, the court held that the zoning board had no authority to grant a variance extending a nonconforming use; the applicant, a seminary, wanted to convert an old fire watchtower to an FM radio transmitter. In the Minnesota case, the court held that the board of adjustment had the authority to issue a variance that would expand a nonconforming boathouse, despite language in the enabling act stating that "no variance may be granted that would allow any use that is prohibited in the zoning district." Also see Burbridge v. Governing Body of the Twp. of Mine Hill, 117 N.J. 376, 568 A.2d 527 (1990), where the court held that a variance to expand a nonconforming use could be granted on the ground that the final result would be more aesthetic (the nonconforming use was an auto body repair shop).

(2) Special Use Permit Case

CITY OF CHICAGO HEIGHTS v. LIVING WORD OUTREACH FULL GOSPEL

Supreme Court of Illinois, 2001.
196 Ill.2d 1, 749 N.E.2d 916, 255 Ill.Dec. 434.

JUSTICE MCMORROW delivered the opinion of the court:

* * *

Under the City's zoning ordinance, the authority to grant or deny an application for a special use permit is reserved to the city council. Prior to the council taking action on an application for a special use permit, the City's zoning board of appeals and the City's plan commission must review the application and make a recommendation. These recommendations are forwarded to the city council, which then decides whether to approve or deny the application. The City's zoning ordinance states that the zoning board of appeals may recommend to the city council that a special use be allowed only if the following six criteria are satisfied:

> "(a) That the establishment, maintenance or operation of the special use will not be unreasonably detrimental to or endanger the public health, safety, morals, comfort or general welfare;
>
> (b) That the special use will not be injurious to the use and enjoyment of other property in the immediate vicinity for the purposes already permitted nor substantially diminish and impair property values within the neighborhood;
>
> (c) That the establishment of the special use will not impede the normal and orderly development and improvement of surrounding property for uses permitted in the district;
>
> (d) That adequate utilities, access roads, drainage and/or other necessary facilities have been or are being provided;
>
> (e) That adequate measures have been or will be taken to provide ingress and egress so designed as to minimize traffic congestion in public streets;
>
> (f) That the special use shall in all other respects conform to the applicable regulations of the district in which it is located, except as such regulations may in each instance be modified by the city council pursuant to the recommendations of the zoning board of appeals." Chicago Heights Municipal Code, app. A, Zoning, § 12–6.6 (1973).

In January 1996, after taking possession of the property at 400 West Lincoln Highway, Living Word submitted an application to the City for a special use permit. A public hearing was held before the City's zoning board of appeals on March 13, 1996. After the hearing, the board forwarded Living Word's application to the City's plan commission. On March 27, 1996, the plan commission recommended that Living Word's application for a special use permit be denied. On April 3, 1996, the zoning board of appeals also recommended that the application be denied. Finally, on April 15, 1996, the city council agreed with the recommendations of the plan commission and the zoning board of appeals and denied Living Word's application for a special use permit.

The city council ultimately denied Living Word's application based upon a comprehensive development plan adopted by the City in December 1995. This plan targeted West Lincoln Highway, the area in which the church is located, for development as a commercial corridor. The concern of the council was that granting a special use permit for a noncommercial use, such as a church, would be at odds with the goals of the comprehensive plan.

Although the city council denied Living Word's application for a special use permit, the church continued to hold services in the building at 400 West Lincoln Highway. Eventually, the City filed suit in the circuit court of Cook County, seeking to permanently enjoin the church from continuing its services. Living Word responded with 14 affirmative defenses which were later refiled in a 14–count counterclaim. Three of the counts in the counterclaim are relevant here. Count VI of the counterclaim alleged that the city council's denial of Living Word's application for a special use permit violated Living Word's right to the free exercise of religion under the first and fourteenth amendments of the United States Constitution. Count XIII alleged that Living Word was merely continuing the Masons' permitted nonconforming use of the property. Count XIV alleged that the city council's denial of Living Word's application for a special use permit was "arbitrary, capricious and unreasonable in light of [*sic*] fact that use of the property by [Living Word] meets standards (a) through (f) of section 12–6.6 of the zoning code of the City."

A bench trial was held in December 1997. During this trial, the court heard testimony from several witnesses, including Maria Arbeen, a real estate appraiser. Arbeen testified that, in her opinion, Living Word had satisfied all the criteria for obtaining a special use permit listed in the City's zoning ordinance.

The court also heard testimony from Joseph Christofanelli, the city planner for the City of Chicago Heights. Christofanelli stated that the City was suffering economic problems and was approximately $57 million in debt. Because of this, Christofanelli explained, the City needed to concentrate on developing commercial areas that would generate real estate and sales taxes. The West Lincoln Highway corridor was of particular importance to the City because that corridor was the City's best commercial, tax-revenue-generating area. Christofanelli stated that permitting any noncommercial use within the West Lincoln Highway corridor would be detrimental to surrounding commercial properties because these properties would miss out on the "spill-over effect" whereby customers patronize more than one business in an area. Christofanelli stated that Living Word's application for a special use permit was denied because "the church was something we had not envisioned for that particular corridor, and here, again, that's based upon the Comprehensive Plan."

The court heard testimony similar to Christofanelli's from Steven Albert, a real estate appraiser. Albert stated that any noncommercial use in the West Lincoln Highway corridor would be incompatible with, and detrimental to, the goals of the City's comprehensive plan. In addition to the foregoing testimony, the circuit judge also reviewed several exhibits, including the City's zoning ordinance, the City's comprehensive plan, the City's official zoning map, Living Word's special use application, minutes from city council meetings, minutes from meetings of the City's zoning board of appeals, minutes from a meeting of the City's plan commission, and numerous diagrams and letters.

* * *

[The trial court denied the city's request for a permanent injunction against the church, finding that the church had met all applicable standards for the special use permit. This ruling was vacated for jurisdictional reasons by the appellate court which then decided the case in the city's favor under the Illinois Religious Freedom Restoration Act, finding that the Act was not violated by the denial of the permit. The church appealed on several grounds including that the city's denial of its application was arbitrary and capricious as a matter of general zoning law. Portions of the case applicable to other claims of the church are omitted.]

ADMINISTRATIVE ACTION

In general, a "special use" is a type of property use that is expressly permitted within a zoning district by the controlling zoning ordinance so long as the use meets certain criteria or conditions. "The purpose of special uses is to provide for those uses that are either necessary or generally appropriate for a community but may require special regulation because of unique or unusual impacts associated with them." S. Connor, *Zoning,* in Municipal Law & Practice § 13.17 (Ill. Inst. for Cont. Legal Educ. 2000). A church may be an appropriate special use because, depending upon its size and location, it may create traffic or parking problems within the neighborhood in which it is located. For example, the number of parking spaces needed by a church may vary considerably depending upon the availability of parking spaces in the neighborhood at the time the church holds services. Thus, although a church might be considered a desirable and appropriate use within a zoning district, the municipality may classify it as a special use and may require, for example, that parking problems be resolved before granting a special use permit to a property owner that would allow the owner to use the property as a church. See generally 3 E. Ziegler, Rathkopf's Law of Zoning & Planning, ch. 41 (4th ed. 1992); 3 K. Young, Anderson's American Law of Zoning, ch. 21 (4th ed. 1996). In Illinois, municipal special uses are authorized by section 11–13–1.1 of the Illinois Municipal Code (65 ILCS 5/11–13–1.1 (West 1994)).

Special uses must be clearly distinguished from use variances. "[A] variance is 'authority extended to a property owner to use his property in a manner forbidden by the zoning enactment,' " generally upon a showing of hardship. 3 K. Young, Anderson's American Law of Zoning § 20.03, at 416 (4th ed. 1996), quoting *Mitchell Land Co. v. Planning & Zoning Board of Appeals,* 140 Conn. 527, 532, 102 A.2d 316, 319 (1953). A special use, on the other hand, " 'allows [a property owner] to put his property to a use the enactment expressly permits.' " 3 K. Young, Anderson's American Law of Zoning § 20.03, at 416 (4th ed. 1996), quoting *Mitchell Land Co. v. Planning & Zoning Board of Appeals,* 140 Conn. 527, 532–33, 102 A.2d 316, 319 (1953). In sharp contrast to a variance, the inclusion of a special use within a zoning ordinance " 'is tantamount to a legislative finding that the permitted use is in harmony with the general zoning plan and will not adversely affect the neighborhood.' " 3 K. Young, Anderson's American Law of Zoning § 21.13, at 126 (4th ed. 1999 Supp.), quoting *Twin County Recycling Corp. v. Yevoli,* 90 N.Y.2d 1000, 1001, 665 N.Y.S.2d 627, 688 N.E.2d 501, 502 (1997). "A special exception use is a 'permitted use' when allowed under a special permit. Thus, there has been a local legislative determination that the use, as such, is neither inconsistent with the public's health, safety, morals or general welfare, nor out of harmony with the town's general zoning plan." 3 E. Ziegler, Rathkopf's Law of Zoning & Planning § 41.08, at 41–34 (4th ed. 1992); see also 83 Am.Jur.2d *Zoning & Planning* § 974, at 814 (1992) ("Where a zoning ordinance authorizes a business as a special use, such authorization is tantamont [*sic*] to a legislative conclusion that the use is appropriate in the district"). Thus, in the instant case, the City zoning ordinance's authorization of churches as a special use along West Lincoln Highway constitutes a legislative finding that churches, as such, are compatible with the surrounding property uses in that area.

In the case at bar, the city council's reason for denying Living Word's application for a special use permit is not in dispute. Stated simply, the city council denied Living Word's application because it believed that all noncommercial uses were incompatible uses along West Lincoln Highway. The council based this belief on the City's then recently adopted comprehensive development plan. This plan, adopted by the City approximately one month before Living Word submitted its application for a special use permit, addresses many areas of concern for the City, including demographic and economic trends occurring within the City. One portion of the plan is devoted to land use and highlights the West Lincoln Highway corridor as an area that should be "improved as an auto commercial area oriented to a regional clientele." Relying on this stated goal, the city council concluded that to grant a special use permit for any noncommercial use, including churches, along West Lincoln Highway would frustrate the plan to develop that area as a strong commercial corridor. For this reason, the council denied Living Word's application.

It must be emphasized that the city council's objection to Living Word's application for a special use permit did not center on any attribute of Living Word that is unique to this particular church or its facilities. The council did not conclude, for example, that the church will impede the orderly development of surrounding properties or lower their value because the church building is unusually large, or because the church's congregation generates traffic problems along West Lincoln Highway. Instead, Living Word's application was denied because the council believed that any noncommercial use of property located in the West Lincoln Highway corridor would have a negative effect on the commercial development of that corridor and, therefore, that all noncommercial uses should be completely excluded.

It is clear that the city council's rationale for denying Living Word's special use permit application is at odds with the legislative intent expressed in the City's zoning ordinance. According to the zoning ordinance, and in contrast to the council's explanation for denying Living Word's application, churches are not a *per se* incompatible use along Lincoln Highway. Quite the contrary, the City zoning ordinance's inclusion of churches as a special use in the West Lincoln Highway corridor "is equivalent to a legislative finding that [such a] use is one that is in harmony with the other uses permitted in the district." 3 E. Ziegler, Rathkopf's Law of Zoning & Planning § 41.05, at 41–21 through 41–22 (4th ed. 1992).

In light of the above, the question arises as to whether the city council, in denying Living Word's application for a special use permit, could legitimately set the legislative intent expressed in the zoning ordinance to one side and, instead, rely upon the developmental goals expressed in the comprehensive plan as the basis for its decision. For the following reasons, we believe the answer to this question is no.

* * *

There is nothing of record in this case which would indicate that Living Word's use of its property as a church would have any adverse effects on surrounding properties above and beyond those that would inherently be associated with any church located in the West Lincoln Highway corridor. Accordingly, in the case at bar, if the city council's denial of the permit application is considered an administrative decision, it cannot be upheld.

The existence of the comprehensive plan, and the council's reliance upon that plan, does not alter this conclusion. The special use criteria in the City's zoning ordinance do not include conformance with the comprehensive plan as a requirement that must be met before a special use permit may be granted. See E. Ziegler, Rathkopf's Law of Zoning & Planning § 41.08, at 41–37 (4th ed. 1992) ("Zoning ordinances may expressly provide as a standard for issuance of a special permit that the proposed use at the particular location be compatible with or not negatively impact the local comprehensive zoning plan"). Moreover, the City's zoning ordinance is law; the comprehensive plan is not. As our Municipal Code explains, "[an official comprehensive] plan shall be advisory and in and of itself shall not be construed to regulate or control the use of private property in any way, except as to such part thereof as has been implemented by ordinances duly enacted by the corporate authorities." 65 ILCS 5/11–12–6 (West 1994); see also *Chase v. City of Minneapolis,* 401 N.W.2d 408, 413 (Minn.App.1987) (incompatibility with comprehensive plan insufficient basis for denying conditional use permit); *Amoco Oil Co. v. City of Minneapolis,* 395 N.W.2d 115, 118 (Minn.App.1986) (same). Acting administratively, the city council is bound by the City's zoning ordinance, not the comprehensive plan. Thus, the city council's reliance on the comprehensive plan could not justify the decision to deny Living Word's application for a special use permit.

Legislative Action

Even if one views the city council's decision to deny Living Word's application as a purely legislative act, that decision cannot be sustained under the justification offered by the city council. The City has emphasized that the council's decision to deny Living Word's application for a special use permit was based on a desire to exclude all noncommercial uses from the West Lincoln Highway corridor and not on any objection or ill-will directed to Living Word in particular. Further, as the City has made clear on appeal, the city council does not intend to apply this policy of excluding noncommercial uses from the West Lincoln Highway corridor on an *ad hoc* basis, but will, instead, consistently deny all noncommercial applications for special use permits. It is clear, therefore, that to uphold the rationale offered by the council for denying Living Word's application for a special use permit would result in the effective amendment of the City's zoning ordinance. Adopting the council's reasoning would completely remove churches from the list of special uses set forth in the City's zoning ordinance. Other noncommercial uses which are listed as special uses under the zoning ordinance, such as public parks and public libraries, would also be eliminated. A new zoning district, one exclusively commercial in character, would thus be created in the West Lincoln Highway corridor. Under the present circumstances, this *de facto* amendment of the City's zoning ordinance cannot be allowed.

* * *

In so holding, we do not mean, in any way, to diminish the severity of the economic problems facing the City or the City's need to address these problems by changing its zoning regulations. Our holding is simply that, if the city council wishes to unconditionally remove all noncommercial uses from the West Lincoln Highway corridor, it must amend the City's zoning ordinance to reflect that intent, and it must do so according to the amendment procedures set forth within the zoning ordinance.

* * *

For the foregoing reasons, the appellate court's vacation of the February 26, 1998, order is affirmed; the judgment of the appellate court that the trial court grant the injunctive relief sought by the City is reversed. The judgment of the circuit court denying the City's request for a permanent injunction against Living Word is affirmed; the circuit court's entry of its February 26, 1998, order is reversed, and that order is vacated. The cause is remanded to the circuit court to enter judgment ordering the City to grant Living Word's application for a special use permit.

Appellate court affirmed in part and reversed in part; circuit court vacated in part and affirmed in part; cause remanded.

Notes

1. See "clarifying" language from Novak v. City of Geneva, 2004 WL 2616301 (N.D.Ill.2004), in which the city council denied plaintiffs a special permit for a drive-through window that the council deemed to be incompatible with the surrounding district.

Plaintiffs argue that the use of compatibility and harmony in zoning decisions concerning Special Use permits is improper under Chicago Heights v. Living Word Outreach Full Gospel Church & Ministries, Inc., 196 Ill.2d 1, 749 N.E.2d 916, 255 Ill.Dec. 434 (Ill. 2001). In Living Word, the Court was primarily concerned with the blanket objection made by Chicago Heights to non-commercial uses in their business district. The Court made clear that the Chicago Heights City Council could not make "effective amendments" to Chicago Heights's zoning law by labeling all non-economic Special Uses as incompatible with current zoning, thereby eliminating them from consideration. Id. at 930. The Court's decision, however, was limited to broad-based or blanket decisions not to allow a certain type of Special Use regardless of individual consideration. Thus, it does not extend to those situations, such as the one before me here, where the City Council denies a specific Special Uses permit for reasons related to the use's location ... The standard articulated by the Court focused on the individual nature of each Special Use permit determination and forces the decision maker to articulate reasons why a proposed Special Use is inappropriate given its specific circumstances. This is exactly what the City Council did when it considered Plaintiffs' Special Use permit for a drive-through window. It looked at the list of nine Special Use Standards articulated in § 1002.2 of its Zoning Code and applied them to Plaintiffs' drive-through window. The fact that the City Council made statements concerning the compatibility of this particular drive-through window with the surrounding neighborhood does not mean the City Council violated *Living Word,* which expressly permits administrative bodies to consider compatibility so long as it is done on an individual basis. Id. at 929.

2. In the Living Word case, we encounter a city whose zoning ordinance reserves to the city council the power to issue special use permits. This evinces a decision by the legislative body not to delegate this important function to the board of appeals, the planning board or commission, or other administrative agency. State law in Illinois did not provide the court sufficient guidance to determine whether the city council, in exercising this reserved authority, was acting in a legislative or an administrative capacity. It avoided the issue by finding that the denial was invalid either as an administrative or a legislative act. This illustrates the importance of identifying the capacity in which a local board is acting and determining whether it followed the applicable requirements. The court found that the city council, as a legislative body, could have changed the law and made the church ineligible for the permit, but that it would have had to follow the prescribed rules for amending the zoning ordinance, which it did not.

3. One constitutional principle which is particularly important in conditional use and special permit cases is the principle that the ordinance contain adequate standards for the issuance of the permit so that a reviewing court may ascertain whether the decision-maker stayed within the bounds of delegated authority. See, e.g., Alpha Portland Cement Co. v. Missouri Dept. of Natural Resources, 608 S.W.2d 451 (Mo.App.1980). The absence of standards would make the grant of a special permit or conditional use wholly discretionary with the agency. In Wakelin v. Town of Yarmouth, 523 A.2d 575 (Me.1987), the court struck down an ordinance which specified

that the zoning board should grant a special exception if the proposed use is "compatible with existing uses" defining compatible "with respect to size, visual impact, intensity of use, proximity to other structures, and density of development." The court held that the definition was unconstitutionally vague and constituted an unlawful delegation of authority.

4. A question that arises frequently is whether the planning commission or zoning board can impose special conditions or restrictions on the special permit or conditional use. In Halle Cos. v. Crofton Civic Ass'n, 339 Md. 131, 661 A.2d 682 (1995) the court upheld the authority of the county to condition a special exception allowing a landfill on the applicant's agreement subject to eight conditions, most prominently assenting to an alternate access route. The court indicated that the reason for the special exception device was to enable the local authority to protect nearby properties and to tailor the scope of permission so as to strike a reasonable balance. Also see Nance v. Council of Memphis, 672 S.W.2d 208 (Tenn.Ct.App.1983) (upholding a condition imposing a time limitation for the renewal of a special use permit for a mental health clinic); Paulson v. Zoning Hearing Bd., 712 A.2d 785 (Pa.Cmwlth.Ct.1998) (overruling a restriction on the hours of operation of a go-cart facility on the grounds that the applicable statute did not permit the attachment of conditions to special exception permits); Anza Parking Corp. v. City of Burlingame, 195 Cal.App.3d 855, 241 Cal.Rptr. 175 (Dist.Ct. App.1987) (holding it unlawful for a conditional use permit to be conditioned upon the permittee not having a right to transfer the permit with the land).

5. In Pollard v. Palm Beach County, 560 So.2d 1358 (Fla.App.1990), the court held that an applicant for a special exception who met all the standards specified in the ordinance could not be denied the exception because of neighbors' objections. (The exception was for an adult congregate living facility for the elderly.)

SECTION 4. NONCONFORMING USES

The policy of allowing nonconforming uses to continue originated in concerns that the application of zoning regulations to uses existing prior to the regulations' enactment might be construed as confiscatory and unconstitutional. It was assumed that, by limiting the enlargement and reconstruction of nonconforming uses, they would disappear over time. The allowance of nonconforming uses has been characterized by the courts as a grudging tolerance of them. The right of municipalities to adopt reasonable measures to eliminate them has been recognized. The ultimate goal of the zoning law is to achieve uniformity of property uses within each zoning district which can only be accomplished by the elimination of uses that do not conform to the specifications of district regulations.

A nonconforming use is created when existing land uses, valid when established, are prohibited by a new or amended zoning law. Nonconforming land uses are defined and regulated in most local zoning laws. A typical local ordinance may state, for example: "A nonconforming use is any use, whether of a building or tract of land or both, existing on the effective date of this chapter, which does not conform to the use regulations of the district in which it is located." Nonconforming use issues arise when the zoning law is first adopted. When a district is zoned residential, for example, all existing nonresidential uses in that district are rendered nonconforming. Later amendments to the zoning ordinance may have the same effect.

Often, zoning ordinances will provide automatic relief to owners of vacant residential lots that become nonconforming due to increased minimum area requirements, or upzoning. But see Khan v. Zoning Bd. of Appeals of Village of Irvington, 87 N.Y.2d 344, 639 N.Y.S.2d 302, 662 N.E.2d 782 (1996), where the court refused to adopt a so-called "single and separate ownership" rule as matter of common law; this rule states that one who owns property in single and separate ownership prior to enactment of the ordinance rendering it nonconforming has a vested right to use the property for residential purposes.

When property owners propose the improvement, expansion, rebuilding, or other change in their nonconforming property use, they must be certain to comply with local regulations governing those matters. Normally, these regulations are found in a discrete article of the local zoning law, entitled Nonconforming Uses. The nonconforming use article of the zoning law will prohibit or limit changes in buildings and lot uses that are nonconforming and provide in a variety of ways for the termination of nonconforming uses, such as limiting their expansion or enlargement, prohibiting the reconstruction of damaged structures, disallowing the reestablishment of nonconforming uses after they have been discontinued for a time, or simply terminating them after the passage of a stipulated amount of time.

This section will present the salient considerations developed by the courts in dealing with nonconforming uses and related regulations and the legitimacy of efforts to dispose of such uses. In this connection, several questions most commonly arise in the various cases:

1. Was there an established use at the time of zoning? (In that regard, what if the site for the structure had been surveyed, or an architect employed, or the site graded, or the basement or foundation dug, or construction begun, and so on?) In short, what was the existing situation when zoning was instituted? The question of change of position and good faith by the landowner often enters in.

2. What is the extent of the nonconforming use, and will the terms of the ordinance permit expansion or a change of some sort with respect to such use?

3. Has there been a termination of the nonconforming use due to substantial destruction of the building in which it is housed, or abandonment of the use, or legislative action of one type or another (including the amortization process)?

4. Is the nonconforming use subject to termination as a nuisance through the granting of injunctive relief? In connection with this latter

question, some cases (particularly some of the earlier ones) removed noxious uses which amounted to nuisances or were nuisance-like in character. This was basically the reasoning and result of Hadacheck v. Sebastian and Reinman v. Little Rock.

A. EXPANSION OR EXTENSION

Local laws often prohibit the enlargement, alteration, or extension of a nonconforming use. To allow the expansion of nonconforming uses, which the zoning law wishes to eliminate over time, would defeat that underlying policy. Normally, the law allows the owners of nonconforming land uses to perform property repairs, conduct normal maintenance, and complete internal alterations that do not increase the degree of, or create any new, noncompliance with the locality's zoning regulations. Courts have upheld prohibitions on the construction of an awning over a courtyard outside a restaurant, on the theory that it would create additional space for patrons to congregate and, in this sense, increase the degree of the nonconforming use. Similarly, the prohibition of the conversion of seasonal bungalows to year-round residences has been upheld as an acceptable method of preventing the enlargement of a nonconforming use.

Where nonconforming business operations are proposed to be expanded, the case law is somewhat less clear. Where roads and structures built on a parcel used as a gravel mining operation exhibited the owner's intention to use the entire parcel, the court held that expanding the mining operation to another location on the property was permitted. The addition of a body-toning operation to the premises containing a nonconforming beauty parlor, however, was considered a prohibited extension of the prior nonconforming use. The court's interest in protecting the owner's demonstrated investment in the gravel mining operation could explain the difference between these cases.

Nonconforming use provisions in zoning laws vary considerably from one locality to another. A municipality particularly intent on eliminating nonconforming uses may prohibit any physical expansion of a building; another may favor property use by allowing, for example, the construction of an additional story because it does not increase the footprint, or lot coverage, of the structure.

STATE v. PERRY

Supreme Court of Errors of Connecticut, 1962.
149 Conn. 232, 178 A.2d 279.

SHEA, ASSOCIATE JUSTICE.

The defendant was convicted, after a trial, to the court, of a violation of the zoning regulations of Stamford. He has appealed, claiming that the court erred in finding on all the evidence that he was guilty of the crime charged beyond a reasonable doubt.

The material facts are not disputed. The defendant is president of the Pickwick Ice Cream Company, which has manufactured ice cream for over twenty-five years on premises located on Newfield Avenue in Stamford. Prior to 1951 the premises were in an industrial zone. In that year, the property was rezoned to a commercial neighborhood zone, and the industrial use by the ice cream company became a nonconforming use. Before this change of zone, all of the property was used in connection with the ice cream business, either for manufacture or storage or for the parking of trucks. In January, 1959, the defendant brought to the property a large trailer which was later insulated and equipped with a blower unit. A rubber hose attached to the trailer was connected to pipes leading from the manufacturing plant. Through these pipes, ammonia, as a cooling agent, was conducted to the trailer to refrigerate it. The trailer was kept at a freezing temperature all of the time and was used to store materials connected with the production of ice cream. The company owned a tractor to which it could connect the trailer for transportation purposes. The trailer is roadworthy, has no foundation and may be moved within a few minutes by hooking it up to the tractor. The trailer is not permanently registered with the commissioner of motor vehicles. Temporary registrations have been issued for it, but the last one expired December 24, 1959. Since then, the trailer has remained on the premises, constantly hooked up to the plant. In February, 1959, the zoning enforcement officer in writing, requested the defendant to discontinue the use of the trailer.

The Stamford zoning regulations provide that a nonconforming use may be continued but may not be extended or expanded, or changed to a less restrictive use. Stamford Zoning Regs. § 9(A) (1951, as amended).[1] The intention of the regulations is to abolish nonconforming uses, or to reduce them to conformity, as speedily as justice will permit. This is in accordance with the policy of the law and the spirit of zoning. *Town of Guilford v. Landon*, 146 Conn. 178, 182, 148 A.2d 551; *Salerni v. Scheuy*, 140 Conn. 566, 570, 102 A.2d 528. It is apparent from the evidence that the defendant attempted to provide, through the use of the trailer, additional enclosed space for his freezing and storing operations. Had he attempted to add to the existing building or to erect a new building for these purposes, he could not have done so, because this would have constituted, beyond question, an extension of a nonconforming use. What he cannot do directly he has attempted to do indirectly by the importation of the trailer. The facts clearly show that the trailer, because of its makeup, location and long continued attachment to the pipes leading from the plant, is intended, designed and arranged to be used to expand, enlarge and extend the nonconforming use conducted in the building on the premises. This is a clear violation of the regulation. *Beerwort v. Zoning Board of Appeals*, 144 Conn. 731, 734, 137 A.2d 756;

1. "Section 9—Non-conforming Uses A—Any building or use of land or building legally existing at the time of enactment of this regulation, or of any amendments thereto, or authorized lawful permit issued prior to the adoption of these regulations which does not conform to the provisions of these regulations for the Use Districts in which it is located, shall be designated a non-conforming use. Such use may be continued but may not be extended or expanded, or changed to a less restrictive use as listed in Section 5—Land Use Schedule."

Burmore Co. v. Smith, 124 N.J.L. 541, 547, 12 A.2d 353; 2 Rathkopf, Law of Zoning and Planning (3d Ed.) p. 59–6. It is not a simple case of increasing the size of the defendant's business. Rather, it is an expansion and extension of the use of the premises by adding facilities for storage and the freezing of commodities where such accommodations had not previously existed *Grundlehner v. Dangler*, 51 N.J.Super. 53, 59, 143 A.2d 192, modified on other grounds, 29 N.J. 256, 148 A.2d 806.

There is no error.

In this opinion the other Judges concurred.

Notes

1. There are many interesting cases involving the general subject-matter presented in Perry. Generally speaking, there seems to be no right to expand or enlarge a nonconforming use regardless of whether the local ordinance prohibits it. The theory behind this is readily apparent—the nonconforming use, as such, is contrary to the intent and purposes of zoning.

The problems arise, however, in distinguishing between the extension or enlargement of a nonconforming use and its repair, in determining whether the construction of a new building is permissible, in deciding whether the addition of new equipment amounts to an extension, whether some new service or product is such an addition as to constitute an extension, or whether an increase in the intensity of use or volume of business amounts to a violation. These are only a few of the multitude of problems that arise in regard to changes in nonconforming uses.

Consider these situations:

(a) Plaintiffs expanded their asphalt manufacturing business to include a concrete plant. To prevent further expansion, the town amended its zoning code prohibiting the manufacture of concrete, thus making plaintiffs' concrete plant nonconforming. Plaintiffs wished to add a third concrete mixer to their plant to meet rising demand. Plaintiffs asserted that the additional concrete mixer would use less than twenty percent of the lot already used for the manufacture of concrete and no new use of the property would result. The town opposed such "expansion" of the plaintiffs' nonconforming use. What result? Adding the third concrete mixer was deemed a lawful expansion of a nonconforming use. See Kc2 v. Town of Middletown, 1999 Del. Super. LEXIS 257 (Del.Super.Ct.1999).

(b) The property in question was home to a milk trucking and distribution operation since 1923. The business became a lawful nonconforming use in 1965. As an efficient business practice, decommissioned milk trucks had been, and were still, kept on the property to act as a source of parts for the operable trucks. The county had adopted strict junkyard regulations, and the zoning board of appeals declared that the business' storage of decommissioned milk trucks was unlawful because the site had not been "certified" under the zoning ordinance as a lawful nonconforming use pursuant to these junkyard regulations. Did this storage of decommissioned vehicles amount to an enlargement or extension of the lawful nonconforming use, or was it merely accessory? The Court of Special Appeals of Maryland found the vehicle storage to be incidental and accessory to the lawful nonconforming trucking business and, thus, permitted it. See County Comm'rs of Carroll County v. Zent, 86 Md.App. 745, 587 A.2d 1205 (Md.Ct.Spec.App.1991).

(c) At the time of the zoning ordinance, defendant was using the property for outdoor storage of earthmoving equipment along with some repair and maintenance. Now defendant wishes to build a structure to enclose his operation. The Supreme Court of Minnesota, in a case of first impression, held that the structure would be an expansion or extension of the nonconforming use: "An addition to an existing building is clearly an extension or expansion of a prior nonconforming use. In our judgment, construction of a building where none existed before constitutes an expansion of a nonconforming use in the same manner as an addition to an existing building. Furthermore, the building will prolong the continuation of the nonconforming use and considerably lessen the likelihood that it will be eliminated in the foreseeable future." County of Freeborn v. Claussen, 295 Minn. 96, 203 N.W.2d 323 (1972). Also see Mossman v. City of Columbus, 234 Neb. 78, 449 N.W.2d 214 (1989), where the court interpreted a provision in the ordinance allowing alteration of nonconforming uses, only if no "structural alterations" were made, to prohibit a mobile home owner to replace his mobile home with another one.

(d) The landowners operated a quarry as a lawful nonconforming use for several decades. Then, a zoning amendment permitted the property's use as a quarry, subject to a special permit application. When the landowners' latest permit expired, they continued to operate the quarry, and the town zoning enforcement officer subsequently ordered the cessation of the operation. In Taylor v. Zoning Bd. of Appeals, 65 Conn.App. 687, 783 A.2d 526 (2001), the court stated that the right to continue the nonconforming quarry operation constituted a vested right. However, the court added that the special permit requirement was a reasonable and valid regulation of the nonconforming use based upon the town's police powers.

(e) An asphalt company sought permission to construct a 1000–barrel-capacity asphalt storage tank to replace two 400–barrel underground tanks which had developed leaks. In Nu–Way Emulsions, Inc. v. City of Dalworthington Gardens, 610 S.W.2d 562 (Tex.Civ.App.1980), the court held that the proposal amounted to enlargement and alteration of a nonconforming use rather than repair of an existing use as alleged by the plaintiff. Cf. Feldman v. Zoning Hearing Bd. of City of Pittsburgh, 89 Pa.Cmwlth. 237, 492 A.2d 468 (1985), where the property owner sought to convert an auto repair shop into a convenience store/gas station; Stevens v. Town of Rye, 122 N.H. 688, 448 A.2d 426 (1982), involving conversion of an auto garage into a showroom for plumbing supplies and bath fixtures.

(f) Conversion of an existing nonconforming restaurant into a discotheque was held to be a substantial alteration of the use in Town of Belleville v. Parrillo's, Inc., 83 N.J. 309, 416 A.2d 388 (1980). The court stressed the factors of the changes in hours of operation, clientele, admission policies, facilities, and music. Similarly, conversion of a movie theater to live entertainment was held to be an impermissible expansion of a nonconforming use in Conforti v. City of Manchester, 141 N.H. 78, 677 A.2d 147 (1996). A little closer to the line, perhaps, is Marzocco v. City of Albany, 217 A.D.2d 872, 629 N.Y.S.2d 847 (1995), where the owner of a nonconforming tavern/restaurant catering to the gay population and featuring male strippers changed the character of his business to one offering topless female dancers as entertainment, then giving up his liquor license and establishing a "juice bar" offering totally nude female dancers and "erotic entertainment." The court found that a significant change in use was involved.

(g) A private care facility operated for about four years in a residential zone which permitted nursing homes, but excluded facilities that care for "insane or other mental cases." The facility cared for eight elderly people with mental problems as a nonconforming use. When the facility changed to one which cared for young people with mental problems, the city charged the operator with violating the zoning ordinance. Although the city argued that young people with mental problems are more apt to be violent than elderly people with such infirmities and that the facility was expanding the nonconforming use, the court reasoned that the intensification was permissible because the nature and character of the use remained substantially the same. The court analogized the change as similar to a store which changes its inventory or a factory which changes its product. City of Jewell Junction v. Cunningham, 439 N.W.2d 183 (Iowa 1989).

2. In Hansen Brothers Enterprises, Inc. v. Board of Supervisors of Nevada County, 12 Cal.4th 533, 48 Cal.Rptr.2d 778, 907 P.2d 1324 (1996), the court held that the diminishing asset doctrine required that a mining company be allowed to expand its rock quarrying and aggregate production into other areas of its property. The court said that under the diminishing asset doctrine quarrying cannot be limited to land actually excavated at the time of enactment of a restrictive ordinance because to do so would deprive the landowner of his use of the property as a quarry. Contra: Township of Fairfield v. Likanchuk's, Inc., 274 N.J.Super. 320, 644 A.2d 120 (App.Div. 1994) (diminishing asset doctrine not applicable unless owner can show that the entire tract was dedicated by the owner to the mining activity).

3. In Memory Gardens Cemetery, Inc. v. Village of Arlington Heights, 250 Ill.App.3d 553, 190 Ill.Dec. 238, 621 N.E.2d 107 (1993), a nonconforming cemetery sought a permit to construct an additional mausoleum. (Twelve mausoleums were already on the cemetery property.) After the city denied the permit, the cemetery sought a declaratory judgment that it did not need a permit on the theory that a mausoleum in a cemetery is not a change in use. The plaintiffs put on the testimony of several expert witnesses who all defined a cemetery as including in-ground internment, mausoleum entombment, and inurnment of cremated remains. The court found, however, that under Illinois law, mausoleums are treated distinctly and thus the construction of a mausoleum would be an expansion or enlargement of a nonconforming use (although, apparently, internment of additional bodies in gravesites would not be an expansion or enlargement). Compare Town of Gardiner v. Blue Sky Entertainment Corp., 213 A.D.2d 790, 623 N.Y.S.2d 29 (1995), where the town sought to close down a nonconforming tourist camp that had been used for sky diving, parachuting, and other recreational aviation activities. The court held that an increase in the volume of skydivers, pilots, and campers was not an improper extension of the nonconforming use because there was no change in the nature of the use, just the volume.

B. DISCONTINUANCE

A property owner's right to continue a nonconforming use may be lost by abandonment. Originally, this required a voluntary, completed act of abandonment by the owner. It was said that there must be the concurrence of an intention to abandon and some act, or failure to act, which implies a lack of interest on the part of the owner to retain the use. Time was considered relevant to the issue of abandonment, but not enough, alone, to establish it. Furthermore, the mere failure to continue the nonconforming use was not sufficient to establish abandonment. Although these rules still exist in some jurisdictions, modern zoning laws frequently stipulate that any discontinuance of the nonconforming use for a specified period constitutes abandonment. Courts hold that such provisions are sufficient to establish the owner's intent to abandon the nonconforming use as a matter of law. Where the established period is reasonable, discontinuance of the use for that time amounts to an abandonment of the use. It has been held that local discontinuance periods apply even when the owner can prove that he did not actually intend to abandon the nonconforming use.

STATE EX REL. MOREHOUSE v. HUNT

Supreme Court of Wisconsin, 1940.
235 Wis. 358, 291 N.W. 745.

[A building which could accommodate 20 to 25 students, in the University Heights area of Madison, was used as a fraternity house before the district was zoned for single family residences. The fraternity in the early 1930's deeded the building to its mortgagee. It was then used as a rooming house for over two years. In 1934, it was leased to Dean Garrison of the law school "to be used for the purpose of residence only." Dean Garrison and his family lived in the structure for the initial two year lease period and then for three more years under successive one year leases. Two servants and a student who tended the furnace lived with the Garrisons. From September, 1935, Dean Garrison subleased some extra rooms as a separate apartment.

After Dean Garrison moved out the mortgagee-owner sought a nonconforming use permit permitting renewed use as a fraternity house. The building commissioner refused, but this was reversed by the board of zoning appeals, which wrote an elaborate decision.

Certiorari was brought by neighbors. The circuit judge reversed the zoning board.]

FOWLER, JUSTICE.

* * * The case is certiorari. When certiorari is invoked to review the action of an administrative board, the findings of the board upon the facts before it are conclusive if in any reasonable view the evidence sustains them. *Wisconsin Labor R. Board v. Fred Rueping L. Co.*, 228 Wis. 473, 493, 279 N.W. 673, 117 A.L.R. 398. Under this rule the appeal board's view of the facts, so far as they appear from its decision, must be

accepted as final and conclusive upon the trial court and upon us. The statutory provision for review by certiorari of the board's action, to the effect that the court may take further evidence and may consider it in reaching its determination, may warrant the court's overriding the board's findings of fact if the additional evidence received shows them to be erroneous, but where as here the additional evidence is incompetent it cannot be given that effect however it might be if it were competent. The view of the board that the owner did not intend to abandon the right of use of the building as a fraternity house but that the use of it for a residence was intended to be only temporary until opportunity should arise to sell it for that purpose, must therefore be upheld and given whatever legal effect it has.

* * *

The quotations from the decision of the board above given show that the board concluded as fact that lapse for a year of the nonconforming use before resuming or adopting another lawful nonconforming use, was a reasonable time in which to resume or adopt a lawful nonconforming use; that lapse of the conforming use under either of the above situations is consistent with and does not constitute an abandonment of the nonconforming use, and that under the facts of the instant case the owner by leasing the premises to Dean Garrison and permitting him to use them as a one-family residence for one year did not intend to abandon or discontinue Class B use.

The question remains whether the owner's intent in respect above stated operates to avoid the language of the ordinance declaring that discontinuance of a nonconforming use prevents resumption of that use.

Although the letter of the ordinance is as stated the letter need not necessarily be applied. *State ex rel. Schaetz v. Manders, supra.* "The letter killeth but the spirit giveth life." If the resumption of the nonconforming use is within the spirit of the ordinance, although contrary to its letter, the spirit rather than the letter governs.

That mere cessation of a nonconforming use under the terms of a zoning ordinance does not destroy the right to continue it or prevent resumption of it was held in the *Manders* case, supra. Under the rule of that case, discontinuance involves more than mere cessation. It involves abandonment. Under that rule, had the owner kept the premises vacant, waiting opportunity to rent or sell to a fraternity, the nonconforming use would have continued. Under the reason of that rule, had the owner, under the finding of fact as to the owner's intention, employed a caretaker for the house this would not have operated as a discontinuance. * * *

* * * But the reservation of right to cancel the lease on sale of the premises is indicative of intent to sell for a fraternity house if opportunity arose. Putting in the lease for "residence only" indicates that the lessee should not turn the house into a tearoom or restaurant or a boardinghouse, but it does preclude the idea of making it a two-family

residence, as later was done, to the knowledge and with the implied assent of the owner, and as might have been done forthwith without violating of the ordinance. Whether under all the circumstances the owner's acts constituted a "voluntary relinquishment or abandonment" of the right to devote the premises to a Class B use depends on whether the use of the building as a single-family residence for a year was a reasonable time under all the circumstances, to allow the owner to devote the premises to the Class B use of a two-family residence. The appeal board thought it was. This was a question for the board to decide and its decision should be sustained. * * *

* * * We are of opinion that the judgment of the circuit court should be reversed, and the record remanded with directions to enter judgment affirming the ruling of the board of zoning appeals. * * *

[The dissenting opinion of Wickhem, J., in which two other justices concurred, is not given.]

Note

See State ex rel. Brill v. Mortenson, 6 Wis.2d 325, 96 N.W.2d 603 (1959), limiting this case, in which a woodworking plant became a nonconforming use following a 1949 zoning amendment. Between 1951 and 1956, the building operated as a paint and enamel shop. After the paint shop owner's business failed, it took 22 months to find a new tenant, who wished to operate a meat distributing and processing plant on the subject premises. This new tenant argued that substitution of one nonconforming use (meat distribution and processing) for another (woodworking and paint shops) did not constitute "discontinuance" under the applicable zoning provision. The court discussed:

> This raises the question of the meaning of the words 'discontinued for a period of 12 months' as used in this ordinance and as applied to a substituted nonconforming use. We construe these words to mean termination or cessation of the nonconforming use for the 12 months period. The doctrine of voluntary abandonment as applied in State ex rel. Schaetz v. Manders, 1931, 206 Wis. 121, 238 N.W. 835 and in State ex rel. Morehouse v. Hunt, 1940, 235 Wis. 358, 370, 291 N.W. 745, is not to be extended and applied to substituted nonconforming uses in a county zoning ordinance limiting discontinuance of such nonconforming uses to a definite time limit. The protection of sec. 59.97(7), Stats., is extended only to the particular lawful use for which the building or premises is actually used at the time the ordinance takes effect. It does not extend to protecting other nonconforming uses substituted by virtue of a privilege or right given by county ordinance.

TOYS "R" US v. SILVA

Court of Appeals of New York, 1996.
89 N.Y.2d 411, 654 N.Y.S.2d 100, 676 N.E.2d 862.

KAYE, CHIEF JUDGE.

(1) The New York City zoning laws prohibit continuation of a nonconforming use if, during a two-year period, "the active operation of

substantially all the non-conforming uses * * * is discontinued" (New York City Zoning Resolution § 52–61). This case presents a novel question of statutory construction: what is the appropriate legal standard to determine whether a nonconforming use has been discontinued under the Zoning Resolution? Contrary to the trial court and Appellate Division, we conclude that substantial—rather than complete—discontinuation of the active, nonconforming activity forfeits the nonconforming use, and that the good faith of the owner is irrelevant to that determination.

(2) Here, the Board of Standards and Appeals (BSA) on the facts found minimal warehouse activity following the complete stoppage of operations for 20 months, which failed to preserve nonconforming use status, and it revoked the building permit allowing petitioner to maintain a nonconforming use on the premises. Because the BSA determination was supported by substantial evidence, we reverse the trial court and Appellate Division decisions reinstating the building permit.

1. Facts

At issue here is a portion of a 16–story building located at the northeast corner of Third Avenue and East 80th Street in Manhattan. Built in 1926, the entire premises were situated in a retail zoning district and, in compliance with the certificate of occupancy and applicable zoning regulation, served as a storage and warehouse facility. When Morgan Manhattan Storage and Warehouse Company purchased the building in 1956, it continued to use the structure exclusively as a warehouse.

The 1961 New York City Zoning Resolution changed the neighborhood from a retail zoning district to residential districts overlaid with strips of commercial districts on the avenue (rather than street) blocks. As a result, that portion of the building on Third Avenue presently remains in a commercial (C1–9) zoning district. The portion fronting on 80th Street, however, is now in a residential (R8B) zone. Because warehouse use is no longer permitted as of right in either the commercially or the residentially zoned areas (see, Zoning Resolution art II; §§ 32–00, 32–25), use of the building as a warehouse could continue under the Zoning Resolution only as a nonconforming use (see, Zoning Resolution §§ 12–10, 52–11).

Morgan continued to use the building as a warehouse until August 1989, when it contracted to sell the premises to a real estate developer. At that time, Morgan emptied the building and for the next 20 months ceased all warehouse operations. The sale fell through, and in April 1991 Morgan transferred a limited amount of goods stored in its other warehouses to the 80th Street facility and assigned a property manager there, in an effort to resume nonconforming warehouse use and thereby maintain the value of its property.

In June 1992, Chase Manhattan Bank acquired the premises from Morgan by way of deed in lieu of foreclosure. In response to a request by Chase for advice as to whether nonconforming warehouse use was permissible, the New York City Department of Buildings (DOB) issued an informal opinion that the nonconforming use at the premises had been re-established in April 1991 and could lawfully continue.

Petitioner Toys "R" Us purchased the basement, first and second floors of the building from a subsidiary of Chase in March 1994. Three months later, petitioner filed an application with DOB to convert the purchased premises into a retail toy store. DOB approved the application and in September 1994 issued a building permit authorizing the conversion.

The 38,000 square foot premises occupy both commercially and residentially zoned space. A toy store is permitted as of right in the commercially zoned portion of the premises on Third Avenue but not in the residentially zoned section fronting on 80th Street, which includes the building's loading docks (see, Zoning Resolution art II; §§ 32–00, 32–15). The instant dispute arises out of the DOB authorization to develop and operate this latter segment of the property situated in the residential zoning district as a retail toy store—a nonconforming use.

Respondent-intervenor "Neighbors–R–Us," a coalition of neighborhood and block associations, objected to the building permit and sought its revocation. In October 1994, DOB denied the request. Respondent-intervenor then challenged the issuance of the building permit by way of an administrative appeal to the BSA. It urged that the nonconforming warehouse use had been discontinued during the two-year period from August 1989 to July 1991 and, therefore, the Zoning Resolution only allowed the property to be developed in furtherance of a permitted use.

The BSA held public hearings during a five-month period concerning the nature and extent of warehouse operations during the period between April and July 1991 and conducted a site inspection of the building and the surrounding area.

After reviewing hundreds of pages of documents and hearing testimony from all sides, the BSA, "based on the totality of the evidence presented," found the warehouse activity between April and July 1991 minimal. Concluding that the Zoning Resolution did not require complete cessation of the nonconforming use as a precondition to termination, the BSA determined that the insignificant level of warehouse activity during that period failed to perpetuate the nonconforming warehouse use. Deeming Morgan's clear intent to resume warehouse operations insufficient to preserve the nonconforming use, the BSA revoked petitioner's building permit.

Petitioner commenced a CPLR article 78 proceeding seeking to reinstate the permit. Supreme Court held that the storage of some goods in the warehouse during April to July 1991, coupled with the absence of any bad faith or fraud by Morgan, sufficiently continued the nonconforming use. It thus granted the petition and annulled the BSA determination, allowing petitioner to maintain a nonconforming retail use in the residentially zoned space.

The Appellate Division affirmed, one Justice dissenting. Like the trial court, the Appellate Division applied a good-faith standard and concluded that the concededly minimal storage activity from April to July 1991 sufficed to preserve nonconforming use status under the Zoning Resolution. The Appellate Division granted leave to appeal to this Court, and we now reverse.

* * *

Whether petitioner can use the residential portion of the premises at issue here for nonconforming toy store use depends on whether its predecessor, Morgan, discontinued its nonconforming warehouse operations for two years within the meaning of section 52–61. This Court has never considered the proper legal standard for determining when a nonconforming use is abandoned under this zoning ordinance. In revoking petitioner's building permit, the BSA construed section 52–61 as requiring substantial discontinuation, rather than complete cessation, of the nonconforming use by the property owner for two consecutive years, irrespective of any intent to preserve nonconforming use status.

The BSA, comprised of five experts in land use and planning, is the ultimate administrative authority charged with enforcing the Zoning Resolution (see, NY City Charter §§ 659, 666). Consequently, in questions relating to its expertise, the BSA's interpretation of the statute's terms must be "given great weight and judicial deference, so long as the interpretation is neither irrational, unreasonable nor inconsistent with the governing statute" (*Matter of Trump–Equitable Fifth Ave. Co. v. Gliedman*, 62 N.Y.2d 539, 545; *see, Appelbaum v. Deutsch*, 66 N.Y.2d 975, 977). Its determination, moreover, must be sustained if it has a rational basis and is supported by substantial evidence (*see, Appelbaum v. Deutsch*, 66 N.Y.2d at 977, *supra*; *Matter of Fuhst v. Foley*, 45 NY2d 441, 444). Where, however, the question is one of pure legal interpretation of statutory terms, deference to the BSA is not required (*see, Matter of Teachers Ins. & Annuity Assn. v. City of New York*, 82 N.Y.2d 35, 41–42).

Here, we must resolve two questions. First, we must determine the appropriate legal standard for abandonment under Zoning Resolution § 52–61—a pure legal question that does not mandate deference to the BSA. We must then decide whether the BSA's conclusion that Morgan abandoned nonconforming warehouse use was supported by substantial evidence.

* * *

According to petitioner, New York courts have uniformly required proof that the entire nonconforming use was discontinued as a precondition to termination. Petitioner points to *Matter of Marzella v. Munroe* (69 N.Y.2d 967) in support of this contention. In *Marzella*, the property owner used a parcel of land that had been rezoned to permit only one two-family structure to house four families in two dwellings. When one house remained vacant for 15 years, so that three families rather than four resided on the property, the local zoning board concluded that nonconforming use of the property for four families had been abandoned. This Court disagreed, finding insufficient evidence to establish that the entire nonconforming use had been abandoned (*id.*, at 968).

In doing so, we explained that "[a]bandonment does not occur unless there has been a complete cessation of the nonconforming use" (*id.*, at 968). Notably, however, the local zoning ordinance in Marzella broadly prohibited resumption of any "nonconforming use which has been abandoned" (*see*, Village of Dobbs Ferry Code § 300–81B). The term "abandoned" was not qualified in any way; the statute therefore gave no indication that anything less than complete discontinuation of the nonconforming use would suffice to surrender it.

Similarly, in *Town of Islip v. P.B.S. Marina* (133 A.D.2d 81), also relied upon by petitioner, the relevant zoning ordinance contained absolute terms, providing that "discontinuance of any non[-]conforming use for a period of one year or more terminates such non-conforming use." The Appellate Division thus concluded that " 'discontinuance connotes a complete cessation * * * so that a minimal nonconforming function, of itself, would not constitute an abandonment' " (*id.*, quoting *Baml Realty v. State of New York*, 35 A.D.2d 857). Indeed, in each of the cases cited by petitioner adopting the complete cessation standard, the statutes spoke exclusively in terms of discontinuance, failing to qualify that requirement in any way (*see, e.g., Baml Realty v. State of New York*, 35 A.D.2d 857, *supra*; *City of Binghamton v. Gartell*, 275 App. Div. 457, 459).

Unlike the statutes in these prior cases, however, Zoning Resolution § 52–61 explicitly equates abandonment with something less than discontinuation of the entire nonconforming use. Section 52–61 specifically terminates any further nonconforming use when "the active operation of substantially all the non-conforming uses * * * is discontinued" for a continuous two-year period (emphasis added). To construe this statute as requiring the property owner to discontinue all nonconforming operations—as the courts below did—simply ignores the plain language of the ordinance requiring that the owner merely cease "substantially" all of the nonconforming use.[2] Allowing the slightest nonconforming function to preserve the nonconforming use, moreover, would eliminate the specific language requiring "active" operations to avoid termination.

2. Tellingly, the drafters of section 52–61 rejected a proposed termination provision that omitted the qualifying language "substantially all." In a Zoning Resolution submitted to the City Planning Commission pursuant to a contract with the City of New York, a special planning staff of architects suggested the following regarding termination of nonconforming uses: "If a nonconforming use *discontinues active or continuous operations* for a continuous period of one year, the building or other structure or tract of land where such non-conforming use previously existed shall thereafter be occupied and used only for a conforming use. Intent to resume active operations shall not affect the foregoing" (Voorhees, Walker, Smith and Smith, Report to NY City Planning Commn, Proposed Zoning Resolution § 51–31 [Aug. 1958] [emphasis added]).

The carefully chosen words of section 52–61 thus impose a standard of substantial rather than complete cessation.[3] The language of the statute also contradicts the conclusion of both the trial court and Appellate Division that section 52–61 implicitly contains a good-faith standard, allowing nonconforming activity to continue upon a showing that a property owner, in the absence of bad faith or fraud, intended to resume nonconforming use.

Generally, abandonment of a nonconforming use requires both an intent to relinquish and some overt act or failure to act, indicating that the owner neither claims nor retains any interest in the subject matter of the abandonment (*see*, 1 Anderson's American Law of Zoning § 6.65, at 678 [Young 4th ed]). In New York, however, the inclusion of a lapse period in the zoning provision removes the requirement of intent to abandon—discontinuance of nonconforming activity for the specified period constitutes an abandonment regardless of intent (*see*, *Matter of Prudco Realty Corp. v. Palermo*, 60 N.Y.2d 656, 657–658).

Zoning Resolution § 52–61 provides a specific lapse period—two years—thereby rendering the owner's intent irrelevant to abandonment. Indeed, section 52–61 goes even one step further, expressly stating that "[i]ntent to resume active operations shall not affect" the determination whether a nonconforming use has been discontinued.

Notwithstanding the unique language of this particular zoning provision, petitioner urges that section 52–61 must be interpreted in its favor as the landowner. To be sure, zoning restrictions, being in derogation of common-law property rights, should be strictly construed and any ambiguity resolved in favor of the property owner (*see, Matter of Allen v. Adami*, 39 N.Y.2d 275, 277). Zoning Resolution § 52–61, however, is not ambiguous—its clear language prohibits additional nonconforming activity when "substantially all" of the "active" nonconforming operations are discontinued, and deems the owner's intent irrelevant. Furthermore, public policy specifically supports termination of nonconforming uses, and the Zoning Resolution itself seeks to achieve "a gradual remedy" for "incompatible" nonconforming uses (Zoning Resolution § 51–00). * * *

The Appellate Division's concern that anything less than complete cessation under section 52–61 will lead to arbitrary results warrants comment. Section 52–61 imposes an objective, not subjective, standard: substantial discontinuation of active, nonconforming operations. Stated otherwise, section 52–61 terminates a nonconforming use when only minimal nonconforming activity continues. Whether this standard has been satisfied will, of course, turn on the peculiar facts of each case. All zoning cases are by their nature fact specific, and as a leading authority

3. Petitioner alternatively urges that, because section 52–61 refers to discontinuation of "substantially all the non-conforming uses"—emphasizing the plural "uses"—discontinuation should be measured by whether a majority of the number of nonconforming uses is maintained, regardless of the level of activity devoted to each use. Petitioner, however, overlooks the basic rule of statutory construction that "[w]ords in the singular number include the plural, and in the plural number include the singular" (General Construction Law § 35).

recognizes, the right to a nonconforming use must necessarily be decided "on a case-by-case basis" (1 Anderson's American Law of Zoning § 6.23, at 553 [Young 4th ed]). Certainly, the DOB and BSA, comprised of qualified experts, are capable of making these determinations.

* * *

The BSA's determination that Morgan substantially discontinued nonconforming warehouse use of the property for 24 months must be confirmed if it has a rational basis and is supported by substantial evidence (*Matter of Cowan v. Kern*, 41 N.Y.2d 591, 598). And where substantial evidence exists, a reviewing court may not substitute its judgment for that of the BSA—even if the court might have decided the matter differently (*Matter of Cowan v. Kern*, 41 N.Y.2d at 599, *supra*; *Matter of Collins v. Codd*, 38 N.Y.2d 269, 270). In reaching its conclusion, moreover, the BSA had de novo review power and was not bound by the findings of the DOB (*see*, Zoning Resolution § 72–11).

The BSA's review of warehouse logs for the contested four-month period revealed only eight customer accounts, compared to the 1,500 accounts previously maintained by the company. It further revealed that approximately 19 crates were shipped to the warehouse at that time, which would have occupied only one-tenth of one percent of the entire volume of the building. This extremely low level of activity was corroborated by testimony of the following: an Enviropact employee who, after examining every lobby floor and 75% of the storage lockers, saw only 12 to 15 crates and a few cardboard files; a Chase loan officer who walked through the building and observed about 20 large storage crates; various neighborhood residents who noticed that the building was vacant and unused; and a local real estate agent who found the warehouse to be completely empty, unheated, unlit and infested with pigeons. Based on this evidence, the BSA rejected the testimony of Morgan's president, Jeffrey Morgan, that five percent of the building was used to maintain 40 to 50 customer accounts from April to July 1991.

The BSA's conclusion, however, was premised on more than the drastic reduction in the volume of storage activity. The BSA specifically noted the absence of any standard evidence for the critical four-month period typically available to document a legitimate business operation, such as insurance records, tax documents, advertisements, liability coverage, customer records, employee records, certain directory listings, telephone records or sales receipts. Jeffrey Morgan even acknowledged that the company failed to renew the requisite Department of Consumer Affairs license after it expired in April 1991.

The BSA thus properly considered objective factors regarding the nature and degree of nonconforming warehouse use, and its determination that Morgan's level of warehouse operations from April to July 1991 was too insignificant to preserve nonconforming use status under section 52–61 was supported by substantial evidence. That conflicting inferences may have been drawn from this evidence is of no moment. "[T]he duty of weighing the evidence and making the choice rests solely upon the [administrative agency]. The courts may not weigh the evidence or reject the choice made by [such agency] where the evidence is conflicting and room for choice exists" (*Matter of Stork Rest. v. Boland*, 282 N.Y. 256, 267).

* * *

Accordingly, the order of the Appellate Division should be reversed, with costs, and the petition dismissed.

JUDGES SIMONS, TITONE, BELLACOSA, SMITH, LEVINE and CIPARICK concur.

Notes

1. There is no uniformity of interpretation in situations in which the use has been discontinued and resumption of it is attempted. Some ordinances attempt to spell out specific time periods and provide that the use cannot be resumed after a given period of non-use has elapsed. A Wisconsin provision stated that if the nonconforming use were "*discontinued* for a period of 12 months, any future use of the building and premises shall conform to the ordinance." Did the word, "discontinued," mean a "voluntary abandonment" in the sense of an *intent* to discontinue? In Lessard v. Burnett County Bd. of Adjustment, 256 Wis.2d 821, 649 N.W.2d 728 (Wis.Ct. App.2002), a Wisconsin Court of Appeals affirmed that, "To apply the 'discontinuance' provisions, proof of intent to abandon the nonconforming use is not required." Zoning Bd. of Adjustment v. Davis, 699 So.2d 1264 (Ala.Civ.App.1997) holds, however, that "discontinuance results from the concurrence of an intent to abandon and some overt act or failure to act which carries the implication of abandonment" (citations omitted).

2. The construction by courts of "discontinued" as implying the requirement of an intent to abandon the nonconforming use is rather odd in view of the purpose of zoning. It exacerbates the problem caused by the nonconforming use and increases the difficulty in dealing with it. Some courts look solely at the fact of discontinuance and ignore the intent of the owner. Thus in Badger v. Town of Ferrisburgh, 168 Vt. 37, 712 A.2d 911 (1998), the nonconforming multifamily housing use was terminated even though the owners purchased the building from the United States Department of Housing and Urban Development (HUD) with the intent to use it as a three-family unit. Twenty-two months prior to the owners' purchase, HUD officials had required all tenants to leave the building. The applicable "discontinuance" ordinance set a time limit of 1 year and specifically stated that "[i]ntent to resume a nonconforming use shall not confer the right to do so." Ferrisburgh, Vt., Zoning Ordinance § 512(2). Also see Martin v. Beehan, 689 S.W.2d 29 (Ky.App.1985), where the court found a nonconforming hotel abandoned despite intermittent attempts to sell the hotel over a 10–year period. The court said the intent of the owner was immaterial, as did the courts in Anderson v. City of Paragould, 16 Ark.App. 10, 695 S.W.2d 851 (1985), and Ka–Hur Enterprises, Inc. v. Zoning Bd. of Appeals of Provincetown, 40 Mass.App.Ct. 71, 661 N.E.2d 120 (1996).

An unusual situation was presented in Sapakoff v. Town of Hague Zoning Bd. of Appeals, 211 A.D.2d 874, 621 N.Y.S.2d 215 (1995), where a nonconforming restaurant and bar was forfeited to the federal government under the drug laws, and the government sold the property at auction to Sapakoff who sought to reinstitute the nonconforming use. The court held that the two-year discontinuance provision was not tolled by virtue of the federal seizure and the permit to resume the previous use was revoked.

3. In Boles v. City of Chattanooga, 892 S.W.2d 416 (Tenn.App.1994), the court held that discontinuance of an adult-oriented establishment while a temporary restraining order was in effect was involuntary, and thus did not constitute discontinuance of a nonconforming use; and, in State ex rel. McArthur v. Board of Adjustment of City of Crestwood, 872 S.W.2d 651 (Mo.App.1994), the court held that the city could not terminate nonconforming use rights of six spaces in a mobile home park that had been vacant for a period of time, because the individual spaces were not lots or parcels, and thus the owner's inability to rent the individual spaces in the park was not a discontinuance.

4. Can a city treat a change of ownership as a discontinuance or termination-triggering event? In Village of Valatie v. Smith, 190 A.D.2d 17, 596 N.Y.S.2d 581 (1993), the court held that a provision in the village code terminating a nonconforming use upon a change in ownership of the property was unconstitutional on its face. The court stated: "[T]he provision at issue appears to run afoul of fundamental rule that zoning deals basically with land use rather than the person who owns or occupies the land." In Caserta v. Zoning Bd. of Appeals of City of Milford, 41 Conn.App. 77, 674 A.2d 855 (1996), the court held that after a change in ownership and an attempt by the new owner to reestablish a discontinued use, reference must be made to the previous owner's intent to reestablish the use. And, in Town of Lyons v. Bashor, 867 P.2d 159 (Colo.App.1993), the court held that the right to maintain a prior nonconforming use of two houses on one lot ran with the land (the lot was put up for sale after a court ordered dissolution of a marriage and had partitioned the land).

5. See Eric J. Strauss and Mary M. Giese, Elimination of Nonconformities: The Case of Voluntary Discontinuance, 25 The Urban Lawyer 159 (1993).

C. DESTRUCTION

MOFFATT v. FORREST CITY

Supreme Court of Arkansas, 1961.
234 Ark. 12, 350 S.W.2d 327.

McFADDIN, JUSTICE.

This litigation involves the application of the Zoning Ordinance of Forrest City, Arkansas. Appellants, Mr. and Mrs. Louie Moffatt, purchased a home in the residential district of Forrest City in 1951. In 1954 they made additions to the home and began operating a meat market and meat processing plant in said additions; and, as business improved, they made other additions and enlargements to the meat market portion of the premises. In 1959, Forrest City adopted a zoning ordinance which classified the area in which the Moffatt premises are located as entirely residential. Moffatt's market was a nonconforming use. The Zoning Ordinance provided: "If a building occupied by a non-conforming use is damaged to the extent of 60 per cent or more of its reproduction value exclusive of foundations, such building may not be restored for any non-conforming use."

On July 20, 1960, there was a fire in which the Moffatt residence quarters were almost entirely destroyed, and the market portion was considerably damaged. When the Moffats undertook to repair the market in order to resume business, the municipality filed this suit in Chancery Court to enjoin them from any reconstruction. The city alleged that the building was more than 60 per cent destroyed, exclusive of foundations, and that because of the Zoning Ordinance the owners could not restore the property for use as a meat market, such being a nonconforming use. The Moffatts resisted the city's claim. There were several hearings in the Chancery Court, and the Chancellor personally viewed the premises. The Chancery decree sustained the city's claim and enjoined the reconstruction of the building, or any building on the premises, for use as a meat market. The Moffatts have appealed. * * *

We agree with the appellants that a zoning ordinance is to be strictly construed in favor of the property holders, since the ordinance is in derogation of the common law and operates to deprive the owner of the property of a use which would otherwise be lawful. *City of Little Rock v. Williams*, 206 Ark. 861, 177 S.W.2d 924, and cases and authorities there cited; see, also *City of West Helena v. Bockman*, 221 Ark. 677, 256 S.W.2d 40. But even giving the Zoning Ordinance of Forrest City a strict construction in favor of the property holders, we must decide the fact question: whether the building on the premises was damaged "to the extent of 60 per cent or more of its reproduction value exclusive of foundations."

The residence and the meat market were housed in one structure. This is shown by the plats and pictures in the transcript. Regardless of the fact that there were additions to the market side of the house, there was only one overall building; and appellants could not have successfully claimed that the market was one building and the residence was another. Such a theory was originally urged, but with becoming candor appellants' learned counsel conceded: " * * * the cause was ultimately submitted on the theory that the market and the residence constituted one structure and that the issue before the Court was 60% destruction of it exclusive of foundations."

There was evidence that the total value of the building before the fire was approximately $15,000; and that to restore the building after the fire would cost approximately $12,000. Five witnesses—some of them building contractors—testified that the damage exceeded 60 per cent. Mr. Moffatt did not dispute the fact that the residence portion of the structure was a total loss; and there was other evidence that the residence portion was 10/15ths of the total value. While there is evidence to the contrary, we cannot say that the preponderance of the evidence is contrary to the Chancellor's conclusions as to the percentage of damage.

Affirmed.

Notes

1. In Stanton v. Town of Pawleys Island, 317 S.C. 498, 455 S.E.2d 171 (1995), the court reversed the denial of a permit to repair a home that had been substantially damaged in a hurricane. The zoning ordinance prohibited ground level living quarters in coastal high hazard areas. Thus Stanton's house was nonconforming. The court held that, as a whole, the house was not more than 50 percent destroyed. Compare Pelham Esplanade v. Village of Pelham Manor Board of Trustees, 154 A.D.2d 599, 546 N.Y.S.2d 427 (1989), where the owner of two apartment buildings sought a permit to rebuild one of the buildings that had undergone fire damage greater than 50 percent. The court held that looking at the "apartment complex as a whole," less than 50 percent was destroyed and the owner was entitled to the permit.

2. In the absence of an ordinance provision to the contrary, the general rule is that a discontinuance of use caused by a fire on the premises does not amount to an abandonment and the building may be repaired and the use resumed. What about discontinuance of the use due to repair of the building, acts of war, government restrictions, foreclosure or condemnation actions, or injunctive relief granted by a court having equity powers?

D. AMORTIZATION—USES AND LIMITATIONS

Some local zoning ordinances require certain nonconforming uses to be amortized over a specified period at the end of which they must be terminated. The term "amortization" is used to describe these provisions because they allow the owner some time during which to recoup his investment in the nonconforming use. Courts may uphold such provisions where the benefit to the public has been deemed of greater moment than the detriment to the property owner and where the property owner's investment is fairly recognized. When an amortization period is reasonable is a question that is answered, typically, in the light of the facts of each particular case. Certainly, a critical factor is the length of the amortization period in relation to the investment. The critical question, however, is whether the public gain achieved by the exercise of the police power outweighs the private loss suffered by the owners of the nonconforming uses. Some state courts take a more expansive view of property rights and make local regulators work harder to allow significant owner investments to be recouped.

Contexts in which amortization provisions are likely to be upheld are:

1. When the common law of nuisance would allow neighboring property owners to enjoin the continuation of the nonconforming use. For example, a gravel pit, auto wrecking operation, or junkyard, harmful to children in a developing residential area, might be enjoined under a private nuisance action. If an amortization provision is challenged, the municipality can show that the owner's property interest is slight

because of her vulnerability to a nuisance action. In this context, however, the label "amortization" is inappropriate. The grace period, if any, allowed by the local statute is gratuitous if, in fact, the owner's use may be enjoined as a nuisance.

2. When the nonconforming use is somewhat noxious and the owner has little investment in it. For example, a provision requiring the owner to cease raising pigeons on the roof or to remove an old outdoor sign might withstand challenge because of the minimal nature of the owner's investment and the significant harm done to the zoning scheme if the owner's activity is allowed to continue. Harder cases are presented when the owner has a significant investment in the use and the public interest in removing it is clear but where the threat to public health and safety is not imminent.

AVR, INC. v. CITY OF ST. LOUIS PARK

Court of Appeals of Minnesota, 1998.
585 N.W.2d 411.

WILLIS, JUDGE.

* * *

AVR owns and operates a ready-mix concrete plant in the City of St. Louis Park. The plant was constructed in 1954. In 1959, the city passed a zoning ordinance permitting ready-mix plants in the area of the city zoned for industrial use but only pursuant to a special use permit. The city did not grant a special use permit to the then-owners of this ready-mix plant, but rather classified the plant as a preexisting nonconforming use, because it was within 400 feet of a residential district.

In 1973, the city amended its zoning code to eliminate ready-mix and concrete block plants as permitted uses in the city. AVR purchased the ready-mix plant in 1974 for $260,000. In May 1980, the city adopted a new comprehensive plan and put AVR on notice that the city intended to phase out the plant and rezone the site for commercial or office use or "as a second choice high density residential use." AVR commenced a declaratory judgment action seeking to invalidate the 1973 zoning ordinance on the ground that it wrongfully eliminated ready-mix plants as permitted uses in industrial zones. The district court declared the ordinance void as applied to AVR, and the city appealed. This court concluded that because the plant was not a public nuisance or a nuisance per se, the city could not legislate it out of existence. *Apple Valley Red–E–Mix v. City of St. Louis Park*, 359 N.W.2d 313, 315 (Minn.App.1984), review denied (Minn. Mar. 21, 1985).

In 1990, the city adopted another new comprehensive plan, which provides that, in the area where the AVR plant is located,

> [h]eavy industrial uses including a concrete ready mix plant and outdoor storage of heavy equipment are to be phased out, and the sites are to be used for high density residential use.

St. Louis Park, Minn., Comprehensive Plan 1990–2010 § 16, at 16–5 (1990). In 1992, the city rezoned AVR's property from I–4 Industrial to R–4 Multifamily Residential. The ordinance provides that the city council

> shall by ordinance amend the Zoning Ordinance to establish an amortization period for individual land uses not permitted in the City. The amortization period shall commence upon publication of the ordinance establishing the length of amortization period.

St. Louis Park, Minn., Code of Ordinances § 14:7–4(D)(4) (1992). The 1992 ordinance required the owners of all properties "that contain a use not permitted in any zoning district [to] register their non-conforming use with the City" within one year of the adoption of the ordinance. *Id.* § 14:7–4(B). The ordinance also required the zoning administrator to meet with such property owners, review each registration application, and determine a reasonable amortization period for each nonconforming use. In determining the length of a reasonable amortization period, the zoning administrator was to consider, at a minimum, the following factors:

> a. Information relating to the structure located on the property;
>
> b. Nature of the use;
>
> c. Location of the property in relation to surrounding uses;
>
> d. Description of the character of and uses in the surrounding neighborhood;
>
> e. Cost of the property and improvements to the property;
>
> f. Benefit to the public by requiring the termination of the non-conforming use;
>
> g. Burden on the property owner by requiring the termination of the non-conforming use;
>
> h. The length of time the use has been in existence and the length of time the use has been non-conforming.

Id. § 14:7–4(D)(2). The city council accepted AVR's registration of the plant property as substantially complete on June 29, 1995.

On July 11, 1995, the city council and planning commission held a joint public hearing for the purpose of adopting an amortization ordinance relating to the AVR plant. City staff presented to the council and planning commission the report and recommendation required by the 1992 ordinance. AVR presented information supporting its position that the plant has an indefinite remaining physical life.

On October 2, 1995, the city amended its zoning ordinance by adopting the following provision:

> The reasonable amortization period applicable to the ready-mix facility owned and operated by [AVR] * * * shall be two (2) years, commencing upon publication of this ordinance. At the conclusion of

> the two-year amortization period, [AVR's] nonconforming ready-mix use shall terminate and cease to operate.

Id. § 14:7–4.1 (1995). In conjunction with the adoption of section 14:7–4.1, the city council adopted a resolution that contained 42 findings of fact supporting the ordinance and that stated:

> The Minnesota Supreme Court has directed, in the *Naegele Outdoor Advertising Co. of Minn. v. Village of Minnetonka* decision, that any amortization period must be "reasonable." Courts in other jurisdictions have identified at least seven (7) factors by which the reasonableness of an amortization period may be evaluated. The St. Louis Park Code of Ordinances incorporates those specific factors in its Amortization Ordinance.

St. Louis Park, Minn., Res. No. 95–131, p. 3 (1995) (citing St. Louis Park, Minn., Code of Ordinances § 14:7–4(D)(2)(a-h) (1992)). The city addressed the factors identified in its amortization ordinance in making findings to support its determination of the length of the amortization period for AVR's plant.

The city also considered the useful life of the plant. To assist it in making that determination, the city retained an accounting firm and a real estate appraisal firm. The accounting firm advised the city that, based on generally accepted accounting principles, the plant's "useful life expired no later than 1994" and that AVR had not only recovered its investment but also had earned a return of approximately 560 percent on its investment. *Id.* p. 37. The city council found that

> [b]ased upon the expert opinions of Arthur Andersen and Patchin, the age of [AVR's] St. Louis Park Facility, AVR's proposal to the City nine years ago to replace the existing St. Louis Park structure, AVR's testimony regarding necessary size of potential relocation sites, and the voluntary relocation and/or new construction actions of other ready-mix businesses in the Twin Cities area, AVR's St. Louis Park Facility has passed its useful life and AVR has had a reasonable opportunity to recover its economic investment.

Id. p.39.

In December 1995, AVR commenced an action seeking a declaration that the city's adoption of the amortization ordinance and the ordinance establishing a two-year amortization period for AVR's plant (1) violate AVR's right to due process of law; (2) violate AVR's right to equal protection of the laws; (3) violate AVR's vested rights by eliminating concrete ready-mix plants as a special or permitted use; and (4) constitute an unconstitutional taking of AVR's property without just compensation. AVR and the city made cross-motions for summary judgment. On January 15, 1998, the district court granted summary judgment to the city and dismissed AVR's complaint. This appeal followed.

* * *

AVR contends that the city's adoption of an amortization ordinance for AVR's plant is equivalent to a decision to grant or deny a variance or special use permit. Therefore, AVR argues, the city's decision is quasi-judicial and the courts should afford it less deference than they would give a legislative zoning decision. Minnesota courts have distinguished

> between zoning matters which are legislative in nature (rezoning) and those which are quasi-judicial (variances and special use permits). Even so, the standard of review is the same for all zoning matters, namely, whether the zoning authority's action was reasonable. Our cases express this standard in various ways: Is there a "reasonable basis" for the decision? or is the decision "unreasonable, arbitrary or capricious"? or is the decision "reasonably debatable"?

Honn v. City of Coon Rapids, 313 N.W.2d 409, 416–17 (Minn.1981). But application of the reasonableness standard depends on the zoning action at issue:

> [I]n legislative zoning, the municipal body is formulating public policy, so the inquiry focuses on whether the proposed use promotes the public welfare. In quasi-judicial zoning, public policy has already been established and the inquiry focuses on whether the proposed use is contrary to the general welfare as already established in the zoning ordinance. Consequently, the reviewing courts, in determining what is reasonable, should keep in mind that the zoning authority is less circumscribed by judicial oversight when it considers zoning or rezoning than when it considers a special use permit or a variance.

Id. at 417. AVR argues that because the amortization ordinance "does not effect a zoning change to unimproved property" but rather "terminat[es] AVR's use of the property" as a ready-mix plant, it is "equivalent to the grant or denial of a special use permit." We disagree. *See Naegele Outdoor Adver. Co. v. Village of Minnetonka*, 281 Minn. 492, 501, 503, 162 N.W.2d 206, 213, 215 (1968) (identifying ordinance establishing amortization period as legislative device and stating power to enact "this type of zoning requirement" is implied); *DI MA Corp. v. City of St. Cloud*, 562 N.W.2d 312, 319–20 (Minn.App.1997) (analyzing validity of amortization ordinance under statute that establishes requirements for amendments to zoning ordinances).

Because zoning or rezoning classifications are legislative acts, courts must uphold them unless

> [their] opponents prove that the classification is unsupported by any rational basis related to promoting the public health, safety, morals, or general welfare, or that the classification amounts to a taking without compensation. This rule applies regardless of the size of the tract of land involved.

State by Rochester Ass'n of Neighborhoods v. City of Rochester, 268 N.W.2d 885, 888 (Minn.1978).

AVR has not shown that the city's adoption of the ordinance establishing an amortization period for AVR's plant is unsupported by any rational basis related to the promotion of the public health, safety, morals, or general welfare. Because the city's establishment of an amortization period for a preexisting nonconforming use was a legislative act, we conclude that the district court did not err in deferring to the city's broad discretion.

AVR contends that the two-year amortization period for its plant is unreasonable. In establishing the length of the amortization period, the city considered the plant's "useful life," a term the Minnesota Supreme Court has used but has not defined. *Naegele*, 281 Minn. at 501, 162 N.W.2d at 213 (stating only "that the useful life of the nonconforming use corresponds roughly to the amortization period"). The city based its determination of useful life on its conclusion that AVR had recouped its original investment and, to a lesser extent, on the fact that the property has been fully depreciated for income tax purposes. In addition, the city considered the other factors it had adopted by ordinance.

AVR argues that the city acted unreasonably in failing to consider "the remaining useful economic or expected life" in determining the length of the amortization period. *See, e.g., City of La Mesa v. Tweed & Gambrell Planing Mill,* 146 Cal.App.2d 762, 304 P.2d 803, 808 (Cal.Dist. Ct.App.1956) (noting estimated 21 years of remaining economic life as one reason for holding five-year amortization period arbitrary and unreasonable). In *Naegele*, the supreme court stated only that the underlying issue in determining the length of an amortization period is whether it is reasonable. 281 Minn. at 501, 162 N.W.2d at 213.

In analyzing the reasonableness of an amortization period, courts in some jurisdictions have considered the property owner's recoupment of its original investment. *See, e.g., Rives v. City of Clarksville*, 618 S.W.2d 502, 510 (Tenn.Ct.App.1981) (considering length of amortization period in relation to property owner's investment); *Town of Islip v. Caviglia*, 73 N.Y.2d 544, 542 N.Y.S.2d 139, 540 N.E.2d 215, 224 (N.Y.1989) (determining reasonableness by examining all facts, including length of amortization period in relation to investment); *City of University Park v. Benners*, 485 S.W.2d 773, 777 (Tex.1972) (noting that termination of nonconforming use after amortization period allowing recoupment of investment is not unconstitutional taking).

Courts also have considered whether the property in question has been fully depreciated for income tax purposes in reviewing the reasonableness of an amortization period, although this factor alone has not been held to be determinative. *See, e.g., Art Neon Co. v. City & County of Denver*, 488 F.2d 118, 122 (10th Cir.1973) (considering depreciation for tax purposes); National Adver. Co. v. County of Monterey, 1 Cal.3d 875, 83 Cal.Rptr. 577, 464 P.2d 33, 35–36 (Cal.1970) (holding that where billboards have been fully depreciated for tax purposes, amortization period was not unreasonable); *Village of Skokie v. Walton on Dempster, Inc.*, 119 Ill.App.3d 299, 74 Ill.Dec. 791, 456 N.E.2d 293, 297 (Ill.App.Ct.

1983) (concluding that amortization period was reasonable where property was completely depreciated for tax purposes); *Philanz Oldsmobile, Inc. v. Keating*, 51 A.D.2d 437, 381 N.Y.S.2d 916, 920 (N.Y.App.Div.1976) (stating that where signs had been fully depreciated for tax purposes, financial loss is nonexistent).

To the extent AVR's contention that the city should have considered the "remaining useful economic or expected life" of AVR's plant is another way of saying that the amortization period should be based on the plant's fair market value or its replacement cost, the argument leads to illogical and contradictory consequences. As one court has recognized:

> [A]pplication of the market-value standard would result in a vicious circle: market value depends on the period of expected nonconforming use, and the period of nonconforming use allowed depends on market value. * * *
>
> Cost of replacing the nonconforming structure, even with an allowance for depreciation, would also provide an unsatisfactory measure of recoupment. A landowner is not permitted to extend the period of nonconforming use by replacements or improvements because [the owner] would be able to extend the nonconforming use indefinitely * * *. To allow replacement cost as a measure of the recoupment allowed would thus allow unjustified extension of the nonconforming use. Moreover, [it] would ignore the factor of obsolescence, which might be substantial * * *.

Murmur Corp. v. Board of Adjustment, 718 S.W.2d 790, 796–97 (Tex. App.1986) (citations omitted).

Here, the city used a combination of recoupment of investment and tax depreciation status as factors in determining the useful life for AVR's plant. The record shows that over the past 23 years the plant provided AVR a return of approximately 560% on its investment and that the plant has been fully depreciated for income tax purposes. These two factors provided the city with a reasonable basis to determine the plant's useful life for purposes of establishing an amortization period.

* * *

Because the ordinance establishing a two-year amortization period for AVR's plant reflects the city's consideration of the plant's useful life and an analysis of other relevant factors adopted by the city, the district court did not err in upholding the city's two-year amortization period.

* * *

Because the city's action was a legislative decision, the district court did not err in deferring to the city's broad discretion to adopt an ordinance establishing a two-year amortization period for AVR's plant. Additionally, because the ordinance establishing an amortization period for AVR's plant is based on the city's consideration of the plant's useful life and application of other relevant factors, the district court did not err in upholding the city's establishment of a two-year amortization period. Finally, because AVR did not demonstrate disparate treatment of similarly situated property owners resulting from the enactment of the amortization ordinance and the ordinance establishing a two-year amortization period for AVR's plant, the district court did not err in concluding that there is no equal protection violation.

Affirmed.

Notes

1. In Akron v. Chapman, 160 Ohio St. 382, 116 N.E.2d 697, 42 A.L.R.2d 1140 (1953), the city required the defendant's nonconforming junkyard to comply with the requirements of the new residential classification specified in the zoning ordinance. The defendant continued to operate his junkyard and the city brought an action to close his business. In holding for the property owner, the court wrote: "What is property? It has been defined as not merely the ownership and possession of lands or chattels but the unrestricted right of their use, enjoyment and disposal. Anything which destroys any of these elements of property, to that extent destroys the property itself. The substantial value of property lies in its use. If the right of use is denied, the value of the property is annihilated and ownership is rendered a barren right. See Spann v. City of Dallas, 111 Tex. 350, 235 S.W. 513, 19 A.L.R. 1387, and O'Connor v. City of Moscow, 69 Idaho 37, 202 P.2d 401, 9 A.L.R.2d 1031. The right to continue to use one's property in a lawful business and in a manner which does not constitute a nuisance and which was lawful at the time it was acquired is within the protection of Section 1, Article XIV, Amendments, Constitution of the United States, and Section 16, Article I of the Ohio Constitution, which provide that no person shall be deprived of life, liberty or property without due process of law."

2. For a case with facts similar to the Akron case but an opposite result, see Collins v. City of Spartanburg, 281 S.C. 212, 314 S.E.2d 332 (1984). The court upheld an ordinance imposing a five-year amortization period on junkyards, auto wrecking yards and auto storage yards, balancing the large public gain from elimination of eyesores against the small private loss. Also see Neighborhood Committee on Lead Pollution v. Board of Adj. of City of Dallas, 728 S.W.2d 64 (Tex.App.1987), where the court upheld a six-year amortization period for a lead smelting and plating operation. Under Texas law, the Board of Adjustment may determine the termination date for nonconforming uses, under the standard of examining the capital investment in the structure by the person owning the land at the time the use became nonconforming. Board of Adjustment of Dallas v. Patel, 882 S.W.2d 87 (Tex.App.1994).

3. In Centaur, Inc. v. Richland County, 301 S.C. 374, 392 S.E.2d 165 (1990), the court upheld a two-year amortization period for sexually-oriented business and limiting their relocation to 16 specified areas in the county.

SECTION 5. ACCESSORY USES

Accessory uses are those uses of land found on the same lot as the principal use and that are subordinate, incidental to, and customarily found in connection with the principal use. For example, a garage is accessory to a residential use of a property because it is customarily found in connection with and is incidental and subordinate to the principal residential use. Generally, zoning laws permit lot owners to use their land for a permitted principal use as well for activities that are accessory to that use.

In order to qualify as accessory, a use must also be incidental and subordinate to the principal use. To be incidental, an accessory use must be reasonably related to the principal use. For instance, a garage or recreational use is reasonably related to the principal residential use and thus deemed incidental. To be subordinate, the accessory use must be proportionately smaller than the principal use. The garage is generally smaller than the house, for instance. An accessory use must also be customarily found in conjunction with its principal use. A use is customary if it commonly, habitually, and by long practice has been reasonably associated with a principal use. A most common example of this is vehicle parking for a residence or business.

Accessory use provisions in zoning laws allow a range of incidental uses of property that owners expect to engage in when they purchase their property for its principal use. By permitting uses customarily incidental and subordinate to the principal activity, zoning ordinances allow property owners additional beneficial use of their property. Regulations which limit the accessory uses allowed in a district also recognize that some neighborhoods should be protected from accessory uses that are not consistent with the expectations of the property owners. This separation of inconsistent uses into zoning districts is part of the original purpose of zoning.

Local ordinances regulate accessory uses in a variety of ways. Within the local zoning law language regulating accessory uses may be found in the definitions of "accessory," "lot," or "use," in separate sections, or in the schedule of regulations for individual districts. There are at least five different approaches a municipality can utilize to regulate accessory uses in its zoning law.

- First, a municipality may simply permit accessory uses by accepting those uses that meet the qualifications of what is customary and incidental. In this case the ordinance does not provide guidelines or expressly state what is or is not an accessory use. Rather, the ordinance simply defines accessory uses as customary, incidental, and subordinate in the definition section and then permits these uses in each district.

- Second, a zoning law may permit certain accessory uses and prohibit all others. The legislature can do this by listing which accessory uses are allowed in each use district. As a matter of statutory construction, those uses not expressly permitted in the list are prohibited unless clearly stated otherwise. This is the most restrictive means of regulation because it limits what qualifies as an accessory use to the legislature's list. It could result in denial of a use that is otherwise incidental, subordinate, and customary to the principal use.

- A more flexible approach is to list and prohibit only problematic accessory uses. This eliminates foreseeable problems with the listed uses while permitting all other accessory uses that are customary, incidental, and subordinate.
- A fourth approach is to provide guidelines that can assist the zoning enforcement officer and zoning board of appeals in interpreting what is an accessory use and by adopting a nonexclusive, illustrative list of acceptable uses. If this approach is used, it is crucial that the law explicitly state that the list is nonexclusive.
- A final regulatory approach is to list some accessory uses that are allowed by special use permit and subject them to certain requirements. This approach can be used by itself or in conjunction with any of the other four approaches.

Permitting accessory uses creates needed flexibility, but can also create problems both for landowners and the municipality. A municipality must be careful when enforcing accessory use regulations against educational institutions and religious organizations. Accessory uses connected to these principal uses are presumed to serve the public interest if they are incidental to the principal use. Although originally intended to permit landowners to use their property fully, the accessory use device is sometimes used to expand greatly the intensity of use, establish a unique or novel use, expand a nonconforming use, or change the use of a property when a variance cannot be obtained. A municipality drafting and enforcing an accessory use provision should be careful to avoid these concerns.

PARKS v. BOARD OF ADJUSTMENT OF THE CITY OF KILLEEN

Court of Civil Appeals of Texas, Third District, 1978.
566 S.W.2d 365.

SHANNON, JUSTICE.

This appeal involves construction and application of the zoning ordinance of Killeen. The issue is whether operation of a music school by a property owner in his residence violates the ordinance. The judgment of the district court of Bell County affirmed the order of the Board of Adjustment of Killeen. That order was to the effect that operation of the school was not in violation of the ordinance. We will affirm the judgment.

Charles E. Baxter and wife, Margaret, own a residence in Killeen. Their property is located in a district zoned single-family residential. The Baxters live in the house and they also conduct a music school there. They teach as many as one hundred-ten student hours each week. Several students are taught different music instruments simultaneously.

The Baxters earn in excess of $20,000 annually from operation of the music school.

Appellant Charles P. Parks owns property near the Baxter residence. Parks initiated proceedings culminating in this appeal in an effort to close down the music school. Parks' position was, and is on appeal, that the operation of the music school was in violation of Subsection 6 of the zoning ordinance. The relevant provisions of Subsection 6 are here set out:

> "Section 6. District 'R–1.' Single-family residential district.
>
> SUBSECTION 6–1. USE REGULATIONS
>
> (M) Accessory buildings and uses, customarily incident to the uses in this subsection 6–1 and located on the same lot therewith, not involving the conduct of a retail business.
>
> (1) The term accessory use shall include customary home occupations such as the office of a milliner, dressmaker, musician or artist, provided that such uses are located in the dwelling used by such a person as his or her private residence, and provided that no assistant not a member of the family residing on the premises is employed, and no window display or sign is used to advertise the same."

Subsection 6–1(M)(1) permits accessory uses customarily incident to single-family dwellings. An examination of Subsection 6–1(M)(1) demonstrates that an accessory use includes customary home occupations. A music school is a "customary home occupation" by the terms of the section. The proof shows that the Baxters use the dwelling as their private residence and that only the Baxters conduct music classes.

By several points of error, appellant insists that the size of the music school and its income are additional limitations which must be considered in the determination whether the music school operation is a "customary home occupation." If the size and income of the school were to be considered, appellant claims that the school could not be viewed as a "customary home occupation."

Appellant's primary authority for argument that a residential music school may lose its "home occupation" status if it becomes too extensive is *Florence v. Turbeville*, 239 S.C. 126, 121 S.E.2d 437 (1961). In *Florence* two hundred-twenty students were instructed six days each week by the owners of the residence. The facts were in that case that the dominant use or purpose of the property was no longer residential but instead commercial. To the contrary, in the case at bar, the evidence supports the district court's presumed conclusion that the property was still used as a residence and the giving of music lessons was but incidental to that use.

Subsection 6–1(M)(1) does not characterize "customary home occupation" in terms of profitability or volume of business. Had the city council desired to so limit the term, "customary home occupation," it could have done so. It is not for the Board of Adjustment or the courts to engraft further limitations upon the ordinance. Accordingly, the Baxter's music school remains a "customary home occupation" even though prosperous and well attended. Appellant's points of error are overruled.

The judgment is affirmed.

GREENTREE v. GOOD SHEPHERD EPISCOPAL CHURCH

Supreme Court, New York County, New York, 1989.
550 N.Y.S.2d 981, 146 Misc.2d 500.

LEONARD N. COHEN, JUSTICE:

"* * * [T]HERE WAS NO ROOM FOR THEM IN THE INN." (LUKE 2:7)

This is a motion by plaintiffs, a unit owner and President of the Board of Managers of a condominium known as Greentree At Murray Hill, located at 248 East 31st Street, New York, New York (the "Condominium") to temporarily enjoin defendants from operating a homeless shelter at Good Shepherd Episcopal Church (the "Church") adjacent to the condominium. By separate notices of cross-motion, the defendant Church, the defendant The Partnership for the Homeless, Inc. (the "Partnership"), and the City defendants, seek dismissal of the complaint for failure to state a cause of action.

"AM I MY BROTHER'S KEEPER?" (GENESIS 4:9)

This action involves important questions regarding who shall be responsible for our less fortunate brothers and sisters. Specifically, the action concerns the extent, if any, to which the court may or should be brought in as arbiter of a dispute involving the right of a church and its parishioners to exercise their religion and to practice Christian charity by temporarily sheltering the homeless and the rights of some of the adjacent property-owning residents who fear crime, drug sales, prostitution and a diminution of property values.

In June 1989, in response to the citywide need for emergency shelters for the thousands of homeless, the Church opened its doors to groups of ten (10) homeless men for temporary emergency shelter three (3) nights a week, in cooperation with the defendant Partnership. The Partnership, a not-for-profit corporation, was founded in August 1982, by lay persons from various religious congregations with leaders of the major religious faith denominations, to provide the major interfaith response to the growing problem of homelessness in New York City. The Partnership presently includes a network of over 380 churches and synagogues in all five boroughs, as well as programs in other major cities across the nation. The Partnership's temporary homeless shelter city network currently embraces 147 church/synagogue shelters, including this Church, providing up to 1600 homeless beds at the height of the winter and over 400,000 individual nights of temporary shelter annually.

Although the Partnership has a contractual relationship with defendant New York City Human Resources Administration ("HRA"), which provides approximately 17 percent of its operating budget, and less than 3 percent of its total budget, the bulk of its operating budget is funded from the private sector. The City, through HRA's contract with the Church, provides only beds, linens, clothing, toiletries and cleaning supplies. The City's Department of Buildings periodically inspects the space for compliance with relevant health and safety regulations. The City does not pay either the Partnership or the Church for its temporary sheltering of the homeless, nor does the City provide for any siting control. Sites for temporary shelters are selected by the Partnership in cooperation with participating churches and/or synagogues. The homeless men who are afforded temporary shelter at the Church are transported there by the City from the John Heuss Center, a drop-in center on Beaver Street in lower Manhattan, established by Trinity Parish. The men arrive between 9:15–9:45 p.m., and are picked up by bus the following morning at approximately 6:00 a.m. From the time of their arrival until their departure the following morning, the men are continually supervised and are not allowed to congregate in the street. The court notes that the Church also has a program which provides food for the hungry on Sundays (following the morning service) and on Fridays at lunchtime. That program—which is not the subject of this lawsuit—distributes bag lunches to approximately 100 guests on Sunday and between 50–75 on Friday. The funds are provided entirely by the Parish and the work is done entirely by parishioners.

In opposition to plaintiff's motion to temporarily enjoin operation of its homeless shelter, and in support of its cross motion to dismiss the complaint, the Church has submitted affidavits by The Right Reverend Richard F. Grein, and Bishop Coadjutor and acting Ecclesiastical Authority of the Diocese of New York of the Episcopal Church, and by the Reverend Vincent Ioppolo, Rector of the Church, attesting to their deep and sincere religious convictions underlying their participation in the homeless shelter program. They cite the teachings of Jesus and the Holy Scriptures and resolutions adopted by the Diocese at its conventions in 1973, 1981, 1983, 1984, 1985 and 1986.

The Bishop states:

> "While others may debate the root causes of hunger and homelessness and who should bear the ultimate responsibility for feeding and housing the victims, as Christians, we do not believe we have the leisure to turn our backs in the meantime on those in our midst who hunger, thirst or have no place to lay their heads."

The Rector of the Church states that:

> "[C]aring for the poor and sheltering the homeless has consistently been part of religion in the Judeo–Christian tradition. The mandate to embrace and to minister to society's outcasts is a lesson learnt [sic] from the Bible."

The Bishop and Rector cite Bible chapter and verse in support of their position that sheltering the homeless is a religious obligation and an important outlet for its ministry.

The Reverend Ioppolo also states that "the religious tradition of giving refuge to persons in need has its roots in Roman, medieval European and English common law. During the Middle Ages every church was a potential sanctuary. Religious sanctuary is an equally well-established practice in this country."

Plaintiffs do not seriously question the sincerity of the religious convictions of the defendant Church or ascribe any but honorable motivations to its conduct in opening up its doors to the handful of homeless men three nights a week. However, they assert that the Church may not house the ten homeless men because such use of the Church would constitute a violation of the applicable Zoning Resolution and the Church's Certificate of Occupancy. Plaintiffs also claim that such use constitutes a public and private nuisance.

* * *

[Portions of the case dealing with other claims of the plaintiffs are omitted]

The plaintiffs argue as to the first and second causes of action that the Church is currently classified as a "Place of Assembly," pursuant to Subchapter 3, § 27–254 of the New York City Charter, and, as such, it may only be used "for religious, recreational, political or social purposes, or for the consumption of food or drink or for similar group activities * * *." They argue that for the premises to be used legally as a shelter, it would have to be classified for "residential use," pursuant to subchapter 3, § 27–264 of the New York City Charter, which applies to "buildings and spaces that are primarily occupied for the shelter and sleeping accommodations of individuals on a day-to-day or week-to-week basis" (emphasis added). Plaintiffs further argue that a new Certificate of Occupancy is required "to ensure that the premises are safe for their intended use" and that the Church is being used as a hotel or motel contrary to the Certificate of Occupancy. They state that a new Certificate of Occupancy is therefore required because such "unauthorized and illegal use threatens not only the people staying within the Church but the adjoining property owners such as the plaintiffs herein."

It has long been held that a church or synagogue may be used for accessory uses and activities which go beyond just prayer and worship (*Community Synagogue v. Bates*, 1 N.Y.2d 445, 453, 154 N.Y.S.2d 15, 136 N.E.2d 488 [1956]). Section 12–10 of the Zoning Resolution defines the term "accessory use" and relevantly states that such use:

> "(a) Is a use conducted on the same zoning lot as the principal use to which it is related (whether located within the same accessory building or other structure, or as an accessory use of land), * * * and

(b) Is a use which is clearly incidental to, and customarily found in connection with, such principal use; and

(c) Is either in the same ownership as such principal use, or is operated and maintained on the same zoning lot substantially for the benefit or convenience of the owner, occupants, employees, customers, or visitors of the principal use."

Such permissible "accessory uses" for a church or synagogue include a Sunday school, men's and women's clubs, youth and community centers (*Id*); a guest house for a Rabbi (*Jewish Reconstructionist Synagogue v. Incorporated Village of Roslyn Harbor*, 38 N.Y.2d 283, 379 N.Y.S.2d 747, 342 N.E.2d 534 [1975], rearg. denied, 39 N.Y.2d 743, 384 N.Y.S.2d 1029, 349 N.E.2d 892 [1976], cert. denied, 426 U.S. 950, 96 S.Ct. 3171, 49 L.Ed.2d 1187); a school and meeting room at a church (*Diocese of Rochester v. Planning Bd. of Town of Brighton*, 1 N.Y.2d 508, 154 N.Y.S.2d 849, 136 N.E.2d 827 [1956]); a day care center (*Unitarian Universalist Church v. Shorten*, 63 Misc.2d 978, 314 N.Y.S.2d 66 [Sup. Ct., Nassau Co 1970]); a drug program (*Slevin v. Long Island Jewish Med. Center*, 66 Misc.2d 312, 319 N.Y.S.2d 937 [Sup.Ct. Nassau Co.1971]) as well as a temporary shelter for the homeless operated by a church, such as in the case at bar (*St. John's Evangelical Lutheran Church v. City of Hoboken*, 195 N.J.Super. 414, 479 A.2d 935 [Hudson Co.1983]).

Therefore, it is clear that the Church's temporary homeless shelter sanctuary program is, as a matter of law, a permissible "accessory use" of the Church which is a protected activity under § 12–10 of the Zoning Resolution and under the Church's current Certificate of Occupancy. Accordingly, plaintiffs' argument that the use of Church property as an emergency temporary shelter for the homeless violates the applicable Zoning Resolution and its Certificate of Occupancy is without merit.

Plaintiffs' argument that the Church is operating a "hotel or motel for transients," contrary to its Certificate of Occupancy and requiring a zoning variance, is also without merit. There is no allegation that living or sleeping accommodations are being rented, or that provisions exist for a 24 hour desk, bellboy or telephone service. Under Zoning Resolution § 12–10, such factors are the sine qua non of a "hotel" (See also, Black's Law Dictionary [rev. 4th ed.], which defines a "hotel" as "a house which is held out to well-behaved members of the traveling public, *who are willing to pay reasonable rates for accommodations*, as a place where they will be received and entertained *as guests for compensation*, and will be furnished with food, drink, and lodging, and everything which they have occasion for while on their way" [emphasis added]).

To the extent that the first and second causes of action allege violations of the Zoning Resolution and Certificate of Occupancy, the court finds, as a matter of law, that such allegations fail to state causes of action. Accordingly, the defendants' cross motions to dismiss those branches of the first and second causes of action are granted.

* * *

DOBO v. ZONING BD. OF ADJUSTMENT OF CITY OF WILMINGTON

Supreme Court of North Carolina, 2003.
576 S.E.2d 324, 356 N.C. 656.

PER CURIAM.

For the reasons stated in the dissenting opinion, the decision of the Court of Appeals is reversed and the case is remanded to the Court of Appeals for further remand to the Superior Court, New Hanover County, for proceedings not inconsistent with the dissenting opinion. REVERSED AND REMANDED; DISCRETIONARY REVIEW IMPROVIDENTLY ALLOWED.

TYSON, JUDGE, * * * I respectfully dissent from part IIA of the majority's opinion as I would hold that petitioners' actual use of the Wood–Mizer portable band saw does not violate the Zoning Ordinance.

IIA.

Petitioners argue that the Board's decision was not supported by competent evidence, and is arbitrary and capricious. I agree. Section 19–6 of the Zoning Ordinance defines the term "accessory use": Accessory use or structure: A use or structure on the same lot with, and of a nature customarily incidental and subordinate to, the principal use or structure (i.e. pump house, home occupation, tool shed, detached garage, storage shed, garage apartment, and other uses as determined by the Code Enforcement Officer).

All of the evidence presented shows that petitioners used the Wood-Mizer saw for non-commercial and non-industrial purposes, as well as for the construction of a fully permitted hobby woodworking shop to be located on their property. I disagree with the majority that because the saw is powered by a forty-horsepower diesel engine; is twenty-six feet four inches in length, six feet six inches wide, seven feet seven inches high; includes the use of a trailer, backhoe, front-end loader, and dump truck; and is capable of cutting logs twenty-one feet long by three inches in diameter automatically converts the use of the Wood–Mizer saw into an industrial use or involves a manufacturing process. Adopting the reasoning of the majority would allow the City to prohibit petitioners' private automobile, with a 200 horsepower engine and a twenty gallon gas tank, because it could be used as a commercial taxicab.

Construction necessarily requires heavy equipment to complete the improvements, such as bulldozers, dump trucks, and front-end loaders for clearing and grading of the land, as well as cranes to set trusses on the structure. Here, the record shows that the backhoe, front-end loader, and dump truck were also legally located on petitioners' 3.2 acre tract, as petitioners legally operate a well drilling business on their property. The Board's and majority's focus is solely on the size and possible uses of the saw, not its actual use by petitioners. Their assertions are insufficient to prohibit petitioners' non-industrial use of their saw.

The conclusion of the Board that "[t]he use of the sawmill on the Dobo property is not a permitted use during the construction of the accessory structure on the property" is not supported by substantial, competent evidence. There is no evidence in the record that petitioners' use of the Wood–Mizer saw to construct a fully permitted woodworking hobby shop is not a permitted use during construction. Testimony by the Code Enforcement Officer that the use of the saw would not be customary is speculative as he further testified that he does not enforce the building code. *See C.C. & J. Enter., Inc. v. City of Asheville,* 132 N.C.App. 550, 553, 512 S.E.2d 766, 769, *disc. review improvidently allowed,* 351 N.C. 97, 521 S.E.2d 117 (1999) (speculative assertions or mere expression of opinion about the possible effects of granting a permit are insufficient to support the findings of a quasi-judicial body).

This Court in *Tucker v. The Mecklenburg Cty. Zoning Bd. of Adjust.,* 148 N.C.App. 52, 557 S.E.2d 631 (2001), addressed a similar issue involving the operation of a dog kennel by respondents on their residentially zoned property. The zoning ordinance in *Tucker* permitted the operation of a private kennel as an accessory use and prohibited the operation of a commercial kennel. While in all respects the kennel operated by respondents could have been used as a commercial kennel, the Board of Adjustment found that because the dogs were adopted and not sold, the kennel was not a commercial kennel but a private kennel permitted as an accessory use under the zoning ordinance. *Id.* at 57–59, 557 S.E.2d at 635–36. This Court agreed and reversed the trial court's order finding the kennel to be a commercial kennel in violation of the zoning ordinance. *Id.* at 57–59, 557 S.E.2d at 636.

Here, the evidence clearly establishes that petitioners used the saw primarily for the construction of a permitted and allowed hobby woodworking shop behind their home and occasionally for the cutting of lumber for friends without charge. There is no evidence that the actual use of the saw by petitioners is for industrial or manufacturing purposes nor that it is not "of a nature that is customarily incidental and subordinate to" the residential use of their property. The actual use of the saw in this case is an accessory use and does not violate the Zoning Ordinance. Counsel for respondent conceded that the construction of the hobby shop is fully permitted and is an allowed accessory use of petitioners' residentially zoned property. Accordingly, I would hold that the Board's decision was not supported by substantial, competent evidence and was arbitrary and capricious.

Petitioners argue that if we scratch the surface facts, it is readily apparent that this action is a thinly veiled attempt by the residents of the adjoining subdivision to impose *de facto* restrictive covenants onto petitioners' property that were never bargained for nor agreed to by petitioners.

The general rule is that a zoning ordinance, being in derogation of common law property rights, should be construed in favor of the free use of property. *See Yancey v. Heafner,* 268 N.C. 263, 266, 150 S.E.2d 440, 443 (1966); *City of Sanford v. Dandy Signs, Inc.,* 62 N.C.App. 568, 569, 303 S.E.2d 228, 230 (1983). Zoning regulations are not a substitute for private restrictive covenants. If the subdivision residents believe that petitioners' use of their property is unreasonable, their remedy is an action in nuisance, not to enlist the City as an accomplice by incessant complaints about their neighbor.

The record shows that petitioners have owned, used, and lived on their property for half a century. The recent addition of an exclusive, walled, and gated subdivision on adjoining property does not convert petitioners' lawful use into an illegal one, simply because petitioners' use is inconsistent with the permitted uses within the adjoining subdivision. Purchasers of lots in a subdivision development, located in formerly rural areas that are rapidly urbanizing, have the duty to inform themselves of uses on adjoining, but unrestricted, property that may not compliment the restrictions and uses that subdivision residents privately covenant among themselves and that apply solely within the confines of their development.

Petitioners further object to the irrelevant statements made by the adjoining neighbors to the Board as to noise and smell from petitioners' property, burning by petitioners on their property, and junk on petitioners' property. The record clearly shows and counsel for respondent conceded that despite numerous visits to petitioners' property, no violation of the penal noise ordinance was found or other ordinances. While there is no indication that the Board's decision was based on this testimony, speculative opinions such as these fail to constitute substantial competent evidence to support a finding that the petitioners' use was not an accessory use. *See C.C. & J.,* 132 N.C.App. at 553, 512 S.E.2d at 769. There is no competent evidence in the record that petitioners' actual use of the Wood–Mizer saw did not constitute an accessory use under the Zoning Ordinance. I would reverse the superior court's order, affirming the 3–2 decision of the Board, and dissent from part IIA of the majority's opinion.

Notes

1. In Collins v. Lonergan, 198 A.D.2d 349, 603 N.Y.S.2d 330 (1993), the court upheld a zoning board of appeals decision that a skate board ramp constructed in conjunction with a single-family home constituted a customary use, despite the fact that skate board facilities were not found on other lots in the community or surrounding suburban towns. The case raises an interesting question about how changing technology affects accessory uses. The decision of the board that the ramp was no more intrusive that a swimming pool or tennis court was not arbitrary or capricious. Collins raises an interesting practice issue: how do you suppose the matter got before the zoning board of appeals in the first place? If the zoning code simply allows accessory uses that are incidental, subordinate, and customary, then how

would a homeowner proceed to get permission to construct a skateboard ramp? Since the jurisdiction of the Zoning Board of Appeals is appellate only with regard to such matters, what decision must have been appealed to it to give it jurisdiction to determine whether the ramp was a permissible accessory use? See Bagko Development Co. v. Damitz, 640 N.E.2d 67 (Ind.App. 4 Dist.1994), where the court upheld a property owner's development and use of a Little League practice facility. The facility was built on a lot adjoining the lot containing their home and did not violate the zoning ordinance. The primary use of the double lot was residential, and use of the practice facility for approximately 8.7 hours per week for about 10 weeks of the year was a subordinate "accessory recreational use" of property.

2. Is a skateboard ramp in 1993 truly a use customarily found in connection with the use of a single-family home? If the Zoning Board of Appeals decided that it was not and, for that reason, denied the homeowner's appeal, what would the effect of that decision be on the ability of homeowners to adopt new recreational uses that evolve with inventions in the recreational segment of the economy? When the ZBA found that skateboard ramps are customarily found in connection with single-family use was it finding that in a literal sense or that recreational uses of this type and intensity are customary in single-family neighborhoods? If you owned the house adjacent to the Collins' home and you had a tennis court in your yard, could you explain the difference in intensity of use between your recreational use and that proposed by your neighbors? What facts would the building inspector need to gather regarding a proposed skateboard ramp to determine whether it met the standards for an accessory use?

3. In Tucker v. Mecklenburg County Zoning Bd. of Adjustment, 148 N.C.App. 52, 557 S.E.2d 631 (2001), the North Carolina Court of Appeals held that respondent's kennel was a permitted accessory use. Respondents established Project HALO Corporation (HALO) as a non-profit organization with the primary goal being the rescue of stray and unwanted dogs. Respondents pay the county licensing and registration fees and taxes. HALO then pays all expenses associated with caring for the dogs. On average, respondents keep approximately 10 to 15 dogs in pens located between their residence and the rear lot line. The animals were not sold, but were either adopted or kept by homeowners, and all animals were owned and licensed by homeowners.

4. Similar to Tucker, the N.J. Superior Court found that a pigeon coop was an accessory use under the zoning code. See Colts Run Civic Ass'n v. Colts Neck Tp. Zoning Board of Adjustment, 315 N.J.Super. 240, 717 A.2d 456 (Law Div.1998). The question before the N.J. Superior Court was whether the maintenance of a "domestic animal shelter," in this case a pigeon coop, as a hobby activity is a permitted accessory use. The zoning district provided for a mixture of residential and agricultural uses. The stated purpose of the zoning plan for this district includes the "continuation of farming." The defendant represented that he raises, trains, and breeds racing pigeons only as a hobby. The pigeons would not be used for business or commercial purposes, and would not be sold, bred, shown, or raced for profit. Ultimately, defendant Board concluded that while the raising of racing pigeons does not serve agricultural purposes in this agriculturally sensitive zoning district, the proposed use is "subordinate" and "incidental"

as an accessory use. The defendant Board reasoned that the raising of racing pigeons "while perhaps not a widely popular hobby, is nevertheless a hobby which is incidental to the residential use of the property in question and is the type of hobby which would customarily be associated with a residential use."

5. An antenna for a wireless mobile telephone system was not a permitted "accessory use" on the top of an apartment building. The court found that the principal use of apartment building was residential, while use of antennae was commercial. The antennae would serve only non-residents and those residents who subscribed to the provider's telephone services. See AWACS, Inc. v. Zoning Hearing Bd. of Newton Tp., Delaware County, 702 A.2d 604 (Pa.Cmwlth.1997).

SECTION 6. HOME OCCUPATIONS

Historically, single-family homes have been used by their occupants for a variety of occupational uses such as beauty parlors, dressmaking, laundries, and day care. Zoning limits single-family homes to residential uses and to those uses that are customarily associated with residential use and incidental and subordinate to that residential use. Does this mean that a single-family homeowner can conduct a particular business in a particular neighborhood, as an accessory use, or is the occupational use prohibited?

In some communities, this question is answered on a case-by-case basis without benefit of any special regulations. The zoning authorities examine the proposed occupational use and determine whether it is customary, incidental, and subordinate to the residential use. Other municipalities define "home occupations" more specifically in their zoning laws, requiring homeowners to conform their occupational uses to those definitions. Some adopt a list of permitted occupational uses of homes while others prohibit a specific list of occupations, while some use a standards approach using signs, traffic, and other activities more in keeping with commercial districts. Thus, a homeowner who trades stocks over the internet from her den does not need a permit while the next door neighbor who takes in children for day care does.

Permitting occupations to be conducted in single-family zoned neighborhoods honors expectations of homeowners that such uses have been permitted historically and are within the bundle of rights purchased with the single-family home. Zoning restrictions limiting the occupational use of homes recognize that residential districts must be protected from home occupations that are out of character with the neighborhood and are not uses that homeowners expect to be affected by when they purchase a home in a single-family area. One of the original purposes of zoning is to separate uses that are inconsistent with one another into distinct zoning districts.

Municipalities use a variety of techniques to regulate home occupations and professional offices:

1. They may let their definition of accessory uses govern the matter, leaving it to the zoning enforcement official to determine, in a given instance, whether a proposed occupational use is customary, incidental, and subordinate to the principal permitted use of a parcel as a single-family home.

2. Local legislatures may adopt a general definition of a home occupation to provide some guidance to enforcement officials to aid their determinations in these matters.

3. They may supplement their general definition of home occupation with a list of permitted occupations, a list of prohibited occupations, and a definition of permitted professional offices.

4. Specified home occupations may be permitted only upon the issuance of a special use permit by a designated reviewing board.

5. Local legislatures may include specific standards that certain occupational uses must meet, such as limiting the percentage of floor area that may be used, prohibiting carrying or selling of merchandise, prohibiting any alteration of the exterior of the building, limiting businesses to those conducted by occupants of the residence, and limiting the number of associates, partners, and employees.

TOWN OF SULLIVANS ISLAND v. BYRUM

Court of Appeals of South Carolina, 1992.
413 S.E.2d 325, 306 S.C. 539.

PER CURIAM

The Plaintiff, Town of Sullivans Island (Town), sought to enjoin the Defendants, Byrums, from using part of their residence as a "Bed & Breakfast" boarding house. The Town also sought to enjoin the Byrums' use of a garage apartment for human habitation. The Town argued that both uses violated the applicable zoning ordinances. The trial judge refused the requested injunctions, and the Town appealed. We reverse and remand for the entry of an order granting both injunctions.

A fire damaged the Byrums' residence in 1983. The Byrums decided to renovate the house and use part of it as a Bed & Breakfast. As a result, the repair work went far beyond the fire damage, including the development of six separate bedrooms and baths. Nothing indicates that the Byrums told the Town of their intended use during the repair process.

At the time of the renovations, § 21–3 of the Town's zoning ordinances defined "permitted home occupation uses" as follows:

> Any use conducted entirely within a dwelling and carried on by the occupants thereof, which use is clearly incidental and secondary to the use of the dwelling for residential purposes and does not change the character thereof, and no person, not a resident of the premises is employed specifically in connection with the activity. Provided, further, that no mechanical equipment is installed or used

except such as is normally used for domestic or professional purposes, and that not over twenty-five (25%) percent of the total floor space of any structure is used for home occupation.

This is the second time these parties have been before this Court regarding the Byrums' Bed & Breakfast operation. In the first case, the Byrums' sought a variance from the twenty-five (25%) per cent limitation on "home occupation" uses. The Board of Adjustment denied the variance on two grounds: (1) a Bed & Breakfast is not a home occupation; and (2) the operation exceeded the twenty-five (25%) per cent limitation on structural usage for home occupations. The Circuit Court reversed both findings on appeal. This Court reversed the Circuit Court and reinstated the Board's denial of the variance, concluding that the Bed & Breakfast operation exceeded the twenty-five (25%) per cent limitation. *Byrum v. Board of Adjustment,* 294 S.C. 114, 362 S.E.2d 890 (Ct.App.1987) (*Byrum* I). This Court did not discuss the first issue.

During the pendency of the appeal before the Circuit Court in *Byrum* I, the Town amended its "home occupation" ordinance and specifically prohibited the use of a residence as a boarding house. At the time of this amendment, the Byrums continued to use more than twenty-five (25%) per cent of the residence in the Bed & Breakfast operation contrary to both the original and the amended ordinance.

After this Court's decision in *Byrum* I, the Byrums continued to operate the Bed & Breakfast but allegedly reduced the structure usage to less than twenty-five (25%) per cent. They applied to the Town for a license, and the Town denied their application. They continued to operate the Bed & Breakfast, and the Town commenced the present action.

* * *

The zoning ordinance defined home occupation as quoted herein above. We conclude that the Bed & Breakfast operation is not "clearly incidental and secondary" to the residential use of the property, and that it changed the character of the residence. The Byrums' renovation of the property included the construction of an apartment within the house where Mr. and Mrs. Byrum would live. This apartment had its own kitchen, bathroom, bedroom, and a small living room. After the renovation, there were five other bedrooms which were used for the Bed & Breakfast. Each bedroom had its own bathroom, water heater, air conditioner, and heater. The second (large) kitchen was used primarily for the preparation of continental breakfasts for the boarders. Under these facts, it is clear that the Bed & Breakfast operation dominated the character and use of the residence and, therefore, it is not a home occupation. It is more like a boarding house than a traditional home occupation, such as a craft shop or dressmaker. The Pennsylvania Commonwealth Court recently reached the same result in a remarkably similar case. *Reynolds v. Zoning Hearing Board of Abington Township,* 134 Pa.Commw. 382, 578 A.2d 629 (1990).

In calculating the percentage of use, the trial judge erred in excluding the square footage of the upstairs hallway or foyer. The record clearly demonstrates that all of the upstairs rooms are part of the present Bed & Breakfast operation. Thus, the only use of the hallway is for the Bed & Breakfast operation. When the square footage of the hallway is added into the trial judge's calculations, the present use clearly exceeds the twenty-five (25%) per cent limitation.

Even if the Bed & Breakfast operation is a home occupation as contemplated by the original ordinance, and the present operation does not exceed the twenty-five (25%) per cent limitation, the amended ordinance is applicable and prohibits any Bed & Breakfast operation. The operation is not a non-conforming use under the amended ordinance, because it was not a conforming use at the time of the amendment, *i.e.*, the Byrums were in violation of the twenty-five (25%) per cent limitation at the time of the amendment. *See Troutman v. Aiken,* 213 Ga. 55, 96 S.E.2d 585 (1957) (A use cannot be a non-conforming use if it was unlawful at the time of the amendment of the ordinance to prohibit the use). This ruling conforms to the law's general disfavor of nonconforming uses.

Nor should the Byrums be entitled to prevail by reason of the law of estoppel.

As a general rule, estoppel does not lie against the government to prevent the due exercise of its police power or to thwart the application of public policy. *South Carolina Dept. of Social Servs. v. Parker,* 275 S.C. 176, 268 S.E.2d 282 (1980). The acts of government agents acting within the scope of their authority can give rise to estoppel against the government, but unauthorized conduct or statements do not give rise to estoppel. *South Carolina Coastal Council v. Vogel,* 292 S.C. 449, 357 S.E.2d 187 (Ct.App.1987), *appeal dismissed,* 294 S.C. 80, 362 S.E.2d 646 (1987). To prove estoppel against the government, the claiming party must show (1) a lack of knowledge and the means of knowledge about the truth of the matter in question, (2) justifiable reliance on the government's conduct, and (3) a prejudicial change in position. *Midlands Utility, Inc. v. South Carolina Dept. of Health and Envtl. Control,* 298 S.C. 66, 378 S.E.2d 256 (1989). When a landowner has actual or constructive notice of a matter, and does not show any misrepresentation or concealment by the government, estoppel will not lie against the government. *South Carolina Pub. Serv. Auth. v. Ocean Forest, Inc.,* 275 S.C. 552, 273 S.E.2d 773 (1981) (power company's easement to cut "danger trees"); *South Carolina State Highway Dept. v. Metts,* 270 S.C. 73, 240 S.E.2d 816 (1978) (right of way over property); *City of Myrtle Beach v. Parker,* 260 S.C. 475, 197 S.E.2d 290 (1973) (existence of a public street).

The Town is not estopped from raising the non-conforming use issue. The record clearly demonstrates that the Town objected to the operation on two grounds at all relevant times. First, it contended that the operation was not a home occupation. Second, it contended that the operation, if permitted as a home occupation, exceeded the twenty-five (25%) per cent limitation on home occupations. Moreover, the Byrums clearly knew at all relevant times that their use exceeded the twenty-five (25%) per cent limitation; that is why they sought a variance in *Byrum* I. Thus, they could not have detrimentally relied on the position taken by the Town, and reliance is a necessary element of estoppel. In addition, nothing indicates that the Byrums changed their position in reliance on any statement or conduct by the Town.

The cases relied upon by the trial judge and the Byrums are not applicable. They involve situations where an official told a property owner that a use was permitted but later reversed that position. Here, the Town never told the Byrums that their Bed & Breakfast operation was a permitted use.

The Town is not estopped from challenging the use of the garage as an apartment. There is no evidence of any statement or conduct by Town that reasonably misled the Byrums into believing the garage apartment was a permitted use, or that the Town would not contest the use. The trial judge found that the Town's building inspector must have known about the construction of the garage apartment. He based this finding on the fact that the inspector visited the residence during the construction. He concluded the inspector must have seen the garage apartment construction and must have had plans showing the garage construction. There is no evidence to support these conclusions.

The building inspector testified he never inspected the garage, never saw any plans, and never knew of the garage apartment construction. No one testified that they showed the garage apartment to the inspector or told him about it.

The Town's administrator testified his search of the Town's records did not reveal any plans on file. He also testified that the Town did not uniformly require plans at the time of the construction. The building permits do not indicate that plans were filed by anyone. No one testified that they submitted any plans. One of the Byrums testified that he assumed the contractor submitted plans, but the contractor did not testify.

Assuming that the building inspector knew of the garage apartment construction, nothing indicates that he had authority to allow such construction or grant a variance to the zoning ordinances.

In summary, we hold the injunctions should be granted. The case is remanded to the Circuit Court of Charleston County for the entry of judgment in accordance with this decision.

REVERSED AND REMANDED.

TOUSSAINT v. TOWN OF HARPSWELL

Supreme Court of Maine, 1997.
1997 ME 189, 698 A.2d 1063.

ROBERTS, JUSTICE.

Jane Waddle appeals from the judgment entered in the Superior Court (Cumberland County, Saufley, J.) on the complaint of Donald and Marietta Toussaint. The court vacated the decision of the Town of Harpswell Zoning Board of Appeals that Waddle's dog kennel is a permitted use as a home occupation. Because we agree with Waddle that her dog kennel qualifies as a home occupation as defined in the Town's shoreland zoning ordinance, we vacate the judgment.

In March 1995 Jane Waddle applied for a building permit to construct an addition to her home in Harpswell. On her application she described the project as "extending the mudroom and adding a garage with indoor-outdoor kennels for our dogs." The code enforcement officer, Roland Mayo, issued a building permit for the project, and construction was completed shortly thereafter. The facility, known as the Great Island Dog Kennel, is a for-profit kennel with 11 indoor-outdoor dog runs and the capacity to board 15 dogs.

The neighborhood surrounding the kennel contains a mixture of year-round homes and summer cottages. The kennel is located in a Commercial Fishing II District as defined in the zoning ordinance. The ordinance permits home occupations in that district subject to the restriction that "[h]ome occupations that provide public restrooms and showers or serve food to the public require a CEO permit." A home occupation is defined in the ordinance as follows:

> an occupation or profession which is customarily conducted on or in a residential structure or property and which is (1) compatible with the residential use of the property and surrounding residential uses; and (2) which employs no more than three (3) persons on site other than family members residing in the home. Home occupations related to commercial fishing in all cases will be acceptable uses. This also includes Bed and Breakfast as a home occupation.

In the fall of 1995, the Toussaints, summer residents of the neighborhood, asked Mayo to enforce the zoning ordinance by prohibiting the continued operation of the kennel. After Mayo refused to take enforcement action, the Toussaints appealed to the zoning board of appeals. The issues presented to the board at its meeting in January 1996 were whether the operation of a dog kennel is customarily conducted on or in a residential structure or property and whether it is compatible with the residential use of the property and surrounding residential uses. At the hearing, five summer residents of the neighborhood, including the Toussaints, objected to the kennel. Each stated that the almost continuous barking by dogs at the kennel was very annoying and disruptive to their enjoyment of the neighborhood. An abutting property owner, but not a resident of the neighborhood, also objected to the kennel. Five year-round residents of the area stated their support for the kennel. They stated that the kennel was not disruptive and that the noise it generated did not add unreasonably to the noise caused by marine-related uses such as lobsterboats, bait trucks, and jet skis, or other noise already present in the area such as the barking of many neighborhood dogs and even the occasional blast from a gun. Finally, to show that dog kennels are customarily conducted on residential property, Waddle submitted a list of kennels operated on residential properties in surrounding communities.

The board denied the appeal by a vote of 2 to 1. The Toussaints sought direct judicial review in the Superior Court. The court set aside the decision as an error of law and remanded to the board for appropriate enforcement action. The court found that a dog kennel is unlike businesses traditionally recognized as home occupations such as dressmaking, hairdressing, and tutoring, and that because such a facility necessarily increases levels of noise, traffic, and odor, it is not compatible with a residential neighborhood, no matter how well it is run. Waddle appeals.

When, as here, the court acts as an intermediate appellate court, we independently examine the record and review the board's decision for an abuse of discretion, error of law, or findings unsupported by substantial evidence in the record. *Cumberland Farms, Inc. v. Town of Scarborough*, 1997 ME 11, ¶ 3, 688 A.2d 914. Because the Toussaints challenged a decision on which they had the burden of proof, they must establish that the evidence compels a contrary result. *Herrick v. Town of Mechanic Falls*, 673 A.2d 1348, 1349 (Me.1996). "If there is relevant evidence in the record to reasonably support the Board's conclusion, the fact that the record contains inconsistent evidence or inconsistent conclusions could be drawn from the evidence does not invalidate the Board's holding." Id. We will not substitute our own judgment for that of the board. *Id.*

I.

Waddle argues that the board determined correctly that a dog kennel is a business customarily conducted on residential property. She contends that a home occupation is more broadly defined in the Harpswell ordinance than in ordinances at issue in cases such as *Baker v. Town of Woolwich*, 517 A.2d 64 (Me.1987), and *Town of Kittery v. Hoyt*, 291 A.2d 512 (Me.1972), in which we determined that certain businesses were not home occupations within the meaning of the local zoning ordinance. She finally contends that the list of other area kennels operated on the same property as the home of the owners establishes that kennels are customarily conducted on residential property, and that the Toussaints failed to establish otherwise. We agree.

We have stated repeatedly that the provisions in a zoning ordinance "should be construed reasonably with regard both to the objects sought to be obtained and to the general structure of the ordinance as a whole" *Christy's Realty Ltd. Partnership v. Town of Kittery*, 663 A.2d 59, 62 (Me.1995). Our review of the Harpswell ordinance reveals that a variety of commercial activities are permitted in the zone where the kennel is located. Those activities include home occupations, bed and breakfasts, and all marine-related commercial activities. The ordinance's definition of home occupation is relatively broad, i.e., rather than limiting home occupations to businesses customarily carried on from a home, as the ordinances at issue in *Baker* and *Hoyt*, the Harpswell ordinance permits businesses that are merely customarily conducted on residential property. The breadth of the term, as used in the Harpswell ordinance, is further revealed by the ordinance's contemplation that home occupations may provide food service to the public, or public restrooms and showers. In light of the breadth of the ordinance and the evidence before the board that many kennels in surrounding communities are operated on residential property, the board concluded properly that a dog kennel qualifies as a business customarily conducted on residential property.

II.

Waddle next contends that the board properly found that her kennel is compatible with the residential use of her property and with surrounding residential uses. Once again, we find no error in the board's decision. Municipal officials possess a familiarity with the neighborhoods in their community that cannot be matched by words in an appellate record. Although there was some dispute whether the operation of the kennel disturbed surrounding neighbors, the record contains relevant evidence to reasonably support the board's determination of compatibility, and we will not substitute our judgment for that of the board.

III.

The final issue that merits our attention involves an alleged conflict of interest of board member Larry Favreau, who voted in favor of Waddle at the meeting in January 1996. Favreau is married to the widow of Waddle's brother and therefore Favreau's two stepchildren are Waddle's niece and nephew. Favreau did not disclose this relationship at the board meeting. After the vote an objection was raised to his participation. In February 1996 the board held a special meeting to consider the Toussaints' request for reconsideration based on Favreau's alleged conflict of interest. The board voted unanimously to deny the Toussaints' request, finding there was no conflict that required Favreau's disqualification.

The Toussaints argue that if we vacate the judgment of the Superior Court they are entitled to a new hearing because Favreau's failure to disclose the conflict of interest denied the board and the public an opportunity to question his participation. We disagree. Although it is prudent for municipal officials to disclose all possible conflicts, even when they are remote, in these circumstances the lack of disclosure does not require a new hearing. The record does not reveal that Favreau had any direct or indirect pecuniary interest in the project under review. Moreover, "[t]he decision as to whether a particular interest is sufficient to disqualify is necessarily a factual one and depends on the circumstances of the particularcase." *Anderson v. Zoning Comm'n of Norwalk*, 157 Conn. 285, 253 A.2d 16 (1968). Here the board voted unanimously to deny reconsideration. On the record before us we cannot say that the decision is clearly erroneous.

The entry is:

Judgment vacated.

Remanded for the entry of a judgment affirming the decision of the Town of Harpswell Zoning Board of Appeals.

Notes

1. Whether a particular home occupation is permitted depends entirely on the exact language of the zoning provisions adopted by the local legislature in each community. Most judicial decisions on the subject involve an attempt on the court's part to determine what types of home occupations are permitted by the specific language of the zoning law and whether that language was interpreted reasonably by the local official or board with delegated authority to make decisions on home occupations. Since zoning regulations are deemed by the courts to be in derogation of common law property rights, they are subject to strict interpretation. Local officers and review boards that decide to deny a property owner the right to an occupational use should base their decisions on specific language in the zoning law and on facts that justify those decisions.

2. In Houghtaling v. Medina Bd. of Zoning Appeals, 134 Ohio App.3d 541, 731 N.E.2d 733 (9th Dist.1999), the Ohio Court of Appeals held that a seven-and-one-half-foot tall anchor erected on front lawn of residence was not considered a "sign" pursuant to a provision of the zoning code that banned signs advertising home occupations. The homeowners operated a travel business that was a permissible home occupation. The court found that the anchor did not "advertise" a home occupation despite evidence showing that the owners used the anchor as a reference point for people who came to their home for business purposes.

3. In Allegheny West Civic Council v. Zoning Bd. of Adjustment, 552 Pa. 541, 716 A.2d 600 (1998), the Supreme Court of Pennsylvania held that an engineering office conducted on the first floor of a home located in a Multiple Family Residence District was not a home occupation and, therefore, was not permitted as an accessory use. The court stated that the use must not only be incidental to, but must also be customarily conducted in, a dwelling. ". . . [Z]oning boards and courts may take notice of what business occupations are customarily conducted in residential dwellings based on general experience and understanding. As local municipalities are free to amend their zoning ordinances to provide for whatever specific uses they deem to be proper for residential property, we see no reason to abandon this approach, where, as here, the zoning ordinance generally provides only for home occupations which are customarily associated with residential dwellings. Turning to the matter before us, we hold that the Commonwealth

Court correctly concluded that Appellants' proposed engineering business is not a use customarily carried on in a dwelling unit."

4. Do you recall the plight of poor Daniel Goldman in the first case presented in this Chapter, Goldman v. Crowther? He was arrested "for repairing, by hand, on an ordinary sewing machine, for hire, used clothing for such patrons as had occasions to require his services," in violation of the use prescriptions of Baltimore's zoning ordinance. The work was done in a four-story residential building that the Goldmans owned and that was located in a zone limited to residential use. Assuming that the Goldmans lived in the building, do you think that this tailoring business should have been allowed as an accessory use? Under modern zoning ordinances, would the business be allowed as a permitted home occupation? How much was the city's zoning scheme benefited by the restriction on tailoring? Was that benefit worth the price of litigation? Is the Goldman v. Crowther case an example of bad facts creating bad law?

Chapter IV

COMMUNITY BUILDING: SUBDIVISION CONTROL AND INFRASTRUCTURE

SECTION 1. REGULATION OF THE SUBDIVISION OF LAND

A. THE ESSENTIAL REASONS FOR AND NATURE OF SUBDIVISION REGULATION

POMEROY, PREFACE TO THE SUBDIVISION OF LAND IN SAN MATEO COUNTY, CALIFORNIA 11

(1932).

A subdivision is not merely a means of marketing land; it is far more, a process of community building. All the flurry of subdivision sales, all the financial considerations involved at the time, all the huge importance of immediate details—these are infinitesimal factors in the ultimate result, which is the addition of an integral part of the community, a part, which, once established in the comparatively short flash of time involved, is fixed as to its physical framework and permanently marked in its character. The fleeting economic effect of the act of subdividing gives way to the permanent, inexorable economic and social effect of the subdivision as a part of the form and life of the community. No subdivision is too small to have character. It may be no more than a particular curve to a street, or the placing of the lots, or the skillful use of setbacks, or the planting plan; but it may give to a mere linear design the impulse of life and set it throbbing with vitality.

MELLI, SUBDIVISION CONTROL IN WISCONSIN

1953 Wis.L.Rev. 389.

Subdivision control, the regulation of the division of raw land into building lots, is a vital component of land-use control. It has become particularly important in the post World War II period as communities have sprung up in previously rural areas. Its importance is not limited to urban communities and their immediate environs. The trend to country living has turned whole sections some distance from large cities into semi-urban areas. The tremendous expansion of recreational areas has created numerous communities along the shores of lakes and rivers. Fortunately, after the ill-fated experience with uncontrolled subdivision in the 1920's, control of that process has become recognized as an integral part of any land-use planning scheme and the statutes of all states, except one, make some sort of provisions for it.

Subdivision control is, of course, only one of the instruments used by a community to regulate the use of privately owned land in the public interest. It is closely related to zoning control in that both are preventive measures intended to avert community blight and deterioration by requiring that new development proceed in defined ways and according to prescribed standards. Zoning relates to the type of building development which can take place on the land; subdivision control relates to the way in which the land is divided and made ready for building development. The two are mutually dependent because the layout of an area is inseparable from the character of the use to be made of the land. * * *

I. Why Have Subdivision Controls?

One of the basic problems involved in any type of governmental control is the justification for that control. Just why, many people ask, should a land owner be compelled to obtain the approval of a governmental agency when he is going to divide a parcel of his land into lots for sale. The answer to this question is not simple because the subdividers are not the only group involved. The home buyer, the mortgage lender and, more importantly, the community as a whole are vitally concerned in the process of subdivision. It is only by understanding the relationship of all of these groups to subdivision control that its validity can be determined.

(1) *The Community.* The most important reason for having subdivision control is to provide an effective instrument for land-use control by the community. The community has a legitimate interest in any new subdivision for a number of reasons.

Permanence of development. The original layout of an area will determine its character for an indefinite period of time. Even though another plan may be clearly more desirable, the cost of changing it once the area has been built up is almost prohibitive. Therefore, whether he realizes it or not the subdivider is setting the pattern for the future community. Many of the perplexing problems facing communities today—traffic congestion, high maintenance costs, cramped school areas, slums—are directly traceable to the manner in which they were originally laid out. Obviously the most practical and economical way of meeting these problems is to provide some method by which the original subdivision of raw land can be suited to the needs of the developing community. The alternative to governmental supervision of the private subdivider is municipal ownership and development of outlying areas. This method has been used successfully by a number of European cities and is sometimes advocated as the solution to the problems of American communities. Whether or not it would be an effective solution is difficult to determine in the absence of experience, but traditionally Americans have preferred the first alternative.

Future services. As society becomes more complex the community is called upon to furnish more services to its residents. Because such services will have to be furnished to any new area the community should have an opportunity to consider each new subdivision in relation to the services it is expected to provide. For example, the community will have to furnish schools and recreational facilities to the area, and it should have notice of where an increase in population is expected so that it can plan accordingly.

Safety considerations. The community will have to provide police and fire protection to the new area. It should have an opportunity to make sure that the streets are wide enough to get fire-fighting apparatus in and that the lots are of sufficient size for safety from fire hazards. It will want to check the layout of the area for traffic control and parking problems. The streets must be adequate for modern traffic. The main thoroughfares should be wide and should link with existing main thoroughfares; there should not be too many streets at an intersection and they should intersect at right angles, particularly on main thoroughfares; the street grades and curves should be safe for modern traffic; adequate off-street parking should be provided for commercial and industrial areas. From the safety angle the community will also want to check the subdivision to be sure that there are adequate places for children to play so that they will not have to play in the streets.

Health considerations. Health is another community consideration. The governing unit will want to be sure that the area is one which will be safe for people to live in. For example, the drainage should be checked to be sure that basements will not flood; an investigation should be made to determine whether the sewage disposal plant of the community is adequate to take care of the new area and, if the area is one which cannot be served by public sewer and water, the community will want to be sure that the lots are of a sufficient size so that private disposal of waste will not create a health problem.

Fiscal considerations. In addition to the services which it is called upon to furnish, the community must always keep in mind the pocketbooks of its citizens and must consider each new development in relation to tax revenues. From this standpoint the community is vitally interested in making sure that new subdivisions will not become blighted areas. Blighted areas from which the tax return is low are one of the biggest problems facing communities today because such areas are unable to pay their way. The cost of services furnished by the community—fire and police protection, schools, recreation facilities, sewage disposal, street repairs—exceeds the revenues obtained from them, and the cost of their services must be borne by higher tax rates which bear heavily on those in the more desirable areas. It is generally agreed that the best means of dealing with blighted areas is to prevent them from developing in the first place by insisting on a desirable layout. Areas with narrow streets and lots and inadequate play space for children deteriorate much more rapidly than others.

Just as important, from a fiscal viewpoint, as the layout of the subdivision is the question of whether it should ever have been subdivided in the first place. The scattering of subdivisions too far from community services such as water and sewer, fire protection, public transportation and schools should be prevented if possible. Subdivisions which are not within reasonable reach of all these services will not only be less desirable places for people to live, but will also tax the resources of the community in attempting to furnish the services. For example, the necessity of extending sewer and water mains a great distance may make the lots so expensive that they will not sell and the community—the taxpayers—will have to shoulder the cost of useless improvements.

Another important question in the determination of whether an area should be subdivided is the problem of whether there are too many lots already available for the demand. An excess of subdivided lots may mean not only that whole areas will end up as dead-land, undeveloped but useless as agricultural land because of divided ownerships, confused titles and high tax assessments, but also that areas will be left only partially developed. This means that in order to furnish the necessary services to the developed lots the community will have to extend sewers, water mains and streets past many vacant lots. Of course, it may be both undesirable and unconstitutional to give a community absolute power to prohibit subdivision only because it may create an excess of subdivided lots. For one thing, the basis for such prohibition is not too sound. Predictions about population trends and economic prosperity have been known to err sadly. But the approving authorities should point out the disadvantages to the subdivider in situations like this.

Accurate records. There is one other reason clearly behind many statutory provisions controlling the subdivision of land. This is the necessity of having a clear and accurate description of the subdivided lots. When land is divided into such small parcels, the awkward and frequently inaccurate metes and bounds description is undesirable. Very early in the history of many states a survey and plat of new subdivisions was required. For example, in Wisconsin the original statutes of 1849 made such a requirement. This means that for purposes of transfer and taxes the parcels can be referred to by block and lot in the subdivision.

(2) *The Home Buyer and Mortgage Lender*

In addition to protecting the community interests subdivision control protects the lot purchaser or home buyer and his mortgage lender. Actually much of his protection arises as an incident of the community supervision because any scheme for orderly land-use development will benefit individuals who have invested in the subdivided lots. For example, subdivisions located too far from fire protection, public transportation and schools are a poor investment for the average home owner. Areas so far from public water and sewer that the cost of extending those services is prohibitive should also be avoided. This is true of subdivisions which, because of an excess of subdivided lots, may never be fully built up. In discouraging the subdivision of these areas the community is protecting the potential buyer.

The purchase of a home is a major investment for the average citizen which he usually amortizes over many years. By requiring that the original layout be of a type that will maintain its character for a long period of years, the community is protecting his investment. Aesthetic considerations, such as the orientation of the subdivision away from near-by areas which are undesirable and the requirement of a certain percentage of curved streets and of planting strips along major traffic ways, are of vital importance here. Any study of real estate values will show that these requirements are not for aesthetic purposes only. They prevent deterioration of the area and preserve property values. They are probably the best protection the home owner has for his investment.

In protecting the investment of the home owner, the mortgage lender and the seller under a land contract are also protected. The great interest shown by the FHA in the original planning of subdivisions in which it may be insuring the mortgages is ample evidence of the fact that the original layout of the subdivision affects the investment of the mortgage lender.

Besides protecting his investment from early obsolescence, community control of subdivision also benefits the home owner in other ways. By requiring a survey and plat of the planned area for official scrutiny, the community provides the buyer with accurate boundary lines thus eliminating costly boundary disputes. In addition when the buyer is purchasing in an undeveloped area the plat gives him an idea of what the area will be like when it is fully developed. For example, the plat shows him what the subdivider's plans are as to street layout, location of commercial and recreational areas, if any, and size of other lots. To a certain extent it also protects him from changes in that development plan. The majority rule is that the sale of lots by reference to a plat showing certain streets and public places estops the subdivider from later changing those streets and public places. There is a possibility that the sale of lots by reference to a plat may also estop the subdivider from later lowering the size of the lots shown on the plat although the majority rule is contra.

(3) *The Subdivider*

Subdivision control by the community also benefits the subdividers themselves. Excessive subdivision and the platting of areas which are too far from community services or which are not good for development frequently spell financial ruin for the subdivider. In discouraging this type of subdivision, the community is therefore protecting his interests as well as those of the public and of potential buyers.

By requiring that the subdivider comply with certain standards, the subdivision control law protects the honest subdivider from the fly-by-night operator. The subdivider who invests the money and time necessary to comply with these requirements is not a speculator who is out to make a quick profit and move on to greener fields. Furthermore, while one subdivider may lay out a very desirable subdivision without any community control, he is being protected from subdividers who without such supervision might surround his development with very undesirable areas which would decrease the value of his subdivision.

This does not mean to say that the subdivider receives only benefit from governmental supervision of subdivision. There are many areas where his interests conflict with the other interests involved. While recognizing that there is legitimate need for control of his business, the fact that certain types of requirements may bear too heavily on him cannot be overlooked. Because the subdivider is so important to the development of the community and because it is so necessary that he be encouraged to develop his land in compliance with the platting laws, a complete discussion of the subdivider and his problems is included in this report. * * *

B. ROLE OF THE PLANNING COMMISSION

The previous reading explains the need for a land use control technique that will help to ensure the orderly growth and development of communities. The following article provides the details on how subdivision controls accomplish these goals, and it also discusses the roles of various players in the land use arena with respect to the review and approval of a subdivision.

MECK, SUBDIVISION CONTROL: A PRIMER FOR PLANNING COMMISSIONERS

The Commissioner (Fall 1996)

Subdivision regulations are land-use controls that govern the division of land into two or more lots, parcels, or sites for building. They provide criteria for the internal design of a land development as well as the standards by which the public improvements in the subdivision are constructed. They protect purchasers of land by ensuring that public improvements are available when it is time to build on the lots and by providing a mechanism for the official recording of lots with the appropriate governmental agency.

State enabling acts or municipal charters give local planning commissions a pivotal role in overseeing subdivision review. Procedures discussed below may vary from state to state and even within states, depending on local practices.

The state enabling legislation or municipal charter will outline the basic steps in processing a subdivision. The legislation may also exempt certain types of land subdivision from detailed local review; this typically occurs when no public improvements or land dedication is required and/or when only two to three lots are created (these are called minor subdivisions or lot splits and an abbreviated approval process will apply to them). The statutes will authorize the local government to adopt the regulations, including design criteria and specific engineering standards. The regulations govern the manner in which the developer submits the subdivision and defines the criteria against which the subdivision will be judged.

In most communities, subdivision review is a two-part process. First, the developer submits a preliminary plan or plat for the initial planning and layout of streets and lots, and type, size, and placement of utilities (water, sanitary and storm sewers, gas, electric, and cable). The preliminary plat shows topographic contour lines—the result of a survey of the site and/or aerial photography—and other site features such as streams and ponds, large trees and other vegetation, flood hazard areas, and existing buildings. Contour lines, typically shown at two-foot intervals, are important because they illustrate land forms such as hills or ravines. By understanding the topography of the site, you can determine whether there will need to be grading changes to ensure that lots will be well-drained and buildable. In addition, you will understand whether or not the streets are laid out to blend with the site's inherent amenities, and whether utilities, such as sanitary sewers, are designed to depend on natural gravity to work.

Often the preliminary plan will cover an area that is larger than the portion that will be initially developed. A developer may wish to improve only that portion of the site that may be sold as lots within one to two years. Consequently, the preliminary plan may show the phasing of the subdivision over a period of several years.

The planning commission is the first governmental agency to officially review the preliminary plan, although the developer may have contacted other agencies before the submission, such as the local government's planning director or professional engineer, and public utility providers. The planning director, if there is one, will have circulated copies of the preliminary plan to other local government agencies for comments, thus ensuring coordination. The planning director will typically submit these comments, along with an analysis of whether the plan meets the design and informational requirements contained in the subdivision regulations and an identification of issues related to the community's comprehensive and functional plans, in a written report to the planning commission. Sometimes a checklist of requirements accompanies the report.

In the preliminary plan stage of review, the basic design issues for the subdivision are resolved. Here are some items a planning commission member should look for in this part of the process:

- Whether the information required by the subdivision regulations is shown on the preliminary plat.

- Whether proposed streets are properly oriented and integrated with existing streets and are of adequate width.
- Whether street intersections are safe and avoid dog-legs that create dangerous jogs.
- Whether proposed lots satisfy area and other dimensional requirements of the zoning code.
- Whether lot layout is sound. For example, odd-angled lots may make it difficult to site a building and still meet yard requirements. Extra-deep lots may need to be provided at corners, in order to satisfy setback and sight distance requirements across intersections, or for sites traversed by ravines or stream valleys, or prone to flooding.
- Whether sites have been dedicated or reserved for parks, or for other public facilities such as schools. Some communities may have mandatory parkland dedication provisions, requiring the dedication of a certain amount of land, or payment of a fee in lieu of dedication, for each lot or dwelling unit, based on a formula in the subdivision regulations. Other communities handle these facilities in a different manner. For example, the local government or school system may decide to purchase land in the proposed subdivision within a certain period of time.
- Whether the plan shows proposed utility easements, such as those for electricity and gas, and whether they are of sufficient depth, located at lot edges if possible, and split between adjoining lots.
- Whether street names are consistent with the local governments policies. For example, it is a good idea to avoid similar street names like Maple Street when there is a "Maple Avenue" that may be confusing to emergency and fire service personnel, as well as the U.S. Postal Service.
- Whether block lengths are excessively long, resulting in uninterrupted straight stretches of road that encourage speeding.
- Whether stormwater detention or retention facilities should be provided onsite or as part of a larger regional facility located offsite. Often, an offsite facility is a better solution to stormwater problems than a smaller, privately owned facility because it will be maintained by the local government.
- Whether the preliminary plan reflects thoroughfares that are proposed in the community's major thoroughfare plan. If the thoroughfare plan calls for a wider right-of-way than a typical residential street to meet community-wide needs (as opposed to those resulting from development of the subdivision), the local government may need to acquire the additional right-of-way to permit future road widenings.

The planning commission will review the proposed subdivision at a public meeting or hearing, listen to the comments of the developer, staff, and interested citizens, and recommend to the legislative body whether to approve, approve with conditions, or deny the preliminary plat. When the recommendation is to approve with conditions, the developer should be required to make changes on the preliminary plan before action by the local legislative body. When the planning commission finds it cannot recommend approval, it should indicate in writing what changes need to be made on the plan before a recommendation for approval can go forward.

The legislative body will take some formal action, such as enactment of an ordinance or resolution, approving the preliminary plan. When that happens, the developer goes ahead with preparation of the final plat, prepared by a surveyor. The final plat is a precise drawing that contains the necessary information that will fix the location of lots and streets with reference to survey markers, such as iron pins driven deep into the ground, and concrete monuments. This information—measurements in tenths of a foot, and angles and bearings—will create the legal land title record for locating the lots. It will also be the means by which the streets and other proposed public improvements are conveyed to and accepted by the local government after the developer constructs them to the government's standards. The final plat is accompanied by engineering drawings and supporting technical analyses, such as those dealing with stormwater or water pressure. These drawings describe the installation of public and private improvements, and other site development modifications such as site grading. Some plats may be accompanied by plans to control erosion and sedimentation during site development, or to address specialized issues such as impact on existing wetlands and their protection or restoration.

The engineering drawings will show proposed vertical and horizontal profiles of streets, water and sewer lines, location of street lights and fire hydrants, sidewalks, design of detention and retention basins, and construction specifications, such as type of concrete or asphalt used and depth of pavement and aggregate base.

The planning commission is again the initial review body, with the staff providing similar backup as in the earlier review stage. In this case, however, the local government's engineer performs a detailed examination of the engineering drawings to ensure that the improvements are properly designed and meet the adopted design and construction standards.

If the final plat is consistent with the approved preliminary plat and any conditions imposed upon it, then the basic design and layout of the subdivision will be agreed upon. Still, the final plat must be checked once again against the requirements in the subdivision regulations and the zoning code for compliance. At this point, the planning commission may find other details that need attention. For example:

- Has the developer provided sidewalks throughout the subdivision that connect with other sidewalks in the area? Sometimes developers resist sidewalk installation, claiming they are not needed or add unnecessarily to a lots costs. But once a subdivision is completed, it is a difficult matter for the local government to construct sidewalks because it must resort to a complicated, often contentious process of special assessments to individual property owners.

- Are curb radii appropriate to the function of the street? The final plat will show the curb radii, which can range anywhere from five to 35 feet, depending on the roads classification. There can be a fair degree of debate about what size radius should be employed and its impact. The larger the curb radius, the faster a vehicle can negotiate a turn. By contrast, the smaller the radius, the slower a vehicle moves, making the intersection safer for a pedestrian.
- Are street lights provided at intersections and, preferably, spaced at regular intervals along streets?
- When a lot is near a flood hazard area or an area with stormwater problems, will the buildable portion of the lot be above the flood elevation? Some final plats specify a pad elevation for the ground floor of the building to ensure that the building will be constructed at a level high enough to prevent flooding.
- Will water pressure be adequate throughout the subdivision? For example, many communities require looped water lines to minimize loss of pressure during large flows of water.
- Will natural areas and stands of old, larger trees that meet certain circumference standards be maintained, albeit in private ownership? Many communities have adopted ordinances to ensure the preservation of mature trees during the subdivision process.
- Are street stubs provided to adjoining vacant tracts of land to allow the future continuation of the internal street system?

The planning commission then reviews the final plat, often along with the engineering plans, at another public meeting and recommends action on it to the local legislative body. Once the local legislative body approves the final plat and the developer makes any additional changes that may be required, the plat is almost ready for recording. However, before the plat may be recorded—at this point it is in the form of a reproducible mylar or linen drawing (although some local governments are requiring that it also be submitted in a computerized format as well)—the developer must either construct the required improvements or post a performance bond to ensure that the improvements will be constructed within the next one or two years. Should the developer fail to complete the improvements within a certain period, the local government may use the performance bond, usually set at 110 to 120 percent of the estimated costs of the improvements, to pay for the installation itself.

If the developer completes the improvements or posts the performance bond, the plat is recorded. Site development work commences and individual lots are ready to be sold. The local government, through its professional engineer, inspects the improvements as they are being constructed. When site development work is completed, the developer requests a release of the performance bond and, if the improvements have been installed properly, the local government releases the bond and accepts responsibility for the improvements. Some communities may also require a maintenance bond for a portion of the cost of the improvements (a figure of around 10 percent) to ensure that the infrastructure will survive one additional building season. The developer may also be required to supply as-built engineering plans, showing the exact location of improvements as they were constructed on the site, so there is a permanent record of the infrastructure. This is especially important as a record for locating underground utilities.

C. GOVERNMENTAL POWER TO REGULATE SUBDIVISIONS

RIDGEFIELD LAND CO. v. DETROIT

Supreme Court of Michigan, 1928.
241 Mich. 468, 217 N.W. 58.

McDonald, J.

The plaintiff has brought certiorari to review the action of the Wayne circuit court in denying a writ of mandamus to compel the defendants to approve a plat. The proposed plat, known as Ridgefield subdivision No. 1, contains 80 acres of land, and is bounded on the north by Pembroke avenue and on the east by Livernois avenue. To conform to the general plan for streets adopted by the city of Detroit, Pembroke avenue ought to be 86 feet wide and Livernois avenue 120 feet wide. In respect to the width of these two streets, the plat did not conform to the general plan. It was submitted to the city plan commission on several occasions, and finally was conditionally approved as follows:

"In order that Mr. Fry may be able to file a plat on the property in question and have his property assessed by lot numbers, the commission agrees to make certain concessions and to approve the plat providing the following changes are made:

1. A 10 foot building line is to be established on Pembroke avenue to conform with property platted to the west.

2. Seventeen feet is to be dedicated for Livernois avenue in addition to the regular 33–foot dedication."

The plaintiff refused to accept the changes, and began this proceeding to compel the approval of the plat as offered.

It is first contended that there is no statute or ordinance authorizing the city plan commission or the city council to require the dedication of an additional 17 feet on Livernois avenue and the establishment of a 10 foot building line on Pembroke avenue as conditions precedent to the approval of this plat.

Under authority of Act No. 279, Pub.Act 1909, as amended (1 Comp.Laws 1915, sec. 3304 et seq.), the city of Detroit provided in its charter for the appointment of a city plan commission of nine members with "power to pass upon the acceptance of all plats of land within and for a distance of three miles beyond the limits of the city."

The authority of the common council with reference to the approval of plats is derived from Act No. 360, Pub.Acts 1925, the applicable portion of which reads as follows:

> "The governing body shall determine as to whether such lands are suitable for platting purposes and shall have the right to require that all streets and private roads shall be graveled or cindered and properly drained, and bridges and culverts installed where necessary, and where lots are platted of a width of 60 feet or less, may require that concrete or gravel walks shall be built and that all highways, streets and alleys conform to the general plan that may have been adopted by the governing body of the municipality for the width and location of highways, streets and alleys; * * * The governing body shall reject said plat if the same does not conform to the provisions of this act."

It thus appears that the common council, which is the governing body referred to in the statute, has power to adopt a general plan for the width of streets and to refuse to approve any plan which does not conform thereto. It adopted such a plan. This plan called the "master plan" was prepared by the city plan commission and rapid transit commission in collaboration with the road commissions of Wayne, Oakland, and Macomb counties and the authorities of the included municipalities. It was adopted by resolution of the common council of the city of Detroit on April 14, 1925. As to width and location, it classifies streets as super-highways, major highways, and secondary thoroughfares. Superhighways are required to be 204 feet wide, major highways are section line roads 120 feet in width, and secondary thoroughfares are quarter section lines 86 feet wide. Livernois avenue is a section line road and Pembroke avenue is a quarter section line road. The proposed plat gives these two streets a width of 66 feet each. The plaintiff concedes that in this respect its plat does not conform to the general street plan but it contends that it does conform to the width of Pembroke and Livernois avenues as dedicated in other plats; that the statute gives the city no power to require a greater width as a condition to the approval of the plat and that if it can be interpreted as conferring such power, it is an infringement on the constitutional rights of the plaintiff in that it compels the dedication of private property for public use without compensation therefor. There is no merit to this contention. The other plats referred to were approved and recorded before the present general street plan was adopted; so it cannot be said that it was not made applicable alike to all persons.

RIDGEFIELD LAND CO. v. DETROIT, 241 MICH. 468, 217 N.W. 58 (1928)

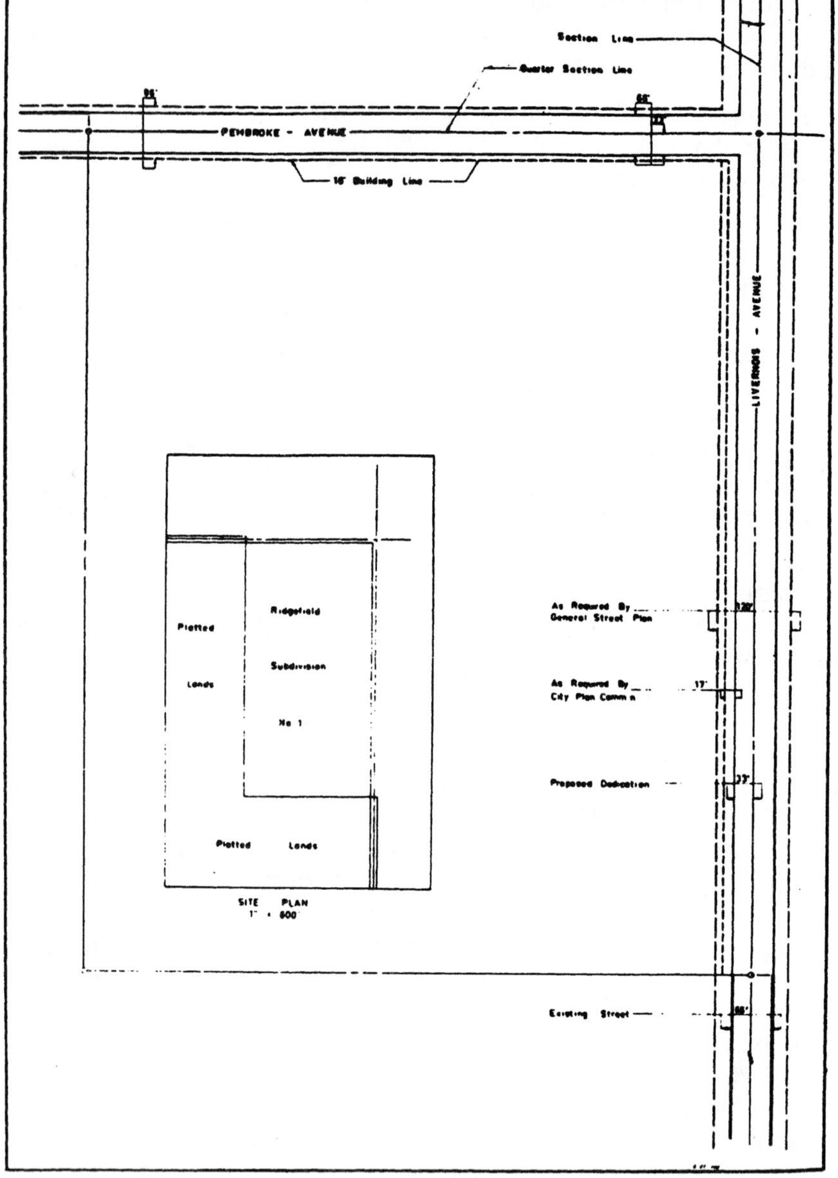

The streets in the city of Detroit, as elsewhere, were originally laid out for the horse and buggy age. They are too narrow for the present traffic conditions. It has become necessary for the general convenience and the public safety to widen them and to prevent others of the same kind from being established. Because of this necessity, there is nothing unreasonable in the demand of the city that the streets designated in the plaintiff's plat shall be of such a width as to conform to the general street plan. It has been determined that streets of a certain width are necessary to accommodate the traffic. They are necessary for the public safety and therefore the right to provide for them is within the police power of the city.

The error in plaintiff's position is the assumption that in requiring an additional dedication and the establishment of a building line to conform to its general plan, the city is exercising power of eminent domain. Its argument would have merit and the authorities cited would have application if this were a case where the plat had been recorded and the city were undertaking to widen the streets or to establish a building line. But this is not such a case. Here the city is not trying to compel a dedication. It cannot compel the plaintiff to subdivide its property or to dedicate any part of it for streets. It can, however, impose any reasonable condition which must be complied with before the subdivision is accepted for record. In theory, at least, the owner of a subdivision voluntarily dedicates sufficient land for streets in return for the advantage and privilege of having his plat recorded. Unless he does so, the law gives him no right to have it recorded. In Ross v. Goodfellow, 7 App.Cas.D.C. 1, 10, 11, it is said:

> It must be remembered that each owner has the undoubted right to lay off his land in any manner that he pleases, or not to subdivide it at all. He cannot be made to dedicate streets and avenues to the public. If public necessity demands parts of his lands for highways, it can be taken only by condemnation and payment of its value. But he has no corresponding right to have his plat of subdivision so made admitted to the records.
>
> In providing for public record, congress can accompany the privilege with conditions and limitations applicable alike to all persons. In providing for such record in the act of 1888, congress sought to conserve the public interest and convenience by requiring practical conformity in all subdivisions of land into squares, streets, and avenues, with the general plan of the city as originally established, and this, regardless of the fact that it might in instances practically coerce the dedication of streets to public use which would otherwise have to be paid for.

In the instant case, the defendants have imposed two conditions with which the plaintiff is required to comply for the privilege of having its plat recorded. They are reasonable and necessary for the public welfare. In the exercise of its power under the statute and its charter, the city had a right to impose them. They do not constitute the taking of private property for public use, and are not an infringement on plaintiff's constitutional rights. The circuit judge was right in holding that the statute conferred power upon the city of Detroit to adopt its present general street plan and to refuse to approve and record all plats that did not conform thereto.

The order is affirmed, with costs to the defendants. * * *

Notes

1. The Ridgefield case has been cited in many jurisdictions over the years for the proposition that subdivision regulation is a fair exchange for the privilege of recording the plat and enabling the subdivider to sell lots by number rather than legal description. Other rationales for subdivision regulation can be found in earlier materials:

A. Consider the following description of the District of Columbia program which ties regulation to public acceptance for maintenance of streets that the subdivider delineates on the proposed plat and offers to dedicate to the public:

Tooke, Methods of Protecting the City Plan in Outlying Districts, 15 Geo.L.J. 127, 137 (1927):

> * * * This third method of protecting the city plan is by a control of the privilege of the owner to dedicate streets and highways in making a subdivision for residential or business purposes. * * * The Act of August 27, 1888, "to regulate the subdivision of land within the District of Columbia" authorized the Commissioners to promulgate general orders regulating the platting and subdividing of all lands within the District and provided that such plats must be approved by them before being admitted to record. Section 5 of the Act laid down that "no future subdivision of land in the District of Columbia, without the limits of the cities of Washington and Georgetown, shall be recorded in the Surveyor's office of the said District, unless made in conformity with the general plan of the city of Washington." In 1893, in order to carry out more completely the same object, Congress passed a supplemental Act providing for a plan for the extension of a permanent system of highways throughout that part of the District lying outside of Washington and Georgetown, which system was to be made as nearly in conformity with the street plan of the city of Washington as the Commissioners should deem advisable and practicable.
>
> The provisions of the second * * * section were as follows:
>
> "Sec. 2. And after any such map shall have been so recorded, no further subdivision of any land included therein shall be admitted to record in the office of the surveyor of said district, or in the office of the recorder of deeds thereof, unless the same be first approved by the Commissioners, and be in conformity to such map. Nor shall it be lawful, when any such map shall have been so recorded, for the Commissioners of the District of Columbia, or any other officer or person representing the United States or the District of Columbia, to thereafter improve, repair or assume any responsibility in regard to any abandoned highway within the area covered by such map, or to accept, improve, repair or assume any responsibility in regard to any highway that any owner of land in such area shall thereafter attempt to lay out or establish, unless such landowner shall first have submitted to the Commissioners a plat of such proposed highway, and the Commissioners shall have found the same to be in conformity to such map, and shall

have approved such plat, and caused it to be recorded in the office of said surveyor."

* * *

The constitutionality of this Act came before the Supreme Court of the United States in 1896 in the case of Bauman v. Ross, 167 U.S. 548, 17 S.Ct. 966, 42 L.Ed. 270, and was unanimously upheld by the Court. The opinion of Gray, J., reviewed not only the history of the legislation on the condemnation of lands for public purposes in the District, but also the adjudications of the Courts of the several States upon similar statutory provisions for the taking of lands by eminent domain. As to section 2, the Court said:

"The recording of the map under section 2 does not constitute a taking of any land, nor in any way interfere with the owner's use and enjoyment thereof. The provision of that section that after the map has been recorded, no further subdivision, not in conformity with the map, shall be admitted to record, goes no further than the earlier acts of Congress of January 12, 1809, c. 8, and August 27, 1888, c. 916, cited at the beginning of this opinion; and is clearly within the authority of Congress to prevent anything being placed upon the public records, which may tend to defeat its object of securing uniformity in the entire system of highways in the District. The provision of section 3, giving to any deed or will, duly recorded, which refers to the subdivision made by the map, the same effect as if such subdivision had been made and recorded by the grantor or testator, tends to promote the same object and benefits rather than injures owners of lands. The provision of section 2, forbidding the Commissioners of the District of Columbia and all other public officers or agents to accept, improve, repair, or assume any responsibility in regard to highways not in conformity with the map, does not touch the rights of owners of lands; but was evidently intended to prevent the District of Columbia from being held responsible to travelers upon such highways, under the law prevailing in the District, as declared by this Court, and suffered to remain unchanged by Congress. The object of the recording of the map is to give notice to all persons of the system of highways proposed to be established by subsequent proceedings of condemnation. It does not restrict in any way the use or improvement of lands by their owners before the commencement of proceedings for condemnation of lands for such highways; nor does it limit the damages to be awarded in such proceedings. The recording of the map, therefore, did not of itself entitle the owners of lands to any compensation or damages."

B. In Trawalter v. Schaefer, 142 Tex. 521, 179 S.W.2d 765 (1944), The Texas Supreme Court upheld the requirement of approval of proposed subdivisions on the theory that such approval was necessary to enable tax assessors to properly locate the newly created lots. Also see Merton v. Dolphin, 28 Wis. 456 (1871).

C. In many jurisdictions the rationale for subdivision regulation is founded on an expansive and general view of the police power. One of the most sweeping statements can be found in Mansfield & Swett, Inc. v. West Orange, 120 N.J.L. 145, 198 A. 225 (1938):

The state possesses the inherent authority—it antedates the constitution—to resort, in the building and expansion of its community life, to such measures as may be necessary to secure the essential common material and moral needs. The public welfare is of prime importance; and the correlative restrictions upon individual rights—either of person or of property—are incidents of the social order, considered a negligible loss compared with the resultant advantages to the community as a whole. Planning confined to the common need is inherent in the authority to create the municipality itself. It is as old as government itself; it is of the very essence of civilized society. A comprehensive scheme of physical development is requisite to community efficiency and progress.

To particularize, the public health, safety, order and prosperity are dependent upon the proper regulation of municipal life. The free flow of traffic with a minimum of hazard of necessity depends upon the number, location and width of streets, and their relation to one another, and the location of building lines; and these considerations likewise enter into the growth of trade, commerce and industry. Housing, always a problem in congested areas affecting the moral and material life of the people, is necessarily involved in both municipal planning and zoning. And it is essential to adequate planning that there be provision for future community needs reasonably to be anticipated. We are surrounded with the problems of planless growth. The baneful consequences of haphazard development are everywhere apparent. There are evils affecting the health, safety and prosperity of our citizens that are well-nigh insurmountable because of the prohibitive corrective cost. To challenge the power to give proper direction to community growth and development in the particulars mentioned is to deny the vitality of a principle that has brought men together in organized society for their mutual advantage. A sound economy to advance the collective interest in local affairs is the primary aim of municipal government.

The police power of the state may be delegated to the state's municipal subdivisions created for the administration of local self-government, to be exerted whenever necessary for the general good and welfare. It reaches to all the great public needs; and the right of property yields to the exercise of this reserve element of sovereignty. The authority is of the essence of the social compact. The genius of organized government is the subordination of individual personal and property rights to the collective interest. In Commonwealth v. Alger, 61 Mass. (7 Cush. 1851) 53, 84, Chief Justice Shaw spoke thus: "We think it is a settled principle, growing out of the nature of well-ordered civil society, that every holder of property, however absolute and unqualified may be his title, holds it under the implied liability that his use of it may be so regulated, that it shall not be injurious to the equal enjoyment of others having an equal right to the enjoyment of their property, not injurious to the rights of the community. All property in this commonwealth is * * * held subject to those general regulations which are necessary to the common good and general welfare. Rights of property, like all other social and conventional rights, are subject to such reasonable limitations in their enjoyment, as shall prevent them from being

> injurious, and to such reasonable restraints and regulations established by law, as the legislature, under the governing and controlling power vested in them by the constitution, may think necessary and expedient. This is very different from the right of eminent domain, the right of a government to take and appropriate private property to public use, whenever the public exigency requires it; which can be done only on condition of providing a reasonable compensation therefor. The power we allude to is rather the police power, the power vested in the legislature by the constitution, to make, ordain and establish all manner of wholesome and reasonable laws, statutes and ordinances, either with penalties or without, not repugnant to the constitution, as they shall judge to be for the good and welfare of the commonwealth, and of the subjects of the same. It is much easier to perceive and realize the existence and sources of this power, than to mark its boundaries, or prescribe limits to its exercise." * * *

2. An important area of federal regulation that has a great impact on land subdivision is The Interstate Land Sales Full Disclosure Act, 15 U.S.C.A. §§ 1701–1720, which requires developers of residential subdivisions of fifty or more lots to register the subdivision with the Department of Housing and Urban Development, prepare a detailed "property report" which must be provided to every would-be purchaser of a lot, and refrain from certain advertising practices. A cause of action for damages for misrepresentation or omission in the property report is given to the purchaser (§ 1709), and a limited right to revoke a purchase agreement is provided (§ 1703(b)). Among other information required in the property report, is

> "(5) a statement of the present condition of access to the subdivision, the existence of any unusual conditions relating to noise or safety which affect the subdivision and are known to the developer, the availability of sewage disposal facilities and other public utilities (including water, electricity, gas, and telephone facilities) in the subdivision, the proximity in miles of the subdivision to nearby municipalities, and the nature of any improvements to be installed by the developer and his estimated schedule for completion." 15 U.S.C.A. § 1705.

The coverage provisions of the act, § 1702, exempt many of the typical urban and suburban subdivisions of more than fifty lots; however, the coverage of the act is still widespread. An indication of the importance and implications of the act can be gathered from the letter that was widely circulated in 1973 by the Office of Interstate Land Sales Registration of the U.S. Department of Housing and Urban Development (HUD):

> Re: Interstate Land Sales Full Disclosure Act
>
> Dear Member:
>
> The purpose of this letter is to alert you to consequences which may ensue from your failure to understand fully the Interstate Land Sales Full Disclosure Act and its implementing regulations.
>
> The 1968 Interstate Land Sales Full Disclosure Act became effective April 28, 1969, and has now been operative for nearly four years. Although the Office of Interstate Land Sales Registration (OILSR) has processed thousands of registrations on both domestic and foreign

subdivisions, it is nevertheless likely that an even larger number of subdivisions covered by this Act are still unregistered.

Unless exempt, any developer having 50 or more lots or parcels of subdivided land who sells these lots by using the U.S. mails or any other instruments of interstate commerce, without first registering with OILSR and providing the purchaser in advance of sale with an approved property report, is in violation of the law and may be sentenced to a jail term of 5 years or a $5,000 fine, or both.

In addition, all such contracts are voidable at the absolute and unconditional election of the purchaser. Besides refunding the purchase price of the lot, the developer may be required to pay the reasonable costs of all improvements on the lot or lots. Once an unregistered developer is faced with the wholesale repurchasing of properties previously sold, many of which have already been improved, his bankruptcy is more than a remote possibility. All developers should be forewarned to reassess their positions on the need for registration before it is too late. Attorneys who have developers as clients have a professional responsibility to familiarize themselves with the provisions of the Interstate Land Sales Full Disclosure Act and its implementing regulations, and to advise their clients accordingly.

In addition to the direct penalties that the developer may face, there may be serious derivative consequences for the accountants, bankers and title companies, and even the real estate brokers of unregistered developers under certain circumstances.

We urge you to read and study the Interstate Land Sales Full Disclosure Act and the OILSR Regulations. We are ready at all times to answer any questions from concerned parties.

Sincerely,
George K. Bernstein
Interstate Land Sales Administrator

The Interstate Land Sales Full Disclosure Act has been held to apply to condominium developments. See, Winter v. Hollingsworth Properties, Inc., 777 F.2d 1444 (11th Cir. 1985); Schatz v. Jockey Club Phase III, Ltd., 604 F.Supp. 537 (S.D. Fla. 1985). See also, Becherer v. Merrill Lynch, Pierce, Fenner & Smith, 127 F.3d 478 (6th Cir.1997), affirming the proposition that condominiums are subject to the Interstate Land Sales Full Disclosure Act, but holding that hotel interests were not condominiums.

3. The preceding materials all deal with the question of the validity and scope of enabling legislation authorizing municipal regulation of the subdivision of land. In the absence of enabling legislation, could a city regulate subdivisions? See Bella Vista Ranches, Inc. v. City of Sierra Vista, 126 Ariz. 142, 613 P.2d 302 (App.1980) where the court held that a 1966 subdivision ordinance was invalid because the state did not enact enabling legislation until 1974.

DAWE v. CITY OF SCOTTSDALE

Supreme Court of Arizona, In Banc, 1978.
119 Ariz. 486, 581 P.2d 1136.

STRUCKMEYER, VICE CHIEF JUSTICE.

This is an action by appellants to have the recorded plat of the Palo Verde Terrace declared a legally existing subdivision, for a declaration that the City of Scottsdale's annexation of the property covered by the plat and its ordinance adopted after the plat was recorded did not affect the validity of the subdivision plan or the owners' right to develop the property, and to compel Scottsdale to issue certain construction permits. The Superior Court entered a judgment in favor of Scottsdale, declaring Scottsdale's zoning applicable to the Palo Verde Terrace and denying appellants' construction permits. The Court of Appeals reversed, 119 Ariz. 493, 581 P.2d 1143 (App.1978). We accepted review. Opinion of the Court of Appeals vacated. Judgment of the Superior Court affirmed.

* * *

* * * During the time when the county was without any zoning, appellants' predecessors in interest, in order to avoid the 35,000 square-foot minimum lot size requirements of the prior zoning ordinance and the ordinance adopted on February 27, 1960, recorded the Palo Verde Terrace subdivision plat. This plat provided for 120 lots of a maximum 10,000 square feet each. No attempt was made to improve the property and it has remained vacant and unimproved from the date the subdivision was recorded in 1960 through the date of the filing of this action, January 17, 1975. In the year 1963, Scottsdale annexed an area which included the Palo Verde Terrace. Scottsdale's zoning permitted a minimum size of 35,000 square feet per lot in the annexed area.

The principal question at issue is whether the appellants have had since 1963 a vested right to develop substandard lots within the City of Scottsdale because of the recording of their plat. We think not.

It has been repeatedly held that subdivision ordinances apply to lots on prior recorded maps which were unsold at the time of the ordinance's enactment. Ziman v. Village of Glencoe, 1 Ill.App.3d 912, 275 N.E.2d 168 (1971); Sherman–Colonial Realty Corp. v. Goldsmith, 155 Conn. 175, 230 A.2d 568 (1967); Blevens v. City of Manchester, 103 N.H. 284, 170 A.2d 121 (1961); State ex rel. Mar–Well, Inc. v. Dodge, 113 Ohio App. 118, 177 N.E.2d 515 (1960); Caruthers v. Board of Adjustment, 290 S.W.2d 340 (Tex.Civ.App.1956).

* * *

Appellants, however, argue that the case of Robinson v. Lintz, 101 Ariz. 448, 420 P.2d 923 (1966), holds that a subdivision lot becomes legally established as to size and description when it is properly recorded and that it is unaffected by subsequent zoning enactments or amendments. Robinson v. Lintz is authority for the proposition that a subdivision lot becomes legally established as to size and description when a plat containing it is recorded. But it does not hold that such a lot is unaffected by subsequent zoning enactments.

* * *

* * * *Robinson* did not concern itself with the problem we must decide here; namely, whether the filing of a plat immunizes a parcel of real estate from subsequent zoning regardless of how urgent the need for regulation might be.

A. Rathkopf, in The Law of Zoning and Planning, Ch. 71, § 11, page 93 (4th ed. 1978), states:

> "* * * whether the subdivider has the right to continue the development of his subdivision as planned in the face of changed rules and regulations of the planning board, or an amendment to the zoning ordinance which changes the permitted uses or the nonuse restrictions of land covered by the plat, is in great measure governed by the same considerations which determine vested rights under a building permit."

We have held that where the amount of work which was done toward the construction of a service station was of small consequence, the permittee acquired no vested right to complete the construction of the building if the board of supervisors exercised its power to rezone the property and revoked the building permit. Verner v. Redman, 77 Ariz. 310, 271 P.2d 468 (1954).

* * *

Judgment of the Superior Court affirmed.

Notes

1. Does this case indicate that any new subdivision requirement may be applied retroactively to the development of land that was platted at an earlier time? The problem of retroactive subdivision regulation is not unusual, but the case law is sparse. See Brous v. Smith, 304 N.Y. 164, 106 N.E.2d 503 (1952); Town of Seabrook v. Tra–Sea Corp., 119 N.H. 937, 410 A.2d 240 (1979); Lampton v. Pinaire, 610 S.W.2d 915 (Ky.App.1980); Williamson Pointe Venture v. City of Austin, 912 S.W.2d 340 (Tex.App.1995); State ex rel. Dreher v. Fuller, 257 Mont. 445, 849 P.2d 1045 (1993).

Presumably, if the new requirements are within the police power, the community may impose them through the building permit or similar administrative process as well as by way of subdivision plat approval. However, if the landowner has changed his position in reliance on old requirements or the absence of requirements, some courts might approach the problem by finding a vested right in the landowner to proceed without meeting the new conditions. Some cases which shed light on the vested right theory are Gruber v. Mayor and Twp. Committee of Raritan Twp., 39 N.J. 1, 186 A.2d 489 (1962); Spindler Realty Corp. v. Monning, 243 Cal.App.2d 255, 53 Cal.Rptr. 7 (1966), certiorari denied 385 U.S. 975, 87 S.Ct. 515, 17 L.Ed.2d 437 (1966) and Western Land Equities, Inc. v. City of Logan, 617 P.2d 388

(Utah 1980).[1] In Town of Orangetown v. Magee, 88 N.Y.2d 41, 643 N.Y.S.2d 21, 665 N.E.2d 1061 (1996) the court upheld a $5 million dollar verdict for a developer whose building permit was wrongfully revoked in mid-project. The trial court found that the developer had spent over $4 million on preparation and land clearing before work was halted by the town. A similar case is Reserve, Ltd. v. Town of Longboat Key, 17 F.3d 1374 (11th Cir.1994) where after spending $6 million the developer's permit was revoked under an ordinance provision providing for revocation of a permit if, after construction was commenced, no substantial work was accomplished in any thirty day period.

2. In Prince George's County v. Sunrise Development Limited Partnership, 330 Md. 297, 623 A.2d 1296 (1993) the court set out the following factual situation:

> In this case the developer of a proposed twelve-story apartment building contends that the project was sufficiently advanced on May 1, 1990, to prevent downzoning. The developer's vested rights argument ultimately rests on a single footing, one that was placed in the ground during the preceding December for a proposed column at a proposed outside corner of a proposed portico.
>
> * * *
>
> [The court accepted the Maryland rule as embodying a two-prong test, (1) a manifest commencement of labor on the ground which everyone can readily see and recognize as the commencement of a building, and (2) the work must have been begun with the intention to continue the work until completion of the building.]
>
> Turning from semantics to the merits of this controversy, the question is whether the Board acted arbitrarily, capriciously or without substantial evidence in concluding that the footing in the middle of the 9.9591 acre site was not readily visible or recognizable on May 1, 1990, as the commencement of a highrise apartment building. The footing's dimensions, as reflected by the Board, result in an area of four square feet. A four square foot footing occupies 9/1,000,000 of the R–10 zone, considered in two dimensions. The footing occupies none of the air space of the R–10 zone, if it is considered in three dimensions. The Board did not err in declining to conclude that this swatch of cement would alert persons who came on the property that construction of a building had begun under the R–10 use.

Also see Lake Bluff Housing Partners v. South Milwaukee, 197 Wis.2d 157, 540 N.W.2d 189 (1995) holding that a change in zoning during the developer's activities did not upset the developer's vested rights. The state bar association is apparently drafting legislation to provide for development

1. In California, where judicial rulings have consistently rejected the vested right argument, the legislature, in 1979, enacted a provision authorizing cities and developers to enter into development agreements. Cal.Govt.Code § 65864 et seq. For analysis of this legislation, see Hagman, Development Agreements, 3 Zoning and Planning Law Report Nos. 9 and 10 (Oct., Nov.1980). In the Utah case the court held that a developer's rights should vest at the time of application for a building permit; the court discusses several alternative theories in the opinion.

agreements in Wisconsin in order to overcome the uncertainties created by the case.

3. With the principal case, compare Selby Realty Co. v. City of San Buenaventura, 10 Cal.3d 110, 109 Cal.Rptr. 799, 514 P.2d 111 (1973). Also see State ex rel. Craven v. City of Tacoma, 63 Wash.2d 23, 385 P.2d 372 (1963).

4. Does the reasoning in the principal case suggest that compulsory subdivision is within the police power? If so, what becomes of the theory that subdivision is a privilege that can be conditioned on the dedication of land for streets and other amenities? Should the classic theory be modified to one which allows any kind of land development to be subjected to conditions and permits? Consider the following case and the notes thereafter.

CITY OF CORPUS CHRISTI v. UNITARIAN CHURCH OF CORPUS CHRISTI

Court of Civil Appeals of Texas, 1968.
436 S.W.2d 923, refused n.r.e.

NYE, JUSTICE.

The Unitarian Church of Corpus Christi as the owner of certain property, applied to the City of Corpus Christi for a building permit to improve its property for church purposes. The church was told by a city department employee that the church property would have to be platted prior to the issuance of the permit. The church prepared a plat of the property, outlining the boundaries of its lot, designating utility easements and submitted it to the City Planning Commission for approval. After a hearing on the church's application, the Commission conditionally approved the church's plat. Approval was subject to the church dedicating a strip of their land, 25 feet by 630 feet for the purpose of widening an easement so that an existing street could be extended. The church was dissatisfied and appealed this decision to the City Council seeking approval of their plat without the requirement of street dedication. After a hearing, the City Council denied the relief sought by the church. The church then filed suit in the district court seeking a declaratory judgment: that the City had no authority under the applicable statutes, charters, and ordinances to require the church to file a map or plat of its property as a condition to granting the building permit. The church sought additionally, the issuance of a writ of mandamus to compel the City to approve their submitted plat. The trial was had before the court without a jury, resulting in a judgment granting the writ of mandamus against the City and ordering approval of the plat as submitted by the church. * * *

The church's lot faces a major dedicated city street (Carroll Lane) on the southeast side. The lot was and is presently served with public utilities. Adjoining the church's property on the northeast side is a tract of land (also 2½ acres) called the Hancock Tract which has heretofore been platted. The owners of the Hancock Tract had dedicated to the City a strip of land 25 feet by 630 feet, being one half of the proposed extension of Kay Street. The City by its present action would require the church to dedicate the other half of the Kay Street extension as a condition to the approval of the plat and the subsequent granting of a building permit. See the following diagram.

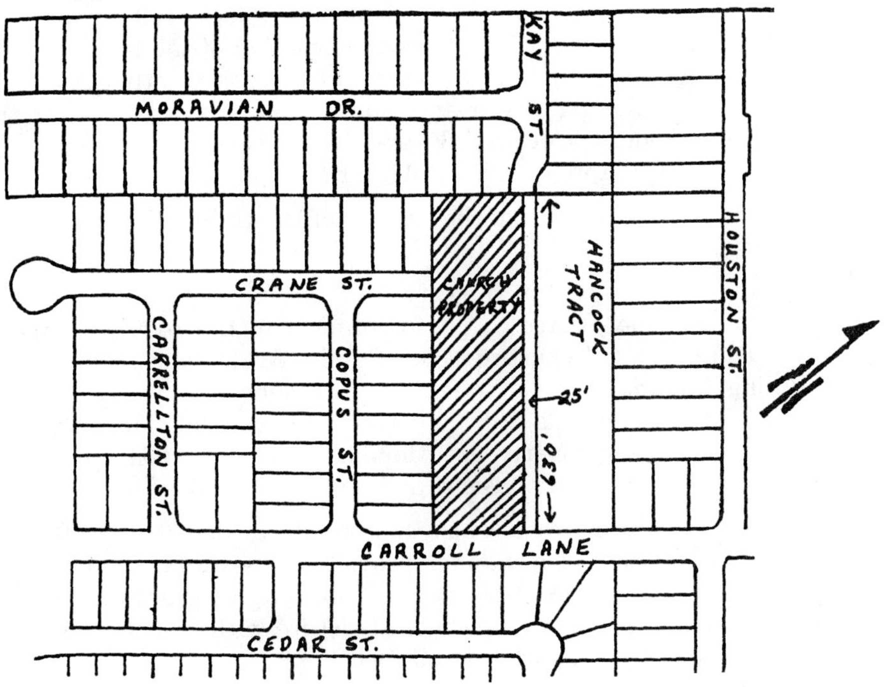

The church is the owner of the property within the City that is not now platted into lots and blocks. The charter of the City of Corpus Christi provides that the City "* * * shall never grant any permit to construct or repair any house or structure within such area (unplatted property) until such map shall be so approved and filed * * *." It follows as we discuss this point in more detail later, that it would be necessary that as a condition precedent to the granting of a building permit by the City, that the church must file a plat of its unplatted property. It is likewise proper for a city to require a property owner to obtain a building permit prior to the erection of a building. This requirement is a valid exercise of a municipality's police power. * * *

This is a limited type law suit involving a single lot owner whose unplatted property was annexed into the City. The property owner wishes to obtain a building permit to build in connection with the entire lot, understanding that such lot would not now or ever, under its proposed plat, be subdivided into two or more lots.

If the statutes, charter provisions or ordinances pertaining to the City of Corpus Christi do not impose upon the church a legal obligation to dedicate a portion of its land for street purposes under these facts, or if such statutes, charter provisions or ordinances do not authorize the

City to require a property owner to make such dedication, then the issuance of a mandamus will be proper. Where the church has done all that the statutes and law demands, the authorized granting of a building permit becomes a mere ministerial duty, the performance of which may be compelled by mandamus. Thus where the City itself or by and through its planning commission, in its construction of the law, deprives a citizen of an unquestionable legal right and there is no other adequate remedy, the court having power to issue mandamus may review the matter. Commissioners' Court v. Frank Jester Development Co., 199 S.W.2d 1004 (Tex.Civ.App.—Dallas 1947, n.r.e.)

* * * Article V, Section 6 of the charter of the City of Corpus Christi provides in part as follows:

> "Any property within the City * * * *not now platted into blocks and lots,* shall be platted * * * to conform to the requirements of * * * (the) * * * Department of Public Works and Zoning and Planning Commission. Its owners, before such property is laid off and *subdivided* shall file * * * a correct map thereof. The City shall never pay for the property used for streets * * * within any such subdivision, * * * " (emphasis supplied)
>
> "* * * After approval such map shall be filed in the office of the County Clerk in the manner provided by law. The head of the engineering * * * (Department) * * * shall never grant any permit to construct or repair any house or structure within such area until such map shall be so approved and filed * * *."

The City, by ordinance adopted in part the rules and regulations governing the platting of land into subdivisions as provided in Art. 974a, Vernon's Ann.Civ.St. Section 1 of such article provides in part as follows:

> "Hereafter every owner of any tract of land situated within the corporate limits * * * who may hereafter *divide* the same in two or more parts *for the purpose of laying out any subdivision* of any tract of land or any addition to any * * * city, or for laying out suburban lots or building lots, * * * shall cause a plat to be made thereof * * *." (emphasis supplied).

The City's ordinance above referred to a defined a subdivision as follows:

> "C. *SUBDIVISION.* A subdivision *is the division* of any lot, tract or parcel of land *into two or more parts,* lots or sites, *for the purpose,* whether immediate or future *of sale or division of ownership.* This definition also includes the resubdivision of land or lots which are a part of a previously recorded subdivision * * *." (emphasis supplied).
>
> "D. *SUBDIVIDER AND/OR DEVELOPER.* The terms 'subdivider' and 'developer' are synonymous and used interchangeably, and shall include any person, * * * who does, or participates in the *doing of, any act toward the subdivision of land* within the intent, scope, and

purview of this ordinance. The singular shall include the plural, and the plural shall include the singular." (emphasis supplied).

The language of Section 1 of Art. 974 is plural and relates to a division of property into parts. The same is true of the City charter and the applicable provisions of its ordinances. It contemplates subdivision for subdivision development purposes. The City's argument that the singular and plural include each other is not applicable to the provisions. A municipal charter is to be read as a whole and every word, phrase, and expression must be considered and interpreted as if deliberately chosen and used for a purpose. 39 Tex.Jur.2d, § 45, Municipal Corporations, p. 397. The church does not propose to divide its property into two or more parts or to lay out a subdivision as stated in Art. 974a and the City's charter.

We believe that the applicability of the language in Art. 974a is controlled by the word "divide". The statute states that "every owner of any tract of land * * * who may hereafter *divide* the same in two or more parts * * *" controls the disposition of those who are affected thereby.

The City relies upon the case of Ayres v. City Council of Los Angeles, 34 Cal.2d 31, 207 P.2d 1, 11 A.L.R.2d 503 (1949) and Southern Pacific Company v. City of Los Angeles, 242 Cal.App.2d 38, 51 Cal.Rptr. 197 (1966). However, in each of these cases an ordinance or statute gave the authority required of them.

It is urged upon us that since the City's platting ordinance provides that whenever a half street has already been provided for, adjacent to a tract "*to be subdivided,*" the other remaining half street shall be platted in such *subdivision* in accordance with Section VI–A of the ordinance. (emphasis supplied). This platting ordinance refers to subdivisions and the emphasis is on "subdivide". The City summarizes the record and contends that the overwhelming evidence shows that the trial court erred and abused its discretion in ordering a writ of mandamus to issue against the City to approve the church's plat in the face of the statutes, charter and ordinance which govern the approval of such plats. This is not a discretionary matter. There is no statute, charter or ordinance which would require the church as a single lot owner to dedicate a portion of its property for streets in order to get approval of its plat to obtain a building permit, where the church does not propose to subdivide the lot into smaller lots or otherwise divide it into a subdivision.

We have no quarrel with the trial court's judgment that the various articles and ordinances make the reasonable requirement that the church must file a plat of its unplatted lot. However, the withholding of a building permit upon the condition that a portion (amounting to 15%) of the church's property be dedicated to public use as a condition for the approval of such plat, is not by law authorized in this case.

* * *

We have considered all of appellant's points of error and they are overruled.

The judgment of the trial court is affirmed.

Notes

1. Is the problem in the principal case that the city had geared all of its required exactions to the concept of "subdivision" and failed to anticipate the problem of "development" of a large parcel without dividing it into two or more lots? Is the cure for the problem to define the city's power in a way which would include more than just the division of land? Some enabling statutes do just that. The Arkansas statute, for example, provides in Ark. Code Ann. § 14–56–417: "Following adoption and filing of a master street plan, the planning commission may prepare and shall administer, after approval of the legislative body, regulations controlling the development of land. The development of land includes, but is not limited to the provision of access to lots and parcels, the extension or provision of utilities, the subdividing of land into lots and blocks, and the parceling of land resulting in the need for access and utilities." Compare with the principal case Bethlehem Evangelical Lutheran Church v. City of Lakewood, 626 P.2d 668 (Colo.1981).

In Village of Lake Bluff v. Jacobson, 118 Ill.App.3d 102, 73 Ill.Dec. 637, 454 N.E.2d 734 (1983), the court held that a village could enforce its subdivision ordinance to enjoin construction of an apartment building on non-subdivided property outside the city limits but within the statutory planning jurisdiction.

Two Texas decisions in 1985 held that the development of mobile home parks, with spaces leased to individual mobile home owners, constituted subdivisions. See, Cowboy Country Estates v. Ellis County, 692 S.W.2d 882 (Tex. App. 1985) and City of Weslaco v. Carpenter, 694 S.W.2d 601 (Tex. App. 1985). Similar conclusions were reached more recently in Kentucky and New Mexico. See, Sizemore v. Madison County Fiscal Court, 58 S.W.3d 887 (Ky.App.2000); and Sandoval County Bd. of Commissioners v. Ruiz, 119 N.M. 586, 893 P.2d 482 (1995).

2. In those states where the enabling legislation is tied to the subdivision plat as the triggering event for regulation or exactions, the problem of how to deal with avoidance of regulation through metes and bounds sales arises. By not subdividing into lots and blocks, can the developer avoid all regulation?

The metes and bounds problem plagues land planners almost everywhere. By selling off individual parcels without benefit of recorded plat, the subdivider avoids meeting the conditions that he knows would be imposed if he presented a formal plat for approval. If a great many metes and bounds parcels are created, attempts at public planning of land development are frustrated, and prospective subdividers become less and less willing to subject themselves to regulations which so many neighbors have escaped. One approach to the problem is that of a statute which would refuse a building permit to the metes and bounds owner, unless reasonable planning conditions (like construction of a road) are met. Of course this may penalize the innocent purchaser instead of the fellow who schemed to avoid the law. What about providing by law for a right to avoid the sale?

Another approach is to define "subdivision" as the dividing of any parcel into two or more lots. Then every land division (a division always produces at least two parcels) would potentially trigger a survey, plat, and plat approval. Although some states use this definitional approach, it can at times be overly burdensome for smaller municipalities to regulate. Therefore, in certain situations, particularly in rural areas where there tend to be owners of larger parcels of land (e.g., farmers), some municipalities may exempt certain divisions from full local review. For example, a municipality may exempt a limited number of divisions for transfer to an immediate family member. Of course, this is not without problems where family members then choose to further subdivide the property for other purposes, or transfer the parcel(s) for perhaps unintended uses.

A further approach is not to require a formal survey or plat, for divisions into just a few lots, but to insist nevertheless on planning commission approval on the deeds of transfer. This approach is evidenced by the following Oklahoma statute:[2]

> "* * * [W]hoever, being the owner or agent of the owner of any parcel of ground, transfers, or sells, or agrees to sell, or negotiates to sell any tract of land of two and one half (2½) acres or less where such tract was not shown of record in the office of the County Clerk as separately owned at the effective date of the regulations hereinafter provided for and not located within a subdivision approved according to law and filed of record in the office of the County Clerk, or if so located, not comprising at least one (1) entire lot as recorded, without first obtaining the written approval of the Commission by its endorsement on the instrument of transfer, shall be subject to the penalties of this Act provided; and such transaction shall be unlawful and the deed or other instrument of transfer shall not be valid, and if recorded, shall not import notice; and the description of such lot or parcel by metes and bounds, in the instrument of transfer or other document used in the process of selling or transferring, shall not exempt the transaction or the parties from such penalties or from the remedies in this Act provided.
>
> "In its consideration of such transfers, referred to as 'lot-splits', the Commission shall apply the same regulations as are applied to subdivisions in order to accomplish the purposes of planning as herein provided."[3]

Compare with this approach the case of State ex rel. Anaya v. Select Western Lands, Inc., 94 N.M. 555, 613 P.2d 425 (App.1979).

3. Can a testamentary devise establish a subdivision? See In re Estate of Sayewich, 120 N.H. 237, 413 A.2d 581 (1980). How about a judicial partition of land? See Mount Laurel Twp. v. Barbieri, 151 N.J.Super. 27, 376 A.2d 541 (1977). A Minnesota statute enables counties with subdivision regulations to require review of all real estate transfer agreements for compliance with subdivision regulations. 1977 Minn.Laws Ch. 189. Is this a workable solution to the metes and bounds problem? In Hyler v. Town of Blue Hill, 570 A.2d 316 (Me.1990) the court found that execution of seven

2. Okl.Stat. Tit. 19, § 863.10 (1962).

3. Little seems to be known about the actual operation of this statute. See 19 Okl. Bar J. 933 (1948).

deeds dividing a parcel of land among family members, after the grantor had failed to get a subdivision approved, was an attempt to evade the subdivision ordinance. (Maine has a statute exempting gifts to family members from subdivision regulation).

4. In Town of Tuftonboro v. Lakeside Colony, Inc., 119 N.H. 445, 403 A.2d 410 (1979), the court held that conversion of an existing colony of rental cottages to a condominium development constituted a subdivision requiring the developer to comply with the subdivision ordinance.

Compare Ivy Club Investors v. City of Kennewick, 40 Wash.App. 524, 699 P.2d 782 (1985), where the court held that the city could not condition approval of a conversion of apartments to condominiums upon the payment of park fees as prescribed in the subdivision ordinance.

D. CLUSTER ZONING

CHRINKO v. SOUTH BRUNSWICK TWP. PLANNING BD.

Superior Court of New Jersey, Law Division, 1963.
77 N.J.Super. 594, 187 A.2d 221.

FURMAN, J.S.C.

This prerogative writ action contests the validity of two ordinances of South Brunswick Township in Middlesex County permitting cluster or open space zoning. By their terms a subdivision developer may reduce minimum lot sizes by 20% or 30% and minimum frontages by 10% or 20% upon his concurrently deeding 20% or 30% of the subdivided tract for parks, school sites and other public purposes, with the approval of the planning board.

South Brunswick Township is in the western section of Middlesex County abutting Somerset and Mercer Counties. Its land area is over 41 square miles. The New Jersey Turnpike, three main arterial highways and the main line of the Pennsylvania Railroad bisect the township. Once predominantly agricultural, with settled communities at Kingston, Dayton, Monmouth Junction and Deans, South Brunswick has experienced an estimated doubling of its population in the three years between 1957 and 1960 and an onrush of new industry and commercial establishments, particularly along the highways.

Downtown New York and downtown Philadelphia are within a radius of 35 miles, drawn from South Brunswick Township. The urban sprawl from the New York metropolitan area reaches within a few miles of the township on the north and east. Residential developments for the wage earners of Philadelphia, Trenton and vicinity are pushing towards South Brunswick from the south and west. Kendall Park, which was developed recently for one-family housing on lots approximating 13,500 square feet, now holds about 40% of the population of South Brunswick Township in an area slightly over one square mile along the northern boundary.

A similar project, Brunswick Acres, is proposed for a 235–acre tract in the Residential 20 Zone in the northeast corner of the township. This development is intertwined with the legal and factual issues before the court. The plaintiffs contend that the cluster or open space ordinances were enacted for the special benefit of the owner, Yenom Corporation. The defendants' position is that they responded with reasonable legislation, general in effect, to the problem of large subdivision developments without land areas available for schools, recreation areas and green spaces.

Facing multiple housing developments and a population upsurge, the South Brunswick Planning Board authorized a master plan report from a firm of planning consultants in 1960. The master plan report, which recommended balanced growth, was submitted in late 1961. No master plan has been adopted. On the subject of cluster or open space zoning, the master plan report suggested an optional system parallel to that enacted in the zoning ordinances under attack here, but applicable only in zones with a minimum lot size of 45,000 square feet and allowing reductions of minimum lot sizes but not minimum frontages. The planning consultants label this recommended scheme "density zoning," stressing that no more homes can be built in a subdivision despite smaller size lots, because the land thus saved must be deeded to the municipality.

The need for preserving woods and parklands in a natural state, as well as lands adequate for other public purposes, is widely recognized. The voters of this State approved by referendum in 1961 the expenditure of $60,000,000 for the acquisition of so-called "green acres" by the State or political subdivisions. L.1961, c. 45, N.J.S.A. 13:8A–1 et seq. Technical Bulletin 42 of the Urban Land Institute, published in 1961, endorses density zoning, which it designates as organic zoning for planned residential developments. Other discussions of the various governmental techniques for acquiring or maintaining recreation and park areas are found in Krasnowiecki & Paul, "Preservation of Open Space in Metropolitan Areas," 110 U.Pa.L.Rev. 179 (1961); Comment, "Techniques for Preserving Open Spaces," 75 Harv.L.Rev. 1622 (1962); Comment, "Control of Urban Sprawl or Securing Open Space: Regulation by Condemnation or by Ordinance?" 50 Cal.L.Rev. 483 (1962).

The cluster or open space zoning ordinance of South Brunswick Township was adopted as No. 19–62, an amendment to the zoning ordinance of 1958. Its main pertinent provisions are as follows:

> "Section 2. The purpose of this subsection is to provide a method of development of residential land which will nevertheless preserve desirable open spaces, school sites, recreation and park areas and lands for other public purposes.
>
> "Section 3. At the discretion of the Planning Board, a subdivider may be allowed to reduce the minimum lot size and dimension requirements in accordance with the provisions of this Ordinance, provided the following conditions are met:

(a) The resulting net lot density of the area to be subdivided shall be no greater than the net lot density of the said area without regard to the provisions of this Ordinance.

(b) All lands within the subdivision other than streets, building lots and private recreational areas shall be deeded to the Township for public purposes simultaneously with the granting of final subdivision approval.

(c) The lands to be deeded for public purposes shall be located, shaped and improved as required by the Planning Board, which shall consider the suitability, physical condition and location of the lands with regard to its proposed uses and to the needs of the Township, in reaching its determination. The Planning Board shall, prior to reaching its determination, cause at least one of its members to confer with the Board of Education, Recreation Commission, Shade Tree Commission, Municipal Utilities Authority, Engineer and other interested municipal agencies as to the potential uses and advisability of accepting the lands offered to be donated.

(d) A portion of the land to be donated for public purposes shall be at least a usable single five acre tract.

(e) With the exception of minimum lot sizes and lot dimension requirements, the subdivision must comply with all other provisions of the Zoning Ordinance, such as front, rear and side setbacks, size of buildings, etc.

(f) There must exist approved plans for public water and public sewer systems which shall be available to all lots in the subdivision prior to the issuance of any Certificates of Occupancy.

(g) A developer may apply to the Planning Board for permission to reduce lot sizes and donate lands to the Township in accordance with this Ordinance at any time prior to applying for final subdivision approval.

"Section 4. If the tract to be subdivided is located in a zone which requires a minimum lot size of 20,000 square feet or less, the developer must donate, exclusive of open drainage water courses, 20% of the tract to the Township; if the tract to be subdivided is located in a zone which requires a minimum lot size in excess of 20,000 square feet, the developer must donate, exclusive of open drainage water courses, 30% of the tract to the Township. The area of the tract shall be determined from a certified outline survey submitted by the subdivider.

"Section 5. If the minimum lot size requirement of the tract to be subdivided be 20,000 square feet or less, the minimum lot size requirement shall be reduced 20% and the minimum frontage requirement shall be reduced 10%. If the minimum lot size requirement of the tract to be subdivided be in excess of 20,000 square feet, the minimum lot size requirement shall be reduced 30% and the minimum frontage requirement shall be reduced 20%."

A companion zoning ordinance amendment, No. 20–62, also challenged in this litigation, amplifies previous requirements concerning performance guarantees by developers to cover specifically improvements to lands to be deeded to the township for public purposes.

* * *

Although the state zoning law does not in so many words empower municipalities to provide an option to developers for cluster or density zoning, such an ordinance reasonably advances the legislative purposes of securing open spaces, preventing overcrowding and undue concentration of population, and promoting the general welfare. Nor is it an objection that uniformity of regulation is required within a zoning district. N.J.S.A. 40:55–31. Such a legislative technique accomplishes uniformity because the option is open to all developers within a zoning district, and escapes the vice that it is compulsory. Midtown Properties, Inc. v. Madison Tp., 68 N.J.Super. 197, 210, 172 A.2d 40 (Law Div.1961).

Zoning ordinances in rapidly growing municipalities may be founded on an outmoded concept that houses will be built one at a time for individual owners in accordance with zoning regulations, with latitude for variances in hardship or other exceptional cases, and that the municipality can take steps whenever warranted to acquire school, park and other public sites. Such a gradual and controlled development is not practicable in many municipalities today. Confronted with a subdivision plan for several hundred homes in a tract meeting all water drainage, sanitation and other conditions, a municipality must anticipate school needs but without lands set aside for that purpose; it must anticipate a large population concentration without recreation areas, parks or green spaces, or lands for firehouses or other public purposes. Cluster or density zoning is an attempted solution, dependent, as set up in the South Brunswick zoning ordinance, upon the agreement of the large-scale developer whose specific monetary benefit may be only that he saves on street installation costs.

* * *

The benefits to Yenom Corporation, other than a saving in street construction costs, are obscure. The same number of homes may be constructed, but on smaller lots. Lands acceptable to the planning board, including at least one five-acre parcel, must be deeded to the municipality. The paramount concern of the municipal officials, as one of them graphically described, was to avoid a "bad deal," the Brunswick Acres plan for 526 homes on 13,500–square–foot lots with only ten acres reserved for public use. Such an objective is valid, if enacted as ordinance No. 19–62 was enacted, as general, not special legislation.

* * *

The proofs in this litigation establish adequate consideration of cluster or density zoning by the South Brunswick Township Planning Board, including four new members who took office on July 1, 1962; specific approval of the concept in the resolutions dated August 25 and September 11, 1962; and endorsement of the ordinances under attack on September 18, 1962, within two weeks of their final adoption.

* * *

For all the foregoing reasons decision is in favor of the defendants.

ORINDA HOMEOWNERS COMMITTEE v. BOARD OF SUPERVISORS

California Court of Appeals, 1970.
11 Cal.App.3d 768, 90 Cal.Rptr. 88.

DEVINE, PRESIDING JUSTICE.

Appellants sought unsuccessfully to gain invalidation by the superior court of a rezoning ordinance of Contra Costa County, in the unincorporated Orinda area. Injunction and writ of mandate were denied and judgment was rendered against plaintiffs. Although a question of standing exists as to some of the plaintiffs, we have no doubt that three of the plaintiffs, homeowners, are qualified because Contra Costa County Ordinance No. 1975, section 2205.10, gives standing to appeal from decisions of the County Planning Commission to anyone whose property rights are adversely affected. It seems to have been taken for granted in the trial court, and understandably so, that the property rights of the homeowners would be adversely affected to a certain extent by the rezoning of the adjacent property, and the question whether rezoning conformed with the general plan was an issue in the case. There is no need, therefore, to make a problem of this matter, and when we refer to plaintiffs, or appellants, herein, we mean the three property owners. We take note, however, of the fact that the litigation is of personal interest to many others in the Orinda area.

Plaintiffs are homeowners upon lands adjacent to a parcel of 187 acres which is owned by real party in interest. The Board of Supervisors of Contra Costa County, on recommendation of the County Planning Commission, rezoned the 187–acre parcel from R–20 (single family residential) to P–1 (planned unit development). The plan called for development of "residential clusters" as well as single family residential lots. The maximum density of the clusters would be eight units per acre. Approximately 345 dwelling units would be constructed, of which about 236 would be located in clusters. The actual number of units is subject to change, but "in no case shall the total number of dwelling units exceed 368." The density of the entire property would not exceed two residential units per acre, which is within the density requirements of the master plan previously adopted by the county. The plan provided for approval by the County Director of Planning of the design of all clusters.

Planned Unit Development

In Hagman, Larson & Martin, California Zoning Practice (Cont.Ed.Bar) p. 236, it is said that a "planned unit development might be described as a tract of land absolved from conventional zoning to permit clustering of residential uses and perhaps compatible commercial and industrial uses, and permitting structures of differing heights." Although planned unit development (which in professional zoning circles has attained the dignity of alphabetical titles—PD or PUD) is often regarded as synonymous with cluster development, "[i]t is more accurate to define cluster development as a device for grouping dwellings to increase dwelling densities on some portions of the development area in order to have other portions free of buildings." (Id., at p. 240.) Since the ordinance in the present case permits as well as regulates residential units only, the term "cluster development" probably fits the situation better than the broader term "planned unit development." But whatever title be given to the concept, the plan is to devise a better use of undeveloped property than that which results from proceeding on a lot-to-lot basis. Control of density in the area to be developed is an essential part of the plan. The reservation of green, or at least open, spaces in a manner differing from the conventional front or back yard is another ingredient. Conformity to good landscaping, as the planners devise it, is also an objective. We do not mean to give a treatise on the subject of planned unit development, however. An excellent description of this species of zoning and a compendium of the literature on the subject is to be found in 114 Pa.L.Rev. 3–170.

Government Code, Section 65852

Appellants contend that the planned unit development or cluster development, as enacted by the ordinance, conflicts with Government Code, section 65852, which provides: "All such regulations shall be uniform for each class or kind of building or use of land throughout each zone, but the regulation in one type of zone may differ from those in other types of zones." It is remarked in Hagman, Larson & Martin, California Zoning Practice (Cont.Ed.Bar) p. 237, that no California court has passed on the validity of the planned unit development, although it was presumed to be valid in Millbrae Ass'n for Residential Survival v. City of Millbrae, 262 Cal.App.2d 222, 69 Cal.Rptr. 251, and the authors cite possible nonconformity with Government Code, section 65852.

We hold that a residential planned unit development (a cluster development) does not conflict with section 65852 merely by reason of the fact that the units are not uniform, that is, they are not all single family dwellings and perhaps the multi-family units differ among themselves. Section 65852 provides that the *regulations* shall be uniform for each class or kind of building or use of land through-out the zone. It does not state that the units must be alike even as to their character, whether single family or multi-family. In conventional zoning, where apartment houses are permitted in a particular zone, single family dwellings, being regarded (whether rightly or wrongly) as a "higher" use, are also allowed. This causes no conflict with section 65852.

We find nothing to indicate that the Legislature's policy, as expressed in the section, was to prevent county planning agencies and boards of supervisors from applying the concept of planned unit development for the use that is best and most harmonious for the area as the planners and the county legislators conceive it to be. In Cheney v. Village 2 at New Hope, Inc., 429 Pa. 626, 241 A.2d 81, a leading case sustaining planned unit development, it was observed that large scale residential developments, particularly in suburban areas, have resulted in more efficient and aesthetic use when there are not inflexible rules applying to individual lots.

In fact, section 65852 seems to have been discussed but once, in Scrutton v. County of Sacramento, 275 Cal.App.2d 412, 417, 79 Cal.Rptr. 872, 877. In that case, appellant contended that rezoning of her property from agricultural to multiple family residential use, upon condition that she pave an adjoining street at her own expense, violated the section. But the court rejected this, holding that section 65852 "aims at the general objective of uniform land use within each land zone," and that the conditional zoning which had been enacted did not conflict with the code section. In Desert Outdoor Advertising, Inc. v. County of San Bernardino, 255 Cal.App.2d 765, 63 Cal.Rptr. 543, an ordinance which prohibited billboards, except in certain areas and under certain conditions, was upheld because it was uniform in application wherever equal conditions existed. It had been contended by appellant in that case that former section 65802, the predecessor to present section 65852, of the Government Code had been violated. No other cases involving these sections (or their predecessor, Government Code, section 38697) have been found. These sections were derived from section 2 of the Standard State Zoning Enabling Act, and it is said in 1 Anderson, American Law of Zoning, § 5.17, p. 288, that the purpose of the section was mainly a political rather than a legal one, namely, to give notice to property owners that there shall be no improper discriminations. This was useful in the early days of zoning. Professor Anderson suggests that the fact that the section is an expression of policy may be the reason for the scarcity of judicial construction of the uniformity requirement.

* * *

Appellants complain that the ordinance leaves to the Planning Agency the matter of density within a zone. But the rezoning resolution provides, in paragraph 10, for the maximum number of dwelling units for the entire property. Although variations from the estimated number of dwelling units are permissible within the maximum, these are not to be made by the Planning Director solely, but only upon approval by the Planning Commission after a hearing. We discern no unlawful delegation of legislative power.

The case is different from that of People v. Perez, 214 Cal.App.2d Supp. 881, 882, 29 Cal.Rptr. 781, cited by appellants, in which a zone was created which nominally was for agricultural use, but which was made subject to varying types of residential use by special permit, no guides being given to the planning body save the most general (the identical standards given to the city council by the Government Code). In the case before us, a single use, residential, is projected.

* * *

The judgment is affirmed.

Notes

1. See Creative Environments, Inc. v. Estabrook, 491 F.Supp. 547 (D.Mass. 1980) where the court held that plaintiff had no constitutional right to construct a development utilizing the cluster concept; Croteau v. Planning Bd. of Hopkinton, 40 Mass.App.Ct. 922, 663 N.E.2d 583 (1996) where the court upheld denial of a cluster development plan because the open space would not be of public significance.

2. The basic aim of the cluster plan is to make suburbia more attractive by eliminating row on row of blocks of similar houses, located on lots of similar size, each an equal distance from the street and approximately an equal distance from one another. This type of suburban planning creates something that has all the charm of a high-rent army camp. The cluster type of planning seeks to retain the attractiveness of country living in urban or semi-urban areas by eliminating conformity and standardization and by placing a high priority on diversity of lot sizes, house locations and by placing a premium on open spaces, trees and natural beauty.

Today, a number of municipalities are enacting "conservation subdivision" laws, often intended to accomplish the same goals as cluster subdivision. Conservation Subdivision Design (CSD) has been described as "a green development strategy that can help communities preserve open space and natural areas in residential housing developments. By reformulating the approach to conventional subdivision design, CSD strategically concentrates home construction on the development site in order to protect sensitive and valuable open space, habitat, and other environmental resources." See, Smart Communities Network at: http://www.smartcommunities.ncat.org/greendev/subdivision.shtml. The Georgia Quality Growth Partnership has published a toolkit, including a model local CSD ordinance. See, http://www.dca.state.ga.us/toolkit/ToolDetail.asp?GetTool=31.

3. New Hampshire, like many other states, permits cluster development and encourages its use as an innovative land use control. N.H. Rev.Stat.Ann. § 674:21. Under this authority, the Town of Peterborough, New Hampshire adopted a cluster development provision in its zoning code which seeks to "permit greater flexibility in the design of housing projects; discourage development sprawl; facilitate the economical and efficient provision of public services; [and] preserve more usable space, agricultural land, recreational areas, and scenic vistas." Code of the Town of Peterborough, New Hampshire, § 245–26(A). Peterborough permits residential clustering as a special exception in its General Residence and Rural Districts and as-of-right in its Retirement Commu-

nity District. The maximum number of dwelling units permitted in a clustered development may not exceed the density allowed in the zoning district where the parcel is located. The town's cluster development provision requires that a minimum of 30% of the total land area be dedicated as common open space. Code of the Town of Peterborough, New Hampshire, § 245–26(C)(8). To insure that the open space remains undeveloped, title to the open space must be deeded to a neighborhood association or to the town or to a conservation organization. The regulations require that the development be situated so as to minimize alteration of the parcel's natural features and to protect the surrounding landscape and the character of adjacent development. Code of the Town of Peterborough, New Hampshire, § 237–22.

Montana enacted provisions to encourage cluster development based on findings that agricultural land is being taken out of production; farmers are being forced to sell their land to generate income; and that cluster development could facilitate farmland preservation while reducing government infrastructure and services. See Mont. Code Ann., § 76–3–509 (2002) which provides:

> (1) If the governing body has adopted a growth policy that meets the requirements of 76–1–601, the governing body may adopt regulations to promote cluster development and preserve open space under this section.

4. Carlson v. Town of Smithfield, 723 A.2d 1129, (R.I. 1999) held that a statute allowing, but not obligating, municipalities to provide for cluster development did not prevent an ordinance from requiring approval of both the planning board and the zoning board for cluster developments. In this case the Carlsons argued that the zoning ordinance, which required approval of both the planning and zoning boards, violated the enabling statute, R.I. Gen. 1956, § 45–24–47(B), which provides that the planning board must approve any land developments. The Carlsons unsuccessfully argued that this gave the planning board exclusive jurisdiction to approve cluster developments (the planning board had approved the development while the zoning board had not). The court further held that the Carlsons had not exhausted their administrative remedies.

5. Consider how the Planned Unit Development (PUD) and the cluster development are different and similar. Although the terminology is sometimes used interchangeably and there is an obvious relationship, they are different planning and land use control techniques.

E. SUBDIVISION EXACTIONS AND OTHER REGULATION ISSUES

Can a local unit require as a condition to subdivision plat approval:

a. Installation of public improvements such as street grading, street surfacing, sanitary and storm sewers, water mains, curb and gutter, sidewalks, street trees and street signs; or

b. Dedication of subdivision streets and widening strips along existing boundary streets; or

c. Imposition of restrictive covenants dictated by the local unit but promised by the developer; or

d. Dedication of land (or first rights of purchase) for park, playground, school, police or fire station, sites; or

e. Payment of fees in lieu of such dedication; or

f. Written findings by the local school board that school facilities will be adequate to take care of the children from the proposed subdivision; or

g. A "contract" by the developer to contribute a substantial sum for school construction, a water or sewerage or other public facility?

These pose issues faced by developers on the growth fringes of many of America's urban areas. Obviously, answers to many if not most of the questions may turn on factual variables, not stated. How wide a widening strip? What restrictive covenants? Is the fee for a neighborhood park or one that is city-wide? Clearly also, in analyzing such issues in particular cases, a first step is to ascertain whether the applicable enabling statute authorizes the action taken. Here, admittedly, the attitude a court brings to the task of construing the statute may make a major difference. But also, the action may be ultra vires and void even on the most liberal construction. Thus, to get to issues of constitutionality, we must assume sufficient enabling delegation. Notice that we talk about what would happen if the particular action were reviewed in a court. Actually, dozens of conditions of doubtful validity imposed on developers are as a practical fact accepted by them and not contested in court. The developer is, after all, a businessperson anxiously awaiting the day when she can begin realizing on her substantial investment by selling lots or lots and houses. A court review may delay that day for a long time. In addition, she may be quite anxious not to arouse the antagonism of the very local officials before whom she may again be shortly reappearing and asking approval for another subdivision. Finally, she may be able to pass the additional cost of the imposed condition on to her customer. In fact, the developer may even be able to charge a profit on the additional cost.

An undeniable fact stands out. The subdivider is in a business that places costs (externalities) onto the community at large. How do we measure these costs? And once measured can they be charged back, regardless of the manner of charge? And can the charging back be premised on rough and ready estimates or must there be precise cost-benefit analyses? What if any role does municipal past practice play? Police stations have always been paid for out of general taxes; small parks are sometimes paid for through special assessments. Are such facts significant?

(1) Traditional Exactions

PETTERSON v. CITY OF NAPERVILLE

Supreme Court of Illinois, 1956.
9 Ill.2d 233, 137 N.E.2d 371.

[The plaintiff obtained a declaratory judgment from the trial court declaring the city of Naperville's subdivision control ordinance void. The case is up on direct appeal from this judgment. Plaintiff's land is located in Du Page County outside Naperville but within its 1½ mile extraterritorial plat approval jurisdiction. Du Page County approved the plat under its subdivision control ordinance requiring bituminous streets only 20 feet wide, without curbs and gutters. On its review the Naperville city planning commission under the city's ordinance required bituminous streets 25 feet wide and plaintiffs agreed to provide these. But the planning commission also required curbs and gutters and suitable storm water drainage facilities. These it was estimated, would cost $19,000 more than the county approved scheme, and the plaintiff refused to provide them. The planning commission then refused to approve the plat. Plaintiff claims the commission's action is (1) ultra vires as to the enabling statutes and (2) arbitrary and unreasonable and therefore unconstitutional.]

MR. JUSTICE DAVIS [after reviewing the facts and analyzing the applicable Illinois statutes]:

* * * A consideration of the above statutes and their amendatory provisions reveals the clear intention of our legislature to grant to municipalities adopting an official plan exclusive control and jurisdiction over the subdivision of lands located not more than one and one-half miles beyond the corporate limits of the municipality. Cities ordinarily have no jurisdiction beyond their corporate limits, and municipal ordinances are confined in their application to the territory of the municipality adopting them. Dean Milk Co. v. City of Elgin, 405 Ill. 204, 90 N.E.2d 112; City of Rockford v. Hey, 366 Ill. 526, 9 N.E.2d 317. But the legislature may, if it sees fit, confer special extraterritorial powers on municipalities, and when it does so the courts recognize and give effect to them. City of West Frankfort v. Fullop, 6 Ill.2d 609, 129 N.E.2d 682; Chicago Packing and Provision Co. v. City of Chicago, 88 Ill. 221. The exercise of such extraterritorial powers by a municipality is, of course, always subject to the requirement that the ordinance passed pursuant to legislative authority constitutes a valid exercise of the police power, and bears a reasonable and substantial relation to the public health, safety or general welfare. City of Park Ridge v. American Nat. Bank and Trust Co., 4 Ill.2d 144, 122 N.E.2d 265, 50 A.L.R.2d 900. It is true that the legislature has given to counties certain powers relative to maps, plats and subdivisions. This power was first conferred in 1915 (Laws of 1915, p. 334–335) and enlarged in 1949. (Ill.Rev.Stat. 1949, ch. 34, par. 25.09.) However, there is nothing in these legislative provisions relative to the powers of counties which indicates that it was not the intention of the

legislature to give exclusive control in those areas within one and one-half miles outside the territorial limits of a municipality to municipalities which have an official plan in effect in such territory. Thus, even though the county of Du Page adopted a resolution regulating subdivisions in the county, the lands in question here, being within the limits prescribed by the City Plan Commission Act and the subdivision control ordinance, are subject to the exclusive control and jurisdiction of the city of Naperville so far as the subdivision of lands and the approval of maps and plats of such subdivisions are concerned.

Plaintiffs contend that the ordinance as drawn is void as an exercise of power by the defendant beyond the grant of the statute; that the statute by granting the right to include "reasonable requirements with reference to streets, alleys, and public grounds," does not contemplate that a city may include such requirements as curbs and gutters or the other improvements prescribed by the ordinance. In this connection the plaintiffs rely on those cases which hold that the legislative powers of cities are strictly construed, and if there is any reasonable doubt as to the existence of the power, the doubt must be resolved against the municipality. But the primary object of statutory construction is to ascertain and give effect to legislative intent. In ascertaining legislative intent, the courts should consider the reason or necessity for the enactment and the meaning of the words, enlarged or restricted, according to their real intent. Likewise the court will always have regard to existing circumstances, contemporaneous conditions, and the object sought to be obtained by the statute. People ex rel. Holvey v. Kapp, 355 Ill. 596, 189 N.E. 920; Chicago Packing and Provision Co. v. City of Chicago, 88 Ill. 221.

Subsection 2 of section 2 of the City Plan Commission Act (Ill.Rev. Stat.1953, ch. 24, par. 53–2(2)) in force at the time of the adoption of the subdivision control ordinance, grants to planning commissions in municipalities of more than 500,000 inhabitants, or in municipalities lying wholly or partly within a radius of thirty miles from the corporate limits of municipalities of more than 500,000 inhabitants, the power to recommend to the corporate authorities a plan or plans for the development and redevelopment of the municipality and contiguous unincorporated territory not more than one and one-half miles beyond the corporate limits of the municipality, and further empowers the commission "To provide for the health, safety, comfort and convenience of the inhabitants of the municipality and contiguous territory, such plan or plans may establish reasonable standards of design for subdivisions and for resubdivisions of unimproved land and of areas subject to redevelopment, including reasonable requirements for public streets, alleys, ways for public service facilities, parks, playgrounds, school grounds, and other public grounds." We believe that the power to prescribe reasonable requirements for public streets in the interest of the health and safety of the inhabitants of the city and contiguous territory includes more than a mere designation of the location and width of streets as plaintiffs seem to contend. The legislature undoubtedly had in mind the complex problems connected with the development of territory contiguous to cities as bearing on the health and safety of all inhabitants within and without the municipality; that in such territory, in the interest of uniformity, continuity, and of public health and safety, the streets should be constructed in such a way as to afford reasonably safe passage to the traveling public and provide reasonable drainage in the interests of health. Plaintiffs made no objection to the paving requirements set forth in the ordinance and agreed to comply with those provisions, apparently considering them to be within the powers granted. Considering the expressed object and purpose of the legislation, it is our conclusion that the provisions of the ordinance requiring curbs and gutters and proper drainage are within the powers conferred by the statute.

The trial court found that the ordinance, as applied to plaintiffs and their property, was arbitrary, unreasonable and discriminatory and had no reasonable relation to the public health, safety or general welfare, and that it was therefore unconstitutional and void. The only proof offered to sustain this finding was evidence which compared the cost of complying with the county regulations and the cost of complying with the requirements of the subdivision control ordinance, together with some testimony that the surface waters drained westward to the river and not toward the city. The fact alone that the cost of curbs and gutters and the drainage facilities prescribed by the subdivision control ordinance would be greater than the cost of open ditches and culverts forms no basis for the finding that the ordinance is arbitrary, unreasonable or discriminatory. There is no proof whatever to show that the ordinance affects plaintiffs' property any differently than other property within the area in question or that it imposes unreasonable or excessive burdens upon the plaintiffs. One who challenges the validity of an ordinance as arbitrary and unreasonable must prove by clear and affirmative evidence that the ordinance constitutes arbitrary, capricious and unreasonable municipal action; that there is no permissible interpretation which justified its adoption, or that it will not promote the safety and general welfare of the public. First Nat. Bank of Lake Forest v. County of Lake, 7 Ill.2d 213, 130 N.E.2d 267. The fact alone that the ordinance may operate to impose burdens or restrictions on the property which would not have existed without the enactment of the ordinance is never determinative of the question of validity. Miller Brothers Lumber Co. v. City of Chicago, 414 Ill. 162, 111 N.E.2d 149. The privilege of the individual to use his property as he pleases is subject always to a legitimate exercise of the police power under which new burdens may be imposed upon property and new restrictions placed upon its use when the public welfare demands. 2700 Irving Park Bldg. Corp. v. City of Chicago, 395 Ill. 138, 69 N.E.2d 827. Plaintiffs offered no convincing proof to support their contention that the ordinance bears no reasonable relation to the public health, safety or general welfare. Such proof as was adduced on this question was introduced by defendant and supports the opposite conclusion. The trial court erred in holding the ordinance unconstitutional on the ground that it was arbitrary, unreasonable and confiscatory and without proper relation to the legitimate objects of the police powers.

* * *

Plaintiffs further urge that the subdivision control ordinance is unconstitutional because it amounts to either taxation without the consent of the taxpayers, or to an exercise of the power of eminent domain without providing compensation to the property owner for the property taken for public use; that if the statute is construed as providing for a form of taxation or special assessment for local improvements, it is void as violating the constitutional provision for uniformity of taxation; and that if the power exercised thereunder is a power of eminent domain, it violates the constitutional requirement that private property shall not be taken for public use without just compensation. This argument ignores the fact that this is not a proceeding initiated by the city for the construction of a local improvement, or to take property under the law of eminent domain. It is a lawsuit in which the plaintiffs seek approval of a proposed plat of a subdivision under an ordinance which exacts compliance with certain requirements as a condition precedent to approval. They cite in support of this contention the case of City of Chicago v. Larned, 34 Ill. 203, followed in 34 Ill. 283, which involved an assessment for improvements made by the city council on the basis of the frontage of the lots upon the street to be improved. There the court held that under the provisions of the constitution of 1848, then in effect, all taxes were subject to the principles of equality and uniformity, and since this special assessment violated these constitutional provisions, it was not a tax, but an exercise of the power of eminent domain for which just compensation must be made; that though compensation could be made by benefits, when these were exhausted it then became a question of taxation, and the principles of equality and uniformity must apply; that the assessment of injuries and benefits is a judicial proceeding not to be made by a city council and that the purported assessment was void. Since the adoption of our present constitution, however, the power to levy and collect special assessments is regarded as a branch of the taxing power and the assessment is regarded as a species of taxation. Chicago and Alton Railroad Co. v. City of Joliet, 153 Ill. 649, 654, 39 N.E. 1077. The case at bar does not involve the imposition of a tax by the municipal authorities, but rather involves the imposition of regulatory provisions by way of the exercise of the police power through an ordinance requiring certain conditions precedent to the subdivision of lands and the approval of plats thereof. The validity of the ordinance is to be tested, neither by the principle of uniformity of taxation nor by the law of eminent domain, but rather by the settled rules of law applicable to cases involving the exercise of police powers. The fact that the exercise of such powers imposes certain burdens, or prevents the most profitable use of the property in private hands, does not of itself render the legislation invalid as a taking of the property without just compensation. City of West Frankfort v. Fullop, 6 Ill.2d 609, 129 N.E.2d 682. The imposition of reasonable regulations as a condition precedent to the subdivision of lands and the recording of plats thereof is not a violation of the constitutional requirement of uniformity of taxation or tantamount to the taking of private property for public use without just compensation.

We find that the judgment of the circuit court of Du Page County was erroneous and it must be reversed.

Notes

1. With the principal case compare, Ayres v. City Council of City of Los Angeles, 34 Cal.2d 31, 207 P.2d 1, 11 A.L.R.2d 503 (1949). The court upheld as valid conditions to the approval of a 13 acre subdivision:

(1) Dedication of a 10 foot strip, 1500 feet along an important traffic artery;

(2) Reservation of an additional 10 foot strip along the same street for trees and shrubs to assure non-access to the artery;

(3) Dedication of an 80 foot, rather than a proffered 60 foot, width for a new street across the subdivision; and,

(4) Dedication of a triangular shaped parcel 12½ x 75 feet to eliminate a traffic hazard.

(With regard to the first two conditions, similar dedications and reservations had been required of earlier subdivisions along the artery.)

The state legislature had given the city of Los Angeles subdivision control powers in its city charter and had by the so-called "Map Act" also empowered cities generally to control subdividing. The city had enacted a subdivision ordinance, but the subdivider contended the conditions, particularly the one requiring dedication of land along an existing street, were not expressly provided for either in the state legislation or in the local ordinance. Said the California court (two judges dissenting):

> The status of an autonomous city, Const. Art. XI, sec. 6; West Coast Advertising Co. v. San Francisco, 14 Cal.2d 516, 95 P.2d 138 (1939); City of Oakland v. Williams, 15 Cal.2d 542, 103 P.2d 168 (1940), is recognized by express references to city ordinances in the Subdivision Map Act. Where as here no specific restriction or limitation on the city's power is contained in the Charter, and none forbidding the particular conditions is included either in the Subdivision Map Act, or the city ordinances, it is proper to conclude that conditions are lawful which are not inconsistent with the Map Act and the ordinances and are reasonably required by the subdivision type and use as related to the character of local and neighborhood planning and traffic conditions.

Compare Rohn v. City of Visalia, 214 Cal.App.3d 1463, 263 Cal.Rptr. 319 (1989) where the court held that a required dedication of 14 per cent of the land to correct a street alignment was an invalid taking.

AYRES v. CITY COUNCIL OF CITY OF LOS ANGELES, 34 CAL.2d 31, 207 P.2d 1 (1949)

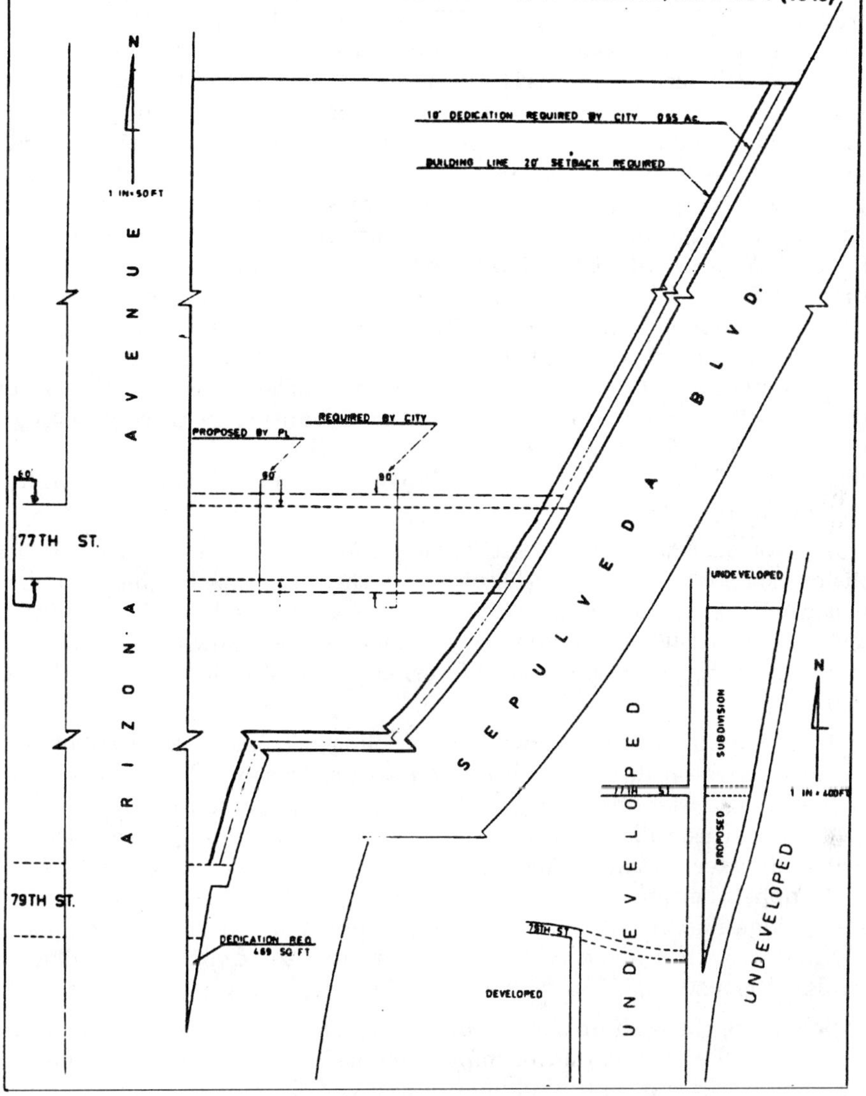

2. The Ayres case involved a "home rule" municipality in a state with a strong tradition of municipal home rule. In states where the powers of municipal corporations are strictly construed, the question of whether the requirements imposed on subdivision approval are *ultra vires* with regard to the enabling legislation is frequently litigated. For example, in State ex rel. Strother v. Chase, 42 Mo.App. 343 (1890), the court held that the city could not require the subdivider to plat an alley extension through his adjacent unplatted land as a condition of subdivision approval. For other cases strictly limiting the approving body to the standards or conditions specified in the enabling legislation, see Tuxedo Homes v. Green, 258 Ala. 494, 63 So.2d 812 (1953) (City engineer in absence of statutory authorization could not require

installation of a lift pump for sewage, but the city might later refuse street dedications); People ex rel. Jackson & Morris, Inc. v. Smuczynski, 345 Ill.App. 63, 102 N.E.2d 168 (1951) (Village, having failed to adopt a subdivision ordinance for its guidance as required by statutes, must approve plat as a "ministerial" act); State ex rel. Lewis v. City Council of Minneapolis, 140 Minn. 433, 168 N.W. 188 (1918) (Could not require grading under a statute referring only to direction and width of streets); Rahway v. Raritan Homes, Inc., 21 N.J.Super. 541, 91 A.2d 409 (1952) (No power to regulate subdividing until city complied with state statute requiring appointment of planning board and adoption of local ordinance); Magnolia Development Co. v. Coles, 10 N.J. 223, 89 A.2d 664 (1952) (No power to require sidewalks, curbs, gutters and gravel roadway in absence of enabling authority); In re Lake Secor Development Co., 141 Misc. 913, 252 N.Y.S. 809 (1931) (Could not force installation of water system under statute referring only to streets, light and air); Eyde Const. Co. v. Charter Twp. of Meridian, 149 Mich.App. 802, 386 N.W.2d 687 (1986) (Township lacked authority to condition plat approval on provision of recreational facilities). See also Annot., Validity and Construction of Regulations as to Subdivision Maps or Plats, 11 A.L.R.2d 524, 535 (1950).

3. Not all conditions on subdivision approvals are subdivision dedications or exactions. For a good discussion of the difference between common-law dedications which benefit the public at-large, and subdivision conditions which simply limit the manner in which a property owner may use the parcel, see, City of Annapolis v. Waterman, 357 Md. 484, 745 A.2d 1000 (2000).

4. Assuming a carefully worded enabling act, and a local subdivision ordinance based on it, there is little doubt that "reasonable" improvements can be required. Mefford v. City of Tulare, 102 Cal.App.2d 919, 228 P.2d 847 (1951) upheld as valid requirements that a profile map be furnished and sewer and water installed. Allen v. Stockwell, 210 Mich. 488, 178 N.W. 27 (1920) upheld ordinance provisions requiring grading and graveling of streets; sidewalks; installation of surface drains and sanitary sewers, apparently under general home rule delegations. Also see Colborne v. Village of Corrales, 106 N.M. 103, 739 P.2d 972 (1987).

Bolstering the position these courts have taken are (1) widespread use of requirements for installation of improvements or submission of a bond for their installation and (2) the findings of many of the studies of free and easy subdividing in the roaring 20's when to "develop" a subdivision one drove a few stakes, mounted some flags, and perhaps erected a pair of grotesque gate posts.[4]

4. Reference may be had, in this regard, to the following:

Adams, VII Regional Survey of New York and Environs (1929);

Cornick, Premature Subdivision and Its Consequences (1938)—Also published by N.Y. Division of State Planning under title "Problems created by premature Subdivision of Urban Lands in Selected Metropolitan Districts";

Fisher, Real Estate Subdividing Activity and Population Growth in Nine Urban Areas (1928)—Deals with Detroit, Cleveland, Milwaukee, Toledo, Birmingham, Grand Rapids, Flint and Ann Arbor areas;

Monchow, Seventy Years of Real Estate Subdividing in the Region of Chicago (1939);

Usually the developer is offered the following alternatives:

(1) Install the improvements before the final plat approval—(usually here he will be relying on approval of his preliminary plat); or,

(2) Furnish escrow money to cover the cost of the improvements; i.e., the plat is approved, and the escrow money is released in installments as the improvements are put in; or

(3) Furnish a surety bond guaranteeing installation of improvements.

Small developers complain about the additional capital required to be risked where improvements must be installed. Large developers know that improvements make lots and houses more saleable and are quite willing to install them, particularly in the typical modern development which involves mass production of houses on the subdivided land. Their complaint is that often the municipal requirements are unreasonable in that the streets required are too wide, the pavement too thick, the sewer too big, etc. See Urban Land Institute, The Community Builders Handbook 39–40 (1954 ed.). We have little or no case law on such questions as these:

(1) Considering the subdivision alone a 10 inch sewer would be adequate, but considering probable development on other lands further out, the developer is required to install and pay for a 15 inch sewer. Is this a valid requirement? See Wright Development, Inc. v. City of Wellsville, 608 P.2d 232 (Utah 1980).

(2) How wide should the roadway of a minor residential street be? The developer says 26 feet, the city says 33 feet?

(3) Is a sidewalk on one side of the street enough?

Improvement requirements should vary with density, topography, soil and whether or not the subdivision is a quiet backwater or is in the mainstream of development. In addition, as we cease to be exclusively concerned with residential subdivisions and begin to regulate subdivisions for commercial and industrial uses, we recognize that improvement requirements must differ. In California, for example, exactions for major thoroughfares is a problem. See Committee of Seven Thousand v. Superior Court, 45 Cal.3d 491, 247 Cal.Rptr. 362, 754 P.2d 708 (1988).

5. The question of what is a "reasonable" improvement, especially in regard to expensive utility or drainage installations, is sometimes litigated. In Texas, for example, subdividers may be required to pay the entire cost of installing water mains which must subsequently be donated to the city water and sewer authority. See Crownhill Homes, Inc. v. City of San Antonio, 433 S.W.2d 448 (Tex.Civ.App. 1968) and Johnson v. Benbrook Water and Sewer Auth., 410 S.W.2d 644 (Tex.Civ.App.1966). Compare Reid Development Corp. v. Parsippany–Troy Hills Twp., 10 N.J. 229, 89 A.2d 667 (1952); Reid

Smith and Fisher, Land Subdividing and the Rate of Utilization (1932)—Intensive study of Grand Rapids area making use of techniques learned in previous study; Whitten, A Research into the Economics of Land Subdivision (1927); New Jersey State Planning Board, Land Subdivision in New Jersey (1938); and, New Jersey State Planning Board, Premature Land Subdivision a Luxury (1941)—Tax Delinquency, Municipal Debt and Premature Subdivision in New Jersey.

Development Corp. v. Parsippany–Troy Hills Twp., 31 N.J.Super. 459, 107 A.2d 20 (1954); Lake Intervale Homes, Inc. v. Parsippany–Troy Hills, 28 N.J. 423, 147 A.2d 28 (1958).

6. If the developer pays his fair share of fees for the water and sewer system and then is forced to abandon his project because of financial difficulties, can the developer get a refund? In McNair v. City of Cedar Park, Texas, 993 F.2d 1217 (5th Cir.1993) the city determined that a major capital expansion of its water system was necessary to accommodate any new development. It imposed a community impact fee of $2,400 per living unit, payable by developers at the time of obtaining subdivision approval. The city, in turn, obligated itself to provide water and sewer services to all new developments. McNair had 100 acres of land, purchased for $1.65 million; he planned an upscale trailer park for 1,600 new residents. After some negotiation with the city, McNair paid the city $1.3 million based on the $2,400 fee for 542 units. Subsequently, McNair abandoned his project and sought a refund of the water fee, plus accrued interest, but by that time, Cedar Park was well into a five-year plan to construct a new system, having already spent $2 million and committed an additional $8 million. The city refused the refund and McNair sued the city alleging unjust enrichment and assumpsit; the case was removed to federal court after McNair added federal law claims. The court held for the city: "The City's retention of the fee is fundamentally fair when one considers that McNair received exactly what he bargained for. He has paid his share of the systemic water and sewer expansion costs and cannot be asked to pay same again. His tract of land is entitled to those city services. At the same time, the City has incurred a substantial expense and obligation. Equity and the controlling law demand that the agreement between the City and McNair be honored. Nothing more; nothing less."

7. What if the developer fails to install the improvements? In Vale Dean Canyon Homeowners Ass'n v. Dean, 100 Or.App. 158, 785 P.2d 772 (1990) the court held that lot owners were third-party beneficiaries of the contract to install roadway improvements made between the developer and the county, and could bring a breach of contract action against the developer.

8. Expensive water and sewer facilities may, however, give rise to a challenge that the city is using the exaction for revenue raising purposes or that the fees are not based on an equitable formula. In Lafferty v. Payson City, 642 P.2d 376 (Utah 1982), the court held that a $1,000 impact fee imposed on a single family dwelling was out of line with the actual costs and was really a revenue raising device. In Southern Nevada Homebuilders Ass'n, Inc. v. Las Vegas Valley Water Dist., 101 Nev. 99, 693 P.2d 1255 (1985) the court struck down a fee imposed on new customers to expand the sewer system because a portion of the fee was used to make improvements in the existing system. Also see Southern Nevada Homebuilders Ass'n v. City of North Las Vegas, 112 Nev. 297, 913 P.2d 1276 (1996) where the court held that imposition of money exactions for expansion of fire and emergency medical services was ultra vires. The enabling statute permitted exactions only for capital improvements or facility expansion necessitated by and attributable to new development.

181 INC. v. SALEM COUNTY PLANNING BD.

Superior Court of New Jersey, Law Division, 1975.
133 N.J.Super. 350, 336 A.2d 501, modified on appeal
140 N.J.Super. 247, 356 A.2d 34 (1976).

MILLER, J.C.C., Temporarily Assigned.

Plaintiff challenges, as unconstitutional, actions of the Salem County Planning Board compelling it to dedicate to the county a portion of land, owned by it, bordering upon a county road, as a condition precedent to approval by the county of a site plan submitted for the construction of a law office. * * *

Plaintiff is the owner of a tract of land in Woodstown, Salem County. The tract abuts on Elm Street (County Road 40) and on U.S. 40 and is irregular in shape. Following its purchase in December 1971 plaintiff applied to the Salem County Planning Board for site plan approval. The site plan review committee recommended approval subject, among other things, to the dedication of 8.25%C along its border on Elm Street, to be used for a proposed widening of Elm Street from 49.5%C to 66%C pursuant to the official map. The time of such widening is indefinite.

* * *

The original site plan review resolution was adopted January 21, 1970 by the board of freeholders pursuant to N.J.S.A. 40:27–6.6. It provided in § 8 that, "As a condition to the approval of a site plan, the planning board *shall* require the dedication of additional right of way * * * " (emphasis supplied). It was this mandatory feature to which plaintiff objected. * * *

* * *

The vice in the county's resolution is that it sets up a blanket policy of taking frontage along every county road without regard to present need, imminency of proposed use or, indeed, of any standard whatsoever. To then expect a landowner to prove himself outside the perimeter of so nebulously defined an area makes it impossible for him to meet his burden. A perusal of the record in this case and an analysis of the testimony which was necessarily adduced by the plaintiff illustrates the predicament of the landowner.

In order, therefore, for the county to place upon the landowner the burden of proof * * * the county must first make its position clear. This must be done, not in generalities, but in specifics applicable to the land sought to be obtained. While obviously there should be the adoption of an official map and a master plan, this is not enough. There should be, at the bare minimum, a proposal for the imminent use of the land, not a mere "banking" for unscheduled future use. While it is true that road appropriations are made on an annual basis it is also true that plans for road work involve "lead time." If the county does not intend to use the land proposed to be taken within such "lead time," to take it without compensation merely because opportunity presents itself runs afoul of the Constitution.

The planning board felt that there was a sufficient rational *nexus* between the proposed use and the widening *in futuro* of Elm Street to justify the requirement of a compulsory dedication. This finding constitutes error.

* * *

In Brazer v. Mountainside, 55 N.J. 456, 465–466, 262 A.2d 857 (1970), the court said that statutory and ordinance provisions for a compulsory dedication could only be valid where the proposed street bears a realistic relation to or is reasonably made necessary by the subdivision. See also Princeton Res. Lands v. Princeton Tp., 112 N.J.Super. 467, 474, 475, 271 A.2d 719 (App.Div.1970), holding that a developer may not be compelled to donate land to increase the width of an existing abutting street.

The constitutional basis of the nexus requirement is neither strange nor novel. It appears in the earlier zoning cases, for instance, Grosso v. Millburn Tp. Adjustment Bd., 137 N.J.L. 630, 633, 61 A.2d 167 (Sup.Ct. 1948), which held that "lands may not be taken for highway use, presently or in futuro, without just compensation." Grosso, supra at 633, 61 A.2d at 169. See also Lomarch Corp. v. Mayor of Englewood, 51 N.J. 108, 237 A.2d 881 (1968). And Battaglia v. Wayne Tp. Planning Board, 98 N.J.Super. 194, 236 A.2d 608 (App.Div.1967), is particularly apposite since, like the instant case, it involved a site plan approval:

> Unlike the case of a land subdivision, no new streets are necessitated by the plaintiff's planned use; there are no purchasers to whom the cost of the improvements can be passed, and plaintiff's land receives no discernible benefit from compliance with the imposed conditions. [at 200, 236 A.2d at 611]

Had Battaglia not applied for official action, Wayne Township could not have imposed upon him the obligations sought to be imposed. The same logic is inescapable here.

* * *

Since the case must go back, the board of freeholders should revise the site plan (and subdivision) standards, eliminating automatic dedication and limiting compulsory taking to those occasions when it meets the rational nexus test and the county's proposed use is specific and imminent. For example, most (although certainly not all) minor subdivisions will probably be found not to meet the rational nexus test as defined herein.

The actions of the planning board are reversed. The case is remanded to the planning board * * *. Jurisdiction is retained. No costs.

Notes

1. Compare with the principal case Sparks v. Douglas County, 127 Wash.2d 901, 904 P.2d 738 (1995). In this case the developer sought approval for four separate small plats in an "in-fill" situation. The county planning commission found that the existing road abutting the proposed developments was substandard and would, after the developer's building, require widening and structural rebuilding; the county asked for dedication of right-of-way for the future widening of the streets. The developer appealed and ultimately the Supreme Court of Washington held that the facts established a sufficient nexus between the developer's activity and the need for road improvements; even though the maximum possible development proposed would be sixteen houses or thirty-two duplex units, that amount of development would nearly double the amount of traffic on the road and would accelerate the need for widening and rebuilding. Also see Pengilly v. Multnomah County, 810 F.Supp. 1111 (D.Or.1992) where the court upheld a county requirement that home builders dedicate several feet of additional right-of-way as a condition of receiving a building permit on the ground that the requirement promoted aesthetics and traffic efficiency.

2. Similar to the principal case are Simpson v. City of North Platte, 206 Neb. 240, 292 N.W.2d 297 (1980); Howard County v. JJM, Inc., 301 Md. 256, 482 A.2d 908 (1984); Lee County v. New Testament Baptist Church, 507 So.2d 626 (Fla.App. 2 Dist.1987); Middlemist v. City of Plymouth, 387 N.W.2d 190 (Minn.App.1986); Unlimited v. Kitsap County, 50 Wash.App. 723, 750 P.2d 651 (1988); Board Of Supervisors of West Marlborough Twp. v. Fiechter, 129 Pa.Cmwlth. 537, 566 A.2d 370 (1989).

3. In addition to holding that compulsory dedications of portions of the landowner's property for future widening is invalid, courts have utilized the same reasoning when the governing entity seeks to require the landowner to improve an existing road which abuts his property. See Hylton Enterprises v. Board of Supervisors, 220 Va. 435, 258 S.E.2d 577 (1979); Charter Twp. of Harrison v. Calisi, 121 Mich.App. 777, 329 N.W.2d 488 (1982). In Luxembourg Group, Inc. v. Snohomish County, 76 Wash.App. 502, 887 P.2d 446 (1995) the court held that requiring a landowner to dedicate an access road not necessary for his development in order to provide access to a neighbor's landlocked parcel was a taking without compensation.

4. Several right-of-way dedication cases involve the conversion of existing gasoline service stations into the ubiquitous and fast-spreading combination convenience store/gasoline station type of business. In Amoco Oil Co. v. Village of Schaumburg, 277 Ill.App.3d 926, 214 Ill.Dec. 526, 661 N.E.2d 380 (1995), app. denied 167 Ill.2d 549, 217 Ill.Dec. 662, 667 N.E.2d 1055, cert. denied 519 U.S. 976, 117 S.Ct. 413, 136 L.Ed.2d 325 (1996) the court held that a demanded dedication of a forty by forty foot triangular section of the landowner's property to rebuild and improve traffic safety at a busy intersection constituted a taking. The dedication would have amounted to about twenty percent of the owner's property and the current defects in the intersection were due to poor original design, not the gas station's activities. Also see William J. (Jack) Jones Insurance Trust v. City of Fort Smith, 731 F.Supp. 912 (W.D.Ark.1990).

(2) Off-Site Improvements and Impact Fees

DIVAN BUILDERS, INC. v. PLANNING BD. OF TWP. OF WAYNE

Supreme Court of New Jersey, 1975.
66 N.J. 582, 334 A.2d 30.

PASHMAN, J.

* * *

* * * Divan's proposal contemplated the construction of 31 single family dwellings in a residential zone of the Township. Because a substantial portion of the building site was covered by a pond, the developer's plan called for its draining and the construction of a conduit which would pipe the water from its upstream source through the development and into an existing drainage facility on the downstream border of the site.

* * *

On June 21, 1972, the Wayne governing body amended its subdivision ordinance by adopting Ordinance No. 69–1972. The ordinance establishes procedures to be followed when off-site improvements are deemed necessary to service a subdivision. The ordinance provides in part that:

> "Prior to the granting of final approval of all subdivisions hereafter submitted to the Planning Board, and prior to the issuance of any building permits for any land use, including land uses which require site plan approval * * * and any residence or other use of property on an unimproved street or where any off-site improvements have not then been installed, the subdivider or other named type of applicant * * * shall have installed, posted a performance bond, or made cash payments, in the manner provided in Section 5 below, with respect to the immediate or ultimate installation of any required off-site improvements."

Off-site improvements include the installation of new, or the extension or modification of existing improvements made necessary in whole or in part by the subdivision which will be benefited by the improvement. The ordinance also provides that the cost of off-site improvements shall be allocated between the applicant, other property owners, or any one or more of them. The cost allocation is based upon such factors as the benefit conferred upon the subdivision, the cost of the improvement, and the extent to which the improvement is necessary to protect neighboring property under the proposed plan.

On June 26, 1972, the Planning Board recommended final approval of plaintiff's remaining 26 lots subject to certain conditions, including the following:

> [T]hat the applicant contribute to the Township of Wayne a sum of $20,000 as their share of improving the downstream conditions of the stream which carries the drainage from the subdivision.

In July 1972 plaintiff received final approval for the remaining portion of its subdivision on the condition that it pay the Township $20,000. This sum represented approximately 8% of the estimated $250,000 cost of the off-site improvement deemed necessary to serve the entire drainage basin. Only one other developer, however, was required to contribute a similar sum pursuant to the ordinance.

* * *

It is clear * * * that a municipality may condition subdivision approval upon the developer's installation of those improvements which the local governing body finds necessary for the protection of the public interest. The problem, of course, is that the statutory scheme makes no specific reference to off-site improvements in this context.

In our view, however, this omission does not preclude a determination that the Planning Act authorizes municipalities to adopt both on-site and off-site improvement ordinances. * * * In our judgment, the constitutional and legislative direction to resolve questions of municipal authority broadly in favor of the local unit, compels the conclusion that, by necessary implication, N.J.S.A. 40:55–1.21 empowers a planning agency to require both on-site and off-site improvements of the physical character and type referred to in N.J.S.A. 40:55–1.20 and N.J.S.A. 40:55–1.21, including off-site improvements made necessary by reason of the subdivision's effect on lands other than the subdivision property, provided that the agency acts pursuant to a valid local ordinance containing suitable standards governing construction and installation of improvements. See Deerfield Estates v. Twp. of East Brunswick, 60 N.J. 115, 286 A.2d 498 (1972).

* * *

We have heretofore recognized that a municipality may utilize three principal ways to finance an off-site improvement. In Deerfield Estates, supra, the defendant municipality refused to install water mains to serve plaintiff's lots. As a threshold question, the Court held that a municipality which had created a planning board and adopted an adequate subdivision ordinance could validly condition subdivision approval upon installation of necessary water mains. 60 N.J. at 122, 286 A.2d 498.

Proceeding to the question of financing the water main extension, Justice Mountain set forth three principal ways in which the municipality could defray the cost of the improvements:

> "First, it may be undertaken entirely at municipal cost and expense. * * * In the second place the municipality may undertake the project as a local improvement and assess the cost against the owners of the properties benefited pursuant to the procedure outlined in N.J.S.A. 40:56–1, et seq.

"The third course is to require that the work be done at the expense of the developer either with or without a formula providing for partial or total reimbursement. Recourse to this third alternative, as to which there has hitherto existed some question, may be had only where appropriate local legislation permits the imposition and when it is fair and equitable that this be done." [60 N.J. at 131, 286 A.2d at 507; footnote omitted].

* * *

Because the need for the off-site improvement was so created, the municipality in recognition of that fact may, in any event, fairly and properly call upon the subdivider to pay the difference between the cost of the improvement and the total amount by which all properties served thereby, including the subdivision, have been specially benefited by the improvement.

Further, but only if the off-site improvement is to be constructed as a "local improvement," * * * with all properties specially benefited thereby to be assessed for the amount of special benefits accruing to each—the subdivider may be called upon to pay in addition to the amount above set forth the amount by which the subdivision property was specially benefited by the improvement.

If the off-site improvement is to be constructed by the municipality as a general improvement—no part of the cost of which may be specially assessed on properties specially benefited thereby—or if the off-site improvement is to be constructed by the subdivider with a provision for later reimbursement by the municipality, then the subdivider may not be charged with the amount by which the subdivision property was specially benefited. To do so would result in patent discrimination in the treatment afforded the subdivision property as contrasted with the other properties specially benefited by the improvement. * * *

We pass now from the question of cost allocation to a consideration of how provision therefor may be made at the time subdivision approval is granted, a date antecedent to the actual construction of the improvement.

It is at once apparent that before the stated conditions are actually imposed on the applicant for subdivision approval, the governing body must decide whether the off-site improvement is to be constructed (1) by the municipality as a general improvement or (2) as a local improvement or (3) whether it is to be done by the developer with a formula providing for partial reimbursement if the improvement specially benefits properties other than the subdivision.

Once that decision has been made, the planning agency should be required to estimate, with the aid of the municipal engineer and such other persons having pertinent information or expertise (a) the cost of the improvement and (b) the amount by which all properties to be serviced thereby, including the subdivision property, will be specially benefited therefrom.

When that has been determined, the subdivider may be required to provide, as a condition for approval of his subdivision application, a bond (or a cash deposit, in lieu thereof) to insure payment to the municipality of one of the following amounts:

(a) If the improvement is to be constructed by the municipality as a general improvement, an amount equal to the difference between the estimated cost of the improvement and the estimated total amount by which all properties to be serviced thereby, including the subdivision property, will be specially benefited by the improvement;

(b) If the improvement is to be constructed by the municipality as a local improvement, then in addition to the amount referred to in (a) the estimated amount by which the subdivision property will be specially benefited by the improvement; or

(c) If the improvement is to be constructed by the subdivider, an amount equal to the estimated cost of the improvement.

If the subdivider should deem that any of the amounts so estimated by the planning agency are unreasonable, it may challenge them and seek to have them revised in appropriate proceedings brought to compel subdivision approval.

Further, since the amounts are only estimated amounts, they should be redetermined once the improvement is completed to the end that the subdivider will be required to pay his appropriate and only his appropriate share of the cost thereof. If the municipality and the subdivider cannot agree with respect thereto, the dispute will have to be decided in a judicial proceeding or proceedings. * * *

It is evident that neither Ordinance 69–1972 nor the action taken by the municipality here conformed to the controlling principles herein set forth. Further, it *prima facie* appears—although defendants deny it—that there has been a disregard of the fundamental principle prohibiting discrimination in cost apportionment in requiring plaintiff to pay $20,000 and allocating no part of the cost to the other properties allegedly specially benefited by [the] improvement, which was constructed as a general improvement.

* * *

To that end, since the improvement was constructed by the municipality as a general improvement, the judgment is reversed and the cause remanded to the trial court for a determination at a trial, following appropriate discovery proceedings and a pretrial conference, of the difference between the cost of the improvement and the total amount by which all properties served thereby were specially benefited therefrom. That difference is fairly chargeable, under the circumstances indicated by the record, in equal shares to plaintiff and the other developer who made a $20,000 payment since their subdivisions created the need for the off-site improvement. Plaintiff will then be entitled to recover from the municipality only that portion, if any of the $20,000 it paid which exceeds the amount fairly chargeable to it.

Reversed and remanded.

POLICY GUIDE ON IMPACT FEES

(ratified by the Board of Directors of the American Planning Association in October 1988 (see, www.planning.org))

Impact fees are payments required by local governments of new development for the purpose of providing new or expanded public capital facilities required to serve that development. The fees typically require cash payments in advance of the completion of development, are based on a methodology and calculation derived from the cost of the facility and the nature and size of the development, and are used to finance improvements offsite of, but to the benefit of the development.

Local governments throughout the country are increasingly using impact fees to shift more of the costs of financing public facilities from the general taxpayer to the beneficiaries of those new facilities. As a general matter, impact fees are capitalized into land values, and thus represent an exaction on the incremental value of the land attributable to the higher and better use made possible by the new public facilities. Some commentators have argued that, under certain circumstances, others may instead bear the incidence of the fee (these may include the original landowner, the developer, or the consumer). There has been little to demonstrate that the imposition of a fee system has stifled development. The fees supplement local government resources that otherwise have decreased because of diminished state and federal transfers of funds. Local governments have also used impact fees to delay or as a substitute for general property tax increases.

Impact fees, when based on a comprehensive plan and used in conjunction with a sound capital improvement plan, can be an effective tool for ensuring adequate infrastructure to accommodate growth where and when it is anticipated. It is important that communities rely on zoning and other land use regulations, consistent with a comprehensive plan, to influence patterns of growth and to more accurately predict new infrastructure needs. However, in areas facing development moratoria because of the lack of adequate public facilities, impact fees may be viewed not as growth stopping measures, but rather as growth facilitators. Impact fees should not be considered a panacea for the funding of general capital improvements, nor should they be used to "stop growth." They can do neither.

Local government experimentation with impact fees has been paralleled by increasing state court involvement in the review of these fees. A general trend in the state courts has been to require a "rational nexus" between the fee and the needs created by development and the benefits incurred by the development. This analysis is a moderate position between a standard that requires that the fee be "specifically and uniquely attributable" to the needs created by new development, and the relaxed standard that the fee be "reasonably related" to the needs created by development.

Impact fees have been criticized as being an inequitable means to finance public facilities. By requiring new development to pay for new facilities without benefiting from existing facility capacity, local governments may be bypassing the traditional practice of intergenerational contribution toward public facilities. Some commentators have argued that, when set at high levels, impact fees may also tend to be regressive. Certain public facilities may be considered "public goods" that should be financed by the entire community, such as general government, police, or schools. To the extent that impact fees are paid by those who are most likely to benefit from the public facilities provided therefrom, however, impact fees are equitable.

Many local communities have expanded the use of impact fees to finance a wide variety of public facilities. The most widespread use of these fees is for sewer and water facilities, parks, and roads. Impact fees are also being used for schools, libraries and public facilities. In recent years, rulings at the state court level have defined how impact fees may be applied and utilized. Thus, there are numerous standards and guidelines available to assist local and regional governmental agencies on the planning processes that must be undertaken to develop a legally defensible impact fee program. Approximately half the states have enacted enabling legislation for impact fees, some of which have specifically included language that governs how these programs are to be implemented. To be most effective and legally valid, impact fees must be carefully designed and documented.

Based on these findings, the American Planning Association adopted the following policies:

1. Support state enabling legislation that establishes clear and concise standards for the adoption and use of impact fees consistent with this policy.

2. Encourage consideration of the use of impact fees as a means to provide additional resources for an adequate public infrastructure and services only as they relate to the needs of new development.

3. Support the use of impact fees as a standardized method for ensuring that new development pays its fair share of the cost of public infrastructure.

4. Encourage the use of impact fees to pay for facilities where a rational nexus can be established.

5. Impact fees should be used in the context of community-wide plans and programs for financing public facilities and services, and ensure the adequacy of public facilities to serve future development.

6. Oppose requiring voter approval to establish fees for mitigation of impacts on public facilities and services where such fees are imposed pursuant to a legislatively approved program in compliance with APA standards for the adoption and use of impact fees.

7. Support continued dialogue between local planning agencies, the general public, and the development community to discuss the public costs associated with new development, reaching an understanding on the calculation of such costs, and establishing alternative means for financing these costs, including the use of impact fees.

8. As a framework for imposing fees, local jurisdictions are encouraged to develop, adopt, and implement capital improvement programs consistent with an adopted comprehensive plan with consideration given to other funding alternatives.

IMPACT FEE STANDARDS

- The imposition of a fee must be rationally linked (the "rational nexus") to an impact created by a particular development and the demonstrated need for related capital improvements pursuant to a capital improvement plan and program.
- Some benefit must accrue to the development as a result of the payment of a fee.
- The amount of the fee must be a proportionate fair share of the costs of the improvements made necessary by the development and must not exceed the cost of the improvements.
- A fee cannot be imposed to address existing deficiencies except where they are exacerbated by new development.
- Funds received under such a program must be segregated from the general fund and used solely for the purposes for which the fee is established.
- The fees collected must be encumbered or expended within a reasonable timeframe to ensure that needed improvements are implemented.
- The fee assessed cannot exceed the cost of the improvements, and credits must be given for outside funding sources (such as federal and state grants, developer initiated improvements for impacts related to new development, etc.) and local tax payments which fund capital improvements, for example.
- The fee cannot be used to cover normal operation and maintenance or personnel costs, but must be used for capital improve-

ments, or under some linkage programs, affordable housing, job training, child care, etc.

- The fee established for specific capital improvements should be reviewed at least every two years to determine whether an adjustment is required, and similarly the capital improvement plan and budget should be reviewed at least every 5 to 8 years.
- Provisions must be included in the ordinance to permit refunds for projects that are not constructed, since no impact will have manifested.
- Impact fee payments are typically required to be made as a condition of approval of the development, either at the time the building or occupancy permit is issued.

Compare the position of the American Planning Association to that of the National Association of Homebuilders below (available at http://www.nahb.org):

Impact Fee Policy

The financing of off-site infrastructure that serves or has the potential for serving more than one project should be based on community-wide or broader funding sources, rather than impact fees/taxes on new housing.

Background

Federal funding of infrastructure—for new roads, highways, sewer and water, other facilities and federal assistance for maintaining old infrastructure—has steadily decreased. This has significantly increased pressure on local governments to find alternative sources of funding. More and more jurisdictions are imposing impact fees on developers and, through developers, on new housing consumers, as a way to pay for improvements beyond that necessary for new development. These exactions, which now exceed $15,000 per home in many areas and even more in some areas, have worsened the nation's housing affordability problems. A more equitable and affordable approach to infrastructure financing assures that impact fees cover only costs that are directly attributable or beneficial to new home construction. Credits for other fees and revenues, such as permit fees, connection fees and sales, income and property taxes, as the result of new home building must be accounted for before imposing new fees and taxes. Costs of facilities that serve the entire community should be spread over the entire community.

Solutions

- Seek and support legislation to provide mechanisms for facilitating broad-based infrastructure finance.

- Support the use of community-wide resources such as property taxes, sales taxes, transfer taxes, and income taxes to support infrastructure finance.
- Encourage government accountability of current and available funding sources before assessing any fee.

Notes

1. The rational nexus test has been utilized by most jurisdictions facing the problem of imposing on developers the requirement of dedicating land outside the proposed subdivision for future improvements or the actual construction of improvements outside the boundaries of the subdivision. As in the principal case, courts are suspicious of schemes that require a developer to pay the total cost of an off-site improvement. See Baltica Construction Co., Inc. v. Planning Board of Franklin Twp., 222 N.J.Super. 428, 537 A.2d 319 (1988); Longridge Builders, Inc. v. Planning Board of Princeton Twp., 52 N.J. 348, 245 A.2d 336 (1968); Kode Harbor Dev. Assoc. v. County of Atlantic, 230 N.J.Super. 430, 553 A.2d 858 (1989); Christopher Lake Development Co. v. St. Louis County, 35 F.3d 1269 (8th Cir.1994). Where the town conditioned subdivision approval on the improvement of an abutting road, even though the road was in good condition, the court, using the rational nexus test, found that the exaction was a taking. Town of Flower Mound v. Stafford Estates L.P., 135 S.W.3d 620 (Tex.2004).

2. Even where developers are asked only to pay a pro rata share of necessary off-site improvements, the rational nexus test must be carefully applied. In New Jersey Builders Association v. Mayor and Twp. Committee of Bernards Twp., 108 N.J. 223, 528 A.2d 555 (1987), the court held requiring new developments to pay a pro rata share of the township's long-range $20 million road improvement plan was ultra vires. Also see Albany Area Builders Association v. Town of Guilderland, 74 N.Y.2d 372, 547 N.Y.S.2d 627, 546 N.E.2d 920 (1989), where the town's Transportation Impact Fee Law was held to have been preempted by the state statutes dealing with road improvements and financing. In Land/Vest Properties, Inc. v. Town of Plainfield, 117 N.H. 817, 379 A.2d 200 (1977), the court upheld the theory of off-site road improvements, but struck down the proposed exaction for failure to establish the rational nexus. Compare KBW, Inc. v. Town of Bennington, 115 N.H. 392, 342 A.2d 653 (1975).

3. In Arrowhead Development Co. v. Livingston County Road Commission, 413 Mich. 505, 322 N.W.2d 702 (1982), the court found that a requirement that the developer regrade an existing county road to eliminate a dangerous condition which would be exacerbated by the development exceeded the commission's statutory powers.

4. In Northwest Land and Investment, Inc. v. City of Bellingham, 31 Wash.App. 742, 644 P.2d 740 (1982), the developer brought a tort action against the city for unlawfully requiring him to install off-site improvements; the court denied relief because the developer did not pursue a challenge to the requirement, and thus, the proximate cause of his loss was his compliance.

Village Square No. 1, Inc. v. Crow–Frederick, 77 Md.App. 552, 551 A.2d 471 (1989) was a case involving a "recapture agreement," a common device used in off-site or in oversized on-site improvements that will, in the future, benefit subsequent developers. The usual agreement provides for the city to calculate how much of the improvement installed by a developer will benefit future nearby developments, a provision that the city will charge the future development(s) that portion of previously installed improvement that benefits the new development, and a promise to reimburse the original developer that amount. As you might expect, a lot of guesswork goes into this process, and there is no guarantee that the original developer will ever see any money. In addition to the Maryland case, where the original developer lost, see Beneficial Development Corp. v. City of Highland Park, 161 Ill.2d 321, 204 Ill.Dec. 211, 641 N.E.2d 435 (1994). In this case the court upheld the recapture agreement while limiting the amount recoverable by the developer. Also see Fischer v. Dover, 131 N.H. 469, 554 A.2d 1293 (1989), cert. denied 502 U.S. 899, 112 S.Ct. 276, 116 L.Ed.2d 228 (1991), where a developer who had installed a road with a recapture agreement received $8,000 ten years later when another developer came along. The installing developer argued, without success, that he should receive an additional sum to represent the inflation in road costs over the ten year period.

5. Put yourself in the position of a planning commissioner or other local official of a unit on the growth fringe of an urban area. Yours is one of the toughest jobs in government. Your town or borough, or village, or satellite city is perhaps reasonably well-equipped with "paper" legal powers. But it is woefully weak in terms of revenue sources and technical competence to wrestle with the problems of urban growth that plague it. There are pressures on you to slow down development so it will not outstrip the community's ability to finance demanded services, especially schools. Other pressure from "old timers" push for preservation of neighborhood "amenities" and the character of the community, by which may be meant, "keep the little houses with their swarms of kids out" or "let's have big lots and big houses only and, for goodness sakes, no trailer camps." Other strong-minded citizens will be pushing hard for "getting some industry in to take some of the property tax load off us householders." And every citizen, even the one who has just moved in last week, will agree that in the future you should make all newcomers "pay their own way." There will be little pressure on you to do what is best in terms of the needs of the metropolitan region; instead you will be asked to wear intellectual blinders and do what is "best" for your political entity and let neighboring units take the consequences.

So, for example, who should pay for the increased costs of public infrastructure related to the new development? Should the cost of a new water filtration system necessitated by the increased number of houses on the system be borne by the community as a whole since each resident will benefit, or should the costs be borne solely by the new residents/homeowners who created the need for the upgrade? Impact fees, or development fees to fund certain off-site improvements, have been a controversial source of revenue for local governments over the last ten years as evidenced in the policy positions of the American Planning Association and the National Association of Home Builders set forth above. With approximately half of the states providing statutory authorization and guidelines for the adoption of local impact fee laws, the

American Planning Association's Legislative Guidebook offers model state statutory language as well as a discussion of elements of a good impact fee statute. See, American Planning Association, *Growing Smart Legislative Guidebook: Model Statutes for Planning and the Management of Change* (Stuart Meck, ed.) (2002) at Chapter 8 (http://www.planning.org/guidebookhtm/chapter_eight_1.htm.).

(3) Non-traditional Exactions

PIONEER TRUST & SAV. BANK v. VILLAGE OF MOUNT PROSPECT

Supreme Court of Illinois, 1961.
22 Ill.2d 375, 176 N.E.2d 799.

MR. JUSTICE HERSHEY delivered the opinion of the court:

Plaintiffs brought a mandamus proceeding in the circuit court of Cook County to compel the corporate authorities of the village of Mount Prospect to approve a plat of subdivision which complied with all the provisions of the official plan of the municipality except that requiring a dedication of land for public use. The case was submitted to the court on an agreed statement of facts. The court entered an order finding the land dedication requirements of the village's official plan invalid and directed the issuance of a writ of mandamus commanding the corporate authorities to approve the plat. The trial court has certified that the validity of a municipal ordinance is involved and that the public interest requires a direct appeal.

Article 53 of the Revised Cities and Villages Act authorizes municipalities to establish plan commissions with authority to recommend to the corporate authorities the adoption of an official plan. Section 53–2 (Ill.Rev.Stat.1959, c. 24, par. 53–2) provides that the plan may "establish reasonable standards of design for subdivisions and for resubdivisions of unimproved land and of areas subject to redevelopment, including reasonable requirements for public streets, alleys, ways for public service facilities, parks, playgrounds, school grounds, and other public grounds." Section 53–3 provides that no plat of subdivision "shall be entitled to record or shall be valid unless the subdivision shown thereon provides for streets, alleys, * * * and public grounds in conformity with the applicable requirements of the official plan."

The village of Mount Prospect has established a plan commission and has adopted by ordinance an official plan as recommended by the commission. Section 6 of article II of that plan contains a requirement for the dedication of public grounds as follows:

> "Dedication of Lands for Public Use: The plat shall have lettered upon it a statement of dedications properly conveying all usable lands dedicated for such public uses as streets, public schools, parks or any other public use, and there shall be attached to the plat a certificate of title certifying the ownership of all such lands to be

so dedicated by said plat. Public grounds, other than streets, alleys and parking areas, shall be dedicated in appropriate locations by the plat (a) at the rate of at least one (1) acre for each sixty (60) residential building sites or family living units, which may be accommodated under the restrictions applying to the land; or (b) at the rate of at least one-tenth (1/10) acre for each one (1) acre of business or industrial building sites which may be accommodated under the restrictions applying to the land."

Plaintiff Salvatore Dimucci is engaged in the business of subdividing real estate for residential purposes and caused a plat of the subdivision to be submitted to the plan commission for approval which complied in all respects with the aforesaid ordinance except as to the dedication of some 6.7 acres of land which would be required under the language of section 6 of article II quoted above. The plaintiffs have refused to dedicate land, and, in view of that refusal, the village board has refused to approve the plat of the subdivision. It is established in the record that the 6.7 acres of land sought to be required to be dedicated or donated would be for the use of an elementary school and for the use of the Mount Prospect Park District as an elementary school site and a secondary use as a playground. The proposed subdivision shows some 250 residential units.

The issue here presented for determination is the validity of the quoted section of the ordinance, and no provision of the ordinance other than that requiring the dedication is under attack by the plaintiffs in this proceeding.

The statute from which the village derives its authority has been before us on two previous occasions. Petterson v. City of Naperville, 9 Ill.2d 233, 137 N.E.2d 371; Rosen v. Village of Downers Grove, 19 Ill.2d 448, 167 N.E.2d 230. In each of these cases the issue presented for decision was narrowly circumscribed, and in neither case did we pass upon the precise point that is involved here. The Petterson case did not involve any question of required dedication of land, but rather concerned the reasonableness of a requirement that the subdivider provide curbs and gutters for the streets of the subdivision. We sustained the validity of such a requirement, stating that "the power to prescribe reasonable requirements for public streets in the interest of the health and safety of the inhabitants of the city and contiguous territory includes more than a mere designation of the location and width of streets." The Rosen case involved a portion of an ordinance of the village of Downers Grove which required subdividers to dedicate land for educational facilities but also provided that if the plan commission should deem that the dedication of such land would not of itself meet the reasonable requirements of providing educational facilities for the proposed subdivision, then the plan commission might require any additional means for providing reasonable facilities. Acting under this ordinance, the municipality attempted to require subdividers to pay a certain sum per lot for educational purposes. We held this attempt invalid because the specific technique employed was not authorized by the statute, and also because the term "educational purposes" was broader than the language of the statute. The Downers Grove ordinance did contain a paragraph, similar to that involved in the instant case, requiring the dedication for public grounds of at least one acre of land for each 75 family living units; but this particular provision was not directly involved in the litigation and we refused to pass on its validity.

Our opinion in the Rosen case thus specifically left undecided the question that is now presented for decision. It did, however, suggest some basic principles for distinguishing between permissible and forbidden requirements. We stated in the Rosen case that the statutory provisions with respect to reasonable requirements for streets and public grounds were based upon the theory that "the developer of a subdivision may be required to assume those costs which are specifically and uniquely attributable to his activity and which would otherwise be cast upon the public." We further observed: "But because the requirement that a plat of subdivision be approved affords an appropriate point of control with respect to costs made necessary by the subdivision, it does not follow that communities may use this point of control to solve all of the problems which they can foresee. The distinction between permissible and forbidden requirements is suggested in Ayres v. The City Council of Los Angeles, 34 Cal.2d 31, 207 P.2d 1, 11 A.L.R.2d 503, which indicates that the municipality may require the developer to provide the streets which are required by the activity within the subdivision but can not require him to provide a major thoroughfare, the need for which stems from the total activity of the community." It is in the light of these basic principles that the reasonableness of the requirement sought to be imposed by the defendant village must be determined. If the requirement is within the statutory grant of power to the municipality and if the burden cast upon the subdivider is specifically and uniquely attributable to his activity, then the requirement is permissible; if not, it is forbidden and amounts to a confiscation of private property in contravention of the constitutional prohibitions rather than reasonable regulation under the police power.

* * *

There can be no controversy about the obvious fact that the orderly development of a municipality must necessarily include a consideration of the present and future need for school and public recreational facilities. Neither the plaintiffs nor the defendants in this case take the negative side of the question as to the desirability either of education or recreation. The question is not one of the desirability of education or recreation, nor of the desirability to improve the public condition, but, rather, the question presented here is one of determining who shall pay for such improvements. Is it reasonable that a subdivider should be required under the guise of a police power regulation to dedicate a portion of his property to public use; or does this amount to a veiled exercise of the power of eminent domain and a confiscation of private property behind the defense of police regulations?

That the addition by this subdivision of some 250 residential units to the municipality would of course aggravate the existing need for additional school and recreational facilities is admitted by the parties to this cause. No complaint is made by the plaintiff in this cause that the land required to be dedicated for such purposes by subdivision control ordinance is unnecessary. The sole question thus presented here is whether the state of law is such that a mandatory dedication of the land without cost to the public may be sustained in the regulation of proposed subdivision when it is admitted that such land may well be needed.

However, this record does not establish that the need for recreational and educational facilities in the event that said subdivision plat is permitted to be filed, is one that is specifically and uniquely attributable to the addition of the subdivision and which should be cast upon the subdivider as his sole financial burden. The agreed statement of facts shows that the present school facilities of Mount Prospect are near capacity. This is the result of the total development of the community. If this whole community had not developed to such an extent or if the existing school facilities were greater, the purported need supposedly would not be present. Therefore, on the record in this case the school problem which allegedly exists here is one which the subdivider should not be obliged to pay the total cost of remedying, and to so construe the statute would amount to an exercise of the power of eminent domain without compensation. Sanitary District of Chicago v. Chicago and Alton R. Co., 267 Ill. 252, 108 N.E. 312, and cases there cited; Ridgemont Develop. Co. v. City of East Detroit, 358 Mich. 387, 100 N.W.2d 301.

Section 6 of article II of the defendant village ordinance imposes an unreasonable condition precedent for the approval of a plat of a subdivision and purports to take private property for public use without compensation. The circuit court of Cook County was correct in so holding, and the judgment of that court is affirmed.

JORDAN v. VILLAGE OF MENOMONEE FALLS

Supreme Court of Wisconsin, 1965.
28 Wis.2d 608, 137 N.W.2d 442, appeal dismissed
385 U.S. 4, 87 S.Ct. 36, 17 L.Ed.2d 3 (1966).

Action by plaintiffs Martin A. Jordan and James F. McMicken and their wives against defendant village to recover $5,000 paid by plaintiffs as an equalization fee in lieu of dedicating land as required by defendant's ordinance governing the subdivision of lands within the village.

In October, 1959, Jordan and McMicken (hereinafter "plaintiffs") commenced negotiations for the purchase of a 7.85 acre tract of land in defendant village for the purpose of subdividing it into lots and selling the lots. While negotiating, plaintiffs became aware that defendant had enacted an ordinance in March, 1959, which required subdividers to either dedicate a portion of their land or pay a fee in lieu thereof. Pertinent sections of the ordinance are:

"In order that adequate open spaces and sites for public uses may be properly located and preserved as the community develops; and in order that the cost of providing the public school, park, and recreation sites and facilities necessary to serve the additional families brought into the community by subdivision development may be most equitably apportioned on the basis of the additional need created by the individual subdivision development, the following provisions are established:

"8.01. Reservation of Potential Sites.

"(1) In the design of the plat, consideration shall be given to the adequate provision of and correlation with such public sites or open areas.

"(2) Where it is determined by the plan commission that a portion of the plat is required for such public sites or open spaces, the subdivider may be required to reserve such area for a period not to exceed three years, after which the Village shall either acquire the property or release the reservation.

"8.02. Dedication of Sites.

"(1) Within the corporate limits of the Village, where feasible and compatible with the comprehensive plan for development of the community, the subdivider shall provide and dedicate to the public adequate land to provide for the school, park and recreation needs of the subdivision.

"(2) The amount of land to be provided shall be determined on the basis of an amount equal in value to $200.00 per residential lot created by the subdivision. Such value shall be determined by the Village assessor on the basis of full and fair market value of the land. If the owner is not satisfied with such appraisal, he may appeal such determination, in which case an appraisal board consisting of one appraiser selected by the Village at its own expense, one selected by the property owner at his own expense and a third selected by the two other appraisers at Village expense, shall determine the value.

"8.03. Proportionate Payment in Lieu of Dedication.

"(1) Where such dedication is not feasible or compatible with the comprehensive plan, the subdivider shall in lieu thereof pay to the Village a fee equivalent to the value of the required dedication. Such fee shall be distributed as follows:

'A. $120.00 per residential lot created by the subdivision to be held in a non-lapsing fund for the benefit of the school district or districts in which the plat lies, on the basis of proper apportionment between districts where the plat is in more than one district, and to be made available to the appropriate district or districts upon their request.

'B. $80.00 per residential lot created by the subdivision to be placed in a non-lapsing fund to be used for park and recreation area development.'

"(2) Such fees shall be used exclusively for immediate or future site acquisition or capital improvement. * * *

"8.05. Determination of Feasibility.

"The determination as to the feasibility of dedication shall be made by the Village Plan Commission. The subdivider shall however have the option of choosing to make payment in lieu of dedication."

With full knowledge of the ordinance, plaintiffs purchased the property for $22,000. Plaintiff Jordan did once voice an informal objection to Gottlieb, village commissioner, stating that he thought the ordinance was unconstitutional. Because of the small area and the particular layout of the subdivision planned, it did not occur to plaintiffs to dedicate any land for school or park sites. They proceeded on the assumption that they would pay the $5,000 equalization fee in lieu of land dedication, which fee they paid by check September 12, 1960, and typed "paid under protest" on the check. Plaintiffs then proceeded to complete the subdivision at a total cost of $73,896.98, including the $5,000 platting fee. All 25 lots were sold between September, 1961, and April, 1963, for a total sum of $100,000.

On October 26, 1962, plaintiffs served on defendant a formal demand and claim for return of the payment, which was denied by defendant.

Plaintiffs alleged that the payment was a tax which the village could not levy because (1) it did not have authorization from the legislature and (2) it was an unconstitutional taking of property without just compensation. Trial was to the court and judgment was entered February 12, 1965, for plaintiffs, requiring defendants to repay to plaintiffs the $5,000 plus interest from September 12, 1960.

Defendant has appealed.

* * *

CURRIE, CHIEF JUSTICE.

The issue on this appeal is the constitutionality of the ordinance pursuant to which the $5,000 equalization fee was paid. Defendant asserts that the ordinance is a valid exercise of its police power in controlling subdivision development to assure its burgeoning population adequate parks and schools. Plaintiffs contend that section 8.03 of the ordinance levies a tax which is not authorized by the legislature and unconstitutional.

* * *

Preliminary to considering the constitutionality of the equalization fee provisions of the ordinance, we deem it advisable to pass on the requirement that the subdivider, where practicable, be required to dedicate a portion of the subdivision for sites for school, park and recreational needs of a value of $200 per residential lot. If this provision of the ordinance is unconstitutional, then of course the provision for payment of a cash fee in lieu of dedicating land for school, park and recreational sites would of necessity also be unconstitutional.

No claim has been asserted in this litigation that the $200 per lot value of land required to be dedicated by the subdivision owner is unreasonable in amount. Nelson, defendant's municipal planning expert, testified that the experience of municipal planners throughout the country has shown that for a good environment for human habitation, for each family in the area, there must be a minimum of 3,000 square feet of land devoted to park and school purposes. After some study of average land values in the village, the village planning commission and the village board determined that land valued at $200 would by and large provide the added park and school lands required for each family brought into the village by creation of the subdivision.

The grounds of the attack upon the land dedication requirement is that it is not authorized by statute and is an unconstitutional taking of private property for public use without just compensation.

Upon careful analysis of sec. 236.45, Stats., we conclude that it does authorize the land dedication requirement of the instant ordinance. Sub. (1) of this statute declares that the purposes of the statute include facilitating "adequate provision for transportation, water, sewerage, schools, parks, playgrounds and other public requirements." The common practice of providing for transportation in a subdivision is for municipal platting ordinances to require dedication of land for streets by the subdivider. Likewise the accepted way to provide water and sewerage facilities for a proposed subdivision is to require the subdivider to provide the same as a condition to the municipality approving the proposed plat. In Zastrow v. Village of Brown Deer[5] this court stated:

> "The Village could require as a condition of its approval of a plat that the subdivider make and install any public improvements reasonably necessary, including a water system, and it could require as a condition for accepting the dedication that the designated facilities previously constructed and provided be without cost to the Village, and that such facilities be according to the Village's specifications and under its inspection, including water mains and laterals."

Similarly it would seem to follow that the way to facilitate provision for schools, parks, and playgrounds to serve the subdivision would be to require the subdivider to dedicate a portion of the subdivision for such

5. 9 Wis.2d 100, 100 N.W.2d 359 (1960).

purposes. Sec. 236.13(2)(a) and (b), Stats.,[6] which apply statewide to all municipalities, irrespective of whether they have planning commissions, grants to municipalities the right to require the subdivider to pay for such public improvements as water and sewer mains, and to dedicate land for public streets, as a condition to the municipality approving the proposed subdivision plat. Sec. 236.45 was intended by the legislature to vest additional authority in those municipalities which had created planning commissions to impose further requirements upon the subdivider. In addition to the aforequoted language spelling out legislative purpose in sub. (1) of this statute, the first sentence of sub. (2)(a), of sec. 236.45, makes clear this intent. The third sentence of this subsection reads, "Such ordinances may make applicable to such divisions any of the provisions of this chapter, or may provide other surveying, monumenting, mapping and approving requirements for such division." Standing alone the statutory words "other * * * approving requirements" would normally be confined to requirements of the same general nature as the antecedent enumerated specific words "surveying, monumenting, mapping." We reject such a restrictive interpretation in favor of the broader one which will encompass the objectives stated in sub. (1). We are further motivated in favor of such a broad interpretation by the direction of sub. (2)(b) requiring a liberal construction of sec. 236.45.

Having concluded that sec. 236.45, Stats., does authorize the land dedication provisions of the instant ordinance, we turn now to the question of whether they constitute an unconstitutional taking of private property for a public purpose. The Illinois supreme court in Pioneer Trust & Sav. Bank v. Village of Mt. Prospect laid down this test of the constitutionality of a requirement placed upon a subdivider, as a condition for approval of the subdivision plat:

> "If the requirement is within the statutory grant of power to the municipality and if the burden cast upon the subdivider is specifically and uniquely attributable to his activity, then the requirement is permissible; if not, it is forbidden and amounts to a confiscation of private property in contravention of the constitutional prohibitions rather than reasonable regulation under the police power."

We deem this to be an acceptable statement of the yardstick to be applied, provided the words "specifically and uniquely attributable to his activity" are not so restrictively applied as to cast an unreasonable burden of proof upon the municipality which has enacted the ordinance under attack. In most instances it would be impossible for the municipal-

6. These subsections provide: "(a) As a further condition of approval, the governing body of the town or municipality within which the subdivision lies may require that the subdivider make and install any public improvements reasonably necessary or that he execute a surety bond to insure that he will make those improvements within a reasonable time.

"(b) Any city or village may require as a condition for accepting the dedication of public streets, alleys or other ways, * * * that designated facilities shall have been previously provided without cost to the municipality, * * *"

ity to prove that the land required to be dedicated for a park or a school site was to meet a need solely attributable to the anticipated influx of people into the community to occupy this particular subdivision. On the other hand, the municipality might well be able to establish that a group of subdivisions approved over a period of several years had been responsible for bringing into the community a considerable number of people making it necessary that the land dedications required of the subdividers be utilized for school, park and recreational purposes for the benefit of such influx. In the absence of contravening evidence this would establish a reasonable basis for finding that the need for the acquisition was occasioned by the activity of the subdivider. Possible contravening evidence would be a showing that the municipality prior to the opening up of the subdivisions, acquired sufficient lands for school, park and recreational purposes to provide for future anticipated needs including such influx, or that the normal growth of the municipality would have made necessary the acquisition irrespective of the influx caused by opening up of subdivisions.

There also may be situations, unlike the instant one, where there is no substantial influx from the outside and the proposed subdivision only fulfills a purely local need within the community. In those situations it may be more difficult to adduce proof sufficient to sustain a land dedication requirement.

We conclude that a required dedication of land for school, park or recreational sites as a condition for approval of the subdivision plat should be upheld as a valid exercise of police power if the evidence reasonably establishes that the municipality will be required to provide more land for schools, parks and playgrounds as a result of approval of the subdivision.

* * *

We do not consider the fact that other residents of the village as well as residents of the subdivision may make use of a public site required to be dedicated by subdivider for school, park or recreational purposes is particularly material to the constitutional issue. This is also true of land required to be dedicated for public street purposes.

* * *

We turn now to the issue of the constitutionality of the equalization fee provision contained in section 8.03 of the ordinance whereby the subdivider is required to pay a total of $200 per lot in lieu of dedicating land of that value for school, park or recreational needs where the village planning commission finds dedication of land for such purposes is not feasible. In respect to this provision, the question which poses the greater difficulty is not whether there is an attempted illegal taking which cannot be justified as a reasonable exercise of the police power, but whether the legislature has authorized such a provision.

* * *

Is the equalization fee such a concomitant of the land dedication provision of the ordinance that its authorization can be found in the language of subs. (1) and (2) of sec. 236.45 hereinbefore relied upon to sustain the land dedication requirement of the ordinance? We conclude that it is.

Where a comparatively small tract of land is subdivided, as in the instant situation, and there is no adjoining land already devoted to school park, or playground purposes to which a portion of the proposed subdivision might be attached, it usually would be impracticable to require dedication of any land of the subdivision. The two alternatives are either to relieve the subdivider from any obligation whatever in this direction, or to require payment of an equalization fee of the nature of that here imposed. The latter is in keeping with the stated purpose of the statute.

While section 8.03(2) of the ordinance permits use of the proceeds of the equalization fee for capital improvement of schools, parks and recreation areas in addition to site acquisition, nevertheless the making of these capital improvements is encompassed by the words of sub. (1) of sec. 236.45 which declare that the purposes of the statute include facilitating "adequate provision for * * * schools, parks, playgrounds and other public requirements."

The equalization fee exacted pursuant to the ordinance is not a property tax. It is not imposed upon the land in the subdivision as such but is imposed on the transaction of obtaining approval of the plat. Thus, if a tax, it partakes of the nature of an excise tax and does not violate the uniformity clause found in sec. 1, art. VIII of the Wisconsin constitution.

While plaintiffs do not openly contend that the equalization fee is in the nature of a special assessment, they employ arguments that tend in that direction. Thus they point to the fact that the ordinance does not require that park and school sites purchased with funds paid in lieu of dedication bear any relationship to the subdivision providing the funds. This argument would be pertinent if the equalization fee's validity were dependent on justifying it as a special assessment. The argument, however, does have some pertinency on the previously considered issue of unconstitutional taking of private property for a public purpose as opposed to a reasonable exercise of police power.

To conclude, we determine that the imposition of the instant $5,000 equalization fee is not invalid as unconstitutional. In so holding we are cognizant that this result is contra to the conclusions reached by the Illinois and Kansas courts in the well considered cases of Rosen v. Village of Downers Grove[7] and Coronado Development Co. v. City of McPherson[8] with respect to the issue of the validity of the attempted exercise of the police power. While we have great respect for these courts, we believe that there is a reasonable basis for upholding the exercise of the police power voiced in the instant ordinance.

7. 19 Ill.2d 448, 167 N.E.2d 230 (1960).

8. 189 Kan. 174, 368 P.2d 51 (1962).

Judgment reversed and cause remanded with directions to dismiss the complaint.

HALLOWS, JUSTICE (dissenting).

* * *

By analogy, any dedication of land for parks and school purposes or money in lieu thereof should be governed by the same rules which apply to public roads and sewer and water in the subdivision. When land is dedicated for public streets or for the furnishing of water mains and sewers, their location insures some definite benefit to the rest of the land in the plat. While these are of special benefit to the lots, they are, of course, incidentally of benefit to the community at large.

In respect to the alternative provision for the payment of money in lieu of land for school and park purposes, I find no authority for the municipality to enact such an alternative and no restriction or requirement that the money be used for parks and schools in the vicinity of the subdivision. The money may be used anywhere in the municipality and is not restricted for the direct benefit of the subdivision. Consequently, this requirement of the payment of a fee which a municipality has the option to demand in lieu of land is nothing more than a revenue-raising device for the general welfare of the municipality and as such is in the nature of a tax and cannot be justified as an exercise of the police power. City of Milwaukee v. Milwaukee & S.T. Corp., 6 Wis.2d 299, 94 N.W.2d 584 (1959); 51 Am.Jur., Taxation, p. 35, sec. 3, and p. 46, sec. 12. I think the trial court was correct in finding the requirement to be in the nature of a tax and the village had no power and was not authorized by the legislature to impose it. Whitney v. Department of Taxation, 16 Wis.2d 274, 114 N.W.2d 445 (1962). There is no implementing authorization conferring the power to impose such a tax nor does the Home–Rule Amendment (sec. 3, Art. XI, Wis. Const.) authorize it since a tax is not a local matter. City of Plymouth v. Elsner, 28 Wis.2d 102, 135 N.W.2d 799 (1965). Being in the nature of a tax it makes no difference whether the tax is a property tax bound by the uniformity requirement or an excise tax not so restricted.

It is quite apparent the so-called equalizing fee bears no reasonable relationship to the subdivision since it is not restricted to its benefit. The placing of such payments in the general treasury of the municipality cannot be justified on the theory that parks and schools will eventually be built or have been built in the subdivision area out of the general fund. Such a view ignores the vital distinction between the taxing power and the police power.

* * *

I would affirm.

Notes

1. For cases holding park or school site dedications or fees in lieu of dedications invalid because unauthorized by enabling statutes see: Rosen v.

Village of Downers Grove, 19 Ill.2d 448, 167 N.E.2d 230 (1960); Coronado Development Co. v. City of McPherson, 189 Kan. 174, 368 P.2d 51 (1962); and Haugen v. Gleason, 226 Or. 99, 359 P.2d 108 (1961), all of which are cited in support of the dissent in the Jordan case. Other cases striking down such exactions include City of Montgomery v. Crossroads Land Co., Inc., 355 So.2d 363 (Ala.1978); Admiral Development Corp. v. City of Maitland, 267 So.2d 860 (Fla.App.1972); Sanchez v. City of Santa Fe, 82 N.M. 322, 481 P.2d 401 (1971); Frank Ansuini, Inc. v. City of Cranston, 107 R.I. 63, 264 A.2d 910 (1970); Berg Development Co. v. City of Missouri City, 603 S.W.2d 273 (Tex.Civ.App.1980); J.E.D. Associates, Inc. v. Town of Atkinson, 121 N.H. 581, 432 A.2d 12 (1981); Kamhi v. Planning Bd. of Yorktown, 59 N.Y.2d 385, 465 N.Y.S.2d 865, 452 N.E.2d 1193 (1983); City of Fayetteville v. IBI, Inc., 280 Ark. 484, 659 S.W.2d 505 (1983); and Town of Longboat Key v. Lands End, Ltd., 433 So.2d 574 (Fla.App.1983). Compare Gulest Associates v. Town of Newburgh, 25 Misc.2d 1004, 209 N.Y.S.2d 729 (1960) and Midtown Properties v. Township of Madison, 68 N.J.Super. 197, 172 A.2d 40, 47 (1961), affirmed 78 N.J.Super. 471, 189 A.2d 226 (1963). See also Reps and Smith, Control of Urban Land Subdivision, 14 Syracuse L.Rev. 405, 411 (1963), and Comment, Requiring Dedication of Park Land, 1961 Wis.L.Rev. 310.

In Haugen v. Gleason, supra, the court reversed the lower court and invalidated a $37.50 per lot fee for park purposes. It treated the fee as a tax upon subdividers for public purposes and held that such a tax was not authorized by any enabling legislation.

In Gulest, supra, the enabling act expressly authorized fees in an amount to be determined by the town board, "which amount shall be available for use by the town for neighborhood park, playground or recreation purposes including the acquisition of property." Nevertheless, the Supreme Court of Orange County, New York annulled a $50.00 per lot fee because (1) the fee could be used in any section of the town and thus was for the benefit, not of subdivision residents, but of the town as a whole, and (2) the statute failed to set out standards or tests.

On the basis of the Gulest case, the developer in Jenad, Inc. v. Village of Scarsdale, 38 Misc.2d 658, 238 N.Y.S.2d 156 (1963) tried unsuccessfully to recover fees he had paid voluntarily in lieu of land dedications. "Plaintiff had a preliminary remedy had it felt aggrieved * * * and no facts have been presented to the court to indicate that plaintiff would have been deprived of the reasonable use of its lands during the pendency of a lawsuit to attack the legality or constitutionality of the Scarsdale regulation before it paid the money in question. Everything before the court points to a business arrangement entered into between plaintiff and the village, and concluded in an amicable fashion resulting in plaintiff thanking the Village Attorney for his 'cooperation' in the matter." Also see Joseph v. Yorktown Planning Bd., 140 A.D.2d 670, 529 N.Y.S.2d 17 (1988). In Video Aid Corp. v. Town of Wallkill, 85 N.Y.2d 663, 628 N.Y.S.2d 18, 651 N.E.2d 886 (1995), a developer paid a $27,000 sewer and water connection fee only after the town indicated it would not grant a building permit unless the fee was paid; the developer then contested the fee as an unconstitutional exaction and sought reimbursement. The New York Court of Appeals held, in a four to three decision that even though the exaction was unconstitutional, the developer could not claim coercion and obtain a refund. The majority concluded that the developer had not even taken the simple step of making a notation on the check that the payment was under protest, and that some indication of protest is necessary when making such payments in order to permit public agencies to operate on a sound fiscal basis and that such agencies need to be made aware when collected funds may have to be refunded. The majority also indicated that an exception to the rule would be recognized in cases where payments are made under duress, but that exception would be applied very narrowly. The message of this case is that in every case where a developer may think that an exaction is excessive, exaction payments should be made under protest; such a practice might also be wise in jurisdictions other than New York.

On the other hand, several cases have followed the holding in the Jordan case and have upheld equalization assessments or dedications for park purposes. See Aunt Hack Ridge Estates, Inc. v. Planning Comm'n of the City of Danbury, 160 Conn. 109, 273 A.2d 880 (1970); Associated Home Builders of Greater East Bay, Inc. v. City of Walnut Creek, 4 Cal.3d 633, 94 Cal.Rptr. 630, 484 P.2d 606 (1971), appeal dismissed 404 U.S. 878, 92 S.Ct. 202, 30 L.Ed.2d 159 (1971); Cimarron Corp. v. Board of County Comm'rs, 193 Colo. 164, 563 P.2d 946 (1977); Collis v. City of Bloomington, 310 Minn. 5, 246 N.W.2d 19 (1976); Home Builders Ass'n of Greater Kansas City v. City of Kansas City, 555 S.W.2d 832 (Mo.1977); Call v. City of West Jordan, 614 P.2d 1257 (Utah 1980); Town of Auburn v. McEvoy, 131 N.H. 383, 553 A.2d 317 (1988) (overruling the J.E.D. Associates case, supra); Messer v. Town of Chapel Hill, 59 N.C.App. 692, 297 S.E.2d 632 (1982), appeal dismissed 307 N.C. 697, 301 S.E.2d 390 (1983); City of College Station v. Turtle Rock Corp., 680 S.W.2d 802 (Tex.1984); and Bayswater Realty and Capital Corp. v. Planning Bd., 76 N.Y.2d 460, 560 N.Y.S.2d 623, 560 N.E.2d 1300 (1990). Also see the annotation in 43 A.L.R.3d 862. In the Walnut Creek case, the court rejected arguments that: (1) the exaction discriminated in favor of apartment builders (the court said that apartment development does not diminish the available supply of open land to the same extent as the activity of subdividers); (2) the exaction amounted to double taxation, once in the higher cost to the lot purchaser, and again in subsequent property taxes to maintain the parks.

Two cases from Florida, both intermediate appellate court decisions, reached opposite conclusions on the validity of money exactions. Compare Broward County v. Janis Development Corp., 311 So.2d 371 (Fla.App.1975) with City of Dunedin v. Contractors and Builders Ass'n of Pinellas County, 312 So.2d 763 (Fla.App.1975) quashed 329 So.2d 314 (1976). See Rhodes, Impact Fees: The Cost–Benefit Dilemma in Florida, 27 Land Use Law & Zoning Dig. 7 (No. 10, 1975). Also see City of Key West v. R.L.J.S. Corp., 537 So.2d 641 (Fla.App.1989), review denied 545 So.2d 1367 (1989) where the court upheld retroactive sewer impact fees for units already sold by a condominium developer (the city had held back occupancy permits for newly-sold units until the fees were paid for units previously sold).

In Riegert Apartments Corp. v. Planning Bd., 105 Misc.2d 298, 432 N.Y.S.2d 43 (1979), a trial court upheld a money exaction in addition to a compulsory land dedication for flood control purposes. The Court of Appeals reversed. 57 N.Y.2d 206, 455 N.Y.S.2d 558, 441 N.E.2d 1076 (1982). Compare Hillis Homes, Inc. v. Snohomish County, 97 Wash.2d 804, 650 P.2d 193 (1982).

2. For a comprehensive discussion of the rationale of exactions see, Heyman and Gilhool, The Constitutionality of Imposing Increased Community Costs on New Suburban Residents Through Subdivision Exactions, 73 Yale L.J. 1119 (1964) and Johnston, Constitutionality of Subdivision Control Exactions: The Quest for a Rationale, 52 Cornell L.Q. 871 (1967). For a practical overview, see Delaney and Smith, Development Exactions: Winners and Losers, Land Use Law, Nov. 1989, p. 3. A review of state enabling legislation regarding impact fees is found in Morgan, State Impact Fee Legislation: Guidelines for Analysis, Land Use Law, Mar. 1990, p. 3 (Part I) and Apr. 1990, p. 3 (Part II). Also see Eastern Diversified Properties, Inc. v. Montgomery County, 319 Md. 45, 570 A.2d 850 (1990); Blaesser & Kentopp, Impact Fees: The "Second Generation," 38 Wash.U.J.Urb. & Contemp.L. 55 (1990). For a current comparison of state enabling statutes, including citations, see John G. Rappa, "Comparison of State Development Impact Fee Statutes," (State of Connecticut, Office of Legislative Research, 2002). Available at: http://www.cga.ct.gov/2002/olrdata/pd/rpt/2002–R–0842.htm. In Idaho Bldg. Contractors Ass'n v. Coeur d'Alene, 126 Idaho 740, 890 P.2d 326 (1995) the court struck down an ordinance imposing a development impact fee on all new construction, holding that the act was inapplicable and the city was really using the fee as a revenue raising device. Also see, Arthur C. Nelson, Development Impact Fees: The Next Generation, 26 The Urban Lawyer 541 (1994).

3. Compare Miller v. City of Beaver Falls, 368 Pa. 189, 82 A.2d 34 (1951) with In re Lake Secor Development Co., 141 Misc. 913, 252 N.Y.S. 809 (1931). In Miller an attempt to require the subdivider in effect to grant the city a three year first right of purchase of park land was declared invalid. The city did not pass the contested ordinance until after the council knew of the intention to subdivide, and the ordinance applied to 4½ acres of the subdivider's total of sixteen acres. Construction of twelve houses had been commenced prior to the ordinance on part of the sixteen acres, but not on the 4½ acre portion. Said Justice Bell for the Pennsylvania Court:

> "The city is not without remedy, but cannot eat its cake and have its penny too. If it desires plaintiff's land for a park or playground which it considers desirable or necessary for its future progress, it can readily and lawfully obtain this land in accordance with the Constitution which, we repeat, is the Supreme Law of the land * * * All that is required is that just compensation be paid therefor."

In the Secor case the planning board denied approval of a 138–acre (2000 lot) subdivision for several reasons, among them "insufficient park area." There is no indication how large a dedication the planning board demanded. The court, after first holding that the planning board had exceeded its enabling authority by insisting on a water system, said at page 812:

> "The demand of the planning board for additional park area is reasonable. The argument that 'all Putnam County is a park' advanced by the petitioner is without merit. The apparent purpose of the petitioner is to establish a summer colony. It must dedicate to public use

sufficient area to provide for the ultimate use to be made of this plat. It argues that the residents there can trespass upon other lands for recreational purposes. The mere statement of the proposition is its answer."

4. In connection with park and school site dedication problems recall that it is constitutional under appropriate legislation to require the subdivider to dedicate, free of charge, all land needed for new streets of ordinary width within the subdivision. (Recall the cross street in the Ayres case, supra.) And the requirement seems universal even though the land may amount to twenty or twenty-five percent of the total area where a gridiron street pattern is used.

As was seen from the Ridgefield case and the Ayres case, supra, there is also authority sustaining required dedications of strips for the purpose of widening existing streets abutting in the subdivision. See also Newton v. American Sec. Co., 201 Ark. 943, 148 S.W.2d 311 (1941).

5. Consider Board of Educ. of Community Consol. Sch. Dist. No. 59 v. E.A. Herzog Constr. Co., 29 Ill.App.2d 138, 172 N.E.2d 645 (1961). Herzog on May 9, 1957 in writing agreed to pay $95,000 toward the cost of a school and the board of education agreed to hold a special referendum to approve the school and to begin construction no later than July 15, 1958. The next day, on May 10, 1957, the county commissioner rezoned Herzog's land and authorized his project. On August 27, 1958, the original agreement was amended with the board of education acknowledging that its delay in commencing construction had undoubtedly affected Herzog's sales and consequently his revenues. Herzog's commitment to pay the $95,000 was restated but the time for payment was postponed until completion of the school. The school was completed. Herzog refused to pay and the board sued. Herzog claimed the agreements were void as against public policy as contracts "for the purchase of influence upon the action of public officers." He also charged that the board of education conspired with members of the county board to withhold rezoning until Herzog agreed to contribute to the cost of the school. The court took judicial notice that the school district has no control over the actions of the county board, brushed aside "these wild and irresponsible charges" and affirmed judgment against Herzog. Said the court:

> "The defendant voluntarily agreed to pay the $95,000 toward construction of the building, as it realized that the proposed school building was essential to its sales program. Having accepted the benefits of the agreement, it is now attempting to renege on its voluntary agreement to contribute money to the school board. It will not be permitted to do so."

Compare Midtown Properties v. Township of Madison, 68 N.J.Super. 197, 172 A.2d 40 (1961), affirmed 78 N.J.Super. 471, 189 A.2d 226 (1963) where a detailed contract between subdivider and a local unit was set aside as an attempt to do by contract what can only be done by following statutory procedures.

6. In Quirk v. Town of New Boston, 140 N.H. 124, 663 A.2d 1328 (1995) the court upheld a requirement that campground developments provide a 200 foot buffer zone around the perimeter of the property. The owner of an existing campground who had invested considerably in installa-

tion of oversized septic systems was denied a permit for a new recreation hall that would have encroached on the buffer zone. The court found that the regulation was akin to a setback requirement, that it was not arbitrary, and that the campground owner had not suffered a taking.

7. For a discussion of ways in which exactions in the land approval process rise to the level of unconstitutional takings of private property because they lack an essential nexus or rough proportionality between the exaction and the projected impact of the proposed development, see the Nollan and Dolan cases discussed in Chapter V.

(4) Denial of Subdivision Approval

COFFEY v. MARYLAND–NATIONAL CAPITAL PARK AND PLANNING COMMISSION

Court of Appeals of Maryland, 1982.
293 Md. 24, 441 A.2d 1041.

SMITH, JUDGE.

* * *

Appellant, Wade S. Coffey, owns 15.85 acres of land on Riverdale Road in Prince George's County, located approximately 1,800 feet east of that road's intersection with the Baltimore–Washington Parkway. The land is zoned R–T (Townhouse Development). This permits a maximum development density of 8.0 to 11.9 units per acre. The master plan for that area, approved in December 1980 by the District Council for Prince George's County, restricts density to 2.7 to 3.5 dwelling units per acre. Almost immediately after adoption of the plan, in January 1981, Coffey submitted an application for approval of a preliminary plan of subdivision. The planning for the subdivision had been in progress for some time. He proposed 117 townhouse units on the tract, a density of 7.38 dwelling units per acre.

Prince George's County Code § 24–103(a)(1) requires subdivision plats to conform to the master plan. Relying upon our decision in *Board of County Comm'rs v. Gaster,* 285 Md. 233, 401 A.2d 666 (1979), the Prince George's County Planning Board of the Maryland–National Capital Park and Planning Commission (the Commission) rejected the proposed subdivision because of noncompliance with the master plan. The Circuit Court for Prince George's County affirmed. Coffey then appealed to the Court of Special Appeals. Because we have not previously addressed such an issue under Art. 66D, we issued the writ of certiorari ex mero motu prior to consideration of the appeal by the intermediate appellate court.

* * *

Coffey's argument runs that prior to *Gaster* planning boards regarded master plans as only a set of recommendations, that *Gaster* was the first case where noncompliance with a master plan caused rejection of a proposed subdivision, and that noncompliance with the master plan constituted insufficient grounds for disapproval of a proposed subdivision. Cases making statements relative to master plans being guides have arisen in the context of an attempted piecemeal change in zoning. For instance, in *Chapman v. Montgomery County,* 259 Md. 641, 643, 271 A.2d 156 (1970), Judge Finan said for the Court, "A 'Master Plan' is not to be confused as a substitute for a comprehensive zoning or rezoning map, nor may it be equated with it in legal significance." No opinion of this Court has made a statement relative to master plans acting only as guides in the context of the facts here involved.

At oral argument, counsel for the Commission said that its past practice had been to treat the master plan as a guide in zoning matters. Counsel further stated, however, that the Commission regarded the master plan as binding in subdivision matters subsequent to the enactment of the regulation requiring proposed subdivisions to conform to the master plan.

* * *

As the author points out in 4 R. Anderson, *American Law of Zoning 2d* § 23.20, at 89 (1977), "Subdivision controls are imposed for the purpose of implementing a comprehensive plan for community development. To achieve this end, plats submitted to a planning commission for approval must be examined in relation to the official map and the master plan." Moreover, as the court observed in *Popular Refreshments, Inc. v. Fuller's Milk Bar, etc.,* 85 N.J.Super. 528, 537, 205 A.2d 445 (1964), petition for certification denied, 44 N.J. 409, 209 A.2d 143 (1965), "If planning boards had no alternative but to rubber-stamp their approval on every subdivision plat which conformed with the zoning ordinance, there would be little or no reason for their existence. While planning and zoning complement each other and serve certain common objectives, each represents a separate municipal function and neither is a mere rubber-stamp for the other," citing *Levin v. Livingston Tp.,* 35 N.J. 500, 506, 173 A.2d 391 (1961).

In this regard, the language used by the court in *Shoptaugh v. County Comm.,* 37 Colo.App. 39, 543 P.2d 524 (1975), *cert. denied* (1976), is significant here. The court there said:

> "Here, the landowner argues that since the proposed use of the land was a use of right under the zoning laws, the Board had no alternative but to either change the zoning or approve the plat. This argument fails to take into consideration that a subdivider must first meet the zoning regulations and then additionally must comply with the state and county subdivision regulations." 37 Colo.App. at 41–42, 543 P.2d 524.

The process of comprehensive zoning or rezoning is a time consuming one. It would be virtually impossible to adopt comprehensive rezoning changes calculated to impose the same density requirements as the master plan which would become effective simultaneously with the adoption of a new master plan that called for lower density development than the preceding plan.

Here we have a regulation duly enacted by the legislative body for Prince George's County which specifies that the planning board shall not approve a subdivision plat not in compliance with the master plan. This subdivision regulation is as much entitled to obedience as any other legislative enactment. The need for the regulation specifying that a subdivision plan must conform to the master plan can be illustrated by comparison to the putting of water in a teacup drop by drop. After a period of time there comes the drop which will cause the cup to overflow. By analogy, developing some of the lots in conformity with the existing zoning will not disrupt the master plan. Concentrated use and development, however, will disrupt it. The legislative body wished to avoid this when it specified that subdivisions must comply with the master plan. Accordingly, the Commission was justified in rejecting Coffey's proposed subdivision for his failure to conform that proposal with the master plan.

Judgment affirmed; Appellant to pay the costs.

MARYLAND–NAT'L CAPITAL PARK AND PLANNING COMM'N v. ROSENBERG

Court of Appeals of Maryland, 1973.
269 Md. 520, 307 A.2d 704.

McWilliams, Judge.

In this appeal, stemming from the confrontation of a landowner and the appellant (the Commission), we are asked to consider what is known in Prince George's County as the "Adequate Public Facilities Ordinance." * * * As we see this case the single issue is whether the action of the Commission was arbitrary and capricious. We think it was. However, before we undertake to relate the facts, we shall set forth the pertinent parts of both the enabling act (Code of Public Local Laws of Prince George's County, § 59 76 (1963)), and the ordinance (Code of Ordinances and Resolutions of Prince George's County, § 3(a) 16 (1967)):

> "* * * The regulations may provide for (1) the harmonious development of the district; (2) the coordination of roads within the subdivision with other existing, planned or platted roads or with other features of the district or with the commission's general plan or with any road plan adopted or approved by the commission as part of the commission's general plan; (3) adequate open spaces for traffic, recreation, light, and air by dedication or otherwise, and the dedication to public use or conveyance of areas designated for such dedication under the provisions of zoning regulations relating to average lot size or planned community subdivision and for the payment of a monetary fee in lieu of dedication, not to exceed five percent of the total assessed value of the land, to be used by the commission to purchase such open spaces for the use and benefit of

the subdivision in cases where dedication would be impractical; (4) the reservation of lands for schools and other public buildings and for parks, playgrounds, and other public purposes, provided no reservation of land for traffic, recreation or any other public purposes as herein provided shall continue for longer than three (3) years without the written approval of all persons holding or otherwise owning any legal or equitable interest in said property; and provided further that such properties so reserved for public use as hereinbefore provided shall be exempt from all state, county and local taxes during such period; (5) the conservation of or production of adequate transportation, water, drainage and sanitary facilities; (6) the preservation of the location of and the volume and flow of water in and other characteristics of natural streams and other waterways; (7) the avoidance of population congestion; (8) the avoidance of such scattered or premature subdivision of land as would involve danger or injury to health, safety or welfare by reason of the lack of water supply, drainage, transportation or other public services or necessitate an excessive expenditure of public funds for the supply of such services; (9) conformity of resubdivided lots to the character of lots within the existing subdivision with respect to area, frontage and alignment to existing lots and streets; (10) control of subdivision or building (except for agricultural or recreational purposes) in flood plain areas or streams and drainage courses, and on unsafe land areas; (11) preservation of outstanding natural or cultural features and historic sites or structures; or (12) other benefits to the health, comfort, safety or welfare of the present and future population of the regional district."

"16. Before preliminary approval may be granted for any subdivision plat the Planning Board must find that: sufficient public facilities and services exist or are programmed for the area. It is the intent of this section that public facilities and services should be adequate to preclude danger or injury to the health, safety and welfare and excessive expenditure of public funds.

"i. The Planning Board shall give due weight to the potential of the proposed subdivision in relation to the surroundings, including the nature, extent and size of the proposed subdivision; the estimated increase in population; the anticipated timing of the development of the land proposed for subdivision; and the degree of urbanization or development within a reasonable distance of the subject property; and the following factors:

"The availability of existing or programmed sewerage or water mains.

"The potential effect of the proposed subdivision on the efficient and economic operation of existing or programmed public facilities.

"The distance of any necessary extension of sewerage and water facilities through unsubdivided lands which are indicated for eventual development on an approved plan.

"The location of the proposed subdivision in respect to the approved Ten Year Water and Sewerage Plan, or in any future plan which designated the timing of construction of facilities.

"The availability of access roads adequate to serve traffic which would be generated by the subdivision, or the presence of a proposal for such road(s) on an adopted Master Plan and in the current Capital Improvement Program or the State Roads Commission program.

"The availability within a reasonable distance, and the adequacy of school, fire, police, utility, and park and recreation services."

The 31 acre tract of land (the property) with which we shall be concerned abuts the northwest side of the Pennsylvania Railroad which at that point serves also as one side of an equilateral triangle; the northeast side is the Capital Beltway (Interstate Rte 495); the south side is the John Hanson Highway (U.S. Rte 50). The property lies within the development known as West Lanham Hills which is about four miles northeast of the District line. Except for the land inside the triangle one can safely say the area surrounding the property is fully developed. Since 1964 the zoning classification of the property has been R–18 (Multiple Family, Medium Density, Residential), a classification with which the owner (appellee) seems content. It is said that a six acre strip has been or will be acquired to serve as the site for the Metro's Ardmore station.

In June 1971 the appellee submitted to the Commission for its approval, as required by the subdivision regulations, a preliminary plan for the subdivision of two parcels of the property. The Commission referred the application to its staff which, in turn, sent it to various county agencies for review and comment. The Board of Education was one of the agencies whose comment was solicited. It referred the matter to its Office of Population Analysis. On 16 June the Office of Population Analysis sent a memorandum to F. Harris Allen, Principal Development Coordinator of the Commission. The memorandum indicated a "Projected Pupil Yield" of 134 for the West Lanham Hills Elementary School, the capacity of which was 640 and which, at the time, had an actual enrollment of 657.

Several weeks later there came into existence an "adequate public facilities check sheet" apparently prepared by someone on the Commission's technical staff. Allen said he used this "in the course of the review of preliminary plans." This check sheet, dated 6 July 1971, indicates that the property had a "potential" of 651 units and that, fully developed and occupied, it would yield 175.8 pupils. The Office of Population Analysis, it will be recalled, developed a figure of 134. The September 1970 enrollment at the West Lanham Hills Elementary School was stated, in the check sheet, to be 668 pupils or 11 more than the enrollment reported by the Office of Population Analysis. There appears also, in the check sheet, the following notation:

> There are no additions in the CIP [Capital Improvement Program] which would increase the capacity of this school *or any other elementary schools in the vicinity.* (Emphasis added.)

It is conceded that the technical staff of the Commission recommended approval of the appellee's application. It was considered by the Prince George's County Planning Board of the Commission on 9 August and disapproved the same day. A letter from Allen to the appellee, dated 13 August, states, in part:

> "* * * West Lanham Hills Elementary School which would serve this property is currently operating over its listed capacity and there are no plans for any elementary schools in the Capital Improvements Program which would relieve this situation. The property, if developed in accordance with the allowable density, would generate approximately 134 elementary school children which would further overload the existing school.
>
> "It was therefore the opinion of the Planning Board that since adequate public facilities are neither existing or programmed to serve the area the proposed subdivision should be denied."

* * *

Nothing in the record suggests the Board held any kind of a hearing and Allen's testimony makes it quite clear that the only evidence or information before the Board when it denied the appellee's application was the check sheet sent up from the technical staff. All the Board could have learned from the check sheet was that last year's (September 1970) enrollment at West Lanham Hills Elementary was 28 pupils in excess of its capacity and that the property could yield 651 dwelling units. * * * The Board could also have learned that an increase in the capacity of West Lanham Hills *"or any other elementary schools in the vicinity"* was not contemplated. What is meant by "vicinity" or which "other elementary schools" the staff had in mind is anyone's guess. We are not to be persuaded that the Board could have given "due weight * * * [to] [t]he availability within a reasonable distance, and the adequacy of school * * * services," in the light of such trivial and inaccurate evidence.

In Baltimore Planning Commission v. Victor Development Co., 261 Md. 387, 275 A.2d 478 (1971), we chose not to deal with the question whether the (Baltimore) Commission had "the power to formulate a rule dealing with the effect of subdivisions upon schools," although we hinted there might be some question about it. Here we choose not to deal with the question whether public schools are "public services" as that expression is used in the enabling act. The appellee urges that the principle of ejusdem generis should apply because of the juxtaposition of "public services" with "lack of water supply, drainage, transportation, or other public services," and it is, to be sure, not a wholly unattractive argument.

The subdivision regulation does not undertake to restrict pupils to the school within the boundaries of the service area in which they reside.

The only limitation is that there must be an adequate school available "within a reasonable distance." Nor do the school authorities consider the boundaries of the service areas to be static and inflexible. Panor, it will be recalled, testified that they have "from year to year changed literally—practically all service areas of all existing schools." Reflecting upon Panor's testimony that the schools in the four contiguous areas have a capacity of 2,300 pupils and that the enrollment as of September 1972 was 251 less than capacity, one need not be especially perceptive to suppose that the area boundaries could readily be adjusted to take care of the 45 pupils said to be in excess of the capacity of West Lanham Hills Elementary School. One must, of course, assume the instant development and occupancy of the appellee's project, but one need not assume that it has been in the R–18 classification since 1964. That is a fact. The regulation does not define "reasonable distance" but we do not think the Board can be heard to say that a mile, or even a mile and one-half, is not a "reasonable distance."

Since we are fully persuaded that the Board's refusal to approve the appellee's preliminary plan was arbitrary and capricious the order of the trial court will be affirmed.

Order affirmed. Costs to be paid by the appellant.

Notes

1. In Corona–Norco Unified School Dist. v. City of Corona, 13 Cal. App.4th 1577, 17 Cal.Rptr.2d 236 (1993) the court held that a school district could not enjoin a city from giving subdivision approval for two projects on the ground of inadequate school facilities. The court based its decision on state statutes that allow school districts to impose exactions on developments for school purposes and concluded that the complex statutory scheme precluded denial of subdivision approval. Also see Grupe Development Co. v. Superior Court, 4 Cal.4th 911, 16 Cal.Rptr.2d 226, 844 P.2d 545 (1993).

In Cherokee Water & Sanitation Dist. v. El Paso County, 770 P.2d 1339 (Colo.App.1988), the court upheld a county regulation requiring all developers to demonstrate a 300 year water supply prior to subdivision approval. The case was a declaratory judgment action presenting a facial challenge to the regulation. The court said:

> Nor have the plaintiffs shown an unconstitutional taking of property. As the challenge is facial, plaintiffs must prove that the mere enactment deprived them of all reasonable use of their property. Landmark Land Co. v. City & County of Denver, 728 P.2d 1281 (Colo.1986), appeal dismissed sub nom., Harsh Investment Corp. v. City & County of Denver, 483 U.S. 1001, 107 S.Ct. 3222, 97 L.Ed.2d 729 (1987). Plaintiffs were unable to demonstrate that the regulation will prevent even residential development on their property, let alone any other reasonable use. Thus, no taking occurred by enactment of the regulation.
>
> Nor are we convinced that the regulation is arbitrary or capricious. Plaintiffs bore the burden of proving beyond a reasonable doubt that the regulations are not rationally and reasonably related to a valid governmental interest. Sellon v. City of Manitou Springs, 745 P.2d 229 (Colo.

1987). The evidence presented by the county demonstrates that the regulation is designed to insure that no development take place where there are not adequate water supplies for the future. Such an interest is valid, and the regulation is rationally and reasonably related thereto, thus satisfying both the federal and state constitutional requirements.

Also see Christianson v. Gasvoda, 242 Mont. 212, 789 P.2d 1234 (1990) where the court upheld denial of a subdivision because it would exacerbate drainage and flooding problems in flatlands below the developer's land. The same developer had previously developed three subdivisions in the uplands area, and the court said the problems created by the previous development justified rejection of the proposed subdivision. A similar case from Connecticut involved a steep slope development. Krawski v. Planning and Zoning Comm'n of Town of South Windsor, 21 Conn.App. 667, 575 A.2d 1036 (1990). And in Wood v. City of Madison, 260 Wis.2d 71, 659 N.W.2d 31 (2003) the court upheld denial of a subdivision because the commercial portion was incompatible with nearby agricultural uses, rejecting the argument that plat approval was being used to perform a zoning function.

In Beach v. Planning and Zoning Comm'n, 141 Conn. 79, 103 A.2d 814 (1954), the commission denied subdivision plat approval for a 145–lot subdivision for the following reasons: "(1) This land is adjacent to a new development which will contain 79 homes. (2) The Council has stated that the financial situation of the town is such that no schools could be built in this area for some time. (3) The additional Police and Fire protection which would be needed in this area cannot now be provided due to the financial situation of the town. (4) The report of the school superintendent shows that the new school in this area will be inadequate to provide for the children already living in this area soon after it opens." The court held that neither the enabling statute nor the subdivision ordinance authorized rejection of plat approval on those grounds and that the rejection was ultra vires. Compare Fallen Leaf Protection Ass'n v. South Tahoe Public Utility Dist., 46 Cal.App.3d 816, 120 Cal.Rptr. 538 (1975) which upheld an absolute prohibition of septic tanks and cesspools for waste disposal. Also compare Board of County Comm'rs of Cecil County v. Gaster, 285 Md. 233, 401 A.2d 666 (1979), where the court upheld denial of a subdivision because of traffic congestion in an area not programmed for new roads until 1990. And see Batch v. Town of Chapel Hill, 326 N.C. 1, 387 S.E.2d 655 (1990) where the court upheld denial of a subdivision plat for failure to coordinate with the town's transportation plan.

In Wolff v. Mooresville Plan Comm'n, 754 N.E.2d 589 (Ind.App.2001), the Court upheld the planning commission's denial of preliminary primary plat approval for a single-family residential subdivision of approximately 278 lots based upon the following findings: that the Plat as filed "failed to address issues concerning the treatment of sanitary waste in a sufficient manner to guarantee that there is a capacity to serve the proposed number of homes on the initial Plat; the applicant failed to provide sufficient information on drainage issues relating to the topography of the ground; health and safety issues concerning roadways and entryways due to topography (evidence presented that the Plat is not suitable due to topography problems, roadway problems and healthy and safety issues concerning sewer and water); and problems with access, sight distances and County approval of the access.''

2. In Walls v. Planning and Zoning Comm'n, 176 Conn. 475, 408 A.2d 252 (1979), the court held that adjacent property owners had no standing to challenge the approval of a subdivision. In State ex rel. Menkhus v.City of Pevely, 865 S.W.2d 871 (Mo.App.1993) the court held a property owner whose subdivision plat met all the requirements of the ordinance could not be denied approval, and in Ex Parte Pine Brook Lakes, Inc., 617 So.2d 1014 (Ala.1992) the court held that the county board improperly denied subdivision approval by merely referring to some possible future road construction in the area.

3. In the 1980's two developments made an impact on the conventional wisdom surrounding subdivision exactions. The twin forces of rapid inflation and the property tax revolt made more people aware of the fact that subdivision exactions have a powerful role in the cost of housing. In those states that have adopted limitations on the property tax, notably California through Proposition 13, one result was an increase in subdivision exactions and permit fees. Cities saw the loss of property tax revenues as reducing funding for municipal services that could be made up only by increasing revenues from other sources. Subdivision exactions, in this sense, would be a hidden tax imposed on new residents, reflected in the cost of housing. However, when coupled with rapid inflation, the increase in exactions became a more visible factor in housing costs. In some communities estimates were that exactions and other development regulations accounted for as much as twenty-five percent of the cost of a single-family dwelling. One result of this problem has been increased attention to ways in which the cost of housing can be lowered. See U.S. Dept. Housing and Urban Development, Reducing the Development Costs of Housing: Actions for State and Local Governments (1979); Ellickson, Suburban Growth Controls: An Economic and Legal Analysis, 66 Yale L.J. 385 (1977). In many communities, even in states without property tax revolt problems, inflationary forces have induced developers to seek reductions in exactions in order to keep the cost of housing down. Even traditional exactions have come under attack. Developers are questioning the necessity of sidewalks in residential subdivisions and the established street widths. They may ask for elimination of curb and gutter requirements, reduction of minimum lot sizes, and revision of building codes, all in the name of making housing affordable (and, incidentally, keeping them in business). In some cities developers are seeking permission to develop single-family and multi-family areas with private drives, rather than streets constructed to city standards and dedicated to the public. If a community resists the pressure for reduction of exactions, developers will frequently raise the spectre that they will pick up and move their operations to nearby cities where the regulatory costs are lower, leaving the community without a housing industry. No easy answers to these problems are available. However, some questions may be posed. Should exactions be standardized at the state level, rather than delegated to local government as is the present practice? Presumably, exactions are a result of the police power, delegated in the enabling legislation. Does the health, safety, morals and general welfare of the public justify thirty-foot wide streets with curb and gutter in the residential subdivisions of City A and twenty-five foot wide streets without

curb or gutter in City B? Would it be better and cheaper to have a standard set of exactions and codes for the entire state? Would such a change be politically feasible? Further, what is the relationship, if any, between growth controls, exactions, inflation and the cost of housing? See Patricia E. Salkin, Barriers to Affordable Housing: Are Land–Use Controls the Scapegoat?, Land Use Law (April 1993) p. 3. Also see Jerry Cheslow, Impact Fees Re-examined in California, N.Y. Times, Apr. 4, 1993, p. 31; this article discusses how impact fees can stunt growth in a financial recession.

SECTION 2. THE OFFICIAL MAP AND PUBLIC STREETS

In 1925, Philip Nichols and Frank B. Williams debated whether to use eminent domain or the police power to prevent building in officially mapped streets. See the 1925 Proceedings, National City Planning Conference 378 and following. Mr. Nichols argued for eminent domain, pointing to the quaint Yankee custom of exactly off-setting damages for eminent domain taking with the special benefits to the rest of the land. Mr. Williams took the police power position urging a board of adjustment to take care of hardship cases. It was pointed out that William Penn laid out a system of checkerboard streets for Philadelphia and that the official map has been popular in Pennsylvania ever since. The Randall map for New York City was authorized in 1807, and an official map for Baltimore in 1817. Mr. Williams said (at 396):

> The age of Washington was the age of city planning. The street plan of New York City, [way out to 155th street] already referred to, was protected by a state law providing that a property owner, when the city was ready to lay out the street and took the land necessary for the purpose, could recover no damages for improvements which he had made in the bed of a mapped street; and there were similar laws in other states. For many years these laws remained unchallenged in our statute books and were generally regarded as valid. But, before our Civil War, in 1861, a change of attitude occurred, and today except in the State of Pennsylvania, all these laws are, under decisions of our highest state courts, held to be a taking of property rights without compensation contrary to our state constitutions.

Kucirek and Beuscher, Wisconsin's Official Map Law, 1957 Wis. L.Rev. 176, 177, state:

> In essence the official map is a simple device. It is one way, but not the only way, to fix building lines. The official map may plat future as well as existing streets. Where future streets are mapped, subdividers must conform to the mapped street lay-out, unless they can prevail upon the proper officials to amend the map. Public sewer and water will be installed only in the bed of the mapped streets. Even more important, a landowner who builds in the bed of the mapped street may be refused compensation for his building when the street is ultimately opened and the mapped land taken. To guard against this drastic consequence, official map laws now customarily

require the landowner to obtain a building permit before proceeding with construction.

The official map of future streets has obvious advantages in terms of the public coffers. It assures that land needed for future streets will be available at bare land prices. Mapping of future streets also gives direction and pattern to future growth of the community, though some feel that the map casts the mold too inflexibly, especially if minor as well as major streets are mapped.

Where existing streets have been officially mapped, the map will often set widening lines (set-backs) warning that new structures must be located in conformance with their lines, and these also have obvious advantages in cutting costs of street widening. Again, a building permit is usually used to assure compliance.

The official map is not the only means of establishing building lines. Other familiar methods are:

(1) Set-back provisions in zoning ordinances;

(2) Set-back ordinances as such—ordinances stating that for prescribed streets no buildings are to be built any closer to the street line than a specified distance;

(3) Set-backs established on plats as a condition to subdivision approval;

(4) Set-back provisions in privately established deed restrictions (restrictive covenants);

(5) The now virtually obsolete method of purchasing set-back easements through eminent domain proceedings.

(6) In the subdivision process, as we have already seen, subdividers may be required to honor the master street plan insofar as that plan indicates street locations; and, of course, the subdivider may be required to install the street at his expense and in compliance with published standards.

The name "official map" is not universal. In Pennsylvania and California for instance, the same planning device is there referred to as "confirmed map" and "precise map" respectively. The name "official map" seems to have originated with Edward M. Bassett and Frank B. Williams, who wrote New York's 1926 act and in 1935 published a model official map act. They distinguished the "official map" sharply from the "master plan":

> A master plan embraces many features not included in an official map. The master plan, therefore, does not usually show precise data founded in careful surveys, while the official map, upon which the details of both public and private works must be based, should be capable of accurate interpretation. The master plan, therefore, may be characterized as plastic, the official map as rigid.

In other words, under the Bassett–Williams scheme, the master plan is not binding upon landowners; the official map is. The master plan is the general formulation, often reflected by non-precise maps, of the results of planning studies—studies not only of the circulatory system, but also of land use districts, location of parks and recreation areas, sites for public buildings and facilities, location of public utilities and other matters. The official map is intended to reflect some aspects of the master plan in a precise, accurate and legally binding manner.

Nonetheless, it is easy to overemphasize in practical terms the differences to the landowner between the officially enacted map on one hand and the commission-approved "unofficial" street plan on the other. Knowledgeable landowners are not apt to build in the bed of an "unofficially" mapped street or other proposed public site. True, the owner may know that he is entitled to compensation for his building when the land is ultimately taken for the public purpose. But he knows of the vagaries of valuation juries and in any case, compensation or no compensation, he does not want to build a structure only to have it torn down, perhaps only a short time later. Consequently many cities successfully guide development along future streets through master street plans, not backed by any legal sanctions except subdivision plat approval. Such plans are less successful in achieving voluntary set-backs along existing streets. Here the legal sanctions of a set-back ordinance or a precise official map are needed to keep the uncooperative owner "in line."

Another point of comparison between a master plan and an official map needs to be made. Even though the master plan is not backed by legal sanctions, it may blight the market for mapped real estate quite as effectively as an official map. If a would-be buyer learns that the land has been marked with a "green spot" on the master plan for a park or has been "master planned" as the bed of a proposed street or thoroughway, he will be as reluctant to buy as if the land had been officially mapped. He does not want to buy and develop land for his private use when he knows that it is earmarked for public taking.

HEADLEY v. CITY OF ROCHESTER

Court of Appeals of New York, 1936.
272 N.Y. 197, 5 N.E.2d 198.

LEHMAN, J.

The plaintiff since 1918 has been the owner of premises in the city of Rochester which are bounded on the south by East avenue and on the west by North Goodman street. East avenue and North Goodman street have been, for more than twenty years, public streets or highways. In 1931, pursuant to article 3 of the General City Law (Cons.Laws, ch. 21), the Council of the city of Rochester passed an ordinance which amended, changed and added to an official map or plan previously adopted by the Council "so as to correct and revise said established Official Map or Plan and to lay out new streets and highways and to widen existing highways." In that map or plan the southerly twenty-five feet of plaintiff's said premises are included in East avenue, as widened, and a strip of plaintiff's premises extending along its westerly edge is included in North Goodman street, as widened. The plaintiff has brought an action to obtain a judgment declaring "that the ordinance and map and plan adopted by the said City of Rochester as aforesaid is unconstitutional and void." At Special Term the complaint was dismissed. The Appellate Division reversed and granted judgment "declaring that the ordinance, map and plan herein involved, are void and ineffectual to create any limitations or restrictions upon the use or conveyance of plaintiff's property."

By chapter 690 of the Laws of 1926 the Legislature added article 3, entitled "Official Maps and Planning Boards," to the General City Law. That article empowers the legislative body of every city to establish an official map or plan of the city showing the streets, highways and parks theretofore laid out and established by law. (Sec. 26.) It empowers such legislative body "whenever and as often as it may deem it for the public interest, to change or add to the official map or plan of the city so as to lay out new streets, highways or parks, or to widen or close existing streets, highways or parks." (Sec. 29.) It further empowers the legislative body of the city to create a planning board of five members and it requires that before making any addition or change in an official map in accordance with section 29 "the matter shall be referred to the planning board for report thereon." The planning board is given "power and authority to make such investigations, maps and reports and recommendations in connection therewith relating to the planning and development of the city as to it seems desirable." (Sec. 31.)

The adoption or revision of a general map pursuant to the provisions of the General City Law does not have the effect of divesting the title of the owner of land in the bed of a street as shown on the map; it does not have the effect of placing upon the city a duty to begin, presently, condemnation proceedings to acquire such land. Article 3 of the statute provides the machinery for intelligent planning in advance for the needs of the city as the city is expected to grow in the future. Only time can prove whether the city has wisely gauged the future, and the city is under no compulsion to open any street shown on the map unless and until the legislative body of the city decides that it is actually needed.

The mere adoption of a general plan or map showing streets and parks to be laid out or widened in the future, without acquisition by the city of title to the land in the bed of the street, can be of little benefit to the public if the development of the land abutting upon and in the bed of the proposed streets proceeds in a haphazard way, without taking into account the general plan adopted and, especially, if permanent buildings are erected on the land in the bed of the proposed street which would hamper its acquisition or use for its intended purpose. So long as the owners of parcels of land which lie partly in the bed of streets shown on such a map are free to place permanent buildings in the bed of a proposed street and to provide private ways and approaches which have no relation to the proposed system of public streets, the integrity of the plan may be destroyed by the haphazard or even malicious development of one parcel or tract to the injury of other owners who may have developed their own tracts in a manner which conforms to the general map or plan.

A statutory requirement that a city must acquire title to the land in the bed of the streets shown on the general map or plan, and to provide compensation for the land taken, would create practical difficulties which would drastically limit, if, indeed, they did not render illusory, any power conferred upon the city to adopt a general map or plan which will make provision for streets which will be needed only if present anticipations of the future development of the city are realized. On the other hand, to leave the land in private ownership, and, without compensation to the owner, incumber it with restrictions upon its use which would result in diminution in its value might be inequitable and perhaps even beyond the power of the State. To meet the difficulty, the Legislature has provided in section 35 of the General City Law that "for the purpose of preserving the integrity of such official map or plan no permit shall hereafter be issued for any building in the bed of any street or highway shown or laid out on such map or plan, provided, however, that if the land within such mapped street or highway is not yielding a fair return on its value to the owner, the board of appeals or other similar board in any city which has established such a board having power to make variances or exception in zoning regulations shall have power in a specific case * * * to grant a permit for a building in such street or highway which will as little as practicable increase the cost of opening such street or highway, or tend to cause a change of such official map or plan, and such board may impose reasonable requirements as a condition of granting such permit, which requirements shall inure to the benefit of the city." The sole complaint of the plaintiff is that so long as that section remains in force the effect of the ordinance adopted by the city is to restrict the use to which the plaintiff may put his land in the bed of the street and to that extent constitutes a taking of his property, and that, since the city is not required to pay any compensation to him unless or until at some time in the indefinite future it may choose to take title to the land, the effect of the ordinance is to deprive him of his property without due process of law.

Not every restriction placed by authority of the State upon the use of property for the general welfare of the State, without payment of compensation, constitutes a deprivation of property without due process of law. This court has sustained a reasonable restriction upon the height of signs on roofs, saying: "Compensation for such interference with and restriction in the use of property is found in the share that the owner enjoys in the common benefit secured to all."

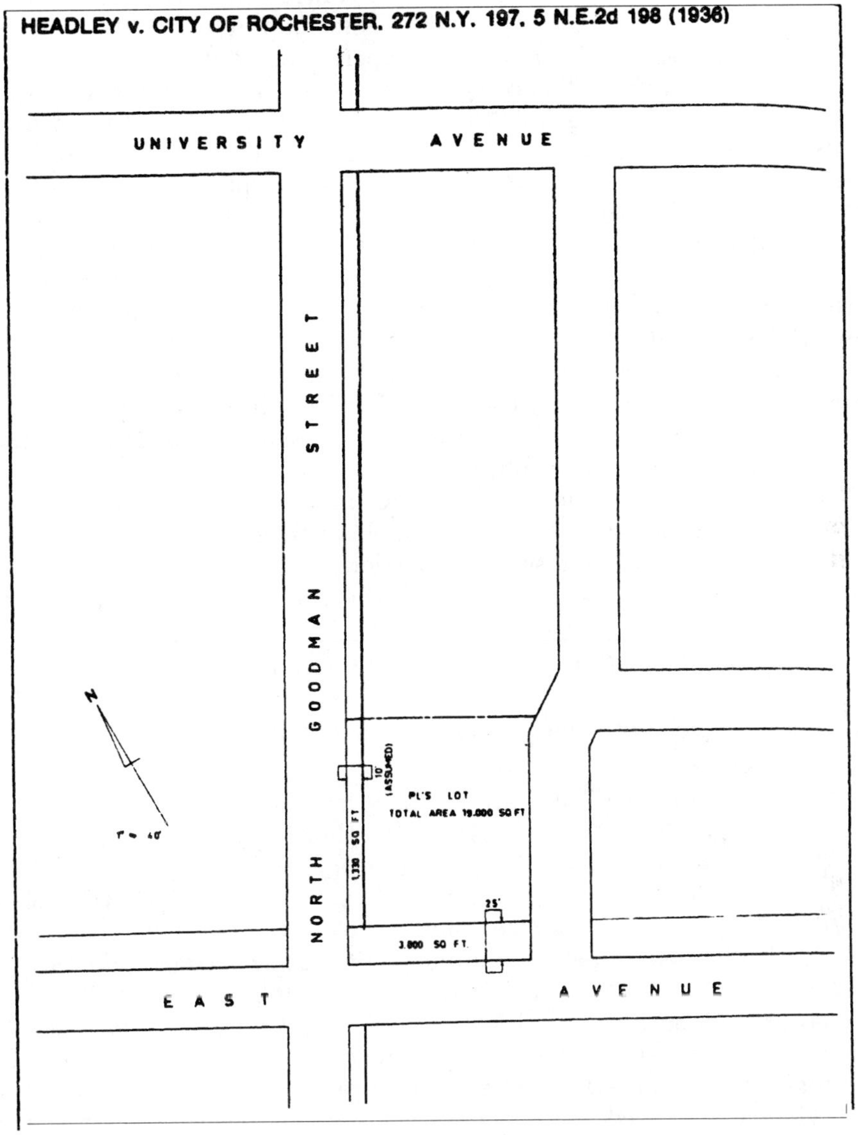

People ex rel. M. Wineburgh Adv. Co. v. Murphy, 195 N.Y. 126, 131, 88 N.E. 17. Under the provisions of the General City Law the owner of land in the bed of the street shown in a map remains as free to alien the land or to use it as he sees fit as he was before the map was adopted, except in one respect. If he desires to improve the property by erecting a building for which a permit is required, the grant of such a permit is surrounded by drastic conditions or restrictions which will in many cases act as an obstacle to such use of the land.

* * *

* * * The complaint alleges only the conclusion of the pleader that by reason of the filing of the ordinance and map or plan "the plaintiff has been, and is, deprived of his property without the payment of compensation therefor." The complaint is silent as to how the plaintiff is injured by the ordinance and the map. The stipulation of facts upon which the case was submitted for decision again fails to indicate in what manner the ordinance has caused damage to the plaintiff or interferes with any use to which the plaintiff desires to put the land. On the contrary, it appears from the stipulated facts that "the plaintiff has at present no plans for the use of said premises nor any particular desire as to the purposes for which he expects to use the same" and "that the plaintiff, because of the claim of the defendant under said ordinance and map, is undecided as to whether he shall endeavor to build upon said premises or endeavor to sell the same." It may be added, incidentally, that the stipulated facts fail to show that there is at present any actual controversy with the city as to the use to which the property may be put, and it appears "that the plaintiff has made no application to the Planning Board, Board of Appeals or Supervisor of Zoning of the City of Rochester for a permit to use those portions of his property included in said map as widened streets or to build thereon or to alter any existing structures therein."

Regardless of the form of action in which relief is sought, the courts will not declare a statute unconstitutional unless and until such relief is necessary for the protection of some right of the suitor guaranteed by the Constitution. * * *

The opinion of the Appellate Division leans heavily upon Forster v. Scott, 136 N.Y. 577, 32 N.E. 976, as authority for its decision. The analogy between the cases is quite illusory and the principles here involved are not touched by that case. There the city of New York, in accordance with the provisions of chapter 681 of the Laws of 1886, filed a map of a proposed street or avenue which as the court pointed out *"covers the entire lot"* of the plaintiff. The statute provided that "no compensation shall be allowed for any building, erection or construction which at any time, subsequent to the filing of the maps, plans, or profiles mentioned in section six hundred and seventy-two of the act, may be built, erected or placed in part or in whole upon or through any street, avenue, road, public square or place exhibited upon such maps, plans or profiles." (p. 582.) The plaintiff made a contract to sell his land to the defendant. He agreed to convey a good title to the land "in fee simple free from any lien or encumbrance." The defendant refused the title, claiming that the filing of the map created an incumbrance upon the property. The validity of the title was submitted to the court upon stipulated facts. It appeared from them that no building was erected on the plaintiff's land and "the same is a vacant lot which derives almost its entire value from the possibility of being used for building purposes. If the lot cannot now be built upon without the house being destroyed, without compensation in the event of the street being opened as prescribed by the statutes above set forth, the lot is not worth what defendant agreed to pay, whereas if it can be used for building purposes it is worth at least $5,000." In other words, the statute purported to give the city the right at some indefinite time in the future to appropriate the land of the plaintiff shown on the map without paying for it the value it would then have if, pending such appropriation, its owner chose to improve it for the only purpose for which it had substantial value.

The court there said: "An encumbrance is said to import every right to or interest in the land, which may subsist in another, to the diminution of the value of the land, but consistent with the power to pass the fee by a conveyance." (p. 582.) If the statute was valid the land "could not be used for building purposes, except at the risk to the owner of losing the cost of the building at some time in the future." (p. 583.) The value of the land was derived from its availability for building purposes and that value would be drastically reduced if the owner could not obtain compensation for the improvements put upon the land. Since these facts were stipulated it could hardly be doubted that the statute attempted to create a public right or interest in the land which diminished its value and would, therefore, constitute an incumbrance as defined by the court. Then in an action between vendor and vendee under a contract of sale, the court was bound to pass upon the validity of the statute.

Every element which led the court to find in that case that the filing of the map, in accordance with the statute there challenged, created, if the statute were valid, an incumbrance upon the property, is wanting in the case now under review. The statute here does not purport to give to the city the right to appropriate the plaintiff's land or any part of it for less than the full value of the lands with the improvements thereon erected at the time of such appropriation. The only restrictions upon the use of any part of the plaintiff's land while title thereto remains in the plaintiff result indirectly from the conditions which the statute attaches to the grant thereafter of a permit to erect a building upon the small portion of plaintiff's land which, as shown on the map, will lie in the bed of the street on which the plaintiff's land abuts, if or when at some time in the future the city may desire to carry out its intention to widen the street. Since it is affirmatively shown that the plaintiff has no plans at present for the use of the premises it seems plain that what this court said and decided in the case of Forster v. Scott (supra) cannot possibly be regarded as any precedent, for the grant of a judgment declaring the statute invalid, unless from the facts here presented the court as matter of law would be constrained to draw the inference that the conditions which the Legislature has sought to impose upon the grant of a permit for the use of a small part of plaintiff's land, creates a limitation upon its use "to the diminution of the value of the land."

No inference of law, indeed no inference of fact, that the attempted condition has affected or will affect the use to which the plaintiff's land will be put or has diminished the value of the land, may be drawn from the stipulated facts. There is no suggestion that a plot of nineteen thousand square feet cannot be suitably improved and put to the most profitable use by the erection of a building which does not encroach upon the small portions which may be used hereafter to widen the street. Sometimes land owners in a particular district assume mutual obligations to set back buildings some distance from the streets. Sometimes such obligations are imposed by zoning ordinance. Sometimes an owner does so voluntarily because he believes that such a setback is the best use for the land immediately abutting on the street. The plaintiff or any successor in title to the property could use the land within the bed of the widened street for such purpose even without a permit. It may be the best use to which that land could be put, even if no map had been adopted, and there were no probability that the city would in time widen the street. Certainly it cannot be said that owners of property do not receive any benefit from the adoption of general maps or plans for the development of city streets, if they can develop their land with some assurance that other owners will not be permitted to frustrate the plan, maliciously or unreasonably. Whether the State may impose conditions for the issuance of permits in order to protect the integrity of the plan of a city where it appears that such conditions interfere with a reasonable use to which the land would otherwise be put or diminishes the value of the land, should not now be decided. Without proof that the imposition of such conditions has deprived an owner of land of some benefit he would otherwise derive from the land, there can be no deprivation of property for which compensation should be made.

Solicitude for the protection of the rights of private property against encroachment by government for a supposed public benefit does not justify the courts in declaring invalid a public law which serves a public purpose, because ten years after it has been on the statute books a single owner, without proof, or even claim, of actual injury, asserts that he has been deprived of his property.

The judgment of the Appellate Division should be reversed and that of the Special Term affirmed, with costs in this court and in the Appellate Division.

NIGRO v. PLANNING BOARD OF THE BOROUGH OF SADDLE RIVER

Supreme Court of New Jersey, 1991.
122 N.J. 270, 584 A.2d 1350.

Garibaldi, J.

In this case, we consider the binding nature of a municipality's official map on local planning board decisions regarding subdivision approvals.

The Demarest family owns a twenty-seven-acre farm in Saddle River. Plaintiff, James Nigro, entered into a contract with the Demarests to purchase ten acres of their property. The subject property was landlocked. In his subdivision application, Nigro proposed an access road servicing the proposed lots through an additional piece of property fronting on Twin Brooks Road that he bought for that purpose. The official map of Saddle River showed no road on Nigro's property but showed a "proposed street" on the portion of the Demarest property not sold to Nigro but retained by the Demarests for farming.

In March 1988, defendant, the Saddle River Planning Board ("Planning Board" or "Board"), denied Nigro's application for preliminary approval of a major subdivision. Admitting that the case presented "a close question," the Board ruled that Nigro's application failed to conform to the intent of the Saddle River master plan, and that the location of the subdivision access road on Nigro's property conflicted with the proposed street on the official map, located on the Demarest property, which the Board deemed "conclusive" and binding under N.J.S.A. 40:55D–32. That statute provides, in part, that a town's "official map shall be deemed conclusive with respect to the location ... of streets ..., whether or not such streets ... are improved or unimproved or are in actual physical existence." * * *

George Demarest and his wife, Elizabeth, own a 27.2–acre plot of land that the family has farmed for over a century. The Demarests want to continue to farm some property, but, as Mr. Demarest testified, since they are getting older, they want to sell some of their acreage. They decided to sell ten acres in the southerly portion of their property and to continue farming their remaining land. Mr. Demarest further testified that he refused Nigro's offer to purchase the entire tract. He explained that it would be impossible to bring a road in from Glenwood Drive and farm in the back of the tract. Finally, he stated that he and his family are still active, do not want to give up farming, and have a son and daughter-in-law who desire to continue farming.

Accordingly, Nigro contracted to purchase approximately ten acres that constitute the southwest corner of the Demarest family farm. The entire farm is circumscribed by the rear portions of developed residential properties along Glenwood Drive to the north and along Twin Brooks Road to the south. Nigro's plot abuts no streets currently in existence; it is effectively landlocked. For the sole purpose of gaining access to the ten acres, Nigro purchased for $1,900,000 an adjacent property fronting Twin Brooks Road.

Thereafter, on January 14, 1988, Nigro applied to the Planning Board for preliminary approval of a major subdivision of his plot, providing for four residential lots. The Board had rejected Nigro's previous application for subdivision of the same property in October 1987. The lots proposed in the 1988 application conformed to the required areas and frontages of local zoning laws. Nigro's plan proposed an access road (hereinafter "access road") from Twin Brooks Road, running north into the ten-acre plot, and ending in a cul-de-sac on the property he is acquiring. However, the official map shows the only proposed street in the area (hereinafter "proposed street") as running south and west from Glenwood Drive across the Demarest Farm and ending in a cul-de-sac.

On March 22, 1988, the Planning Board denied Nigro's application because it failed to conform to the intent of the master plan in that it proposed two cul-de-sacs, whereas the master plan indicated only one. The Board also stressed that the proposal for a new street in the plan could not be approved because it deviated from the proposed street on the official map layout, which the Board deemed conclusive under N.J.S.A. 40:55D–32.

The basic conflict arises in creating a public street in an area where single family residential homes exist where no street was ever contemplated, and in a location not conforming to the planning process of the municipality which clearly contemplated development from Glenwood Drive. [Planning Board Resolution, Mar. 22, 1989.]

Both the access road and the proposed street end in cul-de-sacs, the access road's cul-de-sac being located entirely on the property to be acquired by Nigro. * * *

In reviewing the question of whether the location of proposed streets shown on an official map is conclusive and binding on a planning board, we first review the history of official maps and master plans in New Jersey as the contextual background for our consideration of the statutory scheme of the Municipal Land Use Law (MLUL). N.J.S.A. 40:55D–1 to –129.

A. History of the Official Map

The term "official map" was first used by Basset and Williams in their model "County Planning Enabling Act" published in 1935. Anderson, Law of Zoning in New Jersey § 24.01 (1989). Although an official map is a precise map, showing the existing and proposed streets, highways, drainage systems, and other public improvements, it is essentially a tool of planning, rather than zoning. An official map "does not portray the zoning districts or relate to the zoning plan except insofar as both the zoning Scheme and the official map undertake to implement a common plan for the development of land." Ibid.

Originally, official maps were regarded as mere descriptions of future plans for public improvements. Their function was one of simple notification. In an early case, the United States Supreme Court explained:

> The object of the recording of the map is to give notice to all persons of the system of highways proposed to be established by subsequent proceedings of condemnation. It does not restrict in any way the use or improvement of lands by their owners before the commencement of proceedings for condemnation of lands for such highways, nor does it limit the damages to be awarded in such proceedings. [Bauman v. Ross, 167 U.S. 548, 597, 17 S.Ct. 966, 985, 42 L.Ed. 270, 291 (1897).]

Later views, however, have given more authority to the plans proposed in official maps. "If an official map were no more than a graphic expression of a plan for future development its legal effect would be negligible and its practical impact might be slight.'' Anderson, Law of Zoning in New Jersey, supra, at § 24.10. The contemporary view of the official map as a land-use control device thus accords weight to the legal effect of the official map's adoption.

The major premise underlying the adoption of the official map is to provide for orderly municipal growth at the least cost to the taxpayer. 6A Powell on Real Property P 874[2] (1990 Supp.). An official map enables a municipality to limit development of lands designated or delineated for future public use and thereby reduce the cost of eventual condemnation and shift some of the cost of public improvements to the developer in connection with the approval process. "The purpose of the official map [is] to insure the proper location and economical acquisition of streets . . .'' Anderson, Law of Zoning in New Jersey, supra, at § 24.02. Once an official map is adopted, it may be used to demonstrate a municipality's determination of the location of streets, parks, and other municipal improvements. The legislation enabling municipalities to adopt official maps may provide for sanctions to limit development on the lands on which public facilities are proposed, and establish the official map as a standard for developmental approval. See id. at § 24.06; N.J.S.A. 40:55D–32, –34.

However, the official map does not "interpose an insuperable barrier to approval of a plat which shows some alteration of streets . . . which are shown on such map.'' Anderson, American Law of Zoning, § 24.08 (1986). "[S]treets, highways, parks, and other proposed public improvements shown on the official map do not prevent the platting and dedication or reservation of new streets, highways and parks . . .'' Ibid. A proposed plat may be approved and filed so long as it "adds streets and makes changes in mapped streets which serve the overall purpose of the community plan . . .'' Ibid.

2. New Jersey Statutory Scheme

New Jersey's statutory scheme generally follows that outlined above. Article 5, containing the official-map sections of the Municipal Land Use Law (MLUL), establishes that a municipality's governing body "may by ordinance adopt or amend an official map of the municipality, which shall reflect the appropriate provisions of any municipal master plan . . .'' N.J.S.A. 40:55D–32. The official map is defined by the MLUL simply as a map adopted by ordinance pursuant to article 5. N.J.S.A. 40:55D–5.

N.J.S.A. 40:55D–32, particularly the second paragraph, is the focus of this appeal. The governing body may by ordinance adopt or amend an official map of the municipality . . .

* * * The official map shall be deemed conclusive with respect to the location and width of streets and public drainage ways and the location and extent of flood control basins and public areas, whether or not such streets, ways, basins or areas are improved or unimproved or

are in actual physical existence. Upon receiving an application for development, the municipality may reserve for future public use, the aforesaid streets, ways, basins, and areas in the manner provided in [N.J.S.A. 40:55D–44]. [L.1975, c. 291, § 32, eff. Aug. 1, 1976.]

Until now, we have not directly considered this statute. * * *

In contrast to official maps, master plans have received extensive consideration from legal commentators and the courts. In New Jersey, the master plan is the centerpiece of land use planning. Pursuant to the MLUL, it is "a composite of one or more written or graphic proposals for the development of the municipality." N.J.S.A. 40:55D–5. It may be adopted by a municipal planning board only after a public hearing. N.J.S.A. 40:55D–28. Its required contents are numerous and detailed. Ibid. Its influence is also far-reaching; indeed, the land use and housing elements of a master plan must be adopted before a municipality adopts a zoning ordinance, N.J.S.A. 40:55D–62, and a zoning ordinance inconsistent with or not designed to effectuate the land use and housing plan elements of the master plan must be accompanied by a resolution explaining the inconsistency. Id. * * *

Various provisions of the MLUL, including a requirement that the master plan be examined and updated regularly, N.J.S.A. 40:55D–89, reflect the continuing importance of the master plan.

Against this background for assessing the conclusiveness of official maps and master plans, we now address the situation in Saddle River. The 1979 Saddle River master plan was developed from master plans that had been prepared in 1950 and 1968. The 1968 master plan was the first to include a proposed street into the Demarest property. That proposed street ran from Glenwood Drive. The official map of the municipality provides that development of the property in question should be serviced by a roadway from Glenwood Drive; that roadway is identical to the proposed street in the master plan. Indeed, the official map is identical with the street layout depicted on the master plan. The official map has been amended only once, over ten years ago, since its adoption almost two decades ago.

The Saddle River Planning Board held hearings regarding the proposed Nigro subdivision on February 9, 1988, and March 8, 1988. Several of those who took part in the municipality's planning process testified at the hearings, including Robert Strong, the planner who prepared the 1979 Saddle River master plan, and George Demarest. Both Demarest and Strong stated that the proposed street's origin at Glenwood Drive rather than Twin Brooks Road reflects historical happenstance rather than scrupulous planning. Likewise, both Demarest and Strong testified that Twin Brooks was always the most feasible access to the Demarest tract but that Mr. Demarest was unable to secure the right-of-way to Twin Brooks. Mr. Demarest testified:

> Back in about 1966, I was called by the Mayor and Council or Planning Board of Saddle River and there was a subdivision going in north of me, which is now Glenwood, and they wanted me to come

> over because if they approved it without Me getting a right-of-way, the farm would be landlocked the way it was set up on the maps. The only way that the fire department or police department could have gotten in, if they approved the subdivision without any entrance would have been through Hillsdale and the governing body, which is proper, didn't want to have to send any equipment through Hillsdale to get back into Saddle River.
>
> So I purchased a right-of-way, the 50 foot right-of-way that everybody talks about off Glenwood.... There was no access of [sic] Twin Brooks. But when I was there at the meeting, the planners and the Mayor and Council said the best way to have come in would have been off Twin Brooks and asked me if there was any way I could get an easement or right-of-way in from Twin Brooks.
>
> Anyway, I couldn't get a right-of-way in from Twin Brooks, so my only other alternative was to buy the easement off of Glenwood.

Mr. Demarest's testimony was supported by that of Robert Strong, a professional planner, who was a consultant to the Saddle River Planning Board from the late 1960s through the adoption of the Master Plan in 1978.

> At that time in 1978 there appeared to be only one alternative. The only available alternative was an easement ... on Glenwood Drive.... That is the way the master plan showed the development of the site because that was the only alternative that was available.

Throughout his testimony Mr. Strong emphasized that Glenwood was chosen not because it was the best but because it was the only available access. * * *

Further, Mr. Strong testified that the master plan depicted an arrangement of minor streets merely to illustrate the character of earlier streets in Saddle River so that the remaining undeveloped lands would preserve the area's quiet and safe residential character by creating additional streets free from through traffic. The design was meant to be illustrative but not binding on any specific piece of property. Mr. Strong reinforced the view that the master plan should not be read as though it is cast in stone. Referring specifically to the 1978 master plan, Mr. Strong testified:

> Obviously the key here is "possible location." This was not meant to be the only location. What was important, insofar as the master plan was concerned, was to achieve subdivision design which would meet the intent and purpose of the plan. That intent and purpose was to assure the continuance of quiet, safe residential streets.

In Mr. Strong's opinion this subdivision "is totally in accord with the 1978 Master Plan." Moreover, in his opinion, access on Twin Brooks is "actually preferable" to access on Glenwood. Mr. Strong emphasized that the Twin Brooks access was not available in 1978. He noted two considerations that support approval of Nigro's plan.

One is that this arrangement which is shown, including the future extensions of it, provide shorter cul-de-sacs than that which would be required if the only access would be off Glenwood Drive. That inherently is from a planning standpoint a more desirable way to design in this kind of street system. Cul-de-sacs, which provide lots of benefits for residential areas, also produce lots of problems in terms of municipal services to the area. The shorter they are, the better off the municipality is. You provide the same basic advantages for the residences and you don't provide as many disadvantages to the municipality.

Secondly, and equally important, is that by starting access to the Demarest property at this point, we're starting at the lowest elevation on the property, whereas the scheme that is illustrated on the master plan would start from a relatively high elevation on the property. From a standpoint of engineering design, particularly with respect to drainage and certainly with regard to other potential utility services, this is a far more preferable place to start the development of the entire tract.

Likewise, Mr. Doolittle, the professional engineer and land surveyor who prepared the Nigro subdivision plan, testified that the access road with a grade of seven percent was "absolutely" safer than the proposed street with a grade of twelve to thirteen percent. * * *

Following testimony by Strong, Demarest, Doolittle, several area residents, mainly from Twin Brooks Road, and others, the Planning Board denied Nigro's application on two separate grounds. First, the Board concluded that the application undercut the goals of the master plan and did not represent good planning because it created too many cul-de-sacs. Nigro's proposal necessitated two separate roads for the development of the entire Demarest farm while the official proposed street could service the entire farm property. The trial court disagreed, finding that sound planning reasons supported approval of the access road. The court specifically noted that safety considerations favored approval of Nigro's proposal because the grade of the Twin Brooks access road would be significantly less steep than the proposed street from Glenwood (6.91 degrees versus 12.85 degrees). The Appellate Division found that this qualitative evaluation of planning rationale was not "relevant to the principal issue in this case" and did not address the comparative benefits of the two proposals. 237 N.J.Super. at 307 n. 1, 567 A.2d 1010.

Second, the Planning Board concluded that N.J.S.A. 40:55D–32 prevented it from approving Nigro's application because of its finding that the location of the access road conflicted with the site of the proposed street. The Board acknowledged that "[t]he case might be different if there was no other access available to the property in question." In our view, the Board's conclusion that Nigro's access road was "in conflict" with the proposed street constitutes the critical flaw in the Planning Board's analysis of the case. There is no other access available to Mr. Nigro. The Board, despite Mr. Demarest's testimony that he would not sell Nigro the portion of his property traversed by the proposed street, persisted in its determination that only the Glenwood street would be approved, effectively preventing Nigro from subdividing the property he proposed to acquire.

The resolution also reveals other flaws in the Board's reasoning. By insisting on adherence to streets proposed on the official map for purposes of subdivision approval, the Board appeared to assume that streets shown on the official map are immutable. That assumption is unfounded, particularly when an official map is infrequently amended or updated, as is the case with Saddle River. Moreover, Nigro points to the two recent decisions by the Saddle River Planning Board granting subdivision approval to applications that contained streets not shown on the official map as support for the view that even the Planning Board does not consider the official map street designations to be binding and exclusive.

In reaching our decision, we consider the nature of an official map. We acknowledge that an official map "is more than a chart to guide future development." Anderson, Law of Zoning in New Jersey, supra, at P 24.06. With respect to the designation of major streets, drainage facilities, flood control basins, and public areas, a municipality may properly insist on substantial adherence to the planning choices reflected on its official map, allowing deviations in subdivision or site plan proposals only when reasonably justified by the particular conditions and circumstances. But with respect to its designation of minor roadways, such as the proposed street on the Demarest tract, a municipality should not insist on rigid compliance with its official map. To adopt Saddle River's position would be to elevate the official map to the status of uncompromising forecaster of future development within a municipality. Such a strict view does not comport with the underlying goal of municipal planning: to promote the general welfare. Planning must ultimately be a flexible process, and the fact that the location of a proposed street on an official map differs from that of a street proposed by a developer does not by itself allow or require a planning board to withhold approval of a development proposal. The Board's position unnecessarily restricts the planning process. * * *

We also find that N.J.S.A. 40:55D–32 does not prohibit a planning board from approving a subdivision application that proposes an access road not shown on the official map. Here, the official map showed only one access to the entire twenty-seven-acre farm. Only ten acres of that farm were sold, and those ten acres do not abut the proposed street or any other existing street. The purchaser who bought an adjacent lot fronting an existing street is not categorically prohibited by N.J.S.A. 40:55D–32 from creating a new access road not shown on the official map to enter his ten acres.

The proposed street and the access road now serve two distinct properties owned by two parties. The proposed street provides access to the Demarest property and the Nigro access road to the Nigro property. To freeze the development of the entire twenty-seven-acre tract on the basis of proposals in the official map would effectively force the Demarests to sell or retain the entire parcel.

Planning connotes both flexibility and stability. Under the MLUL, a planning board has the power to exercise control over development of roads proposed in a subdivision. In a case where the location of a proposed road directly conflicts with a critical element of a town's planning, such as a major county thoroughfare, a planning board should consider denying approval of the subdivision. Indeed, an official map deserves the highest degree of deference in such situations.

But where there is no direct conflict between the access road and the proposed street, where there is no other access available to the property owner, where the access road arguably reflects planning comparable to that of the proposed street, then the board should work with the owner and suggest modifications to mitigate any perceived problems. The board cannot deny the property owner's subdivision and have the land remain forever landlocked.

In conclusion, we hold that an official map deserves substantial but not absolute deference in planning board decision-making regarding subdivision approvals. Although a clear conflict with a street proposed on a municipality's official map may provide a basis for a planning board to reject a subdivision application, the official map should not be seen as immutable. Certainly, the statutory requirements for adoption and amendment of an official map suggest that streets proposed on an official map should receive substantial consideration.

However, to fulfill its duty of "guid[ing] the appropriate use or development of all lands ... in a manner which will promote the public health, safety, morals and general welfare," N.J.S.A. 40:55D–2(a), a planning board should not automatically reject applications that do not conform entirely with officially-proposed streets. * * *

LAKE CITY CORPORATION v. CITY OF MEQUON

Supreme Court of Wisconsin, 1997.
207 Wis.2d 155, 558 N.W.2d 100.

N. Patrick Crooks, J.

The City of Mequon (Mequon) seeks review of a published decision of the court of appeals, which reversed and remanded a judgment of the Circuit Court for Ozaukee County, Joseph D. McCormack, Judge. The court of appeals held that, under Wis. Stat. § 236.13(1)(c) (1991–92) a local master plan is consistent with an official map only to the extent the master plan reflects issues encompassed in the official map. Accordingly, the court of appeals held that Mequon's Plan Commission (Plan Commission) improperly denied preliminary plat approval to Lake City Corporation (Lake City) on the grounds that the plat conflicted with an element contained only in the master plan. We conclude that, under § 236.13(1)(c), a master plan is consistent with an official map if any common elements contained in both the master plan and official map are not contradictory. We further conclude that a master plan is consistent with an official map even if the master plan contains additional elements that the official map does not. We therefore hold that a city plan commission may rely on an element contained solely in a master plan to reject plat approval. Thus, we reverse the decision of the court of appeals.

However, it does not necessarily follow that a master plan is inconsistent with an official map if the master plan contains elements that the official map does not. A master plan, pursuant to Wis. Stat. § 62.23(2), is likely to contain additional elements. Yet, a master plan is not incompatible with an official map simply because the master plan contains additional elements. So long as any issues addressed in both a master plan and an official map are not contradictory, the master plan is consistent with the official map.

We additionally accept Mequon's interpretation because it gives effect to the words "master plan" in Wis. Stat. § 236.13(1)(c), whereas Lake City's interpretation does not. Under Lake City's interpretation, a plan commission can rely on a master plan only to the limited extent that it reflects issues contained in an official map. Accordingly, the words "master plan" are rendered superfluous, because the master plan serves as nothing more than a conduit to the official map. If the legislature had intended such a result, it need not have included the words "master plan" in the statute; it could have simply included the words "official map."

We further reject Lake City's proffered interpretation because it leads to an illogical result. Under Wis. Stat. § 236.11, a final plat is entitled to approval only if it "conforms substantially ... to local plans ... adopted as authorized by law...." The reference in § 236.11 to local (master) plans is not qualified by reference to an official map. Accordingly, if we were to accept Lake City's interpretation, this would result in the following: under § 236.11 a plan commission would have authority to deny final plat approval based on any element contained in a master plan, whereas under § 236.13(1)(c) it would have authority to deny preliminary plat approval based on an element contained in a master plan only if the element was similarly contained in an official map. Not only is this result absurd, but it also directly contradicts § 236.13(1)(c). Section 236.13(1)(c) explicitly applies to preliminary and final plats, and therefore indicates that a plan commission's authority to review both preliminary and final plats under ch. 236 should be substantially similar.

Application of Lake City's interpretation would lead to an additional illogical result. Pursuant to Wis. Stat. §§ 62.23(2), (3), and (6)(b), a city is not required to have an official map, nor is a municipality prohibited from having a master plan in the absence of an official map. Under Lake City's interpretation of Wis. Stat. § 236.13(1)(c), if a municipality has only a master plan, then the master plan could never serve as the basis for the denial of preliminary plat approval, since none of the issues addressed in the master plan would be similarly addressed in the (non-existent) official map. Therefore, in these circumstances, § 236.13(1)(c) would be rendered a nullity. Again, this result defies common sense, because the plan commission could then deny final plat approval based upon any element contained in the master plan under Wis. Stat. § 236.11. * * *

Finally, we conclude that the 1957 interpretive commentary to Wis. Stat. § 236.13 supports Mequon's interpretation of this statute. The interpretive commentary states: "The master plan standing alone has no legal teeth. But for plat approval purposes 236.13(1) puts legal teeth into the relatively few master plans that do exist in this state." Jacob H. Beuscher, Interpretive Commentary [1957], Wis. Stat. Ann. § 236.13 (West 1987 & Supp.1996). Mequon's interpretation is consistent with the legislature's intent to put "legal teeth" into master plans, because it allows city plan commissions to continue to rely on master plans to deny plat approval. * * *

III.

In Chapter 236, the legislature has delegated the power to approve subdivision plats to municipalities. * * * In particular, the legislature has given municipalities the discretion to delegate their plat approval power to city plan commissions. Where a municipality has delegated such power, as is the case here, the city plan commission has the power to deny plat approval based on an element contained in a master plan under Wis. Stat. § 236.13(1)(c).

However, in Wis. Stat. § 236.13(1)(c), the legislature did not indicate that a plan commission's ability to rely on a master plan is limited by zoning ordinances. If the legislature had intended this, it could have easily qualified the language in § 236.13(1)(c) by requiring that a master plan be consistent with zoning ordinances in order to serve as a basis for denial of plat approval. It is clear that the legislature knew how to accomplish this goal, since it included similar qualifying language in this very same statute. See § 236.13(1)(c). Furthermore, the legislature also has specified that its grant of zoning power to city councils "may not be deemed a limitation on any power granted elsewhere." Wis. Stat. § 62.23(7)(a). Thus, because the statutes do not indicate that the legislature intended zoning ordinances to limit a city plan commission's authority to deny plat approval based on a master plan, we are not persuaded by Lake City's argument.

* * *

Zoning regulations and subdivision controls are not only adopted and administered by separate agencies, but are authorized by separate enabling acts which may be unlike in their requirements for enactment of regulations and their procedure for enforcement or relief. Thus, the authority of the agency assigned to plat review may not be limited by the zoning regulations.

Accordingly, the court held that "[a]s long as the regulation is authorized by and within the purposes of ch. 236, the fact that it may also fall under the zoning power does not preclude a local government from enacting the regulation pursuant to the conditions and procedures of ch. 236." Thus, * * * the power of a plan commission which is authorized to review plats is not limited or detracted by zoning regulations. * * *

In summary, we hold that Wis. Stat. § 236.13(1)(c) authorizes a city plan commission to deny approval of a plat that conflicts with a local master plan, so long as any common elements contained in both the master plan and official map are not contradictory. We further conclude that a master plan is consistent with an official map even if the master plan contains additional elements that the official map does not. We therefore hold that a city plan commission may rely on an element contained solely in a master plan to reject plat approval. Applying this holding to the present case, we conclude that the Plan Commission had the authority to deny approval of Lake City's proposed preliminary plat, because this plat conflicted with Mequon's newly revised master plan. The cause is remanded to the circuit court for the purpose of reinstatement of its judgment.

The decision of the court of appeals is reversed and cause remanded.

Notes

1. The Bartholomew street map for Rochester, N.Y., was involved in Vangellow v. City of Rochester, 190 Misc. 128, 71 N.Y.S.2d 672 (Sup.Ct. 1947). There, old buildings were built right up to the street line. The map required a ten foot setback. Plaintiffs, who proposed to tear down and reconstruct the buildings, wanted to build showrooms right up to the street line. They brought this action for a declaratory judgment declaring the map invalid as applied to the plaintiffs. Held: The official map as applied to the plaintiffs was not totally void and the court had no jurisdiction until the plaintiffs had exhausted their administrative review remedy before the Rochester zoning board of appeals. See also S.S. Kresge Co. v. City of New York, 194 Misc. 645, 87 N.Y.S.2d 313 (Sup.Ct.1949); Jensen v. City of New York, 42 N.Y.2d 1079, 399 N.Y.S.2d 645, 369 N.E.2d 1179 (1977); St. Luke's German Evangelical Lutheran Church v. City of Rochester, 115 Misc.2d 199, 453 N.Y.S.2d 1012 (1982).

In Ward v. Bennett, 79 N.Y.2d 394, 583 N.Y.S.2d 179, 592 N.E.2d 787 (1992) the New York Court of Appeals held that a landowner denied a building permit to construct a single-family house in the bed of a mapped but unopened street could bring a takings claim for compensation even though the city argued that the owner had not exhausted the available remedy of seeking to have the street de-mapped; the court said that the case was "ripe" for judicial review. This holding seems inconsistent with that in the Vangellow case, supra.

See also, Allyson Phillips, "The Official Map," 5 New York Zoning Law & Practice Report 1 (May/June 2005) for a more recent discussion of the use of the official map in New York. This article also discusses the legal uncertainties surrounding the reservation of lands for certain purposes on the official map and claims of unconstitutional takings.

2. In Grosso v. Board of Adjustment, 137 N.J.L. 630, 61 A.2d 167 (1948) the official map as hastily amended after the plaintiff applied for a building permit placed plaintiff's entire property in the bed of a proposed street. The court had little difficulty holding that the map was invalid as applied to the plaintiff. Compare Barsel v. Woodbridge Twp. Zoning Bd. of Adjustment, 189 N.J.Super. 75, 458 A.2d 1303 (1983). Also see Barile v. City of Port Republic, 186 N.J.Super. 587, 453 A.2d 284 (1982).

3. In a report prepared for the U.S. Bureau of Public Roads, Professors Daniel Mandelker and Graham Waite summarize official map enabling acts for the twenty-eight states that have such statutes. (Mandelker and Waite, A Study of Future Acquisition and Reservation of Highway Rights-of-Way (Mimeo prepared under Contract CPR 11–8006, 1963) Charts 2 and 3, Part I, Appendix). In general these statutes are built on one of three models: (1) the so-called Standard Act; (2) the Bettman model; and (3) the Bassett–Williams model.

The Standard Act calls for payment for the reserved rights-of-way from the time of reservation. As might be expected, little use has been made of this procedure in the four states that have enacted it into law.

Both the Bettman and Bassett–Williams acts authorize the mapping of future streets and widening lines through exercise of the police power. Both include provisions intended to take care of hardship cases, but hardship is defined differently in the two acts.

The Bettman act requires a showing (1) that a reasonable return cannot be earned from the property including the mapped part, or (2) that balancing the interests of the municipality against the interests of the owner, considerations of equity and justice dictate the grant of a permit.

The Bassett–Williams model requires not only a showing that the land in the bed of the mapped street is not yielding a fair return, but it also authorizes refusal of a building permit where the applicant will not be substantially damaged by placing his building outside the mapped street. See, for example, State ex rel. Miller v. Manders, 2 Wis.2d 365, 86 N.W.2d 469 (1957).

These hardship standards should be compared with the standards for zoning variances taken up in Chapter VII. It may be that a city is well advised to use its zoning power to establish set-back lines, rather than establish widening lines under the official map act. See Kucirek and Beuscher, Wisconsin's Official Map Act, 1957 Wis.L.Rev. 176, 196–197 and Phillips v. Board of Adjustment, 44 N.J.Super. 491, 130 A.2d 866 (1957).

Notice the hardship provisions of the Bettman and the Bassett–Williams acts are phrased in terms of *new* buildings. Nothing is said about alterations of buildings which were already in place when the land was mapped. See

Golden v. Aldell Realty Corp., 70 N.Y.S.2d 341 (Sup.Ct.Queens 1947); Agliata v. D'Agostino, 124 N.Y.S.2d 212 (Sup.Ct.Queens 1953); and Kucirek and Beuscher, Wisconsin's Official Map Law, 1957 Wis.L.Rev. 176, 208–210.

Though based generally on the Bassett–Williams or Bettman models the following states have enabling acts that do not classify neatly under one or the other: California, Connecticut, Kentucky (Jefferson County), Maine, Michigan, Minnesota, Missouri, North Carolina, Oklahoma, South Carolina, Texas and Washington. Other states' enabling acts can be grouped as follows:

Standard Act	Bettman	Bassett–Williams
Alabama	Alabama (for counties over 400,000)	Delaware
Colorado	Georgia	Massachusetts
Kentucky	New Hampshire	New Jersey
Maryland	New Mexico	New York
	Tennessee	Pennsylvania (for 2nd class townships)
	Utah	Wisconsin
	Wyoming	

Instead of providing variance procedures for hardship cases, it is also possible to map future streets and widening lines and protect them by a "first right of refusal." Such statutes exist in at least twelve states and unlike hardship laws several of them apply to the mapping of major highways in the open country. Under right of refusal statutes, the governing unit has a specified period of time, thirty, sixty or ninety days, for example, after the owner seeks a building permit or indicates an intention to sell within which to buy him out on a voluntary basis or bring condemnation. See Mandelker and Waite, "A Study of Future Acquisition and Reservation of Highway Rights-of-Way" (Mimeo, prepared under Contract CPA 11–8006, 1963) Chart 3, Appendix I. For an illustrative statute of this type, see Wis.Stat. § 84.295 (1961); and see Miller v. City of Beaver Falls, 368 Pa. 189, 82 A.2d 34 (1951).

4. Is a person suing for breach of covenants in a warranty deed charged with knowledge or notice of the official map? See Bibber v. Weber, 199 Misc. 906, 102 N.Y.S.2d 945 (1951), affirmed 278 App.Div. 973, 105 N.Y.S.2d 758 (1951).

5. In 2000, the Utah Legislature adopted H.B. 165, the "Transportation Corridor Preservation Act." Among other things, the Act authorizes the adoption of official maps as part of the previously required general plans. The statute defines "official map" as "a map, drawn by government authorities and recorded in county recording offices that ... shows actual and proposed rights-of-way, centerline alignments, and setbacks for highways and other transportation facilities." Utah Code Ann. Sec. 72–5–401 (4). Why did it take so long for Utah to recognize the "official map" for transportation planning purposes? See, Recent Legislative Development VI. Governmental Law, 2000 Utah L. Rev. 953 (2000).

SECTION 3. DEVELOPER AGREEMENTS AND VESTED RIGHTS

A. VESTED RIGHTS

American Planning Association, Growing Smart Legislative Guidebook: Model Statutes for Planning and the Management of Change

(Stuart Meck, ed.) (2002).

EXCERPT FROM CHAPTER 8

Several states have "vesting" statutes intended to protect the legal status of rights obtained at various points in the development review process. Vesting statutes are laws that create criteria for determining when a landowner has achieved or acquired a right to develop his or her property in a particular manner, which cannot be abolished or restricted by regulatory provisions subsequently enacted. This is called a vested right because it is a right that has become fixed ("vested") and cannot be eliminated or amended. Such laws are not the same as "takings" or "property rights" statutes, which either provide for review of regulatory statutes for potential taking effects or lower the threshold amount by which property must be diminished in value by enforcement of a regulation for there to be a compensable taking.

Vesting statutes are also not the same as development agreement statutes. Though the effect of a development agreement is to fix the government's right to regulate the property in question, the method used is an agreement in which the landowner typically agrees to at least some restrictions that the government could not generally obtain in exchange for his or her obligations becoming fixed (and for other favorable variances from land development regulations). Vesting statutes, in contrast, apply to the generally applicable regulations of land use, and no agreement is needed for the landowner to be able to assert a vested right to develop.

There is a common thread through most existing vesting statutes. For the development rights to be vested, the government must have made a decision and the landowner must have, in good faith, relied, to his or her detriment, on that decision by making some improvement to the land or some other commitment of resources. It is not surprising that these elements are found so frequently, either expressly or implicitly, for the common law has for hundreds of years included the doctrine of estoppel. Estoppel means that when someone does something with the intent that you will rely on their action or statement, and you indeed rely in good faith on that action or statement demonstrate that reliance by some action to your detriment (not a mere statement that you will rely on it), the original party is legally bound by that action or statement. While the doctrine of estoppel is most commonly applied in private disputes, it has also been used by some courts in land-use cases to create a vested right to develop which is protected by the federal and state constitutions. However, some state courts have restricted or denied the applicability of the estoppel doctrine to land-use cases. In some cases, these courts have stated that granting vested rights at all would be an improper restriction on the police power. In other cases, they have ruled that the landowner must demonstrate that the local official upon whose statement or decision he or she relied was within authority to make the statement or decision, as the government is not bound by an official's unauthorized acts. Even where estoppel is applied to land-use decisions and a vested right was recognized, there is a difference of opinion on what sort of government acts and what level of reliance triggers estoppel. It is almost universal across the case law that the reliance must be in the form of "substantial" or "extensive" expenditures or actual construction, but these terms are rarely defined, instead being left to a case-by-case analysis. Also decided on an ad-hoc basis is the more fundamental issue of what sort of government statement, action, or decision could be the basis of estoppel. Is a statement by an official that one will receive approval sufficient? Preliminary approval of a site plan? Final approval of a site plan? Issuance of a building permit?

Further confusing an examination of the case law is the issue of "last-minute" amendments to land development regulations. Some state courts have decided that a development permit application may be subject to an ordinance that was pending in the local legislative process at the time the application was submitted. Courts in some other states have applied estoppel to such pending ordinances, and have not allowed a new or amended regulation to apply to a development permit application where the applicant had made a substantial investment in good-faith reliance on the ordinances in place at the time of application. And some state courts have found that an applicant who was entitled to a development permit under the regulations in place at the time of application could not be denied a permit based on amended regulations even where there was no substantial investment or reliance by the applicant landowner. "Where a project is caught in a change in the law due to denials of successive applications or delays in processing, the court might look askance at a denial based exclusively on the new law." In such states, courts are especially willing to ignore post-application amendments where the court finds that the local government amended its regulations after the application, or delayed the application until the ordinance became effective, with the intent of barring the application.

AVCO COMMUNITY DEVELOPERS, INC. v. SOUTH COAST REGIONAL COMMISSION

Supreme Court of California, 1976.
17 Cal.3d 785, 132 Cal.Rptr. 386, 553 P.2d 546.

MOSK, J.

We are confronted with the apparently irreconcilable conflict between the interests of a land developer who seeks to avoid compliance with a recently enacted law regulating its project, and the interests of the public in assuring development of the property in a manner consistent with the requirements of current law. Specifically, we must decide whether the developer of a subdivision may acquire a vested right to construct buildings on its land without a permit from the California Coastal Zone Commission (the commission) if it has subdivided and graded the property and made certain improvements on the land, such as installing utilities, but had not applied for or received a building permit for any structures on the land before February 1, 1973.

Section 27400 of the California Coastal Zone Conservation Act of 1972 hereinafter called the Act, provides that on or after February 1, 1973, any person desiring to perform any development within the coastal zone must obtain a permit from the commission. Section 27404, at the time relevant to the events in the present case, qualified this requirement by allowing a builder to proceed after February 1 if he had obtained a vested right to do so by having secured a building permit and in good faith diligently commenced construction and performed substantial work in reliance thereon before the effective date of the Act.

Petitioner, Avco Community Developers, Inc. (Avco) owns 7,936 acres of land in Orange County which it is developing as the Laguna Niguel Planned Community. Of this total, 836 acres, known as the Capron property, was purchased by Avco in 1968. Approximately 473 acres of the Capron property lies within the coastal zone. Our concern in this proceeding is with 74 acres of the land within the permit area, designated as tract 7479.

In 1971, the county, at the instance of Avco, zoned 5,234 acres of the Laguna Niguel project, including tract 7479, as a "Planned Community Development" containing a total of 18,925 residential units. The development was to proceed according to "Planned Community District Regulations" enacted by the county. In 1972, a final map was approved for tract 7479, dividing it into 27 parcels, devoted largely to multiple residential uses. In that year the county issued a rough grading permit which did not refer to grading for any specific building site.

Avco undertook a number of studies for the development of the tract, and proceeded to subdivide and grade the property. By February 1, 1973, pursuant to approvals issued for such purposes by the county, Avco had completed or was in the process of constructing storm drains, culverts, street improvements, utilities, and similar facilities for the tract as well as for the remainder of the Capron property. Under the county's building code, a permit could not be obtained until grading had been completed. Avco had not completed the rough grading by February 1, 1973, and it neither submitted building plans for the tract nor obtained a permit to construct any structures. Before that date, the company had spent $2,082,070 and incurred liabilities of $740,468 for the development of the tract; it is losing $7,113.46 a day, largely due to loss of anticipated rental value, as a result of its inability to proceed with construction of buildings on the tract.

Avco applied to the commission for an exemption from the permit requirements of the Act, claiming that it had a vested right to complete development, and, when its application was denied, sought a writ of mandate to compel the commission to grant the exemption. The trial court, after a hearing in which the evidence consisted entirely of the record of the proceedings before the commission, declined to issue the writ.

The court found that the approvals granted by the county for the development of tract 7479 led Avco to reasonably expect that it would be allowed to construct buildings on the tract "without further discretionary governmental approval," and that the subdivision improvements were installed in good faith reliance upon the county's actions. The court also found that Avco had a detailed plan for the buildings to be constructed on the tract. A model of the structures intended to be built on the tract had been completed in July 1971, and the court found that the maximum number, size and type of buildings "allowable" on the tract could be ascertained by reference to the tract map, the planned community district regulations, and the model.

Although the court opined that fairness suggested Avco be allowed to complete development of the tract in accordance with the map, the regulations and the model, nevertheless because Avco did not have a building permit the trial court felt compelled to hold that it did not have a vested right to construct the buildings, and thus was not exempt from the permit requirement of the Act. Avco asserts that it had a vested right to construct buildings on tract 7479, that the commission is estopped to claim otherwise, and that the Act is unconstitutional.

Vested Rights

It has long been the rule in this state and in other jurisdictions that if a property owner has performed substantial work and incurred substantial liabilities in good faith reliance upon a permit issued by the government, he acquires a vested right to complete construction in accordance with the terms of the permit. Once a landowner has secured a vested right the government may not, by virtue of a change in the zoning laws, prohibit construction authorized by the permit upon which he relied. Here Avco asserts that it had a vested right to construct buildings on tract 7479 without permission from the commission because prior to February 1, 1973, when the coastal permit requirement took effect, it spent large sums of money to construct subdivision improvements and grade the tract, in reliance on several county authorizations, and that these improvements were undertaken and approvals issued for the purpose of constructing buildings. Thus, Avco relies upon the doctrine of vested rights as defined in the common law and in the Act itself.

VESTED RIGHTS UNDER COMMON LAW

Evaluation of this claim requires a determination of the point in the development process at which a landowner can be said to have acquired a vested right to construct buildings on his land. The commission contends, subject to an exception to be discussed infra, that a builder may not acquire a vested right prior to the issuance of a building permit, whereas Avco asserts that in the context of a subdivision a developer's right to construct buildings vests when it has subdivided the land and installed subdivision improvements such as roads and utilities pursuant to governmental authorization. * * *

[N]either the existence of a particular zoning nor work undertaken pursuant to governmental approvals preparatory to construction of buildings can form the basis of a vested right to build a structure which does not comply with the laws applicable at the time a building permit is issued. By zoning the property or issuing approvals for work preliminary to construction the government makes no representation to a landowner that he will be exempt from the zoning laws in effect at the subsequent time he applies for a building permit or that he may construct particular structures on the property, and thus the government cannot be estopped to enforce the laws in effect when the permit is issued.

With commendable candor, the commission concedes that it does not deem a building permit to be an absolute requirement under all circumstances for acquisition of a vested right. It suggests that in rare situations the government may grant another type of permit, such as a conditional use permit, which affords substantially the same specificity and definition to a project as a building permit, and that in such instances a builder might acquire a vested right even though the document was not designated a "building permit." * * * Not only had Avco failed to apply to the county for permits for specific buildings by the date the requirements of the Act became effective, but the county was not advised of such elementary details as the dimension or height of the buildings to be constructed on tract 7479. The trial court's finding that "the maximum number, size and type of buildings that would be allowable to be constructed upon Tract 7479" could be ascertained by reference to the tract map, the regulations, and the model of the buildings does not support a conclusion to the contrary.

The model was prepared by Avco for its own use and was not submitted to the county. An examination of the tract map and the regulations fails to disclose the number and size of the buildings to be constructed on the tract. The map merely designates certain areas for multiple residential use; the regulations for multiple residential structures are stated in the most general terms, and they do not refer to any identifiable buildings to be constructed on any specific lots.

Thus, on the date the Act became effective, the county did not know, much less had it approved, plans indicating such matters as the placement of the buildings to be built on the tract, the size of the proposed buildings, the number of apartments of specified size, or how high the buildings would rise, there being no legal height limitation for multiple residential units. Indeed, it was not even clear how many units would be built on the tract.

Under these circumstances, it would be impossible to determine the precise scope of any purported right to construct buildings on the tract, and we would be compelled to deny the claim of a common law vested right * * *

* * *

The contention that Avco was entitled to a building permit because the county would have been compelled to issue it upon mere application has no merit. The Orange County Building Code (§ 302(a)) provides that a building permit may not issue unless the plans conform not only to the structural requirements of the code but to "other pertinent laws and ordinances." This provision codifies the general rule that a builder must comply with the laws which are in effect at the time a building permit is issued, including the laws which were enacted after application for the permit. A landowner which has not even applied for a permit cannot be in a better position merely because it had previously received permission to subdivide its property and made certain improvements on the land.

* * *

Avco insists that the existence and scope of vested rights is a question of fact for the trial court, that we must accept the court's findings as true, and that they lead inevitably to the conclusion that it has acquired a vested right to construct buildings on tract 7479 without a permit from the commission.

Even if we assume arguendo that a building permit is not required in order to acquire a vested right to construct particular buildings in every case, Avco cannot prevail. As we have seen, although the trial court found that Avco had a detailed plan for the buildings to be erected on the tract, the county was not aware of and had not approved such a plan, and the preliminary approvals which it did grant did not refer to any identifiable buildings. In view of this central premise, the further findings of the trial court that Avco reasonably expected that it would be allowed to construct "buildings" on the tract "without further discretionary governmental approval" and that by granting the preliminary approvals the county represented to Avco that it would be permitted to construct "buildings ... upon obtaining building permits" are not sufficient to sustain a conclusion that Avco had secured a vested right to build structures which the county did not approve and as to which it had no detailed information. * * *

If we were to accept the premise that the construction of subdivision improvements or the zoning of the land for a planned community are sufficient to afford a developer a vested right to construct buildings on the land in accordance with the laws in effect at the time the improvements are made or the zoning enacted, there could be serious impairment of the government's right to control land use policy. In some cases the inevitable consequence would be to freeze the zoning laws applicable to a subdivision or a planned unit development as of the time these events occurred.

Thus tracts or lots in tracts which had been subdivided decades ago, but upon which no buildings have been constructed could be free of all zoning laws enacted subsequent to the time of the subdivision improvement, unless facts constituting waiver, abandonment, or opportunity for amortization of the original vested right could be shown. In such situations, the result would be that these lots, as well as others in similar subdivisions created more recently or lots established in future subdivisions, would be impressed with an exemption of indeterminate duration from the requirements of any future zoning laws. To illustrate: let us hypothesize that because of mounting costs, decreasing demand or innumerable other potential causes, Avco does not build multiple residential units on tract 7479 for a number of years. If we were to accept its premise, the tract would be exempted not only from the current requirements of the Act, but from all zoning laws enacted for an indefinite period in the future. It is no response to these inherent evils to assert that this builder presently intends to construct its multiple residential units expeditiously.

* * *

The judgment is affirmed.

B. DEVELOPER AGREEMENTS

American Planning Association, Growing Smart Legislative Guidebook: Model Statutes for Planning and the Management of Change

(Stuart Meck, ed.) (2002).

EXCERPT FROM CHAPTER 8

A development agreement is "a statutorily authorized, negotiated agreement between a local government and a private developer that establishes the respective rights and obligations of each party with respect to certain planning issues or problems related to a specific proposed development or redevelopment project." (Erin J. Johnson, "Development Agreements: Planning Perspectives," in Development Agreements: Analysis, Colorado Case Studies, Commentary, 3) There are times when a local government and a developer may both wish to vary in some way from the development and land use choices possible under the existing land development regulations and have those variations be fully enforceable. A development agreement allows both flexibility and certainty. It permits flexibility by allowing terms and conditions that are different from and more detailed than the requirements of land development regulations and the statutes authorizing them. It brings certainty by making all elements of the agreement enforceable, against the local government as well as the developer. Thus, it is superior to informal agreements that are only worth as much as the good faith of the parties.

BOLLECH v. CHARLES COUNTY, MARYLAND

United States Court of Appeals, Fourth Circuit, 2003.
69 Fed.Appx. 178 (unpublished).

PER CURIAM.

Appellants Bollech, Haapala, Mesisinger and Winson (the "Trustees") own land on which they planned to develop residential units. In 1989, the Trustees entered into a Development Agreement with Charles County and the Cliffton Potomac Associates Ltd. Partnerships I–X (the "Newburg Station Owners") for the residential development of land.

The Development Agreement's purpose was to assure the timely and orderly provision of water and sanitary sewer facilities to support (1) the proposed residential development on the Trustees' land (the "Potomac Cliffs") and land owned by the Newburg Station Owners (the "Newburg Station"), and (2) a portion of existing developments on adjacent land. The Trustees and the Newburg Station Owners (collectively, the "Property Owners") were allowed under the Development Agreement to develop residential units in prescribed stages. In return, the Property Owners agreed to construct, within a certain amount of time, adequate public facilities (including upgrading, repairing and expanding the existing sewer plant) to serve the proposed residential development and a portion of the existing development on adjacent property.

In 1999, the Trustees submitted an application for a preliminary plan for development. The County refused to accept the application because amendments to the local zoning regulations prevented the County from approving the application. The Trustees claim the Development Agreement provides that the Trustees may develop the residential units on their land irrespective of changes in County land use regulations. In response, the County claims that the County is no longer obligated under the Development Agreement to approve the Trustees' development applications for building permits.

The Trustees brought suit against the County for (1) impairment of the obligation of contract in violation of the Contracts Clause, U.S. Const. Art. I, § 10, cl. 1; and (2) breach of contract. The district court entered an order granting the County's motion for summary judgment and denying the Trustees' cross-motion for summary judgment. In a memorandum opinion, the district court stated that the Development Agreement no longer imposed an enforceable obligation on the County because the Trustees did not ensure the provision of adequate sewer and water facilities within the time period required by the Development Agreement.

* * *

The Contracts Clause states that "No State shall ... pass any ... Law impairing the Obligation of Contracts." U.S. Const. Art. I, § 10, cl. 1. In order to prove a violation of the Contracts Clause, a plaintiff must first prove that there is an enforceable contract that the government has impaired in some manner. If there is no enforceable contract, there is no violation of the Contracts Clause.

If there is an enforceable contractual obligation that has been impaired, the plaintiff must prove that the impairment was substantial. If the impairment is substantial, the court then determine [sic] if the government action giving rise to the substantial impairment was reasonable and necessary to protect an important public interest.

The County claims there was no enforceable contractual obligation to the Trustees at the time of the alleged impairment, 1999. * * * The language of the Development Agreement indicates (1) that the Trustees had an obligation to expand and repair the existing sewage treatment plant as a predicate for development of the proposed residential units and (2) that the development of Potomac Cliffs was to take place by a specified date in 1994. In return, the County promised, among other things, to issue building permits upon application and upon compliance with applicable regulations, in accordance with the schedule set out in the Development Agreement.

The Development Agreement unambiguously imposes obligations on the Trustees. For instance, the Development Agreement states in § 4 .1:

> The development of the property shall be supported by adequate levels of public facilities, including sanitary sewer facilities, water facilities, roadway facilities, stormwater management facilities.... All public facilities necessary to meet adequacy requirements shall be provided and initially financed by the property owners. Owners ... of the Potomac Cliffs Tract generally are responsible for providing public facilities to be situated on that tract.

Under § 4.2.3 of the Development Agreement, the Newburg Station Owners had primary responsibility for the construction of sewer and water facilities, but § 4.2.2(c) states that the Trustees had responsibility for the construction of the facilities if the Newburg Station Owners failed to construct the facilities and the Trustees still planned to develop Potomac Cliffs.

In addition, § 3.2 of the Development Agreement requires the property owners to develop their property in phases. Section 3.2(a) details the schedule of construction phases in which Potomac Cliffs was to be developed. Full development of Potomac Cliffs by the Trustees was scheduled to be completed in 1994.

There is no factual dispute as to whether the Trustees developed Potomac Cliffs by 1994; not only had the Trustees failed to develop Potomac Cliffs by the specified date, but the Trustees failed to ensure the development of adequate sewer and water facilities as required by the Development Agreement in Section 4.2.6(a), which states, in part: "Construction of the additional capacity [to the existing sewer facility] shall be pursued in a timely and reasonable manner, subject to timely approval by the appropriate authorities, so as to meet the schedule for development set forth in Section 3.2 of this Agreement."

The Trustees' failure to meet their obligation under the Development Agreement released the County from the County's obligations under the Agreement. * * * A material failure to perform by one party "prevents performance of [the other party's remaining duties] from becoming due, at least temporarily, and it discharges those duties if it has not been cured during the time in which performance can occur." Restatement (Second) of Contracts § 237 cmt. a. The County was discharged from any enforceable contractual obligation after the Trustees failed to perform within the time period specified in the Development Agreement. * * *

The Trustees argue that the district court erred in finding that the Development Agreement imposes a six-year termination date. The Trustees point out that the Development Agreement expressly required construction to extend over a period of ten years. In addition, the Trustees argue that because the Development Agreement had no express termination date, the Development Agreement is valid for a reasonable amount of time.

The district court did not find that the Development Agreement terminated after six years. The district court recognized that the Trustees were obligated to develop the residential units on their property within the time specified in the Development Agreement under § 3.2. Section 3.2(a) requires that the Potomac Cliffs area be developed by August 12, 1994. In addition, § 4.2.6(a) requires the construction of additional capacity at the existing sewer facility in time to meet the schedule in Section 3.2. Section 4.2.6(a) also requires that the design documents for the construction of additional capacity be submitted for approval to the appropriate authorities no later than six months after the effective date of the Agreement. The Trustees did not meet their obligations within the specified time periods. The Trustees' failure to perform released the County from the County's obligations after the specified time periods elapsed.

The reference to the ten year construction period does not extend the period in which the Trustees can perform. Section 3.2 states that "[t]he construction schedule shall extend over a period of a minimum of ten (10) years, commencing, for the purpose of this Agreement, August 12, 1988." This language applies to the development of both Potomac Cliffs and Newbury Station as a unit. Section 3.2 lays out the phases, within the ten year period, in which each property must be developed.

Section 3.2(a) lays out the plan for Potomac Cliffs, which involves five phases, the last ending in August 1994. Section 3.2(b) lays out the plan for Newbury Station, which involves nine phases, the last ending in August 1998.

The County's obligation to the Trustees were [sic] discharged after August 1994. The district court correctly held that there was no enforceable contract obligation between the County and the Trustees at the time the alleged violation occurred.

* * *

The district court held that there was no breach of contract for the same reason there was no Contracts Clause violation: at the time of the alleged violation, there was no enforceable contractual obligation against the County. The above analysis validates the district court's decision. * * *

AFFIRMED.

Notes

1. Developers typically invest a substantial amount of capital into subdivisions and other types of developments. Is it appropriate at any point in the land development process—which can take years from initial preliminary and final plat approvals to application for the last of the building permits—for developers to know for certain that they will be able to fully build-out their project as envisioned? Why or why not? See, Terry D. Morgan, "Vested Rights Legislation," 34 The Urban Lawyer 131 (Winter 2002).

2. A number of states have adopted statutes to grant vested rights to developers at various stages in the approval process. A key issue is to determine what permit(s) and/or what type of approval(s) will trigger a vested right. For examples of different approaches, see, Ariz. Rev. Stat. § 9–1201, et. seq.; Cal. Gov't Code § 66498.1 et seq.; Colo. Rev. Stat. § 24–68–102, et. seq.; Kan. Stat. § 12–764; N.J. Stat. § 40:55D–49; Or. Rev. Stat. § 227.178; and Va. Code § 15.2–2307. For many states, the answer to this question is found in the common-law of the state. States' approaches are typically categorized as either "early vesting" or "late vesting," depending upon when in the process the right to develop vests. Some states, such as New York, require that substantial work be completed, e.g., "having the shovel in the ground." See, Downey v. Incorporated Village of Ardsley, 3 A.D.2d 663, 158 N.Y.S.2d 306 (1957) and Hasco Electric Corp. v. Dassler, 144 N.Y.S.2d 857, aff'd 1 A.D.2d 889, 150 N.Y.S.2d 552 (1956). See also, City of Suffolk ex rel. Herbert v. Board of Zoning Appeals for the City of Suffolk, 266 Va. 137, 580 S.E.2d 796 (2003).

3. Because of the uncertainties of vested rights, beginning with California in 1979 states began to enact statutes authorizing local governments to enter into developer agreements. California's statute followed on the heels of the decision in Avco Community Developers, Inc. v. South Coast Regional Commission. For a fuller discussion of the policy issues surrounding developer agreements, see, Douglas R. Porter and Lindell L. Marsh, eds., *Develop-*

ment Agreements: Practice, Policy, and Prospects (the Urban Land Institute, 1989). See also, David L. Callies and Julie A. Tappendorf, "Unconstitutional Land Development Conditions and the Development Agreement Solution: Bargaining for Public Facilities After Nollan and Dolan," 51 Case W. Res. L. Rev. 663 (2001) for an excellent discussion of the legal and constitutional challenges of using developer agreements. David L. Callies, Daniel J. Curtin, Jr. and Julie A. Tappendorf, Bargaining for Development: A Handbook on Development Agreements, Annexation Agreements, Land Development Conditions, Vested Rights and the Provision of Public Facilities (Environmental Law Institute, 2003). For a specific case study on Maryland, see, John J. Delaney, "The Maryland Experience," SH018 ALI–ABA 585 (ALI–ABA Land Use Institute: Planning, Regulation, Litigation, Eminent Domain, and Compensation, August 2002). In Legacy Group v. City of Wasco, 106 Cal.App.4th 1305, 131 Cal.Rptr.2d 460 (2003) the court held that a claim for breach of a development agreement was subject to the same statute of limitations as for contract claims.

4. One of the controversial issues surrounding the use of development agreements is whether the agreement amounts to the unconstitutional "contracting away" of the municipal police power. See, SMART v. County of San Luis Obispo, 84 Cal.App.4th 221, 100 Cal.Rptr.2d 740 (2000) where the area residents' association argued that since the County entered into a development agreement freezing zoning for a five-year period for a project before the project was ready for construction, the county improperly contracted away its zoning authority. The Court found that the development freeze was not a surrender of the police power but instead it "advance[d] the public interest by preserving future options." For similar holdings see, Stephens v. City of Vista, 994 F.2d 650 (9th Cir. 1993) and 108 Holdings Ltd. v. City of Rohnert Park, 136 Cal.App.4th 186, 38 Cal.Rptr.3d 589 (2006). But, see Trancas Property Owners Association v. City of Malibu, 138 Cal.App.4th 172, 41 Cal.Rptr.3d 200 (2006) where the Court said that although a city may freeze zoning regulations, numerous procedural and substantive limitations attend the making and performance of a "development agreement." Since the City did not follow the statutory development agreement process, the Court found that the City's actions were invalid on the basis that it contracted away its right to exercise the police power.

Chapter V

FIFTH AMENDMENT LIMITS TO LAND USE REGULATIONS

A. INTRODUCTION: THE BASIC CONSTITUTIONAL CONSIDERATIONS

All land use regulations must conform to the Fifth Amendment of the U.S. Constitution. They are not valid if they deprive any person of property without due process of law and they cannot constitute takings of real property unless just compensation is paid. The structure of the relevant provision of the Fifth Amendment is interesting to study. It reads as follows:

> No person shall be ... deprived of life, liberty, or property, without due process of law; nor shall private property be taken for a public use, without just compensation.

Notice that there is a strategically placed semicolon in this critical constitutional provision. It separates the "due process clause" from the "takings" clause. The first prohibits the federal Congress from passing any laws that do not substantially advance legitimate state interests. This means that a land use regulation is invalid if it does not in fact further a legitimate public purpose. The second requires that, if private land is taken or conscripted for a public use, just compensation must be paid. These clauses are the principal source of the property rights that courts protect from undue interference by legislatures and land use regulators.

The Fourteenth Amendment passes these proscriptions on to the states and the local governments to which state legislatures have delegated the authority to adopt and enforce land use regulations. It specifies that:

> No State shall make or enforce any law which shall abridge the privileges or immunities of citizens of the United States; nor shall any State deprive any person of life, liberty, or property, without due process of law; nor deny to any person within its jurisdiction the equal protection of the laws.

In a 1897 case, Chicago, B. & Q. R. Co. v. Chicago, 166 U.S. 226, 17 S.Ct. 581, 41 L.Ed. 979 (1897), the Supreme Court held that the Fourteenth Amendment incorporates the Fifth Amendment protections of property and applies them as limitations on state law as well as local governmental regulations, since local governments are considered legal instrumentalities of the states. All local zoning, subdivision, site plan, and other land use regulations, under this analysis, are subject to and limited by due process and the takings clause. This chapter explores the extent to which these critical clauses limit the authority of government to adopt and enforce land use regulations.

The first two cases demonstrate that the courts have been wrestling for a long time with Fifth Amendment questions that arise when private property is regulated.

MUGLER v. KANSAS

Supreme Court of the United States, 1887.
123 U.S. 623, 8 S.Ct. 273, 31 L.Ed. 205.

[The state had enacted legislation banning the sale and manufacture of spirituous beverages. Petitioner was owner of a brewery located in the state.]

MR. JUSTICE HARLAN:

* * *

Upon this ground—if we do not misapprehend the position of defendants—it is contended that, as the primary and principal use of beer is as a beverage; as their respective breweries were erected when it was lawful to engage in the manufacture of beer for every purpose; as such establishments will become of no value as property, or, at least, will be materially diminished in value, if not employed in the manufacture of beer for every purpose; the prohibition upon their being so employed is, in effect, a taking of property for public use without compensation, and depriving the citizen of his property without due process of law. In other words, although the State, in the exercise of her police powers, may lawfully prohibit the manufacture and sale, within her limits, of intoxicating liquors to be used as a beverage, legislation having that object in view cannot be enforced against those who, at the time, happen to own property, the chief value of which consists in its fitness for such manufacturing purposes, unless compensation is first made for the diminution in the value of their property, resulting from such prohibitory enactments.

This interpretation of the Fourteenth Amendment is inadmissible. It cannot be supposed that the States intended, by adopting that Amendment, to impose restraints upon the exercise of their powers for the protection of the safety, health, or morals of the community.

* * *

It is supposed by the defendants that the doctrine for which they contend is sustained by *Pumpelly v. Green Bay Co.*, 13 Wall. 168. But in that view we do not concur. That was an action for the recovery of damages for the overflowing of the plaintiff's land by water, resulting from the construction of a dam across a river. The defence was that the dam constituted a part of the system adopted by the State for improving the navigation of Fox and Wisconsin rivers; and it was contended that as the damages of which the plaintiff complained were only the result of the improvement, under legislative sanction, of a navigable stream, he was not entitled to compensation from the State or its agents. The case, therefore, involved the question whether the overflowing of the plaintiff's land, to such an extent that it became practically unfit to be used, was a taking of property, within the meaning of the constitution of Wisconsin, providing that "the property of no person shall be taken for public use without just compensation therefore." This court said it would be a very curious and unsatisfactory result, were it held that, "if the government refrains from the absolute conversion of real property to the uses of the public, it can destroy its value entirely, can inflict irreparable and permanent injury to any extent, can, in effect, subject it to total destruction, without making any compensation, because, in the narrowest sense of that word, it is not *taken* for the public use. Such a construction would pervert the constitutional provision into a restriction upon the rights of the citizen, as those rights stood at the common law, instead of the government, and make it an authority for the invasion of private right under the pretext of the public good, which had no warrant in the laws or practices of our ancestors." pp. 177, 178.

These principles have no application to the case under consideration. The question in *Pumpelly v. Green Bay Company* arose under the State's power of eminent domain; while the question now before us arises under what are, strictly, the police powers of the State, exerted for the protection of the health, morals, and safety of the people. That case, as this court said in *Transportation Co. v. Chicago*, 99 U.S. 635, 642, was an extreme qualification of the doctrine, universally held, that "acts done in the proper exercise of governmental powers, and not directly encroaching upon private property, though these consequences may impair its use," do not constitute a taking within the meaning of the constitutional provision, or entitle the owner of such property to compensation from the State or its agents, or give him any right of action. It was a case in which there was a "permanent flooding of private property," a "physical invasion of the real estate of the private owner, and a practical ouster of his possession." His property was, in effect, required to be devoted to the use of the public, and, consequently, he was entitled to compensation.

As already stated, the present case must be governed by principles that do not involve the power of eminent domain, in the exercise of which property may not be taken for public use without compensation. A prohibition simply upon the use of property for purposes that are declared, by valid legislation, to be injurious to the health, morals, or safety of the community, cannot, in any just sense be deemed a taking or an appropriation of property for the public benefit. Such legislation does not disturb the owner in the control or use of his property for lawful purposes, nor restrict his right to dispose of it, but is only a declaration by the State that its use by any one, for certain forbidden purposes, is prejudicial to the public interests. Nor can legislation of that character come within the Fourteenth Amendment, in any case, unless it is apparent that its real object is not to protect the community, or to promote the general well-being, but, under the guise of police regulation, to deprive the owner of his liberty and property, without due process of law. The power which the States have of prohibiting such use by individuals of their property as will be prejudicial to the health, the morals, or the safety of the public, is not—and, consistently with the existence and safety of organized society, cannot be—burdened with the condition that the State must compensate such individual owners for pecuniary losses they may sustain, by reason of their not being permitted, by a noxious use of their property, to inflict injury upon the community. The exercise of the police power by the destruction of property which is itself a public nuisance, or the prohibition of its use in a particular way, whereby its value becomes depreciated, is very different from taking property for public use, or from depriving a person of his property without due process of law. In the one case, a nuisance only is abated; in the other, unoffending property is taken away from an innocent owner.

PENNSYLVANIA COAL CO. v. MAHON

Supreme Court of the United States, 1922.
260 U.S. 393, 43 S.Ct. 158, 67 L.Ed. 322.

MR. JUSTICE HOLMES delivered the opinion of the Court.

* * *

The statute forbids the mining of anthracite coal in such way as to cause the subsidence of, among other things, any structure used as a human habitation, with certain exceptions, including among them land where the surface is owned by the owner of the underlying coal and is distant more than one hundred and fifty feet from any improved property belonging to any other person. As applied to this case the statute is admitted to destroy previously existing rights of property and contract. The question is whether the police power can be stretched so far.

Government hardly could go on if to some extent values incident to property could not be diminished without paying for every such change in the general law. As long recognized, some values are enjoyed under an implied limitation and must yield to the police power. But obviously the implied limitation must have its limits, or the contract and due process clauses are gone. One fact for consideration in determining such limits is the extent of the diminution. When it reaches a certain magnitude, in most if not in all cases there must be an exercise of eminent domain and compensation to sustain the act. So the question depends upon the particular facts. The greatest weight is given to the judgment of the legislature, but it always is open to interested parties to contend that the legislature has gone beyond its constitutional power.

This is the case of a single private house. No doubt there is a public interest even in this, as there is in every purchase and sale and in all that happens within the commonwealth. Some existing rights may be modified even in such a case. *Rideout v. Knox*, 148 Mass. 368. But usually in ordinary private affairs the public interest does not warrant much of this kind of interference. A source of damage to such a house is not a public nuisance even if similar damage is inflicted on others in different places. The damage is not common or public. *Wesson v. Washburn Iron Co.*, 13 Allen, 95, 103. The extent of the public interest is shown by the statute to be limited, since the statute ordinarily does not apply to land when the surface is owned by the owner of the coal. Furthermore, it is not justified as a protection of personal safety. That could be provided for by notice. Indeed the very foundation of this bill is that the defendant gave timely notice of its intent to mine under the house. On the other hand the extent of the taking is great. It purports to abolish what is recognized in Pennsylvania as an estate in land—a very valuable estate—and what is declared by the Court below to be a contract hitherto binding the plaintiffs. If we were called upon to deal with the plaintiffs' position alone, we should think it clear that the statute does not disclose a public interest sufficient to warrant so extensive a destruction of the defendant's constitutionally protected rights.

But the case has been treated as one in which the general validity of the act should be discussed. The Attorney General of the State, the City of Scranton, and the representatives of other extensive interests were allowed to take part in the argument below and have submitted their contentions here. It seems, therefore, to be our duty to go farther in the statement of our opinion, in order that it may be known at once, and that further suits should not be brought in vain.

It is our opinion that the act cannot be sustained as an exercise of the police power, so far as it affects the mining of coal under streets or cities in places where the right to mine such coal has been reserved. As said in a Pennsylvania case, "For practical purposes, the right to coal consists in the right to mine it." *Commonwealth v. Clearview Coal Co.*, 256 Pa.St. 328, 331. What makes the right to mine coal valuable is that it can be exercised with profit. To make it commercially impracticable to mine certain coal has very nearly the same effect for constitutional purposes as appropriating or destroying it. This we think that we are warranted in assuming that the statute does.

* * *

The rights of the public in a street purchased or laid out by eminent domain are those that it has paid for. If in any case its representatives have been so short sighted as to acquire only surface rights without the right of support, we see no more authority for supplying the latter without compensation than there was for taking the right of way in the first place and refusing to pay for it because the public wanted it very much. The protection of private property in the Fifth Amendment presupposes that it is wanted for public use, but provides that it shall not be taken for such use without compensation. A similar assumption is made in the decisions upon the Fourteenth Amendment. * * * When this seemingly absolute protection is found to be qualified by the police power, the natural tendency of human nature is to extend the qualification more and more until at last private property disappears. But that cannot be accomplished in this way under the Constitution of the United States.

The general rule at least is, that while property may be regulated to a certain extent, if regulation goes too far it will be recognized as a taking. It may be doubted how far exceptional cases, like the blowing up of a house to stop a conflagration, go—and if they go beyond the general rule, whether they do not stand as much upon tradition as upon principle. * * * In general it is not plain that a man's misfortunes or necessities will justify his shifting the damages to his neighbor's shoulders. * * * We are in danger of forgetting that a strong public desire to improve the public condition is not enough to warrant achieving the desire by a shorter cut than the constitutional way of paying for the change. As we already have said, this is a question of degree—and therefore cannot be disposed of by general propositions. But we regard this as going beyond any of the cases decided by this Court. * * *

We assume, of course, that the statute was passed upon the conviction that an exigency existed that would warrant it, and we assume that an exigency exists that would warrant the exercise of eminent domain. But the question at bottom is upon whom the loss of the changes desired should fall. So far as private persons or communities have seen fit to take the risk of acquiring only surface rights, we cannot see that the fact that their risk has become a danger warrants the giving to them greater rights than they bought.

Decree reversed.

MR. JUSTICE BRANDEIS, dissenting.

The Kohler Act prohibits, under certain conditions, the mining of anthracite coal within the limits of a city in such a manner or to such an extent "as to cause the * * * subsidence of any dwelling or other structure used as a human habitation, or any factory, store, or other industrial or mercantile establishment in which human labor is employed." Coal in place is land; and the right of the owner to use his land is not absolute. He may not so use it as to create a public nuisance; and uses, once harmless, may, owing to changed conditions, seriously threaten the public welfare. Whenever they do, the legislature has power to prohibit such uses without paying compensation; and the power to prohibit extends alike to the manner, the character and the purpose of the use. Are we justified in declaring that the Legislature of Pennsylvania has, in restricting the right to mine anthracite, exercised this power so arbitrarily as to violate the Fourteenth Amendment?

Every restriction upon the use of property imposed in the exercise of the police power deprives the owner of some right theretofore enjoyed, and is, in that sense, an abridgement by the State of rights in property without making compensation. But restriction imposed to protect the public health, safety or morals from dangers threatened is not a taking. The restriction here in question is merely the prohibition of a noxious use. The property so restricted remains in the possession of its owner. The State does not appropriate it or make any use of it. The State merely prevents the owner from making a use which interferes with paramount rights of the public. Whenever the use prohibited ceases to be noxious,—as it may because of further change in local or social conditions,—the restriction will have to be removed and the owner will gain be free to enjoy his property as heretofore.

The restriction upon the use of this property cannot, of course, be lawfully imposed, unless its purpose is to protect the public. But the purpose of a restriction does not cease to be public, because incidentally some private persons may thereby receive gratuitously valuable special benefits. Thus, owners of low buildings may obtain through statutory restrictions upon the height of neighboring structures, benefits equivalent to an easement of light and air. * * * Furthermore, a restriction, though imposed for a public purpose, will not be lawful, unless the restriction is an appropriate means to the public end. But to keep coal in place is surely an appropriate means of preventing subsidence of the surface; and ordinarily it is the only available means. Restriction upon use does not become inappropriate as a means, merely because it deprives the owner of the only use to which the property can then be profitably put. The liquor and the oleomargarine cases settled that. *Mugler v. Kansas*, 123 U.S. 623, 668, 669, 8 S.Ct. 273, 31 L.Ed. 205; *Powell v. Pennsylvania*, 127 U.S. 678, 682, 8 S.Ct. 992, 994, 32 L.Ed. 253. See also *Hadacheck v. Sebastian*, 239 U.S. 394, 36 S.Ct. 143, 60 L.Ed. 348; *Pierce Oil Corporation v. City of Hope*, 248 U.S. 498, 39 S.Ct. 172, 63 L.Ed. 381. Nor is a restriction imposed through exercise of the police power inappropriate as a means, merely because the same end might be effected through exercise of the power of eminent domain, or otherwise at public expense. Every restriction upon the height of buildings might be secured through acquiring by eminent domain the right of each owner to build above the limiting height; but it is settled that the State need not resort to that power. Compare *Laurel Hill Cemetery v. San Francisco*, 216 U.S. 358, 30 S.Ct. 301, 54 L.Ed. 515; *Missouri Pacific Ry. Co. v. Omaha*, 235 U.S. 121, 35 S.Ct. 82, 59 L.Ed. 157. If by mining anthracite coal the owner would necessarily unloose poisonous gasses, I suppose no one would doubt the power of the State to prevent the mining, without buying his coal fields. And why may not the State, likewise, without paying compensation, prohibit one from digging so deep or excavating so near the surface, as to expose the community to like dangers? In the latter case, as in the former, carrying on the business would be a public nuisance.

It is said that one fact for consideration in determining whether the limits of the police power have been exceeded is the extent of the resulting diminution in value; and that here the restriction destroys existing rights of property and contract. But values are relative. If we are to consider the value of the coal kept in place by the restriction, we should compare it with the value of all other parts of the land. That is, with the value not of the coal alone, but with the value of the whole property. The rights of an owner as against the public are not increased by dividing the interests in his property into surface and subsoil. The sum of the rights in the parts cannot be greater than the rights in the whole. The estate of an owner in land is grandiloquently described as extending *ab orco usque ad coelum*. But I suppose no one would contend that by selling his interest above one hundred feet from the surface he could prevent the State from limiting, by the police power, the height of structures in a city. And why should a sale of underground rights bar the State's power? For aught that appears the value of the coal kept in place by the restriction may be negligible as compared with the value of the whole property, or even as compared with that part of it which is represented by the coal remaining in place and which may be extracted despite the statute. * * *

* * *

A prohibition of mining which causes subsidence of such structures and facilities is obviously enacted for a public purpose; and it seems, likewise, clear that mere notice of intention to mine would not in this connection secure the public safety. Yet it is said that these provisions of the act cannot be sustained as an exercise of the police power where the right to mine such coal has been reserved. The conclusion seems to rest upon the assumption that in order to justify such exercise of the police power there must be "an average reciprocity of advantage" as between the owner of the property restricted and the rest of the community; and that here such reciprocity is absent. Reciprocity of advantage is an important consideration, and may even be an essential, where the State's power is exercised for the purpose of conferring benefits upon the property of a neighborhood, as in drainage projects, *Wurts v. Hoagland*, 114 U.S. 606, 5 S.Ct. 1086, 29 L.Ed. 229; *Fallbrook Irrigation District v. Bradley*, 164 U.S. 112, 17 S.Ct. 56, 41 L.Ed. 369; or upon adjoining owners, as by party wall provisions, *Jackman v. Rosenbaum Co.*, *ante*, 22. But where the police power is exercised, not to confer benefits upon property owners, but to protect the public from detriment and danger, there is, in my opinion, no room for considering reciprocity of advantage. There was no reciprocal advantage to the owner prohibited from using his oil tanks in 248 U.S. 498; his brickyard, in 239 U.S. 394, 36 S.Ct. 143, 60 L.Ed. 348; his livery stable, in 237 U.S. 171, 35 S.Ct. 511, 59 L.Ed. 900; his billiard hall, in 225 U.S. 623, 32 S.Ct. 697, 56 L.Ed. 1229; his oleomargarine factory, in 127 U.S. 678, 8 S.Ct. 992, 1257, 32 L.Ed. 253;

his brewery, in 123 U.S. 623, 8 S.Ct. 273, 31 L.Ed. 205; unless it be the advantage of living and doing business in a civilized community. That reciprocal advantage is given by the act to the coal operators.

Notes

1. Pennsylvania Coal gave birth to the concept of a "regulatory taking." Soon after Pennsylvania Coal, the Supreme Court was faced with the question of the validity of comprehensive zoning ordinances that dictated the permissible land uses in zoning districts. In Village of Euclid v. Ambler Realty Co., 272 U.S. 365, 47 S.Ct. 114, 71 L.Ed. 303 (1926), the Court upheld comprehensive zoning, despite the owner's argument that placing some of its land in a residential district devalued it quite heavily as potential industrial land. Mr. Justice Sutherland, speaking for the Court, set forth rules for cases, like Euclid, where the landowner alleges that the land use regulation, on its face, is invalid. Ambler Realty's argument was that the very existence of the zoning law constituted a present and irreparable injury and should be enjoined. Faced with a facial challenge of this type, the Court used due process language to decide the case. Reviewing the arguments in favor of zoning advanced by a battery of "commissions and experts[,]" the Court noted that "[I]f these reasons, thus summarized, do not demonstrate the wisdom or sound policy in all respects of those restrictions which we have indicated as pertinent to the inquiry, at least, the reasons are sufficiently cogent to preclude us from saying, as it must be said before the ordinance can be declared unconstitutional, that such provisions are clearly arbitrary and unreasonable, having no substantial relation to the public health, safety, morals, or general welfare." See Chapter III and its discussion of this matter.

After the Euclid case, the Court, in a unanimous opinion by Mr. Justice Sutherland, reversed a judgment denying an injunction against the enforcement of a zoning ordinance as to a particular piece of property. In Nectow v. Cambridge, 277 U.S. 183, 48 S.Ct. 447, 72 L.Ed. 842 (1928), the property had been placed in a residential zone, and after reviewing the facts, Mr. Justice Sutherland noted: "It is made pretty clear that because of the industrial and railroad purposes to which the immediately adjoining lands to the south and east have been devoted and for which they are zoned, the locus is of comparatively little value for the limited uses permitted by the ordinance." The Nectow case became the basis for the customary manner of attacking zoning—that the ordinance, as applied to a particular tract of land, is arbitrary and unreasonable and amounts to a violation of due process. The court invalidated the provision because "it does not bear a substantial relation to the public health, safety, morals, or general welfare." The plaintiff in Nectow proved that its land could not be used for the residential use it was assigned under the zoning. Including plaintiffs property in the residential zoning district would therefore not accomplish the community's general plan, rendering it an unreasonable restriction on land use.

2. In Keystone Bituminous Coal Ass'n v. DeBenedictis, 480 U.S. 470, 107 S.Ct. 1232, 94 L.Ed.2d 472 (1987), the Court upheld the Pennsylvania Bituminous Mine Subsidence and Land Conservation Act, distinguishing Pennsylvania Coal in its opinion. Justice Steven's opinion for the Court

stated that the 1922 decision did not implicitly overrule cases like Mugler, and that the Subsidence Act was a valid exercise of the police power:

> We reject petitioners' implicit assertion that *Pennsylvania Coal* overruled these cases which focused so heavily on the nature of the state's interest in the regulation. Just five years after the *Pennsylvania Coal* decision, Justice Holmes joined the Court's unanimous decision in Miller v. Schoene, 276 U.S. 272, 48 S.Ct. 246, 72 L.Ed. 568 (1928), holding that the Takings Clause did not require the State of Virginia to compensate the owners of cedar trees for the value of the trees that the State had ordered destroyed. The trees needed to be destroyed to prevent a disease from spreading to nearby apple orchards, which represented a far more valuable resource. In upholding the state action, the Court did not consider it necessary to "weigh with nicety the question whether the infected cedars constitute a nuisance according to common law; or whether they may be so declared by statute." Id., at 280, 48 S.Ct., at 247. Rather, it was clear that the State's exercise of its police power to prevent the impending danger was justified, and did not require compensation. See also Euclid v. Ambler Realty Co., 272 U.S. 365, 47 S.Ct. 114, 71 L.Ed. 303 (1926); Omnia Commercial Co. v. United States, 261 U.S. 502, 509, 43 S.Ct. 437, 438, 67 L.Ed. 773 (1923). Other subsequent cases reaffirm the important role that the nature of the state action plays in our takings analysis.
>
> * * *
>
> The second factor that distinguishes this case from *Pennsylvania Coal* is the finding in that case that the Kohler Act made mining of "certain coal" commercially impracticable. In this case, by contrast, petitioners have not shown any deprivation significant enough to satisfy the heavy burden placed upon one alleging a regulatory taking. For this reason, their takings claim must fail. * * *
>
> Petitioners thus face an uphill battle in making a facial attack on the Act as a taking. The hill is made especially steep because petitioners have not claimed, at this stage, that the Act makes it commercially impracticable for them to continue mining their bituminous coal interests in western Pennsylvania. Indeed, petitioners have not even pointed to a single mine that can no longer be mined for profit. * * *
>
> Because our test for regulatory taking requires us to compare the value that has been taken from the property with the value that remains in the property, one of the critical questions is determining how to define the unit of property "whose value is to furnish the denominator of the fraction." Michelman, Property, Utility, and Fairness: Comments on the Ethical Foundations of "Just Compensation" Law, 80 Harv. L.Rev. 1165, 1192 (1967). * * *
>
> The parties have stipulated that enforcement of the DER's 50% rule will require petitioners to leave approximately 27 million tons of coal in place. Because they own that coal but cannot mine it, they contend that Pennsylvania has appropriated it for the public purposes described in the Subsidence Act.

This argument fails for the reason explained in *Penn Central* and *Andrus*. The 27 million tons of coal do not constitute a separate segment of property for takings law purposes. Many zoning ordinances place limits on the property owner's right to make profitable use of some segments of his property. A requirement that a building occupy no more than a specified percentage of the lot on which it is located could be characterized as a taking of the vacant area as readily as the requirement that coal pillars be left in place. Similarly, under petitioners' theory one could always argue that a set-back ordinance requiring that no structure be built within a certain distance from the property line constitutes a taking because the footage represents a distinct segment of property for takings law purposes. Cf. Gorieb v. Fox, 274 U.S. 603, 47 S.Ct. 675, 71 L.Ed. 1228 (1927) (upholding validity of set-back ordinance) (per Holmes, J.). There is no basis for treating the less than 2% of petitioners' coal as a separate parcel of property. * * *

Pennsylvania property law is apparently unique in regarding the support estate as a separate interest in land that can be conveyed apart from either the mineral estate or the surface estate. Petitioners therefore argue that even if comparable legislation in another State would not constitute a taking, the Subsidence Act has that consequence because it entirely destroys the value of their unique support estate. It is clear, however, that our takings jurisprudence forecloses reliance on such legalistic distinctions within a bundle of property rights. * * *

Thus, in practical terms, the support estate has value only insofar as it protects or enhances the value of the estate with which it is associated. Its value is merely a part of the entire bundle of rights possessed by the owner of either the coal or the surface. Because petitioners retain the right to mine virtually all of the coal in their mineral estates, the burden the Act places on the support estate does not constitute a taking. Petitioners may continue to mine coal profitably even if they may not destroy or damage surface structures at will in the process.

But even if we were to accept petitioners' invitation to view the support estate as a distinct segment of property for "takings" purposes, they have not satisfied their heavy burden of sustaining a facial challenge to the Act. Petitioners have acquired or retained the support estate for a great deal of land, only part of which is protected under the Subsidence Act, which, of course, deals with subsidence in the immediate vicinity of certain structures, bodies of water, and cemeteries. See n. 6, supra. The record is devoid of any evidence on what percentage of the purchased support estates, either in the aggregate or with respect to any individual estate, has been affected by the Act. Under these circumstances, petitioners' facial attack under the takings clause must surely fail.

Justice Rehnquist's dissent (joined by Justices Powell, O'Connor and Scalia) stated that " * * * petitioner's interests in particular coal deposits have been completely destroyed. By requiring that defined seams of coal remain in the ground * * * the Subsidence Act has extinguished any interest one might want to acquire in this property. * * * Application of the nuisance exception in these circumstances would allow the State not merely to forbid one 'particular use' of property with many uses but to extinguish all beneficial uses of petitioners' property."

GOLDBLATT v. TOWN OF HEMPSTEAD, N.Y.

Supreme Court of the United States, 1962.
369 U.S. 590, 82 S.Ct. 987, 8 L.Ed.2d 130.

MR. JUSTICE CLARK delivered the opinion of the Court.

The Town of Hempstead has enacted an ordinance regulating dredging and pit excavating on property within its limits. Appellants, who engaged in such operations prior to the enactment of the ordinance, claim that it in effect prevents them from continuing their business and therefore takes their property without due process of law in violation of the Fourteenth Amendment. * * *

Appellant Goldblatt owns a 38–acre tract within the Town of Hempstead. At the time of the present litigation appellant Builders Sand and Gravel Corporation was mining sand and gravel on this lot, a use to which the lot had been put continuously since 1927. Before the end of the first year the excavation had reached the water table leaving a water-filled crater which has been widened and deepened to the point that it is now a 20–acre lake with an average depth of 25 feet. The town has expanded around this excavation, and today within a radius of 3,500 feet there are more than 2,200 homes and four public schools with a combined enrollment of 4,500 pupils.

The present action is but one of a series of steps undertaken by the town in an effort to regulate mining excavations within its limits. A 1945 ordinance, No. 16, provided that such pits must be enclosed by a wire fence and comply with certain berm and slope requirements. Although appellants complied with this ordinance, the town sought an injunction against further excavation as being violative of a zoning ordinance. This failed because appellants were found to be "conducting a prior nonconforming use on the premises. * * *" 135 N.Y.L.J., issue 52, p. 12 (1956). The town did not appeal.

In 1958 the town amended Ordinance No. 16 to prohibit any excavating below the water table[1] and to impose an affirmative duty to refill any excavation presently below that level. The new amendment also made the berm, slope, and fence requirements more onerous.

In 1959 the town brought the present action to enjoin further mining by the appellants on the grounds that they had not complied with the ordinance, as amended, nor acquired a mining permit as required by it.[2] Appellants contended, inter alia, that the ordinance was unconstitutional because (1) it was not regulatory of their business but

1. Specifically the ordinance provides that "[n]o excavation shall be made below two feet above the maximum ground water level at the site."

2. Under the ordinance the town may deny a permit if the proposed excavation will violate any of the provisions of the ordinance.

completely prohibitory and confiscated their property without compensation, (2) it deprived them of the benefit of the favorable judgment arising from the previous zoning litigation, and (3) it constituted ex post facto legislation. However, the trial court did not agree, and the appellants were enjoined from conducting further operations on the lot until they had obtained a permit and had complied with the new provisions of Ordinance No. 16.

Concededly the ordinance completely prohibits a beneficial use to which the property has previously been devoted. However, such a characterization does not tell us whether or not the ordinance is unconstitutional. It is an oft-repeated truism that every regulation necessarily speaks as a prohibition. If this ordinance is otherwise a valid exercise of the town's police powers, the fact that it deprives the property of its most beneficial use does not render it unconstitutional. * * * Nor is it of controlling significance that the "use" prohibited here is of the soil itself as opposed to a "use" upon the soil, *cf. United States v. Central Eureka Mining Co.*, 357 U.S. 155, 78 S.Ct. 1097, 2 L.Ed.2d 1228 (1958), or that the use prohibited is arguably not a common-law nuisance, *e.g., Reinman v. Little Rock, supra.*

This is not to say, however, that governmental action in the form of regulation cannot be so onerous as to constitute a taking which constitutionally requires compensation. Pennsylvania Coal Co. v. Mahon, 260 U.S. 393, 43 S.Ct. 158, 67 L.Ed. 322 (1922); *see United States v. Central Eureka Mining Co., supra.* There is no set formula to determine where regulation ends and taking begins. Although a comparison of values before and after is relevant, *see Pennsylvania Coal Co. v. Mahon, supra,* it is by no means conclusive, *see Hadacheck v. Sebastian, supra,* where a diminution in value from $800,000 to $60,000 was upheld. How far regulation may go before it becomes a taking we need not now decide, for there is no evidence in the present record which even remotely suggests that prohibition of further mining will reduce the value of the lot in question.[3] Indulging in the usual presumption of constitutionality, * * * we find no indication that the prohibitory effect of Ordinance No. 16 is sufficient to render it an unconstitutional taking if it is otherwise a valid police regulation.

The question, therefore, narrows to whether the prohibition of further excavation below the water table is a valid exercise of the town's police power. The term "police power" connotes the time-tested conceptional limit of public encroachment upon private interests. Except for the substitution of the familiar standard of "reasonableness," this Court has generally refrained from announcing any specific criteria. The classic statement of the rule in *Lawton v. Steele*, 152 U.S. 133, 137, 14 S.Ct. 499, 38 L.Ed. 385 (1894), is still valid today:

> "To justify the State in * * * interposing its authority in behalf of the public, it must appear, first, that the interests of the public

3. There is a similar scarcity of evidence relative to the value of the processing machinery in the event mining operations were shut down.

> * * * require such interference; and, second, that the means are reasonably necessary for the accomplishment of the purpose, and not unduly oppressive upon individuals."

Even this rule is not applied with strict precision, for this Court has often said that "debatable questions as to reasonableness are not for the courts but for the legislature. * * *" *E.g., Sproles v. Binford*, 286 U.S. 374, 388, 52 S.Ct. 581, 76 L.Ed. 1167 (1932).

The ordinance in question was passed as a safety measure, and the town is attempting to uphold it on that basis. To evaluate its reasonableness we therefore need to know such things as the nature of the menace against which it will protect, the availability and effectiveness of other less drastic protective steps, and the loss which appellants will suffer from the imposition of the ordinance.

A careful examination of the record reveals a dearth of relevant evidence on these points. One fair inference arising from the evidence is that since a few holes had been burrowed under the fence surrounding the lake it might be attractive and dangerous to children. But there was no indication whether the lake as it stood was an actual danger to the public or whether deepening the lake would increase the danger. In terms of dollars or some other objective standard, there was no showing how much, if anything, the imposition of the ordinance would cost the appellants. In short, the evidence produced is clearly indecisive on the reasonableness of prohibiting further excavation below the water table.

Although one could imagine that preventing further deepening of a pond already 25 feet deep would have a de minimis effect on public safety, we cannot say that such a conclusion is compelled by facts of which we can take notice. Even if we could draw such a conclusion, we would be unable to say the ordinance is unreasonable; for all we know, the ordinance may have a de minimis effect on appellants. Our past cases leave no doubt that appellants had the burden on "reasonableness." * * * This burden not having been met, the prohibition of excavation on the 20–acre–lake tract must stand as a valid police regulation.

We now turn our attention to the remainder of the lot, the 18 acres surrounding the present pit which have not yet been mined or excavated. Appellants themselves contend that this area cannot be mined. They say that this surface space is necessary for the processing operations incident to mining and that no other space is obtainable. This was urged as an important factor in their contention that upholding the depth limitation of the ordinance would confiscate the entire mining utility of their property. However, we have upheld the validity of the prohibition even on that supposition. If the depth limitation in relation to deepening the existing pit is valid, it follows a fortiori that the limitation is constitutionally permissible as applied to prevent the creation of new pits. We also note that even if appellants were able to obtain suitable processing space the geology of the 18–acre tract would prevent any excavation. The water table, appellants admit, is too close to the ground surface to permit commercial mining in the face of the depth restrictions of the ordinance. The impossibility of further mining makes it unnecessary for us to decide to what extent the berm and slope of such excavation could be limited by the ordinance.

Affirmed.

Notes

1. State courts have followed the lead of the Supreme Court in Goldblatt in holding that loss of value alone is not sufficient to cause a taking. See, e.g., Pennington v. Rockdale County, 244 Ga. 743, 262 S.E.2d 59 (1979). An excellent presentation of this view is also found in William C. Haas & Co., Inc. v. City and County of San Francisco, 605 F.2d 1117 (9th Cir.1979).

2. Students and judges have been confounded by the issue of how a land use regulation, adopted as a police power prohibition on the use of private property, can become a "regulatory taking." Return to the Fifth Amendment where it is said that no person shall be deprived of property without due process of law and, separately, that property shall not be taken for a public use without just compensation. For the court to find that a regulation violates due process, one would think, the court would have to find that it did not properly advance a legitimate governmental purpose. We do not hold our property subject to arbitrary, unreasonable, or capricious public regulations. Any regulation that is unreasonable would therefore be invalidated and the landowner freed from its application. For a regulation to be a taking, it should have other characteristics, such as constituting such a severe burden on the owner's property rights as to amount to a constructive taking of title, value, or possession. In a regulatory taking case, then, the court would examine the extent of the burden, to see if a regulation constituted a de facto taking and, if it did, award compensation. This distinction was obscured in Agins v. Tiburon, 447 U.S. 255, 100 S.Ct. 2138, 65 L.Ed.2d 106 (1980), which held that a zoning provision could be a regulatory taking if it "does not substantially advance [a] legitimate state interest" or if it "denies an owner economically viable use of his land." This was designed by the Court as a disjunctive test, meaning that if either of its two prongs is violated by a land use regulation, that regulation constitutes a taking. A land use regulation, under this formulation, could be found to be a taking if it failed to substantially advance a legitimate state interest which sounds like a violation of due process. This seeming contradiction festered for a quarter of a century before being resolved by the Court in the following case.

LINGLE v. CHEVRON U.S.A. INC.

Supreme Court of the United States, 2005.
544 U.S. 528, 125 S.Ct. 2074, 161 L.Ed.2d 876.

[Chevron, challenged a Hawaii Statute that placed a cap on the amount of rent an oil company may charge its lessee-dealers. Hawaii enacted Act 257 in June of 1997 in order to protect gasoline prices from inflation due to the effects of market concentration. Chevron filed suit in the United States District Court for the District of Hawaii claiming the Act affected a taking of its property; the company sought a declaratory judgment and an injunction against the application of the rent cap to its stations.

The parties stipulated that Chevron, under Act 257, was earning a return on its investment on its lessee-dealer stations in Hawaii that satisfies the constitutional standard; Act 257 did not effect a taking because it deprived Chevron of an economically viable use of its property. The lower courts held that Act 257 is a taking because it fails to meet the Agins "substantially advances" test. These courts held that the Act did not substantially advance the legitimate state interest of controlling gasoline prices. In arriving at its conclusion, the district court weighed the reasonableness of two opposing economists who testified on behalf of the opposing litigants; it found the view of Chevron's expert more persuasive than those of the other and concluded that Act 257 would not achieve the objective of controlling gasoline prices and, therefore, constituted a regulatory taking. The Supreme Court now grants certiorari.]

MRS. JUSTICE O'CONNOR delivered the opinion of the Court.

On occasion, a would-be doctrinal rule or test finds its way into our case law through simple repetition of a phrase—however fortuitously coined. A quarter century ago, in *Agins v. City of Tiburon*, 447 U.S. 255, 65 L.Ed.2d 106, 100 S.Ct. 2138 (1980), the Court declared that government regulation of private property "effects a taking if [such regulation] does not substantially advance legitimate state interests. . . ." 447 U.S., at 260, 65 L.Ed.2d 106, 100 S.Ct. 2138. Through reiteration in a half dozen or so decisions since *Agins*, this language has been ensconced in our Fifth Amendment takings jurisprudence. See *Monterey v. Del Monte Dunes at Monterey, Ltd.*, 526 U.S. 687, 704, 143 L.Ed.2d 882, 119 S.Ct. 1624 (1999) (citing cases).

In the case before us, the lower courts applied Agins' "substantially advances" formula to strike down a Hawaii statute that limits the rent that oil companies may charge to dealers who lease service stations owned by the companies. The lower courts held that the rent cap effects an uncompensated taking of private property in violation of the Fifth and Fourteenth Amendments because it does not substantially advance Hawaii's asserted interest in controlling retail gasoline prices. This case requires us to decide whether the "substantially advances" formula announced in *Agins* is an appropriate test for determining whether a regulation effects a Fifth Amendment taking. We conclude that it is not.

* * *

II

A

The Takings Clause of the Fifth Amendment, made applicable to the States through the Fourteenth, see *Chicago, B. & Q. R. Co. v. Chicago*, 166 U.S. 226, 41 L.Ed. 979, 17 S.Ct. 581 (1897), provides that private property shall not "be taken for public use, without just compensation." As its text makes plain, the Takings Clause "does not prohibit the taking of private property, but instead places a condition on the exercise of that power." *First English Evangelical Lutheran Church of Glendale v. County of Los Angeles*, 482 U.S. 304, 314, 96 L.Ed.2d 250, 107 S.Ct. 2378 (1987). In other words, it "is designed not to limit the governmental interference with property rights per se, but rather to secure compensation in the event of otherwise proper interference amounting to a taking." 482 U.S., at 315, 96 L.Ed.2d 250, 107 S.Ct. 2378 (emphasis in original). While scholars have offered various justifications for this regime, we have emphasized its role in "barring Government from forcing some people alone to bear public burdens which, in all fairness and justice, should be borne by the public as a whole." *Armstrong v. United States*, 364 U.S. 40, 49, 4 L.Ed.2d 1554, 80 S.Ct. 1563 (1960); see also *Monongahela Nav. Co. v. United States*, 148 U.S. 312, 325, 37 L.Ed. 463, 13 S.Ct. 622 (1893).

The paradigmatic taking requiring just compensation is a direct government appropriation or physical invasion of private property. See, e.g., *United States v. Pewee Coal Co.*, 341 U.S. 114, 95 L.Ed.809, 71 S.Ct. 670, 119 Ct.Cl. 851 (1951) (Government's seizure and operation of a coal mine to prevent a national strike of coal miners effected a taking); *United States v. General Motors Corp.*, 323 U.S. 373, 89 L.Ed. 311, 65 S.Ct. 357 (1945) (Government's occupation of private warehouse effected a taking). Indeed, until the Court's watershed decision in *Pennsylvania Coal Co. v. Mahon*, 260 U.S. 393, 67 L.Ed. 322, 43 S.Ct. 158 (1922), "it was generally thought that the Takings Clause reached only a 'direct appropriation' of property, or the functional equivalent of a 'practical ouster of [the owner's] possession.' " *Lucas v. South Carolina Coastal Council*, 505 U.S. 1003, 1014, 120 L.Ed.2d 798, 112 S.Ct. 2886 (1992) (citations omitted and emphasis added; brackets in original); see also 505 U.S., at 1028, n. 15, 120 L.Ed.2d 798, 112 S.Ct. 2886 ("Early constitutional theorists did not believe the Takings Clause embraced regulations of property at all").

Beginning with *Mahon*, however, the Court recognized that government regulation of private property may, in some instances, be so onerous that its effect is tantamount to a direct appropriation or ouster—and that such "regulatory takings" may be compensable under the Fifth Amendment. In Justice Holmes' storied but cryptic formulation, "while property may be regulated to a certain extent, if regulation goes too far it will be recognized as a taking." 260 U.S., at 415, 67 L.Ed.2d 322, 43 S.Ct. 158. The rub, of course, has been—and remains—how to discern how far is "too far." In answering that question, we must remain cognizant that "government regulation—by definition—involves the adjustment of rights for the public good," *Andrus v. Allard*, 444 U.S. 51, 65, 62 L.Ed.2d 210, 100 S.Ct. 318 (1979), and that "Government hardly could go on if to some extent values incident to property could not be diminished without paying for every such change in the general law," *Mahon*, supra, 260 U.S., at 413, 67 L.Ed. 322, 43 S.Ct. 158.

Our precedents stake out two categories of regulatory action that generally will be deemed per se takings for Fifth Amendment purposes.

First, where government requires an owner to suffer a permanent physical invasion of her property—however minor—it must provide just compensation. See *Loretto v. Teleprompter Manhattan CATV Corp.*, 458 U.S. 419, 73 L.Ed.2d 868, 102 S.Ct. 3164 (1982) (state law requiring landlords to permit cable companies to install cable facilities in apartment buildings effected a taking). A second categorical rule applies to regulations that completely deprive an owner of "all economically beneficial use" of her property. *Lucas*, 505 U.S., at 1019, 120 L.Ed.2d 798, 112 S.Ct. 2886 (emphasis in original). We held in Lucas that the government must pay just compensation for such "total regulatory takings," except to the extent that "background principles of nuisance and property law" independently restrict the owner's intended use of the property. 505 U.S., at 1026–1032, 120 L.Ed.2d 798, 112 S.Ct. 2886.

Outside these two relatively narrow categories (and the special context of land-use exactions discussed below, * * *), regulatory takings challenges are governed by the standards set forth in *Penn Central Transp. Co. v. New York City*, 438 U.S. 104, 57 L.Ed.2d 631, 98 S.Ct. 2646 (1978). The Court in *Penn Central* acknowledged that it had hitherto been "unable to develop any 'set formula' " for evaluating regulatory takings claims, but identified "several factors that have particular significance." Id., 438 U.S., at 124, 57 L.Ed.2d 631, 98 S.Ct. 2646. Primary among those factors are "the economic impact of the regulation on the claimant and, particularly, the extent to which the regulation has interfered with distinct investment-backed expectations." Ibid. In addition, the "character of the governmental action"—for instance whether it amounts to a physical invasion or instead merely affects property interests through "some public program adjusting the benefits and burdens of economic life to promote the common good"—may be relevant in discerning whether a taking has occurred. Ibid. The Penn Central factors—though each has given rise to vexing subsidiary questions—have served as the principal guidelines for resolving regulatory takings claims that do not fall within the physical takings or Lucas rules. See, e.g., *Palazzolo v. Rhode Island*, 533 U.S. 606, 617–618, 150 L.Ed.2d 592, 121 S.Ct. 2448 (2001); 533 U.S., at 632–634, 150 L.Ed.2d 592, 121 S.Ct. 2448 (O'CONNOR, J., concurring).

Although our regulatory takings jurisprudence cannot be characterized as unified, these three inquiries (reflected in *Loretto*, *Lucas*, and *Penn Central*) share a common touchstone. Each aims to identify regulatory actions that are functionally equivalent to the classic taking in which government directly appropriates private property or ousts the owner from his domain. Accordingly, each of these tests focuses directly upon the severity of the burden that government imposes upon private property rights. The Court has held that physical takings require compensation because of the unique burden they impose: A permanent physical invasion, however minimal the economic cost it entails, eviscerates the owner's right to exclude others from entering and using her property—perhaps the most fundamental of all property interests. See *Dolan v. City of Tigard*, 512 U.S. 374, 384, 129 L.Ed.2d 304, 114 S.Ct.

2309 (1994); *Nollan v. California Coastal Comm'n*, 483 U.S. 825, 831–832, 97 L.Ed.2d 677, 107 S.Ct. 3141 (1987); *Loretto*, supra, 458 U.S., at 433, 73 L.Ed.2d 868, 102 S.Ct. 3164; *Kaiser Aetna v. United States*, 444 U.S. 164, 176, 62 L.Ed.2d 332, 100 S.Ct. 383 (1979). In the *Lucas* context, of course, the complete elimination of a property's value is the determinative factor. See *Lucas*, supra, 505 U.S., at 1017, 120 L.Ed.2d 798, 112 S.Ct. 2886 (positing that "total deprivation of beneficial use is, from the landowner's point of view, the equivalent of a physical appropriation"). And the Penn Central inquiry turns in large part, albeit not exclusively, upon the magnitude of a regulation's economic impact and the degree to which it interferes with legitimate property interests.

B

In *Agins v. City of Tiburon*, a case involving a facial takings challenge to certain municipal zoning ordinances, the Court declared that "the application of a general zoning law to particular property effects a taking if the ordinance does not substantially advance legitimate state interests, see *Nectow v. Cambridge*, 277 U.S. 183, 188, 72 L.Ed. 842, 48 S.Ct. 447 (1928), or denies an owner economically viable use of his land, see *Penn Central Transp. Co. v. New York City*, 438 U.S. 104, 138, n. 36, 57 L.Ed.2d 631, 98 S.Ct. 2646 (1978)." 447 U.S., at 260, 65 L.Ed.2d 106, 100 S.Ct. 2138. Because this statement is phrased in the disjunctive, Agins' "substantially advances" language has been read to announce a stand-alone regulatory takings test that is wholly independent of Penn Central or any other test. Indeed, the lower courts in this case struck down Hawaii's rent control statute as an "unconstitutional regulatory taking," 198 F.Supp.2d, at 1193, based solely upon a finding that it does not substantially advance the State's asserted interest in controlling retail gasoline prices. See supra, at 6–7. Although a number of our takings precedents have recited the "substantially advances" formula minted in *Agins*, this is our first opportunity to consider its validity as a freestanding takings test. We conclude that this formula prescribes an inquiry in the nature of a due process, not a takings, test, and that it has no proper place in our takings jurisprudence.

There is no question that the "substantially advances" formula was derived from due process, not takings, precedents. In support of this new language, Agins cited Nectow v. Cambridge, 277 U.S. 183, 72 L.Ed. 842, 48 S.Ct. 447, a 1928 case in which the plaintiff claimed that a city zoning ordinance "deprived him of his property without due process of law in contravention of the Fourteenth Amendment," 277 U.S., at 185, 72 L.Ed. 842, 48 S.Ct. 447. Agins then went on to discuss Village of Euclid v. Ambler Realty Co., 272 U.S. 365, 71 L.Ed. 303, 47 S.Ct. 114, 4 Ohio Law Abs. 816(1926), a historic decision holding that a municipal zoning ordinance would survive a substantive due process challenge so long as it was not "clearly arbitrary and unreasonable, having no substantial relation to the public health, safety, morals, or general welfare." 272 U.S., at 395, 71 L.Ed. 303, 47 S.Ct. 114 (emphasis added); see also

Nectow, supra, 277 U.S., at 188, 72 L.Ed. 842, 48 S.Ct. 447 (quoting the same "substantial relation" language from Euclid).

When viewed in historical context, the Court's reliance on Nectow and Euclid is understandable. Agins was the Court's first case involving a challenge to zoning regulations in many decades, so it was natural to turn to these seminal zoning precedents for guidance. See Brief for United States as Amicus Curiae in Agins v. City of Tiburon, O. T. 1979, No. 602, pp. 12–13 (arguing that Euclid "set out the principles applicable to a determination of the facial validity of a zoning ordinance attacked as a violation of the Takings Clause of the Fifth Amendment"). Moreover, Agins' apparent commingling of due process and takings inquiries had some precedent in the Court's then-recent decision in Penn Central. See 438 U.S., at 127, 57 L.Ed.2d 631, 98 S.Ct. 2646 (stating in dicta that "it is . . . implicit in Goldblatt [v. Hempstead, 369 U.S. 590, 8 L.Ed.2d 130, 82 S.Ct. 987 (1962),] that a use restriction on real property may constitute a 'taking' if not reasonably necessary to the effectuation of a substantial public purpose, see Nectow v. Cambridge, supra"). But see Goldblatt, supra, 369 U.S., at 594–595, 8 L.Ed.2d 130, 82 S.Ct. 987 (quoting " 'reasonably necessary' " language from Lawton v. Steele, 152 U.S. 133, 137, 38 L.Ed. 385, 14 S.Ct. 499 (1894), a due process case, and applying a deferential " 'reasonableness' " standard to determine whether a challenged regulation was a "valid exercise of the . . . police power" under the Due Process Clause). Finally, when Agins was decided, there had been some history of referring to deprivations of property without due process of law as "takings," see, e.g., Rowan v. United States Post Office Dep't, 397 U.S. 728, 740, 25 L.Ed.2d 736, 90 S.Ct. 1484 (1970), and the Court had yet to clarify whether "regulatory takings" claims were properly cognizable under the Takings Clause or the Due Process Clause, see Williamson County Regional Planning Comm'n v. Hamilton Bank of Jefferson City, 473 U.S. 172, 197–199, 87 L.Ed.2d 126, 105 S.Ct. 3108 (1985).

Although Agins' reliance on due process precedents is understandable, the language the Court selected was regrettably imprecise. The "substantially advances" formula suggests a means-ends test: It asks, in essence, whether a regulation of private property is effective in achieving some legitimate public purpose. An inquiry of this nature has some logic in the context of a due process challenge, for a regulation that fails to serve any legitimate governmental objective may be so arbitrary or irrational that it runs afoul of the Due Process Clause. See, e.g., *County of Sacramento v. Lewis*, 523 U.S. 833, 846, 140 L.Ed.2d 1043, 118 S.Ct. 1708 (1998) (stating that the Due Process Clause is intended, in part, to protect the individual against "the exercise of power without any reasonable justification in the service of a legitimate governmental objective"). But such a test is not a valid method of discerning whether private property has been "taken" for purposes of the Fifth Amendment.

In stark contrast to the three regulatory takings tests discussed above, the "substantially advances" inquiry reveals nothing about the magnitude or character of the burden a particular regulation imposes upon private property rights. Nor does it provide any information about how any regulatory burden is distributed among property owners. In consequence, this test does not help to identify those regulations whose effects are functionally comparable to government appropriation or invasion of private property; it is tethered neither to the text of the Takings Clause nor to the basic justification for allowing regulatory actions to be challenged under the Clause.

Chevron appeals to the general principle that the Takings Clause is meant " 'to bar Government from forcing some people alone to bear public burdens which, in all fairness and justice, should be borne by the public as a whole.' " Brief for Respondent 17–21 (quoting *Armstrong*, 364 U.S., at 49, 4 L.Ed.2d 1554, 80 S.Ct. 1563). But that appeal is clearly misplaced, for the reasons just indicated. A test that tells us nothing about the actual burden imposed on property rights, or how that burden is allocated cannot tell us when justice might require that the burden be spread among taxpayers through the payment of compensation. The owner of a property subject to a regulation that effectively serves a legitimate state interest may be just as singled out and just as burdened as the owner of a property subject to an ineffective regulation. It would make little sense to say that the second owner has suffered a taking while the first has not. Likewise, an ineffective regulation may not significantly burden property rights at all, and it may distribute any burden broadly and evenly among property owners. The notion that such a regulation nevertheless "takes" private property for public use merely by virtue of its ineffectiveness or foolishness is untenable.

Instead of addressing a challenged regulation's effect on private property, the "substantially advances" inquiry probes the regulation's underlying validity. But such an inquiry is logically prior to and distinct from the question whether a regulation effects a taking, for the Takings Clause presupposes that the government has acted in pursuit of a valid public purpose. The Clause expressly requires compensation where government takes private property "for public use." It does not bar government from interfering with property rights, but rather requires compensation "in the event of otherwise proper interference amounting to a taking." *First English Evangelical Lutheran Church*, 482 U.S., at 315, 96 L.Ed.2d 250, 107 S.Ct. 2378 (emphasis added). Conversely, if a government action is found to be impermissible—for instance because it fails to meet the "public use" requirement or is so arbitrary as to violate due process—that is the end of the inquiry. No amount of compensation can authorize such action.

Chevron's challenge to the Hawaii statute in this case illustrates the flaws in the "substantially advances" theory. To begin with, it is unclear how significantly Hawaii's rent cap actually burdens Chevron's property rights. The parties stipulated below that the cap would reduce Chevron's aggregate rental income on 11 of its 64 lessee-dealer stations by about $207,000 per year, but that Chevron nevertheless expects to receive a return on its investment in these stations that satisfies any constitutional standard. See supra, at 4. Moreover, Chevron asserted below, and the

District Court found, that Chevron would recoup any reductions in its rental income by raising wholesale gasoline prices. See supra, at 5. In short, Chevron has not clearly argued—let alone established—that it has been singled out to bear any particularly severe regulatory burden. Rather, the gravamen of Chevron's claim is simply that Hawaii's rent cap will not actually serve the State's legitimate interest in protecting consumers against high gasoline prices. Whatever the merits of that claim, it does not sound under the Takings Clause. Chevron plainly does not seek compensation for a taking of its property for a legitimate public use, but rather an injunction against the enforcement of a regulation that it alleges to be fundamentally arbitrary and irrational.

Finally, the "substantially advances" formula is not only doctrinally untenable as a takings test—its application as such would also present serious practical difficulties. The Agins formula can be read to demand heightened means-ends review of virtually any regulation of private property. If so interpreted, it would require courts to scrutinize the efficacy of a vast array of state and federal regulations—a task for which courts are not well suited. Moreover, it would empower—and might often require—courts to substitute their predictive judgments for those of elected legislatures and expert agencies.

Although the instant case is only the tip of the proverbial iceberg, it foreshadows the hazards of placing courts in this role. To resolve Chevron's takings claim, the District Court was required to choose between the views of two opposing economists as to whether Hawaii's rent control statute would help to prevent concentration and supracompetitive prices in the State's retail gasoline market. Finding one expert to be "more persuasive" than the other, the court concluded that the Hawaii Legislature's chosen regulatory strategy would not actually achieve its objectives. See 198 F.Supp.2d, at 1187–1193. Along the way, the court determined that the State was not entitled to enact a prophylactic rent cap without actual evidence that oil companies had charged, or would charge, excessive rents. See id., at 1191. Based on these findings, the District Court enjoined further enforcement of Act 257's rent cap provision against Chevron. We find the proceedings below remarkable, to say the least, given that we have long eschewed such heightened scrutiny when addressing substantive due process challenges to government regulation. See, e.g., *Exxon Corp. v. Governor of Maryland*, 437 U.S. 117, 124–125, 57 L.Ed.2d 91, 98 S.Ct. 2207 (1978); *Ferguson v. Skrupa*, 372 U.S. 726, 730–732, 10 L.Ed.2d 93, 83 S.Ct. 1028 (1963). The reasons for deference to legislative judgments about the need for, and likely effectiveness of, regulatory actions are by now well established, and we think they are no less applicable here.

For the foregoing reasons, we conclude that the "substantially advances" formula announced in *Agins* is not a valid method of identifying regulatory takings for which the Fifth Amendment requires just compensation. Since Chevron argued only a "substantially advances" theory in support of its takings claim, it was not entitled to summary judgment on that claim.

III

We emphasize that our holding today—that the "substantially advances" formula is not a valid takings test—does not require us to disturb any of our prior holdings.

* * *

Twenty-five years ago, the Court posited that a regulation of private property "effects a taking if [it] does not substantially advance [a] legitimate state interest." *Agins*, supra, 447 U.S., at 260, 65 L.Ed.2d 106, 100 S.Ct. 2138. The lower courts in this case took that statement to its logical conclusion, and in so doing, revealed its imprecision. Today we correct course. We hold that the "substantially advances" formula is not a valid takings test, and indeed conclude that it has no proper place in our takings jurisprudence. In so doing, we reaffirm that a plaintiff seeking to challenge a government regulation as an uncompensated taking of private property may proceed under one of the other theories discussed above—by alleging a "physical" taking, a Lucas-type "total regulatory taking," a *Penn Central* taking, or a land-use exaction violating the standards set forth in *Nollan* and *Dolan*. Because Chevron argued only a "substantially advances" theory in support of its takings claim, it was not entitled to summary judgment on that claim. Accordingly, we reverse the judgment of the Ninth Circuit and remand the case for further proceedings consistent with this opinion.

It is so ordered.

Note

The Lingle Court defines four categories of regulatory takings cases where governmental regulations have the effect of taking the property rights of the plaintiff; in these cases the remedy is just compensation. The first two categories are called per se takings and are represented by Loretto v. Teleprompter Manhattan CATV Corp., 458 U.S. 419, 102 S.Ct. 3164, 73 L.Ed.2d 868 (1982), and Lucas v. South Carolina Coastal Council, 505 U.S. 1003, 112 S.Ct. 2886, 120 L.Ed.2d 798 (1992). In Loretto, an apartment building owner who had not applied for any land use permit or approval was forced by a local law to permit a cable company to attach its transmission lines to her property. Even though the invasion of her right to exclude the public from her property was minimal, it constituted a taking. Government is authorized to condemn property rights such as an affirmative easement to permit utility connections, but if it tries to accomplish this by regulatory means, it risks judicial determination that it has committed a regulatory taking. In Lucas, the trial court found that a beachfront management act prevented the property owner from carrying out any economically viable use on his land: a total taking. When this occurs, the land use regulation effects the equivalent of a physical appropriation and, unless the proscribed use of the land is also prohibited under state nuisance doctrine or other background principles of state law, the regulation constitutes a taking.

The third category tucked into the Court's narrative involves adjudicative land use exactions. These occur when, in the course of approving an owner's application for project approval, a land use board imposes a condition on an approval that requires the owner to let the public enter upon and use the owner's land. Since these conditions violate the fundamental right of an owner to exclude third parties from her land, they are subject to a higher level of scrutiny by the courts. Students should pay close attention to the judicial tests that the Court creates to determine whether land use exactions of this type violate the Fifth Amendment's Takings Clause. The fourth category of regulatory takings cases include all other land use disputes that fail to fit into the per se or exactions categories. In these cases, the court uses a multifactor balancing test articulated in Penn Central Transp. Co. v. New York City, 438 U.S. 104, 98 S.Ct. 2646, 57 L.Ed.2d 631 (1978). These categories of regulatory takings cases are followed and explored in the presentation of the cases and notes that follow.

B. PER SE REGULATORY TAKINGS

LUCAS v. SOUTH CAROLINA COASTAL COUNCIL

Supreme Court of the United States, 1992.
505 U.S. 1003, 112 S.Ct. 2886, 120 L.Ed.2d 798.

JUSTICE SCALIA delivered the opinion of the Court.

In 1986, petitioner David H. Lucas paid $975,000 for two residential lots on the Isle of Palms in Charleston County, South Carolina, on which he intended to build single-family homes. In 1988, however, the South Carolina Legislature enacted the Beachfront Management Act, S.C.Code § 48–39–250 et seq. (Supp.1990) (Act), which had the direct effect of barring petitioner from erecting any permanent habitable structures on his two parcels. See § 48–39–290(A). A state trial court found that this prohibition rendered Lucas's parcels "valueless." This case requires us to decide whether the Act's dramatic effect on the economic value of Lucas's lots accomplished a taking of private property under the Fifth and Fourteenth Amendments requiring the payment of "just compensation." U.S. Const., Amdt. 5.

I

A

South Carolina's expressed interest in intensively managing development activities in the so-called "coastal zone" dates from 1977 when, in the aftermath of Congress's passage of the federal Coastal Zone Management Act of 1972, 86 Stat. 1280, as amended, 16 U.S.C.A. § 1451 et seq., the legislature enacted a Coastal Zone Management Act of its own. See S.C.Code § 48–39–10 et seq. (1987). In its original form, the South Carolina Act required owners of coastal zone land that qualified as a "critical area" (defined in the legislation to include beaches and immediately adjacent sand dunes, § 48–39–10(J)) to obtain a permit from the newly created South Carolina Coastal Council (respondent here) prior to committing the land to a "use other than the use the critical area was devoted to on [September 28, 1977]." § 48–39–130(A).

In the late 1970's, Lucas and others began extensive residential development of the Isle of Palms, a barrier island situated eastward of the City of Charleston. Toward the close of the development cycle for one residential subdivision known as "Beachwood East," Lucas in 1986 purchased the two lots at issue in this litigation for his own account. No portion of the lots, which were located approximately 300 feet from the beach, qualified as a "critical area" under the 1977 Act; accordingly, at the time Lucas acquired these parcels, he was not legally obliged to obtain a permit from the Council in advance of any development activity. His intention with respect to the lots was to do what the owners of the immediately adjacent parcels had already done: erect single-family residences. He commissioned architectural drawings for this purpose.

The Beachfront Management Act brought Lucas's plans to an abrupt end. Under that 1988 legislation, the Council was directed to establish a "baseline" connecting the landward-most "point[s] of erosion ... during the past forty years" in the region of the Isle of Palms that includes Lucas's lots. § 48–39–280(A)(2) (Supp.1988). In action not challenged here, the Council fixed this baseline landward of Lucas's parcels. That was significant, for under the Act construction of occupiable improvements was flatly prohibited seaward of a line drawn 20 feet landward of, and parallel to, the baseline, § 48–39–290(A) (Supp.1988). The Act provided no exceptions.

B

Lucas promptly filed suit in the South Carolina Court of Common Pleas, contending that the Beachfront Management Act's construction bar effected a taking of his property without just compensation. Lucas did not take issue with the validity of the Act as a lawful exercise of South Carolina's police power, but contended that the Act's complete extinguishment of his property's value entitled him to compensation regardless of whether the legislature had acted in furtherance of legitimate police power objectives. Following a bench trial, the court agreed. Among its factual determinations was the finding that "at the time Lucas purchased the two lots, both were zoned for single-family residential construction and ... there were no restrictions imposed upon such use of the property by either the State of South Carolina, the County of Charleston, or the Town of the Isle of Palms." The trial court further found that the Beachfront Management Act decreed a permanent ban on construction insofar as Lucas's lots were concerned, and that this prohibition "deprive[d] Lucas of any reasonable economic use of the lots, ... eliminated the unrestricted right of use, and render[ed] them valueless." The court thus concluded that Lucas's properties had been "taken" by operation of the Act, and it ordered respondent to pay "just compensation" in the amount of $1,232,387.50.

The Supreme Court of South Carolina reversed. It found dispositive what it described as Lucas's concession "that the Beachfront Management Act [was] properly and validly designed to preserve ... South Carolina's beaches." 304 S.C. 376, 379, 404 S.E.2d 895, 896 (1991).

Failing an attack on the validity of the statute as such, the court believed itself bound to accept the "uncontested ... findings" of the South Carolina legislature that new construction in the coastal zone—such as petitioner intended—threatened this public resource. Id., at 383, 404 S.E.2d, at 898. The Court ruled that when a regulation respecting the use of property is designed "to prevent serious public harm," id., at 383, 404 S.E.2d, at 899 (citing, *inter alia*, *Mugler v. Kansas*, 123 U.S. 623, 8 S.Ct. 273, 31 L.Ed. 205 (1887)), no compensation is owing under the Takings Clause regardless of the regulation's effect on the property's value.

Two justices dissented. They acknowledged that our *Mugler* line of cases recognizes governmental power to prohibit "noxious" uses of property—i.e., uses of property akin to "public nuisances"—without having to pay compensation. But they would not have characterized the Beachfront Management Act's "*primary* purpose [as] the prevention of a nuisance." 304 S.C., at 395, 404 S.E.2d, at 906 (Harwell, J., dissenting). To the dissenters, the chief purposes of the legislation, among them the promotion of tourism and the creation of a "habitat for indigenous flora and fauna," could not fairly be compared to nuisance abatement. Id., at 396, 404 S.E.2d, at 906. As a consequence, they would have affirmed the trial court's conclusion that the Act's obliteration of the value of petitioner's lots accomplished a taking.

* * *

III

A

Prior to Justice Holmes' exposition in *Pennsylvania Coal Co. v. Mahon*, 260 U.S. 393, 43 S.Ct. 158, 67 L.Ed. 322 (1922), it was generally thought that the Takings Clause reached only a "direct appropriation" of property, *Legal Tender Cases*, 12 Wall. 457, 551, 20 L.Ed. 287 (1871), or the functional equivalent of a "practical ouster of [the owner's] possession." *Transportation Co. v. Chicago*, 99 U.S. 635, 642, 25 L.Ed. 336 (1879). *See also Gibson v. United States*, 166 U.S. 269, 275–276, 17 S.Ct. 578, 580, 41 L.Ed. 996 (1897). Justice Holmes recognized in *Mahon*, however, that if the protection against physical appropriations of private property was to be meaningfully enforced, the government's power to redefine the range of interests included in the ownership of property was necessarily constrained by constitutional limits. 260 U.S., at 414–415, 43 S.Ct., at 160. If, instead, the uses of private property were subject to unbridled, uncompensated qualification under the police power, "the natural tendency of human nature [would be] to extend the qualification more and more until at last private property disappear[ed]." Id., at 415, 43 S.Ct., at 160. These considerations gave birth in that case to the oft-cited maxim that, "while property may be regulated to a certain extent, if regulation goes too far it will be recognized as a taking." *Ibid.*

Nevertheless, our decision in *Mahon* offered little insight into when, and under what circumstances, a given regulation would be seen as going "too far" for purposes of the Fifth Amendment. In 70–odd years of succeeding "regulatory takings" jurisprudence, we have generally eschewed any " 'set formula' " for determining how far is too far, preferring to "engag[e] in ... essentially ad hoc, factual inquiries," *Penn Central Transportation Co. v. New York City*, 438 U.S. 104, 124, 98 S.Ct. 2646, 2659, 57 L.Ed.2d 631 (1978) (quoting *Goldblatt v. Hempstead*, 369 U.S. 590, 594, 82 S.Ct. 987, 990, 8 L.Ed.2d 130 (1962)). See Epstein, Takings: Descent and Resurrection, 1987 Sup.Ct. Rev. 1, 4. We have, however, described at least two discrete categories of regulatory action as compensable without case-specific inquiry into the public interest advanced in support of the restraint. The first encompasses regulations that compel the property owner to suffer a physical "invasion" of his property. In general (at least with regard to permanent invasions), no matter how minute the intrusion, and no matter how weighty the public purpose behind it, we have required compensation. For example, in *Loretto v. Teleprompter Manhattan CATV Corp.*, 458 U.S. 419, 102 S.Ct. 3164, 73 L.Ed.2d 868 (1982), we determined that New York's law requiring landlords to allow television cable companies to emplace cable facilities in their apartment buildings constituted a taking, id., at 435–440, 102 S.Ct., at 3175–3178, even though the facilities occupied at most only 1 1/2 cubic feet of the landlords' property, see id., at 438, n. 16, 102 S.Ct., at 3177. *See also United States v. Causby*, 328 U.S. 256, 265, and n. 10, 66 S.Ct. 1062, 1067, and n. 10, 90 L.Ed. 1206 (1946) (physical invasions of airspace); *cf. Kaiser Aetna v. United States*, 444 U.S. 164, 100 S.Ct. 383, 62 L.Ed.2d 332 (1979) (imposition of navigational servitude upon private marina).

The second situation in which we have found categorical treatment appropriate is where regulation denies all economically beneficial or productive use of land. *See Agins*, 447 U.S., at 260, 100 S.Ct., at 2141; *see also Nollan v. California Coastal Comm'n*, 483 U.S. 825, 834, 107 S.Ct. 3141, 3147, 97 L.Ed.2d 677 (1987); *Keystone Bituminous Coal Assn. v. DeBenedictis*, 480 U.S. 470, 495, 107 S.Ct. 1232, 1247, 94 L.Ed.2d 472 (1987); *Hodel v. Virginia Surface Mining & Reclamation Assn., Inc.*, 452 U.S. 264, 295–296, 101 S.Ct. 2352, 2370, 69 L.Ed.2d 1 (1981). As we have said on numerous occasions, the Fifth Amendment is violated when land-use regulation "does not substantially advance legitimate state interests *or denies an owner economically viable use of his land.*" Agins, supra, 447 U.S., at 260, 100 S.Ct., at 2141 (citations omitted) (emphasis added).

We have never set forth the justification for this rule. Perhaps it is simply, as Justice Brennan suggested, that total deprivation of beneficial use is, from the landowner's point of view, the equivalent of a physical appropriation. *See San Diego Gas & Electric Co. v. San Diego*, 450 U.S., at 652, 101 S.Ct., at 1304 (Brennan, J., dissenting). "[F]or what is the land but the profits thereof[?]" 1 E. Coke, Institutes ch. 1, § 1 (1st Am. ed. 1812). Surely, at least, in the extraordinary circumstance when no productive or economically beneficial use of land is permitted, it is less realistic to indulge our usual assumption that the legislature is simply "adjusting the benefits and burdens of economic life," *Penn Central Transportation Co.*, 438 U.S., at 124, 98 S.Ct., at 2659, in a manner that secures an "average reciprocity of advantage" to everyone concerned. *Pennsylvania Coal Co. v. Mahon*, 260 U.S., at 415, 43 S.Ct., at 160. And the *functional* basis for permitting the government, by regulation, to affect property values without compensation—that "Government hardly could go on if to some extent values incident to property could not be diminished without paying for every such change in the general law," id., at 413, 43 S.Ct., at 159—does not apply to the relatively rare situations where the government has deprived a landowner of all economically beneficial uses.

On the other side of the balance, affirmatively supporting a compensation requirement, is the fact that regulations that leave the owner of land without economically beneficial or productive options for its use—typically, as here, by requiring land to be left substantially in its natural state—carry with them a heightened risk that private property is being pressed into some form of public service under the guise of mitigating serious public harm. *See, e.g., Annicelli v. South Kingstown*, 463 A.2d 133, 140–141 (R.I.1983) (prohibition on construction adjacent to beach justified on twin grounds of safety and "conservation of open space"); *Morris County Land Improvement Co. v. Parsippany–Troy Hills Township*, 40 N.J. 539, 552–553, 193 A.2d 232, 240 (1963) (prohibition on filling marshlands imposed in order to preserve region as water detention basin and create wildlife refuge). As Justice Brennan explained: "From the government's point of view, the benefits flowing to the public from preservation of open space through regulation may be equally great as from creating a wildlife refuge through formal condemnation or increasing electricity production through a dam project that floods private property." *San Diego Gas & Elec. Co., supra*, 450 U.S., at 652, 101 S.Ct., at 1304 (Brennan, J., dissenting). The many statutes on the books, both state and federal, that provide for the use of eminent domain to impose servitudes on private scenic lands preventing developmental uses, or to acquire such lands altogether, suggest the practical equivalence in this setting of negative regulation and appropriation. See, e.g., 16 U.S.C.A. § 410ff–1(a) (authorizing acquisition of "lands, waters, or interests [within Channel Islands National Park] (including but not limited to scenic easements)"); § 460aa–2(a) (authorizing acquisition of "any lands, or lesser interests therein, including mineral interests and scenic easements" within Sawtooth National Recreation Area); §§ 3921–3923 (authorizing acquisition of wetlands); N.C. Gen.Stat. § 113A–38 (1990) (authorizing acquisition of, inter alia, " 'scenic easements' " within the North Carolina natural and scenic rivers system); Tenn.Code Ann. §§ 11–15–101—11–15–108 (1987) (authorizing acquisition of "protective easements" and other rights in real property adjacent to State's historic, architectural, archaeological, or cultural resources).

We think, in short, that there are good reasons for our frequently expressed belief that when the owner of real property has been called upon to sacrifice *all* economically beneficial uses in the name of the common good, that is, to leave his property economically idle, he has suffered a taking.

B

The trial court found Lucas's two beachfront lots to have been rendered valueless by respondent's enforcement of the coastal-zone construction ban. Under Lucas's theory of the case, which rested upon our "no economically viable use" statements, that finding entitled him to compensation. Lucas believed it unnecessary to take issue with either the purposes behind the Beachfront Management Act, or the means chosen by the South Carolina Legislature to effectuate those purposes. The South Carolina Supreme Court, however, thought otherwise. In its view, the Beachfront Management Act was no ordinary enactment, but involved an exercise of South Carolina's "police powers" to mitigate the harm to the public interest that petitioner's use of his land might occasion. 304 S.C., at 384, 404 S.E.2d, at 899. By neglecting to dispute the findings enumerated in the Act or otherwise to challenge the legislature's purposes, petitioner "concede[d] that the beach/dune area of South Carolina's shores is an extremely valuable public resource; that the erection of new construction, inter alia, contributes to the erosion and destruction of this public resource; and that discouraging new construction in close proximity to the beach/dune area is necessary to prevent a great public harm." Id., at 382–383, 404 S.E.2d, at 898. In the court's view, these concessions brought petitioner's challenge within a long line of this Court's cases sustaining against Due Process and Takings Clause challenges the State's use of its "police powers" to enjoin a property owner from activities akin to public nuisances. *See Mugler v. Kansas*, 123 U.S. 623, 8 S.Ct. 273, 31 L.Ed. 205 (1887) (law prohibiting manufacture of alcoholic beverages); *Hadacheck v. Sebastian*, 239 U.S. 394, 36 S.Ct. 143, 60 L.Ed. 348 (1915) (law barring operation of brick mill in residential area); *Miller v. Schoene*, 276 U.S. 272, 48 S.Ct. 246, 72 L.Ed. 568 (1928) (order to destroy diseased cedar trees to prevent infection of nearby orchards); *Goldblatt v. Hempstead*, 369 U.S. 590, 82 S.Ct. 987, 8 L.Ed.2d 130 (1962) (law effectively preventing continued operation of quarry in residential area).

It is correct that many of our prior opinions have suggested that "harmful or noxious uses" of property may be proscribed by government regulation without the requirement of compensation. For a number of reasons, however, we think the South Carolina Supreme Court was too quick to conclude that that principle decides the present case. The "harmful or noxious uses" principle was the Court's early attempt to describe in theoretical terms why government may, consistent with the Takings Clause, affect property values by regulation without incurring an obligation to compensate—a reality we nowadays acknowledge explicitly with respect to the full scope of the State's police power. * * *

The transition from our early focus on control of "noxious" uses to our contemporary understanding of the broad realm within which government may regulate without compensation was an easy one, since the distinction between "harm-preventing" and "benefit-conferring" regulation is often in the eye of the beholder. It is quite possible, for example, to describe in *either* fashion the ecological, economic, and aesthetic concerns that inspired the South Carolina legislature in the present case. One could say that imposing a servitude on Lucas's land is necessary in order to prevent his use of it from "harming" South Carolina's ecological resources; or, instead, in order to achieve the "benefits" of an ecological preserve. Compare, e.g., *Claridge v. New Hampshire Wetlands Board*, 125 N.H. 745, 752, 485 A.2d 287, 292 (1984) (owner may, without compensation, be barred from filling wetlands because landfilling would deprive adjacent coastal habitats and marine fisheries of ecological support), with, e.g., *Bartlett v. Zoning Comm'n of Old Lyme*, 161 Conn. 24, 30, 282 A.2d 907, 910 (1971) (owner barred from filling tidal marshland must be compensated, despite municipality's "laudable" goal of "preserv[ing] marshlands from encroachment or destruction"). Whether one or the other of the competing characterizations will come to one's lips in a particular case depends primarily upon one's evaluation of the worth of competing uses of real estate. See Restatement (Second) of Torts § 822, Comment g, p. 112 (1979) ("[p]ractically all human activities unless carried on in a wilderness interfere to some extent with others or involve some risk of interference"). A given restraint will be seen as mitigating "harm" to the adjacent parcels or securing a "benefit" for them, depending upon the observer's evaluation of the relative importance of the use that the restraint favors. See Sax, Takings and the Police Power, 74 Yale L.J. 36, 49 (1964) ("[T]he problem [in this area] is not one of noxiousness or harm-creating activity at all; rather it is a problem of inconsistency between perfectly innocent and independently desirable uses"). Whether Lucas's construction of single-family residences on his parcels should be described as bringing "harm" to South Carolina's adjacent ecological resources thus depends principally upon whether the describer believes that the State's use interest in nurturing those resources is so important that *any* competing adjacent use must yield.

When it is understood that "prevention of harmful use" was merely our early formulation of the police power justification necessary to sustain (without compensation) *any* regulatory diminution in value; and that the distinction between regulation that "prevents harmful use" and that which "confers benefits" is difficult, if not impossible, to discern on an objective, value-free basis; it becomes self-evident that noxious-use logic cannot serve as a touchstone to distinguish regulatory "takings"—which require compensation—from regulatory deprivations that do not require compensation. *A fortiori* the legislature's recitation of a noxious-use justification cannot be the basis for departing from our categorical rule that total regulatory takings must be compensated. If it were, departure would virtually always be allowed. The South Carolina Supreme Court's approach would essentially nullify *Mahon*'s affirmation of limits to the noncompensable exercise of the police power. * * *

Where the State seeks to sustain regulation that deprives land of all economically beneficial use, we think it may resist compensation only if the logically antecedent inquiry into the nature of the owner's estate shows that the proscribed use interests were not part of his title to begin with. This accords, we think, with our "takings" jurisprudence, which has traditionally been guided by the understandings of our citizens regarding the content of, and the State's power over, the "bundle of rights" that they acquire when they obtain title to property. It seems to us that the property owner necessarily expects the uses of his property to be restricted, from time to time, by various measures newly enacted by the State in legitimate exercise of its police powers; "[a]s long recognized, some values are enjoyed under an implied limitation and must yield to the police power." *Pennsylvania Coal Co. v. Mahon*, 260 U.S., at 413, 43 S.Ct., at 159. And in the case of personal property, by reason of the State's traditionally high degree of control over commercial dealings, he ought to be aware of the possibility that new regulation might even render his property economically worthless (at least if the property's only economically productive use is sale or manufacture for sale), *see Andrus v. Allard*, 444 U.S. 51, 66–67, 100 S.Ct. 318, 327, 62 L.Ed.2d 210 (1979) (prohibition on sale of eagle feathers). In the case of land, however, we think the notion pressed by the Council that title is somehow held subject to the "implied limitation" that the State may subsequently eliminate all economically valuable use is inconsistent with the historical compact recorded in the Takings Clause that has become part of our constitutional culture.

Where "permanent physical occupation" of land is concerned, we have refused to allow the government to decree it anew (without compensation), no matter how weighty the asserted "public interests" involved, *Loretto v. Teleprompter Manhattan CATV Corp.*, 458 U.S., at 426, 102 S.Ct., at 3171—though we assuredly would permit the government to assert a permanent easement that was a pre-existing limitation upon the landowner's title. Compare *Scranton v. Wheeler*, 179 U.S. 141, 163, 21 S.Ct. 48, 57, 45 L.Ed. 126 (1900) (interests of "riparian owner in the submerged lands . . . bordering on a public navigable water" held subject to Government's navigational servitude), with *Kaiser Aetna v. United States*, 444 U.S., at 178–180, 100 S.Ct., at 392–393 (imposition of navigational servitude on marina created and rendered navigable at private expense held to constitute a taking). We believe similar treatment must be accorded confiscatory regulations, i.e., regulations that prohibit all economically beneficial use of land: Any limitation so severe cannot be newly legislated or decreed (without compensation), but must inhere in the title itself, in the restrictions that background principles of the State's law of property and nuisance already place upon land ownership. A law or decree with such an effect must, in other words, do no more than duplicate the result that could have been achieved in the courts—by adjacent landowners (or other uniquely affected persons) under the State's law of private nuisance, or by the State under its complementary power to abate nuisances that affect the public generally, or otherwise.

On this analysis, the owner of a lake bed, for example, would not be entitled to compensation when he is denied the requisite permit to engage in a landfilling operation that would have the effect of flooding others' land. Nor the corporate owner of a nuclear generating plant, when it is directed to remove all improvements from its land upon discovery that the plant sits astride an earthquake fault. Such regulatory action may well have the effect of eliminating the land's only economically productive use, but it does not proscribe a productive use that was previously permissible under relevant property and nuisance principles. The use of these properties for what are now expressly prohibited purposes was *always* unlawful, and (subject to other constitutional limitations) it was open to the State at any point to make the implication of those background principles of nuisance and property law explicit. See Michelman, Property, Utility, and Fairness, Comments on the Ethical Foundations of "Just Compensation" Law, 80 Harv.L.Rev. 1165, 1239–1241 (1967). In light of our traditional resort to "existing rules or understandings that stem from an independent source such as state law" to define the range of interests that qualify for protection as "property" under the Fifth (and Fourteenth) amendments, * * * this recognition that the Takings Clause does not require compensation when an owner is barred from putting land to a use that is proscribed by those "existing rules or understandings" is surely unexceptional. When, however, a regulation that declares "off-limits" all economically productive or beneficial uses of land goes beyond what the relevant background principles would dictate, compensation must be paid to sustain it.

The "total taking" inquiry we require today will ordinarily entail (as the application of state nuisance law ordinarily entails) analysis of, among other things, the degree of harm to public lands and resources, or adjacent private property, posed by the claimant's proposed activities, see, e.g., Restatement (Second) of Torts §§ 826, 827, the social value of the claimant's activities and their suitability to the locality in question, see, e.g., id., §§ 828(a) and (b), 831, and the relative ease with which the alleged harm can be avoided through measures taken by the claimant and the government (or adjacent private landowners) alike, see, e.g., id., §§ 827(e), 828(c), 830. The fact that a particular use has long been engaged in by similarly situated owners ordinarily imports a lack of any common-law prohibition (though changed circumstances or new knowledge may make what was previously permissible no longer so), see Restatement (Second) of Torts, supra, § 827, comment *g*. So also does the fact that other landowners, similarly situated, are permitted to continue the use denied to the claimant.

It seems unlikely that common-law principles would have prevented the erection of any habitable or productive improvements on petitioner's land; they rarely support prohibition of the "essential use" of land, *Curtin v. Benson*, 222 U.S. 78, 86, 32 S.Ct. 31, 33, 56 L.Ed. 102 (1911). The question, however, is one of state law to be dealt with on remand.

We emphasize that to win its case South Carolina must do more than proffer the legislature's declaration that the uses Lucas desires are inconsistent with the public interest, or the conclusory assertion that they violate a common-law maxim such as *sic utere tuo ut alienum non laedas*. As we have said, a "State, by *ipse dixit*, may not transform private property into public property without compensation. . . ." *Webb's Fabulous Pharmacies, Inc. v. Beckwith*, 449 U.S. 155, 164, 101 S.Ct. 446, 452, 66 L.Ed.2d 358 (1980). Instead, as it would be required to do if it sought to restrain Lucas in a common-law action for public nuisance, South Carolina must identify background principles of nuisance and property law that prohibit the uses he now intends in the circumstances in which the property is presently found. Only on this showing can the State fairly claim that, in proscribing all such beneficial uses, the Beachfront Management Act is taking nothing.

* * *

The judgment is reversed and the cause remanded for proceedings not inconsistent with this opinion.

JUSTICE KENNEDY, concurring in the judgment.

* * *

The finding of no value must be considered under the Takings Clause by reference to the owner's reasonable, investment-backed expectations. * * * The Takings Clause, while conferring substantial protection on property owners, does not eliminate the police power of the State to enact limitations on the use of their property. *Mugler v. Kansas*, 123 U.S. 623, 669, 8 S.Ct. 273, 301, 31 L.Ed. 205 (1887). The rights conferred by the Takings Clause and the police power of the State may coexist without conflict. Property is bought and sold, investments are made, subject to the State's power to regulate. Where a taking is alleged from regulations which deprive the property of all value, the test must be whether the deprivation is contrary to reasonable, investment-backed expectations.

There is an inherent tendency towards circularity in this synthesis, of course; for if the owner's reasonable expectations are shaped by what courts allow as a proper exercise of governmental authority, property tends to become what courts say it is. Some circularity must be tolerated in these matters, however, as it is in other spheres. * * * The definition, moreover, is not circular in its entirety. The expectations protected by the Constitution are based on objective rules and customs that can be understood as reasonable by all parties involved.

In my view, reasonable expectations must be understood in light of the whole of our legal tradition. The common law of nuisance is too narrow a confine for the exercise of regulatory power in a complex and interdependent society. *Goldblatt v. Hempstead*, 369 U.S. 590, 593, 82 S.Ct. 987, 989, 8 L.Ed.2d 130 (1962). The State should not be prevented from enacting new regulatory initiatives in response to changing conditions, and courts must consider all reasonable expectations whatever their source. The Takings Clause does not require a static body of state property law; it protects private expectations to ensure private investment. I agree with the Court that nuisance prevention accords with the most common expectations of property owners who face regulation, but I do not believe this can be the sole source of state authority to impose severe restrictions. Coastal property may present such unique concerns for a fragile land system that the State can go further in regulating its development and use than the common law of nuisance might otherwise permit.

The Supreme Court of South Carolina erred, in my view, by reciting the general purposes for which the state regulations were enacted without a determination that they were in accord with the owner's reasonable expectations and therefore sufficient to support a severe restriction on specific parcels of property. See 304 S.C. 376, 383, 404 S.E.2d 895, 899 (1991). The promotion of tourism, for instance, ought not to suffice to deprive specific property of all value without a corresponding duty to compensate. Furthermore, the means as well as the ends of regulation must accord with the owner's reasonable expectations. Here, the State did not act until after the property had been zoned for individual lot development and most other parcels had been improved, throwing the whole burden of the regulation on the remaining lots. This too must be measured in the balance. *See Pennsylvania Coal Co. v. Mahon*, 260 U.S. 393, 416, 43 S.Ct. 158, 160, 67 L.Ed. 322 (1922).

With these observations, I concur in the judgment of the Court.

[Dissenting opinions omitted]

Notes

1. The Court remanded the Lucas case to the state courts where it was determined that nuisance law and other background principles of law in South Carolina did not prevent the development proscribed by the Beachfront Management Act's regulations. Lucas v. South Carolina Coastal Council, 309 S.C. 424, 424 S.E.2d 484 (1992). Following this decision, the regulations were amended to create a hardship exemption for land unduly burdened by the Act's provisions. The state paid Lucas full value for the taking affected by the regulation, granted the two parcels a hardship exemption, and then sold them to recoup what it had paid. Hardship exemptions, called variances, are contained in nearly all zoning ordinances to resolve practical difficulties and extreme hardships that result from the literal application of zoning provisions to particular parcels. Do you think that all land use regulations, even those that protect critical environmental areas, should contain hardship exemption provisions as a matter of course? What are the pros and cons? Since the Lucas total takings doctrine will apply to environmental regulations that prevent all economically viable use of the land, is there a downside to including such exemptions?

2. How should courts interpret the language in Lucas that permits restrictions on property that "inhere in the title itself," (restrictions that background principles of the state's law of property and nuisance already place upon land ownership in terms of the state law that defines title)?

Consider the case of Hunziker v. State, 519 N.W.2d 367 (Iowa 1994), cert. denied 514 U.S. 1003, 115 S.Ct. 1313, 131 L.Ed.2d 195 (1995). A developer sold a lot in his subdivision to a buyer who planned to build a home. Before construction could begin, the state archaeologist discovered a Native American burial mound on the property, and pursuant to a state statute, prohibited disinterment of the mound and required a buffer zone around the mound for protection. The developer refunded the price of the lot and took it back; he then brought an action for compensation for a regulatory taking. The court ruled against the developer, holding that, under Lucas, "the 'bundle of rights' the plaintiffs acquired by their fee simple title did not include the right to use the land contrary to the provisions [of the statutes denying permission to disinter human remains determined to have state and national significance from an historical or scientific standpoint]. * * * The plaintiffs took title to the land in question subject to the provisions of these sections. These sections and their resulting prohibitions concerning the use of the land ran—so to speak—with the land."

Also see Kim v. New York City, 90 N.Y.2d 1, 659 N.Y.S.2d 145, 681 N.E.2d 312 (1997), where the court held that a property owner's duty to maintain lateral support for roads that abut his property was a prevailing rule of property law inhering in his title, so that placement of fill by the city on the private property was not a taking. The dissenting opinion declared that the placement of fill was a physical taking for a public use—to shore up a roadway. In Esplanade Properties, LLC v. City of Seattle, 307 F.3d 978 (9th Cir. 2002), the court held that a developer who was denied permission to develop some shoreland houses on platforms did not suffer a taking because under Washington law the public trust doctrine regarding tidelands was inherent in the title to private property. Same, as to tidewater land, McQueen v. South Carolina Coastal Council, 354 S.C. 142, 580 S.E.2d 116 (2003). See also James Reginald Benjamin Jr., Rith Energy, Inc. v. United States "The Best of Both Worlds": Use of Common Law and Statutory Law Together in Applying the Nuisance Exception to Defend a Takings Claim, 11 Fed. Circuit B.J. 855 (2002).

3. In Gulf Power Co. v. United States, 187 F.3d 1324 (11th Cir.1999), the court of appeals agreed with seven electric utility companies that the United States government's "mandatory access" provision of the Pole Attachments Act (as part of the Telecommunications Act of 1996) constituted a per se taking. Electric utilities amass a vast network of poles, conduits, and rights-of-way as a function of their semi-public identity as a state-created and sanctioned monopoly. This provision requires utilities to permit cable television and telecommunications carriers "nondiscriminatory access" to the utilities' aforementioned infrastructure. The court ruled, "Under § 224(f), a utility has no choice but to permit a cable company or telecommunication carrier to permanently occupy physical space on its poles, ducts, conduits and rights-of-way ... Such a permanent, physical occupation of property falls squarely within the Loretto rule."

4. An interesting application of the nuisance exception in the Lucas case appears in Colorado Dept. of Health v. The Mill, 887 P.2d 993 (Colo. 1995). The Mill, a mining concern, brought a takings action challenging the Department's imposition of use restrictions on the site as a uranium mill operation. The Colorado Supreme Court held that The Mill should have

known that "the right to make any use of the property that would create a hazard to the public health by spreading radioactive contamination was excluded from The Mill's title at the onset." In coming to the conclusion that the use limitations fell under the Lucas nuisance exception and did not constitute a compensable taking, the Colorado court referred to the regulatory environment governing radioactive materials. This included Colorado common law nuisance, state nuisance statutes, the Department's regulations, and federal standards contained in the Uranium Mill Tailings Radiation Control Act. See also Darack v. Mazrimas, 5 Mass.L.Rptr. 469 (Super.Ct.1996), where the court used the Lucas nuisance doctrine to find that a denial of use of flood-prone property was not a total taking.

5. In Tahoe–Sierra Preservation Council, Inc. v. Tahoe Regional Planning Agency, 535 U.S. 302, 337, 122 S.Ct. 1465, 152 L.Ed.2d 517 (2002), the court rejected the landowners' assertion that a moratorium on development constitutes a temporal taking per se. See the discussion in Chapter VII on development moratoria and the Tahoe–Sierra case.

C. EXACTIONS

A careful reading of the Lingle case reveals that exactions constitute a separate category of regulatory takings doctrine. Lingle refers to "the special category of land use exactions." It defines these as "adjudicative land use exactions—specifically, government demands that a landowner dedicate an easement allowing public access to her property as a condition of obtaining a development permit." The special tests applied by the Court when land use exactions are challenged are created and explained in the next two principal cases.

NOLLAN v. CALIFORNIA COASTAL COMMISSION

Supreme Court of the United States, 1987.
483 U.S. 825, 107 S.Ct. 3141, 97 L.Ed.2d 677.

JUSTICE SCALIA delivered the opinion of the Court.

The Nollans own a beachfront lot in Ventura County, California. A quarter-mile north of their property is Faria County Park, an oceanside public park with a public beach and recreation area. Another public beach area, known locally as "the Cove," lies 1,800 feet south of their lot. A concrete seawall approximately eight feet high separates the beach portion of the Nollans' property from the rest of the lot. The historic mean high tide line determines the lot's oceanside boundary.

The Nollans originally leased their property with an option to buy. The building on the lot was a small bungalow, totaling 504 square feet, which for a time they rented to summer vacationers. After years of rental use, however, the building had fallen into disrepair, and could no longer be rented out.

The Nollans' option to purchase was conditioned on their promise to demolish the bungalow and replace it. In order to do so, under California Public Resources Code §§ 30106, 30212, and 30600 (West 1986), they were required to obtain a coastal development permit from the California Coastal Commission. On February 25, 1982, they submitted a permit application to the Commission in which they proposed to demolish the existing structure and replace it with a three-bedroom house in keeping with the rest of the neighborhood.

The Nollans were informed that their application had been placed on the administrative calendar, and that the Commission staff had recommended that the permit be granted subject to the condition that they allow the public an easement to pass across a portion of their property bounded by the mean high tide line on one side, and their seawall on the other side. This would make it easier for the public to get to Faria County Park and the Cove. The Nollans protested imposition of the condition, but the Commission overruled their objections and granted the permit subject to their recordation of a deed restriction granting the easement.

On June 3, 1982, the Nollans filed a petition for writ of administrative mandamus asking the Ventura County Superior Court to invalidate the access condition. They argued that the condition could not be imposed absent evidence that their proposed development would have a direct adverse impact on public access to the beach. The court agreed, and remanded the case to the Commission for a full evidentiary hearing on that issue.

On remand, the Commission held a public hearing, after which it made further factual findings and reaffirmed its imposition of the condition. It found that the new house would increase blockage of the view of the ocean, thus contributing to the development of "a 'wall' of residential structures" that would prevent the public "psychologically * * * from realizing a stretch of coastline exists nearby that they have every right to visit." The new house would also increase private use of the shorefront. These effects of construction of the house, along with other area development, would cumulatively "burden the public's ability to traverse to and along the shorefront." Therefore the Commission could properly require the Nollans to offset that burden by providing additional lateral access to the public beaches in the form of an easement across their property. The Commission also noted that it had similarly conditioned 43 out of 60 coastal development permits along the same tract of land, and that of the 17 not so conditioned, 14 had been approved when the Commission did not have administrative regulations in place allowing imposition of the condition, and the remaining 3 had not involved shorefront property.

The Nollans filed a supplemental petition for a writ of administrative mandamus with the Superior Court, in which they argued that imposition of the access condition violated the Takings Clause of the Fifth Amendment, as incorporated against the States by the Fourteenth Amendment. The Superior Court ruled in their favor on statutory grounds, finding, in part to avoid "issues of constitutionality," that the California Coastal Act of 1976, Cal.Pub.Res.Code Ann. § 30000 et seq., authorized the Commission to impose public access conditions on coastal development permits for the replacement of an existing single-family home with a new one only where the proposed development would have an adverse impact on public access to the sea. In the Court's view, the administrative record did not provide an adequate factual basis for concluding that replacement of the bungalow with the house would create a direct or cumulative burden on public access to the sea. Accordingly, the Superior Court granted the writ of mandamus and directed that the permit condition be struck.

The Commission appealed to the California Court of Appeal. * * *

The Court of Appeal reversed the Superior Court. 177 Cal.App.3d 719, 223 Cal.Rptr. 28 (1986). It disagreed with the Superior Court's interpretation of the Coastal Act, finding that it required that a coastal permit for the construction of a new house whose floor area, height or bulk was more than 10% larger than that of the house it was replacing be conditioned on a grant of access. Id., at 723–724, 223 Cal.Rptr., at 31; see Cal.Pub.Res.Code § 30212. It also ruled that the requirement did not violate the Constitution under the reasoning of an earlier case of the Court of Appeal, Grupe v. California Coastal Comm'n, 166 Cal.App.3d 148, 212 Cal.Rptr. 578 (1985). In that case, the court had found that so long as a project contributed to the need for public access, even if the project standing alone had not created the need for access, and even if there was only an indirect relationship between the access exacted and the need to which the project contributed, imposition of an access condition on a development permit was sufficiently related to burdens created by the project to be constitutional. * * * The Court of Appeal ruled that the record established that that was the situation with respect to the Nollans' house. * * * It ruled that the Nollans' taking claim also failed because, although the condition diminished the value of the Nollans' lot, it did not deprive them of all reasonable use of their property. * * * Since, in the Court of Appeal's view, there was no statutory or constitutional obstacle to imposition of the access condition, the Superior Court erred in granting the writ of mandamus. The Nollans appealed to this Court, raising only the constitutional question.

II

Had California simply required the Nollans to make an easement across their beachfront available to the public on a permanent basis in order to increase public access to the beach, rather than conditioning their permit to rebuild their house on their agreeing to do so, we have no doubt there would have been a taking. To say that the appropriation of a public easement across a landowner's premises does not constitute the taking of a property interest but rather, (as Justice Brennan contends) "a mere restriction on its use," is to use words in a manner that deprives them of all their ordinary meaning. Indeed, one of the principal uses of the eminent domain power is to assure that the government be able to require conveyance of just such interests, so long as it pays for them. Perhaps because the point is so obvious, we have never been confronted with a controversy that required us to rule upon it, but our cases' analysis of the effect of other governmental action leads to the same conclusion. We have repeatedly held that, as to property reserved by its owner for private use, "the right to exclude [others is] 'one of the most essential sticks in the bundle of rights that are commonly characterized as property.'" *Loretto v. Teleprompter Manhattan CATV Corp.*, 458 U.S. 419, 433, 102 S.Ct. 3164, 3175, 73 L.Ed.2d 868 (1982), quoting *Kaiser Aetna v. United States,* 444 U.S. 164, 176, 100 S.Ct. 383, 391, 62 L.Ed.2d 332 (1979). In *Loretto* we observed that where governmental action results in "[a] permanent physical occupation" of the property, by the government itself or by others, "our cases uniformly have found a taking to the extent of the occupation, without regard to whether the action achieves an important public benefit or has only minimal economic impact on the owner." We think a "permanent physical occupation" has occurred, for purposes of that rule, where individuals are given a permanent and continuous right to pass to and fro, so that the real property may continuously be traversed, even though no particular individual is permitted to station himself permanently upon the premises.[4]

* * *

Given, then, that requiring uncompensated conveyance of the easement outright would violate the Fourteenth Amendment, the question becomes whether requiring it to be conveyed as a condition for issuing a land use permit alters the outcome. We have long recognized that land use regulation does not effect a taking if it "substantially advance[s] legitimate state interests" and does not "den[y] an owner economically viable use of his land," *Agins v. Tiburon,* 447 U.S. 255, 260, 100 S.Ct. 2138, 2141, 65 L.Ed.2d 106 (1980). See also *Penn Central Transportation Co. v. New York City,* 438 U.S. 104, 127, 98 S.Ct. 2646, 2660, 57 L.Ed.2d 631 (1978) ("a use restriction may constitute a 'taking' if not reasonably necessary to the effectuation of a substantial government purpose"). Our cases have not elaborated on the standards for determining what constitutes a "legitimate state interest" or what type of connection between the regulation and the state interest satisfies the requirement that the former "substantially advance" the latter. They have made clear, however, that a broad range of governmental purposes and regulations satisfies these requirements. * * * The Commission argues that among these permissible purposes are protecting the public's ability to see the beach, assisting the public in overcoming the "psychological barrier" to using the beach created by a developed shorefront, and preventing congestion on the public beaches. We assume, without deciding, that this is so—in which case the Commission unquestionably would be able to deny the Nollans their permit outright if their new house (alone, or by reason of

4. The holding of *PruneYard Shopping Center v. Robins,* 447 U.S. 74, 100 S.Ct. 2035, 64 L.Ed.2d 741 (1980), is not inconsistent with this analysis, since there the owner had already opened his property to the general public, and in addition permanent access was not required. The analysis of *Kaiser Aetna v. United States,* 444 U.S. 164, 100 S.Ct. 383, 62 L.Ed.2d 332 (1979), is not inconsistent because it was affected by traditional doctrines regarding navigational servitudes. Of course neither of those cases involved, as this one does, a classic right-of-way easement.

the cumulative impact produced in conjunction with other construction) would substantially impede these purposes, unless the denial would interfere so drastically with the Nollans' use of their property as to constitute a taking.

The Commission argues that a permit condition that serves the same legitimate police-power purpose as a refusal to issue the permit should not be found to be a taking if the refusal to issue the permit would not constitute a taking. We agree. Thus, if the Commission attached to the permit some condition that would have protected the public's ability to see the beach notwithstanding construction of the new house—for example, a height limitation, a width restriction, or a ban on fences—so long as the Commission could have exercised its police power (as we have assumed it could) to forbid construction of the house altogether, imposition of the condition would also be constitutional. Moreover (and here we come closer to the facts of the present case), the condition would be constitutional even if it consisted of the requirement that the Nollans provide a viewing spot on their property for passersby with whose sighting of the ocean their new house would interfere. Although such a requirement, constituting a permanent grant of continuous access to the property, would have to be considered a taking if it were not attached to a development permit, the Commission's assumed power to forbid construction of the house in order to protect the public's view of the beach must surely include the power to condition construction upon some concession by the owner, even a concession of property rights, that serves the same end. If a prohibition designed to accomplish that purpose would be a legitimate exercise of the police power rather than a taking, it would be strange to conclude that providing the owner an alternative to that prohibition which accomplishes the same purpose is not.

The evident constitutional propriety disappears, however, if the condition substituted for the prohibition utterly fails to further the end advanced as the justification for the prohibition. When that essential nexus is eliminated, the situation becomes the same as if California law forbade shouting fire in a crowded theater, but granted dispensations to those willing to contribute $100 to the state treasury. While a ban on shouting fire can be a core exercise of the State's police power to protect the public safety, and can thus meet even our stringent standards for regulation of speech, adding the unrelated condition alters the purpose to one which, while it may be legitimate, is inadequate to sustain the ban. Therefore, even though, in a sense, requiring a $100 tax contribution in order to shout fire is a lesser restriction on speech than an outright ban, it would not pass constitutional muster. Similarly here, the lack of nexus between the condition and the original purpose of the building restriction converts that purpose to something other than what it was. The purpose then becomes, quite simply, the obtaining of an easement to serve some valid governmental purpose, but without payment of compensation. Whatever may be the outer limits of "legitimate state interests" in the takings and land use context, this is not one of them. In short, unless the permit condition serves the same governmental purpose as the development ban, the building restriction is not a valid regulation of land use but "an out-and-out plan of extortion." *J.E.D. Associates, Inc. v. Atkinson,* 121 N.H. 581, 584, 432 A.2d 12, 14–15 (1981). * * *

III

The Commission claims that it concedes as much, and that we may sustain the condition at issue here by finding that it is reasonably related to the public need or burden that the Nollans' new house creates or to which it contributes. We can accept, for purposes of discussion, the Commission's proposed test as to how close a "fit" between the condition and the burden is required, because we find that this case does not meet even the most untailored standards. The Commission's principal contention to the contrary essentially turns on a play on the word "access." The Nollans' new house, the Commission found, will interfere with "visual access" to the beach. That in turn (along with other shorefront development) will interfere with the desire of people who drive past the Nollans' house to use the beach, thus creating a "psychological barrier" to "access." The Nollans' new house will also, by a process not altogether clear from the Commission's opinion but presumably potent enough to more than offset the effects of the psychological barrier, increase the use of the public beaches, thus creating the need for more "access." These burdens on "access" would be alleviated by a requirement that the Nollans provide "lateral access" to the beach.

Rewriting the argument to eliminate the play on words makes clear that there is nothing to it. It is quite impossible to understand how a requirement that people already on the public beaches be able to walk across the Nollans' property reduces any obstacles to viewing the beach created by the new house. It is also impossible to understand how it lowers any "psychological barrier" to using the public beaches, or how it helps to remedy any additional congestion on them caused by construction of the Nollans' new house. We therefore find that the Commission's imposition of the permit condition cannot be treated as an exercise of its land use power for any of these purposes. Our conclusion on this point is consistent with the approach taken by every other court that has considered the question, with the exception of the California state courts. * * * We view the Fifth Amendment's property clause to be more than a pleading requirement, and compliance with it to be more than an exercise in cleverness and imagination. As indicated earlier, our cases describe the condition for abridgement of property rights through the police power as a "*substantial* advanc[ing]" of a legitimate State interest. We are inclined to be particularly careful about the adjective where the actual conveyance of property is made a condition to the lifting of a land use restriction, since in that context there is heightened risk that the purpose is avoidance of the compensation requirement, rather than the stated police power objective.

We are left, then, with the Commission's justification for the access requirement unrelated to land use regulation:

> "Finally, the Commission notes that there are several existing provisions of pass and repass lateral access benefits already given by past Faria Beach Tract applicants as a result of prior coastal permit decisions. The access required as a condition of this permit is part of a comprehensive program to provide continuous public access along Faria Beach as the lots undergo development or redevelopment." App. 68.

That is simply an expression of the Commission's belief that the public interest will be served by a continuous strip of publicly accessible beach along the coast. The Commission may well be right that it is a good idea, but that does not establish that the Nollans (and other coastal residents) alone can be compelled to contribute to its realization. Rather, California is free to advance its "comprehensive program," if it wishes, by using its power of eminent domain for this "public purpose," see U.S. Const., Amdt. V; but if it wants an easement across the Nollans' property, it must pay for it.

Reversed.

[Dissenting opinions omitted.]

DOLAN v. CITY OF TIGARD

Supreme Court of the United States, 1994.
512 U.S. 374, 114 S.Ct. 2309, 129 L.Ed.2d 304.

CHIEF JUSTICE REHNQUIST delivered the opinion of the Court.

Petitioner challenges the decision of the Oregon Supreme Court which held that the city of Tigard could condition the approval of her building permit on the dedication of a portion of her property for flood control and traffic improvements. 317 Ore. 110, 854 P.2d 437 (1993). We granted certiorari to resolve a question left open by our decision in *Nollan v. California Coastal Comm'n*, 483 U.S. 825 (1987), of what is the required degree of connection between the exactions imposed by the city and the projected impacts of the proposed development.

I

The State of Oregon enacted a comprehensive land use management program in 1973. Ore. Rev. Stat. §§ 197.005–197.860 (1991). The program required all Oregon cities and counties to adopt new comprehensive land use plans that were consistent with the statewide planning goals. §§ 197.175(1), 197.250. The plans are implemented by land use regulations which are part of an integrated hierarchy of legally binding goals, plans, and regulations. §§ 197.175, 197.175(2)(b). Pursuant to the State's requirements, the city of Tigard, a community of some 30,000 residents on the southwest edge of Portland, developed a comprehensive plan and codified it in its Community Development Code (CDC). The CDC requires property owners in the area zoned Central Business

District to comply with a 15% open space and landscaping requirement, which limits total site coverage, including all structures and paved parking, to 85% of the parcel. CDC, ch. 18.66, App. to Pet. for Cert. G16–G17. After the completion of a transportation study that identified congestion in the Central Business District as a particular problem, the city adopted a plan for a pedestrian/bicycle pathway intended to encourage alternatives to automobile transportation for short trips. The CDC requires that new development facilitate this plan by dedicating land for pedestrian pathways where provided for in the pedestrian/bicycle pathway plan.

The city also adopted a Master Drainage Plan (Drainage Plan). The Drainage Plan noted that flooding occurred in several areas along Fanno Creek, including areas near petitioner's property. The Drainage Plan also established that the increase in impervious surfaces associated with continued urbanization would exacerbate these flooding problems. To combat these risks, the Drainage Plan suggested a series of improvements to the Fanno Creek Basin, including channel excavation in the area next to petitioner's property. Other recommendations included ensuring that the floodplain remains free of structures and that it be preserved as greenways to minimize flood damage to structures. The Drainage Plan concluded that the cost of these improvements should be shared based on both direct and indirect benefits, with property owners along the waterways paying more due to the direct benefit that they would receive. * * *

Petitioner Florence Dolan owns a plumbing and electric supply store located on Main Street in the Central Business District of the city. The store covers approximately 9,700 square feet on the eastern side of a 1.67–acre parcel, which includes a gravel parking lot. Fanno Creek flows through the southwestern corner of the lot and along its western boundary. The year-round flow of the creek renders the area within the creek's 100–year floodplain virtually unusable for commercial development. The city's comprehensive plan includes the Fanno Creek floodplain as part of the city's greenway system.

Petitioner applied to the city for a permit to redevelop the site. Her proposed plans called for nearly doubling the size of the store to 17,600 square feet, and paving a 39–space parking lot. The existing store, located on the opposite side of the parcel, would be razed in sections as construction progressed on the new building. In the second phase of the project, petitioner proposed to build an additional structure on the northeast side of the site for complementary businesses, and to provide more parking. The proposed expansion and intensified use are consistent with the city's zoning scheme in the Central Business District.

The City Planning Commission granted petitioner's permit application subject to conditions imposed by the city's CDC. The CDC establishes the following standard for site development review approval:

> "Where landfill and/or development is allowed within and adjacent to the 100–year floodplain, the city shall require the dedication of

sufficient open land area for greenway adjoining and within the floodplain. This area shall include portions at a suitable elevation for the construction of a pedestrian/bicycle pathway within the floodplain in accordance with the adopted pedestrian/bicycle plan."

Thus, the Commission required that petitioner dedicate the portion of her property lying within the 100–year floodplain for improvement of a storm drainage system along Fanno Creek and that she dedicate an additional 15–foot strip of land adjacent to the floodplain as a pedestrian/bicycle pathway. The dedication required by that condition encompasses approximately 7,000 square feet, or roughly 10% of the property. In accordance with city practice, petitioner could rely on the dedicated property to meet the 15% open space and landscaping requirement mandated by the city's zoning scheme. The city would bear the cost of maintaining a landscaped buffer between the dedicated area and the new store.

Petitioner requested variances from the CDC standards. Variances are granted only where it can be shown that, owing to special circumstances related to a specific piece of the land, the literal interpretation of the applicable zoning provisions would cause "an undue or unnecessary hardship" unless the variance is granted. Rather than posing alternative mitigating measures to offset the expected impacts of her proposed development, as allowed under the CDC, petitioner simply argued that her proposed development would not conflict with the policies of the comprehensive plan. The Commission denied the request.

The Commission made a series of findings concerning the relationship between the dedicated conditions and the projected impacts of petitioner's project. First, the Commission noted that "[i]t is reasonable to assume that customers and employees of the future uses of this site could utilize a pedestrian/bicycle pathway adjacent to this development for their transportation and recreational needs." The Commission noted that the site plan has provided for bicycle parking in a rack in front of the proposed building and "[i]t is reasonable to expect that some of the users of the bicycle parking provided for by the site plan will use the pathway adjacent to Fanno Creek if it is constructed." In addition, the Commission found that creation of a convenient, safe pedestrian/ bicycle pathway system as an alternative means of transportation "could offset some of the traffic demand on [nearby] streets and lessen the increase in traffic congestion."

The Commission went on to note that the required floodplain dedication would be reasonably related to petitioner's request to intensify the use of the site given the increase in the impervious surface. The Commission stated that the "anticipated increased storm water flow from the subject property to an already strained creek and drainage basin can only add to the public need to manage the stream channel and floodplain for drainage purposes." Based on this anticipated increased storm water flow, the Commission concluded that "the requirement of dedication of the floodplain area on the site is related to the applicant's plan to intensify development on the site." The Tigard City Council approved the Commission's final order, subject to one minor modification; the City Council reassigned the responsibility for surveying and marking the floodplain area from petitioner to the city's engineering department.

Petitioner appealed to the Land Use Board of Appeals (LUBA) on the ground that the city's dedication requirements were not related to the proposed development, and, therefore, those requirements constituted an uncompensated taking of their property under the Fifth Amendment. In evaluating the federal taking claim, LUBA assumed that the city's findings about the impacts of the proposed development were supported by substantial evidence. * * * Given the undisputed fact that the proposed larger building and paved parking area would increase the amount of impervious surfaces and the runoff into Fanno Creek, LUBA concluded that "there is a 'reasonable relationship' between the proposed development and the requirement to dedicate land along Fanno Creek for a greenway." With respect to the pedestrian/bicycle pathway, LUBA noted the Commission's finding that a significantly larger retail sales building and parking lot would attract larger numbers of customers and employees and their vehicles. It again found a "reasonable relationship" between alleviating the impacts of increased traffic from the development and facilitating the provision of a pedestrian/bicycle pathway as an alternative means of transportation.

The Oregon Court of Appeals affirmed, rejecting petitioner's contention that in *Nollan v. California Coastal Comm'n*, 483 U.S. 825 (1987), we had abandoned the "reasonable relationship" test in favor of a stricter "essential nexus" test. 113 Ore.App. 162, 832 P. 2d 853 (1992). The Oregon Supreme Court affirmed. 317 Ore. 110, 854 P.2d 437 (1993). The court also disagreed with petitioner's contention that the *Nollan* Court abandoned the "reasonably related" test. Id., at 118, 854 P. 2d, at 442. Instead, the court read *Nollan* to mean that an "exaction is reasonably related to an impact if the exaction serves the same purpose that a denial of the permit would serve." Id., at 120, 854 P.2d, at 443. The court decided that both the pedestrian/bicycle pathway condition and the storm drainage dedication had an essential nexus to the development of the proposed site. Id., at 121, 854 P.2d, at 443. Therefore, the court found the conditions to be reasonably related to the impact of the expansion of petitioner's business. * * *

II

* * *

Petitioner contends that the city has forced her to choose between the building permit and her right under the Fifth Amendment to just compensation for the public easements. Petitioner does not quarrel with the city's authority to exact some forms of dedication as a condition for the grant of a building permit, but challenges the showing made by the city to justify these exactions. She argues that the city has identified "no special benefits" conferred on her, and has not identified any "special quantifiable burdens" created by her new store that would justify the particular dedications required from her which are not required from the public at large.

III

In evaluating petitioner's claim, we must first determine whether the "essential nexus" exists between the "legitimate state interest" and the permit condition exacted by the city. *Nollan*, 483 U.S., at 837. If we find that a nexus exists, we must then decide the required degree of connection between the exactions and the projected impact of the proposed development. We were not required to reach this question in *Nollan*, because we concluded that the connection did not meet even the loosest standard. 483 U.S., at 838. Here, however, we must decide this question.

A

We addressed the essential nexus question in *Nollan*. * * * We resolved, however, that the Coastal Commission's regulatory authority was set completely adrift from its constitutional moorings when it claimed that a nexus existed between visual access to the ocean and a permit condition requiring lateral public access along the Nollan's beachfront lot. How enhancing the public's ability to "traverse to and along the shorefront" served the same governmental purpose of "visual access to the ocean" from the roadway was beyond our ability to countenance. The absence of a nexus left the Coastal Commission in the position of simply trying to obtain an easement through gimmickry, which converted a valid regulation of land use into "an out-and-out plan of extortion."

No such gimmicks are associated with the permit conditions imposed by the city in this case. Undoubtedly, the prevention of flooding along Fanno Creek and the reduction of traffic congestion in the Central Business District qualify as the type of legitimate public purposes we have upheld. It seems equally obvious that a nexus exists between preventing flooding along Fanno Creek and limiting development within the creek's 100-year floodplain. Petitioner proposes to double the size of her retail store and to pave her now-gravel parking lot, thereby expanding the impervious surface on the property and increasing the amount of stormwater run-off into Fanno Creek.

The same may be said for the city's attempt to reduce traffic congestion by providing for alternative means of transportation. In theory, a pedestrian/bicycle pathway provides a useful alternative means of transportation for workers and shoppers: "Pedestrians and bicyclists occupying dedicated spaces for walking and/or bicycling . . . remove potential vehicles from streets, resulting in an overall improvement in total transportation system flow." A. Nelson, Public Provision of Pedestrian and Bicycle Access Ways: Public Policy Rationale and the Nature of Private Benefits 11, Center for Planning Development, Georgia Institute of Technology, Working Paper Series (Jan. 1994). See also, Intermodal

Surface Transportation Efficiency Act of 1991, Pub. L. 102–240, 105 Stat. 1914; (recognizing pedestrian and bicycle facilities as necessary components of any strategy to reduce traffic congestion).

B

The second part of our analysis requires us to determine whether the degree of the exactions demanded by the city's permit conditions bear the required relationship to the projected impact of petitioner's proposed development. * * *

The city required that petitioner dedicate "to the city as Greenway all portions of the site that fall within the existing 100–year floodplain [of Fanno Creek] ... and all property 15 feet above [the floodplain] boundary." In addition, the city demanded that the retail store be designed so as not to intrude into the greenway area. The city relies on the Commission's rather tentative findings that increased stormwater flow from petitioner's property "can only add to the public need to manage the [floodplain] for drainage purposes" to support its conclusion that the "requirement of dedication of the floodplain area on the site is related to the applicant's plan to intensify development on the site."

The city made the following specific findings relevant to the pedestrian/bicycle pathway:

> "In addition, the proposed expanded use of this site is anticipated to generate additional vehicular traffic thereby increasing congestion on nearby collector and arterial streets. Creation of a convenient, safe pedestrian/bicycle pathway system as an alternative means of transportation could offset some of the traffic demand on these nearby streets and lessen the increase in traffic congestion."

The question for us is whether these findings are constitutionally sufficient to justify the conditions imposed by the city on petitioner's building permit. Since state courts have been dealing with this question a good deal longer than we have, we turn to representative decisions made by them.

* * *

We think the "reasonable relationship" test adopted by a majority of the state courts is closer to the federal constitutional norm than either of those previously discussed. But we do not adopt it as such, partly because the term "reasonable relationship" seems confusingly similar to the term "rational basis" which describes the minimal level of scrutiny under the Equal Protection Clause of the Fourteenth Amendment. We think a term such as "rough proportionality" best encapsulates what we hold to be the requirement of the Fifth Amendment. No precise mathematical calculation is required, but the city must make some sort of individualized determination that the required dedication is related both in nature and extent to the impact of the proposed development.

* * *

We turn now to analysis of whether the findings relied upon by the city here, first with respect to the floodplain easement, and second with respect to the pedestrian/bicycle path, satisfied these requirements.

It is axiomatic that increasing the amount of impervious surface will increase the quantity and rate of storm-water flow from petitioner's property. Therefore, keeping the floodplain open and free from development would likely confine the pressures on Fanno Creek created by petitioner's development. In fact, because petitioner's property lies within the Central Business District, the Community Development Code already required that petitioner leave 15% of it as open space and the undeveloped floodplain would have nearly satisfied that requirement. But the city demanded more—it not only wanted petitioner not to build in the floodplain, but it also wanted petitioner's property along Fanno Creek for its Greenway system. The city has never said why a public greenway, as opposed to a private one, was required in the interest of flood control.

The difference to petitioner, of course, is the loss of her ability to exclude others. As we have noted, this right to exclude others is "one of the most essential sticks in the bundle of rights that are commonly characterized as property." Kaiser Aetna, 444 U.S., at 176. It is difficult to see why recreational visitors trampling along petitioner's floodplain easement are sufficiently related to the city's legitimate interest in reducing flooding problems along Fanno Creek, and the city has not attempted to make any individualized determination to support this part of its request.

The city contends that recreational easement along the Greenway is only ancillary to the city's chief purpose in controlling flood hazards. It further asserts that unlike the residential property at issue in *Nollan*, petitioner's property is commercial in character and therefore, her right to exclude others is compromised. * * *

Admittedly, petitioner wants to build a bigger store to attract members of the public to her property. She also wants, however, to be able to control the time and manner in which they enter. The recreational easement on the Greenway is different in character from the exercise of state-protected rights of free expression and petition that we permitted in *PruneYard*. In *PruneYard*, we held that a major private shopping center that attracted more than 25,000 daily patrons had to provide access to persons exercising their state constitutional rights to distribute pamphlets and ask passersby to sign their petitions. We based our decision, in part, on the fact that the shopping center "may restrict expressive activity by adopting time, place, and manner regulations that will minimize any interference with its commercial functions." By contrast, the city wants to impose a permanent recreational easement upon petitioner's property that borders Fanno Creek. Petitioner would lose all rights to regulate the time in which the public entered onto the Greenway, regardless of any interference it might pose with her retail store. Her right to exclude would not be regulated, it would be eviscerated.

If petitioner's proposed development had somehow encroached on existing greenway space in the city, it would have been reasonable to require petitioner to provide some alternative greenway space for the public either on her property or elsewhere. * * * But that is not the case here. We conclude that the findings upon which the city relies do not show the required reasonable relationship between the floodplain easement and the petitioner's proposed new building.

With respect to the pedestrian/bicycle pathway, we have no doubt that the city was correct in finding that the larger retail sales facility proposed by petitioner will increase traffic on the streets of the Central Business District. The city estimates that the proposed development would generate roughly 435 additional trips per day. Dedications for streets, sidewalks, and other public ways are generally reasonable exactions to avoid excessive congestion from a proposed property use. But on the record before us, the city has not met its burden of demonstrating that the additional number of vehicle and bicycle trips generated by the petitioner's development reasonably relate to the city's requirement for a dedication of the pedestrian/bicycle pathway easement. The city simply found that the creation of the pathway "could offset some of the traffic demand . . . and lessen the increase in traffic congestion."

As Justice Peterson of the Supreme Court of Oregon explained in his dissenting opinion, however, "[t]he findings of fact that the bicycle pathway system '*could* offset some of the traffic demand' is a far cry from a finding that the bicycle pathway system *will*, or is *likely to*, offset some of the traffic demand." 317 Ore., at 127, 854 P.2d, at 447 (emphasis in original). No precise mathematical calculation is required, but the city must make some effort to quantify its findings in support of the dedication for the pedestrian/bicycle pathway beyond the conclusory statement that it could offset some of the traffic demand generated.

IV

Cities have long engaged in the commendable task of land use planning, made necessary by increasing urbanization particularly in metropolitan areas such as Portland. The city's goals of reducing flooding hazards and traffic congestion, and providing for public greenways, are laudable, but there are outer limits to how this may be done. "A strong public desire to improve the public condition [will not] warrant achieving the desire by a shorter cut than the constitutional way of paying for the change." *Pennsylvania Coal*, 260 U.S., at 416.

The judgment of the Supreme Court of Oregon is reversed, and the case is remanded for further proceedings consistent with this opinion.

[Dissent omitted.]

Notes

1. The essential nexus and rough proportionality tests adopted by Nollan and Dolan are said to apply a higher level of judicial scrutiny to conditions imposed on land use approvals that require a landowner to

dedicate an easement allowing the public access to the land. In Dolan, the Court writes "the city must make some sort of individualized determination that the required dedication is related both in nature and extent to the impact of the proposed development." In due process cases, courts defer to governmental decisions, assume that they meet the Constitution's requirements, and impose the burden of proving regulations unreasonable on the challenger. Note how in Nollan and Dolan, this higher level of scrutiny imposes a burden on the government of proving the essential nexus and roughly proportionate relationship that they require. Similarly, in Lucas v. South Carolina Coastal Council, 505 U.S. 1003, 112 S.Ct. 2886, 120 L.Ed.2d 798 (1992), the government regulator must show that, where there is a total taking of all economic value, background principles of state law, including nuisance, proscribe the land use prohibited by the land use regulation.

2. Justice Stevens, in a dissent in the Dolan case, joined by Blackmun and Ginsburg, strongly disagrees with the majority's shifting of the burden of proof to the government. "In our changing world one thing is certain: uncertainty will characterize predictions about the impact of new urban developments on the risks of floods, earthquakes, traffic congestion, or environmental harms. When there is doubt concerning the magnitude of those impacts, the public interest in averting them must outweigh the private interest of the commercial entrepreneur. If the government can demonstrate that the conditions it has imposed in a land-use permit are rational, impartial and conducive to fulfilling the aims of a valid land-use plan, a strong presumption of validity should attach to those conditions. The burden of demonstrating that those conditions have unreasonably impaired the economic value of the proposed improvement belongs squarely on the shoulders of the party challenging the state action's constitutionality. That allocation of burdens has served us well in the past. The court has stumbled badly today by reversing it." Id. at 411.

3. In crafting its new judicial tests in Dolan, the Court reviewed the judicial tests applied by a handful of state courts to land use exactions, not limited to those that require the owner to dedicate an affirmative easement to the public. The Court found that these tests range from very general reasonable connection standards to highly exacting, directly proportional, requirements. In adopting an intermediate standard of proof (rough proportionality), the Court found that it was closer to the "federal constitutional norm."

4. A critical question is whether the Nollan and Dolan tests are limited to conditions that impose public access easements, involved in both cases, or apply to a larger range of land use conditions, such as requirements to provide off site capital improvements or pay for other public benefits. The question was addressed by the Court in City of Monterey v. Del Monte Dunes, Ltd., 526 U.S. 687, 119 S.Ct. 1624, 143 L.Ed.2d 882 (1999). There, the Court noted that "we have not extended the rough-proportionality test of Dolan beyond the special context of exactions—land use decisions conditioning approval of development on the dedication of property to public use." Prior to the Monterey decision, the California Supreme Court held that Dolan does apply in certain money exaction cases. In Ehrlich v. City of Culver City, 12 Cal.4th 854, 50 Cal.Rptr.2d 242, 911 P.2d 429 (1996), the court, applying Dolan, held that a $280,000 fee imposed on a developer to

mitigate the loss of community recreational facilities (the proposed development would replace a failed private tennis club with luxury condominiums), was not shown by the city to be roughly proportional to the impact of the proposed development; on the other hand, a requirement that the developer provide for art reasonably accessible to the public in connection with a generally applicable exaction requirement was upheld in the case. The court said:

> [I]t is not at all clear that the rationale (and the heightened standard of scrutiny) of Nollan and Dolan applies to cases in which the exaction takes the form of a generally applicable development fee or assessment . . . But when a local government imposes special, discretionary permit conditions on development by individual property owners—as in the case of the recreational fee at issue in this case—Nollan and Dolan require that such conditions, whether they consist of possessory dedications or monetary exactions, be scrutinized under the heightened standard.

5. State courts seem less likely to apply Dolan's rough proportionality standard to impact fees that are imposed generally as opposed to those imposed on particular developers. See Blue Jeans Equities West v. City and County of San Francisco, 3 Cal.App.4th 164, 4 Cal.Rptr.2d 114 (1992), cert. denied 506 U.S. 866, 113 S.Ct. 191, 121 L.Ed.2d 135 (1992), in which the court refused to apply the "heightened scrutiny" rule of Nollan where the municipality imposed a "generally applicable development fee[,]" in the form of a traffic impact fee, upon all developers building new office space in downtown San Francisco in order to fund the metro railway's efforts to accommodate increased ridership. See also Home Builders Ass'n of Central Arizona v. City of Scottsdale, 187 Ariz. 479, 930 P.2d 993 (1997), where the plaintiffs challenged a water resources development fee imposed by the city in order to obtain new water in the future. The court considered the Dolan case and found it inapplicable because under the Arizona enabling act a reasonable relationship between the fee and the public burden is required and that standard was met in this case. Also, the court said that a money exaction is a considerably more benign form of regulation than a demand that land be ceded to the city. In Northern Illinois Home Builders Ass'n, Inc. v. County of Du Page, 165 Ill.2d 25, 208 Ill.Dec. 328, 649 N.E.2d 384 (1995), the court upheld one of two state enabling statutes that authorized counties to create schedules of exactions for transportation impacts. The court found that Dolan was no impediment to the imposition of transportation impact fees because of the state police power concern over traffic congestion and the continued adherence of Illinois to the "specifically and uniquely attributable" test for exactions.

6. Does Lingle v. Chevron affect the Nollan and Dolan doctrines? In Lingle, the Court rejected the notion that regulatory takings challenges involve the issue of whether the regulation substantially advances a legitimate public purpose as articulated in Agins v. Tiburon, 447 U.S. 255, 100 S.Ct. 2138, 65 L.Ed.2d 106 (1980). Isn't that what the essential nexus and rough proportionality tests are based on? The Court, in Lingle, states that its rejection of the substantially advances test in takings jurisprudence "does not require us to disturb any of our prior holdings." The Lingle Court admits that Nollan and Dolan quoted the Agins language but not to

determine whether the exaction would substantially advance some legitimate interest and thus survive a due process challenge. "Rather, the issue in the regulatory takings context was whether the exactions substantially advanced the same interests that land-use authorities asserted would allow them to deny the permit altogether." The Court noted that it was dealing with conditions "so onerous that, outside the exactions context, they would be deemed per se physical takings." In these cases, a person may not be required to give up a constitutional right in exchange for a benefit that "has little or no relationship to the property." Circling back to the issue raised in the previous note, do you think that the terms "so onerous" and "constitutional right" limit the holdings of Nollan and Dolan to land use conditions that require the owner to give up her fundamental constitutional right to exclude all others from her property?

D. AD HOC FACTUAL INQUIRIES

PENN CENTRAL TRANSP. CO. v. NEW YORK CITY

Supreme Court of the United States, 1978.
438 U.S. 104, 98 S.Ct. 2646, 57 L.Ed.2d 631.

[Under New York City's Landmarks Preservation Law, Grand Central Terminal, owned by Petitioner, was designated as a landmark. After the agency charged with enforcing the law denied permission to build a multi-story office building in the air rights over the existing structure (on grounds that the proposed tower would impair the aesthetic quality of the terminal's existing facade), Petitioner brought suit claiming that the application of the law constituted a taking of its property.]

MR. JUSTICE BRENNAN delivered the opinion of the Court.

* * *

Before considering appellants' specific contentions, it will be useful to review the factors that have shaped the jurisprudence of the Fifth Amendment injunction "nor shall private property be taken for public use, without just compensation." The question of what constitutes a "taking" for purposes of the Fifth Amendment has proved to be a problem of considerable difficulty. While this Court has recognized that the "Fifth Amendment's guarantee [is] designed to bar Government from forcing some people alone to bear public burdens which, in all fairness and justice, should be borne by the public as a whole," *Armstrong v. United States*, 364 U.S. 40, 49, 80 S.Ct. 1563, 1569, 4 L.Ed.2d 1554 (1960), this Court, quite simply, has been unable to develop any "set formula" for determining when "justice and fairness" require that economic injuries caused by public action be compensated by the Government, rather than remain disproportionately concentrated on a few persons. *See Goldblatt v. Hempstead*, 369 U.S. 590, 594, 82 S.Ct. 987, 990, 8 L.Ed.2d 130 (1962). Indeed, we have frequently observed that whether a particular restriction will be rendered invalid by the Government's failure to pay for any losses proximately caused by it depends largely "upon the particular circumstances [in that] case." *United States v. Central Eureka Mining Co.*, 357 U.S. 155, 168, 78 S.Ct. 1097, 1104, 2 L.Ed.2d 1228 (1958); *see United States v. Caltex, Inc.*, 344 U.S. 149, 156, 73 S.Ct. 200, 203, 97 L.Ed. 157 (1952).

In engaging in these essentially ad hoc, factual inquiries, the Court's decisions have identified several factors that have particular significance. The economic impact of the regulation on the claimant and, particularly, the extent to which the regulation has interfered with distinct investment backed expectations are of course relevant considerations. *See Goldblatt v. Hempstead*, *supra*, 369 U.S., at 594, 82 S.Ct., at 990. So too is the character of the governmental action. A "taking" may more readily be found when the interference with property can be characterized as a physical invasion by Government, *see, e.g., United States v. Causby*, 328 U.S. 256, 66 S.Ct. 1062, 90 L.Ed. 1206 (1946), than when interference arises from some public program adjusting the benefits and burdens of economic life to promote the common good.

"Government could hardly go on if to some extent values incident to property could not be diminished without paying for every such change in the general law," *Pennsylvania Coal Co. v. Mahon*, 260 U.S. 393, 413, 43 S.Ct. 158, 159, 67 L.Ed. 322 (1922), and this Court has accordingly recognized, in a wide variety of contexts, that Government may execute laws or programs that adversely affect recognized economic values. Exercises of the taxing power are one obvious example. A second are the decisions in which this Court has dismissed "taking" challenges on the ground that, while the challenged Government action caused economic harm, it did not interfere with interests that were sufficiently bound up with the reasonable expectations of the claimant to constitute "property" for Fifth Amendment purposes. * * *

More importantly for the present case, in instances in which a state tribunal reasonably concluded that "the health, safety, morals or general welfare" would be promoted by prohibiting particular contemplated uses of land, this Court has upheld land use regulations that destroyed or adversely affected recognized real property interests. *See Nectow v. City of Cambridge*, 277 U.S. 183, 188, 48 S.Ct. 447, 448, 72 L.Ed. 842 (1928). Zoning laws are of course the classic example, *see Euclid v. Ambler Realty Co.*, 272 U.S. 365, 47 S.Ct. 114, 71 L.Ed. 303 (1926) (prohibition of industrial use); *Gorieb v. Fox*, 274 U.S. 603, 608, 47 S.Ct. 675, 677, 71 L.Ed. 1228 (1927) (requirement that portions of parcels be left unbuilt); *Welch v. Swasey*, 214 U.S. 91, 29 S.Ct. 567, 53 L.Ed. 923 (1909) (height restriction), which have been viewed as permissible governmental action even when prohibiting the most beneficial use of the property. * * *

Zoning laws generally do not affect existing uses of real property, but taking challenges have also been held to be without merit in a wide variety of situations when the challenged governmental actions prohibited a beneficial use to which individual parcels had previously been devoted and thus caused substantial individualized harm.

* * *

In contending that the New York City law has "taken" their property in violation of the Fifth and Fourteenth Amendments, appellants make a series of arguments, which, while tailored to the facts of this case, essentially urge that any substantial restriction imposed pursuant to a landmark law must be accompanied by just compensation if it is to be constitutional. Before considering these, we emphasize what is not in dispute. Because this Court has recognized, in a number of settings, that States and cities may enact land use restrictions or controls to enhance the quality of life by preserving the character and desirable aesthetic features of a city, *see City of New Orleans v. Dukes*, 427 U.S. 297, 96 S.Ct. 2513, 49 L.Ed.2d 511 (1976); *Young v. American Mini Theatres, Inc.*, 427 U.S. 50, 96 S.Ct. 2440, 49 L.Ed.2d 310 (1976); *Village of Belle Terre v. Boraas*, 416 U.S. 1, 9–10, 94 S.Ct. 1536, 39 L.Ed.2d 797 (1974); *Berman v. Parker*, 348 U.S. 26, 33, 75 S.Ct. 98, 102, 99 L.Ed. 27 (1954); *Welch v. Swasey, supra*, 214 U.S., at 108, 29 S.Ct., at 571, appellants do not contest that New York City's objective of preserving structures and areas with special historic, architectural, or cultural significance is an entirely permissible governmental goal. They also do not dispute that the restrictions imposed on its parcel are appropriate means of securing the purposes of the New York City law. Finally, appellants do not challenge any of the specific factual premises of the decision below. They accept for present purposes both that the parcel of land occupied by Grand Central Terminal must, in its present state, be regarded as capable of earning a reasonable return, and that the transferable development rights afforded appellants by virtue of the Terminal's designation as a landmark are valuable, even if not as valuable as the rights to construct above the Terminal. In appellants' view none of these factors derogate from their claim that New York City's law has effected a "taking."

* * *

Stated baldly, appellants' position appears to be that the only means of ensuring that selected owners are not singled out to endure financial hardship for no reason is to hold that any restriction imposed on individual landmarks pursuant to the New York scheme is a "taking" requiring the payment of "just compensation." Agreement with this argument would of course invalidate not just New York City's law, but all comparable landmark legislation in the Nation. We find no merit in it.

It is true, as appellants emphasize, that both historic district legislation and zoning laws regulate all properties within given physical communities whereas landmark laws apply only to selected parcels. But, contrary to appellants' suggestions, landmark laws are not like discriminatory, or "reverse spot," zoning: that is, a land use decision which arbitrarily singles out a particular parcel for different, less favorable treatment than the neighboring ones. See 2 Rathkopf, The Law of Zoning and Planning 26–4 and 26–4–26–5, n. 6 (2d Ed.1977). In contrast to discriminatory zoning, which is the antithesis of land use control as part of some comprehensive plan, the New York City law embodies a comprehensive plan to preserve structures of historic or aesthetic interest wherever they might be found in the city, and as noted, over 400 landmarks and 31 historic districts have been designated pursuant to this plan.

Equally without merit is the related argument that the decision to designate a structure as a landmark "is inevitably arbitrary or at least subjective because it basically is a matter of taste" * * *. [A]ppellants not only did not seek judicial review of either the designation or of the denials of the certificates of appropriateness and of no exterior effect, but do not even now suggest that the Commission's decisions concerning the Terminal were in any sense arbitrary or unprincipled. But, in any event, * * * there is no basis whatsoever for a conclusion that courts will have any greater difficulty identifying arbitrary or discriminatory action in the context of landmark regulation than in the context of classic zoning or indeed in any other context.

Next, appellants observe that New York City's law differs from zoning laws and historic district ordinances in that the Landmarks Law does not impose identical or similar restrictions on all structures located in particular physical communities. It follows, they argue, that New York City's law is inherently incapable of producing the fair and equitable distribution of benefits and burdens of governmental action which is characteristic of zoning laws and historic district legislation and which they maintain is a constitutional requirement if "just compensation" is not to be afforded. It is of course true that the Landmarks Law has a more severe impact on some landowners than on others, but that in itself does not mean that the law effects a "taking." Legislation designed to promote the general welfare commonly burdens some more than others. The owners of the brickyard in *Hadacheck*, of the cedar trees in *Miller v. Schoene*, and of the gravel and sand mine in *Goldblatt v. Hempstead*, were uniquely burdened by the legislation sustained in those cases. Similarly, zoning laws often impact more severely on some property owners than others but have not been held to be invalid on that account. For example, the property owner in *Euclid* who wished to use his property for industrial purposes was affected far more severely by the ordinance than his neighbors who wished to use their land for residences.

In any event, appellants' repeated suggestions that they are solely burdened and unbenefited is factually inaccurate. This contention overlooks the fact that the New York City law applies to vast numbers of structures in the city in addition to the Terminal—all the structures contained in the 31 historic districts and over 400 individual landmarks, many of which are close to the Terminal. Unless we are to reject the judgment of the New York City Council that the preservation of landmarks benefit all New York citizens and all structures, both economically and by improving the quality of life in the city as a whole—which we are unwilling to do—we cannot conclude that the owners of the Terminal have in no sense been benefited by the Landmarks Law. Doubtless appellants believe they are more burdened than benefited by the law, but that must have been true too of the property owners in *Miller*, *Hadacheck*, *Euclid*, and *Goldblatt*.

Appellants' final broad-based attack would have us treat the law as an instance, like that in *United States v. Causby*, *supra*, in which Government, acting in an enterprise capacity, has appropriated part of their property for some strictly governmental purpose. Apart from the fact that *Causby* was a case of invasion of airspace that destroyed the use of the farm beneath and this New York City law has in no wise impaired the present use of the Terminal, the Landmarks Law neither exploits appellants' parcel for city purposes nor facilitates nor arises from any entrepreneurial operations of the city. The situation is not remotely like that in *Causby* when the airspace above the Terminal was in the flight pattern for military aircraft. The Landmarks Law's effect is simply to prohibit appellants or anyone else from occupying portions of the airspace above the Terminal, while permitting appellants to use the remainder of the parcel in a gainful fashion. * * *

Rejection of appellants' broad arguments is not however the end of our inquiry, for all we thus far have established is that the New York law is not rendered invalid by its failure to provide "just compensation" whenever a landmark owner is restricted in the exploitation of property interests, such as air rights, to a greater extent than provided for under applicable zoning laws. We now must consider whether the interference with appellants' property is of such a magnitude that "there must be an exercise of eminent domain and compensation to sustain [it]." *Pennsylvania Coal Co. v. Mahon*, 260 U.S., at 413, 43 S.Ct., at 159. That inquiry may be narrowed to the question of the severity of the impact of the law on appellants' parcel, and its resolution in turn requires a careful assessment of the impact of the regulation on the Terminal site.

Unlike the governmental acts in *Goldblatt*, *Miller*, *Causby*, *Griggs*, and *Hadacheck*, the New York City law does not interfere in any way with the present uses of the Terminal. Its designation as a landmark not only permits but contemplates that appellants may continue to use the property precisely as it has for the past 65 years: as a railroad terminal containing office space and concessions. So the law does not interfere with what must be regarded as Penn Central's primary expectation concerning the use of the parcel. More importantly, on this record, we must regard the New York City law as permitting Penn Central not only to profit from the Terminal but to obtain a "reasonable return" on its investment.

Appellants, moreover, exaggerate the effect of the Act on its ability to make use of the air rights above the Terminal in two respects. First, it simply cannot be maintained, on this record, that appellants have been prohibited from occupying any portion of the airspace above the Terminal. While the Commission's actions in denying applications to construct an office building in excess of 50 stories above the Terminal may indicate that it will refuse to issue a certificate of appropriateness for any comparably sized structure, nothing the Commission has said or done suggests an intention to prohibit any construction above the Terminal. The Commission's report emphasized that whether any construction would be allowed depended upon whether the proposed addition "would harmonize in scale, material, and character with [the Terminal]." * * * Since appellants have not sought approval for the construction of a smaller structure, we do not know that appellants will be denied any use of any portion of the airspace above the Terminal.

Second, to the extent appellants have been denied the right to build above the Terminal, it is not literally accurate to say that they have been denied all use of even those pre-existing air rights. Their ability to use these rights has not been abrogated; they are made transferable to at least eight parcels in the vicinity of the Terminal, one or two of which have been found suitable for the construction of new office buildings. Although appellants and others have argued that New York City's transferable development rights program is far from ideal, the New York courts here supportably found that, at least in the case of the Terminal, the rights afforded are valuable. While these rights may well not have constituted "just compensation" if a "taking" had occurred, the rights nevertheless undoubtedly mitigate whatever financial burdens the law has imposed on appellants and, for that reason, are to be taken into account in considering the impact of regulation. *Cf. Goldblatt v. Hempstead*, *supra*, 369 U.S., at 594 n. 3, 82 S.Ct., at 990 n. 3.

On this record we conclude that the application of New York City's Landmarks Preservation Law has not effected a "taking" of appellants' property. The restrictions imposed are substantially related to the promotion of the general welfare and not only permit reasonable beneficial use of the landmark site but afford appellants opportunities further to enhance not only the Terminal site proper but also other properties.

Affirmed.

MR. JUSTICE REHNQUIST, with whom THE CHIEF JUSTICE and MR. JUSTICE STEVENS join, dissenting.

* * *

Appellees do not dispute that valuable property rights have been destroyed. And the Court has frequently emphasized that the term "property" as used in the Taking Clause includes the entire "group of rights inhering in the citizen's [ownership]." *United States v. General Motors Corp.*, 323 U.S. 373, 65 S.Ct. 357, 89 L.Ed. 311 (1945). The term is not used in the

> vulgar and untechnical sense of the physical thing with respect to which the citizen exercises rights recognized by law. [Instead, it] denotes the *group of rights* inhering in the citizen's relation to the physical thing, *as the right to possess, use and dispose of it.* * * * The constitutional provision is addressed to *every sort of interest* the citizen may possess. Id., at 377–378, 65 S.Ct., at 359 (emphasis added).

While neighboring landowners are free to use their land and "air rights" in any way consistent with the broad boundaries of New York zoning, Penn Central, absent the permission of appellees, must forever maintain its property in its present state. The property has been thus subjected to a nonconsensual servitude not borne by any neighboring or similar properties.

Appellees have thus destroyed—in a literal sense, "taken"—substantial property rights of Penn Central. While the term "taken" might have been narrowly interpreted to include only physical seizures of property rights, the construction of the phrase has not been so narrow. * * * Because "not every destruction or injury to property by governmental action has been held to be a 'taking' in the constitutional sense," *Armstrong v. United States*, 364 U.S. 40, 48, 80 S.Ct. 1563, 1568, 4 L.Ed.2d 1554 (1960), however, this does not end our inquiry. But an examination of the two exceptions where the destruction of property does *not* constitute a taking demonstrates that a compensable taking has occurred here.

As early as 1887, the Court recognized that the government can prevent a property owner from using his property to injure others without having to compensate the owner for the value of the forbidden use.

* * *

Thus, there is no "taking" where a city prohibits the operation of a brickyard within a residential city, *see Hadacheck v. Sebastian*, 239 U.S. 394, 36 S.Ct. 143, 60 L.Ed. 348 (1915), or forbids excavation for sand and gravel below the water line, *see Goldblatt v. Town of Hempstead*, 369 U.S. 590, 82 S.Ct. 987, 8 L.Ed.2d 130 (1962). Nor is it relevant, where the government is merely prohibiting a noxious use of property, that the government would seem to be singling out a particular property owner. *Hadacheck*, 239 U.S., at 413, 36 S.Ct., at 146.

* * *

Appellees are not prohibiting a nuisance. The record is clear that the proposed addition to the Grand Central Terminal would be in full compliance with zoning, height limitations, and other health and safety requirements. Instead, appellees are seeking to preserve what they believe to be an outstanding example of Beaux Arts architecture. Penn Central is prevented from further developing its property basically because it did *too good* of a job in designing and building it. The city of New York, because of its unadorned admiration for the design, has decided that the owners of the building must preserve it unchanged for the benefit of sightseeing New Yorkers and tourists.

Unlike in the case of land use regulations, appellees are not *prohibiting* Penn Central from using its property in a narrow set of noxious ways. Instead, appellees have placed an *affirmative* duty on Penn Central to maintain the Terminal in its present state and in "good repair." Appellants are not free to use their property as they see fit within broad outer boundaries but must strictly adhere to their past use except where appellees conclude that alternative uses would not detract from the Landmark. While Penn Central may continue to use the Terminal as it is presently designed, appellees otherwise "exercise complete dominion and control over the surface of the land," *United States v. Causby*, 328 U.S. 256, 262, 66 S.Ct. 1062, 1066, 90 L.Ed. 1206 (1946), and must compensate the owner for his loss. Ibid. "Property is taken in the constitutional sense when inroads are made upon an owner's use of it to an extent that, as between private parties, a servitude has been acquired." *United States v. Dickinson*, 331 U.S. 745, 748, 67 S.Ct. 1382, 1385, 91 L.Ed. 1789 (1947). See also *Dugan v. Rank*, 372 U.S. 609, 625, 83 S.Ct. 999, 1009, 10 L.Ed.2d 15 (1963).

Even where the government prohibits a noninjurious use, the Court has ruled that a taking does not take place if the prohibition applies over a broad cross section of land and thereby "secure[s] an average reciprocity of advantage." *Pennsylvania Coal Co. v. Mahon*, 260 U.S. 393, 415, 43 S.Ct. 158, 160, 67 L.Ed. 322 (1922). It is for this reason that zoning does not constitute a "taking." While zoning at times reduces *individual* property values, the burden is shared relatively evenly and it is reasonable to conclude that on the whole an individual who is harmed by one aspect of the zoning will be benefited by another.

Here, however, a multimillion dollar loss has been imposed on appellants; it is uniquely felt and is not offset by any benefits flowing from the preservation of some 500 other "Landmarks" in New York. Appellees have imposed a substantial cost on less than one one-tenth of one percent of the buildings in New York for the general benefit of all its people. It is exactly this imposition of general costs on a few individuals at which the "taking" protection is directed. * * *

As Justice Holmes pointed out in *Pennsylvania Coal Co. v. Mahon*, "the question at bottom" in an eminent domain case "is upon whom the loss of the changes desired should fall." 260 U.S., at 416, 43 S.Ct., at 160. The benefits that appellees believe will flow from preservation of the Grand Central Terminal will accrue to all the citizens of New York. There is no reason to believe that appellants will enjoy a substantially greater share of these benefits. If the cost of preserving Grand Central Terminal were spread evenly across the entire population of the city of New York, the burden per person would be in cents per year—a minor cost appellees would surely concede for the benefit accrued. Instead, however, appellees would impose the entire cost of several million dollars per year on Penn Central. But it is precisely this sort of discrimination that the Fifth Amendment prohibits.

Appellees in response would argue that a taking only occurs where a property owner is denied *all* reasonable value of his property. The Court has frequently held that, even where a destruction of property rights would not *otherwise* constitute a taking, the inability of the owner to make a reasonable return on his property requires compensation under the Fifth Amendment. *See, e.g., United States v. Lynah*, 188 U.S. 445,

470, 23 S.Ct. 349, 357, 47 L.Ed. 539 (1903). But the converse is not true. A taking does not become a noncompensable exercise of police power simply because the government in its grace allows the owner to make some "reasonable" use of his property. "[I]t is the character of the invasion, not the amount of damage resulting from it, so long as the damage is substantial, that determines the question whether it is a taking." * * *

Notes

1. Does the Court in Penn Central adopt a higher level of scrutiny for these "ad hoc factual inquiries" that apply outside the per se and exaction categories of regulatory takings? Does its approach in any way differ from how the Court approaches a government regulation alleged to violate due process rights, where it defers to the government, presumes the constitutionality of the law, and places a heavy burden of proof on the challenger? The Penn Central Court engages in what it calls "inquiries," where it determines, based on the proofs submitted, whether the regulation constitutes a taking. The plaintiff and the Court admit that historic preservation is a legitimate public purpose and that the city's landmark regulations advance that interest. Regarding these matters, the Court exercises deference in favor of the lawmaker. With respect to the claim that the regulation constitutes a regulatory taking, it conducts an investigation to determine the extent of the regulation's economic impact, its interference with distinct investment backed expectations, and the nature of the regulation itself.

2. Much of the Court's emphasis is on gauging the economic impact of the regulation on the plaintiff: the present uses of the property are not affected and the parties stipulate that the plaintiff is earning a reasonable return on its investment. Further, the regulation does not prevent the plaintiff from building in the air rights above the station. The Landmarks law requires landmark owners to apply for and receive a certificate of appropriateness for any alteration done to the historic building and for any additions to it. The plaintiffs applied to build a modernistic fifty story tower over the station, to greatly alter the historic façade, and to demolish the grand interior lobby. The architect of the original Grand Central Station designed a shorter, but still substantial, skyscraper over the building that conformed with its scale, materials, and character. Presumably, a proposal that conformed to this original design would be approved. Finally, the Court pointed to the economic benefit of transferable development rights in the landmark legislation, finding that they "undoubtedly mitigate whatever financial burdens the law has imposed on" the plaintiffs.

3. How can a court determine whether a land use regulation interferes with the investment backed expectations of a property owner? One helpful way to think about this is to consider the due diligence investigations that precede the purchase of land by an investor. In most parts of the country, pre-purchase due diligence investigations include an extremely thorough analysis of the property and its condition and the regulatory environment of the area in which the land is located. After considering these facts, the buyer purchases the land at a price that reflects its condition, existing regulations, and potential changes in regulations in the relevant jurisdiction. This affects

the value of the land in the hands of the existing owner. Where a land use regulation is subsequently adopted, the regulatory takings question posed by Penn Central is "the extent to which the regulation has interfered with distinct investment backed expectations." Based on its review of the facts presented by the parties, the Court will inquire as to whether the regulation was within the contemplation of a buyer or the owner of the regulated land.

4. The Court's statement in Penn Central that there is no "set formula" for distinguishing regulations that are takings from those that are not is borne out by post-Penn Central decisions of state courts. There is no discernable pattern among these cases that makes it clear when investment backed expectations are, in fact, frustrated by a regulation. This creates an opportunity for lawyers on both sides to use real estate principles and the circumstances of each case to convince state court judges that a landowner's expectations were, or were not, frustrated. What did the landowner pay for the land? Was that price reasonable? What rate of return on the investment in the property is the owner making? Is that rate of return reasonable given prevailing real estate industry standards and expectations? Can the owner demonstrate the extent of lost profits caused by the regulation? Under the regulation, will the value of the property appreciate? How much? Recall that the Penn Central factors are to be balanced with one another. One of the factors is the "character of the governmental action." What this means precisely and how this factor is to be balanced with "the economic impact of the regulation on the claimant," and the extent of interference "with distinct investment backed expectations" is equally opaque and provides additional opportunities for clever advocacy.

5. What if a land purchaser buys a property subject to an existing land use regulation? Presumably the price she pays for the land would be discounted to reflect the diminished value of the property caused by the regulation. How could she claim that the regulation frustrated her investment-backed expectations? On the other hand, what about the claim of the seller that the regulation, when adopted during his period of ownership, frustrates his legitimate investment-backed expectations? Does this claim simply evaporate upon the sale? Do regulations in existence at the time of the purchase of land bear any relationship to the investment backed expectations? Should they be considered in the Court's inquiry into those expectations? This matter is taken up in the next case and, as you will see from reading the concurring opinions by O'Connor and Scalia, the Court is divided on how this dilemma is to be resolved.

PALAZZOLO v. RHODE ISLAND

Supreme Court of the United States, 2001.
533 U.S. 606, 121 S.Ct. 2448, 150 L.Ed.2d 592.

JUSTICE KENNEDY delivered the opinion of the Court.

Petitioner Anthony Palazzolo owns a waterfront parcel of land in the town of Westerly, Rhode Island. Almost all of the property is designated as coastal wetlands under Rhode Island law. After petitioner's development proposals were rejected by respondent Rhode Island Coastal Resources Management Council (Council), he sued in state court, asserting the Council's application of its wetlands regulations took the property without compensation in violation of the Takings Clause of the Fifth Amendment, binding upon the State through the Due Process Clause of the Fourteenth Amendment. Petitioner sought review in this Court, contending the Supreme Court of Rhode Island erred in rejecting his takings claim.

* * *

Petitioner filed an inverse condemnation action in Rhode Island Superior Court, asserting that the State's wetlands regulations, as applied by the Council to his parcel, had taken the property without compensation in violation of the Fifth and Fourteenth Amendments. The suit alleged the Council's action deprived him of "economically, beneficial use" of his property, resulting in a total taking requiring compensation under *Lucas v. South Carolina Coastal Council,* 505 U.S. 1003, 112 S.Ct. 2886, 120 L.Ed.2d 798 (1992). He sought damages in the amount of $3,150,000, a figure derived from an appraiser's estimate as to the value of a 74–lot residential subdivision. The State countered with a host of defenses. After a bench trial, a justice of the Superior Court ruled against petitioner, accepting some of the State's theories.

The Rhode Island Supreme Court affirmed. 746 A.2d 707 (2000). Like the Superior Court, the State Supreme Court recited multiple grounds for rejecting petitioner's suit. * * * In addition to holding petitioner could not assert a takings claim based on the denial of all economic use, the court concluded he could not recover under the more general test of *Penn Central Transp. Co. v. City New York,* 438 U.S. 104, 98 S.Ct. 2646, 57 L.Ed.2d 631 (1978). On this claim, too, the date of acquisition of the parcel was found determinative, and the court held he could have had "no reasonable investment-backed expectations that were affected by this regulation" because it predated his ownership, 746 A.2d, at 717; see also *Penn Central, supra,* at 124, 98 S.Ct. 2646.

We disagree with the Supreme Court of Rhode Island as to the first two of these conclusions; and, we hold, the court was correct to conclude that the owner is not deprived of all economic use of his property because the value of upland portions is substantial. We remand for further consideration of the claim under the principles set forth in Penn Central.

II

* * *

B

We turn to the second asserted basis for declining to address petitioner's takings claim on the merits. When the Council promulgated its wetlands regulations, the disputed parcel was owned not by petitioner but by the corporation of which he was sole shareholder. When title was transferred to petitioner by operation of law, the wetlands regulations were in force. The state court held the postregulation acquisition of title was fatal to the claim for deprivation of all economic use, 746 A.2d, at 716, and to the *Penn Central* claim, 746 A.2d, at 717. While the first holding was couched in terms of background principles of state property law, see *Lucas,* 505 U.S., at 1015, 112 S.Ct. 2886, and the second in terms of petitioner's reasonable investment-backed expectations, see *Penn Central,* 438 U.S., at 124, 98 S.Ct. 2646, the two holdings together amount to a single, sweeping, rule: A purchaser or a successive title holder like petitioner is deemed to have notice of an earlier-enacted restriction and is barred from claiming that it effects a taking.

The theory underlying the argument that postenactment purchasers cannot challenge a regulation under the Takings Clause seems to run on these lines: Property rights are created by the State. See, *e.g., Phillips v. Washington Legal Foundation,* 524 U.S. 156, 163, 118 S.Ct. 1925, 141 L.Ed.2d 174 (1998). So, the argument goes, by prospective legislation the State can shape and define property rights and reasonable investment-backed expectations, and subsequent owners cannot claim any injury from lost value. After all, they purchased or took title with notice of the limitation.

The State may not put so potent a Hobbesian stick into the Lockean bundle. The right to improve property, of course, is subject to the reasonable exercise of state authority, including the enforcement of valid zoning and land-use restrictions. See *Pennsylvania Coal Co.,* 260 U.S., at 413, 43 S.Ct. 158 ("Government hardly could go on if to some extent values incident to property could not be diminished without paying for every such change in the general law"). The Takings Clause, however, in certain circumstances allows a landowner to assert that a particular exercise of the State's regulatory power is so unreasonable or onerous as to compel compensation. Just as a prospective enactment, such as a new zoning ordinance, can limit the value of land without effecting a taking because it can be understood as reasonable by all concerned, other enactments are unreasonable and do not become less so through passage of time or title. Were we to accept the State's rule, the postenactment transfer of title would absolve the State of its obligation to defend any action restricting land use, no matter how extreme or unreasonable. A State would be allowed, in effect, to put an expiration date on the Takings Clause. This ought not to be the rule. Future generations, too, have a right to challenge unreasonable limitations on the use and value of land.

Nor does the justification of notice take into account the effect on owners at the time of enactment, who are prejudiced as well. Should an owner attempt to challenge a new regulation, but not survive the process of ripening his or her claim (which, as this case demonstrates, will often take years), under the proposed rule the right to compensation may not be asserted by an heir or successor, and so may not be asserted at all. The State's rule would work a critical alteration to the nature of property, as the newly regulated landowner is stripped of the ability to transfer the interest which was possessed prior to the regulation. The

State may not by this means secure a windfall for itself. See *Webb's Fabulous Pharmacies, Inc. v. Beckwith,* 449 U.S. 155, 164, 101 S.Ct. 446, 66 L.Ed.2d 358 (1980) ("[A] State, by *ipse dixit,* may not transform private property into public property without compensation"); cf. Ellickson, Property in Land, 102 Yale L.J. 1315, 1368–1369 (1993) (right to transfer interest in land is a defining characteristic of the fee simple estate). The proposed rule is, furthermore, capricious in effect. The young owner contrasted with the older owner, the owner with the resources to hold contrasted with the owner with the need to sell, would be in different positions. The Takings Clause is not so quixotic. A blanket rule that purchasers with notice have no compensation right when a claim becomes ripe is too blunt an instrument to accord with the duty to compensate for what is taken.

Direct condemnation, by invocation of the State's power of eminent domain, presents different considerations from cases alleging a taking based on a burdensome regulation. In a direct condemnation action, or when a State has physically invaded the property without filing suit, the fact and extent of the taking are known. In such an instance, it is a general rule of the law of eminent domain that any award goes to the owner at the time of the taking, and that the right to compensation is not passed to a subsequent purchaser. See *Danforth v. United States,* 308 U.S. 271, 284, 60 S.Ct. 231, 84 L.Ed. 240 (1939); 2 Sackman, Eminent Domain, at § 5.01[5][d][i] ("It is well settled that when there is a taking of property by eminent domain in compliance with the law, it is the owner of the property *at the time of the taking* who is entitled to compensation"). A challenge to the application of a land-use regulation, by contrast, does not mature until ripeness requirements have been satisfied, under principles we have discussed; until this point an inverse condemnation claim alleging a regulatory taking cannot be maintained. It would be illogical, and unfair, to bar a regulatory takings claim because of the post-enactment transfer of ownership where the steps necessary to make the claim ripe were not taken, or could not have been taken, by a previous owner.

There is controlling precedent for our conclusion. *Nollan v. California Coastal Comm'n*, 483 U.S. 825, 107 S.Ct. 3141, 97 L.Ed.2d 677 (1987), presented the question whether it was consistent with the Takings Clause for a state regulatory agency to require oceanfront landowners to provide lateral beach access to the public as the condition for a development permit. The principal dissenting opinion observed it was a policy of the California Coastal Commission to require the condition, and that the Nollans, who purchased their home after the policy went into effect, were "on notice that new developments would be approved only if provisions were made for lateral beach access." *Id.*, at 860, 107 S.Ct. 3141 (Brennan, J., dissenting). A majority of the Court rejected the proposition. "So long as the Commission could not have deprived the prior owners of the easement without compensating them," the Court reasoned, "the prior owners must be understood to have transferred their full property rights in conveying the lot." *Id.*, at 834, n. 2, 107 S.Ct. 3141.

It is argued that *Nollan's* holding was limited by the later decision in *Lucas v. South Carolina Coastal Council*, 505 U.S. 1003, 112 S.Ct. 2886, 120 L.Ed.2d 798 (1992). In *Lucas* the Court observed that a landowner's ability to recover for a government deprivation of all economically beneficial use of property is not absolute but instead is confined by limitations on the use of land which "inhere in the title itself." *Id.*, at 1029, 112 S.Ct. 2886. This is so, the Court reasoned, because the landowner is constrained by those "restrictions that background principles of the State's law of property and nuisance already place upon land ownership." Ibid. It is asserted here that Lucas stands for the proposition that any new regulation, once enacted, becomes a background principle of property law which cannot be challenged by those who acquire title after the enactment.

We have no occasion to consider the precise circumstances when a legislative enactment can be deemed a background principle of state law or whether those circumstances are present here. It suffices to say that a regulation that otherwise would be unconstitutional absent compensation is not transformed into a background principle of the State's law by mere virtue of the passage of title. This relative standard would be incompatible with our description of the concept in *Lucas,* which is explained in terms of those common, shared understandings of permissible limitations derived from a State's legal tradition, see *id.,* at 1029–1030, 112 S.Ct. 2886. A regulation or common-law rule cannot be a background principle for some owners but not for others. The determination whether an existing, general law can limit all economic use of property must turn on objective factors, such as the nature of the land use proscribed. See *id.,* at 1030, 112 S.Ct. 2886 ("The 'total taking' inquiry we require today will ordinarily entail ... analysis of, among other things, the degree of harm to public lands and resources, or adjacent private property, posed by the claimant's proposed activities"). A law does not become a background principle for subsequent owners by enactment itself. *Lucas* did not overrule our holding in *Nollan,* which, as we have noted, is based on essential Takings Clause principles.

For reasons we discuss next, the state court will not find it necessary to explore these matters on remand in connection with the claim that all economic use was deprived; it must address, however, the merits of petitioner's claim under Penn Central. That claim is not barred by the mere fact that title was acquired after the effective date of the state-imposed restriction.

* * *

For the reasons we have discussed, the State Supreme Court erred in finding petitioner's claims were unripe and in ruling that acquisition of title after the effective date of the regulations barred the takings claims. The court did not err in finding that petitioner failed to establish a deprivation of all economic value, for it is undisputed that the parcel retains significant worth for construction of a residence. The claims under the *Penn Central* analysis were not examined, and for this purpose the case should be remanded.

The judgment of the Rhode Island Supreme Court is affirmed in part and reversed in part, and the case is remanded for further proceedings not inconsistent with this opinion.

It is so ordered.

JUSTICE O'CONNOR, concurring.

I join the opinion of the Court but with my understanding of how the issues discussed in Part II–B of the opinion must be considered on remand.

Part II–B of the Court's opinion addresses the circumstance, present in this case, where a takings claimant has acquired title to the regulated property after the enactment of the regulation at issue. As the Court holds, the Rhode Island Supreme Court erred in effectively adopting the sweeping rule that the preacquisition enactment of the use restriction *ipso facto* defeats any takings claim based on that use restriction. Accordingly, the Court holds that petitioner's claim under *Penn Central Transp. Co. v. City of New York,* 438 U.S. 104, 98 S.Ct. 2646, 57 L.Ed.2d 631 (1978), "is not barred by the mere fact that title was acquired after the effective date of the state-imposed restriction." *Ante,* at 2464.

The more difficult question is what role the temporal relationship between regulatory enactment and title acquisition plays in a proper *Penn Central* analysis. Today's holding does not mean that the timing of the regulation's enactment relative to the acquisition of title is immaterial to the *Penn Central* analysis. Indeed, it would be just as much error to expunge this consideration from the takings inquiry as it would be to accord it exclusive significance. Our polestar instead remains the principles set forth in *Penn Central* itself and our other cases that govern partial regulatory takings. Under these cases, interference with investment-backed expectations is one of a number of factors that a court must examine. Further, the regulatory regime in place at the time the claimant acquires the property at issue helps to shape the reasonableness of those expectations.

* * *

The Rhode Island Supreme Court concluded that, because the wetlands regulations predated petitioner's acquisition of the property at issue, petitioner lacked reasonable investment-backed expectations and hence lacked a viable takings claim. 746 A.2d 707, 717 (2000). The court erred in elevating what it believed to be "[petitioner's] lack of reasonable investment-backed expectations" to "dispositive" status. Investment-backed expectations, though important, are not talismanic under *Penn Central.* Evaluation of the degree of interference with investment-backed expectations instead is *one* factor that points toward the answer to the question whether the application of a particular regulation to particular property "goes too far." *Pennsylvania Coal Co. v. Mahon,* 260 U.S. 393, 415, 43 S.Ct. 158, 67 L.Ed. 322 (1922).

Further, the state of regulatory affairs at the time of acquisition is not the only factor that may determine the extent of investment-backed expectations. For example, the nature and extent of permitted development under the regulatory regime vis-a-vis the development sought by the claimant may also shape legitimate expectations without vesting any kind of development right in the property owner. We also have never held that a takings claim is defeated simply on account of the lack of a personal financial investment by a postenactment acquirer of property, such as a donee, heir, or devisee. Cf. *Hodel v. Irving,* 481 U.S. 704, 714–718, 107 S.Ct. 2076, 95 L.Ed.2d 668 (1987). Courts instead must attend to those circumstances which are probative of what fairness requires in a given case.

If investment-backed expectations are given exclusive significance in the *Penn Central* analysis and existing regulations dictate the reasonableness of those expectations in every instance, then the State wields far too much power to redefine property rights upon passage of title. On the other hand, if existing regulations do nothing to inform the analysis, then some property owners may reap windfalls and an important indicium of fairness is lost. As I understand it, our decision today does not remove the regulatory backdrop against which an owner takes title to property from the purview of the *Penn Central* inquiry. It simply restores balance to that inquiry. Courts properly consider the effect of existing regulations under the rubric of investment-backed expectations in determining whether a compensable taking has occurred. As before, the salience of these facts cannot be reduced to any "set formula." *Penn Central,* 438 U.S., at 124, 98 S.Ct. 2646 (internal quotation marks omitted). The temptation to adopt what amount to *per se* rules in either direction must be resisted. The Takings Clause requires careful examination and weighing of all the relevant circumstances in this context. The court below therefore must consider on remand the array of relevant factors under *Penn Central* before deciding whether any compensation is due.

JUSTICE SCALIA concurring.

I write separately to make clear that my understanding of how the issues discussed in Part II–B of the Court's opinion must be considered on remand is not JUSTICE O'CONNOR'S.

The principle that underlies her separate concurrence is that it may in some (unspecified) circumstances be "[un]fai[r]," and produce unacceptable "windfalls," to allow a subsequent purchaser to nullify an unconstitutional partial taking (though, inexplicably, not an unconstitutional total taking) by the government. The polar horrible, presumably, is the situation in which a sharp real estate developer, realizing (or indeed, simply gambling on) the unconstitutional excessiveness of a development restriction that a naive landowner assumes to be valid, purchases property at what it would be worth subject to the restriction, and then develops it to its full value (or resells it at its full value) after getting the unconstitutional restriction invalidated.

This can, I suppose, be called a windfall-though it is not much different from the windfalls that occur every day at stock exchanges or antique auctions, where the knowledgeable (or the venturesome) profit at the expense of the ignorant (or the risk averse). There is something to be said (though in my view not much) for pursuing abstract "fairness" by requiring part or all of that windfall to be returned to the naive original owner, who presumably is the "rightful" owner of it. But there is nothing to be said for giving it instead to the government-which not only did not lose something it owned, but is both the cause of the miscarriage of "fairness" and the only one of the three parties involved in the miscarriage (government, naive original owner, and sharp real estate developer) which acted unlawfully-indeed unconstitutionally. Justice O'CONNOR would eliminate the windfall by giving the malefactor the benefit of its malefaction. It is rather like eliminating the windfall that accrued to a purchaser who bought property at a bargain rate from a thief clothed with the indicia of title, by making him turn over the "unjust" profit to the thief.

In my view, the fact that a restriction existed at the time the purchaser took title (other than a restriction forming part of the "background principles of the State's law of property and nuisance," Lucas v. South Carolina Coastal Council, 505 U.S. 1003, 1029, 112 S.Ct. 2886, 120 L.Ed.2d 798 (1992)) should have no bearing upon the determination of whether the restriction is so substantial as to constitute a taking. The "investment-backed expectations" that the law will take into account do not include the assumed validity of a restriction that in fact deprives property of so much of its value as to be unconstitutional. Which is to say that a Penn Central taking, see Penn Central Transp. Co. v. City of New York, 438 U.S. 104, 98 S.Ct. 2646, 57 L.Ed.2d 631 (1978), no less than a total taking, is not absolved by the transfer of title.

JUSTICE STEVENS concurring in part and dissenting in part.

In an admirable effort to frame its inquiries in broadly significant terms, the majority offers three pages of commentary on the issue of whether an owner of property can challenge regulations adopted prior to her acquisition of that property without ever discussing the particular facts or legal claims at issue in this case. While I agree with some of what the Court has to say on this issue, an examination of the issue in the context of the facts of this case convinces me that the Court has oversimplified a complex calculus and conflated two separate questions. Therefore, while I join Part II–A of the opinion, I dissent from the judgment and, in particular, from Part II–B.

* * *

[Dissenting opinions omitted]

Notes

1. Obscured by the many nuances of the Palazzolo opinion is this language. "[W]e hold [that the Rhode Island Supreme Court] ... was correct to conclude that the owner is not deprived of all economic use of his property because the value of the upland portions is substantial. We remand for further consideration of the claim under the principles set forth in Penn Central." The trial court accepted as uncontested the fact that Palazzolo's two acre upland property would have a value of $200,000 if developed. The Rhode Island Coastal Resources Management Council officials testified that they would have allowed him to build a single residence on the upland parcel. Most of the eighty acres that Palazzolo owned were fragile tidal wetlands where development would have been costly and environmentally damaging. Palazzolo submitted evidence that the land was appraised at over $3 million under a seventy-four lot subdivision proposal he had submitted for approval; subsequently he has asked for approval to build a large private beach club. Both of these applications were denied. In the Court's holding it is clear that the regulatory prohibition of the lion's share of this land is not a per se taking under Lucas and that the $200,000 value of the one developable lot is "substantial."

2. The Rhode Island Supreme Court had held that Palazzolo could have no reasonable investment-backed expectations because the state tidal wetlands regulations applicable to his land predated his acquisition of title. Its opinion was that as a *per se* matter an owner could not have reasonable investment-backed expectations to develop land in a way that violates regulations in place at the time of purchase: so-called "pre-existing regulations." The Court rejected this *per se* notion but disagreed as to whether pre-existing regulations are a factor to be used in determining whether an owner's expectations are reasonable. Reread the concurrences of O'Connor and Scalia on this matter. Do you find one more persuasive than the other? The debate on this matter was taken up by the Court the following year in Tahoe–Sierra Preservation Council v. Tahoe Regional Planning Agency, 535 U.S. 302, 122 S.Ct. 1465, 152 L.Ed.2d 517 (2002). A six-Justice majority in that case, which held that a thirty-two month moratorium on development is not a *per se* taking under Lucas, also affirmed O'Connor's concurrence in Palazzolo regarding investment backed expectations. Justice Kennedy's opinion on behalf of the majority affirmed this language from O'Connor's concurrence in Palazzolo: "Our polestar instead remains the principles set forth in Penn Central itself and our other cases that govern partial regulatory takings. Under these cases, interference with investment-backed expectations is one of a number of factors that a court must examine."

3. That the tidal wetlands regulations of the state in the Palazzolo case do not constitute a total taking was affirmed, in the decision of the Rhode Island Superior Court on remand. Palazzolo v. State of Rhode Island, 2005 WL 1645974 (R.I.Super). The court held that the state's public trust doctrine was part of the background principles of common law in the state. Under that doctrine, Palazzolo had no right to develop the coastal marshlands in the first place. Further, the court found, any development on them would have been so costly that Palazzolo would have lost money attempting to fill, reinforce, and build on the tidal wetland basin which constituted most of his

acreage. Under Penn Central his investment backed expectations were not frustrated. Under Lucas, the regulations were not a total taking.

E. EQUAL PROTECTION

Cases involving claims that property owners have been denied equal protection in the application or enforcement of land use regulations are fairly common. These include instances where owners allege selective application of land use regulations, harassment of the property owner, or discrimination among types of properties. See, Cutting v. Muzzey, 724 F.2d 259 (1st Cir.1984), alleging racial animus against the developer's purchasers, all of whom had Italian surnames; Sylvia Development Corp. v. Calvert County, Maryland, 48 F.3d 810 (4th Cir.1995), alleging discrimination against a developer because he was born in Czechoslovokia, or, in the alternative, that he was from outside the county; Rodrigues v. Village of Larchmont, New York, 608 F.Supp. 467 (S.D.N.Y.1985), alleging harassment of nurseryman by denying him access to the village dump and arbitrary denial of a variance.

Selective enforcement of land use regulations poses a more difficult equal protection issue. In Shelton v. City of College Station, 754 F.2d 1251 (5th Cir.1985), the property owner claimed that the denial of a variance, in a situation where every other like applicant received a variance, violated the Equal Protection Clause of the 14th Amendment. If the evidence supports such a claim, should the court order the issuance of a variance? In considering how to answer the question look at the following case.

VILLAGE OF WILLOWBROOK v. OLECH

Supreme Court of the United States, 2000.
528 U.S. 562, 120 S.Ct. 1073, 145 L.Ed.2d 1060.

PER CURIAM.

Respondent Grace Olech and her late husband Thaddeus asked petitioner Village of Willowbrook (Village) to connect their property to the municipal water supply. The Village at first conditioned the connection on the Olechs granting the Village a 33–foot easement. The Olechs objected, claiming that the Village only required a 15–foot easement from other property owners seeking access to the water supply. After a 3–month delay, the Village relented and agreed to provide water service with only a 15–foot easement.

Olech sued the Village, claiming that the Village's demand of an additional 18–foot easement violated the Equal Protection Clause of the Fourteenth Amendment. Olech asserted that the 33–foot easement demand was "irrational and wholly arbitrary"; that the Village's demand was actually motivated by ill will resulting from the Olechs' previous filing of an unrelated, successful lawsuit against the Village; and that the Village acted either with the intent to deprive Olech of her rights or in reckless disregard of her rights.

The District Court dismissed the lawsuit pursuant to Federal Rule of Civil Procedure 12(b)(6) for failure to state a cognizable claim under the Equal Protection Clause. Relying on Circuit precedent, the Court of Appeals for the Seventh Circuit reversed, holding that a plaintiff can allege an equal protection violation by asserting that state action was motivated solely by a " 'spiteful effort to "get" him for reasons wholly unrelated to any legitimate state objective.' " 160 F.3d 386, 387 (1998) (quoting *Esmail v. Macrane,* 53 F.3d 176, 180 (C.A.7 1995)). It determined that Olech's complaint sufficiently alleged such a claim. 160 F.3d, at 388. We granted certiorari to determine whether the Equal Protection Clause gives rise to a cause of action on behalf of a "class of one" where the plaintiff did not allege membership in a class or group.

Our cases have recognized successful equal protection claims brought by a "class of one," where the plaintiff alleges that she has been intentionally treated differently from others similarly situated and that there is no rational basis for the difference in treatment. See *Sioux City Bridge Co. v. Dakota County,* 260 U.S. 441, 43 S.Ct. 190, 67 L.Ed. 340 (1923); *Allegheny Pittsburgh Coal Co. v. Commission of Webster Cty.,* 488 U.S. 336, 109 S.Ct. 633, 102 L.Ed.2d 688 (1989). In so doing, we have explained that " '[t]he purpose of the equal protection clause of the Fourteenth Amendment is to secure every person within the State's jurisdiction against intentional and arbitrary discrimination, whether occasioned by express terms of a statute or by its improper execution through duly constituted agents.' " *Sioux City Bridge Co., supra,* at 445, 43 S.Ct. 190 (quoting *Sunday Lake Iron Co. v. Township of Wakefield,* 247 U.S. 350, 352, 38 S.Ct. 495, 62 L.Ed. 1154 (1918)).

That reasoning is applicable to this case. Olech's complaint can fairly be construed as alleging that the Village intentionally demanded a 33–foot easement as a condition of connecting her property to the municipal water supply where the Village required only a 15–foot easement from other similarly situated property owners. See *Conley v. Gibson,* 355 U.S. 41, 45–46, 78 S.Ct. 99, 2 L.Ed.2d 80 (1957). The complaint also alleged that the Village's demand was "irrational and wholly arbitrary" and that the Village ultimately connected her property after receiving a clearly adequate 15–foot easement. These allegations, quite apart from the Village's subjective motivation, are sufficient to state a claim for relief under traditional equal protection analysis. We therefore affirm the judgment of the Court of Appeals, but do not reach the alternative theory of "subjective ill will" relied on by that court.

It is so ordered.

JUSTICE BREYER, concurring in the result.

The Solicitor General and the village of Willowbrook have expressed concern lest we interpret the Equal Protection Clause in this case in a way that would transform many ordinary violations of city or state law into violations of the Constitution. It might be thought that a rule that looks only to an intentional difference in treatment and a lack of a rational basis for that different treatment would work such a transformation. Zoning decisions, for example, will often, perhaps almost always, treat one landowner differently from another, and one might claim that, when a city's zoning authority takes an action that fails to conform to a city zoning regulation, it lacks a "rational basis" for its action (at least if the regulation in question is reasonably clear).

This case, however, does not directly raise the question whether the simple and common instance of a faulty zoning decision would violate the Equal Protection Clause. That is because the Court of Appeals found that in this case respondent had alleged an extra factor as well—a factor that the Court of Appeals called "vindictive action," "illegitimate animus," or "ill will." 160 F.3d 386, 388 (C.A.7 1998). And, in that respect, the court said this case resembled *Esmail v. Macrane,* 53 F.3d 176 (C.A.7 1995), because the *Esmail* plaintiff had alleged that the municipality's differential treatment "was the result not of prosecutorial discretion honestly (even if ineptly—even if arbitrarily) exercised but of an illegitimate desire to 'get' him." 160 F.3d, at 388.

In my view, the presence of that added factor in this case is sufficient to minimize any concern about transforming run-of-the-mill zoning cases into cases of constitutional right. For this reason, along with the others mentioned by the Court, I concur in the result.

Notes

1. The Olech case expands the possibility of federal review of local land use decisions. For a thorough discussion of this case and how lower federal courts have reacted to it, see Michael S. Giaimo, Ill Will and Class of One: Equal Protection Claims after the Olech Decision, Land Use Law & Zoning Digest, Feb. 2003, p. 3.

2. In City of Cleburne, Texas v. Cleburne Living Center, 473 U.S. 432, 105 S.Ct. 3249, 87 L.Ed.2d 313 (1985), the city denied a special use permit for the operation of a group home for the mentally retarded, acting pursuant to a municipal zoning ordinance requiring permits for such homes. The Supreme Court held, in an opinion by Justice White, that the mentally retarded did not comprise a "suspect class" so as to trigger the highest level of equal protection scrutiny. However, applying the "traditional" equal protection analysis, White found that the special use permit denial was arbitrary and irrational because the "City does not require a special use permit in an R–3 zone for apartment houses, multiple dwellings, boarding and lodging houses, fraternity or sorority houses, dormitories, apartment hotels, hospitals, sanitariums, nursing homes for convalescents or the aged (other than for the insane or feeble-minded or alcoholics or drug addicts), private clubs or fraternal orders, and other specified uses." Also see Arrington v. Urban Redevelopment Authority of the City of Pittsburgh, 822 A.2d 135 (Pa.Cmwlth.2003), where the court found that excluding owner-occupied housing and churches from an urban redevelopment taking in a blighted area did not violate the equal protection clause because rational reasons for the exceptions could be found; a dissenting opinion stated that no rational reasons for those exclusions existed.

F. REMEDIES

FIRST ENGLISH EVANGELICAL LUTHERAN CHURCH v. LOS ANGELES COUNTY

Supreme Court of the United States, 1987.
482 U.S. 304, 107 S.Ct. 2378, 96 L.Ed.2d 250.

CHIEF JUSTICE REHNQUIST delivered the opinion of the Court.

* * *

In 1957, appellant First English Evangelical Lutheran Church purchased a 21–acre parcel of land in a canyon along the banks of the Middle Fork of Mill Creek in the Angeles National Forest. The Middle Fork is the natural drainage channel for a watershed area owned by the National Forest Service. Twelve of the acres owned by the church are flat land, and contained a dining hall, two bunkhouses, a caretaker's lodge, an outdoor chapel, and a footbridge across the creek. The church operated on the site a campground, known as "Lutherglen," as a retreat center and a recreational area for handicapped children.

In July 1977, a forest fire denuded the hills upstream from Lutherglen, destroying approximately 3,860 acres of the watershed area and creating a serious flood hazard. Such flooding occurred on February 9 and 10, 1978, when a storm dropped 11 inches of rain in the watershed. The runoff from the storm overflowed the banks of the Mill Creek, flooding Lutherglen and destroying its buildings.

In response to the flooding of the canyon, appellee County of Los Angeles adopted Interim Ordinance No. 11,855 in January 1979. The ordinance provided that "[a] person shall not construct, reconstruct, place or enlarge any building or structure, any portion of which is, or will be, located within the outer boundary lines of the interim flood protection area located in Mill Creek Canyon * * *." The ordinance was effective immediately because the county determined that it was "required for the immediate preservation of the public health and safety * * *." The interim flood protection area described by the ordinance included the flat areas on either side of Mill Creek on which Lutherglen had stood.

The church filed a complaint in the Superior Court of California a little more than a month after the ordinance was adopted. As subsequently amended, the complaint alleged two claims against the county and the Los Angeles County Flood Control District. The first alleged that the defendants were liable under Cal. Gov't Code Ann. § 835 (West 1980) for dangerous conditions on their upstream properties that contributed to the flooding of Lutherglen. As a part of this claim, appellant also alleged that "Ordinance No. 11,855 denies [appellant] all use of Lutherglen." The second claim sought to recover from the Flood District in inverse condemnation and in tort for engaging in cloud seeding during the storm that flooded Lutherglen. Appellant sought damages under each count for loss of use of Lutherglen. * * *

* * * Appellant asks us to hold that the Supreme Court of California erred in *Agins v. Tiburon* in determining that the Fifth Amendment, as made applicable to the States through the Fourteenth Amendment, does not require compensation as a remedy for "temporary" regulatory takings—those regulatory takings which are ultimately invalidated by the courts. Four times this decade, we have considered similar claims and have found ourselves for one reason or another unable to consider the merits of the *Agins* rule. *See MacDonald, Sommer & Frates v. Yolo County*, 477 U.S. 340 (1986); *Williamson County Regional Planning Comm'n v. Hamilton Bank*, 473 U.S. 172 (1985); *San Diego Gas & Electric Co., supra*; *Agins v. Tiburon, supra*. For the reasons explained below, however, we find the constitutional claim properly presented in this case, and hold that on these facts the California courts have decided the compensation question inconsistently with the requirements of the Fifth Amendment.

* * *

Consideration of the compensation question must begin with direct reference to the language of the Fifth Amendment, which provides in relevant part that "private property [shall not] be taken for public use, without just compensation." As its language indicates, and as the Court has frequently noted, this provision does not prohibit the taking of private property, but instead places a condition on the exercise of that power. *See Williamson County*, 473 U.S., at 194; *Hodel v. Virginia Surface Mining & Reclamation Assn., Inc.*, 452 U.S. 264, 297, n. 40 (1981); *Hurley v. Kincaid*, 285 U.S. 95, 104 (1932); *Monongahela Navigation Co. v. United States*, 148 U.S. 312, 336 (1893); *United States v. Jones*, 109 U.S. 513, 518 (1883). This basic understanding of the Amendment makes clear that it is designed not to limit the governmental interference with property rights per se, but rather to secure compensation in the event of otherwise proper interference amounting to a taking. Thus, government action that works a taking of property rights necessarily implicates the "constitutional obligation to pay just compensation." *Armstrong v. United States*, 364 U.S. 40, 49 (1960).

We have recognized that a landowner is entitled to bring an action in inverse condemnation as a result of " 'the self-executing character of the constitutional provision with respect to compensation * * *.' " *United States v. Clarke*, 445 U.S. 253, 257 (1980), quoting 6 P. Nichols, Eminent Domain § 25.41 (3d rev. ed. 1972). As noted in JUSTICE BRENNAN's dissent in *San Diego Gas & Electric Co.*, 450 U.S., at 654–655, it has been established at least since Jacobs v. United States, 290 U.S. 13 (1933), that claims for just compensation are grounded in the Constitution itself:

> "The suits were based on the right to recover just compensation for property taken by the United States for public use in the exercise of its power of eminent domain. That right was guaranteed by the Constitution. The fact that condemnation proceedings were not instituted and that the right was asserted in suits by the owners did

> not change the essential nature of the claim. The form of the remedy did not qualify the right. It rested upon the Fifth Amendment. Statutory recognition was not necessary. A promise to pay was not necessary. Such a promise was implied because of the duty to pay imposed by the Amendment. The suits were thus founded upon the Constitution of the United States." Id., at 16. (Emphasis added.)

Jacobs, moreover, does not stand alone, for the Court has frequently repeated the view that, in the event of a taking, the compensation remedy is required by the Constitution. *See, e.g., Kirby Forest Industries, Inc. v. United States*, 467 U.S. 1, 5 (1984); *United States v. Causby*, 328 U.S. 256, 267 (1946); *Seaboard Air Line R. Co. v. United States*, 261 U.S. 299, 304–306 (1923); *Monongahela Navigation, supra*, at 327.

* * *

While the Supreme Court of California may not have actually disavowed this general rule in *Agins*, we believe that it has truncated the rule by disallowing damages that occurred prior to the ultimate invalidation of the challenged regulation. The Supreme Court of California justified its conclusion at length in the *Agins* opinion, concluding that:

> "In combination, the need for preserving a degree of freedom in the land-use planning function, and the inhibiting financial force which inheres in the inverse condemnation remedy, persuade us that on balance mandamus or declaratory relief rather than inverse condemnation is the appropriate relief under the circumstances." *Agins v. Tiburon*, 24 Cal.3d, at 276–277, 598 P.2d, at 31.

We, of course, are not unmindful of these considerations, but they must be evaluated in the light of the command of the Just Compensation Clause of the Fifth Amendment. The Court has recognized in more than one case that the government may elect to abandon its intrusion or discontinue regulations. *See, e.g., Kirby Forest Industries, Inc. v. United States, supra*; *United States v. Dow*, 357 U.S. 17, 26 (1958). Similarly, a governmental body may acquiesce in a judicial declaration that one of its ordinances has effected an unconstitutional taking of property; the landowner has no right under the Just Compensation Clause to insist that a "temporary" taking be deemed a permanent taking. But we have not resolved whether abandonment by the government requires payment of compensation for the period of time during which regulations deny a landowner all use of his land.

* * *

These cases reflect the fact that "temporary" takings which, as here, deny a landowner all use of his property, are not different in kind from permanent takings, for which the Constitution clearly requires compensation. *Cf. San Diego Gas & Electric Co.*, 450 U.S., at 657 (BRENNAN, J., dissenting) ("Nothing in the Just Compensation Clause suggests that 'takings' must be permanent and irrevocable"). It is axiomatic that the Fifth Amendment's just compensation provision is "designed to bar Government from forcing some people alone to bear public burdens which, in all fairness and justice, should be borne by the public as a whole." *Armstrong v. United States*, 364 U.S., at 49. *See also Penn Central Transportation Co. v. New York City*, 438 U.S., at 123–125; *Monongahela Navigation Co. v. United States*, 148 U.S., at 325. In the present case the interim ordinance was adopted by the County of Los Angeles in January 1979, and became effective immediately. Appellant filed suit within a month after the effective date of the ordinance and yet when the Supreme Court of California denied a hearing in the case on October 17, 1985, the merits of appellant's claim had yet to be determined. The United States has been required to pay compensation for leasehold interests of shorter duration than this. The value of a leasehold interest in property for a period of years may be substantial, and the burden on the property owner in extinguishing such an interest for a period of years may be great indeed. *See, e.g., United States v. General Motors, supra.* Where this burden results from governmental action that amounted to a taking, the Just Compensation Clause of the Fifth Amendment requires that the government pay the landowner for the value of the use of the land during this period. *Cf. United States v. Causby*, 328 U.S., at 261 ("It is the owner's loss, not the taker's gain, which is the measure of the value of the property taken"). Invalidation of the ordinance or its successor ordinance after this period of time, though converting the taking into a "temporary" one, is not a sufficient remedy to meet the demands of the Just Compensation Clause.

* * *

Nothing we say today is intended to abrogate the principle that the decision to exercise the power of eminent domain is a legislative function " 'for Congress and Congress alone to determine.' " *Hawaii Housing Authority v. Midkiff*, 467 U.S. 229, 240 (1984), quoting *Berman v. Parker*, 348 U.S. 26, 33 (1954). Once a court determines that a taking has occurred, the government retains the whole range of options already available—amendment of the regulation, withdrawal of the invalidated regulation, or exercise of eminent domain. Thus we do not, as the Solicitor General suggests, "permit a court, at the behest of a private person, to require the * * * Government to exercise the power of eminent domain * * *." Brief for United States as Amicus Curiae 22. We merely hold that where the government's activities have already worked a taking of all use of property, no subsequent action by the government can relieve it of the duty to provide compensation for the period during which the taking was effective.

We also point out that the allegation of the complaint which we treat as true for purposes of our decision was that the ordinance in question denied appellant all use of its property. We limit our holding to the facts presented, and of course do not deal with the quite different questions that would arise in the case of normal delays in obtaining building permits, changes in zoning ordinances, variances, and the like which are not before us. We realize that even our present holding will undoubtedly lessen to some extent the freedom and flexibility of land-use planners and governing bodies of municipal corporations when enacting land-use regulations. But such consequences necessarily flow from any decision upholding a claim of constitutional right; many of the provisions of the Constitution are designed to limit the flexibility and freedom of governmental authorities, and the Just Compensation Clause of the Fifth Amendment is one of them. As Justice Holmes aptly noted more than 50 years ago, "a strong public desire to improve the public condition is not enough to warrant achieving the desire by a shorter cut than the constitutional way of paying for the change." *Pennsylvania Coal Co. v. Mahon*, 260 U.S., at 416.

Here we must assume that the Los Angeles County ordinance has denied appellant all use of its property for a considerable period of years, and we hold that invalidation of the ordinance without payment of fair value for the use of the property during this period of time would be a constitutionally insufficient remedy. The judgment of the California Court of Appeal is therefore reversed, and the case is remanded for further proceedings not inconsistent with this opinion.

[Dissent omitted]

Notes

1. After remand the California Court of Appeal held that the property had not been "taken" in the first instance because the regulation was necessary to protect public health and safety, and the cause of action for inverse condemnation was properly dismissed. First English Evangelical, Lutheran Church of Glendale v. County of Los Angeles, 210 Cal.App.3d 1353, 258 Cal.Rptr. 893 (1989), certiorari denied 493 U.S. 1056, 110 S.Ct. 866, 107 L.Ed.2d 950 (1990). The net result is that while a property owner may be constitutionally entitled to compensation for an interim or temporary taking, she must first establish that a taking has, in fact, occurred. The following cases focus our attention again on the definition of what is a regulatory taking.

2. In San Diego Gas & Electric Co. v. City of San Diego, 450 U.S. 621, 101 S.Ct. 1287, 67 L.Ed.2d 551 (1981), the Supreme Court again skirted the issue of the inverse condemnation remedy for regulatory takings by dismissing the appeal on the ground that the California Supreme Court judgment denying damages was not a final judgment. In a dissenting opinion by Justice Brennan, joined by three other Justices, and approvingly referred to in Justice Rehnquist's concurring opinion, five Justices indicated that invalidation of a land use regulation so oppressive as to amount to a taking is an inadequate remedy and that a landowner in such a situation might be entitled to monetary relief for a "temporary taking" with damages to be measured from the time of the adoption of the oppressive regulation to the time of invalidation. Justice Brennan cited for support of this idea Hagman & Misczynski, Windfalls for Wipeouts 296–297 (1978) and Bosselman, The Third Alternative in Zoning Litigation, 17 Zoning Dig. 113, 114–119 (1965). Also see Duerksen & Mantell, Interim Damages: A Remedy in Land Use Cases?, 33 Land Use Law & Zoning Dig. 6 (April 1981).

3. Precisely what just compensation means in takings jurisprudence is, at best, cloudy. This is particularly the case with temporary takings of the type encountered by First English. Had the state court found that a taking

had occurred and invalidated the regulation, the task for the court would have been to calculate the damage to the property owner due to the imposition of the regulation from its adoption to its invalidation. This is an obviously formidable valuation task. Courts have long resisted adopting standard real estate industry valuation methods as the proper measure of damages. In United States v. 50 Acres of Land, 469 U.S. 24, 105 S.Ct. 451, 83 L.Ed.2d 376 (1984), for example, the court excluded consequential damages and lost profits from the calculation. United States v. 564.54 Acres of Land, 441 U.S. 506, 99 S.Ct. 1854, 60 L.Ed.2d 435 (1979), excluded non-transferable values from just compensation. Compare these with Loveladies Harbor, Inc. v. United States, 28 F.3d 1171 (Fed.Cir.1994), where the Court of Appeals sustained a claims court judgment that permitted the landowner to recover the full pre-regulation value of the property even though the parcel retained some residual value after the taking. See also, Del Monte Dunes at Monterey v. City of Monterey, 920 F.2d 1496 (9th Cir.1990), where demonstrated bad faith on the part of city planners had resulted in a succession of denials of plaintiff's good faith development proposals. The court, in awarding damages, adopted a valuation mechanism that seemingly accounted for the hostility of the agency; it upheld a jury award that included an interest rate on plaintiff's losses that exceed the average rate of return in the industry. This removed from the calculation the plaintiff's risks that the development might not have been completed as planned or might have resulted in a below average success.

4. In Wheeler v. City of Pleasant Grove (Wheeler III), 833 F.2d 267 (11th Cir.1987), the court of appeals expanded on First English, by examining how damages for temporary takings should be determined in inverse condemnation proceedings. In this case, a landowner sold a piece of property in the City of Pleasant Grove to a developer who planned to build a 120–unit apartment building on the site. After finding that the proposed land use complied with applicable zoning ordinances, the Pleasant Grove Planning Commission issued a building permit, and the plaintiffs began work in preparation for construction. Following strong public opposition to the project, and a referendum that confirmed that a majority of the city residents were against it, the City Council passed an ordinance that outlawed the construction of apartment complexes in the city limits and stopped plaintiffs' construction. In a prior decision, the court found that the ban on apartment development and the stop work order under these circumstances constituted a regulatory taking. In this case, it turned to the determination of the appropriate measure of damages owed to the plaintiffs.

The court began its damage analysis by pointing out that "the owner's loss is measured by the extent to which governmental action has deprived him of an interest in property," and that "the value of that interest, in turn, is determined by isolating it as a component of the overall fair market value of the affected property. When, as here, a temporary taking is at issue, the court looked at whether there was an effect on the property's potential for producing income or on an expected profit. The court remanded the case with instructions that the appropriate measure of damages should be the loss in income-producing potential suffered over the sixteen months that the ordinance was in effect.

Upon remand, the district court ruled that the plaintiffs were not entitled to a damage award because their injury did not arise from the unconstitutional enactment of the ordinance, but rather from the prior withdrawal of the building permit under the city's misinterpretation of the ordinance, and the case was again appealed to the circuit court. In Wheeler v. City of Pleasant Grove (Wheeler IV), 896 F.2d 1347 (11th Cir.1990), the court overturned the district court, affirming that the plaintiff's injury was caused by the unconstitutional ordinance. It then again set out to determine the appropriate level of damages. Using the formula articulated by the court in Wheeler III, it awarded damages based on the "market rate of return computed over the period of the temporary taking on the difference between the property's fair market value without the regulatory restriction and its fair market value with the restriction."

5. A very unusual compensation problem was presented in Board of County Supervisors of Prince William County, Virginia v. United States, 48 F.3d 520 (Fed.Cir.1995). A real estate developer proposed to develop 550 acres of land adjacent to Manassas Battlefield Park, a historic Civil War site. As a part of the rezoning process the developer presented the local government with a proffer of amenities he would provide, including storm drains, a community trail system, a community center and swimming pool, tennis courts, a ballfield, and a commitment to contribute a sum of money to the county for school purposes, plus five acres for a fire station and commuter parking lot; in addition to the proffer, the developer deeded several acres of his land to the county for road improvements. After a public outcry about the potential harm to the battlefield site, Congress enacted a statute to take the 550 acres, add them to the Manassas Battlefield National Park, and to pay just compensation to the owners of any property taken. The United States paid the developer, but the county sued in the Court of Claims demanding compensation for the value of the proffers accepted by the county, and for the sixteen acres of land the developer had conveyed to the county for road improvements in connection with the proposed development. The appellate court held that the proffers made to the county were not "property" for the purposes of the Takings Clause, but that the county was entitled to compensation for the land that the developer had previously conveyed to the county for road improvements, it reasoned that even though the land was dedicated for public roads that now would not be built, there was some residual value in the land; the case was remanded for determination of that value.

6. In Del Oro Hills v. City of Oceanside, 31 Cal.App.4th 1060, 37 Cal.Rptr.2d 677 (1995), the court held that a developer who sought taking damages from a city after the city's growth control ordinance was found invalid, could not simply allege an invalid regulation and claim per se damages. The court found that the developer had sold all of his development, albeit not at the highest price he might have obtained (according to the developer's allegations) and that his land had enjoyed viable economic uses during the period the invalid ordinance was in effect. And, in Ellison v. County of Ventura, 265 Cal.Rptr. 795 (Cal.App.1990), the court found that amendments to a zoning ordinance could not be a taking because the value of the property had doubled despite the more restrictive zoning provisions adopted after the owner had purchased the property. See Donald L. Elliot, Givings and Takings, Land Use Law (Jan. 1996) p. 3, for a proposal that courts look to the values added to property by governmental actions as a factor in measuring governmental takings.

Chapter VI

OTHER CONSTITUTIONAL AND STATUTORY LIMITS ON LAND USE REGULATION

SECTION 1. FEDERAL INFLUENCE

The federal impact on state and local land use planning and zoning is most apparent where specific statutory language preempts local government's ability to make certain land use decisions. Beginning in the late 1980's, a series of federal laws addressing housing discrimination, discrimination based upon disability, discrimination based on religious beliefs, and access to the airwaves for the siting of cellular and wireless towers, have had a profound impact on local government's ability to control the location of various types of land uses, as well as to prohibit municipalities from excluding certain uses from their borders. There are a number of reasons why the federal government has inserted its power into the local land use process. Among these are the inability of many local officials to effectively respond to the concerns of the community that represent NIMBY (Not In My Back Yard) for uses often believed to be LULUs (Locally Unwanted Land Uses) and the attitudes of those in the community who take a BANANA (Build Absolutely Nothing Anywhere Near Anyone) perspective on future development around them. Perhaps it is because too many local officials adopted a NIMTOO (Not In My Term Of Office) approach to land use planning and zoning decisions that advocacy organizations and business leaders were successful in realizing strong federal legislation designed to limit local control. As you read through the cases and the notes in this chapter, consider whether the federal laws highlighted are necessary, whether they are accomplishing their stated purpose, and whether these laws have a positive or negative effect on community development in general. In addition, this chapter highlights First Amendment issues that impact the ability of government to regulate in the area of religious uses and adult uses. First Amendment considerations relating to the regulation of signs and billboards is discussed later in Chapter 10.

In her article, Federalism and the Public Good: The True Story Behind the Religious Land Use and Institutionalized Persons Act, 78

Ind. L. J. 311 (2003), Professor Marci A. Hamilton sets forth an argument as to why state and local governance in land use is preferable to federal governance by using the Religious Land Use and Institutionalized Persons Act, enacted in October 2000, and its legislative history to make her point. Her article also demonstrates the effectiveness of the influence of lobbyists and special interest advocacy before Congress. Below is an excerpt from her article (citations omitted):

> RLUIPA is the quintessential legislative product—it is a compromise bill, stripped of other elements, containing oddly paired issues: land use and institutionalized persons involving religious individuals and institutions. One cannot understand RLUIPA without also knowing what happened with its precursors, the Religious Freedom Restoration Act and the Religious Liberty Protection Act bills.
>
> 1. The Religious Freedom Restoration Act ("RFRA")
>
> * * * This is not the Article to go into too many details, but in a nutshell, religious lobbyists prevailed upon Congress to expand religious liberty and civil rights guarantees beyond what the Court interpreted the Constitution to require in Smith. Thus, in effect, they argued that religious claimants should not be subject to the rule of law, and that a handful of cases preceding Smith that had instituted strict scrutiny in the unemployment context should be extended across all laws. Congress was eager to acquiesce, and enacted the RFRA of 1993, which instituted strict scrutiny of every law substantially burdening a religious individual or institution. It was invalidated less than four years later in City of Boerne v. Flores. * * *
>
> No less than 405 pages of legislative history were devoted to castigating the Court for its decision in Smith. RFRA meant that state laws traditionally in the realm of the states, from family law, including adoption and medical neglect standards, to immunization exemptions to land use law, would be altered through its application. Neither state nor local officials were called in to consult on its impact. Nor was there any effort by Congress itself to assess the potential impact of RFRA on the states. The takeover of state authority was simply not part of the legislative calculus.
>
> 2. The Religious Liberty Protection Act Bills ("RLPA")
>
> After City of Boerne v. Flores invalidated the Religious Freedom Restoration Act, Congress introduced the Religious Liberty Protection Acts of 1998 and 1999 * * * After it became clear that RLPA could not be passed—as a result primarily of lobbying by children's advocates, civil rights advocates concerned about fair housing laws, and conservative Christian organizations concerned about the principles of federalism—many believed that its momentum could not be revived. They were wrong. Those organizations lobbying for land use privileges, led by Rev. Gary Dobson, and for greater authority to

thwart prison administrators, led by Charles Colson, head of Prison Ministries Fellowship, continued to push for their particular elements of the bill. The ACLU, along with the Department of Justice, drafted a land use/prison bill, which was transformed in the hands of the ACLU into a land use/institutionalized persons bill. No hearings were held on RLUIPA per se; rather, the hearings on RLPA generally addressing land use law were supposed to stand in as hearings in support of RLUIPA. There was little in the RLPA hearings addressing "institutionalized persons." * * *

The hearings for RLPA involving land use, which then became the sole legislative history for RLUIPA, did not even as a cursory matter take into account the law of land use. No land use expert, either in the government or in the universities, was asked to testify to explain either prevailing legal principles in the field or to analyze RLPA's potential impact in the field. Nor was there any attempt to investigate the existing principles applied to landowners and religious landowners in the land use process.

1. Land Use: A Tradition of Deference to State and Local Governments

Land use law has always been a creature of state and local law. The reason for this is three-fold. First, the permanent nature of land—its immovability—makes its uses far more relevant to those who are nearby than those who are far away. Second, how land is used is an essential ingredient for communities to develop their character and to pursue shared purposes. Land use law is one of the key ways that communities come together to set priorities, to establish their character, and to meet fiscal, aesthetic, and lifestyle needs. Third, by keeping land use law local, citizens have more direct access to their representative (than if those representatives were national) and a proportionally larger voice in the land use process that directly affects them. Land use law is enacted by the state and local governing bodies and implemented by locally elected or appointed boards, with publicized public hearings an integral component in altering the law and in applying it.

The Supreme Court has consistently recognized "the States' traditional and primary power over land and water use." There is no indication in the Court's case law that these principles become inapplicable when the landowner is a religious entity or individual. To the contrary, the Court dismissed an appeal as lacking a substantial federal question brought by a church claiming the right to locate in a residential district, and later characterized that dismissal as follows:

> When the effect of a statute or ordinance upon the exercise of First Amendment freedoms is relatively small and the public interest to be protected is substantial, it is obvious that a rigid test requiring a showing of imminent danger to the security of

the Nation is an absurdity. We recently dismissed for want of substantiality an appeal in which a church group contended that its First Amendment rights were violated by a municipal zoning ordinance preventing the building of churches in certain residential areas.

The federal courts' recognition that land use law is a state and local power has meant that each state has been left to develop its own land use jurisprudence and that the federal courts have "emphasize[d their] reluctance to substitute [their] judgment for that of local decisionmakers, particularly in matters of such local concern as land-use planning. . . ." * * *

The value of federalism as a means of permitting individual communities to shape their goals, and as a means of permitting experimentation in achieving the elusive public good, is crystal clear in land use law. The states do not share a monolithic set of principles regarding land use by religious landowners, or any other landowners for that matter. Instead, they have been permitted to develop a wide variety of land use approaches that are keyed to the values, land, and public good sought in each particular community. * * *

[T]here is no state that gives religious landowners complete carte blanche under land use laws. Every state applies at least some elements of its land use law to religious landowners, whether it is zoning or use restrictions, or both. * * * There is also more to land use law than the mere fact of 50 governing jurisdictions. Within each jurisdiction, there are many categories of land use permits and restrictions, from setback to height and dimensional requirements, to occupancy limitations, as well as zoning. Traffic and the requisite parking is a dominant concern, as is bringing together compatible uses. Fire safety requirements, noise abatement, water usage, and environmental concerns also must be factored in. Some jurisdictions emphasize some elements more than others, but there is in general an attempt to find the right mix of factors to maximize optimal and harmonious use. Thus, focusing on any one element or zoning district in any one jurisdiction will not do justice to the entire balance of landowner rights and responsibilities in that particular jurisdiction, or the possibilities for location within that jurisdiction.

The universe of land use law is quite impressive and complex, though utterly missing from the RLPA history. For example, there are approximately 122,955,000 housing units in the United States. There are also approximately 268,254 houses of worship, approximately 92,012 public elementary and secondary schools, and 27,223 private elementary and secondary schools in the United States, 21,334 of which are religious schools. These statistics do not include other potentially relevant numbers, for example, the number of day care centers, religiously affiliated or otherwise, the number of homeless shelters, the number of religious gatherings held in private residential homes, or the number of church-run activity centers and camps.

There is no suggestion in the RLPA history that the Supreme Court has ever addressed the issue of zoning and land use, though, of course, it had addressed it as early as 1926, where it accurately predicted the necessity of increasing land use regulation:

> Building zone laws are of modern origin.... Until recent years, urban life was comparatively simple; but, with the great increase and concentration of population, problems are developed, and constantly are developing, which require, and will continue to require, additional restrictions in respect of the use and occupation of private lands in urban communities. Regulations, the wisdom, necessity and validity of which, as applied to existing conditions, are so apparent that they are now uniformly sustained, a century ago, or even half a century ago, probably would have been rejected as arbitrary and oppressive. Such regulations are sustained, under the complex conditions of our day, for reasons analogous to those which justify traffic regulations, which, before the advent of automobiles and rapid transit street railways, would have been condemned as fatally arbitrary and unreasonable. And in this there is no inconsistency, for, while the meaning of constitutional guaranties never varies, the scope of their application must expand or contract to meet the new and different conditions which are constantly coming within the field of their operation.

Nor did Congress study the changing nature of houses of worship.

The traditional concept of a small church serving the immediately neighboring community undoubtedly had something to do with the idea that such use was an integral part of community life in "the best and most open localities." However the establishment of a modern church, not dependent upon local residents as its communicants, and in some instances attracting people from far distances, the inevitable use of the automobile in connection therewith and the increased activities of the church for social and community functions having only a remote connection with its primary function, all present a different zoning picture.

Religious landowners regularly submit plans for multi-use buildings in the tens of thousands of square feet—and some hundreds of thousands—offering not just worship, but also religious education, elementary and high school education, banquet halls for religious celebrations, including weddings and bar and bat mitzvahs, coffee houses, motion picture theaters, fitness centers, all-night volleyball courts, child and senior day care centers, and social services, such as homeless shelters, soup kitchens, and drug and alcohol abuse treatment. Indeed, this trend has culminated in a move toward all-inclusive religious communities, from megachurches that are on the scale of a sizable shopping mall to planned communities that encompass not just a house of worship, but many social services and even private homes. This is a trend toward buildings that have greater negative secondary effects on neighbors, whether residential or commercial, and that raises issues properly and regularly considered by land use authorities in creating Master Plans or in the day-to-day determination of permit and variance requests.

A. RELIGIOUS LAND USES

GURU NANAK SIKH SOCIETY OF YUBA CITY v. COUNTY OF SUTTER

United States Court of Appeals, Ninth Circuit, 2006.
456 F.3d 978.

BEA, C. J.:

I. FACTS AND BACKGROUND

A. Denial of Guru Nanak's First CUP Application

Guru Nanak is a non-profit organization dedicated to fostering the teachings and practices of the Sikh religion. In 2001, Guru Nanak attempted to obtain a conditional use permit (CUP) for the construction of a Sikh temple—a gurudwara—on its 1.89–acre property on Grove Road in Yuba City ("the Grove Road property"). The proposed use included about 5,000 square feet dedicated to an assembly area and related activities. The proposed temple site would have held religious ceremonies for no more than seventy-five people at a time. The Grove Road property was in an area designated for low-density residential use (R–1), intended mainly for large lot single family residences; churches and temples are only conditionally permitted in R–1 districts, through issuance of a CUP.

The Sutter County Planning Division, part of the County Community Services Department, issued a report recommending that the Planning Commission grant a CUP for the Grove Road property. The report stated that while the permit presented potential conflicts with established residences in the area, the conflicts could be minimized by specifically recommended conditions that would be consistent with the General Plan of Sutter County. However, at a public meeting, the Planning Commission voted unanimously to deny the CUP. The denial was based on citizens' voiced fears that the resulting noise and traffic would interfere with the existing neighborhood. Following the Commission's denial, Guru Nanak began searching for a different parcel of property for the proposed temple.

B. Denial of Guru Nanak's Second CUP Application

In 2002, Guru Nanak acquired the property at issue in this case, a 28.79–acre parcel located on George Washington Boulevard in an unincorporated area of the County, to build a temple there. The site is zoned "AG" (general agricultural district) in the Sutter County Zoning Code. As in R–1 districts, churches and temples are only conditionally permitted in AG districts, through issuance of a CUP. The parcel includes a walnut orchard and an existing 2,300 square foot single family residence, which Guru Nanak proposed to convert into a Sikh temple by increasing the size of the building by approximately 500 square feet. All of the surrounding properties have identical zoning designations and have orchards. The nearest residence to the property is at least 200 feet north of the parcel's northern boundary. The residence to be converted into the temple is located 105 feet south of that northern boundary.

Another Sikh temple already exists on a ten-acre parcel of land zoned "agricultural" located next to Bogue Road, less than a mile southeast from the proposed temple's parcel. Within Yuba City's sphere of influence, the Bogue Road Sikh temple is surrounded by land zoned "agricultural."

Guru Nanak filed an application for a CUP to build a temple limited to approximately 2,850 square feet on the proposed site. The proposed use of the property was for a Sikh temple, assembly hall, worship services, and weddings. As with the Grove Road property, the proposed facility was intended to accommodate religious services of no more than seventy-five people at a time. Various county and state departments reviewed Guru Nanak's application and added a variety of conditions regarding the environmental impact of the proposed use including a twenty-five foot "no development" buffer along the north side of the property, a requirement that ceremonies remain indoors, and required landscaping.

Guru Nanak had to accept these conditions to receive the Planning Division's recommendation to the Planning Commission. The Planning Division issued a "mitigated negative declaration" (i.e. that the proposed temple would not create a significant environment impact) because "although the proposed [temple] could have a significant impact on the environment[,] . . . the recommended mitigation measures would reduce the possible impacts to a less-than-significant level." The Planning Division cited the temple's maximum attendance of 75 people, minor building conversion, and stipulated mitigation measures as reasons for finding a less-than-significant impact on the environment.

The Planning Commission held a public meeting to consider Guru Nanak's permit application. A member of Guru Nanak testified that while its previous application was for a 1.9–acre lot in a residential area, the subject application pertained to a 28.8–acre lot that did not border anyone's front or back yard. He also stated that Guru Nanak would accept all the Planning Division's proposed conditions on the land's use. Various potential neighbors spoke against the proposed temple, complaining mainly that the temple would increase traffic and noise, interfere with the agricultural use of their land, and lower property values. The Commission approved the application 4–3, subject to the conditions required by the Planning Division and stipulated to by Guru Nanak, with the commissioners echoing the reasoning voiced by both sides.

Several neighbors filed timely appeals to the Sutter County Board of Supervisors. The Planning Division filed another report in response to the appeals, addressing the specific complaints of the concerned neighbors and continuing to recommend approval of Guru Nanak's CUP application. Subject to revised mitigation conditions including an expanded one-hundred foot setback, the Planning Division found that the proposed temple's effect on neighbors' pesticide spraying, nearby traffic, and noise levels would be minimal.

The Board of Supervisors held a public hearing on the appeals. People attending the hearing reiterated claims regarding effects upon the agricultural use of surrounding land, traffic, and property values. In addition, several people complained that the initial plan for a seventy-five person temple was only a starting point for more ambitious facilities and this piece-meal approval process violated the California Environmental Quality Act (CEQA).

The four-member Board of Supervisors unanimously reversed the Planning Commission's approval and denied Guru Nanak's application. Supervisor Kroon flatly rejected the project based on the "right to farm": the property had been agricultural and should remain so. He argued that long-time farmers should not be affected by someone who wishes to change the use of the property. Supervisor Nelson stated that he was concerned that Guru Nanak's proposed use "was too far away from the city" and would not promote orderly growth. He commented that such development is detrimental to the surrounding agricultural uses and that Guru Nanak should locate its church nearer to his and other existing churches. Supervisors Munger and Silva agreed that the proposed temple site's separation from existing infrastructure, termed "leapfrog development," was a poor idea and denied the application on that ground.

C. Local Land Use Law

The Sutter County General Plan is a long-term guide for physical development of land within the County. The Plan empowers the County's Community Services Department to ensure that "new development adjacent to agricultural areas be designed to minimize conflicts with adjacent agricultural uses." [citation omitted]. The Plan disfavors development not contiguous to areas currently designated for urban or suburban uses leapfrog development–because it "has the potential to create land use conflicts and, in most instances, make[s] the provision of services more difficult." [citation omitted.]

The Sutter County Zoning Code designates twenty-two types of districts. Within each of these districts, the Code categorizes uses as "permitted" as a matter of right, uses that require a "zoning clearance," or uses that require a use permit. Zoning clearance uses need only the review and approval of the Community Services Director. Conditional use permit uses require a more comprehensive review through the Sutter County Planning Commission, and require a public hearing. A church must apply for a CUP to locate within any district available to it. Six of the twenty-two types of districts are made available to churches through the Zoning Code: general agricultural (AG); food processing, agricultural and recreation combining (FPARC); one-family residence (R–1), two-family residence (R–2), neighborhood apartment (R–3), and general apartment (R–4).

D. The Decision Below

The district court granted summary judgment for Guru Nanak because it concluded the County substantially burdened Guru Nanak's religious exercise, and that the County did not proffer evidence of compelling interests to justify such burden. Guru Nanak Sikh Soc'y of Yuba City, 326 F.Supp.2d at 1152–54. The district court reasoned that "[t]o meet the 'substantial burden 'standard, the governmental conduct being challenged must actually inhibit religious activity in a concrete way, and cause more than a mere inconvenience." Id. at 1152. Applying its definition of the substantial burden standard to the facts, the district court held that "the denial of the use permit, particularly when coupled with the denial of [Guru Nanak's] previous application, actually inhibits [Guru Nanak's] religious exercise." Id. The court also found that Congress did not overstep its constitutional bounds under Section Five of the Fourteenth Amendment when enacting RLUIPA because the statute targets documented religious discrimination. Id. at 1156–61. The court rejected the County's CEQA claim because the County's Planning Division had already found that the proposed temple, subject to stipulated mitigation measures, would create "a less-than-significant level" of environmental impacts. Id. at 1148–49. Accordingly, the district court invalidated the County's denial of Guru Nanak's CUP application and enjoined the County to approve immediately the CUP. Id. at 1161–63.

II. Analysis

* * *

We decide that the County made an individualized assessment of Guru Nanak's CUP, thereby making RLUIPA applicable, and that the County's denial of Guru Nanak's CUP application constituted a substantial burden, as that phrase is defined by RLUIPA. Because RLUIPA applies to this case, we address RLUIPA's constitutionality pursuant to Section Five of the Fourteenth Amendment, and decide that RLUIPA is a congruent and proportional exercise of congressional power pursuant to the Fourteenth Amendment.

A. Statutory Claim under RLUIPA

RLUIPA is Congress's latest effort to protect the free exercise of religion guaranteed by the First Amendment from governmental regulation. In Employment Division, Department of Human Resources of

Oregon v. Smith, 494 U.S. 872, 878–82, 110 S.Ct. 1595, 108 L.Ed.2d 876 (1990), the Supreme Court decided that the Free Exercise Clause of the First Amendment "does not inhibit enforcement of otherwise valid laws of general application that incidentally burden religious conduct." Cutter v. Wilkinson, 544 U.S. 709, 125 S.Ct. 2113, 2118, 161 L.Ed.2d 1020 (2005).

In 1993, Congress enacted the Religious Freedom and Restoration Act of [sic] (RFRA) in response to the Supreme Court's decision in Smith. RFRA "prohibit[ed] '[g]overnment' from 'substantially burden[ing]' a person's exercise of religion even if the burden results from a rule of general applicability unless the government [could] demonstrate the burden '(1) [was] in furtherance of a compelling governmental interest; and (2) [was] the least restrictive means of furthering that compelling governmental interest.' " City of Boerne v. Flores, 521 U.S. 507, 515–16, 117 S.Ct. 2157, 138 L.Ed.2d 624 (1997) (second and third alterations in original) (quoting 42 U.S.C. § 2000bb–1). In City of Boerne, though, the Supreme Court invalidated RFRA, deciding that it was an unconstitutional exercise of congressional power pursuant to Section Five of the Fourteenth Amendment because of a "lack of proportionality or congruence between the means adopted and the legitimate end to be achieved." Id. at 533, 117 S.Ct. 2157.

Congress enacted RLUIPA in response to the constitutional flaws with RFRA identified by City of Boerne. "RLUIPA 'replaces the void provisions of RFRA[,]' and prohibits the government from imposing 'substantial burdens' on 'religious exercise' unless there exists a compelling governmental interest and the burden is the least restrictive means of satisfying the governmental interest." San Jose Christian, 360 F.3d at 1033–34 (quoting Wyatt v. Terhune, 315 F.3d 1108, 1112 (9th Cir.2003) (citation omitted). To avoid RFRA's fate, Congress wrote that RLUIPA would apply only to regulations regarding land use and prison conditions. See Cutter, 125 S.Ct. at 2118.

RLUIPA applies only if one of three conditions obtain: (1) If the state "program or activity receives Federal financial assistance," 42 U.S.C. § 2000cc(2)(A), implicating congressional authority pursuant to the Spending Clause; (2) if the substantial burden imposed by local law "affects . . . [or] would affect, commerce with foreign nations, among the several States, or with Indian tribes," id. § 2000cc(2)(B), implicating congressional power pursuant to the Commerce Clause; (3) or, as Guru Nanak argues here, if "the substantial burden is imposed in the *implementation of a land use regulation* or system of land use regulations, under which a government makes, or has in place formal or informal procedures or practices that permit the government to make, *individualized assessments* of the proposed uses for the property involved," 42 U.S.C. § 2000cc(2)(C) (emphasis added).

1. Individualized Land Use Assessments

Before we apply the terms of RLUIPA, of course, we first must determine if RLUIPA even applies, by examining whether the actions of the County are "individualized assessments of the proposed uses for the property involved." Id. The County argues that its denial of Guru Nanak's second CUP application falls outside the legislative scope of RLUIPA because its use permit process is a neutral law of general applicability. However, the plain meaning of 2000cc(2)(C), quoted above, belies this contention. RLUIPA applies when the government may take into account the particular details of an applicant's proposed use of land when deciding to permit or deny that use.

The Sutter County Zoning Code does not permit churches as a matter of right in any of the six types of zoned areas available for church construction. Rather, an entity intending to build a church must first apply for a CUP and be approved by the County. The Zoning Code states, "The County realizes that certain uses ... may have the potential to negatively impact adjoining properties and uses. Such uses therefore require a more comprehensive review and approval procedure in order to evaluate and mitigate any potentially detrimental impacts." §§ 1500–8210. The Zoning Code also outlines how the Sutter County Planning Commission, which has original jurisdiction over such use applications, should determine whether to approve or reject an application: The Planning Commission may approve or conditionally approve a use permit if it finds that the establishment, maintenance, or operation of the use or building applied for will or will not, under the circumstances of the particular case, be detrimental to the health, safety, and general welfare of persons residing or working in the neighborhood of such proposed use, or be detrimental or injurious to property and improvement in the neighborhood or to the general welfare of the County. Additionally, the Commission shall find that the use or activity approved by the use permit is consistent with the General Plan [of Sutter County]. §§ 1500–8216 (emphasis added). The County Board of Supervisors reviews the Planning Commission's conditional use decisions "de novo and all applications, papers, maps, exhibits and staff recommendations made or presented to the Planning Commission may be considered." Id. § 1500–312(f). The Sutter County Zoning Code directs the Planning Commission and the Board of Supervisors to "implement [its] system of land use regulations [by making] individualized assessments of the proposed uses of the land involved." 42 U.S.C. § 2000cc.

By its own terms, it appears that RLUIPA does not apply directly to land use regulations, such as the Zoning Code here, which typically are written in general and neutral terms. However, when the Zoning Code is applied to grant or deny a certain use to a particular parcel of land, that application is an "implementation" under 42 U.S.C. § 2000cc(2)(C). See Kaahumanu v. County of Maui, 315 F.3d 1215, 1220–23 (9th Cir.2003) (concluding in a RLUIPA case that a similar permit process resulted in an administrative, rather than legislative, action because it "was based on the circumstances of the particular case and did not effectuate policy"); Freedom Baptist Church of Delaware County v. Twp. of Middletown, 204 F.Supp.2d 857, 868–69 (E.D.Pa.2002) ("No one contests that zoning ordinances must by their nature impose individual assessment regimes. That is to say, land use regulations through zoning codes necessarily involve case-by-case evaluations of the propriety of proposed activity against extant land use regulations."). RLUIPA therefore governs the actions of the County in this case.

2. *Substantial Burden Under RLUIPA*

We next turn to the issue whether the County's denial of Guru Nanak's CUP application substantially burdened its religious exercise within the meaning of RLUIPA. The statute states, in relevant part:

> (a) Substantial burdens
>
> (1) General rule
>
> No government shall impose or implement a land use regulation in a manner that imposes *a substantial burden on the religious exercise* of a person,including a religious assembly or institution, unless the government demonstrates that imposition of the burden on that person, assembly, or institution (A) is in furtherance of a compelling governmental interest; and (B) is the least restrictive means of furthering that compelling governmental interest. 42 U.S.C. § 2000cc (emphasis added).

Guru Nanak bears the burden to prove the County's denial of its application imposed a substantial burden on its religious exercise. Id. § 2000cc–2(b).

The Supreme Court's free exercise jurisprudence is instructive in defining a substantial burden under RLUIPA. The Supreme Court has held that various unemployment compensation regulations imposed a substantial burden on adherents' religious exercise, and thereby were subject to strict scrutiny, because the regulations withheld benefits based on adherents' following their religious tenets. See Sherbert v. Verner, 374 U.S. 398, 406, 83 S.Ct. 1790, 10 L.Ed.2d 965 (1963). This choice between unemployment benefits or religious duties imposed a burden because it exerted "substantial pressure on an adherent to modify his behavior and to violate his beliefs." Thomas v. Review Bd. of the Ind. Employment Sec. Div., 450 U.S. 707, 717–18, 101 S.Ct.1425, 67 L.Ed.2d 624 (1981); see also Lyng v. Nw. Indian Cemetery Protective Ass'n, 485 U.S. 439, 450–51, 108 S.Ct. 1319, 99 L.Ed.2d 534 (1988) (explaining that to trigger strict scrutiny under the First Amendment a governmental burden must have a "tendency to coerce individuals into acting contrary to their religious beliefs"). These cases demonstrate "that a 'substantial burden' must place more than an inconvenience on religious exercise." See Midrash Sephardi, Inc. v. Town of Surfside, 366 F.3d 1214, 1227 (11th Cir.2004).

Accordingly, interpreting RLUIPA, this court has held: "[F]or a land use regulation to impose a 'substantial burden,' it must be 'oppressive' to a 'significantly great' extent. That is, a 'substantial burden' on 'religious exercise' must impose a significantly great restriction or onus upon such exercise." San Jose Christian, 360 F.3d at 1034(quoting Merriam–Webster's Collegiate Dictionary 1170 (10th ed.2002)). Applying

San Jose Christian's definition of a substantial burden to the particular facts here, we find the district court correctly granted summary judgment for Guru Nanak. Most important to us the history behind Guru Nanak's two CUP application processes, and the reasons given for ultimately denying these applications, to a significantly great extent lessened the possibility that future CUP applications would be successful. See Saints Constantine & Helen Greek Orthodox Church, Inc. v. City of New Berlin, 396 F.3d 895, 899–900 (7th Cir.2005) ("Saint Constantine") (finding that, to prove a substantial burden under RLUIPA, a religious group need not "show that there was no other parcel of land on which it could build its church"). We need not and do not decide that failing to provide a religious institution with a land use entitlement for a new facility for worship necessarily constitutes a substantial burden pursuant to RLUIPA. At the same time, we do decide the County imposed a substantial burden here based on two considerations: (1) that the County's broad reasons given for its tandem denials could easily apply to all future applications by Guru Nanak; and (2) that Guru Nanak readily agreed to every mitigation measure suggested by the Planning Division, but the County, without explanation, found such cooperation insufficient.

The Zoning Code permits churches in six types of districts. Churches must apply for a CUP within any or all of the six available districts. Each of the district classifications available to churches is intended to provide an area for a distinct form of development. The CUP application process is intended to ensure that a religious group's proposed property use conforms with the type of development that the particular district contemplates.

Guru Nanak initially applied for a CUP to construct a Sikh temple on a 1.89–acre property in an R–1 (One Family Residence) District. The Sutter County Community Services Department had recommended approval of the proposed use because mitigation measures, agreed to by Guru Nanak, would have minimized conflicts with surrounding land. Nevertheless, the County Planning Commission unanimously rejected the application, citing neighbors' complaints regarding increased noise and traffic.

Guru Nanak predictably responded to these voiced complaints by attempting to locate its temple on property far from residents who would be bothered by noise and traffic. The County's stated reasons for denying Guru Nanak's first application implied to Guru Nanak that it should not attempt to locate its temple in higher density districts (two-family residence, neighborhood apartment, general apartment, and the combining district) where nearby neighbors would be similarly bothered.

Accordingly, Guru Nanak proposed a smaller temple, with the same seventy-five person capacity, on a much larger parcel of agricultural land. The agricultural parcel left much more space between the temple and adjacent properties; that space mitigated the temple's noise and traffic impact on surrounding persons. Both the Community Services

Department and the Planning Commission approved this second application because the parcel's size, along with additional setback and use conditions, adequately addressed the noise, traffic, and other complaints related to the temple's possible impact on surrounding agricultural uses.

The County Board of Supervisors' denial of Guru Nanak's second application frustrated Guru Nanak's attempt to comply both with the reasons given for the County's first denial and the Planning Division's various requirements for Guru Nanak to locate a temple on land zoned "agricultural." The Board's primary reason for denying Guru Nanak's second application was that the temple would contribute to "leapfrog development." Although the Zoning Code conditionally permits churches and other non-agricultural activities within agricultural districts, the County could use its concern with leapfrog development effectively to deny churches access to all such land; a great majority of agriculturally zoned land near Yuba City is separated from existing urban development. Moreover, many other churches already exist on agriculturally zoned land, including another Sikh temple located on Bogue Road less than a mile away from the proposed temple. The Bogue Road Sikh temple's parcel of land, like Guru Nanak's land, is surrounded by other agricultural parcels of land, to the extent such parcels are within Yuba City's sphere of influence. Hence, the County inconsistently applied its concern with leapfrog development to Guru Nanak. At the very least, such inconsistent decision-making establishes that any future CUP applications for a temple on land zoned "agricultural" would be fraught with uncertainty. See id. at 901(finding a substantial burden where a church's future efforts to locate another parcel of property or file new land use applications would result in "delay, uncertainty, and expense").

In denying the second CUP application, the Board of Supervisors disregarded, without explanation, the Planning Division's finding that Guru Nanak's acceptance of various mitigation conditions would make the proposed temple have a less-than-significant impact on surrounding land uses. We "cannot view [the denial of the second CUP application] 'in isolation'; [rather, it] must be viewed in the context of [Guru Nanak's permit process] history.'" See Westchester Day Sch. v. Vill. of Mamaroneck, 417 F.Supp.2d 477, 548 (S.D.N.Y.2006) (quoting Living Water Church of God v. Charter Twp. of Meridian, 384 F.Supp.2d 1123, 1134 (W.D.Mich.2005)). In Westchester Day School, the district court found a substantial burden where the zoning board denied the religious day school's land use application despite the day school having "worked for over one-and-a-half years to address the [zoning board's] concerns and offered to make changes to, inter alia, parking, the size of [the proposed construction,] landscaping, [the] enrollment cap[, and] a bus departure management plan to mitigate the traffic impact." Id.; see also Living Water, 384 F.Supp.2d. at 1134 (finding a substantial burden where the Township denied the church's land use proposal after the church had "worked diligently and in good faith with the Township to address its concerns before submitting a revised ... proposal"). Similarly, during both of its CUP application processes, Guru Nanak agreed to every mitigation condition the Planning Division found necessary to recommend the land entitlements. Regarding the second application in particular, Guru Nanak agreed to a host of conditions proposed specifically to allay the County's concerns with leapfrog development-including a one-hundred foot setback to allow for pesticide spraying, and that all its religious ceremonies be held indoors and limited to seventy-five people. Nevertheless, in denying the second application, the Board of Supervisors neither related why any of such mitigation conditions were inadequate nor suggested additional conditions that would render satisfactory Guru Nanak's application.

While the Zoning Code conditionally permits churches in residential and higher density districts, noise and traffic concerns would likely preclude constructing any other proposed temple on a small parcel of land. Likewise, Guru Nanak would understandably be hesitant to propose a temple on another large, agricultural parcel of land for fear that the County would yet again deny that application because of leapfrog development. Even if Guru Nanak were once again to follow the Planning Division's detailed requirements on mitigating impacts on nearby land, history shows such extensive efforts could very well be in vain. The net effect of the County's two denials-including their underlying rationales and disregard for Guru Nanak's accepted mitigation conditions-is to shrink the large amount of land theoretically available to Guru Nanak under the Zoning Code to several scattered parcels that the County may or may not ultimately approve. Because the County's actions have to a significantly great extent lessened the prospect of Guru Nanak being able to construct a temple in the future, the County has imposed a substantial burden on Guru Nanak's religious exercise.

Our decision contrasts with the facts present in San Jose Christian, where we found the plaintiff had not suffered a substantial burden because the city's actions had not lessened the possibility that the college could find a suitable property. In San Jose Christian, we considered it centrally important that there was no evidence to suggest that the religious institution desired by San Jose Christian College could not be obtained merely by "submit[ing] a complete application." San Jose Christian, 360 F.3d at 1035; see also id. ("Should College comply with this request, it is not at all apparent that its re-zoning application will be denied."). Moreover, we noted that even if its complete application were denied, the college had no reason to believe another application would be rejected. Id. ("[There is] no evidence in the record demonstrating that College was precluded from using other sites within the city."). * * *

3. *Compelling Interests*

The County effectively concedes that it has no compelling interest, much less that the restrictions are narrowly tailored to accomplish such interest. The County presents no such argument in its briefs. Because the County "shall bear the burden of persuasion," 42 U.S.C. § 2000cc–2(b), to prove narrowly tailored, compelling interests, we hold that the district court properly invalidated the County's denial of Guru Nanak's CUP application.

B. Constitutionality of RLUIPA's Individual Land Use Assessments Provision

We now turn to the issue of whether RLUIPA as applied to the facts of this case is constitutional. It is axiomatic that "[t]he powers of the legislature are defined and limited; and that those limits may not be mistaken, or forgotten." Marbury v. Madison, 1 Cranch 137, 176, 5 U.S.137, 2 L.Ed. 60 (1803). We must therefore find an affirmative grant of power provided to Congress to enact a law such as RLUIPA. Because RLUIPA applies in this case due to the County's "individualized assessment" of Guru Nanak's application, the statute's constitutionality depends on Congress's power to "enforce, by appropriate legislation, the provisions of [the Fourteenth Amendment]." U.S. Const. amend. XIV, § 5. RLUIPA will be deemed constitutional only if there is "a congruence and proportionality between the injury to be prevented or remedies and the means adopted to that end." City of Boerne, 521 U.S. at 520, 117 S.Ct. 2157. We hold that RLUIPA is constitutional because it addresses documented, unconstitutional government actions in a proportional manner.

* * *

In this case, RLUIPA targets only "individualized governmental assessment[s]" subject to strict scrutiny under the Supreme Court's free exercise jurisprudence. Congress has power to enforce the Free Exercise Clause, as recognized in Cantwell v. Connecticut, 310 U.S. 296, 60 S.Ct. 900, 84 L.Ed. 1213 (1940), because the "fundamental concept of liberty embodied in [the Fourteenth Amendment's Due Process Clause] embraces the liberties guaranteed by the First Amendment," id. at 303, 60 S.Ct. 900. The Supreme Court decided in Smith that whereas neutral laws of general applicability do not implicate free exercise-based constitutional concerns, laws "len[ding themselves] to individualized governmental assessment of the reasons for the relevant conduct," 494 U.S. at 884, 110 S.Ct. 1595 (emphasis added), are subject to higher scrutiny because they may be unevenly applied against actions premised on religious exercise, see id. ("[A] distinctive feature of unemployment compensation programs is that their eligibility criteria invite consideration of the particular circumstances behind an applicant's unemployment."). When such regulations involving individualized assessments impose substantial burdens on religious exercise, they are subject to strict scrutiny to protect and vindicate the right to free exercise of religion from governmental encroachment. See id.

As we decided earlier, here the County assessed the particular details behind Guru Nanak's application and weighed these particular facts against broad criteria. Therefore, because RLUIPA attempts to protect the free exercise of religion by targeting only regulations subject to strict scrutiny, "it [is] easier for Congress to show a pattern of state constitutional violations" sufficient to justify RLUIPA's enactment. Hibbs, 538 U.S. at 736, 123 S.Ct. 1972.

After we identify the precise right—here, the free exercise of religion in the face of individualized governmental assessments subject to strict scrutiny—being protected by congressional legislation, "we examine whether Congress identified a history and pattern of unconstitutional [regulation] by the States against [religious groups]." See Garrett, 531 U.S. at 368, 121 S.Ct. 955. In nine hearings preceding the enactment of RLUIPA, Congress compiled a substantial amount of statistical and anecdotal data demonstrating that governmental entities nationwide purposefully exclude unwanted religious groups by denying them use permits through discretionary and subjective standards and processes. See H.R.Rep. No. 106–219, 18–24 (summarizing the evidence from these hearings). For instance, "[r]eligious groups accounting for only 9% of the population account for 50% of the reported litigation involving location of churches, and 34% of the reported litigation involving accessory uses at existing churches." Id. at 20–21. Congress also heard persuasive anecdotal evidence regarding a trend of denying newcomer religious groups CUPs in buildings that formerly housed non-religious assemblies or which had housed widely accepted religious groups. Id. at 21–22.

The nature of the regulatory action RLUIPA targets and the evidence which demonstrated that such regulations often violated the Free Exercise Clause may empower Congress to stem such violations pursuant to its Section Five authority. See City of Boerne, 521 U.S. at 530, 117 S.Ct. 2157 ("Strong measures appropriate to address one harm may be an unwarranted response to another, lesser one."). With that backdrop, we must determine if there is "a congruence and proportionality between the injury to be prevented or remedied and the means adopted to that end." See id. at 520, 117 S.Ct. 2157. We find it central to our decision that "[u]nlike [RFRA] at issue in City of Boerne ... which applied broadly," Hibbs, 538 U.S. at 738, 123 S.Ct. 1972, RLUIPA applies more narrowly.

Unlike RFRA, the predecessor to RLUIPA, RLUIPA applies solely to regulations affecting land use and prison conditions, and therefore does not "displac[e] laws and prohibit[ ] official actions of almost every description and regardless of subject matter.... [nor does it] appl[y] to all federal and state law." See City of Boerne, 521 U.S. at 532, 117 S.Ct. 2157. RLUIPA has nowhere near the "universal coverage," id. at 516, 117 S.Ct. 2157, the Supreme Court found unacceptable in City of Boerne. See also Cutter, 125 S.Ct. at 2118 (stating that RLUIPA is "[l]ess sweeping than RFRA"). As with the statutes the Supreme Court has found to be valid as constitutional exercises of Congress's Section Five authority, RLUIPA solely includes "remedies aimed at areas where ... discrimination has been most flagrant." See South Carolina v. Katzenbach, 383 U.S. 301, 315, 86 S.Ct. 803, 15 L.Ed.2d 769 (1966). RLUIPA is a congruent and proportional response to free exercise violations because it targets only regulations that are susceptible, and have been shown, to violate individuals' religious exercise. Therefore, Congress constitutionally enacted RLUIPA pursuant to its enforcement power within Section Five of the Fourteenth Amendment.

* * *

We AFFIRM the district court's order granting summary judgment for Guru Nanak and enjoining the County immediately to approve and grant Guru Nanak's CUP application. * * *

FIFTH AVENUE PRESBYTERIAN CHURCH v. CITY OF NEW YORK

United States Court of Appeals, Second Circuit, 2002.
293 F.3d 570.

STRAUB, Circuit Judge.

Presbyterian is located at the corner of Fifth Avenue and 55th Street in Manhattan. For several years, homeless persons have chosen to sleep on the Church's outdoor property. In February 1999, the Church officially designated two areas on its outdoor property upon which homeless persons are permitted to sleep at night. The first of these areas encompasses the landings at the tops of the staircases leading into the Church's main sanctuary on Fifth Avenue and into its 55th Street entrance. The landings are contained within arched entryways and are recessed approximately five to ten feet from the sidewalk and raised approximately six feet above the sidewalk. The second designated area is a strip of land adjacent to the Church's southern wall that extends approximately five feet to the public sidewalk.

The Church views its outdoor space as a sanctuary for the service-resistant homeless who prefer not to sleep in shelters. Homeless persons are welcome on the Church's outdoor property between 8:00 p.m. and 7:00 a.m. They are not permitted to set up their sleeping area or lie down until 9:00 p.m. Persons taking advantage of the Church's invitation to sleep on its outdoor property are given a list of rules, which includes instructions to clean up after themselves and a prohibition on begging, loud music, disruptive behavior, and foul language.

In November 2001, the City notified Presbyterian that it would no longer permit the homeless to sleep on the Church's outdoor property. Thereafter, on three occasions in early December 2001, city police removed the homeless from the Church's property during the night. Presbyterian claims that the police threatened the homeless with arrest if they refused to leave.

On December 17, 2001, Presbyterian brought suit under 42 U.S.C. § 1983, the First Amendment, the common law of trespass, the Religious Land Use and Institutionalized Persons Act of 2000 ("RLUIPA"), 42 U.S.C. § 2000cc, *et. seq.*, and for deprivation of due process and violation of Article 1, Section 3 of the New York State Constitution. Presbyterian sought injunctive relief preventing the City from entering onto Church property and dispersing the homeless. Focusing primarily on the

Church's cause of action under the Free Exercise Clause of the First Amendment, the City argued that allowing the homeless to sleep on the sidewalk and on Church grounds does not constitute protected religious activity, and that the Church had violated applicable laws or regulations in four ways: (1) operating a shelter without a license; (2) creation of a public nuisance; (3) allowing persons to sleep on a sidewalk that is subject to City regulation; and (4) allowing the use of boxes, tents, and similar materials on the sidewalk in violation of City codes.

Following a hearing, the District Court issued a memorandum and order granting in part the Church's request for a preliminary injunction. In ruling on the Church's application, the District Court concluded that allowing homeless persons to sleep on the Church's private property constitutes protected religious activity because doing so enables the Church to interact with and assist the homeless in bettering their lives. The court rejected the City's arguments that the Church is operating a *de facto* shelter, and that the presence of the homeless amounts to a public nuisance. The court agreed with the City that it is permitted to regulate the presence of sleeping persons, as well as cardboard shelters and tents, on the Church's land adjacent to the sidewalk on 55th Street. Accordingly, the District Court entered a preliminary injunction prohibiting the City from interfering with homeless persons who are sleeping on the Church steps and landings above sidewalk level. The court denied the application with regard to those sleeping on Church property adjacent to the public sidewalk.

* * *

We agree with the District Court that on the present record, the Church has demonstrated a likelihood of success in establishing that its provision of outdoor sleeping space for the homeless effectuates a sincerely held religious belief and therefore is protected under the Free Exercise Clause. *Cf. Stuart Circle Parish v. Bd. of Zoning Appeals of the City of Richmond,* 946 F.Supp. 1225, 1236 (E.D.Va.1996); *Western Presbyterian Church v. Bd. of Zoning Adjustment of the District of Columbia,* 862 F.Supp. 538, 544–46 (D.D.C.1994). Further, we assume, without deciding, that the City's actions in dispersing the homeless substantially burden the Church's protected religious activity, a proposition with which the City has not argued. Accordingly, absent a demonstration that a neutral law of general applicability justifies the City's actions, the City must assert a compelling interest in preventing the homeless from sleeping on Church property that would suffice to overcome the Church's free exercise rights, and that the means it has adopted to fulfill that interest are narrowly tailored. *See Church of Lukumi Babalu Aye,* 508 U.S. at 546, 113 S.Ct. 2217; *Wisconsin v. Yoder,* 406 U.S. 205, 214–15, 92 S.Ct. 1526, 32 L.Ed.2d 15 (1972).

The City points to several laws or policies that it claims support its actions. First, the City argues that Presbyterian is operating a homeless shelter without a license and in contravention of state regulations. Pursuant to 18 N.Y.C.R.R. §§ 485.1 & 491.1, the operator of a shelter for adults must obtain certification from the New York State Department of Social Services and comply with its applicable regulations. A shelter is defined as "an adult care facility established and operated for the purpose of providing temporary residential care, room, board, supervision, information *and* referral...." *Id.* § 491.2 (emphasis added). We agree with the District Court that an invitation to the homeless to sleep on outdoor property does not fall within the ambit of these regulations, which contemplate an indoor facility and the provision of comprehensive social services for the homeless. *See, e.g., id.* § 491.10 (setting forth detailed requirements for shelters pertaining to building and fire codes, furniture, amenities and housekeeping).

As an alternative justification for its actions, the City argues that it is empowered to enforce minimum standards of habitability for privately-run shelters in the absence of applicable regulations. In support of this proposition, the City cites the New York Court of Appeals' decision in *McCain v. Koch,* 70 N.Y.2d 109, 517 N.Y.S.2d 918, 511 N.E.2d 62 (1987). *McCain* held that the New York Supreme Court has the equitable power to require a minimum standard of care for city-run emergency housing so long as the standard of care does not conflict with applicable state or city regulations. *McCain's* holding was premised on the principle that once the City has undertaken to provide emergency housing, it has a duty to ensure certain minimum standards of habitability. *Id.* at 119–20, 517 N.Y.S.2d 918, 511 N.E.2d 62. We decline to extend *McCain's* holding beyond the context of government-administered housing on these facts. Moreover, *McCain* addressed *a court's* equitable power to issue an injunction requiring the City to provide particular amenities; it did not address the City's power to devise and enforce equitable standards of its own making. Nor did the Court of Appeals in *McCain* express any opinion as to the substance of the injunction in that case—*i.e.,* whether the specific requirements in that injunction were in fact the minimum acceptable standards of habitability for a shelter.

The City argues that its power to enforce equitable standards of care for homeless shelters derives from its ability to enforce public nuisance laws. The District Court ruled below that the City had not established the existence of a nuisance, and the City does not challenge that particular holding on appeal. Therefore, we need not consider this argument. The City also claims, in its reply brief, that it has a "policy of regarding the provision of subminimal shelter as a nuisance." Not only is this argument untimely raised, *see Thomas v. Roach,* 165 F.3d 137, 145–46 (2d Cir.1999), but the City has not adequately demonstrated the existence or general applicability of such a policy, or that it applies to the Church's activities.

Finally, the City argues for the first time on appeal that the Church is in violation of New York City Zoning Resolution Section 12–10 because its outdoor sanctuary is not a permissible "accessory" use of its property. Because this argument was not raised below and refusing to consider it will not result in "manifest injustice" in light of the posture of the case, and because adjudication of zoning disputes over accessory uses entails an inherently factual inquiry, *see New York Botanical Garden v. Bd. of Standards & Appeals,* 91 N.Y.2d 413, 420, 671 N.Y.S.2d 423, 694 N.E.2d 424 (1998), we decline to consider the City's argument here. *See Coogan v. Smyers,* 134 F.3d 479, 486–87 (2d Cir.1998). Nor, therefore, need we express any opinion on the plaintiffs' argument, also raised for the first time on appeal, that the Religious Land Use and Institutionalized Persons Act of 2000 ("RLUIPA"), 42 U.S.C. § 2000cc, *et. seq.*, subjects the City's application of its Zoning Resolution to strict scrutiny.

Thus, at the present time, the City has not sufficiently shown the existence of a relevant law or policy that is neutral and of general applicability, and that would therefore justify its actions in dispersing the homeless from the Church's landings and steps. For the first time in its reply brief, the City argues that its dispersal of the homeless from Presbyterian's property is justified by a compelling state governmental interest, namely, "preventing the Church from providing inadequate shelter nightly and encouraging homeless persons to avoid a safer, more civilized alternative." Although arguments raised for the first time in a reply brief need not be considered, *see Thomas,* 165 F.3d at 145–46, we note that the homeless who take advantage of the Church's offer, ten of whom are plaintiffs in this action, do so voluntarily. Moreover, common sense, in addition to evidence put forth by the homeless plaintiffs, suggests that the majority of these homeless will not go to shelters if the City is permitted to disperse them; rather, they will find another place on the street upon which to sleep. Thus, it is doubtful that the "ends" support the City's "means," nor has the City attempted to show that police dispersal in the middle of the night is the least restrictive means of accomplishing its goal of ensuring that the homeless have appropriate sleeping quarters. *See Yoder,* 406 U.S. at 215, 92 S.Ct. 1526.

For the foregoing reasons, we find that the District Court did not abuse its discretion in concluding that Presbyterian has demonstrated a likelihood of success on the merits of its free exercise claim. The opinion and order of the District Court entering a preliminary injunction in favor of Presbyterian is hereby AFFIRMED.

Notes

1. Litigation surrounding RLUIPA claims has increased exponentially over the last few years. While there have been some attempts to bring facial challenges to a municipality's zoning framework alleging that based upon the local law, it would be impossible to locate a religious use in the jurisdiction (See, Civil Liberties for Urban Believers (C.L.U.B) v. City of Chicago, 342 F.3d 752 (7th Cir.2003) where the plaintiffs argued that the City's zoning laws were unconstitutional because religious uses were required to apply for special use permits to locate in business and commercial districts and because religious uses were excluded from manufacturing districts), the overwhelming number of cases focus on as applied challenges, or site specific zoning decisions. For a current listing of cases challenging the application of RLUIPA to planning and zoning decisions, see www.RLUIPA.org, a site maintained by The Beckett Fund for Religious Liberty, and

organization that provides litigation support to organizations and individuals seeking to protect religious liberties.

2. What constitutes a religious use under RLUIPA? School facilities when used for religious and secular purposes? (See, Westchester Day School v. Village of Mamaroneck, ___ F.3d ___, 2007 WL 3011061 (2nd Cir. 2007); A building to be used as a spiritual retreat? (see, DiLaura v. Ann Arbor, 30 Fed.Appx. 501, 2002 WL 273774 (6th Cir.2002)) Church day care facilities? (For differing views see, Living Water Church of God v. Meridian, 2005 WL 3447668 (W.D.Mich.2005) and Grace United Methodist Church v. City of Cheyenne, 451 F.3d 643 (10th Cir. 2006)). A church operated assisted living facility? (See, Greater Bible Way Temple of Jackson v. City of Jackson, 478 Mich. 373, 733 N.W.2d 734 (2007)).

3. Should religious uses be allowed to locate in any zoning district? See, Petra Presbyterian Church v. Village of Northbrook, 489 F.3d 846 (7th Cir.2007) and Vineyard Christian Fellowship of Evanston, Inc. v. City of Evanston, 250 F.Supp.2d 961 (N.D. Ill. 2003). Does the application of building codes to churches violate RLUIPA? See, Peace Lutheran Church & Academy v. Village of Sussex, 246 Wis.2d 502, 631 N.W.2d 229 (App.2001).

4. Is eminent domain a "land use" for purposes of RLUIPA? See, St. John's United Church of Christ v. City of Chicago, 401 F.Supp.2d 887 (N.D. Ill. 2005); Cottonwood Christian Center v. Cypress Redevelopment Agency, 218 F.Supp.2d 1203 (C.D.Cal.2002); and Faith Temple Church v. Town of Brighton, 405 F.Supp.2d 250 (W.D.N.Y.2005).

5. There is an increasing amount of litigation in the federal courts surrounding the applicability of RLUIPA to various planning and zoning decisions. Does RLUIPA give a congregation the right to intervene in land use proceeding to block the siting of a cellular tower where the congregation believes that the placement of the tower will block their view through the windows when they are in the sanctuary praying? See, Omnipoint Communications, Inc. v. City of White Plains, 175 F.Supp.2d 697 (S.D.N.Y.2001).

6. How far does a municipality have to go in accommodating the development needs of a religious institution? See, Prater v. City of Burnside, 289 F.3d 417 (6th Cir.2002) (holding that the City's decision to develop a previously laid-out roadway between two church-owned parcels did not give rise to a claim under RLUIPA). See, McGann v. Incorporated Village of Old Westbury, 293 A.D.2d 581, 741 N.Y.S.2d 75 (2nd Dept. 2002) (finding that a cemetery owned by the Roman Catholic Diocese is a religious use and that although it is entitled to preferential treatment, a proposed use of land as a ninety-seven acre cemetery is subject to environmental review under state law). Are religious institutions always compatible with every other type of land use? See, Boyajian v. Gatzunis, 212 F.3d 1 (1st Cir.2000) and Congregation Kol Ami v. Abington Township, 309 F.3d 120 (3d Cir.2002) suggesting perhaps different answers.

7. The U.S. Department of Justice has taken an active interest in enforcing RLUIPA on behalf of individuals and organizations who believe that their religious liberties have been violated. On February 20, 2007, Attorney General Alberto Gonzalez released a report on the Justice Department's First Freedom Project (see, www.firstfreedom.gov). This follows on the heels of the appointment of a Special Counsel for Religious Discrimina-

tion in 2002 and the creation of a department-wide Religious Freedom Task Force. The Attorney General has also announced a series of training programs and educational materials for religious organizations, civil rights groups and community leaders. Does RLUIPA and/or the actions of the Attorney General violate the Constitutional mandate of separation of church and state?

B. HOUSING DISCRIMINATION

(1) Racial Discrimination in Housing

UNITED STATES v. CITY OF BLACK JACK, MISSOURI

United States Court of Appeals, Eighth Circuit, 1974.
508 F.2d 1179, certiorari denied 422 U.S. 1042,
95 S.Ct. 2656, 45 L.Ed.2d 694 (1975).

[In 1970 the Black Jack area was unincorporated, and was under the St. Louis County master plan. The plan designated 67 acres for multi-family housing, only 15 of which had been developed. In 1969, the Inter–Religious Center for Urban Affairs obtained an option on 12 acres for the purpose of creating housing for low and moderate income persons living in economically depressed and deteriorated areas of St. Louis. In 1970, the area residents succeeded in having Black Jack incorporated as a city. After its incorporation, an ordinance was passed prohibiting the construction of any new multiple-family dwellings and making existing ones nonconforming uses. The United States brought an action to enjoin enforcement of the ordinance under Title VIII of the Civil Rights Act of 1968, 42 U.S.C.A. § 3601 et seq. The District Court held the plaintiff had failed to establish a racially discriminatory purpose or effect and it dismissed the case. Further facts appear in the opinion.]

HEANEY, CIRCUIT JUDGE.

* * *

The racial composition of Black Jack and the surrounding area was set forth by the District Court in its opinion, and is not contested by the parties:

> "Statistical information submitted shows that at the relevant time the area which is now the City of Black Jack was virtually all white, with a black population of between 1% and 2%. The area of St. Louis County north of Interstate Highway 270, which includes Black Jack, is approximately 99% white. * * *
>
> "The virtually all-white character of Black Jack was in marked contrast to the racial composition of other parts of the St. Louis area. In 1970, the pupil population of the City of St. Louis School District was 65.6% black. * * * In 1970, the Kinloch School District, which is only two miles from the nearest boundary of the Hazelwood School District [of which Black Jack is a part], had 1,245 students, all of whom were black.

> "The percentage of blacks in St. Louis County has increased only slightly overall from 4.1% in 1950 to 4.8% in 1970. During the same period, the percentage of blacks in the City of St. Louis more than doubled from 17.9% to 40.9%.
>
> "Between 1950 and 1970, the population of the city declined * * * [by] 27%, while the population of the county more than doubled * * *. From 1960 to 1970, there were approximately 102,-298 new housing starts in the county, and 15,348 in the city, a ratio of almost 7 to 1. During the same period, the city had a net decrease of 24,548 housing units, while the county had a net increase of 84,169. * * *
>
> "The concentration of blacks in the city and in pockets in the county is accompanied by the confinement of a disproportionate number of them in overcrowded or substandard accommodations. The 1970 census reveals that in St. Louis city and county approximately 40% of the black families, as compared with 14% of the white families, lived in overcrowded units. * * *"

United States v. City of Black Jack, Missouri, supra, 372 F.Supp. at 325.

The District Court further found that the average cost of a home in the City of Black Jack in 1970 was approximately $30,000, and that the average income of Black Jack families is approximately $15,000 per year. It found that Park View Heights was designed to meet the housing needs of families making between $5,528 and $10,143 per year.

* * *

We turn then to the merits of the decision below. Congress has declared that the purpose of the Fair Housing Act of 1968 is "to provide, within constitutional limitations, for fair housing throughout the United States." 42 U.S.C.A. § 3601. The Act was passed pursuant to congressional power under the Thirteenth Amendment to eliminate the badges and incidents of slavery. In construing the Civil Rights Act of 1866, also founded on that power, the Supreme Court has declared that

> * * * when racial discrimination herds men into ghettos and makes their ability to buy property turn on the color of their skin, then it too is a relic of slavery.

Jones v. Mayer Co., 392 U.S. 409, 442–443, 88 S.Ct. 2186, 2205, 20 L.Ed.2d 1189 (1968).

Title VIII is designed to prohibit "all forms of discrimination, sophisticated as well as simple-minded." *Williams v. Matthews Co.*, 499 F.2d 819, 826 (8th Cir.1974). Just as Congress requires

> * * * the removal of artificial, arbitrary, and unnecessary barriers to employment when the barriers operate invidiously to discriminate on the basis of racial or other impermissible classification[,]

Griggs v. Duke Power Co., 401 U.S. 424, 430–431, 91 S.Ct. 849, 853, 28 L.Ed.2d 158 (1971), such barriers must also give way in the field of housing. The discretion of local zoning officials, recently recognized in

Village of Belle Terre v. Boraas, 416 U.S. 1, 94 S.Ct. 1536, 39 L.Ed.2d 797 (1974), must be curbed where "the clear result of such discretion is the segregation of low-income Blacks from all White neighborhoods." *Banks v. Perk*, 341 F.Supp. 1175, 1180 (N.D.Ohio, 1972), aff'd in part & rev'd in part without opinion, 473 F.2d 910 (6th Cir.1973).

The burden of proof in Title VIII cases is governed by the concept of the "prima facie case." *Williams v. Matthews Co., supra* 499 F.2d at 826. To establish a prima facie case of racial discrimination, the plaintiff need prove no more than that the conduct of the defendant actually or predictably results in racial discrimination; in other words, that it has a discriminatory effect. See id.; *United Farmworkers of Florida Housing Project, Inc. v. City of Delray Beach*, 493 F.2d 799, 808 (5th Cir.1974); *Hawkins v. Town of Shaw, Mississippi*, 461 F.2d 1171, 1172 (5th Cir.1972) (en banc); *Kennedy Park Homes Ass'n v. City of Lackawanna, supra* 436 F.2d at 114; *Dailey v. City of Lawton, Oklahoma*, 425 F.2d 1037, 1039 (10th Cir.1970); *Norwalk CORE v. Norwalk Redevelopment Agency*, 395 F.2d 920, 931 (2d Cir.1968). The plaintiff need make no showing whatsoever that the action resulting in racial discrimination in housing was racially motivated.[1] See *Williams v. Matthews Co., supra* 499 F.2d at 826; *United Farmworkers of Florida Housing Project, Inc. v. City of Delray Beach, supra* 493 F.2d at 808; *Kennedy Park Homes Ass'n v. City of Lackawanna, supra* 436 F.2d at 114; *Citizens Committee for Faraday Wood v. Lindsay, supra* 362 F.Supp. at 658; *Banks v. Park, supra* 341 F.Supp. at 1180. Effect, and not motivation, is the touchstone, in part because clever men may easily conceal their motivations, but more importantly, because

> * * * [w]hatever our law was once, * * * we now firmly recognize that the arbitrary quality of thoughtlessness can be as disastrous and unfair to private rights and the public interest as the perversity of a willful scheme.

Hobson v. Hansen, 269 F.Supp. 401, 497 (D.D.C.1967), aff'd sub nom. *Smuck v. Hobson*, 132 U.S.App.D.C. 372, 408 F.2d 175 (1969) (en banc)

1. The United States contends that the ordinance ought also be enjoined because it was enacted for the purpose of excluding blacks. There is evidence in the record to support that contention. Opposition to Park View Heights was repeatedly expressed in racial terms by persons whom the District Court found to be the leaders of the incorporation movement, by individuals circulating petitions, and by zoning commissioners themselves. Racial criticism of Park View Heights was made and cheered at public meetings. The uncontradicted evidence indicates that, at all levels of opposition, race placed a significant role, both in the drive to incorporate and the decision to rezone. We agree with the Tenth Circuit's conclusion that improper purpose may be shown circumstantially:

> * * * If proof of a civil right violation depends on an open statement by an official of an intent to discriminate, the Fourteenth Amendment offers little solace to those seeking its protection. In our opinion it is enough for the complaining parties to show that the local officials are effectuating the discriminatory designs of private individuals. * * *

Dailey v. City of Lawton, 425 F.2d 1037, 1039 (10th Cir.1970).

Nevertheless, we do not base our conclusion that the Black Jack ordinance violates Title VIII on a finding that there was an improper purpose.

Once the plaintiff has established a prima facie case by demonstrating racially discriminatory effect, the burden shifts to the governmental defendant to demonstrate that its conduct was necessary to promote a compelling governmental interest.

The District Court concluded that the ordinance had no discriminatory effect. It based this conclusion on its finding that, because Park View Heights was designed to meet the needs of families earning between $5,000 and $10,000 per year—a class including 32 percent of the black population in the metropolitan area and 29 percent of the white population—the ordinance had no measurably greater effect on blacks than on whites. The court's conclusion was in error. It failed to take into account either the "ultimate effect" or the "historical context" of the City's action. See *United Farmworkers of Florida Housing Project, Inc. v. City of Delray Beach, supra* 493 F.2d at 810; Kennedy Park Homes Ass'n v. City of Lackawanna, supra 436 F.2d at 112. The ultimate effect of the ordinance was to foreclose 85 percent of the blacks living in the metropolitan area from obtaining housing in Black Jack, and to foreclose them at a time when 40 percent of them were living in substandard or overcrowded units.

The discriminatory effect of the ordinance is more onerous when assessed in light of the fact that segregated housing in the St. Louis metropolitan area was

> * * * in large measure the result of deliberate racial discrimination in the housing market by the real estate industry and by agencies of the federal, state, and local governments. * * *

United States v. City of Black Jack, Missouri, supra 372 F.Supp. at 326.

Black Jack's action is but one more factor confining blacks to low-income housing in the center city, confirming the inexorable process whereby the St. Louis metropolitan area becomes one that "has the racial shape of a donut, with the Negroes in the hole and with mostly Whites occupying the ring." *Mahaley v. Cuyahoga Metropolitan Housing Authority*, 355 F.Supp. 1257, 1260 (N.D.Ohio, 1973), rev'd, 500 F.2d 1087 (6th Cir.1974). See also *Crow v. Brown*, 332 F.Supp. 382, 384 (N.D.Ga., 1971), aff'd per curiam, 457 F.2d 788 (5th Cir.1972). Park View Heights was particularly designed to contribute to the prevention of this prospect so antithetical to the Fair Housing Act. The Board of Directors of the Park View Housing Corporation was one-half white and one-half black. Affirmative measures were planned to assure that members of the black community would be aware of the opportunity to live in Park View Heights. There was ample proof that many blacks would live in the development, and that the exclusion of the townhouses would contribute to the perpetuation of segregation in a community which was 99 percent white.

It having been established that the ordinance had a discriminatory effect, it follows that the United States had made out a prima facie case under Title VIII, and the burden shifted to the City to demonstrate that a compelling governmental interest was furthered by that ordinance. We turn to that question. The City asserted primarily the following governmental interests to justify the ban on further apartments:

(1) Road and traffic control;

(2) Prevention of overcrowding of schools;

(3) Prevention of devaluation of adjacent single-family homes.

Several other interests were also alluded to in the record, including exclusion of apartments where there were already too many and where there was no need for them.

In determining whether any of these rise to the level of a compelling governmental interest, we must examine: first, whether the ordinance in fact furthers the governmental interest asserted; second, whether the public interest served by the ordinance is constitutionally permissible[2] and is substantial enough to outweigh the private detriment caused by it;[3] and third, whether less drastic means are available whereby the stated governmental interest may be attained. See *Shapiro v. Thompson*, 394 U.S. 618, 637, 89 S.Ct. 1322, 22 L.Ed.2d 600 (1969); Note, Exclusionary Zoning and Equal Protection, 84 Harv.L.Rev. 1645, 1651 (1971).

We need not go beyond the first step in the inquiry, for we find that there is no factual basis for the assertion that any one of the three primary interests asserted by the City is in fact furthered by the zoning ordinance, and we find that the other asserted interests—at least on the facts of this case—are clearly not substantial in relation to the housing opportunities foreclosed. To paraphrase the Supreme Court in *Shapiro v. Thompson, supra* at 638, 89 S.Ct. 1322, we conclude that the City does not use and has no need to use the ordinance for the governmental purposes suggested.

* * *

We hold that Zoning Ordinance No. 12 of the City of Black Jack violates Title VIII, because it denies persons housing on the basis of race, in violation of § 3604(a), and interferes with the exercise of the right to equal housing opportunity, in violation of § 3617. The remedy for this violation of the Fair Housing Act is provided in § 3615:

> * * * any law of a State, a political subdivision, or other such jurisdiction that purports to require or permit any action that would be a discriminatory housing practice under this subchapter shall to that extent be invalid.

2. This portion of the analysis is essentially a qualitative one. For example, *Shapiro v. Thompson, supra* 394 U.S. at 629–631, 89 S.Ct. 1322, 22 L.Ed.2d 600, held that it was constitutionally impermissible for a state to inhibit migration by needy persons into the state, because such migration was a constitutional right. That case further held that limiting payment of welfare benefits to those who had "contributed" to the state in the past through taxes was constitutionally impermissible. Id. at 633, 89 S.Ct. 1322.

3. This portion of the analysis is essentially quantitative. For example, preservation of the public peace and welfare by avoiding racial conflict was held insufficient to validate a zoning ordinance restricting racial integration in *Buchanan v. Warley*, 245 U.S. 60, 38 S.Ct. 16, 62 L.Ed. 149 (1917).

We, therefore, reverse and remand with instructions to the District Court to enter a permanent injunction upon receipt of this Court's order, enjoining the enforcement of the ordinance. The mandate of this Court shall be issued forthwith.

Reversed and remanded.

Notes

1. The sponsors of the project in the principal case also sued the City of Black Jack. In Park View Heights Corp. v. City of Black Jack, 467 F.2d 1208 (8th Cir.1972) (pre-dating the principal case), the court found the zoning ordinance to be exclusionary, ordered reclassification of all land zoned for multi-family use prior to the offending ordinance to a multi-family designation, ordered affirmative action to permit the construction of the particular project, and, after the principal case, approved a consent settlement of $450,000 damages. The affirmative action portion of the decree was further litigated, and in Park View Heights Corp. v. City of Black Jack, 454 F.Supp. 1223 (E.D.Mo.1978), the district court denied injunctive relief requiring the city to ensure construction of the project and additional damages because the project had become economically infeasible due to inflation and new property standards established by HUD. The Eighth Circuit Court of Appeals reversed, 605 F.2d 1033 (8th Cir.1979), holding that notwithstanding the earlier damage settlement and the present economic infeasibility of the project, the city is subject to a continuing, enforceable duty to affirmatively promote moderately priced, interracial housing equivalent to that which would have been built but for the racially discriminatory zoning. In February, 1982, a consent decree was entered which permanently enjoins the city from engaging in discriminatory actions depriving persons of equal access to housing. At one point during the protracted Black Jack litigation, a local woman with a large number of children ran for mayor, campaigning in Ku Klux Klan regalia; she lost in the primary.

2. See also, Macone v. Town of Wakefield, 277 F.3d 1 (1st Cir.2002) where the Court found a lack of evidence and/or history of discrimination, and refused to rely on the fact that Wakefield was a predominantly white community, or that the community was not racially integrated to automatically trigger a Fair Housing Act violation. How should the court weigh public comments that suggest opposition to housing projects based on discrimination? See, Hallmark Developers, Inc. v. Fulton County, Ga., 466 F.3d 1276 (11th Cir.2006).

VILLAGE OF ARLINGTON HEIGHTS v. METROPOLITAN HOUSING DEVELOPMENT CORP.

Supreme Court of the United States, 1977.
429 U.S. 252, 97 S.Ct. 555, 50 L.Ed.2d 450.

MR. JUSTICE POWELL delivered the opinion of the Court.

In 1971 respondent Metropolitan Housing Development Corporation (MHDC) applied to petitioner, the Village of Arlington Heights, Ill., for the rezoning of a 15–acre parcel from single-family to multiple-family classification. Using federal financial assistance, MHDC planned to build 190 clustered townhouse units for low- and moderate-income tenants. The Village denied the rezoning request. MHDC, joined by other plaintiffs who are also respondents here, brought suit in the United States District Court for the Northern District of Illinois. They alleged that the denial was racially discriminatory and that it violated, inter alia, the Fourteenth Amendment and the Fair Housing Act of 1968, 82 Stat. 81, 42 U.S.C.A. § 3601 et seq. Following a bench trial, the District Court entered judgment for the Village, 373 F.Supp. 208 (1974), and respondents appealed. The Court of Appeals for the Seventh Circuit reversed, finding that the "ultimate effect" of the denial was racially discriminatory, and that the refusal to rezone therefore violated, inter alia, the Fourteenth Amendment. 517 F.2d 409 (1975). We granted the Village's petition for certiorari, 423 U.S. 1030, 96 S.Ct. 560, 46 L.Ed.2d 404 (1975), and now reverse.

* * *

The planned development did not conform to the Village's zoning ordinance and could not be built unless Arlington Heights rezoned the parcel to R–5, its multiple-family housing classification. Accordingly, MHDC filed with the Village Plan Commission a petition for rezoning, accompanied by supporting materials describing the development and specifying that it would be subsidized under § 236. The materials made clear that one requirement under § 236 is an affirmative marketing plan designed to assure that a subsidized development is racially integrated. MHDC also submitted studies demonstrating the need for housing of this type and analyzing the probable impact of the development. To prepare for the hearings before the Plan Commission and to assure compliance with the Village building code, fire regulations, and related requirements, MHDC consulted with the Village staff for preliminary review of the development. The parties have stipulated that every change recommended during such consultations was incorporated into the plans.

During the spring of 1971, the Plan Commission considered the proposal at a series of three public meetings, which drew large crowds. Although many of those attending were quite vocal and demonstrative in opposition to Lincoln Green, a number of individuals and representatives of community groups spoke in support of rezoning. Some of the comments, both from opponents and supporters, addressed what was referred to as the "social issue"—the desirability or undesirability of introducing at this location in Arlington Heights low- and moderate-income housing, housing that would probably be racially integrated.

Many of the opponents, however, focused on the zoning aspects of the petition, stressing two arguments. First, the area always had been zoned single-family, and the neighboring citizens had built or purchased there in reliance on that classification. Rezoning threatened to cause a measurable drop in property value for neighboring sites. Second, the Village's apartment policy, adopted by the Village Board in 1962 and amended in 1970, called for R–5 zoning primarily to serve as a buffer between single-family development and land uses thought incompatible, such as commercial or manufacturing districts. Lincoln Green did not meet this requirement, as it adjoined no commercial or manufacturing district.

At the close of the third meeting, the Plan Commission adopted a motion to recommend to the Village's Board of Trustees that it deny the request. The motion stated: "While the need for low- and moderate-income housing may exist in Arlington Heights or its environs, the Plan Commission would be derelict in recommending it at the proposed location." Two members voted against the motion and submitted a minority report, stressing that in their view the change to accommodate Lincoln Green represented "good zoning." The Village Board met on September 28, 1971, to consider MHDC's request and the recommendation of the Plan Commission. After a public hearing, the Board denied the rezoning by a 6–1 vote.

* * *

[The Seventh Circuit Court of Appeals] first approved the District Court's finding that the defendants were motivated by a concern for the integrity of the zoning plan, rather than by racial discrimination. Deciding whether their refusal to rezone would have discriminatory effects was more complex. The court observed that the refusal would have a disproportionate impact on blacks. Based upon family income, blacks constituted 40% of those Chicago area residents who were eligible to become tenants of Lincoln Green, although they composed a far lower percentage of total area population. The court reasoned, however, that under our decision in James v. Valtierra, 402 U.S. 137, 91 S.Ct. 1331, 28 L.Ed.2d 678 (1971), such a disparity in racial impact alone does not call for strict scrutiny of a municipality's decision that prevents the construction of the low-cost housing.

There was another level to the court's analysis of allegedly discriminatory results. Invoking language from *Kennedy Park Homes Assn. v. City of Lackawanna*, 436 F.2d 108, 112 (C.A.2 1970), cert. denied, 401 U.S. 1010, 91 S.Ct. 1256 (1971), the Court of Appeals ruled that the denial of rezoning must be examined in light of its "historical context and ultimate effect." 517 F.2d, at 413. Northwest Cook County was enjoying rapid growth in employment opportunities and population, but it continued to exhibit a high degree of residential segregation. The court held that Arlington Heights could not simply ignore this problem. Indeed, it found that the Village had been "exploiting" the situation by allowing itself to become a nearly all-white community. Id., at 414. The Village had no other current plans for building low-and moderate-income housing, and no other R–5 parcels in the Village were available to MHDC at an economically feasible price.

Against this background, the Court of Appeals ruled that the denial of the Lincoln Green proposal had racially discriminatory effects and could be tolerated only if it served compelling interests. Neither the buffer policy nor the desire to protect property values met this exacting standard. The court therefore concluded that the denial violated the Equal Protection Clause of the Fourteenth Amendment.

* * *

Our decision last Term in *Washington v. Davis*, 426 U.S. 229, 96 S.Ct. 2040, 48 L.Ed.2d 597 (1976), made it clear that official action will not be held unconstitutional solely because it results in a racially disproportionate impact. "Disproportionate impact is not irrelevant, but it is not the sole touchstone of an invidious racial discrimination." Id., at 242. Proof of racially discriminatory intent or purpose is required to show a violation of the Equal Protection Clause. * * *

* * * In making its findings on this issue, the District Court noted that some of the opponents of Lincoln Green who spoke at the various hearings might have been motivated by opposition to minority groups. The court held, however, that the evidence "does not warrant the conclusion that this motivated the defendants." 373 F.Supp., at 211.

On appeal the Court of Appeals focused primarily on respondents' claim that the Village's buffer policy had not been consistently applied and was being invoked with a strictness here that could only demonstrate some other underlying motive. The court concluded that the buffer policy, though not always applied with perfect consistency, had on several occasions formed the basis for the Board's decision to deny other rezoning proposals. "The evidence does not necessitate a finding that Arlington Heights administered this policy in a discriminatory manner." 517 F.2d, at 412. The Court of Appeals therefore approved the District Court's findings concerning the Village's purposes in denying rezoning to MHDC.

We also have reviewed the evidence. The impact of the Village's decision does arguably bear more heavily on racial minorities. Minorities constitute 18% of the Chicago area population, and 40% of the income groups said to be eligible for Lincoln Green. But there is little about the sequence of events leading up to the decision that would spark suspicion. The area around the Viatorian property has been zoned R–3 since 1959, the year when Arlington Heights first adopted a zoning map. Single-family homes surround the 80–acre site, and the Village is undeniably committed to single-family homes as its dominant residential land use. The rezoning request progressed according to the usual procedures. The Plan Commission even scheduled two additional hearings, at least in part to accommodate MHDC and permit it to supplement its presentation with answers to questions generated at the first hearing.

The statements by the Plan Commission and Village Board members, as reflected in the official minutes, focused almost exclusively on the zoning aspects of the MHDC petition, and the zoning factors on which they relied are not novel criteria in the Village's rezoning decisions. There is no reason to doubt that there has been reliance by some neighboring property owners on the maintenance of single-family zoning in the vicinity. The Village originally adopted its buffer policy long before MHDC entered the picture and has applied the policy too consistently for us to infer discriminatory purpose from its application in this case. Finally, MHDC called one member of the Village Board to the stand at trial. Nothing in her testimony supports an inference of invidious purpose.

In sum, the evidence does not warrant overturning the concurrent findings of both courts below. Respondents simply failed to carry their burden of proving that discriminatory purpose was a motivating factor in the Village's decision. This conclusion ends the constitutional inquiry. The Court of Appeals' further finding that the Village's decision carried a discriminatory "ultimate effect" is without independent constitutional significance.

Respondents' complaint also alleged that the refusal to rezone violated the Fair Housing Act of 1968, 42 U.S.C.A. § 3601 et seq. They continue to urge here that a zoning decision made by a public body may, and that petitioners' action did, violate § 3604 or § 3617. The Court of Appeals, however, proceeding in a somewhat unorthodox fashion, did not decide the statutory question. We remand the case for further consideration of respondents' statutory claims.

Reversed and remanded.

[Concurring and dissenting opinions are omitted.]

Notes

1. The effect of the Arlington Heights decision was to alert attorneys that a statistical showing of discriminatory impact of land use decisions discouraging subsidized multi-family housing would not be enough to invoke the equal protection clause of the Fourteenth Amendment. However, as the Black Jack, Missouri case indicates and as the closing paragraph of Arlington Heights suggests, a statistical presentation might be sufficient to establish a violation of the Fair Housing Act. This distinction was taken up by the Seventh Circuit upon the remand of the Arlington Heights case. In Metropolitan Housing Development Corp. v. Village of Arlington Heights, 558 F.2d 1283 (7th Cir.1977), certiorari denied 434 U.S. 1025, 98 S.Ct. 752, 54 L.Ed.2d 772 (1978), the court held that Arlington Heights had a statutory obligation under the Fair Housing Act to refrain from zoning policies that had the effect of foreclosing construction of low-cost housing within its boundaries. The Court of Appeals remanded the case to the District Court. In 1978, MHDC and the Village of Arlington Heights reached a settlement that provided for construction of low-cost housing on an alternate twenty-six acre site in an unincorporated area abutting the village. A nearby suburb, Mount Prospect, and a civic association sought intervention to protest the approval of the consent decree. The Seventh Circuit upheld the decree in Metropolitan Housing Development Corp. v. Village of Arlington Heights, 616 F.2d 1006 (7th Cir.1980). Also see Creek v. Village of Westhaven, 80 F.3d 186 (7th Cir.1996).

The Seventh Circuit opinion was adopted by the Supreme Court in Town of Huntington, New York v. Huntington Branch, NAACP, 488 U.S. 15, 109 S.Ct. 276, 102 L.Ed.2d 180 (1988) (*per curiam* opinion).

2. May cities make a zoning decision that is unfavorable to a developer of low income housing? May a city defend a negative decision by showing good faith use of traditional zoning principles plus no racially discriminatory motive plus other nearby opportunities for low income housing? For authority that the answer to the first question is no and the answer to the second question is yes, see Confederacion de la Raza Unida v. City of Morgan Hill, 324 F.Supp. 895 (N.D.Cal.1971) and Ybarra v. Town of Los Altos Hills, 503 F.2d 250 (9th Cir.1974). Compare Southern Alameda Spanish Speaking Organization v. City of Union City, California, 424 F.2d 291 (9th Cir.1970).

(2) Federal Fair Housing Act Amendments of 1988

The following excerpt from Professor Peter W. Salsich, Jr.'s article, Federal Influence on Local Land Use Decisions: The Fair Housing Act, 9 J. Affordable Housing & Community Dev. L. 228 (2000) explains the applicability of the Federal Fair Housing Act Amendments of 1988 to local land use planning and zoning decisions.

> The Fair Housing Act does not specifically refer to local land use laws. Section 3604(a), as amended, makes it unlawful to "refuse to sell or rent . . . or otherwise make unavailable or deny, a dwelling to any person because of race, color, religion, sex, familial status, or national origin." The phrase "or otherwise make unavailable or deny" has long been held to include local land use regulations.
>
> In Huntington Branch NAACP v. Town of Huntington, the Second Circuit applied the disparate impact test of Title VII employment discrimination cases to strike down a refusal to rezone for multifamily housing. Under this test, discriminatory effect rather than discriminatory intent is the standard. If the plaintiff establishes a prima facie case that a land use regulation has a discriminatory effect, the burden shifts to the defendant municipality to "prove that its actions furthered, in theory and in practice, a legitimate, bona fide governmental interest and that no alternative would serve that interest with less discriminatory effect."
>
> Applying the effect test, the court concluded that the refusal to rezone in order to enable a multifamily subsidized housing development to be located outside the urban renewal area to which such projects were restricted by the local zoning ordinance created "a strong prima facie showing of discriminatory effect" because of its "disproportionate impact" on minorities and its "segregative impact on the entire community." The court then reviewed the town's justifications for its decisions, dividing those reasons into "plan-specific" and "site-specific" reasons.
>
> "Plan-specific" objections, such as parking and fire protection problems, proximity to a railroad station and a utility substation, inadequate recreation and play areas, and undersized and unrealistic

units, "could presumably have been solved with reasonable design modifications ... and proper landscaping," the court asserted. "Site-specific" objections, such as traffic problems and health concerns relating to sewage disposal and proximity to a utility substation, are more problematic. However, the court dismissed these objections because town officials did not focus on these concerns at the land use regulatory stage, but only after the suit was filed. Thus, they amounted to "[p]ost hoc rationalizations by administrative agencies (that) should be afforded 'little deference' by the courts."

Fair Housing Amendments Act

The Fair Housing Amendments Act of 1988 added significant provisions to the Fair Housing Act that affect local land use regulations. The amendments expanded the protections against discrimination in the Fair Housing Act to persons with disabilities and families with children under the age of eighteen. * * *

Important definitions include "handicapped," which means "with respect to a person—(1) a physical or mental impairment which substantially limits one or more of such person's major life activities, (2) a record of having such an impairment, or (3) being regarded as having such an impairment, but such term does not include current, illegal use of or addiction to a controlled substance (as defined in section 102 of the Controlled Substances Act (21 U.S.C. § 802))."

"Familial status" means "one or more individuals (who have not obtained the age of eighteen years) being domiciled with—(1) a parent or another person having legal custody of such individual or individuals; or (2) the designee of such parent or other person having such custody, with the written permission of such parent or other person." The familial status protection also applies to pregnant women and persons securing legal custody of children under eighteen years of age.

Provisions Affecting Local Land Use Regulations

The amendments extend the § 3604 coverage to familial status and disabled status, which impact zoning through apartment and group home controversies.

The second way in which the Fair Housing Amendments Act is made applicable to local land use regulations is contained in the provision adding disabled status as a protective class. Prohibited discrimination against that class includes "... a refusal to make reasonable accommodations in rules, policies, practices, or services, when such accommodations may be necessary to afford such person equal opportunity to use and enjoy a dwelling."

Exemptions from Coverage

Important qualifications to the application of the Fair Housing Amendments Act to local land use regulations include: (a) a statement that the amendments are not intended to invalidate or limit any law that "requires dwellings to be designed and constructed in a manner that affords handicapped persons greater access than is required by this sub-chapter," and (b) a provision that dwellings do not have to be made available to individuals "whose tenancy would constitute a direct threat to the health and safety of other individuals or whose tenancy would result in substantial physical damage to the property of others."

The amendments also exempt from coverage "any reasonable local, State, or Federal restrictions regarding the maximum number of occupants permitted to occupy a dwelling." In addition, the amendments exempt housing for older persons from the familial status discrimination prohibitions. Finally, § 3607(b)(4) denies the protections of the Act to persons convicted of the illegal manufacture or distribution of a controlled substance. * * *

Notes

1. Not every impediment placed in the path of the developer of racially integrated, low-income housing is a violation of equal protection or the Fair Housing Act. Not every denial of a building permit or refusal to rezone land for higher density development can be shown to be a case of exclusionary zoning based on race. See Cowart v. City of Ocala, 478 F.Supp. 774 (M.D.Fla.1979), where the developer failed to modify his plan to comply with local ordinances, resulting in official withdrawal of approval of the project and denial of a building permit. Also see Des Vergnes v. Seekonk Water Dist., 601 F.2d 9 (1st Cir.1979), vacated 454 U.S. 807, 102 S.Ct. 81, 70 L.Ed.2d 76 (1981); Angell v. Zinsser, 473 F.Supp. 488 (D.Conn.1979); Lake Bluff Housing Partners v. City of South Milwaukee, 197 Wis.2d 157, 540 N.W.2d 189 (1995). Also see Brandt v. Village of Chebanse, Illinois, 82 F.3d 172 (7th Cir.1996) where the court held that the Fair Housing Act was not applicable to a developer who wanted a variance to build four-unit apartment buildings with the first floor apartments wheelchair accessible. The court noted that developers are required to make apartments accessible to the handicapped:

> So what Brandt proposes to build is essentially the minimum required by federal law. If such a proposal obliges a government to waive its single-family zoning rules, then four (or more) unit buildings can be erected anywhere a developer pleases. Those who find zoning laws unjustifiable limitations on the use of property would be cheered; but it is unlikely that the Fair Housing Act was designed to abolish single-family zoning for all developers who comply with the requirement that first-floor apartments be accessible to handicapped tenants.

2. The Fair Housing Act and the concomitant development of the discriminatory effect doctrine, and the Fourteenth Amendment suit alleging discriminatory intent, are not the only legal remedies available to rectify alleged acts of local officials that result in housing discrimination. A conspiracy theory under 42 U.S.C.A. § 1985(3) was recognized by a federal court in Fralin & Waldron, Inc. v. County of Henrico, Virginia, 474 F.Supp. 1315 (E.D.Va.1979). In that case the developers optioned a tract of land that was

zoned to permit medium density residential development. After making extensive preparations to build a low- to moderate-income housing project, the county officials downzoned the land to exclude the type of project that was planned. The plaintiffs asked for injunctive and monetary relief and the court, in denying defendants' motion to dismiss, found sufficient allegations of conspiracy to deny constitutional rights. The court also discussed the extent of immunity which some of the individual defendants might claim under the civil rights statutes.

3. Virtually all the cases litigating the issue of housing discrimination under the Fair Housing Act involve municipal defendants and challenges to land use policies on the ground of their discriminatory intent or discriminatory effect. Does the Fair Housing Act apply to a private landlord who takes some action regarding his property that has the effect of reducing the available housing stock for minority persons within the community? See the case of Dreher v. Rana Management, Inc., 493 F.Supp. 930 (E.D.N.Y.1980), where tenants sued the landlord under the Fair Housing Act to enjoin conversion of the building into housing for college students. The plaintiffs alleged that ninety percent of the occupants were black and that after conversion ninety percent of the occupants would be white, thus reducing the housing stock available to black persons in the community. The court granted defendants' motion for a summary judgment.

A case striking down a private landlord's policy excluding families with children (the policy was to limit occupancy of one-bedroom apartments in the complex to one person) is United States v. Badgett, 976 F.2d 1176 (8th Cir.1992).

CITY OF EDMONDS v. OXFORD HOUSE, INC.

Supreme Court of the United States, 1995.
514 U.S. 725, 115 S.Ct. 1776, 131 L.Ed.2d 801.

JUSTICE GINSBURG delivered the opinion of the Court.

The Fair Housing Act (FHA or Act) prohibits discrimination in housing against, inter alios, persons with handicaps. Section 807(b)(1) of the Act entirely exempts from the FHA's compass "any reasonable local, State, or Federal restrictions regarding the maximum number of occupants permitted to occupy a dwelling." 42 U.S.C. § 3607(b)(1). This case presents the question whether a provision in petitioner City of Edmonds' zoning code qualifies for § 3607(b)(1)'s complete exemption from FHA scrutiny. The provision, governing areas zoned for single-family dwelling units, defines "family" as "persons [without regard to number] related by genetics, adoption, or marriage, or a group of five or fewer [unrelated] persons." Edmonds Community Development Code (ECDC) § 21.30.010 (1991).

The defining provision at issue describes who may compose a family unit; it does not prescribe "the maximum number of occupants" a dwelling unit may house. We hold that § 3607(b)(1) does not exempt prescriptions of the family-defining kind, i.e., provisions designed to foster the family character of a neighborhood. Instead, § 3607(b)(1)'s absolute exemption removes from the FHA's scope only total occupancy limits, i.e., numerical ceilings that serve to prevent overcrowding in living quarters.

I

In the summer of 1990, respondent Oxford House opened a group home in the City of Edmonds, Washington (City), for 10 to 12 adults recovering from alcoholism and drug addiction. The group home, called Oxford House–Edmonds, is located in a neighborhood zoned for single-family residences. Upon learning that Oxford House had leased and was operating a home in Edmonds, the City issued criminal citations to the owner and a resident of the house. The citations charged violation of the zoning code rule that defines who may live in single-family dwelling units. The occupants of such units must compose a "family," and family, under the City's defining rule, "means an individual or two or more persons related by genetics, adoption, or marriage, or a group of five or fewer persons who are not related by genetics, adoption, or marriage." ECDC § 21.30.010. Oxford House–Edmonds houses more than five unrelated persons, and therefore does not conform to the code.

Oxford House asserted reliance on the Fair Housing Act, 102 Stat. 1619, 42 U.S.C. § 3601 et seq., which declares it unlawful "[t]o discriminate in the sale or rental, or to otherwise make unavailable or deny, a dwelling to any buyer or renter because of a handicap of ... that buyer or renter." § 3604(f)(1)(A). The parties have stipulated, for purposes of this litigation, that the residents of Oxford House–Edmonds "are recovering alcoholics and drug addicts and are handicapped persons within the meaning" of the Act.

Discrimination covered by the FHA includes "a refusal to make reasonable accommodations in rules, policies, practices, or services, when such accommodations may be necessary to afford [handicapped] person[s] equal opportunity to use and enjoy a dwelling." § 3604(f)(3)(B). Oxford House asked Edmonds to make a "reasonable accommodation" by allowing it to remain in the single-family dwelling it had leased. Group homes for recovering substance abusers, Oxford urged, need 8 to 12 residents to be financially and therapeutically viable. Edmonds declined to permit Oxford House to stay in a single-family residential zone, but passed an ordinance listing group homes as permitted uses in multifamily and general commercial zones. * * *

II

The sole question before the Court is whether Edmonds' family composition rule qualifies as a "restrictio[n] regarding the maximum number of occupants permitted to occupy a dwelling" within the meaning of the FHA's absolute exemption. 42 U.S.C. § 3607(b)(1). In answering this question, we are mindful of the Act's stated policy "to provide, within constitutional limitations, for fair housing throughout the United States." § 3601. We also note precedent recognizing the FHA's "broad and inclusive" compass, and therefore according a "generous construction" to the Act's complaint-filing provision. *Trafficante v. Metropolitan Life Ins. Co.,* 409 U.S. 205, 209, 212, 93 S.Ct. 364, 366–367, 368, 34 L.Ed.2d 415 (1972). Accordingly, we regard this case as an instance in which an exception to "a general statement of policy" is sensibly read "narrowly in order to preserve the primary operation of the [policy]." *Commissioner v. Clark,* 489 U.S. 726, 739, 109 S.Ct. 1455, 1463, 103 L.Ed.2d 753 (1989).

A

Congress enacted § 3607(b)(1) against the backdrop of an evident distinction between municipal land-use restrictions and maximum occupancy restrictions.

Land-use restrictions designate "districts in which only compatible uses are allowed and incompatible uses are excluded." D. Mandelker, Land Use Law § 4.16, pp. 113–114 (3d ed.1993) (hereinafter Mandelker). These restrictions typically categorize uses as single-family residential, multiple-family residential, commercial, or industrial. See, e.g., 1 E. Ziegler, Jr., Rathkopf's The Law of Zoning and Planning § 8.01, pp. 8–2 to 8–3 (4th ed.1995); Mandelker § 1.03, p. 4; 1 E. Yokley, Zoning Law and Practice § 7–2, p. 252 (4th ed.1978).

Land use restrictions aim to prevent problems caused by the "pig in the parlor instead of the barnyard." *Village of Euclid v. Ambler Realty Co.,* 272 U.S. 365, 388, 47 S.Ct. 114, 118, 71 L.Ed. 303 (1926). In particular, reserving land for single-family residences preserves the character of neighborhoods, securing "zones where family values, youth values, and the blessings of quiet seclusion and clean air make the area a sanctuary for people." *Village of Belle Terre v. Boraas,* 416 U.S. 1, 9, 94 S.Ct. 1536, 1541, 39 L.Ed.2d 797 (1974); see also *Moore v. East Cleveland,* 431 U.S. 494, 521, 97 S.Ct. 1932, 1947, 52 L.Ed.2d 531 (1977) (Burger, C.J., dissenting) (purpose of East Cleveland's single-family zoning ordinance "is the traditional one of preserving certain areas as family residential communities"). To limit land use to single-family residences, a municipality must define the term "family"; thus family composition rules are an essential component of single-family residential use restrictions.

Maximum occupancy restrictions, in contradistinction, cap the number of occupants per dwelling, typically in relation to available floor space or the number and type of rooms. See, e.g., International Conference of Building Officials, Uniform Housing Code § 503(b) (1988); Building Officials and Code Administrators International, Inc., BOCA National Property Maintenance Code §§ PM–405.3, PM–405.5 (1993) (hereinafter BOCA Code); Southern Building Code Congress, International, Inc., Standard Housing Code §§ 306.1, 306.2 (1991); E. Mood, APHA–CDC Recommended Minimum Housing Standards § 9.02, p. 37 (1986) (hereinafter APHA–CDC Standards). These restrictions ordinarily apply uniformly to all residents of all dwelling units. Their purpose is to protect health and safety by preventing dwelling overcrowding. See, e.g., BOCA Code §§ PM–101.3, PM–405.3, PM–405.5 and commentary; Abbott, Housing Policy, Housing Codes and Tenant Remedies, 56 B.U.L.Rev. 1, 41–45 (1976).

We recognized this distinction between maximum occupancy restrictions and land-use restrictions in *Moore v. East Cleveland,* 431 U.S. 494, 97 S.Ct. 1932, 52 L.Ed.2d 531 (1977). In *Moore,* the Court held unconstitutional the constricted definition of "family" contained in East Cleveland's housing ordinance. East Cleveland's ordinance "select[ed] certain categories of relatives who may live together and declare[d] that others may not"; in particular, East Cleveland's definition of "family" made "a crime of a grandmother's choice to live with her grandson." Id., at 498–499, 97 S.Ct., at 1935 (plurality opinion). In response to East Cleveland's argument that its aim was to prevent overcrowded dwellings, streets, and schools, we observed that the municipality's restrictive definition of family served the asserted, and undeniably legitimate, goals "marginally, at best." Id., at 500, 97 S.Ct., at 1936 (footnote omitted). Another East Cleveland ordinance, we noted, "specifically addressed . . . the problem of overcrowding"; that ordinance tied "the maximum permissible occupancy of a dwelling to the habitable floor area." Id., at 500, n. 7, 97 S.Ct., at 1936, n. 7; accord, id., at 520, n. 16, 97 S.Ct., at 1939, n. 16 (STEVENS, J., concurring in judgment). Justice Stewart, in dissent, also distinguished restrictions designed to "preserv[e] the character of a residential area," from prescription of "a minimum habitable floor area per person," id., at 539, n. 9, 97 S.Ct., at 1937, n. 9, in the interest of community health and safety.

Section 3607(b)(1)'s language—"restrictions regarding the maximum number of occupants permitted to occupy a dwelling"—surely encompasses maximum occupancy restrictions. But the formulation does not fit family composition rules typically tied to land-use restrictions. In sum, rules that cap the total number of occupants in order to prevent overcrowding of a dwelling "plainly and unmistakably," *see A.H. Phillips, Inc. v. Walling,* 324 U.S. 490, 493, 65 S.Ct. 807, 808, 89 L.Ed. 1095 (1945), fall within § 3607(b)(1)'s absolute exemption from the FHA's governance; rules designed to preserve the family character of a neighborhood, fastening on the composition of households rather than on the total number of occupants living quarters can contain, do not.

B

Turning specifically to the City's Community Development Code, we note that the provisions Edmonds invoked against Oxford House, ECDC §§ 16.20.010 and 21.30.010, are classic examples of a use restriction and complementing family composition rule. These provisions do not cap the number of people who may live in a dwelling. In plain terms, they direct that dwellings be used only to house families. Captioned "USES," ECDC § 16.20.010 provides that the sole "Permitted Primary Us[e]" in a single-family residential zone is "[s]ingle-family dwelling units." Edmonds itself recognizes that this provision simply "defines those uses permitted in a single family residential zone."

A separate provision caps the number of occupants a dwelling may house, based on floor area:

> "Floor Area. Every dwelling unit shall have at least one room which shall have not less than 120 square feet of floor area. Other habitable rooms, except kitchens, shall have an area of not less than 70 square feet. Where more than two persons occupy a room used for sleeping purposes, the required floor area shall be increased at the rate of 50 square feet for each occupant in excess of two." ECDC § 19.10.000 (adopting Uniform Housing Code § 503(b) (1988)).

Edmonds nevertheless argues that its family composition rule, ECDC § 21.30.010, falls within § 3607(b)(1), the FHA exemption for maximum occupancy restrictions, because the rule caps at five the number of unrelated persons allowed to occupy a single-family dwelling. But Edmonds' family composition rule surely does not answer the question: "What is the maximum number of occupants permitted to occupy a house?" So long as they are related "by genetics, adoption, or marriage," any number of people can live in a house. Ten siblings, their parents and grandparents, for example, could dwell in a house in Edmonds' single-family residential zone without offending Edmonds' family composition rule.

Family living, not living space per occupant, is what ECDC § 21.30.010 describes. Defining family primarily by biological and legal relationships, the provision also accommodates another group association: Five or fewer unrelated people are allowed to live together as though they were family. This accommodation is the peg on which Edmonds rests its plea for § 3607(b)(1) exemption. Had the City defined a family solely by biological and legal links, § 3607(b)(1) would not have been the ground on which Edmonds staked its case. It is curious reasoning indeed that converts a family values preserver into a maximum occupancy restriction once a town adds to a related persons prescription "and also two unrelated persons."

Edmonds additionally contends that subjecting single-family zoning to FHA scrutiny will "overturn Euclidian zoning" and "destroy the effectiveness and purpose of single-family zoning." This contention both ignores the limited scope of the issue before us and exaggerates the force of the FHA's antidiscrimination provisions. We address only whether Edmonds' family composition rule qualifies for § 3607(b)(1) exemption. Moreover, the FHA antidiscrimination provisions, when applicable, require only "reasonable" accommodations to afford persons with handicaps "equal opportunity to use and enjoy" housing. §§ 3604(f)(1)(A) and (f)(3)(B).

* * *

The parties have presented, and we have decided, only a threshold question: Edmonds' zoning code provision describing who may compose a "family" is not a maximum occupancy restriction exempt from the FHA under § 3607(b)(1). It remains for the lower courts to decide whether

Edmonds' actions against Oxford House violate the FHA's prohibitions against discrimination set out in §§ 3604(f)(1)(A) and (f)(3)(B). For the reasons stated, the judgment of the United States Court of Appeals for the Ninth Circuit is

Affirmed.

JUSTICE THOMAS, with whom JUSTICE SCALIA and JUSTICE KENNEDY join, dissenting. [Dissenting opinion omitted.]

HOWARD v. CITY OF BEAVERCREEK

United States Court of Appeals, Sixth Circuit, 2002.
276 F.3d 802.

SILER, CIRCUIT JUDGE.

Plaintiff Joseph L. Howard brought suit against the defendant City of Beavercreek ("Beavercreek") alleging that the denial of his request for a variance to Beavercreek's zoning law to accommodate his handicap violated 42 U.S.C. § 3604(f)(3)(B) of the Fair Housing Amendments Act of 1988 ("FHAA") and subsections 4112.02(H)(1), (4), (18), and (19) of the Ohio Revised Code. Howard appeals the district court's order granting summary judgment in favor of Beavercreek. For the reasons that follow, we AFFIRM the district court's judgment.

Howard owns a home in Beavercreek, Ohio, where he has lived with his wife and children since 1984. The home is located on a lot which is 255 feet deep and 110 feet wide. Howard's lot is separated from the adjacent lots on both sides by a split rail fence that is less than five feet eight inches in height. There is also a chain link fence, at least four feet high, that runs across the back of Howard's lot about thirty feet from the rear property line.

In 1996, Howard became concerned that the neighbors who lived on the west side of his property were spying on his family. Howard suffers from post traumatic stress disorder ("PTSD") and a heart condition. Because of the conditions at his home with regard to his neighbors, Howard felt that his medical and psychological conditions were being exacerbated. Thus, he wanted to erect a six-foot privacy fence along the west side of his property to block his neighbors' view. He believed that this would eliminate any undue stress on his medical and psychological conditions and, in addition, would block leaves from blowing into his yard which he no longer could rake due to his heart condition.

The fence Howard intended to construct would run seventy feet from the southwest corner of his property to the street. Under Beavercreek's zoning ordinance, Howard was prohibited from erecting a six-foot fence along the first forty feet of the west property line running from the right-of-way to his house without first obtaining a variance. The zoning ordinance, however, would permit him to build a six-foot fence along the remainder of his property without a variance. He applied for a variance in 1997. In support of his application, Howard provided a statement from his treating physician which detailed his medical and psychological conditions. After a public hearing in May 1998, the Board of Zoning Appeals for the City of Beavercreek denied Howard's request.

In December 1998, Howard filed suit against Beavercreek seeking damages under the FHAA, 42 U.S.C. § 3604(f)(3)(B), and damages, declaratory judgment and injunctive relief under Ohio law, Ohio Revised Code § 4112.02. He alleged that Beavercreek had discriminated against him, as a person who suffers from a handicap, by failing to consider his request for a reasonable accommodation to its zoning rules, when such an accommodation was necessary to afford him an equal opportunity to use and enjoy his dwelling.

The district court * * * granted summary judgment in favor of Beavercreek on Howard's claim under the FHAA and his state law claims for declaratory and injunctive relief. * * * The court went on to find that although fact issues existed as to whether Howard's request for a variance was a reasonable accommodation under the FHAA, the city's denial of his request did not deny him the right to live in the neighborhood of his choice and, thus, did not violate the FHAA. Since the applicable sections of the Ohio Revised Code had language similar to that of the FHAA, the court used the same analysis when it reviewed and rejected Howard's state law claims for declaratory and injunctive relief. The court also determined that there was a second basis for granting summary judgment in favor of Beavercreek on Howard's FHAA claim. Because the "uncontroverted evidence" showed that the six-foot fence would cause a threat to pedestrian and vehicular traffic, the court held that Beavercreek was not required under § 3604(f)(9) of the FHAA to grant Howard's request for a variance. See 42 U.S.C. § 3604(f)(9). * * *

The FHAA makes it unlawful to discriminate against a person with a handicap by refusing "to make reasonable accommodations in rules, policies, practices, or services, when such accommodations may be necessary to afford such person equal opportunity to use and enjoy a dwelling." 42 U.S.C. § 3604(f)(3)(B). This creates an affirmative duty on municipalities, like Beavercreek, to afford its disabled citizens reasonable accommodations in its municipal zoning practices if necessary to afford such persons equal opportunity in the use and enjoyment of their property. *See Smith & Lee Assocs., Inc. v. City of Taylor,* 102 F.3d 781, 794–795 (6th Cir.1996) (holding that city had violated the FHAA by failing to allow adult foster care homes to operate in areas zoned only for single-family neighborhoods*); City of Edmonds v. Washington State Bldg. Code Council,* 18 F.3d 802, 806 (9th Cir.1994), aff'd, 514 U.S. 725, 115 S.Ct. 1776, 131 L.Ed.2d 801 (1995) ("The FHAA imposes an affirmative duty to reasonably accommodate handicapped people.").

When analyzing whether an accommodation is required under this Act, the three operative elements are "reasonable," "equal opportunity" and "necessary." See Smith, 102 F.3d at 794. An accommodation is "reasonable" when it imposes no "fundamental alteration in the nature of the program" or "undue financial and administrative burdens." Id. at 795 (quoting *Southeastern Community College v. Davis,* 442 U.S. 397,

410, 412, 99 S.Ct. 2361, 60 L.Ed.2d 980 (1979)). "Equal opportunity" under the FHAA is defined as "giving handicapped individuals the right to choose to live in single-family neighborhoods, for that right serves to end the exclusion of handicapped individuals from the American mainstream." Id. at 794–95. Linked to the goal of equal opportunity is the term "necessary." Id. at 795. In order to prove that an accommodation is "necessary," "[p]laintiffs must show that, but for the accommodation, they likely will be denied an equal opportunity to enjoy the housing of their choice." Id. (citing *Bronk v. Ineichen,* 54 F.3d 425, 429 (7th Cir.1995) ("[T]he concept of necessity requires at a minimum the showing that the desired accommodation will affirmatively enhance a disabled plaintiff's quality of life by ameliorating the effects of the disability.")).

Howard argues that the district court erred when it held that the requested accommodation was not necessary under the FHAA, because Howard had enjoyed the housing of his choice without the fence since 1984, and he continued to live in his home after the problems with his neighbors began in 1996. Howard asserts that the requested variance would ameliorate the exacerbation of his handicap satisfying the necessity requirement in § 3604(f)(3)(B), as defined in Smith and Bronk. We conclude that the district court was correct in its decision that under the FHAA Howard failed to prove that his requested accommodation was necessary to afford him the equal opportunity to enjoy the housing of his choice.

In his deposition, Howard stated that because of his medical conditions he needed to avoid being upset. He explained that by erecting a six-foot fence, he could avoid being upset by precluding his neighbors from viewing his property from their lot. In addition, he felt that the fence would prevent leaves from blowing into his yard, which he could no longer rake because of his heart condition. Without the fence, Howard stated that he may be forced to move. In addition, one of his treating physicians stated only that "[i]t is feasible that the installation of the privacy fence may relieve this undue stress and allow Mr. Howard to return to his baseline status." This evidence combined with the fact that Howard has lived in his home for several years without the requested variance illustrates that the denial of Howard's variance request has not denied him an equal opportunity to enjoy the housing or community of his choice. See Robinson v. City of Friendswood, 890 F.Supp. 616, 622 (S.D.Tex.1995) ("The Plaintiff had the same disabilities and lived in the same house for years before he constructed the carport indicates that the ordinance did not prevent him from obtaining housing of his choice nor from living in the community of his choice.").

"The Act is intended to prohibit the application of special requirements through land-use regulations, restrictive covenants, and conditional or special use permits that have the effect of limiting the ability of [handicapped] individuals to live in the residence of their choice in the community." H.R.Rep. No. 100–711, at 24 (1988), U.S.Code Cong. & Admin.News 1988, p. 2173, 2185. Thus, local governments are prohibited from "applying land use regulations in a manner that will exclude people with disabilities entirely from zoning neighborhoods, particularly residential neighborhoods, or that will give disabled people less opportunity to live in certain neighborhoods than people without disabilities." *Smith,* 102 F.3d at 795 (citation omitted). Although the requested variance may have reduced some of the stress Howard reportedly was subjected to, Beavercreek's denial of Howard's variance request has neither excluded Howard from the neighborhood or residence of his choice, nor has it created less opportunity for Howard, as a handicapped person, to live in his neighborhood.

In sum, because Howard failed to present sufficient evidence to create a genuine issue of material fact as to whether the variance he requested was a necessary accommodation under § 3604(f)(3)(B), the district court correctly granted summary judgment in favor of Beavercreek on Howard's FHAA claim. Because we find that the district court correctly granted summary judgment based on the "necessary" prong of the Act, we need not address whether the district court was also correct in finding a second basis for granting summary judgment based on the safety hazard posed by the fence. * * *

AFFIRMED.

Note

An interesting case involved a suit against a homeowners group for interfering with the purchase of a home for use as a group home. In United States v. Wagner, 930 F.Supp. 1148 (N.D.Tex.1996), the federal government sued several homeowners in a subdivision who had filed a lawsuit in state court seeking to prevent a neighbor from selling a house for use as a group home for mentally disabled children. The trial court held that the neighbors violated the Fair Housing Act and awarded damages to the intervening homeowner who had tried to sell the property for a group home ($7,500 for emotional distress and $8,000 in punitive damages). Also, the attorney for the homeowner was awarded over $46,000 in attorney's fees and expenses for the intervention in the federal suit to establish the FHA violation (he had already been awarded more than $3,500 for defending in the state court lawsuit).

(3) Age Discrimination in Housing

COLONY COVE ASSOCIATES v. BROWN

California Court of Appeal, 1990.
220 Cal.App.3d 195, 269 Cal.Rptr. 234.

BOREN, ASSOCIATE JUSTICE.

Respondent, owner of a mobile home park, enacted a park rule restricting residency to senior citizens, age 55 or older. Respondent then sought to evict appellants, tenants in the park, because appellants' children, minors born after the park's enactment of its age restriction, were not "grandfathered" as were their parents, who had resided in the park prior to the rule. Appellants appeal following summary judgments granted in unlawful detainer actions brought by respondent. We hold that the enforcement of the mobile home park's senior citizen, age 55 or older, resident restriction does not run afoul of constitutional proscriptions, relevant state statutes, or the Fair Housing Amendments Act of 1988.

* * *

I. Constitutional Concerns

In Schmidt v. Superior Court (1989) 48 Cal.3d 370, 256 Cal.Rptr. 750, 769 P.2d 932, the Supreme Court held that a mobile home park rule limiting residence to adults 25 years or older was not unconstitutional. The *Schmidt* court assumed arguendo the existence of state action such as to warrant applying constitutional concerns to private conduct (id. at pp. 388–389, fn. 14, 389, 256 Cal.Rptr. 750, 769 P.2d 932), and concluded that the mobile home park rule was not, as or when applied, either irrational or arbitrary and did not violate the constitutional rights to equal protection or familial privacy. (Id. at pp. 390–391, 256 Cal.Rptr. 750, 769 P.2d 932.)

In sustaining the constitutionality of the mobile home park rule, the court reasoned as follows: "[A]lthough the constitutional right of 'familial privacy' undoubtedly encompasses a parent's right to live with his or her child (see, e.g., Moore [v. East Cleveland (1977)] 431 U.S. 494, 500–506 [97 S.Ct. 1932, 1936–1939, 52 L.Ed.2d 531]), the mobile home park's 25–years–or–older policy at issue here does not, of course, purport to compel the separation of parent and child or to preclude the family from living together in an entire city (cf., e.g., Moore, supra, 431 U.S. 494 [97 S.Ct. 1932]; Molino v. Mayer and Council of Bor. of Glassboro (1971) 116 N.J.Super. 195 [281 A.2d 401]) or neighborhood (cf. [City of Santa Barbara v.] Adamson [1980] 27 Cal.3d 123 [164 Cal.Rptr. 539, 610 P.2d 436]), but simply denies the family access to a limited number of housing units. In Bynes v. Toll (2d Cir.1975) 512 F.2d 252, 254–256, the Second Circuit upheld a state university regulation excluding married students with children from university housing, explaining that the students' unquestioned constitutional right to procreate and to bring up their children did not mean that the university was 'constitutionally mandated to provide them campus housing to perform their protected prerogatives' (512 F.2d at p. 255), and, on similar grounds, courts of other states which have considered the validity of age-based housing regulations comparable to the rule at issue here—in the absence of a legislative measure barring such age restrictions—uniformly upheld the general constitutional validity of such rules. [Citations.] Particularly in light of the distinct characteristics of mobile home parks—e.g., the generally greater percentage of older residents, the smaller size of the units, the more substantial potential lack of privacy and the greater expense that might have to be incurred in rendering such a park safe for children residents—we agree with the conclusion of the above cited cases that such an age-based regulation is neither irrational nor arbitrary or otherwise vulnerable to constitutional attack." (Schmidt v. Superior Court, supra, 48 Cal.3d at pp. 389–390, 256 Cal.Rptr. 750, 769 P.2d 932, fns. omitted.)

The reasoning in *Schmidt* is particularly compelling here in the context of not merely an adult-only but a senior citizen age restriction rule. In view of the recognized desirability of special living environments and services providing communal educational and recreational facilities which meet the physical and social needs of senior citizens (see Civ.Code, §§ 51.2, subd. (a) and 51.3, subd. (a); cf. Huntington Landmark Adult Community Assn. v. Ross (1989) 213 Cal.App.3d 1012, 1018–1019, 261 Cal.Rptr. 875), respondent's age-based discrimination is "neither irrational nor arbitrary or otherwise vulnerable to constitutional attack." (Schmidt v. Superior Court, supra, 48 Cal.3d at p. 390, 256 Cal.Rptr. 750, 769 P.2d 932.)

II. State Statutory Provisions

Relevant California statutes do not preclude the establishment and enforcement of a senior citizen age qualification rule in a private mobile home park. In analyzing relevant state statutes, Schmidt v. Superior Court, supra, 48 Cal.3d 370, 256 Cal.Rptr. 750, 769 P.2d 932 held that a private mobile home park rule which limited residence in the park to persons 25 years or older, as permitted by Civil Code section 798.76,[4] did not violate the broad antidiscrimination policy embodied in the Unruh Civil Rights Act (Civ.Code, § 51 et seq.), even though the park rule operated to exclude families with children younger than 25 years of age. Most significantly, the amendments to the Unruh Act which address age-based discrimination in housing, Civil Code sections 51.2 and 51.3,[5] reflect a legislative intent specifically to exclude mobile home parks from the reach of the act. * * *

The amendments to the Unruh Act were enacted in response to a prior judicial expression of the appropriateness of age-based discrimination favoring senior citizens. In Marina Point, Ltd. v. Wolfson (1982) 30

4. Civil Code section 798.76 provides as follows:

> "The management may require that a purchaser of a mobile home which will remain in the park, comply with any rule or regulation limiting residence to adults only."

5. Civil Code section 51.2 provides, in pertinent part, as follows: "(a) Section 51 shall be construed to prohibit a business establishment from discriminating in the sale or rental of housing based upon age. Where accommodations are designed to meet the physical and social needs of senior citizens, a business establishment may establish and preserve such housing for senior citizens, pursuant to Section 51.3 of the Civil Code."

Civil Code section 51.3 provides, in pertinent part, as follows: "(a) The Legislature finds and declares that this section is essential to establish and preserve specially designed accessible housing for senior citizens. There are senior citizens who need special living environments and services, and find that there is an inadequate supply of this type of housing in the state. (b) The Legislature finds and declares that different age limitations for senior citizens housing are appropriate in recognition of the size of a development in relationship to the community in which it is located. (c) For the purposes of this section, the following definitions apply: * * * (4) 'Dwelling unit' or 'housing' means any residential accommodation other than a mobile home."

Cal.3d 721, 180 Cal.Rptr. 496, 640 P.2d 115, where the court held the general provisions of the Unruh Act prohibited an ordinary apartment complex from adopting a rule which excluded all families with children from the complex, the court emphasized that the age-based exclusionary policy which it proscribed was distinguishable from "the age-limited admission policies of retirement communities or housing complexes reserved for older citizens." (Id. at p. 742, 180 Cal.Rptr. 496, 640 P.2d 115.) As the court observed, "In light of the public policy reflected by [legislation allowing for adults-only housing in mobile home parks (Civ. Code, § 798.76)], age qualifications as to a housing facility reserved for older citizens can operate as a reasonable and permissible means under the Unruh Act of establishing and preserving specialized facilities for those particularly in need of such services or environment. [Citations.] Such a specialized institution designed to meet a social need differs fundamentally from the wholesale exclusion of children from an apartment complex otherwise open to the general public." (Id. at pp. 742–743, 180 Cal.Rptr. 496, 640 P.2d 115, fns. omitted.)

With the declared intent "to clarify the holdings in Marina Point, Ltd. v. Wolfson[, supra]" (Civ.Code, § 51.2, subd. (b)), and another related decision, the Legislature enacted Civil Code sections 51.2 and 51.3. (See Schmidt v. Superior Court, supra, 48 Cal.3d at pp. 383–384, 256 Cal.Rptr. 750, 769 P.2d 932.) * * *

III. The Fair Housing Amendments Act of 1988

The contention that the Fair Housing Amendments Act of 1988 (Pub.L. No. 100–430 (Sept. 13, 1988) 102 Stat. 1619, 1988 U.S.Code Cong. & Admin.News, No. 8), effective March 1989, invalidates respondent's adults-only policy and proscribes eviction proceedings on familial status grounds is unavailing. In applying federal legislation to the present situation (see Gulf Offshore Co. v. Mobil Oil Corp. (1981) 453 U.S. 473, 477–478, 101 S.Ct. 2870, 2874–2875, 69 L.Ed.2d 784), it is apparent that the Fair Housing Amendments Act makes it generally unlawful to discriminate in the sale or rental of housing or to make a "dwelling" otherwise unavailable on the basis of "familial status," as well as on the previously forbidden grounds of race, color, religion, sex or national origin. (42 U.S.C.A. § 3604.) The definition of the term "dwelling" in the Fair Housing Act includes mobile home sites. (See, e.g., United States v. Warwick Mobile Homes Estates, Inc. (4th Cir.1976) 537 F.2d 1148; United States v. Grooms (M.D.Fla.1972) 348 F.Supp. 1130, 1133.) The term "familial status" is defined as families which include children under the age of 18. (42 U.S.C.A. § 3602(k).)

While the amendment to the Fair Housing Act thus generally bars discrimination in mobile home housing against families with children under 18, it also, however, creates an exception for "housing for older persons" in which discrimination on the basis of familial status is not prohibited. (42 U.S.C.A. § 3607(b)(1).) "Housing for older persons" is legislatively defined to include, in part, housing which is (1) "intended for, solely occupied by, persons 62 years of age or older," or (2) "intended and operated for occupancy by at least one person 55 years of age or older per unit." (42 U.S.C.A. § 3607(b)(2)(B) and (b)(2)(C).)

In determining whether "housing for older persons" qualifies within the meaning of the latter category involving "occupancy by at least one person 55 years of age or older per unit," the amendment to the Fair Housing Act requires that "the Secretary [of Housing and Urban Development (HUD)] shall develop regulations which include at least the following requirements: (i) the existence of significant facilities and services specifically designed to meet the physical or social needs of older persons, or if the provision of such facilities and services is not practicable, that such housing is necessary to provide important housing opportunities for older persons; and (ii) that at least 80 percent of the units are occupied by at least one person 55 years of age or older per unit; and (iii) the publication of, and adherence to, policies and procedures which demonstrate an intent by the owner or manager to provide housing for persons 55 years of age or older." (42 U.S.C.A. § 3607(b)(2)(C)(i to iii).)

The amendment further contains a "grandfather clause" in section 3607(b)(3)(A). That section provides that housing will not be disqualified as "housing for older persons" merely because "persons residing in such housing as of September 13, 1988," do not meet the requirements under either the 62 or 55 years of age or older categories, so long as any new occupants meet the age requirements under either of those two categories, as specified in section 3607(b)(2)(B) or (b)(2)(C).

* * *

It is sufficient for our purpose in reviewing the grant of a motion for summary judgment that the mobile home park, as indicated by its age restriction regulation, was "intended and operated for occupancy by at least one person 55 years of age or older per unit." (42 U.S.C.A. § 3607(b)(2)(C).) Moreover, as a matter of law, to the extent that units in the park are occupied by persons not in that category, "The act also contains a 'grandfather clause,' providing that persons under the applicable age limits who were residing in housing when the federal act was enacted will not disqualify the housing from the statutory exemption for housing for older persons so long as the applicable age requirements are applied to all new occupants. (42 U.S.C.A. § 3607(b)(3).)" (Schmidt v. Superior Court, supra, 48 Cal.3d at p. 375, fn. 4, 256 Cal.Rptr. 750, 769 P.2d 932.) Accordingly, there were no triable issues of material fact, and summary judgment was appropriate. (See AARTS Productions, Inc. v. Crocker National Bank (1986) 179 Cal.App.3d 1061, 1064–1065, 225 Cal.Rptr. 203; Code Civ.Proc., § 437c, subd. (c).)

* * *

IV. Conclusion

We are aware of the plight of young couples with children who seek affordable housing. We also recognize the unique difficulties which arise when a mobile home owner is forced to vacate a mobile home park rental space. The Legislature has also acknowledged the critical importance of adequate housing for families. (See Health & Saf. Code, §§ 50001, 50003, 50003.3, 50004; Gov.Code, § 65913; Marina Point, Ltd. v. Wolfson, supra, 30 Cal.3d at p. 743, 180 Cal.Rptr. 496, 640 P.2d 115.) Discrimination against children in housing is at odds with fundamental notions of humanity. "A society that sanctions wholesale discrimination against its children in obtaining housing engages in a suspect activity. Even the most primitive society fosters the protection of its young; such a society would hardly discriminate against children in their need for shelter * * *." (Marina Point, Ltd. v. Wolfson, supra, 30 Cal.3d at p. 744, 180 Cal.Rptr. 496, 640 P.2d 115.)

Nonetheless, as discussed above, our legislative bodies have also addressed the competing interests and housing needs of older persons in our society. Consistent with our constitutional and legislative analysis, appellants' legitimate housing needs cannot be satisfied by the present attack upon legislation which provides for the establishment of senior citizen mobile home parks.

Disposition

The judgments are affirmed. Respondent's request for sanctions is denied.

Lucas, P.J., and Ashby, J., concur.

Notes

1. Another case that gives a full discussion of the reasons for allowing mobile home parks dedicated to the elderly is Taxpayers Ass'n of Weymouth Twp., Inc. v. Weymouth Twp., 80 N.J. 6, 364 A.2d 1016 (1976), appeal dismissed 430 U.S. 977, 97 S.Ct. 1672, 52 L.Ed.2d 373 (1977). Also see Seifred v. Zabel, 369 N.W.2d 571 (Minn.App.1985); Metro. Dade County Fair Housing and Employment Appeals Bd. v. Sunrise Village Mobile Home Park, Inc., 485 So.2d 865 (Fla.App. 3 Dist.1986).

2. A leading case contrary to the position of allowing zoning for the elderly is Hinman v. Planning and Zoning Comm'n, 26 Conn.Sup. 125, 214 A.2d 131 (1965). The court ruled that a rural town of less than 5,000 population did not have authority under the enabling act to create a new zoning classification (Senior Citizen Planned Community District) for development on tracts of 400 or more acres. In New York, the courts have allowed such zoning. See Maldini v. Ambro, 36 N.Y.2d 481, 369 N.Y.S.2d 385, 330 N.E.2d 403 (1975), appeal dismissed 423 U.S. 993, 96 S.Ct. 419, 46 L.Ed.2d 367 (1975); Campbell v. Barraud, 58 A.D.2d 570, 394 N.Y.S.2d 909 (1977); Apfelbaum v. Town of Clarkstown, 104 Misc.2d 371, 428 N.Y.S.2d 387 (1980); but see the unusual case of Central Management Co. v. Town Bd. of Oyster Bay, 47 Misc.2d 385, 262 N.Y.S.2d 728 (1965), where the town board rejected a proposed high rise apartment building for the elderly because it was to be built in an area remote from medical and shopping facilities on a plot of land which was virtually an island between two expressways, and the

court held that the board could not take into account the age of the proposed residents and the rejection was thus arbitrary.

3. Prior to the decision in the principal case, the California legislature passed a resolution (S.J.R. 1, 1989) requesting that the President and the Congress amend the Fair Housing Act Amendments of 1988 to clarify the rules concerning mobile home parks for the elderly. The resolution states that most California mobile home parks have adults-only restrictions and that the HUD regulations are ambiguous as to what is required for a mobile home park to operate with age restrictions without violating the act. The resolution also notes that the cost of senior citizen housing in mobile home parks might be increased by the cost of installation of facilities to meet the physical or social needs of the residents as stated in the act. Federal courts have been reluctant to find exceptions for elder residences that lack special facilities. In Lanier v. Fairfield Communities Inc., 776 F.Supp. 1533 (M.D.Fla.1990) the court held that the exception was not available where the residential community was two miles from the nearest shopping and medical facilities, provided no transportation, no emergency call buttons, and no congregate dining or health facilities. Also see Park Place Home Brokers v. P–K Mobile Home Park, 773 F.Supp. 46 (N.D.Ohio 1991) (off-site facilities and services could not be considered in determining whether the mobile home park could claim the exemption); Hooker v. Weathers, 990 F.2d 913 (6th Cir.1993) (burden of proof is on the owner of the residences to establish the older persons exemption). In 1995 Congress amended the act to strike out the section requiring significant facilities to serve the elderly as a condition for exemption, P.L. 104–76, § 2.

4. Perhaps the most controversial part of the Fair Housing Act Amendments of 1988 is the rule against discrimination in the rental of apartment housing on the basis of familial status (i.e., children under 18). The Congressional intent is clearly to prohibit adults-only apartment buildings, a widespread practice across the nation. This provision became effective in March, 1989. See, e.g., United States v. Badgett, 976 F.2d 1176 (8th Cir.1992); United States v. Tropic Seas, Inc., 887 F.Supp. 1347 (D.Haw.1995). Also, federal courts have seen a number of cases brought under the provision in the Fair Housing Act Amendments prohibiting discrimination in housing on the basis of handicap. See, e.g., Larkin v. State of Michigan Dept. of Social Services, 89 F.3d 285 (6th Cir.1996). Also see James Brooke, Young Unwelcome in Retirees' Haven, N.Y. Times, Feb. 16, 1997, p. 10.

5. In Betsey v. Turtle Creek Associates, 736 F.2d 983 (4th Cir.1984), the court found a violation of the Fair Housing Act where an adults-only rental policy had a disparate racial impact on minority tenants.

6. For further reading on senior housing issues, see Helen L. Edmonds and Dwight H. Merriam, Zoning and the Elderly: Issues for the 21st Century, Land Use Law (Mar. 1995), p. 3; Devinder Brar and Bridget Holohan, Housing Options for an Aging Population: Options for Reform (Government Law Center 1999) available at www.governmentlaw.org/files/Housing_Alternatives_For_An_Aging_Population.pdf; and Patricia E. Salkin, "Where Will the Aging Baby Boomers Go? Planning and Zoning for an Aging Population," 32 Real Estate L. J. 181 (Fall 2003).

C. AMERICANS WITH DISABILITIES ACT

INNOVATIVE HEALTH SYSTEMS v. CITY OF WHITE PLAINS

United States Court of Appeals, Second Circuit, 1997.
117 F.3d 37.

HEANEY, SENIOR CIRCUIT JUDGE:

In December 1992, plaintiff-appellee Innovative Health Systems, Inc. ("IHS"), an outpatient drug- and alcohol-rehabilitation treatment center, began efforts to relocate to a building in downtown White Plains. After over a year of seeking permission from the city, IHS was ultimately denied the necessary building permit by the White Plains Zoning Board of Appeals ("ZBA"). On November 14, 1995, plaintiffs-appellees, IHS and five individual clients, initiated this action against the City of White Plains; Mayor S.J. Schulmann; the ZBA; Chair of the ZBA, Terrence Guerrier; the White Plains Planning Board; and Chair of the Planning Board, Mary Cavallero, (collectively, "the City"), alleging that the ZBA's zoning decision violated both Title II of the Americans with Disabilities Act, 42 U.S.C. §§ 12131–12165 (1994), and section 504 of the Rehabilitation Act of 1973, 29 U.S.C. § 794 (1994). The plaintiffs-appellees moved for a preliminary injunction to prevent the City from interfering with IHS's occupation of the new site. The City cross-moved to dismiss the complaint. In a detailed and thorough opinion, the United States District Court for the Southern District of New York (Barrington D. Parker, Jr., Judge) granted the preliminary injunction and denied the motion to dismiss, except with respect to Mayor Schulmann. *Innovative Health Sys. v. City of White Plains,* 931 F.Supp. 222 (S.D.N.Y.1996). The remaining defendants appeal. We affirm except with respect to one individual client, Martin A.

In 1992, Dr. Ross Fishman, Executive Director of IHS, decided that the program should move from its current facility to a building located in downtown White Plains. The new site was more than five times as large as the current site and was closer to a bus line and to other service providers that IHS clients frequently visit. Dr. Fishman planned to expand the services offered by IHS at the new site to include a program for children of chemically dependent persons. Therefore, IHS predicted an increase in the number of clients it would serve.

In December 1992, the Deputy Commissioner of Building for the City of White Plains informed IHS that its proposed use of the downtown site—counseling offices with no physicians on staff for physical examinations or dispensing of medication—qualified as a business or professional office under White Plains' zoning ordinance and thus would be permissible in the zoning district. In January 1994, Dr. Fishman signed a lease for the new space. IHS paid a monthly rent of $8,500 from July 1, 1994 to June 30, 1995 and has paid $6,000 per month since July 1995. The leased space includes a section that formerly had been used as retail space. Dr. Fishman initially intended to renovate the former retail space for the treatment program and sub-lease the remaining space, which had previously been used as an office. In April 1994, IHS filed an application with the White Plains Department of Building for a building permit. Because the application requested a change of use from "retail" to "office," the Commissioner of Building ("Commissioner") referred it to the Planning Board for approval as required by the local zoning ordinance.

The application provoked tremendous opposition from the surrounding community, including Cameo House Owners, Inc. ("Cameo House"), a co-operative association representing resident-owners who lived in the remainder of the downtown building in which IHS sought to relocate, and Fashion Mall Partners, L.P. ("Fashion Mall"), the owner of a shopping mall located near the proposed IHS site. The Planning Board held two public meetings on the proposed use at which the opponents expressed their concern about the condition and appearance of people who attend alcohol- and drug-dependence treatment programs and the effect such a program would have on property values. Opponents also argued that the proposed use constituted a "clinic" and that, therefore, under the zoning ordinance, the use was a "hospital or sanitarium," an impermissible use in the zoning district. In response to this argument, at the Planning Board's request, the Commissioner reconsidered and reaffirmed his previous determination that the proposed site constituted permitted "office" use.

Because continued opposition caused delay and additional costs, IHS withdrew its application from the Planning Board. It instead applied to the Commissioner for a permit to renovate the former retail section of the downtown site, which did not involve a change of use or the Planning Board's approval. Again, however, the application was vehemently opposed by members of the surrounding community.

To resolve the dispute, the Commissioner sought review of his decision by the White Plains Corporation Counsel. In his written opinion, the Corporation Counsel stated that, absent compelling authority to the contrary, the Commissioner's decision should stand. The Corporation Counsel considered the opponents' argument under the zoning ordinance and concluded that the Commissioner's interpretation was correct. Accordingly, the Commissioner issued his final determination that the use was permitted and the Department of Building issued the building permit to IHS.

Cameo House and Fashion Mall immediately appealed the Commissioner's decision to the ZBA, requesting an interpretation of the zoning ordinance that an alcohol-treatment facility is not permitted in the relevant zoning district. The ZBA conducted a two-day public hearing on the matter, at which community members continued to voice strong opposition to having a drug- and alcohol-dependency treatment center in the downtown location. They again focused largely on fears of jeopardized safety and falling property values. The opposition also pressed the same zoning arguments rejected by the Commissioner and the Corporation Counsel. IHS relied on the reasoning of the previous decisions and urged the ZBA to consider their consistency with already-permitted uses in the same zoning district. Specifically, IHS reminded the board that the zoning district of its former location also excludes "hospitals and sanitaria" and that several other mental health professionals and social workers practiced in the district of the proposed site.

On July 5, 1995, the ZBA voted four-to-one to reverse the Commissioner's decision. The Board did not issue a written resolution, as required by the zoning ordinance, but rather stated on the record that, based on its understanding of the services IHS provides, it is better classified as a clinic than an office. Absent in their discussion, however, was any reference to the zoning ordinance or the Commissioner's interpretation.

IHS and five individual clients initiated this action against the City, alleging that the revocation of the building permit constituted discrimination and differential treatment based on a disability as against both the individual clients and the program that assisted them. They also claimed that even if the zoning decision was not discriminatory, the City should have permitted the relocation as a reasonable accommodation. In February 1996, they moved for a preliminary injunction against the City to prevent it from interfering with the occupation of the downtown site.

The City opposed the motion and moved for dismissal, arguing: (1) zoning decisions do not fall within the scope of the ADA or the Rehabilitation Act, (2) the appellees lack standing under the ADA, (3) the federal statutes do not accord preferential treatment to persons with disabilities, and (4) neither IHS nor the individual clients have demonstrated irreparable harm or a likelihood of success on the merits. The district court granted the preliminary injunction and denied the motion to dismiss, except as against the Mayor. The City now appeals, raising essentially the same arguments.

* * *

B. Likelihood of Success on the Merits

The City also challenges the district court's determination that the appellees have demonstrated a likelihood of success on the merits, arguing primarily: (1) neither the ADA nor the Rehabilitation Act covers zoning decisions, (2) the appellees lack standing under both the ADA and the Rehabilitation Act, and (3) appellees have not stated a claim under either statute. We address each argument in turn.

1. *Application of Discrimination Statutes to Zoning*

Both Title II of the ADA and section 508 of the Rehabilitation Act prohibit discrimination based on a disability by a public entity. The ADA provides:

> [N]o qualified individual with a disability shall, by reason of such disability, be excluded from participation in or be denied the benefits

> of the services, programs, or activities of a public entity, or be subjected to discrimination by any such entity. 42 U.S.C. sec. 12132(1994).

The Rehabilitation Act contains the following similar prohibition:

> No otherwise qualified individual with a disability ... shall, solely by reason of her or his disability, be excluded from the participation in, be denied the benefits of, or be subjected to discrimination under any program or activity receiving Federal financial assistance.... 29 U.S.C. sec. 794(a)(1994).

It is undisputed that both anti-discrimination provisions govern the City. What the City contests is the application of either statute to its zoning decisions because it contends that zoning does not constitute a "service, program, or activity." We disagree.

The ADA does not explicitly define "services, programs, or activities." Section 508 of the Rehabilitation Act, however, defines "program or activity" as "all of the operations" of specific entities, including "a department, agency, special purpose district, or other instrumentality of a State or of a local government." 29 U.S.C. § 794(b)(1)(A) (1994). Further, as the district court recognized, the plain meaning of "activity" is a "natural or normal function or operation." *Innovative Health Sys.*, 931 F.Supp. at 232 (quoting Webster's Third New International Dictionary (1993)). Thus, as the district court held, both the ADA and the Rehabilitation Act clearly encompass zoning decisions by the City because making such decisions is a normal function of a governmental entity. Id. Moreover, as the district court also noted, the language of Title II's anti-discrimination provision does not limit the ADA's coverage to conduct that occurs in the "programs, services, or activities" of the City. Rather, it is a catch-all phrase that prohibits all discrimination by a public entity, regardless of the context, and that should avoid the very type of hair-splitting arguments the City attempts to make here.

In its analysis, the district court also looked to the ADA's legislative history and the Department of Justice's regulations and Technical Assistance Manual, all of which support the court's interpretation of the plain language of the statute. With respect to Title II of the ADA, the House Committee on Education and Labor stated:

> The Committee has chosen not to list all the types of actions that are included within the term "discrimination", as was done in titles I and III, because this title essentially simply extends the anti-discrimination prohibition embodied in section 504 to all actions of state and local governments....
>
> Title II of the bill makes all activities of State and local governments subject to the types of prohibitions against discrimination against a qualified individual with a disability included in section 504 (nondiscrimination).

H.R.Rep. No. 101–485(II), at 84, 151 (1990), reprinted in 1990 U.S.C.C.A.N. 303, 367, 434 (emphasis added). As the preamble to the

Department of Justice regulations explains, "[T]itle II applies to anything a public entity does.... All governmental activities of public entities are covered." 28 C.F.R. pt. 35, app. A at 456 (1996). The Department of Justice's Technical Assistance Manual, which interprets its regulations, specifically refers to zoning as an example of a public entity's obligation to modify its policies, practices, and procedures to avoid discrimination. The Americans with Disabilities Act: Title II Technical Assistance Manual § II–3.6100, illus. 1 (1993) ("TA Manual").

Although it gives lip service to the importance of looking to the statutory language to glean legislative intent, the City does not point to specific language in either statute to explain the exemption it seeks to create for zoning decisions. We decline to draw an arbitrary distinction—to prohibit public entities from discriminating against persons with disabilities in some of their activities and not in others—without a reasoned basis for such a distinction. The only authority for the City's interpretation of Title II are several lower court decisions that hold that the ADA does not apply to zoning decisions. After careful review of the cited authority, we agree with the district court that none of the cases adequately analyzed the language of the ADA. Similarly, we find no direction from any other circuit on this issue. Without persuasive authority to the contrary, we affirm the district court's sound and thorough analysis.

The City also challenges IHS's standing to sue under either the ADA or the Rehabilitation Act. Although the City does not contest that IHS can meet the constitutional standing requirements of injury-in-fact, causation, and redressability, see *Valley Forge Christian College v. Americans United for Separation of Church & State,* 454 U.S. 464, 472, 102 S.Ct. 752, 758, 70 L.Ed.2d 700 (1982) (setting forth the Article III requirements), it argues that prudential standing requirements bar IHS from asserting a claim under either statute. *See Warth v. Seldin,* 422 U.S. 490, 499, 95 S.Ct. 2197, 2205, 45 L.Ed.2d 343 (1975) (generally, a party "must assert his own legal rights and interests, and cannot rest his claim to relief on the legal rights or interests of third parties"). Specifically, the City argues that the discrimination statutes confer rights on a narrow class of persons, namely "qualified individual[s] with a disability," as set forth in both statutes' definitions of discrimination by public entities. See 42 U.S.C. § 12132; 29 U.S.C. § 794; see also *Kessler,* 876 F.Supp. at 653 (holding that an entity that serves the disabled lacks standing under the ADA).

At first blush, this argument has appeal. The City appropriately looks to the statutory language to determine whether Congress granted an express right of action to persons who otherwise would be barred by prudential standing rules. *See Warth,* 422 U.S. at 501, 95 S.Ct. at 2206 (as long as constitutional requirements met, Congress may grant standing to seek relief on the basis of the legal rights and interests of others). The City's analysis falls short, however, in its selective analysis of the statutes. It stops at the definitions of discrimination, which set forth a substantive, legal right of persons with disabilities to be free from discrimination. That IHS is not granted legal rights under the statutes, however, "hardly determines whether they may sue to enforce the ... rights of others." *See Gladstone, Realtors v. Village of Bellwood,* 441 U.S. 91, 103 n. 9, 99 S.Ct. 1601, 1609 n. 9, 60 L.Ed.2d 66 (1979). Rather, we must look to whether the statutes "grant [ ] persons in the plaintiff's position a right to judicial relief." *Warth,* 422 U.S. at 500, 95 S.Ct. at 2206.

Looking to the enforcement provisions of each statute, we agree with the district court that IHS has standing under both Title II of the ADA and the Rehabilitation Act. Title II's enforcement provision extends relief to "any person alleging discrimination on the basis of disability." 42 U.S.C. § 12133 (1994). Similarly, the Rehabilitation Act extends its remedies to "any person aggrieved" by the discrimination of a person on the basis of his or her disability. 29 U.S.C. § 794a(a)(2). As the district court noted, the use of such broad language in the enforcement provisions of the statutes "evinces a congressional intention to define standing to bring a private action under 504 [and Title II] as broadly as is permitted by Article III of the Constitution." See *Innovative Health Sys.,* 931 F.Supp. at 237 (quoting *Nodleman v. Aero Mexico,* 528 F.Supp. 475, 485 (D.C.Cal.1981) (citing *Trafficante v. Metropolitan Life Ins. Co.,* 409 U.S. 205, 209, 93 S.Ct. 364, 366–67, 34 L.Ed.2d 415 (1972))).

With respect to Title II, the City further argues that we should respect the different language Congress chose to employ in Titles I and III, which define discrimination to include conduct directed at an entity based on its relationship or association with disabled persons. See 42 U.S.C. § 12112(b)(4) (Title I); 42 U.S.C. § 12182(b)(1)(E) (Title III). According to the City, because Title II does not contain similar language, Congress intended to prevent standing based on association under this section. Although courts generally should be reluctant to conclude that the omission of language in one part of a statute that is included in another is unintentional, see e.g., *City of Chicago v. Environmental Defense Fund,* 511 U.S. 328, 337–38, 114 S.Ct. 1588, 1593, 128 L.Ed.2d 302 (1994), there is extensive support in this instance to read the specific examples of discrimination from the other two titles into Title II.

As a starting point, Title II sets out only a general definition of discrimination. By listing specific examples of discriminatory behavior in the other two titles, Congress surely did not intend to excuse similar discriminatory conduct by a public entity simply because such conduct is not spelled out in Title II. This common-sense interpretation of Title II is confirmed by the legislative history. The House Committee on Education and Labor indicated that Title II's prohibitions are to be "identical to those set out in the applicable provisions of titles I and III of this legislation." H.R.Rep. No. 101–485(II), at 84 (1990), reprinted in 1990 U.S.C.C.A.N. 303, 367. More specifically, the House Report on the ADA states that the prohibitions of discrimination on the basis of association from Titles I and III should be incorporated in the regulations implementing Title II. *Id.;* H.R.Rep. No. 485(III), at 51 (1990), *reprinted in* 1990 U.S.C.C.A.N. 445, 474; *see also Kinney v. Yerusalim,* 9 F.3d 1067,

1073 n. 6 (3d Cir.1993) (legislative history indicates that Titles II and III are to be read consistently).

As directed by the House Report, the regulations implementing Title II provide:

> A public entity shall not exclude or otherwise deny equal services, programs, or activities to an individual or entity because of the known disability of an individual with whom the individual or entity is known to have a relationship or association. 28 C.F.R. sec. 35.130(g).

The preamble to section 35 acknowledges that the regulation is based on the relevant sections from Titles I and III and that "[t]his paragraph was not contained in the proposed rule." 28 C.F.R. pt. 35, app. A at 470. Based on the inconsistency between the rule and the regulation, the City argues persuasively that we should not give the regulation "controlling weight." In light of the specific congressional mandate to include this paragraph in the regulations, however, and the fact that this particular construction of discrimination is not "manifestly contrary" to Title II's general discrimination prohibition, we give the regulation the weight to which it is due. See *Chevron,* 467 U.S. at 844, 104 S.Ct. at 2782–83. * * *

In any event, because we have already determined that Title II provides relief to "any person alleging discrimination," it is irrelevant whether Title II directly proscribes discrimination based on association with disabled persons. Accordingly, we affirm the district court's determination that IHS has standing to assert a claim under both the ADA and the Rehabilitation Act.

Assuming that the discrimination statutes apply to zoning decisions and that the appellees have standing, the City contends that the district court erred in concluding the appellees will likely be successful on the merits of their discrimination claims. The City argues that the appellees' claims will fail because (1) IHS's clients are not "qualified individuals with a disability" because they are not drug-free, (2) the appellees were not denied the benefits of the City's zoning activity, and (3) the City's zoning decision was not based on bias against chemically-dependent persons. We address each argument in turn.

The City claims that IHS has admitted that some of its clients are not drug-free and that therefore, under either statute the clients are excluded from the definition of "qualified individuals with a disability." See 42 U.S.C. § 12210(a) (term "does not include an individual who is currently engaging in the illegal use of drugs, when the covered entity acts on the basis of such use"); 29 U.S.C. § 706(8)(C)(i) (same). Although, we are not convinced that IHS has admitted that its clients are not drug-free, the program indisputably does not tolerate drug use by its participants. An inevitable, small percentage of failures should not defeat the rights of the majority of participants in the rehabilitation program who are drug-free and therefore disabled under both statutes. See 42 U.S.C. § 12210(b)(2); 29 U.S.C. § 706(8)(C)(ii)(II).

The City also argues that the appellees have not been denied the benefits of the City's zoning activity because they were able to participate in every step of the process: They were given full consideration by the Commissioner, the Corporation Counsel, the Planning Board, and the ZBA. In so arguing, the City has misconstrued the nature of the appellees' complaint. The appellees' claim is not premised on the denial of the right to participate in the zoning approval process. Rather, they allege that they have been denied the benefit of having the City make a zoning decision without regard to the disabilities of IHS's clients. They have therefore made a claim cognizable under both statutes of discrimination.

The City additionally contends that the appellees have not produced any evidence of the City's discriminatory motives in denying the building permit to IHS. There is little evidence in the record to support the ZBA's decision on any ground other than the need to alleviate the intense political pressure from the surrounding community brought on by the prospect of drug- and alcohol-addicted neighbors. The public hearings and submitted letters were replete with discriminatory comments about drug- and alcohol-dependent persons based on stereotypes and general, unsupported fears. * * * Although the City certainly may consider legitimate safety concerns in its zoning decisions, it may not base its decisions on the perceived harm from such stereotypes and generalized fears. As the district court found, a decision made in the context of strong, discriminatory opposition becomes tainted with discriminatory intent even if the decisionmakers personally have no strong views on the matter. *Innovative Health Sys.*, 931 F.Supp. at 243 (quoting *Association of Relatives & Friends of AIDS Patients v. Regulations & Permits Admin.*, 740 F.Supp. 95, 104 (D.P.R.1990)); see also *Support Ministries for Persons with AIDS, Inc. v. Village of Waterford, N.Y.*, 808 F.Supp. 120, 134 (N.D.N.Y.1992) (zoning officials who "bowed to political pressure" by those with animus against people with alcohol- and drug-related disabilities violated Fair Housing Act).

We also find the ZBA's decision to be highly suspect in light of the requirements set forth in the zoning ordinance. The Commissioner and the Corporation Counsel carefully reviewed IHS's application and gave detailed explanations for their approval. The Corporation Counsel analyzed the definition of "hospital or sanitaria" and concluded that because IHS was not an "institution for the purpose of serving general medical, surgical, psychiatric, physical therapy and rehabilitation purposes," it did not fall under this classification. The ZBA, on the other hand, simply stated, without explanation, that IHS was a clinic and thus an impermissible use in the downtown site. The ZBA ignored the requirements of the "hospital or sanitaria" classification and did not explain why it declined to follow the Corporation Counsel's straightforward analysis. Further, although made aware of other similar uses in the same district, the ZBA did not explain the distinction between IHS's proposed use and the other mental health professionals and social workers who do not work exclusively with chemically-dependent persons.

On appeal, the City states that the ZBA's decision was "amply supported by legal arguments" without setting forth any of the supposed "legal arguments" for our consideration. The lack of a credible justification for the zoning decision raises an additional inference that the decision was based on impermissible factors, namely the chemical-dependent status of IHS's clients. Accordingly, we see no reason to disturb the district court's finding of likelihood of success on the merits.

* * *

Accordingly, we affirm the district court's grant of a preliminary injunction in favor of appellees, except with respect to Martin A., who lacks standing to pursue this claim.

Notes

1. Since the required accommodations are pretty much the same, plaintiffs tend to bring challenges alleging violations of the FHAA, the ADA and the Rehabilitation Act in their lawsuits. See, e.g., Dadian v. Village of Wilmette, 269 F.3d 831 (7th Cir.2001). Also see First Step, Inc. v. City of New London, 247 F.Supp.2d 135 (D.Conn.2003) with facts very similar to the principal case.

2. It is often left to the courts to figure out what constitutes a "reasonable accommodation" under the acts. In Regional Economic Community Action Program, Inc. v. City of Middletown, 294 F.3d 35 (2d Cir.2002) the Court said, "...a proper reasonable accommodation might assert that the zoning authority should have waived or modified its rule against elevators in residential dwellings to permit those who need them to use them and thereby have full access to and enjoyment of residences there." See, Oconomowoc Residential Programs v. City of Milwaukee, 300 F.3d 775 (7th Cir.2002) (a variance from the City zoning ordinance restricting group homes from operating within 2,500 feet of each other is a reasonable accommodation under both the ADA and the FHAA); but see, Harding v. City of Toledo, 433 F.Supp.2d 867 (N.D. Ohio, 2006) where the Court uphold a city ordinance requiring a 500 ft. buffer separating adult group homes. The Court said such requirement did not violate either the ADA nor the FHAA.

3. The requirement for a reasonable accommodation imposes an affirmative duty to modify local requirements when they discriminate against the handicapped. See, Liddy v. Cisneros, 823 F.Supp. 164, 176 (S.D.N.Y. 1993). The Courts have broadly defined what constitutes a "handicap" under the Act. For example, the following conditions have been found to be covered under the definition: alcoholism and drug addition (see, e.g., Oxford House v. Township of Cherry Hill, 799 F.Supp. 450 (D.N.J. 1991)); emotional problems and mental illness (see, e.g., Association for Advancement of the Mentally Handicapped, Inc. v. City of Elizabeth, 876 F.Supp. 614 (D.N.J. 1994); old age (see, e.g., United States v. Commonwealth of Puerto Rico, 764 F.Supp. 220 (D.P.R.1991)); AIDS and HIV (see, e.g., Support Ministries for Persons With AIDS, Inc. v. Village of Waterford, 808 F.Supp. 120 (N.D.N.Y. 1992)); and homelessness (see, Stewart B. McKinney Foundation v. Town of Fairfield, 790 F.Supp. 1197 (D.Conn.1992)).

D. TELECOMMUNICATIONS ACT OF 1996

The following introduction to Professor Carol A. Goforth's article, "A Bad Call: Preemption of State and Local Authority to Regulate Wireless Communication Facilities on the Basis of Radio Frequency Emissions," 44 N.Y. L. Sch. L. Rev. 311 (2001) provides a good overview of the status of local governments' ability to regulate the siting of wireless towers after the enactment of the Telecommunications Act of 1996 (citations omitted).

> Early in 1996, Congress enacted a complicated piece of federal legislation entitled the Telecommunications Act of 1996 (the "Telecom Act"). When President Clinton signed the Telecom Act into law on February 8, 1996, he characterized it as "truly revolutionary legislation that [would] bring the future to our doorstep." The legislation was promoted as being "pro-competitive," and "deregulatory," and supporters claimed that it would offer consumers lower prices, better service, and faster access to new technologies.
>
> The Telecom Act applies broadly to the entire telecommunications industry, and many of its provisions are of unquestioned benefit to the American public. However, buried among the many complicated provisions of the statute is a section which precludes state and local governments from regulating the placement of "personal wireless facilities" on the basis of the "environmental effects" of radio-frequency emissions, to the extent that such emissions are within the Federal Communication Commission's safety guidelines. Although it may not be obvious, the technical phrase "personal wireless facilities" refers primarily to the towers which cellular and personal communications services (PCS) providers have been building in ever-increasing numbers. In addition, "environmental effects" is a euphemism which was apparently intended to encompass any impact that radio-frequency emissions may have on human health. Unfortunately, even though the FCC has promulgated exposure guidelines for such emissions, the Commission has never claimed to be an expert in human health matters and generally relies on industry to set the standards. The effects of radio-frequency (RF) emissions are only now being studied, and everyone acknowledges that the scientific data is far from complete.
>
> As a practical matter, this seemingly trivial section in the massive Telecom Act removes from state and local governments power to make decisions about where cellular and PCS towers should be located in order to protect citizens from possible health risks. The potential magnitude of this problem becomes apparent when one considers the number of towers being built by the telecommunications industry.
>
> By now, virtually every community in the country has been touched by the phenomenon which has been called "the pin-cushioning of America." Some commentators have complained that towers which provide space for the PCS and/or cellular antennas have been

appearing "like mushrooms after the rain." It is predicted that 100,000 new towers will be needed in the next few years to accommodate the growing needs of these industries.

While state and local governments generally retain the ability to regulate the placement of such facilities on the basis of considerations such as aesthetics, they cannot promulgate zoning regulations or ordinances based on any potential health risks from the RF emissions from these towers. Moreover, in at least one state, the courts have found that the language in the Telecom Act also precludes individual citizens from presenting evidence about health risks in private litigation.

Industry claims such preemption is necessary in order to enable them to build out their systems, which they say everyone wants and needs. They argue that state and local regulation is both unnecessary and counter-productive because the FCC is already regulating RF exposure. On the other hand, critics complain that the Telecom Act, by preempting state and local regulation in this manner, has created "a serious threat to our health and environment in ways that Congress simply did not understand when they passed the Telecommunications Act of 1996." * * *

SPRINT SPECTRUM v. WILLOTH

United States Court of Appeals, Second Circuit, 1999.
176 F.3d 630.

JOHN M. WALKER, JR., CIRCUIT JUDGE:

* * *

On or about May 5, 1996, Sprint presented its proposal to build three cell sites to representatives from Ontario as part of its plan to provide PCS services to the town. * * * The Planning Board first considered Sprint's three applications at its public meeting on June 11, 1996. At the meeting, Sprint generally described the PCS technology and reviewed its plans. The Board decided to hold a public hearing on Sprint's application on July 9, 1996, and asked Sprint to submit a Full Environmental Assessment Form ("FEAF") and visual addendum for each application so that the Planning Board could determine whether Sprint was required to file an environmental impact statement ("EIS") pursuant to New York's State Environmental Quality Review Act ("SEQRA").

SEQRA requires agencies to evaluate whether pending actions have significant environmental consequences, and if so, requires the agency to go through an EIS procedure beginning with a draft EIS ("DEIS") and continuing through a final EIS ("FEIS") aimed at ferreting out the environmental consequences of approving a project as well as practicable mitigating measures.

Following the public hearing, the Board met to review Sprint's applications on August 13, 1996 in accordance with SEQRA's requirements. That meeting primarily revolved around alternative sites and network designs for the Town of Ontario which the Board had asked Sprint to consider. The discussions included whether two 250 foot towers located in the industrial or industrial transitional zone would meet Sprint's needs, and whether it would be feasible for Sprint's proposed towers to be lower.

At a special meeting held on September 3, 1996, the Board adopted a resolution "to declare a positive environmental impact" pursuant to SEQRA regarding the three proposed sites. The resolution indicated that there might be some potentially significant adverse environmental impact associated with Sprint's proposals, roughly described as impact on property values, visual impact and "cumulative impacts" of the proposed facilities and possible future facilities * * *

At its May 20, 1997 meeting, the Board accepted the DEIS as complete, and, after a public hearing on July 8, 1997, Sprint submitted a FEIS to the Board on August 8, 1997. * * *

On September 25, 1997, the Board, faced with a choice between three towers or none, concluded that Sprint had failed to mitigate the environmental impact to the largest extent practicable and denied the application.

Sprint challenged the Board's decision under the Telecommunications Act as well as under New York State law * * *

The Telecommunications Act of 1996 ("TCA"), codified at 47 U.S.C. § 151 et seq., is an omnibus overhaul of the federal regulation of communications companies, intended:

> to provide for a pro-competitive, de-regulatory national policy framework designed to accelerate rapidly private sector deployment of advanced telecommunications and information technologies and services ... by opening all telecommunications markets to competition....

H.R. Conf. Rep. No. 104–458, at 113 (1996). In furtherance of this goal, Congress enacted 47 U.S.C. § 332(c)(7) which limits the state and local government's authority to deny construction of wireless telecommunications towers, see id. § 332(c)(7)(B)(i), and regulates how such decisions must be made, see id. §§ 332(c)(7)(B)(ii)–(iv). Although the TCA preserves local zoning authority in all other respects over the siting of wireless facilities, id. § 332(c)(7)(A), "the method by which siting decisions are made is now subject to judicial oversight. Therefore, denials subject to the TCA are reviewed by this court more closely" than are other types of zoning decisions to which federal courts generally accord great deference.

The two principal limitations on local zoning authority, both of which are at issue in this case, are found in subsection B(i), which provides that state and local regulation of "the placement, construction, and modification of personal wireless service facilities ... (I) shall not unreasonably discriminate among providers of functionally equivalent services; and (II) shall not prohibit or have the effect of prohibiting the provision of personal wireless services." 47 U.S.C. § 332(c)(7)(B)(i).

A denial of a request to build wireless facilities must be "in writing and supported by substantial evidence contained in a written record," id. § 332(c)(7)(B)(iii), and not contrary to the limits on town authority set forth in id. § 332(c)(7)(B)(i). Whether a decision is supported by substantial evidence must be determined according to " 'the traditional standard used for judicial review of agency actions.' " *Cellular Tel. Co.,* 166 F.3d at 494. Substantial evidence requires evaluation of the entire record, including opposing evidence, and requires a decision to be supported by "less than a preponderance but more than a scintilla of evidence. 'It means such relevant evidence as a reasonable mind might accept as adequate to support a conclusion.' " *Cellular Tel. Co.,* 166 F.3d at 494.

Sprint claims it has been subjected to unreasonable discrimination in violation of subsection B(i)(I) because its application was treated less favorably than that of Frontier Corp., a cellular provider whose application for a single tower in the town's industrial area was approved by the Town Board in 1993. The record is sparse on this issue, but Sprint appears to base its claim on two grounds. First, Sprint asserts, and the Planning Board concedes, that Frontier did not have to undergo the extensive environmental review process with which Sprint had to contend. Second, Sprint points out that Frontier was permitted to construct a tower, consistent with its coverage plan, that allows it to provide in-building coverage, whereas Sprint's application for the three towers it requires to provide in-building coverage was denied.

Sprint has produced no direct evidence that Frontier provides greater coverage than Sprint would be able to if it were to site one or two towers in less sensitive parts of town. Sprint only points out that PCS systems (like Sprint's) require more towers than do analog cellular systems (like Frontier's) to provide the same level of service. * * *

We assume, arguendo, that the Board's treatment of Sprint's application could be construed as discriminatory because (1) Sprint, but not Frontier, was required to undergo a time-consuming and costly environmental quality review procedure, and (2) the Board's denial of Sprint's three tower application could disable Sprint from matching Frontier's level of coverage. Even so, we think that the Planning Board's actions still would not be "unreasonable" within the meaning of subsection B(i)(I). "[T]he Act explicitly contemplates that some discrimination among providers of functionally equivalent services is allowed. Any discrimination need only be reasonable." *AT & T Wireless PCS, Inc. v. City Council of Va. Beach,* 155 F.3d 423, 427 (4th Cir.1998). The legislative history of the TCA contemplated that the very form of discrimination asserted by Sprint would occur and should be permitted.

[T]he phrase "unreasonably discriminate among providers of functionally equivalent services" will provide localities with the flexibility to treat facilities that create different visual, aesthetic, or safety concerns differently to the extent permitted under generally applicable zoning requirements even if those facilities provide functionally equivalent services. For example, the conferees do not intend that if a State or local government grants a permit in a commercial district, it must also grant a permit for a competitor's 50–foot tower in a residential district.

In other words, local governments may reasonably take the location of the telecommunications tower into consideration when deciding whether: (1) to require a more probing inquiry, and (2) to approve an application for construction of wireless telecommunications facilities, even though this may result in discrimination between providers of functionally equivalent services. See *AT & T Wireless PCS,* 155 F.3d at 427 (discrimination based on traditional bases of zoning regulation such as preserving character of neighborhood and avoiding aesthetic blight is not unreasonable). As far as the record reveals, that is what occurred in this case. Thus, we reject Sprint's unreasonable discrimination claim.

Sprint claims that the Planning Board's refusal to approve its application to construct three towers "prohibit[s] or [has] the effect of prohibiting the provision of personal wireless services" in violation of subsection (B)(i)(II).

The essence of Sprint's argument is that it has the right under this provision of the TCA to construct any and all towers that, in its business judgment, it deems necessary to compete effectively with other telecommunications providers, wireless or not. Otherwise, Sprint argues in substance, the effect will be to "prohibit ... the provision of personal wireless services." This untenable position founders on the statutory language. Since Sprint admits it would never propose to build towers it deems unnecessary to compete successfully, a fact which undoubtedly will hold true for most service providers, such a rule would effectively nullify a local government's right to deny construction of wireless telecommunications facilities, a right explicitly contemplated in 47 U.S.C. § 332(c)(7)(B)(iii). See *AT & T Wireless PCS,* 155 F.3d at 428.

In support of its claim to provide services as it sees fit, Sprint points to the TCA's purposes "[t]o promote competition and reduce regulation in order to secure lower prices and higher quality services for American telecommunications consumers and encourage the rapid deployment of new telecommunications technologies." Pub.L. No. 104–104, 100 Stat. 56, preamble (1996). Sprint also argues correctly that some of the competition contemplated by the TCA may come from personal wireless services, since such services can be a substitute for traditional land-line based systems. See 47 U.S.C. § 332(c)(3)(A) (commercial mobile service providers not exempt from state-imposed universal availability requirements "where such services are a substitute for land line telephone exchange service for a substantial portion of the communications within such State").

We do not read the TCA to allow the goals of increased competition and rapid deployment of new technology to trump all other important considerations, including the preservation of the autonomy of states and municipalities. In the context of constructing a national wireless telecommunications infrastructure, Congress chose to preserve all local zoning authority "over decisions regarding the placement, construction, and modification of personal wireless service facilities," 47 U.S.C. § 332(c)(7)(A), subject only to the limitations set forth in section 332(c)(7)(B). Sprint's ability to compete with land-line based services simply is not part of the inquiry under subsection B. Subsection B(i)(I) speaks only to Sprint's ability to compete with "functionally equivalent services," which does not include land-line services. Because subsection B(i)(II) only considers whether a town's decision will have the effect of prohibiting personal wireless services in a given area, Sprint's reliance on that subsection to contend that it cannot be prohibited from competing effectively with land-line systems is misplaced.

* * *

The Planning Board's principal argument to the contrary is equally untenable. * * * Absent an explicit policy banning personal wireless services, the Board contends, courts can only consider whether in aggregate a town's repeated denials of applications have the effect of a general ban. Since Ontario does not have a general ban in effect, as evidenced by its earlier approval of Frontier's application and professed willingness to accept some level of PCS service, the Board insists its actions must necessarily be in conformance with subsection B(i)(II). We disagree with this reasoning.

The Planning Board's interpretation would essentially convert subsection B(i)(II) into a simple directive to consider applications on a case-by-case basis. * * * Since the Planning Board's interpretation would run counter to the TCA's stated goals, and since the plain language of the statute compels a solution that accommodates the TCA's purposes and that does not render any portion of subsection B(i)(II) superfluous, we refuse to adopt the Board's interpretation.

Construing subsection B(i)(II) to apply only to general bans would lead to the conclusion that, in the absence of an explicit anti-tower policy, a court would have to wait for a series of denied applications before it could step in and force a local government to end its illegal boycott of personal wireless services. That solution does not fit well or easily within the statutory scheme of expedited appeal set forth in subsection B(v) and the preferred remedy of imposing injunctive relief on local governments that impermissibly deny tower construction applications.

Interpreting subsection B(i)(II) as only prohibiting general bans also would lead to the untenable result that once personal wireless services are available somewhere within the jurisdiction of a state or local government, whether by virtue of a facility located outside or inside its borders, the state or local government could deny any further applications with impunity. * * * We believe that what is meant by the Act's proscription that local government regulation of wireless service facilities "shall not prohibit or have the effect of prohibiting the provision of personal wireless services" lies between the extreme positions argued by

Sprint and the Planning Board. The question for us to resolve is what Congress meant by "personal wireless services." The plain statutory language of subsection B(i)(II) read in conjunction with the appropriate definitions set forth in the TCA provides the answer.

"It would be [a] gross understatement to say that the Telecommunications Act of 1996 is not a model of clarity." *AT & T Corp. v. Iowa Utils. Bd.*, 525 U.S. 366, 119 S.Ct. 721, 738, 142 L.Ed.2d 835 (1999). Our task, regrettably, requires a detailed parsing of the statutory language, including layers of highly technical definitions. From this exercise, however, we conclude that the parameters of the statutory proscription of local government's prohibition of "personal wireless services" in the context of this case depends upon a conception of "personal wireless services" that is the equivalent of the ability of mobile, handheld telephones to reach a cell site that provides access to a land-line exchange and allows phone calls to be made to and from the national telephone network.

"Personal wireless services" is defined, if somewhat opaquely, as "[1] commercial mobile services, [2] unlicensed wireless services, and [3] common carrier wireless exchange access services." 47 U.S.C. § 332(c)(7)(C)(i). Each of the three individual terms are further defined in the TCA, although some of the definitions are lacking in both clarity and apparent usefulness. Each will be considered in turn.

1. "Commercial mobile services" is essentially defined as mobile service for profit that makes interconnected service available to the public. See id. § 332(d)(1). "Interconnected service" is in turn defined as "service that is interconnected with the public switched network...." Id. § 332(d)(2). The FCC defines "public switched network," as "[a]ny common carrier switched network, whether by wire or radio, including local exchange carriers, interexchange carriers, and mobile service providers, that use the North American Numbering Plan in connection with the provision of switched services," 47 C.F.R. § 20.3, which in plain language means the public telephone network. See id. § 68.2. "Mobile service" is defined in pertinent part as "a radio communication service carried on between mobile stations or receivers and land stations." 47 U.S.C. § 153(27). "Commercial mobile services" therefore means a for profit radio communication services carried on between mobile stations or receivers and land stations that are connected to the national telephone network.

2. "Unlicensed wireless services," is defined as "the offering of telecommunications services using duly authorized devices which do not require individual licenses...." Id. § 332(c)(7)(C). Since Sprint's PCS network requires a license, that part of the definition is not relevant to this case.

3. "Common carrier wireless exchange access services," as with other definitions in this statutory maze, consists of several individually defined terms. Sprint is a "common carrier" as defined in id. § 153(10), because it offers its common carrier services for hire, and this definition

therefore is pertinent to this case. "Exchange access" is defined as "the offering of access to telephone exchange services or facilities for the purpose of the origination or termination of telephone toll services." Id. § 153(16). In other words, this part of the definition of "personal wireless services" deals with the ability to make and receive telephone calls using wireless equipment.

For the reader who has chosen to follow this exercise, the end is near. Putting together the first and third components of the definition of "personal wireless services," those relevant to this case, we can conclude that the local government is proscribed from prohibiting for-profit radio communication services carried on between mobile stations or receivers and land stations that (1) are connected to the national telephone network and that (2) provide wireless phones with access to telephone exchange services or facilities for the purpose of the origination or termination of telephone toll services.

By speaking in terms of communications between land stations (cell sites that connect directly to land-lines) and mobile stations (wireless telephones) and access to facilities necessary to make and receive phone calls, the plain focus of the statute is on whether it is possible for a user in a given remote location to reach a facility that can establish connections to the national telephone network. In our view, therefore, the most compelling reading of subsection B(i)(II) is that local governments may not regulate personal wireless service facilities in such a way as to prohibit remote users from reaching such facilities. In other words, local governments must allow service providers to fill gaps in the ability of wireless telephones to have access to land-lines.

The Planning Board argues that our interpretation would render illusory the town's right to deny applications, a right contemplated in subsection B(iii). We disagree.

A local government may reject an application for construction of a wireless service facility in an under-served area without thereby prohibiting personal wireless services if the service gap can be closed by less intrusive means. There are numerous ways to limit the aesthetic impact of a cell site. It may be possible to select a less sensitive site, to use a preexisting structure or to camouflage the tower and/or antennae * * * A local government may also reject an application that seeks permission to construct more towers than the minimum required to provide wireless telephone services in a given area. A denial of such a request is not a prohibition of personal wireless services as long as fewer towers would provide users in the given area with some ability to reach a cell site.

Furthermore, once an area is sufficiently serviced by a wireless service provider, the right to deny applications becomes broader: State and local governments may deny subsequent applications without thereby violating subsection B(i)(II). The right to deny applications will still be tempered by subsection B(i)(I), which prohibits unreasonable discrimination. However, it is not unreasonably discriminatory to deny a subsequent application for a cell site that is substantially more intrusive than existing cell sites by virtue of its structure, placement or cumulative impact. We hold only that the Act's ban on prohibiting personal wireless services precludes denying an application for a facility that is the least intrusive means for closing a significant gap in a remote user's ability to reach a cell site that provides access to land-lines.

Turning to Sprint's application in this case, the evidence in the record establishes that two towers and possibly even a single tower would allow Sprint to provide in-vehicle coverage throughout the entire town of Ontario, and in-building coverage throughout most of it, including the more densely populated areas. Where the holes in coverage are very limited in number or size (such as the interiors of buildings in a sparsely populated rural area, or confined to a limited number of houses or spots as the area covered by buildings increases) the lack of coverage likely will be de minimis so that denying applications to construct towers necessary to fill these holes will not amount to a prohibition of service.

Because there is substantial evidence in the record to support the conclusion that virtually all of Ontario could be serviced with fewer than three towers, the Planning Board did not violate subsection B(i)(II)'s ban on prohibiting personal wireless services by rejecting Sprint's all or nothing application. See Town of Amherst, 173 F.3d at 14 (no prohibition of personal wireless services where "lower towers could be used (and possibly resited)").

The TCA imposes limits on the authority of state and local governments to restrict personal wireless services. The TCA itself does not provide the legal basis to deny an application to construct a personal wireless facility. That authority must be found in state or local law. In this case, it is state law that prescribes the Planning Board's obligation to deny a site plan that does not satisfy SEQRA's substantive and procedural requirements.

* * *

Aesthetics is generally a valid subject of municipal regulation and concern both under the Planning Board's review of a site plan. While there are times when "the inclusion of a permitted use in a local zoning ordinance is tantamount to a legislative finding that the permitted use is in harmony with the general zoning plan and will not adversely affect the local community," *WEOK Broad. Corp.*, 79 N.Y.2d at 383, 583 N.Y.S.2d 170, 592 N.E.2d 778, the fact that the towers constitute a permitted use is "by no means determinative," id. A local zoning ordinance permitting a specific type of structure, such as radio or television towers, may give rise to a presumption "that the aesthetic visual impact of the towers was . . . considered at the time that radio and television towers were included as permitted uses in the . . . zone." Id. But no such presumption is warranted here because the pertinent zoning ordinance permits "utility substations," a term encompassing a multitude of structures. This general term does not support the inference that the Ontario Town Board considered and accepted the aesthetic impact of telecommunications towers. To the contrary, a natural reading of the applicable zoning ordinance is that the Town Board left open for future consideration by the Planning Board on a case-by-case basis the compatibility between a proposed structure and the affected neighborhood. Consequently, the Planning Board is neither precluded from evaluating the aesthetic impact of Sprint's proposal, nor must it overcome a presumption that Sprint's towers are in conformance with the neighborhood character.

The Board's decision to reject Sprint's application on aesthetic grounds will be impervious to attack in the courts where "the Board ... has made a reasoned elaboration resulting from its 'hard look' pursuant to SEQRA review such that it can be concluded that its findings and determination are supported by substantial evidence," id. and is not otherwise "affected by an error of law, or its decision was not rational, or is arbitrary or capricious...." Id.

* * *

Sprint's contrary assertions notwithstanding, the evidence in the record before us is more than adequate to support the Planning Board's conclusion that Sprint's three tower proposal would have a significant negative aesthetic impact. Sprint submitted information about minimum tower height requirements and photographic simulations, admitting that "[b]y necessity, the tower will be visible from a wide area surrounding the site." The real estate experts consulted by the Planning Board stated that the towers would have a stigmatizing effect based in part on aesthetics which would reduce the buyer pool, leading to a 10% to 25% reduction in property values. The stigmatizing effect is substantiated by a letter written by Sprint's attorney to the neighboring town of Walworth's planning board, explaining Sprint's difficulties in finding alternate property sites. A real estate expert hired by Sprint even admitted that "a diminished supply of potential buyers ... concededly may exist for a property which views or is in the vicinity of a nearby tower installation," but predicted that the property value would not be affected. The Planning Board was, of course, entitled to disregard that prediction where two of its own real estate experts concluded otherwise.

* * *

The Planning Board also found that approving Sprint's application would set a precedent that could "result [in] ... a large number of towers in the town," and concluded that "the cumulative impact of multiple towers would have a significant environmental impact on the Town of Ontario." Sprint challenges this analysis, arguing that the Planning Board could not consider the cumulative impact of future applicants because no applications were currently pending. We disagree. * * * Given the Planning Board's correct determination that it could not discriminate between providers, the nexus between Sprint's application and the identified cumulative effects is so close that the Planning Board acted well within its discretion in considering the cumulative effects of Sprint's application.

* * *

Affirmed.

Note

A large number of cases can be found interpreting the Telecommunications Act of 1996. See, for some representative examples, Independent Wireless One Corp. v. Town of Charlotte, 242 F.Supp.2d 409 (D.Vt.2003); USCOC of Virginia RSA #3, Inc. v. Montgomery County, 343 F.3d 262 (4th Cir.2003).

Further Notes on Federal Preemption

Normally, we do not think of the federal government setting out to override local land use regulations, and indeed that issue is rarely discussed in the formulation of federal law or regulations. However, in recent years more and more instances appear to conflict—or apparently conflict—between local land use ordinances and federal statutes or regulations. Cataloging all such conflicts is impossible, however, the previous sections highlighted the issues that are currently heavily litigated. Other examples of federal preemption in the land use arena include:

1. The Federal Railway Safety Act has been held to preempt all local railroad safety legislation (except state law in an area where the Secretary of Transportation has not issued a regulation or order, and stricter state law is necessary). CSX Transportation, Inc. v. City of Plymouth, 86 F.3d 626 (6th Cir.1996). In this case the court held that a local ordinance prohibiting trains from obstructing streets for more than five minutes was preempted by the federal act. The reasoning was that compliance with the local ordinance would require railroads to schedule shorter, more frequent trains, with a concomitant effect on train traffic accident rates. Many communities where railroads still operate have ordinances like the one held preempted.

2. In Payless ShoeSource, Inc. v. Town of Penfield, New York, 934 F.Supp. 540 (W.D.N.Y.1996), the court considered the application of a town sign ordinance that required all commercial signs in a particular area to be either yellow, red, or white. The owner of a retail shoe store claimed that the sign ordinance conflicted with a federally registered trademark. The trademarked sign was yellow with two orange-colored "O"s. The court held that the sign ordinance was not preempted by the federal Lanham Act provision prohibiting a state or one of its subdivisions from requiring "alteration" of a federally registered mark.

3. Local regulation of television satellite dishes and antennas was specifically preempted by FCC regulation. 47 C.F.R. § 25.104 et seq. This specific preemption came about as a result of widespread aesthetic concerns, particularly in suburban communities, when satellite receiving dishes became popular in the 1970's and thereafter. See Loschiavo v. City of Dearborn, 33 F.3d 548 (6th Cir.1994), holding that the FCC regulation precluding enforcement of zoning restrictions regulating satellite dishes created a private right of action under 42 U.S.C. § 1983. But see Camco Cable

Services, Inc. v. City of Lauderhill, 13 F.Supp.2d 1329 (S.D.Fla.1998) holding that the federal regulation protecting the right of antenna users to receive satellite signals does not confer a federal right upon a cable services company, and therefore does not confer standing to bring § 1983 action.

4. The National Manufactured Housing and Safety Standards Act, 42 U.S.C. §§ 5401–5426 has been held to preempt city ordinances imposing greater safety requirements for mobile or manufactured homes. Scurlock v. City of Lynn Haven, Florida, 858 F.2d 1521 (11th Cir.1988); but the act does not preempt zoning of mobile home locations, King v. City of Bainbridge, 276 Ga. 484, 577 S.E.2d 772 (2003).

5. The Stewart B. McKinney Homeless Assistance Act, 42 U.S.C.A. § 11301 et seq. requires federal agencies to make surplus and underutilized federal property available to lease to organizations wishing to provide housing for homeless persons. This act was held to preempt local zoning ordinances in United States v. Village of New Hempstead, New York, 832 F.Supp. 76 (S.D.N.Y.1993).

6. CERCLA (Comprehensive Environmental Response, Compensation and Liability Act) has been held to preempt conflicting state or local regulation ("conflict preemption"). See, e.g., United States v. Denver, 100 F.3d 1509 (10th Cir.1996). This case pitted a local zoning restriction on maintenance of hazardous waste in industrial zones against an EPA order requiring the owner of a site in the city to do on-site solidification of soils contaminated with radioactive waste.

7. Environmental Justice is the fair treatment and meaningful involvement of all people regardless of race, color, national origin, or income with respect to the development, implementation, and enforcement of environmental laws, regulations, and policies. Fair treatment means that no group of people, including a racial, ethnic, or a socioeconomic group, should bear a disproportionate share of the negative environmental consequences resulting from industrial, municipal, and commercial operations or the execution of federal, state, local, and tribal programs and policies. Meaningful involvement means that: (1) potentially affected community residents have an appropriate opportunity to participate in decisions about a proposed activity that will affect their environment and/or health; (2) the public's contribution can influence the regulatory agency's decision; (3) the concerns of all participants involved will be considered in the decision making process; and (4) the decision makers seek out and facilitate the involvement of those potentially affected. In sum, environmental justice is the goal to be achieved for all communities and persons across this Nation. Environmental justice is achieved when everyone, regardless of race, culture, or income, enjoys the same degree of protection from environmental and health hazards and equal access to the decision-making process to have a healthy environment in which to live, learn, and work. A federal Interagency Working Group on Environmental Justice (IWG) was established in 1994 pursuant to Executive Order 12898. The National Environmental Justice Advisory Council (NEJAC) is a federal advisory committee established by charter on September 30, 1993, to provide independent advice, consultation, and recommendations to the Administrator of the U.S. Environmental Protection Agency (EPA) on

matters related to environmental justice. See, www.epa.gov/compliance/environmentaljustice.

Although there is no federal statute or specific regulation entitled "environmental justice," advocates successfully utilize the authority of the Civil Rights Act of 1964 to enforce environmental justice principles. A recent study by the National Academy of Public Administration, Addressing Community Concerns: How Environmental Justice Relates to Land Use Planning and Zoning (July 2003), clearly signals that planning and zoning decision makers need to be more aware of environmental concerns (the report is available at www.napawash.org/pubs/ej.pdf). There is likely to be a flurry of lawsuits over the next decade challenging the decisions and actions of local officials relative to land use matters and environmental justice. For an excellent summary of the various land use planning and zoning techniques that impact environmental justice concerns, see Craig Anthony Arnold, Planning Milagros: Environmental Justice and Land Use Regulation, 76 Denv. U. L. Rev. 1 (1998).

For some recent examples of how the public is using environmental justice principles in litigation, see, In the Matter of the Application of Rhino Environmental Services, Colonias Development Council v. Rhino Environmental Services, 138 N.M. 133, 117 P.3d 939 (Sup.Ct.2005) (Holding that in reviewing a permit for an application to operate a landfill, the New Mexico Environment Department is required to consider public opinion at a public hearing including testimony regarding the proposed landfill's adverse impact on a community's quality of life); and Coliseum Square Ass'n, Inc. v. Jackson, 465 F.3d 215 (5th Cir.2006). In this case, the Circuit Court found that the environmental justice study performed by HUD was neither capricious nor arbitrary in its choice of methodology. While the court cited Executive Order 12898, it did not interpret the order as granting the appellants a private right of action, defaulting to the APA's deferential "arbitrary and capricious" standard. The court saw "no administrative insensitivity to racial or economic inequality" and concluded there was no reason to find that HUD's determination that local zoning changes would create a significantly detrimental environmental impact.

In September 2006, the Office of the Inspector General of the U.S. EPA released a follow-up evaluation report on the U.S. Environmental Protection Agency's performance in the conduct of environmental justice reviews of programs, policies and activities. Among other things, the report found that "EPA senior management has not sufficiently directed program and regional offices to conduct environment justice reviews in accordance with Executive Order 12898. Consequently, the majority of respondents reported their programs or offices have not performed environmental justice reviews. Though some offices may not be subject to an environmental justice review, the respondents expressed a need for further guidance to conduct reviews, including protocols, a framework, or additional directions. Until these program and regional offices perform environmental justice reviews, the Agency cannot determine whether its programs cause disproportionately high and adverse human health or environmental effects on minority and low-income populations." The full report and recommendations can be accessed at: www.epa.gov/oigearth/reports/2006/20060918–2006–P–00034.pdf.

For an excellent fifty-state survey on how environmental justice is being implemented across the country at the state and local level, see Environmental Justice for All A Fifty State Survey of Legislation, Policies and Cases, Third Edition, available at www.uchastings.edu/?pid=1353. The report explains: "Beginning with New Hampshire's pioneering EJ policy in 1993, at least thirty-two states and the District of Columbia have adopted formal environmental justice statutes, executive orders, or policies. (citations omitted) In addition, ten additional states either employ full-time environmental justice officers or personnel, or have active EJ programs. Viewed collectively, the efforts of these forty-one states demonstrate significant and increased attention to the issue of environmental justice at the level of state government."

8. The Endangered Species Act of 1973, 16 U.S.C. §§ 1531–1544 provides "for conservation, protection and propagation of endangered species ... by Federal action and by encouraging the establishment of State endangered species conservation programs." S. Rep. No. 307, 93rd Cong., 1st Sess., 1, reprinted in 1973 U.S. Code Cong. & Admin. News 2989–90. Section 9 of the ESA prohibits "any person or agency" from "taking" an endangered species of fish or wildlife. This is where local land use decisionmaking is implicated. See, Comment, The Scope of Federal Authority Under the Endangered Species Act: Implications for Local Land Use Planning, 65 Alb. L. Rev. 497 (2001); Coggins & Russell, Beyond Shooting Snail Darters in Pork Barrels: Endangered Species and Land Use in America, 70 Geo. L.J. 1433 (1982); and Michael Cassidy and Michael Donohue, "The Endangered Species Act and Land Use Planning," 29 No. 9 Zoning and Planning Law Report 1 (September 2006).

E. REGULATING ADULT BUSINESS USES

A variety of ordinary commercial uses may be excluded from communities as municipalities exercise their zoning power to safeguard the public health and welfare. The desire of local officials to exclude adult business uses, however, has proved more difficult since the regulation of adult entertainment facilities and sexually-oriented businesses is subject to First Amendment considerations. In one of the leading cases on this issue, Young v. American Mini Theatres, Inc., 427 U.S. 50, 96 S.Ct. 2440, 49 L.Ed.2d 310 (1976), the Supreme Court upheld a zoning ordinance that prohibited any "adult" movie theater, book store, and similar establishments within 1000 feet of any other such establishment, or within 500 feet of a residential area, after finding that the regulation did not violate the First Amendment. In reaching this conclusion, the court stressed that, although the First Amendment protects sexually explicit forms of communication from total suppression, municipalities have the power to place reasonable restrictions on the time, place, and manner in which these materials are showcased or sold, if the regulations are necessary to further some significant governmental interest. In Young, the Supreme Court upheld the exclusionary ordinance finding that the regulation was needed to develop an overall plan for the community and to regulate the use of commercial property within its borders.

Secondary effects studies have become an essential condition precedent to the enactment of local adult use ordinances to support the legitimate governmental interest in regulating these uses. City of Renton v. Playtime Theaters, Inc., 475 U.S. 41, 106 S.Ct. 925, 89 L.Ed.2d 29 (1986), as well as City of Erie v. Pap's A.M., 529 U.S. 277, 120 S.Ct. 1382, 146 L.Ed.2d 265 (2000), make it clear that municipalities may rely on similar studies in other jurisdictions to support their regulations. Justice O'Connor, however, warned in City of Los Angeles v. Alameda Books, Inc., 535 U.S. 425, 122 S.Ct. 1728, 152 L.Ed.2d 670 (2002) that municipalities cannot get away with shoddy data or reasoning and that "the municipality's evidence must fairly support the municipality's rationale for its ordinance."

SECRET DESIRES LINGERIE, INC. v. CITY OF ATLANTA

Supreme Court of Georgia, 1996.
266 Ga. 760, 470 S.E.2d 879.

THOMPSON, JUSTICE.

On October 4, 1993, the City of Atlanta enacted an ordinance to regulate lingerie modeling studios. Appellants challenged the constitutionality of the ordinance, seeking declaratory and injunctive relief. Following a trial, the superior court upheld the constitutionality of the ordinance. This appeal followed.

Appellants assert the City did not rely upon relevant evidence of the undesirable secondary effects of lingerie modeling studios when it enacted the ordinance and that, therefore, the ordinance cannot pass constitutional muster. We agree.

When a governing body enacts an ordinance regulating adult entertainment establishments because of their purported undesireable secondary effects, it must rely upon specific evidence showing a correlation between such establishments and the undesirable secondary effects the governing body seeks to control. *Chambers v. Peach County*, 266 Ga. 318, 320, 467 S.E.2d 519 (1996). The governing body can rely on evidence in the form of studies performed by other governmental units. *City of Renton v. Playtime Theatres*, 475 U.S. 41, 51, 106 S.Ct. 925, 930–31, 89 L.Ed.2d 29 (1986); *Discotheque v. City Council of Augusta*, 264 Ga. 623, 624, 449 S.E.2d 608 (1994). It can rely on evidence in the form of its own formal studies, see *World Famous Dudley's v. City of College Park*, 265 Ga. 618, 619, 458 S.E.2d 823 (1995), and it may rely on evidence not contained in formal studies. See *Parker v. Whitfield County*, 265 Ga. 829, 463 S.E.2d 116 (1995) (county relied upon studies of other communities as well as formal and informal meetings between members of the board, county sheriff's department, county residents and commissioners of other counties). The studies need not be perfect, *World Famous Dudley's v. City of College Park, supra*, but they must be considered before the ordinance is passed in order for the ordinance to be considered as one enacted for the purpose of combating the undesirable secondary effects of sexually explicit businesses. *Chambers v. Peach County, supra.* In a lawsuit challenging the constitutionality of an ordinance regulating adult business establishments, the governing body must be able to offer evidence of the studies it relied upon in enacting the ordinance. Id. If it cannot do so, the ordinance cannot be deemed constitutional.

At trial, the City introduced the testimony of three of its vice squad officers who opined that there is a correlation between lingerie modeling studios and prostitution. But the City did not even show that members of the city council were aware of the officers' conclusions, much less that the ordinance was enacted on the basis of those conclusions. And the ordinance itself sheds no light on this issue.

Compare *World Famous Dudley's v. City of College Park, supra,* in which the preamble of an ordinance regulating adult business establishments recited that it was based on the experiences of certain cities.

The City is unable to point to any evidence demonstrating that it considered specific studies of the pernicious secondary effects of lingerie modeling studios before enacting the ordinance. Although the trial court found that the City had knowledge of the police officers' conclusions prior to the enactment of the ordinance, the trial court's finding is clearly erroneous. There is not a scintilla of evidence demonstrating that the police officers (or their superiors) alerted the city council to the problems they uncovered.

The trial court erred in upholding the constitutionality of the ordinance. *Chambers v. Peach County, supra.*

Judgment reversed.

All the Justices concur, except FLETCHER, P.J., and HUNSTEIN, J., who dissent.

FLETCHER, PRESIDING JUSTICE, dissenting.

The trial court found that the City of Atlanta had knowledge of the secondary effects of lingerie modeling studios "prior to and at the time" the city council enacted the challenged ordinance. Because this factual finding is not clearly erroneous and the city's ordinance does not violate free speech, I dissent.

* * *

The police officers testified that they had investigated complaints of criminal activity in lingerie modeling studios; had seen acts of prostitution, simulated sex, and public indecency in the establishments; and had arrested one patron for engaging in sexual intercourse with an employee. The officers explained the difficulties they encountered in making arrests and their discussions with their supervisors about how best to curtail the crimes occurring in lingerie modeling shops and other adult entertainment establishments. This testimony shows that the city did not need to collect studies from other cities; it could rely on its own relevant experience in passing the ordinance to prevent crime. After two days of testimony, the trial court found that "acts of public indecency have been taking place in such establishments for several years" and the city was "aware of criminal activities taking place in lingerie modeling studios prior to and at the time the ordinance was enacted." A review of the record shows that the trial court was not clearly erroneous in finding the city relied on its own experience in enacting the ordinance.

In reversing, the majority opinion ignores the rationale for evaluating city ordinances to determine if they impermissibly infringe on free speech. Instead, it collapses federal first amendment law to a single test: whether the city council relied on "specific studies" of secondary effects before enacting the ordinance. Just as a governing body is not required to consider a "study" before adopting regulations that restrict leafletting at a state park or seeking an injunction that restricts demonstrations on public streets and sidewalks outside facilities offering abortions, a city is not required under either the United States Constitution or the Georgia Constitution to consider a "study" before enacting an ordinance that regulates lingerie modeling studios. All the first amendment requires is that a city rely on evidence that it reasonably believes is relevant to its important governmental interests. This court should not require more.

We have never addressed whether lingerie modeling is expressive conduct entitled to the protection of the free speech clause of the United States and Georgia Constitutions. Assuming that it is, this court must determine whether the law furthers an important government interest, the government interest is unrelated to the suppression of speech, and the incidental restriction of speech is no greater than is essential to further the government interest. The Atlanta ordinance meets this test. First, the trial court found that acts of public indecency had occurred in lingerie modeling establishments for years and that the city was aware of these criminal activities in enacting the ordinance. Second, the city's interest in preventing crime is unrelated to the suppression of expressive conduct. Third, the restrictions in the ordinance are no greater than is essential to further the city's interest in crime prevention. Unlike the total ban on private modeling sessions that was challenged in *Quetgles*, [264 Ga. at 708, 450 S.E.2d 677] the challenged ordinance here merely imposes reasonable regulations. The ordinance requires each establishment to obtain a license and employee permits, prohibits locking devices that hinder police inspection, and establishes reasonable closing hours. Because the city's ordinance does not restrict protected expression in violation of the federal or state constitutions, the trial court properly concluded that the ordinance was constitutional. Therefore, I would affirm.

I am authorized to state that Justice Hunstein joins in this dissent.

VOYEUR DORM, L.C. v. CITY OF TAMPA

United States Court of Appeals, Eleventh Circuit, 2001.
265 F.3d 1232.

DUBINA, Circuit Judge:

This appeal arises from Voyeur Dorm L.C.'s ("Voyeur Dorm") alleged violation of Tampa's City Code based on the district court's characterization of Voyeur Dorm as an adult entertainment facility. Because we conclude the district court misapplied Tampa's City Code when it erroneously found that Voyeur Dorm offered adult entertainment to the public at the residence in question, we reverse the judgment of the district court.

As alleged in its complaint, Voyeur Dorm is a Florida limited liability company that maintains offices and conducts its business in Hillsborough County, Florida. Voyeur Dorm operates an internet based web site that provides a 24 hour a day internet transmission portraying the lives of the residents of 2312 West Farwell Drive, Tampa, Florida. Throughout its existence, Voyeur Dorm has employed 25 to 30 different women, most of whom entered into a contract that specifies, among other things, that they are "employees," on a "stage and filming location," with "no reasonable expectation of privacy," for "entertainment purposes." Subscribers to "voyeurdorm.com" pay a subscription fee of $34.95 a month to watch the women employed at the premises and pay an added fee of $16.00 per month to "chat" with the women. From August 1998 to June 2000, Voyeur Dorm generated subscriptions and sales totaling $3,166,551.35.

In 1998, Voyeur Dorm learned that local law enforcement agencies had initiated an investigation into its business. In response, counsel for Voyeur Dorm sent a letter to Tampa's Zoning Coordinator requesting her interpretation of the City Code as it applied to the activities occurring at 2312 West Farwell Drive. In February of 1999, Tampa's Zoning Coordinator, Gloria Moreda, replied to counsel's request and issued her interpretation of the City Code, concluding in relevant part:

> The following generally describes the activities occurring on the property:
>
> 1. 5 unrelated women are residing on the premises.
>
> 2. 30 Internet cameras are located in various rooms in the house; such as the bedrooms, bathrooms, living rooms, shower and kitchen.
>
> 3. For a fee, internet viewers are able to monitor the activities in the different rooms.
>
> 4. The web page address is *http://www.voyeurdorm.com/*
>
> 5. The web page shows various scenes from the house, including a woman with exposed buttocks. Statements on the page describe activities that can be viewed such as "the girls of Voyeur Dorm are fresh, naturally erotic and as young as 18. Catch them in the most intimate acts of youthful indiscretion."
>
> The web page can be found by going to Yahoo! and entering "Voyeurdorm" on the search. The name of the website is, itself, advertising the adult nature of the entertainment. Voyeur is defined in the *American Heritage Dictionary,* Second College Edition as "A [sic] person who derives sexual gratification from observing the sex

organs or sexual acts of others, especially from a secret vantage point."

It is my determination that the use occurring at 2312 W. Farwell Dr., as described in your letter, is an adult use. Section 27–523 defines adult entertainment as: "Any [sic] premises, except those businesses otherwise defined in this chapter, on which is offered to members of the public or any person, for a consideration, entertainment featuring or in any way including specified sexual activities, as defined in this section, or entertainment featuring the displaying or depicting of specified anatomical areas, as defined in this section; 'entertainment' as used in this definition shall include, but not be limited to, books, magazines, films, newspapers, photographs, paintings, drawings, sketches or other publications or graphic media, filmed or live plays, dances or other performances distinguished by their display or depiction of specified anatomical areas or specified anatomical activities, as defined in this section."

Please be aware that the property is zoned RS–60 Residential Single Family, and an adult use business is not permitted use. You should advise your client to cease operation at that location.

Thereafter, in April of 1999, Dan and Sharon Gold Marshlack appealed the Zoning Coordinator's decision to Tampa's Variance Review Board. On or about July 13, 1999, the Variance Review Board conducted a hearing. At the hearing, Voyeur Dorm's counsel conceded the following: that five women live in the house; that there are cameras in the corners of all the rooms of the house; that for a fee a person can join a membership to a web site wherein a member can view the women 24 hours a day, seven days a week; that a member, at times, can see someone disrobed; that the women receive free room and board; that the women are part of a business enterprise; and that the women are paid. At the conclusion of the hearing, the Variance Review Board unanimously upheld the Zoning Coordinator's determination that the use occurring at 2312 West Farwell Drive was an adult use. Subsequently, Mr. and Mrs. Marshlack filed an appeal from the decision of the Variance Review Board to the City Council. The Tampa City Council held a hearing in August of 1999, at the conclusion of which the City Council unanimously affirmed the decision of the Variance Review Board.

* * *

The threshold inquiry is whether section 27–523 of Tampa's City Code applies to the alleged activities occurring at 2312 West Farwell Drive. Because of the way we answer that inquiry, it will not be necessary for us to analyze the thorny constitutional issues presented in this case.

Section 27–523 defines adult entertainment establishments as

[a]ny premises, except those businesses otherwise defined in this chapter, on which is offered to members of the public or any person, for a consideration, entertainment featuring or in any way including

specified sexual activities, as defined in this section, or entertainment featuring the displaying or depicting of specified anatomical areas, as defined in this section; "entertainment" as used in this definition shall include, but not be limited to, books, magazines, films, newspapers, photographs, paintings, drawings, sketches or other publications or graphic media, filmed or live plays, dances or other performances either by single individuals or groups, distinguished by their display or depiction of specified anatomical areas or specified sexual activities, as defined in this section.

Tampa argues that Voyeur Dorm is an adult use business pursuant to the express and unambiguous language of section 27–523 and, as such, cannot operate in a residential neighborhood. In that regard, Tampa points out: that members of the public pay to watch women employed on the premises; that the Employment Agreement refers to the premises as "a stage and filming location"; that certain anatomical areas and sexual activities are displayed for entertainment; and that the entertainers are paid accordingly. Most importantly, Tampa asserts that nothing in the City Code limits its applicability to premises where the adult entertainment is actually consumed.

In accord with Tampa's arguments, the district court specifically determined that the "plain and unambiguous language of the City Code . . . does not expressly state a requirement that the members of the public paying consideration be *on* the premises viewing the adult entertainment." *Voyeur Dorm, L.C., et al. v. City of Tampa, Fla.*, 121 F.Supp.2d 1373 (M.D.Fla.2000) (order granting summary judgment to Tampa). While the public does not congregate to a specific edifice or location in order to enjoy the entertainment provided by Voyeur Dorm, the district court found 2312 West Farwell Drive to be "a premises on which is offered to members of the public for consideration entertainment featuring specified sexual activities within the plain meaning of the City Code." *Id.*

Moreover, the district court relied on Supreme Court and Eleventh Circuit precedent that trumpets a city's entitlement to protect and improve the quality of residential neighborhoods. *See City of Renton v. Playtime Theatres, Inc.*, 475 U.S. 41, 50, 106 S.Ct. 925, 89 L.Ed.2d 29 (1986) ("[A] city's 'interest in attempting to preserve the quality of urban life is one that must be accorded high respect.' ") (quoting *Young v. American Mini Theatres, Inc.*, 427 U.S. 50, 71, 96 S.Ct. 2440, 2453, 49 L.Ed.2d 310 (1976)); *Sammy's of Mobile, Ltd. v. City of Mobile*, 140 F.3d 993, 996–97 (11th Cir.1998) (noting that it is well established that the regulation of public health, safety, and morals is a valid and substantial state interest); *Corn v. City of Lauderdale Lakes*, 997 F.2d 1369, 1375 (11th Cir.1993) (noting that the "Supreme Court has held [that] restrictions may be imposed to protect 'family values, youth values and the blessings of quiet seclusion' ") (internal citations omitted).

In opposition, Voyeur Dorm argues that it is not an adult use business. Specifically, Voyeur Dorm contends that section 27–523 applies to locations or premises wherein adult entertainment is actually offered to the public. Because the public does not, indeed cannot, physically attend 2312 West Farwell Drive to enjoy the adult entertainment, 2312 West Farwell Drive does not fall within the purview of Tampa's zoning ordinance. We agree with this argument.

The residence of 2312 West Farwell Drive provides no "offer[ing] [of adult entertainment] to members of the public." The offering occurs when the videotaped images are dispersed over the internet and into the public eye for consumption. The City Code cannot be applied to a location that does not, itself, offer adult entertainment to the public. As a practical matter, zoning restrictions are indelibly anchored in particular geographic locations. Residential areas are often cordoned off from business districts in order to promote a State's interest. *See, e.g., City of Renton,* 475 U.S. at 50, 106 S.Ct. 925 ("A city's interest in attempting to preserve the quality of urban life is one that must be accorded high respect."). It does not follow, then, that a zoning ordinance designed to restrict facilities that offer adult entertainment can be applied to a particular location that does not, at that location, offer adult entertainment. Moreover, the case law relied upon by Tampa and the district court concerns adult entertainment in which customers *physically attend* the premises wherein the entertainment is performed. Here, the audience or consumers of the adult entertainment do not go to 2312 West Farwell Drive or congregate anywhere else in Tampa to enjoy the entertainment. Indeed, the public offering occurs over the Internet in "virtual space." While the district court read section 27–523 in a literal sense, finding no requirement that the paying public be *on the premises,* we hold that section 27–523 does not apply to a residence at which there is no public offering of adult entertainment. Accordingly, because the district court misapplied section 27–523 to the residence of 2312 West Farwell Drive, we reverse the district court's order granting summary judgment to Tampa. Since the resolution of this threshold issue obviates the need for further analysis, we do not reach the remaining issues regarding the constitutionality of Tampa's zoning restrictions as applied to Voyeur Dorm.

Notes

1. Generally, municipalities may not prohibit adult businesses entirely. City of Renton v. Playtime Theatres, Inc., 475 U.S. 41, 106 S.Ct. 925, 89 L.Ed.2d 29 (1986), however, some sexually oriented uses may be considered so "obnoxious" that total exclusion will be upheld. See, e.g., Wigginess Inc. v. Fruchtman, 482 F.Supp. 681 (S.D.N.Y.1979), upholding a zoning ordinance provision prohibiting the operation of adult physical culture establishments offering massages by members of the opposite sex to their customers, and Northend Cinema, Inc. v. City of Seattle, 90 Wash.2d 709, 585 P.2d 1153 (1978), certiorari denied sub nom. Apple Theatre, Inc. v. City of Seattle, 441 U.S. 946, 99 S.Ct. 2166, 60 L.Ed.2d 1048 (1979), upholding a zoning ordinance prohibiting "adult movie" theaters in all neighborhoods but the downtown district.

2. Although courts will generally uphold ordinances that restrict adult uses to certain zoning districts (see for example, Union Twp. Bd. of Trustees v. Old 74 Corp., 137 Ohio App.3d 289, 738 N.E.2d 477 (2000) and Buzzetti v. City of New York, 140 F.3d 134 (2nd Cir. 1998), courts do sometimes strike down locational zoning for adult businesses. See Topanga Press, Inc. v. City of Los Angeles, 989 F.2d 1524 (9th Cir.1993). Some adult business ordinances falter on the definitions that trigger restrictions. For example, in Triplett Grille, Inc. v. City of Akron, 816 F.Supp. 1249 (N.D.Ohio 1993) the ordinance was struck down as overbroad because it applied to performances which included nudity of any kind, not just erotic entertainment. Also see Barnes v. Glen Theatre, Inc., 501 U.S. 560, 111 S.Ct. 2456, 115 L.Ed.2d 504 (1991), and City of Renton v. Playtime Theatres, 475 U.S. 41, 106 S.Ct. 925, 89 L.Ed.2d 29 (1986). Courts also uphold regulations that require adult uses to be separated from one another. These distancing or dispersal requirements can even apply to existing adult businesses. See, World Wide Video of Washington, Inc. v. City of Spokane, 368 F.3d 1186 (9th Cir. 2004) and N.W. Enterprises Inc. v. City of Houston, 372 F.3d 333 (5th Cir.2004). But, the regulations may not be so restrictive that they constitute essentially preclusion. See, Brookpark News & Books, Inc. v. City of Cleveland, 66 Ohio App.3d 613, 585 N.E.2d 908 (1990).

3. The Voyeur Dorm, L.C. v. City of Tampa case raises the importance of clarity in the drafting of zoning ordinances, particularly when it comes to regulating adult uses. It is not uncommon for adult use restrictions to be voided for vagueness. For example, in Harris Books, Inc. v. City of Santa Fe, 98 N.M. 235, 647 P.2d 868 (1982) adult bookstores and theaters were prohibited within 1,000 feet of a "residential area." The ordinance failed to define "residential area" and the court found the term impermissibly vague. Municipal attempts to define adult uses based on the amount of stock in trade or merchandise are often unsuccessful (see, World Wide Video, Inc. v. City of Tukwila, 117 Wash.2d 382, 816 P.2d 18 (1991) and Encore Videos, Inc. v. City of San Antonio, 330 F.3d 288 (5th Cir.2003), *cert. denied*, 540 U.S. 982, 124 S.Ct. 466, 157 L.Ed.2d 372 (2003), *clarified*, 352 F.3d 938 (5th Cir.2003)).

4. May municipalities restrict the number of adult uses in a building? See, City of Los Angeles v. Alameda Books, Inc., 535 U.S. 425, 122 S.Ct. 1728, 152 L.Ed.2d 670 (2002).

SECTION 2. STATE PREEMPTION

The previous section demonstrated areas where the federal government has intervened through statute and/or regulation to preempt or limit local control over certain types of land uses. The state governments may also play a significant role in limiting or restricting local decision-making control in certain areas. Consider the cases below and the notes that follow.

A. MINING

GERNATT ASPHALT PRODUCTS, INC. v. TOWN OF SARDINIA

New York Court of Appeals, 1996.
87 N.Y.2d 668, 642 N.Y.S.2d 164, 664 N.E.2d 1226.

SIMONS, J.

Petitioner challenges the legality of amendments to the Town of Sardinia's Zoning Ordinance which eliminated mining as a permitted use throughout the Town. The principal issues presented are whether: (1) the Town violated various statutory provisions relating to referral and public notice of the amendments when it enacted some but not all of the amendments that were proposed; (2) the New York State Mined Land Reclamation Law supersedes the Town's authority to amend its Zoning Ordinance in a manner that eliminates mining as a permitted use throughout the Town; and (3) the Town's action constituted impermissible exclusionary zoning. * * *

The Town of Sardinia is a small rural community located in western New York. Farming is the economic mainstay but it is rich in deposits of extractable minerals. Eight mines, covering over 600 acres, are presently located within the Town. These mining uses were lawful under the Town Zoning Ordinance adopted in 1969, which permitted mining in all R–A districts and, by incorporation, in all other districts in the Town. Town Board approval of a mining site was required, however, and approval was conditioned on consideration of the possible nuisance to neighbors of the proposed site and the miner's plan to restore the land after mining operations ceased.

Petitioner Gernatt has conducted mining operations at several sites within the Town for many years and presently owns three operating mines. In 1989, it acquired a 400–acre parcel of land known as the Gabel Thomas property. It has applied to the Department of Environmental Conservation (DEC) for the necessary State permit to mine the site but has not yet received one. Following petitioner's purchase of the Gabel Thomas site, the Town became concerned about the effect its development might have on this rural community, and took a number of steps to regulate the expansion of mining within its borders.

This litigation focuses on three ordinances introduced by the Town Board at its meeting August 18, 1993. The first two were adopted. Section 6.02(A)(5) of the existing Zoning Ordinance made quarries, clay, sand and gravel pits permitted uses in R–A districts, and the first ordinance adopted at the August meeting repealed that section. The second ordinance repealed section 7.07 which required approval of the Town Board to excavate. The third proposal, which designated quarries, clay, sand and gravel pits as specially permitted uses but only at sites currently authorized by DEC, was tabled for further study.

It is important to note three points about the Town's actions and the three proposed amendments: (1) the amendments as enacted did not *prohibit* or terminate existing mining operations throughout the Town—they continued as lawful, but nonconforming uses; (2) the only functional difference between the amendments as proposed and as enacted is the legal status of currently operating mines: while mining on existing sites is now a nonconforming use under the Town's Zoning Ordinance, had the amendments been adopted as proposed mining on existing sites would have been a specially permitted use; and (3) even if all three proposed amendments had been enacted, *new* mining would not have been permitted in the Town, because proposed section 7.07 authorized special permits only for mining sites permitted by the DEC at the time the legislation was enacted.

Petitioner instituted this special proceeding seeking to annul the Board's adoption of the "repealer" amendments and to enjoin the Town from enforcing the nonconforming use provision of its Zoning Ordinance. * * * On appeal, the Appellate Division concluded * * * that the adopted amendments were inconsistent with and preempted by the New York State Mined Land Reclamation Law * * *.

II. The Mined Land Reclamation Law

The Mined Land Reclamation Law (ECL 23–2701 et seq. [the MLRL]) is a comprehensive legislative scheme which broadly empowers the Department of Environmental Conservation to regulate the mining industry in this State. The policies underlying the statute are to foster and encourage an economically sound and stable mining and minerals industry, to manage well depletable mineral resources, and to provide for the reclamation of mined land (see, ECL 23–2703[1] [as originally enacted, L 1974, ch. 1043, and as amended, L 1991, ch. 166]). The Legislature sought to achieve those purposes by replacing the existing patchwork of local regulatory ordinances with "standard and uniform restrictions and regulations" and by addressing the environmental issues related to reclamation of abandoned mining sites (*Matter of Frew Run Gravel Prods. v. Town of Carroll,* 71 N.Y.2d 126, 131–133, 524 N.Y.S.2d 25, 518 N.E.2d 920). As originally enacted, the provisions of the statute expressly superseded "all other state and local laws relating to the extractive mining industry * * * [except] local zoning ordinances or other local laws which impose stricter mined land reclamation standards or requirements than those found herein" (ECL 23–2703 [former (2)]).

In *Frew Run,* we addressed whether the MLRL preempted a municipality's zoning ordinance when the DEC had issued a permit to operate a sand and gravel mine at a site that lay within a zoning district in which mining was not a permitted use. We noted that under the MLRL, the preemption question was one of statutory construction, not a search for implied preemption, because the Legislature included within the MLRL an express supersession clause. We concluded that the MLRL did not preempt the local zoning ordinance which limited mining activities to certain zoned districts (see, *Matter of Frew Run,* 71 N.Y.2d, at 130–131, 524 N.Y.S.2d 25, 518 N.E.2d 920, supra).

The supersession clause of the MLRL has since been amended (see, ECL 23–2703[2], amended by L 1991, ch 166, § 228), and we must now determine whether the amendments to the Zoning Ordinance of the Town of Sardinia which eliminated mining as a permitted use in all zoning districts are preempted by the Mined Land Reclamation Law. Relying on the amendment to the MLRL as a restatement of the policy in favor of fostering and promoting the mining industry in this State, and contending that our holding in Frew Run leaves municipalities with the limited authority to determine in which zoning districts mining may be conducted but not the authority to prohibit mining in all zoning districts, petitioner contends that the "repealer provisions" enacted by the Town of Sardinia are invalid because they are preempted by the Mined Land Reclamation Law. Neither the Mined Land Reclamation Law as amended nor the holding in *Frew Run* leads to that conclusion.

In *Frew Run,* we distinguished between zoning ordinances and local ordinances that directly regulate mining activities. Zoning ordinances, we noted, have the purpose of regulating land use generally. Notwithstanding the incidental effect of local land use laws upon the extractive mining industry, zoning ordinances are not the type of regulatory provision the Legislature foresaw as preempted by Mined Land Reclamation Law; the distinction is between ordinances that regulate property uses and ordinances that regulate mining activities (see, *Matter of Frew Run,* 71 N.Y.2d, at 131, 524 N.Y.S.2d 25, 518 N.E.2d 920, supra; see also, *Matter of Hunt Bros. v. Glennon,* 81 N.Y.2d 906, 597 N.Y.S.2d 643, 613 N.E.2d 549; compare, *Matter of Briarcliff Assocs. v. Town of Cortlandt,* 144 A.D.2d 457, 534 N.Y.S.2d 215, lv. denied 74 N.Y.2d 611, 546 N.Y.S.2d 555, 545 N.E.2d 869; *Matter of Northeast Mines v. State of New York Dept. of Envtl. Conservation,* 113 A.D.2d 62, 494 N.Y.S.2d 914, lv. denied 68 N.Y.2d 612, 510 N.Y.S.2d 1026, 503 N.E.2d 123). In *Frew Run,* we concluded that nothing in the plain language, statutory scheme, or legislative purpose of the Mined Land Reclamation Law suggested that its reach "was intended to be broader than necessary to preempt conflicting regulations dealing with mining operations and reclamation of mined lands" (id., at 133, 524 N.Y.S.2d 25, 518 N.E.2d 920 [emphasis added]), and that in the absence of a clear expression of legislative intent to preempt local control over land use, the statute could not be read as preempting local zoning authority.

The express supersession provision of the MLRL (ECL 23–2703), was amended in 1991. It now provides:

"For the purposes stated herein, this title shall supersede all other state and local laws relating to the extractive mining industry; provided, however, that nothing in this title shall be construed to prevent any local government from * * * enacting or enforcing local zoning ordinances or laws which determine permissible uses in zoning districts" (ECL 23–2703[2] [b]).

The patent purpose of the 1991 amendment was to withdraw from municipalities the authority to enact local laws imposing land reclamation standards that were stricter than the State-wide standards under the MLRL. The language of this amended provision accords with the distinction drawn in Frew Run between zoning ordinances and local ordinances that regulate mining activities, and there is nothing in the sparse legislative history of the amendment to the statute suggesting that the Legislature intended the MLRL to go further and limit municipalities' broad authority to govern land use.

Petitioner contends that the amendments to the Zoning Ordinance prohibit mining throughout the Town. In its view the amendments necessarily regulate mining and are therefore preempted by the MLRL because they conflict with the statute's stated purpose of fostering the mining industry in this State. It relies on this Court's observation in *Frew Run* that while the Town of Carroll prohibited mining in one district, it allowed mining by special permit in another. At bottom, petitioner's argument is that if the land within the municipality contains extractable minerals, the statute obliges the municipality to permit them to be mined somewhere within the municipality.

Nothing in the MLRL imposes that obligation on municipalities, nor has the Legislature broadened the preemptive reach of the statute to restrict municipal authority to regulate permissible uses of land within the municipality. Rather, in amending ECL 23–2703 in 1991, the Legislature expressly excluded that authority from its preemptive reach. Thus, we conclude that the MLRL does not preempt the Town's authority to determine that mining should not be a permitted use of land within the Town, and to enact amendments to the local zoning ordinance in accordance with that determination.

* * *

The municipality's authority to amend its Zoning Ordinance to eliminate mining as a permitted use in the municipality is not preempted by the Mined Land Reclamation Law, because that statute specifically exempts local zoning enactments from its preemptive reach. * * *

Accordingly, the order of the Appellate Division should be reversed, with costs, and the order and judgment of Supreme Court, Erie County, reinstated.

KAYE C.J., and TITONE, BELLACOSA, SMITH, LEVINE and CIPARICK, JJ., concur.

B. AGRICULTURAL USES

CRAIG v. COUNTY OF CHATHAM

Supreme Court of North Carolina, 2002.
356 N.C. 40, 565 S.E.2d 172.

LAKE, CHIEF J.

The issues raised here on review require the interpretation of the North Carolina General Statutes and application of North Carolina case law governing the question of preemption of county ordinances by the State. Specifically, the primary issues presented, defendants' first and second issues, relate to the validity of two Chatham County ordinances passed by the Chatham County Board of Commissioners and certain rules passed by the Chatham County Board of Health, all regulating swine farms.

On 6 April 1998, the Chatham County Board of Commissioners enacted the "Chatham County Ordinance Regulating Swine Farms" (the Swine Ordinance) and "An Ordinance to Amend the Chatham County Zoning Ordinance to Provide for Regulation of Swine Farms" (the Zoning Ordinance). The Swine Ordinance regulates swine farms "raising 250 or more animals of the porcine species," through a permitting system which affects currently existing farms and those which expand in the future. The Swine Ordinance is applicable to all such swine farms without regard to whether the farm is served by an animal waste management system having a design capacity of 600,000 pounds "steady state live weight" or greater. Under the Swine Ordinance, the owners of swine farms are assigned the financial responsibility for future contaminations that might occur, which responsibility is ensured through both a written agreement with the Chatham County Health Department and some form of financial security. The Swine Ordinance also provides requirements for setback distances and buffer zones for farms and sprayfields, and semiannual testing of wells on the farm.

The Zoning Ordinance is applicable only to swine farms that are "served by an animal waste management system having a design capacity of 600,000 pounds steady state live weight (SSLW) or greater." The Zoning Ordinance limits swine farms to areas of the county which are zoned either "Light Industrial" or "Heavy Industrial." The Zoning Ordinance further requires the swine farmer to obtain a conditional use permit, with issuance contingent upon a showing of compliance with the Swine Ordinance.

On 28 April 1998, the Chatham County Board of Health enacted the "Chatham County Board of Health Swine Farm Operation Rules" (Health Board Rules), which apply to all swine farms raising "250 or more animals of the porcine species," without regard to the design capacity of the farm's animal waste management system. The Health Board Rules are virtually identical to the Swine Ordinance.

On 2 September 1998, Timothy H. Craig and the Chatham County Agribusiness Council (CCAC) filed a complaint against defendants in superior court seeking a declaration that the Swine Ordinance, Zoning Ordinance and Health Board Rules were not legally valid. On 2 September 1999, CCAC filed a motion for partial summary judgment, and in September 1999, defendants filed an answer and a motion for summary judgment. The trial court granted defendants' motion for summary judgment and denied CCAC's motion for partial summary judgment. Plaintiffs appealed to the Court of Appeals, which affirmed in part and reversed in part the ruling of the trial court, holding that the Health Board Rules and the Swine Ordinance are preempted by state law but holding that the trial court was correct in granting summary judgment to defendants as to the Zoning Ordinance. This Court subsequently allowed defendants' petition for discretionary review and plaintiffs' conditional petition for discretionary review as to an additional issue.

Defendants first contend that the Court of Appeals erred in concluding that state law preempts the regulation of swine farms and thus prevents county commissioners and a local board of health from adopting an ordinance and rules regulating swine farms.

The enactment and operation of a general, statewide law does not necessarily prevent a county from regulating in the same field. However, preemption issues arise when it is shown that the legislature intended to implement statewide regulation in the area, to the exclusion of local regulation. See N.C.G.S. § 160A–174(b)(5) (2001). " '[M]unicipal by-laws and ordinances must be in harmony with the general laws of the State, and whenever they come in conflict with the general laws, the by-laws and ordinances must give way.' " *State v. Williams,* 283 N.C. 550, 552, 196 S.E.2d 756, 757 (1973) (quoting *Town of Washington v. Hammond,* 76 N.C. 33, 36 (1877)). The law of preemption is grounded in the need to avoid dual regulation. See, e.g., id. at 554, 196 S.E.2d at 759.

Counties are creatures of the General Assembly and have no inherent legislative powers. *High Point Surplus Co. v. Pleasants,* 264 N.C. 650, 654, 142 S.E.2d 697, 701 (1965); *De Loatch v. Beamon,* 252 N.C. 754, 757, 114 S.E.2d 711, 714 (1960). They are instrumentalities of state government and possess only those powers the General Assembly has conferred upon them. *Harris v. Board of Comm'rs of Washington Cty.,* 274 N.C. 343, 346, 163 S.E.2d 387, 390 (1968); *High Point Surplus,* 264 N.C. at 654, 142 S.E.2d at 701. Hence, we look to the North Carolina General Statutes to see what powers the General Assembly has delegated broadly to counties on a statewide basis or more specifically to counties such as Chatham in the area of swine farm regulation.

The General Assembly, in N.C.G.S. § 153A–121, has delegated to counties the power and authority to enact ordinances. That statute provides in part:

> A county may by ordinance define, regulate, prohibit, or abate acts, omissions, or conditions detrimental to the health, safety, or welfare of its citizens. N.C.G.S. § 153A–121(a) (2001).

However, N.C.G.S. § 160A–174, as interpreted and applied by our case law, provides limitations on the exercise of this power.

The relevant portions of N.C.G.S. § 160A–174 state:

> A city ordinance shall be consistent with the Constitution and laws of North Carolina and of the United States. An ordinance is not consistent with State or federal law when:

* * *

> (5) The ordinance purports to regulate a field for which a State or federal statute clearly shows a legislative intent to provide a complete and integrated regulatory scheme to the exclusion of local regulation.

This Court has held that N.C.G.S. § 160A–174 is applicable to counties as well as cities. *State v. Tenore,* 280 N.C. 238, 185 S.E.2d 644 (1972).

> N.C.G.S. § 130A–39 delegates power to the local board of health to adopt a more stringent rule in an area regulated by the Commission for Health Services or the Environmental Management Commission where, in the opinion of the local board of health, a more stringent rule is required to protect the public health. N.C.G.S. § 130A–39(b) (2001).

The Commission for Health Services and the Environmental Management Commission (EMC) are state agencies. The governor appoints all members serving on the EMC and a majority of the members serving on the Commission for Health Services. N.C.G.S. § 143B–283(a) (1999) (amended in 2001); N.C.G.S. § 130A–30(a) (2001). A local board of health is limited in its rule-making powers in that the regulation must be "related to the promotion or protection of health." *City of Roanoke Rapids v. Peedin,* 124 N.C.App. 578, 587, 478 S.E.2d 528, 533 (1996).

In holding that the Swine Ordinance and the Health Board Rules were preempted by state law, the Court of Appeals reasoned that the Chatham County Board of Commissioners and the Chatham County Board of Health sought to regulate an area in which the General Assembly had provided a "complete and integrated regulatory scheme" of swine farm regulations. *Craig v. County of Chatham,* 143 N.C.App. 30, 545 S.E.2d 455 (2001); see also N.C.G.S. § 160A–174(b)(5). We concur in this assessment.

In determining if the General Assembly intended to provide statewide regulation to the exclusion of local regulation, we must decide if it has shown a clear legislative intent to provide such a "complete and integrated regulatory scheme."

Defendants argue that when the General Assembly intends to preempt the field, it will do so through an express statement of intent. Furthermore, they argue that without such an expression of intent, this Court would be merely imposing its own judgment for that of the General Assembly in finding that the General Assembly preempted the field. We disagree.

If the General Assembly were required to provide an express statement of intent, N.C.G.S. § 160A–174(b)(5) would be meaningless. The General Assembly can create a regulatory scheme which, though not expressly exclusory, is so complete in covering the field that it is clear any regulation on the county level would be contrary to the statewide regulatory purpose.

In determining the purpose and intent of the General Assembly in adopting the swine regulation statutes, we must primarily look to " 'the spirit of the act[ ] and what the act seeks to accomplish.' " *State v. Anthony,* 351 N.C. 611, 615, 528 S.E.2d 321, 323 (2000) (quoting *Taylor v. Taylor,* 343 N.C. 50, 56, 468 S.E.2d 33, 37 (1996)). Where legislative intent is not readily apparent from the act, it is appropriate to look at various related statutes in pari materia so as to determine and effectuate the legislative intent. *Brown v. Flowe,* 349 N.C. 520, 523–24, 507 S.E.2d 894, 896 (1998).

* * *

In *Greene v. City of Winston–Salem,* 287 N.C. 66, 213 S.E.2d 231 (1975), this Court found upon review of an ordinance enacted by the City of Winston–Salem that there was a legislative intent to preempt. The City of Winston–Salem enacted an ordinance which required sprinkler systems in high-rise buildings. Id. at 67, 213 S.E.2d at 232. The City referred to a state law which required sprinkler systems in certain buildings in support of its argument that state law did not give the State Building Code Council sole regulatory authority in the area. Id. at 75, 213 S.E.2d at 237. This Court noted that the General Assembly does not have to delegate all or sole authority in the particular regulatory field to one state agency in order to establish that there is a "complete and integrated regulatory scheme." Id.

There are two components to the statewide swine farm regulations found in the North Carolina General Statutes, the "Swine Farm Siting Act" and the "Animal Waste Management Systems." In examining each of these, we will look to any statement of "purpose" and "intent" in an effort to determine if the General Assembly has created a "complete and integrated system" for swine farm regulation in the state.

The Swine Farm Siting Act, N.C.G.S. §§ 106–800 to –805 (2001), governs the placement of swine farms and lagoons, and provides in its section designated "Purpose" the following:

> [C]ertain limitations on the siting of swine houses and lagoons for swine farms can assist in the development of pork production, which contributes to the economic development of the State, by lessening the interference with the use and enjoyment of adjoining property. N.C.G.S. § 106–801.

This expression of intent is significant in that it notes pork production is important to the economic stability of the state, yet recognizes that adjoining landowners have a right to the use and enjoyment of their land. This stated intent also shows that the General Assembly was trying to reach a balance between two very important interests, the economy of North Carolina and the right of a landowner to enjoy his land with minimal interference. If each of North Carolina's one hundred counties is free to create its own particularized regulations for swine farms, the overall balance which the General Assembly has reached within a uniform plan for the entire state will be lost. The result could well be that the rights of adjacent landowners in each individual county would be substantially elevated above the rights of swine farmers to workable, nonexcessive regulations. Swine farms would be forced to comply with both state and county regulations. Furthermore, a swine farmer with a large farm that crossed the boundaries of one or more counties in North Carolina conceivably would have to conform the farm to the regulations established by various counties and those established by the state. Ultimately, such farms could be forced to adapt to differing, even conflicting, regulations. Any such dual regulation would present an excessive burden on swine farmers and the pork production industry as a whole.

The Animal Waste Management Systems component of the statewide regulations, N.C.G.S. §§ 143–215.10A to 215.10M (2001) (§ 143–215.10C altered in 1999; § 143–215.10B altered in 2001), provides in pertinent part: "It is the intention of the State to promote a cooperative and coordinated approach to animal waste management among the agencies of the State." N.C.G.S. § 143–215.10A (emphasis added). This unequivocal statement makes it clear that the purpose for creating these statutes was to regulate animal waste management at the state level. If each county were allowed to enact its own waste management guidelines, there could be no statewide "coordinated approach." Notably also, the agencies designated to implement the Animal Waste Management Systems statutes are exclusively state agencies. N.C.G.S. §§ 143–215.10A to –215.10M (permitting, inspection, and enforcement are vested in the Division of Water Quality, while the Soil and Water Conservation Commission is in charge of designating the technical specialists responsible for inspecting the waste management plans). The expression of intent further provides that one of the goals of the Act is "minimizing the regulatory burden." N.C.G.S. § 143–215.10A. Certainly, the stated goal of limiting or minimizing the burden of the regulatory scheme for waste management systems on swine farms would not be attainable if counties could impose additional burdens on swine farmers to comply with varying regulations.

Thus, from our review of the expressed "purpose" and "intent" of the Swine Farm Siting Act and the Animal Waste Management statutes, we conclude that these two components of North Carolina's swine farm regulations show an intention to cover the entire field of swine farm regulation in North Carolina.

* * *

The Animal Waste Management Systems component regulates swine farms even more extensively than the Swine Farm Siting Act. The Animal Waste Management Systems component creates a "permitting program" which requires swine farm owners to obtain a permit before constructing or operating any waste management system. N.C.G.S. § 143–215.10C(a). An "animal waste management system" is defined as practices "that provide for the collection, treatment, storage, or land application of animal waste." N.C.G.S. § 143–215.10B(3). To obtain the necessary permit, swine farm owners must submit to the EMC their waste management system plan, which has been approved by a technical specialist. N.C.G.S. § 143–215.10C(d). The Animal Waste Management Systems has detailed specifications as to how each farm's animal waste management system shall be designed, constructed and operated so as to prevent pollution. N.C.G.S. § 143–215.10C. It also provides a time limit upon which the EMC must approve or deny the permit after a new permit has been applied for or a renewal permit is sought. N.C.G.S. § 143–215.10C(c). In the event the EMC does not act in the required ninety days, the permit is considered to be approved. Id. The Animal Waste Management Systems component provides an extensive list of necessary parts for all animal waste management plans, such as provisions regarding periodic testing of waste products used on the farm as nutrient sources and a checklist of potential odor sources and management practices which are designed to minimize the source of the odor. N.C.G.S. § 143–215.10C(e). Any established swine farm waste management plan must require at least annual testing of the soil at crop sites where the waste has been applied to the land. N.C.G.S. § 143–215.10C(e)(6).

We conclude from the foregoing specifications that North Carolina's swine farm regulations, the Swine Farm Siting Act and the Animal Waste Management Systems statutes are so comprehensive in scope that the General Assembly must have intended that they comprise a "complete and integrated regulatory scheme" on a statewide basis, thus leaving no room for further local regulation.

Turning now to the Health Board Rules enacted by the Chatham County Board of Health, we note that they contain more stringent rules than those established in the EMC regulations. However, N.C.G.S. § 130A–39 specifically grants local boards of health the power to enact rules which are more strict when they are "required to protect the public health." N.C.G.S. § 130A–39(b). In an effort to protect the environment, the EMC has created a system of permitting and inspection which regulates waste management systems on farms, including swine farms of more than 250 swine. See 15A NCAC 2H.0217(a)(1)(A) (Sept.2001).

* * *

When we look at the Swine Farm Siting Act, the Animal Waste Management Systems statutes, and the EMC's regulation together, as parts of an overall scheme, we conclude that the Swine Ordinance and the Health Board Rules are incompatible with state law in that they purport to regulate a field in which the State has provided a "complete and integrated regulatory scheme" to the exclusion of local regulation. We therefore affirm the Court of Appeals in this regard.

We next address the issue of the ordinance to amend the Zoning Ordinance, which is before us upon plaintiffs' petition for discretionary review as to an additional issue. Plaintiffs contend the Court of Appeals erred in upholding the Zoning Ordinance. We agree.

"Counties have no inherent authority to enact zoning ordinances." *Jackson v. Guilford Cty. Bd. of Adjust.*, 275 N.C. 155, 162, 166 S.E.2d 78, 83 (1969). N.C.G.S. § 153A–340 is the statutory grant of power which provides counties with the authority to zone. There is, however, a specific limitation on this grant of power as it relates to swine farms:

> A county may adopt zoning regulations governing swine farms served by animal waste management systems having a design capacity of 600,000 pounds steady state live weight (SSLW) or greater provided that the zoning regulations may not have the effect of excluding swine farms served by an animal waste management system having a design capacity of 600,000 pounds SSLW or greater from the entire zoning jurisdiction. N.C.G.S. § 153A–340(b)(3) (2001).

The Zoning Ordinance, as amended, enacted by Chatham County requires all swine farms served by an animal waste management system having a design capacity of 600,000 pounds SSLW or greater, regardless of the actual number of swine, to be located in either a "Light" or "Heavy Industrial" district. The Zoning Ordinance further compels applicants to obtain a Construction/Expansion permit "as required by the [Swine Ordinance]."

Plaintiffs contend that in light of the Court of Appeals' determination that the Swine Ordinance is invalid, the Zoning Ordinance's express incorporation of the Swine Ordinance causes the Zoning Ordinance to fail as well. Specifically, plaintiffs argue that state preemption of the Swine Ordinance, as it is incorporated in the Zoning Ordinance, invalidates the Zoning Ordinance.

The Zoning Ordinance is not per se invalid. However, in this case, as written, the Zoning Ordinance cannot stand.

The sole restriction on zoning swine farms is that they "may not have the effect of excluding swine farms served by an animal waste management system having a design capacity of 600,000 pounds SSLW or greater from the entire zoning jurisdiction." N.C.G.S. § 153A–340(b)(3). Chatham County's Zoning Ordinance does not exclude all farms with an animal waste management system of 600,000 SSLW or greater, but merely restricts these farms to "Light" or "Heavy Industrial" districts within the county. The Zoning Ordinance complies with the restrictions established in section 153A–340(b)(3).

However, the requirement in the Zoning Ordinance that the applicant must have a Construction/Expansion permit obtained through compliance with the Swine Ordinance proves to be fatal. The Zoning Ordinance requires compliance with only a portion of the Swine Ordinance; however, that specific portion of the Swine Ordinance requires compliance with all other sections of the Swine Ordinance, to the extent the other sections are applicable to swine farms.

As we noted above, the Swine Ordinance cannot stand because it seeks to impose regulations on swine farmers where the State has shown an intent to cover the field of swine farm regulation. The Zoning Ordinance's attempt to incorporate the Swine Ordinance prevents us from sustaining its validity. Accordingly, we conclude that the Zoning Ordinance's incorporation of the Swine Ordinance invalidates the Zoning Ordinance.

* * *

AFFIRMED IN PART; REVERSED IN PART.

C. GROUP HOMES FOR THE MENTALLY ILL

JENNINGS v. NEW YORK STATE OFFICE OF MENTAL HEALTH

Court of Appeals of New York, 1997.
90 N.Y.2d 227, 660 N.Y.S.2d 352, 682 N.E.2d 953.

SMITH, J.

New York State policy has long favored the establishment of residential housing facilities to deinstitutionalize the treatment of mentally disabled persons. However, some residents of the Pine Hills community in the City of Albany (the City) believed that their neighborhood was already overcrowded with such facilities. The present dispute arose when the City filed an objection to the siting of the newest housing residence proposed for the area pursuant to Mental Hygiene Law § 41.34. Following a hearing, the Acting Commissioner of the New York State Office of Mental Health (the Commissioner) found that the proposed facility would not substantially alter the nature or character of the neighborhood in question.[1] We conclude that the determination of the Commissioner is supported by substantial evidence and dismiss the City's CPLR article 78 petition against the Commissioner's decision.

In December of 1994, Rehabilitation Support Services, Inc. (RSS), a private sponsor of residential facilities for disabled adults, notified the City that it wished to renovate an abandoned structure at 117 South Lake Avenue and open a community residential facility for the mentally disabled at that location. Gerald D. Jennings, the Mayor of the City of Albany, wrote the Commissioner "to formally object to the siting of a community residence proposed for the premises located at 117 South

1. Mental Hygiene Law § 41.34(c)(5) provides: "In the event the municipality objects to establishment of a facility in the municipality because to do so would result in such a concentration of community residential facilities for the mentally disabled or combination of such facilities and other facilities licensed by other state agencies that the nature and character of areas within the municipality would be substantially altered; or the sponsoring agency objects to the establishment of a facility in the area or areas suggested by the municipality; or in the event that the municipality and sponsoring agency cannot agree upon a site, either the sponsoring agency or the municipality may request an immediate hearing before the commissioner to resolve the issue. The commissioner shall personally or by a hearing officer conduct such a hearing within fifteen days of such a request. * * * The commissioner shall sustain the objection if he determines that the nature and character of the area in which the facility is to be based would be substantially altered as a result of establishment of the facility. The commissioner shall make a determination within thirty days of the hearing."

Lake Avenue." Without suggesting an alternative site for the proposed facility, Mayor Jennings requested a hearing pursuant to Mental Health Law § 41.34(c)(5) to resolve the dispute. It was the first time that the City had objected "under the Mental Hygiene Law to [the] siting of a facility."

At the hearing, the Director of Program Development for RSS testified that the proposed facility would provide transitional housing for 10 mentally disabled adults who had been recently discharged from an institutional psychiatric hospital. The RSS representative testified that the facility would offer a "supportive natural setting" for the residents to organize their lives, set goals and prepare "for [a] more long-term housing setting where they would then continue their progress in their rehabilitation and using a variety of community services to help them do that." She testified that residents would attend school or work during the day. In the evenings, residents would dine together "family style" and engage in various activities, such as homework or household chores, before retiring.

Licensed by the New York State Office of Mental Health, the facility would be supervised around the clock by a nonresident staff working in shifts. At most times, one or two staff members would be on duty but up to three staff members could share supervisory responsibilities during the busiest part of the day. Persons who are in immediate danger to themselves or others, are chemically dependent upon drugs or alcohol or have acute medical needs that require on-site medical supervision would not be permitted to reside in the house.

A representative of the Albany County Department of Mental Health testified that according to the estimates of the Albany County Discharge Facilitation Program, there were around 90 people receiving inpatient care who were presently in need of a community residential placement such as the one proposed. There was also evidence that, at the time, there was "only one other similar residential program" providing a short-term placement option for the mentally disabled in the process of "reentering and integrating themselves into the community." The need for the proposed facility was apparently exacerbated by the mandated "depletion of inpatient services" at area State psychiatric hospitals. In a written statement, the Albany County Department of Mental Health professed its support of the proposed facility "in the hopes of offsetting potential increases in homelessness, recidivism, and overall disenfranchisement that could result within our community." The City did not dispute the need for the proposed facility.

The City's Director of Planning testified that the decrepit building where the new facility was to be established was currently a "blighting influence" on the community. The witness acknowledged that the planned renovation "might be a physical improvement in terms of the exterior of the building." Nevertheless, the Planning Director and the City's remaining witnesses still argued against the establishment of the proposed residence because the area was already over concentrated with such housing facilities.

According to the City's witnesses, the prevalence of special needs housing already in the neighborhood had a negative effect on property values which made it difficult for people to sell and to attract others to the area. One witness claimed to have heard of a real estate agent who would not show houses in the area because the neighborhood had become known as "where all the nuts live." Others testified that some parents in the neighborhood would not let their children play on the front yard of their homes. Another witness testified to "erratic, annoying, [and] disturbing behavior" by residents of facilities already established in the neighborhood.

The Hearing Officer's report is dated June 20, 1995. She defined the relevant area to examine. Some witnesses had testified about the boundaries encompassed by the Pine Hills Neighborhood Association. The City's Director of Planning had submitted maps showing special needs housing facilities within varying concentric circles around 117 South Lake Avenue, the site of the proposed facility. However, the Hearing Officer delineated the relevant area as that within the boundaries suggested by the residents living closest to 117 South Lake. These residents, who testified on behalf of the City, testified about their understanding of the boundaries of their immediate neighborhood. The Hearing Officer stated that her "visit to the site and its environs verified this testimony."

Within this 13–block area, the Hearing Officer found four similar facilities already in existence. Some facilities were not considered because they were located outside the immediate neighborhood. One residence within the relevant area was not considered because its housing capacity was over 14, the maximum defined under Mental Hygiene Law § 41.34.

Finally, the Hearing Officer did not factor in the presence of Oxford House, "an unlicensed self-selecting group of adults recovering from addictions living together in a residence" located within the neighborhood. The fact that Oxford House was not licensed by the State was significant in her decision to exclude it in her analysis of over concentration. As she stated "[t]he development of better neighborhood housing for the developmentally and mentally disabled should not be stymied by the presence of housing developed by unrelated adults banding together for 'moral support and counseling.' "

The Hearing Officer concluded that the "siting of the proposed facility at 117 South Lake Avenue will not result in such a concentration of community residential facilities of this type in this municipality that the nature and character of the area would be substantially altered." The Hearing Officer further opined that the "real issue driving this hearing" could be "laid squarely at the doorstep of the Alcohol Crisis Center, a 40 bed shelter for alcoholics located within CDPC [Capital District Psychiatric Center] * * *. A drunk tank can not be added to a residential mix without negatively affecting all the other facilities in the area, and dampening the welcome historically given by the neighbors."

The Commissioner concurred with the Hearing Officer's recommendation and concluded that the establishment of the residence would not result in a substantial change in the nature and character of the neighborhood. The Commissioner rejected the testimony about "inappropriate behavior" as vague and unassignable "to persons who reside in programs such as that proposed." The Commissioner noted that testimony about diminished property values was irrelevant to the issue of substantial alteration to the area. He also noted that "perceptions about persons with mental disabilities cannot be used to bar housing for [those] persons * * * just as perceptions about persons based on their race, religion and ethnicity cannot be used to keep such persons from residing in a neighborhood."

The Commissioner adopted the delineation of the relevant area recommended by the Hearing Officer. In his examination of the facilities already within the neighborhood, the Commissioner found "ten residential programs which must be considered on the issues of over concentration and substantial alteration." These included the four considered by the Hearing Officer and the one facility excluded by the Hearing Officer as too large. Also included for consideration were five one- or two-bedroom residence apartments licensed by either the Office of Mental Health (OMH) or the Office of Mental Retardation and Developmental Disabilities (OMRDD).

Eight facilities were excluded as "located outside of the determined neighborhood." Two facilities were rejected due to their location and their size and functional dissimilarities with the proposed facility. The latter ground alone was sufficient to exclude two other facilities from consideration, the CDPC (a 210–bed inpatient hospital) and the Alcoholism Receiving Center (a 40–bed detoxification facility). Finally, the Commissioner did not consider Oxford House because it was not licensed by OMH or OMRDD.

The Commissioner noted that the "Site Selection Law is not concerned with over concentration alone" and further stated that "evidence of nearby facilities cannot sustain the municipality's objection without sufficient proof of substantial alteration which would result from the latter." The Commissioner found that such evidence was lacking in this case. In so holding, the Commissioner acknowledged the apprehensions of the City's witnesses as "subjectively genuine" but concluded that the residents' primary concern had to do with the behavior of persons who utilized the Alcoholism Receiving Center, just as the Hearing Officer had also noted. However, the Commissioner found that "the testimony that these behaviors may be continued and expanded on by individuals residing in the proposed program is wholly speculative and not convincing in any manner. Such conjectural testimony cannot support a conclusion that the proposed residence would substantially alter the area."

The City filed this article 78 proceeding seeking to annul the Commissioner's decision. The City's primary argument concerned the "area" examined. According to the City, the Commissioner arbitrarily excluded several facilities from consideration by limiting his analysis to the "neighborhood" rather than the "area."

The Appellate Division compared the 13–block area examined by the Commissioner with the maps prepared by the City that depicted the number of special needs housing within a three-fourths-mile radius of 117 South Lake Avenue. The Court found that the Commissioner's delineation of the affected area was arbitrary and capricious and annulled the Commissioner's approval of the residence: "Although we recognize there can be no precise definition of an 'area,' and the Commissioner's findings in this regard are entitled to great deference, in this unique situation where there is a high concentration of similar facilities that impact upon the subject area, we find that the Commissioner's delineation of the neighborhood boundaries to exclude a number of other residential facilities in close proximity to the site in question was arbitrary and capricious, and that an additional community residence would only serve to continue the substantial alteration of the nature and character of the area" (220 A.D.2d 148, 151–152, 644 N.Y.S.2d 844).

* * *

Mental Hygiene Law § 41.34 was enacted and designed "to facilitate the establishment of community residences" (Governor's Approval Mem., L. 1978, chs. 468, 469, 470, 1978 McKinney's Session Laws of N.Y., at 1821; see also, *Crane Neck Assn., Inc. v. New York City/Long Is. County Servs. Group,* 61 N.Y.2d 154, 472 N.Y.S.2d 901, 460 N.E.2d 1336). As Governor Carey wrote in approving the bill, the law was a legislative attempt "to encourage a process of joint discussion and accommodation between the providers of care and services to the mentally disabled and representatives of the community" (1978 McKinney's Session Laws of N.Y., at 1821). In creating a balance between these potentially competing interests, the Legislature set forth a specific mechanism for the resolution of disputes involving the placement of community residences for the mentally disabled. A sponsoring agency intending to establish or operate a community residential facility for the disabled must provide notice of such intention to the chief executive officer of the municipality (Mental Hygiene Law § 41.34[c][1]). The municipality, in turn, may either approve of the recommended site, suggest alternatives within the jurisdiction, or outright object to the proposal. The Commissioner of the department responsible for licensing the proposed facility must hold a hearing to resolve any dispute (Mental Hygiene Law § 41.34[c][5]).

In reviewing any objection to the facility, the Commissioner must consider the need for the facility and the concentration of similar facilities already established in the area (id.). Nevertheless, the only ground provided in the statute to justify sustaining the objection is if the Commissioner determines "that the nature and character of the area in which the facility is to be based would be substantially altered as a result of establishment of the facility" (Mental Hygiene Law § 41.34[c][5]). Thus, while over concentration is certainly relevant, whether the nature and character of an area will be substantially altered by the establishment of the proposed facility is the dispositive inquiry.

Here, the Commissioner's delineation of the area to be affected by the establishment of the proposed residence is rational and supported by the evidence adduced at the hearing. The Commissioner determined that the relevant "area" was the neighborhood beginning "at Morris Street * * * east to Robin Street, south to Myrtle Avenue, west to South Lake, south to its intersection with New Scotland and Woodlawn Avenues, west on Woodlawn Avenue to Ontario Street and north again to Morris Street." The larger area urged by the City is delineated by a circle within a three-fourths-mile radius from 117 South Lake. This boundary has no relation to physical or subjective neighborhood limits. In contrast, the Commissioner relied upon boundaries created by parks and main thoroughfares which residents were not likely to cross on foot.

The Commissioner's determination rationally adopts the boundaries of the neighborhood as defined by the City's own witnesses. It was the neighbors closest to 117 South Lake Avenue who testified about the boundaries of their neighborhood and it is in that neighborhood where the proposed facility would be located. Such evidence is of paramount importance under the State policy, which is geared towards incorporating the mentally disabled into "the life of the community which is expected to provide them with sustenance" (Governor's Approval Mem., 1978 McKinney's Session Laws of N.Y., at 1821). Accordingly, the Commissioner may properly focus on the potential impact upon direct "neighbors" (id.).

The Appellate Division's choice of a different area was simply that—a different choice. The record contains evidence relating to zoning districts, zip code districts and census districts as well as boundaries within concentric circles radiating out from the site of the proposed facility in varying one-fourth-mile increments. Although the relevant area might reasonably have been determined in a variety of ways, the dispositive inquiry is whether the establishment of the subject facility will substantially alter the nature or character of the area in which the facility will be located and there is little evidence of this beyond speculation. If the proposed facility would not "substantially alter" its immediate neighborhood, it is difficult to find fault with the conclusion that adjacent areas would be little affected. In sum, the Commissioner's decision to examine the potential impact of the proposed facility upon its immediately surrounding community is entitled to deference as rational and supported by the record.

The City argues primarily that, upon consideration of a larger area, more facilities would be encompassed within the analysis. That a larger area includes more facilities is not surprising. However, the inverse corollary is also true. More facilities would be found over a larger area. Here, there is no indication that the larger area considered by the Appellate Division would be any more "saturated" than the smaller neighborhood examined by the Commissioner. In fact, the maps prepared by the City support the opposite conclusion.

It should be noted that one of the goals of the statute is to avoid over concentration of such facilities in any one area. Nevertheless, as the Commissioner noted, the mere number of "special needs" facilities within an area is not dispositive.

Here, the evidence strongly supports the conceded need for the proposed residence and the City suggested no alternative site. The mere presence of other facilities already situated in a particular area cannot be the sole basis for denying the establishment of a similar new facility when such need for that facility is demonstrated. This is precisely the balance reached by the statute in which concentration is relevant but secondary to a determination that the nature and character of an area will be "substantially altered." Thus, it was reasonable for the Commissioner to require proof of more than a mere recitation of the number of other facilities located in the same area to sustain the City's objection.

Finally, the Commissioner's decision to limit his examination to certain facilities was not arbitrary. The Mental Hygiene Law only requires the Commissioner to consider

> "the existing concentration of such facilities and other similar facilities licensed by other state agencies in the municipality or in the area in proximity to the site selected and any other facilities in the municipality or in the area in proximity to the site selected providing residential services to a significant number of persons who have formerly received in-patient mental health services in facilities of the office of mental health or the office of mental retardation and developmental disabilities" (Mental Hygiene Law § 41.34[c][5] [emphasis supplied]).

Thus, under section 41.34, only facilities which are licensed by a State agency or which house former patients of OMH/OMRDD services must be considered. In contrast, the City argues that all "special needs" facilities should be taken into account regardless of licensing status, size or function. Such a sweeping position is not the one adopted by the Legislature and the Commissioner's conclusions in this regard are rational.

Judging from the testimony of the residents, it appears that many of the concerns may be traced to the Alcoholism Receiving Center and the nonlicensed Oxford House. The proposed residence at issue, however, is for individuals who suffer from mental disabilities, not addiction. Concerns about behavior of those receiving treatment for addiction must not obfuscate the primary issue before us. The record supports the Commissioner's conclusion that the addition of a residence housing 10 mentally disabled adults would neither result in an over concentration of similar facilities nor substantially alter the nature and character of the neighborhood.

Accordingly, the judgment of the Appellate Division should be reversed, with costs, and the petition dismissed.

KAYE, C.J., and TITONE, BELLACOSA, LEVINE, CIPARICK and WESLEY, JJ., concur.

Notes

1. The first case in this section dealing with mining presents an example of how state governments may not entirely preempt local governments from controlling certain land uses, but rather how the state may regulate certain activities that occur on the land. In these situations, the local governments may, for example, decide whether to allow mining to occur in a particular zoning district, but once the activity is a permitted use, the state preempts local control regarding regulating how the mining operation is conducted. But see, San Pedro Mining Corp. v. Board of County Commissioners of Santa Fe County, 121 N.M. 194, 909 P.2d 754 (1995) and River Springs Limited Liability Company v. Board of County Commissioners of the County of Teton, 899 P.2d 1329 (Wyo.1995) where courts have held that the states' mining law did not preempt all local regulation of mining activities. What are the reasons why state government would want to regulate the mining industry? For a discussion of the preemption of local zoning control over mining activities on federal public lands see, South Dakota Min. Ass'n, Inc. v. Lawrence, 155 F.3d 1005, 29 Envtl. L. Rep. 20,043 (8th Cir.1998).

2. In his article, Local Land Use Regulation of Extractive Industries: Evolving Judicial and Regulatory Approaches, 14 UCLA J. Envtl. L. & Pol'y 41 (1995/96), Professor Bruce Kramer offers the following observation:

> Regulation of the extractive industries antedates the regulation of urban development through comprehensive zoning and planning. The trend towards not only suburban, but rur-urban, development will undoubtedly increase local political pressure to further regulate and restrict the extractive industries. In addition, counties are being empowered to engage in zoning and planning regulation. These two developments will undoubtedly lead to further confrontation between those who make their living extracting minerals and those who want a "quiet place to live." Traditional land use doctrines can be applied to the industry, but a number of courts have recognized the unique locational circumstances of the industry. Other courts treat the extractive industry as any other use, subject to the police power, constrained only by constitutional limitations. The recent spate of appellate court opinions indicates that the confrontation between the various interests involved has become a reality and is likely to continue into the future.

Professor Kramer also discusses the overlapping and potentially conflicting state and local regulation of the industry. Can different levels of government effectively regulate different aspects of land use and activities that occur on land? If so, who benefits? What are the potential economic impacts of dual regulation?

3. Similar to the challenges of the confrontation between newer suburban and rural homeowners with the mining industries, farmers and agribusiness often face bitter NIMBY stand-offs with neighbors who may complain about odors, timing of farm operations and related noise, and farm related traffic. The growing political influence of the surrounding landowners, who often out-number the farmer in votes, has changed the landscape of local government regulation of agribusinesses. As a result, states have increasingly adopted regulations in the area of agricultural activities, sometimes supporting the farming industry (e.g., right to farm laws) and other times regulating farming operations out of public health and safety concerns. Which level of government is most appropriate to regulate the activities that occur on farms, the state government or the local government where the farming operation is located? See, Christopher A. Novack, Agriculture's New Environmental Battleground: The Preemption of County Livestock Regulations, 5 Drake J. A. L. 429 (2000).

4. Should state government require that local governments permit the siting of group homes for the mentally ill? While the Federal Fair Housing Act discussed in the previous section would cover group homes as well, why have state governments enacted their own preemptive regulations? Can and should local government officials ever get past the pressures of NIMBY when it comes to siting locally unwanted land uses? What would support a mayor's decision to oppose the siting of group homes on non-discriminatory grounds? Should local governments be required to permit somewhere within their borders all types of imaginable housing and uses?

5. When local governments fail to take reasonable decisive actions, which may be politically unpopular due to the "not in my back yard" ("NIMBY") syndrome, the private sector and non-profit advocacy organizations eventually plead to a higher level of government. Many local land use decisions are difficult. Millions of dollars may be at risk, as well as real or perceived public health and welfare issues. It is uncomfortable for zoning board members and local legislators to listen to their constituents, neighbors, and friends oppose proposed projects for what may amount to NIMBY and fail to support constituent desires. Although local officials could debate the differences between representative and delegate theories of governance, the bottom line is that progress is delayed, economic development is stalled, and needed housing alternatives to accommodate all members of the community are prohibited. When this happens, it naturally begs the point that, "There must be a better way." See, Patricia E. Salkin, The Politics of Land Use Reform in New York: Challenges and Opportunities, 73 St. John's L. Rev. 1041 (1999). What level of government is most appropriate to regulate land use?

SECTION 3. INTERGOVERNMENTAL CONFLICTS

A. STATE–LOCAL CONFLICTS

BROWN v. KANSAS FORESTRY, FISH AND GAME COMM'N

Court of Appeals of Kansas, 1978.
2 Kan.App.2d 102, 576 P.2d 230.

FOTH, CHIEF JUDGE:

The issue presented in this appeal is whether, in the absence of any clear legislative direction one way or the other, a state agency must conform its land use to local zoning regulations. It is an issue which has not been squarely answered by the courts of this state.

The agency involved here is the state forestry, fish and game commission. In 1975 it purchased two lots in the middle of a twenty-three lot subdivision near Manhattan, Kansas, which had been zoned for single family residences. The commission intended to use the land for a public parking lot, complete with toilet facilities, for the convenience of its patrons using a fishing and recreation facility on the adjacent Big Blue River.

The plaintiffs own and reside on fourteen of the twenty-one other lots in the subdivision. They brought this action to enjoin the commission from its proposed use of its land, alleging that such use would violate both Riley county zoning regulations and certain restrictive covenants governing the subdivision. After a hearing, and upon the parties' stipulation that the commission's proposed use would violate the zoning regulations, the trial court temporarily enjoined the use. It further ordered that the injunction would be made permanent unless the commission promptly perfected an appeal or applied for rezoning. Rather than seek rezoning the commission elected to take this appeal.

In this court, as in the court below, the commission argues that it is exempt from local zoning regulations for two reasons. First it says that as an agency of the state itself, performing a governmental function, it is immune from regulation by a mere political subdivision in the absence of a legislative declaration to the contrary. Second, it relies on its possession of the power of eminent domain as indicating a legislative intent that its use of land not be subject to control by local authorities.

A concise review of the terms in which courts have traditionally analyzed conflicts between governmental agencies over land use regulations is found in City of Temple Terrace v. Hillsborough Ass'n, Etc., 322 So.2d 571 (Fla.App.1975), affirmed on opinion below, Hillsborough Ass'n, Etc. v. City of Temple Terrace, 332 So.2d 610 (Fla.1976). The Florida Court of Appeals there noted:

"* * * In deciding this type of case, the courts have used varying tests. One approach utilized by a number of courts is to rule in favor of the superior sovereign. Thus, where immunity from a local zoning ordinance is claimed by an agency occupying a superior position in the governmental hierarchy, it is presumed that immunity was intended in the absence of express statutory language to the contrary. E.g., Aviation Services, Inc. v. Board of Adjustment, 1956, 20 N.J. 275, 119 A.2d 761. A second test frequently employed is to determine whether the institutional use proposed for the land is 'governmental' or 'proprietary' in nature. If the political unit is found to be performing a governmental function, it is immune from the conflicting zoning ordinance. E.g., City of Scottsdale v. Municipal Court, 1962, 90 Ariz. 393, 368 P.2d 637. On the other hand, when the use is considered proprietary, the zoning ordinance prevails. E.g., Taber v. City of Benton Harbor, 1937, 280 Mich. 522, 274 N.W. 324. Where the power of eminent domain has been granted to the governmental unit seeking immunity from local zoning, some courts have concluded that this conclusively demonstrates the unit's superiority where its proposed use conflicts with zoning regulations. E.g., Mayor of Savannah v. Collins, 1954, 211 Ga. 191, 84 S.E.2d 454. Other cases are controlled by explicit statutory provisions dealing with the question of whether the operation of a particular governmental unit is subject to local zoning. E.g., Mogilner v. Metropolitan Plan Commission, 1957, 236 Ind. 298, 140 N.E.2d 220.

"When the governmental unit which seeks to circumvent a zoning ordinance is an arm of the state, the application of any of the foregoing tests has generally resulted in a judgment permitting the proposed use. This has accounted for statements of hornbook law to the effect that a state agency authorized to carry out a function of the state is not bound by local zoning regulations. 2 Anderson, American Law of Zoning § 9.06 (1968); 8 McQuillin, Municipal Corporations § 25.15 (1965)." (p. 574.)

* * *

There being no "explicit statutory provision" applicable here, the commission relies on the other three common tests: in its first argument it combines the "superior sovereign" with the "governmental-proprietary" test; in its second it asserts the "eminent domain" test. All have been subject to scholarly criticism as too simplistic, avoiding the kind of analysis needed for rational resolution of the complex issues posed by land use problems in a modern, urban-oriented society. See, Comment, "The Applicability of Zoning Ordinances to Governmental Land Use," 39 Tex.L.Rev. 316 (1961); Note, "Municipal Power to Regulate Building Construction and Land Use by Other State Agencies," 49 Minn.L.Rev. 284 (1964); Comment, "The Inapplicability of Municipal Zoning Ordinances to Governmental Land Uses," 19 Syracuse L.Rev. 698 (1968); Note, "Governmental Immunity From Local Zoning Ordinances," 84 Harv.L.Rev. 869 (1971).

Recent judicial pronouncements are increasingly in the same vein. Thus in State v. Kopp, 330 S.W.2d 882 (Mo.1960), the question was whether a city had to comply with county zoning ordinances in building a sewage disposal plant outside the city limits. The court viewed the question as one of legislative intent, "not to be resolved simply by applying the 'governmental vs. proprietary' test." (p. 887.) The court went on to find that the grant of eminent domain power to the city evinced a legislative intent that it not be subject to county zoning. Just two years later, however, the same court, in St. Louis County v. City of Manchester, 360 S.W.2d 638 (Mo.1962), found that a city's possession of eminent domain power did not grant automatic immunity from the county's zoning power in locating its disposal plant. Rather, the court sought to reconcile the two powers and held that the eminent domain statutes "do not purport to give the city the right to select the exact location in St. Louis County, and the public interest is best served in requiring it to be done in accordance with the zoning laws." (p. 642.) Missouri thus has abandoned as controlling both the governmental-proprietary and the eminent domain tests, looking instead to legislative intent and the public interest.

The Missouri court relied in part on City of Richmond v. County Board, 199 Va. 679, 101 S.E.2d 641 (1958), where a statute authorizing the city to establish a jail outside the city limits was held not to authorize a location in violation of the county's zoning regulation. Rather than rely on any automatic test, and specifically rejecting the "governmental-proprietary" test, the Virginia court also sought to reconcile the two enactments and give each full play. * * *

Pennsylvania has employed a similar analysis. In Wilkinsburg–Penn Jt. W.A. v. Churchill B., 417 Pa. 93, 207 A.2d 905 (1965), a municipal water authority sought to build a water tower in violation of borough zoning restrictions. When the borough refused a variance the authority brought suit to enjoin the borough from interfering with the proposed structure. The court viewed the question as one of statutory construction; the fact that the authority was given the power to determine its services "exclusively" did not make it immune from the zoning power of the borough. "The initial service decisions remain with the Authority, but they must be made within the framework of other applicable laws, unless the Legislature directs otherwise." (p. 101, 207 A.2d p. 909.) The two grants of authority—to build and to zone—could be reconciled. Should there be an improper exercise of the zoning power as to the authority's land use, the court said, it could be challenged in the same manner as other zoning decisions.

Later, in City of Pittsburgh v. Commonwealth, 468 Pa. 174, 360 A.2d 607 (1976), the same court decided a zoning dispute between the state's bureau of corrections and a city over the location of a pre-release center for women convicts. It commenced its analysis by observing:

> "Resolving the conflict simply by saying that the 'state' agency must prevail because it is exercising the power of the sovereign overlooks

that the zoning power the city seeks to exercise is also a sovereign power. Such a resolution ignores the interests the state seeks to promote by legislative grants of powers to municipalities. Interests such as those fostered by comprehensive land use planning statutes are too important not to be recognized as involving exercises of state power.'' (p. 180, 360 A.2d p. 610.)

The court resolved the question by again reconciling the grants of authority. The city's zoning, which would permit pre-release centers in other parts of the city, was held not to be arbitrary. Finding that "suitable alternatives exist to accommodate both the community's interest in maintaining the integrity of low-density, residential zoning and the needs of the Bureau'' (p. 187, 360 A.2d p. 614), the court held that the state agency's use was subject to the city's zoning ordinance.

Pennsylvania's way in this area was indicated by the leading case in the new wave of intergovernmental zoning decisions, Rutgers v. Piluso, 60 N.J. 142, 286 A.2d 697 (1972). There the question was whether Rutgers, the state university, could build student housing units in excess of the maximum number permitted by a township zoning ordinance. * * *

After recognizing the three common tests (asserted by the commission here) and reviewing its own prior decisions, the court formulated its own test:

> "The rationale which runs through our cases and which we are convinced should furnish the true test of immunity in the first instance, albeit a somewhat nebulous one, is the legislative intent in this regard with respect to the particular agency or function involved. That intent, rarely specifically expressed, is to be divined from a consideration of many factors, with a value judgment reached on an overall evaluation. All possible factors cannot be abstractly catalogued. The most obvious and common ones include [1] the nature and scope of the instrumentality seeking immunity, [2] the kind of function or land use involved, [3] the extent of the public interest to be served thereby, [4] the effect local land use regulation would have upon the enterprise concerned and [5] the impact upon legitimate local interests. * * * In some instances one factor will be more influential than another or may be so significant as to completely overshadow all others. No one, such as the granting or withholding of the power of eminent domain, is to be thought of as ritualistically required or controlling. And there will undoubtedly be cases, as there have been in the past, where the broader public interest is so important that immunity must be granted even though the local interests may be great. The point is that there is no precise formula or set of criteria which will determine every case mechanically and automatically.'' (pp. 152–53, 286 A.2d p. 702. Numbers inserted.)

The court went on to find that the state university performed an essential governmental function for the benefit of all the people of the state, and that the legislature would not intend its growth to be subject to restriction or control by local land use regulation. After observing that the same reasoning would generally be true of all state functions and agencies, the court added the following caveat:

> "It is, however, most important to stress that such immunity in any situation is not completely unbridled. Even when it is found to exist, it must not, as this court said in Washington Township v. Village of Ridgewood, supra, 26 N.J. [578] at 584–586, 141 A.2d 308, be exercised in an unreasonable fashion so as to arbitrarily override all important legitimate local interests. This rule must apply to the state and its instrumentalities as well as to lesser governmental entities entitled to immunity. For example, it would be arbitrary, if the state proposed to erect an office building in the crowded business district of a city where provision for off-street parking was required, for the state not to make some reasonable provision in that respect. And, at the very least, even if the proposed action of the immune governmental instrumentality does not reach the unreasonable stage for any sufficient reason, the instrumentality ought to consult with the local authorities and sympathetically listen and give every consideration to local objections, problems and suggestions in order to minimize the conflict as much as possible. * * *" (pp. 153–54, 286 A.2d p. 703.)

The test applied in *Rutgers* has come to be known as the "balancing of interests" test. In Kunimoto v. Kawakami, 56 Haw. 582, 545 P.2d 684 (1976), the state university of Hawaii was permitted to condemn land for a use which would violate Honolulu's zoning ordinances. The finding of immunity was based on the overriding statewide concern for higher education expressed in the Hawaii constitution and the university's enabling legislation. The court, however, expressly reserved the question of whether the "balancing of interest" test expounded in *Rutgers* would apply to other state projects.

In another state university case, City of Newark v. University of Delaware, 304 A.2d 347 (Del.Ch.1973), the court reached the same result—i.e., the university's immunity—by expressly following the *Rutgers* rationale. A legislative intent that the university be immune from local zoning was inferred from the vital role it plays in the state's public mission, although such immunity would not prevail if the university's action were shown to be unreasonable or arbitrary in a given instance.

Minnesota adopted a "balancing of interests" test in Town of Oronoco v. City of Rochester, 293 Minn. 468, 197 N.W.2d 426 (1972), at about the same time as and apparently quite independently of the *Rutgers* decision, which was not cited. In that case the city's proposed sanitary landfill would violate a township zoning ordinance. The court recognized that under the "general rule" the city would be immune because it possessed eminent domain powers and would be exercising a governmental function. It declined to follow the general rule, saying:

"* * * However, the trend is to limit such freedom from regulation, a trend which we believe is well within the dictates of the public interest, principally because the pungent realities of urban sprawl and overpopulation have accentuated the need for land-use planning and control that serves as foundation for the exercise of police power in the area of zoning. Consequently, in order to support the principle of enlightened land-use control, we decline to adopt in Minnesota the general rule of governmental exemption from zoning regulation.

"The exigencies of the present matter, however, illustrate the core of wisdom in that general rule and the danger in too readily assuming enlightenment where none in fact may exist in the implementation of a particular local zoning policy. Therefore, we adopt a balancing-of-public-interests test for the resolution of conflicts which arise between the exercise by governmental agencies of their police power and their right of eminent domain. This is preferable to adherence to a less flexible 'general rule' based simply on the form of the opposing parties rather than the substance of their conflict." (p. 471, 197 N.W.2d p. 429. Footnotes omitted.)

Balancing the city's urgent need to replace its present disposal system against the marginal impact on the proposed area for the new facility, the court found immunity should prevail under the facts of that case.

The Florida Court of Appeals, in City of Temple Terrace v. Hillsborough Ass'n, Etc., supra, after describing the traditional tests in the language quoted above, rejected them one by one. It adopted in their stead the *Rutgers* "balancing of interests" test, justifying its decision by saying:

"The old tests were adopted at a time when state government was much smaller. The myriad of agencies now conducting the functions of the state have necessarily resulted in a diminution of centralized control. The decision of a person administering an outlying function of a state agency with respect to the site where this function should be performed is not necessarily any better than the decision of the local authorities on the subject of land use. The adoption of the balancing of interests test will compel governmental agencies to make more responsible land-use decisions by forcing them to consider the feasibility of other sites for the facility as well as alternative methods of making the use of the proposed site less detrimental to the local zoning scheme.

"Our burgeoning population and the rapidly diminishing available land make it all the more important that the use of land be intelligently controlled. This can only be done by a cooperative effort between interested parties who approach their differences with an open mind and with respect for the objectives of the other. When the state legislature is silent on the subject, the governmental unit seeking to use land contrary to applicable zoning regulations should have the burden of proving that the public interests favoring the proposed use outweigh those mitigating against a use not sanctioned by the zoning regulations of the host government." (322 So.2d at 578–79.)

In adopting the Court of Appeals opinion in that case as its own the Florida Supreme Court noted a further policy consideration:

> "An ancillary benefit in resolving inter-governmental disputes results from our adoption of the City's view. By requiring state agencies to seek local approval for non-conforming uses, an administrative solution is always present in the form of zoning appeals. In contrast, if the state were not required to seek local approval, the city would always be forced to litigate its disagreement, as happened here. It serves the public's benefit to resolve these controversies in a way which does not mandate the most expensive and least expeditious way of settling intergovernmental disputes." (Hillsborough Ass'n, Etc. v. City of Temple Terrace, supra at 612, n. 3.)

Finally, among foreign cases, we note Matter of Suntide Inn Motel, 563 P.2d 125 (Okl.1977), cited to us by the commission at oral argument. It does not support the kind of automatic immunity urged on us by the commission. The issue in that case was whether the state department of corrections was required to have city planning commission approval for the location of a community treatment center. Three justices in the majority found that such approval was not necessary, basically because the state, as the superior sovereign, was not bound by local regulation in the absence of an express legislative declaration. Four justices dissented, urging that the *Rutgers* balancing test should be adopted, and that under such a test the state agency should seek local approval. * * *

Two justices were in between. They concurred in the finding of immunity, but only because they thought the result of balancing tipped in favor of the state agency. * * *

* * *

In our own analysis we start with the premise that the legislature has not spoken directly on the subject, any more than has our Supreme Court. * * * There is nothing in the statutes which says the commission is subject to local zoning, nor is there anything which grants it immunity.

We therefore regard the question as open in this state. Given the choice, we think this case aptly illustrates why the balancing of interests test better promotes the public's interest than any of the traditional mechanical tests.

* * * The real questions are where the decision-making authority should be lodged, and if a claim of arbitrariness is to be made who should have the presumption of reasonableness and who the burden of proof.

Dealing with the specifics of this case, we are not talking about establishing a public hunting or fishing facility in an area zoned for agriculture. The merits of such a case appear clear, at least on the surface. Here, we are dealing with an all-night parking lot with toilet facilities in the middle of a residential subdivision. The commission anticipates that the recreational facility will be used at a rate of 10,000 man days per year. At least some of those users will employ the proposed parking lot. The merits of this proposal are not nearly so clear. * * *

If we look at the factors suggested as relevant by the Rutgers court we find: (1) The instrumentality seeking immunity is a state agency, and its judgment is entitled to considerable deference. (2) The general function being performed—promoting recreation—is one of recognized public utility but hardly on a level of importance with public education. The specific use, providing parking space near but not in a recreation area, is of a more marginal public interest. (3) While there is public interest in the proposed use in that some people will find this parking lot more convenient than other available lots, the segment of the population affected is relatively small. (4) Regulation, if rezoning is refused, would have the effect of requiring the parking lot to be located in some area other than a residential subdivision. Such a move might make the lot less convenient, but would probably not substantially impair the usefulness of the recreation area. (5) The proposed use would, prima facie at least, have a substantial adverse impact on the surrounding householders and on the existing land use plan.

* * * [T]hese factors were not weighed on the basis of evidence either by a zoning body or by the court below, and our observations are based on a skimpy record and our own general knowledge. The commission simply asserted its immunity, without attempting to justify the reasonableness of its decision, while the court looked no further than the admitted violation of the zoning regulation.

It seems to us that, on balance, the initial decision on reasonableness in this case can be made more expeditiously and with greater discernment by the local zoning authority—here the county. That being so, we infer a legislative intent that the responsibility should be imposed on that body. If rezoning is arbitrarily denied, that decision can be reviewed by the courts at the commission's behest through normal channels. If, on the other hand, we were to hold that the commission's status as superior sovereign immunizes it from the normal zoning processes as it urges, then the burden of going forward with a lawsuit would fall on either the county or the affected landowners. In such a suit they would be required to show arbitrariness on the part of the commission. While it is true the landowners would have much the same burden if dissatisfied by an order *granting* rezoning, that would be because two administrative agencies at different levels have concurred in finding the proposed use appropriate. The zoning route strikes us as cheaper and faster, and it puts the local land use decision in local hands where, in this case, it belongs.

In this case the district court ordered the commission to seek rezoning. It can still do so. In our opinion that is the proper course for it to take, and the trial court properly so ordered.

Affirmed.

Notes

1. Two years after the principal case, the Supreme Court of Kansas was faced with the question of whether the state Board of Regents was required to obtain a building permit and follow city building codes in constructing a new facility at the University of Kansas Medical Center. In State ex rel. Schneider v. City of Kansas City, 228 Kan. 25, 612 P.2d 578 (1980), the court quoted extensively from the principal case, and then, enigmatically, stated: "Whatever may be the merits of such a balancing of interest approach to the use of land by a state agency under city or county zoning laws, we do not feel such a test would be feasible or practical as applied to local building codes and proposed construction by the Board of Regents." (A similar case involving local building codes and a state university is Regents of Univ. of California v. City of Santa Monica, 77 Cal.App.3d 130, 143 Cal.Rptr. 276 (1978). Compare Varnado v. Southern University at New Orleans, 621 So.2d 176 (La.App.1993) holding that the university was bound by the local zoning ordinance as to the use of off-campus property.) Ten years later the Kansas court felt that the balancing test should apply to a state agency charged with the construction of prisons. In Herrmann v. Board of County Comm'rs, 246 Kan. 152, 785 P.2d 1003 (1990) the court held the agency not to be immune from local zoning, but found that the balancing test favored the construction of a correctional facility because a prison is a major project of compelling state interest; moreover, a federal court had ordered a new prison or, if the state failed, court-ordered release of felons.

2. The Temple Terrace case from Florida, relied on by the court in the principal case, dealt with the issue of whether a non-profit corporation performing what would otherwise be a state function in operating a home for the mentally retarded, was immune from a local zoning ordinance. See City of Muskegon Heights v. Moseler, 178 Mich.App. 609, 444 N.W.2d 145 (1989), reversed without opinion 433 Mich. 918, 448 N.W.2d 721 (1989).

3. Courts in many states have taken up the question of which test to use in resolving intergovernmental zoning conflicts. Although the superior sovereign and eminent domain tests still appear to prevail, the trend of decisions is clearly in the direction of the balancing of interests approach. See, e.g., City of Ames v. Story County, 392 N.W.2d 145 (Iowa 1986). The issue in this case is becoming very common—whether a city is subject to county regulations in locating a waste disposal facility. See City of Fargo v. Harwood Twp., 256 N.W.2d 694 (N.D.1977); City of Everett v. Snohomish County, 112 Wash.2d 433, 772 P.2d 992 (1989). But see City of Washington v. Warren County, 899 S.W.2d 863 (Mo. 1995) where the court espoused the eminent domain test and held that a city was immune from the county's zoning ordinance in connection with an airport; Macon–Bibb County Hospital Authority v. Madison, 204 Ga.App. 741, 420 S.E.2d 586 (1992), holding that the county hospital was immune from local zoning regulations as regards placement of roof signs on its medical center.

4. Several cases dealing with intergovernmental immunity involve the applicability of local zoning ordinances to construction of correctional facili-

ties by state agencies. This type of public use is almost certain to provoke neighbors and local communities to protest and litigate the question. In Dearden v. City of Detroit, 403 Mich. 257, 269 N.W.2d 139 (1978), the court held that the state department of corrections was immune from local zoning ordinances, and to hold otherwise would thwart state policy to locate correctional facilities in community settings. To the same effect, see City of New Orleans v. State of Louisiana, 364 So.2d 1020 (La.1978); County Commissioners of Bristol v. Conservation Comm'n of Dartmouth, 380 Mass. 706, 405 N.E.2d 637 (1980); Lane v. Zoning Bd. of Adjustment of City of Talladega, 669 So.2d 958 (Ala.Civ.App.1995). With these cases, compare City of Pittsburgh v. Commonwealth of Pennsylvania, 468 Pa. 174, 360 A.2d 607 (1976) and Matter of Suntide Inn Motel, 563 P.2d 125 (Okl.1977) (overruled by Independent School Dist. No. 89 v. City of Oklahoma City, 722 P.2d 1212 (Okl.1986) (adopting balancing test)), both discussed in the principal case. In Peter Garrett Gunsmith v. City of Dayton, 98 S.W.3d 517 (Ky. 2002) the court held that a state statute prohibiting local control of guns did not preempt local zoning restrictions pertaining to location of gun shops.

Also see City of Hattiesburg v. Region XII Comm'n on Mental Health and Retardation, 654 So.2d 516 (Miss.1995); Taylor v. State, Dept. of Rehabilitation and Correction, 43 Ohio App.3d 205, 540 N.E.2d 310 (1988) where the court held the state should make "reasonable efforts" to comply with local land use restrictions in siting correctional facilities, but need not follow local zoning procedures. And in City of Louisville Bd. of Zoning Adjustment v. Gailor, 920 S.W.2d 887 (Ky.App.1996) the court held that a private corporation seeking to construct and operate a correctional facility in downtown Louisville enjoyed the same immunity from local zoning regulations as a public entity. Contra to the Kentucky decision is Freedom Ranch, Inc. v. Board of Adjustment of City of Tulsa, 878 P.2d 380 (Okl. 1994), cert. denied 513 U.S. 1043, 115 S.Ct. 636, 130 L.Ed.2d 543.

5. What if the intergovernmental dispute involves a "foreign" government? In Town of Groton v. Laird, 353 F.Supp. 344 (D.Conn.1972) the court stated that the Navy was exempt from the local zoning ordinance. In Township of Middletown v. N/E Regional Office, United States Postal Service, 601 F.Supp. 125 (D.N.J.1985) the court held that the Postal Service was not subject to local zoning laws. And, in U.S. Postal Service v. Town of Greenwich, Connecticut, 901 F.Supp. 500 (D.Conn.1995) the court held that the state building code could not be applied to a post office construction project under the Supremacy Clause. Compare Pan American Health Organization v. Montgomery County, 338 Md. 214, 657 A.2d 1163 (1995) where the court held the international health organization was not exempt from the local zoning rules. This problem is discussed in 3 Williams, American Land Planning Law § 81.01 (1986).

6. If the ultimate issue in zoning conflicts between various levels of state government is that of legislative intent, do you think the best solution might be a statute spelling out the proper relationships? Along this line see City and County of Denver v. Board of County Commissioners, 782 P.2d 753 (Colo.1989) discussing the 1974 Land Use Act which allows both state and local government to regulate land uses that might have an impact beyond the immediate scope of the project. The case involved site selection and construction of major water and sewage treatment systems.

In South Carolina, S.C. Code Ann. § 6–7–830 (Supp. 1991) provides: "All agencies, departments and subdivisions of this State that use real property, as owner or tenant, in any county or municipality in this State shall be subject to the zoning ordinance thereof." See City of Charleston v. South Carolina State Ports Authority, 309 S.C. 118, 420 S.E.2d 497 (1992) (ports authority had to obtain architectural approval by city board of architectural review before constructing a building).

7. Of course, a statutory solution might not be viable in heading off conflicts between two cities or two counties. Consider, for example, City of Kirkwood v. City of Sunset Hills, 589 S.W.2d 31 (Mo. 1979) dealing with the issue of one municipality acquiring a municipal swimming pool in a neighboring town without complying with a zoning ordinance.

B. LOCAL–LOCAL CONFLICTS

CITY OF BRIDGETON v. CITY OF ST. LOUIS

Missouri Court of Appeals, E.D., 2000.
18 S.W.3d 107.

ROBERT G. DOWD, JR., JUDGE.

The City of Bridgeton (Bridgeton) appeals from a judgment in a court-tried civil case in an action for declaratory judgment and injunction which seeks to prevent the City of St. Louis (St. Louis) from proceeding with its plan, W–1W, for the expansion of Lambert–St. Louis International Airport (Lambert Airport) and St. Louis's counterclaim which seeks a declaration that St. Louis is not required to comply with Bridgeton's zoning ordinances.* * *

Bridgeton is a constitutional charter city under Missouri Constitution, Art. VI, Section 19, located in St. Louis County, Missouri. The City of St. Louis is a special constitutional charter city under Missouri Constitution, Art. VI, Section 31. St. Louis has owned and operated Lambert Airport since the 1920's. Lambert Airport is located outside of St. Louis, in Bridgeton and other adjacent cities in northwest St. Louis County.

In 1993, it was determined that the Master Plan for the airport needed to be updated. St. Louis proposed to add a runway and terminals to Lambert Airport. The proposed W–1W plan would extend the runway into an area of Bridgeton that is not zoned for an airport. The new runway is needed to allow for simultaneous landing of aircraft during inclement weather. The Federal Aviation Administration (FAA) requires runways to be 3,400 feet apart in order to have simultaneous instrument landings. Currently, the two major runways at Lambert Airport are less than 1,400 feet apart. At Lambert Airport, simultaneous instrument landings are not possible during inclement weather which creates delays to passengers in St. Louis and other destinations. The costs of these delays to the national economy is reflected in the FAA's Record of Decision which predicted a savings (based on the construction of the W–1W Project) of $1.9 billion at Lambert Airport and $5.1 billion to the

National Air Transportation System during 2005 to 2015. There are also predicted savings to passengers from reduced delays of $1.4 billion at Lambert Airport and $9.5 billion nationally. The FAA, after considering several plans, approved the W–1W plan as the only possible, prudent and practicable alternative.

Bridgeton sued St. Louis to prevent the expansion of the airport into Bridgeton in contravention of Bridgeton's zoning laws. The trial court found for St. Louis. This appeal follows.

In its first point, Bridgeton claims the trial court erred when it held Section 305.200(3), did not prohibit St. Louis from expanding Lambert Airport in Bridgeton without first obtaining Bridgeton's zoning approval. Bridgeton argues the plain language of the statute prohibits the construction of the new runway in violation of Bridgeton's Zoning Ordinance.

This same issue was litigated and decided in *City of St. Louis v. City of Bridgeton,* 705 S.W.2d 524 (Mo.App. E.D.1985) (hereinafter *Bridgeton I*). In *Bridgeton I,* St. Louis wanted to construct an airport employee parking lot in Bridgeton on land St. Louis owned. The area was not zoned for this use. After the Bridgeton City Council unanimously rejected a proposed ordinance granting St. Louis permission to construct the lot under a section of the zoning ordinance applicable to off-street parking, St. Louis sought declaratory and injunctive relief seeking immunity from Bridgeton's zoning. In its opinion, this court analyzed Section 305.200(3). The pertinent part of Section 305.200(3) states:

> ... no airport or landing field shall be established or located in any county, city or city under special charter in violation of any plan or master airport plan or zoning regulation restricting the location of an airport or landing field adopted by the planning commission of any such county, city or city under special charter.

Judge Reinhard, writing for this court, found in analyzing this portion of Section 305.200(3) that "[t]his provision relates to the establishment of a new airport in a new location, not the operation of an existing one, and we find it inapplicable here." *Bridgeton I,* 705 S.W.2d at 528. We further note the absence of, or specific legislative silence related to, any statutory language regarding expansion or addition in Section 305.200(3). In Chapter 305, the term "establish" patently refers to an action undertaken at the outset of an airport's existence; wherein the act of establishing an airport or landing field is an act separate from acquiring, leasing or setting apart real property for such purpose. Section 305.210. Further, paragraph three of Section 305.200 states, "no airport or landing field shall be established or located in any county, city or city under special charter...."; whereas paragraph one of Section 305.200 provides that a county, city or special charter city can acquire property "for an airport or landing field or *addition* thereto...." (emphasis added.) It may be reasonably concluded that this language evinces a legislative intent to distinguish between a new airport and the expansion of existing facilities; thereby avoiding the situation where no surrounding municipalities would allow expansion within their boundaries; and thereby render expansion an impossibility and potentially, as a result, doom a viable airport, as well as the economic well-being of the dependent region.

The addition of a runway to Lambert Airport is not the establishment of a new airport in a new location; it is the operation and expansion of an existing airport. Lambert Airport is an established airport. The proposed runway addition would enhance facilities already located there. The runway is meant to be an addition to existing facilities. We find W–1W is the expansion of an existing and operating airport. We again find Section 305.200(3) is inapplicable to this case. Point denied.

In its second point, Bridgeton claims the trial court erred when it ruled a new runway was not a "landing field" under Section 305.200(3). Bridgeton argues the construction of a new runway is a "landing field" under Section 305.200(3), and it cannot be built without zoning approval.

The language of the statute prohibits the establishment or location of a landing field or airport. We found under Bridgeton's first point that St. Louis is expanding an existing airport. St. Louis is not establishing or locating an airport or a landing field. Section 305.200(3) again is inapplicable. Point denied.

In its third point, Bridgeton claims the trial court erred when it held St. Louis did not first have to apply to Bridgeton for zoning approval. Bridgeton argues the Bridgeton Zoning Ordinance and the Intergovernmental Zoning Immunity Ordinance are valid exercises of Bridgeton's authority and the evidence did not establish facts which would invalidate the ordinances. Bridgeton argues that even if Section 305.200(3) does not prohibit the airport expansion into Bridgeton, the basic principles of home rule embodied in Article VI, Section 19(a) of the Missouri Constitution should bar St. Louis from moving forward with W–1W. Bridgeton claims St. Louis must seek zoning approval from Bridgeton or establish that it is immune. St. Louis argues the determination of whether or not St. Louis is immune from Bridgeton's zoning regulations is a question of law for the courts, not a question for a city council to decide. Bridgeton argues St. Louis must exhaust administrative remedies by first seeking immunity under the Ordinance before seeking judicial relief. * * *

Here, the question is whether or not St. Louis is immune from Bridgeton's zoning ordinances—a question of law. We find it is not necessary for St. Louis to exhaust administrative remedies before asking the court in its counterclaim to determine immunity. If the question had been "Is the area zoned R–1 or R–2?," it would be a question requiring the special expertise within the scope of the administrative agency's responsibility. Bridgeton's City Council has special knowledge and expertise in determining the zoning in areas of Bridgeton. Instead the question to be resolved here is whether or not St. Louis is immune from

Bridgeton's zoning ordinances. We find it is not necessary for St. Louis to exhaust administrative remedies. Point denied. * * *

Both parties pleaded facts which were relevant to a balancing of interests test. Bridgeton specifically pleaded the negative effects the airport expansion would have on the community of Bridgeton. Bridgeton was aware intergovernmental immunity was at issue if the court found the Intergovernmental Immunity Ordinance was invalid. St. Louis asserts in its counterclaim that Bridgeton's Zoning Ordinance cannot be applied to prevent St. Louis from proceeding with its planned expansion of the Airport under the W–1W Project. St. Louis also stated in its counterclaim that a justiciable controversy exists between the parties as to whether St. Louis is subject to Bridgeton's Zoning Ordinance in connection with St. Louis's plan to expand the airport under the W–1W Project. Consequently, St. Louis would not be subject to Bridgeton's Zoning Ordinance if it had intergovernmental immunity. We find this issue was sufficiently pleaded to put Bridgeton on notice that the balancing of interests test would be used to show St. Louis's intergovernmental immunity. Point denied. * * *

We also find the trial court properly applied the balance of interests test. The trial court heard evidence from both parties considering the impact of the Airport expansion. In resolving claims of governmental immunity from zoning regulations, Missouri courts have applied two tests: (1) the "power of eminent domain" test, and (2) the "balancing of interests" test. *City of Washington v. Warren County,* 899 S.W.2d 863, 865–66 (Mo.1995).

The court in Bridgeton I detailed factors to consider when evaluating immunity under the balancing of interests test. "The factors the court considered were the nature and scope of the instrumentality seeking immunity, the kind of function or land use involved, the extent of the public interest to be served thereby, the effect local land use regulation would have upon the enterprise concerned and the impact upon legitimate local interest." *Bridgeton I,* 705 S.W.2d at 529. "In some instances one factor will be more influential than another or may be so significant as to completely overshadow all others." Id. "And there will undoubtedly be cases, as there have been in the past, where the broader public interest is so important that immunity must be granted even though the local interests may be great." Id.

Here, the trial court evaluated the interests of the parties using the balancing of interests test. In its analysis, the trial court concluded St. Louis was immune from Bridgeton's zoning ordinances because the importance of expanding Lambert Airport pursuant to the W–1W plan outweighed Bridgeton's interest in enforcing its zoning ordinances as to St. Louis.

The trial court considered Lambert Airport's current inadequate capacity which might endanger its status as a hub airport. The trial court considered Lambert Airport's inability to accommodate traffic during inclement weather. The trial court also considered the savings to passengers because of reduced delays. There was also evidence of the regional and statewide importance of expanding Lambert Airport. Lambert Airport's location west of St. Louis provides important access to Jefferson City, the State capitol, and its location benefits the St. Louis region concentrated westward of St. Louis City. Delay or impediment to Lambert Airport's expansion would be detrimental to the economic development of the State of Missouri. Additionally, there was credible testimony that airports generate significant regional economic growth in terms of jobs and commercial activity, including in those communities in close proximity to the Airport.

The trial court also heard evidence of Bridgeton's interest in maintaining their community. The acquisition for the expansion would require over 18% of Bridgeton's total land area including more than 1,900 residential parcels, 6 schools, at least 2 parks, 6 churches and 75 businesses. After considering all of the evidence, the court found the expansion would benefit not only citizens of St. Louis, but citizens in Bridgeton, the entire metropolitan area, and the State of Missouri.

The trial court examined copious amounts of evidence and determined St. Louis is immune from Bridgeton's zoning ordinances using the balancing of interests test. The substantial benefits conferred by the operation of the airport on the public clearly outweigh the interests of Bridgeton. The expansion of Lambert Airport is essential to its survival. We find there was substantial evidence to support the trial court's finding, the finding was not against the weight of the evidence, and the trial court did not erroneously declare or apply the law. Point denied. * * *

Judgment affirmed.

CITY OF NEW ROCHELLE v. TOWN OF MAMARONECK

United States District Court, Southern District of New York, 2000.
111 F.Supp.2d 353.

McMAHON, DISTRICT JUDGE.

For some months, two shore communities in lower Westchester County have been embroiled in debate over a proposal to build an IKEA, the Swedish home furnishings superstore, on a 16.4–acre area on the eastern border of the City of New Rochelle, New York. Within New Rochelle, the matter has generated an extraordinary amount of dissension. City officials view the proposal as vital to urban redevelopment, while residents of the stable working-class neighborhood that would be destroyed if the City acquired the property needed for construction of the store oppose the project. But the highly publicized debate is not confined to the City's borders. Fearing that the store would create serious traffic congestion on its nearby streets, the adjacent Town of Mamaroneck has actively opposed the IKEA project. When it became clear that New Rochelle intended to proceed with condemnation of the property, Mamaroneck's Town Board passed an ordinance, known as the Local Impact Review Law ("Local Law"), which requires that its Town Board review the impact of certain major development projects in an area outside of, but adjacent to, Mamaroneck. The Law provides that a permit must be granted upon a showing that the impact of the development on the Town will be mitigated.

New Rochelle commenced an action in the New York State Supreme Court for declaratory and injunctive relief and damages as a result of the passage of the Local Law. It asserts several constitutional and statutory claims under both Federal and State law. Defendants timely removed the action to this Court pursuant to 28 U.S.C. § 1441(b), on the ground that this Court has original jurisdiction over the federal claims in suit. Defendants now move to dismiss the complaint on various substantive grounds, including lack of standing, lack of ripeness and failure to state a federal claim. Plaintiff opposes that motion and has cross-moved to remand the action to state court.

For the reasons stated below, Defendants' motion is granted in part and denied in part. The state law claims are remanded to New York State Supreme Court. Plaintiff's remaining federal claim is stayed pending resolution of the issues of New York statutory and constitutional law that are paramount in this very local matter. * * *

"Whether a claimant has standing is 'the threshold question in every federal case, determining the power of the court to entertain the suit.'" *In re Gucci,* 126 F.3d 380, 387–88 (2d Cir.1997). To establish standing to bring a complaint, a plaintiff must allege a personal stake in the outcome of the case and a "distinct and palpable" injury by way of "specific, concrete facts." *Duke Power Co. v. Carolina Environmental Study Group, Inc.,* 438 U.S. 59, 72, 98 S.Ct. 2620, 57 L.Ed.2d 595 (1978). Mamaroneck argues that, because the Local Law imposes an environmental review requirement on "developers" and "development," but imposes no obligation on any municipal entities, including New Rochelle, New Rochelle lacks standing to challenge the law. Mamaroneck is wrong.

Contrary to Mamaroneck's contention, the Local Law does not limit its provisions to "developers" or "development," but rather applies to any "project" that is "undertaken" that "abuts, adjoins or is adjacent to a Town street." (Local Law at §§ 130–2, 130–3.) Nothing in the plain language of the statute limits its applicability to "developers." Nor does the Local Law explicitly exclude municipalities or municipally-sponsored projects from the permit requirements. It is thus reasonable to conclude that New Rochelle's current undertaking of a major urban renewal project within the Fifth Avenue Redevelopment Area involving the "physical alteration of 10 acres or more" would fall well within the Defendants' new Local Law. I therefore find that New Rochelle has sufficiently alleged an "injury in fact" or such a personal stake in the outcome of the litigation as to warrant invocation of the Court's jurisdiction.

New Rochelle shares a 3.5 mile border with Mamaroneck. The proposed Fifth Avenue Urban Renewal Area abuts Mamaroneck. New Rochelle is in the midst of a comprehensive environmental review and other deliberations involving the Urban Renewal Area and the adoption of an Urban Renewal Plan. Indeed, Defendants have on several occasions conceded that the passage of the Local Law and its timing was directed at forcing New Rochelle to abandon its redevelopment efforts in the Fifth Avenue Area, specifically, the assemblage of property necessary for the development of the IKEA site. For example, the Local Law was adopted after New Rochelle rejected Mamaroneck's request that Mamaroneck be granted "equal approver" status over the project under SEQRA. New Rochelle clearly has a sufficient legal interest and direct stake in being able to undertake redevelopment projects within its own borders without subjecting itself to the independent jurisdiction of the Town of Mamaroneck. And as Mamaroneck's efforts were specifically aimed at stalling New Rochelle's redevelopment plans, it is disingenuous, at best, for Mamaroneck to claim that New Rochelle is "attempting to assert the rights that actually belong, if at all, to the developer or owner of property that may be subject to the Local Law."

Aside from the Urban Renewal Plan, New Rochelle also alleges that it owns roads and other properties within the area affected by the Local Law. Even if the law were not aimed specifically at the IKEA project (which it clearly is), New Rochelle would have sufficient allegations of injury to its own real property to confer standing upon it in this matter. * * *

Defendants further contend that, even if Plaintiff has standing to challenge the Local Law, New Rochelle's claims are speculative and premature because neither New Rochelle nor any developer has made an application under the Local Law. New Rochelle alleges that it suffered impairment of its state and federal rights at the moment the law was passed. To the extent that Count V of the complaint can be read to allege a taking of New Rochelle's real property in violation of the Due Process Clause, Defendants are correct; that claim is not ripe for review. All other claims, however, are ripe. * * *

Mamaroneck moves to dismiss Count IV on the ground that the Local Law is a local quality of life ordinance that has no identifiable impact on interstate commerce. New Rochelle counters that the complaint pleads a Commerce Clause violation by alleging that the Local Law will "[i]mpede the free flow of commerce and discriminate against businesses or developments desiring to locate in the City, thus causing it economic loss." New Rochelle also contends that its allegation that the "Local Law jeopardizes any major development in New Rochelle that borders Mamaroneck, specifically the Urban Renewal Project, provides a disincentive for any developer to come into New Rochelle, and has the potential of depressing the City's economy and harming the well-being of its residents," states a claim for violation of the Commerce Clause.

The Commerce Clause provides that "[t]he Congress shall have Power ... To regulate Commerce ... among the several States...." U.S. Const., Art. I, § 8, cl. 3. The so-called dormant Commerce Clause, the scope of which has been defined through judicial opinions, forbids States and their subdivisions to regulate interstate commerce. The Supreme Court has generally distinguished between two types of impermissible state or local regulations: (1) those that discriminate against out-of-state interests; and (2) those that do not discriminate against out-of-state interests, but have an incidental effect on interstate commerce. The first category of laws receive strict scrutiny, and are virtually per se violations of the Commerce Clause. *See Oregon Waste Sys., Inc. v. Department of Envtl. Quality,* 511 U.S. 93, 99, 114 S.Ct. 1345, 128 L.Ed.2d 13 (1994). In analyzing the second category of laws, courts balance the burden imposed on interstate commerce against the benefits provided to local interests. *See Pike v. Bruce Church, Inc.,* 397 U.S. 137, 142, 90 S.Ct. 844, 25 L.Ed.2d 174 (1970). Under this balancing test, the law will be held valid unless the burden on interstate commerce is clearly excessive in relation to the putative local benefits. See id. See also *C & A Carbone, Inc. v. Clarkstown,* 511 U.S. 383, 402, 114 S.Ct. 1677, 128 L.Ed.2d 399 (1994) (O'Connor, J. concurring) (internal citations omitted). But the Court has recognized that the line between per se violations and those that require a balancing of considerations is not always clear. Thus, the critical consideration in determining whether a statute is a constitutionally permissible regulation "is the overall effect of the statute on both local and interstate activity." *Brown–Forman Distillers Corp. v. New York State Liquor Authority,* 476 U.S. 573, 579, 106 S.Ct. 2080, 90 L.Ed.2d 552 (1986).

Turning first to whether the complaint alleges a per se violation of the Commerce Clause, I conclude that it does not. Mamaroneck asserts that the Local Law was enacted solely to protect the environment and living conditions in and around Mamaroneck. New Rochelle counters that the Law was intended and designed to impede the Urban Redevelopment Project. The complaint alleges discrimination against non-local, i.e. non-Mamaroneck, commerce. It does not, however, allege discrimination against out-of-state interests. * * *

A local ordinance that discriminates against non-local interests but does not explicitly discriminate against out-of-state economic interests may nonetheless implicate the dormant commerce clause. Legislation relating to "health and safety" and to the "protection of the environment and conservation of natural resources" is a legitimate exercise of state and local authority. *Gary D. Peake Excavating Inc. v. Town Bd. of Hancock,* 93 F.3d 68 (2d Cir.1996). Defendants contend that, because the Local Law concerns itself exclusively with environmental, health and safety matters, and because the benefits of the law redound to the locality and local residents, it cannot be said to violate the Commerce Clause. However, if there is any effect on interstate commerce, no matter how incidental, I am required to weigh the magnitude of the effect on interstate commerce against the local benefits. See *Pike,* 397 U.S. 137, 90 S.Ct. 844, 25 L.Ed.2d 174.

* * *

Because the Local Law is an economically protectionist law, New Rochelle argues that it represents an impediment to the free flow of goods in interstate commerce. I find Plaintiff's argument that the Local Law has an incidental effect on interstate commerce, because many of the builders and contractors who would be engaged in construction in the redevelopment zone come from out of state and use products that travel in interstate commerce, to be insufficient. This sort of "house that Jack built" argument is far too attenuated to support a conclusion of interference in interstate commerce and fails as a matter of law. (Indeed, accepting such an argument would be to accept that every nearly every municipal zoning regulation is a Commerce Clause violation.)

However, the Local Law may have other potential effects on interstate commerce. For example, discovery might reveal that the law was, in fact, aimed solely at preventing national or international retail "superstores" from being built in the area. Or it might be revealed that Mamaroneck was looking to keep out streams of shoppers from across the Connecticut border, which lies just ten miles from the redevelopment area.* * *

I therefore deny Defendants' motion to dismiss the Commerce Clause claim.

Counts V and VI allege due process and equal protection violations. Plaintiff's due process claim consists of three grounds: (1) the Local Law constitutes a taking of New Rochelle's property without due process; (2) the Local Law, on its face, represents an unlawful taking of New Rochelle's property interest in its own permitting process; and (3) the Local Law is unconstitutionally vague. New Rochelle's equal protection claim alleges that the Local Law "will inhibit new construction in the City of New Rochelle, and shift development away from the City and to [Mamaroneck], as well as cause economic benefit to existing businesses within [Mamaroneck] by stifling competition." Additionally, Plaintiff argues that the Local Law creates a statutory classification insofar as it applies to those properties that fall within the Local Law's parameters: (a) "the construction of 250 or more residential units," (b) "the physical alteration of ten acres or more," (c) "the construction of a facility with more than 100,000 square feet," of (d) a project that "involves parking for more than 1,000 vehicles," provided (e) said development project "abuts, adjoins or is adjacent to a Town street within or upon the border of the Town of Mamaroneck. . . ." (citing Local law No. 4–2000.) Plaintiff contends that the Law is unconstitutional because such classification—which treats different property owners differently—lacks any rational justification.

The threshold issue, which neither party has addressed, is whether New Rochelle, a municipal corporation organized under the laws of New

York State, can maintain a suit challenging the Local Law on the basis that its rights to due process and equal protection were infringed. While the Second Circuit has not yet spoken on this issue, I conclude that New Rochelle cannot maintain a claim under these Clauses.

It has long been the case that a municipality may not invoke the protections of the Fourteenth Amendment against its own state. *See City of Newark v. New Jersey,* 262 U.S. 192, 196, 43 S.Ct. 539, 67 L.Ed. 943 (1923). A municipality is thus prevented from attacking state legislation on the grounds that the law violates the municipality's own rights. See, e.g., *City of New Orleans v. New Orleans Water–Works Co.,* 142 U.S. 79, 89–91, 12 S.Ct. 142, 35 L.Ed. 943 (1891); *Hunter v. City of Pittsburgh,* 207 U.S. 161, 28 S.Ct. 40, 52 L.Ed. 151 (1907). Moreover, while municipalities or other state political subdivisions may challenge the constitutionality of state legislation on certain grounds and in certain circumstances, these do not include challenges brought under the Due Process or Equal Protection Clauses of the Fourteenth Amendment. See, e.g., *Rogers v. Brockette,* 588 F.2d 1057 (5th Cir.), cert. denied, 444 U.S. 827, 100 S.Ct. 52, 62 L.Ed.2d 35 (1979). This is because "a municipal corporation, in its own right, receives no protection from the Equal Protection or Due Process Clauses vis-a-vis its creating state." *South Macomb Disposal Authority v. Township of Washington,* 790 F.2d 500, 505 (6th Cir.1986). * * *

In *South Macomb,* the Sixth Circuit addressed the question of whether a municipal corporation could sue another township within the same state on the ground that the township imposed certain waste disposal permitting requirements in violation of the municipal corporation's right to due process and equal protection. Applying the same reasoning that has led federal courts to bar municipalities from bringing due process and equal protection claims against their own states, the Sixth Circuit concluded:

> [T]he Fourteenth Amendment simply does not prescribe guidelines and impose restriction upon one political subdivision vis-a-vis another political subdivision. The relationship between the entities is a matter of state concern; the Fourteenth Amendment protections and limitations do not apply.

I agree with the holding of *South Macomb,* and dismiss Counts V and VI to the extent they allege a violation of New Rochelle's rights as a governmental entity.

* * *

In order to plead a violation of its due process rights under the Fifth and Fourteenth Amendments, a plaintiff must allege that it has a protectable property interest, that it was deprived of that property interest by the adoption of the Local Law; and that the deprivation occurred without due process of law or the payment of just compensation. See *Board of Regents v. Roth,* 408 U.S. 564, 576–77, 92 S.Ct. 2701,

33 L.Ed.2d 548 (1972); *Brady v. Town of Colchester,* 863 F.2d 205, 211 (1988).

As noted above, any real property takings claim is not presently justiciable because New Rochelle has not applied for approval through the Local Law. With its alternative theory, Plaintiff argues that Mamaroneck has interfered with its jurisdiction and control over the Urban Renewal project, and has thereby interfered with its ability as a sovereign municipality to bestow various "forms of largess"—including land use approvals and permits—upon private applicants within its own municipal boundaries. New Rochelle contends that it maintains a property interest in the power to grant permits, and that any derogation of that power is a deprivation of its property.

* * *

New Rochelle's claim that the Local Law represented a taking of that property in violation of the Fifth and Fourteenth Amendments, * * * would be non-justiciable until Mamaroneck actually rendered a final decision under the law. Second, the holding of Macomb compels me to conclude that, where the authority to grant "largess" is conferred by the state, it is matter of state law to resolve any alleged infringements on that authority. It is simply not a question of the property rights of a "person" as contemplated by the Due Process Clause.

Plaintiff's allegation of an equal protection violation likewise fails. Where a statute challenged under equal protection does not burden a fundamental right or draw a distinction based on suspect classification, the statute will be upheld if it is rationally related to a legitimate government purpose. See *Nicholas v. Tucker,* 114 F.3d 17, 20 (2d Cir.1997). * * * I find that Mamaroneck had a legitimate governmental purpose in determining that developments of a certain size and location required additional environmental review.

Plaintiff next argues that the Local Law distinguishes between "applicable projects that are adjoining or adjacent to a Town street, but not similar projects that are adjoining or adjacent to a State or County road located within the Town of Mamaroneck." It further argues that the Law impermissibly distinguishes between residents and non-residents of Mamaroneck. The first argument is silly, as the Law clearly states it is concerned about a specific area adjoining Mamaroneck's border; I do not read Mamaroneck's use of the terms "town road" as making any distinction between types of roads within Mamaroneck. In any event, neither of these arguments, however, is enough to meet the high threshold for equal protection challenges to economic regulations. The purposes of the Local Law are stated in the law itself and clearly establish the relationship between the law and Mamaroneck's interest in the health, safety, welfare, comfort and convenience of its residents.

* * *

The state law claims, Counts I, II, III, IV and VIII, are hereby remanded to the New York State Supreme Court. Counts V and VI are dismissed. Count IV, the Commerce Clause claim, is stayed pending resolution of the State law claims.

Notes

1. Can a local unit rule its provincial world and ignore the effects of its zoning upon "outsiders"? If not, how can these outside interests be heard and be protected? Note that these may be interests of immediate neighbors as in Borough of Cresskill v. Borough of Dumont, 15 N.J. 238, 104 A.2d 441 (Sup. Ct.1954), or wider metropolitan regional interests as in State ex rel. Anshe Chesed Congregation v. Bruggemeier, 97 Ohio App. 67, 115 N.E.2d 65 (1953), where a satellite village of 1,800 was required to take a metropolitan-wide synagogue with 5,000 members. Or there may be state-wide interest as in the case of zoning affecting the state highways or the state's public waters. Or the interests might be national, as where local zoning has impact on national defense activities, national parks or forests or national transportation routes. See, e.g., MacDonald v. Board of County Comm'rs for Prince George's County, 238 Md. 549, 210 A.2d 325 (1965) which involved the national interest in protecting the view from Mt. Vernon from a proposed high-rise apartment building across the river in Maryland. Also see United States v. Board of Supervisors, 611 F.2d 1367 (4th Cir.1979), holding that the United States had standing to seek an injunction to restrain construction of high-rise office buildings across the Potomac from the capitol. The interest of the government was its proprietary interest in the capitol and protecting the symmetry of its skyline and the setting of its monuments. The gravamen of the complaint was the ultra vires action of defendant in granting a special use permit.

Will the courts always act to protect such interest? If so, on what substantive legal basis? The statutory requirement of a "comprehensive plan"? Due process and its prolific offspring, "general welfare"? Equal protection? And what about party-in-interest rules on the procedural side? Are these such that interested outside groups, local units, the state or the federal government can intervene in local zoning proceedings and insist on judicial review? Would an administrative appeals procedure to a state agency or to a joint local-state board be a better solution?

2. In Wrigley Properties, Inc. v. City of Ladue, 369 S.W.2d 397 (Mo. 1963), a city which lay in the path of better residential development and representing about the finest residential development in the entire St. Louis metropolitan area refused to change its residential zoning so as to authorize a ten acre shopping center. The question, said the court, was fairly debatable. One of the reasons cited by the court as possibly sustaining the council's refusal to rezone was "that the proposed use as a shopping center appears to be *more for the benefit of other cities and towns than for the benefit of Ladue.*" (Emphasis supplied.) Compare this with Duffcon Concrete Products v. Cresskill, 1 N.J. 509, 64 A.2d 347, 9 A.L.R.2d 678 (1949), where the New Jersey court concluded that a densely settled suburb could properly exclude industry if it has some other place to go in the general area, but nevertheless, where the following general standard was announced:

> What may be the most appropriate use of any particular property depends not only on all the conditions, physical, economic and social,

prevailing within the municipality and its needs, present and reasonably prospective, but also on the nature of the entire region in which the municipality is located and the use to which the land in that region has been or may be put most advantageously. The effective development of a region should not and cannot be made to depend upon the adventitious location of municipal boundaries, often prescribed decades or even centuries ago and based in many instances on considerations of geography, of commerce, or of politics that are no longer significant with respect to zoning.

See Haar, Regionalism and Realism in Land Use Planning, 105 U.Pa. L.Rev. 5 (1957), and Note, Zoning Against the Public Welfare: Judicial Limitations on Municipal Parochialism, 71 Yale L.J. 720 (1962).

3. On this question of regional considerations, what about the following: A town in the state of New York adopted a law which rezoned part of the town, including an area contiguous to the New Jersey border, from a residential district of one-acre plots to an "office park" district. At the time the law was passed, the land which was rezoned was "mostly wooded" and sloped up from a river. The new zoning provision made possible the construction of a large office-research complex. A municipal corporation of the State of New Jersey brought an action in federal court complaining with respect to the action taken by the adjoining New York community. The New Jersey community argued that it would be injured by reduction in revenues which would result from depreciation in the value of its property and by the need for additional expenditures "to provide for adequate traffic and other related expenses." It sought damages in excess of $10,000 and declaratory relief. The New York town moved for summary judgment alleging that the complaint failed to state a cause of action. Aside from the merits of the claim, does the New Jersey township have standing to sue? See Township of River Vale v. Town of Orangetown, 403 F.2d 684 (2d Cir.1968). Compare Orange Fibre Mills, Inc. v. City of Middletown, 94 Misc.2d 233, 404 N.Y.S.2d 296 (1978). Also see Village of Barrington Hills v. Village of Hoffman Estates, 81 Ill.2d 392, 43 Ill.Dec. 37, 410 N.E.2d 37 (1980), certiorari denied, 449 U.S. 1126, 101 S.Ct. 943, 67 L.Ed.2d 112 (1981), where the court held that one municipality had standing to challenge another's zoning decision to allow construction of an open-air music theatre near the residential areas in the plaintiff village, and City of Thornton v. Board of County Comm'rs, 42 Colo.App. 102, 595 P.2d 264 (1979), where the city was allowed standing to challenge the county rezoning of property adjacent to city-owned land from agricultural to planned unit development. In Town of Mesilla v. City of Las Cruces, 120 N.M. 69, 898 P.2d 121 (1995) the court held that a town was a "person aggrieved" and had standing to challenge rezoning of the neighboring city that allegedly resulted in aesthetic and economic injury to the plaintiff town.

4. A common problem in recent years, involves the shopping center developer who secures relatively inexpensive undeveloped land near a city which is usually subject to less onerous county regulation and the developer proposes a "regional" shopping center which may have a harmful economic impact on city plans to either preserve or redevelop a viable downtown retail district or to establish a regional shopping center at a different location.

Does the city have any basis for blocking the proposed development? Consider the following cases:

a. Save a Valuable Environment (SAVE) v. City of Bothell, 89 Wash.2d 862, 576 P.2d 401 (1978): The city rezoned a 141 acre farm to permit construction of a major regional shopping center. SAVE, a nonprofit environmental protection organization, challenged the rezoning as having a detrimental effect on both the environment and the economy of the area. After holding that SAVE had standing, the court stated:

> * * * Bothell may not act in disregard of the effects outside its boundaries. Where the potential exists that a zoning action will cause a serious environmental effect outside jurisdictional borders, the zoning body must serve the welfare of the entire affected community. If it does not do so it acts in an arbitrary and capricious manner. * * *
>
> The action was arbitrary and capricious [in this case] in that it failed to serve the welfare of the community as a whole. Specifically, adverse environmental effects and potentially severe financial burdens on the affected community have been completely disregarded. * * *
>
> We do not hold that a city proposing a rezone which will affect neighboring jurisdictions must engage in inter-jurisdictional planning. It is clear, however, that such coordinated planning is desirable and might have avoided the result in this case.

b. Carmel Estates, Inc. v. Land Conservation and Development Commission, 51 Or.App. 435, 625 P.2d 1367 (1981). The Board of County Commissioners approved rezoning 26.5 acres of agricultural land for the construction of a shopping center halfway between the cities of Sandy and Gresham. The city of Sandy and the Metropolitan Service District challenged the proposed rezoning as inconsistent with several goals of the existing comprehensive plan, most particularly the goal prohibiting conversion of agricultural land to urban uses without a showing of necessity. In the report of the hearing officer (which was adopted by the Commission), after stating that to allow this development would frustrate the very purpose of urban growth boundaries and render the plan useless in controlling urban sprawl, the following comment appears:

> According to the testimony, this development would seriously frustrate urban-level utilization of lands in Sandy. Mr. Roger Jordan, city manager, testified that '* * * a development of this magnitude only three or four miles away from our incorporated boundaries, when we have made all the investments to accommodate growth within our boundaries, would have a drastic effect.' * * * Mr. Jack Hammond, the city attorney stated that a consultant hired by the city found that [the proposed] shopping center would reduce retail sales in Sandy by 17.7 percent * * * In response to this undisputed evidence, the Board of County Commissioners found:

"The City of Sandy has presented argument that it will suffer economic injury because of increased competition to its existing and planned commercial enterprises. The Board has weighed the detriment to the city against the public benefit of the proposed uses and finds that the proposed uses outweigh the detriment to the City of Sandy." Findings, p. 6.

This finding ignores applicable law. Proof that rural development will injure a city is proof of a Goal 14 violation. Cities and counties are not in competition for urban developments. Cities are the housing, employment, shopping, and service centers and providers. * * * The whole point of Goal 14 is that rural lands are not available to satisfy the state's housing, shopping, nonresource employment, and other non-farm and non-forest related needs.

5. Sometimes the shopping center dispute involves two cities which are vying for the large shopping center so as to increase the tax base. This problem is typified by the case of City of Rohnert Park v. Harris, 601 F.2d 1040 (9th Cir.1979), cert. denied sub nom. City of Rohnert Park v. Landrieu, 445 U.S. 961, 100 S.Ct. 1647, 64 L.Ed.2d 236 (1980). Here two towns, seven miles apart, each wanted to develop a regional shopping center. When one of the towns lined up a developer and anchor tenants, the other town sued alleging violation of antitrust laws, HUD regulations (selling urban renewal land at under market value to the developer) and the federal administrative procedure act. The court found no cause of action.

Chapter VII

SMART GROWTH AND GROWTH MANAGEMENT

SECTION 1. INTRODUCTION

A. LOCAL LAND USE CONTROLS THAT ACHIEVE SMART GROWTH

"Smart Growth" admits of no clear definition. It provides a popular label for a growth strategy that addresses current concerns about traffic congestion, disappearing open space, non-point source pollution, the high cost of housing, increasing local property taxes, longer commutes, and the diminishing quality of community life. To accomplish smart growth, government must take two related actions. The first is the designation of discrete geographical areas into which private market growth pressures are directed. The second is the designation of other areas for recreation, conservation, and environmental protection. This reduces a complicated subject to its two most essential features and leaves much for further discussion. This focus, however, permits a precise description of how smart growth can be implemented, if a consensus for it is developed.

The balance between land development and conservation that is a standard component of most smart growth and growth management strategies is reflected in this chapter and Chapter IX which discusses local environmental law. In this chapter we touch on the imposition of moratoriums on development, which create time to think under pressure and revise the local land use regime; local and statewide growth management strategies; efforts to preserve agricultural land in rural areas; and a few of the more popular innovative land use tools such as floating zones, planned unit development districts, overlay zones, incentives, and performance zoning. These latter techniques are sometimes referred to as neo-Euclidian measures: designed to breathe flexibility into the rigid uniformity of the district-bound zoning approved in Euclid v. Ambler Realty. Chapter IX covers the many types of laws localities are adopting to protect natural resources from the adverse impacts of development. Together, these chapters give the student an introduction to the full range of techniques being used to achieve smart growth objectives.

What is accomplished by directing development to growth areas? The aspiration is to create a sense of community, promote economically viable development, ensure the ease of movement and safety of residents, and preserve open space, natural resources, and sustainable habitats. In 1979, a growth boundary encompassing Portland and 23 surrounding towns was established to comply with Oregon's innovative growth management law.[1] Fifteen miles from city hall, outside the bounded growth area, is the Willamette River Valley, where growth is limited to small-scale development consistent with the predominately agricultural use of the land. Maryland's novel smart growth spending law directs state infrastructure improvements into settled communities and "priority funding areas," which are growth areas designated by county governments.[2]

Concentrating development in designated growth areas, bounded in some specific way, is a necessary factor in the smart growth equation. Bounded growth, however, is not a novel concept. Local governments have traditionally drawn blueprints for growth in the design of their zoning codes. Zoning's primary characteristic is the creation of hard-edged districts that separate land uses into residential, commercial, and industrial zones. Traditional zoning districts separate land uses to advance a number of public purposes. The architects of zoning thought that this approach to community planning protected children in residential districts from commercial and industrial traffic, for example, and protected residential property values by placing noxious and inconsistent uses in distant locations. The zoning enabling acts in most states enable local governments to divide the community into zoning districts and to regulate the density of population, the use of land, and the size, shape, and location of buildings within each district. Although this authority has been used in some communities to impose a grid type of development pattern on the land, with residences separated from retail and commercial areas, zoning itself may be used to designate a variety of growth districts to carry out a local smart growth agenda. Municipalities have designated large parcels of land for mixed-use zones, planned unit development districts, planned residential development areas, and floating zones, as well as conservation areas.

1. American Planning Association, Planning Communities for the 21st Century 49–50 (1999). In 1973, the Oregon legislature passed Senate Bill 10, OR. REV. STAT. §§ 197.000—197.860 (1991), requiring municipal and county governments to adopt comprehensive plans consistent with state goals. *Id.* at §§ 197.005(3), 197.010. The growth management objectives of the state's plan are to "geographically bound urban development, provide adequate housing and urban development within the boundaries, and prevent urban encroachment on important natural resource lands outside the boundaries." John M. DeGrove, Lincoln Inst. of Land Policy, Planning & Growth Management in the States, 117–120 (1993).

2. MD. CODE ANN., STATE FIN. & PROC. § 5–7B–01 (1995 & Supp. 2000). This legislation (Smart Growth and Neighborhood Conservation Act) encourages bounded development by pledging the state to concentrate its infrastructure and development project funding in "priority funding areas" to ensure that growth occurs in and around existing and carefully planned growth areas. This is balanced by the Rural Legacy Program, MD. CODE ANN., NAT. RES. § 5–9A–01 (2000), which directs other state resources to protect agricultural, forest, and natural resource lands.

Perhaps we are moving into an era of "smarter growth," where public policy encourages more compact and integrated land uses to accomplish a number of contemporary public interests, such as the reduction of car travel and air pollution and the rate of consumption of farmland, natural resources, and environmentally sensitive areas. Smart growth advocates see the designation of areas for more compact, mixed-use development as a present imperative, a necessary change in the zoning blueprint needed to address the concerns addressed by the Oregon and Maryland growth management initiatives.

If local governments are to design the basic blueprint for smart growth, how should they proceed? State law provides numerous planning tools for municipalities to use in designating growth and conservation areas. The principal among these, of course, is the comprehensive plan, the ideal document to account for the rational allocation of land use. Local comprehensive plans usually include a statement of goals and objectives regarding the community's physical development and describe the specific actions to be taken to provide for the long-range growth and development of the locality.

Comprehensive plans can, in fact, be quite detailed, incorporating maps, graphs, and studies that can precisely locate designated growth areas and spell out the techniques to be used to encourage development in those areas. This authority is highly elastic, and can be stretched to fit all development contexts, from urban and suburban to rural, where communities wish to control growth. Growth control measures, including goals, objectives, and techniques contained in the comprehensive plan—then adopted into a variety of local laws—were validated over thirty years ago by the Court of Appeals in New York in Golden v. Ramapo.

GOLDEN v. PLANNING BOARD OF TOWN OF RAMAPO

Court of Appeals of New York, 1972.
30 N.Y.2d 359, 334 N.Y.S.2d 138, 285 N.E.2d 291, appeal dismissed 409 U.S. 1003, 93 S.Ct. 440, 34 L.Ed.2d 294 (1972).

SCILEPPI, JUDGE.

Both cases arise out of the 1969 amendments to the Town of Ramapo's Zoning Ordinance. * * *

Experiencing the pressures of an increase in population and the ancillary problem of providing municipal facilities and services, the Town of Ramapo, as early as 1964, made application for grant under section 801 of the Housing Act of 1964 (78 U.S.Stat. 769) to develop a master plan. The plan's preparation included a four-volume study of the existing land uses, public facilities, transportation, industry and commerce, housing needs and projected population trends. The proposals appearing in the studies were subsequently adopted pursuant to section 272–a of the Town Law, Consol.Laws, c. 62, in July, 1966 and implemented by way of a master plan. The master plan was followed by the adoption of a comprehensive zoning ordinance. Additional sewage district and drainage studies were undertaken which culminated in the adoption of a capital budget, providing for the development of the improvements specified in the master plan within the next six years. Pursuant to section 271 of the Town Law, authorizing comprehensive planning, and as a supplement to the capital budget, the Town Board adopted a capital program which provides for the location and sequence of additional capital improvements for the 12 years following the life of the capital budget. The two plans, covering a period of 18 years, detail the capital improvements projected for maximum development and conform to the specifications set forth in the master plan, the official map and drainage plan.

Based upon these criteria, the Town subsequently adopted the subject amendments for the alleged purpose of eliminating premature subdivision and urban sprawl. Residential development is to proceed according to the provision of adequate municipal facilities and services, with the assurance that any concomitant restraint upon property use is to be of a "temporary" nature and that other private uses, including the construction of individual housing, are authorized.

The amendments did not rezone or reclassify any land into different residential or use districts, but, for the purposes of implementing the proposals appearing in the comprehensive plan, consist, in the main, of additions to the definitional sections of the ordinance, section 46–3, and the adoption of a new class of "Special Permit Uses", designated "Residential Development Use." "Residential Development Use" is defined as "The erection or construction of dwellings on any vacant plots, lots or parcels of land" (§ 46–3, as amd.); and, any person who acts so as to come within that definition, "shall be deemed to be engaged in residential development which shall be a separate use classification under this ordinance and subject to the requirement of obtaining a special permit from the Town Board" (§ 46–3, as amd.).

The standards for the issuance of special permits are framed in terms of the availability to the proposed subdivision plat of five essential facilities or services: specifically (1) public sanitary sewers or approved substitutes; (2) drainage facilities; (3) improved public parks or recreation facilities, including public schools; (4) State, county or town roads—major, secondary or collector; and, (5) firehouses. No special permit shall issue unless the proposed residential development has accumulated 15 development points, to be computed on a sliding scale of values assigned to the specified improvements under the statute. Subdivision is thus a function of immediate availability to the proposed plat of certain municipal improvements; the avowed purpose of the amendments being to phase residential development to the Town's ability to provide the above facilities or services.

Certain savings and remedial provisions are designed to relieve of potentially unreasonable restrictions. Thus, the board may issue special permits vesting a present right to proceed with residential development in such year as the development meets the required point minimum, but in no event later than the final year of the 18–year capital plan. The approved special use permit is fully assignable, and improvements scheduled for completion within one year from the date of an application are to be credited as though existing on the date of the application. A prospective developer may advance the date of subdivision approval by agreeing to provide those improvements which will bring the proposed plat within the number of development points required by the amendments. And applications are authorized to the "Development Easement Acquisition Commission" for a reduction of the assessed valuation. Finally, upon application to the Town Board, the development point requirements may be varied should the board determine that such a variance or modification is consistent with the on-going development plan.

The undisputed effect of these integrated efforts in land use planning and development is to provide an over-all program of orderly growth and adequate facilities through a sequential development policy commensurate with progressing availability and capacity of public facilities. While its goals are clear and its purposes undisputably laudatory, serious questions are raised as to the manner in which these ends are to be effected, not the least of which relates to their legal viability under present zoning enabling legislation, particularly sections 261 and 263 of the Town Law. The owners of the subject premises argue, and the Appellate Division has sustained the proposition, that the primary purpose of the amending ordinance is to control or regulate population growth within the Town and as such is not within the authorized objectives of the zoning enabling legislation. We disagree.

In enacting the challenged amendments, the Town Board has sought to control subdivision in all residential districts, pending the provision (public or private) at some future date of various services and facilities. A reading of the relevant statutory provisions reveals that there is no specific authorization for the "sequential" and "timing" controls adopted here. That, of course, cannot be said to end the matter, for the additional inquiry remains as to whether the challenged amendments find their basis within the perimeters of the devices authorized and purposes sanctioned under current enabling legislation. Our concern is, as it should be, with the effects of the statutory scheme taken as a whole and its role in the propagation of a viable policy of land use and planning.

* * *

Of course, zoning historically has assumed the development of individual plats and has proven characteristically ineffective in treating with the problems attending subdivision and development of larger parcels, involving as it invariably does, the provision of adequate public services and facilities. To this end, subdivision control (Town Law, §§ 276, 277) purports to guide community development in the directions outlined here, while at the same time encouraging the provision of adequate facilities for the housing, distribution, comfort and convenience of local residents (*Village of Lynbrook v. Cadoo*, 252 N.Y. 308, 314, 169 N.E. 394, 396). It reflects in essence, a legislative judgment that the development of unimproved areas be accompanied by provision of essential facilities (*Matter of Brous v. Smith*, 304 N.Y. 164, 106 N.E.2d 503; see, also, 3 Rathkopf, The Law of Zoning and Planning [3d ed.], pp. 71–1 to 71–7; Cutler, Legal and Illegal Methods for Controlling Community Growth on the Urban Fringe, 1961 Wis.L.Rev. 370). And though it may not, in a definitional or conceptual sense be identified with the power to zone, it is designed to complement other land use restrictions, which, taken together, seek to implement a broader, comprehensive plan for community development (see Haar, The Master Plan: An Impermanent Constitution, 20 Law & Contemp.Probs. 353).

It is argued, nevertheless, that the timing controls currently in issue are not legislatively authorized since their effect is to prohibit subdivision absent precedent or concurrent action of the Town, and hence constitutes an unauthorized blanket interdiction against subdivision.

It is, indeed, true that the Planning Board is not in an absolute sense statutorily authorized to deny the right to subdivide. That is not, however, what is sought to be accomplished here. The Planning Board has the right to refuse approval of subdivision plats in the absence of those improvements specified in section 277, and the fact that it is the Town and not the subdividing owner or land developer who is required to make those improvements before the plat will be approved cannot be said to transform the scheme into an absolute prohibition any more than it would be so where it was the developer who refused to provide the facilities required for plat approval.[3] Denial of subdivision plat approval,

3. The difference between the ordinary situation and the situation said to subsist here resides in the fact that where plat approval is denied for want of various improvements, the developer is free to provide those improvements at his own expense. In the ordinary case where the proposed improvements will not be completed before the plat is filed the developer's obligation is secured by a performance bond (Town Law, § 277; see, also, Control of Land Subdivision, Office of Planning Coordination [1968 ed.], p.32). On the other hand, in the present case, plat approval is conditioned upon the Town's obligation to undertake improvements in roads, sewers, and recreational facilities. As the town may not be held to its program, practices do vary form year to year "and fiscal needs cannot be frozen beyond review and recall" (concurring opn. Hopkins, J. 37 A.D.2d at 244, 324 N.Y.S.2d at 187), the "patient owner" who relied on the capital program for qualification then is said to face the prospect that the improvements will be delayed and the impediments established by the ordinance further extended by the Town's failure to adhere to its own schedule.

The reasoning, as far as it goes, cannot be challenged. Yet, in passing on the validity of the ordinance on its face, we must assume not only the Town's good faith, but its assiduous adherence to the program's scheduled implementation. We cannot, it is true, adjudicate in a vacuum and we would be remiss not to consider the substantial risk that the Town may eventually default in its obligations. Yet, those are future events, the staple of clairvoyant, not of court deliberations. The threat of default is not so imminent or likely that it would warrant our prognosticating and striking down these amendments as invalid on their face. When and if the danger should materialize, the aggrieved landowner can seek relief by way of an article 78 proceeding, declaring the ordinance unconstitutional as applied to his property. Alternatively, should it arise at some future point in time that the Town must fail in its enterprise, an action for a declaratory judgment will indeed prove the most effective vehicle for relieving property owners of what would constitute absolute prohibitions.

invariably amounts to a prohibition against subdivision, albeit a conditional one (Real Property Law, Consol.Laws, c. 50, §§ 334–a, 335; see, also, 3 Rathkopf, Law of Zoning and Planning [3d ed.], pp. 71–122, supra); and to say that the Planning Board lacks the authority to deny subdivision rights is to mistake the nature of our inquiry which is essentially whether development may be conditioned pending the provision by the municipality of specified services and facilities. Whether it is the municipality or the developer who is to provide the improvements, the objective is the same—to provide adequate facilities, off-site and on-site; and in either case subdivision rights are conditioned, not denied.

* * *

Recognition of communal and regional interdependence, in turn, has resulted in proposals for schemes of regional and State-wide planning, in the hope that decisions would then correspond roughly to their level of impact (see, e.g., Proposed Land Use and Development Planning Law, §§ 2–101, 4–101, 4–102; ALI, A Model Land Development Code, art. 7). Yet, as salutary as such proposals may be, the power to zone under current law is vested in local municipalities, and we are constrained to resolve the issues accordingly. What does become more apparent in treating with the problem, however, is that though the issues are framed in terms of the developer's due process rights, those rights cannot, realistically speaking, be viewed separately and apart from the rights of others " 'in search of a [more] comfortable place to live.' " (*Concord Twp. Appeal*, 439 Pa. 466, 474, n. 6, 268 A.2d 765, 768, supra; *National Land & Inv. Co. v. Easttown Twp. Bd. of Adj.*, 419 Pa. 504, 527–528, 215 A.2d 597, supra; see, generally, Sager, Tight Little Islands: Exclusionary Zoning, Equal Protection and the Indigent, 21 Stan.L.Rev. 767; Roberts, Demise of Property Law, 57 Cornell L.Rev. 1).

There is, then, something inherently suspect in a scheme which, apart from its professed purposes, effects a restriction upon the free mobility of a people until sometime in the future when projected facilities are available to meet increased demands. Although zoning must include schemes designed to allow municipalities to more effectively contend with the increased demands of evolving and growing communities, under its guise, townships have been wont to try their hand at an array of exclusionary devices in the hope of avoiding the very burden which growth must inevitably bring (*see National Land & Inv. Co. v. Easttown Twp. Bd. of Adj.*, 419 Pa. 504, 532, 215 A.2d 597, supra; *Girsh Appeal*, 437 Pa. 237, 263 A.2d 395; *Concord Twp. Appeal*, 439 Pa. 466, 268 A.2d 765, supra; see, also, Roberts, Demise of Property Law, 57 Cornell L.Rev. 1, 5). Though the conflict engendered by such tactics is certainly real, and its implications vast, accumulated evidence, scientific and social, points circumspectly at the hazards of undirected growth and the naive, somewhat nostalgic imperative that egalitarianism is a function of growth. (See, generally, Lewis, Ecology and Politics: II, *New York Times*, March 6, 1972, p. 33, cols. 1, 2).

Of course, these problems cannot be solved by Ramapo or any single municipality, but depend upon the accommodation of widely disparate interests for their ultimate resolution. To that end, Statewide or regional control of planning would insure that interests broader than that of the municipality underlie various land use policies. Nevertheless, that should not be the only context in which growth devices such as these, aimed at population assimilation, not exclusion, will be sustained; especially where, as here, we would have no alternative but to strike the provision down in the wistful hope that the efforts of the State Office of Planning Coordination and the American Law Institute will soon bear fruit.

Hence, unless we are to ignore the plain meaning of the statutory delegation, this much is clear: phased growth is well within the ambit of existing enabling legislation. And, of course, it is no answer to point to emergent problems to buttress the conclusion that such innovative schemes are beyond the perimeters of statutory authorization. These considerations, admittedly real, to the extent which they are relevant, bear solely upon the continued viability of "localism" in land use regulation; obviously, they can neither add nor detract from the initial grant of authority, obsolescent though it may be. The answer which Ramapo has posed can by no means be termed definitive; it is, however, a first practical step toward controlled growth achieved without forsaking broader social purposes.

* * *

The subject ordinance is said to advance legitimate zoning purposes as it assures that each new home built in the township will have at least a minimum of public services in the categories regulated by the ordinance. The Town argues that various public facilities are presently being constructed but that for want of time and money it has been unable to provide such services and facilities at a pace commensurate with increased public need. It is urged that although the zoning power includes reasonable restrictions upon the private use of property, exacted in the hope of development according to well-laid plans, calculated to advance the public welfare of the community in the future (*Arverne Bay Constr. Co. v. Thatcher*, 278 N.Y. 222, 229, 15 N.E.2d 587, 590; *Hesse v. Rath*, 249 N.Y. 436, 438, 164 N.E. 342), the subject regulations go further and seek to avoid the increased responsibilities and economic burdens which time and growth must ultimately bring (see *National Land & Inv. Co. v. Easttown Twp. Bd. of Adj.*, 419 Pa. 504, 532, 215 A.2d 597, supra; *Girsh Appeal*, 437 Pa. 237, 263 A.2d 395, supra; *Concord Twp. Appeal*, 439 Pa. 466, 268 A.2d 765, supra).

* * *

What we will not countenance, then, under any guise, is community efforts at immunization or exclusion. But, far from being exclusionary, the present amendments merely seek, by the implementation of sequential development and timed growth, to provide a balanced cohesive community dedicated to the efficient utilization of land. The restrictions conform to the community's considered land use policies as expressed in its comprehensive plan and represent a bona fide effort to maximize population density consistent with orderly growth. True other alternatives, such as requiring off-site improvements as a prerequisite to subdivision, may be available, but the choice as how best to proceed, in view of the difficulties attending such exactions (see Heyman & Gilhool, The Constitutionality of Imposing Increased Community Costs on New Suburban Residents through Subdivision Exactions, 73 Yale L.J. 1119; see, also, ALI, A Model Land Development Code, § 3–104, subd. [6]), cannot be faulted.

Perhaps even more importantly, timed growth, unlike the minimum lot requirements recently struck down by the Pennsylvania Supreme Court as exclusionary, does not impose permanent restrictions upon land use (see *National Land & Inv. Co. v. Easttown Twp. Bd. of Adj.*, 419 Pa. 504, 215 A.2d 597, supra; *Concord Twp. Appeal*, 439 Pa. 466, 268 A.2d 765, supra). Its obvious purpose is to prevent premature subdivision absent essential municipal facilities and to insure continuous development commensurate with the Town's obligation to provide such facilities. They seek, not to freeze population at present levels but to maximize growth by the efficient use of land, and in so doing testify to this community's continuing role in population assimilation. In sum, Ramapo asks not that it be left alone, but only that it be allowed to prevent the kind of deterioration that has transformed well-ordered and thriving residential communities into blighted ghettos with attendant hazards to health, security and social stability—a danger not without substantial basis in fact.

* * *

The proposed amendments have the effect of restricting development for onwards to 18 years in certain areas. Whether the subject parcels will be so restricted for the full term is not clear, for it is equally probable that the proposed facilities will be brought into these areas well before that time. Assuming, however, that the restrictions will remain outstanding for the life of the program, they still fall short of a confiscation within the meaning of the Constitution.

An ordinance which seeks to permanently restrict the use of property so that it may not be used for any reasonable purpose must be recognized as a taking: The only difference between the restriction and an outright taking in such a case "is that the restriction leaves the owner subject to the burden of payment of taxation, while outright confiscation would relieve him of that burden" (*Arverne Bay Constr. Co. v. Thatcher*, 278 N.Y. 222, 232, 15 N.E.2d 587, 592, supra). An appreciably different situation obtains where the restriction constitutes a *temporary* restriction, promising that the property may be put to a profitable use within a reasonable time. The hardship of holding unproductive property for some time might be compensated for by the ultimate benefit inuring to the individual owner in the form of a substantial increase in valuation; or, for that matter, the landowner might be compelled to chafe under the temporary restriction, without the benefit of such compensation, when that burden serves to promote the public good (*cf. Arverne Bay Constr. Co. v. Thatcher*, 278 N.Y. 222, 232, 15 N.E.2d 587, 592, supra).

We are reminded, however, that these restrictions threaten to burden individual parcels for as long as a full generation and that such a restriction cannot, in any context, be viewed as a temporary expedient. The Town, on the other hand, contends that the landowner is not deprived of either the best use of his land or of numerous other appropriate uses, still permitted within various residential districts, including the construction of a single-family residence, and consequently, it cannot be deemed confiscatory. Although no proof has been submitted on reduction of value, the landowners point to obvious disparity between the value of the property, if limited in use by the subject amendments and its value for residential development purposes and argue that the diminution is so considerable that for all intents and purposes the land cannot presently or in the near future be put to profitable or beneficial use, without violation of the restrictions.

* * *

Without a doubt restrictions upon the property in the present case are substantial in nature and duration. They are not, however, absolute. The amendments contemplate a definite term, as the development points are designed to operate for a maximum period of 18 years and during that period, the Town is committed to the construction and installation of capital improvements. The net result of the on-going development provision is that individual parcels may be committed to a residential development use prior to the expiration of the maximum period. Similarly, property owners under the terms of the amendments may elect to accelerate the date of development by installing, at their own expense, the necessary public services to bring the parcel within the required number of development points. While even the best of plans may not always be realized, in the absence of proof to the contrary, we must assume the Town will put its best effort forward in implementing the physical and fiscal timetable outlined under the plan. Should subsequent events prove this assumption unwarranted, or should the Town because of some unforeseen event fail in its primary obligation to these landowners, there will be ample opportunity to undo the restrictions upon default. For the present, at least, we are constrained to proceed upon the assumption that the program will be fully and timely implemented (n. 7, p. 373, 334 N.Y.S.2d p. 148, 285 N.E.2d p. 298, supra).

* * *

In sum, where it is clear that the existing physical and financial resources of the community are inadequate to furnish the essential services and facilities which a substantial increase in population requires, there is a rational basis for "phased growth" and hence, the challenged ordinance is not violative of the Federal and State Constitutions. Accordingly, the order appealed from should be reversed and the actions remitted to Special Term for entry of a judgment declaring section 46–13.1 of the Town Ordinance constitutional.

BREITEL, JUDGE (dissenting). The limited powers of district zoning and subdivision regulation delegated to a municipality do not include the power to impose a moratorium on land development. Such conclusion is dictated by settled doctrine that a municipality has only those powers, and especially land use powers, delegated or necessarily implied.

But there is more involved in these cases than the arrogation of undelegated powers. Raised are vital constitutional issues, and, most important, policy issues trenching on grave domestic problems of our time, without the benefit of a legislative determination which would reflect the interests of the entire State. The policy issues relate to needed housing, planned land development under government control, and the exclusion in effect or by motive, of walled-in urban populations of the middle class and the poor. The issues are raised by a town ordinance, which, as one of the Appellate Division Justices noted below, reflect a parochial stance without regard to its impact on the region or the State, especially if it becomes a valid model for many other towns similarly situated.

* * *

It is important to note how radically the Ramapo scheme differs from those used and adopted under existing enabling acts. The zoning acts, starting from 50 years ago, based on national models, provided simply for district zoning to control population density and some planning to protect preferred uses of land, such as single-family dwellings, from other uses considered less desirable or even harmful to residential living or environmental balance. Since the beginning, in this State and elsewhere, by amendment to the enabling acts by the Legislature, provision has been made for subdivision planning and, in some instances, planned unit development, to prevent large-scale developers from dumping homes wholesale in raw land areas without private and, to some extent, public facilities essential to the use of the homes. In more recent years, since World War II, the need for a much enlarged kind of land planning has become critical. The evils of uncontrolled urban sprawl on the one hand, and the suburban and exurban pressure to exclude urban population on the other hand, have created a massive conflict, with social and economic implications of the gravest character. Throughout the nation the conflict has risen or threatened and solutions are being sought in careful intensive examination of the problem affecting those within and those without the localities to be regulated.

* * *

Decisive of the present appeals, however, is the absence in the town of legislative authorization to postpone growth, let alone to establish unilaterally phased population levels, through the expedient of barring residential development for scheduled periods of up to 18 years. It has always been the rule that a municipality has only those land use powers delegated or necessarily implied (1 Anderson, American Law of Zoning, § 3.10). Existing enabling legislation does not grant the power upon which the Ramapo ordinance rests. And for policy reasons, one should not strain the reading of the enabling acts, even if straining would avail, to distort them, beyond any meaning ever attributed to them, except by the ingenious draftsmen of the Ramapo ordinance.

* * *

Going beyond district zoning, the statute provides for subdivision platting (§ 276 et seq.). It does not provide support for the procedures essayed in the Ramapo ordinance. But what is important is that even intensive subdivision regulation was required to be authorized by statute before towns could control subdivision developers. Statutory authorization was all the more important because the then drastic regulation required the developers to provide private and public facilities for the wholesale distribution of homes and to provide moneys and bonds to make sure that they performed as promised. Notably, no developer is forbidden to develop for a period of years.

The urgent need to control the tempo and sequence of land development has been recognized by courts, government commissions, and commentators (see Cutler, Legal and Illegal Methods of Controlling Community Growth, 1961 Wis.L.Rev. 370; Fagin, Regulating the Timing of Urban Development, 20 Law & Contemp.Prob. 298; Report of National Commission on Urban Problems, pp. 245, 251; New York State, Office of Planning Coordination, Planning Law Revision Study, Draft Outline, pp. 13, 17). Techniques to control the rate, nature and sequence of community development are plentiful although not all are presently authorized or comport with constitutional limitations. Thus, in *Albrecht Realty Co. v. Town of New Castle*, 8 Misc.2d 255, 167 N.Y.S.2d 843, the Town of New Castle in Westchester County sought to control growth by placing a moratorium on the issuance of building permits for unspecified periods and with no apparent object other than controlling growth. The measure was voided because the enabling act did not authorize "a direct regulation of the rate of growth" (at p. 256, 167 N.Y.S.2d at p. 844). For another technique, in California the purchase of "development rights" or a time-limited easement by the local government reportedly has been employed. The community is saved the expense of purchasing the fee simple of the owner. It obtains flexibility by the power to release land for development while landowners are compensated. The method is also said to justify assessing or taxing the owner at a lower rate (see Cutler, op. cit., supra, at p. 394). A similar approach is followed in England and has been recently recommended by the President's National Commission on Urban Problems (Report, at p. 251; Mandelker, Notes from the English: Compensation in Town and County Planning, 49 Cal.L.Rev. 699; see, also, Ann., Zoning—With Compensation, 41 ALR3d 636).

* * *

The exclusionary effect of local efforts to preserve the country's Edens has been largely noted. Professor Roberts, in an important essay, explores the conditions bedevilling places like Ramapo but also assesses the calamitous effects of ill-advised parochial devices (E.F. Roberts, The Demise of Property Law, 57 Cornell L.Rev. 1). The problems of development of the larger community run so deep, he suggests that: " 'Snob zoning,' of course, may best be 'solved' by the legislature. This really is the lesson contained in *Girsh* which seems, moderately enough, to suggest that a regional planning mechanism should be devised to create a pluralist suburbia in which each class could find its proper place. More interest, however, is being generated by the notion of statewide land-use planning which presumably would allow each class its niche outside center city. Whether this interest in formulating state planning derives from a concern for the lower orders or reflects instead an irritation at the lack of order when a multitude of tiny hamlets makes any planning impossible, is difficult to tell." (at p. 37). To leave vital decisions controlling the mix and timing of development to the unfettered discretion of the local community invites disaster.

* * *

A glance at history suggests that Ramapo's plan to have public services installed in advance of development is unrealistic. Richard Babcock, the distinguished practitioner in land development law, some years ago addressed himself to the natural desire of communities to stay development while they caught up with the inexorable thrust of population growth and movement. He observed eloquently that this country was built and is still being built by people who moved about, innovated, pioneered, and created industry and employment, and thereby provided both the need and the means for the public services and facilities that followed (Babcock, The Zoning Game, at pp. 149–150). Thus, the movement has not been in the other direction, first the provision of public and utility services and then the building of homes, farms, and businesses. This court has said as much, in effect, in *Westwood Forest Estates v. Village of South Nyack*, 23 N.Y.2d 424, 297 N.Y.S.2d 129, 244 N.E.2d 700, supra, unanimously and in reliance on commonplace authority and precedent.

As said earlier, when the problem arose outside the State the judicial response has been the same, frustrating communities, intent on walling themselves from the mainstream of development, namely, that the effort was invalid under existing enabling acts or unconstitutional (*National Land & Inv. Co. v. Easttown Twp. Bd. of Adj.*, 419 Pa. 504, 215 A.2d 597, supra; Girsh Appeal, 437 Pa. 237, 263 A.2d 395, supra; *Bristow v. City of Woodhaven*, 35 Mich.App. 205, 192 N.W.2d 322, supra; *Lakeland Bluff v. County of Will*, 114 Ill.App.2d 267, 252 N.E.2d 765, supra; *Concord Twp. Appeal*, 439 Pa. 466, 268 A.2d 765, supra; *Oakwood at Madison v. Township of Madison*, 117 N.J.Super. 11, 283 A.2d 353 supra). The response may not be charged to judicial conservatism or self-restraint. In short, it has not been illiberal. It has indeed reflected the larger understanding that American society is at a critical crossroads in the accommodation of urbanization and suburban living, with effects that are no longer confined, bad as they are, to ethnic exclusion or "snob" zoning (see Roberts, op. cit., supra, at pp. 36–49). Ramapo would preserve its nature, delightful as that may be, but the supervening question is whether it alone may decide this or whether it must be decided by the larger community represented by the Legislature. Legally, politically, economically, and sociologically, the base for determination must be larger than that provided by the town fathers.

Accordingly, I dissent and vote to affirm the orders in both cases.

FULD, C.J., and BURKE, BERGAN and GIBSON, JJ., concur with SCILEPPI, J.

BREITEL, J., dissents and votes to affirm in a separate opinion in which JASEN, J., concurs.

Notes

1. Golden is the seminal case establishing the authority of local governments to adopt phased growth control ordinances. What are the elements of the Ramapo strategy that achieved its objective of phased growth?

2. Can you follow the majority's thinking as it traces the delegated authority of the Town of Ramapo and concludes that the authority includes growth control measures? What statutes does it point to in coming to this conclusion? What do these statutes provide that justify the court's conclusion?

3. Golden is one of the first cases to examine the issue of urban sprawl and its antidote: managed growth, currently called smart growth. With 1600 local governments in New York alone, how can individual municipalities, acting independently and in a policy vacuum, establish growth control systems that properly direct regional marketplace and population pressures? Is the court content to leave this issue in the hands of municipal governments? What are its options?

4. Does Golden articulate the view that communities must accept population growth subject only to reasonable restrictions that phase that growth so that municipal services may be provided? How does that square with the views of those who argue that, in the interest of protecting biodiversity and the environmental context of natural resources, localities should prevent the development of large-scale landscapes rich in habitat, wetlands, woods, and water resources? How should advocates of natural resource preservation or conservation, or adherents to the deep ecology movement, respond?

5. A collection of articles presented on the 30th anniversary of the Golden case is contained in the Urban Lawyer, Vol. 35, No. 1, Winter 2003.

6. The local officials in Ramapo responsible for the town's growth control laws knew they were vulnerable. If small groups of residents in discrete parts of town grew discontent with the town's land use laws, they had the power to form their own villages, adopt their own land use laws, and abandon the carefully sculpted town-wide approach. At the time the growth

control law was adopted, there were six independent villages within the town and their growth and zoning were carefully incorporated into the town's proposals.[4] In 1967, the town board adopted a local law that limited the creation of villages under New York's law that allowed village secession from towns. This law provided that every petition for the incorporation of additional villages within town boundaries should comply with all the requirements of the applicable provisions of the state's village incorporation law and contain allegations that the proposed incorporation was in the overall public interest of the proposed village, the rest of the town, and any school or fire district affected by the incorporation.

The constitutionality of this law was challenged in Marcus v. Baron, 57 N.Y.2d 862, 456 N.Y.S.2d 39, 442 N.E.2d 437 (1982). The petitioners claimed that the law was inconsistent with the state-adopted village incorporation law. The New York Court of Appeals found nothing in state law to sustain town authority to govern village secession: no express or implied authority, no legislative intent, and no evidence of this authority in the constitution or other municipal statute. The result was the invalidation of the controlled secession law. Since the Marcus v. Baron decision, several villages have been formed and assumed land use jurisdiction from the town. As a result, there is today very little contiguous land left in Ramapo for the town's comprehensive plan and inventive zoning controls to regulate.

SECTION 2. MORATORIA

A moratorium on development suspends the right of property owners to obtain development approvals while the community takes time to consider, draft, and adopt land use plans or rules to respond to new or changing circumstances not adequately dealt with by its current laws. At the local level, moratoria figure into growth management and smart growth by giving communities experiencing growth pressures time to rethink their land use plan and laws and adopt a new, smarter approach that more properly manages growth.

A moratorium is sometimes used, for example, by a community just prior to adopting its first comprehensive plan and zoning law or undertaking a comprehensive revision of its plan and zoning. The moratorium prevents developers and property owners from rushing to develop their land under current land use rules that the community is in the process of changing. By so doing, it helps to accomplish the purpose of the new rules by giving them the broadest possible applicability and preventing development that is inconsistent with them. Moratoria are also used to prevent development for a time while the government agency decides whether to acquire land for a public use or until capital improvements are made, as in the Golden case.

A moratorium can be seen as the most extreme land use action that a regulatory agency can take, because it suspends completely the rights

4. These six villages were: Suffern, Spring Valley, Hillburn, Sloatsburg, New Square, and Pomona.

of owners to use their property. In this light, regulators are advised to precede the adoption of a moratorium by findings that confirm the necessity of this action. What are the conditions that mandate the imposition of a moratorium? Are there no available alternatives less burdensome on property rights? Why are the existing land use plans and ordinances not adequate? What recent circumstances have occurred that justify the adoption of the moratorium? How serious and urgent are these circumstances? What hard evidence is there to document the necessity of the moratorium? Does the regulatory agency, in fact, have the legal authority to declare a moratorium? For how long? Under what circumstances?

In the case of Tahoe–Sierra Preservation Council, Inc. v. Tahoe Regional Planning Agency, 535 U.S. 302, 122 S.Ct. 1465, 152 L.Ed.2d 517 (2002), the U.S. Supreme Court held that a moratorium on all development lasting 32 months was not, by itself, a regulatory taking. At issue in the Tahoe case was the validity of a moratorium on development adopted by the Tahoe Regional Planning Agency to protect the unique environment and tourist-based economy of the Lake Tahoe region. The purpose of the moratorium was to give the Agency time to deal with the threat posed by construction and land development to the clarity of Lake Tahoe, which had begun to cloud as early as the late 1950's. The problem addressed was the construction of buildings, mostly homes, in the steeper drainage areas near streams and wetlands. These resources act as filters for much of the nitrogen, phosphorous, and other pollution that water runoff carries.

By 1980, it was obvious that the initial land use regulations adopted by the Agency had failed. After the withdrawal of support by the State of California, the Agency's structure was redefined by amendments to the compact law that year. The Agency was directed by the two states to develop environmental threshold carrying capacities including standards for air quality, water quality, soil conservation, vegetation preservation, and noise. This new legislation halted temporarily all development in critical environmental areas in the region, giving the Agency the time it required to consider, draft, adopt, and implement needed new regulations. That moratorium lasted for 32 months.

The legal challenge to this moratorium was launched by a nonprofit corporation representing 400 owners of land in the critical environmental areas of the Basin who had purchased their parcels prior to the 1980 changes in the compact legislation. They claimed that the moratorium on the development of their properties was a regulatory taking. Their essential argument was that, even though the regulation does not take the future right to develop, the temporary taking of all development rights, for the 32–month period, itself violates the Constitution. The landowners argued for a categorical rule which would classify a development moratorium as a taking without considering the moratorium's length, the severity of the problems addressed, the good faith of the agency involved, or what it did to conduct the required studies, analyze the underlying problems, and draft appropriate new regulations.

The U.S. Supreme Court rejected the plaintiffs' arguments and refused to declare that a moratorium is a categorical taking, regardless of the circumstances. It held that a moratorium, like most other land use regulations, is subject to an ad hoc inquiry that considers the circumstances of the case such as the character of the regulation, the public interest to be achieved, the extent to which it interferes with the owner's investment-backed expectations, and how severely they are affected by the regulation. In other words, a moratorium may be a taking, under the circumstances of a particular case, but is not categorically so. In the Tahoe case, the Court noted that the lower federal courts had concluded that the 32–month period was not unreasonable and that the Agency had acted in good faith during that time to do what needed to be done before the moratorium could be lifted. It further recognized that the consensus of land use planners is that moratoria are an essential tool of successful development.

Moratoria, the Court noted, prevent landowners from rushing to develop, causing inefficient and ill-conceived growth before a comprehensive plan can be adopted. They prevent regulators from making hasty decisions which would disadvantage landowners as well as the public. The Court recognized that land values can actually increase during a moratorium and that the public and all landowners are reciprocally benefited by moratoria because they protect everyone's interest against immediate construction that might be inconsistent with the provisions of the plan that is ultimately adopted. Of course, moratoria can be enacted that are not reasonable in these ways and they are vulnerable, under Tahoe, to challenge.

MARYLAND–NAT'L CAPITAL PARK AND PLANNING COMM'N v. CHADWICK

Court of Appeals of Maryland, 1979.
286 Md. 1, 405 A.2d 241.

MURPHY, CHIEF JUDGE.

The central issue in this case is whether the appellant, Maryland–National Capital Park and Planning Commission (the Commission), by placing the appellees' land in public "reservation" without their consent for a period not to exceed three years, as authorized by * * * the Montgomery County Code * * *, unconstitutionally deprived the landowners of the use of their property without payment of just compensation.

* * *

Under § 7–115(a), the Commission's approval is required before any subdivision plat within the regional district may be recorded in the land records of Montgomery or Prince George's Counties. The Commission is empowered under § 7–116(a)(4) to prepare subdivision regulations which may provide for

> "the reservation of lands for schools and other public buildings and for parks, playgrounds, and other public purposes, provided no reservation of land for traffic, recreation or any other public purposes as herein provided shall continue for longer than three years without the written approval of all persons holding or otherwise owning any legal or equitable interest in the property; and provided further that the properties reserved for public use shall be exempt from all State, county, and local taxes during the period."

Pursuant to the state enabling legislation, Montgomery County adopted an ordinance authorizing the placement of land in public reservation. Under the provisions of the ordinance * * * the Commission's Planning Board for Montgomery County, which is authorized to administer subdivision regulations in that jurisdiction, is required to "refer all preliminary subdivision plans to the general plan or parts thereof, adopted or proposed or studies related thereto, or shall otherwise determine the need for reserving for public use any of the land included in the preliminary subdivision plan." The ordinance specifies that reservations "for a period of three years may be required for road or street rights of way, public school and building sites, parks, playgrounds or other recreational areas or other public purposes." The ordinance also provides that placement of land in public reservation shall be by resolution of the Commission, which shall state the time, not over three years, that the reservation will be effective.

Under the provisions of the ordinance, property in reservation is exempt from all state, county and local taxes * * *. It is also subject to restrictions on its use, as detailed in § 50–31(a)(5):

> "(5) PRESERVATION. During the reservation period, no building or structure shall be erected upon the land so reserved. No trees, topsoil or cover shall be removed or destroyed; no grading shall be done; no storm drainage structure shall be so built as to discharge water on the reservation except for storm drainage construction in accordance with a storm drainage plan approved by the department of public works or the Washington Suburban Sanitary Commission; *nor shall any land so reserved be put to any use whatsoever, except upon written approval of the board.* Nothing in this section shall be construed as prohibiting the owner from removing weeds or trash from property so reserved, nor from selling when approved by the board such parts of the land as may be necessary for water, sewer or road right of way for public agencies." (Emphasis added.)

Nothing in the state enabling act, or in Montgomery County's implementing ordinance, obligates the Commission to acquire property placed by it in reservation, either during or at the expiration of the reservation period. No provision is made for payment of compensation to the property owner for the time that his property is held in reservation, whether or not it is ultimately acquired by the Commission.

* * *

On April 25, 1978, the Chadwicks filed suit in the Circuit Court for Montgomery County, seeking the issuance of a writ of mandamus directing the Commission to approve their preliminary subdivision plan, and requesting a declaratory judgment that the reservation of their property and any statute requiring such reservation were unconstitutional as a taking of property without payment of just compensation. The court (McAuliffe, J.) held that the Commission's resolution placing the Chadwicks' property in public reservation under § 50–31 of the County Code was unconstitutional and it ordered the Commission to approve the preliminary subdivision plan. * * *

* * * Our cases have recognized and applied the distinction between a compensable taking under the eminent domain power and a noncompensable regulation under the police power. * * * We have consistently upheld regulations which may have, as an incidental effect, the diminution of value of property, so long as those regulations have been shown to be fair exercises of the police power. * * * A regulation which prohibits a beneficial use of private property constitutes a fair exercise of the police power if the public interest generally requires it and the regulation is reasonably necessary to achieve the public goal without being unduly oppressive upon individuals. * * * However, we have recognized that a governmental action, while not rising to the status of a compensable "taking" of property, may amount to an invalid deprivation of property rights without due process of law, either because the purpose of the action was improper, see, e.g., *Hoyert v. Bd. of County Comm'rs*, 262 Md. 667, 278 A.2d 588 (1971) (attempt to depress value of property in anticipation of subsequent condemnation); *Carl M. Freeman, Inc. v. St. Rds. Comm'n*, 252 Md. 319, 250 A.2d 250 (1969) (sole purpose of ordinance is to freeze land values) or because the means chosen were too burdensome on the individual property owner. See, e.g., *Spaid v. Board of Co. Comm'rs*, 259 Md. 369, 269 A.2d 797 (1970) ("buffer zoning" to establish a border of vacant property around a residential neighborhood). * * *

* * *

The present case does not involve a valid exercise of the police power regulating, in the public interest, a mere beneficial use of private property for which compensation need not be paid to the affected landowner. On the contrary, we think the Commission's resolution placing appellees' land in reservation for a period up to three years stripped the landowners, for that extended period of time, of all reasonable use of their property and was tantamount to a "taking" without compensation as the lower court declared. In so concluding, we recognize the commendable governmental objective sought to be achieved by placing the land in reservation but, as was said in *Pennsylvania Coal Co. v. Mahon,* supra (260 U.S. at 416, 43 S.Ct. at 160), "a strong public desire to improve the public condition is not enough to warrant achieving the desire by a shorter cut than the constitutional way of paying for the change."

We construe the ordinance under which the Commission acted as not permitting the landowner to make, as a matter of right, any use of the property placed in reservation (other than to remove trash and weeds). We further construe the ordinance as not authorizing the planning board to permit, upon the landowner's application, any use of the reserved property which conflicts with the flat prohibition contained in the ordinance against grading the land, erecting any structures thereon, or removing trees, top soil or other cover. Restrictions of such totality upon the use of property placed in reservation *for a three-year period* bring this case within the principle, so well illustrated in *Pennsylvania Coal,* that a governmental restriction imposed on the use of land may be so onerous as to constitute a taking which constitutionally requires the payment of just compensation.

* * *

Considered together, *Pennsylvania Coal* and *Penn Central* provide ample guidance for determining whether a governmental restriction on the use of land, sought to be imposed under the police power, is of such magnitude as to constitute a taking in the constitutional sense. As we have indicated, the Commission's resolution placing appellees' land in reservation for a period of up to three years, with no reasonable uses permitted, amounts to a virtual "freeze" on the use of the property in its entirety. The resolution does not merely circumscribe a beneficial use of the property; it inhibits all beneficial use for up to three years, without any guarantee that the property will be acquired in the future. That the Commission's resolution is tantamount to a taking is, we think, clearly buttressed by cases in other jurisdictions.

In *Miller v. Beaver Falls*, 368 Pa. 189, 82 A.2d 34 (1951), Pennsylvania's Supreme Court invalidated a state law and implementing city ordinance which allowed a municipality to designate private property as parklands for up to three years, but which imposed no duty upon the municipality to acquire the designated property. The enactments provided that no compensation for improvements located on the property after notice was given of its placement in reservation would be paid if the property was subsequently acquired for public use. While the court conceded the desirability of the purpose to be achieved (establishment of parks for public use), it said that the city's action "in plotting [the] ground for a park or playground and freezing it for three years is, in reality, a taking of property by possibility, contingency, blockade and subterfuge, in violation of the clear mandate of our Constitution that property cannot be taken * * * without just compensation having been first made and secured." 82 A.2d at 37.

* * *

* * * See also *Gordon v. City of Warren Plan. & Urb. Renew. Comm'n*, 388 Mich. 82, 199 N.W.2d 465 (1972); *Peacock v. County of Sacramento*, 271 Cal.App.2d 845, 77 Cal.Rptr. 391 (1969). Compare *Washington Sub. San. Comm'n v. Nash*, 284 Md. 376, 396 A.2d 538

(1979); *Hoyert v. Bd. of County Comm'rs*, 262 Md. 667, 278 A.2d 588 (1971); *Carl M. Freeman, Inc. v. St. Rds. Comm'n*, 252 Md. 319, 250 A.2d 250 (1969).

The Commission, supported by a well-prepared amicus curiae brief filed by the Attorney General, urges that we apply the rationale of cases like *Headley v. City of Rochester*, 272 N.Y. 197, 5 N.E.2d 198 (1936), and *State v. Manders*, 2 Wis.2d 365, 86 N.W.2d 469 (1957), sustaining the constitutionality of so-called official map laws—statutes which establish the location of existing and planned streets and place restrictions on the issuance of permits to build structures in the bed of proposed roadways. These statutes restricting development in the bed of mapped streets contained provisions for variances to assure the landowner of a reasonable return on affected property, including the granting of a building permit to prevent substantial damage accruing to the owner where that course of action is required by justice and equity. Maryland's statute controlling development in mapped streets is similar to those involved in *Headley* and *Manders*. * * *

The facts of the present case clearly distinguish it from the cited cases involving the reservation of street locations. As in those cases, we recognize the need to promote intelligent planning by placing reasonable restrictions on the improvement of land scheduled to be acquired for public use. We do not, therefore, condemn as beyond the police power the enactment of reservation statutes which are reasonable in their application both as to duration and severity. Our holding today is a narrow one, limited to the facts before us. We conclude only that the Commission's resolution passed pursuant to * * * the County Code, placing appellees' land in reservation for up to three years, without any reasonable uses permitted as of right, was tantamount to a "taking" in the constitutional sense. Because the Commission's resolution did not provide for the payment of just compensation, it was unconstitutional as applied to the appellees' property and was thus of no effect. Consequently, the trial judge correctly ruled, in accordance with the requested prayer for relief, that the Commission's resolution was a nullity and that the Commission was required to forthwith approve appellees' preliminary subdivision plan.

JUDGMENT AFFIRMED WITH COSTS.

Notes

1. Was Chadwick overruled by Tahoe? The plaintiff's argument in Tahoe was that a moratorium suspending all development rights applied to a large area of environmental significance was, *per se*, a regulatory taking. Did the Court in Tahoe hold that moratoria cannot be takings? Are the circumstances in the Chadwick case sufficiently different from those in Tahoe to merit a different result, as applied to that situation?

2. Regulations that have the effect of preventing any development of land so as to make future acquisition by condemnation less costly are almost invariably held to be takings. One example is Joint Ventures, Inc. v. Department of Transportation, 563 So.2d 622 (Fla.1990), where the Depart-

ment reserved a portion of petitioner's vacant land for stormwater drainage to accommodate widening of a highway, rendering that portion undevelopable. The Court invalidated as unconstitutional the statutory provisions authorizing such reservations of private land by a state authority, stating, "[T]he statutory scheme [constitutes] a thinly veiled attempt to 'acquire' land by avoiding the legislatively mandated procedural and substantive protections of the [eminent domain procedure statute]." See also Department of Transportation v. Weisenfeld, 617 So.2d 1071 (Fla. 5th Dist.Ct. App.1993).

3. Many land use enabling statutes have provisions similar to the one litigated in the principal case. However, most such statutes provide for a shorter period of time for the public to decide whether or not to condemn. The typical time period is one year. Would such a provision have saved the Maryland scheme? The court in Chadwick acknowledged a distinction between temporary restrictions on development (valid regulation) and tying up land for a long period (taking), but relied in part on a New Jersey case invalidating a one-year reservation scheme. Perhaps one reason for judicial mistrust of reservation schemes is that the way they typically work in practice is that just when the landowner is ready to develop, his land is put into limbo while the public decides whether it can afford to buy him out.

DROSTE v. BOARD OF COUNTY COMM'RS OF COUNTY OF PITKIN

Supreme Court of Colorado, 2007.
159 P.3d 601.

JUSTICE HOBBS delivered the Opinion of the Court.

* * *

I.

The petitioners in this case include several members of the Droste family ("Drostes"). The Drostes own approximately 925 acres of land lying between the City of Aspen and the Town of Snowmass Village commonly known as the Droste Ranch. In March of 1974 Pitkin County (the "County") zoned the Droste Ranch AF–1, a zoning designation that permitted single-family dwellings "by right" on lots of ten acres or more. In 1975 the County designated the Droste Ranch as an area containing or having a significant impact on natural resources of statewide importance, but did not alter the zoning.

In 1996 the County purchased a conservation easement for approximately 100 acres of the Droste Ranch for $480,000. The County purchased an additional conservation easement covering 500 acres of the Droste Ranch in 1999 for $7.5 million. In both conservation easements the parties agreed to preserve critical wildlife habitats, particularly elk migration corridors.

In 2000 and 2002 the Drostes applied for approval of three separate development projects, each of which was denied. In February of 2003 a representative of the Drostes conferred with a representative of the

County regarding three potential new applications for development, but the Drostes did not file any applications at that time.

The Board of County Commissioners for Pitkin County (the "Board") adopted Ordinance Number 13–2003, confirmed through a public hearing on April 9, 2003. This resolution imposed a moratorium on all land use applications effective March 12, 2003. The moratorium's stated purpose was to allow the County time to conduct a comprehensive study of the area, including sensitive environmental areas and significant wildlife habitats. This study was necessary as part of the process of adopting a master plan by January 8, 2004, as required of Pitkin County by section 30–28–106(4)(b).

The Board's ordinance includes the following findings:

3. The State of Colorado has mandated that all areas of unincorporated Pitkin County be subject to a master plan by no later than January of 2004. Much of the moratorium area has never been subject to a master planning effort. The anticipated master planning process will create a master plan for Owl Creek Valley and appropriate amendments to the Downvalley Master Plan concerning the lower Brush Creek Valley.

4. The Owl Creek Planning area is currently being examined by the County Planning staff and the Owl Creek Caucus to produce a comprehensive Master Plan. This existing caucus and planning area is contiguous to areas in the lower Brush Creek Valley, which share many of the same physical and neighborhood characteristics and are experiencing the same pressure for development. This area lies between United States Forest Service land and Wildcat Ranch within the Town of Snowmass Village, which in many circumstances contains critical wildlife habitat and migratory corridors for deer and elk between the United States Forest Service land and the preserved open space of Wildcat Ranch.

5. The moratorium is to allow time to conduct a comprehensive study of what appropriate zoning and development regulations should be imposed as a result of the Master Plan process. This study shall examine what appropriate development density and development intensity should be approved in the moratorium area. The intent of the [Board] in enacting this moratorium is to allow sufficient time to conclude the County Master Plan process and enact appropriate zoning regulations to implement the adopted Master Plan.

6. There is an emergency that warrants the enactment of this ordinance and temporary moratorium. Failure to impose proper regulations will allow development to proceed, which may be out of character with the community and will negatively affect the cultural, environmental and neighborhood qualities of the moratorium area. It is anticipated by the Board of County Commissioners that an appropriate analysis of the area and adoption of necessary zoning regulations can be accomplished within sixty (60) days.

The Board adopted a second ordinance, confirmed through a public hearing, to provide for a moratorium through the first week of January 2004 in order to complete the master plan process. The second ordinance recited steps the planning staff had taken since adoption of the first ordinance, including "determination of the basic parameters for wildlife protection" and a work program for "completion of the Master Plan review process and drafting of the final Master Plan" by January 1, 2004. In total, the moratorium lasted approximately ten months.

The Drostes filed suit against the Board on May 14, 2003, seeking a declaratory judgment that the County lacked authority to impose the moratorium, and praying for injunctive relief. The parties filed cross motions for summary judgment. The County argued that it had the power to enact moratoria under the Areas and Activities of State Interest Act, section 24–65.1–101, et seq., C.R.S. (2006)("H.B.1041") and the County's general police power. The Drostes countered that the only authority to impose moratoria in Colorado land use law is found in section 30–28–121, which limits such regulation to (1) the context of zoning plan adoption and (2) a duration of up to six months only.

The trial court granted summary judgment to the County, finding that it had authority to enact the moratorium at issue pursuant to H .B. 1041 and its general police power. In November of 2003 the Drostes filed a motion for the trial court to amend its judgment. Relying on *Droste v. Board of County Commissioners*, 85 P.3d 585 (Colo.App.2003), the Drostes pointed out that the court of appeals' recent decision in their favor held that H.B. 1041 did not apply to lands zoned prior to May 17, 1974.

Neither party disputes that the Droste Ranch was zoned prior to May 17, 1974. The trial court amended its earlier judgment to add that the County had authority to impose the moratorium for the purpose of preparing a master plan under its general police power and the Local Government Land Use Control Enabling Act of 1974, sections 29–20–101 to–107 ("Land Use Enabling Act"), as well as H .B. 1041.

The Drostes appealed and the court of appeals affirmed. Without addressing H.B. 1041 or general police powers as possible sources of authority, the court of appeals ruled that the County had authority to impose the moratorium at issue in this case pursuant to the Land Use Enabling Act. We uphold the judgment of the court of appeals.

II.

We hold that Pitkin County had authority under sections 29–20–101 to–107 to adopt ordinances, confirmed through public hearings, imposing a temporary moratorium on land use application reviews that lasted approximately ten months, while it prepared its master plan.

A.

Standard of Review

The standard for review of this land use case is set forth in another of our land use decisions, *Board of County Commissioners v. Bainbridge,*

929 P.2d 691, 699 (Colo.1997). Counties have only those powers that are expressly granted to them by the Colorado Constitution or by the General Assembly. *Pennobscot v. Bd. of County Comm'rs*, 642 P.2d 915, 918 (Colo.1982). Those powers include all of the implied powers reasonably necessary to the proper exercise of the delegated powers. *Id.*

Statutes are to be construed as a whole to give a consistent, harmonious, and sensible effect to all of their parts. *Bainbridge*, 929 P.2d at 699. When we interpret a comprehensive legislative scheme, we must give meaning to all portions thereof and construe the statutory provisions to further the legislative intent. *Id.* In construing a statute, we look first to the plain language of the statute and the words should be given their plain and ordinary meaning. *Id.* If the statutory language is clear and unambiguous, the statute must be interpreted as written. *Id.*

B.

The Land Use Enabling Act of 1974

* * *

The Land Use Enabling Act broadly empowers local governments to plan for and regulate land use within their jurisdictions:

> The general assembly hereby finds and declares that in order to provide for planned and orderly development within Colorado and a balancing of basic human needs of a changing population with legitimate environmental concerns, the policy of this state is to clarify and provide broad authority to local governments to plan for and regulate the use of land within their respective jurisdictions.

§ 29–20–102(1), C.R.S. (2006) (emphasis added). The statute expressly includes a number of provisions identifying particular examples of allowable land use regulation, culminating in a catch-all provision that confers comprehensive local authority to make land use decisions, subject to the constitutional rights of the property owner:

> (b) Protecting lands from activities which would cause immediate or foreseeable material danger to significant wildlife habitat and would endanger a wildlife species;
>
> ....
>
> (e) Regulating the location of activities and developments which may result in significant changes in population density;
>
> ....
>
> (g) Regulating the use of land on the basis of the impact thereof on the community or surrounding areas; and
>
> (h) Otherwise planning for and regulating the use of land so as to provide planned and orderly use of land and protection of the environment in a manner consistent with constitutional rights.

§ 29–20–104, C.R.S. (2006). The statutory definition of "local government" includes counties. § 29–20–103(1.5), C.R.S. (2006).

The Land Use Enabling Act also contains a provision that we have construed as codifying the familiar rule that a specific provision controls over a more general provision. *Bainbridge*, 929 P.2d at 707; see also *Pennobscot*, 642 P.2d at 919. Section 29–20–107 provides "where other procedural or substantive requirements for the planning for or regulation of the use of land are provided by law, such requirements shall control."

In the field of land use regulation, moratoria are often employed to preserve the status quo in a particular area while developing a long-term plan for development. *Tahoe-Sierra Pres. Council, Inc. v. Tahoe Reg'l Planning Agency*, 535 U.S. 302, 337, 122 S.Ct. 1465, 152 L.Ed.2d 517 (2002) (citations omitted). The moratorium is an "essential tool of successful development." *Id.* at 337–38 (citations omitted). It counters the incentive of landowners to develop their land quickly to avoid the consequences of an impending land use plan for the jurisdiction. *Id.* at 339.

* * *

Our General Assembly has made clear its explicit intent to promote well-planned growth through the Land Use Enabling Act, sections 29–20–101 to–107. In section 30–28–106(4)(b), the legislature required Pitkin County to adopt a master plan: "the counties of . . . Pitkin shall adopt a master plan within two years after January 8, 2002." Section 30–28–107 mandates that, in preparation of a county or regional master plan, a county or regional planning commission shall make careful and comprehensive surveys and studies of the existing conditions and probable future growth of the territory within its jurisdiction: * * *

§ 30–28–107. The question in this case is whether, in light of all the applicable provisions of Colorado's land use statutes, the General Assembly's grant of land use authority to local government necessarily implies the authority to adopt temporary moratoria that suspend review of development applications for a reasonable period of time necessary to prepare master plans. We conclude that it does.

C.

The Power to Impose Moratoria Granted by the Enabling Act Is Not Limited by the County Planning and Building Codes

The Drostes argue that a provision of the County Planning and Building Codes grants counties the authority to impose moratoria only in the context of zoning plan approval and then only for a period of up to six months. We disagree.

* * *

Section 30–28–121 provides that a board of county commissioners, without holding a public hearing, may adopt a temporary moratorium for no more than six months in the context of zoning plan adoption:

* * *

We conclude that section 30–28–121 of the planning and building statutes does not apply to this case. It pertains to temporary moratoria adopted without a public hearing in connection with the adoption of a zoning plan. We construe this provision as an additional grant of authority to local government in the context of zoning plan adoption, i.e., that the local government may adopt a moratorium for a six month duration, without a public hearing. This section does not conflict with, preempt, or control the local government's necessarily implied authority to adopt a reasonable moratorium of sufficient duration to prepare a master plan.

In conclusion, the case before us involves a moratorium of ten months duration confirmed through a public hearing and adopted in connection with a master plan. The Land Use Enabling Act includes the necessarily implied authority of the local government to impose, through a public hearing process, a moratorium of limited duration to halt further development pending adoption of a master plan. The length and conditions of a moratorium are subject to the protection of property owners against uncompensated takings as provided by sections 29–20–201 to –204.

III.

Accordingly we affirm the judgment of the court of appeals.

Notes

1. In Toll Brother's Inc. v. West Windsor Township, 712 A.2d 266, 312 N.J.Super. 540 (1998), the Township of West Windsor adopted an ordinance that created timed growth districts, the purpose of which was to slow growth. New Jersey's Municipal Land Use Law (N.J. Stat. Ann. § 40:55D–90) prohibits "the prohibition of development in order to prepare a master plan and development regulations" in addition to moratoria on applications for development or interim zoning ordinance * * * except * * * where the municipality demonstrates * * * clear imminent danger to the health of inhabitants * * * and in no cases shall exceed a six-month term." The court held that the township's timed growth controls constituted a prohibited moratorium because in order to immediately develop, 40 percent of the allowable density was foregone. The state supreme court decision in this case is in Chapter VI. Also see New Jersey Shore Builders Association v. Mayor and Township Committee of Township of Middletown, 234 N.J.Super. 619, 561 A.2d 319 (1989), where the court invalidated a moratorium ordinance "because it was based on a health officer's opinion that lacked the factual basis to demonstrate the existence of a 'clear imminent danger to the health of inhabitants.'" For additional background, see Peter A. Buchsbaum, Timed Growth Ordinances Rejected in New Jersey, 31 The Urban Lawyer 823 (1999).

2. Most situations involving moratoria on development because of water or sewer system emergencies pit developers against a state-level agency, usually an environmental agency. This type of moratorium is not litigated frequently because the state's police power interest in public health and safety is easily defended. See, e.g., Ungar v. State, 63 Md.App. 472, 492

A.2d 1336 (1985); Friel v. Triangle Oil Co., 76 Md.App. 96, 543 A.2d 863 (1988). In Estate of Scott v. Victoria County, 778 S.W.2d 585 (Tex.App.1989), the property owner sought compensation for a taking due to a sewer moratorium. The court held that a property owner has no property right in sewer extensions, merely an expectancy of service. In Foster v. Board of Comm'rs of Warrick County, 647 N.E.2d 1147 (Ind.App.1995), the court upheld a moratorium on further building permits in a previously approved subdivision because earlier construction by the developer caused severe drainage problems affecting nearby residents; the county board imposed the moratorium until the inadequate drainage system previously installed by the developer was corrected. And in McNaughton Co. v. Witmer, 149 Pa.Cmwlth. 307, 613 A.2d 104 (1992), the court held that a developer could not recover damages for delay in his project for the period during which a validly enacted sewer connection moratorium was in effect.

The New York Times reported on November 20, 1989 (page B 6), a two-year-old moratorium on all new sewer mains from Mt. Kisco to Yonkers, New York: "Much of the county's new construction has come to a halt. Although individual home builders can still hook up to existing sewer mains, dozens of developers, who must extend the mains before erecting homes now own land they can neither build on nor sell." Also see Kawaoka v. City of Arroyo Grande, 17 F.3d 1227 (9th Cir.1994), where the court upheld a city's temporary water moratorium against charges of spot zoning, differential treatment, and racial bias against persons of Japanese ancestry; Gilbert v. State, 218 Cal.App.3d 234, 266 Cal.Rptr. 891 (1990), upholding a moratorium on new water connections.

3. Sometimes a moratorium is enacted specifying one particular land use. In Duncanson v. Board of Supervisors of Danville Twp., 551 N.W.2d 248 (Minn.App.1996), the court upheld a moratorium on feedlots despite the fact that the plaintiff's proposed feedlot was the only project known to be affected by the moratorium. And in First Bet Joint Venture v. City of Central City, 818 F.Supp. 1409 (D.Colo.1993), a moratorium on zoning permits for future gaming facilities was upheld (the plaintiff's taking claim was held not ripe). See Wendy U. Larsen and Marcella Larsen, Moratoria as Takings Under Lucas, Land Use Law (June 1994), p. 3.

4. Another type of moratorium is one that halts development for a temporary period pending adoption of a new comprehensive plan or new zoning ordinance. The validity of this type of moratorium depends upon interpretation of the state's enabling statutes, which may or may not expressly grant such power to municipalities. See, e.g., Noghrey v. Acampora, 152 A.D.2d 660, 543 N.Y.S.2d 530 (1989). In Naylor v. Township of Hellam, 773 A.2d 770, 565 Pa. 397 (2001), the Supreme Court of Pennsylvania held that the municipality lacked the authority to impose a moratorium on subdivision approvals while revising its comprehensive plan because the Municipal Planning Code (MPC) 53 §§ 10101–11202 does not expressly authorize moratoria and therefore the power to suspend development is not implicit or incidental to the powers expressly conferred. This case demonstrates that the outcome of a moratorium is closely related to a municipality's home rule authority.

Where municipalities do have the power to adopt moratoria while creating or revising their comprehensive plan or zoning law, moratoria may be invalid because of their duration or other defect. In Duke v. Huntington, 153 Misc.2d 521, 581 N.Y.S.2d 978 (Sup.Ct.1991), for example, plaintiff wished to construct a timber dock along one of the town's waterways, but his efforts were stalled by a town ordinance "temporarily" restricting construction along waterways until the town could promulgate a new waterfront revitalization plan. The process to revamp the waterfront revitalization plan began in 1984, and "temporary" moratoria had impeded plaintiff's plans for more than three years. Although the court generally approved of so-called "stop-gap" moratoria to allow for the enactment of new or amended comprehensive plans or zoning laws, it found the development delays in the case at hand to be excessive and indefinite in duration and, thus, unconstitutionally void.

SECTION 3. GROWTH MANAGEMENT

INTRODUCTION: WHO SHOULD DECIDE?

The case of Golden v. Planning Bd. of Ramapo, 30 N.Y.2d 359, 334 N.Y.S.2d 138, 285 N.E.2d 291 (1972), which began this chapter on smart growth and growth management, set in motion three decades of debate over which level of government should dictate such matters. In Golden, the court's ambivalence over the predominant authority of local governments in land use was palpable: New York's zoning regime, it said, "is burdened by the largely antiquated notion which deigns that the regulation of land use and development is uniquely a function of local government * * *."[5]

At precisely the same time, a revolution to wrest land use control from local governments was begun. It was fueled by the understanding that local control of land use creates serious inefficiencies and inequities. A report entitled The Quiet Revolution, prepared for the Council of Environmental Quality in 1971, contained a powerful statement of the problems caused by the delegation of land use control to towns, villages, boroughs, cities, and townships: "This country is in the midst of a revolution in the way we regulate land * * *. The *ancien regime* being overthrown is the feudal system under which the entire pattern of land development has been controlled by thousands of individual local governments, each seeking to maximize its tax base and minimize its social problems, and caring less what happens to all the others."[6]

5. Golden, 30 N.Y.2d 359, 334 N.Y.S.2d 138, 285 N.E.2d at 299.

6. Fred Bosselman & David Callies, Council on Envtl. Quality, The Quiet Revolution in Land Use Control 1 (1972). See also Michael Allan Wolf, The Prescience and Centrality of Euclid v. Ambler, in Zoning and The American Dream: Promises Still to Keep 252, 253 (Charles M. Haar & Jerold S. Kayden eds., 1989) (specifying the problems identified in Euclid of assigning control over land use to local governments as "exclusion, anti-competitiveness, parochialism, and aestheticism"). To these must be added the propensity of local governments, most of which rely heavily on local property taxes, to favor economic development over environmental protection. See Paul E. Peterson, The Price of Federalism 36–37, 69–75 (Brookings, 1995).

The revolution has not succeeded, despite all the attention given to the efforts of states to create statewide counter-regimes under the rubrics of growth management, sustainable development, and, recently, smart growth. After analyzing recent state planning and smart growth legislation, a preeminent practitioner and scholar concludes that one of the major problems in fighting sprawl today is "the states' failure to reclaim some of their authority delegated early on to localities in the land use field * * *."[7]

In this section, we examine a number of cases challenging the attempts of single municipalities in burgeoning regions to control growth, and then turn to the efforts of state legislatures to guide and direct local prerogatives in the interests of growth management.

A. LOCAL REGULATION OF URBAN GROWTH

CONSTRUCTION INDUSTRY ASS'N OF SONOMA COUNTY v. CITY OF PETALUMA

United States Court of Appeals, Ninth Circuit, 1975.
522 F.2d 897, certiorari denied 424 U.S. 934,
96 S.Ct. 1148, 47 L.Ed.2d 342 (1976).

CHOY, CIRCUIT JUDGE:

The City of Petaluma (the City) appeals from a district court decision voiding as unconstitutional certain aspects of its five-year housing and zoning plan. We reverse.

STATEMENT OF FACTS

The City is located in southern Sonoma County, about 40 miles north of San Francisco. In the 1950's and 1960's, Petaluma was a relatively self-sufficient town. It experienced a steady population growth from 10,315 in 1950 to 24,870 in 1970. Eventually, the City was drawn into the Bay Area metropolitan housing market as people working in San Francisco and San Rafael became willing to commute longer distances to secure relatively inexpensive housing available there. By November 1972, according to unofficial figures, Petaluma's population was at 30,500, a dramatic increase of almost 25 per cent in little over two years.

The increase in the City's population, not surprisingly, is reflected in the increase in the number of its housing units. From 1964 to 1971, the following number of residential housing units were completed:

1964	270	1968	379
1965	440	1969	358
1966	321	1970	591
1967	234	1971	891

In 1970 and 1971, the years of the most rapid growth, demand for housing in the City was even greater than above indicated. Taking 1970

7. Robert H. Freilich, From Sprawl to Smart Growth 240 (A.B.A. 1999).

and 1971 together, builders won approval of a total of 2000 permits although only 1482 were actually completed by the end of 1971.

Alarmed by the accelerated rate of growth in 1970 and 1971, the demand for even more housing, and the sprawl of the City eastward, the City adopted a temporary freeze on development in early 1971. The construction and zoning change moratorium was intended to give the City Council and the City planners an opportunity to study the housing and zoning situation and to develop short and long range plans. The Council made specific findings with respect to housing patterns and availability in Petaluma, including the following: That from 1960–1970 housing had been in almost unvarying 6000 square-foot lots laid out in regular grid patterns; that there was a density of approximately 4.5 housing units per acre in the single-family home areas; that during 1960–1970, 88 per cent of housing permits issued were for single-family detached homes; that in 1970, 83 per cent of Petaluma's housing was single-family dwellings; that the bulk of recent development (largely single-family homes) occurred in the eastern portion of the City, causing a large deficiency in moderately priced multi-family and apartment units on the east side.

To correct the imbalance between single-family and multi-family dwellings, curb the sprawl of the City on the east, and retard the accelerating growth of the City, the Council in 1972 adopted several resolutions, which collectively are called the "Petaluma Plan" (the Plan).

The Plan, on its face limited to a five-year period (1972–1977),[8] fixes a housing development growth rate not to exceed 500 dwelling units per year.[9] Each dwelling unit represents approximately three people. The 500–unit figure is somewhat misleading, however, because it applies only to housing units (hereinafter referred to as "development-units") that are part of projects involving five units or more. Thus, the 500–unit figure does not reflect any housing and population growth due to construction of single-family homes or even four-unit apartment buildings not part of any larger project.

The Plan also positions a 200 foot wide "greenbelt" around the City,[10] to serve as a boundary for urban expansion for at least five years, and with respect to the east and north sides of the City, for perhaps ten

8. The district court found that although the Plan is ostensibly limited to a five-year period, official attempts have been made to perpetuate the Plan beyond 1977. Such attempts include the urban extension line (see text infra) and the agreement to purchase from the Sonoma County Water Agency only 9.8 million gallons of water per day through the year 1990. This flow is sufficient to support a population of 55,000. If the City were to grow at a rate of about 500 housing units per year (approximately three persons per unit), the City would reach a population of 55,000 about the year 1990. The 55,000 figure was mentioned by City officials as the projected optimal (and maximum) size of Petaluma. See, e.g., R.T. at 135–43, 145–46.

9. The allotment for each year is not an inflexible limitation. The Plan does provide for a 10 percent variance (50 units) below or above the 500 unit annual figure, but the expectation of the Council is that not more than 2500 units will be constructed during the five-year period.

10. At some points this urban extension line is about one-quarter of a mile beyond the present City limits.

to fifteen years. One of the most innovative features of the Plan is the Residential Development Control System which provides procedures and criteria for the award of the annual 500 development-unit permits. At the heart of the allocation procedure is an intricate point system, whereby a builder accumulates points for conformity by his projects with the City's general plan and environmental design plans, for good architectural design, and for providing low and moderate income dwelling units and various recreational facilities. The Plan further directs that allocations of building permits are to be divided as evenly as feasible between the west and east sections of the City and between single-family dwellings and multiple residential units (including rental units),[11] that the sections of the City closest to the center are to be developed first in order to cause "infilling" of vacant area, and that 8 to 12 per cent of the housing units approved be for low and moderate income persons.

In a provision of the Plan, intended to maintain the close-in rural space outside and surrounding Petaluma, the City solicited Sonoma County to establish stringent subdivision and appropriate acreage parcel controls for the areas outside the urban extension line of the City and to limit severely further residential infilling.

Purpose of the Plan

The purpose of the Plan is much disputed in this case. According to general statements in the Plan itself, the Plan was devised to ensure that "development in the next five years will take place in a reasonable, orderly, attractive manner, rather than in a completely haphazard and unattractive manner." The controversial 500–unit limitation on residential development-units was adopted by the City "[i]n order to protect its small town character and surrounding open space."[12] The other features of the Plan were designed to encourage an east-west balance in development, to provide for variety in densities and building types and wide ranges in prices and rents, to ensure infilling of close-in vacant areas, and to prevent the sprawl of the City to the east and north. The Construction Industry Association of Sonoma County (the Association) argues and the district court found, however, that the Plan was primarily enacted "to limit Petaluma's demographic and market growth rate in housing and in the immigration of new residents." *Construction Industry Ass'n v. City of Petaluma*, 375 F.Supp. 574, 576 (N.D.Cal.1974).

11. By providing for the increase of multi-family dwellings (including townhouses as well as rental apartments), the Plan allows increased density. Whereas, during the years just preceding the Plan, housing density was about 4.5 units per acre, under the Plan single-family housing will consist of not only low (4.5 units per acre) but also medium density (4.5 to 10 units per acre). And multi-family housing, to comprise about half of the housing under the Plan, will be built at a density of 10 or more units per acre.

12. After the appellees initiated this suit, the City attempted to show that the Plan was implemented to prevent the overtaxing of available water and sewage facilities. We find it unnecessary, however, to consider the claim that sewage and water problems justified implementation of the Plan.

Market Demand and Effect of the Plan

In 1970 and 1971, housing permits were allotted at the rate of 1000 annually, and there was no indication that without some governmental control on growth consumer demand would subside or even remain at the 1000–unit per year level. Thus, if Petaluma had imposed a flat 500–unit limitation on *all* residential housing, the effect of the Plan would clearly be to retard to a substantial degree the natural growth rate of the City. Petaluma, however, did not apply the 500–unit limitation across the board, but instead exempted all projects of four units or less. Because appellees failed to introduce any evidence whatsoever as to the number of exempt units expected to be built during the five-year period, the effect of the 500 *development-unit* limitation on the natural growth in housing is uncertain. For purposes of this decision, however, we will assume that the 500 development-unit growth rate is in fact below the reasonably anticipated market demand for such units and that absent the Petaluma Plan, the City would grow at a faster rate.

According to undisputed expert testimony at trial, if the Plan (limiting housing starts to approximately 6 per cent of existing housing stock each year) were to be adopted by municipalities throughout the region, the impact on the housing market would be substantial. For the decade 1970 to 1980, the shortfall in needed housing in the region would be about 105,000 units (or 25 per cent of the units needed). Further, the aggregate effect of a proliferation of the Plan throughout the San Francisco region would be a decline in regional housing stock quality, a loss of the mobility of current and prospective residents and a deterioration in the quality and choice of housing available to income earners with real incomes of $14,000 per year or less. If, however, the Plan were considered by itself and with respect to Petaluma only, there is no evidence to suggest that there would be a deterioration in the quality and choice of housing available there to persons in the lower and middle income brackets. Actually, the Plan increases the availability of multi-family units (owner occupied and rental units) and low-income units which were rarely constructed in the pre-Plan days.

Court Proceedings

Two landowners (the Landowners) and the Association instituted this suit under 28 U.S.C.A. §§ 1331, 1343 and 42 U.S.C.A. § 1983 against the City and its officers and council members, claiming that the Petaluma Plan was unconstitutional. The district court ruled that certain aspects of the Plan unconstitutionally denied the right to travel insofar as they tended "to limit the natural population growth of the area." 375 F.Supp., at 588. The court enjoined the City and its agents from implementing the unconstitutional elements of the Plan, but the order was stayed by Justice Douglas pending this appeal.

* * *

Appellees claim that the Plan is arbitrary and unreasonable and, thus, violative of the due process clause of the Fourteenth Amendment.

According to appellees, the Plan is nothing more than an exclusionary zoning device,[13] designed solely to insulate Petaluma from the urban complex in which it finds itself. The Association and the Landowners reject, as falling outside the scope of any legitimate governmental interest, the City's avowed purposes in implementing the Plan—the preservation of Petaluma's small town character and the avoidance of the social and environmental problems caused by an uncontrolled growth rate.

In attacking the validity of the Plan, appellees rely heavily on the district court's finding that the express purpose and the actual effect of the Plan is to exclude substantial numbers of people who would otherwise elect to move to the City. 375 F.Supp. at 581. The existence of an exclusionary purpose and effect reflects, however, only *one* side of the zoning regulation. Practically all zoning restrictions have as a purpose and effect the *exclusion* of some activity or type of structure or a certain density of inhabitants. And in reviewing the reasonableness of a zoning ordinance, our inquiry does not terminate with a finding that it is for an exclusionary purpose. We must determine further whether the *exclusion* bears any rational relationship to a *legitimate state interest.* If it does not, then the zoning regulation is invalid. If, on the other hand, a legitimate state interest is furthered by the zoning regulation, we must defer to the legislative act. Being neither a super legislature nor a zoning board of appeal, a federal court is without authority to weigh and reappraise the factors considered or ignored by the legislative body in passing the challenged zoning regulation. The reasonableness, not the wisdom, of the Petaluma Plan is at issue in this suit.

In determining whether the City's interest in preserving its small town character and in avoiding uncontrolled and rapid growth falls within the broad concept of "public welfare," we are considerably assisted by two recent cases. *Belle Terre,* supra, and *Ybarra v. Town of Los Altos Hills*, 503 F.2d 250 (9th Cir.1974) each of which upheld as not unreasonable a zoning regulation much more restrictive than the Petaluma Plan, are dispositive of the due process issue in this case.

In *Belle Terre* the Supreme Court rejected numerous challenges to a village's restricting land use to one-family dwellings excluding lodging

13. "Exclusionary zoning" is a phrase popularly used to describe suburban zoning regulations which have the effect, if not also the purpose, of preventing the migration of low and middle-income persons. Since a large percentage of racial minorities fall within the low and middle income brackets, exclusionary zoning regulations may also effectively wall out racial minorities. See generally Aloi, Goldberg & White, Racial and Economic Segregation by Zoning: Death Knell for Home Rule?, 1969 U.Tol.L.Rev. 65 (1969); Bigham & Bostick, Exclusionary Zoning Practices: An Examination of the Current Controversy, 25 Vand.L.Rev. 1111 (1972); Davidoff & Davidoff, Opening the Suburbs: Toward Inclusionary Land Use Controls, 22 Syracuse L.Rev. 509 (1971); Note, Exclusionary Zoning and Equal Protection, 84 Harv.L.Rev. 1645 (1971).

Most court challenges to and comment upon so-called exclusionary zoning focus on such traditional zoning devices as height limitations, minimum square footage and minimum lot size requirements, and the prohibition of multi-family dwellings or mobile homes. The Petaluma Plan is unique in that although it assertedly slows the growth rate it replaces the past pattern of single-family detached homes with an assortment of housing units, varying in price and design.

houses, boarding houses, fraternity houses or multiple-dwelling houses. By absolutely prohibiting the construction of or conversion of a building to other than single-family dwelling, the village ensured that it would never grow, if at all, much larger than its population of 700 living in 220 residences. Nonetheless, the Court found that the prohibition of boarding houses and other multi-family dwellings was reasonable and within the public welfare because such dwellings present urban problems, such as the occupation of a given space by more people, the increase in traffic and parked cars and the noise that comes with increased crowds. According to the Court,

> "A quiet place where yards are wide, people few, and motor vehicles restricted are legitimate guidelines in a land-use project addressed to family needs. This goal is a permissible one within Berman v. Parker, supra. The police power is not confined to elimination of filth, stench, and unhealthy places. It is ample to lay out zones where family values, youth values, and the blessings of quiet seclusion, and clean air make the area a sanctuary for people."

416 U.S. at 9, 94 S.Ct. at 1541. While dissenting from the majority opinion in *Belle Terre* on the ground that the regulation unreasonably burdened the exercise of First Amendment associational rights, Mr. Justice Marshall concurred in the Court's express holding that a local entity's zoning power is extremely broad:

> "[L]ocal zoning authorities may properly act in furtherance of the objectives asserted to be served by the ordinance at issue here: *restricting uncontrolled growth,* solving traffic problems, keeping rental costs at a reasonable level, and making the community attractive to families. The police power which provides the justification for zoning is not narrowly confined. And, it is appropriate that we afford zoning authorities *considerable latitude in choosing the means by which to implement such purposes.*"

416 U.S. at 13–14, 94 S.Ct. at 1543 (Marshall, J., dissenting) (emphasis added) (citations omitted).

Following the *Belle Terre* decision, this court in *Los Altos Hills* had an opportunity to review a zoning ordinance providing that a housing lot shall contain not less than one acre and that no lot shall be occupied by more than one primary dwelling unit. The ordinance as a practical matter prevented poor people from living in Los Altos Hills and restricted the density, and thus the population, of the town. This court, nonetheless, found that the ordinance was rationally related to a legitimate governmental interest—*the preservation of the town's rural environment*—and, thus, did not violate the equal protection clause of the Fourteenth Amendment. 503 F.2d at 254.

Both the Belle Terre ordinance and the Los Altos Hills regulation had the purpose and effect of permanently restricting growth; nonetheless, the court in each case upheld the particular law before it on the ground that the regulation served a legitimate governmental interest falling within the concept of the public welfare: the preservation of quiet family neighborhoods (Belle Terre) and the preservation of a rural environment (Los Altos Hills). Even less restrictive or exclusionary than the above zoning ordinances in the Petaluma Plan which, unlike those ordinances, does not freeze the population at present or near-present levels.[14] Further, unlike the Los Altos Hills ordinance and the various zoning regulations struck down by state courts in recent years, the Petaluma Plan does not have the undesirable effect of walling out any particular income class nor any racial minority group.[15]

Although we assume that some persons desirous of living in Petaluma will be excluded under the housing permit limitation and that, thus, the Plan may frustrate some legitimate regional housing needs, the Plan is not arbitrary or unreasonable. We agree with appellees that unlike the situation in the past most municipalities today are neither isolated nor wholly independent from neighboring municipalities and that, consequently, unilateral land use decisions by one local entity affect the needs and resources of an entire region. See, e.g., *Golden v. Planning Board of Town of Ramapo*, 30 N.Y.2d 359, 334 N.Y.S.2d 138, 285 N.E.2d 291, appeal dismissed, 409 U.S. 1003, 93 S.Ct. 436, 34 L.Ed.2d 294 (1972); *National Land & Investment Co. v. Kohn*, 419 Pa. 504, 215 A.2d 597 (1965); Note, Phased Zoning: Regulation of the Tempo and Sequence of Land Development, 26 Stan.L.Rev. 585, 605 (1974). It does not necessarily follow, however, that the *due process* rights of builders and landowners are violated merely because a local entity exercises in its own self-interest the police power lawfully delegated to it by the state. See *Belle Terre,* supra; *Los Altos Hills,* supra. If the present system of delegated

14. Under the Petaluma Plan, the population is expected to increase at the rate of about 1500 persons annually. This rate approximates the rate of growth in the 1960's and represents about a 6 per cent increase per year over the present population.

15. Although appellees have attempted to align their business interests in attacking the Plan with legitimate housing needs of the urban poor and racial minorities, the Association has not alleged nor can it allege, based on the record in this case, that the Plan has the purpose and effect of excluding poor persons and racial minorities. Cf. Board of County Supervisors of Fairfax County v. Carper, 200 Va. 653, 107 S.E.2d 390 (1959). Contrary to the picture painted by appellees, the Petaluma Plan is "inclusionary" to the extent that it offers new opportunities, previously unavailable, to minorities and low and moderate-income persons. Under the pre-Plan system single family, middle-income housing dominated the Petaluma market, and as a result low and moderate income persons were unable to secure housing in the area. The Plan radically changes the previous building pattern and requires that housing permits be evenly divided between single-family and multi-family units and that approximately eight to twelve per cent of the units be constructed specifically for low and moderate income persons.

In stark contrast, each of the exclusionary zoning regulations invalidated by state courts in recent years impeded the ability of low and moderate income persons to purchase or rent housing in the locality. See, e.g., Southern Burlington County NAACP v. Township of Mount Laurel, 67 N.J. 151, 336 A.2d 713 (Mar. 24, 1975) (zoned exclusively for single-family detached dwellings and multi-family dwellings designed for middle and upper income persons); Oakwood at Madison, Inc. v. Township of Madison, 117 N.J.Super. 11, 283 A.2d 353 (1971) (minimum one or two acre requirement and severe limitation on multi-family units); Appeal of Kit–Mar Builders, Inc., 439 Pa. 466, 268 A.2d 765 (1970) (two to three acre minimum lot size); Appeal of Girsh, 437 Pa. 237, 263 A.2d 395 (1970) (prohibition of apartment buildings); National Land & Investment Co. v. Kohn, 419 Pa. 504, 215 A.2d 597 (1965) (four acre minimum lot); Board of County Supervisors of Fairfax County v. Carper, 200 Va. 653, 107 S.E.2d 390 (1959) (rezoning to minimum two acre lots with the effect of keeping poor in another section of municipality).

zoning power does not effectively serve the state interest in furthering the general welfare of the region or entire state, it is the state legislature's and not the federal courts' role to intervene and adjust the system. As stated supra, the federal court is not a super zoning board and should not be called on to mark the point at which legitimate local interests in promoting the welfare of the community are outweighed by legitimate regional interests. See Note, supra, at 608–11.

We conclude therefore that under *Belle Terre* and *Los Altos Hills* the concept of the public welfare is sufficiently broad to uphold Petaluma's desire to preserve its small town character, its open spaces and low density of population, and to grow at an orderly and deliberate pace.[16]

COMMERCE CLAUSE

The district court found that housing in Petaluma and the surrounding areas is produced substantially through goods and services in interstate commerce and that curtailment of residential growth in Petaluma will cause serious dislocation to commerce. 375 F.Supp. at 577, 579. Our ruling today, however, that the Petaluma Plan represents a reasonable and legitimate exercise of the police power obviates the necessity of remanding the case for consideration of appellees' claim that the Plan unreasonably burdens interstate commerce.

It is well settled that a state regulation validly based on the police power does not impermissibly burden interstate commerce where the regulation neither discriminates against interstate commerce nor operates to disrupt its required uniformity. *Huron Cement Co. v. Detroit*, 362 U.S. 440, 448, 80 S.Ct. 813, 4 L.Ed.2d 852 (1960). * * *

* * *

Consequently, since the local regulation here is rationally related to the social and environmental welfare of the community and does not discriminate against interstate commerce or operate to disrupt its required uniformity, appellees' claim that the Plan unreasonably burdens commerce must fail.[17]

Reversed.

16. Our decision upholding the Plan as not in violation of the appellees' due process rights should not be read as a permanent endorsement of the Plan. In a few years the City itself for good reason may abandon the Plan or the state may decide to alter its laws delegating its zoning power to the local authorities; or to meet legitimate regional needs, regional zoning authorities may be established. See, e.g., Cal.Gov.Code §§ 66600 et seq. (San Francisco Bay Conservation and Development Commission); Cal.Gov.Code §§ 66801, 67000 et seq. (Tahoe Regional Planning Agency); Public Resources Code §§ 27000 et seq. (California Coastal Zone Conservation Commission). To be sure, housing needs in metropolitan areas like the San Francisco Bay Area are pressing and the needs are not being met by present methods of supplying housing. However, the federal court is not the proper forum for resolving these problems. The controversy stirred up by the present litigation, as indicated by the number and variety of amici on each side, and the complex economic, political and social factors involved in this case are compelling evidence that resolution of the important housing and environmental issues raised here is exclusively the domain of the legislature.

17. Our decision today conforms with others which have upheld reasonable state environmental legislation despite some burden incidentally placed on interstate commerce. See, e.g., *Huron Cement Co. v. Detroit*, supra (air pollution statute); *Procter*

Notes

1. Local governments have invented many ways to manage growth while preserving the community character or natural resources. The City of Aspen, Colorado, Growth Management Quota System (Aspen Municipal Code Chapter 26.470) is designed to limit growth to 30,000 people, including visitors, in order to protect community character and ensure adequate delivery of municipal services. To accomplish this, the Growth Management Quota System allows a maximum annual growth rate of 2 percent per year, which limits the amount of development of residential housing, tourist accommodations, and commercial and office development. A scoring system that includes bonus points for affordable housing among other amenities is used to determine which development projects will be granted a permit in a given year.

2. The Ramapo and Petaluma cases focused nationwide interest on the techniques of growth control. Despite the concerns expressed in the dissenting opinion in Ramapo and the district court opinion in Petaluma about local parochialism and the need for addressing the problem on a regional or statewide basis, most of the development in the area has continued to focus on individual communities and local plans. As you read the next principal case, determine whether the majority adequately deals with the issue of local parochialism in the context of regional housing needs and regional welfare.

ASSOCIATED HOME BUILDERS OF THE GREATER EASTBAY, INC. v. CITY OF LIVERMORE

Supreme Court of California, 1976.
18 Cal.3d 582, 135 Cal.Rptr. 41, 557 P.2d 473.

TOBRINER, JUSTICE.

We face today the question of the validity of an initiative ordinance enacted by the voters of the City of Livermore which prohibits issuance of further residential building permits until local educational, sewage disposal, and water supply facilities comply with specified standards. Plaintiff, an association of contractors, subdividers, and other persons interested in residential construction in Livermore, brought this suit to enjoin enforcement of the ordinance. The superior court issued a permanent injunction, and the city appealed.

* * *

[At this point the court reversed the trial court in holding that notice and hearing requirements in the zoning enabling legislation also applied to initiatives. These were held to be inapplicable to enactments by the voters. The court also reversed a trial court finding that the ordinance was unconstitutionally vague.]

& Gamble Co. v. City of Chicago, 509 F.2d 69 (7th Cir.), certiorari denied, 421 U.S. 978, 95 S.Ct. 1980, 44 L.Ed.2d 470 (1975) (ban on phosphate detergents); *American Can Co. v. Oregon Liquor Control Commission*, 15 Or.App. 618, 517 P.2d 691 (1973) (ban on non-returnable beverage containers).

Finally, we reject plaintiff's suggestion that we sustain the trial court's injunction on the ground that the ordinance unconstitutionally attempts to bar immigration to Livermore. Plaintiff's contention symbolizes the growing conflict between the efforts of suburban communities to check disorderly development, with its concomitant problems of air and water pollution and inadequate public facilities, and the increasing public need for adequate housing opportunities. We take this opportunity, therefore, to reaffirm and clarify the principles which govern validity of land use ordinances which substantially limit immigration into a community; we hold that such ordinances need not be sustained by a compelling state interest, but are constitutional if they are reasonably related to the welfare of the region affected by the ordinance. Since on the limited record before us plaintiff has not demonstrated that the Livermore ordinance lacks a reasonable relationship to the regional welfare, we cannot hold the ordinance unconstitutional under this standard.

1. Summary of Proceedings

The initiative ordinance in question was enacted by a majority of the voters at the Livermore municipal election of April 11, 1972, and became effective on April 28, 1972. The ordinance, set out in full in the margin,[18] states that it was enacted to further the health, safety, and welfare of the citizens of Livermore and to contribute to the solution of air pollution. Finding that excessive issuance of residential building permits has caused school overcrowding, sewage pollution, and water rationing, the ordinance prohibits issuance of further permits until three standards are met: "1. EDUCATIONAL FACILITIES—No double sessions in the schools nor overcrowded classrooms as determined by the California

18. The initiative provides as follows: "INITIATIVE ORDINANCE RE BUILDING PERMITS

"An ordinance to control residential building permits in the City of Livermore:

"A. The people of the City of Livermore hereby find and declare that it is in the best interest of the City in order to protect the health, safety, and general welfare of the citizens of the city, to control residential building permits in the said city. Residential building permits include single-family residential, multiple residential, and trailer court building permits within the meaning of the City Code of Livermore and the General Plan of Livermore. Additionally, it is the purpose of this initiative measure to contribute to the solution of air pollution in the City of Livermore.

"B. The specific reasons for the proposed position are that the undersigned believe that the resulting impact from issuing residential building permits at the current rate results in the following problems mentioned below. Therefore no further residential permits are to be issued by the said city until satisfactory solutions, as determined in the standards set forth, exist to all the following problems:

"1. EDUCATIONAL FACILITIES—No double sessions in the schools nor overcrowded classrooms as determined by the California Education Code.

"2. SEWAGE—The sewage treatment facilities and capacities meet the standards set by the Regional Water Quality Control Board.

"3. WATER SUPPLY—No rationing of water with respect to human consumption or irrigation and adequate water reserves for fire protection exist.

"C. This ordinance may only be amended or repealed by the voters at a regular municipal election.

"D. If any portion of this ordinance is declared invalid the remaining portions are to be considered valid."

Education Code. 2. SEWAGE—The sewage treatment facilities and capacities meet the standards set by the Regional Water Quality Control Board. 3. WATER SUPPLY—No rationing of water with respect to human consumption or irrigation and adequate water reserves for fire protection exist."

Plaintiff association filed suit to enjoin enforcement of the ordinance and for declaratory relief. After the city filed its answer, all parties moved for judgment on the pleadings and stipulated that the court, upon the pleadings and other documents submitted, could determine the merits of the cause. On the basis of that stipulation the court rendered findings and entered judgment for plaintiff. The city appeals from that judgment.

* * *

[The portion of the decision dealing with the conflict between the notice and hearing provisions of the zoning enabling act and the initiative procedures act is omitted.]

3. THE LIVERMORE ORDINANCE IS NOT VOID FOR VAGUENESS

The trial court found the ordinance unconstitutionally vague on two grounds: (1) that the ordinance did not contain sufficiently specific standards for the issuance or denial of building permits, and (2) that it did not specify what person or agency was empowered to determine if the ordinance's standards have been met. We disagree with both rationales and find the ordinance sufficiently specific to fulfill constitutional requirements.

The controversy concerning the specificity of the ordinance centers upon the standard as to education. The ordinance prohibits issuance of residential building permits until a "satisfactory solution" has been evolved to the problem of "Educational Facilities"; it defines a satisfactory solution as one characterized by "No double sessions in the schools nor overcrowded classrooms as determined by the California Education Code."

The term "double sessions" is sufficiently specific; as stated by Professor Deutsch, it "can be defined by reference to common practice, since the term is frequently used to refer to a situation where different groups of students in the same grade are attending the same school at different times of the day because of a lack of space." (Deutsch, op. cit., supra, pp. 22–23.) The phrase "overcrowded classrooms as determined by the California Education Code," however, is less clear, since nowhere in the Education Code does there appear a definition of "overcrowded classrooms."

The City of Livermore, however, points out that the ordinance does not refer to a definition of "overcrowded classrooms" contained in the Education Code, but to a determination of that subject. The language, it contends—and plaintiff does not dispute the contention—was intended to refer to resolution 3220, adopted by the board of the Livermore Valley

Joint School District on January 18, 1972, in which that board, pursuant to authority granted it by Education Code section 1052, established clear and specific standards for determining whether schools are overcrowded.[19]

Rather than interpret the ordinance in a manner which would expose it to the charge of unconstitutional vagueness, we adopt the suggestion of the city and construe the ordinance's standard on education to incorporate the specific guidelines established in board resolution 3220. In so doing we conform to the rule that enactments should be interpreted when possible to uphold their validity * * * and the corollary principle that courts should construe enactments to give specific content to terms that might otherwise be unconstitutionally vague. * * *

* * *

The ordinance's standards relating to sewage and water supply present no constitutional difficulties. The sewage provision incorporates the "standards set by the Regional Water Quality Control Board"; that agency has in fact established specific and detailed standards of water purification and sewage disposal. The water supply provision describes a "satisfactory solution" as one in which water is not rationed, and "adequate water reserves for fire protection exist." The existence of rationing is an objective fact which can be ascertained by inquiry to the agencies having authority to ration. Although individuals may differ as to the adequacy of reserves for fire protection, the considered judgment of the agencies responsible for fire protection would provide a reliable guide.

Although we have determined that the ordinance's standards meet constitutional requirements of certainty, plaintiff argues, and the trial

19. Board Resolution 3220 provides as follows:

"ADEQUACY OF SCHOOLS

"1. Sufficient instructional space shall be determined to exist when:

a. For elementary schools:

(1) All students can be housed in single session classes in affected schools.

(2) At least 900 square feet of functional instructional area are available for each classroom or teaching station.

(3) Class sizes average 30 students or less throughout the District.

b. For secondary schools:

(1) All students can be housed within the capacity of existing schools on regular day session. Capacity will be determined by applying State Department of Education criteria in keeping with maximum class size.

"2. Minimum support services exist when:

a. Sufficient shelf and cabinet space is provided to accommodate books and equipment normally associated with a classroom.

b. A faculty workroom exists.

c. Off-street parking for each teaching station is provided.

d. Sufficient playground area and playground equipment is provided to support outdoor play activity.

e. Sufficient furniture and equipment for each classroom to accommodate all students and teachers.

f. A library is established equivalent to at least one classroom for each 600 students.

"3. School construction and outfitting, in terms of classroom space, architectural layout, space relationship, outdoor facilities, utilities, grounds development, and furniture and equipment, shall meet or exceed State Bureau of Education standards."

court held, that the ordinance is void because it fails to designate what agency or person determines whether these standards have been achieved. We question plaintiff's underlying assumption that an ordinance or statute is void if it does not specify on its face the agency that is to adjudge disputes concerning its application; by such a test most of the civil and criminal laws of this state would be invalidated. In any event, we believe that the Livermore ordinance, read in the light of the structure of Livermore's city government and the applicable judicial decisions, does indicate the method by which disagreements concerning the ordinance's standards are resolved.

The Livermore ordinance establishes standards to govern the issuance or denial of residential building permits. These standards must be directed in the first instance to the city building inspector, the official charged with the duty of issuing or denying such permits. Since the duties of this official are ministerial in character, his decisions can be reviewed by writ of mandamus. * * * Thus the ultimate decision as to compliance with the standards will be rendered by the courts. * * *

4. ON THE LIMITED RECORD BEFORE US, PLAINTIFF CANNOT DEMONSTRATE THAT THE LIVERMORE ORDINANCE IS NOT A CONSTITUTIONAL EXERCISE OF THE CITY'S POLICE POWER

Plaintiff urges that we affirm the trial court's injunction on a ground which it raised below, but upon which the trial court did not rely. Plaintiff contends that the ordinance proposes, and will cause, the prevention of nonresidents from migrating to Livermore, and that the ordinance therefore attempts an unconstitutional exercise of the police power, both because no compelling state interest justifies its infringement upon the migrant's constitutionally protected right to travel, and because it exceeds the police power of the municipality.

The ordinance on its face imposes no absolute prohibition or limitation upon population growth or residential construction. It does provide that no building permits will issue unless standards for educational facilities, water supply and sewage disposal have been met, but plaintiff presented no evidence to show that the ordinance's standards were unreasonable or unrelated to their apparent objectives of protecting the public health and welfare. Thus, we do not here confront the question of the constitutionality of an ordinance which limits or bars population growth either directly in express language or indirectly by the imposition of prohibitory standards; we adjudicate only the validity of an ordinance limiting building permits in accord with standards that reasonably measure the adequacy of public services.

* * * [T]he limited record here prevents us from resolving that constitutional issue. We deal here with a case in which a land use ordinance is challenged solely on the ground that it assertedly exceeds the municipality's authority under the police power; the challenger eschews any claim that the ordinance discriminates on a basis of race or wealth. Under such circumstances, we view the past decisions of this

court and the federal courts as establishing the following standard: the land use restriction withstands constitutional attack if it is fairly debatable that the restriction in fact bears a reasonable relation to the general welfare. For the guidance of the trial court we point out that if a restriction significantly affects residents of surrounding communities, the constitutionality of the restriction must be measured by its impact not only upon the welfare of the enacting community, but upon the welfare of the surrounding region. We explain the process by which the court can determine whether or not such a restriction reasonably relates to the regional welfare. Since the record in the present case is limited to the pleadings and stipulations, and is devoid of evidence concerning the probable impact and duration of the ordinance's restrictions, we conclude that we cannot now adjudicate the constitutionality of the ordinance. Thus we cannot sustain the trial court judgment on the ground that the ordinance exceeds the city's authority under the police power; that issue can be resolved only after trial.

* * *

We therefore reaffirm the established constitutional principle that a local land use ordinance falls within the authority of the police power if it is reasonably related to the public welfare. Most previous decisions applying this test, however, have involved ordinances without substantial effect beyond the municipal boundaries. The present ordinance, in contrast, significantly affects the interests of nonresidents who are not represented in the city legislative body and cannot vote on a city initiative. We therefore believe it desirable for the guidance of the trial court to clarify the application of the traditional police power test to an ordinance which significantly affects nonresidents of the municipality.

When we inquire whether an ordinance reasonably relates to the public welfare, inquiry should begin by asking *whose* welfare must the ordinance serve. In past cases, when discussing ordinances without significant effect beyond the municipal boundaries, we have been content to assume that the ordinance need only reasonably relate to the welfare of the enacting municipality and its residents. But municipalities are not isolated islands remote from the needs and problems of the area in which they are located; thus an ordinance, superficially reasonable from the limited viewpoint of the municipality may be disclosed as unreasonable when viewed from a larger perspective.

These considerations impel us to the conclusion that the proper constitutional test is one which inquires whether the ordinance reasonably relates to the welfare of those whom it significantly affects. If its impact is limited to the city boundaries, the inquiry may be limited accordingly; if, as alleged here, the ordinance may strongly influence the supply and distribution of housing for an entire metropolitan region, judicial inquiry must consider the welfare of that region.

* * *

We explain the process by which a trial court may determine whether a challenged restriction reasonably relates to the regional welfare. The first step in that analysis is to forecast the probable effect and duration of the restriction. In the instant case the Livermore ordinance posits a total ban on residential construction, but one which terminates as soon as public facilities reach specified standards. Thus to evaluate the impact of the restriction, the court must ascertain the extent to which public facilities currently fall short of the specified standards, must inquire whether the city or appropriate regional agencies have undertaken to construct needed improvements, and must determine when the improvements are likely to be completed.

The second step is to identify the competing interests affected by the restriction. We touch in this area deep social antagonisms. We allude to the conflict between the environmental protectionists and the egalitarian humanists; a collision between the forces that would save the benefits of nature and those that would preserve the opportunity of people in general to settle. Suburban residents who seek to overcome problems of inadequate schools and public facilities to secure "the blessing of quiet seclusion and clean air" and to "make the area a sanctuary for people" (*Village of Belle Terre v. Boraas*, supra, 416 U.S. 1, 9, 94 S.Ct. 1536, 1541, 39 L.Ed.2d 797) may assert a vital interest in limiting immigration to their community. Outsiders searching for a place to live in the face of a growing shortage of adequate housing, and hoping to share in the perceived benefits of suburban life, may present a countervailing interest opposing barriers to immigration.

Having identified and weighed the competing interests, the final step is to determine whether the ordinance, in light of its probable impact, represents a reasonable accommodation of the competing interests. We do not hold that a court in inquiring whether an ordinance reasonably relates to the regional welfare, cannot defer to the judgment of the municipality's legislative body. But judicial deference is not judicial abdication. The ordinance must have a *real and substantial* relation to the public welfare. (*Miller v. Board of Public Works, supra*, 195 Cal. 477, 490, 234 P. 381.) There must be a reasonable basis in fact, not in fancy, to support the legislative determination. (*Consolidated Rock Products Co. v. City of Los Angeles* (1962) 57 Cal.2d 515, 522, 20 Cal.Rptr. 638, 370 P.2d 342.) Although in many cases it will be "fairly debatable" (*Euclid v. Ambler Co.*, supra, 272 U.S. 365, 388, 47 S.Ct. 114, 71 L.Ed. 303) that the ordinance reasonably relates to the regional welfare, it cannot be assumed that a land use ordinance can *never* be invalidated as an enactment in excess of the police power.

The burden rests with the party challenging the constitutionality of an ordinance to present the evidence and documentation which the court will require in undertaking this constitutional analysis. Plaintiff in the present case has not yet attempted to shoulder that burden. Although plaintiff obtained a stipulation that as of the date of trial the ordinance's goals had not been fulfilled, it presented no evidence to show the likely duration or effect of the ordinance's restriction upon building permits.

We must presume that the City of Livermore and appropriate regional agencies will attempt in good faith to provide that community with adequate schools, sewage disposal facilities, and a sufficient water supply; plaintiff, however, has not presented evidence to show whether the city and such agencies have undertaken to construct the needed improvements or when such improvements will be completed. Consequently we cannot determine the impact upon either Livermore or the surrounding region of the ordinance's restriction on the issuance of building permits pending achievement of its goals.

With respect to the competing interests, plaintiff asserts the existence of an acute housing shortage in the San Francisco Bay Area, but presents no evidence to document that shortage or to relate it to the probable effect of the Livermore ordinance. Defendants maintain that Livermore has severe problems of air pollution and inadequate public facilities which make it reasonable to divert new housing, at least temporarily, to other communities but offer no evidence to support that claim. Without an evidentiary record to demonstrate the validity and significance of the asserted interests, we cannot determine whether the instant ordinance attempts a reasonable accommodation of those interests.

In short, we cannot determine on the pleadings and stipulations alone whether this ordinance reasonably relates to the general welfare of the region it affects. The ordinance carries the presumption of constitutionality; plaintiff cannot overcome that presumption on the limited record before us. Thus the judgment rendered on this limited record cannot be sustained on the ground that the initiative ordinance falls beyond the proper scope of the police power.

* * *

The judgment of the superior court is reversed, and the cause remanded for further proceedings consistent with the views expressed herein.

WRIGHT, C.J. and MCCOMB, SULLIVAN and RICHARDSON, JJ., concur.

* * *

[A dissenting opinion by JUSTICE CLARK is omitted.]

MOSK, JUSTICE (dissenting).

I dissent.

Limitations on growth may be justified in resort communities, beach and lake and mountain sites, and other rural and recreational areas; such restrictions are generally designed to preserve nature's environment for the benefit of all mankind. They fulfill our fiduciary obligation to posterity. As Thomas Jefferson wrote, the earth belongs to the living, but in usufruct.

But there is a vast qualitative difference when a suburban community invokes an elitist concept to construct a mythical moat around its perimeter, not for the benefit of mankind but to exclude all but its fortunate current residents.

* * * Where I part company with the majority is in its substantive holding that a total exclusion of new residents can be constitutionally accomplished under a city's police power.

The majority, somewhat desultorily, deny that the ordinance imposes an absolute prohibition upon population growth or residential construction. It is true that the measure prohibits the issuance of building permits for single-family residential, multiple residential and trailer residential units until designated public services meet specified standards. But to see such restriction in practicality as something short of total prohibition is to employ ostrich vision.

First of all, the ordinance provides no timetable or dates by which the public services are to be made adequate. Thus the moratorium on permits is likely to continue for decades, or at least until attrition ultimately reduces the present population. Second, it is obvious that no inducement exists for *present* residents to expend their resources to render facilities adequate for the purpose of accommodating *future* residents. It would seem more rational, if improved services are really contemplated for any time in the foreseeable future, to admit the new residents and compel them to make their proportionate contribution to the cost of the educational, sewage and water services. Thus it cannot seriously be argued that Livermore maintains anything other than total exclusion.

The trial court found, inter alia, that the ordinance prohibited the issuance of building permits for residential purposes until certain conditions are met, but the measure does not provide that any person or agency is required to expend or commence any efforts on behalf of the city to meet the requirements. Nor is the city itself obliged to act within any specified time to cure its own deficiencies. Thus, in these circumstances procrastination produces its own reward: continued exclusion of new residents.

The significant omissions, when noted in relation to the ordinance preamble, reveal that the underlying purpose of the measure is "to control residential building permits in the City of Livermore"—translation: to keep newcomers out of the city—and not to solve the purported inadequacies in municipal educational, sewage and water services. Livermore concedes no building permits are now being issued and it relates no current or prospective schedule designed to correct its defective municipal services.

A municipal policy of preventing acquisition and development of property by nonresidents clearly violates article I, sections 1 and 7, subdivisions (a) and (b), of the Constitution of California.

Exclusion of unwanted outsiders, while a more frequent phenomenon recently, is not entirely innovative. The State of California made an abortive effort toward exclusivity back in the 1930s as part of a scheme to stem the influx of poor migrants from the dust bowl states of the southwest. The additional burden these indigent new residents placed on California services and facilities was severely aggravated by the great depression of that period. In *Edwards v. California* (1941) 314 U.S. 160, 62 S.Ct. 164, 86 L.Ed. 119, the Supreme Court held, however, that the nature of the union established by the Constitution did not permit any one state to "isolate itself from the difficulties common to all of them by restraining the transportation of persons and property across its borders." The sanction against immigration of indigents was invalidated.

If California could not protect itself from the growth problems of that era, may Livermore build a Chinese Wall to insulate itself from growth problems today? And if Livermore may do so, why not every municipality in Alameda County and in all other counties in Northern California? With a patchwork of enclaves the inevitable result will be creation of an aristocracy housed in exclusive suburbs while modest wage earners will be confined to declining neighborhoods, crowded into sterile, monotonous, multi-family projects, or assigned to pockets of marginal housing on the urban fringe. The overriding objective should be to minimize rather than exacerbate social and economic disparities, to lower barriers rather than raise them, to emphasize heterogeneity rather than homogeneity, to increase choice rather than limit it.

* * *

One thing emerges with clarity from the foregoing and from numerous related cases: access to housing is regarded by the Supreme Court as a matter of serious social and constitutional concern. While this interest has generally been manifest in the context of racial discrimination, there is no valid reason for not invoking the principle when persons of all races and of all economic groups are involved. There are no invariable racial or economic characteristics of the goodly numbers of families which seek social mobility, the opportunities for the good life available in a suburban atmosphere, and access to types of housing, education and employment differing from those indigenous to crowded urban centers.

There is a plethora of commentary on efforts, in a variety of contexts, of local communities to discourage the influx of outsiders. In virtually every instance, however, the cities limited availability of housing; until now it has never been seriously contemplated that a community would attempt total exclusion by refusing all building permits. * * *

* * *

In sum, I realize the easiest course is for this court to defer to the political judgment of the townspeople of Livermore, on a they-know-what's-best-for-them theory (*Eastlake v. Forest City Enterprises, Inc.* (1976) 426 U.S. 668, 96 S.Ct. 2358, 49 L.Ed.2d 132; *James v. Valtierra* (1971) 402 U.S. 137, 91 S.Ct. 1331, 28 L.Ed.2d 678). But conceptually, when a locality adopts a comprehensive, articulated program to prevent any population growth over the foreseeable future, it places its public policy intentions visibly on the table for judicial scrutiny and constitutional analysis.

Communities adopt growth limits from a variety of motives. There may be conservationists genuinely motivated to preserve general or specific environments. There may be others whose motivation is social exclusionism, racial exclusion, racial discrimination, income segregation, fiscal protection, or just fear of any future change; each of these purposes is well served by growth prevention.

Whatever the motivation, total exclusion of people from a community is both immoral and illegal. (Cal. Const. art. I, §§ 1, 7, subds. (a) & (b).) Courts have a duty to prevent such practices, while at the same time recognizing the validity of genuine conservationist efforts.

The problem is not insoluble, nor does it necessarily provoke extreme results. Indeed, the solution can be relatively simple if municipal agencies would consider the aspirations of society as a whole, rather than merely the effect upon their narrow constituency. (See, e.g., A.L.I. Model Land Development Code, art. 7.) Accommodation between environmental preservation and satisfaction of housing needs can be reached through rational guidelines for land-use decision-making. Ours, of course, is not the legislative function. But two legal inhibitions must be the benchmark of any such guidelines. First, any absolute prohibition on housing development is presumptively invalid. And second, local regulations, based on parochialism, that limit population densities in growing suburban areas may be found invalid unless the community is absorbing a reasonable share of the region's population pressures.

Under the foregoing test, the Livermore ordinance is fatally flawed. I would affirm the judgment of the trial court.

Notes

1. In light of the decision in the principal case, how might a court respond to a local referendum or initiated ordinance expressing either an absolute cap on population or a specific limit on the number of building permits to be issued? In City of Boca Raton v. Boca Villas Corp., 371 So.2d 154 (Fla.App.1979), certiorari denied 449 U.S. 824, 101 S.Ct. 86, 66 L.Ed.2d 27 (1980), the court affirmed a trial court judgment holding invalid an initiated ordinance adopted by the citizens of Boca Raton establishing a limit of 40,000 dwelling units in the city. The court stated that a determination that the ordinance was confiscatory was not necessary in that the trial court found that the ordinance bore no rational relationship to the general welfare. The court stated:

> Our study of the briefs and record convinces us that there is substantial competent evidence to support the finding of an absence of a rational relationship regarding the charter amendment and zoning ordinance. That being the case, we need not reach the question of confiscation vel non because the finding that there is no compelling need justifying an exercise of the police power burdening private property is sufficient to warrant striking down the legislative act. * * * That is not to say there must be an absolute necessity requiring the enactment of

> certain zoning restrictions before they can be tolerated as a proper exercise of the police power. But, as here, an excessive restriction on the use of private property which does not contribute substantially to the public health, morals, safety and welfare is arbitrary and unreasonable and thus unconstitutional. * * * The trial court found, and the record supports such finding, that the charter amendment and implementing ordinances bore no such rational relationship to the requisite purposes.
>
> We would concede that most of the cases where judicial invalidation of zoning laws has been upheld have in some measure involved the issue of confiscation. Those cases hold that as applied to the property involved the zoning ordinance was unreasonable because it deprived a property owner of the beneficial use of his property. We suggest the reason that the confiscation issue is so pervasive in the case law on this subject is because someone's ox is getting gored. Who is going to institute litigation but the person who feels his property rights infringed upon by excessive restrictions upon the use thereof?
>
> There are cases, however, which support the principle that zoning which unnecessarily restricts property, zoning which bears no rational relationship to the public health, safety, morals and welfare is unconstitutional without raising the confiscation issue.
>
> * * *
>
> In view of our conclusion that an otherwise valid attack may be made upon the charter amendment and implementing ordinances, we need not consider the trial judge's findings that the cap and implementing ordinances are so drastic and restrictive as to be confiscatory as applied to appellees' property.

2. Compare the *Boca Raton* case above to City of Hollywood v. Hollywood, Inc., 432 So.2d 1332 (Fla. Dist.Ct.App. 4th Dist. 1983), in which the municipality imposed a 3000–unit density cap in order to slow growth. In upholding the cap, the court stated:

> We cannot conclude the subject of a unit cap without addressing this court's recent decision in City of Boca Raton v. Boca Villas Corp., 371 So.2d 154 (Fla. 4th DCA 1979), wherein we upheld the trial court's conclusion that a 40,000 unit cap for the entire city "[did] not contribute substantially to the public health, morals, safety and welfare [and was therefore] arbitrary and unreasonable." However, the facts in that Boca Raton case reveal that the cap was established by public referendum, the City planning department was never even consulted and when examined, the Boca Raton City Planning Director knew of no compelling reason for imposing this fixed limitation. In the case before us now, the City did not adopt any such Alice-in-Wonderland approach. The record is replete with comprehensive plans, studies, reports, public meetings and actual discussions with the developer over a period of years. Unlike the *Boca Raton* case, the City of Hollywood did not present its community purpose in the abstract, but presented a more than adequate case for the proposition that the proposed cap would contribute substantially to the public health, morals, safety and welfare of its citizens. The record also supports the proposition that the City has been attempting to accom-

plish a density slash since 1971 and that the developer has owned most of its holdings for fifty years. As a consequence, this was no sudden municipal zoning karate chop such as transpired in the *Boca Raton* case.

3. After the decision in the Livermore case, several California cities and towns experienced initiated growth limitation ordinances. In 1987, the California Evidence Code § 669.5 was amended to provide that—in cases involving an ordinance which numerically limits residential construction permits—the city "shall bear the burden of proof that the ordinance is necessary for the protection of the public health, safety, or welfare of the population * * * " This provision is discussed in Building Industry Ass'n of San Diego v. Superior Court, 211 Cal.App.3d 277, 259 Cal.Rptr. 325 (1989). Also see Lesher Communications, Inc. v. City of Walnut Creek, 52 Cal.3d 531, 277 Cal.Rptr. 1, 802 P.2d 317 (1990), where the court struck an initiated growth control ordinance challenged as inconsistent with the existing general plan, finding that the ordinance was not labeled as, or intended to be viewed as, an amendment to the plan.

STEEL HILL DEVELOPMENT, INC. v. TOWN OF SANBORNTON

United States Court of Appeals, First Circuit, 1972.
469 F.2d 956.

COFFIN, CHIEF JUDGE.

Located in the rolling hills of Belknap County, New Hampshire is the tiny town of Sanbornton with a year-round population of approximately 1,000 persons living in some 330 regular homes. Long popular as a major recreational and resort area, Belknap County commenced to share its rural beauty with visitors in considerably greater degree with the opening in the 1960's of Interstate Highway 93 which funneled droves of touring urbanites from the Boston area, one hundred miles away, into towns like Sanbornton. Since Sanbornton borders Lake Winnisquam, is within easy reach of Lake Winnipesaukee and affords simple access to most New Hampshire ski areas, it is no surprise that its summer population is about 2,000 persons, that it has around 400 seasonal homes, and now is afforded the unique opportunity to serve as a seasonal second home paradise for persons who would buy the proposed 500 to 515 family units planned by appellant Steel Hill Development, Inc. In short, as the district court stated, "this case reflects the current clash between those interested in opening up new and hitherto undeveloped land for sale and profit and those wishing to preserve the rural character of Northern New England and shield it from the relentless pressure of an affluent segment of our society seeking new areas for rest, recreation and year round living." *Steel Hill Development, Inc. v. Town of Sanbornton*, 338 F.Supp. 301, 302 (D.N.H.1972).

Steel Hill acquired its 510 acres in December 1969 and immediately began surveying the land, mapping the topography and creating plans for conventional and "cluster" development. At that time, and until March 9, 1971 the entire Steel Hill tract was zoned as General Residence and Agricultural, requiring a minimum lot size of 35,000 square feet, or about three-fourths of an acre. Desirous of effectuating the "cluster" plan which appellant knew would require amending the zoning ordinance, appellant engaged in extensive and cordial negotiations with the town planning board during 1970. In order to permit some development while the "cluster" concept was under consideration, the board accepted a plan for 50 conventional lots meeting the 35,000 square feet requirement and scheduled, according to usual practice, a public hearing on the matter. About one hundred townsfolk attending the meeting on November 13, 1970 expressed opposition to any development by Steel Hill. Nevertheless, the planning board later approved the subdivision plan for thirty-seven lots, in the face of a petition, presented by about thirty town residents, for zoning the entire town as six acre minimum lots. Because public interest had been heightened in preserving Sanbornton's "charm as a New England small town", the planning board then proposed amendments to the zoning ordinance designed to enlarge the Forest Conservation areas, and to establish separate General Residential Districts and Agricultural Districts, with increased minimum acreage requirements in these districts and in the Historical Preservation and the Recreational Districts. These were passed.

As a result of the re-zoning, approximately 70 per cent of appellant's land is in the Forest Conservation District and 30 per cent in the Agricultural District. Clearly, its plans for "cluster" or conventional development are inconsistent with the new zoning ordinance. Appellant filed suit in the district court alleging that the three and six acre minimum lot size requirements are unconstitutional because they bear no rational relationship to the health, safety, morals or general welfare of the community and are therefore violative of N.H. R.S.A. 31:60 and the due process clause of the Fourteenth Amendment; that the rezoning greatly reduced the value of its land so as to constitute a taking without compensation; and that the classification of its land was violative of the equal protection clause of the Fourteenth Amendment because it was arbitrary and discriminatory in the restrictions imposed on development. The district court found adversely to appellant on all counts.

* * *

New Hampshire, like most states, has granted authority to localities to zone in order to promote public health, safety, morals and general welfare. N.H. R.S.A. 31:60. A zoning ordinance under such a statute may not be declared unconstitutional unless its "provisions are clearly arbitrary and unreasonable, having no substantial relation to the public health, safety, morals, or general welfare." *Village of Euclid v. Ambler Realty Co.*, 272 U.S. 365, 47 S.Ct. 114, 71 L.Ed. 303 (1926); *Gorieb v. Fox*, 274 U.S. 603, 47 S.Ct. 675, 71 L.Ed. 1228 (1927). Thus a court does not sit as a super zoning board with power to act *de novo,* but rather has, in the absence of alleged racial or economic discrimination, a limited role of review.

The district court found that, as the Sanbornton Planning Board had itself determined, topography and soil conditions posed severe problems of pollution, improper sewage disposal, poor drainage and erosion to large-scale development of the Steel Hill Tract, justifying imposition of the three-acre minimum lot size requirement in accordance with the public health. We have carefully read the conflicting trial testimony of the various experts who expressed an opinion on these matters and cannot say that the court's finding is clearly erroneous. In any event, appellant does not seem to challenge that ruling, but rather directs its argument to the unreasonableness of the six acre lot requirement.

The district court stated that it could not find the six acre requirement reasonable if only health and safety were considered, but that such requirement was reasonably related to the promotion of the general welfare of the community. N.H. R.S.A. 31:60. The court considered the pollution of Lake Winnisquam, possible interference with smelt spawning in Black Brook, increased traffic problems inherent in large-scale development, and increased air pollution. Testimony of planning board members and citizens opposed to Steel Hill's plans additionally reveals a desire to discourage density of population, and most importantly, a fear of premature development which was manifested in this effort to provide for orderly growth of the unspoiled areas of the town in a logical way. Several witnesses testified that not only would the town's rural character be destroyed by Steel Hill's massive plans, which would, in effect, double the town's population, but that there could be immeasurable ecological harm.

* * * [A]ppellant here does not seek to satisfy an already existing demand for suburban expansion, but rather seeks to create a demand in Sanbornton on behalf of wealthy residents of Megalopolis who might be willing to invest heavily in time and money to gain their own haven in bucolic surroundings. Note, 57 Iowa L.Rev. 126, 127 (1972). These different problems of suburban and rural expansion, their scientific and legal analyses, and their appropriate solutions cannot so easily be equated.

More appropriate to appellant's argument, and not cited to us, is *Kavanewsky v. Zoning Board of Appeals of Town of Warren*, 160 Conn. 397, 279 A.2d 567 (1971), where the town, when threatened with rapid development, increased minimum lot size requirements from one to two acres, an increase which the court found motivated by a "demand of the people to keep Warren a rural community with open spaces and keep undesirable businesses out", id. at 570, a goal not within the general welfare. In contrast, perhaps, is *Confederacion de la Raza Unida v. City of Morgan Hill*, 324 F.Supp. 895 (N.D.Cal.1971), which permitted a restriction, imposed by a zoning ordinance, on the development of a charming mountainous area of a city because of esthetic and environmental concerns. Yet even *Kavanewsky,* so far as appears, was dealing with an effort to keep out permanent residents and businesses, not to damp down a promoter's goal of doubling the housing in a small town by its large-scale second home plans. If, however, appellant has failed to present us with any controlling authority, neither have appellees. *Morgan Hill* involved a more detailed ordinance regulating density which resulted in a minimum lot size of only one half acre on the average. *County Commissioners of Queen Anne's County v. Miles*, 246 Md. 355, 228 A.2d 450 (1967), involved the upholding of a five acre minimum lot size requirement. The affected land comprised only 6.7 per cent of the county and the zoning was done pursuant to a long-range plan to preserve an unusually beautiful country estate section of a river. While we note that it is not within judicial competence to say that the forests in Sanbornton are any less worth preserving than country river estates, we do find it significant that the six acre requirement extends to approximately 50 per cent of the town, including the only area currently under any sort of development.

In short, no precedent compels its application to the case before us. We are faced with "a local legislative determination that the general welfare will be promoted by exclusion of an unwanted use from a non-metropolitan community [which exclusion] is not likely to conflict with a regional need for local space for that use." 57 Iowa L.Rev. at 140. We recognize, as within the general welfare, concerns relating to the construction and integration of hundreds of new homes which would have an irreversible effect on the area's ecological balance, destroy scenic values, decrease open space, significantly change the rural character of this small town, pose substantial financial burdens on the town for police, fire, sewer, and road service, and open the way for the tides of weekend "visitors" who would own second homes. If the federal government itself has thought these concerns to be within the general welfare, see, e.g., 42 U.S.C.A. § 4321, et seq., we cannot say that Sanbornton cannot similarly consider such values and reflect them in its zoning ordinance. Though some courts may have rejected them within the suburban zoning context, as in *Kohn,* and its progeny, or where permanent first homes are involved, as in *Kavanewsky,* but cf. *Morgan Hill,* we think they are persuasive in the case before us. "Many environmental and social values are involved in a determination of how land would best be used in the public interest. The choice of the voters of [the city] is not lacking in support in this regard." *Southern Alameda Spanish Speaking Organization v. City of Union City*, 424 F.2d 291 (9th Cir.1970).

Yet, though it may be proper for Sanbornton to consider the foregoing factors, we think the town has done so in a most crude manner. We are disturbed by the admission here that there was never any professional or scientific study made as to why six, rather than four or eight, acres was reasonable to protect the values cherished by the people of Sanbornton. On reviewing the record, we have serious worries whether the basic motivation of the town meeting was not simply to keep outsiders, provided they wished to come in quantity, out of the town. We cannot think that expansion of population, even a very substantial one, seasonal or permanent, is by itself a legitimate basis for permissible objection. Were we to adjudicate this as a restriction for all time, and were the evidence of pressure from land-deprived and land-seeking outsiders more real, we might well come to a different conclusion. Where there is natural population growth it has to go somewhere, unwelcome as it may be, and in that case we do not think it should be channelled by the happenstance of what town gets its veto in first. But, at this time of uncertainty as to the right balance between ecological and population pressures, we cannot help but feel that the town's ordinance, which severely restricts development, may properly stand for the present as a legitimate stop-gap measure.

In effect, the town has bought time for its citizens not unlike the action taken in referendum by the City of Boulder, Colorado to restrict growth on an emergency basis until an adequate study can be made of future needs. 60 Georgetown L.J. 1363 (1972). *See also Golden v. Planning Board of Town of Ramapo*, 30 N.Y.2d 359, 334 N.Y.S.2d 138, 285 N.E.2d 291 (1972), appeal dismissed 409 U.S. 1003, 93 S.Ct. 440, 34 L.Ed.2d 294 (1972). It was evident to the zoning board, and the district court, that haphazard and uncontrolled development of the town's hill areas would be inimical to present and future Sanbornton residents, *see Candlestick Properties, Inc. v. San Francisco Bay Conservation & Development Comm.*, 11 Cal.App.3d 557, 89 Cal.Rptr. 897 (1970), and that if the zoning laws do become "permanent barriers", then as the district court said, resort to the courts is always possible. *Steel Hill Development,* supra, 338 F.Supp. at 307. The zoning ordinance here in question has been in existence less than two years. Hopefully, Sanbornton has begun or soon will begin to plan with more precision for the future taking advantage of numerous federal or state grants for which it might qualify. Additionally, the New Hampshire legislature, to the extent it expects small towns like Sanbornton to cope with environmental problems posed by private developments, might adopt legislation similar to the federal National Environmental Policy Act, 42 U.S.C.A. § 4321 et seq. and thereby require developers to submit detailed environmental statements, if such power does not already reside within the town's arsenal of laws. Thus, while we affirm the district court's determination at the present time, we recognize that this is a very special case which cannot be read as evidencing a general approval of six-acre zoning, and that this requirement may well not indefinitely stand without more homework by the concerned parties.

Lastly, we find little merit to appellant's contentions that the zoning ordinance has resulted in a taking of appellant's property without just compensation or that it is discriminatory. As the district court found, appellant still has the land and buildings for which it paid $290,000. The estimated worth, had Steel Hill's original plans been approved, is irrelevant. Though the value of the tract has been decreased considerably, it is not worthless or useless so as to constitute a taking. *Hadacheck v. Sebastian,* 239 U.S. 394, 36 S.Ct. 143, 60 L.Ed. 348 (1915); *Sibson v. State, N.H.*, 282 A.2d 664 (1971). *Cf. State v. Johnson*, 265 A.2d 711 (Me.1970); *Bartlett v. Zoning Comm. of Town of Old Lyme*, 161 Conn. 24, 282 A.2d 907 (1971). As to appellant's claim of discrimination, we note that its land, like all other land zoned six acres, is essentially virgin forest. It is adjacent to, and its March 1971 re-zoning represented an extension of, the Forest Conservation District created in 1970. Thus the ordinance cannot be said to discriminate unreasonably against Steel Hill, be it the only developer in the town.

Affirmed.

Notes

1. For the subsequent history of the Steel Hill case, see Steel Hill Development, Inc. v. Town of Sanbornton, 392 F.Supp. 1134, and 392 F.Supp. 1144 (D.N.H.1974).

2. Do you think that a rural community far from the expanding metropolis is in a better legal position to preserve its "way of life" by preventing virtually all large developments than a rural community right in the path of the growing urban area? See Ybarra v. Town of Los Altos Hills, 503 F.2d 250 (9th Cir.1974), in which the court validated an ordinance that set a one-acre minimum lot size for residential lots and, thus, precluded the plaintiffs, low-income Mexican–Americans, from constructing multifamily dwellings, all in the name of preserving the town's "rural environment." See also Sturges v. Town of Chilmark, 380 Mass. 246, 402 N.E.2d 1346 (1980), in which the court upheld restrictive "rate of development" ordinances on Martha's Vineyard.

3. In New Hampshire, the courts have held that growth control ordinances must comply with the zoning enabling statutes. See Britton v. Town of Chester, 134 N.H. 434, 595 A.2d 492 (N.H. 1991), and Stoney–Brook Development Corp. v. Town of Pembroke, 118 N.H. 791, 394 A.2d 853 (1978). After these decisions, the legislature passed enabling legislation authorizing towns and cities to enact growth control ordinances. See N.H.Rev.Stat.Ann. 31:62–a and 31:62–b.

In Stoney–Brook Development Corp. v. Town of Fremont, 124 N.H. 583, 474 A.2d 561 (1984), the town had set a three percent growth rate which was challenged by the developer (who had received only three of the four building permits it sought). The court ruled for the developer holding that growth controls must be the product of careful study and must be constantly reviewed with a general view of relaxing the controls. Under this test, the court found the town's three percent figure to be arbitrary and artificial.

B. DENIAL OF ACCESS TO INFRASTRUCTURE

DATELINE BUILDERS, INC. v. CITY OF SANTA ROSA

California Court of Appeal, First District, 1983.
146 Cal.App.3d 520, 194 Cal.Rptr. 258.

WHITE, PRESIDING JUSTICE.

On this appeal by Dateline Builders, Inc. (Builders) from a judgment in favor of the City of Santa Rosa (City), the major question is whether the City was required to connect its existing sewer trunk line to Builders' proposed "leap frog" housing development beyond the City's boundaries. For the reasons set forth below we have concluded that the City reasonably exercised its police power because Builders' proposed housing development was not consistent with the City's compact land use and development policy as set forth in the City and County's previously adopted General Plan.

The pertinent facts substantially as found below and revealed by the record are as follows: Builders, a California corporation, held an option on a parcel of real property located beyond the limits of the city boundary, on Todd Road in an undeveloped rural area known as the Santa Rosa Plain. The City is a charter city located in Sonoma County (County).

The County Board of Supervisors determined that: 1) there was a need for development of sewer facilities in the Santa Rosa Plain; 2) it was in the public interest to avoid the proliferation of small and scattered un-unified sewer treatment facilities by a cooperative effort with the City to create a single regional facility to be owned and operated by the City. On October 17, 1964 the City and County entered into the "Plains Agreement," a mutual expression of policy and intent to exercise their police powers cooperatively for the orderly development of the Santa Rosa Plain, and to prevent a proliferation of fragment sewer districts and systems.

Paragraph 10 of the Plains Agreement provided that both the City and County would adopt a policy that the areas in the Santa Rosa Plain adaptable to urban type development, would be developed consistent with the City and County's General Plan and with the development standards of the City. To implement this policy the City and County agreed to enact subdivision, building, zoning and other property development regulations "to prevent haphazard or substandard property development." Paragraph 10 further provided that any development proposal in the Santa Rosa Plain be accompanied by proof that the proposed development was consistent with the City and County's joint General Plan and consistent with the City's development standards and regulations.

To implement one of the policies of the Plains Agreement the City Council adopted a procedure that required the proponent of a development to apply for and receive a certificate of compliance (certificate) prior to the extension of new service outside the city; the certificate then served as proof of compliance with the city's development standards.

* * *

Builders' application for a certificate was reviewed by the City for consistency with its plan, and development policies and standards. The City determined that Builders' proposed development in an agricultural area well beyond the city boundaries represented "leap-frog" development inconsistent with the city's plans, policies and standards. On December 9, 1971, the City denied the request without prejudice; Builders never submitted a subsequent or renewed application for a certificate. Builders appealed the determination to the City Council. On January 4, 1972 the City Council heard the appeal and refused to issue the certificate, on the same grounds, i.e., inconsistent with the City's General Plan and standards for compact development.

* * *

Builders rely on and urge us to follow, *Robinson v. City of Boulder* (1976) 190 Colo. 357, 547 P.2d 228 and *Delmarva Enterprises, Inc. v. Mayor and Council of the City of Dover* (Del.1971) 282 A.2d 601. In both *Robinson* and *Delmarva, supra,* the owners of property outside of the city limits successfully argued that each city had unlawfully discriminated against them by refusing to hook up their properties to the city's exclusive water and sewer services. Both the Delaware and Colorado courts reasoned that: 1) as the exclusive supplier of these services, each city acting in a proprietary capacity as a public utility, was held to the same standards as a private utility, and therefore could refuse to do so only for utility-based reasons, such as insufficient capacity; and 2) each city was bound by the rule that a municipality is without jurisdiction over territory beyond its limits in the absence of legislation. In *Boulder, supra,* 547 P.2d at 230–231, however, the court did not reach the City's argument that the rules applicable to private utilities should not apply to a governmental utility authorized to implement governmental objectives such as the adoption of a Master-plan. The City of Boulder and the county in which it was located had jointly developed and adopted a Boulder Valley comprehensive plan to provide for discretionary land use decisions. The court specifically noted that the proposed Boulder development complied with the county zoning regulations and that the county, rather than the city, had the ultimate responsibility for the approval of the proposed development.

Builders argue that the *Boulder* case, *supra,* is on all fours with the facts of the instant case. Builders, however, ignore the fact that its Todd Road project had the tentative approval of the county conditioned, inter alia, upon a change in zoning and other conditions with which Builders admittedly did not attempt to comply. However, we do not base our holding only on this factual distinction. By failing to seek rezoning from the County or meet the other 23 conditions imposed by the County in its tentative approval of the subdivision map, and then pursuing this action against the City, Builders was trying to play off against each other, the City and County who had agreed to cooperative planning. Basically, Builders argues that because a City cannot exercise its police power beyond its boundaries, the City was prevented from using the denial of the sewer hookup as a planning tool.

Builders ignores the joint policy of the City and County as expressed in the Plains Agreement, for orderly growth in conformance with the guidelines of the jointly adopted General Plan. Agreements such as that here in issue that lead to joint planning by cities and counties should and have been encouraged by the Legislature. The complex economic, political and social factors involved in land use planning are compelling evidence that resolution of the important housing and environmental issues raised here, is the domain of the Legislature. (Cf. *Construction Ind. Ass'n, Sonoma Co. v. City of Petaluma, supra,* 522 F.2d fn. 17 at 909.) Unfortunately, the experience of many communities in this state has been that when planning is left to developers, the result is urban sprawl. The City's express and reiterated reason for denying the certificate was that Builders' proposed development violated its policy of orderly compact development from the urban core, and would result in a "leap-frog" development and "urban sprawl." A municipality cannot be forced to take a stake in the developer's success in the area. (Cf. *Reid Dev. Corp. v. Parsippany–Troy Hills Tp.* (1954) 31 N.J.Super. 459, 107 A.2d 20, at 23.) Neither common law nor constitutional law inhibits the broad grant of power to local government officials to refuse to extend utility service so long as they do not act for personal gain nor in a wholly arbitrary or discriminatory manner. (See authorities cited in *Control of the Timing and Location of Government Utility Extensions* (1974) 26 Stanford L.Rev. 945–963.)

Builders rely on the line of California authorities holding that where a municipality provides a public utility service "[g]enerally it is true that where the scope of a project transcends the boundaries of a municipality it ceases to be for a municipal purpose." (*Santa Barbara etc. Agency v. All Persons* (1957) 47 Cal.2d 699, 710, 306 P.2d 875, revd. on other grounds (1958) 357 U.S. 275, 78 S.Ct. 1174, 2 L.Ed.2d 1313, dealing with a county water agency.) The California Supreme Court in upholding the right of a charter city to issue notices of sale for revenue bonds for sewerage improvements applied the above principle to sewer systems: "* * * sewer projects may transcend the boundaries of one or several municipalities * * *. In such circumstances the project 'ceases to be a municipal affair and comes within the proper domain and regulation of the general laws of the state.' (*Wilson v. City of San Bernadino* (1960) 186 Cal.App.2d 603, 604, 611 [9 Cal.Rptr. 431] * * *)" (*City of Santa Clara v. Von Raesfeld* (1970) 3 Cal.3d 239, 246, 90 Cal.Rptr. 8, 474 P.2d 976; see also *Pixley v. Saunders* (1914) 168 Cal. 152, 160, 141 P. 815.) These authorities, of course, predate *Associated Home Builders etc., Inc. v. City of Livermore, supra,* 18 Cal.3d 582, 601, 135 Cal.Rptr. 41, 557 P.2d 473. We agree with the City that unlike the situation in the past, most municipalities today are neither isolated nor wholly independent from neighboring entities, and consequently, land use decisions by one local unit affect the needs and resources of the entire region. The Plains Agreement and the General Plan demonstrate that the City and County were aware of these realities.

Builders recognize that in this state, as elsewhere, publicly owned municipal utilities are not regulated by the Public Utilities Commission (PUC) or any other supervisory agency in the absence of a legislative grant of authority while privately owned utilities are. (*American Microsystems, Inc. v. City of Santa Clara* (1982) 137 Cal.App.3d 1037, 1042–1043, 187 Cal.Rptr. 550.) It has long been the rule in this state that when operating a municipal utility, a city retains its character as a municipal corporation. Reasons must be found for holding it liable to the same extent as a private utility corporation. (*Pasadena v. R.R. Com.* (1920) 183 Cal. 526, 530, 192 P. 25.) Builders here argue that there were sufficient reasons here because the City was the only supplier, could not act beyond its boundaries and could not use sewer hookup as a planning device. We do not agree.

In *Associated Home Builders, etc., Inc. v. City of Livermore, supra,* 18 Cal.3d 582, 601, 135 Cal.Rptr. 41, 557 P.2d 473, our Supreme Court intimated that in California a city may enact restrictions that are effective beyond its boundaries. *Associated Home Builders* also reiterated the desirability of regional planning. As to a city's alleged inability to act beyond its boundaries, we note that Government Code section 65859 set forth below, a part of the same enactment as Government Code section 65300 and 65302 * * * expressly provides otherwise.

Builders' contention that denial of the certificate could not be used as a planning device overlooks a fundamental distinction between such a decision as an improper initial use of the police power, and as here, a necessary and proper exercise of the power once the planning decision had been made. Here, of course, the adoption of the General Plan with its policy of orderly and compact growth to avoid urban sprawl was made in 1967. The policy was a proper exercise of the police power for the general welfare (*Associated Home Builders, supra,* 18 Cal.3d 601, 135 Cal.Rptr. 41, 557 P.2d 473; cf. *Wilson v. Hidden Valley Mun. Water Dist.* (1967) 256 Cal.App.2d 271, 288, 63 Cal.Rptr. 889) previously adopted by the City Council and the County. (Cf. *Golden v. Ramapo* (1972) 30 N.Y.2d 359, 334 N.Y.S.2d 138, 285 N.E.2d 291, app. dism. 409 U.S. 1003, 93 S.Ct. 440, 34 L.Ed.2d 294.) Builders' argument that only zoning may be used for planning sits poorly in its mouth as they never sought to rezone the property or meet any of the County's other conditions.

The judgment is affirmed.

Note

In County of Del Norte v. City of Crescent City, 71 Cal.App.4th 965, 84 Cal.Rptr.2d 179 (Ct.App. 1st Dist., Div. 4, 1999), the appellate court upheld the city's policy to refuse water service connections to all development outside of its political borders. Already experiencing wastewater and capacity issues, the court also found justification for the city's policy in *Dateline Builders*: "It is not against the law or public policy to use utilities as a tool to manage growth."

CHARLES v. DIAMOND

Court of Appeals of New York, 1977.
41 N.Y.2d 318, 392 N.Y.S.2d 594, 360 N.E.2d 1295.

JASEN, JUDGE.

Petitioner, a landowner in the Village of Camillus, planned to construct three apartment buildings, totaling 36 units, on his property.

Village law required that such buildings had to be connected to the village sewage system. On May 9, 1972, the village board authorized issuance of a building permit. However, on May 22, 1972, the State Department of Environmental Conservation informed petitioner that he could not connect into the village sewage system until "the Village undertakes a program to correct the deficiencies of their sewage system". The State likewise directed the Onondaga County Health Department not to authorize the petitioner to connect into the existing system until the present deficiencies were corrected. Thereafter, in June, 1972, petitioner commenced this article 78 proceeding against the State Commissioner of Environmental Conservation, the Deputy Commissioner, Onondaga County Department of Health, and the Village of Camillus, contending that the actions of the State, county and village were arbitrary and capricious, resulting in an unconstitutional appropriation of his property without compensation. Petitioner sought a judgment directing the respondents to approve the village connection to his property, requiring the village to take appropriate steps so that the State and county would allow petitioner to use the village sewer system and awarding damages in the amount of $50,000 for damages already sustained. Alternatively, petitioner sought damages in the amount of $100,000 for the appropriation of his property in the event "that sewers are not approved * * * and he is not allowed to build the apartments on his property".

* * *

At the threshold, we note that this case does not involve the potentially troublesome issue of whether mere failure to provide municipal services can result in an inverse condemnation for which the municipality must pay compensation. Much more is involved here than merely an asserted failure to provide a service due equally to all members of the community. It is, of course, old law that a municipality is under no obligation to furnish sewers to particular property owners. Municipal corporations have ample opportunity to provide sewers "but it is not their duty to make every sewer or drain which may be desired by individuals, or which a jury might even find to be necessary and proper." * * * Although municipal sewage disposal obligations have been discussed at great length in the tort realm, and little mentioned elsewhere, it is virtually beyond question that an individual property owner has no right to insist that the municipality provide him with a system, at least where the problem is unique to his land and can be remedied at his expense. Article 14 of the Village Law provides for the optional construction of sewers in a village, with the cost to be borne entirely by the village, entirely by the owners of the property benefited or by the village and the property owners jointly, at the option of the village. It is also old law that once a municipality has acted to provide a sewer and its improvement causes damage, the municipality is liable to compensate for the injuries sustained. * * *

In this case, it is undisputed that the village provided a sewage disposal system and that local law requires that if a sewer is provided, it must be used. Moreover, the local law requires sewer-connected toilet facilities if the property is intended for any human use. The vice of the situation is that the municipality requires the use of public sewers if the property is to be developed for human use and yet has not provided an adequate system for meeting the requirement imposed by the ordinance. Hence, the claim is more than an undifferentiated demand for municipal service due to all citizens equally. The contention, stripped to its essence, is that the sewer ordinance is being applied unconstitutionally to petitioner's property, thereby frustrating nearly all reasonable development.

* * *

A police power regulation to be reasonable must be kept within the limits of necessity. * * * In *Matter of Belle Harbor Realty Corp. v. Kerr,* 35 N.Y.2d 507, 364 N.Y.S.2d 160, 323 N.E.2d 697, we established a three-pronged test for measuring whether necessity limits have been exceeded. "To justify interference with the beneficial enjoyment of property the municipality must establish that it has acted in response to a dire necessity, that its action is reasonably calculated to alleviate or prevent the crisis condition, and that it is presently taking steps to rectify the problem." * * * In that case, the municipality revoked a building permit on the ground that evidence uncovered since the issuance of the permit revealed that sewers were "grossly inadequate" for present use and new sewer connections were not advisable. The builder contended that the city had not acted because of sewer inadequacy but in response to community opposition to the planned development. We authorized the commencement of a proceeding to determine whether the revocation was a necessary health measure or was, in fact, motivated by political considerations. However, there was no contention that the developer would be entitled to money damages for any delay, whether justified by health requirements or not.

Similarly, in [*Westwood Forest Estates v. Village of South Nyack,* 23 N.Y.2d 424, 297 N.Y.S.2d 129, 244 N.E.2d 700 (1969)], we struck down a village zoning ordinance that prohibited all apartment house construction. The ordinance was purportedly justified by the fact that the village had inadequate sewage treatment facilities and new multiple dwellings would increase pollution of the Hudson River. Yet the sewage problem was not caused by the nature of the plaintiff's land but was general to the community. It was, we concluded, impermissible to single out one landowner to bear a heavy financial burden caused by a general community condition. * * * We were careful to note that the village, while it could not blanketly prohibit development, could impose moratoriums or other temporary measures in order to deal with the problem. * * * Indeed, we have sustained development restrictions, pursuant to a general community plan, for periods as long as 18 years. (See *Matter of Golden v. Planning Bd. of Town of Ramapo,* 30 N.Y.2d 359, 334 N.Y.S.2d 138, 285 N.E.2d 291, app. dsmd., 409 U.S. 1003, 93 S.Ct. 436, 34 L.Ed.2d

294.) However, the crucial factor, perhaps even the decisive one, is whether the ultimate economic cost of the benefit is being shared by the members of the community at large, or, rather, is being hidden from the public by the placement of the entire burden upon particular property owners. (See *French Investing Co. v. City of New York,* 39 N.Y.2d 587, 596–597, 385 N.Y.S.2d 5, 10–11, 350 N.E.2d 381, 386–387, *supra.*)

* * *

In this case, the delay, as measured from the time the difficulty first surfaced, has been substantial. Petitioner has been through a tortured course of litigation and appeal. Yet the reasons, if any, for apparent municipal inactivity in the face of sewage difficulties have never been explained. The present record, even after two appeals to the Appellate Division, is woefully silent. While it is true that the municipality has not submitted any justification for the delay, we also note that the property owner has not submitted any proof, apart from his conclusory allegations, that the municipal delay has exposed him to, or has caused him, significant economic injury of some sort. It is, of course, the property owner that must come forward with such proof in support of the claim that the zoning ordinance is being applied to the property unconstitutionally, in order to put the municipality to the task of justifying its action. * * * On this inadequate record, it would be inappropriate for us to determine the constitutionality of the municipal action. Both parties have not submitted the proof necessary for an intelligent and conclusive judicial evaluation of their respective claims. Since the parties should be given an opportunity, which neither has yet had, to submit their proof on trial, any temporary relief, short of a final declaration on the constitutionality of the village action, would be an idle gesture.

* * *

Assuming that the landowner has been prejudiced by an unreasonable delay on the part of the municipality, the question of proper constitutional remedy is reached. Of course, in the event that unreasonable delay is established, the landowner is entitled to a declaration that the ordinance, insofar as it requires the use of public sewers, may not be constitutionally applied to him. * * * Thus, this petitioner would be constitutionally free from the requirement that his property be tied into the public sewer system. The property could be developed by the use of private sewer disposal systems, provided compliance is made with pertinent provisions of local law. He should have that option.

A permit for the construction of a private sewage disposal system may be obtained by the owner. Of course, the proposed facility must comply with all relevant State health and sanitary requirements and is subject to village inspection. In addition, the property owner would be required to operate and maintain the facility in a sanitary manner at all times.

* * *

The order of the Appellate Division should be modified and, as modified, affirmed, without costs.

Order modified, without costs, and the matter remitted to Supreme Court, Onondaga County, for further proceedings in accordance with the opinion herein and, as so modified, affirmed.

BREITEL, C.J., and GABRIELLI, JONES, WACHTLER, FUCHSBERG and COOKE, JJ., concur.

Note

Also see Walz v. Town of Smithtown, 46 F.3d 162 (2d Cir.1995), where homeowners brought a successful civil rights action against the town and the town's superintendent of highways for denial of a permit to connect their home to the public water system after the failure of their well. The court upheld a jury verdict of $102,000 in compensatory damages against the town, $9,500 in punitive damages against the superintendent, and over $48,000 in attorney's fees.

C. STATE GROWTH MANAGEMENT LEGISLATION

The legislatures of all 50 states have developed statewide approaches to growth management. The adoption of the zoning and planning enabling acts, in the first instance, evidences a policy of delegating much of the responsibility for managing private land development to the local or county level of government. What is known as state growth management legislation refers to additional statutes that provide further guidance to, or impose limitations on, local land use authority. Even under these statutes, local governments play a significant, if somewhat more tethered, role in land use regulation.

Growth management statutes have been enacted to create fairer, more efficient, or more environmentally sound land use patterns. Much of the attention in the literature is focused on state statutes that define urban growth boundaries or that provide for state or regional plans which local comprehensive plans must consider or with which they must conform. But other approaches exist that guide or limit local land use authority in the interest of achieving better results. These include, for example, statutes that create regional land use review boards to which specified local decisions can be referred, affordable housing goals and mandates, regional agencies that exercise extraordinary power over a single area, state agency power over regional impact projects, and programs designed to obtain local compliance with one or more state growth management objectives. With continuing population pressures and the persistence of urban sprawl, it is likely that state statutes will continue to be adopted that attempt to influence, if not replace, local hegemony in this field. For the foreseeable future, however, it is not likely that the central role of local governments will be replaced.

An interesting example of a law that limits local land use authority is Connecticut's Affordable Housing Appeals Act. The Act makes it difficult for town land use commissions to turn down an affordable housing proposal unless ten percent of their housing stock is already affordable to low and moderate income households. (See Conn. Gen. Stat. § 8–30g). The Act requires the municipality to carry the burden of proving that the denial is in the public interest. This reverses the presumption of validity used by the courts to review challenges to other local land use decisions. The local commission must show that its decision was supported by substantial evidence on the record, that the rejection was necessary to protect substantial public interests in health or safety, and that those interests clearly outweigh the need for affordable housing and cannot be protected by reasonable changes to the proposed affordable housing development.

The positions of scholars and advocates on the issue of regional planning differ greatly. Three popular views are that regional planning agencies should preempt local land use authority to the extent necessary to serve regional interests; that regional agencies should be set up to mediate inter-local matters in the region's best interest; and that localities should be encouraged to form intermunicipal land use compacts to meet their own needs, which are increasingly interdependent and regional in nature. Some states have adopted enabling acts to form regional agencies which may or may not preempt some aspect of local control. Others provide funding or assistance to facilitate the formation of voluntary regional councils or agencies, often for the purpose of securing federal transportation or planning funds.

The Standard City Planning Enabling Act, promulgated by the Hoover Commission in 1928, provided for regional planning by authorizing local planning commissions to petition the governor to establish a regional planning commission and to prepare a master plan for the region's physical development. Provisions were included in the planning enabling act for communication between the regional and municipal planning commissions with the objective of achieving a certain degree of consistency between local and regional plans. In 1968, the Douglas Commission, appointed by President Johnson, issued its Report on Urban Problems, Building the American City, which reinforced regional planning. The Commission recommended that each state create a state agency for land use planning and prepare state and regional land use plans. In other words, regional consciousness has been with us since the early days of American zoning.

Much of the country, at one time or another, has been brought within the jurisdiction of some form of regional planning organization due to a variety of influences. The most powerful of these was the promise of funding for regional efforts under housing, water, and public works programs of the federal government. Predominant among these organizations were voluntary areawide regional councils of government, multi-state river basin compacts, and regional economic development organizations.

With few exceptions, these regional bodies have stopped far short of preemptive land use planning and regulation. They have become, however, effective vehicles for communication, education, collaboration, and networking. Among their most significant contributions is the effect they have of educating local land use officials. In these regional bodies, local representatives learn about the common problems and mutual dependence of localities that share the same economic or housing market area or that have regulatory power over river basins and watersheds that cannot be protected without intermunicipal cooperation.

Several states have adopted statutes that create urban growth areas. These statutes aim to achieve the essential goal of smart growth: to contain growth in defined and serviceable districts. They are guided by various objectives, including the creation of cost-effective centers, preservation of agricultural districts, promotion of affordable housing, protection of significant landscapes containing critical environmental assets, and the preservation of open lands for the future. Not all of these state growth management statutes are regional in nature. Maine requires local land use plans to identify areas suitable for absorbing growth and other areas for open space protection. Minnesota authorizes, but does not require, localities to designate urban growth areas in local and county comprehensive plans. Oregon and Maryland take a more direct approach, requiring the creation of growth and preservation districts and taking effective action to see that local governments conform their regulatory activities to established state land use objectives.

The Maryland statute, adopted in 1997, establishes priority funding areas and denies state agency funding for growth-related projects outside those designated areas. The state makes it clear that it will not fund growth inducing projects in rural areas not served by water and sewer systems. This is an incentive based program intended to slow down the conversion of agricultural and rural lands and to create growth areas that are serviceable in a cost-effective manner.

The Oregon growth management statute, adopted in 1973, is the most directive of its kind. It creates a state agency known as the Land Conservation and Development Commission (LCDC), articulates a number of statewide land use planning goals, requires local governments to adopt comprehensive plans that contain urban growth boundaries, and requires local plans to be approved by the Commission. The statute also created the Metropolitan Service District (Metro) to supervise the intermunicipal urban growth boundary in the greater Portland area. In 1979, the statute was amended to create the Land Use Board of Appeals (LUBA) to review local land use decisions. Litigation under this regime has not attacked its legality, but mainly the validity of particular planning decisions that affect individual parcels.

Goal 14 of the Oregon land use planning statute—the urbanization goal—classifies land into three categories: rural, urbanizable, and urban. Rural lands are agricultural, forest, or open space lands, or other land suitable for sparse settlement, with few public services. Urbanizable lands are to be contained within an urban growth boundary and are deemed suitable for future urban uses: lands that can be served by infrastructure and that are needed for the expansion of an urban area. Urban areas are within or adjacent to existing cities with concentrations of population and supporting public facilities and services. The statute provides for the orderly conversion of rural land to urban, based on the consideration of a number of factors including the need to accommodate population growth through the provision of housing, jobs, and infrastructure.

HAVILAND v. LAND CONSERVATION AND DEVELOPMENT COMMISSION

Court of Appeals of Oregon,1980.
45 Or.App. 761, 609 P.2d 423.

BUTTLER, PRESIDING JUDGE.

Petitioners appeal from an order of the Land Conservation and Development Commission (LCDC or Commission) in which that agency concluded that the City of Medford and Jackson County had not violated statewide planning goals in establishing the urban growth boundaries of Medford which excluded petitioners' property.

In Spring, 1978, the city and county amended their comprehensive plans, which have not yet been acknowledged by LCDC, by passing ordinances each establishing an urban growth boundary around the city of Medford. The boundaries were drawn in order to comply with LCDC Statewide Planning Goal 14. To the end of providing for "an orderly and efficient transition from rural to urban land use," Goal 14 requires that "urban growth boundaries shall be established to identify and separate urbanizable land from rural land."

The ordinances adopted by the city and county differ; the city urban growth boundary is more inclusive than that of the county but both versions exclude petitioners' property.

Petitioners sought review of the ordinances by LCDC, as authorized by former ORS 197.300(1)(d),[20] which requires the Commission to review, upon "(p)etition by any person or group of persons whose interests are substantially affected, a comprehensive plan provision * * * or other ordinance or regulation alleged to be in violation of statewide planning goals * * *." The LCDC properly limited its review to consideration of whether the local planning authority properly applied the Commission's goals in light of facts found by it and supported by the record. Former ORS 197.305.

That section limits the Commission's review to the record, and former ORS 197.310(3) directs the Commission to enter a final order which must include "a clear statement of findings setting forth the basis

20. ORS 197.300, 197.305, 197.310 and 197.315 were repealed by Oregon Laws 1979, chapter 772, section 26, effective November 1, 1979. That chapter establishes a Land Use Board of Appeals and provides new procedures for the review of land use decisions. The extent to which the appealability of local decisions, or the scope of review by the board, the commission and this court, must abide the event.

for the commission's determination in the proceeding." Under former ORS 197.310(5) the order of the commission may be appealed in the manner provided in ORS 183.480 for appeals from final orders in contested cases. Subsection (2) of that section provides that our review of such orders shall be solely as provided in ORS 183.482 (among other sections).

Our review, then, is of the Commission's order, including the findings and conclusions supporting it. If those findings are supported by the evidence from the record on which the Commission relied, and the conclusions are supported by those findings, we may not disturb the order solely because we might reach a different conclusion. See ORS 183.482(8)(a).

On this appeal, petitioners contend that there are inadequate facts in the record to support the population projection arrived at by the planning staffs, that the city and county erred in failing to adopt site-specific findings explaining why petitioners' land was excluded from the urban growth boundary, that petitioners' land had been committed to urbanization and therefore should have been included within the boundary and that inadequate consideration had been given to Goal 14, the urbanization goal of the statewide planning goals, and also Goals 2, 3, 5, 6, 9, 10, 11 and 12.

Taking the last contention first, the Commission, in its opinion and final order, determined that in establishing an urban growth boundary, which is only a preliminary step in adopting a comprehensive plan, only Goal 14 need be directly considered. When a comprehensive plan is adopted and submitted to the Commission for acknowledgment the other goals must be addressed. Until that time, the other planning goals apply only indirectly through the seven factors of Goal 14.[21]

We accept the agency's determination on the scope and applicability of the goals drafted by it, as we would accept as authoritative an agency's interpretation of a regulation promulgated by it. See *McPherson v. Employment Division*, 285 Or. 541, 549, n. 6, 591 P.2d 1381 (1979).

The Commission properly viewed a challenge to an urban growth boundary under former ORS 197.300(1)(d) in limiting its role to consideration of whether the local planning authorities had properly applied Goal 14 in light of facts found by the planning authorities and supported

21. Goal 14 requires that "(e)stablishment and change of the boundaries shall be based upon consideration of the following factors:

"(1) Demonstrated need to accommodate long-range urban population growth requirements consistent with LCDC goals;

"(2) Need for housing, employment opportunities, and livability;

"(3) Orderly and economic provision for public facilities and services;

"(4) Maximum efficiency of land uses within and on the fringe of the existing urban area;

"(5) Environmental, energy, economic and social consequences;

"(6) Retention of agricultural land as defined, with Class I being the highest priority for retention and Class VI the lowest priority; and,

"(7) Compatibility of the proposed urban uses with nearby agricultural activities."

in the record. The Commission viewed Goal 14 criteria as "accountability safeguards" to provide a means for assessing urbanization decisions, stating that if it appears that

> "the planning body fully considered all of the urbanization criteria, and the facts pertinent to the application of those criteria, and if the facts reported have support in the record, the local decision should be upheld even though the Commission or a court might have balanced the criteria differently or drawn a different conclusion from the facts presented."

The Commission proceeded to review each of the Goal 14 criteria in light of the record and found that each of them was considered and that the findings relating to those criteria are supported by the record. Based on that review, the Commission entered its own findings with specific reference to the record supporting them. Those findings are supported by the record and support the Commission's order. No useful purpose would be served by detailing them here, except to note the disposition of the specific contentions made by petitioners here.

The LCDC found that petitioners' challenge to the population projection did not manifest a violation of Goal 14. The first two criteria of Goal 14, consideration of "(d)emonstrated need to accommodate long-range urban population growth requirements consistent with LCDC goals" and of "(n)eed for housing, employment opportunities and livability" necessitate an estimation of the area's future population. Petitioners contend that the city and county population projections for the year 2000 are too low and that more land will be needed to meet the criteria than found by the city and county. The Commission, however, found that there was substantial evidence in the record to support the conclusion that, if anything, the amount of land included within the urban growth boundary exceeded the needs of the future population as estimated by the city and county, and, in fact, was in excess of the needs of the future population as projected by petitioners.[22] There is substantial evidence in the record to support this finding.

Petitioners next argue that site-specific findings should have been made to explain the exclusion of their land because of their extensive participation, including attendance at all planning commission hearings and presentation of oral and written testimony, which made them parties to the proceeding. Although decisions that result from judicial or quasi-judicial proceedings may require specific findings relating to each party involved, the Commission properly concluded that these proceedings were essentially legislative and do not require findings regarding the specific property of each landowner affected. See *Culver v. Dagg*, 20 Or.App. 647, 532 P.2d 1127, rev. den. (1975).

Moreover, LCDC points out that the record does contain findings with respect to the area of land which includes petitioners' property,

22. The hearings officer calculated that the amount of vacant land included within the urban growth boundary would support a growth rate of 4.3%, a higher rate "than seriously contended for by any of the petitioners."

which findings refute petitioners' additional contention that their property must be included because of its commitment to urbanization. The city and county considered that criterion for inclusion of property, but were aware that the drawing of an urban growth boundary involved, in addition, consideration of the seven Goal 14 criteria. A certain amount of land was included based upon an estimate of the future need for urban land and the findings reflect a concern that the inclusion of more land, including the area in which petitioners' property is located, within the boundary would violate Goal 14 by including more land than was warranted by that estimate. Absent evidence that the need for urbanizable land cannot be filled without including either committed lands or, for example, class I–IV agricultural lands, there is no reason why land committed to urban use may not be excluded for reasons which outweigh the commitment factor. The judgment is essentially a legislative one, subject to compliance with Goal 14.

The Commission's findings that the city and county considered Goal 14 are supported by substantial evidence in the record. We affirm its conclusion and final order.

Affirmed.

RESIDENTS OF ROSEMONT v. METRO

Court of Appeals of Oregon, 2001.
173 Or.App. 321, 21 P.3d 1108.

DEITS, C.J.

Petitioners Rosemont Property Owners Assoc., Kuhl and Eiselius (petitioners) seek review of, and respondents City of Lake Oswego and City of West Linn (cities) cross-petition from, LUBA's decision remanding Metro's decision that amended its urban growth boundary (UGB) to add an 830–acre area. We affirm on the petition and reverse and remand on the cross-petition.

The parties agree that the facts are correctly stated in LUBA's opinion:

> "On March 6, 1997, Metro designated 18,579 acres of land as urban reserves pursuant to OAR chapter 660, division 21, including lands in the Stafford area of Clackamas County. That area included five urban reserve study areas (URSAs) numbered 30, 31, 32, 33 and 34. On February 25, 1999, LUBA remanded Metro's decision in *D.S. Parklane Development, Inc. v. Metro*, 35 Or. LUBA 516 (1999) (*Parklane I*), *aff'd* 165 Or.App. 1, 994 P.2d 1205 (2000) (*Parklane II*).
>
> "In 1998, Metro began proceedings to consider expanding its UGB in order to comply with a state mandate to provide a 20–year supply of residential land within the UGB. ORS 197.296. Pursuant to ORS 197.299, Metro was required to add to the UGB half of the amount of land needed to comply with ORS 197.296 by December 1998. Metro planning staff conducted various analyses that nar-

rowed potential expansion sites to 26 URSAs, and then conducted further analyses that ranked those 26 URSAs as candidates for urbanization."

"On December 3, 1998, while the decision appealed in *Parklane I* was before LUBA, the Metro Council considered proposals to expand the UGB to include all of URSAs 31, 32, 33 and 34. The Council voted to remove more than half of the land in those URSAs from consideration, and approved an expansion of the UGB to include 830 acres of land in URSAs 31, 32 and 33, hereafter the 'expansion area' or the 'Rosemont area.' Proponents of including the Rosemont area in the UGB had developed a concept plan, the Rosemont Village Concept Plan (RVCP), proposing development in accordance with the requirements of Metro's 2040 Growth Concept. The 830–acre expansion area includes approximately 762 acres of land zoned for exclusive farm use (EFU), with the remainder consisting of exception lands, *i.e.,* lands for which an exception to Statewide Planning Goal 3 (Agricultural Lands) had previously been taken. The soils on the EFU-zoned lands are predominantly Class III and IV soils.

"On December 17, 1998, the Council adopted Ordinance No. 98–782C, approving the challenged UGB expansion." (Footnotes omitted.)

The cities, among others, brought these consolidated appeals to LUBA, challenging various aspects of Metro's decision. Petitioners intervened in the LUBA proceeding to assert positions that generally supported the local decision. Although LUBA resolved many of the cities' critical arguments in their favor, it rejected their contention that Metro erred in basing the LUBA amendment on a "subregional need" for "affordable housing" in the general area of the cities and the proximate Stafford area, rather than determining the need for urban land by reference to the entire Metro region. In their cross-petition, which we address first, the cities' only assignment of error challenges that adverse ruling by LUBA.

The cities argue that it is inconsistent with Statewide Planning Goal 14 for a planning body to expand its UGB based on a need for housing or other urban facilities in only a part of its territory, at least without considering "whether that need could be accommodated outside of the identified subregion."[23] This court has not previously decided the question that the cities raise. However, in *1000 Friends of Oregon v. Metro Service Dist.*, 18 Or. LUBA 311, 324 (1989), LUBA was presented with at least part of the question and concluded that,

23. The cities also make arguments that, even assuming our rejection of their underlying contention, the "factual base" for and evidence supporting Metro's designation of the Stafford–Rosemont subregion were inadequate and that the Rosemont Village Concept Plan was insufficient to ensure that the subregional need would be met. We do not reach those secondary arguments. As the parties and LUBA do, we will use the term "subregion" to refer to localized areas within a planning jurisdiction, as distinct from the "region" that constitutes all of the planning body's territory.

> "within the Metro UGB a subregional need could also constitute a regional need for purposes of Goal 14 factors 1 and 2. * * * [W]e reject petitioner's contention that, as a matter of law, a subregional need could never provide a basis for amending Metro's regional UGB."

For the reasons that follow, we agree with LUBA that a subregional need may, in some circumstances, constitute need for purposes of satisfying factors 1 and 2 of Goal 14. We also conclude, however, that LUBA erred in affirming Metro's decision here, because, in deciding that factors 1 and 2 of Goal 14 were satisfied, Metro focused solely on what it identified as a subregional need without any consideration of this need in the regional context or any explanation of how this area was identified as a subregion or why the needs of this area should be viewed in isolation.

* * *

Considering the text and context of the pertinent laws, we believe that LUBA was correct in holding that it cannot be said, as a matter of law, that a subregional need will *never* satisfy the need factors of Goal 14. However, we also conclude that there is nothing in the text or context of Goal 14 or those portions of the Metro Code implementing Goal 14 that provides authority for a subregional need alone to serve as the basis for a UGB expansion without consideration being given to the "regional context." As LUBA explained in an early decision on this subject:

> "As a regional urban growth boundary, Metro's boundary looks to growth trends on a regional basis and is designed to accommodate regional growth. Changes within jurisdictions served by Metro may be necessary to accommodate that regional growth, *but the Board does not agree with the petitioner that only the growth in Clackamas County is relevant in deciding whether the urban growth boundary in Clackamas County needs to be amended*. Without a showing by petitioner as to how the Clackamas County urban growth boundary is critical to the regional urban growth boundary in some manner requiring it to be viewed by itself, we believe we would be doing more harm than good by accepting petitioner's proposition." *Home Builders Ass'n v. Metropolitan Service District*, 2 Or LUBA 25, 30 (1980) (emphasis added).

In order to satisfy the need factors of Goal 14, a subregional need must be identified and evaluated in the context of the regional needs. *See 1000 Friends of Oregon v. Metro*, 38 Or. LUBA 565 (2000) (slip op at 3–14) (LUBA concluded that Metro properly identified a subregional need for housing and considered the role that need plays in the context of the entire UGB and regional need).

Here, Metro's decision to expand the UGB in the Stafford–Rosemont area appears to have been based *solely* on subregional considerations of the kind reflected in factor 2. As the cities argue:

"Metro's decision in this case was based solely on a determination of need for affordable housing within three or six miles of the Stafford and Rosemont intersection, and did not consider whether that need could be accommodated outside of the identified subregion." (Footnotes omitted.)

We agree with the cities that Metro erred in that respect and that LUBA accordingly erred in affirming that aspect of Metro's decision. To illustrate, there might be some *a priori* logic to the proposition that persons employed on the rural fringe of Clackamas County cannot be adequately accommodated by housing on the urban fringes of Multnomah and Washington Counties. However, there is no corresponding logic to the proposition that Metro appears to have found decisive here, *i.e.,* that a determinative housing need could be established solely by reference to areas in close proximity to the preselected site of the proposed UGB expansion and without *any* consideration of other parts of the regional planning territory. Metro's decision does not explain why the affordable housing must lie within a six-mile radius of the Stafford–Rosemont intersection, let alone why that intersection may appropriately be treated as the nucleus of an identifiable subregion or of the subregion to which virtually exclusive consideration was given as the site of the expansion. We hold that Metro's present supportive showing for its decision does not satisfy Goal 14 in this regard.

* * *

Notes

1. In Benjfran Development Inc. v. Metropolitan Service Dist., 95 Or.App. 22, 767 P.2d 467 (1989), landowners challenged the refusal of the Metropolitan Service District to allow 500 acres to be developed as an industrial park. The District was created to administer the urban growth boundary program in the greater Portland area. The landowner's argument was that the state economic development planning goal—Goal 9—and another parallel state statute should be given precedence over the urbanization goal—Goal 14. The court deferred to the decision of the District to disallow the development of the acreage for industrial purposes. See also Port of St. Helens v. Land Conservation & Development Comm'n, 165 Or.App. 487, 996 P.2d 1014 (2000).

2. Consider how radically the Oregon growth management statute changed the historical balance of power between local, regional, and state agencies regarding the regulation of land use. Is there something unique about the legal system or the political culture in Oregon that enabled state lawmakers to effect such a drastic change? If local governments are created by the states and given their legislative authority primarily through state enabling acts, why can't their land use authority be taken away in the interest of achieving statewide or regional objectives?

3. On November 2, 2004, Oregon voters passed Ballot Measure 37 by a margin of 61%. The initiative, which has the same effect as a statutory enactment, entities property owners to compensation for any decreases in property values caused by land use regulations. To avoid having to compen-

sate owners, the government enacting the regulation may elect to waive its application to a particular property. The impact of the Measure on Oregon's growth management program was immediate and severe. Within two years of the Measure's adoption over 7,500 claims were filed threatening over 125,000 acres of prime farmland in Willamette Valley. The adverse effect of the Measure on the landscape and the government's treasury triggered efforts within the state legislature to pass legislation softening its impacts.

4. In 1973, in Bedford v. Mount Kisco, 33 N.Y.2d 178, 351 N.Y.S.2d 129, 306 N.E.2d 155 (1973), the Court of Appeals heard the Town of Bedford's complaint that a rezoning by the Village of Mount Kisco from single-family to multi-family use of a parcel bounded on three sides by the town would have an undue impact on the town. The Court of Appeals found for Mount Kisco noting that "the [village] Board of Trustees considered the welfare and economic stability of Mount Kisco, as its first concern * * *. Bedford understandably differed from the conclusion reached, but that difference must be regarded as the necessary result of conflicting zoning policies that are confronted at the edge of every municipality." Bedford v. Mount Kisco represents the settled judicial doctrine in New York: that the state courts will not serve as the mediating mechanism for these border disputes in the ordinary circumstance.

5. Local sovereignty in land use matters has been established and generally reinforced since zoning was declared constitutional. In Euclid v. Ambler Realty Co., the court recognized the principle of local self-determinism in land use control with these words: "although physically a suburb of Cleveland, Euclid has powers of its own." However, federal and state preemption of local control does limit local sovereignty regarding particular matters of concern to these higher levels of government. See Chapter VI.

6. In Wambat Realty Corp. v. State of New York, 41 N.Y.2d 490, 362 N.E.2d 581, 393 N.Y.S.2d 949 (1977), the Court of Appeals upheld the Adirondack Park Agency Act. The Adirondack Park Agency was authorized to govern land use decisions in twelve counties containing 105 local towns and villages. Its jurisdiction contains six million acres of private land, over twenty percent of the state. It is a classic example of top-down regionalism. The statute creating the APA allows local control over land use only after communities adopt land use plans and regulations that conform to the Agency's plan and regulatory regime, which preempted the land use authority of localities in the Adirondack region to various degrees. The plaintiff in Wambat claimed that the Act, "which set forth a comprehensive zoning and planning program for all of the public and private lands within the park, together with other restrictions on local land use contained in the act, unconstitutionally deprive[d] the Town of Black Brook of its own zoning and planning powers." The court disagreed, holding that the preservation of the area was a paramount state concern.

7. In 1970, the New York legislature was presented with the Statewide Comprehensive Planning Act, which provided for the creation of state, regional, county, and local plans—all cross certified and consistent, another classic top-down approach. At the time, this was the nation's most far-reaching attempt to guide and constrain the parochial effects of local land use decision-making. The perceived threat to local control was clear, and the

political reaction was predictable, swift, and definitive. The bill was withdrawn, and the New York Office of Planning Coordination—the agency that proposed it—was voted out of existence by the state legislature.

8. Despite this stunning political defeat, the state's highest court, the Court of Appeals, took a remarkably strong position regarding the need for regional mechanisms to make sense out of "insular" land use decisions. Refer back to Golden v. Town of Ramapo, 30 N.Y.2d 359, 334 N.Y.S.2d 138, 285 N.E.2d 291 (1972), where the court upheld the Town of Ramapo's novel growth management legislation. In so doing, it recognized the limitations of planning a region one community at a time, stating that "only at the regional level can the pitfall of idiosyncratic municipal action be avoided." The court called for a system of "statewide or regional control of land use planning" to "insure that interests broader than that of the municipality underlie various land use policies." It went on to say that "zoning enabling legislation is burdened by the largely antiquated notion which deigns that the regulation of land use and development is uniquely a function of local government." It found that this system suffers from "pronounced insularism" and that "questions of broader public interest have commonly been ignored" by it. In the absence of any regional or statewide planning framework, however, the decision simply sanctioned local growth management, allowing one suburb in the path of metropolitan development to adopt an ordinance in a contextual vacuum.

9. Since the creation of the Adirondack Park Agency and the Golden decision, nine voluntary, relatively weak regional councils, organized by local governments, focusing mostly on data gathering, research, grant getting, and technical assistance to local communities, have been New York's approach to regionalism in land use planning in most of the state. These regional councils are not guided by any statewide plan or development and conservation guidelines, paralleling the situation in most states. After a twenty year respite from regional legislation, the state legislature adopted the Hudson River Greenway Act in 1991, creating the Hudson River Greenway Communities Council and providing for a voluntary regional planning process based on local plans and county compacts that adhere to a few greenway planning principles. The Greenway is enjoying some success with a majority of the 242 communities in the regions voting to become participating localities in the Greenway compact.

10. Strong regionalism has not prevailed in New York for the same reason it has not prevailed in the majority of states. Former Speaker of the House Thomas P. O'Neill Jr., once quipped that "all politics is local." All reform efforts aimed at constraining local control must overcome this political reality. The danger in advocating top-down, statewide land use solutions is that it identifies local control as the problem to be solved, rather than the base on which to build an intermunicipal process, responsive to regional needs. The challenge for advocates of a regional approach to land use planning and control is to identify effective regional processes that respect the critical role that local governments play in land use decision-making. To be politically palatable, these solutions must be perceived not as methods of imposing a state or regional body's will on local governments but as means of communicating effectively about regional and local needs,

balancing those interests, and arriving at mutually beneficial decisions over time.

SECTION 4. SMART GROWTH TECHNIQUES

A. POST–EUCLIDIAN ZONING

The essence of traditional zoning is the division of the community into zoning districts and the separation of land uses among those districts. In Euclid v. Ambler Realty, the 1926 U.S. Supreme Court case which upheld the constitutional validity of zoning, the key question was whether the separation of uses served a legitimate public purpose. The Court held that it did and traditional, or Euclidian, zoning has been characterized ever since as zoning that mandates the separation of residential, retail, commercial, and industrial land uses among zoning districts.

Post–Euclidian, or Neo–Euclidian, zoning encompasses a variety of techniques designed to allow regulatory flexibility that some suggest is not permitted under the Euclidian approach. That use separation is a valid police power objective does not mean that mixed-use zoning is not. That Euclidian zoning prescribed uniform height, lot coverage, and setback standards does not mean that localities may not waive those bulk and area restrictions to serve sound community planning objectives. For decades, localities have been inventing techniques that provide them more flexibility in placing development on the land. Since these newer techniques tend to use higher densities, mixed-uses, and cost-effective design, they may also be called smart growth techniques. What smart growth aspires to do is to aggregate development in more cost-effective arrangements so that it is more cost and energy efficient, more affordable, and more environmentally sound. To accomplish these objectives is difficult in some states using the prescriptions of Euclidan zoning.

Breaking out of the mold, however, has not been easy. The local governments that have invented smart growth techniques, and the courts that have reviewed their validity when challenged, have had to examine whether the enabling acts of the states permitted such flexibility. The original zoning enabling act, which was followed often literally in the original acts adopted by the states, delegated permission to localities to "divide the municipality into districts of such number, shape, and area as may be deemed best suited to carry out the purposes of this act." It further specified that "all such regulations shall be uniform for each class or kind of buildings throughout each district." (See Chapter III) The purposes of zoning originally included accomplishing the objectives of the comprehensive plan, promoting the general welfare, preventing the overcrowding of land, avoiding undue concentration of population, and facilitating the adequate provision of service and infrastructure. The standard zoning enabling act ended its purpose clause with these critical words: "Such [zoning] regulations shall be made with reasonable consideration, among other things, the character of the district and its peculiar suitability for particular uses, and with a view to conserving the value of buildings and encouraging the most appropriate use of land throughout such municipality."

Do these words allow local governments to adopt techniques such as floating zones, overlay districts, clustered subdivisions, bonus or incentive zoning, transfer of development rights, or performance zoning? These and similar techniques have been adopted by localities to do a better job of arranging permitted densities on individual sites and to create a better overall pattern of land development in the community. In some states, whether localities have the legal authority to adopt smart growth techniques depends on how expansively the courts view the delegation of zoning authority to local governments. Localities, it is said, have only those powers expressly delegated to them or those necessarily implied to accomplish the stated legislative goals. So, for example, can a local legislature authorize its planning board to cluster the density permitted under the zoning applicable to a particular parcel on 70 percent of the land in order to preserve open space and protect the community's character? Would this violate the uniformity requirement of the zoning enabling act? Is this the creation of a new district that amounts to illegal spot zoning? Does it serve any of the purposes for which zoning may be adopted?

Why do neighboring property owners object when a locality, using a smart growth zoning technique, permits a mixed-use development or a clustered development in a single-family residential zone? What are the investment-backed expectations of a home purchaser who buys a home in a Euclidian zoning district? Do purchasers have vested rights in the zoning of the surrounding area or does the local legislature retain the right to amend the rules when the public interest requires? Consider the objections of the plaintiff in the following case to the Village of Tarrytown's early adoption of floating zoning.

RODGERS v. VILLAGE OF TARRYTOWN

Court of Appeals of New York, 1951.
302 N.Y. 115, 96 N.E.2d 731.

FULD, JUDGE.

This appeal, here by our permission, involves the validity of two amendments to the General Zoning Ordinance of the Village of Tarrytown, a suburban area in the County of Westchester, within twenty-five miles of New York City.

Some years ago, Tarrytown enacted a General Zoning Ordinance dividing the village into seven district or zones Residence A for single family dwellings, Residence B for two-family dwellings, Residence C for multiple dwellings and apartment houses, three business districts and an industrial zone. In 1947 and 1948, the board of trustees, the village's legislative body, passed the two amendatory ordinances here under attack.

The 1947 ordinance creates a new district or class of zone * * * (to) be called 'Residence B–B', in which, besides one-and two-family dwellings, buildings for multiple occupancy of fifteen or fewer families were permitted. The boundaries of the new type district were not delineated in the ordinance but were to be 'fixed by amendment of the offical [sic] village building zone map, at such times in the future as such district or class of zone is applied, to properties in this village.' The village planning board was empowered to approve such amendments and, in case such approval was withheld, the board of trustees was authorized to grant it by appropriate resolution. In addition, the ordinance erected exacting standards of size and physical layouts for Residence B–B zones: a minimum of ten acres of land and a maximum building height of three stories were mandated; setback and spacing requirements for structures were carefully prescribed; and no more than 15% of the ground area of the plot was to be occupied by buildings.

A year and a half after the 1947 amendment was enacted, defendant Elizabeth Rubin sought to have her property, consisting of almost ten and a half acres in the Residence A district, placed in a Residence B–B classification. After repeated modification of her plans to meet suggestions of the village planning board, that body gave its approval, and, several months later, in December of 1948, the board of trustees, also approving, passed the second ordinance here under attack. In essence, it provides that the Residence B–B district 'is hereby applied to the (Rubin) property * * * and the district or zone of said property is hereby changed to 'Residence B–B' and the official Building Zone Map of the Village of Tarrytown is hereby amended accordingly (by specification of the various parcels and plots involved)'.

Plaintiff, who owns a residence on a six acre plot about a hundred yards from Rubin's property, brought this action to have the two amendments declared invalid and to enjoin defendant Rubin from constructing multiple dwellings on her property. The courts below, adjudging the amendments valid and the action of the trustees proper, dismissed the complaint. We agree with their determination.

While stability and regularity are undoubtedly essential to the operation of zoning plans, zoning is by no means static. Changed or changing conditions call for changed plans, and persons who own property in a particular zone or use district enjoy no eternally vested right to that classification if the public interest demands otherwise. Accordingly, the power of a village to amend its basic zoning ordinance in such a way as reasonably to promote the general welfare cannot be questioned. Just as clearly, decision as to how a community shall be zoned or rezoned, as to how various properties shall be classified or reclassified, rests with the local legislative body; its judgment and determination will be conclusive, beyond interference from the courts, unless shown to be arbitrary, and the burden of establishing such arbitrariness is imposed upon him who asserts it. In that connection, we recently said in *Shepard v. Village of Skaneateles*, 300 N.Y. 115, 118, 89 N.E.2d 619, 620: 'Upon parties who attack an ordinance * * * rests the burden of showing that the regulation assailed is not justified under the police power of the state by any reasonable interpretation of the facts. 'If the validity of the legislative classification for zoning purposes be fairly debatable, the legislative judgment must be allowed to control.' *Village of Euclid v. Ambler Realty Co.*, 272 U.S. 365, 388, 47 S.Ct. 114, 118, 71 L.Ed. 303; see, also, *Town of Islip v. F.E. Summers Coal & Lbr. Co.*, 257 N.Y. 167, 169, 170, 177 N.E. 409, 410; *Matter of Wulfsohn v. Burden*, 241 N.Y. 288, 296–297, 150 N.E. 120, 121–122, 43 A.L.R. 651.'

By that test, the propriety of the decision here made is not even debatable. In other words, viewing the rezoning in the case before us, as it must be viewed, in the light of the area involved and the present and reasonably foreseeable needs of the community, the conclusion is inescapable that what was done not only accorded with sound zoning principles, not only complied with every requirement of law, but was accomplished in a proper, careful and reasonable manner.

The Tarrytown board of trustees was entitled to find that there was a real need for additional housing facilities; that the creation of Residence B–B districts for garden apartment developments would prevent young families, unable to find accommodations in the village, from moving elsewhere; would attract business to the community; would lighten the tax load of the small home owner, increasingly burdened by the shrinkage of tax revenues resulting from the depreciated value of large estates and the transfer of many such estates to tax exempt institutions; and would develop otherwise unmarketable and decaying property.

The village's zoning aim being clear, the choice of methods to accomplish it lay with the board. Two such methods were at hand. It could amend the General Zoning Ordinance so as to permit garden apartments on any plot of ten acres or more in Residence A and B zones (the zones more restricted) or it could amend that Ordinance so as to invite owners of ten or more acres, who wished to build garden apartments on their properties, to apply for a Residence B–B classification. The board chose to adopt the latter procedure. That it called for separate legislative authorization for each project presents no obstacle or drawback and so we have already held. See, e.g., *Nappi v. La Guardia*, 184 Misc. 775, 781, 55 N.Y.S.2d 80, 86, per Froessel, J. *affirmed* 269 App.Div. 693, 54 N.Y.S.2d 722, *affirmed* 295 N.Y. 652, 64 N.E.2d 716; *Matter of Green Point Sav. Bank v. Board of Zoning Appeals*, 281 N.Y. 534, 539, 24 N.E.2d 319, 321. Whether we would have made the same choice is not the issue; it is sufficient that the board's decision was neither arbitrary nor unreasonable.

As to the requirement that the applicant own a plot of at least ten acres, we find nothing therein unfair to plaintiff or other owners of smaller parcels. The board undoubtedly found, as it was privileged to find, that garden apartments would blend more attractively and harmoniously with the community setting, would impose less of a burden upon village facilities, if placed upon larger tracts of land rather than scattered about in smaller units. Obviously, some definite acreage had to be chosen, and, so far as the record before us reveals, the choice of ten acres as a minimum plot was well within the range of an unassailable legislative judgment. See, e.g., *Nappi v. LaGuardia, supra*, 295 N.Y. 652, 64 N.E.2d 716, affirming 269 App.Div. 693, 54 N.Y.S.2d 722, affirming 184 Misc. 775, 55 N.Y.S.2d 80, wherein the qualifying acreage was also fixed at ten.

Nor did the board, by following the course which it did, divest itself or the planning board of power to regulate future zoning with regard to garden apartments. The mere circumstance that an owner possesses a ten-acre plot and submits plans conforming to the physical requirements precribed [sic] by the 1947 amendment will not entitle him, ipso facto, to a Residence B–B classification. It will still be for the board to decide, in the exercise of a reasonable discretion, that the grant of such a classification accords with the comprehensive zoning plan and benefits the village as a whole. And while no such question is here presented we note that the board may not arbitrarily or unreasonably deny applications of other owners for permission to construct garden apartments on their properties. The action of the board must in all cases be reasonable and, whether a particular application be granted or denied, recourse may be had to the courts to correct an arbitrary or capricious determination. See, e.g., *Nappi v. La Guardia, supra*, 184 Misc. 775, 781, 55 N.Y.S.2d 80, 86, affirmed 269 App.Div. 693, 54 N.Y.S.2d 722, affirmed 295 N.Y. 652, 64 N.E.2d 716; *Matter of Green Point Sav. Bank v. Board of Zoning Appeals*, supra, 281 N.Y. 534, 539, 24 N.E.2d 319; *Arverne Bay Const. Co. v. Thatcher,* 278 N.Y. 222, 232, 15 N.E.2d 587, 591, 117 A.L.R. 1110; *Dowsey v. Village of Kensington*, 257 N.Y. 221, 231, 177 N.E. 427, 430, 86 A.L.R. 642; *Matter of Larkin Co. v. Schwab*, 242 N.Y. 330, 334, 336, 151 N.E. 637, 638, 639; *City of Little Rock v. Joyner*, 212 Ark. 508, 206 S.W.2d 446; *Frink v. Orleans Corp.*, 159 Fla. 646, 32 So.2d 425.

The charge of illegal 'spot zoning' leveled at the creation of a Residence B–B district and the reclassification of defendant's property is without substance. Defined as the process of singling out a small parcel of land for a use classification totally different from that of the surrounding area, for the benefit of the owner of such property and to the detriment of other owners, see *Harris v. City of Piedmont*, 5 Cal.App.2d 146, 152, 42 P.2d 356; *Cassel v. Mayor & City Council of Baltimore, Md.*, 73 A.2d 486, 488–489; *Board of Co. Comrs. of Anne Arundel County v. Snyder*, 186 Md. 342, 345–346, 46 A.2d 689; *Leahy v. Inspector of Bldgs. of New Bedford*, 308 Mass. 128, 134, 31 N.E.2d 436; *Page v. City of Portland*, 178 Or. 632, 641, 165 P.2d 280; *Weaver v. Ham*, Tex.Sup., 232 S.W.2d 704, 709; see, also, Yokley, Zoning Law and Practice (1948), s 85; *cf. People v. Cohen*, 272 N.Y. 319, 5 N.E.2d 835, 'spot zoning' is the very antithesis of planned zoning. If, therefore, an ordinance is enacted in accordance with a comprehensive zoning plan, it is not 'spot zoning,' even though it (1) singles out and affects but one small plot *see, e.g., Shepard v. Village of Skaneateles, supra*, 300 N.Y. 115, 89 N.E.2d 619, or (2) creates in the center of a large zone small areas or districts devoted to a different use. *See Nappi v. LaGuardia, supra,* 295 N.Y. 652, 64 N.E.2d 716, affirming 269 App.Div. 693, 54 N.Y.S.2d 722, affirming 184

Misc. 775, 55 N.Y.S.2d 80–business area in residence zone; *Marshall v. Salt Lake City*, 105 Utah 111, 126–127, 141 P.2d 704, 149 A.L.R. 282 business district in residence zone; *Higbee v. Chicago, B. & Q. R. R. Co.*, 235 Wis. 91, 98–99, 292 N.W. 320, 128 A.L.R. 734 railraod station in residence zone; *see, also, Avery v. Village of La Grange*, 381 Ill. 432, 442, 45 N.E.2d 647; *Town of Marblehead v. Rosenthal*, 316 Mass. 124, 126, 55 N.E.2d 13; Rathkopf, Law of Zoning and Planning (2d ed. 1949), p. 72 et seq. Thus, the relevant inquiry is not whether the particular zoning under attack consists of areas fixed within larger areas of different use, but whether it was accomplished for the benefit of individual owners rather than pursuant to a comprehensive plan for the general welfare of the community. Having already noted our conclusion that the ordinances were enacted to promote a comprehensive zoning plan, it is perhaps unnecessary to add that the record negates any claim that they were designed solely for the advantage of defendant or any other particular owner. Quite apart from the circumstance that defendant did not seek the benefit of the 1947 amendment until eighteen months after its passage, the all-significant fact is that that amendment applied to the entire territory of the village and accorded each and every owner of ten or more acres identical rights and privileges.

By the same token, there is no basis for the argument that "what has been done by the board of trustees" constitutes a device for "the granting of a variance", opinion of Conway, J., 302 N.Y. p. 129, 96 N.E.2d at 738. As we have already shown, the village's zoning aim, the statute's purpose, was not to aid the individual owner but to permit the development of the property for the general welfare of the entire community. That being so, the board of trustees followed approved procedure by changing the General Zoning Ordinance itself. See, e.g., *Matter of Clark v. Board of Zoning Appeals*, 301 N.Y. 86, 91, 92 N.E.2d 903, 905. Accordingly, when the board was called upon to consider the reclassification of the Rubin property under the 1947 amendment, it was concerned, not with any issue of hardship, but only with the question of whether the property constituted a desirable location for a garden apartment.

We turn finally to the contention that the 1947 ordinance is invalid because, in proclaiming a Residence B–B district, it set no boundaries for the new district and made no changes on the building zone map. The short answer is that, since the ordinance merely prescribed specifications for a new use district, there was no need for it to do either the one or the other. True, until boundaries are fixed and until zoning map changes are made, no new zone actually comes into being, and neither property nor the rights of any property owner are affected. But it was not the design of the board of trustees by that enactment to bring any additional zone into being or to affect any property or rights; the ordinance merely provided the mechanics pursuant to which property owners might in the future apply for the redistricting of their property. In sum, the 1947 amendment was merely the first step in a reasoned plan of rezoning, and specifically provided for further action on the part of the board. That action was taken by the passage of the 1948 ordinance which fixed the boundaries of the newly created zone and amended the zoning map accordingly. It is indisputable that the two amendments, read together as they must be, fully complied with the requirements of the Village Law and accomplished a rezoning of village property in an unexceptionable manner.

In point of fact, there would have been no question about the validity of what was done had the board simply amended the General Zoning Ordinance so as to permit property in Residence A and Residence B zones or, for that matter, in the other districts throughout the village to be used for garden apartments, provided that they were built on ten-acre plots and that the other carefully planned conditions and restrictions were met. It may be conceded that, under the method which the board did adopt, no one will know, from the 1947 ordinance itself, precisely where a Residence B–B district will ultimately be located. But since such a district is simply a garden apartment development, we find nothing unusual or improper in that circumstance. The same uncertainty as to the location of the various types of structures would be present if a zoning ordinance were to sanction garden apartments as well as one-family homes in a Residence A district and yet there would be no doubt as to the propriety of that procedure. *See Nappi v. LaGuardia, supra,* 295 N.Y. 652, 64 N.E.2d 716, affirming 269 App.Div. 693, 54 N.Y.S.2d 722, affirming 184 Misc. 775, 55 N.Y.S.2d 80. Consequently, to condemn the action taken by the board in effectuating a perfectly permissible zoning scheme and to strike down the ordinance designed to carry out that scheme merely because the board had employed two steps to accomplish what may be, and usually is, done in one, would be to exalt form over substance and sacrifice substance to form.

Whether it is generally desirable that garden apartments be freely mingled among private residences under all circumstances, may be arguable. In view, however, of Tarrytown's changing scene and the other substantial reasons for the board's decision, we cannot say that its action was arbitrary or illegal. While hardships may be imposed on this or that owner, 'cardinal is the principle that what is best for the body politic in the long run must prevail over the interests of particular individuals.' *Shepard v. Village of Skaneateles, supra*, 300 N.Y. 115, 118, 89 N.E.2d 619, 620.

The judgment of the Appellate Division should be affirmed, with costs.

CONWAY, JUDGE (dissenting).

The decision here made gives judicial sanction to a novel and unprecedented device whereby the board of trustees of a village may, in the exercise of its discretion, authorize the erection of multiple family dwellings on property, located wholly within established districts theretofore uniformly zoned for use as one- or two-family dwellings, by the simple expedient of declaring, upon the application of individuals owning a certain acreage, that henceforth such property shall constitute a new and separate zoning district. The device may have much to commend it in the way of administrative convenience, but it most assuredly is not 'zoning', as that term has previously been understood. We think the action of the board of trustees of the village of Tarrytown is unauthorized by the Village Law of this State, which is the sole source of the board's power to act. Moreover, we feel that the board's action, here approved, is completely at odds with all sound zoning theory and practice, and may well prove to be the opening wedge in the destruction of effective and efficient zoning in this State.

First of all, we think the board had no power to create the so-called 'Residence B–B' district by the basic ordinance of 1947. Section III of that ordinance provided as follows: 'The boundaries of said newly created district or class of zone will be fixed by amendment of the official village building zone map, at such times in the future as such district or class of zone is applied to properties in this village.' That language can, in no sense, be considered as validly creating a new district or class of zone. It is essential to the creation of a zoning district that its physical boundaries be established in advance; otherwise there is no 'district', there is merely the possibility that a district may one day be delineated. *Matter of Kensington–Davis Corp. v. Schwab*, 239 N.Y. 54, 58–59, 145 N.E. 738, 739. Section 176 of the Village Law, entitled 'Districts', provides that '* * * the board of trustees may divide the village into districts of such number, shape and area as may be deemed best suited to carry out the purposes of this act * * *' (emphasis supplied). The plain import of that language is that after the board has exercised its power to 'divide the village into districts', there should result a number of physically ascertainable districts, each having a definite 'shape' and 'area'. Obviously, the board of trustees, in enacting the 1947 ordinance, did not 'divide' the village into district; the board merely assigned a name or title to a district which might some day be created. As a result of that ordinance, no one could tell whether there would ever be any 'Residence B–B districts', or, if so, what their number, shape and area might be. Thus, the reference in the ordinance to 'districts' or 'zones' is meaningless, for it is impossible to have a true 'district' or 'zone' without specified boundaries. As we said in the *Kensington* case, *supra*, 239 N.Y. at page 58, 145 N.E. at page 739, 'Power was given under that law 'to divide the city into districts.' This clearly contemplated fixed areas with defined boundaries.' The key to any zoning ordinance is the map showing the boundaries of the areas affected. No map showing the location of the new Residence B–B district was, or could have been, made and filed with the 1947 ordinance which was therefore defective. *Village of Williston Park v. Israel*, 301 N.Y. 713, 95 N.E.2d 208, affirming 276 App.Div. 968, 94 N.Y.S.2d 921, affirming 191 Misc. 6, 76 N.Y.S.2d 605. All that the language of the 1947 ordinance means is that, from time to time, in the future, the board may, upon the application of individuals owning ten acres, set aside certain property in the village and assign to it the 'Residence B–B' designation. That, we submit, is 'spot zoning', if it may be classified as zoning at all, and is unauthorized under our statutes.

Under the mandate of section 177 of the Village Law, the regulations of the board of trustees, including the division of the village into districts, 'shall be made in accordance with a comprehensive plan'. The action of the board in the case at bar cannot, under any view of the facts, be considered as taken 'in accordance with a comprehensive plan'. The board takes no action on its own initiative. It makes no investigation to determine which areas of the village are suitable for the erection of multiple family dwellings, and which are not. With relation to the type of construction here involved, the board has adopted no plan, comprehensive or otherwise. Under the ordinance, the board merely waits for some individual, owning ten acres of land or who has acquired ten acres of land, to make an application to have it declared a 'Residence B–B' district; then the board accepts or rejects the application. That is not comprehensive planning by the board; it is just the opposite. It is spot zoning at the request of landed interests who may happen to find favor with the board. As a result of this decision, it is possible that there will be found in the residential areas of Tarrytown multiple family dwellings scattered (or spotted) haphazardly throughout the village without any studied, overall plan. How may the board adopt a comprehensive plan with respect to these multiple family dwellings when it is impossible for it to know the names, number and location of individuals who own or who may acquire ten-acre parcels and who may wish to avail themselves of the ordinance. This is an ordinance which benefits those who can meet a property qualification and is thus undemocratic.

We are adjured by the prevailing opinion, 302 N.Y. p. 126, 96 N.E.2d at 736, not 'to exalt form over substance and sacrifice substance to form', yet we think the decision of the majority has done just that. Essentially and basically, what has been done by the board of trustees in the instant case is to permit a nonconforming use in an established zone. Heretofore, such action has always been referred to as the granting of a 'variance', yet the board has here sought to cloak its ultimate objective under the label and form of 'rezoning'. In order to protect and preserve our zoning systems from the frequent and inevitable attacks of interested parties who seek to avoid zoning laws for their own purposes, this court has imposed strict and severe limitations upon the granting of variances. Two recent illustrations are *Matter of Taxpayers' Ass'n v. Board of Zoning Appeals*, 301 N.Y. 215, 93 N.E.2d 645, and *Matter of Clark v. Board of Zoning Appeals*, 301 N.Y. 86, 92 N.E.2d 903. It cannot be denied that the individual respondent here would never have been able to secure a variance permitting the erection of multiple family dwellings in Residence A or B districts under the rules stated in those two cases. Nevertheless, the identical result has here been reached by denominating the action of the board as 'rezoning'. In that fashion, the board of trustees, which, incidentally, does not even have the power to grant a variance, since that power resides in the board of appeals, Village Law, § 175, has successfully avoided the long-established and stringent limitations upon the granting of variances, merely by adopting a procedure under the name of 'rezoning'. Now, instead of making the required showing that (1) the land cannot yield a reasonable return if used only for a purpose allowed in that zone, (2) that the plight of the owner is due to unique circumstances and not to the general conditions of the neighborhood, and (3) that the use sought will not alter the essential character of the neighborhood *Matter of Taxpayers' Ass'n v. Board of Zoning Appeals, supra*, 301 N.Y. at page 218, 93 N.E.2d at page 647, all a property owner need do is to show that he possesses ten acres of land and the board becomes authorized to permit a nonconforming use thereon. That, we submit, is truly exalting form over substance.

The case of *Nappi v. LaGuardia*, 295 N.Y. 652, 64 N.E.2d 716, affirming 269 App.Div. 693, 54 N.Y.S.2d 722, affirming 184 Misc. 775, 55 N.Y.S.2d 80, is clearly distinguishable from the case at bar. In the *Nappi* case, the New York City zoning resolution did not purport to establish a new district; it merely added a further permitted use to the uses already authorized in certain residence districts in the city. The distinction is obvious and important. A person purchasing property in New York City in the designated residence districts would be on notice that the additional use was authorized. He may examine the zoning ordinance and discover, with certainty, all the permitted uses to which the adjoining property could be put. On the contrary, a person purchasing property in Tarrytown in a Residence A or B district to bring up his children now has no way of knowing whether the property next to his may or may not become the site of a multiple family dwelling with the attendant increases in population, traffic dangers, commerce and congestion.

Finally, it seems to us specious to argue that since the ultimate objective of the board might have been accomplished in a different and legal manner, that the procedure actually used should therefore be sustained. The question remains whether the particular method adopted by the board was in conformity with the legislative requirements found in the Village Law, and whether it accorded with sound, proper zoning theory and practice. In this case, we feel that the board's action must fall on both counts. That being so, it is of no moment that the same result might have been reached through the employment of approved legal procedures. Zoning methods are determined by the Legislature and not by the ingenuity of local boards of trustees or by the courts. In short, we think the end cannot here justify the means used.

The judgments below should be reversed and the case remitted to Special Term for the entry of a judgment in plaintiff's favor in accordance with this opinion.

LOUGHRAN, C.J., and LEWIS, DYE and FROESSELL, JJ., concur with FULD, J.

CONWAY, J., dissents in opinion in which DESMOND, J., concurs.

Judgment affirmed.

Notes

1. The New York Town, Village, and General City Law, in authorizing local legislatures to create zoning districts require that "[a]ll such regulations shall be uniform for each class or kind of buildings, throughout such district but the regulations in one district may differ from those in other districts." See § 7–702 Village Law. How does the majority opinion in Rodgers square with this statutory requirement?

2. Why is the dissenting judge so upset? He says that what the village has done here is not zoning. In the process he calls the floating zoning mechanism "spot zoning," a "nonconforming use," and a "variance." Consider those terms carefully and compare them to the floating zone technique that is sustained by the majority opinion.

3. Consider the meaning of this quote from the majority opinion in Rodgers: "Changed or changing conditions call for changed plans, and persons who own property in a particular zone or use district enjoy no eternally vested right to that classification if the public interest demands otherwise." Imagine you are advising a client who has just found that she lives next to a ten acre parcel that has just been rezoned for garden apartments under a floating zone provision of the zoning ordinance. Read these words to her and try to anticipate her reaction. What security does existing zoning give to a landowner or neighbor? What changes in circumstances are sufficient to authorize a legislative body to change zoning uses, for example, from single family to multi-family or from residential to industrial?

4. In Bellemeade Company v. Priddle, Ky., 503 S.W.2d 734 (Ky.1973), the Kentucky Supreme Court upheld the floating zone provision that resulted in the construction of a motel within a neighborhood zoned residential and in Cetrulo v. City of Park Hills, Ky., 524 S.W.2d 628 (Ky.1975), the same court upheld a planning commission's approval of a "Planned Unit Development" (PUD) consisting of a seven-story condominium on a seven-and-a-half acre tract within a neighborhood zoned for single family residences.

5. Recognizing that the city had numerous abandoned properties that were non-conforming uses in the neighborhoods where they were located, the City of Cumberland, Maryland, created a Rehabilitation and Redevelopment Floating Zone. The purpose of this floating zone is to "allow and provide incentives for the reuse, rehabilitation, and redevelopment of such structures in a manner that will allow them to be restored to the active tax roles and inventory of land in the City, while preserving the integrity of the neighborhood in which they are located." Zoning Ordinance of the City of Cumberland, Maryland, § 5.01.12. To ensure that proposed rehabilitation and redevelopment of such properties are compatible with adjacent residential areas, the city included protective performance standards. The requirements first establish that the floating zone may be located only in areas designated by the city's comprehensive plan, or within four specific zoning districts: Urban Residential, Residential–Office, Gateway–Commercial District, and Gateway–Industrial District. § 6.14.01. The property owner seeking to create the floating zone must submit a petition to the city's zoning administrator. The ordinance contains permitted and prohibited uses in the four designated districts. For example, in the Urban Residential District,

although not normally permitted in the district, uses such as retail/accessory light manufacturing, food and beverage manufacturing, packaging, and processing are permitted where the property will be designated a Rehabilitation and Redevelopment Floating Zone. § 6.14.02. The ordinance protects adjacent properties through performance standards. § 6.14.04. These standards include regulations governing the preservation of natural site amenities; the control of smoke, dust, noise, fumes, and vibrations; proper lighting, waste management, and parking; and appropriate landscape buffers.

B. SMARTER SITE PLANNING: CLUSTERING AND ENVIRONMENTAL IMPACT REVIEW

One approach to smart growth is to do a better job of site planning. Euclidian zoning combined with typical subdivision regulations forces local planners to approve cookie-cutter subdivisions. Under the traditional approach, the entire parcel is divided into lots and a single-family home is built on each lot. Every home is sited in a similar fashion, a result achieved by applying uniform setback, lot coverage, and height requirements to its design, and requiring that all streets, curbs, gutters, lighting, and landscaping follow set standards. In many communities this results in monotonous uniformity, car dependent living, the disappearance of open space, and high cost housing.

Many states have adopted amendments to their zoning enabling laws that delegate authority to localities to permit clustering of their residential developments. Clustering is discussed in detail in Chapter IV, as part of the residential subdivision process. We note it here as a smart growth technique because, in its application, clustering has been used to preserve open space, protect valuable agriculture soils, promote housing affordability, and avoid development of critical environmental areas: all objectives of smart growth land use strategies.

In a number of states, local governments are allowed by law to control the development of individual parcels by conducting environmental impact reviews and imposing conditions on land use approvals in order to mitigate environmental impacts. The state legislatures in California, Massachusetts, Minnesota, New York, and Washington have delegated express authority to local governments to conduct environmental impact reviews on proposed land use projects. This allows local land use agencies to require that subdivision and site plans take into consideration and mitigate the adverse impacts of the proposed development on environmental resources.

In other states, the authority to protect the environment while reviewing and approving development plans for individual sites is found to be implied in the zoning enabling act. This is the case in South Carolina where localities may adopt environmental review procedures as part of their land use review process. The legal situation in South Carolina illustrates how a broad view of local authority can help communities in their efforts to adopt smart growth land use and planning strategies.

South Carolina—Flexibility Provisions

In South Carolina, municipalities derive their land use powers from both home rule authority and enabling statutes. The South Carolina Constitution authorizes the legislature to provide for "the structure and organization, powers, duties, functions and responsibilities of the municipalities * * * by general law." S.C. Const. art. VIII, § 8. The constitution says that "[t]he provisions of [the] Constitution and all laws concerning local government shall be liberally construed in their favor," and that any powers granted to local government by the constitution and laws "shall include those fairly implied and not prohibited by [the] Constitution." S.C. Const. art. VIII, § 17. See also *Southern Bell Telephone and Telegraph Co. v. City of Aiken*, 279 S.C. 269, 306 S.E.2d 220 (1983) (holding that Article VIII of the South Carolina Constitution was completely revised for the purpose of accomplishing home rule and granted renewed autonomy to local government).

This broad grant of local authority was statutorily implemented by the South Carolina Legislature by provisions such as the following: "All counties of the State * * * have authority to enact regulations, resolutions, and ordinances * * * respecting any subject as appears to them necessary and proper for the security, general welfare, and convenience of counties or for preserving health, peace, order, and good government in them." S.C. Code Ann. § 4–9–25. "State legislation provides that the powers of a municipality shall be liberally construed in favor of the municipality and the specific mention of particular powers shall not be construed as limiting in any manner the general powers of such municipalities." S.C. Code Ann. § 5–7–10, see *Williams v. Town of Hilton Head Island*, 311 S.C. 417, 429 S.E.2d 802 (1993) (holding that the South Carolina Legislature intended to abolish the former rule of strict construction when enacting S.C. Code Ann. §§ 5–7–10 et seq.).

These provisions enlarge the scope of local government authority. Under home rule, local governments in South Carolina "may enact regulations deemed necessary and proper for the general welfare unless such regulations are actually inconsistent with the Constitution or general law of the state." Douglas T. Kendall, Preserving South Carolina's Beaches: The Role of Local Planning in Managing Growth in Coastal South Carolina, 1 S.C. Envt'l L.J. 61, 68 (2000). For a general discussion of South Carolina Home Rule, see *Hospitality Ass'n v. County of Charleston*, 320 S.C. 219, 464 S.E.2d 113 (1995).

Local governments in South Carolina derive their express zoning and planning powers from the South Carolina Local Government Planning Enabling Act. S.C. Code Ann. § 6–29–310–1200. Enacted in 1994, the purpose of the Act was to consolidate the local planning and zoning statutes in a comprehensive law and recognize new planning and zoning powers. See Kendall, at 65. The Act provides that a local government may create a planning commission, whose duty and function is to create "plans and programs * * * designed to promote public health, safety, morals, convenience, prosperity, or the general welfare." S.C. Code Ann.

§ 6–29–340(A). Comprehensive plans must include, but are not limited to, seven elements: (1) population, (2) economic development, (3) natural resources, (4) cultural resources, (5) community facilities, (6) housing, and (7) land use. § 6–29–510. The Act notes that "specific planning elements must be based upon careful and comprehensive surveys and studies of existing conditions and probable future development and include recommended means of implementation." § 6–29–340. All zoning and land use regulations must be in accordance with the comprehensive plan. 6–29–720(B). The Act also authorizes specific zoning techniques such as cluster development, floating zones, and planned development districts. 6–29–720(C). However, it makes clear that "any other planning and zoning techniques may be used." When making revisions to the zoning ordinance, the municipality is authorized to consider "the protection of * * * ecologically sensitive areas." S.C. Code Ann. § 6–29–710.

The South Carolina Local Government Planning Act extends the planning and zoning authority of local governments and emphasizes protection of the environment. This specific authority, state rules indicating that local authority is to be interpreted broadly, and a deepening concern for the environment persuaded the town of Mount Pleasant to adopt a local environmental review ordinance. Mount Pleasant, South Carolina, Code of Ordinances, § 156.264.

The purpose of the ordinance is to provide a basis for assessing the impacts of significant development proposals on the "town's overall environment and infrastructure, natural ecology, and economic, historic, social, and related public resources." § 156.264(A). The ordinance requires an impact assessment for development projects that meet certain thresholds. The developer must provide a general description of the project, and identify data about the impacts upon municipal facilities, services, and resources. The town planning director reviews the impact assessment and may conduct independent field investigations for verification. If negative impacts are identified, the town council determines whether the impacts are "acceptable and in the public interest." § 156.264(G). If not, the council has the authority to request the developer to mitigate negative impacts.

The Mount Pleasant impact assessment process requires extensive review of the impacts of individual development projects. Developers must submit information concerning the impacts upon "public services and facilities, the environment, natural resources, historical and archaeological resources, local housing needs, the local economy and other areas affecting the health, safety, general welfare and quality of life in the town." § 156.264(E).

There is an extensive traffic impact assessment process, which requires the developer to submit a Transportation Impact Assessment Data Form. § 156.264(2)(d). The impact assessment must address the negative effects the development will have on marshes, creeks, rivers, plant and animal habitats, and buffer zones and must describe the steps taken to mitigate the negative effects and to protect the natural resources. This local law provides its local boards extensive authority to review and condition land development projects so that their adverse impacts on the environment are minimized.

C. SMARTER PATTERNS OF GROWTH: FLEXIBILITY TECHNIQUES

While better site planning is an important objective, the real flaw in Euclidian zoning, from the smart growth perspective, is that it allows development—usually at relatively low densities—throughout the community. The traditional zoning district map provides a downtown core district, some neighborhood commercial zones, industrial districts along rail lines, highways, or rivers, allows multi-family housing in or close to some of these districts, and then puts the majority of the land in single-family zoning districts with different minimum lot sizes, ranging from a quarter-acre to five-acre lots.

In developing suburban and fringe communities, smart growth advocates that the densities of land uses permitted by the Euclidian zoning ordinance be arranged differently. The suggestion is to identify growth districts, allow mixed-use higher density zoning at the core of such districts, and arrange a mix of housing types around the core in a sufficiently dense pattern so that residents can walk to shop, to recreate, and, for some, to work. As older suburbs develop their remaining vacant land or, with older cities, redevelop blighted, underdeveloped, or abandoned areas, smart growth suggests that similar planning principles be applied. How precisely to approach new development and redevelopment of large tracts of land in any particular community will, of course, depend on the idiosyncrasies of the place. The question is whether there are strategies available under state law that allow them to create new and different land use patterns. In all cases however local planners need to know whether they have the tools necessary to arrange development and conservation of the land in a cost-effective, environmentally-friendly, and affordable fashion. The remainder of this chapter describes and illustrates some of the smart growth techniques available to arrange development at the areawide level.

D. PERFORMANCE ZONING

(Citations for the material in this section are available in John R. Nolon, *Golden* and Its Emanations: The Surprising Origins of Smart Growth, The Urban Lawyer, Vol. 35, No. 1, Winter, 2003.)

Performance zoning is a land use invention that emerged in the late 1960s. It gained widespread attention in 1973 in Bucks County, Pennsylvania, which advocated its use by localities to provide developers more flexibility in site and building design while protecting open space and natural resources. The model was adopted, at least in part and for a time, by most of the communities in Bucks County.

The Bucks County model regulates development not by using traditional dimensional and use standards but by reference to performance standards that measure the impact of a development on a particular site. In Bucks County, performance zoning was limited to housing development: all types of housing were permitted in all zoning districts and were regulated by impact measures regarding impervious coverage, retained open space, and protection of wetlands, watercourses, and other natural resources.

Some aspects of traditional zoning—such as zoning districts and certain use prescriptions—were retained in the Bucks County model. Each was governed, however, by performance standards: an open space ratio, intensity factors such as building volume, transportation impacts, impervious coverage, and landscaping. Dense buffering was required between incompatible uses, and a site capacity calculation was used to limit development impacts on each parcel and its surroundings. Traffic impact analyses were used, density transfers were allowed to prevent hardships, and bonus densities were allowed to encourage affordable housing.

Despite its promise and growing relevance due to current interest in smart growth, performance zoning has not gained wide acceptance. The approach is thought to be less predictable and somewhat harder to administer than the classic use-and dimension-based approach. Its principal contribution to local land use practice has been to encourage the gradual insinuation of performance standards into traditional mechanisms such as zoning ordinances and subdivision regulations. Many localities have become accustomed to administering complex and flexible environmental reviews of their land use decisions and enforcing a growing number of standards that they have adopted. These developments challenge the criticisms of performance zoning as too complex and indeterminate. The gradual adoption of other Post–Euclidian techniques may have proceeded far enough to merit a fresh look at performance zoning and its practicality.

Hyde Park, New York—Performance Zoning

The Town of Hyde Park, in New York, took such a look and drafted an interesting set of performance standards capable of reshaping the development pattern prescribed by local zoning. The Hyde Park approach to performance-based land use regulation begins with a division of the town into six areas: a greenbelt, the Hudson River waterfront, 10 neighborhoods, four hamlets, a planned development district, and a town center. Within the neighborhood, hamlet, and town center districts, core areas are established where mixed-use, higher density development is encouraged. In the waterfront district, there are five landing districts where higher density development of water-related land uses is encouraged. The planned development district connects the nationally-known Franklin and Eleanor Roosevelt sites, a national park, and the Culinary Institute of America. The PDD encourages a mix of tourism-related development and open space amenities that aspire to attract a large number of visitors, fuel the local economy, and strengthen the tax base. Major subdivision of land is discouraged in the waterfront and greenbelt districts. This is the regulatory base on which the more specific performance standards rest. This overall community design appears in, and is taken from, the adopted comprehensive plan of the community.

The organizing principle of the proposed Hyde Park zoning ordinance is to encourage "organic growth in community centers." The ordinance establishes three additional "strategic directions": enhancement of community identity, economic expansion, and civic cohesion. The zoning is calculated to encourage a pattern of land use in which mixed uses and development with higher density, scale, and intensity of use occur in community centers supported by infrastructure and services. "Outlying areas" are reserved for lower density, scale, and intensity of use and for the maintenance of open space and natural resources. Among the purposes of the new zoning are pedestrian orientation, orderly expansion of existing centers, integrity of Hudson River views, historic preservation, affordable housing, and reduction of traffic congestion.

A trilogy of performance standards guides development permitting under the ordinance: density, intensity, and scale factors. "Density" refers to the relative compactness or closeness of a land use, expressed in dwelling units per acre or employment units per acre. An employment unit is one to three persons simultaneously engaged in the conduct of a business, trade, or occupation. A business employing six persons constitutes two employment units. "Intensity" references the amount of traffic caused by the proposed land use, expressed as the number of daily vehicle trips generated. "Scale" is the size or bulk of the proposed structures, calculated in gross square feet of floor area in all buildings, excluding parking.

A list of land uses is permitted in various districts; it includes six residential, 16 non-residential, and nine "community" uses. These 31 uses may be combined: the ordinance encourages mixed uses in the core areas of all districts "provided that the scale, density, and intensity of all uses" complies with the standards established for each district. Bulk regulations are established including height, size, lot coverage, and yards.

Site design requirements regulate parking, ingress and egress, separate pedestrian ways and bicycle paths, landscaping, architectural features, stormwater management, erosion control, lighting, and infrastructure. Central water and sewer systems are required for all major developments proposed in the neighborhood, hamlet, town center and landing districts, including their core areas. Site standards list a variety of environmental performance factors, including wetland, stream, and natural area protection. The segmentation of any significant natural habitat or wildlife corridor is to be avoided. Protected open space is to be contiguous with that on adjacent lots and designed as a cohesive whole. Historic and scenic overlay districts are created.

The Hyde Park zoning ordinance proposes the use of site plan review to achieve its four strategic objectives. In neighborhood core areas, for example, residential densities up to eight units per acre, multi-family residences, bed and breakfast establishments, and commercial and community uses serving the neighborhood are encouraged. Low-intensity industrial uses close to the center of the core are deemed appropriate, as are small front yards, and common and connected open space with associated commercial and community gathering places. Buildings should incorporate attractive bays, balconies, and porches, use traditional building forms and natural materials, and building facades should vary, but not dramatically. Design consistency along streets is encouraged.

In the four designated hamlet districts, residential uses at a density of up to six units per acre are permitted along with limited non-residential uses. In the hamlet core area, densities of up to 10 dwelling units per acre are allowed along with more extensive commercial uses. In the core, residential subdivision is limited to multi-family housing purposes. In the rest of the hamlet district, subdivision of land is encouraged, as is mixed residential development that gradually decreases density from the hamlet core areas outward to the district's edge. Expressed in performance terms, parcels in core areas of hamlets are limited to a maximum of 12,000 gross square feet, 10 dwelling units, 20 employment units, and 5,480 daily vehicle trips per acre. The preservation of contiguous open space is encouraged in hamlet districts. A variety of other provisions are included that protect the environment. Notable among them is a 500–foot wetland buffer within which land uses are to be limited to those that are consistent with high quality wetlands.

The Hyde Park zoning draft contains guidelines for site plan review in the designated town center. In the core of the town center, performance maximums are 32,000 gross square feet, 24 dwelling units, 50 employment units, and 10,970 daily vehicle trips per acre. Non-residential uses in the core are encouraged that serve the needs of local residents and the tourist trade the plan aspires to support. In this district, only multi-family residential development is allowed. Open space standards are aimed at creating a public realm—parks, commons, and plazas that serve as public and private sector gathering points and amenities. All development is to be pedestrian friendly and designed to incorporate landscaping and building separations that diminish the visual dominance of automobiles and stark paved spaces.

In the Bellefield planned development district, immediately to the south of the town center district, development is encouraged that promotes tourism-related businesses while complementing the Roosevelt park, library, and homes, including a non-vehicular trail linking these sites through an environmentally sensitive area that is to be preserved. All subdivision of land must be consistent with a comprehensive plan and vision for the roughly 1,000–acre district, clustering of development is required to create small centers of development, and no more than 50 percent of the gross floor area of all development may consist of residences. Together, the town center and Bellefield PDD promise sensitively sited economic development to serve the economic needs of the residents and build a significant tax base for the community. The

Bellefield PDD is to be the gateway to the town as well as a regional hub serving the tourism industry.

The zoning map that accompanies the zoning proposals depicts the size and location of all these districts. It appears that approximately seventy percent of the land area of the town is located in the greenbelt and waterfront districts. In these two districts, the performance standards allow a maximum density of one dwelling unit per four acres, a relatively low density development pattern that assures a rural context for the well-defined districts and cores. A species of relief is offered to landowners in these low density districts, as well as the other districts, should they wish to exceed the scale, density, and intensity standards. The zoning draft contains a special exception permit provision. Applications for this permit must demonstrate how the proposed development conforms with the four strategic objectives of the ordinance. Approval authority for this special use permit is given to the Zoning Board of Appeals.

In accompanying subdivision regulations, it is strongly recommend that all land subdivision in the Greenbelt and Waterfront districts be clustered to maintain the rural appearance and environmental resources of the town. The objective of these cluster provisions is to leave "substantial portions" of subdivided land undeveloped. The planning board is authorized to mandate clustering for any particular subdivision that may have a significant adverse impact on the community's rural landscape or its natural resources. Interestingly, mixed uses are permitted, including non-residential development. A net acreage method of determining maximum allowable density on a particular parcel is provided that avoids the time-consuming process of analyzing how many units would be permitted under a conventional subdivision. The open space to be preserved must have a conservation value which insures that preserved land will serve specific ecological, recreational, or agricultural purposes. To the extent that these provisions exceed the authority localities have to permit and require clustering, the draft regulations express an intent to supersede the Town Law provisions, using authority to supersede generally applicable state law under Section 10 of the Municipal Home Rule Law.

The Hyde Park model can be understood as a community-wide smart growth strategy, transferring mixed-use higher density development rights to defined cores comprising approximately one third of the community and greatly restricting development in designated environmental areas. The use of detailed site plan standards and of three impact factors (density, intensity, and scale) serve the same purpose as project-by-project environmental reviews: they mitigate the environmental impact of specific developments. They accomplish more by allowing developers in designated districts and their cores great flexibility to mix uses, achieve multi-family housing development, and build at greater densities.

Notes

1. See Kendig, Performance Zoning (American Planning Ass'n 1980). The prototypical ordinance presented in this publication contains eight zoning districts, Agricultural, Rural, Estate, Development, Urban Core, Neighborhood Conservation, Commercial Conservation, and Holding. Five general use categories are either permitted, denied or conditionally permitted in these districts (the five categories are agriculture, residential, institutional, commercial, and industrial). The heart of the ordinance is the performance standards provisions which provide minimum standards for open space, density, impervious surface coverage, and lot area. The publication contains detailed illustrations as well as a model ordinance with commentary. Also see Porter, Phillips & Lassar, Flexible Zoning: How It Works (Urban Land Inst.1988).

2. Performance zoning can be used to ensure that individual projects do not have a negative environmental effect on surrounding properties. It is the lack of such standards in many zoning, subdivision, and site plan laws that limits the ability of land use approval agencies to approve development proposals, while protecting surrounding properties. In DeCoals v. Board of Zoning Appeals of Westover, 168 W.Va. 339, 284 S.E.2d 856 (1981), the court upheld extensive performance standards that prevented the emanation of dust and noise from industrial sites. The ordinance prohibited the escape of dust of any kind from the property and noise was allowed to equal but not exceed the decibel level of traffic sounds in the street during a normal work day.

3. The Florida Growth Management Act, § 163.3202, encourages municipalities to adopt innovative land use techniques including performance zoning as well as planned-unit development, impact fees, incentive zoning, and the transfer of development rights.

E. PLANNED UNIT DEVELOPMENT ZONING

To achieve greater flexibility, some localities have adopted a planned unit development (PUD) ordinance as part of their zoning law. Under some PUD laws, the owners of several adjacent parcels may apply for a special permit to create a higher density, mixed-use development, with considerable design flexibility. This type of PUD provides for the development of new neighborhoods of different sizes and land uses. It also allows underutilized or deteriorated sites to be assembled and redeveloped in older communities. PUD ordinances may provide bonus density and design flexibility as incentives to developers and require that the developer provide infrastructure investments, affordable housing, or open space and environmental benefits in exchange.

The PUD device can be used to combine several smaller parcels into one large parcel and to locate improvements on appropriate portions of the larger parcel to provide more cost-effective development and to conserve the larger site's sensitive environmental features. This technique provides the economic and environmental benefits of clustering development, but on a larger scale.

Although the types and requirements of PUDs vary, there are three characteristics that are common to most PUD ordinances. First, PUDs must conform to the local comprehensive or master plan. In Bridger Canyon Property Owners' Association, Inc. v. Planning and Zoning Commission, 270 Mont. 160, 890 P.2d 1268 (1995) a local homeowners' association challenged the local planning and zoning commission's conditional approval of a PUD application. In overturning the commission's PUD approval, the Supreme Court of Montana determined that the commission exceeded its authority when it approved the PUD, which failed to comply with the community's general plan for zoning. Large-scale, mixed-use development with significant environmental benefits can easily be provided for in a comprehensive plan as a means of accommodating appropriate types of development.

Second, to create a PUD most local governments require that the land to be developed as a PUD be under single ownership or be controlled by a single entity. For example, the city of Robbinsdale, Minnesota, PUD provision states that the "property shall be in single ownership or under the management or supervision of a central authority or otherwise subject to such supervisory lease or ownership control." Code of the City of Robbinsdale, Minnesota, § 530.05(2)(a). This requirement allows the community to impose responsibility for establishing and maintaining the site's environmental features on a reliable and durable entity.

Third, the PUD permits the relaxation of underlying density and area requirements by clustering development in certain areas while preserving other areas as open space. By permitting increased density in certain portions of the PUD property, housing, businesses, and other amenities, such as restaurants, may be combined near one another, permitting residents to walk from one destination to another and reducing dependence on automobiles. This larger-scale shift of development away from the environmentally sensitive portion of the site allows truly significant landscapes to be preserved.

Because the creation of a PUD usually effects a change in the expectations of the property owners in the nearby areas, legal challenges are brought claiming that PUDs violate the uniformity requirement of the zoning enabling act or are beyond the scope of municipal land use authority. Although most state courts hold that the PUD is itself a zoning district, or is an acceptable means of effecting the most appropriate use of the land, some states have amended their enabling acts to expressly authorize the use of PUDs. Recall that in Rodgers v. Tarrytown, found at the beginning of this section, the court reasoned that "[t]he village's zoning aim being clear, the choice of methods to accomplish it lay with the board."

Great Falls, Montana—PUD Ordinance

The PUD ordinance of the City of Great Falls, Montana, is an example of a PUD provision that gives significant design discretion to the PUD developer, while requiring that significant benefits be provided to the community. The purpose of the Great Falls PUD ordinance is "to allow and provide for the imaginative and efficient utilization of land through large-scale development, greater design flexibility, the consolidation of open spaces, the clustering of buildings, and the integration of compatible uses." Code of the City of Great Falls, Montana, § 17.63.010. The process begins with a pre-application conference between the developer and the city's planning director and appropriate city officials to review preliminary plans. Within two weeks after the pre-application conference, the planning director must furnish the developer with written comments regarding the proposed PUD and provide recommendations to inform and assist the developer in preparing the PUD application. The formal PUD process begins when the developer submits a preliminary development plan to the local planning board, which must include a description of the number and type of dwelling units, proposed lot coverage, total open space, usable open space, and the type and amount of nonresidential development planned. The preliminary development plan must also include a map showing the natural features of the PUD property.

The Great Falls PUD law does not prescribe specific design, density, and setback requirements. (In contrast to the Great Falls PUD provisions, the city of Robbinsdale, Minnesota, prescribes specific requirements such as minimum project size, required frontage, yard setbacks, height restrictions, and density bonuses. Code of the City of Robbinsdale, Minnesota, § 530.05(5).) Instead, such matters are left to be negotiated between the developer and the planning board. The PUD ordinance provides that "PUDs are characterized by cluster developments and common open space. Only by proper design can the traditional values of privacy, light, air and ventilation be preserved. It is not practical to set specific standards that would be applicable to all PUD's for these items, but it is incumbent upon the developer and the Planning Board to consider these items in the design and review of the PUD." § 17.63.140. By providing significant design discretion to the developer, the design and development of each PUD in Great Falls can conform to the physical, economic, and social character of the area where a PUD is to be located.

The Great Falls ordinance is more prescriptive regarding open space requirements and the incorporation of environmental design. To ensure that the required open space is preserved, the PUD ordinance requires that the open space be protected by restrictive covenants or other legal agreements acceptable to the City of Great Falls. With respect to environmental design, the ordinance requires the developer to submit a landscaping plan that protects existing natural features and vegetation by minimizing the impact of the PUD development on these resources. § 17.63.210. The planning board may require measures to mitigate the PUD's impact on natural resources. Finally, the ordinance requires that the developer provide financial guarantees to the city to ensure that the PUD is developed in accordance with the submitted plans and according to the construction schedule provided by the developer. If, for example, the approved environmental conservation plans are violated, the city can remedy the problem and charge the costs to the developer, using the financial guarantee.

F. TRADITIONAL NEIGHBORHOOD DISTRICTS

New urbanists, sometimes called neo-traditionalists, advocate zoning and land use regulations that allow for the creation of traditional urban neighborhoods. They point out that, under conventional zoning and subdivision laws, most traditional neighborhoods found in urban areas can no longer be replicated. The corner drugstore or deli in a residential neighborhood is not allowed, apartments cannot exist above stores, and houses cannot be built close to the sidewalk, nor cars parked in garages that front on alleys that kids use as playgrounds. If cookie-cutter subdivisions are the result of standards contained in zoning and subdivision ordinances, the new urbanists ask, why can't such regulations be modified to create different, more flexible neighborhoods? See Jonathan Barnett, What's New About New Urbanism?, in Charter of the New Urbanism 5 (2000).

Neo-traditionalists and many smart growth advocates argue that a new type of land development pattern is needed—one that is more concentrated and that creates a quality of neighborhood in which residents feel comfortable living. One such approach is to create mixed-use neighborhoods where housing types are varied, retail and commercial services are available within walking distance of residences, public green space is provided, visual and recreational amenities exist nearby, and pedestrian and bicycle travel is actively encouraged. Houses in such a neighborhood district can be allowed on smaller lots, retail and commercial uses can be mixed with residential uses, a variety of housing types can be allowed, and accessible open space can be created and dedicated to the use of all the neighbors.

Traditional Neighborhood Development (TND) is a zoning mechanism that has emerged in recent years as a method of achieving such objectives and as a promising alternative to conventional zoning. TND zoning districts are more friendly than conventional zoning to environmental conservation, pedestrian movement, and compact development. This device is similar to Planned Unit Development, but is focused more closely on achieving traditional spatial relationships.

City of Austin, Texas—TND Ordinance

The City of Austin's zoning code contains a Traditional Neighborhood District (TND) that illustrates how the mechanism works. The purpose of the Austin TND ordinance is to "encourage mixed-use, compact development that is sensitive to the environmental characteristics of the land and facilitates the efficient use of services." (§ 13–9–2.) The organizing principle behind a TND district is the neighborhood, which is characterized by diverse and integrated land uses existing in close proximity to each other. The TND neighborhood contains several well-defined areas within walking distance of the neighborhood center (typically a quarter-mile or a five-minute walk) connected by a network of thoroughfares that service both cars and pedestrians. To create recognizable areas within the larger integrated neighborhood, TND provisions govern the type, location, and amount of particular land uses in each area with an eye toward how they interact. TNDs also closely regulate the design standards for streetscapes, landscapes, and architecture that foster a sense of place among the residents.

Conventional zoning generally divides a municipality into zones with predetermined use, dimension, and density requirements. In contrast, Austin's TND ordinance:

- creates neighborhoods that are modest in size and pedestrian-oriented;
- allows a diversity of housing types, jobs, shopping, services, and public facilities within the district;
- integrates residences, shops, workplaces, and civic buildings all within close proximity;
- designs a neighborhood that respects and preserves unique natural features and open spaces;
- coordinates a more equitable transportation system with facilities for pedestrians, bicycles, public transit, and cars;
- creates well-configured squares, plazas, greens, landscaped streets, preserves, greenbelts, and parks woven into the pattern of the neighborhood and dedicated to the collective social activity, recreation, and visual enjoyment of the populace;
- provides for civic buildings, open spaces, and other visual features that act as landmarks, symbols, and focal points for community identity;
- contains design standards to provide for compatible building arrangement, bulk, form, character, and landscaping to establish a livable, harmonious, and diverse environment;
- forms a distinct edge and defines the border between the public street and the private block interior; and
- provides for architecture and landscape that respond to the unique character of the region.

(§ 13–9–2(B))

While continuing to regulate size, dimension, and use, the primary concern of the TND is the harmonious integration of land uses within the neighborhood. The two essential areas of Austin's TND exemplify this concern with integrating uses:

1. Neighborhood Center Area: TND districts have one Neighborhood Center Area that is generally not less than 5% of the gross land area within the district and is within easy walking distance of most of the lots in the adjacent Mixed Residential Area. This

Neighborhood Center Area serves as the focal point of the district and usually contains a central square adjacent to which are generally located retail, commercial, civic and public services. Within this area, land uses are allocated as follows:

not less than 20% to townhouse, condo, multi-family residential,

not less than 20% to commercial, and

not less than 5% to civic uses.

2. Mixed Residential Area: The adjacent Mixed Residential Area includes a variety of residential land uses and open spaces. Retail and commercial uses are allowed, but required to blend into the residential character of the neighborhood. Streets must be designed to promote pedestrian activity while providing for safe and efficient movement of vehicular traffic. The land in this area is allocated as follows:

not less than 50% and not more than 80% to single family residential,

not more than 10% to duplex housing,

not less than 10% to townhouse, condo, multi-family residential,

not less than 1% and not more than 2% to commercial uses, and

not less than 2% to civic uses.

A TND district in Austin can contain a Neighborhood Edge Area along the perimeter of the district that is less dense than the Mixed Residential Area and between 100–250 feet in width. Only single-family residential dwellings, with larger lots and setbacks, are permitted here. A TND can also include a Workshop and Employment Center Area of not more than 10% of gross land area, where commercial and light industrial uses not appropriate in a Neighborhood Center or Mixed Residential Area can be located. Austin's TND ordinance contains these areas. (§ 13–9–45 Land Use Allocations.) The Austin TND ordinance also pays close attention to civic uses, such as community halls and open space, as they relate to residential and commercial development.

Austin's TND develops land in a purposeful manner in order to create a "sustainable, long-term community that provides economic opportunity and environmental and social equity for the residents." (§ 13–9–2 (A).) Integration of uses, pedestrian scale of development, diversity of building types, social interactions, and environmental sensitivity are the principles that guide the TND ordinance. The TND approach to creating compact, mixed-use development allows for better natural resource protection. Because a TND is limited in size, it encourages infill rather than the "leap-frog" development characteristic of suburban land development. Open space provided in the TND can be situated to link with other green spaces within the community.

Notes

1. Traditional Neighborhood Districts have been enacted by local governments in several states, without express enabling legislation. Some states, especially those whose courts have narrowly interpreted the requirement that zoning provisions must be uniform within zoning districts, may need to pass TND enabling statutes before localities will attempt its use. TND enabling legislation in Connecticut, Pennsylvania, and Wisconsin provides support and guidance for local TND regulations. (Sitkowski, R.J. et al. "Enabling Legislation for Traditional Neighborhood Development Regulations" Land Use Law & Zoning Digest October 2001 p. 3.)

2. In 2000, the Pennsylvania state legislature amended its Municipalities Planning Code to add the authority for localities to adopt TND provisions. (Act 68 of 2000; Article VII–A of the Act contains TND enabling legislation.)

3. See Wis. Stat. § 66.034(3) for a more comprehensive approach to getting local governments to use the TND technique. The purpose of the law is to give developers an alternative and more sustainable approach to development. Cities and villages may enact the TND as a zoning district designation, an overlay zone, a floating zone, or as a modified approach to PUDs. The Wisconsin law provides for the University of Wisconsin Extension to prepare a model traditional neighborhood development ordinance. Wis. Stat. § 66.034(2)(a).

4. The Belmont, North Carolina, Traditional Neighborhood Development law, § 4.11.1 et seq., states that its purpose "is to minimize traffic congestion, suburban sprawl, infrastructure costs, and environmental degradation." The ordinance contains design standards for public and civic areas and privately constructed or rehabilitated structures.

G. TRANSFER OF DEVELOPMENT RIGHTS

Like the other techniques explored in this section, the transfer of development rights provides a mechanism for channeling growth to those areas of a community where the infrastructure and services needed to support additional development may be provided cost-effectively. New York statutes define transfer of development rights (TDR) as "the process by which development rights are transferred from one lot, parcel, or area of land in a sending district to another lot, parcel, or area of land in one or more receiving districts." N.Y. Town Law § 261–a; N.Y. Village Law § 7–701; N.Y. Gen. City Law § 20–f.

A 1997 survey of 3,500 local governments and a review of planning literature found 107 TDR programs in 25 states. John B. Bredin, Transfer of Development Rights: Cases, Statutes, and a Model, 2000 APA National Planning Conference, http://www.asu.edu/caed/proceedings00/BREDIN/bredin.htm.

The programs have been established in rural communities and in some of the country's largest cities, including New York City and Chicago.

The comprehensive plan for the Long Island Pine Barrens, for example, allocates development credits to land in the fragile pine barrens aquifer, based on the land's development yield under local zoning, and greatly restricts development in these "sending districts." (Central Pine Barrens Comprehensive Land Use Plan, ch. 6 (adopted June 28, 1995)). The plan establishes "receiving districts" into which these development credits may be transferred. Developers who own land in these receiving districts may purchase credits from landowners in sending districts. Each purchased credit allows the developer to build one housing unit over that permitted by the receiving district's zoning.

There are three basic elements to a TDR program: the sending district, the receiving district, and the TDR credits themselves. The sending district consists of the area to be protected from development. The receiving district is located where additional density can be absorbed and supported with existing or expanded infrastructure and services. The TDR credits are a legal representation of the abstract development rights that will be severed from property in the sending district and grafted onto property in the receiving district. The TDR credits can be traded in a free market or a TDR bank can be established to facilitate exchanges. When a TDR credit is purchased from a property owner in the sending district, that property owner records a deed restriction prohibiting development on the property. The TDR credit can then be applied to property in the receiving district as a density bonus. In New York's Long Island Pine Barrens' TDR program, a 52,500–acre sending district and a 47,500–acre receiving district were established that crossed the jurisdictions of three towns and two villages.

Sarasota, Florida—TDR Program

The TDR program in Sarasota County, Florida was enacted for the purpose of preventing sprawl and preserving open space, agricultural lands, and environmentally sensitive areas. County of Sarasota, Florida, Transfer of Development Rights Ordinance, Ordinance No. 82–61 (1982). Under the program, there are two sending overlay zones: a Residential Sending Zone (RSZ), and a Conservation Sending Zone (CSZ). For a property to be designated as an RSZ, the parcel must be: (i) in a platted subdivision and fail to conform to the county's development regulation because of a lack of paved streets or drainage, or some other deficiency; (ii) in an environmentally sensitive area, including lands identified by the county as having high ecological value; (iii) in an area which is needed for agricultural, open space, or other conservation use; (iv) have historical or archeological significance; or (v) be located on a barrier island. County of Sarasota, Florida, Zoning Ordinance, § 7.20(a)(1). For a property to be designated as a CSZ it must contain at least 500 acres and either (i) be designated by the county as a site of high ecological value; (ii) be in a flood hazard zone; (iii) be in a storm surge area; or (iv) contain an important watercourse with associated wetlands. Sarasota County's TDR ordinance established four receiving overlay zones which allow urban-style densities for landowners or developers who acquire development rights from the sending districts.

The owners of land in the sending districts must apply to have their parcels included in the program and must agree to grant a conservation easement to the county that limits property development to agricultural or open space. § 7.20(c)(4). If the application is approved by the county planning commission and the board of commissioners, the owner receives a transfer permit for a specified number of development rights. These rights may then be sold to the owners of land in a designated receiving district. To use the development rights, the purchaser must submit a copy of the transfer permit along with an application for a permit to develop the property. If the applicant receives approval for the proposed development, the applicant may use the transferred development rights in addition to the rights allowed under the existing zoning on the receiving parcel.

SUITUM v. TAHOE REGIONAL PLANNING AGENCY

Supreme Court of the United States, 1997.
520 U.S. 725, 117 S.Ct. 1659, 137 L.Ed.2d 980.

JUSTICE SOUTER delivered the opinion of the Court.

Petitioner Bernadine Suitum owns land near the Nevada shore of Lake Tahoe. Respondent Tahoe Regional Planning Agency, which regulates land use in the region, determined that Suitum's property is ineligible for development but entitled to receive certain allegedly valuable "Transferable Development Rights" (TDR's). Suitum has brought an action for compensation under Rev. Stat. § 1979, 42 U.S.C. § 1983, claiming that the agency's determinations amounted to a regulatory taking of her property. While the pleadings raise issues about the significance of the TDR's both to the claim that a taking has occurred and to the constitutional requirement of just compensation, we have no occasion to decide, and we do not decide, whether or not these TDR's may be considered in deciding the issue whether there has been a taking in this case, as opposed to the issue whether just compensation has been afforded for such a taking. The sole question here is whether the claim is ripe for adjudication, even though Suitum has not attempted to sell the development rights she has or is eligible to receive. We hold that it is.

In 1969, Congress approved the Tahoe Regional Planning Compact between the States of California and Nevada, creating respondent as an interstate agency to regulate development in the Lake Tahoe basin. See *Lake Country Estates, Inc. v. Tahoe Regional Planning Agency*, 440 U.S. 391, 394, 99 S.Ct. 1171, 1173, 59 L.Ed.2d 401 (1979). After the 1969 compact had proven inadequate for protection of the lake and its environment, the States proposed and Congress approved an amendment in 1980, requiring the agency to adopt a plan barring any development exceeding such specific "environmental threshold carrying capacities" as the agency might find appropriate. Pub.L. 96–551, Arts. I(b), V(b), V(g), 94 Stat. 3234, 3239–3241.

In 1987, the agency adopted a new Regional Plan providing for an "Individual Parcel Evaluation System" (IPES) to rate the suitability of vacant residential parcels for building and other modification. Tahoe Regional Planning Agency Code of Ordinances, ch. 37 (TRPA Code). Whereas any property must attain a minimum IPES score to qualify for construction, *id.*, § 37.8.E; App. 145, an undeveloped parcel in certain areas carrying runoff into the watershed (known as "Stream Environment Zones" (SEZ's)) receives an IPES score of zero, TRPA Code § 37.4.A(3). With limited exceptions not relevant here, the agency permits no "additional land coverage or other permanent land disturbance" on such a parcel. *Id.*, § 20.4.

Although the agency's 1987 plan does not provide for the variances and exceptions of conventional land-use schemes, it addresses the potential sharpness of its restrictions by granting property owners TDR's that may be sold to owners of parcels eligible for construction, *id.*, §§ 20.3.C, 34.0 to 34.3. There are three kinds of residential TDR's. An owner needs both a "Residential Development Right" and a "Residential Allocation" to place a residential unit on a buildable parcel, *id.*, §§ 21.6.C, 33.2.A; the latter permits construction to begin in a specific calendar year, but expires at year's end, *id.*, § 33.2.B(3)(b). An owner must also have "Land Coverage Rights" for each square foot of impermeable cover placed upon land. App. 145; see also TRPA Code, ch. 20. All owners of vacant residential parcels that existed at the effective date of the 1987 plan (July 1, 1987), including SEZ parcels, automatically receive one Residential Development Right, *id.*, § 21.6.A; owners of SEZ property may obtain and transfer bonus points equivalent to three additional Residential Development Rights, *id.*, §§ 35.2.C, 35.2.D. SEZ property owners also receive Land Coverage Rights authorizing coverage of an area equal to 1% of the surface area of their land. *Id.*, §§ 20.3.A, 37.11. Finally, SEZ owners, like other property owners, may apply for a Residential Allocation, awarded by local jurisdictions in random drawings each year. *Id.*, § 33.2.B; App. 98–99. All three kinds of TDR's may be transferred for the benefit of any eligible property in the Lake Tahoe region, subject to approval by the agency based on the eligibility of the receiving parcel for development. TRPA Code §§ 20.3.C, 34.1 to 34.3.

In 1972, Suitum and her late husband bought an undeveloped lot in Washoe County, Nevada, within the agency's jurisdiction, and 17 years later, after adoption of the 1987 Regional Plan, Suitum obtained a Residential Allocation through Washoe County's annual drawing. When she then applied to the agency for permission to construct a house on her lot, the agency determined that her property was located within a SEZ, assigned it an IPES score of zero, and denied permission to build. Suitum appealed the denial to the agency's governing board, which itself denied relief.

After the agency turned down the request for a building permit, Suitum made no effort to transfer any of the TDR's that were hers under the 1987 plan, and there is no dispute that she still has the one Residential Development Right that owners of undeveloped lots automatically received, plus the Land Coverage Rights for 183 square feet that she got as the owner of 18,300 square feet of SEZ land. It is also common ground that Suitum has the right to receive three "bonus" Residential Development Rights. Although Suitum has questioned the certainty that she would obtain a new Residential Allocation if she sought one, the agency has represented to this Court that she undoubtedly [sic] would. (citation omitted)

Instead, Suitum brought this 42 U.S.C. § 1983 action alleging that in denying her the right to construct a house on her lot, the agency's restrictions deprived her of "all reasonable and economically viable use" of her property, and so amounted to a taking of her property without just compensation in violation of the Fifth and Fourteenth Amendments. App. 15, 16. The agency responded by objecting, among other things, that Suitum's takings claim was not ripe due to her "failure to obtain a final decision by TRPA as to the amount of development * * * that may be allowed by" the agency. *Id.*, at 10. On cross-motions for summary judgment, the District Court ordered supplemental briefing on the nature of Suitum's TDR's, including "what [TDR's] can be transferred in [Suitum's] case and the procedures, prerequisites and value of such transfer as applicable in this case." *Id.*, at 89. The agency introduced an affidavit from a real estate appraiser, whose opinion was that the Residential Development Right that Suitum already has, and the three more to which she is entitled, have a market value between $1,500 and $2,500 each; that her Land Coverage Rights can be sold for $6 to $12 per square foot ($1,098–$2,196 total); and that her lot devoid of all TDR's would sell for $7,125 to $16,750. *Id.*, at 131–132. The appraiser also said that if Suitum were to obtain a Residential Allocation and sell it with a Development Right, together they would bring between $30,000 and $35,000. *Ibid.* As if in spite of the figures supplied by its own affidavit, however, the agency maintained that the "*actual* benefits of the [TDR] program for [Suitum] * * * can only be known if she pursues an appropriate [transfer] application," with the result that Suitum's claim was not ripe for adjudication. *Id.*, at 91. For her part, Suitum insisted that trying to transfer her TDR's would be an " 'idle and futile act' " because the TDR program is a "sham," and she supplied the affidavit of one of the agency's former employees whose view was that "there is little to no value to [Suitum's TDR's] at the present time as * * * either [there is] no market for them or the procedure for transferring one particular right would restrict the opportunity to transfer a remaining right." *Id.*, at 135.

* * *

The only issue presented is whether Suitum's claim of a regulatory taking of her land in violation of the Fifth and Fourteenth Amendments is ready for judicial review under prudential ripeness principles. * * *

The agency nonetheless argued below, and the lower courts agreed, see *supra*, at 1664, that there remains a "final decision" for the agency to make: action on a possible application by Suitum to transfer the

TDR's to which she is indisputably entitled. This is not, however, the type of "final decision" required by our *Williamson County* precedents. Those precedents addressed the virtual impossibility of determining what development will be permitted on a particular lot of land when its use is subject to the decision of a regulatory body invested with great discretion, which it has not yet even been asked to exercise. No such question is presented here. The parties agree on the particular TDR's to which Suitum is entitled, and no discretionary decision must be made by any agency official for her to obtain them or to offer them for sale. The only decision left to the agency is approval of a particular transfer of TDR's to make certain that a given potential buyer may lawfully use them. But whether a particular sale of TDR's may be completed is quite different from whether TDR's are salable; so long as the particular buyer is not the only person who can lawfully buy, the rights would not be rendered unsalable even if the agency were to make a discretionary decision to kill a particular sale. And the class of buyers is not even arguably so limited here, where there is no question so far as the law is concerned that TDR's may be bought and used for the benefit of all sorts of land parcels and lots.

The agency's argument that Suitum's case is not ripe because no " 'values attributable to [Suitum's TDR's] are known,' " Brief for Respondent 23 (quoting No. CV–N–91–040–ECR (D.Nev., Mar. 30, 1994, App. to Pet. for Cert. C–4), is just a variation on the preceding position, and fares no better. First, as to Suitum's rights to receive TDR's that she may later sell, we have already noted that little or no uncertainty remains. Although the value of a Residential Development Right may well be greater if it is offered together with a Residential Allocation, and although Suitum must still enter the lottery for the latter, there is no discretionary decision to be made in determining whether she will get one; in fact, the probability of her getting one is "100 percent" according to the agency, see Tr. of Oral Arg. 40, since there are fewer applications than available allocations, see *id.*, at 39–40. But even if that were not the case, as it probably will not always be, it would be unreasonable to require Suitum to enter the drawing in order to ripen her suit. The agency does not, and surely could not, maintain that if the odds of success in the allocation lottery were low, Suitum's takings claim could be kept at bay from year to year until she actually won the drawing; such a rule would allow any local authority to stultify the Fifth Amendment's guarantee. Rather, in such circumstances, the value attributable to the allocation Suitum might or might not receive in the drawing would simply be discounted to reflect the mathematical likelihood of her obtaining one.

Second, as to Suitum's right to transfer her TDR's, the only contingency apart from private market demand turns on the right of the agency to deny approval for a specific transfer on grounds that the buyer's use of the TDR's would violate the terms of the scheme or other local land-use regulation, and the right of a local regulatory body to deny transfer approval for the latter reason. See TRPA Code §§ 20.3.C, 34.2,

34.3. But even if these potential bars based on a buyer's intended use of TDR's should turn out to involve the same degree of discretion assumed in the *Williamson County* ripeness requirement, that discretion still would not render the value of the TDR's nearly as unknowable as the chances of particular development being permitted on a particular parcel in the absence of a zoning board decision that could quite lawfully be either yes or no. While a particular sale is subject to approval, salability is not, and the agency's own position assumes that there are many potential, lawful buyers for Suitum's TDR's, whose receipt of those rights would unquestionably be approved.

The valuation of Suitum's TDR's is therefore simply an issue of fact about possible market prices, and one on which the District Court had considerable evidence before it, see *supra*, at 1663–1664. Of course, as the agency appears to be saying, see, *e.g.*, Brief for Respondent 22–23, the very best evidence of the value of Suitum's TDR's might be their actual selling price (assuming, of course, that the sale were made in good faith and at arm's length). But similar determinations of market value are routinely made in judicial proceedings without the benefit of a market transaction in the subject property. See, *e.g.*, *United States v. 819.98 Acres of Land, More or Less, Located in Wasatch and Summit Counties*, 78 F.3d 1468, 1469–1470 (C.A.10 1996) (upholding valuation of condemned land based on expert testimony relating to comparable sales and discounted cash flow); *United States v. L.E. Cooke Co.*, 991 F.2d 336, 338–339 (C.A.6 1993) (same with respect to valuation of mineral rights leases); see also 5 J. Sackman, Nichols' Law of Eminent Domain § 23–01, p. 23–6 (rev. 3d ed. 1997) ("[I]t is well established that the value of * * * land taken or injured by the exercise of the power of eminent domain may be shown by opinion evidence"); see generally 4 *id.*, § 12.02 (discussing establishment of market value of condemned land). While it is true that market value may be hard to calculate without a regular trade in TDR's, if Suitum is ready to proceed in spite of this difficulty, ripeness doctrine does not block her. In fact, the reason for the agency's objection is probably a concern that without much market experience in sales of TDR's, their market values will get low estimates. But this is simply one of the risks of regulatory pioneering, and the pioneer here is the agency, not Suitum.

* * *

Because we find that Suitum has received a "final decision" consistent with *Williamson County's* ripeness requirement, we vacate the judgment of the Court of Appeals and remand for further proceedings consistent with this opinion.

It is so ordered.

Notes

1. In Suitum, the regulatory agency prevented all development on the property owner's lot which was located in a critical environmental area of national importance. If this is found to be a regulatory taking, is it possible

that the Court could find that the TDR credits to which Suitum is entitled are adequate compensation for that taking?

2. In Fred F. French Investing Co., Inc. v. City of New York, 39 N.Y.2d 587, 350 N.E.2d 381, 385 N.Y.S.2d 5 (1976), the Court of Appeals declared that the city was unable to use the transfer development rights (TDR) of airspace from the regulated parcel to other receiving areas as a means of validating the rezoning of the petitioner's land as a public park. The court noted that the development rights that were transferred had a "value so uncertain and contingent, as to deprive the property owner of their practical usefulness." Notwithstanding the ineffectiveness of the TDR mechanism in this context, the court held that a TDR provision "may not be disregarded in determining whether the ordinance has destroyed the economic value of the underlying property." See W.J.F. Realty Corp. v. State, 176 Misc.2d 763, 672 N.Y.S.2d 1007 (Sup.Ct., Suffolk Co.1998), in which the court distinguished the Long Island Pine Barrens Protection Act (discussed above) from the TDR program in *Fred F. French*, and validated the Act as promoting a legitimate government interest.

3. TDR is used in a number of smart growth contexts where the goal is to shift zoned development potential from conservation areas, as in Suitum, to more appropriate areas for development. In 1999, an Oregon law was adopted that creates a transferable development credit. The statute allows municipalities to establish receiving locations for denser development using these credits to conform to land use planning goals of the Oregon growth management statute. Consider the Dover, Maryland, Zoning Code, § 170–27.2. Transfer of Development Rights enacted to protect areas of high conservation value by concentrating development in appropriate areas and protecting land in areas with high natural resource values. [Added 10–31–90 by Ord. No. 16–90; amended 01–22–03 by Ord. 35–02] The City of Seattle and King County, Washington, have entered into an interlocal agreement and adopted local laws to establish a program of transferring development rights from rural unincorporated King County to downtown Seattle. The agreement acknowledges that there are mutual benefits to the City and the County in preserving the natural environment in rural King County, particularly by helping protect salmon species which are a federally listed threatened species. King County Ordinance 13274 and Ordinance 13974 and Seattle Ordinance 119365.

H. OVERLAY ZONING DISTRICTS

Overlay zoning can be used to protect large-scale critical environmental areas from development or to promote growth in areas that support higher density development. A simple strategy for achieving smart growth in a community is to identify one or two conservation overlay zones and one or two development overlay zones and implement them at the same time.

Overlay zoning is a flexible alternative to traditional zoning. To create an overlay zone, a mapped district is superimposed on one or more established zoning districts. Property within the overlay district is then subject to two sets of regulations and stipulations: those contained in the underlying zoning district provisions and those provided for by the overlay zone itself. Communities may create overlay zones as a smart growth strategy both to encourage appropriate development in a designated development district and to protect critical natural resource areas, such as a watershed or a large landscape, or important natural features, such as steep slopes, wildlife habitats, or wetlands. Overlay districts can also be used to protect and enhance urban neighborhoods and historic districts in all communities.

In Franchise Developers, Inc. v. City of Cincinnati, 30 Ohio St.3d 28, 505 N.E.2d 966 (1987), the Supreme Court of Ohio upheld the denial of a permit for a Wendy's restaurant in a commercial neighborhood designated for preservation and enhancement. The city council had adopted an overlay zone, called an environmental quality district, with special standards designed to prevent businesses from locating in designated urban neighborhoods where the characteristics of the environment are of significant public value and are vulnerable to damage by development permitted under conventional zoning. The court found support for the denial in the city's adopted Urban Design Plan which provided that fast food restaurants were not appropriate in this district. By reading the underlying zoning provisions, the standards of the environmental quality district, and the adopted plan together, the court found that the property owner was put on notice of the restriction and that the restriction, plan, and ordinance accomplished a valid public purpose of preserving the quality of this urban neighborhood.

Albuquerque, New Mexico, created a Historic Overlay Zone and an Urban Conservation Overlay Zone as a means of preserving areas that have high artistic value. Areas in the Historical Overlay are suitable for preservation for historical, architectural, or cultural reasons. Areas in the Urban Conservation Overlay have "distinctive characteristics that are worthy of conservation." For both types of overlay district the ordinance requires that the city council identify the area's distinctive characteristics and general preservation guidelines. Specific development guidelines must be adopted by the landmarks and urban conservation commission, which must also issue a certificate of appropriateness before any development activity begins. An application for an Urban Conservation Overlay can be made only by property owners in the area where the overlay is applied. Fifty-one percent of those property owners must agree in writing to the application before it can be submitted.

Development overlay zones are targeted for infrastructure expansion, urban park development, incentive zoning, traditional neighborhood district zoning, transfer of development rights, floating zones, and other programs that support appropriate development patterns. Local zoning can designate these development zones as the receiving districts under a TDR program and as eligible areas for bonus densities under incentive zoning. Supplemental design regulations can be adopted and recreational facilities targeted to ensure the quality of the denser development districts.

The overlay district is most often used as a technique for conserving fragile natural resources. The underlying zoning may permit the subdivision of all land in such an area for residential purposes—a plan that, without further safeguards, might destroy the natural resource. To accomplish a more appropriate land use pattern, an overlay district can be adopted that contains special clustering, setback provisions, or other standards that protect environmentally constrained areas. In conservation overlay districts, additional standards must be met to protect identified environmental assets.

If wildlife habitat is to be protected in an overlay district, for example, the provisions of the overlay zone will require that habitat areas are to be designated and that development of an affected parcel is to be regulated to avoid harm to the habitat. Quite often this is done by requiring developments that affect protected resources to secure a special permit. The special permit will contain conditions that protect the natural features by the way that buildings and improvements are located on the site. Additional provisions can be added to the overlay district's standards that are not typically found in zoning ordinances, such as provisions for grading or for landscape restoration, or limitations on the development of steep slopes. Consider the approach taken by the municipal regulator in the next principal case.

GLISSON v. ALACHUA COUNTY

District Court of Appeal of Florida, First District, 1990.
558 So.2d 1030.

JOANOS, JUDGE.

This appeal concerns land use regulations adopted by the Alachua County Board of County Commissioners which will impact on appellants' future use of their property.

* * *

Pursuant to the provisions of its comprehensive plan, Alachua County designated the Cross Creek region as a special study area. The Cross Creek Special Study Area includes 3,100 acres lying on either side of Cross Creek, between Orange Lake and Lake Lochloosa in southeast Alachua County. The area contains the site of the Marjorie Kinnan Rawlings house (a State of Florida Historic Site). There is little development in the area, and it is surrounded by the Lochloosa Wildlife Management Area and the two lakes. The two lakes and the Cross Creek body of water have been designated as Outstanding Florida Waters. *See* § 403.061(27)(a), Fla.Stat. (1987).

Appellants are eighteen landowners in the Cross Creek Special Study Area. Their holdings range from less than one acre to 522 acres, held by Mr. Ernest Southward, as trustee for several investors in the property. Appellants Southward and Brown purchased property in the Cross Creek area for development purposes. Other appellants are long-term residents or property owners in or near Cross Creek.

On August 13, 1985, the Alachua County Board of County Commissioners adopted CPA–5–85 as an amendment to the Alachua County Comprehensive Plan. The amendment established specific development guidelines for the Cross Creek area, and was the culmination of the special study of the Cross Creek area. The study contained three general sets of guidelines or policies for the Village Center development area and the Village periphery development area, four resource protection areas, and general development guidelines. The resource protection areas are the wetlands, exceptional upland habitat, hammock zones, and active use zones.

The wetland areas are restricted from all construction activity, except minor accessory uses. Under the regulations, permitted density could be transferred at a rate of one unit per five acres, where there was appropriate contiguous property under the same ownership. Areas designated as exceptional upland habitat are considered conservation areas, where only one dwelling unit per five acres is permitted. Lot sizes are reduced to one acre and the remaining four acres of the area are to be protected in their natural state. Removal of the existing indigenous vegetation is discouraged, except for bona fide agricultural practices on existing farm lands. The hammock zones are designated as areas which will serve as wildlife habitats of secondary value and generally act as transitional zones to buffer the conservation areas. In the Village periphery, one dwelling unit per five acres is permitted on lot sizes of one acre, clustered so as to preserve the most sensitive or unique areas. The active use zones are designated as areas having comparatively little ecological value, and will be the focus of future development. No active use is permitted within a radius of 750 feet of an eagle nest. Within an additional 750 feet, all residential density has to be transferred to appropriate contiguous property under the same ownership.

CPA–5–85 existed without change or amplification until December 22, 1987, when the Commission adopted Ordinance 87–25. Ordinance 87–25 modified CPA–5–85 by adding provisions for variance applications and created a system for transfer of development rights (TDR's) within the study area to qualifying property within an urban cluster. Under CPA–5–85, if TDR's were issued, they could only be used outside the Cross Creek area, because no urban cluster is located in Cross Creek. With the passage of Ordinance 87–25 two years later, a property owner could transfer density in a restricted use zone to appropriate contiguous property under the same ownership, or to appropriate adjoining property not under the same ownership if all the affected properties were presented for development as a planned unit development (PUD).

Evidence adduced at trial indicated that the areas designated as exceptional upland habitat and hammock are found throughout Alachua County, and are not unique to the Cross Creek area. In addition, there was evidence that many of these areas had been disturbed, either by timbering or by agricultural activities, and that only six of the forty-five active eagles' nests in Alachua County are located in the Cross Creek area. Expert testimony indicated that farming, and cattle grazing are not economically feasible in the Cross Creek area. According to the expert witness, the restrictions imposed under Ordinance 87–25 and CPA–5–85 make it unlikely that a prospective buyer would consider purchasing the property for agricultural purposes. In addition, testimony from a land planner and developer indicated that the value of the individual parcels of property in Cross Creek had been seriously reduced as a result of Ordinance 87–25, and that individual property owners had been denied beneficial uses of their property. The record reflects that appellants Southward, Glisson, and Brown expended varying sums of money prior to passage of CPA–5–85 to prepare their land for residential development. Although Mr. Glisson's plan had received conceptual approval, after passage of CPA–5–85, he was advised by the County Attorney's office that conceptual approval did not entitle a property owner to obtain a permit of any kind. Due to the advice he received from the county attorney, and his personal knowledge of the unsuccessful development approval efforts of Mr. Southward and Mr. Brown, Mr. Glisson considered that any further expenditures for obtaining development permits would be futile.

The county agrees that appellants' property located in the special study area would be more valuable if appellants were free to develop it for use as recreational vehicle and mobile home parks, condominiums, or at suburban intensities. On the other hand, the record reflects that only one appellant has applied for development approval since the adoption of CPA–5–85, and that his application was approved, and the subdivided lots were sold for a substantial sum.

* * *

The first issue concerns appellants' contention that the land use regulations promulgated by the county constitute an attempt to exercise the power of eminent domain, disguised as an exercise of the police power. In support of this contention, appellants assert that the language of the comprehensive plan amendments and zoning ordinance 87–25, together with trial testimony concerning specific details of the regulations and their impact on appellants' property, demonstrate that the Cross Creek plan constitutes the creation of a "public benefit." Appellants further assert that the evidence demonstrates that the boundaries for application of the Cross Creek plan were drawn on the assumption that the state would buy and preserve the surrounding area, and restrictions were accordingly imposed in the Cross Creek area to conform land uses in the area to those uses in the surrounding areas which are under state ownership. In essence, appellants contend that as owners of property in the Cross Creek area, they are entitled to compensation because the regulations require them to maintain the status quo with regard to present uses of their property, in order to preserve an area as a benefit to be enjoyed by the public at large.

At the outset, it is well settled that the state may, by regulation or condemnation, restrict the use of private property. The fifth amendment was not designed "to limit the governmental interference with property rights per se, but rather to secure compensation in the event of otherwise proper interference amounting to a taking." *First English Evangelical Lutheran Church of Glendale v. County of Los Angeles, Cal.,* 482 U.S. 304, 107 S.Ct. 2378, 2386, 96 L.Ed.2d 250 (1987). *See also Department of Agriculture v. Mid–Florida Growers, Inc.,* 521 So.2d 101, 103 (Fla.), *cert. denied,* 488 U.S. 870, 109 S.Ct. 180, 102 L.Ed.2d 149 (1988). There is no set formula or test for determining where legitimate government regulation ends and taking begins, in the sense that the regulation has gone too far. *MacDonald, Sommer & Frates v. Yolo County,* 477 U.S. 340, 106 S.Ct. 2561, 2566, 91 L.Ed.2d 285 (1986); *Penn Central Transportation Co. v. New York City,* 438 U.S. 104, 124, 98 S.Ct. 2646, 2659, 57 L.Ed.2d 631 (1978); *Goldblatt v. Hempstead,* 369 U.S. 590, 594, 82 S.Ct. 987, 990, 8 L.Ed.2d 130 (1962); *Graham v. Estuary Properties, Inc.,* 399 So.2d 1374, 1380 (Fla.), *cert. denied, sub nom., Taylor v. Graham,* 454 U.S. 1083, 102 S.Ct. 640, 70 L.Ed.2d 618 (1981). Not surprisingly, the difficulty has always been in defining "too far," i.e., in distinguishing "the point at which regulation becomes so onerous that it has the same effect as an appropriation of the property through eminent domain or physical possession." *MacDonald, Sommer & Frates v. Yolo County,* 106 S.Ct. at 2566. "The general rule * * * is that while property may be regulated to a certain extent, if regulation goes too far it will be recognized as a taking." *Pennsylvania Coal Co. v. Mahon,* 260 U.S. 393, 43 S.Ct. 158, 160, 67 L.Ed. 322 (1922).

The propriety of a land use regulation which requires a property owner to maintain the status quo with respect to land use was decided adversely to appellants' position in *Graham v. Estuary Properties, Inc.* In *Graham,* the court reaffirmed the rule that the "exercise of the state's police power must relate to health, safety, and welfare of the public and may not be arbitrarily and capriciously applied." 399 So.2d at 1379. *See also Sarasota County v. Barg,* 302 So.2d 737, 741 (Fla.1974); *Davis v. Sails,* 318 So.2d 214, 217 (Fla. 1st DCA 1975); *City of Sunrise v. D.C.A. Homes, Inc.,* 421 So.2d 1084, 1085 (Fla. 4th DCA 1982); *Moviematic Industries Corp. v. Board of County Commissioners of Metropolitan Dade County,* 349 So.2d 667, 669 (Fla. 3d DCA 1977). The issue in *Graham* was whether the denial of an application for approval of a development of regional impact (DRI) constituted a taking. The permit was denied primarily to prevent the destruction of a large mangrove forest as called for by the development plan. The court reviewed the question primarily on the basis of a harm-benefit test involving the following factors:

(1) whether there has been a physical invasion of the property;

(2) the diminution in value of the property, i.e., whether the regulation precludes all economically reasonable use of the property;

(3) whether the regulation confers a public benefit or prevents a public harm;

(4) whether the regulation promotes the health, safety, welfare, or morals of the public;

(5) whether the regulation was applied arbitrarily and capriciously; and

(6) the extent to which the regulation has curtailed investment-backed expectations.

Graham, 399 So.2d at 1380–1381.

In *Graham,* the court held that the restrictions on development constituted a valid exercise of the police power. The court concluded that denial of a DRI permit prevented a public harm in that the proposed development would pollute the surrounding bays. While recognizing the public would be benefited because the bays would remain clean, the benefit was not deemed compensable because it was "in the form of maintaining the status quo." *Graham,* 399 So.2d at 1382.

The interests purportedly protected by the regulations at issue in this case are appropriate subjects for exercise of the police power. For example, among the interests deemed legitimate for exercise of the state's police power are such matters as: (1) protection of aesthetic interests, *City of Sunrise v. D.C.A. Homes,* 421 So.2d at 1085, *Moviematic v. County Commissioners,* 349 So.2d at 669; (2) preservation of residential or historical character of a neighborhood, *Moviematic,* 349 So.2d at 669; and (3) protection of environmentally sensitive areas and pollution control, *Graham v. Estuary Properties,* 399 So.2d at 1381; *Moviematic,* 349 So.2d at 669. Under certain circumstances, a regulation may meet the standards necessary for exercise of the police power, but still result in a taking which requires compensation. *See Department of Agriculture v. Mid–Florida Growers,* 521 So.2d at 103; *Dade County v. National Bulk Carriers, Inc.,* 450 So.2d 213, 215 (Fla.1984); *Joint Ventures v. Department of Transportation,* 519 So.2d 1069, 1070 (Fla. 1st DCA 1988).

To succeed in a regulatory taking claim, a property owner must demonstrate (1) that a regulation is unreasonable or arbitrary, or (2) that it denies a substantial portion of the beneficial use of the property. *Joint Ventures v. Department of Transportation,* 519 So.2d at 1070. *See also Nollan v. California Coastal Commission,* 483 U.S. 825, 107 S.Ct. 3141, 97 L.Ed.2d 677 (1987); *First English Evangelical Lutheran Church v. Los Angeles County,* 107 S.Ct. at 2386; *MacDonald, Sommer & Frates v. Yolo County,* 106 S.Ct. at 2566; *Herrington v. Sonoma County,* 834 F.2d 1488, 1497 (9th Cir.1987), *cert. denied,* 489 U.S. 1090, 109 S.Ct. 1557, 103 L.Ed.2d 860 (1989). A police power regulation is not invalid simply because it denies the highest and best use of the property, *Penn Central Transportation Co. v. New York City,* 438 U.S. 104, 125, 98 S.Ct. 2646, 2659–2660, 57 L.Ed.2d 631 (1978); *Goldblatt v. Town of Hempstead,* 369 U.S. 590, 82 S.Ct. 987, 8 L.Ed.2d 130 (1962); *Graham v. Estuary Properties,* 399 So.2d at 1382, or because it dramatically diminishes the value of the property. *Hadacheck v. Sebastian,* 239 U.S. 394, 36 S.Ct. 143, 60 L.Ed. 348 (1915); *Graham v. Estuary Properties,* 399 So.2d at 1382. Rather, "[i]f the regulation is a valid exercise of the police power, it is not a taking if a reasonable use of the property remains."

Agins v. City of Tiburon, 447 U.S. 255, 100 S.Ct. 2138, 2141, 65 L.Ed.2d 106 (1980); *American Savings & Loan Association v. Marin County,* 653 F.2d 364, 368 (9th Cir.1981).

Courts considering the police power/taking dichotomy have held that a taking issue is not ripe for determination until such time as the property owner has received a final determination from the government as to the permissible uses of the property. *Joint Ventures v. Department of Transportation,* 519 So.2d at 1073–1074, J. Ervin, specially concurring; *Moviematic,* 349 So.2d at 671. *See also MacDonald, Sommer & Frates v. Yolo County,* 106 S.Ct. at 2566. In other words, "an essential prerequisite to a taking claim is a final decision by the government as to what use of the property will be allowed." *MacDonald, Sommer & Frates,* 106 S.Ct. at 2566; *Unity Ventures v. Lake County,* 841 F.2d 770, 774 (7th Cir.1988). A final decision may be shown by (1) a rejected development plan, and (2) a denial of a variance. *Unity Ventures,* 841 F.2d 770, 774 (7th Cir.1988); *Kinzli v. City of Santa Cruz,* 818 F.2d 1449 (9th Cir.1987), *cert. denied,* 484 U.S. 1043, 108 S.Ct. 775, 98 L.Ed.2d 861 (1988). Although the final decision prerequisite also may be satisfied by proof that attempts to comply would be futile, futility is not established until at least one meaningful application has been filed. *Unity Ventures,* 841 F.2d at 775; *Kinzli,* 818 F.2d at 1454.

Where, as in the instant case, a taking claim arises in the context of a facial challenge rather than in the context of a concrete controversy concerning the effect of a regulation on a specific parcel of land, the only issue is whether the mere enactment of the regulation constitutes a taking. *Keystone Bituminous Coal Association v. DeBenedictis,* 480 U.S. 470, 107 S.Ct. 1232, 1247, 94 L.Ed.2d 472 (1987); *Agins v. City of Tiburon,* 100 S.Ct. at 2141. The test to be applied in considering a facial challenge is relatively straightforward, i.e., "[a] statute regulating the uses that can be made of property effects a taking if it 'denies an owner economically viable use of his land. * * * ' " *Keystone Bituminous Coal Association v. DeBenedictis,* 107 S.Ct. at 1247, quoting *Hodel v. Virginia Surface Mining and Reclamation Assn., Inc.,* 452 U.S. 264, 101 S.Ct. 2352, 69 L.Ed.2d 1 (1981). In determining whether a development restriction denies a landowner economically viable use of his property, the focus is on the existence of permissible uses. *Hodel v. Virginia Surface Mining and Reclamation Act; Agins v. City of Tiburon; Lake Nacimiento Ranch Co. v. San Luis Obispo County,* 830 F.2d 977, 982 (9th Cir.1987). To prevail, the landowner must show that there is no available beneficial use of his property under the land use ordinance. *Nacimiento,* 830 F.2d at 982. *See also Penn Central,* 98 S.Ct. at 2662.

* * * Application of the test for determining the facial validity of a regulation demonstrates that in this case, the contested regulations substantially advance legitimate state interests, in that the regulations are directed to protection of the environment and preservation of historic areas. Furthermore, because the regulations permit most existing uses of the property, and provide a mechanism whereby individual landowners may obtain a variance or a transfer of development rights, the

regulations on their face do not deny individual landowners all economically viable uses of their property. The county concedes that the regulations have diminished the value of appellants' property by restricting some of the more economically rewarding uses to which the property may be put. However, diminution in value of the property is not the test. Rather, it is incumbent upon appellants to demonstrate that they have been denied all or a substantial portion of the beneficial uses of their property, and this they have failed to do.

Furthermore, we note that the "status quo" test set forth in *Graham v. Estuary Properties* imposes a more stringent test for recovery than the traditional balancing test. *See,* generally, *Keystone Bituminous Coal Association v. DeBenedictis; City of Miami Beach v. Ocean & Inland Co.,* 147 Fla. 480, 3 So.2d 364 (1941). In *Graham,* the court determined that reducing the amount of the property to be developed by one-half, did not so diminish the value of the property or the owner's investment-backed expectations as to render the exercise of the police power unreasonable. On the basis of the record before us, even if a proposed development plan had been pursued to a final determination, it is arguable whether under *Graham,* appellants could show a sufficient diminution in value or loss of investment-backed expectations, to warrant a finding that the contested land use regulations are unreasonable, hence invalid.

* * *

In summary, we conclude that the challenged amendments and regulations are not facially unconstitutional, and that the amendments and regulations properly address conservation concerns, as mandated by section 163.3177(6)(d), Florida Statutes (1987). Furthermore, the new restrictions on their face do not constitute a taking. However, since the restrictions have not been applied to a specific land use proposal, the taking issue cannot be determined as a factual matter. Accordingly, the amended final judgment is affirmed in all respects.

ERVIN and BARFIELD, JJ., concur.

Notes

1. What precisely were the appellant landowners upset about in the principal case? How was their land zoned prior to the adoption of the 1985 and 1987 amendments of their land use plan and regulations? How did these amendments change their rights to develop their property? How are the standards created for protecting the special study area applied and how do they relate to the standards contained in the underlying zoning provisions?

2. In the principal case, notice how the County Commissioners, by adding variance and Transfer of Development Rights features, successfully anticipated the owners' claim that the establishment of the special study area and its implementing provisions constituted a regulatory taking.

3. The Upland Preservation Overlay district adopted by Brookfield, Wisconsin, is intended to preserve "all significant woodlands, wildlife habitat areas, areas of rough topography and related scenic areas." In addition to

maintaining "the natural beauty of the city," the overlay is intended to control erosion and sedimentation and to maintain water quality. The ordinance contains a deed restriction on subdivision plats prohibiting the erection of structures, the removal of vegetation, and any filling or excavating of land within the overlay, which runs with the land in perpetuity. (Brookfield, WI, Municipal Code § 17.96).

4. Limington, Maine, includes an Endangered Species and Critical Areas Overlay in its zoning ordinance to protect plants, fish, and animals in areas identified by the state as habitat for endangered species and for certain waterfowl, wading birds, and shorebirds, as spawning areas for Atlantic salmon, and as deer wintering areas. Except for non-intensive recreational uses, new structures and uses within the overlay require a conditional use permit. A report by a wildlife biologist on the probable effects of the proposed use on habitat and species may be required with as part of the permit application. (Limington, ME, Zoning Ordinance § 6.6.1).

5. The Town of Wallingford, Connecticut's zoning regulations contain two overlay districts that protect hydrological features of the local environment. These include an Aquifer Protection District and a Watershed Protection District. The regulations state that the Aquifer Protection District "shall be superimposed over the primary and secondary recharge areas of the Quinnipiac River Aquifer and the Muddy River Aquifer and all regulations, requirements, and controls of this section shall be in addition to the standard regulations of the underlying zoning district." The Watershed Protection District provisions state that its purpose is "to provide for additional standards for permitted uses of the underlying district in order to protect and maintain the surface waters of the Wallingford Public Water Supply Watershed to a quality consistent with its use as a primary drinking water source for the Town." (Town of Wallingford, CT, Zoning Regulations, § 4.12 B and 4.13 A).

6. Douglas County, Oregon, has adopted a series of overlays to protect specific natural resources: a Mineral Resources Overlay Development Ordinance; a Riparian Vegetation Corridor Overlay; a Peripheral Big Game Habitat Overlay; a Columbian White–Tailed Deer Habitat Overlay; and a Special Bird Habitat Overlay. Douglas County, OR, Land Use and Development Ordinances § 3.32.100. In Benton County, Oregon, a Sensitive Fish and Wildlife Habitat Overlay was applied to areas not protected by other state or local programs where sensitive nesting, roosting, or watering sites have been identified. The overlay applies "to all northern bald eagle nests and roosts, spotted owl nests, osprey nests, great blue heron rookeries, and band-tailed pigeon mineral springs." (Benton County, OR, Development Code, ch. 87).

I. INCENTIVE ZONING

Under the law of several states, local legislatures may allow developers to build at densities greater than those permitted by the existing zoning in exchange for public benefits such as the provision of affordable housing or the preservation of open space. Incentives may also include waivers of setback, lot coverage, and height requirements. In some of these states, the public benefits that municipalities may receive in exchange for zoning are broadly defined. Some states, such as California, Florida, New Jersey, and Oregon, enable localities to provide incentives for affordable housing as part of a statewide housing program. Maryland's incentive zoning enabling statute, permits localities to encourage innovation and promote flexibility, economy, and ingenuity in development and, to this end, to award developers incentives in the form of increased density.

In New York, communities used the standard zoning enabling statute to award incentives for affordable housing years before the legislature adopted a broad enabling act making it clear that localities can use bonus density incentives and waive all dimensional requirements of zoning codes in exchange for a broad range of public benefits, including infrastructure, open space, day care, and affordable housing. The Town of LaGrange, New York for example, awards a 40 percent density bonus when a developer promises to preserve 80 percent of a site for farming purposes. LaGrange, New York, Code ch. 100, art. III, § 100–31C(3). Most often the public benefits received for the incentives awarded are provided directly by the developer as part of the development itself. The New York statute allows communities to receive cash payments in exchange for zoning incentives awarded a developer. This allows localities to use the cash to achieve the public benefit directly. Under this authority, it is possible for the community to purchase development rights, or conservation easements, on valuable open land with the cash contributed by a developer who is granted zoning incentives to build in an appropriate location that can absorb the development impacts.

The City of Suffolk, Virginia, uses incentive zoning to conserve natural resources. Located in the southeast corner of the state along the James River, the city contains 430 square miles of land that includes woods, lakes, rivers, and rolling terrain. Under the city's incentive zoning ordinance, developers may receive density bonuses—in some instances up to 140 percent of the existing density—in exchange for providing a variety of public amenities. Density bonuses may be provided for the creation of public parks; the preservation of open space, agricultural land, or critical environmental areas; the construction of retirement housing; the redevelopment of existing commercial strip centers; the construction of traditional neighborhood development; or clustering. Determination of the density bonus is based upon a formula established under the city's Unified Development Ordinance. Unified Development Ordinance of the City of Suffolk, Virginia, § 31–409.

To obtain the density bonuses provided for by the Unified Development Ordinance, the developer of a parcel must obtain a conditional use permit. § 31–409(a)(3). This requires that the developer submit a conditional use permit application to the city's planning commission. Once the application is complete, the planning commission reviews the application and provides its recommendation to the city council. The city council then holds a public hearing on the permit. Before granting approval for the permit, the city council must be satisfied that the increase in density will not adversely affect the health, safety, or comfort of persons living or working in the neighborhood and that it has no greater impact on the neighborhood than any other use generally permitted in the same district. § 31–306.

In two neighboring communities in New York, incentive zoning is being used as a means of encouraging development in appropriate locations while protecting valuable farmland. The Village and the Town of Warwick, which have independent zoning authority, have entered into an intermunicipal agreement regarding the annexation of land by the village, the use of floating zoning, and the provision of incentive zoning to preserve farmland in the town that lies in the village's watershed and viewshed. Under the agreement, land annexed by the village is brought into the village and its water and sewer district at the same density permitted by town's three-acre single-family zone. A floating zone, allowing densities up to three units per acre, is available upon application by the developer of the annexed land. The floating zone is created as an incentive zone; developers are required to pay $50,000 per unit for each bonus housing unit made possible by the application of the zone to the land. This money is paid into a dedicated trust fund, jointly administered by the village and town. Nearly all of the funds will be used to purchase development rights on farmland in the town, much of it in proximity to the village. This illustrates the creative combination of incentive zoning, annexation, intermunicipal cooperation, and floating zoning to meet the common interests of both communities.

Notes

1. Municipal Art Society of New York v. Koch, 137 Misc.2d 832, 522 N.Y.S.2d 800, (Sup.Ct. N.Y. County 1987), determined that the cash sale of a zoning bonus was an unacceptable application of incentive zoning. "The Coliseum is located in a zone which permits construction as-of-right of floor space up to a maximum of 15 times the square footage of the lot. This [density] is subject to being increased by up to 20% in exchange for the developer agreeing to 'provide major improvements for the adjacent subway stations' provided that 'the zoning lot for the development * * * which a [density] bonus is requested shall be adjacent to the mezzanine or concourse of the subway station for which the improvement is proposed or an existing connecting passageway to the station.'" 137 Misc.2d at 833. Under the development agreement between the city and the developer, the city would be "obtaining not only $35 to $40 million of local subway improvements, but an additional $57 million to be employed for other purposes." Id., at 832. The court determined that the sale was inappropriate because the cash payment to be made to the city was to be employed for purposes other than local improvements. The court held that the "government may not place itself in the position of reaping a cash premium because one of its agencies bestows a zoning benefit upon a developer. Zoning benefits are not cash items." Id., at 838.

2. The court in Asian Americans for Equality v. Koch, 72 N.Y.2d 121, 531 N.Y.S.2d 782, 527 N.E.2d 265 (1988), upheld a zoning amendment that created a special use district. The new zoning provided that development in

the Special Manhattan Bridge District would be "regulated by a system of bonus points permitting increased density in residential buildings for those developers who agree to: 1) donate space for community facilities such as senior citizen or day care centers, educational facilities; 2) construct low-income dwelling units; or 3) rehabilitate existing substandard housing." 72 N.Y.2d at 122. The plaintiffs argued that the incentive zoning scheme provided greater bonuses for educational and senior citizen facilities than it did for low-income housing. They argued that such housing was necessary to combat the effects of gentrification caused by the creation of the special district and that the zoning discouraged developers from building low-income housing. The court concluded that inducing private developers to provide public benefits involves a complex set of considerations. It held that the plaintiffs had not carried their burden of proving that the bonus scheme was clearly arbitrary or capricious or undertaken for an improper purpose.

Chapter VIII

HOUSING AND URBAN DEVELOPMENT

SECTION 1. INTRODUCTION

Demographic experts project that the American population will increase by one hundred million over the next forty years. These additional residents will create a tremendous demand for additional housing and nonresidential development. It is predicted that over seventy million new homes and one hundred billion square feet of nonresidential space will be necessary to accommodate this growth in population. Since many of the new households will comprise young singles and couples, aging empty nesters, and immigrants, a large percentage of these 100 million Americans will be oriented to urban living.

This contrasts with the demand created by population growth over the past half century, which contained a higher proportion of traditional families and resulted in new home construction that emphasized single-family units on individual plots of land. This previous demand for housing along with low interest mortgages and highway expansion combined to attract urban dwellers to the country and fuel urban sprawl, contributing to the deterioration of city neighborhoods and threatening the financial capacity of urban municipalities.

Until recently, much of the debate about the flight of development from cities into the surrounding countryside focused on how spread-out land use patterns consume open space, cause nonpoint source pollution of surface and ground water resources, eliminate habitat, cause flooding, cost more in municipal services, such as water and sewer systems and roads, and increase traffic congestion. Local officials in distressed cities concerned themselves with reducing inner-city poverty, increasing urban tax bases, and stimulating job development.

Currently, planners and scientists are focused on how urban sprawl contributes to greenhouse gas emissions and accelerates climate change and its worrisome consequences. In 2006 and 2007, the Intergovernmental Panel on Climate Change (IPCC) released three reports expressing the consensus of the scientific community that global warming is unequivocal, that its main driver is human activity, and that the consequences of climate alteration are severe: widening droughts, more frequent and serious storm events, increased inland flooding, sea level rise, and consequent inundation of low lying lands. Climate change has provided a sharper focus and deeper emphasis on how population patterns affect society.

City dwellers own fewer cars, take fewer automobile trips, and use less fossil fuel to heat and cool their residences. Less energy is needed to heat, cool, light, and fuel buildings in many cities because they are more densely developed and because residences in cities tend to be smaller than the national average. In addition, the density of the population and the mix of residential and commercial uses make public transit possible and reduce the use of automobiles by urban dwellers.

In many cities, residents are responsible for less than a third of the carbon emissions attributable to their suburban counterparts, many of whom live in large single-family homes on individual parcels of land in exclusively residential neighborhoods. In many affluent suburbs, residents live in homes that routinely exceed the national average of 2,400 square feet. They take up to fifteen automobile trips per household per day to work, shop, and recreate. Simply eliminating the average car trip to work can reduce a commuter's contribution to carbon dioxide emissions by 6,520 pounds per year.

Land use law is implicated in this. It is, after all, zoning that creates the blueprint for land development and dictates the densities and land uses that give some U.S. cities international bragging rights in the struggle to reduce carbon emissions and slow climate change. Urban zoning and market demand in many cities produce relatively smaller residential units, a large proportion of multi-family, high-rise, and mixed-use buildings, and locate retail goods, personal services, and mass transit stations within walking distance for many residents.

How the land is developed to accommodate the next 100 million people in the U.S. is of critical importance. Future land use patterns and human settlements will determine how cost effective, equitable, and environmentally friendly the country will be in the twenty-first century. This chapter explores attempts to accommodate a greater percentage of that population growth in existing built up places, particularly cities and their older suburbs. Its topics include efforts to reverse the flight of middle-income and affluent residents from older urban centers, revitalize urban places, concentrate new development in centers, and prevent developing suburbs from excluding low- and moderate-income households.

The big picture here focuses on metropolitan area settlement patterns. How do cities become more livable, attract back the affluent households they have lost, and develop the tax base they need to support their diverse populations and the cultural, civic, educational, and governmental services they provide their regions? How do older suburbs protect and enhance their aging residential and commercial neighborhoods? How do cities and established suburbs deal with the competition for economic development and high-end residential projects coming from communities on the fringe? How do these fringe communities ensure that cost-effective and inclusive land patterns are created as they develop and change?

The cases and notes in this section illustrate the complexity of these questions while describing the legal authority that localities have to deal with these persistent challenges. They point out the opportunities and difficulties of ordering development. They also raise serious questions about how the legal authority given to localities can be used effectively.

SECTION 2. PREVENTING URBAN DECAY

Land use students may remember Javins v. First National Realty Corp., 428 F.2d 1071 (D.C.Cir.1970), from their first year property class and that, at common law, no warranties with respect to property condition are implied by courts in conveyances, including leases. The landlord in Javins brought an action against tenants for failure to pay rent. The tenants posited a novel argument: they withheld payment of rent because the landlord had violated its warranty of habitability through poor maintenance resulting in approximately 1500 violations of the District of Columbia housing code. In holding for the tenants, the Javins court found that "a warranty of habitability, measured by the standards set out in the Housing Regulations for the District of Columbia, is implied by operation of law into leases of urban dwelling units covered by those Regulations and that breach of this warranty gives rise to the usual remedies for breach of contract, including the withholding of rent."

The case is presented here stripped of some of the rationale that led the court to imply the warranty, leaving those portions that reflect on the realities of urban living for low- and moderate-income families and the efficacy of legal tools such as housing codes to maintain the quality of life in the urban core.

New York City adopted the first urban housing code in 1901: the Tenement House Act. Housing codes aim to ensure that multi-family buildings are safe, sanitary, and efficient. The housing code, like a number of other techniques used to maintain livability and redevelop cities, is not traditionally thought of as a land use technique, but is one of a growing list of tools that community leaders use to accomplish their land use planning objectives. The Javins case illustrates that urban cities, in their struggle to remain livable, do have authority to regulate housing conditions, to enforce housing code standards, and to force building owners to repair, where the funds are available.

JAVINS v. FIRST NATIONAL REALTY CORP.

United States Court of Appeals, District of Columbia Circuit, 1970.
428 F.2d 1071.

J. SKELLY WRIGHT, Circuit Judge.

These cases present the question whether housing code violations which arise during the term of a lease have any effect upon the tenant's obligation to pay rent. The Landlord and Tenant Branch of the District of Columbia Court of General Sessions ruled proof of such violations inadmissible when proffered as a defense to an eviction action for nonpayment of rent. The District of Columbia Court of Appeals upheld this ruling. *Saunders v. First National Realty Corp.*, 245 A.2d 836 (1968).

Because of the importance of the question presented, we granted appellants' petitions for leave to appeal. We now reverse and hold that a warranty of habitability, measured by the standards set out in the Housing Regulations for the District of Columbia, is implied by operation of law into leases of urban dwelling units covered by those Regulations and that breach of this warranty gives rise to the usual remedies for breach of contract.

The facts revealed by the record are simple. By separate written leases, each of the appellants rented an apartment in a three-building apartment complex in Northwest Washington known as Clifton Terrace. The landlord, First National Realty Corporation, filed separate actions in the Landlord and Tenant Branch of the Court of General Sessions on April 8, 1966, seeking possession on the ground that each of the appellants had defaulted in the payment of rent due for the month of April. The tenants, appellants here, admitted that they had not paid the landlord any rent for April. However, they alleged numerous violations of the Housing Regulations as 'an equitable defense or (a) claim by way of recoupment or set-off in an amount equal to the rent claim,' as provided in the rules of the Court of General Sessions. They offered to prove

> 'that there are approximately 1500 violations of the Housing Regulations of the District of Columbia in the building at Clifton Terrace, where Defendant resides some affecting the premises of this Defendant directly, others indirectly, and all tending to establish a course of conduct of violation of the Housing Regulations to the damage of Defendants * * *.'

Settled Statement of Proceedings and Evidence, p. 2 (1966). Appellants conceded at trial, however, that this offer of proof reached only violations which had arisen since the term of the lease had commenced. The Court of General Sessions refused appellants' offer of proof and entered judgment for the landlord. The District of Columbia Court of Appeals affirmed, rejecting the argument made by appellants that the landlord was under a contractual duty to maintain the premises in compliance with the Housing Regulations. *Saunders v. First National Realty Corp., supra*, 245 A.2d at 838.

Since, in traditional analysis, a lease was the conveyance of an interest in land, courts have usually utilized the special rules governing real property transactions to resolve controversies involving leases. However, as the Supreme Court has noted in another context, 'the body of private property law * * *, more than almost any other branch of law, has been shaped by distinctions whose validity is largely historical.' Courts have a duty to reappraise old doctrines in the light of the facts and values of contemporary life—particularly old common law doctrines which the courts themselves created and developed. As we have said before, 'The continued vitality of the common law * * * depends upon its ability to reflect contemporary community values and ethics.'

* * *

A. In our judgment the common law itself must recognize the landlord's obligation to keep his premises in a habitable condition. This conclusion is compelled by three separate considerations. First, we believe that the old rule was based on certain factual assumptions which are no longer true; on its own terms, it can no longer be justified. Second, we believe that the consumer protection cases discussed above require that the old rule be abandoned in order to bring residential landlord-tenant law into harmony with the principles on which those cases rest. Third, we think that the nature of today's urban housing market also dictates abandonment of the old rule.

* * *

It is overdue for courts to admit that these assumptions are no longer true with regard to all urban housing. Today's urban[27] tenants, the vast majority of whom live in multiple dwelling houses, are interested, not in the land, but solely in 'a house suitable for occupation.' Furthermore, today's city dweller usually has a single, specialized skill unrelated to maintenance work; he is unable to make repairs like the 'jack-of-all-trades' farmer who was the common law's model of the lessee. Further, unlike his agrarian predecessor who often remained on one piece of land for his entire life, urban tenants today are more mobile than ever before. A tenant's tenure in a specific apartment will often not be sufficient to justify efforts at repairs. In addition, the increasing complexity of today's dwellings renders them much more difficult to repair than the structures of earlier times. In a multiple dwelling repair may require access to equipment and areas in the control of the landlord. Low and middle income tenants, even if they were interested in making repairs, would be unable to obtain any financing for major repairs since they have no long-term interest in the property.

* * *

27. In 1968 more than two thirds of America's people lived in the 228 largest metropolitan areas. Only 5.2% lived on farms. The World Almanac 1970 at 251 (L. Long ed.). More than 98% of all housing starts in 1968 were non-farm. Id. at 313.

Thus we are led by our inspection of the relevant legal principles and precedents to the conclusion that the old common law rule imposing an obligation upon the lessee to repair during the lease term was really never intended to apply to residential urban leaseholds. Contract principles established in other areas of the law provide a more rational framework for the apportionment of landlord-tenant responsibilities; they strongly suggest that a warranty of habitability be implied into all contracts for urban dwellings.

B. We believe, in any event, that the District's housing code requires that a warranty of habitability be implied in the leases of all housing that it covers. The housing code—formally designated the Housing Regulations of the District of Columbia—was established and authorized by the Commissioners of the District of Columbia on August 11, 1955. Since that time, the code has been updated by numerous orders of the Commissioners. The 75 pages of the Regulations provide a comprehensive regulatory scheme setting forth in some detail: (a) the standards which housing in the District of Columbia must meet; (b) which party, the lessor or the lessee, must meet each standard; and (c) a system of inspections, notifications and criminal penalties. The Regulations themselves are silent on the question of private remedies.

* * *

The District of Columbia Court of Appeals gave further effect to the Housing Regulations in *Brown v. Southall Realty Co.,* 237 A.2d 834 (1968). There the landlord knew at the time the lease was signed that housing code violations existed which rendered the apartment 'unsafe and unsanitary.' Viewing the lease as a contract, the District of Columbia Court of Appeals held that the premises were let in violation of Sections 2304[28] and 2501[29] of the Regulations and that the lease, therefore, was void as an illegal contract. In the light of Brown, it is clear not only that the housing code creates privately enforceable duties as held in Whetzel, but that the basic validity of every housing contract depends upon substantial compliance with the housing code at the beginning of the lease term. The Brown court relied particularly upon Section 2501 of the Regulations which provides:

> 'Every premises accommodating one or more habitations shall be maintained and kept in repair so as to provide decent living accommodations for the occupants. This part of this Code contemplates more than mere basic repairs and maintenance to keep out the elements; its purpose is to include repairs and maintenance designed to make a premises or neighborhood healthy and safe.'

28. 'No person shall rent or offer to rent any habitation, or the furnishings thereof, unless such habitation and its furnishings are in a clean, safe and sanitary condition, in repair, and free from rodents or vermin.'

29. 'The housing and sanitary codes, especially in light of Congress' explicit direction for their enactment, indicate a strong and pervasive congressional concern to secure for the city's slum dwellers decent, or at least safe and sanitary, places to live.' *Edwards v. Habib,* supra Note 44, 130 U.S.App.D.C. at 139, 397 F.2d at 700.

By its terms, this section applies to maintenance and repair during the lease term. Under the Brown holding, serious failure to comply with this section before the lease term begins renders the contract void. We think it untenable to find that this section has no effect on the contract after it has been signed. To the contrary, by signing the lease the landlord has undertaken a continuing obligation to the tenant to maintain the premises in accordance with all applicable law.

This principle of implied warranty is well established. Courts often imply relevant law into contracts to provide a remedy for any damage caused by one party's illegal conduct. In a case closely analogous to the present ones, the Illinois Supreme Court held that a builder who constructed a house in violation of the Chicago building code had breached his contract with the buyer:

> '* * * The law existing at the time and place of the making of the contract is deemed a part of the contract, as though expressly referred to or incorporated in it. * * *'
>
> 'The rationale for this rule is that the parties to the contract would have expressed that which the law implies 'had they not supposed that it was unnecessary to speak of it because the law provided for it.' * * * Consequently, the courts, in construing the existing law as part of the express contract, are not reading into the contract provisions different from those expressed and intended by the parties, as defendants contend, but are merely construing the contract in accordance with the intent of the parties.'

We follow the Illinois court in holding that the housing code must be read into housing contracts—a holding also required by the purposes and the structure of the code itself. The duties imposed by the Housing Regulations may not be waived or shifted by agreement if the Regulations specifically place the duty upon the lessor. Criminal penalties are provided if these duties are ignored. This regulatory structure was established by the Commissioners because, in their judgment, the grave conditions in the housing market required serious action. Yet official enforcement of the housing code has been far from uniformly effective. Innumerable studies have documented the desperate condition of rental housing in the District of Columbia and in the nation. In view of these circumstances, we think the conclusion reached by the Supreme Court of Wisconsin as to the effect of a housing code on the old common law rule cannot be avoided:

> '* * * The legislature has made a policy judgment—that it is socially (and politically) desirable to impose these duties on a property owner—which has rendered the old common law rule obsolete. To follow the old rule of no implied warranty of habitability in leases would, in our opinion, be inconsistent with the current legislative policy concerning housing standards. * * *'

We therefore hold that the Housing Regulations imply a warranty of habitability, measured by the standards which they set out, into leases of all housing that they cover.

* * *

The judgment of the District of Columbia Court of Appeals is reversed and the cases are remanded for further proceedings consistent with this opinion.

So ordered.

Notes

1. What are the economic consequences of the Javins decision? When landlords defer maintenance and housing code violations occur, what will tenants do with the rent if they know about the implied warranty of habitability? Will they pay it? Will they put it in escrow? Will they join forces and contract to make repairs, pay for them with withheld rents, and offset that amount in any non-payment action? How are rents in inner city apartment buildings set? What is their market value? Are these rents enough to pay utilities, insurance, mortgage principal and interest, property taxes, building maintenance personnel and materials, and make capital improvements? If not, can landlords raise rents to cover recurring expenses and needed improvements? What are the consequences to lower-income tenants if rents are raised?

2. The conditions of low- and moderate-income housing in the District of Columbia and many other cities continued to decline even after the adoption of housing codes and the imposition of the warranty of habitability on urban landlords, which was accomplished by statutes in many states. Following the Javins case, more affluent residents poured out into the developing suburbs with modern housing in single-family subdivisions—communities with low crime rates and higher quality schools. This "white flight" left behind serious fiscal and physical conditions in the inner city such as the deterioration and abandonment of the housing stock, which is addressed in the following case.

MOORE v. CITY OF DETROIT

Court of Appeals of Michigan, 1987.
159 Mich.App. 199, 406 N.W.2d 488.

KELLY, J.J.

* * *

Defendants argue that Ord. 556–H authorizes the city to confiscate privately owned property for a public purpose and thus involves the exercise of the city's power of eminent domain rather than its police powers. Defendants then conclude that the omission of a provision in the ordinance requiring just compensation renders the ordinance violative of the property owners' due process rights. * * * We earlier held that Ord. 556–H was enacted under the police powers granted to Detroit as a home rule city. * * * We again conclude that Ord. 556–H represents an exercise of the city's police powers and we reject defendants' reliance on the law of eminent domain.

Section 12–11–46.1 of Ord. 556–H sets forth the legislative findings on which the Detroit City Council relied in enacting the nuisance abatement ordinance:

(a) Scattered throughout the city are a large number of unoccupied dwellings which are constantly broken into, vandalized, used for unsanitary or immoral purposes and are potential fire hazards.

(b) There are many unoccupied dwellings in the city which, because of their vacant status, constitute hazards to the health, safety, and welfare of the public.

(c) Certain vacant dwellings have reached a stage of disrepair and deterioration which create a public nuisance or exert a downgrading or blighting influence on the surrounding neighborhood, resulting in discouraging neighbors from making improvements to properties and thus adversely affecting the tax revenue of the city.

(d) Throughout the city, the number of vacant and deteriorated dwellings constituting public nuisances has become so high that traditional means of abating such nuisances have been ineffectual, and blight and deterioration of emergency proportions have resulted.

(e) Currently, tax delinquent abandoned dwellings revert to the state and are then deeded to the city through the state tax reversion process. However, this process takes several years, during which time many dwellings are lost through vandalism and deterioration.

(f) Permitting families to repair and move into abandoned homes within the city will preserve the residential housing stock of the city, increase neighborhood stability and provide needed homes for Detroit families.

These stated purposes fall within the city's powers to "provide for the public peace and health of its citizenry and promote the safety of persons and properties within its boundaries." * * * Although these goals, if achieved, will no doubt benefit the public, we are not persuaded that the taking authorized under Ord. 556–H is for a "public purpose" as that term has evolved under the law of eminent domain. Most significantly, Ord. 556–H does not impose upon the property owner a burden which should be borne by the public. See *Penn Central Transportation Co. v. New York City*, 438 U.S. 104, 123–124; 98 S.Ct. 2646; 57 L.Ed.2d 631 (1978); * * *. In a disordered society, vacant houses develop into public nuisances, as that term is defined in Ord. 556–H, partly because of the action or inaction of their owners. It is neither unfair nor unjust for the city to impose the burden of abating these nuisances upon the individual owners rather than upon the public as a whole. Neighborhoods don't blight overnight.

Although we reject defendants' reliance on the law of eminent domain, our conclusion that Ord. 556–H represents an exercise of the city's police powers does not entirely resolve the issue of whether the ordinance unconstitutionally deprives property owners of their property interests without adequate compensation. See *Loretto v. Teleprompter Manhattan CATV Corp.*, 458 U.S. 419; 102 S.Ct. 3164; 73 L.Ed.2d 868 (1982); * * *. A statute or ordinance authorizing physical occupancy of property without compensation to the property owner must be reasonable under the surrounding circumstances. * * *. Before considering the reasonableness of the occupancy authorized under Ord. 556–H, we find it helpful to visit a few of its procedural provisions.

Ord. 556–H does not by itself transfer title of property to the city or to the nuisance abatement contractor. Transfer of title must be achieved by the city through an action to quiet title, * * * or through delinquent tax proceedings, * * * Ord. 556–H simply creates a temporary right in third parties to enter, occupy and repair a vacant home which has been declared by lawful authority to be an unlawful nuisance. At the end of the abatement period, the city will have obtained title to the property through prescribed judicial proceedings so that the property may then be sold by the city to the nuisance abatement contractor. * * *. We note that the property owner is notified of the activity on his or her property at all stages of the abatement process and is provided numerous opportunities to assert ownership of the property, thereby terminating the nuisance abatement contract. It is significant that defendants in this case do not assert any due process challenge to the notice and hearing provisions of Ord. 556–H.

Since Ord. 556–H does not authorize permanent occupancy of private property by third persons, defendants' reliance on Loretto, supra, is not dispositive. The Supreme Court in Loretto, repeatedly emphasized that its decision is based upon the permanency of the government-authorized occupancy challenged therein. Defendants' reliance on Loretto stems from an erroneous interpretation of Ord. 556–H as authorizing the city to take title to real property.

Correctly interpreted, Ord. 556–H simply amends the city's original building code and creates an alternative to demolition or costly repairs by government or third persons who do not gain rights to occupy the property. Defendants agree that the city may authorize a third party to enter private property in order to demolish a building identified as a public nuisance and that the property owner has no right to just compensation for this taking. Defendants further admit that just compensation is not required where the city contracts with a third party to repair a building identified as a public nuisance. It is the nuisance abatement contractor's occupancy of the property while making repairs which defendants now challenge as unconstitutional.

Defendants, however, fail to adequately distinguish between a taking authorized under the original building code and the taking authorized under Ord. 556–H. Under both the original building code and Ord. 556–H, third parties are authorized by the city to enter onto private property for the purpose of abating a public nuisance. Although the entry and physical possession authorized under Ord. 556–H extends the duration of the physical occupancy and allows the third party to make general use of the property while abating the nuisance, obviously such possession is not more intrusive than demolition.

In any event, the dispositive inquiry is whether this extended physical possession is reasonable under the circumstances. We believe that it is. As noted by Justice Stevens in Young v. American Mini Theatres, Inc., * * * cities "must be allowed a reasonable opportunity to experiment with solutions to admittedly serious problems." After having determined that existing mechanisms were ineffective in attacking the perils of abandoned homes scarring its neighborhoods, the city's legislative body enacted Ord. 556–H as an alternative method of abating these public nuisances. Defendants have failed to carry their burden of proving that this alternative is unreasonable and, therefore, unconstitutional. * * * Ord. 556–H authorizes only a temporary physical possession of property for the purpose of abating a public nuisance and relies upon other, well-established judicial processes in providing for the transfer of title to property. Built into the ordinance are ample notice and opportunity provisions which protect the right of the property owner to terminate the nuisance abatement contract at any point. Given the nature of the intrusion, the purpose sought to be accomplished and the ease with which a property owner may terminate a nuisance abatement contract, we cannot say that Ord. 556–H constitutes an unreasonable exercise of the city's police powers.

Defendants briefly argue that Ord. 556–H is arbitrary and discriminatory because property owners will be treated differently based on the whims of nuisance abatement contractors regarding which houses will be occupied. While it is true that some houses capable of rehabilitation will be the subject of nuisance abatement contracts while others will be demolished or repaired by nonoccupant third parties, this difference in treatment is neither arbitrary nor unfair. We hold that it is a reasonable effort to solve a difficult problem. It may not work but it should be tried.

* * *

Affirmed.

Note

In Rental Prop. Owners Ass'n v. City of Grand Rapids, 455 Mich. 246, 566 N.W.2d 514 (1997), the Supreme Court of Michigan cited the Moore case and Detroit's nuisance abatement ordinance in confirming the constitutionality of a Grand Rapids ordinance that permits the municipality to proclaim that a building constitutes a public nuisance and close it for a year if it can be shown that the building has housed repetitive illegal drug activity.

DAVIDSON BROS., INC. v. D. KATZ & SONS, INC.

Superior Court of New Jersey, Appellate Division, 1994.
274 N.J.Super. 159, 643 A.2d 642.

D'Annunzio, J.A.D.

Plaintiff Davidson Bros., Inc. (Davidson) appeals from a trial court judgment entered after a bench trial held on remand from the Supreme Court. *Davidson Bros., Inc. v. D. Katz & Sons, Inc.*, 121 N.J. 196, 579 A.2d 288 (1990). Applying the reasonableness test formulated by the Supreme Court, the trial court determined that a covenant prohibiting the use as a supermarket of a property in downtown New Brunswick, New Jersey, was unenforceable. We now affirm.

Davidson operated a number of supermarkets in New Jersey. In 1952, it opened a supermarket of 10,000 square feet on George Street in downtown New Brunswick. In June 1978, Davidson took over an existing supermarket located at Elizabeth Street, also in New Brunswick but approximately two miles from the George Street store (hereinafter George Street), near the border with North Brunswick. Davidson paid $315,000 for the assets of the Elizabeth Street store (hereinafter Elizabeth Street), not including inventory, and made a substantial additional investment for improvements. Davidson leased the Elizabeth Street real property.

Davidson closed George Street in February 1979 because its volume had decreased after Davidson acquired Elizabeth Street. It sold George Street in September 1980 to defendant D. Katz & Sons, Inc. (Katz), a rug merchant. The deed to Katz contained the covenant in issue:

> The lands and premises described herein and conveyed hereby are conveyed subject to the restriction that said lands and premises shall not be used as and for a supermarket or grocery store of a supermarket type, however designated, for a period of forty (40) years from the date of this deed. This restriction shall be a covenant attached to and running with the lands.

The closing of George Street as a supermarket created a hardship for downtown residents, most of whom did not own or have ready access to motor vehicles. In response to their plight, the city government sought to attract another supermarket operator to the downtown area. The city's efforts culminated in the acquisition of George Street from Katz by the defendant New Brunswick Housing Authority, and the leasing of the property, for one dollar a year, to defendant C–Town, on condition that C–Town invest at least $10,000 for improvements and operate George Street as a supermarket.

Davidson commenced this action to enforce the covenant. Davidson appealed from an adverse summary judgment and we affirmed in an unreported opinion, utilizing traditional "touch and concern" analysis applicable to covenants alleged to run with the land. *Davidson Bros., Inc. v. D. Katz & Sons, Inc.*, No. A–5489–86 (App.Div. Sept. 15, 1988). *See generally Caullett v. Stanley Stilwell & Sons, Inc.*, 67 N.J.Super. 111, 116–18, 170 A.2d 52 (App.Div.1961).

Our Supreme Court granted Davidson's petition for certification and reversed and remanded for a trial. In doing so, the Court determined that "rigid adherence" to the "touch and concern" requirement was no longer warranted. *Davidson Bros. Inc., supra*, 121 N.J. at 210, 579 A.2d 288. It held that enforceability of a covenant would depend on its reasonableness, and that the principle of "touch and concern" is "but one of the factors." * * *

* * *

On remand, Davidson no longer sought injunctive relief and abandoned its contention that the one dollar per year lease to C–Town was an unconstitutional use of public property for a private purpose. Those changes in position were caused by Davidson's sale of its Elizabeth Street store to another supermarket operator in 1989 for $687,500. Davidson limited its claim to damages consisting of lost sales and profits during the two year period it competed with C–Town, and the reduced value of its Elizabeth Street store due to C–Town's competition.

Davidson's accountant testified that sales at Elizabeth Street for 1988 and 1989 were $1,452,000 less than they would have been had the George Street store not reopened. He calculated the lost profit on those sales to be $350,000. He also opined that due to the lower sales volume, Davidson sold the Elizabeth Street store for $567,000 less than it should have sold for.

Defendants' accountant disagreed. He testified that although Elizabeth Street may have lost sales due to C–Town's operation of George Street, those lost sales would not have been profitable. Defendants' accountant also testified that the Elizabeth Street store did not lose value as a result of C–Town's competition.

After a lengthy trial, the trial court rendered an oral opinion. Applying the eight factors announced by the Supreme Court, the court found that the 40 year term was unreasonably long * * *; that the covenant imposed an unreasonable restraint of trade * * *; and that it was contrary to the public interest * * *. Regarding [the latter factor] * * *, the court ruled that the covenant adversely impacted the public interest because "there is a substantial public need for the supermarket under the circumstances of this case."

The trial court deemed the damages issue to be moot because of its determination that the covenant was unreasonable and unenforceable. However, the court announced that it was unable to determine from the evidence that Davidson had sustained damages due to C–Town's competition.

We now affirm on the ground that the covenant was so contrary to public policy that it should not be recognized as a valid, enforceable obligation.

The proofs established that New Brunswick is a small city which continues to suffer from many of the maladies affecting the larger cities of New Jersey and the nation, especially in its core downtown area. This area, where George Street is located, has been the focus of a large scale redevelopment and revitalization effort measured in decades. Although this effort's emphasis has been on commercial projects primarily, the downtown area is also the site of many low to moderate income housing projects of the New Brunswick Housing Authority. These were federally funded projects, and many of their residents depended on George Street for their shopping requirements before Davidson closed the store. George Street is within two blocks of four of those housing projects with a total of 726 units.

The testimony of New Brunswick's Director of Policy, Planning and Economic Development, and his report which was introduced into evidence, provided a demographic profile of the city. There are a total of 3,148 households in the downtown area. Twenty-six percent of those households are below the poverty level, compared with seventeen percent in the balance of the city. Of the "family households" downtown, twenty-eight percent are female householders with children, compared with fourteen percent in the balance of the city. Of the female headed households, fifty-four percent are below the poverty level, which is consistent with the balance of the city. Thirty-seven percent of the downtown housing units have no vehicle, almost twice as many as the balance of the city. Seven hundred and forty-three downtown units are occupied by persons sixty-five years and older; twenty-one percent of those seniors are below the poverty level, almost double the proportion in the rest of the city. The downtown area, therefore, contains the city's greatest concentration of disadvantaged persons.

Davidson's closing of George Street further disadvantaged them. No other supermarket was within walking distance. For those who lacked access to motor vehicles, buses, taxis and dependence on others replaced a walk to the supermarket. The problem was especially difficult for female heads of household who used to send their children to the store or have their children accompany them. With the elimination of George Street, getting to the supermarket was a particularly difficult exercise in logistics and child care.

But inconvenience was not the only cost. Dr. James J. O'Connor testified for defendants as an expert in food marketing and distribution. Dr. O'Connor's experience involved hands-on management of his family's wholesale and retail food businesses, followed by academic and government experience in food distribution issues. Shortly before his testimony in this case, Dr. O'Connor had completed a study for the United States Department of Agriculture regarding supermarkets in United States cities. According to Dr. O'Connor, the absence of a supermarket in a low income city neighborhood makes food more expensive and has a negative impact on diet and, therefore, on the inner city population's health.

Dr. O'Connor also stated that the absence of a supermarket contributes to inner city decay, because a supermarket is a retail anchor that attracts other retail operations. Withdrawal of a supermarket tends to force other merchants to leave the same neighborhood. The resulting vacuum is filled by convenience stores or "ma and pa" groceries. They are more expensive and lack variety. They rarely have produce and, if they do have it, it is of poor quality. Moreover, selection of poultry and fish is very limited and very expensive. Dr. O'Connor opined that there is a general lack of inner city supermarkets in the nation, which poses a significant social policy problem.

Dr. O'Connor's uncontradicted testimony is consistent with the conclusions reached by a congressional committee. House Select Comm.

on Hunger, 100th Cong., 1st Sess., Obtaining Food: Shopping Constraints on the Poor (Comm. Print 1987) (hereinafter Report). The committee concluded that "low-income consumers are unable to maximize their limited expendable resources for a basic need-food-because of the barriers of the [sic] location and transportation. Hence, the grip of hunger and poverty tightens around the low-income consumer." *Id.* at 1.

The committee recognized the exacerbating impact of "supermarket migration" on this problem[.]

* * *

The committee also recognized the impact of the inner city consumers' limited shopping choices[.]

* * *

In its Report, the committee noted that experts and organizations addressing the problems of urban living recommended the provision of incentives to bring supermarkets back into the cities. The committee recommended, among other policy options, that "State and local governments should implement tax breaks and other incentives to ... small- and medium-sized grocery, and supermarket chains to encourage their expansion and/or relocation in low-income communities." Id. at 10; see also Urban Grocery Gap: Hearing Before the House Select Comm. on Hunger, 102d Cong., 2d Sess. (1992) (hearing devoted to various initiatives undertaken to encourage supermarket development in inner cities).

New Brunswick's initial efforts to respond to the problem were unsuccessful. It attempted to provide and organize transportation, an option that proved to be ineffective. It also sought to find a downtown property easily adaptable to supermarket use and to attract another supermarket operator to run it. Other than the George street store, however, there was none available.

Senator John Lynch, the Mayor of New Brunswick during the relevant period, testified that initial approaches to supermarket operators were unsuccessful because too much capital was required to rehabilitate and convert other buildings to supermarket use. According to Senator Lynch the "problem was making the bottom line work because of assembling the property, providing relocation costs, dealing with [environmental] laws, all of those things that add cost to the bottom line." Moreover, many properties that had conversion potential were unavailable or had other problems.

On the other hand, George Street, the former supermarket, was capable of being easily reconverted to supermarket use.

New Jersey courts have refused to enforce contracts that violate public policy. *See Vasquez v. Glassboro Service Ass'n, Inc.*, 83 N.J. 86, 104–05, 415 A.2d 1156 (1980) (contract requiring migrant farmworker to leave barracks immediately upon discharge violates public policy). "No contract can be sustained if it is inconsistent with the public interest or detrimental to the common good." *Id.* at 98, 415 A.2d 1156.

"The sources of public policy include federal and state legislation and judicial decisions." *Ibid.* The rehabilitation of our inner cities is a public policy of this State often expressed in relevant legislation.

The New Jersey Economic Development Authority Act (EDA), N.J.S.A. 34:1B–1 to–21, is intended to promote economic development generally throughout the State. As part of the EDA, the Legislature determined that the "provision of buildings, structures and other facilities to increase opportunity for employment in manufacturing, industrial, commercial, recreational, retail and service enterprises in the State is in the public interest." N.J.S.A. 34:1B–2b. The Legislature also specifically addressed the developmental problems of inner cities when it found:

> By virtue of their architectural and cultural heritage, their positions as principal centers of communication and transportation and their concentration of productive and energy efficient facilities, many municipalities are capable of ameliorating the conditions of deterioration which impede sound community growth and development; and that building a proper balance of housing, industrial and commercial facilities and increasing the attractiveness of such municipalities to persons of all income levels is essential to restoring such municipalities as desirable places to live, work, shop and enjoy life's amenities.

[N.J.S.A. 34:1B–2f (emphasis added).]

Similarly, in enacting the New Jersey Urban Enterprise Zones Act, N.J.S.A. 52:27H–60 to –89, the Legislature determined that "there persist in this State, particularly in its urban centers, areas of economic distress characterized by high unemployment, low investment of new capital, blighted conditions, obsolete or abandoned industrial or commercial structures, and deteriorating tax bases." N.J.S.A. 52:27H–61a. The Legislature also noted that revitalization of those areas required "application of the skills and entrepreneurial vigor of private enterprise; and it is the responsibility of government to provide a framework within which encouragement be given to private capital investment in these areas, disincentives to investment be removed or abated, and mechanisms be provided for the coordination and cooperation of private and public agencies in restoring the economic viability and prosperity of these areas." N.J.S.A. 52:27H–61 (emphasis added).

In support of these objectives, the Legislature offered a rich variety of subsidies and incentives to businesses operating in a designated enterprise zone. The City of New Brunswick currently is eligible for Open Competitive Urban Enterprise Zone Designation.

Other laws, too numerous to describe in detail, reveal how urban rehabilitation is imbedded in public policy and the public interest. * * *

Davidson's withdrawal from George Street caused difficulties and hardships of the nature mentioned earlier and made the downtown area a less hospitable and desirable place. Davidson had the right to terminate its George Street operation. In doing so, however, it imposed a restriction on the use of its former property designed to impede the relocation of another supermarket operation to the downtown area. The evidence supports the conclusion that the George Street store was peculiarly suited for supermarket use, and that there were no economically viable substitute locations. Consequently, the covenant, if enforced through injunctive relief or exposure to a judgment for damages, presented a formidable obstacle to remediation of the harm caused by Davidson's withdrawal. *Cf. Cipollone v. Liggett Group, Inc.*, 505 U.S. 2608, 112 S.Ct. 2608, 2620, 120 L.Ed.2d 407, 426 (1992) (obligation to pay damages is an effective method of controlling conduct). By harm, we mean the personal hardship caused by the withdrawal of a supermarket as well as the damage to the ongoing efforts of government and private enterprise to revitalize the city. We are persuaded, therefore, that, in the absence of any equivalent reciprocal benefit to the city, Davidson's scorched earth policy is so contrary to the public interest in these circumstances that the covenant is unreasonable and unenforceable. * * *

Affirmed.

Notes

1. The Davidson case demonstrates the intergovernmental nature of efforts to prevent urban decay and to reverse its serious consequences. It reveals the nature of the urban population left behind when businesses and affluent citizens move and the frustrations of developing strategies to serve that population's housing, health, and economic needs. Reference in the case to the New Jersey Economic Development Authority Act and its emphasis of remedial actions to promote employment in inner cities serves as an introduction to the next section on urban redevelopment.

2. Among the many initiatives of the federal government to help states and local governments build and rehabilitate urban housing and fight urban decay is one that complements the New Jersey program referred to in the note above and demonstrates the intergovernmental nature of these efforts. The Empowerment Zone/Enterprise Community (EZ/EC) program, established in 1993, is a federal initiative designed to create self-sustaining, long-term economic development in neighborhoods experiencing serious poverty and unemployment. The EZ/EC Program offers incentives for programs that provide business assistance, train and educate area residents, improve access to healthcare, and develop transportation. Eligible communities can receive tax incentives, performance grants, and loans.

SECTION 3. REDEVELOPING URBAN AREAS

A. INTRODUCTION

One of the most intriguing questions in municipal law is why one person's private property can be taken under the power of eminent domain to allow another private party to redevelop an area. In Berman v. Parker, 348 U.S. 26, 75 S.Ct. 98, 99 L.Ed. 27 (1954), the U.S. Supreme

Court noted that the public uses for which property may be taken under the power of eminent domain are coextensive with the police power of the state. Since the public welfare is broad and inclusive, the ends that may be achieved by using the power to condemn title to land include stemming blight and deterioration, redeveloping underdeveloped areas, and increasing the economic productivity of an area. The Berman court noted that the role of the judiciary in determining whether that power of eminent domain is being exercised for a public purpose is an extremely limited one.

The plaintiffs in Berman complained that their property, which contained a department store, could not be taken for a slum clearance project aimed at the elimination of squalid housing conditions. How, the plaintiffs asked, does it serve the public interest in stemming housing blight to condemn a commercial building in good repair? The court deferred to the urban renewal authority in the District of Columbia which had decided that area-wide blight could only be cured by an area-wide solution and, thus, it was necessary to take the plaintiffs' building whose existence and use did not conform to the urban renewal plan for the area.

The advocates of urban renewal won a short-lived victory in Berman. The questionable results of slum clearance and redevelopment came under fierce attack only a few years after the decision. The critics held that urban renewal fostered segregation, was responsible for the demolition of historic buildings, dislocated the urban poor, and wasted government resources. With the passage of the Housing and Community Development Act of 1974, federal urban renewal planning and project grants were folded into the special revenue sharing formula of the Community Development Block Grant program. The disappearance of dedicated urban renewal funding and a number of other categorical funding programs for urban areas added to the sense of ambivalence about the ability of cities to revitalize themselves.

This ambivalence has not curtailed the use of the power of eminent domain to take "blighted" property and commit it to redevelopment. Many challenges have been brought against condemnation schemes that take title to moderately blighted or underdeveloped properties so that commercial or industrial developers can acquire title to the land and develop commercial centers, mixed-use marina complexes, shopping plazas, light industrial parks, and other, more intensive, job-producing developments.

The role of the courts in reviewing the propriety of land condemnations is threefold: to be sure the condemning authority followed the procedures required by the state eminent domain law; to be sure the purpose for which the property is taken is a public one which, under Berman, is broadly defined; and to see that just compensation is paid. Condemning authorities do not have to demonstrate that their proposed redevelopment plans, in fact, will be beneficial. "Just" compensation does not mean enough money to reestablish your home or business; the standard is whether the authority paid the price that a willing buyer would pay a willing seller at the time of the condemnation. Since the properties taken are often in declining or underdeveloped areas, this price is sometimes quite modest.

B. DOWNTOWN RETAIL DEVELOPMENT

MINNEAPOLIS COMMUNITY DEVELOPMENT AGENCY v. OPUS NORTHWEST, LLC

Court of Appeals of Minnesota, 1998.
582 N.W.2d 596.

SCHUMACHER, JUDGE.

The city seeks to invoke the power of eminent domain to take two parcels of property located on Nicollet Mall in downtown Minneapolis. The condemnation is being undertaken to serve the city's desire to locate a mid-priced retail store, parking complex, extended skyway access, and an office building in the south Nicollet Mall area. Due to the high cost of downtown property, the city has used tax increment financing to attract a mid-priced retailer to locate downtown.

The city has been unsuccessful for a number of years in bringing development projects to south Nicollet Mall. There has been no large-scale development in the area for a number of years, and the city complains that a lack of skyway connections, insufficient parking, and parcelization of land ownership prevents projects that could improve the tax base and economy of the area. In the mid–1980s, the city designated the area as a redevelopment district and a tax increment financing district. At that time, it made detailed findings supporting those designations. In 1996, before commencing the Ryan–Dayton Hudson project, the city updated and confirmed its earlier findings.

The city is contracting with Ryan Corporation for the development, construction, and eventual ownership of much of the project. The retail store will be owned and operated by the Dayton Hudson Corporation, which will place a Target store on the first and second floors of the building (hereinafter Dayton Hudson and Target collectively referred to as Dayton Hudson).

Opus is the owner of the two parcels being condemned. Before the city and Dayton Hudson chose Ryan, Opus also bid on the project, but it was not chosen because, among other reasons, Opus could not secure a mid-priced retailer as an anchor tenant. Opus now proposes to build a $120 million office building on its property without any government subsidies, however, its current proposal still does not contain a mid-priced anchor retailer. Opus objected to the condemnation proceedings.

Minneapolis ordinances require contractors to file affirmative action plans before doing business with the city. Dayton Hudson has not filed an affirmative action plan with the city. Opus, as a private taxpayer under the tax increment financing statutes, challenges the legality of the overall project.

* * *

From the 19th century to the present, the judiciary's review of condemnation proceedings has remained "very narrow." *State ex rel. Simpson v. Rapp*, 39 Minn. 65, 67, 38 N.W. 926, 928 (1888); *County of Dakota* (C.P.46–06) *v. Lakeville*, 559 N.W.2d 716, 719 (Minn.App.1997). We review only whether the taking serves a public purpose and is necessary. *City of Duluth v. State*, 390 N.W.2d 757, 763, 764 (Minn. 1986).

> Great weight must be given to the determination of the condemning authority, and the scope of review is narrowly limited. If it appears that the record contains some evidence, however informal, that the taking serves a public purpose, there is nothing left for the courts to pass upon. * * * The court is precluded from substituting its own judgment for that of the [public body] as to what may be necessary and proper to carry out the purpose of the plan.

Id. at 763 (quoting *Housing & Redev. Auth. v. Minneapolis Metro. Co.*, 259 Minn. 1, 15, 104 N.W.2d 864, 874 (1960)). Public purpose and necessity are questions of fact, and the district court's decisions on these matters will not be reversed on appeal unless clearly erroneous. *State by Humphrey v. Byers*, 545 N.W.2d 669, 672 (Minn.App.1996).

Opus admits that this court should show deference to the city's legislative condemnation findings but contends that the deference should not be "slavish." Opus argues that "substantial authority" requires that we apply a "heightened scrutiny" to any condemnation that benefits private interests. Opus's foreign authority, however, is distinguishable. *See Wilmington Parking Auth. v. Land With Improvements*, 521 A.2d 227, 230–31 (Del.1986) (government parking authority acted outside its narrow statutory parking power when underlying purpose of condemnation was to benefit newspaper, not create parking); *City of Lansing v. Edward Rose Realty, Inc.*, 442 Mich. 626, 502 N.W.2d 638, 645 (1993) (city sought to condemn apartment building because owner refused to use city's franchised cable company; court held condemnation served no public purpose because there was no statutory grant of power to allow access for cable T.V., and public benefit was not clear and predominant); *Poletown Neighborhood Council v. City of Detroit*, 410 Mich. 616, 304 N.W.2d 455, 457, 459 (1981) (court, despite announcing it was using heightened standard, affirmed Detroit's condemnation of land to allow General Motors to construct assembly plant to increase employment and revitalize economic base of community); *City of Ctr. Line v. Chmelko*, 164 Mich.App. 251, 416 N.W.2d 401, 402 (1987) (city's condemnation was "complete fiction" because city acted as agent for local car dealer and alleged public purposes were not supported by the evidence); *City of*

Jamestown v. Leevers Supermarkets, Inc., 552 N.W.2d 365, 372, 374 (N.D.1996) (case remanded for court to determine if "primary object" was public; court noted trend is to allow broad legislative discretion to use powers of eminent domain for variety of economic development purposes).

Unlike the condemnations criticized in *City of Lansing* and *Wilmington Parking*, the condemnation of Opus's property falls within the city's prescribed authority. Additionally, it appears that the application of a heightened level of scrutiny to review condemnation proceedings, for which Opus cites these foreign cases, is out of touch with the national trend. 2A *Nichols on Eminent Domain*, § 7.06[24][c], at p. 7–242 (Matthew Bender revised 3d ed.1998) (trend is to sanction "broad legislative discretion to use eminent domain for a variety of economic development purposes.").

Finally, Opus's foreign authority is inconsistent with Minnesota caselaw. Minnesota courts have not employed a heightened standard of review in appeals involving governmental condemnation benefiting private parties. *See, e.g., City of Duluth*, 390 N.W.2d at 763–64 (condemnation of Jeno Paulucci's Chun King plant to allow a paper mill to be built); *City of Minneapolis v. Wurtele*, 291 N.W.2d 386, 390 (Minn.1980) (condemnation of private property to construct City Center in downtown Minneapolis). We reject the invitation to change our well-established and limited standard of review.

What constitutes a "public use" or "public purpose" is broadly defined. *City of Duluth*, 390 N.W.2d at 763. As noted, it includes a city's acquisition of private property for use by a different private entity. *Id.* at 763–64. If there is some evidence in the record that the taking serves a public purpose, there is nothing left for the court to decide. *Id.*

Condemnation efforts undertaken to enhance deteriorating urban areas and to create jobs satisfy the public purpose aspect of a condemnation proceeding. *Id.* at 763; *see also Wurtele*, 291 N.W.2d at 390. The legislature has recognized that actions taken to foster new development, including the financing thereof, "in areas of a city that are already built up in order to provide employment opportunities, to improve the tax base, and to improve the general economy of the state * * * are [examples of] a public purpose." Minn.Stat. § 469.124 (1996). In this case, the city presented testimony that the proposed project will have the following benefits: a mid-priced retail store, increased parking, increased employment, increased tax base, extension of the skyway system, unification of the multiple-ownership/parcelization of the area, modernization of outdated and incompatible buildings, and furtherance of the city's ultimate objective of creating an economically viable retail corridor between downtown businesses and the convention/hospitality district. The city also presented evidence that these objectives will not be met by Opus's proposal or without the city's involvement. The finding of public purpose in this case is consistent with the authority granted by the legislature in section 469.124 , and it is not clearly erroneous.

Absolute necessity is not required for a finding of public purpose, rather "[i]t is enough to find that 'the proposed taking is *reasonably necessary* or *convenient* for the furtherance of a proper purpose.' " *City of Duluth*, 390 N.W.2d at 764–65 (quoting *City of Pipestone v. Halbersma*, 294 N.W.2d 271, 274 (Minn.1980)) (emphasis added). A party challenging the necessity of the condemnation of a parcel will not succeed by merely suggesting alternatives to the government's plan. *Id.* at 766. Accordingly, Opus's argument, to the extent that it relies on Opus's own plan to build an alternative tower, is not persuasive.

The heart of Opus's appeal involves challenges to the legality and attainability of the city's condemnation. Any corporation contracting with the City of Minneapolis must have an affirmative action plan filed with the city. Minneapolis, Minn., Code of Ordinances (hereinafter MCO) § 139.50(b), (c) (1997). The city ordinance applies specifically to tax increment financing contracts and to owner-occupants of any project financed through tax increment financing. MCO § 139.50(d) (1997) (citing Minnesota Tax Increment Financing Act). Dayton Hudson will be the eventual owner occupant of the tax-increment-financed, mid-priced retail store. Dayton Hudson, however, does not have an affirmative action plan on record with the city and is not currently permitted to contract with the city for that reason. Opus contends that the condemnation is, therefore, illegal.

Opus relies on three early Minnesota Supreme Court cases in support of its argument. In each of those cases, the supreme court found that the proposed condemnation of rivers and lakes to create a utility plant was illegal and, therefore, the condemnations could not go forward. See *Minnesota Canal & Power Co. v. Fall Lake Boom Co.*, 127 Minn. 23, 31–32, 148 N.W. 561, 564 (1914) (condemnation denied, despite approval by U.S. government, because Minnesota Canal, in order to make its plant work, would need to obtain greater amounts of navigable water than allowed by state statute); *Minnesota Canal & Power Co. v. Pratt*, 101 Minn. 197, 222–23, 112 N.W. 395, 401–02 (1907) (condemnation prohibited because, despite change in state laws, waters in question were also federal and Minnesota Canal did not receive permission from U.S. government); *Minnesota Canal & Power Co. v. Koochiching Co.*, 97 Minn. 429, 443, 107 N.W. 405, 410 (1906) (condemnation prohibited due to absence of state and federal laws allowing alienability of navigable waters).

In sum, the *Minnesota Canal* trilogy stands for the proposition that a condemning authority cannot undertake a public project if the project itself is not permitted by law. The public purposes for the present condemnation (obtaining a mid-priced retail store, increased public parking and employment, etc.) and the means of accomplishment (through tax increment financing for Ryan) are all legal. In the *Minnesota Canal* cases, however, the diversion of lakes and rivers, no matter how attempted, was not permitted by law.

In addition, Opus's challenge to the legality of Dayton Hudson's occupancy is anticipatory. The ordinance requires an owner-occupant of a tax-increment-financed project to file an affirmative action plan with the city. It is contemplated that Dayton Hudson will be the *eventual* owner-occupant of the mid-priced retail store included in this project, but Dayton Hudson is not a *current* owner-occupant and is not now in violation of MCO § 139.50. In its brief and at oral argument, the city argued that the goals for which condemnation was initiated are not dependent on a specific retailer or developer. To date, the city has signed a development contract with Ryan; neither that agreement nor the contemplated building of a mid-priced retail store is illegal. In the event Dayton Hudson violates the city ordinance, a controversy will exist upon which a court can pass judgment. *See Izaak Walton League of Am. Endowment, Inc. v. State, Dep't of Natural Resources*, 312 Minn. 587, 589, 252 N.W.2d 852, 854 (1977) ("The existence of a justiciable controversy is prerequisite to adjudication. The judicial function does not comprehend the giving of advisory opinions."). Because there is no existing illegality affecting the project as a whole, we decline to speculate on the likelihood of a future violation of MCO § 139.50. The condemnation is not barred by the fact that Dayton Hudson does not have an affirmative action plan on file with the city.

Opus also argues that there can be no proper or necessary purpose if the project for which property is condemned is too speculative, relying on a Wisconsin case holding that a private owner is "entitled to have it shown that the taking is for a public use definite and certain of attainment." *Schumm v. Milwaukee County*, 258 Wis. 256, 45 N.W.2d 673, 676 (1951). In *Schumm*, a non-profit group and the county entered into negotiations for condemnation of property upon which the non-profit group intended to construct war memorials. *Id.*, 45 N.W.2d at 674. Without any of the necessary resolutions, the county instructed its counsel to commence condemnation proceedings. *Id.*, 45 N.W.2d at 675. There was no valid contract between the county and the non-profit group. *Id.*, 45 N.W.2d at 676. There were numerous details to be resolved, including the specifications for the memorials, the amount of money required, whether resolutions would be passed, and whether the city in which the proposed memorials were to be placed would grant permission to the county. *Id.*, 45 N.W.2d at 677. The county's agreement with the group was too riddled with uncertainty to justify the taking of private property. *Id.*

Opus suggests that the lack of finality to some details of the development agreement between the city and Ryan render the project similar to that in *Schumm* and too speculative to justify condemnation. This case differs substantially and significantly from *Schumm*. First, the city supports and has passed resolutions directing the project to go forward. Second, there is a written contract between the city and Ryan and Dayton Hudson is committed to the project, assuming that this litigation can be resolved. Third, funding is in place through the tax increment financing plan and Ryan. Fourth, while there have been no negotiations with owners on block 34, this is within the city's control, and there is no need to secure the approval of a distinct governing authority. Finally, the contingencies that exist appear to be normal for this stage and type of development, and Opus has presented no evidence that the Ryan-city contract is out of the ordinary.

The trial court concluded that there was no evidence to suggest that the project would not be completed once the cloud of litigation was removed. The relative certainty of this project stands in marked contrast to the ambiguity and uncertainty of the plans for the property to be condemned by the county in *Schumm*. Considering our standard of review, the trial court's finding that the public purpose of the project is proper and not speculative is supported by the evidence and is not clearly erroneous.

Opus challenges the use of tax increment financing money in this project as a private taxpayer under Minn.Stat. § 469.1771, subd. 1(a) (1996). The statute provides:

> The owner of taxable property located in the city, town, school district, or county in which the tax increment financing district is located may bring suit for equitable relief or for damages, as provided in subdivisions 3 and 4, arising out of a failure of a municipality or authority to comply with the provisions of sections 469.174 to 469.179, or related provisions of this chapter.

Id. This court reviews statutory construction de novo. *Hibbing Educ. Ass'n v. Public Employment Relations Bd.*, 369 N.W.2d 527, 529 (Minn. 1985). Findings of fact and credibility determinations, upon which the trial courts base legal conclusions, will not be set aside unless clearly erroneous. Minn. R. Civ. P. 52.01.

In 1983, the city declared the area in question on the south Nicollet Mall to be a redevelopment district. In 1985, the area in question was designated as tax increment financing District 63. Opus has not challenged the findings supporting either decision. In 1996, before the city condemned Opus's property, it made new, summary findings that updated and confirmed the findings made in 1983 and 1985. At issue is whether the tax increment financing statute required the city's 1996 findings and, if so, whether they were sufficiently detailed. The city's 1996 findings concluded that private investment would not be forthcoming and that tax increment financing would generate higher property values than any purely private investment.

Before a tax increment financing district can be created, a municipality must make the necessary findings. Minn.Stat. § 469.175, subd. 3 (1996). Once the district is properly created, however, a municipality may *modify* a tax increment financing plan with *no specified procedure or findings* unless modification includes an increase in the bonded indebtedness or there are other circumstances identified in the statute and not present here. Minn.Stat. § 469.175, subd. 4 (1996). Specifically, in the absence of changes specified in Minn.Stat. § 469.175, subd. 4, changes to an existing tax increment financing plan constitute "modification" for which no new findings are required and no procedure is prescribed by the statute.

Under Minn.Stat. § 469.175, subd. 1(a)(5)(ii) (1996), an original tax increment financing district plan must include an estimate of the "amount of bonded indebtedness to be incurred." The original tax increment financing plan for this area anticipated that $157 million of indebtedness would be incurred. It appears that only two projects financed by tax increment financing ever drew on the authorized total indebtedness. These projects total $36.4 million. Because the current project is estimated to cost $62 million, the three projects do not exceed the total estimated indebtedness. Accordingly, since the "amount of bonded indebtedness" is not being increased, the 1996 decision is a mere modification of the existing plan and Minn.Stat. § 469.175, subd. 4 does not require the city to issue new, detailed findings. We affirm the trial court's conclusion that Opus failed to establish the existence of a statutory violation.

The trial court's findings of public purpose and necessity are supported by the evidence and are not clearly erroneous. The failure of Dayton Hudson to file an affirmative action plan does not render the project illegal. Further, because the project is supported by the city and is the subject of a contract between the city and Ryan, the condemnation is not based on speculation. Finally, the city was not required to make new findings because the current project does not require an increase in the amount of bonded indebtedness authorized in the original tax increment financing plan.

Affirmed.

Notes

1. Note that Minneapolis designated the Nicollet Mall area a redevelopment district in 1983 and an area eligible for tax increment financing in 1985, in the waning years of federal urban renewal funding. Tax increment financing ("TIF") statutes were adopted in many states to provide an alternative method of financing redevelopment. Earlier Minnesota cases had consistently upheld the tax increment financing approach to redevelopment. In R.E. Short Co. v. City of Minneapolis, 269 N.W.2d 331 (1978), the first Minnesota opinion on tax increment financing, the court stated:

> The purpose of tax-increment financing of urban redevelopment is to create economically productive property where none presently exists by providing inducements to private commercial development. The municipality, either with or without the power of eminent domain, acquires all the property in an area in which the value of real estate is declining or there is a high proportion of underutilized or tax-delinquent land. Pursuant to a development plan for the area, the municipality then delineates a number of new disposition parcels which it markets to private developers. Inducements to such private development include promises to construct certain support facilities or various other types of incentives affording substantial savings to the developer. Once the land becomes productive, the increment over the prior tax revenues is uti-

lized to pay off the interest and principal on the bonds issued to finance the redevelopment, and the municipality retains in its general treasury the amount equal to the former tax revenue from the area. After the bonds are paid off, the area is expected to remain economically productive, providing substantially increased tax revenues for municipal government.

This philosophy of development financing underlays the decision to create the Loring Park Development District just south of downtown Minneapolis. Acting pursuant to L.1971, c. 677, the city council established this district by a resolution dated June 9, 1972. At that time, there were 58 privately owned land parcels, many of which were economically unproductive. The goal of the Loring Park Development District was to renew the area by the private construction of additional residential units, convention and hotel facilities, and various other commercial enterprises. The city also planned to upgrade the public works and beautify the district by constructing the Loring Greenway. All of this development, the city council determined, would provide not only employment during the construction phase of the project but also additional permanent employment, increased tax revenues, and a more productive tax base for the district and the city. In April 1973, the city held the first of four bond sales, and in August it began acquisition of the land, first by purchase and, after April 1974, by eminent domain proceedings. The district was then replatted into 14 disposition parcels which were to be offered to developers willing to construct structures that would conform to the alternative land uses outlined in the development program.

2. Tax increment financing statutes allow cities or redevelopment authorities to issue bonds secured by the increase in property tax revenues that the newly redeveloped land will generate for the city. This projected increase in taxes becomes the revenue stream used to pay the principal and interest on bonds sold to private investors. Because these are considered public bonds, the interest paid to investors is tax exempt and therefore lower than interest paid on private financing from commercial lenders. By issuing and selling these bonds, the authority secures the capital needed, up front, to purchase land, install infrastructure, or lower the cost of the enterprise so that it becomes economically feasible. Often, the TIF program is entwined with a state statutory enterprise zone enabling act that allows cities to offer zoning and tax incentives for redevelopment in the poorest areas of cities.

3. In accord with the principal case is Richards v. Muscatine, 237 N.W.2d 48 (Iowa 1975), which upheld tax increment financing against an attack that alleged a disparate burden on taxpayers outside the redevelopment area for the duration of the project; the court also rejected an argument that the scheme violated a constitutional provision on uniformity of taxation, holding that the private developer pays taxes on his development at the same rate as all other taxpayers. See also Brady v. Dubuque, 495 N.W.2d 701 (Iowa 1993), in which the Iowa Supreme Court confirmed the validity of a tax increment program. Compare Miller v. Covington Development Auth., 539 S.W.2d 1 (Ky.1976), where the court held tax increment financing violative of the state constitution and struck down the statute with State v. Miami Beach Redevelopment Agency, 392 So.2d 875 (Fla.1980),

upholding the Florida statute. Penn v. Florida Def. Fin. & Accounting Serv. Ctr. Auth., 623 So.2d 459 (Fla.1993), constitutes the Supreme Court of Florida's most recent validation of the tax increment financing scheme.

Most of the decisions that consider a broad constitutional attack on the tax increment financing programs have upheld the device. In addition to the principal case and those cited above, see Tax Increment Financing Comm'n of Kansas City v. J.E. Dunn Construction Co., Inc., 781 S.W.2d 70 (Mo.1989); In re Request for Advisory Opinion on Constitutionality of 1986 PA 281, 430 Mich. 93, 422 N.W.2d 186 (1988); City of El Paso v. El Paso Community College Dist., 729 S.W.2d 296 (Tex.1986); Wolper v. City Council of City of Charleston, 287 S.C. 209, 336 S.E.2d 871 (1985); Meierhenry v. City of Huron, 354 N.W.2d 171 (S.D.1984); Oklahoma City Urban Renewal Auth. v. Medical Tech. & Research Auth., 2000 OK 23, 4 P.3d 677 (2000); Kuehn, Tax Increment Financing, Land Use Law (May, 1985) p. 3.

4. The Opus decision pinpoints a critical and ubiquitous problem: parcelization. This term refers to the problem caused by the multiple ownership of many small parcels in a proposed urban redevelopment area. By using eminent domain and working with a qualified and eligible redeveloper, cities can unify parcel ownership, create an efficient scale of operations, and hope to attract investment capital and project funding for truly viable projects. When aided by techniques such as tax increment financing, projects become even more feasible. Is there real hope for urban areas in this blueprint for redevelopment? As land values rise in suburban and fringe areas and as the population sprawls out with attendant property tax increases, open space disappearance, and traffic congestion, do opportunities arise to reinvest in existing urban areas, using these and other revitalization techniques? If the answer is no, then where will new households formed as the population increases settle? How much of the projected increase in the nation's population can be counted on to locate in urbanized areas as opposed to the greenfields farther out? In attempting to answer these questions, one can see more clearly the connection between urban revitalization and suburban settlements and between the forces of economic development and environmental conservation.

C. PROMOTING BROWNFIELD REDEVELOPMENT

Another method of keeping density in the right place and preventing urban sprawl is brownfield redevelopment. In many communities, former industrial properties blight the landscape and remain unrealized economic opportunities. Brownfields are abandoned, idled, or under-used industrial and commercial facilities where expansion or redevelopment is complicated by real or perceived environmental contamination. Nationwide, there are over 450,000 brownfields.

Brownfield redevelopment is an important smart growth technique for a variety of reasons. First, by remediating contaminated properties, the environmental threat presented by these sites is eliminated, thereby protecting the health of the community. Second, when redeveloped, the formerly abandoned sites generate tax revenue for the community. Third, by developing brownfield sites, which are typically located in more urbanized areas, some development pressure is removed from outlying greenfields. Fourth, communities can use brownfields to meet various planning objectives such as the creation of affordable housing or additional commercial development.

Because brownfields are often contaminated from past operations, they present economic and public policy challenges to their host communities. Developers are often reluctant to engage in redevelopment efforts because of the liability that may be imposed upon them under the Comprehensive Environmental Response, Compensation and Liability Act (CERCLA, 42 U.S.C. § 9601 *et seq.*). CERCLA and similar laws adopted by many states impose strict, joint, and several liability upon an owner or operator of a site where contamination is present, regardless of whether that person caused the pollution. Consequently, a developer could be liable for millions of dollars of remediation costs simply by purchasing a site with hazardous contamination. This potential liability causes many brownfield sites to lie fallow.

As a means to encourage the redevelopment of brownfields, a number of states have enacted statutes to reduce liability and have created programs that provide financial incentives to redevelopers. Congress helped as well by adopting the Small Business Liability Relief and Brownfields Revitalization Act. Pub. L. No. 107–118, 115 Stat. 2355 (2002). The law provides some relief from liability for bona fide purchasers who meet certain conditions and contains various funding mechanisms for brownfield revitalization.

The following case involves the acquisition of contaminated parcels by a city redevelopment agency. It illustrates the complex legal issues that arise in this context regarding the high costs of remediation, liability that can arise under CERCLA, and rights to collect from other parties for to cover the costs of cleanup.

EMERYVILLE v. ELEMENTIS PIGMENTS, INC.

United States District Court, N.D. California, 2001.
2001 WL 964230, 52 ERC 1648.

ALSUP, DISTRICT J.

INTRODUCTION

The City of Emeryville paid for the costs of cleaning up the soil and groundwater on land that it obtained, then brought suit against defendants and others to recover its cleanup costs under the Comprehensive Environmental Response, Compensation, and Liability Act, 42 U.S.C. 9601 et. seq. The plaintiffs, the City of Emeryville and the Emeryville Redevelopment Agency proceed on two theories. The City's primary theory is that defendants, Elementis Pigments, Incorporated and Pfizer, Incorporated, are responsible to pay the City for all of its cleanup costs. In the alternative, if the City is unable to sue for cost recovery, it seeks contribution. EPI has counterclaimed against the City for contribution. In a letter to the Court dated March 2, 2001, the City stated that it would "dismiss its second claim for relief (contribution under CERCLA Section 113) if the Court grants [the City's] motion for summary judgment." This order GRANTS the City's motion for summary judgment on EPI's counterclaims, DENIES EPI's motion for summary judgment on the City's cause of action for cost recovery and DISMISSES WITHOUT PREJUDICE the City's cause of action for contribution. The City's state law tort claims shall be addressed in a separate order.

STATEMENT

The property at issue consists of approximately 15 acres located east of Interstate 80, west of the tracks of the Union Pacific Railroad, south of Powell Street, and north of the new IKEA store in Emeryville. A site-map submitted by the City's experts is provided below. At present, the City owns all the areas depicted in the map. * * * Historically, the property at issue in this action was divided into four parcels: the McKinley parcel, the Sepulveda parcel, the Elementis parcel, and the Old Shellmound Street parcel.

Temescal Creek bisects the property and drains westward into the San Francisco Bay. According to the City's experts, the soil and groundwater on the property is contaminated with lead, arsenic, other heavy metals, petroleum hydrocarbons, volatile and semi-volatile organic compounds, pesticides, and a number of other toxins (Doty Decl., Exh. 2).

In 1903, part of the property was occupied by Shell Mound Park. The park consisted of a race track, two dancing pavilions, a bowling alley, shooting galleries, a restaurant, and other entertainment facilities. Industrial operations began around the 1920's (ibid.).

The Sherwin–Williams Company owned the northern third of the site and manufactured pesticides there from approximately the 1920's until the early 1960's. Part of the land Sherwin–Williams used comprises what is now the Elementis parcel. Both sides agree that Sherwin–Williams caused a significant amount of contamination at the site.

In the late 1940's, Sherwin–Williams ceased its pesticide operations on the Sepulveda parcel. From around 1950 until the 1990's, Josephine and Arthur Sepulveda operated A & J Trucking on what is now the Sepulveda parcel. A trust related to them also ran a small trucking business there. In the course of these operations, petroleum hydrocarbons and perhaps solvents were stored in underground tanks, which leaked.

Sherwin–Williams sold the McKinley parcel to Dorothy Warburton in 1965. The McKinley parcel was paved and used as a warehouse for the Artificial Flower Association and a storage area for an electric-sign business. In 1981, she sold the property to Richard McKinley. Under the name Develco, Baker–Hughes operated a machine shop on the McKinley parcel from around 1982 to 1992. Develco generated metal shavings and solvent wastes.

From the 1920's to 1990, Pfizer, Inc. and Pfizer Pigments, Inc. and C.K. Williams manufactured and packaged iron-oxide pigments on the Elementis parcel. C.K. Williams merged into Pfizer in 1962. In 1990, Pfizer sold its land and operations to Harcros Pigments, Inc. In 1992, Harcros changed its name to Elementis. Elementis ceased production in 1998.

* * *

Acquisition of the Property

In 1995, the City began negotiating with the Sepulvedas and Mr. McKinley to acquire their parcels, but the parties were unable to agree. The City then initiated the statutorily-required procedures for taking the land by eminent domain. On May 22, 1998, the City made an offer of just compensation to Mr. McKinley. On August 17, 1998, the City submitted a similar offer to the Sepulvedas, which the City modified on September 17, 1998. Subsequently, the City issued notices of intent to adopt resolutions of necessity for acquisition of both parcels. These notices sought public participation in whether to institute eminent domain proceedings. On October 20, 1998, a public meeting was held, and these resolutions were formally adopted. The resolutions directed the City to file an action in state court to acquire title to the two parcels. Instead, the City purchased the Sepulveda parcel in November of 1998 and the McKinley parcel in February of 1999, expressly reserving the right to sue for cleanup costs.

In the mid-1990's the City began negotiating with EPI to purchase EPI's parcel. According to the City, in November of 1997, the City offered EPI $9.8 million in exchange for EPI's land if EPI would clean the site to the satisfaction of the Department of Toxic Substances Control, a state environmental agency. EPI never responded to the offer, and the City sent EPI an offer of just compensation. On January 14, 1998, EPI filed an inverse condemnation action against the City in state court. On January 22, 1998, the City issued a notice of intent to adopt resolutions of necessity for acquisition of defendants' parcel. The resolution was adopted at a public meeting on February 18, 1998. On February 19, 1998, the City filed an eminent domain action against EPI, seeking title to EPI's parcel.

On the same day that the City filed its eminent domain action, EPI entered into a voluntary cleanup agreement with the DTSC. On June 8, 1998, one of the City's attorneys sent a letter to the DTSC, requesting the DTSC to terminate its agreement with EPI. The letter stated that although EPI "was aware of serious contamination on its site no later than early 1996" it had done nothing to clean up the property. The letter claimed that EPI and Sherwin–Williams wished to pursue less expensive cleanup measures than the ones the City proposed and that EPI and Sherwin–Williams were unduly delaying the cleanup process and preventing the City from obtaining regulatory approval to clean up the adjoining properties. On June 23, 1998, the Alameda Superior Court granted plaintiffs prejudgment possession of EPI's parcel. On June 26, the DTSC terminated EPI's voluntary cleanup agreement. On January 11, 1999, after a hearing, a state court held that the City was "authorized to take the property by eminent domain."

* * *

Cleanup

In 1997, prior to attempting to acquire the land, the City conducted an investigation into contamination at the site. In 1998, it entered into an oversight and consultation agreement with the DTSC. Under DTSC oversight, the City's consultants progressed through the various phases of remediation: they conducted a remedial investigation and prepared health risk assessment, a feasibility study and a draft remedial action plan. With DTSC approval, the remedial action plan was finalized into a final remedial action plan and then a remedial design implementation plan. In 1999, all the buildings on-site were demolished. Beginning in May of 1999, contractors removed and disposed of more than 25,000 cubic yards of contaminated soil and 635,000 gallons of contaminated water. On May 8, 2000, the DTSC sent a letter to the City certifying that the project was complete under state law. The final remedial action plan requires groundwater monitoring for the next five years. If further groundwater contamination is discovered, treatment may be necessary.

* * *

On August 4, 1999, the City filed suit herein against Sherwin–Williams, the Sepulvedas and Sepulveda trustees, Baker–Hughes, Pfizer, and Elementis, seeking relief under CERCLA and state law for cleanup costs. On February 15, 2001, Sherwin–Williams, the Sepulvedas and the Sepulveda trustees, and Baker–Hughes all settled, and their settlement was approved.

ANALYSIS

* * *

The City's Liability

The main issue is whether the City can be held liable under CERCLA for any of the cleanup costs it incurred. Since the City cannot be held liable for the reasons stated below, it is entitled to summary judgment on EPI's counterclaims for contribution, and its cost recovery claim will proceed to trial.

Congress passed CERCLA to ensure the cleanup of hazardous waste. *Wickland Oil Terminals v. Asarco, Inc.*, 792 F.2d 887, 890 (9th Cir.1986). With few exceptions, anyone who has ever polluted a property or who currently owns contaminated real estate can be held liable for the entire cost of cleaning up the land, regardless of fault. While liability is expansive, the statue provides two mechanisms for recovering cleanup costs from those actually responsible: cost recovery under Section 9607 and contribution under Section 9613. When a plaintiff is also a party that can be held liable under CERCLA (for instance, one of many industrial tenants that used the same property), a plaintiff may only sue for contribution under Section 9613. *Pinal Creek Group v. Newmont Mining Corp.*, 118 F.3d 1298, 1306 (9th Cir.1997). This limitation is important, because under Section 9607 (cost recovery), a plaintiff may hold any defendant jointly and severally liable for the entire cleanup cost, whereas under Section 9613 (contribution), a plaintiff may only sue a defendant for that defendant's share of the costs. Ibid.

To establish that a defendant is liable under CERCLA, a plaintiff must prove that there was a "release" of a "hazardous substance" from a "facility," and this caused the plaintiff to incur "response costs." A plaintiff must also prove that a defendant falls within one, or more, of four categories, two of which are relevant here:

> (1) the owner and operator of a vessel or facility,
>
> (2) any person who at the time of disposal of any hazardous substance owned or operated any facility at which such hazardous substances were disposed of....

42 U.S.C. 9607 (a)(1)-(2). There is no dispute that releases of hazardous substances occurred on the properties at issue, and that this has caused plaintiffs to incur response costs. The point of contention is whether the City fits into any of the statutory categories of "responsible parties," namely a prior "owner or operator," or a current "owner." EPI advances several theories of liability, which shall be considered in turn.

(i) Prior Owner

EPI has not established a genuine issue of material fact as to whether the City was a prior "owner" as defined by CERCLA. * * *

* * *

(ii) Prior Operator

Similarly, EPI has not raised a factual issue as to whether the City was ever an operator within the meaning of CERCLA. * * *

* * *

(iii) Current Owner

In response to EPI's contention that the City is liable as a current owner, the City has asserted CERCLA's "innocent landowner" defense. This defense provides complete immunity to current owner liability when (1) the owner did not cause any of the contamination; (2) the contamination was not caused by an agent of the owner; (3) the owner was not in a "contractual relationship" with the person who caused the contamination; (4) the owner exercised "due care" regarding the contamination; and (5) the owner took precautions against foreseeable acts by third persons. 42 U.S.C. 9607 (b)(4). As already noted, EPI has not raised an factual issue as to whether the City or any of its agents caused the contamination. EPI instead directs its attack on the "contractual relationship'' element. The term ''contractual relationship'' is defined to include land purchases, but to exclude when a ''government entity acquire[s] the facility by escheat, or through any other involuntary transfer or acquisition, or through the exercise of eminent domain authority by purchase or condemnation.'' 42 U.S.C. 9601 (35)(A)(ii).

EPI argues that because the City purchased the McKinley and Sepulveda parcels, the City did not exercise its eminent domain authority and cannot assert the innocent landowner defense. In EPI's view, the innocent landowner defense is unavailable unless a municipality obtains a property by filing an action for eminent domain. The Ninth Circuit has not addressed what the phrase ''exercise of eminent domain authority by purchase or condemnation'' means, and the legislative history regarding the meaning of this phrase is silent.

While defenses to CERCLA liability are narrowly circumscribed, EPI's reading of the phrase ''exercise of eminent domain authority by purchase or condemnation'' is too constricted. The statute's plain language does not require any type of eminent domain proceeding. Rather, it uses the broader phrase ''exercise of eminent domain authority.'' Additionally, the words ''by purchase or condemnation'' encompass purchases and do not limit the defense to the result of a judicial proceeding. It is doubtful that Congress intended to require senseless litigation as a prerequisite to the defense or to saddle state courts with unnecessary litigation, as this would frustrate CERCLA's purpose of ensuring ''the prompt and effective cleanup of waste disposal sites.'' *Mardan Corp. v. C.G.C. Music, Ltd.*, 804 F.2d 1454, 1455 (9th Cir.1986) (citing 126 Cong. Rec. 31964 (statement of Rep. Florio)).

* * *

[In California], state law expressly contemplates government entities exercising their ''eminent domain authority'' without resorting to litigation. It is undisputed that the City followed all the eminent domain procedures required by state law. It did everything short of filing a complaint and litigating. It made ''every reasonable effort'' to buy the land, terminating the dispute without a lawsuit, as required by law. The City has duly exercised its eminent domain authority within the meaning of CERCLA Section 9601(35).

The due-care requirement is met when a party promptly attempts to remove the environmental hazards on its land. *State of New York v. Lashins Arcade. Co.*, 91 F.3d 353, 360–61 (2d Cir.1996) (citing H .R. Rep. No. 1016 at 34 (1980)). The numerous remedial plans and reports provided by the City demonstrate that it diligently pursued remediation from the time it obtained the property in 1998 until the time the DTSC certified that the cleanup was complete in May of 2000. EPI claims that Mr. James' testimony creates a material issue of fact about whether the City was aware of the contamination since the 1940's. As already discussed, Mr. James' testimony does not link the City to the contamination or show that the City was aware of it in any way. EPI offers no other evidence to support its contention that the City lacked due care.

Nor does it offer any evidence to contradict the City's evidence that from the initiation of demolition through completion of the soil remediation activities, the site was fenced-off and subject to 24–hour security to prevent foreseeable acts or omissions by third-parties (James Decl. P 5). EPI fails to raise a genuine issue of material fact as to whether the City exercised due care or took precautions against acts of third persons.

Because EPI has established no triable theory under which the City could be held liable for the on-site contamination, the City's motion for summary judgment as to the counterclaims for contribution under CERCLA and California Health and Safety Code Sections 15300 et. seq., which mirrors CERCLA, is granted. Additionally, EPI's motion for summary judgment on the City's cause of action for cost recovery under Section 9607 is denied. The City's cause of action for contribution under Section 9613 is dismissed without prejudice, so that it may "pursue the contribution claims should further proceedings, such as an appeal, result in a determination" that it is liable (Plaintiffs' Letter, dated March 2, 2001).

* * *

Notes

1. The principal case introduces the urban renewal or urban redevelopment agency as a key player in urban revitalization efforts. Such agencies are established by local governments under statutes adopted by state legislatures. Typically, they are independent agencies that operate outside the legal constraints that limit municipalities and give them the ability to be entrepreneurial in pursuit of urban redevelopment and to work closely with private sector redevelopers. These "quasi-public" bodies are controlled to some degree by their local governments. Their boards of directors include ex-officio appointments such as the local mayor or individuals appointed by the mayor or city council. Depending on the state statute, they may be authorized to sell bonds to investors to raise funds for land acquisition, building demolition, remediation, provision of supportive infrastructure, and other project related costs. Typically, they are given the power of eminent domain to condemn land that they cannot acquire at a reasonable price from property owners in designated redevelopment areas.

2. Redevelopment or renewal agencies are typically authorized to use their power of eminent domain in "blighted areas." This raises the question of what constitutes blight. This issue was addressed in Yonkers Community Development Agency v. Morris, a decision of the New York Court of Appeals, 37 N.Y.2d 478, 373 N.Y.S.2d 112, 335 N.E.2d 327 (1975), where the court noted: "As already indicated, on that question the agency's road is made easier by the liberal rather than literal definition of a "blighted" area now universally endorsed by case law. Many factors and interrelationships of factors may be significant. These may include such diverse matters as irregularity of the plots, inadequacy of the streets, diversity of land ownership making assemblage of property difficult, incompatibility of the existing mixture of residential and industrial property, overcrowding, the incidence of crime, lack of sanitation, the drain an area makes on municipal services, fire

hazards, traffic congestion, and pollution. It can encompass areas in the process of deterioration or threatened with it as well as ones already rendered useless, prevention being an important purpose." Blighted property may even include vacant land (Cannata v. City of New York, 11 N.Y.2d 210, 227 N.Y.S.2d 903, 182 N.E.2d 395 (1962)) and air rights (Jersey City Chapter of Prop. Owner's Protective Assn. v. City Council of Jersey City, 55 N.J. 86, 259 A.2d 698 (1969)). Nor is it necessary that the degree of deterioration or precise percentage of obsolescence or mathematical measurement of other factors be arrived at with precision, since the combination and effects of such things are highly variable. (City of Chicago v. R. Zwick Co., 27 Ill.2d 128, 188 N.E.2d 489 (1963)).

3. For a critical review of using "blight" as a basis for condemnation, tax breaks, and financial assistance see Colin Gordon, Blighting the Way: Urban Renewal, Economic Development, and the Elusive Definition of Blight, 31 Fordham Urb. L.J. 305 (2004). "Clearly 'blight' has lost any substantive meaning as either a description of urban conditions or a target for public policy. Blight is less an objective condition than it is a legal pretext for various forms of commercial tax abatement that, in most settings, divert money from schools and county-funded social services. Redevelopment policies originally intended to address unsafe or insufficient urban housing are now more routinely employed to subsidize the building of suburban shopping malls. And such policies (especially state TIF programs) not only ignore the ongoing urban crisis, but by subsidizing sprawl, routinely contribute to blight in the cities under the pretext of fighting it in the suburbs."

4. Industrial Development Agencies (IDA's) are another type of independent "quasi-public" agency created by local governments pursuant to authority contained in state statutes. IDA's possess many of the same powers as urban renewal agencies which are to be exercised in most cases to provide jobs: employment in industrial or commercial development that the agencies assist in a variety of ways. They are authorized to use the power to condemn title to land needed for a job development project. The powers and limits of the authority of IDAs are explored in the following case.

5. In the aftermath of Kelo v. City of New London, which follows below in Section E, the Minnesota legislature adopted a law limiting the scope of eminent domain. It joined 25 other states that enacted some type of legislation in the year following *Kelo*. The Minnesota law, SF 2750, limits the use of eminent domain to a public use or public purpose defined as the possession, occupation, ownership, or enjoyment of property by the general public or a public agency, or for the mitigation of blight which refers to properties that constitute an actual danger to public health and safety. The law provides that the public benefits of economic development, alone, do not constitute a public use or purpose. It also requires good faith negotiations with property owners and increases public notice and hearing requirements. The law exempts from these new limitations the taking of private property in over 2000 Tax Increment Financing Districts in the state.

D. INDUSTRIAL REDEVELOPMENT

SUN CO. v. CITY OF SYRACUSE INDUSTRIAL DEVELOPMENT AGENCY

Supreme Court of New York, Appellate Division, Fourth Department, 1995.
625 N.Y.S.2d 371, 209 A.D.2d 34.

BOEHM, J.

Petitioners, Sun Company, Inc. (Sun), Atlantic Refining & Marketing Company, Inc. (Atlantic), Citgo Petroleum Corporation (Citgo), and Mobil Oil Corporation (Mobil) (collectively, the Oil Companies) and Upstate Milk Cooperatives, Inc. (Upstate) challenge, pursuant to EDPL 207, the findings and determination of respondent, City of Syracuse Industrial Development Agency (SIDA), to condemn property owned by petitioners situated near the south shore of Onondaga Lake in the Oil City area of the City of Syracuse. The purpose of the taking is the proposed development of a retail shopping center to be known as Carousel Landing (Carousel Landing Project). SIDA's determination was made after entering into a Preferred Developer Agreement with Pyramid Companies (Pyramid), a partnership engaged in the development of retail commercial properties. Petitioners contend that the proposed taking of their property is not primarily for a public purpose and that, under the terms of the Preferred Developer Agreement, SIDA illegally "contracted away" its eminent domain power. Petitioners also attack the validity of the condemnation in various other respects. Petitioners contend, inter alia, that the environmental review of the Carousel Landing Project, made under ECL article 8, the State Environmental Quality Review Act (SEQRA), was improperly segmented from other planned development at the Syracuse lakefront and that the environmental review was deficient.

I. THE HISTORY OF THE CAROUSEL LANDING PROJECT

The proposed condemnation of petitioners' properties is the latest in a series of actions dating back to 1987, when SIDA and the City announced a Master Plan for redevelopment of approximately 800 acres of land known as the "Lakefront Area", bounded by Onondaga Lake to the north and by interstate highways on the east, south and west. At that time, in addition to development of a proposed retail shopping mall to be known as "Carousel Center", the Master Plan contemplated the creation of a lakefront park, a light industrial trade zone, cluster multifamily housing, a marina and office park, and mixed commercial and retail uses. In 1990, Pyramid completed construction of Carousel Center, financed with SIDA-issued bonds, in the northern portion of the Lakefront Area. With several other entities, Pyramid also constructed projects in the Franklin Square area, which is located at the southern end of the Lakefront Area.

* * *

In December 1991 the Syracuse Office of Lakefront Development issued an "Action Plan for the Syracuse Lakefront" (Lakefront Plan). The Lakefront Plan was announced as having been prepared for the "citizens of Syracuse" by the Mayor's Lakefront Advisory Committee, comprised of an 11–member Inner Harbor Task Force and a 23–member Strategic Planning Team.

On September 18, 1992, SIDA and Pyramid entered into a "Preferred Developer Agreement", which designated Pyramid as a preferred developer for the Carousel Landing Project to be constructed on property owned by petitioners. The Carousel Landing Project was to be "no less than a 350,000 square foot retail complex." Under the terms of the Preferred Developer Agreement, Pyramid undertook certain financial obligations and, in return, SIDA agreed to acquire "at least those properties within [Oil City] which [Pyramid] commits to acquire from [SIDA] for the development of the [Carousel Landing Project]." Pyramid agreed to pay all costs associated with the acquisition of approximately 65 acres of property and the SEQRA review. In March 1993 consultants hired by Pyramid commenced preparation of a Draft Environmental Impact Statement (DEIS) for the Carousel Landing Project.

In July 1993 representatives of the Oil Companies met with City Officials, including Susan Hopkins, the City's Director of Lakefront Development, to propose alternatives to the Carousel Landing Project. The Oil Companies presented a plan whereby the petroleum facilities would be consolidated on 33 acres of land within Oil City. The Oil Companies' consolidation plan was rejected in a letter from Ms. Hopkins, dated August 3, 1993, in which she stated: "[W]e are bound by a preferred develope[r] agreement with [Pyramid] the terms of which preclude the adoption of the [Oil Companies'] proposal."

* * *

II. The Proceedings Commenced in This Court

In a prior proceeding, Supreme Court denied the motion of the Oil Companies for a preliminary injunction, dismissed their complaint as premature, and granted SIDA's motion for a preliminary injunction enjoining the Oil Companies from restraining SIDA's agents from entering upon petitioners' property for inspection purposes. We affirmed (see, *Sun Co. v. City of Syracuse Indus. Dev. Agency*, 197 A.D.2d 912).

* * *

SIDA's authority to acquire property is derived from General Municipal Law § 858 (4), which provides that a public benefit corporation established as an industrial development corporation (IDA) under article 18–A of the General Municipal Law may "acquire by purchase, grant, lease, gift, pursuant to the provisions of the eminent domain procedure law ... real property or rights or easements therein necessary for its corporate purposes".

The scope of review of a proposed condemnation is limited by EDPL 207 " 'to whether the proceeding was constitutional or within the agency's statutory jurisdiction; whether the agency made its determination and findings in accordance with the procedures set forth in article 2; and whether "a public use, benefit or purpose will be served by the proposed acquisition" '[citations omitted]. If an adequate basis for a determination is shown' and the objector cannot show that the determination was "without foundation", the agency's determination should be confirmed' [citations omitted]" (*Matter of Waldo's, Inc. v. Village of Johnson City*, 74 N.Y.2d 718, 720-721).

III. Petitioners' Challenges Under EDPL 207

Petitioners contend that the statutory condemnation scheme granting an IDA the power to condemn property is facially unconstitutional; that, as applied, the statutory procedure is subject to an agreement with a private commercial entity and is, therefore, unconstitutional; that they have been deprived of due process because Pyramid cannot provide them with a certain and adequate source and manner of payment of just compensation; that the proposed condemnation is not primarily for a public purpose; that SIDA illegally contracted away its eminent domain power; and that the condemnation would violate General Municipal Law § 862. Additionally, Upstate contends that the condemnation of its property is excess to the Carousel Landing Project.

Preliminarily, we reject the contention of petitioners that the statutory condemnation scheme granting an IDA the power to condemn property is facially unconstitutional. It is well established that an IDA is "authorized by statute to exercise the State's eminent domain powers" (*Matter of Northeast Parent & Child Socy. v. City of Schenectady Indus. Dev. Agency*, 114 A.D.2d 741, 742; see, General Municipal Law § 858 [4]). So long as the governmental agency takes the property for a public purpose and provides the owner with just compensation, "[t]he EDPL does not violate substantive due process" (*First Broadcasting Corp. v. City of Syracuse*, 78 A.D.2d 490, 495; see, *Rosenthal & Rosenthal v. New York State Urban Dev. Corp.*, 771 F.2d 44, cert. denied 475 U.S. 1018).

Further, the Preferred Developer Agreement provides petitioners with a certain and adequate source and manner of payment. The Agreement provides: "Prior to the actual date of taking, pursuant to EDPL Section 402 (B) 5, [Pyramid] will initially pay to the [SIDA] the total amount of acquisition damages as determined by the appraisers for those parcels which [Pyramid] commits to acquire from [SIDA]. [SIDA] will, in turn, pay said funds to the affected condemnees as their respective advance payments pursuant to EDPL Section 304 ... [Pyramid] agrees to pay to [SIDA] those amounts determined by the Court to be full compensation including statutory interest, for those parcels which [Pyramid] commits to acquire from [SIDA]."

There is no prohibition against private funding of a public condemnation (*Matter of Waldo's, Inc. v. Village of Johnson City*, 74 N.Y.2d 718,

721, *supra*; *Matter of New York State Urban Dev. Corp.* [TOH Realty Corp.,] 165 A.D.2d 733, 734–735, lv. denied 77 N.Y.2d 810). The provision of the Agreement regarding payment is in accord with statutory procedure (see, EDPL 304) and constitutes a certain and adequate source and manner of just compensation (see, *Matter of New York State Urban Dev. Corp.* [TOH Realty Corp.], *supra*).

General Municipal Law Prohibition

In response to petitioners' objections based upon the General Municipal Law, SIDA argues that the 1993 amendments to General Municipal Law § 862 (L. 1993, ch. 356, § 15) prohibiting IDAs from funding retail projects do not apply because (1) the amendments provide that they shall not apply to projects for which an agency has authorized assistance by the passage of an inducement resolution before the effective date of October 19, 1993, and (2) the amendments exempt tourist destinations and retail establishments in "highly distressed areas".

Although the Preferred Developer Agreement is not the equivalent of an inducement resolution, as SIDA argues, nevertheless, the Carousel Landing Project is exempt from the retail establishment prohibition. That exemption arises out of the fact that "the project is located in a highly distressed area" (General Municipal Law § 862 [2] [b] [iii]).

General Municipal Law § 854 (18) defines a "highly distressed area" as:

> "(a) a census tract or tracts or block numbering areas [sic] or areas or such census tract or block numbering area contiguous thereto which, according to the most recent census data available, has:
>
> > "(i) a poverty rate of at least twenty percent for the year to which the data relates or at least twenty percent of households receiving public assistance; and
> >
> > "(ii) an unemployment rate of at least 1.25 times the statewide unemployment rate for the year to which the data relates".

In an affidavit, William Bush, Director of the Office of Development for the City of Syracuse, states that the census tract where the project is located: "is contiguous to four (4) census tracts which qualify as 'highly distressed areas' as defined in [General Municipal Law] § 854 (18). Each of these four census tracts qualifies as a highly distressed area in that each has a poverty rate of at least 20% for the years to which the data relates or at least 20% of households receiving public assistance and an unemployment rate of at least 1.25 times the statewide unemployment rate for the year to which the data relates. These Census tracts are Census Tracts 5, 13, 22 and 23." A census map is attached to the affidavit. Petitioners do not dispute the accuracy of the location of the census tracts as affecting the property subject to condemnation or that the property is "highly distressed". Accordingly, the exception in General Municipal Law § 862 (2) (b) applies.

Public Purpose

Petitioners further contend that the Carousel Landing Project is nothing more than an ordinary strip shopping center and that there is no unique characteristic of the project that can support the acquisition and forced relocation of petitioners' longstanding and important economic enterprises that provide necessary energy resources for the nonpublic purpose of developing a discount shopping mall. We reject that contention. The Carousel Landing Project is an integral part of an over-all plan to redevelop a unique public asset—the Syracuse lakefront. According to SIDA, acquisition of the Carousel Landing Project site is crucial to that redevelopment plan, which would transform an economically underutilized area limited in development potential by the presence of Oil City and its unsightly oil tanks into an aesthetic asset with a mix of residential, recreational and commercial uses. SIDA determined that acquisition of the Carousel Landing Project site would serve the public purposes of reducing physical blight and improving the aesthetic appearance of the area, improving the infrastructure in the project area, expanding employment opportunities, increasing the tax base and sales tax revenues, and promoting the identification and alleviation of environmental problems in the area. The record supports SIDA's determination that the dominant purposes of the project are to reduce urban physical and economic blight and promote economic revitalization of the acquisition site. Although Pyramid also will benefit privately from the project, that "incidental private benefit will not invalidate an agency's determination so long as the public purpose is dominant [citations omitted]" (*Matter of Waldo's, Inc. v. Village of Johnson City*, 74 N.Y.2d 718, 721, *supra*; see also, *Rosenthal & Rosenthal v. New York State Urban Dev. Corp.*, 771 F.2d 44, 46, *supra*).

We conclude, therefore, that SIDA's stated purposes for the acquisition of petitioners' property support the determination that the Carousel Landing Project serves a legitimate public purpose (see, *Matter of Waldo's, Inc. v. Village of Johnson City*, *supra*; *Matter of Jackson v. New York State Urban Dev. Corp.*, 67 N.Y.2d 400, 424–425; *Matter of Northeast Parent & Child Socy. v. City of Schenectady Indus. Dev. Agency*, 114 A.D.2d 741, *supra*; *Rosenthal & Rosenthal v. New York State Urban Dev. Corp.*, supra).

* * *

Effect of Agreement on SIDA's Eminent Domain Power

There is no merit to the contention of petitioners that, in contracting with Pyramid, SIDA improperly delegated and surrendered its authority to exercise its eminent domain power. Although the Preferred Developer Agreement reflects a cooperative effort between SIDA and Pyramid, it does not surrender the eminent domain power. Pyramid may influence SIDA's decision with respect to what properties will be condemned, but the Preferred Developer Agreement clearly establishes that the condemnation decision is SIDA's and SIDA's alone (see, e.g., P 8). Indeed, the Preferred Developer Agreement provides that other buyers/developers may become involved should Pyramid decline to make use of all property condemned by SIDA. SIDA had control over "the ultimate decision" on the Carousel Landing Project, and thus Pyramid did not acquire SIDA's power of eminent domain.

It is undisputed that the entire area known as Oil City had been targeted for redevelopment as early as 1987, and that the approach to redevelopment was to encourage private development projects. As noted, different projects have already been undertaken in the redevelopment area, including Franklin Square (office buildings and residential units) and Carousel Center. Also under development is the New York State Barge Canal Terminal, a major tourist attraction. The plan to develop the Lakefront Area was accepted in 1991, and the Carousel Landing Project is the type of development that will provide significant public benefit.

There is also no dispute that Pyramid was the only private developer to express interest in the Carousel Landing Project. The steps articulated in the Preferred Developer Agreement were put forth to ensure that SIDA would not condemn petitioners' property unless it had a firm commitment to the project from Pyramid, i.e., to ensure that SIDA would not condemn property without adequate compensatory resources.

After identifying the goals of the parties, the Preferred Developer Agreement provides that SIDA will designate Pyramid as the preferred developer of the Redevelopment Area, and that Pyramid will diligently pursue development of the project known as Carousel Landing. The Preferred Developer Agreement states: "[SIDA] will pursue the acquisition of all properties within the Redevelopment Area pursuant to the Eminent Domain Procedure Law ('EDPL') and the State Environmental Quality Review Act ('SEQRA'), subject to the terms of this Agreement, up to but not including, the making of the formal Determination and Findings pursuant to EDPL § 204. In the event [Pyramid] elects not to proceed with the project or to acquire only selected parcels ... [SIDA] has the right to continue with the acquisition of the Redevelopment Area" (emphasis added).

After discussing Pyramid's financial obligation and ability to opt out in part or in whole, the Preferred Developer Agreement's paragraph 8 states: "[Pyramid] will elect whether to proceed with the Project within 20 days after receipt of the final appraisals and, in no event, later than 5 days before [SIDA]'s meeting at which it intends to make its Determination and Findings pursuant to EDPL § 204 ... In the event [Pyramid] elects to proceed [SIDA] will take all the necessary actions pursuant to EDPL to acquire at least those properties within the Redevelopment Area which [Pyramid] commits to acquire from [SIDA] for the development of this Project" (emphasis added).

In the context of this urban redevelopment project, SIDA and Pyramid did not engage in a quid pro quo whereby SIDA contracted away its power of eminent domain for value given by Pyramid. Here, SIDA intended to condemn the property and entered into an agreement with Pyramid to ensure that the property would be developed in the anticipated beneficial manner. The language of paragraph 8 of the Preferred Developer Agreement, suggesting that SIDA will condemn the properties upon Pyramid's final commitment to the redevelopment project, does not amount to an impermissible bargaining away of the governmental entity's power of eminent domain (see, Matter of Waldo's, Inc. v. Village of Johnson City, supra, at 722).

* * *

E. ECONOMIC DEVELOPMENT

KELO v. CITY OF NEW LONDON

Supreme Court of the United States, 2005.
545 U.S. 469, 125 S.Ct. 2655, 162 L.Ed.2d 439.

STEVENS, JUSTICE.

In 2000, the city of New London approved a development plan that, in the words of the Supreme Court of Connecticut, was "projected to create in excess of 1,000 jobs, to increase tax and other revenues, and to revitalize an economically distressed city, including its downtown and waterfront areas." * * * In assembling the land needed for this project, the city's development agent has purchased property from willing sellers and proposes to use the power of eminent domain to acquire the remainder of the property from unwilling owners in exchange for just compensation. The question presented is whether the city's proposed disposition of this property qualifies as a "public use" within the meaning of the Takings Clause of the Fifth Amendment to the Constitution.

I

The city of New London (hereinafter City) sits at the junction of the Thames River and the Long Island Sound in southeastern Connecticut. Decades of economic decline led a state agency in 1990 to designate the City a "distressed municipality." In 1996, the Federal Government closed the Naval Undersea Warfare Center, which had been located in the Fort Trumbull area of the City and had employed over 1,500 people. In 1998, the City's unemployment rate was nearly double that of the State, and its population of just under 24,000 residents was at its lowest since 1920.

These conditions prompted state and local officials to target New London, and particularly its Fort Trumbull area, for economic revitalization. To this end, respondent New London Development Corporation (NLDC), a private nonprofit entity established some years earlier to assist the City in planning economic development, was reactivated. In January 1998, the State authorized a $5.35 million bond issue to support the NLDC's planning activities and a $10 million bond issue toward the creation of a Fort Trumbull State Park. In February, the pharmaceutical company Pfizer Inc. announced that it would build a $300 million research facility on a site immediately adjacent to Fort Trumbull; local planners hoped that Pfizer would draw new business to the area, thereby serving as a catalyst to the area's rejuvenation. After receiving initial approval from the city council, the NLDC continued its planning activities and held a series of neighborhood meetings to educate the public about the process. In May, the city council authorized the NLDC to formally submit its plans to the relevant state agencies for review. Upon obtaining state-level approval, the NLDC finalized an integrated development plan focused on 90 acres of the Fort Trumbull area.

The Fort Trumbull area is situated on a peninsula that juts into the Thames River. The area comprises approximately 115 privately owned properties, as well as the 32 acres of land formerly occupied by the naval facility (Trumbull State Park now occupies 18 of those 32 acres). The development plan encompasses seven parcels. Parcel 1 is designated for a waterfront conference hotel at the center of a "small urban village" that will include restaurants and shopping. This parcel will also have marinas for both recreational and commercial uses. A pedestrian "riverwalk" will originate here and continue down the coast, connecting the waterfront areas of the development. Parcel 2 will be the site of approximately 80 new residences organized into an urban neighborhood and linked by public walkway to the remainder of the development, including the state park. This parcel also includes space reserved for a new U. S. Coast Guard Museum. Parcel 3, which is located immediately north of the Pfizer facility, will contain at least 90,000 square feet of research and development office space. Parcel 4A is a 2.4–acre site that will be used either to support the adjacent state park, by providing parking or retail services for visitors, or to support the nearby marina. Parcel 4B will include a renovated marina, as well as the final stretch of the riverwalk. Parcels 5, 6, and 7 will provide land for office and retail space, parking, and water-dependent commercial uses. * * *

The NLDC intended the development plan to capitalize on the arrival of the Pfizer facility and the new commerce it was expected to attract. In addition to creating jobs, generating tax revenue, and helping to "build momentum for the revitalization of downtown New London," * * * the plan was also designed to make the City more attractive and to create leisure and recreational opportunities on the waterfront and in the park.

The city council approved the plan in January 2000, and designated the NLDC as its development agent in charge of implementation. See Conn. Gen. Stat. § 8–188 (2005). The city council also authorized the NLDC to purchase property or to acquire property by exercising eminent domain in the City's name. § 8–193. The NLDC successfully negotiated the purchase of most of the real estate in the 90–acre area, but its negotiations with petitioners failed. As a consequence, in November 2000, the NLDC initiated the condemnation proceedings that gave rise to this case.

II

Petitioner Susette Kelo has lived in the Fort Trumbull area since 1997. She has made extensive improvements to her house, which she prizes for its water view. Petitioner Wilhelmina Dery was born in her Fort Trumbull house in 1918 and has lived there her entire life. Her husband Charles (also a petitioner) has lived in the house since they married some 60 years ago. In all, the nine petitioners own 15 properties in Fort Trumbull—4 in parcel 3 of the development plan and 11 in parcel 4A. Ten of the parcels are occupied by the owner or a family member; the other five are held as investment properties. There is no allegation that any of these properties is blighted or otherwise in poor condition; rather, they were condemned only because they happen to be located in the development area.

In December 2000, petitioners brought this action in the New London Superior Court. They claimed, among other things, that the taking of their properties would violate the "public use" restriction in the Fifth Amendment. After a 7–day bench trial, the Superior Court granted a permanent restraining order prohibiting the taking of the properties located in parcel 4A (park or marina support). It, however, denied petitioners relief as to the properties located in parcel 3 (office space). * * *

After the Superior Court ruled, both sides took appeals to the Supreme Court of Connecticut. That court held, over a dissent, that all of the City's proposed takings were valid. It began by upholding the lower court's determination that the takings were authorized by chapter 132, the State's municipal development statute. See Conn. Gen. Stat. § 8–186 *et seq.* (2005). That statute expresses a legislative determination that the taking of land, even developed land, as part of an economic development project is a "public use" and in the "public interest." 268 Conn., at 18–28, 843 A. 2d, at 515–521. Next, relying on cases such as *Hawaii Housing Authority v. Midkiff*, 467 U.S. 229, 81 L. Ed. 2d 186, 104 S. Ct. 2321 (1984), and *Berman v. Parker*, 348 U.S. 26, 99 L. Ed. 27, 75 S. Ct. 98 (1954), the court held that such economic development qualified as a valid public use under both the Federal and State Constitutions. * * *

Finally, adhering to its precedents, the court went on to determine, first, whether the takings of the particular properties at issue were "reasonably necessary" to achieving the City's intended public use, * * * and, second, whether the takings were for "reasonably foreseeable needs," * * *. The court upheld the trial court's factual findings as to parcel 3, but reversed the trial court as to parcel 4A, agreeing with the City that the intended use of this land was sufficiently definite and had been given "reasonable attention" during the planning process. * * *

The three dissenting justices would have imposed a "heightened" standard of judicial review for takings justified by economic development. Although they agreed that the plan was intended to serve a valid public use, they would have found all the takings unconstitutional because the City had failed to adduce "clear and convincing evidence" that the economic benefits of the plan would in fact come to pass. *Id.*, at 144, 146, 843 A. 2d, at 587, 588 (Zarella, J., joined by Sullivan, C. J., and Katz, J., concurring in part and dissenting in part).

We granted certiorari to determine whether a city's decision to take property for the purpose of economic development satisfies the "public use" requirement of the Fifth Amendment. 542 U.S. 965, 159 L.Ed.2d 857, 125 S.Ct. 27 (2004).

III

Two polar propositions are perfectly clear. On the one hand, it has long been accepted that the sovereign may not take the property of *A* for the sole purpose of transferring it to another private party *B*, even though *A* is paid just compensation. On the other hand, it is equally clear that a State may transfer property from one private party to another if future "use by the public" is the purpose of the taking; the condemnation of land for a railroad with common-carrier duties is a familiar example. Neither of these propositions, however, determines the disposition of this case.

As for the first proposition, the City would no doubt be forbidden from taking petitioners' land for the purpose of conferring a private benefit on a particular private party. See *Midkiff,* 467 U.S., at 245, 81 L. Ed. 2d 186, 104 S. Ct. 2321 ("A purely private taking could not withstand the scrutiny of the public use requirement; it would serve no legitimate purpose of government and would thus be void"); *Missouri Pacific R. Co. v. Nebraska,* 164 U.S. 403, 41 L. Ed. 489, 17 S. Ct. 130 (1896). Nor would the City be allowed to take property under the mere pretext of a public purpose, when its actual purpose was to bestow a private benefit. The takings before us, however, would be executed pursuant to a "carefully considered" development plan. 268 Conn., at 54, 843 A.2d, at 536. The trial judge and all the members of the Supreme Court of Connecticut agreed that there was no evidence of an illegitimate purpose in this case. Therefore, as was true of the statute challenged in *Midkiff,* 467 U.S., at 245, 81 L. Ed. 2d 186, 104 S. Ct. 2321, the City's development plan was not adopted "to benefit a particular class of identifiable individuals."

On the other hand, this is not a case in which the City is planning to open the condemned land—at least not in its entirety—to use by the general public. Nor will the private lessees of the land in any sense be required to operate like common carriers, making their services available to all comers. But although such a projected use would be sufficient to satisfy the public use requirement, this "Court long ago rejected any literal requirement that condemned property be put into use for the general public." * * * Indeed, while many state courts in the mid–19th century endorsed "use by the public" as the proper definition of public use, that narrow view steadily eroded over time. Not only was the "use by the public" test difficult to administer (*e.g.*, what proportion of the public need have access to the property? at what price?), but it proved to be impractical given the diverse and always evolving needs of society. Accordingly, when this Court began applying the Fifth Amendment to the States at the close of the 19th century, it embraced the broader and more natural interpretation of public use as "public purpose." See, *e.g.*, *Fallbrook Irrigation Dist. v. Bradley*, 164 U.S. 112, 158–164, 41 L. Ed. 369, 17 S. Ct. 56 (1896). Thus, in a case upholding a mining company's use of an aerial bucket line to transport ore over property it did not own, Justice Holmes' opinion for the Court stressed "the inadequacy of use by the general public as a universal test." *Strickley v. Highland Boy Gold Mining Co.,* 200 U.S. 527, 531, 50 L. Ed. 581, 26 S. Ct. 301 (1906). We have repeatedly and consistently rejected that narrow test ever since.

The disposition of this case therefore turns on the question whether the City's development plan serves a "public purpose." Without exception, our cases have defined that concept broadly, reflecting our longstanding policy of deference to legislative judgments in this field.

In *Berman v. Parker,* 348 U.S. 26, 99 L. Ed. 27, 75 S. Ct. 98 (1954), this Court upheld a redevelopment plan targeting a blighted area of Washington, D. C., in which most of the housing for the area's 5,000 inhabitants was beyond repair. Under the plan, the area would be condemned and part of it utilized for the construction of streets, schools, and other public facilities. The remainder of the land would be leased or sold to private parties for the purpose of redevelopment, including the construction of low-cost housing.

The owner of a department store located in the area challenged the condemnation, pointing out that his store was not itself blighted and arguing that the creation of a "better balanced, more attractive community" was not a valid public use. *Id.*, at 31, 99 L. Ed. 27, 75 S. Ct. 98. Writing for a unanimous Court, Justice Douglas refused to evaluate this claim in isolation, deferring instead to the legislative and agency judgment that the area "must be planned as a whole" for the plan to be successful. *Id.*, at 34, 99 L. Ed. 27, 75 S. Ct. 98. The Court explained that "community redevelopment programs need not, by force of the Constitution, be on a piecemeal basis—lot by lot, building by building." *Id.*, at 35, 99 L. Ed. 27, 75 S. Ct. 98. The public use underlying the taking was unequivocally affirmed:

"We do not sit to determine whether a particular housing project is or is not desirable. The concept of the public welfare is broad and inclusive.... The values it represents are spiritual as well as physical, aesthetic as well as monetary. It is within the power of the legislature to determine that the community should be beautiful as well as healthy, spacious as well as clean, well-balanced as well as carefully patrolled. In the present case, the Congress and its authorized agencies have made determinations that take into account a wide variety of values. It is not for us to reappraise them. If those who govern the District of Columbia decide that the Nation's Capital should be beautiful as well as sanitary, there is nothing in the Fifth Amendment that stands in the way." *Id.*, at 33, 99 L. Ed. 27, 75 S. Ct. 98.

In *Hawaii Housing Authority v. Midkiff*, 467 U.S. 229, 81 L. Ed. 2d 186, 104 S. Ct. 2321 (1984), the Court considered a Hawaii statute whereby fee title was taken from lessors and transferred to lessees (for just compensation) in order to reduce the concentration of land ownership. We unanimously upheld the statute and rejected the Ninth Circuit's view that it was "a naked attempt on the part of the state of Hawaii to take the property of A and transfer it to B solely for B's private use and benefit." *Id.*, at 235, 81 L. Ed. 2d 186, 104 S. Ct. 2321 (internal quotation marks omitted). Reaffirming *Berman*'s deferential approach to legislative judgments in this field, we concluded that the State's purpose of eliminating the "social and economic evils of a land oligopoly" qualified as a valid public use. 467 U.S., at 241–242, 81 L. Ed. 2d 186, 104 S. Ct. 2321. Our opinion also rejected the contention that the mere fact that the State immediately transferred the properties to private individuals upon condemnation somehow diminished the public character of the taking. "[I]t is only the taking's purpose, and not its mechanics," we explained, that matters in determining public use. *Id.*, at 244, 81 L. Ed. 2d 186, 104 S. Ct. 2321.

In that same Term we decided another public use case that arose in a purely economic context. In *Ruckelshaus v. Monsanto Co.,* 467 U.S. 986, 81 L. Ed. 2d 815, 104 S. Ct. 2862 (1984), the Court dealt with provisions of the Federal Insecticide, Fungicide, and Rodenticide Act under which the Environmental Protection Agency could consider the data (including trade secrets) submitted by a prior pesticide applicant in evaluating a subsequent application, so long as the second applicant paid just compensation for the data. We acknowledged that the "most direct beneficiaries" of these provisions were the subsequent applicants, *id.,* at 1014, 81 L. Ed. 2d 815, 104 S. Ct. 2862, but we nevertheless upheld the statute under *Berman* and *Midkiff.* We found sufficient Congress' belief that sparing applicants the cost of time-consuming research eliminated a significant barrier to entry in the pesticide market and thereby enhanced competition. 467 U.S., at 1015, 81 L. Ed. 2d 815, 104 S. Ct. 2862.

Viewed as a whole, our jurisprudence has recognized that the needs of society have varied between different parts of the Nation, just as they have evolved over time in response to changed circumstances. Our earliest cases in particular embodied a strong theme of federalism, emphasizing the "great respect" that we owe to state legislatures and state courts in discerning local public needs. See *Hairston v. Danville & Western R. Co.*, 208 U.S. 598, 606–607, 52 L.Ed. 637, 28 S.Ct. 331 (1908) (noting that these needs were likely to vary depending on a State's "resources, the capacity of the soil, the relative importance of industries to the general public welfare, and the long-established methods and habits of the people"). For more than a century, our public use jurisprudence has wisely eschewed rigid formulas and intrusive scrutiny in favor of affording legislatures broad latitude in determining what public needs justify the use of the takings power.

IV

Those who govern the City were not confronted with the need to remove blight in the Fort Trumbull area, but their determination that the area was sufficiently distressed to justify a program of economic rejuvenation is entitled to our deference. The City has carefully formulated an economic development plan that it believes will provide appreciable benefits to the community, including—but by no means limited to—new jobs and increased tax revenue. As with other exercises in urban planning and development, the City is endeavoring to coordinate a variety of commercial, residential, and recreational uses of land, with the hope that they will form a whole greater than the sum of its parts. To effectuate this plan, the City has invoked a state statute that specifically authorizes the use of eminent domain to promote economic development. Given the comprehensive character of the plan, the thorough deliberation that preceded its adoption, and the limited scope of our review, it is appropriate for us, as it was in *Berman*, to resolve the challenges of the individual owners, not on a piecemeal basis, but rather in light of the entire plan. Because that plan unquestionably serves a public purpose, the takings challenged here satisfy the public use requirement of the Fifth Amendment.

To avoid this result, petitioners urge us to adopt a new bright-line rule that economic development does not qualify as a public use. Putting aside the unpersuasive suggestion that the City's plan will provide only purely economic benefits, neither precedent nor logic supports petitioners' proposal. Promoting economic development is a traditional and long accepted function of government. There is, moreover, no principled way of distinguishing economic development from the other public purposes that we have recognized. In our cases upholding takings that facilitated agriculture and mining, for example, we emphasized the importance of those industries to the welfare of the States in question, see, *e.g.*, *Strickley*, 200 U.S. 527, 50 L. Ed. 581, 26 S. Ct. 301; in *Berman,* we endorsed the purpose of transforming a blighted area into a "well-balanced" community through redevelopment, 348 U.S., at 33, 99 L. Ed. 27, 75 S. Ct. 98; in *Midkiff*, we upheld the interest in breaking up a land oligopoly that "created artificial deterrents to the normal functioning of the State's residential land market," 467 U.S., at 242, 81 L. Ed. 2d 186, 104 S. Ct. 2321; and in *Monsanto,* we accepted Congress' purpose of eliminating a "significant barrier to entry in the pesticide market," 467 U.S., at 1014–1015, 81 L. Ed. 2d 815, 104 S. Ct. 2862. It would be incongruous to hold that the City's interest in the economic benefits to be derived from the development of the Fort Trumbull area has less of a public character than any of those other interests. Clearly, there is no basis for exempting economic development from our traditionally broad understanding of public purpose.

Petitioners contend that using eminent domain for economic development impermissibly blurs the boundary between public and private takings. Again, our cases foreclose this objection. Quite simply the government's pursuit of a public purpose will often benefit individual private parties. For example, in *Midkiff*, the forced transfer of property conferred a direct and significant benefit on those lessees who were previously unable to purchase their homes. In *Monsanto*, we recognized that the "most direct beneficiaries" of the data-sharing provisions were the subsequent pesticide applicants, but benefiting them in this way was necessary to promoting competition in the pesticide market. 467 U.S., at 1014, 81 L. Ed. 2d 815, 104 S. Ct. 2862. The owner of the department store in *Berman* objected to "taking from one businessman for the benefit of another businessman," 348 U.S., at 33, 99 L. Ed. 27, 75 S. Ct. 98, referring to the fact that under the redevelopment plan land would be leased or sold to private developers for redevelopment. Our rejection of that contention has particular relevance to the instant case: "The public end may be as well or better served through an agency of private enterprise than through a department of government—or so the Congress might conclude. We cannot say that public ownership is the sole method of promoting the public purposes of community redevelopment projects." *Id.*, at 34, 99 L. Ed. 27, 75 S. Ct. 98.

It is further argued that without a bright-line rule nothing would stop a city from transferring citizen *A*'s property to citizen *B* for the sole reason that citizen *B* will put the property to a more productive use and thus pay more taxes. Such a one-to-one transfer of property, executed outside the confines of an integrated development plan, is not presented in this case. While such an unusual exercise of government power would certainly raise a suspicion that a private purpose was afoot, the hypothetical cases posited by petitioners can be confronted if and when they arise. They do not warrant the crafting of an artificial restriction on the concept of public use.

Alternatively, petitioners maintain that for takings of this kind we should require a "reasonable certainty" that the expected public benefits will actually accrue. Such a rule, however, would represent an even greater departure from our precedent "When the legislature's purpose is legitimate and its means are not irrational, our cases make clear that empirical debates over the wisdom of takings—no less than debates over the wisdom of other kinds of socioeconomic legislation—are not to be carried out in the federal courts." *Midkiff*, 467 U.S., at 242, 81 L. Ed. 2d 186, 104 S. Ct. 2321. Indeed, earlier this Term we explained why similar practical concerns (among others) undermined the use of the "substantially advances" formula in our regulatory takings doctrine. See *Lingle v. Chevron U.S.A. Inc.*, 544 U.S. 528, 161 L. Ed. 2d 876, 125 S. Ct. 2074 (2005) (noting that this formula "would empower—and might often require—courts to substitute their predictive judgments for those of elected legislatures and expert agencies"). The disadvantages of a heightened form of review are especially pronounced in this type of case. Orderly implementation of a comprehensive redevelopment plan obviously requires that the legal rights of all interested parties be established before new construction can be commenced. A constitutional rule that required postponement of the judicial approval of every condemnation until the likelihood of success of the plan had been assured would unquestionably impose a significant impediment to the successful consummation of many such plans.

Just as we decline to second-guess the City's considered judgments about the efficacy of its development plan, we also decline to second-guess the City's determinations as to what lands it needs to acquire in order to effectuate the project. "It is not for the courts to oversee the choice of the boundary line nor to sit in review on the size of a particular project area. Once the question of the public purpose has been decided, the amount and character of land to be taken for the project and the need for a particular tract to complete the integrated plan rests in the discretion of the legislative branch." *Berman*, 348 U.S., at 35–36, 99 L. Ed. 27, 75 S. Ct. 98.

In affirming the City's authority to take petitioners' properties, we do not minimize the hardship that condemnations may entail, notwithstanding the payment of just compensation. We emphasize that nothing in our opinion precludes any State from placing further restrictions on its exercise of the takings power. Indeed, many States already impose "public use" requirements that are stricter than the federal baseline. Some of these requirements have been established as a matter of state constitutional law, while others are expressed in state eminent domain statutes that carefully limit the grounds upon which takings may be exercised. As the submissions of the parties and their *amici* make clear, the necessity and wisdom of using eminent domain to promote economic development are certainly matters of legitimate public debate. This Court's authority, however, extends only to determining whether the City's proposed condemnations are for a "public use" within the meaning of the Fifth Amendment to the Federal Constitution. Because over a century of our case law interpreting that provision dictates an affirmative answer to that question, we may not grant petitioners the relief that they seek.

JUSTICE KENNEDY, concurring.

I join the opinion for the Court and add these further observations.

This Court has declared that a taking should be upheld as consistent with the Public Use Clause, U.S. Const., Amdt. 5, as long as it is "rationally related to a conceivable public purpose." *Hawaii Housing Authority v. Midkiff*, 467 U.S. 229, 241, 81 L. Ed. 2d 186, 104 S. Ct. 2321 (1984); see also *Berman v. Parker*, 348 U.S. 26, 99 L. Ed. 27, 75 S. Ct. 98 (1954). This deferential standard of review echoes the rational-basis test used to review economic regulation under the Due Process and Equal Protection Clauses, see, e.g., *FCC v. Beach Communications, Inc.*, 508 U.S. 307, 313–314, 124 L. Ed. 2d 211, 113 S. Ct. 2096 (1993); *Williamson v. Lee Optical of Okla., Inc.*, 348 U.S. 483, 99 L. Ed. 563, 75 S. Ct. 461 (1955). The determination that a rational-basis standard of review is appropriate does not, however, alter the fact that transfers intended to confer benefits on particular, favored private entities, and with only incidental or pretextual public benefits, are forbidden by the Public Use Clause.

A court applying rational-basis review under the Public Use Clause should strike down a taking that, by a clear showing, is intended to favor a particular private party, with only incidental or pretextual public benefits, just as a court applying rational-basis review under the Equal Protection Clause must strike down a government classification that is clearly intended to injure a particular class of private parties, with only incidental or pretextual public justifications. See *Cleburne v. Cleburne Living Center, Inc.*, 473 U.S. 432, 446–447, 450, 87 L. Ed. 2d 313, 105 S. Ct. 3249 (1985); *Department of Agriculture v. Moreno*, 413 U.S. 528, 533–536, 37 L. Ed. 2d 782, 93 S. Ct. 2821 (1973). As the trial court in this case was correct to observe: "Where the purpose [of a taking] is economic development and that development is to be carried out by private parties or private parties will be benefited, the court must decide if the stated public purpose—economic advantage to a city sorely in need of it—is only incidental to the benefits that will be confined on private parties of a development plan." * * *

* * *

The trial court concluded, based on these findings, that benefiting Pfizer was not "the primary motivation or effect of this development plan"; instead, "the primary motivation for [respondents] was to take advantage of Pfizer's presence." * * * Likewise, the trial court concluded that "[t]here is nothing in the record to indicate that . . . [respondents] were motivated by a desire to aid [other] particular private entities." * * * Even the dissenting justices on the Connecticut Supreme Court agreed that respondents' development plan was intended to revitalize the local economy, not to serve the interests of Pfizer, Corcoran Jennison, or any other private party. * * * This case, then, survives the meaningful rational basis review that in my view is required under the Public Use Clause.

* * *

For the foregoing reasons, I join in the Court's opinion.

JUSTICE O'CONNOR, with whom the CHIEF JUSTICE, JUSTICE SCALIA, and JUSTICE THOMAS join, dissenting.

* * *

Today the Court abandons this long-held, basic limitation on government power. Under the banner of economic development, all private property is now vulnerable to being taken and transferred to another private owner, so long as it might be upgraded—*i.e.*, given to an owner who will use it in a way that the legislature deems more beneficial to the public—in the process. To reason, as the Court does, that the incidental public benefits resulting from the subsequent ordinary use of private property render economic development takings "for public use" is to wash out any distinction between private and public use of property—and thereby effectively to delete the words "for public use" from the Takings Clause of the Fifth Amendment. Accordingly I respectfully dissent.

* * *

II

Where is the line between "public" and "private" property use? We give considerable deference to legislatures' determinations about what governmental activities will advantage the public. But were the political branches the sole arbiters of the public-private distinction, the Public Use Clause would amount to little more than hortatory fluff. An external, judicial check on how the public use requirement is interpreted, however limited, is necessary if this constraint on government power is to retain any meaning. See *Cincinnati v. Vester*, 281 U.S. 439, 446, 74 L. Ed. 950, 50 S. Ct. 360 (1930) ("It is well established that ... the question [of] what is a public use is a judicial one").

Our cases have generally identified three categories of takings that comply with the public use requirement, though it is in the nature of things that the boundaries between these categories are not always firm. Two are relatively straightforward and uncontroversial. First, the sovereign may transfer private property to public ownership—such as for a road, a hospital, or a military base. See, *e.g.*, *Old Dominion Land Co. v. United States*, 269 U.S. 55, 70 L. Ed. 162, 46 S. Ct. 39 (1925); *Rindge Co. v. County of Los Angeles*, 262 U.S. 700, 67 L. Ed. 1186, 43 S. Ct. 689 (1923). Second, the sovereign may transfer private property to private parties, often common carriers, who make the property available for the public's use—such as with a railroad, a public utility, or a stadium. See, *e.g.*, *National Railroad Passenger Corporation v. Boston & Maine Corp.*, 503 U.S. 407, 118 L. Ed. 2d 52, 112 S. Ct. 1394 (1992); *Mt. Vernon–Woodberry Cotton Duck Co. v. Alabama Interstate Power Co.*, 240 U.S. 30, 60 L. Ed. 507, 36 S. Ct. 234 (1916). But "public ownership" and "use-by-the-public" are sometimes too constricting and impractical ways to define the scope of the Public Use Clause. Thus we have allowed that, in certain circumstances and to meet certain exigencies, takings that serve a public purpose also satisfy the Constitution even if the property is destined for subsequent private use. See, *e.g.*, *Berman v. Parker*, 348 U.S. 26, 99 L. Ed. 27, 75 S. Ct. 98 (1954); *Hawaii Housing Authority v. Midkiff*, 467 U.S. 229, 81 L. Ed. 2d 186, 104 S. Ct. 2321 (1984).

This case returns us for the first time in over 20 years to the hard question of when a purportedly "public purpose" taking meets the public use requirement. It presents an issue of first impression: Are economic development takings constitutional? I would hold that they are not. We are guided by two precedents about the taking of real property by eminent domain. In *Berman*, we upheld takings within a blighted neighborhood of Washington, D. C. The neighborhood had so deteriorated that, for example, 64.3% of its dwellings were beyond repair. 348 U.S., at 30, 99 L. Ed. 27, 75 S. Ct. 98. It had become burdened with "overcrowding of dwellings," "lack of adequate streets and alleys," and "lack of light and air." *Id.,* at 34, 99 L. Ed. 27, 75 S. Ct. 98. Congress had determined that the neighborhood had become "injurious to the public health, safety, morals, and welfare" and that it was necessary to "eliminat[e] all such injurious conditions by employing all means necessary and appropriate for the purpose," including eminent domain. *Id.*, at 28, 99 L. Ed. 27, 75 S. Ct. 98. Mr. Berman's department store was not itself blighted. Having approved of Congress' decision to eliminate the harm to the public emanating from the blighted neighborhood, however, we did not second-guess its decision to treat the neighborhood as a whole rather than lot-by-lot. *Id.*, at 34–35, 99 L. Ed. 27, 75 S. Ct. 98; see also *Midkiff*, 467 U.S., at 244, 81 L. Ed. 2d 186, 104 S. Ct. 2321 ("it is only the taking's purpose, and not its mechanics, that must pass scrutiny").

In *Midkiff*, we upheld a land condemnation scheme in Hawaii whereby title in real property was taken from lessors and transferred to lessees. At that time, the State and Federal Governments owned nearly 49% of the State's land, and another 47% was in the hands of only 72 private landowners. Concentration of land ownership was so dramatic that on the State's most urbanized island, Oahu, 22 landowners owned 72.5% of the fee simple titles. *Id.*, at 232, 81 L. Ed. 2d 186, 104 S. Ct. 2321. The Hawaii Legislature had concluded that the oligopoly in land ownership was "skewing the State's residential fee simple market, inflating land prices, and injuring the public tranquility and welfare," and therefore enacted a condemnation scheme for redistributing title. *Ibid.*

In those decisions, we emphasized the importance of deferring to legislative judgments about public purpose. Because courts are ill-equipped to evaluate the efficacy of proposed legislative initiatives, we rejected as unworkable the idea of courts' " 'deciding on what is and is not a governmental function and . . . invalidating legislation on the basis of their view on that question at the moment of decision, a practice which has proved impracticable in other fields.' " *Id.*, at 240–241, 81 L. Ed. 2d 186, 104 S. Ct. 2321 (quoting *United States ex rel. TVA v. Welch*, 327 U.S. 546, 552, 90 L. Ed. 843, 66 S. Ct. 715 (1946)); see *Berman, supra*, at 32, 99 L. Ed. 27, 75 S. Ct. 98 ("[T]he legislature, not the judiciary, is the main guardian of the public needs to be served by social legislation"); see also *Lingle v. Chevron U.S.A., Inc.*, 544 U.S. 528, 161 L. Ed. 2d 876, 125 S. Ct. 2074 (2005). Likewise, we recognized our inability to evaluate whether, in a given case, eminent domain is a necessary means by which to pursue the legislature's ends. *Midkiff, supra*, at 242, 81 L. Ed. 2d 186, 104 S. Ct. 2321; *Berman, supra*, at 103, 99 L. Ed. 27, 75 S. Ct. 98

Yet for all the emphasis on deference, *Berman* and *Midkiff* hewed to a bedrock principle without which our public use jurisprudence would collapse: "A purely private taking could not withstand the scrutiny of the public use requirement; it would serve no legitimate purpose of government and would thus be void." *Midkiff*, 467 U.S., at 245, 81 L. Ed. 2d 186, 104 S. Ct. 2321; *id.*, at 241, 81 L. Ed. 2d 186, 104 S. Ct. 2321 ("[T]he Court's cases have repeatedly stated that 'one person's property may not be taken for the benefit of another private person without a justifying public purpose, even though compensation be paid' " (quoting *Thompson v. Consolidated Gas Util. Corp.*, 300 U.S. 55, 80, 81 L. Ed. 510, 57 S. Ct. 364 (1937))); see also *Missouri Pacific R. Co. v. Nebraska*, 164 U.S. 403, 417, 41 L. Ed. 489, 17 S. Ct. 130 (1896). To protect that principle, those decisions reserved "a role for courts to play in reviewing a legislature's judgment of what constitutes a public use . . . [though] the Court in *Berman* made clear that it is 'an extremely narrow' one." *Midkiff, supra*, at 240, 81 L. Ed. 2d 186, 104 S. Ct. 2321 (quoting *Berman, supra*, at 32, 99 L. Ed. 27, 75 S. Ct. 98).

The Court's holdings in *Berman* and *Midkiff* were true to the principle underlying the Public Use Clause. In both those cases, the extraordinary, precondemnation use of the targeted property inflicted affirmative harm on society—in *Berman* through blight resulting from extreme poverty and in *Midkiff* through oligopoly resulting from extreme wealth. And in both cases, the relevant legislative body had found that eliminating the existing property use was necessary to remedy the harm. *Berman, supra*, at 28–29, 99 L. Ed. 27, 75 S. Ct. 98; *Midkiff, supra*, at 232, 81 L. Ed. 2d 186, 104 S. Ct. 2321. Thus a public purpose was realized when the harmful use was eliminated. Because each taking *directly* achieved a public benefit, it did not matter that the property was turned over to private use. Here, in contrast, New London does not claim that Susette Kelo's and Wilhelmina Dery's well-maintained homes are the source of any social harm. Indeed, it could not so claim without adopting the absurd argument that any single-family home that might be razed to make way for an apartment building, or any church that might be replaced with a retail store, or any small business that might be more lucrative if it were instead part of a national franchise, is inherently harmful to society and thus within the government's power to condemn.

* * *

It was possible after *Berman* and *Midkiff* to imagine unconstitutional transfers from A to B. Those decisions endorsed government intervention when private property use had veered to such an extreme that the public was suffering as a consequence. Today nearly all real property is susceptible to condemnation on the Court's theory. In the prescient words of a dissenter from the infamous decision in *Poletown*, "[n]ow that we have authorized local legislative bodies to decide that a different commercial or industrial use of property will produce greater public benefits than its present use, no homeowner's, merchant's or manufacturer's property, however productive or valuable to its owner, is immune from condemnation for the benefit of other private interests that will put it to a 'higher' use." 410 Mich., at 644–645, 304 N. W. 2d, at 464 (opinion of Fitzgerald, J.). This is why economic development takings "seriously jeopardiz[e] the security of all private property ownership." *Id.*, at 645, 304 N. W. 2d, at 465 (Ryan, J., dissenting).

Any property may now be taken for the benefit of another private party, but the fallout from this decision will not be random. The beneficiaries are likely to be those citizens with disproportionate influence and power in the political process, including large corporations and development firms. As for the victims, the government now has license to transfer property from those with fewer resources to those with more. The Founders cannot have intended this perverse result. "[T]hat alone is a *just* government," wrote James Madison, "which *impartially* secures to every man, whatever is his *own*." For the National Gazette, Property, (Mar. 29, 1792), reprinted in 14 Papers of James Madison 266 (R. Rutland et al. eds. 1983).

I would hold that the takings in both Parcel 3 and Parcel 4A are unconstitutional, reverse the judgment of the Supreme Court of Connecticut, and remand for further proceedings.

Notes

1. The majority in Kelo made it clear that "a one-to-one transfer of property, executed outside the confines of an integrated development plan, is not presented in this case." What do you make of Justice Kennedy's concurrence? He writes: "The determination that a rational-basis standard of review is appropriate does not, however, alter the fact that transfers intended to confer benefits on particular, favored private entities, and with only incidental or pretextual public benefits, are forbidden by the Public Use Clause." Several pre-Kelo state court decisions that examine takings that transfer title from one private owner to another move in this direction. In 99 Cents Only Stores v. Lancaster Redevelopment Agency, 237 F.Supp.2d 1123 (2001), for example, a federal district court in California invalidated the condemnation of a store to accommodate the interest of an adjacent Costco's expansion plans; it found that the redevelopment agency's only purpose "was to satisfy the private expansion demands of Costco." In Bailey v. Myers, 206 Ariz. 224, 76 P.3d 898 (2003), the state court held that the taking of a brake shop for a hardware store to advance economic development lacked the requisite public use. Donald Trump's attempt to get the Casino Reinvestment Development Authority in New Jersey to condemn the parcels of a few landowners who had refused to sell to expand his hotel and casino was thwarted by the state court; it found that the Authority had given Trump a blank check regarding future development on the site. Casino Reinvestment Development Authority v. Banin, 320 N.J.Super. 342, 727 A.2d 102 (1998).

2. Justice O'Connor's dissent disparages Kennedy's confidence in the rational-basis test as sufficient to ferret out privately motivated takings: "Whatever the details of Justice Kennedy's as-yet-undisclosed test, it is difficult to envision anyone but the 'stupid staff[er]' failing it." The suggestion is that only the most inept administrations could fail to paper over a private deal and make it appear public in nature.

3. The Court dealt with what constitutes a "public use" under the Fifth Amendment as early as 1896 shortly after Congress authorized the war department to condemn private property in and around the Gettysburg battlefield. The Gettysburg Electric Railway Company challenged this act arguing that preventing the completion of its rail line in order to preserve the lines of battle was not a public use as that term is employed in the Fifth Amendment. In United States v. Gettysburg Electric Ry. Co., 160 U.S. 668, 16 S.Ct. 427, 40 L.Ed. 576 (1896), the Court framed the question that the case raised as: whether "the use to which the [government] desires to put the land... is of that kind of public use for which the government of the United States is authorized to condemn land." The Court held that the government "... has authority to do so whenever it is necessary or appropriate to use the land in the execution of any of the powers granted to it by the constitution.... [W]hen the legislature has declared the *use or purpose* to be a public one, its judgment will be respected by the courts ..." (emphasis added).

4. A few years later, the Court decided a case involving a one-to-one transfer between private parties. In Strickley v. Highland Boy Gold Mining Company, 200 U.S. 527, 26 S.Ct. 301, 50 L.Ed. 581 (1906), an easement over the plaintiff's property was condemned and handed over to his neighbor, a private mining company. The complaint was that this was done solely for private gain and benefit and was not, therefore, a public use under the Fifth Amendment. The condemnation was done under a Utah statute which asserted that the public welfare of the state demanded that mining operations in the mountains have access to rail lines in its valleys. Mr. Justice Holmes wrote the opinion of the Court which addressed the sole question of whether the Utah statute is consistent with the constitutional prescriptions regarding the condemnation of property for a public use. His opinion holds as follows: "In the opinion of the state legislature and the Supreme Court of Utah, the *public welfare of that State* demands that aerial lines between the mines on its mountain sides and the railways in the valleys below should not be made impossible by the refusal of a private owner to sell the right to cross his land. The Constitution of the United States does not require us to say that they are wrong" (emphasis added).

5. Critics of the Kelo decision contend that developers often drive public decisions to condemn private land. In New London, however, there was no developer on the scene during the multi-year public decision-making process. The New London Redevelopment Authority, a publicly-created, not for profit corporation, was authorized to purchase and condemn land for the area-wide development project, and following acquisition, to advertise for private redevelopers, select one, and lease the acquired land to that developer.

6. Justice Stevens, in his majority decision, points out that New London "invoked a state statute that specifically authorizes the use of eminent domain to promote economic development in distressed cities. He also indicates that the redevelopment area was not blighted, but that the city was in need of "economic rejuvenation." Critics of the Kelo case argue that economic development is not a public use for which the power of condemnation can be used. Consider these facts: New London is formally designated by the state as a "distressed city." In Connecticut, a state of great disparity

between haves and have nots, New London houses mostly the latter. Its 5.5 square miles were carved out of the affluent town of Waterford, which has a property tax rate forty percent lower than New London's. The city hosts transit facilities, hospitals, colleges, polluting industries, and low-and moderate-income workers: all resources critical to its region's well-being. New London's poverty and unemployment rates are well above the state's average. Because the city lost a naval base and most of its industrial jobs, its tax base declined and it has flirted with municipal bankruptcy.

New London, after years of public discussion and debate, adopted an area-wide redevelopment plan for one of the few relatively low-density parcels left, next to the shuttered naval facility and a state-funded public park. The plan envisioned a small mixed-use, tourist-oriented urban village, with public parking, a renovated marina and river walk open to the public, and some restaurants and shopping. These activities would generate 1,000 new jobs, bring tax revenues to the fiscally strapped city, and enable it to provide better services to its low-and middle-income residents and workers and continued service to the region beyond. Distressed city area-wide redevelopment programs were initiated and continued to deal with a tight knot of despair in cities like New London. These cities were called "places from which men turn" by the unanimous U.S. Supreme Court in Berman v. Parker, which upheld an area-wide urban renewal plan in the District of Columbia in 1954. Countless local, state, and federal programs have struggled to restore inner-city regional centers, to obtain the proper balance of housing, industrial, and commercial facilities, and to increase their attractiveness to persons of all incomes to make them desirable places to live, work, shop, and enjoy life and its urban amenities.

7. In County of Wayne v. Hathcock, 471 Mich. 445, 684 N.W.2d 765 (2004), the Michigan Supreme Court reversed its decision in Poletown Neighborhood Council v. City of Detroit, 410 Mich. 616, 304 N.W.2d 455 (1981). In Poletown, the court held that acquiring land by condemning homes in a working class neighborhood to convey to General Motors for a new automobile plant and related facilities constituted a "public use" under the Michigan Constitution. The Poletown court was impressed by evidence that indicated that if General Motors were not able to expand its current plant, the impoverished City of Detroit would lose over 6,000 jobs and the result would be the relocation of operations to a three million square foot plant in a greenfield location. In Hathcock, the court examined a decision by Wayne County to take private land located near an airport to allow private interests to develop a mixed-use business park, the Pinnacle Project. In contrast to Detroit, Wayne County was experiencing impressive population growth and economic development, with the airport serving as the region's economic engine. The Hathcock majority held that the taking of private property under the circumstances of this case was "wholly inconsistent with the common understanding of 'public use' at the time our Constitution was ratified." In a classic application of the notion that the law arises from the facts, the court examined the contexts in which eminent domain was used in Michigan prior to the time the relevant provision of its constitution was amended in 1963. After taking a look at these circumstances, the court held that the condemnation and subsequent conveyance of land to private properties in the Wayne County context was inconsistent with this historical

understanding in Michigan. The decision recognized three contexts that were proper for the use of condemnation to transfer property to a private entity, as "seen through the eyes of an individual sophisticated in the law at the time of ratification of our 1963 Constitution:"

> (1) where public necessity of the extreme sort requires collective action [highways, railways, public utility infrastructure, etc.]; (2) where the property remains subject to public oversight after transfer to a private entity; and (3) where the property is selected because of facts of independent public significance, rather than the interests of the private entity to which the property is eventually transferred [clear slums and blight to promote public health and safety]. . .

The court concluded that "The exercise of eminent domain at issue here—the condemnation of defendants' properties for the Pinnacle Project and the subsequent transfer of those properties to private entities—implicates none of the saving elements noted by our pre–1963 eminent domain jurisprudence." Prior case law in Michigan and the record of the 1963 constitutional convention indicated that the power of eminent domain it the state was to be exercised only to achieve a "public use" and that efforts to expand the term to include "public purpose" were defeated in the courts prior to Poletown and rejected in the constitutional convention itself. As a term of art, in Michigan, the term "public use" in condemnation law is not coterminous with the term "public purpose" as it seems to be under federal jurisprudence.

8. In City of Norwood v. Horney, 110 Ohio St.3d 353, 853 N.E.2d 1115 (2006), the city moved to condemn private property in an area found to be "deteriorating," rather than "deteriorated." Here the city was approached by a private developer who wanted to acquire the land and build a mixed use development with residences, offices, and retail space and two large public parking facilities to be owned by the city. The project was projected to add two million dollars to the city's annual property tax revenues. Authority for the condemnation of land in "deteriorating areas" was found in the city's code. The condemnees sued and presented a case of first instance to the Ohio Supreme Court: "We have never been asked whether a city may appropriate property that the city determines is in an area that may deteriorate in the future."

Relying on Hathcock, the court noted that economic development by itself is not a sufficient predicate for a taking of private property:

> "Our understanding of the individual's fundamental rights in property, as guaranteed by the Ohio Constitution and our consistent holdings throughout the past two centuries that a genuine public use must be present before the state invokes its right to take, is better reflected by Hathcock's holdings that economic development by itself is not a sufficient public use to satisfy a taking. Although economic benefit can be considered as a factor among others in determining whether there is a sufficient public use and benefit in a taking, it cannot serve as the sole basis for finding such benefit. . . . We hold that an economic or financial benefit alone is insufficient to satisfy the public-use requirement . . . In

light of that holding, any taking based solely on financial gain is void as a matter of law, and the courts owe no deference to a legislative finding that the proposed taking will provide financial benefit to a community."

Turning to whether taking land in an area that is "deteriorating" to prevent the prospect of future deterioration is a sufficient basis for condemnation, the court stated:

"A fundamental determination that must be made before permitting the appropriation of a slum or a blighted or deteriorated property for redevelopment is that the property, because of its existing state of disrepair or dangerousness, poses a threat to the public's health, safety, or general welfare. Although we adhere to a broad construction of "public use," we hold that government does not have the authority to appropriate private property based on mere belief, supposition, or speculation that the property may pose such a threat in the future.... We therefore hold that the use of "deteriorating area" as a standard for determining whether private property is subject to appropriation is void for vagueness and offends due-process rights because it fails to afford a property owner fair notice and invites subjective interpretation. Further, we hold that the term "deteriorating area" cannot be used as a standard for a taking, because it inherently incorporates speculation as to the future condition of the property into the decision on whether a taking is proper rather than focusing that inquiry on the property's condition at the time of the proposed taking."

The court further held that when it reviews an eminent domain statute, it "shall utilize the heightened standard of review employed for a statute or regulation that implicates a First Amendment or other fundamental constitutional right."

SECTION 4. PROTECTING GROWTH DISTRICTS FROM COMPETITION

The cases in this section raise questions about the ability of local governments and their citizens to contain growth in established centers. Market pressures sometimes operate as a centrifugal force: the unfavorable conditions at the urban core repel capital investment outward. The underlying tension in land use policy and lawmaking is the tension between the principle of centered growth and the realities of the market. Can localities use their land use authority to tug at and rein in the momentum of the market? Can zoning be used to prevent competition with businesses in designated growth districts or to keep people from moving far away from established commercial centers? Do commercial property owners in developed districts have standing to sue adjacent municipalities for zoning land to accommodate their competitors? How much control do individual localities have over external market and political forces that frustrate their carefully conceived land use plans?

FORTE v. BOROUGH OF TENAFLY

Superior Court of New Jersey, Appellate Division, 1969.
255 A.2d 804, 106 N.J.Super. 346.

GAULKIN, S.J.A.D.

Defendants (hereafter Tenafly) appeal from a judgment declaring Tenafly's amended zoning ordinance unconstitutional insofar as it forbade the construction of a supermarket upon plaintiffs' lands.

Prior to August 1967 the zoning ordinance permitted such a use in the zone in which plaintiffs' lands were situated. Early in 1967 plaintiffs applied to the building inspector for a permit to build the building, and to the planning board (board) for approval of its site plan and parking area. The board, aided by Kendree and Shepherd, planning consultants, was then engaged in a planning study of the borough with a view toward a comprehensive master plan. The consultants had recommended and the board agreed that the 'central business core' of the borough should not only be preserved as the borough's retail shopping area, but strengthened and improved. This was to be done principally by improving the roads and the traffic pattern in said core to eliminate through-traffic and traffic congestion, and by forbidding retail businesses in the rest of the borough. This the board and its advisers felt would encourage retail businesses in the area to remain and improve and expand their properties, thus improving the appearance and enhancing the value of all properties in the business area, and providing the borough with an inviting 'downtown' center. If retail businesses were allowed to spread along the roads throughout the borough, it was believed the central business area would deteriorate and decay. Therefore, instead of approving plaintiffs' application, the board adopted a resolution asking 'that an interim zoning ordinance amendment be adopted in order to create a new district known as the C–2 District in order to discourage and restrict the spread of retail business beyond the downtown business core * * *.' Shepherd, the borough's planning consultant, testified that 93% of all of the borough's retail business establishments were in the central business core.

The governing body agreed and, on November 28, 1967, passed ordinance #939. The ordinance recited the resolution of the planning board and created the C–2 District, stating

> 'A. Intent—This district is intended for commercial and wholesale services and small local convenience neighborhood service establishments and other businesses not suited to the general retail business zone, and to provide uses which will not have an adverse effect upon the downtown business core.'

The C–2 District included plaintiffs' property.

That portion of the C–2 zone here involved included all the lands previously contained in the business zone on the west side of County Road north of Mahan Street to the Cresskill border. Plaintiffs' lands were on said side of County Road, beginning at Prospect Terrace, the street north of and parallel to Mahan Street. At the time of the passage of the amendment there were a number of businesses in the new C–2 zone. Coming south from the Cresskill border on said side of County Road there was a Robert Hall clothing store. In the next block, between Summit Street and Hudson Avenue there was an Esso Service Station, Midtown County Rambler (selling new and used cars), County Auto Parts, an unoccupied but recently renovated business building and a funeral home. Continuing south, in the next block there was Lamb Studios (manufacturers of ceramics) and property occupied jointly by Stryker Drafting and Manufacturing Company and Poretta Plumbing and Heating Company. Then came plaintiffs' lots. Below Prospect Terrace there was a barber and beauty shop, a tavern with a catering service, a TV repair shop and a small grocery store with living quarters on the second floor. On the easterly side of County Road, opposite the premises in question, (zoned residential), there is a Ford automobile agency at the corner of Summit Street, a gasoline station at the corner of Hudson Avenue, between Hudson and Prospect a dance school and studio, and on the corner of Prospect and County Road a cocktail lounge. The land abutting plaintiffs' property to the rear is in the M–1 industrial zone.

Plaintiffs immediately instituted this action to have the ordinance declared invalid. Defendants contend that the action should have been dismissed because plaintiffs failed to first apply for a variance. Under the circumstances here presented, it would have been futile to apply for a variance and therefore it was proper for plaintiffs to proceed as they did.

After a full trial, the trial court entered the judgment appealed from.

Defendants made some effort before the trial court to justify the elimination of retail stores in the C–2 zone on the ground that such uses would increase traffic on County Road, and so forth. The trial judge ruled, in effect, that since the true reasons were those expressed in the ordinance itself, it was not necessary to pass on the other alleged justifications. We agree, but add that the evidence does not establish any other justification. In other words, if the intention to preserve, rehabilitate and improve the central business area does not sustain the ordinance, it must fall.

The first question, then, is this: May a municipality which wishes to preserve, rehabilitate and improve an established business area devoted chiefly to retail stores, zone the rest of the municipality against retail sales? We hold that it may.

Plaintiffs admit that if Tenafly were writing on a clean slate it could zone one part of the borough for retail stores and forbid all but residential use in the remainder of the borough. However, they argue that here Tenafly did not write on a clean slate; before the amendment of the ordinance they were in the same zone and had the same rights as those in the so-called central business core; much of the land in the C–2 District was already devoted to commercial uses, including retail, and since the ordinance was tailored to permit nearly all of them to continue as nonconforming uses, the amendment was a sham directed against them alone, solely because they wanted to build a supermarket. Plaintiffs insist it was passed for the sole benefit of the merchants in the central business core; therefore it was unlawfully oppressive, discriminatory and unconstitutional. Furthermore, even assuming that Tenafly would have had the right to forbid retail stores in an area not already commercial, it was arbitrary and unreasonable to do so in this area, already largely commercial (including retail) and abutting commercial and industrial zones. They point out that the Robert Hall store sells only at retail, the gas station and the auto parts store are of course retail, and the manufacturers of ceramics may be selling at retail, as may the plumbing and heating and the barber and beauty shops, the tavern and the TV repair store. The small grocery store admittedly sells only at retail.

The trial judge ruled, in effect, that since the avowed purpose of the ordinance was 'to protect the business district' it was invalid. We think that was too narrow a view. Zones are often created or uses therein curtailed in a manner which benefits other zones. The mere fact that this is one of the purposes of the ordinance does not make it invalid. An area desirable for industry may be zoned otherwise because industry would damage a nearby residential or business zone. Conversely, residential uses may be forbidden in or near industrial areas to encourage the full expansion of industrial plants therein without fear of complaint of nuisance. It is true that a municipality may not, by zoning or otherwise, exclude a particular use only because it will compete with an existing business or businesses (179 Duncan Ave. v. Jersey City, 122 N.J.L. 292, 5 A.2d 68 (Sup.Ct.1939)), but if the exclusion of competition happens to be an incident or effect of otherwise valid zoning, it does not invalidate it.

Tenafly has what it considers to be a decaying central business core, choked by poor parking and traffic facilities. We take judicial notice that this is a problem which today faces many municipalities. Tenafly could have permitted the deterioration to continue into blight, hoping that new and desirable retail business areas would develop elsewhere. Instead, it appears that it wishes to make a strong effort to revitalize the present area. It elected to do so upon the recommendation of the planning consultants and the planning board. We hold that it has the right to do so, and the fact that the ordinance may give the central area a virtual monopoly over retail business does not invalidate it.

There is no evidence that Tenafly is trying to keep out supermarkets, or to benefit any particular business or businesses in the central business core. Tenafly is perfectly willing for supermarkets to open in C–1 zones, where such uses are permitted, although it concedes that there may be difficulty in finding or assembling therein the necessary land.

Assuming that the ordinance is generally valid, it leaves the question whether it is unreasonable and therefore invalid insofar as it applies to plaintiffs' property. Plaintiffs contend that it is unreasonable for the ordinance to take away from them the right to sell at retail because nearly every one of their neighbors in the C–2 zone sells at retail—some, like Robert Hall and the grocery, only at retail. They argue that the neighbors will continue to sell at retail either as permitted, accessory or nonconforming uses; hence it is discriminatory, arbitrary and unreasonable not to let them do likewise. But plaintiffs may use their property for the many purposes allowed by the ordinance. If they do, they will have the same rights to make incidental or accessory retail sales as those already carrying on similar businesses in the C–2 zone. The nonconforming retail stores are not so numerous as to make the ordinance unreasonable.

The judgment is reversed.

SWAIN v. COUNTY OF WINNEBAGO

Appellate Court of Illinois, Second District, 1969.
250 N.E.2d 439, 111 Ill.App.2d 458.

DAVIS, ACTING PRESIDING JUSTICE.

This is a declaratory judgment action brought to challenge the validity of a zoning ordinance adopted by the Winnebago County Board of Supervisors, which ordinance rezoned the property of the defendants, David W. Johnson, Helga S. Johnson, Gunnard R. Olson and Myrtle A. Olson, to permit the construction of a shopping center. The plaintiffs' amended complaint was dismissed and they have appealed.

The defendants' property consists of 145 acres of unimproved land located in Winnebago County on East State Street Road, approximately one mile east of Mulford Road. The land had been zoned for agricultural use, and was changed by the ordinance in question to a business zoning classification to permit the development of a regional shopping center. This land is a substantial distance from the downtown Rockford area, and it is outside of the corporate limits of the City of Rockford.

* * *

The plaintiffs challenge the zoning ordinance on two grounds: first, that it did not receive the required vote of the County Board of Supervisors; and second, on the standard constitutional ground that the rezoning was arbitrary and bears no reasonable relationship to the public health, safety and general welfare, and, thus, is void. They concede that their attack is not based upon any statutory remedy, such as a quo warranto; and they assert that they brought this action, as residents, citizens and taxpayers of Winnebago County, and challenge an amendatory zoning ordinance on the grounds above specified.

The plaintiffs are not the owners of the real estate which was rezoned. To have standing to sue, under the circumstances, they have the burden of alleging facts which show that they have suffered special damage as a result of the ordinance, which differ from that suffered by the general public. *Garner v. County of Du Page*, 8 Ill.2d 155, 158, 159, 133 N.E.2d 303 (1956); *Bullock v. City of Evanston*, 5 Ill.2d 22, 33, 34, 123 N.E.2d 840 (1955); *Hughes v. City of Peoria*, 80 Ill.App.2d 392, 394, 395, 225 N.E.2d 109 (1967).

The necessity of showing special damage extends generally to the plaintiffs' right to challenge the validity of the zoning ordinance and not to any particular ground on which the validity is challenged. The special interest that must be shown before a taxpayer may challenge the act of a corporate body is not limited to ordinances affecting zoning. The financial or administrative affairs of the county are not subject to question by the suit of a taxpayer unless his taxes are directly to be affected, or unless he, as opposed to the general public, has some special or distinct interest affected. *Bistor v. Board of Assessors*, 346 Ill. 362, 372, 373, 179 N.E. 120, 78 A.L.R. 686 (1931); 14 I.L.P. Counties § 87, p. 157; 20 C.J.S. Counties § 288.

The reason for such a rule is well stated in *Garner v. County of Du Page*, supra, where the court, on page 159, 133 N.E.2d page 304, said:

> "As stated in 43 C.J.S. Injunctions § 22B, Where a similar rule is expressed in connection with the right of a private individual to seek injunctive relief for a public injury, 'The rule is not a technical and arbitrary one, but has a solid foundation in principle and is sustained by very sound reasons of public policy, its object being to protect defendant against a multiplicity of suits and to secure him in one suit a final determination of all the controverted questions involved.' "

We do not find the allegations in the complaint sufficient to establish the plaintiffs' standing to sue. There is no allegation, and it would seem that there could be none, that the general tax burden would be increased as a result of the rezoning. See: *Garner v. County of Du Page*, supra, 159, 133 N.E.2d 303. The allegations in regard to increased traffic and the use and development of public facilities are not special damages peculiar to the plaintiffs, as opposed to the general public. The remainder of the plaintiffs' allegations, insofar as special damages are concerned, amount to no more than allegations, differently stated, that the plaintiffs will suffer losses by reason of increased competition which will result from the new shopping center.

The property in question is distant from the business properties of the plaintiffs. There is no factual basis in the complaint for assuming that the allegations of loss and depreciation in business interests and value of business properties could result from anything other than the new and increased competition which may result from this zoning.

The plaintiffs contend, however, that *Hughes v. City of Peoria*, supra, establishes their standing to sue in this case. In Hughes, the plaintiffs claimed to represent a number of persons operating businesses in the central business district of Peoria. The land, which had been rezoned to permit a shopping center, was three or four miles from the plaintiffs' businesses and properties. The plaintiffs alleged that they had invested large sums of money in their businesses and properties in reliance upon the existing zoning classifications; and that as a result of the rezoning, their businesses and properties would be greatly depressed and depreciated in value. The trial court found for the defendants on summary judgment.

The Appellate Court acknowledged, on pages 394 and 395, 225 N.E.2d 109, that the plaintiffs had the burden of establishing that they would suffer a special damage by reason of the new use, which would differ from that suffered by the general public, and at page 395, 225 N.E.2d at page 110, the court stated: 'The allegations in the complaint of damages to plaintiffs' businesses and properties are allegations of special damage, *Brown v. County of Lake*, 67 Ill.App.2d 144, 213 N.E.2d 790, * * *. Thus, the Appellate Court concluded that there was no basis for the trial court's finding that the properties of the plaintiffs were located so far distant from the rezoned properties so as to preclude any damage to the plaintiffs.

It is interesting to note, however, that the Appellate Court, at pages 396 and 397, 225 N.E.2d 109, referred to an allegation in the complaint that the plaintiffs would be 'greatly disadvantaged in competition with the new proposed shopping center,' and conceded that such an allegation is not a recognizable special damage. The court further stated that all of the cases which were called to its attention clearly held that increased business competition provides no standing to complain of a zoning change, and at page 397, 225 N.E.2d 109, it cited a number of such cases.

The case of *Brown v. County of Lake*, 67 Ill.App.2d 144, 213 N.E.2d 790 (1966), is not authority for the proposition that losses resulting to businesses and business properties from the increase in competition permitted by a zoning change are special damages giving the injured party standing to sue. Yet, this is what we read the statement in Hughes to mean.

In both *Hughes* and the case at bar, the general allegations of depreciation and loss in value of the plaintiffs' businesses and business properties are mere conclusions which must be supported by specific allegations of fact which show a special damage. *Winston v. Zoning Board of Appeals*, 407 Ill. 588, 594, 95 N.E.2d 864 (1951).

Realistically, however, the only factual basis that can be found (or assumed) to support the conclusions of damage, in both Hughes and the case at bar, is that the new competition will cause the plaintiffs' businesses to suffer.

* * *

From the allegations in the complaint in the case at bar, we do not believe—as apparently the court did in Hughes—that there is any valid basis for a finding of damage to the plaintiffs' businesses or properties, other than as a result of increased competition. It is not the function of the county zoning ordinances to provide economic protection for existing businesses. *Exchange Nat. Bank of Chicago v. Village of Skokie*, 86 Ill.App.2d 12, 21, 229 N.E.2d 552 (1967). Neither the fact that parties may suffer reduced incomes or be put out of business by more vigorous or appealing competition, nor the fact that properties on which such businesses are operated would thus depreciate in value, give rise to a standing to sue. *Cord Meyer Development Company v. Bell Bay Drugs, Inc.*, 20 N.Y.2d 211, 282 N.Y.S.2d 259, 229 N.E.2d 44, 46, 47 (1967); *Whitney Theatre Co. v. Zoning Board of Appeals*, 150 Conn. 285, 189 A.2d 396, 398 (1963); *London v. Planning and Zoning Com'n. of Town of Stratford*, 149 Conn. 282, 179 A.2d 614, 616 (1962); *Kreatchman v. Ramsburg*, 224 Md. 209, 167 A.2d 345, 351 (1961).

Free and open competition has always been a strong pillar in the foundation of our society. A person can have no vested or special property right in either the monopoly or competitive advantage accorded by zoning restictions [sic] at a given time. It is the philosophy of our society that any increased competition which may result from a change in the zoning restrictions will ultimately be beneficial. A competitor who may suffer has no actionable injury. Whether or not the particular zoning is in the best interest of the orderly development of the community is a determination to be made by the legislative body—the Winnebago County Board of Supervisors.

The plaintiffs do not claim a right to represent or speak for the people of the entire county. They claim a special interest in the zoning in question because of their particular properties which are located in a rather small, specified area in the City of Rockford and within the county. The factual allegations of their complaint, however, do not warrant concluding that they have suffered any special damage from the change of zoning, which differed from that of the general public, other than that resulting from the potential increased competition. We deem this insufficient to accord them standing to maintain this suit. See: *Garner v. County of Du Page*, supra, 8 Ill.2d 160, 133 N.E.2d 303.

* * *

For the reasons stated herein, the judgment of the trial court dismissing the complaint is affirmed.

Judgment affirmed.

Notes

1. Plaintiffs in Forte concede that if Tenafly were writing on a clean slate it could create any development pattern it chose in the interest of creating viable economic, mixed-use centers. They urge the court to use the existence of nonconforming uses in the area of their proposed supermarket to hold the denial of their proposal unreasonable, motivated solely to prevent economic competition with stores in the central district. Since the court disagreed and upheld the denial, does the decision support zoning to create

economic centers in newly developing communities, older suburbs, and developed urban areas? If comprehensive plans may include objectives and strategies for the proper economic development of communities, how are such strategies to be implemented if zoning is prohibited from marshalling market forces by directing them into discrete locations?

2. Who are the combatants in the Swain? Are they proxies for those engaged in the ongoing struggle to create rational land development patterns? The City of Rockport and the plaintiff merchants in this sense represent older cities with existing centers and supportive infrastructure. Winnebago County is the outlying suburban jurisdiction seeking desirable tax ratables: projects that bring in more property tax revenue than they cost the municipality in the provision of services. While cost of service studies often demonstrate that agricultural land pays more in property taxes than it costs the municipality in services, how does the county compare the economics of 145 agriculturally zoned acres with the cost-benefit of a regional shopping center? What incentive is there for the county to disapprove the proposed development? Is it enough to say that it will add to the forces of sprawl and hasten the decline of Rockport? Do your answers argue for state intervention in local land use decision-making?

3. Wal–Mart v. Town of North Elba, 238 A.D.2d 93, 668 N.Y.S.2d 774 (1998), is a case in which the court upheld the denial of a permit to build a big box retail outlet outside the town's core commercial district because of its negative impact on the general character and ambience of the community. The petitioner, Wal–Mart, contended that the town had improperly and erroneously come to that conclusion. The court held that the data documenting the decline of the downtown and estimating the store's further adverse influence on that decline were reasonable and sustainable. It held that it was not irrational to conclude that the use, though permitted, is not desirable at the particular location. (Matter of Market Sq. Props. v. Town of Guilderland Zoning Bd. of Appeals, 109 A.D.2d 164, 166, 491 N.Y.S.2d 519 (1985), affd. 66 N.Y.2d 893, 498 N.Y.S.2d 772, 489 N.E.2d 741 (1985)). The court stated that while the town's decision refers to the economic effect the proposed store would be expected to have upon other local businesses, it does so in the context of assessing the probability and extent of the change it would work upon the overall character of the community, as a result of an increased vacancy rate among commercial properties in the downtown area—an entirely proper avenue of inquiry.

4. Wal–Mart was also denied a permit to build a retail outlet in the village of Chadron, Ohio, on twenty-three acres that were zoned C–1: local retail business. The zoning code defined local retail business to include businesses that normally employ fewer than ten people and occupy less than 10,000 square feet. Wal–Mart contended that these provisions failed to advance a legitimate public interest. In Loreto Development Co. v. Village of Chardon, 119 Ohio App.3d 524, 695 N.E.2d 1151 (1996), the Court of Appeals of Ohio upheld the ordinance and the denial. Because of the great deference that courts give to determinations of legislative bodies, the court held that the plaintiff had not carried its burden of proving that no

legitimate public purpose was served by the ordinance. The fact that the legislature wished to protect the residential, small-town character of this part of town was clearly a legitimate interest to be advanced by zoning.

5. The Village Districts Act (Conn. Gen. Stat. § 8–2j) was signed into law on May 22, 1998, as Public Act 98–116, "An Act Authorizing the Establishment of Village Districts" effective October 1, 1998. The Act, an amendment to Connecticut's zoning enabling legislation, authorizes local zoning commissions to protect the distinctive character, landscape, and historic value of the areas under their jurisdiction. The Pennsylvania Municipalities Planning Code (MPC) states that zoning ordinances may permit the preservation of "natural and historic resources and prime agricultural land and activities." 53 PA. Stat. § 10603(b)(5).

SECTION 5. EXCLUSIONARY ZONING

This section considers the legal obligations of suburban communities to provide for a variety of types of housing through their zoning ordinances. Zoning is by nature exclusionary. Since its inception, it has separated land uses by district, excluding all uses except those that are expressly permitted. In adopting a zoning ordinance, the municipal legislature is making a clear statement about the type of community it wants to be. Ideally, this starts with the adoption of a comprehensive plan that reviews the community's place in its region, demographic trends, the need for commercial, industrial, and other land uses, as well as different types of housing.

In most states, there is great diversity of circumstances among municipalities ranging from those that are large and complex to those that are small and uncomplicated. There are urban communities in need of revitalization, older suburbs that are struggling to remain financially viable, newer suburbs facing their first development pressures, and rural communities where there is little demand for development of any kind. To accommodate this diversity, state legislatures typically give municipal decision-makers flexibility to make informed and appropriate choices.

What happens, then, when these leaders elect to exclude all but a small number of land uses and to remain a predominately residential, single-family community? At what point does the exclusion of commercial and multi-family buildings become unconstitutionally exclusionary? What happens when municipal zoning includes commercial, retail, and industrial developments that need moderate-income workers but zones out multi-family buildings and other, more affordable types of housing? Municipal legislators argue that their decisions on these matters should be deferred to by the courts since they make local policy and understand local circumstances. Developers argue that since municipalities get their power to zone from the state, that power must accommodate the interests of the people of the state which include those in search of housing as well as conveniently located goods and services.

A. THE BEDROOM SUBURB

STATE EX REL. CHIAVOLA v. VILLAGE OF OAKWOOD

Court of Appeals of Missouri, Western District, 1994.
886 S.W.2d 74.

Opinion By: HAROLD L. LOWENSTEIN

This appeal stems from a trial court determination that the single zoning ordinance (Ordinance No. 10) of the Village of Oakwood (Oakwood), which allows only single family residential usage in Oakwood: (1) is unconstitutional on due process grounds; and (2) as being infirm because Oakwood failed to develop a comprehensive plan under § 89.040, RSMo 1986. The Appellant, Oakwood, is a small bedroom community located in Clay County, and is a suburb of Kansas City. Oakwood consists of 80 single family dwellings on 80 platted lots.

The Plaintiffs/Respondents (Landowners) filed a multi-count petition. The trial court granted summary judgment on Count I which prayed for a declaration that Ordinance No. 10, and "all zoning ordinances" of Oakwood, were unconstitutional both facially, and as applied to Landowners and for the municipality's failure to have a separate comprehensive plan. The remaining counts, which prayed for damages under several theories, were not reached since they hinged on the ruling of Count I. Pursuant to Rule 74.01(b) the trial court determined the appealability in its declaration that its ruling was final and appealable. The trial court did not take up Landowners' request for attorney fees in Count I, under 42 U.S.C. § 1988 and under Missouri Declaratory Judgment Act §§ 527.010–.130 RSMo 1986, or in any of the other five counts. Landowners have cross-appealed on this non-ruling of attorney fees. Their cross-appeal will be addressed at the end of this opinion.

At the very heart of this appeal lies the issue of whether a Missouri municipality may enact valid zoning ordinances without having first formally adopted a "comprehensive plan," under § 89.040, which provides that regulations on zoning and districts "... shall be made in accordance with a comprehensive plan...."

Summary judgment was granted on the portion of Landowners' petition which sought declaratory relief from Oakwood's only ordinance, Ordinance No. 10, relating to zoning and land use. Ordinance No. 10 was adopted in 1955, shortly after residents of a housing subdivision were incorporated as a village under § 80.020 RSMo 1986. The ordinance limited the use of the 80 lots comprising Oakwood to single-family residential use with a lot size of 30,000 square feet.

Oakwood is now bordered by a major thoroughfare, North Oak Trafficway (North Oak), as well as a portion of Kansas City and other villages in Clay County. North Oak carries approximately 25,000 cars per day and contains many commercial properties in the other municipalities it passes through.

In 1981 the Landowners, Chiavola and Flott purchased a house in Oakwood located on a six acre lot. They sought to rezone the portion of their land which abuts North Oak, approximately 4.7 acres, for commercial use. Oakwood's zoning commission, and later its trustees, denied the rezoning petition. The circuit court reversed, holding among other reasons; Ordinance No. 10 was invalid because Oakwood had not previously adopted a "comprehensive plan" pursuant to chapter 89, and the ordinance would not suffice as both the zoning "plan" and the zoning ordinance. As a result of the demise of Ordinance No. 10 Oakwood presently has no zoning ordinance on any land within its boundaries.

Ordinance No. 10 was the product of an Oakwood Zoning Commission hearing held in February, 1955, which recommended to the Trustees that the boundaries of Oakwood be zoned as "one residential district." Attached to the Commission's report was a description of the 80 lot plats of Oakwood. The report and subsequent ordinances provided for streets and parks but no commercial areas. This ordinance was passed in March, 1955. Although amendments were made to Ordinance No. 10 in 1966 and 1967, Oakwood has limited the land use to single-family dwellings.

There are two arguments which Oakwood, Appellants, presents as error to this court: 1) Ordinance No. 10 is not facially unconstitutional; and 2) it is not statutorily invalid. The parties, in both their briefs and arguments, seem to confuse the issues of constitutionality and statutory validity. This opinion will first outline the constitutional issues, and then the statutory issue. This court finds Ordinance No. 10 to be both constitutionally and statutorily sound and, therefore, reverses the judgment. Landowners cross-appeal is dismissed.

Standard of Review

Since zoning and refusal to rezone are legislative acts, this court reviews de novo any challenges to their validity. * * * This court is to first determine whether or not the legislative judgment was fairly debatable, and if it is, then the decision must stand. *Euclid v. Ambler Realty Co.*, 272 U.S. 365, 71 L. Ed. 303, 47 S. Ct. 114 (1926) * * *. There is a presumption of validity for zoning ordinances; the presumption is rebuttable, but Landowners bear the burden of proving Ordinance No. 10 is unreasonable in order to successfully rebut the presumption. * * * Where there is uncertainty regarding the reasonableness of a zoning regulation, it is to be resolved in the government's favor. * * *

I. Constitutional Attack

A. Reasonableness

The first point on appeal is that the court erroneously held Ordinance No. 10 to be unconstitutional. An ordinance may be either facially unconstitutional or unconstitutional as applied to a particular tract of land. Here it is asserted that on its face, Ordinance No. 10 is unconstitutional. The due process clauses of the Fourteenth Amendment to U.S.

Constitution and the Missouri Constitution, Art. 1 § 10, require zoning "to bear a substantial relationship to health, safety, morals or the public welfare." * * * The constitutional standard is essentially one of reasonableness. * * * Zoning may be unreasonable on its face or as applied to a particular tract of land. In Missouri, courts not only "determine whether application of the zoning is substantially related to the alleged purpose of the zoning, but also the private detriment caused by such application." * * * Therefore, even where the zoning is related to the public welfare, the zoning may be considered unconstitutional where it demonstrates a detriment to private interests which outweighs the public benefit from retaining it. * * *

What is reasonable depends on the requirements of the locality, for what might be reasonable in one place may be unreasonable in another. * * * The fact that economic loss will be sustained if the ordinance is upheld is not controlling; nor is the fact that neighboring or adjoining land is less restrictive, establishes that the regulation is arbitrary or unfairly discriminatory. * * *

Here the zoning regulation, calling for single-family residential use, is facially reasonable. The general plan, as it can be inferred from Ordinance No. 10, its amendments via subsequent ordinances, and the development of Oakwood, was to establish a small bedroom community consisting of 80 homes. The ordinance provided for the single-family homes, churches and community buildings, public parks, and accessory uses customarily incident to the other allowable uses not involving the conduct of business or industry. This court can not say the zoning ordinance does not bear a substantial relationship to public health, safety, morals or general welfare and, therefore, is unreasonable or, that the detriment to Landowners outweighs the public benefits.

B. Comprehensive Single Use Zoning

The judgment also infers the ordinance is facially unconstitutional because it provides for only one type of zoning . . . single-family residential. *McDermott v. Calverton Park*, 454 S.W.2d 577 (Mo. banc 1970), controls on this issue. The Court in *Calverton Park* overruled a portion of its earlier ruling in *Moline Acres v. Heidbreder*, 367 S.W.2d 568 (Mo. 1963), which held a municipality could not adopt a single-use zoning ordinance.

In *Moline Acres*, the city was incorporated as a village and adopted a single-use zoning ordinance. The Court held the Missouri statutes were "never intended . . . to give to a municipality the power to adopt a one use district zoning ordinance encompassing the whole town." *Id.* at 573. Thus, the Court found the village lacked the authority to enact such an ordinance. *Id.*

The Supreme Court of Missouri, in *Calverton Park* specifically overruled the quoted portion of Moline Acres saying, "We have read and reread the applicable statutes and find nothing therein to indicate a legislative intent that, under all circumstances, a municipality must provide for more than one use in its zoning ordinance." *Calverton Park*,

454 S.W.2d at 577. This is especially true for small bedroom communities situated in large metropolitan areas. *Id.* at 581. In *Calverton Park*, the village consisted of approximately 1700 residents and was situated between the cities of Florissant and Ferguson in the St. Louis area. *Id.* at 579. Due to its location, there was an abundance of commercial facilities located within a short distance from the village. *Id.* at 580. The ordinance in question allowed for public buildings, parks, golf courses and four zoning districts, all of which were restricted to single-family residential use. *Id.* at 579.

Clarkson Valley Estates. Inc. v. Clarkson Valley, 630 S.W.2d 151 (Mo. App. 1982) further supports the proposition that single-use zoning is legally permissible. In *Clarkson Valley*, the court held single-family residential zoning for the entire village was "legally permissible and factually justified given the nature of the community involved." *Id.* at 153. The Village of Clarkson Valley was incorporated in 1952 and zoned primarily as single-family residential area. *Id.* at 152. Several years later, a landowner in the village attempted to develop his 25 acres of land commercially and, as a result, the village rezoned his portion of land as commercial. The residents of the village were adamantly opposed to the rezoning. *Id.* at 152. A short time later the village returned to the single-family residential zoning and the landowner was prohibited from any further commercial development. *Id.* at 153.

Under § 89.020 RSMo 1986, the legislative body of Oakwood is permitted to use zoning to promote health, safety, morals, and general welfare of its residents. "Certainly, where commercial and professional services are conveniently available elsewhere, none of those purposes would be enhanced by multiple-use zoning as compared to one-family dwelling use." *Calverton Park*, 454 S.W.2d at 582. In addition, the objectives of 89.040 are to "lessen congestion in the streets; to secure safety from fire, panic and other dangers; to promote health and the general welfare; to provide adequate light and air; to prevent the overcrowding of land; and to avoid undue concentration of population," are better served by a single-use zoning ordinance than they would be from multiple-use zoning in such a small area. *Id.* The Village of Oakwood is a bedroom community which has been divided into 80 lots and borders the neighboring city of Gladstone near North Oak Trafficway, Barry Road and Vivion Road (all heavily traveled thoroughfares). There are numerous commercial facilities located a short distance from Oakwood. Given the nature of the community, it was appropriate for Oakwood to zone all of the land in its boundaries as single-family residential.

C. Comprehensive Plan

Contrary to the assertion by Landowners, there is no requirement for the existence of a separate comprehensive plan in order for a zoning regulation to be constitutional. While the existence of a separate well-delineated plan may might it easier to establish an appropriate use of Oakwood's police power, and the reasonableness of the regulation or ordinance, it is not a constitutional requirement. * * * If it were a constitutional requirement, all zoning prior to the enactment of § 89.040 which requires all zoning to be done "in accordance with the comprehensive plan," would have been unconstitutional. Furthermore, even if it were a constitutional requirement, a plan may be inferred from Ordinance No. 10, and Oakwood's subsequent zoning ordinances (specifically ordinances 33, 46, 48, and 66), that Oakwood planned on being a small residential bedroom community.

II. Statutory Attack

The second part of the appeal is that Ordinance No. 10 is invalid due to Oakwood's failure to provide a comprehensive plan pursuant to § 89.040 RSMo 1986. § 89.040 provides:

> Such regulations shall be made in accordance with a comprehensive plan and designed to lessen congestion in the streets; to secure safety from fire, panic and other dangers; to promote health and the general welfare; to provide adequate light and air.... Such regulations shall be made with reasonable consideration, among other things, to the character of the district and its peculiar suitability for particular uses, and with a view to conserving the values of buildings and encouraging the most appropriate use of land throughout such municipality. (emphasis added).

In their petition, Landowners assert in their petition, since there is not a separate document or documents designated as the "comprehensive plan," Oakwood did not comply with the statute. Remember that the requirement of a plan is based on the premise that zoning regulations are not an end in and of themselves, but are the means to the end to sound planning for the public good. * * * Zoning "does no more than apply the rules of good housekeeping to public affairs. It keeps the kitchen stove out of the parlor, the bookcase out of the pantry, and the dinner table out of the bedroom." * * * The requirement of a comprehensive plan is not a "mere technicality which serves only as an obstacle for public officials to overcome in carrying out their duties" but, rather, is the essence of zoning. *Udell v. Haas*, 21 N.Y.2d 463, 235 N.E.2d 897, 900–901, 288 N.Y.S.2d 888 (N.Y. 1968). Without a plan there can be no rational allocation of land use. Id. The crux of this appeal is the question: what form must a comprehensive plan take in order to comply with § 89.040?

There is no definition of a comprehensive plan in chapter 89, governing zoning and planning of municipalities in Missouri. The language used in the Missouri statute mirrors that used in the Standard State Zoning Enabling Act, which has acted as the model for a majority of the states—i.e., all regulations must be "in accordance with the comprehensive plan." While there is not an exact definition, it can be said that a:

> 'plan' connotes an integrated product of a rational process and 'comprehensive' requires something beyond a piecemeal approach, both to be revealed by the ordinance in relation to the physical facts

and the purposes authorized" by statute. Kozesnik v. Montgomery, Twp., 24 N.J. 154, 131 A.2d 1 (N.J. 1957).

* * *

This court finds the better reasoned cases, as they apply to the fact pattern at hand, are those which do not require a comprehensive plan separate and apart from the zoning ordinance itself. This court holds a comprehensive plan may be validly enacted in an ordinance itself without existing in some form separate from the ordinance. See * * * *Osiecki v. Huntington*, 170 A.D.2d 490, 565 N.Y.S.2d 564 (A.D. 2 Dept. 1991). See * * * Comprehensiveness may be found in the fact the ordinance zones all, or substantially all, of a political subdivision; that it regulates all uses; or that it covers all of the usual factors of land utilization, height area and use. * * *

First, in looking at the statutes themselves, there is no mandate requiring Oakwood to adopt a separate plan as a condition precedent to the enactment of the ordinance. * * * Furthermore, "the general rule has become . . . that, absent specific requirements in enabling legislation, the comprehensive plan need not have a separate physical existence apart for the zoning ordinances, and it need not be in writing, but its design may be found in the scheme apparent in the zoning regulations themselves." * * * Where the enabling statute expressly requires the adoption of a comprehensive plan as a condition precedent to the passage of zoning regulations and ordinances, then a different result must occur. * * *

* * *

* * * [T]his court finds that Oakwood acted in conformance with its comprehensive plan because the preamble to the ordinance indicated an intent to create a single residential district with the same boundaries as the incorporated Oakwood; because there was a meeting by the trustees of the village which appointed a zoning commission to meet and make recommendations regarding regulations. The board met and the notice for a public hearing was given. The commission made its final record at the meeting and recommended the ordinance be enacted. The ordinance was subsequently enacted. The ordinance was comprehensive in scope; setting out both the area, height, and use requirements. Since there is evidence that planning was done, and there is no specific requirement that the village pass a separate comprehensive plan as a condition precedent to the passage of zoning ordinances. This court finds that Ordinance No. 10 was both constitutionally and statutorily valid.

This opinion does not stand for the proposition that a municipality, no matter what its size, does not have to adopt a comprehensive plan separate from the zoning ordinance. What was sufficient for Oakwood in this case, an ordinance which provided comprehensive zoning for a single land use, and which evidenced future plans for the community, will not necessarily suffice for all larger towns or cities. * * * Without a comprehensive plan, courts in situations such (as the case at bar), will have to determine on an ad hoc basis whether their efforts meet the requirement of creating a "general plan to control and direct the use and development of property in a municipality." * * * The summary judgment ruling Ordinance No. 10 invalid is reversed.

Landowners cross-appeal as to their request for attorney's fees is dismissed. The trial judge noted in the judgment, and in a subsequent clarification hearing, that the issue of fees was not being addressed and, therefore, was still an issue to be decided with the balance of the case.

The judgment is reversed, the cross-appeal is dismissed, and the cause is remanded.

Notes

1. The principal case follows an earlier Missouri case, McDermott v. Village of Calverton Park, 454 S.W.2d 577 (Mo. 1970). In Calverton Park, plaintiffs sought to have a zoning ordinance declared invalid which "did not provide for any commercial use" and "limited the use of the land to one-family dwellings." The court held that where adequate commercial services can be obtained nearby it is permissible to exclude commercial structures from the community and that the allowance of only one-family housing promoted the welfare of the community where multiple-use zoning did not. See also, Clarkson Valley Estates, Inc. v. Village of Clarkson Valley, 630 S.W.2d 151 (Mo.App.1982). Also see Cadoux v. Planning and Zoning Commission, 162 Conn. 425, 294 A.2d 582 (1972), certiorari denied 408 U.S. 924, 92 S.Ct. 2496, 33 L.Ed.2d 335 (1972), and the annotation in 54 A.L.R.3d 1282.

2. For the view that single use zoning is invalid, see Dowsey v. Village of Kensington, 257 N.Y. 221, 177 N.E. 427 (1931); Gunderson v. Village of Bingham Farms, 372 Mich. 352, 126 N.W.2d 715 (1964); Hobart v. Collier, 3 Wis.2d 182, 87 N.W.2d 868 (1958); and Matthews v. Board of Zoning Appeals of Greene County, 218 Va. 270, 237 S.E.2d 128 (1977). The Gunderson case in Michigan was modified when a later court explained that towns had to have a minimum of two zones. Compare Countrywalk Condominiums, Inc. v. Oakland Circuit Court City of Orchard Lake Village, 221 Mich.App. 19, 561 N.W.2d 405 (1997), where the court upheld a zoning scheme allowing only single-family, professional offices, and local business. The total exclusion of apartments and condominiums was justified on the basis of an overburdened traffic system.

B. EXCLUSION THROUGH HOUSING AND LOT SIZE PROVISIONS

Zoning also can exclude low, moderate, and middle income households by establishing large minimum lot sizes and allowing (or even requiring) developers to build large homes. Local decision-makers may adopt such provisions to ensure that the assessed value of homes remains high, providing the community with tax assessments and revenues needed to pay the cost of education and municipal services. Zoning is a critical factor in the local municipal finance formula: by deciding what types of land uses to allow, the municipality determines the infrastructure and services it must provide future residents and businesses as well as the values of property it can tax to provide those benefits.

There is a political counterpart to this financial reality of conducting municipal business. Many of the articulate and powerful voters in suburban communities own single-family houses on individual lots. Not only do they want the values of their homes to increase through the construction of new higher priced, large homes, but they do not want land uses in the community that will lower their home values or adversely affect the quality of their suburban experience. These are "private interests" and cannot serve as the legal basis for zoning, no matter how powerful a political force they represent.

Zoning provisions must serve a public purpose; they must advance in some way the public health, safety, welfare, and morals. How are these interests advanced by zoning that provides predominately for large, expensive single-family homes that are beyond the means of a large percentage of a region's households? Does such zoning discriminate in some legally cognizable way against those who are excluded?

NATIONAL LAND AND INVESTMENT CO. v. KOHN

Supreme Court of Pennsylvania, 1965.
419 Pa. 504, 215 A.2d 597.

["Sweetbriar," an 85 acre residential development tract, was worth $260,000 when the lot minimum was one acre. Now that the minimum for the residential area of which "Sweetbriar" is a part has been changed to four acres, the most optimistic estimate is $175,000. The zoning amendment was held unconstitutional by the trial court. The Supreme Court first disposed of a variety of procedural questions to get to the substance of the constitutional issue. Part of the court's analysis of that issue is set out below. Two judges dissented.]

ROBERTS, JUSTICE.* * *

Easttown Township has an area of 8.2 square miles devoted almost exclusively to residential use * * * The township finds itself in the path of a population expansion approaching from two directions. From the east, suburbs closer to the center of Philadelphia are reaching capacity and residential development is extending further west to Easttown. In addition, a market for residential sites is being generated by the fast growing industrial-commercial complex in the King of Prussia–Valley Forge area to the north of Easttown Township.

Easttown's vital statistics provide a good indication of its character. At present, about 60% of the township's population resides in an area of about 20% of the township. The remaining 40% of the population occupies the balance of about 80% of its area. Privately imposed restrictions limit lot areas to four, five and ten acre minimums on approximately 10% of the total area of the township, consisting of land located in the southern and western sections. Of the total 5,157 acres in the township, some 898, or about 17%, have been restricted by the new zoning ordinance to minimum lots of two acres. Approximately 1,565 acres composing about 30% of the township are restricted by the zoning ordinance to lots of four acres minimum area. About 5% of the population live in the areas zoned for two and four acre sites which together constitute about 47% of the township. Some 1,835 acres, representing about 35% of the township, remain unaffected by the new zoning and continue, under the township's original zoning classification, to be zoned for building sites with a minimum area of one acre.

* * *

U.S. Census figures show that Easttown's population grew from 2,307 in 1920 to 6,907 in 1960. As of April, 1963, the population estimate was 8,400. Public school population through the sixth grade grew from 498 in the school year 1955–56 to 1,052 in the school year 1963–64 and, as projected, will be about 1,680 in 1969–70.

New residential construction from 1951 through the first eight months of 1963, a twelve year period, consisted of 1,149 units at an estimated cost of about $21,000,000, with an average of 100 building permits annually. At this rate of growth, allowing four persons per housing unit in Easttown, its population, related to new residences, would grow under the previous one acre minimum zoning at the rate of about 400 persons per annum.

* * *

The task of considering the Easttown Township zoning ordinance and passing upon the constitutionality of its four acre minimum area requirement as applied to appellees' property is not an easy one. In the span of years since 1926 when zoning received its judicial blessing, the art and science of land planning has grown increasingly complex and sophisticated. The days are fast disappearing when the judiciary can look at a zoning ordinance and, with nearly as much confidence as a professional zoning expert, decide upon the merits of a zoning plan and its contribution to the health, safety, morals or general welfare of the community. This Court has become increasingly aware that it is neither a super board of adjustment nor a planning commission of last resort * * * The zoning power is one of the tools of government which, in order to be effective, must not be subjected to judicial interference unless clearly necessary. For this reason, a presumption of validity attaches to a zoning ordinance which imposes the burden to prove its invalidity upon the one who challenges it. * * *

While recognizing this presumption, we must also appreciate the fact that zoning involves governmental restrictions upon a landowner's constitutionally guaranteed right to use his property, unfettered, except in very specific instances, by governmental restrictions. The time must never come when, because of frustration with concepts foreign to their legal training, courts abdicate their judicial responsibility to protect the constitutional rights of individual citizens. Thus, the burden of proof imposed upon one who challenges the validity of a zoning regulation must never be made so onerous as to foreclose, for all practical purposes, a landowner's avenue of redress against the infringement of constitutionally protected rights.

The oft repeated, although ill defined, limitation upon the exercise of the zoning power requires that zoning ordinances be enacted for the health, safety, morals or general welfare of the community. * * *

We turn, then, to the question of the constitutionality of four acre minimum in the factual context of the instant case. Quite obviously, appellees will be deprived of part of the value of their property if they are limited in the use of it to four acre lots. When divided into one acre lots as originally planned, the value of "Sweetbriar" for residential building was approximately $260,000. When the four acre restriction was imposed, the number of available building sites in "Sweetbriar" was reduced by 75% and the value of the land, under the most optimistic appraisal, fell to $175,000. The four acre minimum greatly restricts the marketability of this tract because, with fewer potential lots, the cost of improvements such as curbing, streets and other facilities is thus greater on each lot. In addition, each building lot being larger, the cost per lot is automatically increased. The desire of many buyers not to be burdened with the upkeep of a four acre lot also makes "Sweetbriar," so restricted, less desirable. Although there was some evidence in the record that lots of four acres or more could eventually be sold it is clear that there is not a readily available market for such offerings.

Against this deprivation of value, the alleged public purposes cited as justification for the imposition of a four acre minimum area requirement upon appellees' land must be examined. Appellants contend that the four acre minimum is necessary to insure proper sewage disposal in the township and to protect township water from pollution. * * *

We can not help but note also that the Second Class Township Code provides for establishing sanitary regulations which can be enforced by a "sanitary board" regardless of the zoning for the area. The Code also provides for the installation and maintenance of sewer systems but the township has made no plans in this regard. In addition, under the township subdivision regulations, the zoning officer may require lots larger than the minimum permitted by the zoning ordinance if the result of percolation tests upon the land show that a larger land area is needed for proper drainage and disposal of sewage. These legislatively sanctioned methods for dealing with the sewage problem compel the conclusion that a four acre minimum is neither a necessary nor a reasonable method by which Easttown can protect itself from the menace of pollution.

In addition to the alleged problem of sewage disposal as justifying the four acre minimum, appellants cite the inadequacy of township roads and the burden which continued one acre zoning for the entire township would impose upon that road system.

* * *

According to the experts produced for both sides, Easttown's present road network as a whole is capable, with normal maintenance and improvement, of serving a population up to 13,000. This is 4,600 more than the population of the township in April, 1963. On the basis of the former one acre zoning, resulting in a population increase of 400 persons per year, that figure would not be reached until after 1972 or later.

It can be seen, therefore, that the restriction to four acre lots, so far as traffic is concerned, is based upon possible future conditions. Zoning is a tool in the hands of governmental bodies which enables them to more effectively meet the demands of evolving and growing communities. It must not and can not be used by those officials as an instrument by which they may shirk their responsibilities. Zoning is a means by which a governmental body can plan for the future—it may not be used as a means to deny the future. * * *

It is not difficult to envision the tremendous hardship, as well as the chaotic conditions, which would result if all the townships in this area decided to deny to a growing population sites for residential development within the means of at least a significant segment of the people.

The third justification for rezoning, and one urged upon us most assiduously, deals with the preservation of the "character" of this area. The photographic exhibits placed in the record by appellants attest to the fact that this is an area of great beauty containing old homes surrounded by beautiful pasture, farm and wood land. It is a very desirable and attractive place in which to live.

Involved in preserving Easttown's "character" are four aspects of concern which the township gives for desiring four acre minimum zoning. First, they cite the preservation of open space and the creation of a "greenbelt" which, as most present day commentators impress upon us, are worthy goals. While in full agreement with these goals, we are convinced that four acre minimum zoning does not achieve the creation of a greenbelt in its technical sense and, to the limited extent that open space is so preserved, such zoning as is here involved is not a permissible means to that end.

* * *

If the preservation of open spaces is the township objective, there are means by which this can be accomplished which include authorization for "cluster zoning" or condemnation of development rights with compensation paid for that which is taken. A four acre minimum acreage requirement is not a reasonable method by which the stated end can be achieved.

Next, the township urges us to consider the historic sites in the township and the need to present them in the proper setting. We are unmoved by this contention since it appears to be purely and simply a makeweight. First, an examination of the map of historical sites in the township demonstrates that the overwhelming majority of such sites, located in areas of dense population, can hardly be provided with proper settings by four acre zoning elsewhere in the township. * * *

Closely related to the goal of protecting historic monuments is the expressed desire to protect the "setting" for a number of old homes in Easttown, some dating back to the early days of our Commonwealth. Appellants denominate this goal as falling within the ambit of promoting the "general welfare". Unfortunately, the concept of the general welfare defies meaningful capsule definition and constitutes an exceedingly difficult standard against which to test the validity of legislation. However, it must always be ascertained at the outset whether, in fact, it is the public welfare which is being benefited or whether, disguised as legislation for the public welfare, a zoning ordinance actually served purely private interests.

There is no doubt that many of the residents of this area are highly desirous of keeping it the way it is, preferring, quite naturally, to look out upon land in its natural state rather than on other homes. These desires, however, do not rise to the level of public welfare. This is purely a matter of private desire which zoning regulations may not be employed to effectuate.

* * *

The fourth argument advanced by appellants, and one closely analogous to the preceding one, is that the rural character of the area must be preserved. If the township were developed on the basis of this zoning, however, it could not be seriously contended that the land would retain its rural character—it would simply be dotted with larger homes on larger lots.

Appellants point to the fact that the surrounding townships have similar low density zoning provisions. Although the zoning of the surrounding area is frequently a relevant consideration in assessing the validity of a zoning regulation * * * it is not controlling on the issue presented. This is particularly so when we are dealing with a unique zoning classification such as is involved here. With most zoning classifications, there can be little question as to their suitability in any political subdivision; the only issue concerns their placement. With these classifications, the surrounding zoning is particularly relevant. As the classification itself becomes more questionable, however, similar classifications in surrounding districts become of less significance in supporting the validity of the restriction.

* * *

The township's brief raises (but, unfortunately, does not attempt to answer) the interesting issue of the township's responsibility to those who do not yet live in the township but who are part, or may become part, of the population expansion of the suburbs. Four acre zoning represents Easttown's position that it does not desire to accommodate those who are pressing for admittance to the township unless such admittance will not create any additional burdens upon governmental functions and services. The question posed is whether the township can stand in the way of the natural forces which send our growing population into hitherto undeveloped areas in search of a comfortable place to live. We have concluded not. A zoning ordinance whose primary purpose is to prevent the entrance of newcomers in order to avoid future burdens, economic and otherwise, upon the administration of public services and facilities can not be held valid. Of course, we do not mean to imply that a governmental body may not utilize its zoning power in order to insure that the municipal services which the community requires are provided in an orderly and rational manner.

The brief of the appellant-intervenors creates less of a problem but points up the factors which sometime lurk behind the espoused motives for zoning. What basically appears to bother intervenors is that a small number of lovely old homes will have to start keeping company with a growing number of smaller, less expensive, more densely located houses. It is clear, however, that the general welfare is not fostered or promoted by a zoning ordinance designed to be exclusive and exclusionary. * * *

In light of the foregoing, therefore, we are compelled to conclude that the board of adjustment committed an error of law in upholding the constitutionality of the Easttown Township four acre minimum requirement as applied to appellees' property. We therefore affirm the order of the Court of Common Pleas of Chester County.

Order affirmed.

Notes

1. The Wall Street Journal for August 15, 1966, reported that to avoid the expense of further litigation the town and the builder in the principal case finally compromised on two-acre lots.

2. Compare the principal case with, Bilbar Const. Co. v. Board of Adjustment, 393 Pa. 62, 141 A.2d 851 (1958), which notes that minimum lot areas cannot be so large as to be exclusionary and thereby serve private interests, but finds a one-acre requirement to be reasonable.

3. The Pennsylvania court returned to the problem of large lot zoning in Appeal of Kit–Mar Builders, Inc., 439 Pa. 466, 268 A.2d 765 (1970). In this case the developer contracted to purchase 140 acres contingent on rezoning to permit one-acre homesites. The existing zoning required two acre lots on roadways and three acre lots in the interior. The rezoning was denied on grounds of sewerage problems and the developer appealed. Justice Roberts again wrote the majority opinion, striking down the two and three acre restrictions, and reaffirming National Land: "We once again reaffirm our past authority and refuse to allow the township to do precisely what we have never permitted—keep out people, rather than make community improvements. * * * [C]ommunities must deal with the problems of population growth. They may not refuse to confront the future by adopting zoning regulations that effectively restrict population to near present levels." Justice Roberts keyed his opinion to a judicial stand against exclusionary zoning practices, ruling that a municipality must present an "extraordinary justification" for implementing a minimum lot size requirement of two acres or

more. The same Pennsylvania high court, in C & M Developers v. Bedminster Twp. Zoning Hearing Bd., 573 Pa. 2, 820 A.2d 143 (2002), found this "extraordinary justification" standard nonbinding, yet still struck down an ordinance that had the effect of limiting development to one unit per three acres based upon the traditional standard: substantial relation to a police power purpose.

4. Is a decision striking down two acre zoning to allow a developer to develop homes on one acre sites a judicial blow against exclusionary zoning? Should not the real issue be whether the community is making provisions for low-and moderate-income housing? If a community does provide in its zoning for a variety of housing types, then why does it matter that some zones are set aside for one, two, or five acre lots? Consider these questions in connection with the materials on zoning that excludes multi-family housing in Section E, *infra*.

5. Judges routinely state that they defer to the discretion and decisions of local lawmakers regarding zoning, which is highly sensitive to local circumstances. Does Justice Roberts' decision in the principal case sound deferential to you? What is the difference between accepting the rationale advanced by local planners and lawmakers to justify large-lot residential zoning, and pointing out the flaws in that thinking as the Roberts decision does with precision? As an attorney arguing for or against a zoning provision, how can you convince the court to disregard the stated reasons for local zoning amendments? If the parties engage professional experts to testify on their behalf and the expert opinions differ, how could a court decide to invalidate the zoning?

6. Consider also the case of County Comm'rs of Queen Anne's County v. Miles, 246 Md. 355, 228 A.2d 450 (1967), in which the Maryland Court of Appeals upheld a county zoning ordinance providing for five residential zones, one of which covered a substantial land area and imposed a five-acre minimum lot size. The ordinance was attacked on the basis that "the properties were so zoned in order that they could be disposed of only to 'substantial' people, of 'more than ample' financial resources." The court noted that "there were many criteria considered in the decision" including the fact that many historical sites were located in the area. Other testimony, which the court cited, was to the effect that it was desirable to attract persons "of means" to the community; that tourists could be attracted in this manner; that it was a reasonable use of zoning for a rural county to employ in an otherwise urbanized area to preserve the desired character of the county; and that it would contribute to the health and safety of the county by minimizing sanitation problems, reducing the traffic and channeling the denser population growth into locations nearer the centers of development. The court stated:

> We agree that if the primary purpose or effect of the ordinance is to benefit private interests, rather than the public welfare, the legislation cannot be held valid merely because some of its incidental effects may be for the general good. On the other hand, if the ordinance has a substantial relationship to the general welfare of the community in that it can fairly be taken as a reasonable effort to plan for the future within the framework of the County's economic and social life, it is not

unconstitutional because under it some persons may suffer loss and others be benefited. Courts of other states have had occasion to balance these factors; the decisions, as we read them, turn on the various economic, physical and sociological factors involved in the particular case.

After reviewing a number of these cases, the Maryland court concluded that the ordinance was fair and reasonable and not arbitrary or capricious.

YBARRA v. TOWN OF LOS ALTOS HILLS

United States Court of Appeals, Ninth Circuit, 1974.
503 F.2d 250.

SOLOMON, DISTRICT JUDGE.

Appellants challenge the constitutionality of a large-lot zoning ordinance of the City of the Town of Los Altos Hills ["Los Altos" or "the town"], a California suburban community. The trial court held that the zoning ordinance was constitutional and dismissed the action. We affirm.

Appellants are two Mexican–Americans and the Confederacion de la Raza Unida, an unincorporated association of Mexican–American organizations. Neither of the named individual appellants are residents of Los Altos, but both qualify for federally assisted low-income housing. They brought this action on their own behalf and on behalf of all other persons of Mexican descent whose incomes qualify them for federally assisted housing.

In December, 1970, appellants obtained an option to buy certain lots in Los Altos. They paid a nominal amount for the option but agreed to pay $14,000 per acre if the option were exercised. The option could only be exercised if the land were rezoned for multifamily dwellings and if the Federal Housing Administration approved a low-income housing project for that land.

The zoning ordinance provides that a housing lot shall contain not less than one acre and that no lot shall be occupied by more than one primary dwelling unit. Appellants have not applied for a zoning variance to allow construction of their proposed multifamily project.

Appellants brought this action against the town, its city manager, and the members of the town council. Appellants allege that the zoning ordinance prevents them from constructing a housing project and assert that the ordinance violates the supremacy, due process, and equal protection clauses of the United States Constitution. They seek declaratory and injunctive relief.

* * *

Appellants' principal contention is that the Los Altos zoning ordinance denies them equal protection of the laws. They assert that the ordinance discriminates against Mexican–Americans and the poor and that the town must show a compelling state interest to justify discrimination against "suspect classifications" based on ethnic background and wealth.

Appellants' evidence at trial showed that in Santa Clara County, in which Los Altos is located, there is a high statistical correlation between being Mexican–American and being poor. Mexican–Americans form only 2.1% of the town's population but comprise 17.59% of the county's population.

The trial court found that the ordinance prevented poor people from living in Los Altos. He also found that if Mexican–Americans did not live there, it was because of the poverty and not because of their race. Appellants concede that the ordinance does not bar wealthy Mexican–Americans from living in Los Altos. We agree that discrimination against the poor does not become discrimination against an ethnic minority merely because there is a statistical correlation between poverty and ethnic background.

Appellants also assert that they need not show racial discrimination to void the ordinance and that it is sufficient to show that the ordinance discriminates against the poor. They argue that the town must show a compelling interest to justify the ordinance because wealth is a suspect classification. See *Harper v. Virginia Board of Elections*, 383 U.S. 663, 86 S.Ct. 1079, 16 L.Ed.2d 169 (1966); *Griffin v. Illinois*, 351 U.S. 12, 76 S.Ct. 585, 100 L.Ed. 891 (1956).

In *San Antonio School District v. Rodriguez*, 411 U.S. 1, 93 S.Ct. 1278, 36 L.Ed.2d 16 (1973), the court discussed the conditions under which poverty becomes a suspect classification under the equal protection clause:

> "The individuals, or groups of individuals, who constituted the class discriminated against in our prior cases shared two distinguishing characteristics: because of their impecunity they were completely unable to pay for some desired benefit, and as a consequence, they sustained an absolute deprivation of a meaningful opportunity to enjoy that benefit. 411 U.S. at 20, 93 S.Ct. at 1290."

In our view these two criteria set forth the threshold requirements before a court using traditional tests may consider whether the classification is constitutionally impermissible.

Appellants meet the first criterion because the ordinance prevents them from living in Los Altos because of their poverty. They failed to meet the second criterion because they did not show that they had no "meaningful opportunity" to obtain low-cost housing. The evidence showed that no poor people live or work in Los Altos. Appellants failed to show that adequate low-cost housing was unavailable elsewhere in Santa Clara County in areas accessible to appellants' jobs and social services. In these circumstances the town need not show a compelling interest to justify a zoning ordinance which discriminates against the poor.

Since there is no suspect classification requiring a strict standard of review, the town need only show that the ordinance bears a rational relationship to a legitimate governmental interest. Id. at 40, 93 S.Ct. 1278. Here the ordinance is rationally related to preserving the town's rural environment. See *Village of Belle Terre v. Boraas*, 416 U.S. 1, 94 S.Ct. 1536, 39 L.Ed.2d 797 (1974). The ordinance does not violate the equal protection clause.

Appellants allege that the ordinance violates Section 65302 of the California Government Code, which requires towns to adopt housing plans which "make adequate provision for the housing needs of all economic segments of the community." We believe that the section requires a town to provide housing for its residents but does not require it to provide housing for non-residents, even though the non-residents may live in the broader urban community of which the town is a part.

Appellants' other contentions are without merit. The ordinance does not conflict with the National Housing Act, 42 U.S.C.A. §§ 1401 et seq., and does not violate the supremacy clause. *James v. Valtierra*, 402 U.S. 137, 140, 91 S.Ct. 1331, 28 L.Ed.2d 678 (1971). The ordinance is not arbitrary and does not deny appellants due process. See *Village of Euclid v. Ambler Realty Co.*, 272 U.S. 365, 47 S.Ct. 114, 71 L.Ed. 303 (1926).

The judgment of the district court dismissing the action is affirmed.

Notes

1. Is the legal principle to be gleaned from the preceding case that large lot zoning is definitely exclusionary in regard to low-income groups, but such exclusion is constitutionally legitimate as long as housing opportunities for lower income groups are provided elsewhere in the region? If you think otherwise, then what is the principle? An intermediate appellate court in New York, in Robert E. Kurzius, Inc. v. Incorporated Village of Upper Brookville, 67 A.D.2d 70, 414 N.Y.S.2d 573 (1979), struck down a five acre minimum on the ground that the housing needs of low-and moderate-income persons were not being met within the village. The Court of Appeals rejected that reasoning, stating: "There was no proof that persons of low or moderate incomes were foreclosed from housing in the general region because of an unavailability of properly zoned land." 51 N.Y.2d 338, 434 N.Y.S.2d 180, 414 N.E.2d 680 (1980).

2. In Lionshead Lake, Inc. v. Wayne Township, 10 N.J. 165, 89 A.2d 693 (1952), a minimum house size requirement was upheld because preserving the character of the community was a valid objective and house size could achieve that goal. This was true even where the plaintiff demonstrated that the township was in the path of development. This New Jersey doctrine matured in Home Builders League of South Jersey, Inc. v. Township of Berlin, 81 N.J. 127, 405 A.2d 381 (1979), where plaintiffs attacked a minimum floor area requirement. Even where such a provision can be shown to be reasonably related to a legitimate state interest, it can be invalidated if its adverse consequences become too severe. In this case, the town was unable to establish that the ordinance achieved a legitimate state interest since it failed to show what public purpose was served by it other than achieving economic segregation. The Supreme Court of New Jersey affirmed the lower court's holding that the ordinance was invalid.

C. RESTRICTING NON–TRADITIONAL FAMILIES

A zoning ordinance routinely includes a definitions section and a separate section that lists the types of zoning districts it establishes, including the land uses that are allowed as-of-right or by special permit within each district. Single-family residential districts permit the construction of a single-family homes on individual parcels as-of-right. This provision regulates the construction of the building and limits it, for example, to having one kitchen. The single-family home, as an architectural matter, is designed and built for a single "housekeeping unit."

The mischief explored in this section arises in the ordinance's definitions section. There a "single-family" is defined and the definitions vary from community to community. "Single-family" may be defined as a household whose members are related by blood, marriage, or adoption. Some definitions add households of unrelated individuals, but limit the number of individuals in these non-traditional households to a certain number of persons, ranging from two to five. The definition may require that, to qualify as a family, the non-traditional household must live and cook together as a single housekeeping unit. Some ordinances not only limit non-traditional households to a small number of individuals but require that those individuals must be elderly, exceeding, for example, sixty-one years of age.

What happens when an unmarried couple with children from former marriages takes up residence in a single-family home? Do they constitute a family? They are not all related by blood, marriage, or adoption and they may exceed the numerical limit on the number of unrelated persons allowed. Are their rights, or those of the owner of a home who rents to such a non-traditional family, violated when the municipality determines that they may not live in a single-family zoning district? Similar issues are raised when single-family homes are occupied by a small group of graduate students, or by a couple with foster children.

Zoning was designed primarily to limit the physical impacts of land use. In a single-family district, it serves the public interest to limit traffic, parking, housing overcrowding, noise, water usage, and waste water. Is it legitimate to limit single-family home occupancy to households whose members are related by blood, marriage, or adoption? What public interest does such a limitation serve and is that interest within the interests cognizable by zoning regulation? What federal and state constitutional protections are implicated by such land use limitations and what state and federal statutes are involved?

VILLAGE OF BELLE TERRE v. BORAAS

Supreme Court of the United States, 1974.
416 U.S. 1, 94 S.Ct. 1536, 39 L.Ed.2d 797.

MR. JUSTICE DOUGLAS delivered the opinion of the Court.

Belle Terre is a village on Long Island's north shore of about 220 homes inhabited by 700 people. Its total land area is less than one square mile. It has restricted land use to one-family dwellings excluding lodging houses, boarding houses, fraternity houses, or multiple dwelling houses. The word "Family" as used in the ordinance means, "One or more persons related by blood, adoption or marriage, living and cooking together as a single housekeeping unit, exclusive of household servants. A number of persons but not exceeding two (2) living and cooking together as a single housekeeping unit though not related by blood, adoption, or marriage shall be deemed to constitute a family."

Appellees (Dickmans) are owners of a house in the village and leased it in December, 1971 for a term of 18 months to Michael Truman. Later Bruce Boraas became a colessee. Then Anne Parish moved into the house along with three others. These six are students at nearby State University at Stony Brook and none is related to the other by blood, adoption, or marriage. When the village served the Dickmans with an "Order to Remedy Violations" of the ordinance, the owners plus three tenants thereupon brought this action under 42 U.S.C.A. § 1983 for an injunction declaring the ordinance unconstitutional. The District Court held the ordinance constitutional and the Court of Appeals reversed, one judge dissenting. 2 Cir., 476 F.2d 806. The case is here by appeal, 28 U.S.C.A. § 1254(2); and we noted probable jurisdiction, 414 U.S. 907, 94 S.Ct. 234, 38 L.Ed.2d 145.

* * *

The present ordinance is challenged on several grounds: that it interferes with a person's right to travel; that it interferes with the right to migrate to and settle within a State; that it bars people who are uncongenial to the present residents; that the ordinance expresses the social preferences of the residents for groups that will be congenial to them; that social homogeneity is not a legitimate interest of government; that the restriction of those whom the neighbors do not like trenches on the newcomers' rights of privacy; that it is of no rightful concern to villagers whether the residents are married or unmarried; that the ordinance is antithetical to the Nation's experience, ideology and self-perception as an open, egalitarian, and integrated society.

We find none of these reasons in the record before us. It is not aimed at transients. Cf. Shapiro v. Thompson, 394 U.S. 618, 89 S.Ct. 1322, 22 L.Ed.2d 600. It involves no procedural disparity inflicted on some but not on others such as was presented by Griffin v. Illinois, 351 U.S. 12, 76 S.Ct. 585, 100 L.Ed. 891. It involves no "fundamental" right guaranteed by the Constitution, such as voting, *Harper v. Virginia State Board*, 383 U.S. 663, 86 S.Ct. 1079, 16 L.Ed.2d 169; the right of association, *NAACP v. Alabama ex rel. Patterson*, 357 U.S. 449, 78 S.Ct. 1163, 2 L.Ed.2d 1488; the right of access to the courts, *NAACP v. Button*, 371 U.S. 415, 83 S.Ct. 328, 9 L.Ed.2d 405; or any rights of privacy, cf. *Griswold v. Connecticut*, 381 U.S. 479, 85 S.Ct. 1678, 14 L.Ed.2d 510; *Eisenstadt v. Baird*, 405 U.S. 438, 453–454, 92 S.Ct. 1029, 1038–1039, 31 L.Ed.2d 349. We deal with economic and social legislation where legislatures have historically drawn lines which we respect against the charge of violation of the Equal Protection Clause if the law be "reasonable, not arbitrary" (quoting *F.S. Royster Guano Co. v. Virginia*, 253 U.S. 412, 415, 40 S.Ct. 560, 561, 64 L.Ed. 989) and bears "a rational relationship to a [permissible] state objective." *Reed v. Reed*, 404 U.S. 71, 76, 92 S.Ct. 251, 254, 30 L.Ed.2d 225.

It is said, however, that if two unmarried people can constitute a "family," there is no reason why three or four may not. But every line drawn by a legislature leaves some out that might well have been included. That exercise of discretion, however, is a legislative not a judicial function.

It is said that the Belle Terre ordinance reeks with an animosity to unmarried couples who live together. There is no evidence to support it; and the provision of the ordinance bringing within the definition of a "family" two unmarried people belies the charge.

The ordinance places no ban on other forms of association, for a "family" may, so far as the ordinance is concerned, entertain whomever they like.

The regimes of boarding houses, fraternity houses, and the like present urban problems. More people occupy a given space; more cars rather continuously pass by; more cars are parked; noise travels with crowds.

A quiet place where yards are wide, people few, and motor vehicles restricted are legitimate guidelines in a land use project addressed to family needs. This goal is a permissible one within Berman v. Parker, supra. The police power is not confined to elimination of filth, stench, and unhealthy places. It is ample to lay out zones where family values, youth values, and the blessings of quiet seclusion, and clean air make the area a sanctuary for people.

* * *

Reversed.

MR. JUSTICE MARSHALL, dissenting.

* * *

When separate but equal was still accepted constitutional dogma, this Court struck down a racially restrictive zoning ordinance. *Buchanan v. Warley*, 245 U.S. 60, 38 S.Ct. 16, 62 L.Ed. 149 (1917). I am sure the Court would not be hesitant to invalidate that ordinance today. The lower federal courts have considered procedural aspects of zoning, and acted to insure that land use controls are not used as means of confining minorities and the poor to the ghettos of our central cities. These are limited but necessary intrusions on the discretion of zoning authorities. By the same token, I think it clear that the First Amendment provides some limitation on zoning laws. It is inconceivable to me that we would allow the exercise of the zoning power to burden First Amendment freedoms, as by ordinances that restrict occupancy to individuals adhering to particular religious, political or scientific beliefs. Zoning officials properly concern themselves with the uses of land—with, for example, the number and kind of dwellings to be constructed in a certain neighborhood or the number of persons who can reside in those dwellings. But zoning authorities cannot validly consider who those persons are, what they believe, or how they choose to live, whether they are Negro or white, Catholic or Jew, Republican or Democrat, married or unmarried.

My disagreement with the Court today is based upon my view that the ordinance in this case unnecessarily burdens appellees' First Amendment freedom of association and their constitutionally guaranteed right to privacy. Our decisions establish that the First and Fourteenth Amendments protect the freedom to choose one's associates. *NAACP v. Button*, 371 U.S. 415, 430, 83 S.Ct. 328, 336, 9 L.Ed.2d 405 (1963). Constitutional protection is extended not only to modes of association that are political in the usual sense, but also to those that pertain to the social and economic benefit of the members. The selection of one's living companions involves similar choices as to the emotional, social, or economic benefits to be derived from alternative living arrangements.

The freedom of association is often inextricably entwined with the constitutionally guaranteed right of privacy. The right to "establish a home" is an essential part of the liberty guaranteed by the Fourteenth Amendment. *Meyer v. Nebraska*, 262 U.S. 390, 399, 43 S.Ct. 625, 626, 67 L.Ed. 1042 (1923); *Griswold v. Connecticut*, 381 U.S. 479, 495, 85 S.Ct. 1678, 1687, 14 L.Ed.2d 510 (1965). And the Constitution secures to an individual a freedom "to satisfy his intellectual and emotional needs within the privacy of his own home." *Stanley v. Georgia*, 394 U.S. 557, 564–565, 89 S.Ct. 1243, 1248, 22 L.Ed.2d 542 (1969); see *Paris Adult Theatre I v. Slaton*, 413 U.S. 49, 66–67, 93 S.Ct. 2628, 2640–2641, 37 L.Ed.2d 446 (1973). Constitutionally protected privacy is, in Mr. Justice Brandeis' words, "as against the government, the right to be let alone * * * the right most valued by civilized man." *Olmstead v. United States*, 277 U.S. 438, 478, 48 S.Ct. 564, 572, 72 L.Ed. 944 (1928) (dissenting opinion). The choice of household companions—of whether a person's "intellectual and emotional needs" are best met by living with family, friends, professional associates or others—involves deeply personal considerations as to the kind and quality of intimate relationships within the home. That decision surely falls within the ambit of the right to privacy protected by the Constitution.

The instant ordinance discriminates on the basis of just such a personal lifestyle choice as to household companions. It permits any number of persons related by blood or marriage, be it two or twenty, to live in a single household, but it limits to two the number of unrelated persons bound by profession, love, friendship, religious or political affiliation or mere economics who can occupy a single home. Belle Terre imposes upon those who deviate from the community norm in their choice of living companions significantly greater restrictions than are applied to residential groups who are related by blood or marriage, and comprise the established order with the community. The town has, in effect, acted to fence out those individuals whose choice of lifestyle differs from that of its current residents.

This is not a case where the Court is being asked to nullify a township's sincere efforts to maintain its residential character by preventing the operation of rooming houses, fraternity houses or other commercial or high-density residential uses. Unquestionably, a town is free to restrict such uses. Moreover, as a general proposition, I see no constitutional infirmity in a town limiting the density of use in residential areas by zoning regulations which do not discriminate on the basis of constitutionally suspect criteria. This ordinance, however, limits the density of occupancy of only those homes occupied by unrelated persons. It thus reaches beyond control of the use of land or the density of population, and undertakes to regulate the way people choose to associate with each other within the privacy of their own homes.

* * *

I respectfully dissent.

[A dissenting opinion by Justice Brennan is omitted.]

Notes

1. Also see Palo Alto Tenants Union v. Morgan, 321 F.Supp. 908 (N.D.Cal.1970), affirmed 487 F.2d 883 (9th Cir.1973), certiorari denied 417 U.S. 910, 94 S.Ct. 2608, 41 L.Ed.2d 214 (1974); Westhab, Inc. v. City of New Rochelle, 2004 WL 1171400 (S.D.N.Y.2004).

2. In 1977, the Supreme Court was faced with another "single-family" case. In Moore v. City of East Cleveland, Ohio, 431 U.S. 494, 97 S.Ct. 1932, 52 L.Ed.2d 531 (1977), the ordinance contained a complex definition of family which had the effect of making Mrs. Moore's occupancy of her dwelling along with her son and two grandsons (who were first cousins) illegal. In a plurality opinion by Justice Powell, the Court distinguished Belle Terre by noting that the earlier case affected only unrelated individuals while the East Cleveland ordinance forbade the living together of certain categories of relatives. The Court thus gave "close scrutiny" to the ordinance because of the governmental intrusion into the "family" and found that the city could offer no acceptable justification for such intrusion. The city's argument that the objectives of the ordinance were to avoid overcrowding, traffic congestion and undue burdens on the school system was found by the Court to have, at best, a tenuous relationship to the definition of family and the effect of the ordinance on Mrs. Moore.

Justice Powell explained the Belle Terre case in the following statement:

> The city argues that our decision in Village of Belle Terre v. Boraas, 416 U.S. 1, 94 S.Ct. 1536, 39 L.Ed.2d 797 (1974), requires us to sustain the ordinance attacked here. Belle Terre, like East Cleveland, imposed limits on the types of groups that could occupy a single dwelling unit. Applying the constitutional standard announced in this Court's leading land-use case, Village of Euclid v. Ambler Realty Co., 272 U.S. 365, 47 S.Ct. 114, 71 L.Ed. 303 (1926), we sustained the Belle Terre ordinance

on the ground that it bore a rational relationship to permissible state objectives.

But one overriding factor sets this case apart from Belle Terre. The ordinance there affected only unrelated individuals. It expressly allowed all who were related by "blood, adoption, or marriage" to live together, and in sustaining the ordinance we were careful to note that it promoted "family needs" and "family values." 416 U.S., at 9, 94 S.Ct., at 1541. East Cleveland, in contrast, has chosen to regulate the occupancy of its housing by slicing deeply into the family itself. This is no mere incidental result of the ordinance. On its face it selects certain categories of relatives who may live together and declares that others may not. In particular, it makes a crime of a grandmother's choice to live with her grandson in circumstances like those presented here.

When a city undertakes such intrusive regulation of the family, neither Belle Terre nor Euclid governs; the usual judicial deference to the legislature is inappropriate. "This Court has long recognized that freedom of personal choice in matters of marriage and family life is one of the liberties protected by the Due Process Clause of the Fourteenth Amendment." * * * Of course, the family is not beyond regulation.

* * * But when the government intrudes on choices concerning family living arrangements, this Court must examine carefully the importance of the governmental interests advanced and the extent to which they are served by the challenged regulation.

3. After Belle Terre, would you expect the state courts to accept restrictive definitions of "family" so as to exclude from the single-family district living arrangements other than the traditional family? Consider the following materials.

McMINN v. TOWN OF OYSTER BAY

Court of Appeals of New York, 1985.
66 N.Y.2d 544, 498 N.Y.S.2d 128, 488 N.E.2d 1240.

SIMONS, JUDGE.

Plaintiffs are the owners and tenants of a four-bedroom house in Massapequa in the Town of Oyster Bay, Long Island, which is in violation of the Town zoning ordinance. They commenced this action against defendants, the Town of Oyster Bay, the Town Council and its supervisor and building inspector, for a declaration that that portion of the ordinance restricting "single-family" housing to any number of persons related by blood, marriage or adoption or to two persons not so related but both of whom are 62 years of age or older violates the due process and equal protection clauses of the State Constitution (N.Y. Const., art. I, §§ 6, 11) and Human Rights Law § 296 (Executive Law § 296). Plaintiffs also sought an injunction against further enforcement of the ordinance. Following a trial, Supreme Court concluded that the age requirement for defining two unrelated individuals as a family violated the State constitutional guarantee of equal protection of the laws and that the ordinance also violated Executive Law § 296(5) to the extent it prohibited occupancy of a single-family house by two individuals on the ground of marital status but that the ordinance was in all other respects valid (111 Misc.2d 1046, 445 N.Y.S.2d 859). The combined effect of these rulings was to find the ordinance constitutional insofar as it restricted occupancy of a single-family home to any number of persons related by blood, marriage or adoption or two unrelated persons. On cross appeals, the Appellate Division modified the judgment and declared that the challenged portion of the ordinance was facially unconstitutional under the due process clause of our State Constitution insofar as it prohibits occupancy of one-family homes by persons unrelated by blood, marriage or adoption and that it was constitutional insofar as it limits occupancy of one-family homes to a single housekeeping unit (105 A.D.2d 46, 482 N.Y.S.2d 773).

* * *

Plaintiffs Robert and Joan McMinn purchased their house in 1973. It is in a D Residence district. On June 1, 1976, they leased the house to four unrelated young men between the ages of 22 and 25 who had grown up in the area and wanted to remain near their families but not reside with them. Shortly after the tenants moved in, a criminal information was filed against the McMinns in District Court, Nassau County, charging them with violating the zoning ordinance because the house was occupied by more than one family. The McMinns and the tenants then commenced this action seeking declaratory and injunctive relief and the criminal proceedings have been adjourned pending its disposition. In their complaint, plaintiffs assert only State constitutional and statutory claims and expressly reserve the right to litigate all Federal claims in a Federal forum pursuant to England v. Medical Examiners, 375 U.S. 411, 84 S.Ct. 461, 11 L.Ed.2d 440. They contend that the restrictive definition of "family" contained in the ordinance is facially invalid under Executive Law § 296 and the due process and equal protection clauses of the State Constitution (N.Y. Const., art. I, §§ 6, 11) or, in the alternative, that it violated these statutory and constitutional provisions as applied to them.

* * *

Indisputably, this ordinance was enacted to further several legitimate governmental purposes, including preservation of the character of traditional single-family neighborhoods, reduction of parking and traffic problems, control of population density and prevention of noise and disturbance. The dispute centers on whether the means the local legislature has chosen, the challenged ordinance and more specifically the definition of "family" contained in it, are reasonably related to the achievement of these legitimate purposes.

Manifestly, restricting occupancy of single-family housing based generally on the biological or legal relationships between its inhabitants bears no reasonable relationship to the goals of reducing parking and traffic problems, controlling population density and preventing noise and disturbance (see, *Moore v. East Cleveland*, 431 U.S. 494, 499–500, 97

S.Ct. 1932, 1935–1936, 52 L.Ed.2d 531; id., at p. 520, n. 16, 97 S.Ct. at p. 1946, n. 16 [Stevens, J., concurring]; *City of Santa Barbara v. Adamson*, 27 Cal.3d 123, 164 Cal.Rptr. 539, 544, 610 P.2d 436, 441; *State v. Baker*, 81 N.J. 99, 405 A.2d 368, 373). Their achievement depends not upon the biological or legal relations between the occupants of a house but generally upon the size of the dwelling and the lot and the number of its occupants. Thus, the definition of family employed here is both fatally overinclusive in prohibiting, for example, a young unmarried couple from occupying a four-bedroom house who do not threaten the purposes of the ordinance and the underinclusive in failing to prohibit occupancy of a two-bedroom home by 10 or 12 persons who are related in only the most distant manner and who might well be expected to present serious overcrowding and traffic problems.

* * *

Defendants contend that the scope of protection accorded under the due process clause of our State Constitution is coextensive with the protection provided by the due process clause of the 14th Amendment and that the challenged portion of the ordinance would survive Federal due process scrutiny under *Village of Belle Terre v. Boraas*, 416 U.S. 1, 94 S.Ct. 1536, 39 L.Ed.2d 797, supra. Because the ordinance challenged in this case contains age limitations making it more restrictive than the Belle Terre ordinance and because the Supreme Court did not state in either *Belle Terre* or *Moore v. East Cleveland*, 431 U.S. 494, 97 S.Ct. 1932, 52 L.Ed.2d 531, supra what definition of family is minimally necessary to survive Federal due process scrutiny, those decisions are not determinative of whether the ordinance before us would withstand Federal constitutional analysis. We have no need to consider the issue, however, for it is clear that the definition of family contained in this ordinance is incompatible with our prior decisions in *White Plains* and *Group House*. Although those cases did not involve an explicit adjudication of the homeowner's constitutional rights, they also cannot reasonably be interpreted as relying upon the public policy favoring establishment of group homes found in the Social Services Law (Social Services Law § 374–c). Quite the contrary, in each case the court expressly disavowed any reliance on the homeowner's assertion that enforcement of the restrictive definitions of family contained in the challenged ordinance would contravene the State's Social Services Law and the public policy embodied in it (see, *Group House v. Board of Zoning & Appeals*, 45 N.Y.2d 266, 271, 408 N.Y.S.2d 377, 380 N.E.2d 207, supra; *City of White Plains v. Ferraioli*, 34 N.Y.2d 300, 306, 357 N.Y.S.2d 449, 313 N.E.2d 756, supra; cf. *Crane Neck Assn. v. New York City/Long Is. County Servs. Group*, 61 N.Y.2d 154, 472 N.Y.S.2d 901, 460 N.E.2d 1336). Thus, the reasoning employed in White Plains and Group House is equally applicable to the constitutional issue raised on this appeal and provides ample support for the conclusion reached today.

Accordingly, in view of our holding that the definition of family in article I, § 1 of the Building Zone Ordinance of the Town of Oyster Bay is facially unconstitutional under the due process clause of the New York State Constitution (art. I, § 6), the order of the Appellate Division should be affirmed, with costs.

KAYE, JUDGE (concurring).

[Concurring opinion omitted.]

Note

1. Also see Baer v. Town of Brookhaven, 73 N.Y.2d 942, 540 N.Y.S.2d 234, 537 N.E.2d 619 (1989) where the court struck down a prohibition against more than four unrelated persons in the single-family district. The defendants were five elderly women sharing a house. See also Unification Theological Seminary v. City of Poughkeepsie, 201 A.D.2d 484, 607 N.Y.S.2d 383 (2nd Dept.1994), in which the court upheld a city ordinance that provides a rebuttable presumption that four or more unrelated persons living in a single dwelling do not constitute the functional equivalent of a traditional family.

2. Residential areas near college campuses become crowded with numbers of students who share a house. Many cases review ordinances that seek to control the problem by limiting the number of non-related persons who can occupy a house. Some cases are:

a. Borough of Glassboro v. Vallorosi, 117 N.J. 421, 568 A.2d 888 (1990). The New Jersey Supreme Court struck down a single-family definition that was applied to a group of ten college sophomores leasing a house. The court noted that the ordinance was adopted after "a rowdy weekend celebration by Glassboro State College students." Because the students planned to live in the house for three years and shared housekeeping duties, the court found that they were the functional equivalent of a family.

b. College Area Renters and Landlord Ass'n v. City of San Diego, 43 Cal.App.4th 677, 50 Cal.Rptr.2d 515 (1996). Here the court held that an attempt by the city to restrict the number of unrelated occupants in apartments under a sliding scale relating to square footage, off-street parking, and number of bathrooms violated the state constitution's equal protection provision. Owner-occupied overcrowded housing was exempted from the ordinance, enacted to deal with the problem of "mini dorms" in neighborhoods near college campuses. Another "mini dorm" case is Kirsch v. Prince George's County, 331 Md. 89, 626 A.2d 372 (1993), cert. denied 510 U.S. 1011, 114 S.Ct. 600, 126 L.Ed.2d 565 (1993) (zoning ordinance restricting rental to student groups but not other groups of similar size violates Equal Protection Clause). See also Anderson v. Provo City Corp., 108 P.3d 701 (Utah 2005) (the court upheld a zoning ordinance providing that only occupying owners could rent out apartments accessory to their homes to students in order prevent congestion and nuisance).

c. The Michigan Court of Appeals, on the other hand, upheld an ordinance in Ann Arbor limiting occupancy of single-family houses to not more than six unrelated individuals. Stegeman v. City of Ann Arbor, 213 Mich.App. 487, 540 N.W.2d 724 (1995). Perhaps college students in

Michigan are different than a religious commune, because an earlier Michigan Supreme Court case, Charter Twp. of Delta v. Dinolfo, 419 Mich. 253, 351 N.W.2d 831 (1984) held that a ban against more than six unrelated individuals occupying a single-family house denied due process and was arbitrary as applied to members of The Work of Christ Community living together in a house. The Stegeman court distinguished the ordinance at bar in the Dinolfo case in two respects: first, "Delta Twp ordinance allowed only one unrelated individual to reside in the household in addition to the family, while the instant ordinance allows up to six unrelated individuals to reside together; [s]econd, the Delta Twp ordinance did not provide for a so-called 'functional family' of unrelated individuals, for which the ordinance in the case at bar does provide." Also see Unification Theological Seminary v. City of Poughkeepsie, 201 A.D.2d 484, 607 N.Y.S.2d 383 (1994).

3. A New Jersey case found that an ordinance containing a restrictive definition of family violated the state constitutional provision recognizing the right of privacy. See State v. Baker, 81 N.J. 99, 405 A.2d 368 (1979). Also see City of Chula Vista v. Pagard, 115 Cal.App.3d 785, 171 Cal.Rptr. 738 (1981), where a claim of religious freedom to live communally was at issue; Holy Name Hospital v. Montroy, 153 N.J.Super. 181, 379 A.2d 299 (1977), where the court found that four nuns sharing a house constituted a harmless voluntary family; Children's Home of Easton v. City of Easton, 53 Pa. Cmwlth. 216, 417 A.2d 830 (1980), where the court held that a proposed foster home was the functional equivalent of a biological family and thus distinguishable from Belle Terre.

4. The cases to this point indicate that the problem of allowing unrelated persons to share a house revolves around issues of traffic, overcrowding, noise, and other environmental impacts. However, the next case illustrates that a "moral" component might be important.

CITY OF LADUE v. HORN

Missouri Court of Appeals, 1986.
720 S.W.2d 745.

CRANDALL, JUDGE.

Defendants, Joan Horn and E. Terrence Jones, appeal from the judgment of the trial court in favor of plaintiff, City of Ladue (Ladue), which enjoined defendants from occupying their home in violation of Ladue's zoning ordinance and which dismissed defendants' counterclaim. We affirm.

The case was submitted to the trial court on stipulated facts. Ladue's Zoning Ordinance No. 1175 was in effect at all times pertinent to the present action. Certain zones were designated as one-family residential. The zoning ordinance defined family as: "One or more persons related by blood, marriage or adoption, occupying a dwelling unit as an individual housekeeping organization." The only authorized accessory use in residential districts was for "[a]ccommodations for domestic persons employed and living on the premises and home occupations." The purpose of Ladue's zoning ordinance was broadly stated as to promote "the health, safety, morals and general welfare" of Ladue.

In July, 1981, defendants purchased a seven-bedroom, four-bathroom house which was located in a single-family residential zone in Ladue. Residing in defendants' home were Horn's two children (aged 16 and 19) and Jones's one child (age 18). The two older children attended out-of-state universities and lived in the house only on a part-time basis. Although defendants were not married, they shared a common bedroom, maintained a joint checking account for the household expenses, ate their meals together, entertained together, and disciplined each other's children. Ladue made demands upon defendants to vacate their home because their household did not comprise a family, as defined by Ladue's zoning ordinance, and therefore they could not live in an area zoned for single-family dwellings. When defendants refused to vacate, Ladue sought to enjoin defendants' continued violation of the zoning ordinance. Defendants counterclaimed, seeking a declaration that the zoning ordinance was constitutionally void. They also sought attorneys' fees and costs. The trial court entered a permanent injunction in favor of Ladue and dismissed defendants' counterclaim. Enforcement of the injunction was stayed pending this appeal.

* * *

Capsulated, defendants' attack on Ladue's ordinance is three-pronged. First, the zoning limitations foreclose them from exercising their right to associate freely with whomever they wish. *Roberts v. United States Jaycees*, 468 U.S. 609, 104 S.Ct. 3244, 82 L.Ed.2d 462 (1984). Second, their right to privacy is violated by the zoning restrictions. *Stanley v. Georgia*, 394 U.S. 557, 89 S.Ct. 1243, 22 L.Ed.2d 542 (1969). Third, the zoning classification distinguishes between related persons and unrelated persons. *United States Dept. of Agriculture v. Moreno*, 413 U.S. 528, 93 S.Ct. 2821, 37 L.Ed.2d 782 (1973). Defendants allege that the United States and Missouri Constitutions grant each of them the right to share his or her residence with whomever he or she chooses. They assert that Ladue has not demonstrated a compelling, much less rational, justification for the overly proscriptive blood or legal relationship requirement in its zoning ordinance.

Defendants posit that the term "family" is susceptible to several meanings. They contend that, since their household is the "functional and factual equivalent of a natural family," the ordinance may not preclude them from living in a single-family residential Ladue neighborhood. See, e.g., *McMinn v. Town of Oyster Bay*, 66 N.Y.2d 544, 498 N.Y.S.2d 128, 488 N.E.2d 1240 (Ct.App.1985). Defendants argue in their brief as follows:

> The record amply demonstrates that the private, intimate interests of Horn and Jones are substantial. Horn, Jones, and their respective children have historically lived together as a single family unit. They use and occupy their home for the identical purposes and in the

identical manners as families which are biologically or maritally related.

To bolster this contention, defendants elaborate on their shared duties, as set forth earlier in this opinion. Defendants acknowledge the importance of viewing themselves as a family unit, albeit a "conceptual family" as opposed to a "true non-family," in order to prevent the application of the ordinance.

The fallacy in defendants' syllogism is that the stipulated facts do not compel the conclusion that defendants are living as a family. A man and woman living together, sharing pleasures and certain responsibilities, does not per se constitute a family in even the conceptual sense. To approximate a family relationship, there must exist a commitment to a permanent relationship and a perceived reciprocal obligation to support and to care for each other. See, e.g., *State ex rel. Ellis v. Liddle*, 520 S.W.2d 644, 650 (Mo.App.1975). Only when these characteristics are present can the conceptual family, perhaps, equate with the traditional family. In a traditional family, certain of its inherent attributes arise from the legal relationship of the family members. In a non-traditional family, those same qualities arise in fact, either by explicit agreement or by tacit understanding among the parties.

While the stipulated facts could arguably support an inference by the trial court that defendants and their children comprised a non-traditional family, they do not compel that inference. Absent findings of fact and conclusions of law, we cannot assume that the trial court's perception of defendants' familial status comported with defendants' characterization of themselves as a conceptual family. In fact, if a finding by the trial court that defendants' living arrangement constituted a conceptual family is critical to a determination in defendants' favor, we can assume that the court's finding was adverse to defendants' position. Ordinarily, given our deference to the decision of the trial court, that would dispose of this appeal. We decline, however, to restrict our ruling to such a narrow basis. We therefore consider the broader issues presented by the parties. We assume, arguendo, that the sole basis for the judgment entered by the trial court was that defendants were not related by blood, marriage or adoption, as required by Ladue's ordinance.

* * *

Ladue has a legitimate concern with laying out guidelines for land use addressed to family needs. "It is ample to lay out zones where family values, youth values, and the blessings of quiet seclusion and clean air make the area a sanctuary for people." [Citing the *Belle Terre* case.] The question of whether Ladue could have chosen more precise means to effectuate its legislative goals is immaterial. Ladue's zoning ordinance is rationally related to its expressed purposes and violates no provisions of the Constitution of the United States. Further, defendants' assertion that they have a constitutional right to share their residence with whomever they please amounts to the same argument that was made and found unpersuasive by the court in *Belle Terre.*

* * *

For purposes of its zoning code, Ladue has in precise language defined the term family. It chose the definition which comports with the historical and traditional notions of family; namely, those people related by blood, marriage or adoption. That definition of family has been upheld in numerous Missouri decisions. See, e.g., *London v. Handicapped Facilities Board of St. Charles County*, 637 S.W.2d 212 (Mo.App. 1982) (group home not a "family" as used in restrictive covenant); *Feely v. Birenbaum*, 554 S.W.2d 432 (Mo.App.1977) (two unrelated males not a "family" as used in restrictive covenant); *Cash v. Catholic Diocese*, 414 S.W.2d 346 (Mo.App.1967) (nuns not a "family" as used in a restrictive covenant).

Decisions from other state jurisdictions have addressed identical constitutional challenges to zoning ordinances similar to the ordinance in the instant case. The reviewing courts have upheld their respective ordinances on the ground that maintenance of a traditional family environment constitutes a reasonable basis for excluding uses that may impair the stability of that environment and erode the values associated with traditional family life.

The essence of zoning is selection; and, if it is not invidious or discriminatory against those not selected, it is proper. *Town of Durham v. White Enterprises, Inc.*, 115 N.H. 645, 348 A.2d 706 (1975). There is no doubt that there is a governmental interest in marriage and in preserving the integrity of the biological or legal family. There is no concomitant governmental interest in keeping together a group of unrelated persons, no matter how closely they simulate a family. Further, there is no state policy which commands that groups of people may live under the same roof in any section of a municipality they choose.

The stated purpose of Ladue's zoning ordinance is the promotion of the health, safety, morals and general welfare in the city. Whether Ladue could have adopted less restrictive means to achieve these same goals is not a controlling factor in considering the constitutionality of the zoning ordinance. Rather, our focus is on whether there exists some reasonable basis for the means actually employed. In making such a determination, if any state of facts either known or which could reasonably be assumed is presented in support of the ordinance, we must defer to the legislative judgment. We find that Ladue has not acted arbitrarily in enacting its zoning ordinance which defines family as those related by blood, marriage or adoption. Given the fact that Ladue has so defined family, we defer to its legislative judgment.

The judgment of the trial court is affirmed.

PUDLOWSKI, P.J., and KAROHL, J., concur.

Notes

1. Consider a new type of house originally developed in California called a tandem house, containing two private areas of equal size with a bedroom and bathroom flanking a common area of living room, dining room and kitchen. This house is designed for buyers called "mingles" or "couplets" who may be unrelated persons (neither a traditional nor alternative family) who could not individually afford to buy a house and who by combining assets can share a house. The tandem house is obviously designed to meet the problem of inflationary mortgage and building costs. Should zoning ordinance definitions of family be allowed to inhibit such real estate marketing devices as the tandem house?

2. The definition of single-family is important not only in the context presented in the previous cases—the traditional family as opposed to alternative styles of living—but is also an essential ingredient in the problem of exclusion of group homes and institutional uses in single-family zoning districts.

CITY OF WHITE PLAINS v. FERRAIOLI

Court of Appeals of New York, 1974.
34 N.Y.2d 300, 357 N.Y.S.2d 449, 313 N.E.2d 756.

BREITEL, CHIEF JUDGE.

In an action by the City of White Plains to enforce its zoning ordinance and enjoin use of a single-family house as a "group home" for 10 foster children, defendants, Abbott House, Inc. and the owners of the house, appeal. Abbott House, a private agency licensed by the State to care for neglected and abandoned children, leases the house in an "R–2" single-family zone. The city contends that the group home is not a single-family use, but either a philanthropic institution, allowed only by special permit, or a boarding house, wholly excluded from an "R–2" zone. The city obtained summary judgment in the courts below.

The issue is a narrow one: whether the "group home," consisting of a married couple and their two children, together with 10 foster children, qualifies as a single "family" unit, under the ordinance. It is concluded that the group home, set up in theory, size, appearance and structure to resemble a family unit, fits within the definition of family, for purposes of a zoning ordinance. Hence, the order of the Appellate Division should be reversed and summary judgment granted to defendants.

Abbott House as noted, is a not-for-profit membership corporation licensed by the State to care for neglected and abandoned children. In 1971, legislation was enacted permitting so-called "authorized agencies" like Abbott House to establish "group homes," under strict State regulation and inspection, where from 7 to 12 foster children might live in a simulated family atmosphere (Social Services Law, § 374–c, Consol. Laws, c. 55; L.1971, ch. 677). The group home concept is relatively new; instead of being institutionalized, neglected or abandoned youngsters are divided into small groups and placed in homes with an adult couple, approximating a normal family environment. In this way, it is thought, the children obtain many of the benefits of home life. Siblings may be kept together. Whatever other advantages there are to the group home, it is also less costly than institutionalized care. Abbott House also operates a traditional dormitory-style institution elsewhere in the State which houses over 100 children.

The particular group home in this case consists of an adult couple, the Seards, their two children, and 10 foster children. Of the 10, there are seven siblings, the Bell children ranging in age from 7 to 13, and three unrelated youngsters. The Seards are paid a salary to care for the children and all household expenses are paid by Abbott House, with substantial funding to it by the City of New York. Abbott House has a five-year lease on a house owned by the Ferraiolis who are also defendants. The children, natural and foster, live together as if they were brothers and sisters and the Seards were their common parents. The household is maintained as a family would be in a single housekeeping unit with kitchen facilities.

The Ferraioli house is in an R–2 zone of the city where the principal permitted uses are as a "Single family dwelling for one housekeeping unit only," fire houses, police stations, public schools and churches. As an accessory use, a resident family may include up to two roomers. Welfare uses, including philanthropic institutions, are special uses permitted in R–2 districts or other residential districts only at the discretion of the zoning board of appeals. Abbott House has not sought permission from the board. Rooming houses are permitted in certain residential districts of the city, but not in an R–2 zone.

The zoning ordinance defines a family:

> A "family" is one or more persons limited to the spouse, parents, grandparents, grandchildren, sons, daughters, brothers or sisters of the owner or the tenant or of the owner's spouse or tenant's spouse living together as a single housekeeping unit with kitchen facilities.

It is significant that the group home is structured as a single housekeeping unit and is, to all outward appearances, a relatively normal, stable, and permanent family unit, with which the community is properly concerned. If that be true, the group home is no less qualified to occupy the Ferraioli house than are any of the neighboring families in their respective homes.

The group home is not, for purposes of a zoning ordinance, a temporary living arrangement as would be a group of college students sharing a house and commuting to a nearby school * * *. Every year or so, different college students would come to take the place of those before them. There would be none of the permanency of community that characterizes a residential neighborhood of private homes. Nor is it like the so-called "commune" style of living. The group home is a permanent arrangement and akin to a traditional family, which also may be sundered by death, divorce, or emancipation of the young. Neither the foster parents nor the children are to be shifted about; the intention is that they remain and develop ties in the community. The purpose is to emulate the traditional family and not to introduce a different "life style."

Of course, the Supreme Court of the United States, in the recent *Belle Terre* case, has held that it is a proper purpose of zoning to lay out districts devoted to "family values" and "youth values." Hence, toward that end those uses which conflict with a stable, uncongested single family environment may be restricted. High density uses, for example, may be restricted; so too those uses which are associated with occupancy by numbers of transient persons may be limited. By requiring single family use of a house, the ordinance emphasizes and ensures the character of the neighborhood to promote the family environment. The group home does not conflict with that character and, indeed, is deliberately designed to conform with it.

Thus the city has a proper purpose in largely limiting the uses in a zone to single-family units. But if it goes beyond to require that the relationships in the family unit be those of blood or adoption, then its definition of family might be too restrictive (see *Kirsch Holding Co. v. Borough of Manasquan*, 59 N.J. 241, 250, 281 A.2d 527; *City of Des Plaines v. Trottner*, 34 Ill.2d 432, 216 N.E.2d 116 [per Schaeffer, J.]; *Boston–Edison Protective Assn. v. Paulist Fathers*, 306 Mich. 253, 10 N.W.2d 847). Zoning is intended to control types of housing and living and not the genetic or intimate internal family relations of human beings.

Whether a family be organized along ties of blood or formal adoptions, or be a similarly structured group sponsored by the State, as is the group home, should not be consequential in meeting the test of the zoning ordinance. So long as the group home bears the generic character of a family unit as a relatively permanent household, and is not a framework for transients or transient living, it conforms to the purpose of the ordinance (see *Planning & Zoning Comm. v. Synanon Foundation*, 153 Conn. 305, 308, 216 A.2d 442). Moreover, in no sense is the group home an institutional arrangement, which would be another matter. Indeed, the purpose of the group home is to be quite the contrary of an institution and to be a home like other homes.

In short, an ordinance may restrict a residential zone to occupancy by stable families occupying single-family homes, but neither by express provision nor construction may it limit the definition of family to exclude a household which in every but a biological sense is a single family. The minimal arrangement to meet the test of a zoning provision, as this one, is a group headed by a householder caring for a reasonable number of children as one would be likely to find in a biologically unitary family. * * *

Defendants contend, and the issue raised is not without trouble, that the zoning ordinance, if it prohibits a group home use in an R–2 district, absolutely or without a special permit, contravenes the State's Social Services Law. That law, as discussed above, authorizes licensed agencies to establish group homes in appropriate neighborhoods (Social Services Law, § 374–c). In somewhat analogous circumstances, courts have held local zoning ordinances void as contrary to State policy when they restricted an "agency boarding home," a day care center, and a center for delinquent youths (*Abbott House v. Village of Tarrytown*, 34 A.D.2d 821, 312 N.Y.S.2d 841; *Matter of Unitarian Universalist Church v. Shorten*, 63 Misc.2d 978, 980–981, 314 N.Y.S.2d 66 [Meyer, J.]; Nowack v. Department of Audit & Control, 72 Misc.2d 518, 520, 338 N.Y.S.2d 52). Certainly, by constitutional provision and State policy, the care of neglected and abandoned children is a paramount concern (N.Y.Const., art. VII, § 8, subd. 2; *Matter of Wiltwyck School v. Hill*, 11 N.Y.2d 182, 193, 227 N.Y.S.2d 655, 182 N.E.2d 268). Since it is concluded, however, that a group home is a family, this broader question need not now be resolved by this court.

* * *

Accordingly, the order of the Appellate Division should be reversed, with costs, and summary judgment granted to defendants dismissing the complaint.

Notes

1. The group home is an outgrowth of the principle of deinstitutionalization or normalization, which is based on the policy of rejecting the large custodial institution as a method of dealing with those members of society who are dependent, such as the mentally handicapped, juvenile delinquents and neglected or orphaned children. The group home is designed to provide an environment that approximates that of normal society, which perforce includes the idea of family living. The public and private organizations that promote and operate group homes frequently seek locations in single-family zoning districts; often, a clash between local government or nearby neighbors and the proposed group home results in litigation. Because so many local governments have demonstrated hostility to the location of group homes in single-family districts state legislation became increasingly common as a device for preempting local zoning ordinances restrictive of group homes. For an overview of this problem, see Comment, 24 Kan.L.Rev. 677 (1976); Kressel, The Community Residence Movement: Land Use Conflicts and Planning Imperatives, 5 N.Y.U.Rev.L. & Soc.Change 137 (1975); Lippincott, A Sanctuary for People: Strategies for Overcoming Zoning Restrictions on Community Homes for Retarded Persons, 31 Stan.L.Rev. 767 (1979); Hopperton, A State Legislative Strategy for Ending Exclusionary Zoning of Community Homes, 19 Urb.L.Ann. 47 (1980); Nimby's Legacy: A Challenge to Local Autonomy: Regulating the Sting of Group Homes in New York, 26 Fordham Urb. L.J. 209 (1999); and Residential Group Homes for Nebraska's Troubled Youth: An Attractive Alternative to Institutionalization, 77 Neb. L. Rev. 835 (1998).

2. The majority of cases dealing with zoning of group homes have favored their location in single-family districts. In most of the cases the courts utilize the approach of defining the word family so as to include the surrogate family implicit in the group home concept. See, e.g., Human

Services Consultants, Inc. v. Zoning Hearing Bd., 137 Pa.Cmwlth. 594, 587 A.2d 40 (1991), permitting a group home for three adult retarded persons and their support staff in a single-family district. In Eichlin v. Zoning Hearing Bd. of New Hope Borough, 671 A.2d 1173 (Pa.Cmwlth.1996) the court held that eight unrelated HIV-infected persons were the functional equivalent of a family. However, the courts are not always willing to treat every type of communal living arrangement as a family situation:

In Dinan v. Board of Zoning Appeals, 220 Conn. 61, 595 A.2d 864 (1991), property owners rented out their two-family house to a total of ten unrelated boarders, each under a separate lease. The house was located in a single-family residential zone. The Court denied the owners' ultra vires attack on the town's definition of "family", which included only "individuals related by blood, marriage, or adoption, living together as a single housekeeping unit." The Court explained:

> Traditional families are united not merely by the legal relationships among them but also by the deep affection that arises from a lifetime of sharing not just common facilities or meals in a home, but every aspect of experience. Nontraditional families may have a similar basis for their unity. Such lasting relationships are likely to generate the interest of a family not only in the home it occupies, but in the neighborhood, its schools, parks and other accouterments of urban living. The transient and separate character of residency by the plaintiffs' tenants is not as likely to stimulate on their part similar concerns about the quality of living in the neighborhood for the long term.

Similarly, a Connecticut court held that a halfway home for an average of six men with histories of substance abuse problems did not constitute a single-family home. Meyers v. Zoning Bd. of Appeals, 1997 WL 325816 (Conn.Super.Ct.1997). Also see Albert v. Zoning Hearing Bd., 578 Pa. 439, 854 A.2d 401 (2004). And, in Northern Maine General Hosp. v. Ricker, 572 A.2d 479 (Me.1990) the court held that a prerelease center for adult inmates could be excluded from a single-family district that permitted group homes because it was significantly more objectionable than other types of group homes.

3. Some courts have avoided the "single-family" problem by finding a group home to be a permitted educational facility in the single-family district, e.g., Watros v. Greater Lynn Mental Health & Retardation Ass'n, 421 Mass. 106, 653 N.E.2d 589 (1995); Campbell v. City Council of Lynn, 415 Mass. 772, 616 N.E.2d 445 (1993), or a permitted community center, e.g., Appeal of Fleming, 44 Pa.Cmwlth. 641, 405 A.2d 1309 (1979).

4. Some group home cases do not involve local hostility through the zoning ordinance, but rather a conflict with restrictive covenants limiting use of the proposed group home to single-family dwelling purposes. Here again, the courts generally read the covenants so as to permit the group home. See, e.g., Blevins v. Barry–Lawrence County Assoc. for Retarded Citizens, 707 S.W.2d 407 (Mo.1986), permitting a group home for eight retarded adults and live-in house parents on property burdened by a covenant restricting use to "residential use" and "single-family dwelling." See also, Hill v. Community Of Damien Of Molokai, 121 N.M. 353, 911 P.2d 861 (1996), in which the Supreme Court of New Mexico found that the use of a

home by four unrelated AIDS victims complied with a restrictive covenant prohibiting the property from being used for anything other than a single-family residence. In Clem v. Christole, Inc., 548 N.E.2d 1180 (Ind.App.1990), the court held that a state statute invalidating restrictive covenants which prohibit group homes constituted a taking.

5. Another approach to the group home problem is reflected in cases that find state-operated or state-sponsored group homes are immune from local zoning ordinances. See Hillsborough Ass'n for Retarded Citizens v. City of Temple Terrace, 332 So.2d 610 (Fla.1976); Township of South Fayette v. Commonwealth, 477 Pa. 574, 385 A.2d 344 (1978); City of Baltimore v. State Dept. of Health and Mental Hygiene, 38 Md.App. 570, 381 A.2d 1188 (1978); Region 10 Client Management, Inc. v. Town of Hampstead, 120 N.H. 885, 424 A.2d 207 (1980). Compare Brownfield v. State, 63 Ohio St.2d 282, 407 N.E.2d 1365 (1980) and Macon Ass'n For Retarded Citizens v. Macon–Bibb County Planning & Zoning Commission, 252 Ga. 484, 314 S.E.2d 218 (1984).

6. More than half of the states have adopted legislation since 1970 designed to overcome zoning barriers to the establishment of group homes. The legislation is not uniform and the approach varies from state to state. Typically, the statutes may apply only to certain types of group homes, e.g., those for the developmentally disabled, and may impose maximum residency limits in language such as "up to six [or eight] persons." See Hopperton, A State Legislative Strategy for Ending Exclusionary Zoning of Community Homes, 19 Urban L. Ann. 47 (1980). Also see Adams County Ass'n for Retarded Citizens, Inc. v. City of Westminster, 196 Colo. 79, 580 P.2d 1246 (1978); State ex rel. Thelen v. City of Missoula, 168 Mont. 375, 543 P.2d 173 (1975); Pioneer Subdivision Homeowners Ass'n, Inc. v. Professional Counseling Services, Inc., 2002 WL 31443218 (Tenn.Ct.App. 2002). In Garcia v. Siffrin Residential Ass'n, 63 Ohio St.2d 259, 407 N.E.2d 1369 (1980), the court held the state statute permitting group homes in single-family districts could not operate to preempt a local home rule zoning ordinance excluding such uses.

7. In some cases the zoning ordinance is not exclusionary as to group homes, but such uses may require a special use permit or exception, or may be a conditional use in the single-family district. As to the standards to be applied in such cases, see Warren County Probation Ass'n v. Warren County Zoning Hearing Bd., 50 Pa.Cmwlth. 486, 414 A.2d 398 (1980). Also see State v. City of Bellingham, 25 Wash.App. 33, 605 P.2d 788 (1979); Ayers v. Porter County Plan Comm'n, 544 N.E.2d 213 (Ind.App.1989). In City of Cleburne, Texas v. Cleburne Living Center, 473 U.S. 432, 105 S.Ct. 3249, 87 L.Ed.2d 313 (1985), the Court held that requiring a special use permit for a group home for mentally retarded persons in the city's R–3 district was invalid because the same district did not require special use permits for nursing homes, sanitariums, hospitals, fraternity or sorority houses, boarding houses, dormitories and other similar uses.

8. One unusual case involving group homes is People v. St. Agatha Home for Children, 47 N.Y.2d 46, 416 N.Y.S.2d 577, 389 N.E.2d 1098 (1979), cert. denied 444 U.S. 869, 100 S.Ct. 145, 62 L.Ed.2d 94 (1979), where the plaintiffs charged the operators of a group home with operating a non-secure juvenile detention facility in violation of the criminal provisions of the

zoning ordinance. The court held that the burden of proof requisite in a criminal proceeding had not been met and that the group home was operating under county aegis and was, therefore, immune from the city zoning ordinance.

9. The Fair Housing Amendments Act of 1988 (FHAA), P.L. 100–430, makes discrimination against the handicapped in the sale, lease, or construction of multi-family units a prohibited practice. In Baxter v. City of Belleville, Ill., 720 F.Supp. 720 (S.D.Ill.1989), the court enjoined a city from refusing a special permit to remodel a building to house AIDS patients. In the same vein, see Association of Relatives and Friends of AIDS Patients v. Regulations and Permits Admn., 740 F.Supp. 95 (D.Puerto Rico 1990); Support Ministries for Persons with AIDS, Inc. v. Village of Waterford, New York, 808 F.Supp. 120 (N.D.N.Y.1992); Familystyle of St. Paul, Inc. v. City of St. Paul, 728 F.Supp. 1396 (D.Minn.1990). In Hill v. Community of Damien of Molokai, 121 N.M. 353, 911 P.2d 861 (1996), the court held that a group home for AIDS patients did not violate a restrictive covenant specifying single-family residential uses, and that even if the residents did not constitute a "family" and violated the covenant, the covenant would violate the Fair Housing Act. In United States v. City of Taylor, Michigan, 798 F.Supp. 442 (E.D.Mich.1992), the court found intentional discrimination against the proposed residents of an adult foster care home for twelve elderly disabled persons, and a violation of the Fair Housing Act. In Epicenter of Steubenville, Inc. v. City of Steubenville, 924 F.Supp. 845 (S.D.Ohio 1996), the court held that a city ordinance imposing a one-year moratorium against new adult care facilities violated the FHAA.

In Brandt v. Village of Chebanse, 82 F.3d 172 (7th Cir.1996), the court upheld denial of a variance for an apartment building with handicapped-accessible units to locate in a single-family residential district. The court found that because a permit had been previously denied for a similar non-accessible project, the denial in this case was not based on discrimination against the handicapped. Compare, Larkin v. State of Michigan Dept. of Social Services, 89 F.3d 285 (6th Cir.1996), where the court held that a Michigan statute prohibiting location of group homes within 1500 feet of existing group homes was preempted by the federal act. And in Association for Advancement of the Mentally Handicapped v. City of Elizabeth, 876 F.Supp. 614 (D.N.J.1994), the court held that a city ordinance and the authorizing provision of the state enabling act that automatically denied conditional use permits for group homes for developmentally disabled persons on certain conditions violated the FHAA.

10. In Taylor Home of Charlotte Inc. v. City of Charlotte, 116 N.C.App. 188, 447 S.E.2d 438 (1994), neighbors succeeded in stopping a proposed group home for persons with AIDS. The court approved the local board interpretation of the state enabling legislation for group homes and the city ordinance to define group homes as "sheltered living arrangements primarily for rehabilitation." The court stated: "The Board interpreted that language to require that the residents of a group home be such that some day they could live normal lives. The Board found as a fact that that 'a dictionary commonly defines "rehabilitation" to mean the restoring of a handicapped or delinquent person to a useful life through education and therapy.' " Compare "K" Care, Inc. v. Town of Lac du Flambeau, 181 Wis.2d

59, 510 N.W.2d 697 (1993), where the court considered whether the denial of a permit to construct a facility for elderly residents violated the Fair Housing Act. The town argued that the federal statute only applied to discrimination against the handicapped and by definition the federal act was inapplicable to a home for the elderly. The court held: "We conclude that the proposed residents of the new facility ... are handicapped within the meaning of the FHA. These residents obviously suffer from physical and mental impairments that substantially limit one or more major life activities. They are unable to eat, bathe, walk or use a toilet without assistance. In short, they are no longer able to live independently." Also see City of St. Joseph v. Preferred Family Healthcare, 859 S.W.2d 723 (Mo.App.1993), where the court found that persons recovering from alcohol and drug abuse were not mentally or physically handicapped within the meaning of the federal Rehabilitation Act of 1973, § 504 (29 U.S.C.A. § 794). Also see Daniel R. Mandelker, Zoning Discrimination Against Group Homes Under the Fair Housing Act, Land Use Law (Nov. 1994) p. 3.

D. RESTRICTING MOBILE HOMES AND MANUFACTURED HOUSING

Akin to limiting occupancy of single-family homes to traditional families is the issue of prohibiting construction of non-traditional types of housing in single-family zones: housing that is not built on site or "stick built." The effect of restrictions that prohibit or limit the placement of mobile or modular homes in single-family districts is to discriminate against certain types of housing construction and, sometimes, against certain types of households. What public interest is served by such limitations? Do they violate the due process and equal protection rights of owners and occupants?

Modular or prefabricated housing can be as architecturally distinguished and as expensive as stick built homes. Mobile homes that are built to conform to the National Manufactured Housing Construction and Safety Standards Act administered by the U.S. Department of Housing and Urban Development manifestly protect the health and safety of their occupants. Prohibiting or limiting the location or number of such homes is increasingly difficult to justify as their quality increases. Older, substandard, and truly mobile homes raise legitimate public issues when they are not properly located and regulated, as do trailers and vans designed for transient purposes. The following principal case and the notes raise and discuss these issues.

YURCZYK v. YELLOWSTONE COUNTY

Supreme Court of Montana, 2004.
319 Mont. 169, 83 P.3d 266.

JUSTICE JAMES C. NELSON delivered the Opinion of the Court.

Yellowstone County, the Board of County Commissioners of Yellowstone County, et al. (collectively, the County), appeal from a grant of summary judgment in the Thirteenth Judicial District Court, Yellowstone County, and Francis and Anita Yurczyk (the Yurczyks) cross-appeal. We affirm.

* * *

In March of 1994, the Board of County Commissioners of Yellowstone County (the Board) adopted a resolution that created Zoning District #17 (District 17) and a Planning and Zoning Commission (the Zoning Commission) for District 17 which included the three Board members, James Zeigler (Zeigler), Michael Matthew (Matthew), and William Kennedy (Kennedy); the Yellowstone County Surveyor, James Logan (Logan); and the Yellowstone County Assessor, Max Lennington (Lennington). The following month, a public hearing was held regarding the proposed regulations for District 17 and, at a second public hearing in May, Zeigler, Matthew, Kennedy, and Logan voted to adopt the "Zoning Regulations—Zoning District Number 17" (the Regulations). The Regulations were then executed by all the members of the Zoning Commission.

The Regulations included a provision pertaining to dwelling units. The units could be single family units only; the gross floor area could be no less than 1,500 square feet; only "on-site construction with new materials ... to be completed within one year from date of beginning;" the units had to be "built according to CABO [Counsel of American Building Officials] One & Two Family Dwelling Code currently in use by the State of Montana;"and the unit's foundation had to be "permanent and continuous ... to frost level with or without a full basement." District 17 Zoning Regulations Article 4(C)(4).

In 1998, a resident of District 17, Arthur Weiss (Weiss), requested a zoning clarification from the Yellowstone County Planning Department regarding whether or not modular and mobile homes were allowed in District 17. Kerwin Jensen, senior planner, advised Weiss that modular and manufactured homes were not allowed because they were not consistent with on-site construction.

In December of 1999, the Yurczyks, residents of Thompson Falls, purchased two 40–acre tracts of land in District 17 for investment purposes and with the intent of building a single-family dwelling on one of the tracts and selling the tract and home to their daughter and son-in-law by June of 2000. The Yurczyks bought a Stratford modular home from Bennett Homes and Realty (Bennett Realty) and moved it onto the property in May of 2000. That same day the City of Billings/Yellowstone County Planning Department received a complaint regarding the modular home.

Nicole Cromwell (Cromwell), a planner with the City of Billings/Yellowstone County Planning Department, was assigned to investigate the complaint. After making two visits to the site, speaking with the people placing the home, and determining that the home conformed to the Uniform Building Code and CABO standards, Cromwell sent a letter to Casey Smith, the Yurczyks' son-in-law, advising him that the modular home violated the on-site construction provision of the Regulations and would have to be removed by May 31, 2000. Cromwell also advised Smith that the decision could be appealed to the Yellowstone County Board of Adjustment.

On May 22, 2000, the Yurczyks sent a letter to the Yellowstone County Board of Adjustment requesting a hearing. Cromwell forwarded the letter to the Board of Adjustment for District 17. The Board of Adjustment for District 17 held a hearing on July 11 and affirmed the Planning Department's decision.

Thereafter, the Yurczyks commenced litigation against the County alleging that the Regulations were unenforceable because they were adopted in violation of statutory requirements and that the Board and the Zoning Commission illegally, arbitrarily, and capriciously adopted and enforced the zoning regulations in violation of their substantive due process rights, equal protection rights, and their right to use, enjoy, and develop their property. Both parties filed motions for summary judgment. The court held a hearing on the cross motions and a hearing to determine damages, and attorney's fees and costs.

The court found that the Yurczyks' procedural due process rights were not violated because the Board had substantially complied with statutory procedural requirements; that the Yurczyks' substantive due process rights were violated because the "on-site construction" requirement did "not have a substantial bearing upon the public health, safety, morals, or general welfare of the community" and "was not based upon a legitimate governmental objective;"that the Yurczyks' equal protection rights were violated because the on-site provision treated the Yurczyks differently than similarly situated property owners and it did not have a substantial bearing upon the preservation of property values in District 17; that the on-site regulation was unenforceable because it was void for vagueness; and that the Yurczyks were entitled to $4,450.93 in damages, $1,051 in costs, and $29,250 in attorney's fees. The County appeals the District Court's holding as to substantive due process, equal protection, and void for vagueness, and the award for damages. The Yurczkys cross-appeal, asserting that the court erred in holding that the Board substantially complied with statutory procedural requirements.

Standard of Review

Our standard of review in appeals from summary judgment rulings is de novo. Motarie v. N. Mont. Joint Refuse Disposal (1995), 274 Mont. 239, 242, 907 P.2d 154, 156 (citing Mead v. M.S.B., Inc. (1994), 264 Mont. 465, 470, 872 P.2d 782, 785). When we review a district court's grant of summary judgment, we apply the same evaluation as the district court based on Rule 56, M.R.Civ.P. Bruner v. Yellowstone County (1995), 272 Mont. 261, 264, 900 P.2d 901, 903.

Discussion

* * *

Issue Two

Whether the Yurczyks' substantive due process and equal protection rights were violated and the "on-site construction" regulation was void for vagueness.

A. Substantive Due Process

The County argues that the District Court erred in finding that the Yurczyks' right to substantive due process was violated because the on-site construction provision does have a bearing on the welfare of the community. The County maintains that the regulation helps to preserve property values. The Yurczyks contend that the zoning ordinance does not protect property values, it interferes with their constitutional right to use, enjoy, and develop their property.

Under § 76–2–301, MCA, "local municipal governments in Montana are empowered to enact zoning ordinances restricting the use of property in their jurisdictional area." *Boland v. City of Great Falls* (1996), 275 Mont. 128, 132, 910 P.2d 890, 892–93. We have held that a zoning ordinance enacted pursuant to the aforementioned section "will be found to be a constitutional exercise of police power if it has a substantial bearing upon the public health, safety, morals or general welfare of the community." *Boland*, 275 Mont. at 132, 910 P.2d at 893.

Citing several cases, *FCC v. Beach Communications* (1993), 508 U.S. 307, 113 S. Ct. 2096, 124 L. Ed. 2d 211 ; *Aleman v. Glickman* (9th Cir. 2000), 217 F.3d 1191; *Joseph E. Seagram & Sons, Inc. v. Hostetter* (1966), 384 U.S. 35, 86 S. Ct. 1254, 16 L. Ed. 2d 336, the County argues that we should not ask whether the regulation actually preserved property values but whether the Board members, at the time the ordinance was passed, could have reasonably believed that the regulation would protect property values. As the Yurczyks noted, "those cases involve review of state and federal legislative enactments and corresponding statutory classifications—not local zoning ordinances."

We hold that the zoning regulation at issue here does not have a substantial bearing on the public health, safety, morals, or general welfare of the community as the County asserts. Jeff Bollman (Bollman), a senior planner for the City of Billings/Yellowstone County, who helped draft and create the Unified Zoning Regulations, which combined the City and County zoning regulations, and County Commissioner, Matthew, were both unable to identify any health and only minimal safety concerns that the on-site construction provision addressed. As to general welfare, Matthew testified that he believed the provision advanced the residents' ability to control their environment and Bollman was also unable to determine what kind of general welfare interests the provision protected other than a possible preservation of property values.

While a resident's ability to control his environment and the preservation of property values may implicate legitimate government concerns in some zoning situations, there is nothing in the record here that demonstrates these concerns actually drove the formulation of the regulations at issue. Indeed, the record reflects that the modular home would not have affected property values in the area. Lennington testified that homes built off-site "would have no real bearing upon market values at all ... in this particular setting, [District 17,] because [it] is a rural setting, and it's spread out into large residential acreages." Thus, the "on-site construction" provision does not have a substantial bearing upon the public health, safety, morals, or general welfare of the community. Accordingly, we hold that the District Court did not err in concluding that the Yurczyks' substantive due process rights were violated because the "on-site construction" requirement was not rationally related to a legitimate governmental interest.

B. Equal Protection

In assuming that the Yurczyks' equal protection rights were not violated, the County again argues that the regulation had a rational relationship to the welfare of the community. Because we have already addressed and disposed of that issue, we will not revisit it. Even assuming that Yurczyks were not treated differently than similarly situated groups, the zoning ordinance did not have "a substantial bearing upon the public health, safety, morals or general welfare of the community." *Boland*, 275 Mont. at 132, 910 P.2d at 893. Accordingly, we hold that the District Court did not err in concluding that the regulation violated the Yurczyks' equal protection rights.

* * *

The trial court's decision is affirmed.

Notes

1. Compare the case of Clark v. County of Winnebago, 817 F.2d 407 (7th Cir.1987). The property owner sought to have a portion of his land rezoned to "Mobile Home District." When his request was denied, he brought a due process challenge in federal court on the theory that the requirements for the mobile home district were discriminatory and that the ordinance unconstitutionally discriminated between site-built homes and mobile homes. The court upheld the ordinance, stating: "There was testimony at trial that, despite advances in the mobile home industry, distinctions between mobile homes and site-built homes still exist with respect to design, construction, and general appearance. While some mobile homes may compare favorably with conventional homes, zoning classifications necessarily require that generalizations be made. Mathematical certainty is not required for the ordinance to pass constitutional muster, so long as there is a reasonable basis for the classification chosen." See also Lex, Inc. v. Board of Trustees of Town of Paragon, 808 N.E.2d 104 (Ind.Ct.App.2004) (upholding ban on placement of mobile homes within the municipality if more than five years old).

2. Congress, in P.L. 93–383, provided the basis for federal regulation of construction standards for manufactured homes. See 42 U.S.C. § 5401 et seq.and 24 C.F.R. § 3280 et seq. The federal certification of manufactured homes along with changes in style (such as pitched roofs and non-metal

siding) and the advent of double-wide and triple-wide homes have contributed to more widespread acceptance of manufactured housing in communities around the country. See Colorado Manufactured Housing Ass'n v. Pueblo County, 857 P.2d 507 (Colo.App.1993); Tennessee Manufactured Housing Ass'n v. Metropolitan Government of Nashville, 798 S.W.2d 254 (Tenn.App. 1990); compare Duggins v. Walnut Cove, 63 N.C.App. 684, 306 S.E.2d 186 (1983). In Lauderbaugh v. Hopewell Township, 319 F.3d 568 (3d Cir.2002), the court held that the federal statute may preempt more restrictive local building regulations, but does not deal with location issues.

3. In California a statute, Cal. Govt. Code § 65852.3 provides:

> (a) A city, including a charter city, county, or city and county, shall allow the installation of manufactured homes certified under the National Manufactured Housing Construction and Safety Standards Act of 1974 (42 U.S.C.A. Sec. 5401 et seq.) on a foundation system, pursuant to Section 18551 of the Health and Safety Code, on lots zoned for conventional single-family residential dwellings. Except with respect to architectural requirements, a city, including a charter city, county, or city and county, shall only subject the manufactured home and the lot on which it is placed to the same development standards to which a conventional single-family residential dwelling on the same lot would be subject, including, but not limited to, building setback standards, side and rear yard requirements, standards for enclosures, access, and vehicle parking, aesthetic requirements, and minimum square footage requirements. Any architectural requirements imposed on the manufactured home structure itself, exclusive of any requirement for any and all additional enclosures, shall be limited to its roof overhang, roofing material, and siding material. These architectural requirements may be imposed on manufactured homes even if similar requirements are not imposed on conventional single-family residential dwellings. However, any architectural requirements for roofing and siding material shall not exceed those which would be required of conventional single-family dwellings constructed on the same lot. At the discretion of the local legislative body, the city or county may preclude installation of a manufactured home in zones specified in this section if more than 10 years have elapsed between the date of manufacture of the manufactured home and the date of the application for the issuance of a permit to install the mobile home in the affected zone. In no case may a city, including a charter city, county, or city and county, apply any development standards which will have the effect of precluding manufactured homes from being installed as permanent residences.

Also see 30A Maine Rev. Stat. Ann. § 4358, and Paladac v. City of Rockland, 558 A.2d 372 (Me.1989). A number of states have adopted statutes similar to the one in California. In Tennessee Manufactured Housing Ass'n v. Metropolitan Govt. of Nashville, 798 S.W.2d 254 (Tenn.App.1990), the court construed a statute providing " . . . no power or authority granted by this Code to regulate zoning or land use planning shall be used to exclude the placement of a residential dwelling on land designated for residential use solely because the dwelling is partially or completely constructed in a manufacturing facility; provided, however, that the term 'residential dwelling' as used in this part shall not apply to factory-manufactured mobile homes constructed as a single self-contained unit and mounted on a single chassis . . ." The court held that the proviso did not apply to a double-wide manufactured home, reasoning that the word "and" in the proviso was intended as a conjunctive; thus a double-wide home was not one on a single chassis.

4. In Cannon v. Coweta County, 260 Ga. 56, 389 S.E.2d 329 (1990), the Supreme Court of Georgia held that a per se exclusion of manufactured homes from single-family districts was unconstitutional. The court questioned the trial court's acceptance of the county's arguments that manufactured homes adversely affect the local tax base and that manufactured homes adversely affect the value of nearby site-built homes. In a footnote the court suggested that a local government could regulate manufactured homes in such ways as requiring attachment to a permanent foundation, appropriate lot sizes, and aesthetic standards. But see King v. City of Bainbridge, 276 Ga. 484, 577 S.E.2d 772 (2003), in which the Supreme Court of Georgia overruled Cannon, stating that it is perfectly appropriate for a municipality to restrict the placement of mobile homes based upon reasoning such as aesthetics and neighboring property values. Compare, Grant v. County of Seminole, Fla., 817 F.2d 731 (11th Cir.1987).

5. Because of the general recognition that mobile homes are an essential method of meeting the housing needs of low-and moderate-income residents, courts question the validity of total exclusion of mobile homes or mobile home parks from the entire community. See, e.g., In re Shore, 524 Pa. 436, 573 A.2d 1011 (1990); Guy v. Brandon Twp., 181 Mich.App. 775, 450 N.W.2d 279 (1989); Jensen's, Inc. v. City of Dover, 130 N.H. 761, 547 A.2d 277 (1988); Borough of Malvern v. Jackson, 108 Pa.Cmwlth. 248, 529 A.2d 96 (1987), settlement stipulation approved 521 Pa. 570, 559 A.2d 489 (1989). Compare to Stahl v. Upper Southampton Twp. Zoning Hearing Bd., 146 Pa.Cmwlth. 659, 606 A.2d 960 (1992), appeal denied 533 Pa. 639, 621 A.2d 584 (1993), where the court found a de facto exclusion of mobile home parks invalid where the ordinance permitted such parks with minimum 9,000 square foot lots, density requirements of three units per acre, and a requirement that the park be in single ownership.

E. ZONING THAT EXCLUDES MULTI–FAMILY HOUSING

There are several factors that lead some developing municipalities to adopt zoning restrictions that exclude or greatly limit the amount of land zoned for multi-family housing. These include a desire to protect the value of existing single-family homes, to avoid the costs of providing municipal services, including education, to multi-family housing and its occupants, and the fear that multi-family housing will bring with it households that the majority of current residents would rather not have living in the community. This exclusionary effect is accomplished simply by not zoning any land in the community for multi-family use, by designating one or a few small areas as multi-family districts, or by allowing multi-family housing projects only by special use permit which can be denied in the discretion of the approval board in certain circumstances.

These provisions tend to exclude low-and moderate-income households from living in the community because multi-family housing is more cost effective to build than single-family homes. Under multi-family zoning developers can concentrate more dwelling units on a parcel of land; per unit construction costs can be lower because of common walls, hallways, amenities, and equipment; road and utility costs per unit can be less, and the soft costs involved in securing approval to build and finance construction are divided among more units. Multi-family housing, of course, can be very expensive, exceeding the costs of building single-family homes, so providing for it in the zoning ordinance does not guarantee the construction of affordable housing, but the prospect of it is possible.

Unique legal issues are raised when exclusionary zoning of this type is adopted by developing suburbs whose zoning allows single-family homes and various commercial land uses. New residents and businesses will require the services of lower wage workers. If the community provides no affordable housing, these workers will commute into the community from surrounding municipalities that do provide such housing. In addition, limited-income households such as senior citizens, young families, single-parent families, and the unemployed will be excluded from communities with no affordable housing stock.

From a state constitutional perspective, the legal question this raises is whether the power to zone, which is delegated to the local government by the state itself, can be exercised by a community in a way that excludes people in the state who are in need of housing. Zoning may not be used for the express purpose of excluding growth where development pressures exist. Can communities in growth areas accept types of growth that generate higher property tax revenues or that are more socially desirable, while refusing to accommodate affordable types of housing? Is this a question more properly answered by the courts or the state legislature?

Practice in the fifty states on this issue differs markedly. In New Jersey, the courts have taken the lead, beginning in 1975 when the Supreme Court of the state declared that every municipality through its zoning must make "realistically possible an appropriate variety and choice of housing."

SOUTHERN BURLINGTON COUNTY NAACP v. TOWNSHIP OF MOUNT LAUREL

Supreme Court of New Jersey, 1975.
67 N.J. 151, 336 A.2d 713.

HALL, J.

This case attacks the system of land use regulation by defendant Township of Mount Laurel on the ground that low and moderate income families are thereby unlawfully excluded from the municipality. The trial court so found, 119 N.J.Super. 164 (Law Div.1972), and declared the township zoning ordinance totally invalid. Its judgment went on, in line with the requests for affirmative relief, to order the municipality to make studies of the housing needs of low and moderate income persons presently or formerly residing in the community in substandard housing, as well as those in such income classifications presently employed in the township and living elsewhere or reasonably expected to be employed therein in the future, and to present a plan of affirmative public action designed "to enable and encourage the satisfaction of the indicated needs." Jurisdiction was retained for judicial consideration and approval of such a plan and for the entry of a final order requiring its implementation.

* * *

The implications of the issue presented are indeed broad and far-reaching, extending much beyond these particular plaintiffs and the boundaries of this particular municipality.

There is not the slightest doubt that New Jersey has been, and continues to be, faced with a desperate need for housing, especially of decent living accommodations economically suitable for low and moderate income families. The situation was characterized as a "crisis" and fully explored and documented by Governor Cahill in two special messages to the Legislature—A Blueprint for Housing in New Jersey (1970) and New Horizons in Housing (1972).

Plaintiffs represent the minority group poor (black and Hispanic) seeking such quarters. But they are not the only category of persons barred from so many municipalities by reason of restrictive land use regulations. We have reference to young and elderly couples, single persons and large, growing families not in the poverty class, but who still cannot afford the only kinds of housing realistically permitted in most places—relatively high-priced, single-family detached dwellings on sizeable lots and, in some municipalities, expensive apartments. We will, therefore, consider the case from the wider viewpoint that the effect of Mount Laurel's land use regulation has been to prevent various categories of persons from living in the township because of the limited extent of their income and resources. In this connection, we accept the representation of the municipality's counsel at oral argument that the regulatory scheme was not adopted with any desire or intent to exclude prospective residents on the obviously illegal bases of race, origin or believed social incompatibility.

* * *

I

THE FACTS * * *

[At this point Judge Hall presents an extensive physical description and history of the growth and development of the township.]

* * *

The record thoroughly substantiates the findings of the trial court that over the years Mount Laurel "has acted affirmatively to control development and to attract a selective type of growth" (119 N.J.Super. at 168) and that "through its zoning ordinances has exhibited economic discrimination in that the poor have been deprived of adequate housing and the opportunity to secure the construction of subsidized housing, and has used federal, state, county and local finances and resources solely for the betterment of middle and upper-income persons." (119 N.J.Super. at 178.)

There cannot be the slightest doubt that the reason for this course of conduct has been to keep down local taxes on property (Mount Laurel is not a high tax municipality) and that the policy was carried out without regard for non-fiscal considerations with respect to people, either within or without its boundaries. This conclusion is demonstrated not only by what was done and what happened, as we have related, but also by innumerable direct statements of municipal officials at public meetings over the years which are found in the exhibits. The trial court referred to a number of them. 119 N.J.Super. at 169–170. No official testified to the contrary.

This policy of land use regulation for a fiscal end derives from New Jersey's tax structure, which has imposed on local real estate most of the cost of municipal and county government and of the primary and secondary education of the municipality's children. The latter expense is much the largest, so, basically, the fewer the school children, the lower the tax rate. Sizeable industrial and commercial ratables are eagerly sought and homes and the lots on which they are situate are required to be large enough, through minimum lot sizes and minimum floor areas, to have substantial value in order to produce greater tax revenues to meet school costs. Large families who cannot afford to buy large houses and must live in cheaper rental accommodations are definitely not wanted, so we find drastic bedroom restrictions for, or complete prohibition of, multi-family or other feasible housing for those of lesser income.

This pattern of land use regulation has been adopted for the same purpose in developing municipality after developing municipality. Almost every one acts solely in its own selfish and parochial interest and in effect builds a wall around itself to keep out those people or entities not adding favorably to the tax base, despite the location of the municipality or the demand for varied kinds of housing. There has been no effective intermunicipal or area planning or land use regulation. * * *

II

The Legal Issue

The legal question before us, as earlier indicated, is whether a developing municipality like Mount Laurel may validly, by a system of land use regulation, make it physically and economically impossible to provide low and moderate income housing in the municipality for the various categories of persons who need and want it and thereby, as

Mount Laurel has, exclude such people from living within its confines because of the limited extent of their income and resources. Necessarily implicated are the broader questions of the right of such municipalities to limit the kinds of available housing and of any obligation to make possible a variety and choice of types of living accommodations.

We conclude that every such municipality must, by its land use regulations, presumptively make realistically possible an appropriate variety and choice of housing. More specifically, presumptively it cannot foreclose the opportunity of the classes of people mentioned for low and moderate income housing and in its regulations must affirmatively afford that opportunity, at least to the extent of the municipality's fair share of the present and prospective regional need therefor. These obligations must be met unless the particular municipality can sustain the heavy burden of demonstrating peculiar circumstances which dictate that it should not be required so to do.

We reach this conclusion under state law and so do not find it necessary to consider federal constitutional grounds urged by plaintiffs. We begin with some fundamental principles as applied to the scene before us.

Land use regulation is encompassed within the state's police power. Our constitutions have expressly so provided since an amendment in 1927. That amendment, now Art. IV, § 6, par. 2 of the 1947 Constitution, authorized legislative delegation of the power to municipalities (other than counties), but reserved the legislative right to repeal or alter the delegation (which we take it means repeal or alteration in whole or in part). The legislative delegation of the zoning power followed in 1928, by adoption of the standard zoning enabling act, now found, with subsequent amendments, in N.J.S.A. 40:55–30 to 51.

It is elementary theory that all police power enactments, no matter at what level of government, must conform to the basic state constitutional requirements of substantive due process and equal protection of the laws. These are inherent in Art. I, par. 1 of our Constitution, the requirements of which may be more demanding than those of the federal Constitution. * * *

* * *

It is plain beyond dispute that proper provision for adequate housing of all categories of people is certainly an absolute essential in promotion of the general welfare required in all local land use regulation. Further the universal and constant need for such housing is so important and of such broad public interest that the general welfare which developing municipalities like Mount Laurel must consider extends beyond their boundaries and cannot be parochially confined to the claimed good of the particular municipality. It has to follow that, broadly speaking, the presumptive obligation arises for each such municipality affirmatively to plan and provide, by its land use regulations, the reasonable opportunity for an appropriate variety and choice of housing, including, of course, low and moderate cost housing, to meet the needs, desires and resources of all categories of people who may desire to live within its boundaries. Negatively, it may not adopt regulations or policies which thwart or preclude that opportunity.

* * *

We turn to application of these principles in appraisal of Mount Laurel's zoning ordinance, useful as well, we think, as guidelines for future application in other municipalities.

The township's general zoning ordinance (including the cluster zone provision) permits, as we have said, only one type of housing—single-family detached dwellings. This means that all other types—multi-family including garden apartments and other kinds housing more than one family, town (row) houses, mobile home parks—are prohibited. Concededly, low and moderate income housing has been intentionally excluded. While a large percentage of the population living outside of cities prefers a one-family house on its own sizeable lot, a substantial proportion do not for various reasons. Moreover, single-family dwellings are the most expensive type of quarters and a great number of families cannot afford them. Certainly they are not pecuniarily feasible for low and moderate income families, most young people and many elderly and retired persons, except for some of moderate income by the use of low cost construction on small lots.

As previously indicated, Mount Laurel has allowed some multi-family housing by agreement in planned unit developments, but only for the relatively affluent and of no benefit to low and moderate income families. And even here, the contractual agreements between municipality and developer sharply limit the number of apartments having more than one bedroom. * * *

Mount Laurel's zoning ordinance is also so restrictive in its minimum lot area, lot frontage and building size requirements, earlier detailed, as to preclude single-family housing for even moderate income families. Required lot area of at least 9,375 square feet in one remaining regular residential zone and 20,000 square feet (almost half an acre) in the other, with required frontage of 75 and 100 feet, respectively, cannot be called small lots and amounts to low density zoning, very definitely increasing the cost of purchasing and improving land and so affecting the cost of housing. As to building size, the township's general requirements of a minimum dwelling floor area of 1,100 square feet for all one-story houses and 1,300 square feet for all of one and one-half stories or higher is without regard to required minimum lot size or frontage or the number of occupants (see Sente v. Mayor and Municipal Council of City of Clifton, 66 N.J. 204, 208–209, 330 A.2d 321 (1974)). In most aspects these requirements are greater even than those approved in *Lionshead Lake, Inc. v. Township of Wayne, supra*, 10 N.J. 165, 89 A.2d 693, almost 24 years ago and before population decentralization, outer suburban development and exclusionary zoning had attained today's condition. See also Williams and Wacks, Segregation of Residential Areas Along Economic Lines: Lionshead Lake Revisited, 1969 Wis.L.Rev. 827. Again it is evident these requirements increase the size and so the cost of housing. The conclusion is irresistible that Mount Laurel permits only such middle and upper income housing as it believes will have sufficient taxable value to come close to paying its own governmental way. * * *

Without further elaboration at this point, our opinion is that Mount Laurel's zoning ordinance is presumptively contrary to the general welfare and outside the intended scope of the zoning power in the particulars mentioned. A facial showing of invalidity is thus established, shifting to the municipality the burden of establishing valid superseding reasons for its action and non-action. We now examine the reasons it advances.

* * *

[Judge Hall rejected the reasons advanced by the defendant, which were primarily fiscal and ecological.]

* * *

We have earlier stated that a developing municipality's obligation to afford the opportunity for decent and adequate low and moderate income housing extends at least to "* * * that municipality's fair share of the present and prospective regional need therefor." Some comment on that conclusion is in order at this point. Frequently it might be sounder to have more of such housing, like some specialized land uses, in one municipality in a region than in another, because of greater availability of suitable land, location of employment, accessibility of public transportation or some other significant reason. But, under present New Jersey legislation, zoning must be on an individual municipal basis, rather than regionally. So long as that situation persists under the present tax structure, or in the absence of some kind of binding agreement among all the municipalities of a region, we feel that every municipality therein must bear its fair share of the regional burden. (In this respect our holding is broader than that of the trial court, which was limited to Mount Laurel-related low and moderate income housing needs.)

The composition of the applicable "region" will necessarily vary from situation to situation and probably no hard and fast rule will serve to furnish the answer in every case. Confinement to or within a certain county appears not to be realistic, but restriction within the boundaries of the state seems practical and advisable. (This is not to say that a developing municipality can ignore a demand for housing within its boundaries on the part of people who commute to work in another state.) Here we have already defined the region at present as "those portions of Camden, Burlington and Gloucester Counties within a semicircle having a radius of 20 miles or so from the heart of Camden City." The concept of "fair share" is coming into more general use and, through the expertise of the municipal planning adviser, the county planning boards and the state planning agency, a reasonable figure for Mount Laurel can be determined, which can then be translated to the allocation of sufficient land therefor on the zoning map. See generally, New Jersey Trends, ch. 27, Listokin, Fair Share Housing Distribution: An Idea Whose Time Has Come?, p. 353. We may add that we think that, in arriving at such a determination, the type of information and estimates, which the trial judge (119 N.J.Super. at 178) directed the township to compile and furnish to him, concerning the housing needs of persons of low and moderate income now or formerly residing in the township in substandard dwellings and those presently employed or reasonably expected to be employed therein, will be pertinent.

There is no reason why developing municipalities like Mount Laurel, required by this opinion to afford the opportunity for all types of housing to meet the needs of various categories of people, may not become and remain attractive, viable communities providing good living and adequate services for all their residents in the kind of atmosphere which a democracy and free institutions demand. They can have industrial sections, commercial sections and sections for every kind of housing from low cost and multi-family to lots of more than an acre with very expensive homes. Proper planning and governmental cooperation can prevent over-intensive and too sudden development, insure against future suburban sprawl and slums and assure the preservation of open space and local beauty. We do not intend that developing municipalities shall be overwhelmed by voracious land speculators and developers if they use the powers which they have intelligently and in the broad public interest. Under our holdings today, they can be better communities for all than they previously have been.

III

The Remedy

As outlined at the outset of this opinion, the trial court invalidated the zoning ordinance in toto and ordered the township to make certain studies and investigations and to present to the court a plan of affirmative public action designed "to enable and encourage the satisfaction of the indicated needs" for township related low and moderate income housing. Jurisdiction was retained for judicial consideration and approval of such a plan and for the entry of a final order requiring its implementation.

We are of the view that the trial court's judgment should be modified in certain respects. We see no reason why the entire zoning ordinance should be nullified. Therefore we declare it to be invalid only to the extent and in the particulars set forth in this opinion. The township is granted 90 days from the date hereof, or such additional time as the trial court may find is reasonable and necessary to allow, to adopt amendments to correct the deficiencies herein specified. It is the local function and responsibility, in the first instance at least, rather than the court's, to decide on the details of the same within the guidelines we have laid down. If plaintiffs desire to attack such amendments, they may do so by supplemental complaint filed in this cause within 30 days of the final adoption of the amendments.

We are not at all sure what the trial judge had in mind as ultimate action with reference to the approval of a plan for affirmative public action concerning the satisfaction of indicated housing needs and the entry of a final order requiring implementation thereof. Courts do not build housing nor do municipalities. That function is performed by private builders, various kinds of associations, or, for public housing, by special agencies created for that purpose at various levels of government. The municipal function is initially to provide the opportunity through appropriate land use regulations and we have spelled out what Mount Laurel must do in that regard. It is not appropriate at this time, particularly in view of the advanced view of zoning law as applied to housing laid down by this opinion, to deal with the matter of the further extent of judicial power in the field or to exercise any such power. See, however, *Pascack Ass'n v. Mayor and Council of the Township of Washington*, 131 N.J.Super. 195, 329 A.2d 89 (Law Div.1974), and cases therein cited, for a discussion of this question. The municipality should first have full opportunity to itself act without judicial supervision. We trust it will do so in the spirit we have suggested, both by appropriate zoning ordinance amendments and whatever additional action encouraging the fulfillment of its fair share of the regional need for low and moderate income housing may be indicated as necessary and advisable. (We have in mind that there is at least a moral obligation in a municipality to establish a local housing agency pursuant to state law to provide housing for its resident poor now living in dilapidated, unhealthy quarters.) The portion of the trial court's judgment ordering the preparation and submission of the aforesaid study, report and plan to it for further action is therefore vacated as at least premature. Should Mount Laurel not perform as we expect, further judicial action may be sought by supplemental pleading in this cause.

The judgment of the Law Division is modified as set forth herein. No costs.

[Two concurring opinions are omitted.]

Notes

1. In response to the Mount Laurel I decision and order, the township simply added three new zoning districts, designed to bring itself into compliance with the Mount Laurel doctrine. The township did not attempt to cure those sections of the zoning code declared in Mount Laurel I to be unconstitutional. Upon further appeal to the courts by the plaintiffs, alleging that the township had not done enough to comply, the Supreme Court of New Jersey expressed frustration and a determination to "put some steel in [the Mount Laurel] doctrine." In Southern Burlington County NAACP v. Mt. Laurel, 92 N.J. 158, 456 A.2d 390 (1983), (Mount Laurel II), the Court wrote:

> This is the return, eight years later, of Southern Burlington County N.A.A.C.P. v. Township of Mount Laurel, 67 N.J. 151, 336 A.2d 713 (1975) (Mount Laurel I). We set forth in that case, for the first time, the

doctrine requiring that municipalities' land use regulations provide a realistic opportunity for low and moderate income housing. The doctrine has become famous. The Mount Laurel case itself threatens to become infamous. After all this time, ten years after the trial court's initial order invalidating its zoning ordinance, Mount Laurel remains afflicted with a blatantly exclusionary ordinance. Papered over with studies, rationalized by hired experts, the ordinance at its core is true to nothing but Mount Laurel's determination to exclude the poor. Mount Laurel is not alone; we believe that there is widespread non-compliance with the constitutional mandate of our original opinion in this case.

To the best of our ability, we shall not allow it to continue. This Court is more firmly committed to the original Mount Laurel doctrine than ever, and we are determined, within appropriate judicial bounds, to make it work. The obligation is to provide a realistic opportunity for housing, not litigation. We have learned from experience, however, that unless a strong judicial hand is used, Mount Laurel will not result in housing, but in paper, process, witnesses, trials and appeals. We intend by this decision to strengthen it, clarify it, and make it easier for public officials, including judges, to apply it.

2. Mount Laurel I provided builders a remedy—rezoning of their parcels to multi-family housing. This resulted in a slow and piecemeal process of breaking down zoning barriers, one development application and one law suit at a time. The essence of the Mount Laurel II case was the judicial declaration that municipalities must take affirmative action to provide incentives to developers to provide their fair share of their region's need for affordable housing. Typically, such incentives involve providing developers with a zoning bonus: additional density over the as-of-right zoning density allowed on land they own which provides a financial incentive for them to create housing units within their developments that are affordable to low-and moderate-income households. The difficulties of courts and court appointed masters supervising a process of defining relevant housing regions, determining regional housing needs, allocating those needs to each municipality, and supervising the compliance of local governments are obvious; this is unfamiliar terrain for the judicial branch of government which is accustomed to deferring to local legislative actions and confining remedies to the parties involved in binary lawsuits.

3. The New Jersey state legislature relieved the courts of much of this burden by passing the Fair Housing Act of 1985, N.J. Stat. Ann. §§ 52:27D–301 et seq. (West 2007). Under this statute, these tasks were transferred to the Council on Affordable Housing (COAH) which it created. The Act also allowed suburban municipalities to negotiate Regional Contribution Agreements with "receiving communities" to which they can transfer up to fifty percent of their fair share need in exchange for cash payments or other consideration. The Act also blunted the use of the builder's remedy based on the assumption that it was no longer needed as a method of implementation given the structure established by the Act and the new responsibilities given to COAH. Claiming that this fatally weakened the strategy of protecting the rights of low-and moderate-income households, plaintiffs attacked the Act in Hills Development Co. v. Township of Bernards, 103 N.J. 1, 510 A.2d 621(1986). In Hills, the court upheld the Act but went on to say:

"No one should assume that our exercise of comity today signals a weakening of our resolve to enforce the constitutional rights of New Jersey's lower income citizens. The constitutional obligation has not changed; the judiciary's ultimate duty to enforce it has not changed; our determination to perform that duty has not changed. What has changed is that we are no longer alone in this field. The other branches of government have fashioned a comprehensive statewide response to the Mount Laurel obligation. This kind of response, one that would permit us to withdraw from this field, is what this Court has always wanted and sought. It is potentially far better for the State and for its lower income citizens. . . ."

4. The role of the courts has remained critical to the accomplishment of the objectives of the Mount Laurel I and II decisions. A 1,000 unit ceiling on any individual municipality's fair share goal established by COAH was invalidated in Carlton Homes, Inc. v. COAH, 244 N.J.Super. 438, 582 A.2d 1024 (App.Div.1990). The court also invalidated a regulation by COAH that allowed a community to fill fifty percent of its affordable housing obligation by giving preference to local residents and workers. In re Township of Warren, 132 N.J. 1, 622 A.2d 1257 (1993). In 2002, the court affirmed the continued viability of the builder's remedy in Toll Bros., Inc v. Township of West Windsor, 173 N.J. 502, 803 A.2d 53 (2002). That case concludes with the following words:

"If municipalities believe, as the League of Municipalities contends, that the builder's remedy has become a developer's weapon, it is the municipalities that possess the shield of COAH-afforded protection to ward off builder's remedy litigation. Until practically all municipalities with a significant Mount Laurel obligation use the COAH process, however, the builder's remedy remains a necessary mechanism for the enforcement of constitutional values. Experience demonstrates that absent adequate enforcement, the Mount Laurel doctrine can deliver little more than a vague and hollow promise that a reasonable opportunity for the development of affordable housing will be provided. This case demonstrates that unfortunate fact."

5. In 2004, COAH ceased the practice of certifying state-wide, regional, and local housing needs and substituted for it a "growth share" approach. N.J. Admin. Code tit. 5, § 94 (2004). This new strategy ties the obligation of a community to provide affordable housing to a proportion of its growth. Specifically, for every eight market-rate residential units produced and for every twenty-five jobs created, a locality is obligated to provide one unit of affordable housing. This approach was perceived by some as another retreat from the forceful dictates of the Mount Laurel cases and was immediately challenged.

6. The standards for judging whether zoning ordinances in New York are unconstitutionally exclusionary were first articulated by the state highest court in 1975. Berenson v. Town of new Castle, 38 N.Y.2d 102, 109, 341 N.E.2d 236, 241, 378 N.Y.S.2d 672, 680 (1975). In this first Berenson decision, the New York Court of Appeals clarified certain fundamental principles regarding the delegation and use of the power to zone. First, the court stated that the "primary goal of a zoning ordinance must be to provide

for the development of a balanced, cohesive community which will make efficient use of the town's available land." Second, "in enacting a zoning ordinance, consideration must be given to regional needs and requirements.... There must be a balancing of the local desire to maintain the status quo within the community and the greater public interest that regional [housing] needs be met." Third, that "[a]lthough we are aware of the traditional view that zoning acts only upon the property lying within the zoning board's territorial limits, it must be recognized that zoning often has substantial impact beyond the boundaries of the municipality."

The court established a two-prong test to be applied by the courts when determining the reasonableness of local zoning ordinances attacked as exclusionary. The two factors are: (1) whether the town has provided a properly balanced and well ordered plan for the community—that is, are the present and future housing needs of all the town's residents met; and (2) were regional needs considered. After adopting these guidelines, the state's highest court remanded the case for trial to the Supreme Court in Westchester County. The Berenson case was decided by this lower court on December 6, 1977. After a trial on the issues, Judge Trainor found that New Castle's ordinance violated both prongs of the test. The zoning ordinance was declared invalid to the extent that it failed to allow for multi-family development at densities of at least eight units to the acre. New Castle was directed to issue a building permit for the project and given six months to amend its ordinances to provide for the construction of three thousand five hundred units of multi-family housing over a ten year period. The decision was then appealed by New Castle. That case, decided by the Appellate Division in 1979, follows.

BERENSON v. TOWN OF NEW CASTLE

Supreme Court of New York, Appellate Division, 1979.
67 A.D.2d 506, 415 N.Y.S.2d 669.

GULOTTA, JUSTICE.

The plaintiffs have secured a declaratory judgment invalidating the zoning ordinance of the Town of New Castle to the extent that it fails to make adequate provision for multi-family housing. (At the time this action was commenced, the ordinance totally excluded multi-family residential housing from the list of permitted uses. A subsequent amendment, examined in proposal form at the trial and enacted prior to Special Term's decision, purports to provide for 100–150 units of multi-family housing, as a permitted use, in the central business district of Chappaqua.) The issue on appeal is not whether the Town of New Castle may permissibly exclude multi-family housing from within its borders. The town now concedes that its total exclusion was improper and contends that the interim amendment of its zoning ordinance "is just the beginning of a process of experimentation in accommodating alternative housing forms including multi-family housing." Rather, the issue before us is whether the far-reaching remedial provisions of the judgment may be sustained. We hold that, for the most part, they may not.

* * *

* * * That there does exist an unmet local and regional need for multi-family housing is not seriously contested by the town on appeal, and this finding is amply supported by the evidence. However, instead of merely declaring the ordinance unconstitutional and remanding the matter to the Town Board for passage of an amended zoning ordinance which would pass judicial muster, Special Term went further and awarded the plaintiffs comprehensive affirmative relief. Finding that the town had not merely "failed" to consider local and regional housing needs, but, on the contrary, had "continuously and actively opposed any planning or program that would suggest the assumption by it of any responsibility to meet local or regional housing needs", and that compliance with the standards for local government land use control would not be promoted if made to depend upon repetitive litigation of the basic substantive issues, Special Term promulgated "judicially established housing goals" by declaring that the construction of 3,500 units of multi-family housing over the next 10 years was "the most conservative estimate of what will be required of New Castle * * * to supply its own needs * * * [and] its share of the regional needs", and directed the town to amend its zoning ordinance, land use regulations and planning policies to accommodate the needed housing. The town was given six months within which to comply, and in the absence of timely and satisfactory compliance, Special Term decreed that the traditional presumption of validity attending zoning ordinances would be suspended and applications for rezoning would be granted on an *ad hoc* basis to individual developers whose proposals meet the judicially established housing goals, unless the town is able to establish compelling reasons for denial. Special Term also declared that the zoning ordinance was unconstitutional as it applied to the plaintiffs' property and directed the town to rezone that property for multi-family housing at a density of eight units per acre within six months. In its decision, Special Term stated that a building permit should be issued to the plaintiffs upon the advent of rezoning. To all of this broad, comprehensive relief the town objects, and rightfully so.

* * *

* * * Zoning and land use regulations were deemed to be legislative functions, to be exercised by and within the particular expertise of the *local* legislative body. Thus, with the single exception of discriminatory zoning of similarly situated parcels, in which case the obvious remedy was to treat like parcels alike, a judicial declaration that a zoning ordinance was invalid as applied to a particular piece of property was never accompanied by a declaration which actually rezoned that property or placed it within a particular use classification. * * *

More recently, however, court challenges to exclusionary zoning on behalf of those excluded from the community have come into being, spawned by tremendous economic and social changes and the deterioration of city life. These challenges have not been prompted by the mere growth of the suburbs as attractive, affluent, mainly white collar bedroom communities, for those have been with us for many years. Rather, the critical factor appears to have been the relatively recent flight of blue collar jobs to the suburbs, where housing for the employer, but not his employees, was willingly provided. Moreover, while the early judicial challenges to such exclusionary practices were brought by plaintiff-developers who wished to put their property to a more profitable, higher density use, it was soon recognized that the developers' rights could not realistically be separated from the rights of others, then nonresidents, " 'in search of a comfortable place to live' " (*Concord Township Appeal*, 439 Pa. 466, 474, n. 6, 268 A.2d 765, 768, n. 6) and the cases were decided accordingly. In these cases, the relief sought was generally a declaration of the unconstitutionality of the zoning ordinance and the relief, when granted, consisted of such a declaration and, in some of cases, in a departure from past practices, a direction, in effect, rezoning the plaintiff's land * * *.

[At this point the court reviewed the Pennsylvania and New Jersey exclusionary zoning cases.]

* * *

Turning back now to the case at bar, Special Term found, on the basis of the evidence adduced at the trial that "the most conservative estimate of what will be required of New Castle over the next ten years to supply its own needs for multi-family housing and to meet its share of the regional needs for such housing is not less than 3,500 multi-family housing units," a figure which the court determined was not speculative, but rather "a realistic planning goal that recognized the minimum needs established by the evidence." As previously noted, since it deemed the town to be resistant to the voluntary assumption of its responsibilities in this respect and considered a one-time detailed mandate of specified changes in the zoning ordinance to be superior to expensive and repetitive litigation to achieve zoning relief on a parcel by parcel basis, Special Term simply directed the town to amend its ordinance and accessory regulations to provide for the construction of at least 3,500 units of multi-family housing by the end of 1987. In our opinion, this mandate is unsupported by the evidence, contrary to law, and contrary to sound principles of planning.

* * *

In point of fact then, the multi-family housing quota of 3,500 units, adopted by Special Term as New Castle's "fair share" of regional housing needs is a highly abstract and speculative number, to which the trial court ultimately gave more weight than did its proponents, Levy and Raymond. Further, the court apparently failed to appreciate that the figure itself was referable to the housing market in general, both as to income groups and the type of housing (single-or multi-family) to be provided, and was not directly referable to the needs of the low income groups with which the court was primarily concerned. The use of a "fair share" goal has never been judicially approved in the context of the housing needs of the population at large. Its raison d'etre lies in the housing needs of the low and moderate income groups whose "circumstances of * * * economic helplessness * * * to find adequate housing * * * [combined with] the wantonness of foreclosing them therefrom by [exclusionary] zoning", impelled the New Jersey Supreme Court to adopt the "fair share" doctrine in the first instance (*Pascack Assn. v. Mayor & Council of Township of Washington, Bergen County*, 74 N.J. 470, 480, 379 A.2d 6, 11). Moreover, Special Term's judgment cannot and does not insure that any of the multi-family units to be constructed will be anything other than luxury condominiums, with which the market may already be saturated. While not sufficient to save the zoning ordinance from invalidation, the town's contention that multi-family rental housing (the type most affordable by persons of low and moderate income) cannot be constructed today even with governmental subsidies unless the land is publicly owned or figured at zero cost is not without some merit, especially if we are talking about providing lower income housing in sizeable quantities. Indeed, the New Jersey Supreme Court's subsequent focus upon "least-cost" housing as opposed to low-income housing is attributable to its recognition that it will be virtually impossible to provide large amounts of newly constructed housing for the economically less fortunate in the foreseeable future. * * *

Aside from these evidentiary and practical problems, it is also abundantly clear that Special Term's declaration of a specific, mandatory "fair share" quota for the Town of New Castle is unsupported by case law and contrary to the public policy considerations embodied therein. It will be recalled that the "fair share" doctrine in Pennsylvania never encompassed the judicial specification of a particular number of higher density units to be built or the acreage to be devoted to such usage, and that even in New Jersey, where the doctrine is most highly developed, the Supreme Court has thus far refused to require judicial prescription of a mandatory "fair share" unit quota, concluding in essence, that such a course would be both inappropriate and impracticable. Nor is the decision of the Court of Appeals on the prior Berenson appeal (38 N.Y.2d 102, 378 N.Y.S.2d 672, 341 N.E.2d 236, supra) authority for the adoption of a "fair share" unit quota. Quite to the contrary, in holding that New Castle could validly exclude multi-family housing if its neighboring communities provided a sufficient number of such units, or the land upon which they could be built, to satisfy their own, New Castle's, and the regional needs, the Court of Appeals impliedly held that New Castle per se did not have to bear any "fair share" of any such housing burden. On the other hand, however, we cannot be blind to the fact that were the regional and local needs already being satisfied elsewhere, it is unlikely that we would be presented with the instant lawsuit, as the desire of developers and builders such as the plaintiffs to maximize their profits through more intensive land usage is, after all, dependent upon a market demand for that type of development. In any event, by holding that the courts had no choice, in the absence of meaningful regional planning, but to "assess the reasonableness of what the locality has done" (*Berenson v.*

Town of New Castle, 38 N.Y.2d 102, 111, 378 N.Y.S.2d 672, 682, 341 N.E.2d 236, 243, supra), the Court of Appeals in our view, merely intended to have Special Term determine whether New Castle's exclusion of multi-family dwellings was reasonable in light of present and foreseeable local and regional needs. We do not perceive that the court intended that a finding of unreasonableness, i.e., that there was an unmet local or regional need for multi-family housing which the town had ignored by excluding such housing, would authorize the court to go even further and remedy the deficiency by specific judicial fiat.

Although we therefore, find that Special Term erred in mandating a "fair share" unit goal, there is little doubt but that the record establishes an unsatisfied local and regional need for multi-family housing on the part of what we shall simply call the less affluent residents of the New York City metropolitan area. Indeed, the town does not argue to the contrary. And while multi-family zoning cannot insure that such units will actually be built, or that, if built, they will be affordable by families of modest means, the absence of such zoning, as noted by Special Term, surely precludes any such construction.

As a court of law, we cannot provide any lasting solution for the complex problems posed by cases such as this, but we can and must in appropriate cases require a developing municipality such as the Town of New Castle to cease its policy of immunizing itself from the ordinary incidents of growth and "confront the challenge of population growth with open doors" (*Golden v. Planning Bd. of Town of Ramapo*, 30 N.Y.2d 359, 379, 334 N.Y.S.2d 138, 153, 285 N.E.2d 291, 302, supra). The zoning ordinance thus having been properly declared unconstitutional for failure to make adequate provision for multi-family housing, the judgment should be modified so as to delete the 3,500 unit requirement, but direct that the matter be remanded to the Town Board to remedy its zoning deficiency within six months. Further, Special Term should retain jurisdiction for the purpose of allowing the plaintiffs to challenge the sufficiency of any amended ordinance by supplemental pleadings in this case. It is our expectation that the town will now set about its task with the utmost good faith. However, we feel compelled to note that the interim amendment here, characterized by one of plaintiffs' witnesses as having been drawn with such care as might be exercised if the town had to accept a leper colony into its midst, was not such a good-faith effort. Allegedly designed to provide 100–150 units of multi-family housing in the central business district of Chappaqua (an inadequate number in any event), plaintiffs presented uncontroverted proof that this estimated yield was based solely on spatial capacity and, as a general matter, could not be realized without the conversion of existing commercial space into residential space or the construction of a second floor on the tops of one-story commercial buildings, there being so little vacant land left to develop; as a practical matter, it was stated, the construction of no more than 27 units was realistically possible.

* * *

Judgment of the Supreme Court, Westchester County, entered December 30, 1977, modified, on the law, by deleting the third, fourth, fifth and sixth decretal paragraphs thereof and substituting therefor provisions (1) remanding the matter to the Town Board to remedy its zoning deficiency within a period of six months, (2) directing the Town Board to rezone plaintiffs' property for multi-family use and (3) directing that Special Term retain jurisdiction for the purpose of allowing plaintiffs to challenge the sufficiency and validity of any amended ordinance by supplemental pleadings in this case. As so modified, judgment affirmed, with costs to respondents payable by appellant.

* * *

SHAPIRO, JUSTICE (concurring in part and dissenting in part).

With one exception, I concur in the scholarly and comprehensive opinion of my brother MR. JUSTICE GULOTTA.

The amended zoning ordinance enacted by the Town of New Castle in response to the caveat of *Berenson v. Town of New Castle*, 38 N.Y.2d 102, 378 N.Y.S.2d 672, 341 N.E.2d 236, was a derisive mockery, verging on contempt. * * *

* * *

In a case such as this where the dilatory tactics of the town have prevented the plaintiffs from proceeding with their building project for more than five years, two strikes should be out. The conduct of the town fathers exhibits a flagrant and intentional and malicious policy of disregard for the law which was clearly intended to impede, if not entirely defeat, the rights of the plaintiffs. Thus, the zoning ordinance should be declared invalid with no period of grace. If there is no zoning until the town fathers shoulder their proper responsibilities—so be it. They should not be given leisure time to reform. Enough is enough.

Notes

1. The 1979 Berenson decision was not appealed to the state's highest court. Under court order, the developer's property was rezoned by the town for multi-family housing and the town proceeded to amend its zoning ordinance to provide for a modest amount of additional multi-family and other more affordable types of housing. Can you understand why, under these circumstances, the decision in the principal case was not appealed? The 1979 Berenson decision referred to a doctrine found in the Pennsylvania and New Jersey affordable housing case law: "it was soon recognized that the developers' right could not realistically be separated from the rights of others, then nonresidents in search of a comfortable place to live." If the developer's economic needs are met by the rezoning of its land, then who represents the rights of those in search of housing in appealing cases like this to the state's highest court? Does this help explain why the New Jersey courts required that every municipality must make "realistically possible an appropriate variety and choice of housing."

2. In Britton v. Town of Chester, 134 N.H. 434, 595 A.2d 492 (1991), a New Hampshire court struck down a two-acre minimum lot size restriction when it found that the ordinance had the effect of limiting the total area of the town available for affordable housing to 1.73 percent of its land mass. The court said the ordinance violated the state zoning enabling legislation delegating zoning power for the "general welfare of the community." The court also used the builder's remedy employed by Mt. Laurel and Berenson, but in a less drastic fashion; the court ordered the town to revise its zoning ordinance, and then face a builder's remedy if it did not do so.

3. In its 1975 Berenson decision, the New York Court of Appeals expressed concern over taking an aggressive role regarding these matters:

> "Zoning ... is essentially a legislative act. Thus, it is quite anomalous that a court should be required to perform the tasks of a regional planner. To that end, we look to the Legislature to make appropriate changes in order to foster the development of programs designed to achieve sound regional planning.... Until the day comes when regional, rather than local, governmental units can make such determinations, the courts must assess the reasonableness of what the locality has done."

4. In Connecticut, the state legislature has taken action by adopting the Affordable Housing Land Use Appeals Act of 1990 which expressly reverses the burden of proof when a municipality denies a developer's application to construct affordable housing. (Conn. Gen. Stat. § 8–30g). Under the Act, a municipality that denies a developer's application to construct affordable housing carries the burden of proving that its action is justified by showing that it was necessary to protect substantial public interests and such public interests clearly outweigh the need for affordable housing. If a zoning commission denies a developer's affordable housing proposal, the commission must "prove, based upon evidence in the record compiled before such commission, that the decision is necessary to protect substantial interest in health, safety or other matters which the commission may legally consider; such public interests clearly outweigh the need for affordable housing; and such public interests cannot be adequately protected by reasonable changes to the affordable housing development...." Affordable housing is defined to include developments in which at least thirty percent of the dwelling units are guaranteed to be affordable to households with median incomes who will not pay more than thirty percent of their annual income for housing costs in the development. Connecticut communities in which at least ten percent of the housing stock is affordable to low- and moderate-income families are exempt from the application of this burden shifting statute. Does this approach sound effective to you? What if a developer buys land zoned single-family, applies for approval of an affordable, multi-family housing project, and then negotiates with the zoning commission for a lower-density market rate multi-family project?

5. Another state statutory approach is found in Rhode Island, R.I. Gen. L. § 45–24–30, which provides that the purposes of zoning include:

> (8) Promoting a balance of housing choices, for all income levels and groups, to assure the health, safety and welfare of all citizens and their rights to affordable, accessible, safe and sanitary housing.

(9) Providing opportunities for the establishment of low and moderate income housing.

* * *

(16) Providing opportunities for reasonable accommodations in order to comply with the Rhode Island Fair Housing Practices Act, the United States Fair Housing Amendments Act of 1988 (FHAA), the Rhode Island Civil Rights of Individuals with Handicaps Act, and the Americans with Disabilities Act of 1990 (ADA).

6. The California legislature requires local governments to provide for affordable housing in the adoption and amendment of their zoning ordinances and restricts the ability of local review boards to turn down proposals for affordable housing. California communities must zone "sufficient vacant land for residential use. . . to meet housing needs for all income categories as identified in the housing element of the general plan." Cal. Gov't Code § 65913.1, *et seq.* When developers challenge land use regulations that restrict the supply of housing that may be built, the statute shifts the burden to the local government to establish that the restriction is "necessary for the protection" of public health, safety, or welfare. A further burden of proof is established to justify the denial of permission to build housing projects for low-and moderate-income households. This statutory approach builds on a requirement in the state planning enabling law that requires local governments to include housing components in their comprehensive plans. Cal. Gov't Code § 65580.

SECTION 6. INCLUSIONARY ZONING

Communities in many states have the legal authority to create inclusionary zoning programs. Whether motivated by judicial fiat, legislative direction, or a desire to meet compelling housing needs, communities can take the initiative and use their land use authority to create opportunities for developers to provide affordable housing. Such programs take the form of mandatory requirements contained in local zoning that require developers to provide affordable housing as part of their approved market rate projects, or the provision of incentives to developers who decide voluntarily to produce affordable housing. In California, the legislature has adopted statutes that require municipalities to provide density bonuses to housing developers. Cal. Gov't Code §§ 65580–65589.3. The housing element of the local comprehensive plan, under this provision, must contain an "assessment of housing needs and an inventory of resources and constraints relevant to the meeting of these needs." Interestingly, this local assessment must include the locality's share of regional housing needs; the statute contains an approach for estimating and distributing regional needs. In drafting and adopting a housing element, local officials must analyze governmental constraints on the development of housing, the availability of housing subsidies and financing, and available construction sites with appropriate services for housing. These matters and their legal ramifications are discussed in the following case.

HOME BUILDERS ASSOCIATION OF NORTHERN CALIFORNIA v. CITY OF NAPA

California Court of Appeal, First District, Division 5, 2001.
90 Cal.App.4th 188, 108 Cal.Rptr.2d 60.

JONES, P.J.

* * *

City, like many other localities in California, has a shortage of affordable housing. This shortage has negative consequences for all of City's population, but causes particularly severe problems for those on the lower end of the economic spectrum. Manual laborers, some of whom work in the region's wine or leisure industries, are forced to live in crowded, substandard housing. There is a large, and growing population of homeless, including many families and teenagers. Workers from low-income families increasingly are forced to live greater distances from their places of employment, which causes increased traffic congestion and pollution.

City formed the Napa Affordable Housing Task Force to address these problems. The task force was a broad based community group that included representatives from non-profit agencies, environmental groups, religious institutions, local industries, for-profit developers, and the local chamber of commerce. The purpose of the task force was to "study the issues surrounding affordable housing in the City of Napa and . . . make recommendations to the Housing Authority Commission."

The task force studied housing issues for several months. It formed subcommittees, conducted public hearings, and evaluated affordable housing solutions that had been enacted by other communities. Ultimately the task force recommended that City enact an inclusionary housing ordinance modeled after one that had been enacted by Napa County.

City responded by enacting the inclusionary zoning ordinance that is at issue in the present appeal. The ordinance applies to all development in the city, including residential and non-residential.

The primary mandate imposed by the ordinance on residential developers is a requirement that ten percent of all newly constructed units must be "affordable" as that term is defined. The ordinance offers developers two alternatives. First, developers of single-family units may, at their option, satisfy the so called inclusionary requirement through an "alternative equivalent proposal" such as a dedication of land, or the construction of affordable units on another site. Developers of multi-family units may also satisfy the 10 percent requirement through an "alternative equivalent proposal" if the City Council, in its sole discretion, determines that the proposed alternative results in affordable housing opportunities equal to or greater than those created by the basic inclusionary requirement.

As a second alternative, a residential developer may choose to satisfy the inclusionary requirement by paying an in-lieu fee. Developers of single-family units may choose this option by right, while developers of multi-family units are permitted this option if the City Council, again in its sole discretion, approves. All fees generated through this option are deposited into a housing trust fund, and may only be used to increase and improve the supply of affordable housing in City.

Developments that include affordable housing are eligible for a variety of benefits including expedited processing, fee deferrals, loans or grants, and density bonuses that allow more intensive development than otherwise would be allowed. In addition, the ordinance permits a developer to appeal for a reduction, adjustment, or *complete waiver* of obligations under the ordinance "based upon the absence of any reasonable relationship or nexus between the impact of the development and . . . the inclusionary requirement."

HBA is a non-profit corporation and association of builders, contractors, and related trades and professionals involved in the residential construction industry. In September 1999, HBA filed a complaint against City seeking to have the inclusionary zoning ordinance declared facially invalid. * * *

HBA contends that City's inclusionary zoning ordinance is facially invalid because it violates the taking clauses of the Federal and State Constitutions.

* * *

Here, City's inclusionary zoning ordinance imposes significant burdens on those who wish to develop their property. However the ordinance also provides significant benefits to those who comply with its terms. Developments that include affordable housing are eligible for expedited processing, fee deferrals, loans or grants, and density bonuses. More critically, the ordinance permits a developer to appeal for a reduction, adjustment, or *complete waiver* of the ordinance's requirements. Since City has the ability to waive the requirements imposed by the ordinance, the ordinance cannot and does not, on its face, result in a taking.

HBA contends the ordinance's waiver clause does not preclude a facial challenge because that clause improperly places the burden on the developer to prove that a waiver would be appropriate when the City has not established a justification for the exactions mandated by the ordinance. According to HBA, allocating the burden in this way is inconsistent with *Dolan v. City of Tigard* (1994) 512 U.S. 374, 391, footnote 8, 114 S.Ct. 2309, 129 L.Ed.2d 304. HBA misreads *Dolan.* Quite to the contrary, the Supreme Court stated in *Dolan,* that when evaluating the validity of generally applicable zoning regulations, it is appropriate to place the burden on the party who is challenging the regulation. (*Ibid.*) As we will discuss below, City's inclusionary zoning ordinance is a generally applicable legislative enactment rather than an individualized assessment imposed as a condition of development. Thus, the burden shifting standard described in *Dolan* does not apply.

* * *

Here, HBA contends that City's inclusionary zoning ordinance * * * is invalid because it fails to substantially advance legitimate state interests. We are unpersuaded.

First, we have no doubt that creating affordable housing for low and moderate income families is a legitimate state interest. Our Supreme Court has said that the "assistance of moderate-income households with their housing needs is recognized in this state as a legitimate governmental purpose." (*Santa Monica Beach, Ltd. v. Superior Court* (1999) 19 Cal.4th 952, 970, 81 Cal.Rptr.2d 93, 968 P.2d 993.) This conclusion is consistent with repeated pronouncements from the state Legislature which has declared that "the development of a sufficient supply of housing to meet the needs of *all Californians* is a matter of statewide concern," (Gov.Code, § 65913.9, emphasis added) and that local governments have "a responsibility to use the powers vested in them to facilitate the improvement and development of housing to make adequate provision for the housing needs of *all economic segments of the community*." (Gov.Code, § 65580, subd. (d), emphasis added.) Indeed, Witkin lists 12 separate statutes that are "designed to stimulate the construction of low and moderate income housing by the private sector." (4 Witkin, Summary of Cal. Law (9th ed. 1987) Real Property § 54, p. 275; *id.* (2000 Supp.) § 54, p. 134.)

Second, it is beyond question that City's inclusionary zoning ordinance will "substantially advance" the important governmental interest of providing affordable housing for low and moderate income families. By requiring developers in City to create a modest amount of affordable housing (or to comply with one of the alternatives) the ordinance will necessarily increase the supply of affordable housing. We conclude City's ordinance "substantially advance[s] legitimate state interests." (*Agins v. Tiburon, supra,* 447 U.S. at p. 260, 100 S.Ct. 2138.)

HBA's principal constitutional claim is that City's ordinance is invalid under *Nollan v. California Coastal Comm'n* (1987) 483 U.S. 825, 107 S.Ct. 3141, 97 L.Ed.2d 677, and *Dolan v. City of Tigard, supra,* 512 U.S. 374, 114 S.Ct. 2309, 129 L.Ed.2d 304.

In *Nollan* the court discussed the "substantially advance" test in the context of a governmental requirement that appellant property owners dedicate a portion of their beachfront property to the public as a condition for obtaining a rebuilding permit. In the course of its discussion, the court said there must be an "essential nexus" between a condition imposed on the use of land, and the impacts caused by the proposed use. (*Nollan v. California Coastal Comm'n, supra,* 483 U.S. at p. 837, 107 S.Ct. 3141.)

Dolan also involved dedications of property that were a condition for granting a development permit. There the court said that a "rough proportionality" standard "best encapsulates what we hold to be the requirement of the Fifth Amendment. No precise mathematical calculation is required, but the city must make some sort of individualized determination that the required dedication is related both in nature and extent to the impact of the proposed development." (*Dolan v. City of Tigard, supra,* 512 U.S. at p. 391, 114 S.Ct. 2309.)

HBA contends City's ordinance is invalid under *Nollan* and *Dolan* because there is no "essential nexus" or "rough proportionality" between the exaction required by the ordinance, and the impacts caused by development of property.

We reject this argument because *Nollan* and *Dolan* are inapplicable under the facts of this case. "[T]he intermediate standard of judicial scrutiny formulated by the high court in *Nollan* and *Dolan* is intended to address ... land use 'bargains' between property owners and regulatory bodies—those in which the local government conditions permit approval for a given use on the owner's surrender of benefits which *purportedly* offset the impact of the proposed development. It is in this paradigmatic permit context—where the individual property owner-developer seeks to negotiate approval of a planned development—that the combined *Nollan* and *Dolan* test quintessentially applies." (*Ehrlich v. City of Culver City* (1996) 12 Cal.4th 854, 868, 50 Cal.Rptr.2d 242, 911 P.2d 429.) "But a different standard of scrutiny [applies] to development fees that are generally applicable through legislative action 'because the heightened risk of the "extortionate" use of the police power to exact unconstitutional conditions is not present.' " (*Santa Monica Beach, Ltd. v. Superior Court, supra,* 19 Cal.4th at p. 966, 81 Cal.Rptr.2d 93, 968 P.2d 993, quoting *Ehrlich v. City of Culver City, supra,* 12 Cal.4th at p. 876, 50 Cal.Rptr.2d 242, 911 P.2d 429.) "[I]ndividualized development fees warrant a type of review akin to the conditional conveyances at issue in *Nollan* and *Dolan,* whereas generally applicable development fees warrant the more deferential review that the *Dolan* court recognized is generally accorded to legislative determinations." (*Santa Monica Beach, Ltd. v. Superior Court, supra,* 19 Cal.4th at pp. 966–967, 81 Cal.Rptr.2d 93, 968 P.2d 993.) The justification for these varying levels of scrutiny is founded in the nature of the two types of exactions. "It is one thing for courts to make a government agency adhere to its own justification for requiring the dedication of a particular portion of property as a condition of development; such adherence safeguards against the possibility that the justification is merely a pretext for taking the property without paying compensation.... But it is another thing for courts to require that a complex, generally applicable piece of economic legislation that will have many effects on many different persons and entities accomplish precisely the goals stated in a legislative preamble in order to preserve its constitutionality." (*Santa Monica Beach, Ltd. v. Superior Court, supra,* 19 Cal.4th at p. 972, 81 Cal.Rptr.2d 93, 968 P.2d 993.)

Here, we are not called upon to determine the validity of a particular land use bargain between a governmental agency and a person who wants to develop his or her land. Instead we are faced with a facial challenge to economic legislation that is generally applicable to *all* development in City. We conclude the heightened standard of review described in *Nollan* and *Dolan* is inapplicable under these facts.

* * *

HBA also contends that the inclusionary zoning ordinance is invalid because the lack of housing for low and moderate income families in City is the product of City's own prior restrictive land use policies.

HBA has not cited any authority to support the proposition that a zoning ordinance which tries to solve problems caused by prior legislative decisions is invalid, and case law is directly to the contrary. For example, in *Penn Central Transp. Co. v. New York City* (1978) 438 U.S. 104, the Supreme Court ruled that New York could enact a landmark preservation law that was designed to mitigate the effects of prior policies that permitted "large numbers of historic structures, landmarks, and areas" to be destroyed. (*Id.* at p. 108.) If New York can enact a landmark preservation law to remedy a shortage of historic buildings created by its prior policies, City can enact an inclusionary zoning ordinance even if its prior policies contributed to a scarcity of available land and a shortage of affordable housing.

HBA contends the inclusionary zoning ordinance is facially invalid under the due process clause of the Federal Constitution because it "requires property owners who develop residential housing to sell or rent 10% of their units at prices or rents that are based entirely upon certain fixed percentages of the income levels of lower and very low-income households." Imposing such a requirement violates the due process clause, HBA argues, because "the inclusionary zoning law provides no mechanism to make a fair return for property owners who are forced to sell or rent units at an amount unrelated to market prices."

We doubt seriously that HBA is entitled to a "fair return" under the due process clause. The "fair return" standard is commonly used to evaluate restrictions placed on historically regulated industries such as railroads and public utilities. (See, e.g., *Power Comm'n v. Pipeline Co.* (1942) 315 U.S. 575.) It has also been used to evaluate rent control ordinances. (See e.g. *Fisher v. City of Berkeley* (1984) 37 Cal.3d 644, 679.) However HBA has not cited, and we are not aware of, any case that holds a housing developer is entitled to *"fair return" on his or her investment.*

However we need not base our decision on this ground. First, it is not literally correct to say that City's ordinance "requires property owners who develop residential housing to sell or rent 10% of their units [to low income individuals]." Under the ordinance, any person who does not want to sell or rent a portion of his or her housing unites to low income individuals may choose one of the alternatives, such as donating vacant land or paying an in-lieu fee. Thus HBA's argument is based on an incorrect premise.

Second, and more importantly, HBA's facial due process challenge must necessarily fail. As we have said, " 'A claim that a regulation is *facially* invalid is only tenable if the terms of the regulation will not permit those who administer it to avoid an unconstitutional *application* to the complaining parties.' "(*San Mateo County Coastal Landowners' Assn. v. County of San Mateo, supra,* 38 Cal.App.4th at p. 547, internal citation omitted.) When an ordinance contains provision that allow for administrative relief, we must presume the implementing authorities will exercise their authority in conformity with the Constitution. (See *Fisher v. City of Berkeley, supra,* 37 Cal.3d at p. 684.)

Here, as we have noted, City's ordinance includes a clause that allows city officials to reduce, modify or waive the requirements contained in the ordinance "based upon the absence of any reasonable relationship or nexus between the impact of the development and . . . the inclusionary requirement." Since City has the authority to completely waive a developer's obligations, a facial challenge under the due process clause must necessarily fail.

HBA contends the waiver clause does not preclude a facial challenge because it does not state expressly that a waiver may be granted based on a lack of a "fair return." However the power of an agency to make adjustments to guarantee a fair return is "not limited to those literally granted by the ordinance. . . ." (*City of Berkeley v. City Berkeley Rent Stabilization Bd.* (1994) 27 Cal.App.4th 951, 962.) When this standard is not expressly stated, it is "present by implication." (*Ibid.*)

The judgment is affirmed.

Note

In Villager Pond, Inc. v. Town of Darien, 56 F.3d 375 (2d Cir.1995), the developer of a condominium project sued the town for damages claiming that it had illegally exacted two units in the development to be conveyed to the town for low-and moderate-income people. The court rejected the argument that the developer had a property interest in receiving his zoning permits under the Dolan v. City of Tigard case, but remanded to the trial court for a determination of the developer's property interest under state law.

BUILDING INDUSTRY ASSOCIATION OF SAN DIEGO COUNTY, INC. v. CITY OF SAN DIEGO

Superior Court, San Diego County, California, 2006.
2006 WL 1666822.

MEYER, J.

The City of San Diego enacted an inclusionary zoning ordinance in an effort to help resolve the affordable housing crisis existing in San Diego. The ordinance requires that developers either set aside a share of their projects for lower- or moderate-income households, or pay an "in lieu" fee to the City. [See SDMC §§ 142.1301–1312]

Although a developer may obtain a waiver of the requirements, section 142.1305(d) provides:

> No waiver shall be issue to an applicant unless: (1) Special circumstances, unique to that development justify the grant of the waiver; (2) The development would not be feasible without the waiver; (3) A specific and substantial financial hardship would occur if the waiver were not granted; and (4) No alternative means of compliance are available which would be more effective in attaining the purposes of this Division than the relief requested.

The ordinance enacted by the City of San Diego is similar to those in other areas of California, including the ordinance addressed in *Home Builders Association of Northern California v. City of Napa* (2001) 90 Cal.App.4th 188.

In Home Builders, the Court set forth the appropriate test to determine whether "economic legislation that is generally applicable to all development," such as the subject inclusionary zoning ordinance, survives a facial constitutional challenge.

After determining that the ordinance substantially advanced legitimate state interests, the Home Builders court concluded that not only was there no "taking," but also that the petitioners could not show a facial challenge based upon the due process clause.

> Second, and more importantly, HBA's facial due process challenge must necessarily fail. As we have said, " 'A claim that a regulation is facially invalid is only tenable if the terms of the regulation will not permit those who administer it to avoid an unconstitutional application to the complaining parties. . . ." ' (*San Mateo County Coastal Landowners' Assn. v. County of San Mateo*, supra, 38 Cal.App.4th at p. 547, citation omitted.) When an ordinance contains provisions that allow for administrative relief, we must presume the implementing authorities will exercise their authority in conformity with the Constitution. (See *Fisher v. City of Berkeley*, supra, 37 Cal.3d at p. 684.)
>
> Here, as we have noted, City's ordinance includes a clause that allows city officials to reduce, modify or waive the requirements contained in the ordinance "based upon the absence of any reasonable relationship or nexus between the impact of the development and . . . the inclusionary requirement." Since City has the authority to completely waive a developer's obligations, a facial challenge under the due process clause must necessarily fail. [*Id.*, at 199]

In Home Builders, the "complete waiver" allowed the City of Napa to avoid an unconstitutional application by a determination of an "absence of any reasonable relationship or nexus between the impact of the development and . . . the inclusionary requirement." In other words, the waiver provision set forth an out for a developer when the basic constitutional connection is lacking. The waiver provision in the San Diego ordinance is not the same as the one contained in the Napa ordinance.

The waiver provision enacted by the City of San Diego permits a waiver only upon the determination of four separate findings, all of which must be made.

Accordingly, on its face, the ordinance does not provide for the granting of a waiver solely because of an absence of any reasonable relationship or nexus between the impact of the development and the inclusionary requirement. The City can, therefore, impose the inclusionary requirement on a development not reasonably related to the need for that requirement.

Inasmuch as the waiver provision enacted by the City of San Diego does not allow the City to avoid the unconstitutional application of the ordinance, the ordinance on its face results in an unconstitutional taking.

* * *

Counsel for Petitioner Building Industry Association is hereby directed to prepare a judgment granting a writ a mandate, setting aside the subject ordinance, and remanding the matter to the San Diego City Council in accordance with the views expressed herein.

Notes

1. The New York legislature authorized its local governments to provide zoning incentives to developers to provide affordable housing as well as other public amenities. Town Law § 261–b, Village Law § 7–703, and General City Law § 81–d. Incentive zoning is used to induce land developers to provide affordable housing for senior citizens, local workers, or low- and moderate-income citizens. Under a typical incentive zoning provision, the developer is allowed to build a greater number of homes than is otherwise permitted by the zoning law and to sell or rent some of these "bonus units" at market value. In return, the developer is required to use that profit to reduce the cost of the additional bonus units to make them affordable. These affordable homes must then be rented or sold to persons or families of limited income. Incentives can be provided to developers of raw land or to those who propose the expansion of existing structures, the adaptive reuse of older buildings, or the redevelopment of brownfield sites and other distressed parcels in older, developed areas. The New York statutes allow incentives to be given in exchange for the provision of other community benefits, as well, including open space or parks, day care or elder care, or "other specific physical, social, or cultural amenity of benefit to the residents of the community." Where the community benefit cannot feasibly or practically be provided directly by individual developers, the incentive system can provide for developers to make cash payments to the locality. Such sums must be held in a trust fund to be used exclusively for the community benefits specified.

2. Local inclusionary housing programs implicate the economics of development. By giving bonus densities to developers, the economic difficulties of providing low- and moderate-income housing in unsubsidized, market rate projects are mitigated. If bonus programs are voluntary, allowing developers to opt into them in exchange for providing a percentage of

proposed units as affordable, very few legal issues arise. Experience indicates that voluntary programs are only moderately successful in attracting developers who prefer to aim for the top of the market and avoid the complications of two-tiered marketing. When developers are required to provide affordable housing on-site with market rate units and where bonuses or other incentives are not provided, they often object. They argue that the affordable units constrict their market: fewer affluent residents will be attracted to the development or they will expect to pay less because of the presence of lower income households in the development. Developers may argue that the economic feasibility of their projects is destroyed by the costs of providing affordable units, particularly in flat markets, and that the requirements constitute a regulatory taking. To avoid due process and takings claims, local programs often give developers other options. These include buy-out provisions allowing developers to pay a per unit amount into a local trust fund which is used to subsidize the provision of affordable housing off site. Another approach is to allow developers to provide the required housing in a different building or on a different site: the so-called off-site option.

3. This chapter on Housing and Urban Development provided information at its inception about the prospect of accommodating homes and work places for the 100 million more Americans expected over the next four decades and the importance of this to mitigating climate change and dealing with a variety of other important social and economic objectives. It then examined methods of stemming urban blight and fostering urban revitalization; proceeded to an analysis of the strategic efforts of aging suburban communities to combat competition for tax ratables with newer, developing communities; and ended with a look at judicial and statutory initiatives to prevent exclusionary zoning. What do you make of these attempts to use land use planning, zoning, eminent domain, conditions on developers' project approvals, and other legal techniques to influence market forces to create optimal human settlement patterns? The governor of New Jersey at the time of the Mount Laurel decision chastened the court by saying that there is no reason to make every community a "carbon copy" of other communities, in other words that every community should not have an obligation to provide its fair share of housing to low-and moderate-income housing. The current New Jersey "growth share" approach adopts that approach, imposing the obligation to provide affordable housing only on developing communities. Do you agree with this policy perspective or do you have another view? During your careers, the issues this chapter addresses will become more and more significant. What is the role of lawyers, planners, and other professionals in guiding development by framing policy objectives and ensuring their proper implementation through land use law?

Chapter IX

LOCAL ENVIRONMENTAL LAW

SECTION 1. HISTORICAL OVERVIEW

Environmental law was defined originally by federal statutes adopted in the early 1970s such as the Clean Water Act and the Clean Air Act. Within a few years, well over a dozen such laws were adopted and a new era of environmental cleanup and pollution prevention was launched. Uniform standards were created, aggressive enforcement practices were adopted, and federal and state agencies were employed to preserve threatened natural resources and to protect the public health.

The emphasis in the teaching and practice of environmental law has been on the central role of the federal government as the standard-setter and steward of a healthy environment. This focus all but obscures the importance of the role of local governments in environmental protection. Federal agencies have successfully reduced pollution that emanates from "point sources," such as smokestacks and water pipes. But most environmental damage today is caused by "nonpoint source" pollution that results from land uses that are the legal responsibility of municipal governments. Federal attempts to influence local land use control in the interest of abating nonpoint source pollution have been thwarted by a variety of legal, political, and practical obstacles.

During the last two decades, there has been a remarkable but little noticed trend among local governments to adopt laws that protect natural resources and lessen environmental pollution. These local environmental laws exhibit a number of forms. They include local comprehensive plans expressing environmental values, zoning districts created to protect critical environmental areas, environmental standards contained in subdivision and site plan regulations, and stand-alone environmental laws adopted to protect particular natural features such as ridgelines, wetlands, floodplains, stream banks, existing vegetative cover, and forests. Local governments have creatively used a variety of traditional and modern powers that their state legislatures have delegated to them to address locally occurring environmental problems. This phenomenon is seldom studied in environmental law classes despite the critical legal role that localities play in determining the use of the land.

As earlier chapters demonstrate, our nation's legal system gives local governments a key, if not the principal role, in land use regulation. Local governments may adopt master plans, zoning ordinances, and a variety of community-building regulations that provide for their future development. Comprehensive zoning began as a mechanism for protecting public health and safety by separating incompatible land uses from one another. In its application, zoning became design-oriented, focusing on the layout of streets and highways, the location of public buildings, the ability of fire trucks and firefighters to reach and fight fires, the size and bulk requirements that protect property values, and the infrastructure connections that create a workable community.

Subdivision and site plan regulations emerged to complement zoning and help localities implement their physical plans. Such regulations initially concentrated on the creation of safe intersections; the fluid movement of vehicles; the adequacy of road width, curbs, and sidewalks; the siting of buildings; and the prevention of off-site impacts such as flooding. In Golden v. Ramapo, the leading state court case sustaining local growth management ordinances, New York's highest court referred to subdivision control as a mechanism "to guide community development in the directions outlined here, while at the same time encouraging the provision of adequate facilities for the housing, distribution, comfort and convenience of local residents." Golden, 30 N.Y.2d 359, 334 N.Y.S.2d 138, 285 N.E.2d 291, 298 (1972). At their inception, regulatory tools such as subdivision and site plan regulation were not designed to protect natural resources from degradation. This is not to say that land use regulations designed to protect the health of residents do not achieve environmental benefits, as the following case demonstrates.

DE MARS v. ZONING COMMISSION OF TOWN OF BOLTON

Connecticut Supreme Court, 1955.
142 Conn. 580, 115 A.2d 653.

WYNNE, ASSOCIATE JUSTICE.

The zoning commission of the town of Bolton adopted certain changes of the zoning regulations which had been in effect in that town for more than two years. Six residents of the town have appealed from a judgment of the Court of Common Pleas. That court dismissed an appeal by them from the action of the commission in adopting the changes. The question before us is whether the court erred in holding that the commission did not act arbitrarily, illegally, or in abuse of its discretion.

Following is a summary of the facts: Zoning regulations were adopted in the town on August 1, 1951. They provided for a residence zone A, a residence zone B and business zones. Residence zone A includes almost the entire town. Residence zone B relates to that portion of the town known as the Lake Area. This is primarily a colony of summer cottages surrounding a lake in the town, although some of the cottages have been made suitable for all-the-year occupancy. The business zones are small in area, not yet affected by the surge of out-of-town pressures. On April 19, 1954, a hearing was held by the zoning commission on certain proposals which the commission itself had initiated. These had to do primarily with enlarging lot areas by increasing the minimum dimensions of lots, in residence zone A, from 150 feet in width and 200 feet in depth to 200 by 200 feet; in residence zone B, from 75 feet in width and 150 feet in depth to 150 by 150 feet; and in business zones, from 150 feet in width and 200 feet in depth to 200 by 200 feet.

The plaintiffs' appeal is predicated upon three claims: (1) The commission is without power to change existing regulations unless there has been a substantial change in circumstances and conditions since the adoption of the regulations. (2) Where the commission makes amendments or changes on its own initiative, it must introduce at the public hearing sufficient facts to substantiate a valid reason or reasons for the change. (3) The records of the commission must set forth the facts warranting the commission's finding that a change is necessary.

Section 837 of the General Statutes confers upon zoning commissions the power to adopt regulations among other purposes, 'to promote health and the general welfare.' These regulations must be made upon reasonable consideration of the character of the district and its peculiar suitability for particular purposes and with a view to conserving the value of buildings and encouraging the most appropriate use of land throughout the town. They may be amended and changed. Cum.Sup. 1953, § 282c. A zoning authority is endowed with a wide and liberal discretion. *Bartram v. Zoning Commission*, 136 Conn. 89, 96, 68 A.2d 308. This discretion is to be overruled only when the commission has not acted fairly, with proper motives and upon valid reasons. *Mallory v. Town of West Hartford*, 138 Conn. 497, 505, 86 A.2d 668. It is true that ordinarily a change of zone affecting a small area should be made only when there has been a change in conditions or new considerations have arisen since the previous zoning of the area. *Hills v. Zoning Commission*, 139 Conn. 603, 609, 96 A.2d 212, * * *. In the instant case, the change in the regulations affected a substantial part of the town of Bolton. Even if the requirement was applicable, it has been met adequately. Anticipating that the greatest residential use of land in the town was yet to come, the board concluded that larger lot sizes would provide greater area for the disposal of sewage and would increase the distances between sewage disposal areas and the residential water supply. We cannot say that this purpose of the change in the regulations affecting the size of building lots was so unrelated to the public health and welfare as to be unreasonable. *State v. Hillman*, 110 Conn. 92, 100, 105, 147 A. 294; *Strain v. Mims*, 123 Conn. 275, 286, 193 A. 754. Zoning regulations such as the one here concerned have generally been held valid. *Simon v. Town of Needham*, 311 Mass. 560, 564, 42 N.E.2d 516, 141 A.L.R. 688; 1 Yokley, Zoning Law & Practice (2d Ed.) p. 422. The first claim of the plaintiffs is without merit.

The plaintiffs' second and third claims may be considered together. Section 282c of the 1953 Cumulative Supplement provides that "[w]henever a zoning commission shall make any change in a zoning regulation or the boundaries of a zoning district it shall state upon its records the reason why such change is made." *See Levine v. Zoning Board of Appeals*, 124 Conn. 53, 57, 198 A. 173; *Perdue v. Zoning Board of Appeals*, 118 Conn. 174, 179, 171 A. 26; *Grady v. Katz,* 124 Conn. 525, 530, 1 A.2d 137. However, as we pointed out in *Couch v. Zoning Commission*, 141 Conn. 349, 358, 106 A.2d 173, the members of a zoning commission may well be laymen and cannot be expected to set forth the reasons for their action in language which would satisfy the meticulous criticism of a legal expert. The record of the commission shows that the change was made in the light of expected residential growth, in order to provide larger areas for sewage disposal, and by so doing to lessen the danger to the residential water supply. While the reason for the change was not stated as specifically and in as much detail as it could have been, we cannot say that the commission wholly failed to meet the direction given in the statute. In adopting regulations, the commission acts in a legislative capacity. It is by no means confined to a consideration of only such evidence as may be presented to it, and it is not required to disclose at the public hearing the information upon which it will act. It is entitled to take into consideration facts which may have been learned through personal observation. *Jennings v. Connecticut Light & Power Co.*, 140 Conn. 650, 675, 103 A.2d 535; *Mrowka v. Board of Zoning Appeals*, 134 Conn. 149, 154, 55 A.2d 909. The second and third claims of the plaintiffs are without validity.

There is no error.

Notes

1. Note that the Connecticut Supreme Court mentions that one of the purposes of zoning is to "encourage the most appropriate use of land." That language is in the Connecticut state statutes that delegate the power to zone to cities and towns. It is also contained in the Standard Zoning Enabling Act promulgated by the Hoover Commission in the early 1920s—the model adopted by many of the fifty states. Is this language, by itself, broad enough to authorize local zoning provisions that protect environmental resources and functions such as wetlands and habitats?

2. In most states, it is understood that municipalities have no inherent powers, but can exercise only that authority granted or necessarily implied from, or incident to, the powers expressly granted by the state. Courts vary from state to state in how strictly they construe express delegations of power to municipalities. Some find a broader range of implied or incidental powers within the express language used; others do not. It is for this reason that the power to adopt zoning, subdivision, or site plan regulations may not be sufficient in some states to support a broad range of local environmental laws. Finding authority to adopt such laws requires a careful reading of the express language of existing statutes and an understanding of whether state courts take broad or strict approaches to interpretation. Section 7–148 (c)(8) of the Connecticut General Statutes, for example, delegates separate authori-

ty to cities and towns to pass laws that "provide for the protection and improvement of the environment * * *."

3. In De Mars, the court upheld amendments to zoning regulations based, in part, on protecting the residential water supply pursuant to the municipality's power to adopt zoning laws. How does this court's interpretation of local authority compare to the court's interpretation in the case below?

MORRIS COUNTY LAND IMPROVEMENT CO. v. TOWNSHIP OF PARSIPPANY–TROY HILLS

Supreme Court of New Jersey, 1963.
40 N.J. 539, 193 A.2d 232.

HALL, J.

The fundamental question in this case is the constitutional validity of provisions of defendant township's zoning ordinance which greatly restrict the use of swampland and have for their prime object the retention of the land substantially in its natural state, essentially for public purposes. The provisions not only control land uses in the district, but also strictly regulate any reclamation or improvement of land therein. The Law Division sustained the provisions in a prerogative writ action brought by the plaintiff, a land owner within the area. We certified its appeal on our own motion before it was heard in the Appellate Division.

Parsippany–Troy Hills is a large, sprawling township in Morris County, with a great quantity of vacant land, which has in late years undergone very considerable development activity, accompanied by concomitant increase in population, with the usually resultant problems of planning and zoning. * * *

The particular area here involved is a large swamp of 1500 or more acres known as Troy Meadows. It is located mostly in the southeasterly corner of the township extending to some extent easterly into East Hanover Township and to a slight degree southerly across the boundary of Hanover Township. It and other similar formations in nearby municipalities represent the remaining parts of what was once Lake Passaic, a huge body of water formed eons ago by action of the last glacier in blocking the original channel of the Passaic River. Now, Troy Meadows slowly drains, by means of small streams and man-made ditches running through it, into tributaries of the present Passaic River and forms a portion of that river's basin.

As might be expected, the elevation of the area is low in relation to the surrounding land and considerably below the grade of the roads encircling or running through it. The terrain is typical swampland, with a high water table and marsh grass and cattail vegetation. The surface soil is black or dark brown muck and peat, two to six feet deep, wet and very unstable. The second stratum, from two to four feet in thickness, consists of clay and silt materials which drain poorly and are highly compressible in nature. The bottom layer is composed of sand and gravel, found, on the average, seven or eight feet beneath the surface. The testimony in the case is uncontradicted that the two top layers will not bear structures, are unsuitable for fill and would have to be removed and the land filled with proper material before it could be used for any active purpose, except possibly the raising of fish or the growing of aquatic plants.

At the present time, there are practically no active land uses in the Parsippany–Troy Hills portion of the area. About 75% of it is owned by Wildlife Preserves, Inc. (Wildlife), a private noncommercial, but taxpaying corporation, interested in conservation and preservation of the natural state of the area as a public or quasi-public wildlife sanctuary and nature study refuge. This organization has been energetic and apparently quite influential in urging the local authorities to restrict use of all of the land accordingly. It has even opposed filling of any of the land on the basis that the effect of the fill on the water would be biologically adverse to the conservation of wildlife.

There is no doubt that the area in its present state, acting essentially as a sponge, constitutes a natural detention basin for flood waters in times of very heavy rainfall, which would otherwise run off more quickly and aggravate damaging flood conditions occurring with some frequency in municipalities farther down the Passaic River valley. During such periods, Troy Meadows itself is flooded to some extent, but apparently with little, if any, effect on surrounding higher land.

Plaintiff's property consists of 66 acres in the lower corner of the meadows, fronting several hundred feet on Perrine (or Troy) Road, a dirt highway which is the boundary line in this section with Hanover Township. This acreage is part of a large tract, the balance of which is located across the road in Hanover. The entire parcel was acquired in 1952. The Hanover portion consisted mostly of high land, with a small amount of swamp near the road. At the time of acquisition and since, it has been zoned for industrial use. Plaintiff operates a sand and gravel business at the location in Hanover and has filled in the swampy portion of its property in that township with overburden and other unusable material from the sand and gravel pit.

At the time of acquisition, plaintiff's 66 acres in Parsippany–Troy Hills, along with the rest of Troy Meadows, was zoned, like the high land to the west, in the most restrictive residential classification under the township's original zoning ordinance adopted in 1945. The validity of the inclusion of the swamp in such a zone is indeed most doubtful, but apparently it was never attacked and, since no one would build an expensive home in a marsh, it served the practical purpose of precluding all development.

In 1954 an amendment to the zoning ordinance established "The Indeterminate Zone Classification * * * to cover such parts of the Township as Troy Meadows, where the nature of the land is such that its most appropriate future use is dependent on decisions by others than the government of the Township, such as with respect to flood control, and any change of present use and condition should be subject to special and individual consideration." The amendment forbade any new use, or change in existing use except for agricultural purposes or the growing of fish, water fowl and water plants, and also forbade any dumping or other disposal of material or any change in the natural or existing grade of the land, without the obtaining of a special permit from the Township Committee. From the evidence in the instant case, it is apparent that these almost "freezing" regulations were enacted as a stopgap or interim measure with the expectation or hope that higher governmental authority might well acquire the area as part of a large and much discussed flood control project to benefit the entire Passaic Valley—a project which has not yet come to pass.

Plaintiff attempted no utilization whatever of its Parsippany–Troy Hills land from 1952 until June 1959 when it commenced to fill along the edge of the road with overburden and excess material from the gravel pit operation, without obtaining any permit. Wildlife made a complaint against it in the Municipal Court for violation of the indeterminate zone regulations. While the complaint was pending, plaintiff unsuccessfully applied to the governing body to rezone its property for industrial use. Thereafter, in January 1960, plaintiff was granted a limited permission by the Township Committee to place fill to a depth of 300 feet from Perrine Road at its own risk, since the matter of the revision of land uses in the area was then under study by the township. This permission was conditioned upon submission to, and approval by, the Township Engineer of a sketch showing grades. Plaintiff resumed filling, but did not submit the sketch.

In March 1960, after an extended consideration of the meadows area by planning consultants and township officials, the indeterminate zone provisions were repealed and a new zoning classification created for the area under the title "Meadows Development Zone." The first paragraph of the new regulations set forth the purpose:

> "The Meadows Development Zone classification is established to be applied to areas of the Township with a high water table. These areas can perform a function for the Township of Parsippany–Troy Hills, if they are properly regulated in their uses. Therefore, the following special regulations become necessary to provide for the most appropriate uses of land in the district which will permit development in harmony with its character and the regional requirements for the area."

The new regulations permitted the following uses as of right: agricultural uses; raising of woody or herbaceous plants; commercial greenhouses; raising of aquatic plants, fish and fish food (with a one-family dwelling as an adjunct to any of these uses, provided its lowest floor was a specified distance above flood level); outdoor recreational uses operated by a governmental division or agency; conservation uses "including drainage control, forestry, wildlife sanctuaries and facilities for making same available and useful to the public"; hunting and fishing preserves; public utility transmission lines and substations; radio or television transmitting stations, and antenna towers; and township sewage treatment plants and water supply facilities.

The section went on to provide for what were designated as "uses which may be permitted as special exceptions by the Board of Adjustment under R.S. 40:55–39(b)," with the following preamble:

> "* * * In determining whether a special exception shall be granted, the Board shall apply the standards set forth for each particular use and, in addition, shall determine that in its development and operation the proposed use will conform to the general purposes for which the district is established, and will not impair present or potential use of adjacent properties, as may be permitted under the terms of this section."

These so-called permitted uses amounted, for the most part, to strict regulation of land reclamation in aid of uses allowed as of right. Thus, a special exception, with particular conditions, was required for any permitted use which involved a change in any drainage ditch, for the removal of earth products, such as gravel, sand, fill-dirt and peat, and for the diking, damming or filling of any land within the zone with an existing elevation of less than 175 feet above sea level (apparently this limitation would encompass practically all the land in the zone). The standards and conditions for exceptions to permit removal of earth products and filling included intricate site plan approval by the Planning Board together with studies and reports by other township officials and agencies before favorable action could be taken by the Board of Adjustment. Moreover, no filling was allowed except by the use of material taken from land within the zone. In addition, approval was required of ponds and lakes which would inevitably be created by a filling operation (since the fill had to come from within the zone and the only suitable material was the sand and gravel found below the first two strata of soil).

The removal of earth products from the zone, as a use in itself, previously permitted, became prohibited by an amendment of these provisions in June 1960. This forbade such removal on a commercial or profit basis and completely banned taking earth products beyond the boundaries of the zone.

Plaintiff continued to fill its lands after the adoption of the Meadows Development Zone provisions, without municipal authorization, until further complaints made by Wildlife put an end to the work. By that time the fill extended 1000 feet or more along the road to a depth of 150 feet or greater. It then applied to the Board of Adjustment in August 1960 for a special exception, allegedly in accordance with the ordinance, to fill its lands further as shown on a map submitted, to excavate for an 18–acre reservoir of unspecified depth, to use the material taken therefrom to supply the fill and to sell the excess to defray the cost of the operation. Since the application sought leave to do things forbidden by the ordinance, it amounted also to a request for variance. The application was ultimately denied in January 1961. This suit against the Township and the Board of Adjustment followed.

* * *

[The court first ruled adversely to the plaintiff on claims (1) that the board of adjustment abused its discretion; (2) the court erred in making a visit to the land unaccompanied by counsel; and (3) the plaintiff had established a nonconforming use. The court then continued:]

This brings us to the important and decisive question in the case—the matter of the validity of the 1960 Meadows Development Zone provisions. Plaintiff's attack is full-scale and is not confined to unconstitutional effect of the regulations as applied to its property.

* * *

There cannot be the slightest doubt from the evidence that the prime object of the zone regulations is to retain the land substantially in its natural state. As we have already said, the testimony is uncontradicted that the character of the surface soil is such that it is unsuited for any of the permitted active uses, except possibly the raising of fish and aquatic plants. The first two layers would have to be removed and replaced with proper fill which would support structures where the use involved the construction of buildings, and with appropriate top soil where agriculture and similar soil uses were contemplated. And land reclamation along these lines is, for all practical purposes, rendered impossible. Apart from the matter of having to obtain permission subject to exceedingly difficult conditions, the regulations absolutely prohibit not only the removal of the unusable top two layers of earth from the zone (and, indeed, even from the particular premises within the zone under the amendment to the soil removal ordinance), but also forbid the importation from outside the zone of suitable fill material or soil. As a practical matter, the only available method seems to be to dredge fill material from the bottom stratum of sand and gravel in some other portion of the premises (which, however, does not have the qualities of fertile top soil) and to fill the excavation as far as possible with the unusable upper layers from the area being excavated and filled. Even then it appears that a pond or lake would probably result in the unfilled portion of the excavation because of the high water table. And the regulations also require approval of such a formation. Moreover, the regulations further provide that earth removal will be permitted only if it "will not impair the present and potential use of adjacent properties." This might well become another block to any land reclamation since, it will be recalled, Wildlife has objected to any filling on the ground of an adverse biological effect on the water and the swamp creatures in its sanctuary.

In addition, it will be noted that many of the previously listed permitted uses in the zone are public or quasi-public in nature, rather than of the type available to the ordinary private landowner as a reasonable means of obtaining a return from his property, i.e., outdoor recreational uses to be operated only by some governmental unit, conservation uses and activities, township sewage treatment plants and water facilities and public utility transmission lines, substations and radio and television transmitting stations and towers. All in all, about the only practical use which can be made of property in the zone is a hunting or fishing preserve or a wildlife sanctuary, none of which can be considered productive.

One has to conclude that the uses to which a private landowner may put his property in the zone under the 1960 regulations are little more favorable to him than the almost "freezing" provisions which controlled the area when subject to the stop-gap Indeterminate Zone regulations. One also has the strong feeling that the ordinance changes made in 1960 were adopted essentially, not to benefit the landowner or to permit practical change in the natural state of the area, but rather because it was considered, and quite properly so, that the indeterminate zone provisions were or had become invalid for any number of reasons.

It is equally obvious from the proofs, and legally of the highest significance, that the main purpose of enacting regulations with the practical effect of retaining the meadows in their natural state was for a public benefit. This benefit is twofold, with somewhat interrelated aspects: first, use of the area as a water detention basin in aid of flood control in the lower reaches of the Passaic Valley far beyond this municipality; and second, preservation of the land as open space for the benefits which would accrue to the local public from an undeveloped use such as that of a nature refuge by Wildlife (which paid taxes on it).

This prime public, rather than private, utilization can be clearly implied from the purpose sections of the zone regulations previously quoted. And it is established beyond any question by the testimony of the township's own witnesses. * * * It is fair to conclude from the proofs that any other factors which were taken into consideration in arriving at the detailed regulations were clearly subordinate to these two public purposes.

Private property may not, of course, be taken for public use without just compensation. N.J. Const., Art. I, par. 20. The measures here adopted to accomplish public benefits do not amount to a direct or outright taking, as were those struck down in *Grosso v. Board of Adjustment of Millburn Township*, 137 N.J.L. 630, 61 A.2d 167 (Sup.Ct. 1948), where use of the plaintiff's property was precluded by placing the lot in the bed of a proposed street on the official map; in *Hager v. Louisville & Jefferson County Planning & Zoning Commission*, 261 S.W.2d 619 (Ky.Ct.App.1953), where the plaintiff's land was rendered useless by zoning it as ponding areas for temporary storage basins in accordance with a flood control plan; and in *Miller v. City of Beaver Falls*, 368 Pa. 189, 82 A.2d 34 (Sup.Ct.1951), where private utilization of the tract was inhibited for a period of years, pursuant to a statute, by its inclusion in a territory encompassed by an ordinance adopting a general plan for present and future parks.

* * *

While the issue of regulation as against taking is always a matter of degree, there can be no question but that the line has been crossed where the purpose and practical effect of the regulation is to appropriate private property for a flood water detention basin or open space. These are laudable public purposes and we do not doubt the high-mindedness of their motivation. But such factors cannot cure basic unconstitutionality. Nor is the situation saved because the owner of most of the land in the zone, justifiably desirous of preserving an appropriate area in its natural state as a wetland wildlife sanctuary, supports the regulations. Both public uses are necessarily so all-encompassing as practically to prevent the exercise by a private owner of any worthwhile rights or benefits in the land. So public acquisition rather than regulation is required. *See* Dunham, "*Flood Control Via the Police Power*", 107 U.Pa.L.Rev. 1098 (1959); Krasnowiecki and Paul, "*The Preservation of Open Space in Metropolitan Areas*", 110 U.Pa.L.Rev. 179, 184–189 (1961); Note, "*Techniques for Preserving Open Spaces*", 75 Harv.L.Rev. 1622 (1962); and, generally, Dunham, "*A Legal and Economic Basis for City Planning*", 58 Colum.L.Rev. 650, 658–670 (1958). *Cf. Alford v. Finch*, 155 So.2d 790 (Fla.Sup.Ct.1963). Our statutes empower the State and its subdivisions to purchase or condemn property needed for flood control, see e.g., N.J.S.A. 58:16A–1 et seq., and N.J.S.A. 40:69–4.1 et seq., and that found desirable for open-space, park, playground, conservation and recreation purposes, see e.g., R.S. 40:61–1, N.J.S.A. and N.J.S.A. 13:8A–1 et seq. (New Jersey Green Acres Land Acquisition Act of 1961). And the federal government has provided for grants to states in aid of open space programs. 42 U.S.C.A. §§ 1500–1500e.

We cannot agree with the trial court's thesis that, despite the prime public purpose of the zone regulations, they are valid because they represent a reasonable local exercise of the police power in view of the nature of the area and because the presumption of validity was not overcome. In our opinion the provisions are clearly far too restrictive and as such are constitutionally unreasonable and confiscatory. * * *

The judgment of the Law Division is reversed and the cause remanded for the entry of a judgment consistent with this opinion.

Notes

1. Read the court's description of the physical process that a developer would have to follow to prepare the marshland owned by the plaintiff for productive use. What would the effect of that massive activity be on the site and surrounding ecosystem?

2. The court in Morris County Land recognized that the township's purpose in preventing productive use of the plaintiff's property was "to provide for the most appropriate use of the land * * *." Why wasn't that enough to sustain the township's regulation? What public benefits did the

court understand the regulation to serve? Do you think that, after the loss of hundreds of thousands of acres of wetlands during the ensuing four decades, the courts now have a deeper and more serious understanding of the benefits of wetlands protection? Would this understanding affect the court's interpretation of the reasonable investment-backed expectations of those who purchase this marsh with its high water table, six-foot deep layers of muck and peat, and general unsuitability for productive development use?

SECTION 2. ADVENT OF LOCAL ENVIRONMENTAL LAW

In the modern era, New Jersey courts have disregarded the holding in Morris County Land. In Gardner v. New Jersey Pinelands Comm'n, 125 N.J. 193, 593 A.2d 251 (1991), the court upheld a restriction placing most of an existing farm in a district restricting uses to agricultural with limited possibilities to develop the land. The court rejected the takings claim, finding a lack of investment-backed expectations, and in the course of the opinion disapproved of much of the language in the Morris County case:

> Plaintiff also cites *Morris County Land Improvement Co. v. Parsippany–Troy Hills Township*, 40 N.J. 539, 193 A.2d 232 (1963) (Morris County Land), to support his contention that preservation zoning can constitute a taking if it interferes too greatly with the landowner's use of its property. *Morris County Land* held that a zoning ordinance that maintained an entire swamp area in its natural state, permitting use only for raising fish and aquatic plants and as a flood water detention basin, constituted a taking because the landowner had been deprived of "any worthwhile rights or benefits in the land." *Id.* at 555–56, 193 A.2d 232. We find *Morris County Land* inapposite. Plaintiff does not deny that the uses allowed under the Act and the CMP are "worthwhile rights or benefits in the land." In contrast to the permitted uses in *Morris County Land,* agriculture in the pinelands region is an existing, indeed a longstanding, endeavor that is economically supported locally and nationally. Moreover, the vitality of Morris County Land has declined with the *emerging priority accorded to the ecological integrity of the environment* [emphasis added]. The decision, now nearly thirty years old, arose in a time before the environmental and social harms of indiscriminate and excessive development were widely understood or acknowledged. That the same facts would occasion the same result today is by no means certain. See *AMG Assocs. v. Township of Springfield*, 65 N.J. 101, 112 n. 4, 319 A.2d 705 (1974). Indeed, many more recent decisions have overtly or tacitly failed to follow *Morris County Land* in environmental contexts. E.g., *Loveladies Harbor, Inc.*, supra, 176 N.J.Super. 69, 422 A.2d 107; *Usdin*, supra, 173 N.J.Super. 311, 414 A.2d 280; *New Jersey Builders Ass'n*, supra, 169 N.J.Super. 76, 404 A.2d 320; *Toms River Affiliates*, supra, 140 N.J.Super. 135, 355 A.2d 679; *Sands Point Harbor, Inc.*, supra, 136 N.J.Super. 436, 346 A.2d

612. For example, in *American Dredging Co. v. State*, 161 N.J.Super. 504, 391 A.2d 1265 (Ch.Div.1978), aff'd, 169 N.J.Super. 18, 404 A.2d 42 (App.Div.1979), the Department of Environmental Protection, acting pursuant to the Wetlands Act of 1970, N.J.S.A. 13:9A–1 to–10, issued an order prohibiting the plaintiff from placing dredged material on a portion of its land. The court distinguished *Morris County Land* by explaining, "Where the effect of the governmental prohibition against use is not in furtherance of a governmental activity, such as flood control or preservation of land for a park or recreational area, but rather to preserve the land for ecological reasons in its natural environment without change, the consideration of the reasonableness of the exercise of the police power must be redetermined." *Id.* 161 N.J.Super. at 509, 391 A.2d 1265.

The Gardner case was decided in 1991, nearly 30 years after Morris County Land. The Gardner court states that regulations that preserve the land "for ecological reasons" may be more reasonable than those aimed at flood control or open space preservation. It was during this 30 year period that land use patterns rapidly sprawled beyond urban boundaries and that the damage done to ecosystems became manifest. There is a fundamental difference between the typical local zoning regulation designed to separate one land use from another and the regulation involved in Gardner. The court characterizes it as preserving agricultural land uses for ecological reasons. By the date of the Gardner case, it appears that a discernable environmental ethic had entered land use legislation and jurisprudence.

In the cases below, notice the shift of local regulations from simple Euclidian Zoning to a consideration of environmental protection for purposes of protecting the public's health and welfare.

JUST v. MARINETTE COUNTY

Supreme Court of Wisconsin, 1972.
56 Wis.2d 7, 201 N.W.2d 761.

HALLOWS, CHIEF JUSTICE.

Marinette county's Shoreland Zoning Ordinance Number 24 was adopted September 19, 1967, became effective October 9, 1967, and follows a model ordinance published by the Wisconsin Department of Resource Development in July of 1967. See Kusler, Water Quality Protection For Inland Lakes in Wisconsin: A Comprehensive Approach to Water Pollution, 1970 Wis.L.Rev. 35, 62–63. The ordinance was designed to meet standards and criteria for shoreland regulation which the legislature required to be promulgated by the department of natural resources under sec. 144.26, Stats. These standards are found in 6 Wis.Adm.Code, sec. NR 115.03, May, 1971, Register No. 185. The legislation, secs. 59.971 and 144.26, Stats., authorizing the ordinance was enacted as a part of the Water Quality Act of 1965 by ch. 614, Laws of 1965.

Shorelands for the purpose of ordinances are defined in sec. 59.971(1), Stats., as lands within 1,000 feet of the normal high-water elevation of navigable lakes, ponds, or flowages and 300 feet from a navigable river or stream or to the landward side of the flood plain, whichever distance is greater. The state shoreland program is unique. All county shoreland zoning ordinances must be approved by the department of natural resources prior to their becoming effective. 6 Wis.Adm. Code, sec. NR 115.04, May, 1971, Register No. 185. If a county does not enact a shoreland zoning ordinance which complies with the state's standards, the department of natural resources may enact such an ordinance for the county. Sec. 59.971(6), Stats.

There can be no disagreement over the public purpose sought to be obtained by the ordinance. Its basic purpose is to protect navigable waters and the public rights therein from the degradation and deterioration which results from uncontrolled use and development of shorelands. In the Navigable Waters Protection Act, sec. 144.26, the purpose of the state's shoreland regulation program is stated as being to "aid in the fulfillment of the state's role as trustee of its navigable waters and to promote public health, safety, convenience and general welfare." In sec. 59.971(1), which grants authority for shoreland zoning to counties, the same purposes are reaffirmed. The Marinette County shoreland zoning ordinance in secs. 1.2 and 1.3 states the uncontrolled use of shorelands and pollution of navigable waters of Marinette county adversely affect public health, safety, convenience, and general welfare and impair the tax base.

The shoreland zoning ordinance divides the shorelands of Marinette County into general purpose districts, general recreation districts, and conservancy districts. A "conservancy" district is required by the statutory minimum standards and is defined in sec. 3.4 of the ordinance to include "all shorelands designated as swamps or marshes on the United States Geological Survey maps which have been designated as the Shoreland Zoning Map of Marinette County, Wisconsin or on the detailed Insert Shoreland Zoning Maps." The ordinance provides for permitted uses and conditional uses. One of the conditional uses requiring a permit under sec. 3.42(4) is the filling, drainage or dredging of wetlands according to the provisions of sec. 5 of the ordinance. "Wetlands" are defined in sec. 2.29 as "(a)reas where ground water is at or near the surface much of the year or where any segment of plant cover is deemed an aquatic according to N.C. Fassett's 'Manual of Aquatic Plants.'" Section 5.42(2) of the ordinance requires a conditional-use permit for any filling or grading "Of any area which is within three hundred feet horizontal distance of a navigable water and which has surface drainage toward the water and on which there is: (a) Filling of more than five hundred square feet of any wetland which is contiguous to the water * * * (d) Filling or grading of more than 2,000 square feet on slopes of twelve per cent or less."

In April of 1961, several years prior to the passage of this ordinance, the Justs purchased 36.4 acres of land in the town of Lake along the south shore of Lake Noquebay, a navigable lake in Marinette county. This land had a frontage of 1,266.7 feet on the lake and was purchased partially for personal use and partially for resale. During the years 1964, 1966, and 1967, the Justs made five sales of parcels having frontage and extending back from the lake some 600 feet, leaving the property involved in these suits. This property has a frontage of 366.7 feet and the south one half contains a stand of cedar, pine, various hard woods, birch and red maple. The north one half, closer to the lake, is barren of trees except immediately along the shore. The south three fourths of this north one half is populated with various plant grasses and vegetation including some plants which N.C. Fassett in his manual of aquatic plants has classified as "aquatic." There are also non-aquatic plants which grow upon the land. Along the shoreline there is a belt of trees. The shoreline is from one foot to 3.2 feet higher than the lake level and there is a narrow belt of higher land along the shore known as a "pressure ridge" or "ice heave," varying in width from one to three feet. South of this point, the natural level of the land ranges one to two feet above lake level. The land slopes generally toward the lake but has a slope less than twelve per cent. No water flows onto the land from the lake, but there is some surface water which collects on land and stands in pools.

The land owned by the Justs is designated as swamps or marshes on the United States Geological Survey Map and is located within 1,000 feet of the normal high-water elevation of the lake. Thus, the property is included in a conservancy district and, by sec. 2.29 of the ordinance, classified as "wetlands." Consequently, in order to place more than 500 square feet of fill on this property, the Justs were required to obtain a conditional-use permit from the zoning administrator of the county and pay a fee of $20 or incur a forfeiture of $10 to $200 for each day of violation.

In February and March of 1968, six months after the ordinance became effective, Ronald Just, without securing a conditional-use permit, hauled 1,040 square yards of sand onto this property and filled an area approximately 20–feet wide commencing at the southwest corner and extending almost 600 feet north to the northwest corner near the shoreline, then easterly along the shoreline almost to the lot line. He stayed back from the pressure ridge about 20 feet. More than 500 square feet of this fill was upon wetlands located contiguous to the water and which had surface drainage toward the lake. The fill within 300 feet of the lake also was more than 2,000 square feet on a slope less than 12 percent. It is not seriously contended that the Justs did not violate the ordinance and the trial court correctly found a violation.

The real issue is whether the conservancy district provisions and the wetlands filling restrictions are unconstitutional because they amount to a constructive taking of the Justs' land without compensation. Marinette County and the state of Wisconsin argue the restrictions of the conservancy district and wetlands provisions constitute a proper exercise of the police power of the state and do not so severely limit the use or depreciate the value of the land as to constitute a taking without compensation.

To state the issue in more meaningful terms, it is a conflict between the public interest in stopping the despoliation of natural resources, which our citizens until recently have taken as inevitable and for granted, and an owner's asserted right to use his property as he wishes. The protection of public rights may be accomplished by the exercise of the police power unless the damage to the property owner is too great and amounts to a confiscation. The securing or taking of a benefit not presently enjoyed by the public for its use is obtained by the government through its power of eminent domain. The distinction between the exercise of the police power and condemnation has been said to be a matter of degree of damage to the property owner. In the valid exercise of the police power reasonably restricting the use of property, the damage suffered by the owner is said to be incidental. However, where the restriction is so great the landowner ought not to bear such a burden for the public good, the restriction has been held to be a constructive taking even though the actual use or forbidden use has not been transferred to the government so as to be a taking in the traditional sense. *Stefan Auto Body v. State Highway Comm.* (1963), 21 Wis.2d 363, 124 N.W.2d 319; *Buhler v. Racine County* (1966), 33 Wis.2d 137, 146 N.W.2d 403; *Nick v. State Highway Comm.* (1961), 13 Wis.2d 511, 109 N.W.2d 71, 111 N.W.2d 95; *State v. Becker* (1934), 215 Wis. 564, 255 N.W. 144. Whether a taking has occurred depends upon whether "the restriction practically or substantially renders the land useless for all reasonable purposes." *Buhler v. Racine County, supra.* The loss caused the individual must be weighed to determine if it is more than he should bear. As this court stated in *Stefan*, at pp. 369–370, 124 N.W.2d 319, p. 323, "* * * if the damage is such as to be suffered by many similarly situated and is in the nature of a restriction on the use to which land may be put and ought to be borne by the individual as a member of society for the good of the public safety, health or general welfare, it is said to be a reasonable exercise of the police power, but if the damage is so great to the individual that he ought not to bear it under contemporary standards, then courts are inclined to treat it as a 'taking' of the property or an unreasonable exercise of the police power."

Many years ago, Professor Freund stated in his work on The Police Power, sec. 511, at 546–547, "It may be said that the state takes property by eminent domain because it is useful to the public, and under the police power because it is harmful * * *. From this results the difference between the power of eminent domain and the police power, that the former recognizes a right to compensation, while the latter on principle does not." Thus the necessity for monetary compensation for loss suffered to an owner by police power restriction arises when restrictions are placed on property in order to create a public benefit rather than to prevent a public harm. Rathkopf, The Law of Zoning and Planning, Vol. 1, ch. 6, pp. 6–7.

This case causes us to reexamine the concepts of public benefit in contrast to public harm and the scope of an owner's right to use of his property. In the instant case we have a restriction on the use of a citizen's property, not to secure a benefit for the public, but to prevent a harm from the change in the natural character of the citizen's property. We start with the premise that lakes and rivers in their natural state are unpolluted and the pollution which now exists is man made. The state of Wisconsin under the trust doctrine has a duty to eradicate the present pollution and to prevent further pollution in its navigable waters. This is not, in a legal sense, a gain or a securing of a benefit by the maintaining of the natural status quo of the environment. What makes this case different from most condemnation or police power zoning cases is the interrelationship of the wetlands, the swamps and the natural environment of shorelands to the purity of the water and to such natural resources as navigation, fishing, and scenic beauty. Swamps and wetlands were once considered wasteland, undesirable, and not picturesque. But as the people became more sophisticated, an appreciation was acquired that swamps and wetlands serve a vital role in nature, are part of the balance of nature and are essential to the purity of the water in our lakes and streams. Swamps and wetlands are a necessary part of the ecological creation and now, even to the uninitiated, possess their own beauty in nature.

Is the ownership of a parcel of land so absolute that man can change its nature to suit any of his purposes? The great forests of our state were stripped on the theory man's ownership was unlimited. But in forestry, the land at least was used naturally, only the natural fruit of the land (the trees) were taken. The despoilage was in the failure to look to the future and provide for the reforestation of the land. An owner of land has no absolute and unlimited right to change the essential natural character of his land so as to use it for a purpose for which it was unsuited in its natural state and which injures the rights of others. The exercise of the police power in zoning must be reasonable and we think it is not an unreasonable exercise of that power to prevent harm to public rights by limiting the use of private property to its natural uses.

This is not a case where an owner is prevented from using his land for natural and indigenous uses. The uses consistent with the nature of the land are allowed and other uses recognized and still others permitted by special permit. The shoreland zoning ordinance prevents to some extent the changing of the natural character of the land within 1,000 feet of a navigable lake and 300 feet of a navigable river because of such land's interrelation to the contiguous water. The changing of wetlands and swamps to the damage of the general public by upsetting the natural environment and the natural relationship is not a reasonable use of that land which is protected from police power regulation. Changes and filling to some extent are permitted because the extent of such changes and fillings does not cause harm. We realize no case in Wisconsin has yet dealt with shoreland regulations and there are several cases in other states which seem to hold such regulations unconstitutional; but nothing in this court has said or held in prior cases indicates that destroying the natural character of a swamp or a wetland so as to make that location available for human habitation is a reasonable use of that land when the new use, although of a more economical value to the owner, causes a harm to the general public.

* * *

The Justs rely on several cases from other jurisdictions which have held zoning regulations involving flood plain districts, flood basins and wetlands to be so confiscatory as to amount to a taking because the owners of the land were prevented from improving such property for residential or commercial purposes. While some of these cases may be distinguished on their facts, it is doubtful whether these differences go to the basic rationale which permeates the decision that an owner has a right to use his property in any way and for any purpose he sees fit. In *Dooley v. Town Plan & Zon. Com. of Town of Fairfield* (1964), 151 Conn. 304, 197 A.2d 770, the court held the restriction on land located in a flood plain district prevented its being used for residential or business purposes and thus the restriction destroyed the economic value to the owner. The court recognized the land was needed for a public purpose as it was part of the area in which the tidal stream overflowed when abnormally high tides existed, but the property was half a mile from the ocean and therefore could not be used for marina or boathouse purposes. In *Morris County Land I. Co. v. Parsippany–Troy Hills Tp.* (1963), 40 N.J. 539, 193 A.2d 232, a flood basin zoning ordinance was involved which required the controversial land to be retained in its natural state. The plaintiff owned 66 acres of a 1,500–acre swamp which was part of a river basin and acted as a natural detention basin for flood waters in times of very heavy rainfall. There was an extraneous issue that the freezing regulations were intended as a stop-gap until such time as the government would buy the property under a flood-control project. However, the court took the view the zoning had an effect of preserving the land as an open space as a water-detention basin and only the government or the public would be benefited, to the complete damage of the owner.

In *State v. Johnson* (1970), Me., 265 A.2d 711, the Wetlands Act restricted the alteration and use of certain wetlands without permission. The act was a conservation measure enacted under the police power to protect the ecology of areas bordering the coastal waters. The plaintiff owned a small tract of a salt-water marsh which was flooded at high tide. By filling, the land would be adapted for building purposes. The court held the restrictions against filling constituted a deprivation of a reasonable use of the owner's property and, thus, an unreasonable exercise of the police power. In *MacGibbon v. Board of Appeals of Duxbury* (1970), 356 Mass. 635, 255 N.E.2d 347, the plaintiff owned seven acres of land which were under water about twice a month in a shoreland area. He was denied a permit to excavate and fill part of his property. The purpose of the ordinance was to preserve from despoilage natural features and resources such as salt marshes, wetlands, and ponds. The court took the view the preservation of privately owned land in its natural, unspoiled state for the enjoyment and benefit of the public by preventing the owner from using it for any practical purpose was not within the limit and scope of the police power and the ordinance was not saved by the use of special permits.

It seems to us that filling a swamp not otherwise commercially usable is not in and of itself an existing use, which is prevented, but rather is the preparation for some future use which is not indigenous to a swamp. Too much stress is laid on the right of an owner to change commercially valueless land when that change does damage to the rights of the public. It is observed that a use of special permits is a means of control and accomplishing the purpose of the zoning ordinance as distinguished from the old concept of providing for variances. The special permit technique is now common practice and has met with judicial approval, and we think it is of some significance in considering whether or not a particular zoning ordinance is reasonable.

A recent case sustaining the validity of a zoning ordinance establishing a flood plain district is *Turnpike Realty Co. v. Town of Dedham* (June, 1972), 362 Mass. 221, 284 N.E.2d 891. The court held the validity of the ordinance was supported by valid considerations of public welfare, the conservation of "natural conditions, wildlife and open spaces." The ordinance provided that lands which were subject to seasonal or periodic flooding could not be used for residences or other purposes in such a manner as to endanger the health, safety or occupancy thereof and prohibited the erection of structures or buildings which required land to be filled. This case is analogous to the instant facts. The ordinance had a public purpose to preserve the natural condition of the area. No change was allowed which would injure the purposes sought to be preserved and through the special-permit technique, particular land within the zoning district could be excepted from the restrictions.

The Justs argue their property has been severely depreciated in value. But this depreciation of value is not based on the use of the land in its natural state but on what the land would be worth if it could be filled and used for the location of a dwelling. While loss of value is to be considered in determining whether a restriction is a constructive taking, value based upon changing the character of the land at the expense of harm to public rights is not an essential factor or controlling.

We are not unmindful of the warning in *Pennsylvania Coal Co. v. Mahon* (1922), 260 U.S. 393, 416, 43 S.Ct. 158, 160, 67 L.Ed. 322:

> "* * * We are in danger of forgetting that a strong public desire to improve the public condition is not enough to warrant achieving the desire by a shorter cut than the constitutional way of paying for the change."

This observation refers to the improvement of the public condition, the securing of a benefit not presently enjoyed and to which the public is not entitled. The shoreland zoning ordinance preserves nature, the environment, and natural resources as they were created and to which the people have a present right. The ordinance does not create or improve the public condition but only preserves nature from the despoilage and harm resulting from the unrestricted activities of humans.

* * *

The Judgment in case number 106, dismissing the Justs' action, is modified to set forth the declaratory adjudication that the shoreland zoning ordinance of respondent Marinette County is constitutional; that the Justs' property constitutes wetlands and that particularly the prohibition in the ordinance against the filling of wetlands is constitutional; and the judgment, as so modified, is affirmed. * * *

Notes

1. Other cases that accord with Just are, People ex rel. San Francisco Bay Conservation and Development Commission v. Gianulias, 188 Cal. App.3d 520, 233 Cal.Rptr. 621 (1986) (upholding an injunction to prevent further filling of lands "subject to tidal action"); Holiday Point Marina Partners v. Anne Arundel County, 349 Md. 190, 707 A.2d 829 (1998) (upholding a municipal ordinance limiting the distance between marine facilities and shellfish beds); Karam v. Dep't of Envtl. Prot., 308 N.J. Super. 225, 705 A.2d 225 (1998) (upholding a denial to construct a dock on a river in favor of protecting a "special restricted area" that harbored shellfish habitat); Cottonwood Farms v. Board of County Comm'rs, 763 P.2d 551 (Colo.1988) (upholding denial of a permit to operate a rock quarry in an agriculturally-zoned district); Buechel v. Department of Ecology, 125 Wn.2d 196, 884 P.2d 910 (Wash.1994) (upholding denial of a variance to construct a home on an undersized shoreline lot).

2. At the time of the Just decision, local governments were just beginning to enact laws to protect wetlands and surrounding buffer areas from the impacts of development. In the late 1960's, Massachusetts towns relied on their delegated land use authority to protect locally-defined wetlands. In the early 1970's, the state legislatures in both Massachusetts and Connecticut passed statutes directly authorizing localities to adopt wetland regulations. The Connecticut statute, in fact, obligated local governments to adopt wetlands laws as strict as or stricter than state promulgated standards and to establish local wetland review agencies. Conn. Gen. Stat. §§ 22a–36 et. seq. A 1981 state court decision held that a local wetlands agency has the right to regulate areas adjacent to established wetlands where activities occur that might adversely impact the wetlands themselves. Aaron v. Conservation Comm'n of Redding, 183 Conn. 532, 441 A.2d 30 (1981).

3. State and federal courts have upheld environmental regulations that severely limit the amount of development allowed against charges that they constitute regulatory takings. See Moskow v. Commissioner of the Department of Environmental Management, 384 Mass. 530, 427 N.E.2d 750 (1981). In this case, state inland wetland regulations prevented development on over half of a 297,000 square-foot parcel, prohibiting the development of all but one house on the site. "A single family house is a sufficient practical use to prevent the wetland restrictions from constituting a taking * * *." This

position is sustained in Palazzolo v. Rhode Island, 533 U.S. 606, 121 S.Ct. 2448, 150 L.Ed.2d 592 (2001). Palazzolo owned a 20–acre parcel, most of which was salt marsh subject to tidal flooding. Development would have required significant fill, up to six feet in some places, to support any development. Under the Rhode Island coastal wetland regulations, development on the tidal wetlands portion of this site was prohibited unless the owner secured a special exception permit for an activity that serves a compelling public purpose that benefits the public as a whole. Since the responsible state agency, in denying Palazzolo's application to fill eleven of eighteen tidal wetland acres for a private beach club, made a determination that this type of private development of tidal lands was not eligible for a special use permit, the Court held that the matter was ripe. Palazzolo's property contained two unregulated upland acres and it was agreed that a substantial residence could be built on that land. The Court upheld the Rhode Island Supreme Court's determination that the coastal regulations did not constitute a total taking under Lucas v. South Carolina Coastal Council, 505 U.S. 1003, 112 S.Ct. 2886, 120 L.Ed.2d 798 (1992). Palazzolo presented evidence that the land was appraised at $3,150,000 under a seventy-four lot subdivision proposal he had submitted for approval before his private beach club application. The parties agreed that the upland acres had a value of $200,000 for residential development. The Court noted that the development rights on the upland area did not constitute a token interest. Therefore, the regulations did not leave the land economically idle as must be the case for the Lucas total taking rule to apply.

IN RE SPRING VALLEY DEVELOPMENT

Supreme Judicial Court of Maine, 1973.
300 A.2d 736.

WEATHERBEE, JUSTICE.

Raymond Pond is located in the town of Raymond and is slightly more than one mile in length. Lakesites, Inc. is the owner of a large tract of land containing about 92 acres located on one side of the Pond. Lakesites' development of this land into a residential subdivision has been interrupted by an order of the Environmental Improvement Commission directing it to cease the operation of this development until Lakesites has applied for and received the Commission's approval of its development.

The Commission claims to have derived its authority for this order from 38 M.R.S.A. §§ 481–488, Site Location of Development Law, hereinafter referred to as the Site Location Law. Lakesites' appeal attacks both the Commission's interpretation of the Act as including residential subdivisions and the Act's constitutionality. We conclude that the authority of the Commission does extend to residential subdivisions and that the statute represents a valid exercise of the police power. We deny the appeal.

The agreed statement of facts and the testimony presented at hearing before the Commission reveal that Lakesites' property extends along the shore of the Pond at least 3400 feet. Lakesites has subdivided this tract into 90 lots ranging in size from 20,000 square feet to 53,000 square feet with several other areas reserved from sale. It refers to this property as its Spring Valley Development.

Lakesites has cleared and graded portions of this land, has built a road for ingress and egress and has surveyed the property, marking off the boundaries of the individual lots. While it contemplates that purchasers will build year-round or part-time homes on their lots it does not intend to construct or participate in the construction of the buildings or to control the use of the lots "except insofar as there are any required deed restrictions." No action has been taken with respect to providing services for any of the lots.

Lakesites proposes that the selling of these lots be a profitable venture and it has placed their sale in the hands of licensed real estate brokers.

Lakesites submitted its subdivision plan to the Raymond Planning Board which, after some changes had been made, approved it as satisfying the only subdivision requirement then existing in the town ordinance—that of lot size. The subdivision plan was then recorded in the Cumberland County Registry of Deeds.

There was in effect at this time the Site Location Law the constitutionality of which is under attack. This law required persons intending to construct or operate a development which may substantially affect local environment to notify, before commencing the construction or operation, the Environmental Improvement Commission of their intent and the nature and location of the development. If the Commission determines it to be necessary, a hearing shall be held at which the developer has the burden of satisfying the Commission that the development will not substantially adversely affect the environment or pose a threat to the public's health, safety or general welfare. 38 M.R.S.A. §§ 483, 484.

The Legislature defined developments which may substantially affect environment as meaning

> "* * * [1] any commercial or industrial development which requires a license from the Environmental Improvement Commission, [2] or which occupies a land area in excess of 20 acres, [3] or which contemplates drilling for or excavating natural resources, excluding borrow pits for sand, fill or gravel, regulated by the State Highway Commission and pits of less than 5 acres, [4] or which occupies on a single parcel a structure or structures in excess of a ground area of 60,000 square feet." 38 M.R.S.A. § 482(2).

Although Lakesites' development did occupy a land area in excess of 20 acres, it did not notify the Commission of its intentions. However, the Commission eventually learned of Lakesites' plans and proceeded at once to schedule and conduct a hearing as it is authorized to do by section 485. Notice of the hearing was given Lakesites.

Lakesites was represented at the hearing by its attorney who challenged the Commission's jurisdiction to regulate Lakesites' activity contending that the mere subdivision of land does not constitute a "commercial or industrial development" within the scope of the Site Location Law. The attorney made a formal objection to all testimony other than that relating to jurisdiction. He elected to waive his right to contest as to the merits of the case although he was offered full opportunity to do so, choosing not to offer evidence or to cross-examine witnesses who testified regarding the proposed development.

These witnesses testified at length as to various aspects of the environment which they said would be substantially adversely affected by the proposed development. Later, after consideration of the matter, the Commission made findings of fact and held that Lakesites had failed in its burden to prove that its proposed development meets the standards for approval established by the Legislature in section 4845 and had failed to demonstrate that it had plans that would adequately protect the public's health, safety and general welfare. It issued an order denying Lakesites the right to proceed with its development until such time as it has made a proper application to the Environmental Improvement Commission and has received the Commission's approval.

From this decision of the Commission, Lakesites has appealed to the Supreme Judicial Court sitting as the Law Court, [38 M.R.S.A. § 487] raising specifically the issue as to whether the offering for sale of subdivided lots of the type owned by Lakesites is either a commercial or an industrial development subject to the provisions of 38 M.R.S.A. §§ 481–488 and, secondarily, if the Site Location Law is applied to this developer, are there constitutional violations of Equal Protection and Due Process.

* * *

The Legislature's concise statement of its Findings and Purpose makes clear to us the basis for its conclusion that state action was essential to insure that commercial and industrial developments, which because of their nature or their size, will impose unusually heavy demands upon the natural environment, shall not be located in areas where the environment does not have the capacity to withstand the impact of the development. But did the Legislature intend to bring residential developments within the application of the law? If so, did it intend to include mere subdivisions?

* * *

We think that the use of the word "commercial" was intended to describe the motivation for the development and not the type of activity to be performed on the property after it is developed. We consider that the Legislature chose to distinguish between commercial and non-commercial developments for a sound reason—it doubtless concluded that a greater need for supervision exists in the case of a commercially motivated development where the dominant factor is the hope for profit than in a non-commercial development where land is being prepared for public enjoyment or divided for family distribution or for some other purpose than profit. In other words, commercial residential developments have a propensity for being big, concentrated and exhausting to the resources of the environment.

It seems to us that the business of subdividing large tracts of land and selling the lots must be considered a commercial venture. The Legislature doubtless so viewed it. Certainly, this construction best accords with the purpose of the statute. *Strout v. Burgess*, 144 Me. 263, 275, 68 A.2d 241, 250 (1949).

This interpretation finds support in the history of the legislation we are examining.

* * *

We find it significant in our assessment of legislative intent that the 105th Legislature, aware that the Commission was interpreting the Act to include residential subdivisions, took no affirmative action to indicate a contrary intent, rejected two attempts to remove some residential subdivisions from the operation of the Act and finally acted to add the specific words "including subdivisions."

In our opinion the 104th Legislature intended to include commercial residential developments among those developments which may substantially affect environment. But did the Legislature intend the Act to affect commercial residential developments where the developer merely plots the tract, subdivides it into lots by plan and offers the lots for sale to the public?

* * *

The Appellant argues to us that it was the Legislature's intention to prevent acts being done to the land which would harm the land and that, therefore, the law is directed to the person who will do the act—such as the builder—and not to the person who merely subdivides and sells the land. With this we cannot agree. The Legislature intended the Commission to scrutinize the proposals before the harmful act could be done. The Act is a preventive measure and the injury sought to be avoided can best be prevented as soon as plans for development reveal the harm which will occur upon its completion. We would hardly expect that the Legislature intended to postpone the determination of suitability of an area for a residential development until the lots had been sold to purchasers who will, upon starting construction, discover that they are participants in—as well as victims of—a local environmental disaster.

Furthermore, if a subdivider has sold the lots to numerous individual purchasers each of whom, among other things, is to construct his own building, grade his own land, build his own driveway to the street, and provide for his own sanitary sewage disposal, there would be no one "intending to construct or operate a development" who could be held responsible under the statute. We do not ascribe to the Legislature an intention that legislation so important to the public welfare would suffer from such inherent futility.

We consider that both the legislative intent and the statutory language of the Act encompass residential developments in which the developer merely subdivides the land into lots and offers the lots for sale without any intention to construct buildings or to provide additional improvements or services on the lots. We do not find that the Act as so interpreted and applied is constitutionally impermissible. The subdividing is the initial step in such a development.

The Commission correctly ruled as fact that this particular residential development is a commercial development which may substantially affect environment requiring compliance with the provisions of the Site Location Law.

* * *

CONSTITUTIONALITY OF APPLICATION OF THE ACT TO ONE WHO ONLY SUBDIVIDES

Lakesites does not deny the power of the State to act properly under the police power to protect the environment but urges us that the application of the Act to one who merely subdivides is constitutionally forbidden. It argues that a remedial Act must be designed and applied rationally and reasonably to achieve the purposes for which the Act was devised. The evil to be avoided, the appellant contends, is the damaging impact of the development upon the environment and the impact occurs and the damage is sustained only with the construction and occupation of the premises—not when the land is only subdivided on plans and the lots are sold. Until such activity creating the impact occurs on the land, the appellant argues, there is no burden or impact which can affect the environment and so the application of the Act to a mere subdivider as a prerequisite to his selling his land is not directly related to the Act's purpose.

It is true that the Act and its application under the police power must have a clear, real and substantial relation to the purpose of the Act.

* * *

In our opinion such a connection between the purpose of the Act and its application to the subdivider is clear and reasonable. We have concluded earlier in this opinion that the Legislature intended to empower the Commission to prevent ecological damage before it occurs rather than to permit the occurrence of harm which can then be cured only at great public expense—if at all. It is not unreasonable to place upon the subdivider who plans the number, size and location of the lots to be offered for sale the responsibility for avoiding an inevitable large scale ecological calamity. The subdividing for sale is the first step in a commercial residential development and the Legislature reasonably concluded that the public welfare requires that control be exercised through the subdivider rather than attempting it through (in this case) 90 different purchasers whose properties can perhaps never at that later point—because of sheer weight and concentration of numbers—avoid environmental misadventure.

* * *

Lakesites protests that as it is only a subdivider it cannot accurately foresee the activity to be performed on the lots it sells and so cannot control the future adequacy of provisions relating to pollution control and maintenance of healthful water supplies. To be sure, the Act imposes upon the developer—including the mere subdivider—responsibilities which he has not had in the past. The Legislature has determined that an owner of a large tract of undeveloped land may no longer subdivide it, sell the lots and then walk away from the transaction indifferent to the local catastrophe that may result when construction and occupancy reveal the incapacity of the environment to withstand the impact of the development. It may be that this responsibility can more easily be met by a subdivider who is also a constructor of the buildings but it is equally the responsibility of the subdivider who chooses only to sell the bare lots. The duty is no doubt more burdensome as the land is less suitable and it may be impossible of compliance if the environment is of a type incapable of sustaining the proposed development. In the latter situation the public welfare demands that the land be used for another purpose or that the impact of the same use be diminished. In many situations the subdivider may be able to meet his burden of affirmatively demonstrating to the Commission that he has met the criteria through satisfactory conditions in his instruments of sale. We do not consider the burden to be unreasonable in view of the overriding public interest.

* * *

DOES THE ACT DENY THE DEVELOPER EQUAL PROTECTION OF THE LAW?

Finally, Lakesites argues that the Act denies a developer—and especially it—equal protection under the law. It argues that the subdivider of over 20 acres must receive the Commission's approval while the subdivider of under 20 acres faces no such requirements, and so it contends it is denied equal protection because size, it says, has no rational or reasonable correlation to the environmental impact. A 21 acre subdivision, it argues, may contain 5 residences while one of 19 acres may contain 19 residences. It is elementary that the Legislature may in its judgment create classifications so long as they are not arbitrary and are based upon actual differences in classes which differences bear a substantial rational relation to the public purpose sought to be accomplished by the statute. *In re Milo Water Company*, 128 Me. 531, 149 A. 299 (1930).

The purpose, as we have said, was to control the locations of those commercial and industrial developments which could substantially adversely affect the environment. The Legislature evidently concluded that the size of a development has a distinct relationship to the amount of its potential adverse impact upon the environment and concluded that at this time the public interest could best be served by applying the admittedly severe restrictions of the new law to large developments. The justification of the distinction as to size seems most clear in such legislation as this. For example, in an area with no municipal sewage disposal system, such as in Spring Valley Development, and where much of the soil has a high seasonal water table and is unsuitable for septic tank disposal of domestic sewage, the potential danger to the environment from the discharge of sewage from 90 residences must be greater than the discharge from 2 or from 19. Drawing the line at 20 acres is not a denial of equal protection. * * *

We see no irrational or arbitrary discrimination in the application of the Act to the large mere-subdivider. It is his act of subdividing that initially indicates the volume of the impact likely to fall upon the environment.

The distinction made by the Legislature does not appear to be unreasonable.

* * *

We find that the application of the Act to Lakesites does not offend the provisions of either the state or federal constitutions.

* * *

MOVIEMATIC INDUSTRIES CORP. v. BOARD OF COUNTY COM'RS

Florida Court of Appeal, Third District, 1977.
349 So.2d 667.

HAVERFIELD, JUDGE.

Appellant seeks review of an order denying its petition for writ of certiorari, and upholding the validity of Dade County resolution Z–115–75 rezoning petitioner's property from IU–2 to GU.

Over ten years ago Moviematic Industries Corporation purchased 1,200 acres of undeveloped real property located in a remote area of unincorporated west Dade County zoned for heavy industrial use (IU–2) with a special exception for business airport uses. The property overlies the Biscayne Aquifer which serves as a major source of the drinking water in the county. On March 19, 1974 the county commission imposed a building moratorium on an area consisting of approximately 323 square miles of west Dade County, including petitioner's property, for the express purpose of conducting and preparing a comprehensive study directed to the protection of the fresh water supply and the natural ecosystems which function in this part of the county. Following the study, on April 23, 1975 the county building and zoning department and the planning department jointly recommended to the commission that (1) petitioner's property be rezoned from IU–2 to GU (interim classification which permits single family residential use on minimum five acre lots), and (2) the previously approved special permit for business airport uses be terminated. At a public hearing on this matter, the commission heard expert testimony in support of the recommended GU zoning classification and petitioner's evidence in opposition thereto. At the conclusion of the hearing, the commissioners adopted resolution Z–115–75 which rezoned the subject property from IU–2 to GU and terminated the special permit for business airport uses. Petitioner by way of certiorari sought review of the zoning resolution in the circuit court and after a hearing, the court entered its order of denial.

Appellant basically argues that zoning resolution Z–115–75 is invalid because it bears no reasonable relationship to the public health, safety, morals and welfare and constitutes such an unreasonable restriction on petitioner's right to the beneficial use of its property that the resolution amounts to a taking of real property without compensation in violation of the United States and Florida Constitutions. We cannot agree.

A threshold question to a consideration of this appeal is whether preservation of an adequate drinking water supply and ecological system in a particular area are legitimate objectives of zoning resolutions and ordinances.

Zoning regulations which are reasonably related to the adequacy of governmental services fall within the established purpose of the public health, safety and welfare; water supply relates clearly to the public health. Therefore, zoning ordinances have been sustained because of their tendency to insure that such essential governmental services as water supply will be provided. See Anderson, R.M., American Law of Zoning s 7.26 (2d ed 1968). It is clear that the county commission is empowered under Article 1, Section 1.01(A)(9) and (12) of the Home Rule Charter of Metropolitan Dade County to enact zoning ordinances and resolutions to assure an adequate water supply for the protection of the public. See also Section 2–116.3 et seq. Code of Metropolitan Dade County, Section 23A–1, Code of Metropolitan Dade County.

With respect to the objective of preserving the ecological systems, zoning regulations which tend to preserve the residential or historical character of a neighborhood and/to enhance the aesthetic appeal of a community are considered valid exercises of the public power as relating to the general welfare of the community. *See City of Miami Beach v. Ocean & Inland Co.*, 147 Fla. 480, 3 So.2d 364 (1941); *Merritt v. Peters*, 65 So.2d 861 (Fla.1953); *Sunad, Inc. v. City of Sarasota*, 122 So.2d 611 (Fla.1960); *William Murray, Inc. v. Jacksonville*, 254 So.2d 364 (Fla. 1st DCA 1971); *City of Boca Raton v. Tradewind Hills, Inc.*, 216 So.2d 460 (Fla. 4th DCA 1968); *County of Brevard v. Woodham*, 223 So.2d 344 (Fla. 4th DCA 1969); *Watson v. Mayflower Property, Inc.*, 223 So.2d 368 (Fla 4th DCA 1969); *City of Coral Gables v. Wood*, 305 So.2d 261 (Fla. 3d DCA 1974) and *E. B. Elliott Advertising Co. v. Metropolitan Dade County*, 425 F.2d 1141 (5th Cir. 1970); *Stone v. City of Maitland*, 446 F.2d 83 (5th Cir. 1971); *Maher v. City of New Orleans*, 516 F.2d 1051 (5th Cir. 1975). The above being legitimate concerns within the category of the general welfare, then certainly the irreversible effect on the area's ecological balance as the result of urban development can be and should be considered and reflected in zoning codes. We find the inclusion of ecological considerations as a legitimate objective of zoning ordinances and resolutions is long overdue and hold that preservation of the ecological balance of a particular area is a valid exercise of the police power as it relates to the general welfare. We are not alone in this determination as courts in other jurisdictions have recognized the importance of considering the ecological objectives in zoning matters. See *Nattin Realty, Inc. v. Ludewig*, 67 Misc.2d 828, 324 N.Y.S.2d 668 (Sup.Ct.1971) and *Steel Hill Development, Inc. v. Town of Sanbornton*, 469 F.2d 956 (1st Cir. 1972). *In Nattin Realty, Inc., supra*, 67 Misc.2d 828, 324 N.Y.S.2d at 672, the court summarized this issue most appropriately as follows:

> "Respecting ecology as a new factor, it appears that the time has come if, indeed, it has not already irretrievably passed for the courts, as it were, to take 'ecological notice' in zoning matters."
>
> "(5) * * * the municipality has here presented sufficient evidence to warrant the rezoning of the petitioner's property, for it was prompted to do so by ecological considerations based not upon whim or fancy but upon scientific findings. The definition of 'public health, safety and welfare' surely must now be broadened to include and to provide for these belatedly recognized threats and hazards to the public weal. The Town's decision to forego what, undoubtedly, would be substantial additional tax revenue would appear to constitute a recognition that it as well as an owner must subordinate immediate to long-term interests."
>
> "The Court is not unmindful that zoning changes prompted by such environmental considerations may appreciably limit the uses and profitability of land; yet if both factors were to be placed upon the scales, the pro bono public considerations must prevail. If there is substantial evidence sustaining the municipality's determination to rezone because of ecology, the court should not void such legislative determination."

In view of our determination that ecological considerations are legitimate objectives of a zoning ordinance or resolution, the following summation of evidence presented to the commission substantiates the county's position that resolution Z–115–75 is reasonably related to the public health and welfare and will confer a public benefit upon the citizens of the county:

> "The subject property area overlies one of the most permeable aquifers in the world, the Biscayne Aquifer. This aquifer serves as the source of virtually all drinking water in Dade County and must be protected from contamination. Due to the unique area hydrology and geology, the Biscayne Aquifer, the inland drainage canals, and the conservation area in West Dade County are all directly intercon-

nected. As a result of this interconnection, the bodies must be considered as component parts of the same water supply system."

The composition of the Biscayne Aquifer is mostly limestone and sand. The generally high porosity of the sand and the many passages through the limestone offer very little resistance to flow. The result is that the aquifer responds quickly to slight differences in the water table, with the following consequences:

1. The water table is relatively flat.

2. The yields of wells are large.

3. The ground and surface water regimens have an uncommonly high interrelationship.

4. The water table reacts quickly to rainfall. There is a high rate of rainfall penetration and surface water infiltration and, although annual rainfall is high, there is relatively little runoff as compared with other localities.

5. The coastal areas, which are exposed to Biscayne Bay and the Atlantic Ocean, are highly susceptible to saltwater intrusion.

The property in question contains a blue-green algae mat or periphyton which filters out many pollutants from the ground water. The process, which is referred to as 'biological assimilation', is important in protecting the ground and surface water quality.

Before it may be developed or improved, the subject property must be filled by a minimum of three feet of earth or other suitable fill material to comply with federal flood control criteria. Thus, the natural state of the property would have to be substantially altered before any meaningful development thereon could occur.

Any excavation of the Petitioner's property would remove the natural periphyton 'filtering mat' and would expose the aquifer, from which the drinking water supplies of Dade County are drawn, to a whole range of pollutants. The algae mat involves biological, chemical and physical processes which maintain the area's water quality.

"Rainfall, which varies between 40 and 85 inches per year and averages about 59 inches per year, provides the major water resource of Dade County. Approximately 80% of the annual rainfall occurs during the six-month 'rainy season' from May through October. The sensitivity of the area is unchallenged."

* * *

We conclude that the restrictions imposed by resolution Z–115–75 are reasonable in light of the legislative intent to preserve as nearly as possible an adequate water supply and the ecological balance in the area. However, that is not to say petitioner would be precluded from compensation under the Constitution if at some future date, upon taking positive steps to develop its property, petitioner proves it has been so restricted in its development efforts by the County that it is being deprived of the beneficial use of the property for the purpose of conferring a public benefit.

Affirmed.

Environmental Impact Reviews

In 1970, the federal government adopted the National Environmental Policy Act (NEPA), 42 U.S.C. §§ 4321–4370 (2000), which requires federal agencies to evaluate the impact of their decisions on the environment. NEPA instills environmental values in the agencies' decision-making process by requiring the preparation of an environmental impact statement for all federal actions that significantly affect the quality of the human environment. The heart of NEPA is the requirement that federal agencies conduct an environmental impact review (EIR) prior to initiating their own capital projects, allocating funds to others, or taking other actions that might have environmental impacts. EIR is a process that requires government decision-makers to determine whether projects will have a significant environmental impact and to consider how such impacts can be ameliorated. Federal agencies must prepare a detailed statement on the environmental impact of the proposed action, evaluate any adverse environmental effects, and consider alternatives to the proposed action before undertaking it. 42 U.S.C. § 4332.

NEPA was followed by the enactment of state environmental policy acts (SEPAs) in about half the states. Like NEPA, the state statutes stress the importance of environmental protection and require state agencies to conduct an environmental impact review before undertaking actions that might affect the environment adversely. Most SEPAs apply only to state agency actions. However, in six states—California, New York, Washington, Minnesota, Massachusetts, and Hawaii—the state statutes' EIR requirement applies to the actions of local government agencies as well. This requirement affects a host of local planning and zoning decisions, including the adoption of zoning ordinances and amendments, the grant of zoning variances, subdivision and site plan approvals, issuance of special use permits, and the adoption of comprehensive plans.

Where local land use agencies are required to conduct environmental impact reviews, additional steps are added to the local land use approval process that can conflict with the procedures prescribed for traditional land use reviews. In 1975, New York enacted the State Environmental Quality Review Act (SEQRA). N.Y. Envtl. Conserv. Law §§ 8–0101 to 8–0117 (McKinney 2003). SEQRA requires an environmental impact statement for all government actions that may have a "significant effect on the environment." SEQRA applies to all agencies and instrumentalities of the state, which includes local agencies such as legislatures, planning boards, and zoning boards of appeals. SEQRA gives local land use agencies independent authority to impose conditions on land use approvals to mitigate the potential adverse environmental impacts of proposed projects. It can also be used to extend significantly the time it takes to conduct local land use reviews.

The following case required the judiciary in New York to sort out the conflicting policies of state-enacted land use and environmental statutes and to balance the developer's right to a predictable and timely local review with the public interest in environmental protection expressed in SEQRA.

SUN BEACH REAL ESTATE DEVELOPMENT CORP. v. ANDERSON

New York Supreme Court, Appellate Division, Second Department, 1983.
469 N.Y.S.2d 964, 98 A.D.2d 367.

LAZER, J.

Under the Town Law, a planning board which fails to act on a preliminary subdivision plat application within 45 days is deemed to have approved the preliminary plat (Town Law, § 276, subd. 3). What we now decide is how that rigorous mandate for prompt action interacts with the State Environmental Quality Review Act (SEQRA) (ECL 8–0101 et seq.) requirement that an application for a permit or authorization shall not be deemed complete until a draft environmental impact statement (DEIS) has been accepted by the agency principally responsible for the approval (ECL 8–0109, subd 5).

Having been found in violation of the Town Law time restriction in processing petitioner's 777–acre subdivision plat, East Hampton's Planning Board argues that the 45–day time limit did not even begin to run until the board accepted petitioner's DEIS and that 45 days was too short a time for the board to meet its SEQRA obligations. Victorious at Special Term, the petitioner disagrees, contending that the 45–day time limit is an absolute one and that it is unaffected by any provision of SEQRA. We believe that preliminary plat approval determines important design features of a subdivision and therefore SEQRA's mandate for early meaningful consideration of the environmental consequences of a project requires environmental review to be undertaken when a preliminary plat application is filed. Once the East Hampton Planning Board determined that a DEIS was necessary, the preliminary plat application was not complete until the DEIS was accepted by the board. As a consequence, the time requirements of the Town Law did not commence running until after that acceptance.

On July 29, 1982, Sun Beach Real Estate Development Corp., the owner of a 777–acre tract in the Town of East Hampton, applied to the planning board for preliminary approval of a subdivision plat which showed a proposed development of 188 one-family residences and 143 condominium units. Attached to the application was an environmental assessment form (EAF) intended to assist the planning board in determining the environmental significance of the application (see 6 NYCRR 617.2 [l]). By letter dated September 7, 1982, the planning board informed Sun Beach that its application would be processed when it was complete, i.e., when the board issued a determination that the preliminary approval was of no environmental significance or when it accepted a DEIS if it decided there was environmental significance. Relying on subdivision 3 of section 276 of the Town Law, on October 15, 1982, Sun Beach demanded a certificate from the town clerk granting preliminary plat approval because the planning board had failed to hold a hearing on the plat within 45 days after submission of the application. On October 27, 1982, 90 days after the application had been filed, the planning board determined that the subdivision might significantly affect the environment and accepted as satisfactory a DEIS the applicant had submitted in mid-September, more than 45 days after filing of the application. A hearing was scheduled for December 8, 1982 to consider both the DEIS and the preliminary plat approval application. In January, 1983, Sun Beach brought this proceeding pursuant to CPLR article 78 against the town, the town clerk and the planning board seeking judgment directing issuance of a certificate of preliminary plat approval. Special Term granted the petition and directed the town clerk to issue the certificate. That judgment is at issue here.

There can be no doubt that absent SEQRA's requirements, Sun Beach would have been entitled to the approval certificate because default statutes such as section 276 of the Town Law and similar provisions governing city and village planning authorities (see General City Law, § 32; Village Law, § 7–728) have been uniformly construed to require automatic approval upon the failure to act within the prescribed time limits (*see, e.g., Matter of Pekar v. Town of Veteran Planning Bd.*, 58 A.D.2d 703; *Matter of Wallkill Manor v. Coulter*, 40 A.D.2d 828, affd. 33 N.Y.2d 783; *Matter of Northern Operating Corp. v. Chamberlain*, 34 A.D.2d 686, affd. 31 N.Y.2d 704; *Matter of Fishman v. Arnzen*, 29 A.D.2d 954; *Matter of Scarsdale Meadows v. Smith*, 20 A.D.2d 906; *Matter of Levin v. Thornbury*, 2 A.D.2d 774). None of the cited cases dealt, however, with the co-ordination between existing subdivision approval procedures and the SEQRA process. Recognizing the impact of SEQRA, the town contends that when section 276 of the Town Law is harmonized with SEQRA, the time limits imposed by the Town Law do not commence to run until the planning board has accepted a DEIS.

It is a familiar canon of statutory construction that apparently conflicting statutory provisions should be harmonized in a manner that preserves the essential purposes of both (*Matter of Burger King v. State Tax Comm.*, 51 N.Y.2d 614; *Matter of Lumpkin v. Department of Social Servs.*, 59 A.D.2d 485, affd. 45 N.Y.2d 351; McKinney's Cons Laws of NY, Book 1, Statutes, § 98). Since Sun Beach claims there is no conflict, it is necessary to examine the requirements of SEQRA to see if they can be integrated into existing subdivision approval time limits, and if they cannot, to decide whether there is any reasonable method to reconcile the two statutes.

SEQRA's procedures are intended to minimize to the greatest degree possible the adverse environmental consequences of any project that is approved. In *Glen Head–Glenwood Landing Civic Council v. Town of Oyster Bay* (88 A.D.2d 484, 486–487) we summarized the procedure as follows:

> "As early as possible in the SEQRA process, the agency 'having principal responsibility for carrying out or approving' a given project or activity—the 'lead' agency (ECL 8–0111, subd. 6)—must determine whether an environmental impact statement (EIS) should be prepared with reference to the proposal submitted (ECL 8–0109, subd. 4; 8–0111, subd. 6). If the lead agency determines that the project 'may have a significant effect on the environment', either the agency or the applicant—at the latter's option—must prepare a draft environmental impact statement (DEIS) (ECL 8–0109, subds. 2, 4). If the draft statement is accepted by the agency 'as satisfactory with respect to scope, content and adequacy', it is then circulated to the DEC, other agencies having an interest in the proposal, and 'interested members of the public' (ECL 8–0109, subds. 4, 5; 6 NYCRR 617.8 [b]; 617.10). After allowing a period for comment, the lead agency must prepare a final environmental impact statement (FEIS) and circulate it in the same manner as the draft statement (ECL 8–0109, subds. 4, 5, 6; 6 NYCRR 617.10 [h]). Finally, upon adoption of the environmental-affecting proposal by the lead agency, it is required to make explicit findings that (1) the requirements of SEQRA have been met, and (2) adverse environmental effects revealed in the EIS process will be minimized or avoided to the maximum extent possible (ECL 8–0109, subd. 8; 6 NYCRR 617.9 [c])."

It is undisputed that development of petitioner's 777–acre tract will have environmental reverberations and that the instant subdivision process constitutes an "action" which invokes SEQRA's directives. An action is defined as "projects or activities involving the issuance to a person of a lease, permit, license, certificate or other entitlement for use or permission to act by one or more agencies" (ECL 8–0105, subd. 4, par [i]). By regulation, "actions" also encompass "planning activities of an agency that commit the agency to a definite course of future decisions" (6 NYCRR 617.2 [b] [2]). All of the activities or steps in a capital project (i.e., planning, design, contracting, construction and operation) constitute an action, but only one draft and one final environmental statement are necessary if the statement "address[es] each step at a level of detail sufficient for an adequate analysis of environmental effects" (6 NYCRR 617.2 [b]).

While the imprecision of the statutory language renders it difficult to identify the precise point when a DEIS must be prepared during an "action" (see *Matter of Tri–County Taxpayers Assn. v. Town Bd.*, 55 N.Y.2d 41, 45), the legislative intent is that environmental factors be given consideration "[a]s early as possible in the formulation of a proposal for an action" (ECL 8–0109, subd. 4; see, also, 6 NYCRR 617.1 [c]). The emphasis on early consideration facilitates the underlying purposes of a DEIS—"to relate environmental considerations to the inception of the planning process, to inform the public and other public agencies as early as possible about proposed actions that may significantly affect the quality of the environment'' (ECL 8–0109, subd. 4). This is consistent with the requirement that the SEQRA process "run concurrently with other procedures relating to the review and approval of the action'' (ECL 8–0109, subd. 5). If the DEIS is not prepared at an early stage, modification of a project in light of subsequently discovered environmental problems may become difficult because nonenvironmental considerations may have already been transformed into an over-all proposal (see Orloff, SEQRA: New York's Reformation of NEPA, 46 Albany L. Rev. 1128, 1136). Not only will the sponsors of projects be more likely to resist alteration of proposals which already have received some processing and approval, but institutional bias may result because later governmental decisions may be influenced by prior governmental decisions or commitments (*see Matter of Tri–County Taxpayers Assn. v. Town Bd., supra*; Note, Program Environmental Impact Statements: Review and Remedies, 75 Mich. L. Rev. 107, 111–112; 4 Rohan, Zoning and Land Use Controls, § 27.02 [2]). Indeed, in *Tri–County* (supra, pp. 46–47), the Court of Appeals declared that: "[T]he dynamics and freedom of decision-making with respect to a proposal to rescind a prior action are significantly more constrained than when the action is first under consideration for adoption. Thus, although not legally conclusive the initiatory action by the town board might well have been practically determinative. In effect the purpose of SEQRA is to assure the preparation and availability of an environmental impact statement at the time any significant authorization is granted for a specific proposal.''

It is thus apparent that the DEIS must be prepared at a point " 'where genuine flexibility remains before bureaucratic momentum strips [it] of any real influence on decision-making' '' (*see Mount Sutro Defense Comm. v. Regents of Univ. of Cal.*, 77 Cal.App.3d 20, 34).

With these considerations in mind, we return to the parties' debate as to when it is during the subdivision approval process that the DEIS must be filed. We view preliminary plat approval as so significant a determination during the process that an environmental impact statement must be deemed a prerequisite to the approval. * * *

In determining the temporal position of the DEIS in the subdivision process, the holdings of our sister States are entitled to respect in view of the essential uniformity of environmental legislation (see Robinson, SEQRA's Siblings: Precedents from Little NEPA's in the Sister States, 46 Albany L. Rev. 1155, 1157). Interpreting Washington's State Environmental Policy Act of 1971 (Wash. Rev. Code Ann., ch. 43.21C; SEPA), a statute similar to our own, the Supreme Court of Washington held that preliminary approval of a subdivision requires the preparation of an environmental impact statement (*see Loveless v. Yantis*, 82 Wn.2d 754). The court reasoned that preliminary approval of a plat is a discretionary, non-duplicative decision and preparation of a statement at the time of preliminary approval would facilitate early and meaningful environmental review of the project because that is the stage when the planning body, the developer and the public should be made aware of the environmental consequences of the design matters revealed in the preliminary plat and investment costs would be minimized if the plat were to be abandoned or altered (*Loveless v. Yantis*, *supra*, pp. 765–766).

Our conclusion, then, is that when the planning agency has determined that development of the subdivision might significantly affect the environment, the application for preliminary approval is not complete until a DEIS has been filed and has been accepted by the agency as satisfactory in scope and content (see ECL 8–0109, subd. 5; 6 NYCRR 617.3 [e]). The DEIS should be available when it is still practicable to modify the project so as to mitigate potentially adverse economic effects or to choose a less environmentally damaging alternative (see ECL 8–0109, subds. 2, 8) and before it is too late to influence the basic design of a project already fixed at the preliminary stage (*see* ECL 8–0103, subd. 7; *Glen Head–Glenwood Landing Civic Council v. Town of Oyster Bay*, 88 A.D.2d 484, *supra; Matter of Town of Henrietta v. Department of Environmental Conservation*, 76 A.D.2d 215).

Once the application is complete, the planning board must coordinate its subdivision approval procedures with SEQRA (ECL 8–0109, subd. 5; 8–0103, subd. 6). The 30–day period of comment on the DEIS for involved agencies and the public (6 NYCRR 617.8 [c]) easily fits within the 45–day period for holding a preliminary plat hearing under subdivision 3 of section 276 of the Town Law and it is preferable that a joint hearing be held (6 NYCRR 617.8 [d]). The final environmental impact statement need not be prepared until after the final plat has been submitted since SEQRA requires only one DEIS and one final environmental impact statement to be prepared for a given action (6 NYCRR 617.2 [b]); preparation of a final environmental impact statement need only precede the agency's final decision to approve an action (6 NYCRR 617.9 [c]). Depending on whether significant new information is revealed in the final plat submission, the agency may require the filing of a supplemental DEIS (*see Glen Head–Glenwood Landing Civic Council v. Town of Oyster Bay*, 88 A.D.2d 484, 494–495, *supra*).

Where a DEIS is a requisite to preliminary approval, the 45–day deadline imposed by the Town Law seems too short for planning boards to fulfill their SEQRA requirements. While an agency may vary SEQRA's time limits for "preparation, review and public hearings to coordinate the environmental review process with other procedures relating to review and approval of an action" (ECL 8–0109, subd. 5), provided the periods as varied are "no less protective of environmental values" (6 NYCRR 617.4 [b]), the agency cannot take any further steps until the submission of a DEIS (see ECL 8–0109, subd. 4). If the application does not contain the DEIS, the 45–day period for Town Law action may elapse before the statement has been filed, leaving the agency with the option of granting approval without the DEIS and running the risk of legal challenge to its decision or of denying approval on the ground of inadequate environmental review (Sahm, Project Approval Under the California Environmental Quality Act: It Always Takes Longer Than You Think, 19 Santa Clara L.Rev. 579). Neither alternative is acceptable.

It is apparent that SEQRA's drafters did not take into account some of the idiosyncracies of subdivision procedures (see Marsh, Commentary—Unresolved Issues, 46 Albany L. Rev. 1298, 1304) and it has been left to the judiciary to attempt to co-ordinate the statutes. Resolution of the instant case depends on which statute has preeminence—the 45-day requirement enacted in 1966 to limit the depredations of dilatory planning boards (*see Matter of Mahopac Isle v. Agar*, 39 Misc.2d. 1, *supra*; 1 Anderson, N.Y. Zoning Law and Practice [2d ed.], § 15.07) or SEQRA enacted in 1975 to save the environment and preserve it for future generations (ECL 8–0101, 8–0103, subds. 1, 8). We have no difficulty in according priority to SEQRA because the legislative declaration of purpose in that statute makes it obvious that protection of "the environment for the use and enjoyment of this and all future generations" (ECL 8–0103, subd. 8) far overshadows the rights of developers to obtain prompt action on their proposals. Once SEQRA's priority is recognized, the statute must be read to mandate that a preliminary plat application is not complete until a DEIS has either been dispensed with or accepted and the 45-day limitation in the Town Law does not commence to run until the application is complete (*see Asarco Inc. v. Air Quality Coalition*, 92 Wn.2d 685, 710). Here, the East Hampton Planning Board conducted a hearing on the preliminary plat within 45 days of its acceptance of the DEIS and therefore it acted in a timely manner without default under subdivision 3 of section 276 of the Town Law.

In reaching our conclusion, we are quite aware that SEQRA and its regulations have set no time limits within which a planning board must accept a proposed DEIS (*see Matter of East Clinton Developers v. Town of Clinton*, 88 A.D.2d 416). The danger, of course, is that planning boards may utilize the absence of SEQRA time limitations to resume the type of bureaucratic delay that resulted in the enactment of the 45-day time limitation in 1966. If such consequences are to be avoided, the Legislature and the Commissioner of Environmental Conservation should turn their attention to the problem.

Whatever the future may hold in this respect, however, the instant judgment should be reversed, without costs or disbursements, and proceeding dismissed.

* * *

Notes

1. The California Environmental Quality Act (CEQA), like New York's SEQRA, applies to the granting or denial of permits to private developers. Pub.Res.C. § 2100 et. seq. For a complete discussion on state environmental review acts and corresponding court decisions, see Nicholas Robinson, SEQRA's Siblings: Precedents from Little NEPA's in the Sister States, 46 Alb. L. Rev. 1155 (1982) and Philip Weinberg, A Powerful Mandate: NEPA and State Environmental Review Acts in the Courts, 5 Pace Envtl. L. Rev. 1

(1987). For an overview of state environmental review statutes see Growing Smart Legislative Guidebook, Chapter 12, Appendix B, pp. 12–30 to 12–32 (American Planning Association 2002).

2. Most environmental impact review statutes require the assessment of the impact of government actions on the "environment." Should the "environment" be limited to flora and fauna? In Chinese Staff and Workers Association v. City of New York, 68 N.Y.2d 359, 502 N.E.2d 176, 509 N.Y.S.2d 499 (1986), community residents used SEQRA to challenge the approval of a special use permit for the construction of a high-rise luxury condominium. The petitioners argued that the city's environmental review was arbitrary and capricious because it failed to consider the possible displacement of low-income residents. The court held that it is clear from the express terms of the statute and the regulations that the term environment is broadly defined and expressly includes considerations such as "existing patterns of population concentration, distribution, or growth, and existing community or neighborhood characteristics." Therefore, the court stated that the impact that a proposed project may have on population patterns or community character is a relevant concern in an environmental analysis. In Jackson v. New York State Urban Dev. Corp., 67 N.Y.2d 400, 503 N.Y.S.2d 298, 494 N.E.2d 429 (1986), although the Court of Appeals focused on SEQRA's "attempt to strike a balance between social and economic goals and concerns about the environment," it indicated that "environment" is "defined broadly to include 'land, air, water, minerals, flora, fauna, noise, objects of historic or aesthetic significance, existing patterns of population concentration, distribution, or growth, and existing community or neighborhood character.' "

3. Where the local land use agency makes a determination that no adverse environmental impact is likely and therefore no environmental impact statement is required, the approval deadlines in the underlying land use regulations apply. See Figgie Int'l v. Town of Huntington, 203 A.D.2d 416, 610 N.Y.S.2d 563 (App.Div. 2d Dep't 1994), holding that if a determination is made that no DEIS is necessary, then the city/town/village subdivision/site plan approval ordinance governs, and the fixed time period for government action concerning an application is effective.

Conservation Easements and Land Trusts

A conservation easement is a voluntary agreement between a private landowner and a municipal agency or a qualified not-for-profit corporation to restrict the development, management, or use of the land. The owner of the real property conveys an interest in the land—a conservation easement—to a qualified public or private agency and the deed is placed on the local land records. That agency holds the interest and enforces its restrictions against the transferring owner and all subsequent owners of the land. The purpose of a conservation easement is to preserve or conserve the scenic, open, historic, archaeological, architectural, or natural condition of real property. In addition to restricting land use, conservation easements may permit public access, such as hiking over a trail on the property or biking along a designated path. Existing uses on the property and expansions of uses not inconsistent with the preservation or conservation of these features may be allowed on the restricted parcel.

Conservation easements may be donated, sold at full-market value, or sold at below-market value by the owner of the land. If the easement is donated or is sold at below-market value, the landowner may qualify for an income tax deduction in the year of the donation or bargain sale. Subject to a conservation easement, the land may qualify for a lower estate tax valuation on the death of the owner, thereby reducing the tax burden on the beneficiaries of the owner's estate. Similarly, the local property tax assessments may be lowered, benefiting the landowner on an annual basis thereafter.

A land trust is a local or regional not-for-profit organization, private in nature, organized to preserve and protect the natural and man-made environment by, among other techniques, holding conservation easements that restrict the use of real property. Land trusts usually pursue their own organizational agendas. However, under contract with a local government, a land trust may agree to serve as a vehicle for the negotiation, acquisition, holding, and enforcement of conservation easements agreed to by, or imposed on, landowners as part of the local development review and approval process. The purpose of involving a private land trust in a municipal conservation program is to save the local government the expense and inconvenience of holding, monitoring, and enforcing conservation easements, to insulate the matter from political change, and to take advantage of the land trust's expertise in these matters.

Most states provide statutory authorization for the use of this popular easement. In 1981 the Uniform Conservation Easement Act was adopted, influencing legislation in about half of the states. A copy of the Act is available at www.law.upenn.edu/bill/archives/ulc/fnact99/19805/ucea89.htm. Between 1988 and 1998, land trusts protected approximately 1.4 million acres through conservation easements. According to the Land Trust Alliance, a national organization that seeks to facilitate the land trust movement and maintains a national directory of land trusts. (There are over 1,200 land trusts in the United States). Links to local land trusts are available at the Alliance's web site, www.lta.org.

The interplay of laws that protect the environment and traditional local land use regulations is evident in the following case where the town planning board approved the subdivision of environmentally sensitive land subject to the development being located, or "clustered," on the more buildable portion of the 450 parcel. The petitioners argue that the board allowed excessive density in approving the cluster subdivision because of the existence of a conservation easement that limits severely the development on 240 acres of the tract.

MATTER OF FRIENDS OF THE SHAWANGUNKS v. KNOWLTON

Court of Appeals of New York, 1985.
64 N.Y.2d 387, 476 N.E.2d 988, 487 N.Y.S.2d 543.

MEYER, J.

Lake Minnewaska Mountain Houses, Inc. (Mountain Houses), owns approximately 450 acres of land located on Lake Minnewaska in the Town of Rochester, Ulster County. In 1977, Mountain Houses sold to the Palisades Interstate Park Commission (PIPC) a conservation easement on 240 acres of the land contiguous to the 10,000 acre Minnewaska State Park owned by PIPC. The easement permits the erection of one single family residence, a potable water storage pond and the maintenance of the existing golf course and accessory areas, but otherwise proscribes development of the 240 acres. By agreement dated February 26, 1980, Mountain Houses sold the entire 450 acres to the Marriott Corporation, subject, however, as a condition precedent to closing, to Marriott's obtaining approval of subdivision of the property to permit construction of a hotel and condominium units.

In April 1982, Marriott applied to the Town Planning Board for approval of a plat of the 450 acres calling for construction of a hotel and 300 residential condominium units, the condominium units to be clustered on part of the 210 acres not covered by the conservation easement. The district in which the 450 acres is located requires a plot of one or more acres per residential unit. After notice to interested parties and a public hearing on the application, the Planning Board approved the requested 300 units. PIPC, though given notice, interposed no objection.

Petitioners, eight individual owners of nearby properties and two not-for-profit conservation organizations, then commenced this article 78 proceeding against the Planning Board. Special Term granted Marriott's application to intervene and on the merits dismissed the petition. The Appellate Division reversed, concluding that the 240 acres subject to the conservation easement could not be counted in determining the number of units permissible under the town's cluster zoning resolution, because the conservation easement constituted an "applicable requirement" within the meaning of Town Law § 281(b), the enabling act pursuant to which the cluster zoning provisions of the zoning ordinance were adopted. Both the Planning Board and Marriott appeal as of right.

Town Law § 281 provides in pertinent part that:

> "The town board is hereby empowered by resolution to authorize the planning board, simultaneously with the approval of a plat or plats pursuant to this article, to modify applicable provisions of the zoning ordinance, subject to the conditions hereinafter set forth and such other reasonable conditions as the town board may in its discretion add thereto. Such authorization shall specify the lands outside the limits of any incorporated village to which this procedure

may be applicable. The purposes of such authorization shall be to enable and encourage flexibility of design and development of land in such a manner as to promote the most appropriate use of land, to facilitate the adequate and economical provision of streets and utilities, and to preserve the natural and scenic qualities of open lands. The conditions hereinabove referred to are as follows:

> . . .
>
> "(b) The application of this procedure shall result in a permitted number of building plots or dwelling units which shall in no case exceed the number which could be permitted, in the planning board's judgment, if the land were subdivided into lots conforming to the minimum lot size and density requirements of the zoning ordinance applicable to the district or districts in which such land is situated and conforming to all other applicable requirements.
>
> . . .
>
> "(d) In the event that the application of this procedure results in a plat showing lands available for park, recreation, open space, or other municipal purposes directly related to the plat, then the planning board as a condition of plat approval may establish such conditions on the ownership, use, and maintenance of such lands as it deems necessary to assure the preservation of such lands for their intended purposes. The town board may require that such conditions shall be approved by the town board before the plat may be approved for filing."

The Town of Rochester, pursuant to that authorization, has incorporated in its zoning ordinance provisions for residential cluster development permitting its Planning Board to vary the residential density within a tract provided that the proposed development produces a total acreage density as specified for the district in which located and guarantees permanent retention and maintenance of "open areas."

Petitioners argue (1) that conservation easements are authorized by ECL 49–0301 et seq. and, therefore, that the PIPC easement is an "applicable requirement" within the meaning of Town Law § 281(b), and (2) that because the land covered by the easement is not "legally buildable," it cannot be considered in determining permissible density for a cluster zoning development. We disagree and, therefore, reverse.

II

The use that may be made of land under a zoning ordinance and the use of the same land under an easement or restrictive covenant are, as a general rule, separate and distinct matters, the ordinance being a legislative enactment and the easement or covenant a matter of private agreement (see, *Ginsberg v. Yeshiva of Far Rockaway,* 36 N.Y.2d 706 aff'd. 45 A.D.2d 334, 337–338; 4 Rathkopf, The Law of Zoning and Planning § 57.02 [4th ed.]). Thus, a particular use of land may be enjoined as in violation of a restrictive covenant, although the use is permissible under the zoning ordinance (*Gordon v. Incorporated Vil. of Lawrence,* 56 N.Y.2d 1003, aff'd. 84 A.D.2d 558, 559; *Regan v. Tobin,* 89 A.D.2d 586, 587), and the issuance of a permit for a use allowed by a zoning ordinance may not be denied because the proposed use would be in violation of a restrictive covenant (*People ex rel. Rosevale Realty Co. v. Kleinert,* 204 App.Div. 883, on later appeal 206 App.Div. 712, appeal dismissed 236 N.Y. 605, order resettled 207 App.Div. 828, aff'd. 237 N.Y. 580, writ dismissed 268 U.S. 646; *Matter of 109 Main St. Corp. v. Burns,* 14 Misc.2d 1037; *Matter of Forte v Wolf,* 225 N.Y.S.2d 858; cf. *Matter of Isenbarth v. Bartnett,* 206 App.Div. 546, aff'd. 237 N.Y. 617).

Petitioners seek to distinguish those rules as related only to covenants and easements appurtenant to an interest in real property, whereas a conservation easement, as defined in article 49 of the Environmental Conservation Law, may be held only by a public body or not-for-profit conservation organization (ECL 49–0305[3][a]) and is enforceable notwithstanding that it is of a character wholly distinct from the easements traditionally recognized at common law and notwithstanding defenses that would defeat a common-law easement (ECL 49–0305[5]). The short answer to the argument is that ECL article 49 was not enacted until 1983 and that PIPC does own the adjacent Minnewaska State Park. Thus the easement granted PIPC in 1977 was a common-law easement appurtenant, which, whatever its burden upon intervenor's use of the 240 acres it covered, cannot be construed to be an "applicable requirement" within the meaning of Town Law § 281(b), unless the usual rule that words in a statute are to be construed by reference to words and phrases with which they are associated (McKinney's Cons.Laws of N.Y., Book 1, Statutes § 239[a]) is to be ignored.

More importantly, the present version of Town Law § 281 was enacted by chapter 963 of the Laws of 1963, 20 years before enactment of the Environmental Conservation Law provisions relating to conservation easements (L.1983, ch. 1020). Petitioners point to nothing in the legislative history of either statute to suggest a legislative intent to include within the concept of the "other applicable requirements" referred to in Town Law § 281(b), such an easement rather than other zoning and planning requirements imposed by the Town Law. * * *

* * *

III

The argument that, because the 240 acres subject to the easement cannot be built upon while the easement continues in force, the burdened land may not be counted in determining cluster zoning density is of no greater aid to petitioners. "[I]t is undisputed that the PIPC does not own the land burdened by the easement. It merely has an easement, which is 'a right, distinct from ownership, to use in some way the land of another' " (*Matter of Sierra Club v. Palisades Interstate Park Commn.,* 99 A.D.2d 548, 549, 471 N.Y.S.2d 633, lv. denied 63 N.Y.2d 604).

Mountain Houses, having granted PIPC only an easement, continued to own the underlying fee and with it the right to use the property in any manner not in violation of the easement. Marriott, as Mountain Houses' conditional vendee, proposes to use the land in fulfillment of its obligation under the cluster development provisions of the town zoning ordinance to provide open areas and guarantee their permanent maintenance and retention, a use in furtherance of the purpose declared by Town Law § 281, "to preserve the natural and scenic qualities of open lands" and in no way violative of PIPC's easement.

As the conditional vendee of the fee of the 450–acre tract, Marriott is entitled to have the entire 450 acres considered in determining the permissible number of dwelling units. One of the major purposes of cluster zoning being the preservation of the natural and scenic qualities of open land, it is fundamentally inconsistent with the statutory purpose to hold that because that part of the land that will be thus preserved under a cluster zoning proposal is also subject to an easement that preserves it as open land, it may not be counted in determining density. The more so is this true in light of the case law, discussed above, holding zoning ordinances and restrictive covenants to be separate and distinct matters.

Equally unavailing are petitioners' suggestions (1) that if the property covered by the conservation easement may be counted, density on the adjoining land greater than permissible under conventional zoning will result, threatening the preservation goal of the conservation easement, and (2) that, having granted an easement to PIPC, Mountain Houses should not be permitted to "double dip" by using the underlying fee in computing cluster density. The answer to the first is that the declared purposes of Town Law § 281 contemplate both "flexibility of design and development" and the preservation of "the natural and scenic qualities of open lands." Those purposes are frustrated if the trade-off of increased density on the developed portion of the land in return for preserving undeveloped the remainder of the land is foreclosed by exclusion of the open area from the density computation simply because the developer has agreed with others to keep the open areas open. Moreover, because the PIPC easement makes the burdened land available for use and enjoyment of the public (N.Y. Const., art. XIV, § 4; ECL 49–0301; PRHPL 9.05[5]), it is difficult to understand how the preservation goal of the easement is threatened by inclusion of the open area in the density computation. To read the statutes as necessarily implying the rule of exclusion for which petitioners contend would be to ignore not only the history of Town Law § 281 (see, n. 5, supra;) and the usual rules of statutory construction (*Matter of Kamhi v. Planning Bd.*, 59 N.Y.2d 385, 392; *People v. Graham,* 55 N.Y.2d 144, 152), but also the fact that subdivision (b) of that section makes the number of permitted dwelling units a matter of "the planning board's judgment," which may be overturned only if illegal, arbitrary or an abuse of discretion (CPLR 7803; Town Law § 282).

The double dip argument is essentially addressed to the process of negotiation with PIPC rather than to any provision of either law. Petitioners point to nothing in the Environmental Conservation Law that would prevent PIPC from acquiring an easement over the cluster open areas had cluster approval been sought first, or that requires PIPC when acquiring a conservation easement to proscribe use of the burdened land if the landowner later applies for cluster development approval. Had cluster approval been obtained first, the acquisition price of a conservation easement over the already burdened open area would probably have been less, but even that is not entirely clear when it is remembered that PIPC's purposes include not only obtaining conservation easements (ECL 49–0303[3]), but also the provision of hotel and other facilities for the use of the public (PRHPL 9.05[5]). Whatever the result, the point is that the matter was within the discretion of PIPC and, as already noted, it neither interposed an objection to Marriott's 300–unit application nor included in its conservation easement agreement anything related to use of the burdened area as cluster zone open space.

For the foregoing reasons the order of the Appellate Division should be reversed, with costs, and the judgment of Special Term, Ulster County, should be reinstated.

Chief Judge Wachtler, C.J., and Judges Jasen, Simons, Kaye and Alexander, JJ., concur.

Order reversed, with costs, and judgment of Supreme Court, Ulster County, reinstated.

Notes

1. There is a great deal of common law in the Friends of the Shawangunks case. The conservation easement owned by the Palisades Interstate Park Commission was purchased by PIP before New York adopted its version of the Uniform Conservation Easement Act. PIP owned land that is appurtenant to, and benefited by, the restriction on the burdened, or servient, parcel, and it is allowed under common law principles to enforce the restrictive covenant on the burdened land. Subsequent purchasers of the restricted parcel will be on notice of the covenant when they conduct a title search prior to purchase and discover the deed conveying the "conservation easement" to the Commission. When land trusts enter into conservation easements with landowners, they often do not own land adjacent to the burdened parcels, hence the easements, under common law, cannot be called appurtenant, but would be considered "in gross". The Uniform Conservation Easement Act resolved the question that arose in many states of whether an easement in gross could be enforced by a non-profit land trust or a municipal government and whether the restriction ran with the land to burden subsequent purchasers.

2. The Smith v. Mendon case, 4 N.Y.3d 1, 789 N.Y.S.2d 696, 822 N.E.2d 1214 (2004), illustrates how conservation easements can be used in conjunction with the approval of land use proposals by local planning boards. In Smith, New York's highest court held that a conservation easement

imposed by the town planning board as a condition to site plan approval is not an exaction and is not subject to heightened judicial scrutiny when challenged as a regulatory taking. The Mendon planning board conditioned its approval of the Smiths' proposal to build a single-family home on an environmentally-constrained ten acre parcel. The condition required the Smiths to file a conservation easement covering portions of the parcel located within the Town's environmental protection overlay districts. The Town previously had established four overlay districts that cover sensitive lands that contain steep slopes or border on major creeks, wooded areas, or floodplains. The overlay district provisions prohibit development and other land disturbing activities unless the landowner can show that a proposed activity will not adversely affect the protected resources.

The actual construction of the Smiths' home would not have adversely affected the environment since the proposed development would not occur in the overlay districts. Nonetheless, the Planning Board found that the conservation restriction was needed to put subsequent buyers on notice that the property contains restraints which may limit development within these environmentally sensitive areas and would provide the most meaningful and responsible means of protecting the property in the overlay districts. The conservation restriction mirrors the effect of the overlay district regulations by prohibiting construction on sensitive lands. It adds to those regulations by allowing town inspectors to enter the property, upon 30 days notice, to inspect conditions in the constrained areas. The restriction also encumbers the property in perpetuity, which would survive the town's elimination or relaxation of the overlay district rules. Further, the conservation restriction provides the town with legal ability to bring an injunction to enforce the restriction, adding to its power to issue citations and seek civil and criminal penalties—the normal methods of enforcing land use regulations.

SECTION 3. RESOURCE–SPECIFIC LOCAL LAND USE REGULATIONS

The gradual evolution toward environmental sensitivity in local land use controls has proceeded far enough that a distinct environmental ethic, as opposed to an incidental one, is evident. Local governments have adopted a host of environmental regulations. Local laws addressing the following issues can now be found and studied: cluster development; environmentally sensitive area protection; erosion and sediment control; grading, excavations, and fill; floodplain control; groundwater/aquifer resource protection; landscaping; ridgeline protection; scenic resource protection; soil removal; solid waste disposal; stream and watercourse protection; steep slopes; stormwater management; timber harvesting; tree protection; vegetation removal; and wetlands. Interestingly, many of these ordinances deal with the prevention of nonpoint source pollution, an urgent problem that generally is conceded to be beyond the reach of federal environmental law.

Local governments derive their authority to adopt laws that protect the environment from land use enabling statutes, home rule laws, and special laws directly aimed at environmental protection. In New York, municipalities have been delegated additional authority to protect the environment under the state's home rule law. The home rule provisions of Article IX of the New York Constitution and legislation passed pursuant to it give local governments broad home rule powers. N.Y. Const. Art. IX. The state legislature implemented Article IX with the enactment of the Municipal Home Rule Law (MHRL), the provisions of which are to be "liberally construed." Under the MHRL, localities are given the authority to adopt laws relating to their "property, affairs or government," and for "the protection and enhancement of [their] physical and visual environment."

The MHRL has been regarded as a source of local authority to regulate land use, in addition to the zoning and planning enabling statutes. It also has been interpreted to permit the enactment of purely environmental laws. For example, in Ardizzone v. Elliott, 75 N.Y.2d 150, 551 N.Y.S.2d 457, 550 N.E.2d 906, 908 (1989), the court stated that the municipality had the "power to regulate the freshwater wetlands within its boundaries under the Municipal Home Rule Law." This broad authority is critical to enacting laws that protect resources such as wildlife and wildlife habitat that may not fit squarely within the ambit of traditional zoning laws. The grant of authority encompassed in the MHRL provides a safety net for communities desiring to enact extensive environmental laws. This, combined with the power of local governments to include environmental standards in their zoning and land use regulations, provides ample authority for the state's villages, towns, and cities to create an integrated set of land use laws. Environmental laws may be added to the municipality's suite of land use laws by adopting them under the MHRL, the zoning enabling act, the subdivision or site plan delegation statutes, and by referring to the broad language of the planning enabling acts.

A. WATER RESOURCE PROTECTION

The adverse impact of development on surface waters is dramatically described by the U.S. Supreme Court in Tahoe–Sierra Preservation Council, Inc., et. al. v. Tahoe Regional Planning Agency, 535 U.S. 302, 122 S.Ct. 1465, 152 L.Ed.2d 517 (2002). The case explains the effect of nonpoint source pollution on Lake Tahoe as follows:

> Lake Tahoe's exceptional clarity is attributed to the absence of algae that obscures the waters of most other lakes. Historically, the lack of nitrogen and phosphorous, which nourish the growth of algae, has ensured the transparency of its waters. Unfortunately, the lake's pristine state has deteriorated rapidly over the past 40 years; increased land development in the Lake Tahoe Basin (Basin) has threatened the " 'noble sheet of blue water' " beloved by Twain and countless others. 34 F.Supp.2d, at 1230. As the District Court found, "[d]ramatic decreases in clarity first began to be noted in the late 1950's/early 1960's, shortly after development at the lake began

in earnest." *Id.* at 1231. The lake's unsurpassed beauty, it seems, is the wellspring of its undoing.

The upsurge of development in the area has caused "increased nutrient loading of the lake largely because of the increase in impervious coverage of land in the Basin resulting from that development." *Ibid.* "Impervious coverage—such as asphalt, concrete, buildings, and even packed dirt—prevents precipitation from being absorbed by the soil. Instead, the water is gathered and concentrated by such coverage. Larger amounts of water flowing off a driveway or a roof have more erosive force than scattered raindrops falling over a dispersed area—especially one covered with indigenous vegetation, which softens the impact of the raindrops themselves." Ibid. Given this trend, the District Court predicted that "unless the process is stopped, the lake will lose its clarity and its trademark blue color, becoming green and opaque for eternity."

535 U.S. at 306–08.

Those areas in the Basin that have steeper slopes produce more runoff; therefore, they are usually considered "high hazard" lands. Moreover, certain areas near streams or wetlands known as "Stream Environment Zones" (SEZs) are especially vulnerable to the impact of development because, in their natural state, they act as filters for much of the debris that runoff carries. Because "[t]he most obvious response to this problem * * * is to restrict development around the lake—especially in SEZ lands, as well as in areas already naturally prone to runoff," id., at 1232, conservation efforts have focused on controlling growth in these high hazard areas.

The Tahoe–Sierra decision and the other cases in this section demonstrate how rapidly land use controls are evolving in order to protect water resources from the adverse impacts of land development.

(1) Aquifer/Groundwater Supplies

Some localities use their environmental authority to protect drinking water aquifers by imposing additional regulatory standards on development projects proposed in such areas. The aquifer protection ordinance of Wallingford, Connecticut, prohibits certain land uses in order to protect its groundwater resources. Landowners are not allowed to conduct businesses that use hazardous chemicals, or to use their land for solid waste disposal facilities, junk yards, septage lagoons, hazardous waste drum storage areas, bulk storage piles, surface impoundments, road salt storage, or pipelines that transmit oil, gasoline or other hazardous materials. Other more manageable uses are allowed but restricted, such as above-ground chemical and fuel storage, underground fuel storage, dry cleaning, and new or enlarged manure, fertilizer, pesticide, and herbicide storage sites.

QUICK v. AUSTIN

Supreme Court of Texas, 1998.
7 S.W.3d 109.

JUSTICE ABBOTT delivered the opinion of the Court.

* * *

Frustrated by their perception that the Austin City Council was failing to safeguard Barton Springs adequately, a group of Austin citizens interested in protecting the environment initiated the Save Our Springs Ordinance and placed it on the Austin municipal ballot for a local referendum election. In August 1992, the Austin citizens participating in the referendum election overwhelmingly approved the Ordinance. Two days after the voters approved the Ordinance, the Austin City Council enacted the Ordinance and incorporated it into the City Code.

The purpose of the Ordinance, according to its Declaration of Intent, is to insure water quality control in Barton Creek, Barton Springs, and the Barton Springs Edwards Aquifer. The provisions of the Ordinance apply to those areas within Austin and Austin's extraterritorial jurisdiction that contain watersheds contributing to Barton Springs. The Ordinance limits impervious or non-porous cover on land in the regulated areas to between 15% and 25% of the net site area. The Ordinance also requires that new developments be set back from streams and not contribute to an increase in the amount of pollution constituents commonly found in urban rainfall runoff water. Construction in the "critical water quality zone" of the Barton Creek watershed is prohibited by the Ordinance. The Ordinance provides for no waivers or exceptions unless necessary to avoid conflict with state and federal laws.

Petitioners Jerry J. Quick, Kaira G. Quick, John M. Bryant, Ruth E. Bryant, Joe Cox, Dolores Cox, Florence Turck, and Circle C Land Corporation all own land outside the city limits of Austin but within its extraterritorial jurisdiction. Because their land is within Austin's extraterritorial jurisdiction, any development of their property must comply with the Ordinance. The Petitioners sued the City in Hays County, seeking a declaratory judgment that the Ordinance was void because it was illegally enacted. Additionally, Petitioners challenged the Ordinance under section 26.177(d) of the Texas Water Code, which authorizes a party aggrieved by a water pollution control ordinance to appeal to district court to review whether the ordinance is invalid, arbitrary, unreasonable, inefficient, or ineffective.

Save Our Springs Alliance, Inc., an incorporated association of individuals led by the citizen initiators of the Ordinance, moved to intervene in the suit. The Alliance urged that the City was incapable of adequately advocating the Alliance's interest due to previous hostilities over the Ordinance. *See, e.g., City Council of Austin v. Save Our Springs Coalition*, 828 S.W.2d 340 (Tex.App.—Austin 1992, no writ) (citizens sued City to force election on the Ordinance). The trial court, however, struck the plea in intervention, leaving the City to defend the Ordinance.

The Petitioners and the City proceeded to try the case to a jury. The jury answered "yes" to all the questions in the charge inquiring whether the Ordinance and its impervious cover limitations, its prohibition against increases in pollution constituents, and its failure to contain variances were an unreasonable, arbitrary, and inefficient attempt to control water quality. The jury also found that the Ordinance was not a proper subject for the initiative and referendum process and that the Ordinance regulated the number, use, and size of buildings in the City's extraterritorial jurisdiction (a violation of section 212.003 of the Texas Local Government Code).

Based on the jury's answers, the trial court rendered judgment for the Petitioners declaring the Ordinance null and void. The trial court's final judgment also contained conclusions of law, including that the Ordinance was ineffective because the Texas Natural Resource Conservation Commission had not approved it and that the Ordinance was void because it was enacted without a public hearing in violation of section 212.002 of the Local Government Code. The trial court further decreed that any permit required by Petitioner Circle C Land Corporation to develop its property would be subject only to the law in effect when the original application for preliminary subdivision approval was filed, which, in some cases, pre-dated the enactment of the Ordinance.

The court of appeals reversed and rendered in part and modified in part the trial court's judgment. 930 S.W.2d 678. The appellate court first determined that the trial court did not abuse its discretion in striking the Alliance's plea in intervention. 930 S.W.2d at 683. The court of appeals then concluded that the trial court erred in rendering judgment that the Ordinance was unreasonable, arbitrary, and inefficient pursuant to section 26.177(d) of the Texas Water Code because section 26.177(d) was unconstitutional under article II, section 1 of the Texas Constitution, the separation of powers provision. *Id.* at 685. The court of appeals further held that the Ordinance was not illegally enacted because (1) it did not require approval by the Texas Natural Resource Conservation Commission before it could become effective, (2) it was not subject to sections 212.002 and 212 .003 of the Local Government Code, and (3) it was a proper subject of the initiative and referendum process. *Id.* at 686–91. The appellate court accordingly reversed the trial court's judgment in part and rendered judgment that the Ordinance was a valid legislative act. The court of appeals also modified the trial court's judgment in part, holding that any permit required by Circle C would be considered only under the regulations and ordinances in effect when the original application for preliminary subdivision approval was filed, as long as the permit application was filed after September 1, 1987. *Id.* at 693–94.

Petitioners challenged the court of appeals' judgment by filing an application for writ of error with this Court. Petitioners allege that the court of appeals erred by holding (1) that section 26.177(d) of the Water

Code is unconstitutional as a violation of separation of powers, (2) that the Ordinance is not subject to sections 212.002 and 212.003 of the Local Government Code, (3) that the Ordinance is effective without the City first obtaining the Texas Natural Resource Conservation Commission's approval, (4) that the Ordinance was a proper subject of the initiative and referendum process, and (5) that only Circle C's permit applications filed after September 1, 1987 would be considered on the basis of the regulations and ordinances in effect at that time. The Alliance also filed its own application for writ of error, contending that the court of appeals erred in upholding the trial court's striking of its plea in intervention.

We first consider the constitutionality of section 26.177(d) of the Texas Water Code. Section 26.177(d) provides in pertinent part:

> Any person affected by any * * * ordinance * * * relating to water pollution control and abatement outside the corporate limits of such city adopted pursuant to this section or any other statutory authorization may appeal such action to the [Texas Natural Resource Conservation Commission] or district court * * *. The issue on appeal is whether the action or program is invalid, arbitrary, unreasonable, inefficient, or ineffective in its attempt to control water quality. The commission or district court may overturn or modify the action of the city.

Tex. Water Code § 26.177(d).

The trial court submitted several questions to the jury inquiring whether various provisions of the Ordinance were "unreasonable," "arbitrary," or "inefficient." Based on the jury's affirmative answers to these questions, the court then rendered judgment that the Ordinance was invalid under section 26.177(d).

The court of appeals, however, concluded that section 26.177(d) violates the separation of powers doctrine of the Texas Constitution because it requires a de novo review of a legislative act. The court of appeals reasoned that the trial court conducted a de novo review of the statute as evidenced by the court's charge asking the jury to determine, by a preponderance of the evidence, whether the jury thought the Ordinance was unreasonable, arbitrary, or inefficient. The court of appeals further ruled that section 26.177(d) authorized such an unconstitutional de novo review by permitting the reviewing court to "modify" a legislative act and to determine whether a legislative act was "inefficient" or "ineffective."

* * *

Petitioners urge that the Ordinance's invalidity under the *Comeau* standard is manifest. Petitioners rely upon evidence in the record that, before the passage of the Ordinance, the City already had the most stringent water quality standards in Texas. Moreover, a city engineer and the head of Austin's Environmental Services admitted during trial that no discernible trend of pollution existed in Barton Springs prior to the Ordinance's enactment. Accordingly, Petitioners maintain that the Ordinance was unnecessary and based on flawed data.

Petitioners also complain that it is impossible to comply with the Ordinance. The Ordinance requires that a development not increase annual pollution loadings of thirteen identified constituents. Petitioners contend that the rules implemented by the City of Austin to execute the Ordinance require runoff surface water from a development to have lower average concentrations of some of these constituents than was found in certain rain samples taken in Austin. In fact, Petitioners point out that the Ordinance requires that runoff surface water have less average nitrogen than contained in some name-brand bottled drinking water. Petitioners allege that the Ordinance's practical effect is therefore a preclusion of all development in the watershed areas.

Petitioners also attack the lack of variances in the Ordinance. For instance, even if a landowner could establish that no increase in pollution would result from constructing a greater percentage of impervious cover than allowed under the Ordinance, no variance is permitted.

Finally, Petitioners impugn the Ordinance's financial impact. The City's own expert economist concluded that the Ordinance would, over a fifteen-year period, decrease property values in the watershed areas in the range of $229 million to $379 million. The Petitioners introduced evidence at trial that some land lost ninety percent of its value because of the Ordinance.

The City presented evidence at trial that sharply contradicted the Petitioners' arguments. In response to the Petitioners' evidence regarding the effectiveness of the water control ordinances in place before the Save Our Springs Ordinance, the City provided testimony that the Ordinance was cheaper and easier to administer than earlier measures. Further, the evidence also established that eighty-six percent of all development applications received a variance under the water quality ordinance in effect immediately prior to the Save Our Springs Ordinance. This excessive grant of variances under the prior ordinance, according to the City, obviously undercut its effectiveness.

To rebut the Petitioners' claim that it is impossible to comply with the Ordinance because its rules require that runoff be purer than rain, the City elicited testimony from Stephen Stecher, the project director of the Barton Creek watershed study. He testified that soil and plants on the ground typically capture much of the nitrogen and some other constituents in urban rainfall before the constituents reach a creek or tributary. Accordingly, even assuming that the Petitioners' evidence regarding the rainfall samples was reliable, *see* ante at n. 3, the City contends that compliance with the technical rules is still possible because runoff is naturally less contaminated with certain pollutants than rainfall. In further support of its argument that it is not impossible to comply with the Ordinance, the City presented testimony from two developers that it is not only possible, but actually profitable to develop land in the watershed areas in compliance with the Ordinance. These developers both testified that they were anticipating sizable profits from their developments complying with the strictures of the Ordinance.

Finally, the City offered evidence that the impervious cover limitations in the Ordinance reduce polluting runoff and are a nationally-recognized method of protecting water quality. According to the City, the provisions restricting the pollutant constituents are only a small percentage of the 138 pollutants that the City is required to monitor under federal law. The restrictions on impervious cover and pollutant constituents, the City therefore urges, are clearly related to its goal of protecting the watershed from pollution in order to preserve water quality.

In light of the conflicting evidence presented at trial regarding the Ordinance, we cannot conclude that the Petitioners met their "extraordinary burden" of establishing that reasonable minds could not differ regarding whether the Ordinance was invalid, arbitrary, unreasonable, inefficient, or ineffective in its attempt to control water quality. While Petitioners presented evidence tending to establish that prior water control ordinances were sufficient such that the Ordinance was not necessary, the City's evidence regarding the excessive grant of variances under the prior measure precludes a determination that reasonable minds could not differ on the need for the Ordinance.

The trial testimony conflicts regarding a landowner's ability to comply with the Ordinance. The Petitioners offered scientific testimony attempting to establish that it was virtually impossible to comply with the Ordinance, but this testimony was refuted by the City. Moreover, the City also presented the testimony of two developers that, not only did the City approve their developments under the Ordinance, they actually anticipate profitable returns on their investments. The conflict in this evidence demonstrates that reasonable minds could indeed differ on whether compliance with the Ordinance is possible.

While the Petitioners decry the lack of a variance procedure in the Ordinance, the Ordinance does actually provide a limited variance to keep the Ordinance from running afoul of federal and state laws. Moreover, the Petitioners' complaint regarding the lack of a variance procedure ignores the evidence that the excessive grant of variances under prior water control measures had undercut their effectiveness.

We perceive that the real crux of the Petitioners' complaint is that the Ordinance unreasonably reduces property values and requires excessive expenditures in order to comply with its provisions. The Petitioners established that the Ordinance will result in at least a $225 million decrease in property values in regulated areas, and that the Ordinance has caused some parcels of land to lose ninety percent of their value. The City has not refuted this evidence.

However, in this case, the fact that the Ordinance severely impacts some property values does not make it invalid, arbitrary, unreasonable, inefficient, or ineffective in its attempt to control water quality. While the Ordinance's impervious cover limitations undoubtedly substantially affect the value of some property parcels, such limitations are a nationally-recognized method of preserving water quality. Further, it is indisputable that limiting pollutants in runoff water will aid in preserving water quality. We therefore conclude that the Ordinance's provisions are rationally related to its goal of protecting water quality.

Because we have concluded that the Ordinance is rationally related to the governmental interest in protecting water quality, the City has the right to significantly limit development in watershed areas in furtherance of this interest. *See Day–Brite Lighting, Inc. v. Missouri,* 342 U.S. 421, 424, 72 S.Ct. 405, 96 L.Ed. 469 (1952). * * *

The Petitioners next attack the court of appeals' conclusion that the Ordinance is not void under sections 212.002 and 212.003 of the Local Government Code. Local Government Code section 212.002 provides:

> After a public hearing on the matter, the governing body of a municipality may adopt rules governing plats and subdivisions of land within the municipality's jurisdiction to promote the health, safety, morals, or general welfare of the municipality and the safe, orderly, and healthful development of the municipality. Tex. Loc. Gov't Code § 212.002.

Local Government Code section 212.003 provides in pertinent part:

> (a) The governing body of a municipality by ordinance may extend to the extraterritorial jurisdiction of the municipality the application of municipal ordinances adopted under Section 212.002 and other municipal ordinances relating to access to public roads. However, unless otherwise authorized by state law, in its extraterritorial jurisdiction a municipality shall not regulate:
>
> (1) the use of any building or property for business, industrial, residential, or other purposes;
>
> (2) the bulk, height, or number of buildings constructed on a particular tract of land;
>
> (3) the size of a building that can be constructed on a particular tract of land, including without limitation any restriction on the ratio of building floor space to the land square footage; or
>
> (4) the number of residential units that can be built per acre of land.
>
> *Id.* § 212.003.

Petitioners argue that (1) sections 212.002 and 212.003 govern the Ordinance, (2) the Ordinance was enacted without a public hearing in violation of section 212.002, and (3) the Ordinance effectively violates the prohibitions in section 212.003 by regulating the use, bulk, height, number, or size of buildings. Petitioners accordingly advocate that the trial court correctly held that the Ordinance was void. The City responds that sections 212.002 and 212.003 do not apply because these sections are zoning statutes and the Ordinance is a water pollution control measure. We agree with the City.

By their express terms, sections 212.002 and 212.003 apply to ordinances that "govern plats and subdivisions of land." Further, the statutes' legislative history indicates that they govern a city's zoning authority, not a city's authority to apply water quality requirements. For instance, House Bill 3187, which amended section 212.003, "prohibits the application of zoning regulations in ETJ areas." COMMITTEE ON URBAN AFFAIRS, BILL ANALYSIS, Tex. H.B. 3187, 71st Leg., R.S. (1989). In fact, the Legislature made it clear that section 212.003 was not intended "to affect the ability of a municipality to apply water control requirements" in its extraterritorial jurisdiction. Conference Committee Report, Tex. H.B. No. 3187, 71st Leg., R.S. (1989). We therefore conclude that sections 212.002 and 212.003 apply only to zoning statutes, not water control measures such as the Ordinance.

Petitioners nevertheless assert that the Ordinance is, in effect, a zoning ordinance, not a water control ordinance. Petitioners argue that the Ordinance's impervious cover limitations effectively constitute a regulation on the use, bulk, height, number, and size of buildings in the City's extraterritorial jurisdiction in violation of section 212.003. Petitioners contend that we should consider the actual effect of the Ordinance, not its stated purpose, in determining whether the Ordinance must comply with these statutes.

However, we disagree with Petitioners' assertion that the Ordinance effectively constitutes a zoning regulation. The Ordinance's stated goal is to protect and preserve a "clean and safe drinking water supply" and "to prevent further degradation of the water quality in Barton Creek, Barton Springs, and the Barton Springs Edwards Aquifer." While the Ordinance clearly has effects on land use through its imposition of impervious cover limitations, these cover limitations are typical features in ordinances protecting water quality. Indeed, as discussed previously, such cover limitations are a nationally-recognized method of preserving water quality, and therefore we conclude that the cover limitations further the Ordinance's stated goal. On balance, the Ordinance is not a zoning regulation seeking to shape urban development, but rather is a measure designed to protect water quality. We accordingly hold that the requirements of sections 212.002 and 212.003 are not applicable to the Ordinance, and the Ordinance cannot be invalidated by these statutes.

* * *

For the foregoing reasons, we affirm the court of appeals' judgment holding that the Ordinance is a valid legislative act that need not be approved by the Texas Natural Resource Conservation Commission to become effective and enforceable. We dismiss Circle C's point of error regarding the court of appeals' modification of the trial court's judgment with regard to section 481.143 of the Government Code because Circle C did not obtain final relief prior to the repeal of section 481.143.

* * *

Notes

1. In the Moviematic case, supra, note that the Florida court held that the preservation of an adequate drinking water supply and the ecological system in a particular area are legitimate objectives of zoning laws.

2. Under the Clean Water Act, most local governments in urban areas have an obligation to enact laws that reduce pollutants contained in storm-water runoff. One way of accomplishing this objective is to limit the amount of impervious coverage allowed in new developments approved by local land use review boards. In Quick v. Austin, supra, note how the Austin aquifer protection ordinance uses impervious coverage limitations in the interest of aquifer protection. Consider the court's conclusion that this ordinance was not adopted under the city's delegated zoning authority. If the zoning authority were the source of its legislative authority, would impervious coverage limitations applicable to its extraterritorial jurisdiction have been within its authority to enact? Why?

3. Note how in defending its ordinance, the City of Austin referred to its legal obligations under federal environmental statutes. Did this argument work for the City in rebutting landowners' claims that the ordinance was unreasonable and arbitrary? Does this suggest a strategic link that can be forged between federal and municipal environmental laws?

CONNECTICUT RESOURCES RECOVERY AUTH. v. PLANNING & ZONING COMM'N

Supreme Court of Connecticut, 1993.
225 Conn. 731, 626 A.2d 705.

KATZ, ASSOCIATE JUSTICE.

* * *

The following relevant facts are undisputed. Since 1945, Meriden has owned a 138 acre tract of land in Wallingford. In 1958, Wallingford adopted zoning regulations that placed the tract in a rural district. At that time, a relatively small portion of the tract was being used for solid waste disposal. The largest use of the tract was for sewage lagoons to accommodate overflow from a sewage treatment plant located in Meriden. Other portions of the tract were being used for sand excavation, industrial waste disposal and sludge disposal. Much of the tract was vacant. The parties presented conflicting evidence as to whether one portion of the tract was used for stump and brush disposal or for a sawmill and lumber storage area. The parties agree that sewage treatment facilities and garbage dumps were not permitted uses under the 1958 Wallingford zoning regulations. These regulations provided that while nonconforming uses could be continued, they could not be changed or extended except in very limited circumstances. Wallingford Planning and Zoning Regs. § 11 (1958), "Non-Conforming Buildings and Uses."

By 1982, approximately sixty and one-half acres of the tract were being used for disposal of solid and bulky waste. In 1983, Wallingford adopted zoning regulations that established an aquifer protection district and specifically prohibited solid waste disposal in this district.[1] The district consists of the primary and secondary recharge areas of the Quinnipiac River Aquifer and the Muddy River Aquifer. Wallingford Zoning Regs. § 4.12.B (1985), "Aquifer Protection (APD) District." It includes the tract owned by Meriden. The aquifer protection regulations were codified in September, 1985, at which time they took effect.

In December, 1985, Meriden agreed to lease part of its tract to CRRA for use as a disposal site for ash residue, sludge, bulky waste and solid waste. On November 10, 1988, CRRA and Meriden applied to the commission to delete the regulation prohibiting solid waste disposal in an aquifer protection district. Following a public hearing on January 5, 1989, regarding the application, the commission voted to retain the regulation.

On January 29, 1989, the plaintiffs appealed the commission's decision to the Superior Court pursuant to General Statutes § 8–9. The court held a preliminary hearing on the issue of standing to determine whether CRRA and Meriden had been aggrieved by the commission's decision. The court was concerned that solid waste disposal might be a protected nonconforming use of the tract, in which case the plaintiffs could not be harmed by the regulation prohibiting solid waste disposal in an aquifer protection district. At the hearing, the plaintiffs filed a motion to continue the appeal until they could pursue with local zoning authorities the issue of whether solid waste disposal was a valid nonconforming use of the tract. * * * The court granted the motion.

On February 22, 1990, CRRA and Meriden requested a certificate of zoning compliance from Linda Bush, the Wallingford zoning enforcement officer. By a letter dated March 14, 1990, Bush informed CRRA and Meriden that she would not issue a certificate because use of the tract for solid waste disposal was a nonconforming use that had been unlawfully expanded. CRRA and Meriden appealed Bush's decision to the board. Following a May 21, 1990 public hearing, the board voted to sustain Bush's decision.

The plaintiffs appealed the board's decision to the Superior Court pursuant to General Statutes § 8–8(b). The court granted a motion made by CRRA and Meriden to consolidate this appeal with the first appeal and held a hearing on both appeals on June 11, 1991. In a lengthy memorandum of decision dated January 8, 1992, the trial court rendered judgment for CRRA and Meriden in each appeal. The defendants filed petitions for certification to appeal to the Appellate Court. The Appellate Court granted the petitions, and we transferred the appeals to this court pursuant to Practice Book § 4023 and General Statutes § 51–199(c).

* * *

1. Section 4.12.A of the Wallingford zoning regulations provides: "A major source of Wallingford's drinking water is the Quinnipiac River Aquifer. Protection of this resource is vital to ensure an adequate supply of safe drinking water. This protection can best be achieved by regulations that control pollution within the aquifer recharge area." Section 4.12.F lists nonpermitted uses, including solid waste disposal. Wallingford Zoning Regs. § 4.12.B (1985), "Aquifer Protection (APD) District."

II

We next consider the first case, *Connecticut Resources Recovery Authority v. Planning & Zoning Commission* (Docket No. 14584). The commission claims that the trial court incorrectly determined that: (1) the regulation prohibiting solid waste disposal over an aquifer is an invalid exercise of the town's police power; (2) the regulation is inconsistent with the plan of development; (3) the regulation is preempted by state solid waste and water quality statutes; and (4) the commission's decision was not supported by the record. We consider these arguments in turn.

A

The trial court held that the blanket prohibition of solid waste disposal in an aquifer protection zone is an invalid exercise of the police power. The plaintiffs argue that General Statutes § 8–2 empowers the commission only to regulate land use, not to prohibit certain uses, and that the prohibition of solid waste disposal over an aquifer lacks a reasonable relation to the public health, safety and welfare. We disagree.

To challenge an ordinance successfully, a party must establish the invalidity of the ordinance beyond a reasonable doubt. *Lizotte v. Conservation Commission*, 216 Conn. 320, 337, 579 A.2d 1044 (1990). Section 8–2 authorizes local authorities to regulate land use through zoning, and specifically requires them to do so "with reasonable consideration for the protection of existing and potential public surface and ground drinking water supplies." We have said that "when a statute authorizes a municipality to regulate a certain activity, a prohibition of that activity will be valid if it is rationally related to the protection of the community's public health, safety and general welfare." *Beacon Falls v. Posick*, 212 Conn. 570, 583, 563 A.2d 285 (1989); *see also Lizotte v. Conservation Commission, supra*, 216 Conn. at 336, 579 A.2d 1044.

In *Lizotte v. Conservation Commission, supra*, at 322–23, 579 A.2d 1044, the plaintiffs challenged the validity of a local regulation prohibiting the location of a septic system within 150 feet of an inland wetland or watercourse. They contended that the regulation was invalid because the enabling statute authorized only "necessary" regulations and the blanket prohibition was not necessary. *Id.*, at 336, 579 A.2d 1044. We held that prohibitions of activities are within the police power of a municipality if they are rationally related to the protection of the public health, safety and welfare, and that a municipality may rationally conclude that prohibition of a risky activity is more appropriate than case-by-case analysis. *Id.*, at 334, 337, 579 A.2d 1044. In *Beacon Falls v. Posick, supra*, 212 Conn. at 586, 563 A.2d 285 we concluded that a townwide ban of garbage dumps was a valid exercise of the police power.

The record before the trial court indicated that, at the time it adopted the solid waste prohibition, the commission was aware that the Meriden owned tract was a suspected source of contamination of Wallingford's water supply. A document issued by a regional planning authority in 1980 specifically recommended that solid waste disposal operations over the aquifer should be suspended.

We have long held that "[a]n agency which has the authority to enact regulations is vested with a large measure of discretion, and the burden of showing that the agency has acted improperly rests upon the one who asserts it." *Aaron v. Conservation Commission*, 183 Conn. 532, 537, 441 A.2d 30 (1981); *see also Lizotte v. Conservation Commission, supra*, 216 Conn. at 337, 579 A.2d 1044. Local commissions "are closest to the circumstances and conditions which create the problem and shape the solution * * *. [I]n determining claims of error in such matters, [c]ourts must be scrupulous not to hamper the legitimate activities of civic administrative boards by indulging in a microscopic search for technical infirmities in their action." (Citations omitted; internal quotation marks omitted.) *Frito-Lay, Inc. v. Planning & Zoning Commission*, 206 Conn. 554, 573, 538 A.2d 1039 (1988). We conclude that Wallingford's prohibition of solid waste disposal over an aquifer is a valid exercise of its police power that is rationally related both to protection of the groundwater and to the public health, safety and welfare. Accordingly, we reverse the trial court's holding to the contrary.

B

The trial court also held that the solid waste ordinance was invalid because it did not comply with Wallingford's plan of development. The trial court noted that the town planning document recommends that an aquifer protection district should be created and "[r]estricted to uses which do not present undue risk of groundwater contamination and prohibiting or controlling those which do, such as, the use, storage, treatment or disposal of hazardous materials including storage of road salts or de-icing compounds* * *." Town of Wallingford Proposed Plan of Development Update, Phase 1 and 2—Summary Report, July, 1983, p. 14. The trial court held that because this plan did not specifically list solid waste disposal as an unduly risky activity, and there was no evidence that the commission considered the Meriden tract a threat to the groundwater at the time it adopted the plan of development, there was nothing in the record to indicate that the prohibition complied with the town plan of development.

We reject the trial court's reasoning and the plaintiffs' concomitant claim on appeal that because the plan provision quoted above specifically lists storage of "road salts" and "de-icing compounds" as unduly hazardous uses, the prohibition of solid waste disposal is necessarily inconsistent with this plan. As the trial court noted, a "plan of development is properly called a master plan * * *. The master plan, in its designation of appropriate uses for various areas in a town, is merely advisory." (Citation omitted.) *Dooley v. Town Plan & Zoning Commission*, 154 Conn. 470, 473, 226 A.2d 509 (1967).

General Statutes § 8–2 directs local authorities to regulate land use through zoning "with reasonable consideration for the protection of existing and potential public surface and ground drinking water supplies." It is clear from the record before the trial court that the Wallingford zoning authorities were aware that the Meriden owned tract was a threat to the groundwater and public health at the time they adopted the solid waste prohibition. We conclude that the solid waste prohibition was consistent both with the plan of development and with the comprehensive plan, which is to be found in the scheme of the zoning regulations themselves. *See Protect Hamden/North Haven from Excessive Traffic & Pollution, Inc. v. Planning & Zoning Commission, supra*, 220 Conn. at 551, 600 A.2d 757.

C

The trial court also held that the regulation banning solid waste disposal over an aquifer is preempted by certain state solid waste and water protection statutes. We disagree.

General Statutes § 22a–208a(b), part of the Solid Waste Management Act, provides that "nothing in this chapter or chapter 446e shall be construed to limit the right of any local governing body to regulate, through zoning, land usage for solid waste disposal." In *Beacon Falls v. Posick, supra*, 212 Conn. at 577–79, 563 A.2d 285, we held that this language demonstrated that the legislature did not intend to preempt local zoning regulation of solid waste disposal.

The plaintiffs attempt to distinguish *Beacon Falls v. Posick, supra*, on the grounds that that case involved a private dump whereas this case involves CRRA, a public instrumentality. Their argument is unpersuasive, however, because § 22a–208a(b) references chapter 446e, which is the section of the General Statutes creating CRRA. Further, in Beacon Falls v. Posick, supra, we specifically held "that the legislature intended only to preempt local zoning authority to the extent that it conflicted with the operation of a CRRA facility on property owned by the CRRA prior to May 11, 1984 * * *." *Id.*, at 579, 563 A.2d 285. The lease agreement between CRRA and Meriden was not even formed until late 1985. The trial court therefore incorrectly concluded that the solid waste prohibition was preempted.

D

Finally, we consider the trial court's conclusion that the commission's decision not to delete the solid waste prohibition was not reasonably supported by the record. The commission furnished two reasons for its refusal to delete the solid waste prohibition: (1) compliance with the town plan of development; and (2) protection of the drinking water supply. The commission claims that the trial court, in rejecting both of these reasons, impermissibly weighed the evidence and substituted its judgment for that of the commission. We agree.

We have often said that "[t]he trial court may not substitute its judgment for the wide and liberal discretion vested in the local authority when acting within its prescribed legislative powers." (Internal quotation marks omitted.) *Frito-Lay, Inc. v. Planning & Zoning Commission, supra*, 206 Conn. at 572–73, 538 A.2d 1039; *see also Calandro v. Zoning Commission*, 176 Conn. 439, 442, 408 A.2d 229 (1979). "[I]t is not the function of the court to retry the case. Conclusions reached by the commission must be upheld by the trial court if they are reasonably supported by the record. The credibility of the witnesses and the determination of issues of fact are matters solely within the province of the agency." (Internal quotation marks omitted.) *Protect Hamden/North Haven from Excessive Traffic & Pollution, Inc. v. Planning & Zoning Commission, supra,* 220 Conn. at 542–43, 600 A.2d 757; *Calandro v. Zoning Commission, supra*, 176 Conn. at 440, 408 A.2d 229. "The commission ha[s] the task of weighing th[e] evidence and reaching a conclusion on the merits of the plaintiff's application." *Calandro v. Zoning Commission, supra,* at 441, 408 A.2d 229. "[T]he court may grant relief on appeal only where the local authority has acted illegally or arbitrarily or has abused its discretion." (Internal quotation marks omitted.) *Frito-Lay, Inc. v. Planning & Zoning Commission, supra,* 206 Conn. at 573, 538 A.2d 1039. "[T]he action of the commission should be sustained if even one of the stated reasons is sufficient to support it." *Id.*, at 576, 538 A.2d 1039.

The commission had before it evidence that the Meriden solid waste disposal site was a suspected source of contamination of Wallingford's water supply. Documents from the state department of environmental protection, expert consultants, and a regional planning authority, and testimony from a member of the legislature's environment committee, all recommended that solid waste disposal operations over the aquifer be suspended. There was also testimony that expansion of the solid waste operations might cause further contamination.

We have said that "a local legislative body may consider the effects that are likely to flow from proposed amendments to its zoning regulations, and may decide, within the proper statutory parameters, that it would be unwise policy for the town to countenance those effects." *Protect Hamden/North Haven from Excessive Traffic & Pollution, Inc. v. Planning & Zoning Commission, supra*, 220 Conn. at 548, 600 A.2d 757. The plaintiffs conceded at oral argument that, at most, the evidence they presented at the hearing showed that there was a possibility that a solid waste disposal site could be operated safely over an aquifer. The trial court ruled that because there was a possibility of compatibility between these two uses, it was irrational for the commission to refuse to delete the blanket prohibition. We disagree.

In *Lizotte v. Conservation Commission, supra,* we upheld a blanket prohibition of septic systems within 150 feet of a wetland. We stated: "The commission could reasonably have concluded that, regardless of whether a specific prohibited activity may or may not adversely affect the town's wetlands, the risk of pollution outweighed in all instances the benefits to be gained by allowing case-by-case analysis of each application for a regulated use." *Id.*, at 337, 579 A.2d 1044. In this case, the commission could reasonably have concluded that although there was a possibility that a landfill could be operated safely in the aquifer protection district, the risk to the town's water supply outweighed any possible benefits.

In sum, we conclude that the local zoning authorities acted properly in refusing to delete the solid waste prohibition and in refusing to issue a certificate of zoning compliance.

The judgments are reversed and the cases are remanded with direction to render judgments dismissing the plaintiffs' appeals.

Notes

1. In the Connecticut Resources Recovery case, did the court hold that the state zoning enabling act delegated authority to cities and towns to prohibit solid waste facilities over groundwater aquifer areas? What language is contained in the Connecticut zoning enabling act that is missing in the relevant delegating statute in Texas? How broadly does the Connecticut court interpret the authority granted to local governments under the relevant state enabling act? Can you pinpoint the precise language the court relies on to sustain the local law and can you understand the principles of statutory interpretation that the court followed?

2. The town of North Kingston, Rhode Island, enacted an ordinance whose purpose was to protect the "chemical, physical and biological integrity" of the groundwater from pollutants in order "to ensure the availability of safe and potable drinking water for present and future needs." North Kingston Revised Ord. § 8–120 (1992). Maximum discharge levels of specified inorganic, organic, radioactive, and biologic pollutants are prescribed in the town's regulations. Discharges exceeding these levels are prohibited in areas designated as groundwater reservoir and recharge areas.

(2) Stormwater Management

Stormwater management is the process of controlling and cleansing the excess stormwater runoff so it does not harm natural resources or human health. As more land is covered with impervious surfaces, such as roads, parking lots, and buildings, there is less surface area available for stormwater to infiltrate. Where storm basins do not exist or are not adequate, stormwater finds its way to the nearest water body. Impervious surfaces not only increase the volume and velocity of runoff, but also prevent the natural processing of nutrients, sediments, and other contaminants. Regulation of stormwater runoff through stormwater management also controls floods, reduces erosion and sedimentation, and aids ground water replenishment.

Stormwater runoff control is crucial to the success of the federal Clean Water Act (CWA), 33 U.S.C. §§ 1251–1387(2000). It is one of the most serious causes of water pollution in the United States, exceeding in many locales the contamination caused by sewage and industrial facility discharges. Stormwater runoff carries algae-promoting nutrients, floatable trash, used motor oil, suspended metals, sediments, raw sewage, pesticides, and other toxic contaminants. They flow with stormwater runoff from their source to streams, rivers, lakes, estuaries, and oceans.

The United States Environmental Protection Agency (EPA), pursuant to its authority under the Clean Water Act, promulgated regulations establishing its Stormwater Management Program. EPA set forth a two-phase program. Phase I began regulating medium and large operators of municipal separate storm sewer systems (MS4s) in 1990. Phase I regulations require large cities and municipalities to implement a stormwater management program as a means to control polluted discharges from their MS4s. Phase II of the program, which was established in 1999, extends this coverage to small municipalities that operate MS4s.

Phase II regulates small MS4s as well as small construction activities; *i.e.*, those activities disturbing between one and five acres of land. Pursuant to these rules, municipal operators of regulated MS4s (those operating within a designated urbanized area) are required to obtain either an individual or a general National Pollutant Discharge Elimination System (NPDES) permit. There are three requirements in Phase II of the Stormwater Program: (1) reduce pollution to the maximum extent possible (MEP); (2) protect water quality; and (3) comply with the applicable water quality requirements of the Clean Water Act.

Best management practices are utilized to achieve the goal of reducing pollutants in stormwater. To ensure that operators meet the MEP standard, EPA sets forth six minimum control measures that must be included in a management plan, including public education and participation programs, pollution prevention programs, programs to detect and eliminate illicit discharges, and programs to address stormwater runoff from construction sites and post-construction land uses.

The effect on local land use autonomy is evident in the fine print of the regulations. Local governments that operate stormwater systems are required to adopt erosion and sediment control laws, establish site plan review procedures for projects that will impact water quality, inspect construction activities, and adopt enforcement measures. Post-construction runoff controls are also required for development and redevelopment projects. Redevelopment is defined to include any change in the footprint of existing buildings that disturbs more than one acre of land. EPA has specifically targeted post-construction activities because areas undergoing new development or redevelopment have been shown to significantly increase pollution in receiving water bodies. Developing and implementing programs that minimize pollution in stormwater discharges is an effective approach to stormwater quality management.

Non-structural best management practices noted in the federal regulations include comprehensive planning and zoning ordinances that guide growth away from sensitive areas and that restrict industrial and other intense land uses that compromise water quality. Zoning measures targeted by the regulations include the requirement of buffer strips, designation of riparian preservation zones, and maximization of open space.

This extensive effort by the federal government to influence local land use regulation raises a number of political and legal issues, not the least of which is whether it violates the sovereign right of state governments to control land use without federal interference.

The Ninth Circuit Court of Appeals upheld federal regulations mandating municipalities to obtain Clean Water Act permits for storm sewers. The case below describes the legislative and political tension between local, state, and federal regulations.

ENVIRONMENTAL DEFENSE CENTER, INC. v. UNITED STATES ENVIRONMENTAL PROTECTION AGENCY

United States Court Of Appeals, Ninth Circuit, 2003.
319 F.3d 398.

BROWNING, JAMES. R., CIRCUIT JUDGE.

Petitioners challenge a rule issued by the United States Environmental Protection Agency pursuant to the Clean Water Act, 33 U.S.C. §§ 1251–1387, to control pollutants introduced into the nation's waters by storm sewers.

Storm sewers drain rainwater and melted snow from developed areas into water bodies that can handle the excess flow. Draining stormwater picks up a variety of contaminants as it filters through soil and over pavement on its way to sewers. Sewers are also used on occasion as an easy (if illicit) means for the direct discharge of unwanted contaminants. Since storm sewer systems generally channel collected runoff into federally protected water bodies, they are subject to the controls of the Clean Water Act. In October of 1999, after thirteen years in process, the Environmental Protection Agency ("EPA") promulgated a final administrative rule (the "Phase II Rule" or "the Rule") under § 402(p) of the Clean Water Act, 33 U.S.C. § 1342(p), mandating that discharges from small municipal separate storm sewer systems and from construction sites between one and five acres in size be subject to the permitting requirements of the National Pollutant Discharge Elimination System ("NPDES"), 33 U.S.C. §§ 1311(a), 1342. EPA preserved authority to regulate other harmful stormwater discharges in the future.

In the three cases consolidated here, petitioners and intervenors challenge the Phase II Rule on twenty-two constitutional, statutory, and procedural grounds. We remand three aspects of the Rule concerning the issuance of notices of intent under the Rule's general permitting scheme. We affirm the Rule against all other challenges.

* * *

The Municipal Petitioners' primary contention is that the Phase II Rule compels small MS4s to regulate citizens as a condition of receiving a permit to operate, and that EPA lacks both statutory and constitutional authority to impose such a requirement. * * *

The Municipal Petitioners contend that the Phase II Rule on its face compels operators of small MS4s to regulate third parties in contravention of the Tenth Amendment. We note that a facial challenge must show that there are no circumstances under which the challenged provisions would be constitutional. *Legal Aid Soc'y v. Legal Servs. Corp.*, 145 F.3d 1017, 1023–24 (9th Cir.1998). We conclude that the Rule does not violate the Tenth Amendment, because it directs no unconstitutional coercion.

The Phase II Rule requires any operator of a small MS4 applying for an individual permit or submitting a notice of intent for coverage under a general permit to specify plans for compliance with a series of six minimum control measures designed to protect water quality. 40 C.F.R. § 122.34. These "Minimum Measures" require an applicant to propose programs for: (1) conducting public education and outreach on stormwater impacts, *id.* at § 122.34(b)(1); (2) engaging public participation in the development of stormwater management programs, *id.* at § 122.34(b)(2); (3) detecting and eliminating illicit discharges to the MS4, *id.* at § 122.34(b)(3); (4) reducing pollution to the MS4 from construction activities disturbing one acre or more, *id.* at § 122.34(b)(4); (5) minimizing water quality impacts from development and redevelopment activities that disturb one acre or more, *id.* at § 122.34(b)(5); and (6) preventing or reducing pollutant runoff from municipal activities, *id.* at § 122.34(b)(6).

The Municipal Petitioners contend that the measures regulating illicit discharges, small construction sites, and development activities interfere excessively with local government functions and unconstitutionally compel small MS4 operators to regulate third parties, i.e. upstream dischargers. The Illicit Discharge Detection and Elimination measure requires that a permit seeker prohibit non-stormwater discharges to the MS4 and implement appropriate enforcement procedures. 40 C.F.R. § 122.34(b)(3)(ii)(B). The Construction Site Stormwater Runoff Control measure requires a permit seeker to implement and enforce a program to reduce stormwater pollutants from small construction sites. *Id.* at §§ 122.34(b)(4)(i)–(ii). It mandates erosion and sedimentation controls, site plan reviews that take account of water quality impacts, site inspections, and the consideration of public comment, and requires that construction site operators implement erosion, sedimentation, and waste management best management practices. *Id.* The Post–Construction/New Development measure requires permit seekers to address post-construction runoff from new development and redevelopment projects disturbing one acre or more. *Id.* at § 122.34(b)(5)(ii)(B). Noting that most MS4s are operated by municipal governments, and that "[t]he drainage of a city in the interest of the public health and welfare is one of the most important purposes for which the police power can be exercised," *New Orleans Gaslight Co. v. Drainage Comm'n*, 197 U.S. 453, 460, 25 S.Ct. 471, 49 L.Ed. 831 (1905), the Municipal Petitioners argue that requiring Phase II permit applicants to enact "ordinances or other regulatory measures" amounts to federal commandeering in contravention of the Tenth Amendment. *See New York v. United States*, 505 U.S. 144, 188, 112 S.Ct. 2408, 120 L.Ed.2d 120 (1992).

EPA counters that nothing in the Phase II Rule violates the Tenth Amendment, because it extends to small MS4s a generally applicable regulatory scheme that does not excessively interfere with municipal functions. It argues that the Phase II Rule no more trespasses on state sovereignty than did the Driver's Privacy Protection Act ("DPPA") unanimously upheld in *Reno v. Condon*, 528 U.S. 141, 151, 120 S.Ct. 666, 145 L.Ed.2d 587 (2000), as a rule of general applicability that "incidentally" applied to States—even though the universe of entities to which the DPPA could in fact apply included *only* States. 528 U.S. at 151, 120 S.Ct. 666 (declining to address whether general applicability is a constitutional requirement "because the DPPA is generally applicable"). EPA contends that the federal government need not avoid all requirements that cause States and localities to engage their legislative or executive processes, but only those that would "excessively interfere" with the functioning of those governments. *Printz v. United States*, 521 U.S. 898, 932, 117 S.Ct. 2365, 138 L.Ed.2d 914 (1997). EPA argues that the federal government's great interest in preventing water pollution justifies the "minimal interference" with municipal functions that the Minimum Measures might occasion, and asserts that the Measures by definition could not interfere "excessively" with state or local governments, since MS4s are only required to reduce pollutants to the "maximum extent practicable." 40 C.F.R. § 122.34(a).

The Tenth Amendment provides that "all is retained [by the States] which has not been surrendered [to the federal government]." *New York v. United States*, 505 U.S. at 156, 112 S.Ct. 2408 (internal quotations omitted). If a power is delegated to Congress by the Constitution, the Tenth Amendment expressly disclaims any reservation of that power to the States, and Congress's exercise of that power does not intrude impermissibly on state sovereignty. *Id.*; *Garcia v. San Antonio Metro. Transit Auth.*, 469 U.S. 528, 549, 105 S.Ct. 1005, 83 L.Ed.2d 1016 (1985). But the Tenth Amendment also signals constitutional protection for our system of dual sovereignty, confirming "that the power of the Federal Government is subject to limits that may, in a given instance, reserve power to the States." *New York v. United States*, 505 U.S. at 157, 112 S.Ct. 2408. Among the most important limits implied by the Tenth Amendment are the circumstances under which the federal government may not conscript state and local governments to regulate on its behalf—as petitioners contend EPA has inappropriately done in the Phase II Rule.

* * *

The Tenth Amendment thus requires that we evaluate whether the Phase II Rule coerces state action (leaving a State no choice but to comply with a federal mandate), whether the mandated action forces the State to regulate third parties (as opposed to regulating state activities legitimately subject to generally applicable federal law), and, if the federal law is generally applicable, whether it nevertheless excessively interferes with the functioning of state government.

In conducting this inquiry, however, we are sensitive to the fact that solving pressing environmental problems may require the formation of partnerships between federal and state authorities that the Supreme Court has referred to as "program[s] of cooperative federalism." *Hodel*, 452 U.S. at 289, 101 S.Ct. 2352 ("[T]he Surface Mining Act establishes a program of cooperative federalism that allows the States, within limits established by federal minimum standards, to enact and administer their own regulatory programs, structured to meet their own particular needs * * * "). Although local governments have traditionally enjoyed broad authority over drainage activities, *New Orleans Gaslight Co.*, 197 U.S. at 460, 25 S.Ct. 471, they do not enjoy exclusive sovereign authority over actions that contribute pollutants to the nation's waters.

We conclude that even if the Individual and General Permit options of the Phase II Rule require operators of small MS4s to regulate third parties, the Phase II Rule entails no unconstitutional coercion because operators of small MS4s have two alternatives to the Individual and General Permit options: the option of not discharging and the Alternative Permit option.

* * *

Notes

1. In Environmental Defense Center, the municipal petitioners argued vehemently that the Phase II regulations give them no choice but to regulate construction and post-construction activity. The majority stated that municipalities have alternative means for disposing of collected stormwater, such as recycling it or constructing wetland collectors, and can chose not to accept stormwater discharges running off construction sites. The majority concludes that the requirements of the Phase II regulations involve "minimal interference" with municipal functions. It further calls the stormwater regulatory regime "cooperative federalism" requiring the formation of a partnership between the federal and state authorities. In the dissent, Circuit Judge Tallman vigorously disagreed stating: "The law of gravity is inflexible; the stormwater will run downhill through the municipalities into federal waters whether the sewer system is open or blocked. No matter how much we want to uphold EPA's regulatory scheme, we cannot change the law of gravity." Which side of this debate seems correct to you? Are recycling and wetlands construction adequate, cost-effective solutions to controlling the ravaging runoff of a storm? Can municipalities realistically stop construction site and post-construction runoff from entering their municipal stormwater systems? Is there a difference between "requiring" a partnership and "coercing" state action?

2. Colorado law permits local governments to adopt regulations limiting development in stormwater and floodwater runoff channels. "To the end that adequate safety may be secured, the county planning commission may include in said zoning plan provisions establishing, regulating, and limiting such uses on or along any storm or floodwater runoff channel or basin * * *." Colo. Rev. Stat. § 30–28–111 (1986).

3. The city of Fitchburg, Massachusetts, adopted a stormwater management and erosion control ordinance to prevent and diminish property damage and flooding. *See* Fitchburg, Mass. Code § 154–1 (1999). The ordinance was adopted to prevent or diminish "property damage, flooding, the contamination of drinking water supplies, the loss of recreational opportunities, adverse impacts on fisheries and wildlife, the loss of wetlands, and * * * the loss of valuable agricultural soils."

4. Minneapolis, Minnesota, enacted its stormwater management ordinance "to minimize negative impacts on stormwater runoff rates, volumes, and quality on Minneapolis lakes, streams, wetlands, and the Mississippi River by guiding future significant development and redevelopment activity, and by assuring long-term effectiveness of existing and future stormwater management constructed activities." Minneapolis 99–Or–156, § 1 (1999). The ordinance requires all land-disturbing projects to follow an approved Stormwater Management Plan.

(3) Floodplains

Development activities can destroy floodplains, decrease flood storage, increase runoff, and decrease water quality. Local floodplain regulations can limit the extension of buildings and infrastructure into the flood areas, require that such buildings are built at certain elevations, prevent the obstruction of stream channels, and prohibit the construction of chemical or other hazardous materials storage facilities. The National Flood Insurance Program exerted an early and strong influence on the initiation of local environmental legislation. It required localities to adopt and enforce floodplain management programs as a prerequisite to the eligibility of local property owners for flood disaster insurance and payments.

Irvine, California adopted a Floodplain District Ordinance for the purpose of promoting the public health, safety, and general welfare, and to minimize public and private losses due to flood conditions in specific areas. Irvine, Ca. Zoning Ord. § 5–2–2 (2002). Its floodplain ordinance notes that the flood hazard areas of the city are subject to periodic water inundation, which results in loss of life and property, health and safety hazards, and extraordinary public expenditures. The Flood Hazard Area Ordinance adopted by the city of Detroit is aimed at maintaining stable development patterns that are not subject to the "blighting influence of flood damage." Detroit, Mi. Zoning Ord. § 49.0102(D) (2001). The Floodplain Protection District Ordinance of the town of Penfield, New York, contains extensive provisions to protect the environment and the public from the dangers of flooding. Penfield, NY Zoning Ord. §§ 3–14(A), (F)(1–4) (1987).

APRIL v. CITY OF BROKEN ARROW

Supreme Court of Oklahoma, 1989.
775 P.2d 1347.

DOOLIN, JUSTICE.

The question presented is whether the adoption of two municipal land-use ordinances on their face substantially interfered with landowner's use and enjoyment of his property so as to constitute a permanent "taking" of property without just compensation in violation of the United States and Oklahoma Constitutions. Put another way, the question is, does a taking result if the limitations on the use of owner's property do "not substantially advance legitimate state interests, or denies an owner economical, viable use of his land, [citations omitted]."

I.

Appellee Paul April, M.D., ("Owner"), purchased 40 acres of undeveloped agricultural land, for investment purposes, in the City of Broken Arrow, Tulsa County, Oklahoma ("City"). City is a suburban residential area south of the city of Tulsa. Owner's real property, used as pasture land, is located within an existing 100–year flood plain of Haikey Creek and its tributaries ("Haikey"). Haikey is a "natural water drainage system" in and around City.

Property adjacent to Haikey, including Owner's land which is transversed by three pre-existing wet-weather creeks converging in the flood plain, is naturally subject to flooding following periods of heavy rainfall. Haikey drains over "one square mile" of Owner's property, because the elevation of Owner's property is lower than the elevation of the periodic hundred year flood. City has not made any physical intrusions or entered upon Owner's property. Nor has City diverted any additional water into Haikey's drainage system, or erected any facilities upstream from Owner's property, or granted any building permits altering the natural water flow throughout the topography of the 100–year flood plain.

Owner, intending to sell his land to a developer, requested and was granted R–2 residential single family zoning for his property in 1975, after his previous request for R–6 high density multifamily apartment zoning was denied by City. When R–2 zoning was approved, allowing three family dwellings per acre (theoretically 120 homes), City's planning commission and planning commission staff informed Owner:

> the majority of (your) property is within the 100–year frequency flood and is also within the adopted Flood Hazard Area * * *, (therefore) the developer will be required to build all house pads at least one foot above the 100–year frequency flood elevation * * *.

This was City's only regulatory requirement for development of land within the flood plain. In October 1977, Owner requested his property be rezoned from 40 acres of R–2, residential single family to 20 acres of R–4, duplex and 20 acres of R–5, apartments. Owner's request was denied by City's planning commission and staff.

In January 1978, Owner made another application to the City's planning commission, requesting his property be re-zoned from R–2 single family to R–4, Duplex. City's planning commission and staff again denied Owner's petition for re-zoning, and Owner, for the first time, appealed to the City Council. "[I]n anticipation of the 'floodplain' ordinance being adopted * * *, (Owner) sought relief in the form of a 'waiver' or variance from the * * * City Council on March 13, 1978 which was, * * *, denied. * * *."

On March 20, 1978, the city council enacted "The Flood Damage Protection Ordinance, No. 735", regulating the development of land in Haikey's flood plain, and "The Earth Change Resolution Ordinance No. 736", controlling all excavations and earth modifications throughout the municipality (both hereinafter, "Land–Use Ordinances"). Both land-use ordinances became effective immediately. On May 1, 1978, the city council denied Owner's appeal for rezoning.

Owner initiated the present inverse condemnation suit in December of 1978, alleging, inter alia, City's "overt actions;" that is, adoption of its land-use ordinances, limiting his property to "Flood Tolerant Land Uses," and city's approval of building permits to other developers in the flood plain has resulted in the appropriation of Owner's property for "general public use" as "a detention pond as part of a municipal stormwater drainage system." Owner further alleges City's action prohibits construction on Owner's land by restricting its use to "public or semi-public purposes," that it effectively limits Owner's use of his land as a "horse pasture," and finally that it denies Owner beneficial use of his property by destroying his reasonable "investment-backed expectations." After various motions and pleadings, Owner dismissed three other causes of action.

At trial, Owner asserted his "property lies in the path of (City's) future plans for a public park, Haikey Creek detention reservoir, levee pump station and channel improvements." Owner argued City's land-use ordinance "goes too far," because his property is "economically worthless, as evidenced by the Report of Commissioners," appointed by the trial court. The commissioners' report found the value of Owner's property "taken and damaged," resulting from City's enactment of the land-use ordinances, amounted to $240,000.00.

Before and during trial, City insistently argued two propositions to support its contention that there was no basis in either fact or law for the trial court to determine the constitutionality of the ordinances as applied to Owner's property. One, City's mere enactment of its ordinance regulating the general use of land within the flood plain does not, as a matter of law, constitute substantial interference with nor amount to an overt action exercising dominion and control over Owner's property, because Owner's property floods as a result of a natural phenomenon beyond City's exercise of its police power. Two, Owner has never applied for or been denied a building permit, or a variance under the land-use ordinances, thus, Owner has an adequate remedy at law to determine the beneficial use of his property.

City urged dismissal of Owner's action because the trial court lacked a justiciable issue. However, the jury rendered a verdict in favor of Owner and against City for $240,000.00. Thereafter, the trial court awarded attorney fees, appraisers fees, city engineering-planning fees, and trial cost against City pursuant to 27 O.S.1981 § 12. Owner retains possession of the land in question.

II.

In resolving this appeal we are confronted, as we were in *Mattoon v. City of Norman*, with the following contentions: One, whether a municipality's adoption of a flood plain ordinance constitutes a taking of property without just compensation for which a landowner may seek damages under an action in inverse condemnation. Two, whether the doctrine requiring exhaustion of administrative remedies is applicable to preclude judicial review of the action.

City and its amici argue that opinion does not control the instant case, because *Mattoon* is significantly distinguishable. Owner argues *Mattoon* provides the applicable rule to govern the results of this appeal. Therefore, we deem it important to reiterate, and go further into the statement of our opinion and reasons for our *Mattoon* decision, because due to the procedural posture of that appeal, we found ourselves unable to address the merits of the "taking" question.

In *Mattoon*, city enacted a flood plain ordinance, reserving landowner's (and approximately 500 other similarly situated landowners') property for flood drainage purposes. Landowner filed a class action for inverse condemnation, alleging city adopted its flood plain ordinance unreasonably, neglected and refused to properly maintain its drainage system, and had diverted surface waters into tributaries which crossed and flooded landowner's property. The trial court sustained city's demurrer to landowner's petition by merely finding the ordinance was a valid exercise of city's police power. * * *

We recognized "a valid enactment of a flood plain ordinance is not per se a taking," because "acts done in the proper exercise of the police power which merely impair the use (or value) of property do not constitute a 'taking.' " We held "the test of whether there can be a recovery in inverse condemnation is whether there is a sufficient interference with the landowner's use and enjoyment to constitute a taking." More importantly, we acknowledged governmental land-use regulations may amount to an actual or de facto taking—"(i)f there is an overt act by the governmental agency resulting in an assertion of dominion and control over property." (Emphasis added.)

Two components were implicit in the taking claim advanced by landowner's petition in *Mattoon*. First, landowner had alleged city's unreasonable adoption of its flood plain ordinance had "taken" his property, that is, the ordinance "goes too far," and any proffered compensation was not "just." Thus, landowner's factual contentions adequately alleged a "regulatory taking" claim, by contending city's ordinance was an extreme regulation destroying a major portion of landowner's property value. Second, landowner alleged a "physical taking" of property, that is, city also overtly acted to flood landowner's property by unreasonably diverting surface water, and improperly maintaining its drainage channels.

Accordingly, we reversed and remanded the trial court's judgment with directions to reinstate landowner's action, because first, merely finding an ordinance was validly enacted within city's lawful exercise of its police power, without considering the general principles of due process, does not "absolutely preclude compensation for property taken or damaged by such exercise." Second, landowner's petition alleged a question of fact, the reasonableness of city's diversion of surface water over landowner's property, and such challenge was sufficient to withstand city's demurrer.

* * *

III.

In cases such as this, the nature of the government's action and the type of taking alleged are critical factors in our analysis. Without undertaking to survey the historical intricacies of regulatory zoning ordinances it is fair to say that any local government seeking to participate in the National Flood Insurance Program is required by federal law and authorized by state law to enact land use and regulatory control measures. Other provisions enforcing such measures, (including a building permit and appeal system), are also required in mitigating flood hazards. City's legitimate exercise of its police power, asserted for the public welfare, controls owner's use of his property.

In balancing the private and public interests herein, Owner's potential use of all property, under our system of government, is subordinate to the right of City's reasonable regulations, ordinances, and all similar laws that are clearly necessary and bear a rational relation to preserving the health, safety, and general welfare of the residents of Broken Arrow.

* * *

While asserted with great vigor, Owner's argument that City has appropriated his property for general public use as a detention reservoir, is quite simply untenable under the particular facts of this case. We find no evidence, or persuasive testimony, indicating City has adopted any recommendations with respect to appropriating Owner's land as a detention pond. City has acquired no property interest in Owner's land, has not physically invaded Owner's property, nor has his land been set aside for a public use.

Indeed, Owner stipulated City has not proposed or approved the building of any facilities or taken any action increasing the natural flow of water over Owner's property or flooding his land. We note that as a result of Pre Trial Conference, Sec. 9 thereof, the owner declared and admitted;

"9. (1) That the City of Broken Arrow has *not* constructed or caused to be constructed *any* facilities upstream from plaintiff's property which has increased the waterflow over plaintiff's property." Unlike the extreme factual circumstances found in Mattoon, in the instant case, Owner's property floods following periods of heavy rainfall, and such a natural phenomenon is definitely beyond City's ordinary exercise of its police power.

Furthermore, even if Owner's allegations were substantiated by the record, City's future plans for inclusion of his property for "potential" public use in a flood control plan would not give rise to a cause of action for inverse condemnation. For as Justice Stewart wrote in his concurring opinion in *Hughes v. Washington*: "[T]he Constitution measures a taking of property not by what a state says, or what it intends, but by what it does."

Accepting as we must the general proposition that local public officials must be afforded reasonable "elasticity" in planning and implementing legitimate land-use interests, and given the "particular facts" of this case; we hold such limitations substantially advance City's legitimate goals of; one, reducing risks of loss of life and property; two, protecting the public's interest in health; three, preserving the aesthetic environment and fiscal integrity of Haikey's flood prone areas; four, enabling landowners to develop their property located within the flood plain, as well as allowing landowners to purchase federally-sponsored flood hazard insurance to protect their investments.

Our conclusion that City's land-use ordinances are lawful and valid exercises of its police power does not conclude this matter; for as we explicitly held in *Mattoon*, such a mere finding does not "absolutely preclude compensation for property taken or damaged by such exercises." In this connection, we proceed then to a consideration of whether Owner has been denied economical viable use of his land.

IV

It is relevant at this juncture to recognize Owner merely alleges a "regulatory taking" of property. Given the absence of any administrative decision regarding the application of City's land-use ordinances to Owner's property, City and its amici challenge our appellate jurisdiction and the trial court's adjudicatory authority, arguing Owner's "regulatory taking" claim is premature, because "an essential prerequisite to its assertion is a final and authoritative determination of the type and intensity of development legally permitted on the subject property." We agree.

Owner is completely incorrect when he asserts he has no "adequate" remedy at law. Owner alleged the development of 120 homesites "was permitted by existing zoning" prior to City's adoption of its land-use ordinances. Owner asserts such development "is not consistent with the terms of the ordinance (and) if permitted would seriously undermine the purpose of the ordinances." Owner contends he requested a waiver or variance from the city council by agreeing to reduce the number of dwelling units from 120 to 88. Owner further asserts he asked City to repeal the effect of the ordinance as it pertains to his property. This argument is misleading, and inaccurate.

Owner has never submitted a plan or subdivision plat to use or improve his real property. Nor did he properly seek and receive any concrete and definitive statement from City as to how many single family dwelling units he could build on his land, if the floor of such dwelling units were built one foot above the existing 100–year flood elevation.

Regardless of how many homesites are erected, City's land-use ordinances neither prevent the present and presumably most beneficial use of Owner's property, "nor extinguish a fundamental attribute of ownership." The disputed property, as earlier requested by Owner, is still zoned for single residential family dwellings.

Furthermore, and most significant, Owner has never applied for a building permit to develop his property, or an earth change permit to raise his land out of the flood plain, nor has he ever properly requested a hardship variance under the "established" administrative procedures of the land-use ordinances. In summary, the record indicates Owner failed to submit a plan for development of his property prior to or subsequent to the City's adoption of its land-use ordinances.

* * *

We conclude the trial court was presented with no justiciable issue to hear Owner's regulatory taking claim, because Owner has never applied for a building or earth change permit, has failed to exhaust his administrative remedies, and has presented no competent evidence showing the pursuit of such remedies would be futile or inadequate. We hold there is as yet no concrete controversy regarding the application of City's land-use ordinances to Owner's property, because even though City has denied Owner's increased zoning intensity applications, there are other economically viable uses available to Owner.

Lastly, it is important to note that Owner purchased flood-prone property in Haikey Creek and its tributaries. Even if City had taken no action with regards to flood-damage prevention, Owner's property would continue to flood following periods of heavy rainfall.

The judgment of the trial court is REVERSED, and the cause is REMANDED to the district court WITH DIRECTIONS TO DISMISS Owner's complaint—for want of a justiciable issue.

Notes

1. The National Flood Insurance Act of 1968, 42 U.S.C. § 1601 *et seq.*, requires local governments to enact floodplain regulations prior to making flood insurance available to residents of the community. This act has had a widespread effect in spurring floodplain regulations. See Dinkins, The Federal Zoning Program: Regulation of Floodplain Use Under the National Flood Insurance Act, ABA Law Notes, Spring 1978, Vol. 14, No. 2. An excellent

overview of the Act can be found in Weinstein, Revisiting the National Flood Insurance Program, 48 Land Use Law No. 10 (Oct. 1996), pp. 3–8.

2. What if the owner in the principal case had shown that the city's floodplain regulations prevented all viable and economic use of its property? Do owners of environmentally constrained land have legitimate investment-backed expectations in their development? To what extent? Do owners have an obligation to notice environmental features on land they intend to purchase? How does one discover flood plains? Do 100–year floods leave visible, discoverable marks? How far beyond a physical inspection must a prospective purchaser go in conducting due diligence prior to acquiring a parcel? See Leonard v. Town of Brimfield, 423 Mass. 152, 666 N.E.2d 1300 (1996), where the court held that floodplain restrictions were not a taking; the case takes a hard look at the issue of investment-backed expectations. In Karches v. City of Cincinnati, 38 Ohio St.3d 12, 526 N.E.2d 1350 (1988), the court held a zoning ordinance invalid as applied to property in a floodplain which had been downzoned to Riverfront District, RF–1; the court found that none of the RF–1 uses were economically feasible.

3. Floodplain restrictions were one of the first types of local environmental law enacted by municipalities. The general trend of decisions is to uphold restrictions that prohibit building structures in the floodplain. See Dunham, Flood Control Via the Police Power, 107 U.Pa.L.Rev. 1098 (1959); U.S. Water Resources Council, Regulation of Flood Hazard Areas (1971); American Society of Planning Officials, Regulations for Floodplains, Planning Advisory Service Report No. 277 (1972). Also see Vartelas v. Water Resources Comm'n, 146 Conn. 650, 153 A.2d 822 (1959), upholding the setting of encroachment lines along a stream and a regulation forbidding the placing of buildings within the lines; Turner v. County of Del Norte, 24 Cal.App.3d 311, 101 Cal.Rptr. 93 (1972), upholding an absolute prohibition of structures in a floodplain along the Klamath River; Turnpike Realty Co. v. Town of Dedham, 362 Mass. 221, 284 N.E.2d 891 (1972), upholding floodplain restrictions in a swampy area; Dur–Bar Realty Co. v. City of Utica, 57 A.D.2d 51, 394 N.Y.S.2d 913 (1977), affirmed 44 N.Y.2d 1002, 408 N.Y.S.2d 502, 380 N.E.2d 328 (1978), upholding a "Land Conservation District" which limited uses to farming, marinas, recreational uses, and landfill operations. See generally, Comment, Various Aspects of Floodplain Zoning, 55 N.Dak.L.Rev. 429 (1980).

4. In New City Office Park v. Planning Bd., Town of Clarkstown, 144 A.D.2d 348, 533 N.Y.S.2d 786 (1988), the court upheld denial of final site approval for an office park development located within the 100–year floodplain. The specific basis for the denial was that the project would have required a considerable amount of fill to elevate the buildings above the floodplain and the developer was unable to provide sufficient land for compensatory storage of floodwaters in the event of a 100–year flood.

5. What do you make of the intergovernmental relationship involved in floodplain regulation? A federal law, the National Flood Insurance Program, impacts directly on local governments, denying them and their constituent landowners a federal incentive (flood insurance and payments). Should there be a state role in such matters? If so, what should it be? Is there any benefit to the federal government involving state governments and agencies in these

regulatory relationships? A typical state enabling statute authorizing floodplain regulation is Ariz. Rev. Stat. § 48–3601 et seq. (Floodplain Act of 1973). One possible weakness in such enabling acts is that floodplain regulation is not mandatory for local governments. In some states control of floodplain construction is vested in a state agency. Typical of this approach is the State of Wisconsin. See State v. Trudeau, 139 Wis.2d 91, 408 N.W.2d 337 (1987), cert. denied 484 U.S. 1007, 108 S.Ct. 701, 98 L.Ed.2d 652 (1988), where the state sued the developer and the local government for granting a floodplain variance. Also see City of La Crosse v. Wisconsin Dept. of Natural Resources, 120 Wis.2d 168, 353 N.W.2d 68 (1984). Some states require local governments to adopt regulations protecting floodplains. In Montana, the state legislature passed the Floodway Management Act, designating the Department of Natural Resources and Conservation as the lead agency. MCA § 76–5–301 states that local governments must adopt land use regulations that meet or exceed minimum standards of the department in controlling development in designated floodplains or floodways. If a local government fails to enact such ordinances, the department must enforce its own minimum standards through a state permit system.

(4) Wetlands

Local wetlands regulations restrict activities such as dredging and soil disposal, construction of roads, grading and soil removal, timber harvesting, and placement of buildings and infrastructure on wetlands and their buffer areas. Wetlands exist where there is sufficient water to saturate the soil long enough to support animals and plants suited to wetland environments. In nature, wetlands often include wildlife habitat areas adjacent to watercourses, upland slopes, wooded lands, and other critical environmental features. Some local wetlands laws recognize these connections and attempt to protect the complete ecosystem. The town of Lewisboro, New York, has adopted a local wetlands and watercourse law that contains extensive protections for these resources. Lewisboro, NY Code § 217–1(A) (1999). The city of Concord, New Hampshire, has created a Shoreline Protection District to maintain the quality of surface waters and groundwater, retain flood storage properties, protect wildlife habitat and feeding areas, and protect other unique natural resources. Concord, NH Code ch. 28 § 3–3 (2002).

In Connecticut, state law defines a wetland as an area containing soil types "designated as poorly drained, very poorly drained, alluvial, and floodplain by the National Cooperative Soils Survey, as may be amended from time to time, of the Natural Resources Conservation Service of the United States Department of Agriculture." Conn. Gen. Stat. § 22a–38(15) (2001). Connecticut's Inland Wetlands and Watercourses Act requires all municipalities to establish an inland wetlands agency. Conn. Gen. Stat. § 22a–36 to 22a–45. The agency regulates activities within wetlands designated by the municipalities. A local wetlands agency has the right to regulate not only the land within the established boundaries of a wetland or watercourse, but also any adjacent area where activities might occur that would "use" the wetlands in a prohibited manner. The Act prohibits anyone from conducting a "regulated activity" on any inland wetland or watercourse without a permit. Regulated activities include almost all development and land use activities. The Commissioner of the State Department of Environmental Protection (DEP) may revoke the local wetlands agency's authority to regulate activity in the wetlands if the DEP determines that the local agency has failed to perform its duties. The Commissioner's regulations require that local agencies report to the DEP all permits issued and any other action they have taken. Local wetlands agencies are given the authority to adopt regulations that expand on the Commissioner's regulations, or to add to them if necessary to protect the wetlands.

FAFARD v. CONSERVATION COMMISSION OF BARNSTABLE

Supreme Judicial Court of Massachusetts, 2000.
432 Mass. 194, 733 N.E.2d 66.

ABRAMS, J.

The plaintiffs, Madlyn and Howard Fafard (Fafards), appeal from the Conservation Commission of Barnstable's (commission's) decision denying them permission to build a fixed pier on the Eel River. The commission grounded its decision on town bylaws and pier regulations that claim authority to protect "the interests of recreation and public trust rights."

Pursuant to G.L. c. 249, § 4, the plaintiffs sought review in the nature of certiorari in the Superior Court. The Superior Court judge denied the Fafards' motion for judgment on the pleadings and affirmed the decision of the commission.[2] We granted the Fafards' application for direct appellate review.

The Fafards assert that the bylaws and pier regulations of Barnstable are invalid. According to them, only the Commonwealth may act to further public trust rights. They also argue that G.L. c. 91, which provides for State licensing of structures on coastal lands, preempts the pier regulations on which the commission based its decision. The Fafards also raise the issue of arbitrary and capricious decision-making by the commission, but that issue is not properly before us because it is raised only in their reply brief. See Mass. R.A.P. 16(a)(4), as amended, 367 Mass. 921 (1975).

2. The judge noted in his decision that "[t]he record is unclear as to whether the [town of Barnstable] has been approved by the Department [of Environmental Protection (DEP)] to administer a local permitting program." This issue has been clarified on appeal: Barnstable was not authorized by the DEP to administer a DEP permitting program. Therefore, although we affirm the Superior Court judge's decision, we do so on different grounds.

We also note that a related action, which was consolidated with the instant case but decided separately, remains pending in Superior Court. That action, which is not before us, concerns whether the commission's denial of the Fafards' first notice of intent was untimely. We are concerned with the Fafards' second notice of intent to the commission.

We conclude that only the Commonwealth or its express designee may act to further public trust rights. Therefore, those portions of the bylaw that claim to enforce public trust rights are not a valid exercise of the town's power. Consequently, the town could not grant such authority to the commission. We also conclude that, after the portions of the bylaw that claim public trust authority are struck, the remaining portion of the bylaw and pier regulations are not preempted by State statute. Because the commission also acted under valid portions of the town bylaw, we conclude that the commission's denial of the Fafards' request for a proposed pier was an appropriate exercise of municipal powers. We affirm the decision of the Superior Court.

1. *Facts.* Barnstable enacted a wetlands protection bylaw (wetlands bylaw) in order to regulate work in and around wetlands more strictly than does the State's wetlands protection act. See G.L. c. 131, § 40 (Wetlands Protection Act); Barnstable Bylaws, c. III, art. XXVII, § 12. See generally art. 89, § 6, of the Amendments to the Constitution of the Commonwealth (Home Rule Amendment). The wetlands bylaw also purports to protect "public trust rights in trustlands." Chapter III, art. XXVII, § 1. The wetlands bylaw vests in the commission the authority to issue and to deny permits for a number of specified activities affecting wetlands resources.

Pursuant to its powers under the wetlands bylaw, the commission adopted regulations for private piers and docks (pier regulations). The relevant pier regulations specify that piers may not extend more than twenty per cent of the width of a waterway and that piers serving private interests may not interfere with various water-related activities. The pier regulations also specify that, "[t]hese regulations notwithstanding, the [commission] will consider any and all pier proposals on a site specific basis, disposing of each according to its merit and the degree to which statutory interests have been protected and preserved at the locus."

The trust owns property, which the Fafards use as a seasonal residence, on the Eel River. The Eel River is a narrow coastal tidal inlet, approximately 2,000 feet long, closed at one end. The Fafards' property lies toward the closed end of the river.

In May, 1997, Howard Fafard filed a notice of intent with the commission as required by the wetlands bylaw seeking permission to construct a fixed pier and to install a ramp and floats to provide access from the upland portion of the property to the water. The proposed pier would extend forty-two feet beyond the mean low water mark into an area of the river which is 161 feet wide. Therefore, the planned pier would occupy more than twenty per cent of the width of the river and would stand on "Commonwealth tidelands," or lands below the mean high water mark. See G.L. c. 91, § 1; 310 Code Mass. Regs. § 9.02 (1994). The Fafards also proposed to keep their fifty-five foot twin-screw power boat at the pier, which, with a beam of sixteen feet, would extend another sixteen feet beyond the pier.

The commission held two public hearings and, on September 16, 1997, denied the Fafards' application "in the interest of recreation and public trust rights." In support of the denial, the commission found, inter alia, that (1) the proposed pier did not conform with the pier regulations; (2) the proposed pier would interfere with an existing mooring that had been in continuous use for over ten years; (3) the pier "would pose significant adverse impacts to the interest of recreation (such as navigation) and public trust rights"; and (4) the Fafards had not met their burden of proving that the pier would not have an "unacceptable significant and cumulative effect upon the wetland[s]."

* * *

3. *Preemption.* The Fafards also argue that the unsevered portions of the bylaw, and the pier regulations enacted under those portions of the bylaw, are invalid because they are inconsistent with sections of G.L. c. 91. We disagree.

"Municipalities may not adopt bylaws or ordinances that are inconsistent with State laws." *Boston Gas Co. v. Somerville*, 420 Mass. 702, 703, 652 N.E.2d 132 (1995), and cases cited. As a starting point in determining "whether a local ordinance is inconsistent with a statute, this court has looked to see whether there was * * * an express legislative intent to forbid local activity on the same subject." *Id.* at 704, 652 N.E.2d 132. Nothing in G.L. c. 91 states expressly that municipalities may deny permission to construct piers such as the Fafards proposed or that they may grant permission to construct piers. Therefore, we are confronted with one of the "hard cases * * * in which it is asserted that a legislative intent to bar local action should be inferred in all the circumstances." *Wendell v. Attorney Gen.*, 394 Mass. 518, 524, 476 N.E.2d 585 (1985).

a. *Frustration of purpose.* Legislative intent to bar local action may be inferred where "the local regulation would somehow frustrate the purpose of the statute so as to warrant an inference that the Legislature intended to preempt the subject." *Boston Gas Co. v. Newton*, 425 Mass. 697, 699, 682 N.E.2d 1336 (1997). We examine whether the pier regulations frustrate the three sections of G.L. c. 91 that explicitly address the Commonwealth's powers and responsibilities with respect to the licensing and permitting of piers on Commonwealth tidelands. See G.L. c. 91, §§ 2, 14, 18.

General Laws c. 91, § 2, sets forth the general rubric to be used by the DEP in issuing State permits and licenses for pier construction: "In carrying out its duties * * * the department shall act to preserve and protect the rights in tidelands of the inhabitants of the [C]ommonwealth by ensuring that the tidelands are utilized only for water-dependent uses or otherwise serve a proper public purpose." Section 2 also states that, in issuing licenses and permits, the DEP shall "protect the interests of the [C]ommonwealth." *Id.*

In *Golden v. Selectmen of Falmouth*, 358 Mass. 519, 265 N.E.2d 573 (1970), we considered whether a local bylaw was inconsistent with the State wetlands protection act. See G.L. c. 138, § 27A, as amended through St.1969, c. 406. We concluded that, because the State statute "establishes minimum State-wide standards * * * local communities [are] free to adopt more stringent controls" than those embodied in State law. *Id.* at 526, 265 N.E.2d 573. See *Lovequist v. Conservation Comm'n of Dennis*, 379 Mass. 7, 393 N.E.2d 858 (1979).

Like the statute considered in *Golden v. Selectmen of Falmouth*, supra, G.L. c. 91, § 2, sets forth minimum standards. This section does not address the impact of pier construction on zoning regulations, public safety, the creation of nuisances, or other spheres traditionally within municipal authority. Rather, § 2 specifies that the department may allow construction on Commonwealth tidelands only if that construction would serve a "proper public purpose."

The pier regulations do not usurp the DEP's authority to deny licenses or permits to applicants who seek to build structures that do not serve such a purpose. Rather, the pier regulations require a local permit in addition to the State requirement that applicants obtain a State permit. The existence of a local permitting program alongside the State program in no way interferes with the mandate of § 2. See *Lovequist v. Conservation Comm'n of Dennis, supra*; *Golden v. Selectmen of Falmouth, supra*. Cf. *Crawford v. Building Inspector of Barnstable*, 356 Mass. 174, 180, 248 N.E.2d 488 (1969) ("No special rights accrue * * * because the pier was constructed under a license granted by the Commonwealth's Department of Public Works. The license was 'subject to all applicable Federal, State, County, and Municipal laws, ordinances and regulations' ").

We consider next whether the pier regulations are preempted by G.L. c. 91, §§ 14 and 18. Section 14 authorizes the DEP to "license and prescribe the terms for the construction or extension of [piers and other structures]." Section 14 specifies that the DEP may not permit structures unless they serve "a proper public purpose and * * * said purpose shall provide a greater public benefit than public detriment to the rights of the public." Section 14 thus requires that the DEP balance the public costs against the public benefits of a proposed project.

Section 18 specifies procedures for licensing programs administered by the DEP and provides for notice to local authorities when application for a DEP license is made. Section 18 requires the DEP to "take into consideration the recommendation of the local planning board in making its decision whether to grant a license."

The Fafards argue that, because §§ 14 and 18 authorize the DEP to grant and deny licenses with local authorities acting only in an advisory capacity, we should infer that the Legislature intended to preclude local permitting programs. We disagree.

"The existence of legislation on a subject * * * is not necessarily a bar to the enactment of local ordinances and bylaws exercising powers or functions with respect to the same subject." *Bloom v. Worcester*, 363 Mass. 136, 156, 293 N.E.2d 268 (1973). Even where a statute specifies that local authorities act only in an advisory capacity to State licensing authorities, we need not infer that the Legislature intended to preclude local regulation. See *Golden v. Selectmen of Falmouth, supra* at 525, 265 N.E.2d 573. There, we considered whether a Falmouth zoning bylaw was preempted by G.L. c. 130, § 27A. The State statute at issue required individuals planning to remove, fill, or dredge certain coastal areas to provide notice to local authorities. Municipalities were permitted to make recommendations to the department of public works, which retained ultimate authority over whether the proposed activities would be permitted. See G.L. c. 130, § 27A. We concluded that "[t]he fact that the [statute] confers upon a local board the advisory power to make recommendations concerning the installation of certain protective measures 'as may protect the public interest' does not, we think, preclude the authority of the local board acting under the zoning bylaw to initially authorize or bar a project." *Id.* at 525, 265 N.E.2d 573.

The same reasoning applies here. None of the language in either G.L. c. 91, § 14 or § 18, suggests that, because the statute allows municipalities to provide advice to the DEP, the Legislature intended to preclude local regulation of pier construction on Commonwealth tidelands. "The legislative intent to preclude local action must be clear." *Bloom v. Worcester, supra* at 155, 293 N.E.2d 268.

The bylaws further the interests the Legislature intended to protect in G.L. c. 91. As long as the DEP retains ultimate authority to reject projects for which the public costs do not outweigh the public benefits, Barnstable's local permitting program is not inconsistent with G.L. c. 91, §§ 14 and 18. See *Lovequist v. Conservation Comm'n of Dennis, supra* at 15, 393 N.E.2d 858. Barnstable's permitting program does not frustrate the purpose of the relevant sections of G.L. c. 91.

b. *Field preemption.* Local regulation also may be preempted even where such regulation does not conflict directly with an existing statute: "in some circumstances we can infer that the Legislature intended to preempt the field because legislation on the subject is so comprehensive that any local enactment would frustrate the statute's purpose." *Boston Gas Co. v. Newton*, 425 Mass. 697, 699, 682 N.E.2d 1336 (1997), quoting *Boston Gas Co. v. Somerville*, 420 Mass. 702, 703, 652 N.E.2d 132 (1995).

The sections of G.L. c. 91 that regulate pier construction are by no means comprehensive. As the preceding discussion of the relevant sections demonstrates, the Legislature provided only general principles to be used in regulating construction on Commonwealth tidelands. See G.L. c. 91, § 14. This distinguishes the instant case from those cited by the Fafards in support of their argument. See *Boston Gas Co. v. Newton, supra* (State regulation of public utilities industry, which has long been recognized as thoroughly regulated, see *Boston Edison Co. v. Boston*, 390 Mass. 772–774, 459 N.E.2d 1231 [1984], preempts local ordinance); *Boston Gas Co. v. Somerville, supra* (same).

The Fafards, however, argue that, even if the statutes themselves are not comprehensive, the bylaws and pier regulations frustrate the Legislature's intent to create a centralized authority for managing Commonwealth tidelands. The Fafards suggest that this legislative intent is implicit in regulations promulgated by the DEP. See 310 Code Mass. Regs. § 9.07 (1996). Although regulations adopted by a State agency are not dispositive on the question of the scope of authority granted an agency by statute, "[w]e must uphold the regulation if it can be interpreted in harmony with the act by any reasonable construction." *Massachusetts Auto Body Ass'n, Inc. v. Commissioner of Ins.*, 409 Mass. 770, 777, 570 N.E.2d 147 (1991).

Title 310 Code Mass. Regs. § 9.07(3) establishes procedures for cities or towns seeking to administer "a local permitting program for small structures accessory to residences." Cities or towns authorized by the DEP under this regulation may issue permits in lieu of the DEP, subject to appeal to the DEP. *Id.*

The bylaw and pier regulations do not purport to issue State permits in lieu of the DEP. The bylaw and pier regulations require a local permit in addition to the permit required by the DEP and are not inconsistent with DEP regulations allowing towns and cities to act as local surrogates for the DEP.

The Fafards also complain that the commission "attempts to avoid * * * administrative review of its permitting decisions by DEP." Nothing in G.L. c. 91 "grants to the [DEP] the authority to authorize a project which [a] local board has vetoed." *Golden v. Selectmen of Falmouth, supra* at 525, 265 N.E.2d 573. Further, an individual in the Fafards' position may seek review of the commission's decision. "Such a person has exactly the same remedy * * * as is available under any other * * * by-law[,] an action in the nature of certiorari under G.L. c. 249, § 4." *Lovequist v. Conservation Comm'n of Dennis, supra* at 16, 393 N.E.2d 858.

4. *The commission's decision.* Because the pier regulations are not preempted by State statute, we consider whether, after severing the portions of the bylaw purporting to grant the commission authority to act on behalf of the public trust, the commission had the authority to deny permission to construct the pier. We conclude that it did.

The Legislature has granted local conservation commissions the authority to act to prevent alteration of wetlands in order to preserve certain wetlands values. See G.L. c. 40, § 8C; G.L. c. 131, § 40. Conservation commissions acting under G.L. c. 131, § 40, may take regulatory action to protect, inter alia, the recreational value of wetlands. *Lovequist v. Conservation Comm'n of Dennis, supra* at 12–13, 393 N.E.2d 858. Coastal wetlands subject to municipal regulation under G.L. c. 131, § 40, include "any bank, marsh, swamp, meadow, flat or other lowland subject to tidal action or coastal storm flowage." Thus, local conservation commissions are authorized by the Legislature to protect recreation values by regulating construction on Commonwealth tidelands.

The wetlands bylaw authorizes the commission to act to protect various wetlands values, "including, but not limited to, * * * recreation." Barnstable Bylaws, c. III, art. XXVII, § 1. The pier regulations derive authority from this section of the bylaw, stating that "[t]he Bylaw protects each citizen's enjoyment of [tidelands and waters] by protecting the interests spelled out in [G.L. c. 131, § 40,] and Town of Barnstable Article XXVII," and establishing "performance standards for private piers and docks."

The Fafards' proposed pier and ramp would extend across Commonwealth tidelands, which municipalities may regulate under G.L. c. 131, § 40, into submerged lands seaward of the low water mark. "When analyzing a grant of power to a municipal government we must keep in mind that 'a grant of an express power carries with it all unexpressed, incidental powers necessary to carry it into effect.' " *Greater Boston Real Estate Bd. v. Boston*, 397 Mass. 870, 876–877, 494 N.E.2d 1301 (1986), quoting *Flynn v. Cambridge*, 383 Mass. 152, 158, 418 N.E.2d 335 (1981). Of course, as with other spheres of regulation that do not fall within a municipality's ordinary powers, "no local action may be taken without explicit legislative authorization," and we recognize "only those powers which are expressly conferred by statute or necessarily implied from those expressly conferred." *Greater Boston Real Estate Bd. v. Boston*, *supra* at 877, 494 N.E.2d 1301, quoting *Church v. Boston*, 370 Mass. 598, 601, 351 N.E.2d 212 (1976). Therefore, the commission was authorized to protect recreational values by denying a permit for the pier.

Because of the proposed pier's large size, the commission determined that the pier would have a negative effect on recreation. Specifically, the commission found that the "Eel River in the subject reach is enjoyed by many recreational boaters who cruise the river to its end point and return to West Bay." The commission determined that, "as proposed, the pier would pose significant adverse impact to the interest of recreation" and would interfere with an existing mooring. Based on these findings, the commission cited recreational values as one of the bases for its decision in addition to public trust rights.

The commission's denial of permission to build the pier because it would impair recreational values is supported by the record. The denial is also a legitimate exercise of the commission's authority consistent with powers to protect wetlands granted by the Legislature to municipal conservation commissions. See G.L. c. 131, § 40.

5. *Conclusion.* Although the bylaws and pier regulations are not preempted by G.L. c. 91, they are void insofar as they claim authority to protect public trust rights without a legislative grant of authority or a grant of authority from the DEP. However, because the bylaw was severable and the commission's decision also is sustainable on the basis of powers granted by the Legislature to local conservation commissions, we conclude that the commission did not "substantially err[ ] in a way that materially affected the rights of the parties." *Massachusetts Bay*

Transp. Auth. v. Auditor of the Commonwealth, 430 Mass. 783, 791, 724 N.E.2d 288 (2000).

Judgment affirmed.

Notes

1. Fafard held that only the State of Massachusetts, or its express designee (which did not include Barnstable), can enforce public trust rights. The public trust doctrine has its roots in the Institutes of Justinian in Roman Law. Under English law, the King—or Sovereign—held property rights in the air, running water, and the sea and its shores. British doctrine considered tidelands to be held by the King for the benefit of all commonwealth subjects. This doctrine did not translate precisely to the American federal system: states replaced the Crown as the trustee of community resources and the state legislatures and courts became the principal arbiters of what is held in trust for the people and what enters the realm of private property. At common law, the lands covered and influenced by tidal water were navigable-in-law and preserved in the public trust; navigation rights were held by the public, subjecting riparian owners to a servitude running to members of the public. Coastal state legislatures have enacted tidal wetlands acts to regulate private land uses on coasts, adjacent to tidal estuaries, and along other tidally-influenced areas, including land adjacent to coastal inlets and large water bodies subject to tidal fluctuations.

2. The Fafard court is one of many that interprets broadly the delegation of local wetlands authority. In Danzinger v. Conservation Com'n of Town of Newtown, 29 Conn. L. Rptr. 367 (Conn.Super.Ct.2001), plaintiff challenged the municipal agency's regulations that expanded the area around wetlands that was subject to regulation and added additional definitions to a list of regulated activities. The court was faced with the issue of whether the defendant acted within its statutory authority when it expanded the geographical area and the activities subject to wetlands regulations. "Acting in such a legislative capacity, the defendant has wide and liberal discretion * * * and is free to amend its regulations whenever time, experience, and responsible planning for contemporary or future conditions reasonably indicate the need for a change." The court found that there was sufficient evidence to support the amendments. See also Queach Corp. v. Inland Wetlands Commission of the Town of Branford, 258 Conn. 178, 779 A.2d 134 (2001) (upholding a municipality's amendment increasing a fifty foot buffer protection area to a 100–foot protection area).

B. LAND RESOURCE PROTECTIONS

(1) Erosion and Sedimentation Control

Soil erosion is a major source of nonpoint source pollution. Some erosion occurs naturally, but it is greatly accelerated by urbanization. Erosion control measures are a critical ingredient in local stormwater management plans and floodplain programs. Comprehensive wetland regulations aim to limit erosion in upland development to prevent the effects of sedimentation of wetlands which greatly impairs their function and value to the public and nature.

Local governments can adopt regulations to prevent soil erosion and the deposit of sediments in surface waters that land development projects cause. Undeveloped land contains organic particles that are biologically and chemically active and that, when disturbed and transported to surface waters, can cause serious water quality problems. One local soil protection ordinance observes that its purpose is to safeguard persons, protect property, prevent damage to the environment, and promote the public welfare by guiding, regulating, and controlling the design, use, and maintenance of any development or other activity that disturbs or breaks the surface of soil or results in the movement of earth on land situated in the town.

MARION RD. ASS'N v. WESTPORT PLANNING & ZONING COMMISSION

Connecticut Superior Court, 1994.
1994 WL 592221.

LEVIN, JUDGE.

The plaintiffs, homeowners and a neighborhood association, appeal from the action of the defendant Westport Planning & Zoning Commission (commission) granting with conditions and modifications the application of the defendants Conservative Synagogue and Three Hundred PRW Associates for a special permit and site plan approval to construct a synagogue building on a 4.7 acre parcel in a Residence AA zone. The plaintiffs' appeal enumerates over sixteen claims of error against the commission. In their brief, however, the plaintiffs claim that the commission erred by (1) approving an application which was substantially unchanged from a prior application which it had denied, (2) approving an application which violated the parking and/or coverage requirements in the regulations, (3) approving the application despite uncontroverted expert testimony that the synagogue would have an adverse impact on neighborhood property values, (4) necessarily finding that the application conformed to certain sections of the zoning regulations, (5) accepting and acting on an incomplete and inadequate application, and (6) imposing illegal and improper conditions of approval in its decision. "Issues that were raised in the appeal but not briefed by the plaintiff[s] * * * are considered abandoned." *Grace Community Church v. Planning & Zoning Commission*, 42 Conn.Sup. 256, 259, 615 A.2d 1092 (1992) (Fuller, J.).

* * *

IX

The plaintiffs contend that the commission erred in approving an application that failed to comply with § 37 of the regulations which require the filing of a sediment and control plan.

Section 37–1 states: "The purpose of these Sediment and Erosion Control Regulations is to reduce accelerated soil erosion; reduce the danger from stormwater runoff and to minimize nonpoint sediment pollution resulting from and being developed.'' In furtherance of that purpose, § 37–2 of the regulations provides that a sediment and erosion ''[p]lan shall be submitted with any application for development when the disturbed area of such development is cumulatively more than one-half (1/2) acre.'' Section 37–6 of the regulations provides for the contents and ''standards'' of such a plan.[3] No such plan appears in the record.

The defendants counter that the record reflects that a ''conceptual'' plan was submitted to the Conservation Director who reviewed it and requested that the final plan be submitted together with a ''narrative'' before a zoning permit was issued. The Conservation Commission reviewed this ''plan'' and also required that a final plan be submitted prior to the issuance of a zoning permit. Section 37–4 does provide that ''[a]ll S & E [sediment and control] Plans shall be submitted to the Conservation Director for *recommendation* prior to the filing of any application with either the Planning and Zoning Commission or the Zoning Board of Appeals, as applicable or prior to the issuance of a Zoning Permit. The Conservation Director shall review the plan to determine compliance with Section 37–5 below and shall inform the appropriate authority and the applicant of his/her *recommendation* within thirty (30) days of the date of receipt of said plan. Upon receipt of the Conservation Director's *recommendations* the Zoning Enforcement Officer shall certify that the plan complies with the requirements of this Section.'' (Emphasis added.)

The ''conceptual'' plan, alone, submitted by the applicant, did not comply with the regulations. This conclusion is supported by provisions in the General Statutes. Sediment and erosion control regulations are not unique to this municipality. They are mandated by General Statutes § 22a–329.[4] More, General Statutes § 22a–327(5) states what a soil

3. Section 37–6 of the regulations, entitled ''Standards'', provides that ''[a]ny S & E [soil and erosion] Plan submitted pursuant to this Section shall include but not be limited to the following: a) the cumulative area(s) of disturbance, including areas of excavation, filling or stockpiling of earth material; b) existing and proposed grades or spot elevations; c) location of any inland wetlands, tidal wetlands, watercourses, existing or proposed drainage facilities on or adjacent to the site; d) anticipated start and completion dates; e) agent's name; f) sequence for institution of soil erosion and sediment control measures; g) the minimum Soil Erosion and Sediment Control Plans shall be developed using principles outlines in Chapters #3 & #4 of the Connecticut Guidelines for Soil Erosion and Sediment Control; h) a bond may be required in accordance with Section 43–13 of the Zoning Regulations.''

4. General Statutes ''Sec. 22a–329. Municipal land use. Regulations. (a) The regulations adopted by a municipality pursuant to sections 8–2 and 8–25, on and after July 1, 1985, shall require that: (1) Proper provision be made for soil erosion and sediment control; (2) a soil erosion and sediment control plan be submitted with any application for development when the disturbed area of such development is more than one-half acre; and (3) the municipality or the soil and water conservation district shall certify that the plan complies with regulations adopted pursuant to said sections. Prior to certification, any plan submitted to a municipality may be reviewed by the soil and water conservation districts which may make recommendations concerning such plan, provided such review shall be completed within thirty days of the receipt of such plan. The regulations shall include, but not be limited to, provisions for certification of a plan and inspection of measures being installed pursuant to such plan. A single-family dwelling that is not a part of a subdivision of land shall be exempt from such regulations. The soil and water conservation districts shall assist municipalities erosion and sediment control plan is and shall contain: " 'Soil erosion and sediment control plan' means a scheme that minimizes soil erosion and sedimentation and includes, but is not limited to, a map and narrative. The map shall show topography, cleared and graded areas, proposed area alterations and the location of and detailed information concerning erosion and sediment measures and facilities. The narrative shall describe the project, the schedule of major activities on the land, the application of conservation practices, design criteria, construction details and the maintenance program for any erosion and sediment control facilities that are installed * * * " No such plan was filed by the applicant. To allow the applicant's "conceptual" plan to pass muster would trivialize these requirements into "a consciousness-raising exercise [rather] than as obligatory regulations." Tondro, Connecticut Land Use Regulation (2d Ed.1992), p. 335.

* * *

Notes

1. The Marion Road decision in footnote four mentions that Connecticut state law requires that local zoning ordinances "shall provide that proper provision be made for soil erosion and sediment control pursuant to Section 22a–329." Local zoning laws in Connecticut also must protect existing and potential public surface and groundwater drinking supplies. These substantive mandates illustrate how state legislatures can link federal and local environmental law. In an ideal system, federal environmental standards would be reflected in state law and, where local land use law authority is implicated, state legislatures would provide encouragement and incentives to localities to adopt corresponding standards or, where necessary, mandate local compliance. How would states enforce such mandates? One technique used in federal point source pollution control and coastal zone protection laws is for the state to step in and enforce the standards where localities fail to cooperate. Is it economically feasible for the states to enforce soil and erosion prevention standards, for example, in every one of their municipalities? What does your answer to this question imply about the practicalities of formulating intergovernmental policy?

2. Violations of municipal erosion and sedimentation ordinances can result in the assessment of heavy fines. In City of Asheville v. Woodberry Assoc., 114 N.C.App. 377, 442 S.E.2d 328 (1994), a developer was fined $90,910 for failure "to take protective action to control the erosion and sedimentation which was occurring."

(2) Steep Slope/Ridgeline/Hilltop Protection

Ridgelines and hilltops are valuable for both their scenic and their ecological qualities. Surface runoff from ridgeline development can con-

which so request in developing regulations to comply with this section. Nothing in this section shall be construed as extending the time limits for the approval of any application under chapter 124 or 126.

"(b) Notwithstanding the provisions of subsection (a) of this section, the council may grant an extension of time for the adoption of the regulations on soil and sediment control required under sections 8–2 and 8–25, but not beyond June 30, 1986, to any municipality which makes application to the council before July 1, 1985."

taminate rivers and streams that supply drinking water downstream. Development of septic systems on ridges and hilltops can cause contamination of lower-lying properties. Buildings and roads can disrupt wildlife corridors and critical habitats. Hillsides and ridgelines are inherently unstable and care must be taken to prevent mudslides and other catastrophic movements of earth. Local laws can require that development on ridgelines and hilltop areas blend in with the natural environment and be buffered to preserve particularly valuable viewsheds in the community.

Steep slopes usually are associated with other environmental features such as rock outcrops, shallow soils, bedrock fractures, and groundwater seeps. Excavations or building construction can cause instability through loosening of the soil structure and the removal of trees, vegetation, and rocks. Grading, cutting, and filling—activities associated with preparation of construction sites—can compromise the stability of some slopes. Activities such as agriculture, road and railway construction, house building, and land drainage can be regulated to protect steep slopes. The Town of Cortlandt, New York, has adopted a local law for the purpose of preventing the "improper alteration" of steep slopes. Cortlandt, NY Code § 259.1 (1992). Provisions of this kind can often be found in local ridgeline or hilltop protection ordinances throughout the nation.

The trend in local environmental law is to recognize natural connections on the land and waters by broadening the scope of natural protection laws. Steep slopes, like wetlands, are often found in association with other critical environmental features and perform multiple functions of community value ranging from providing breathtaking vistas, to harboring wildlife in their unique, horizontal ecosystems, to protecting down-slope landowners and water bodies from flooding, erosion, and sedimentation. In Harris v. Zoning Com'n of the Town of Milford, 259 Conn. 402, 788 A.2d 1239 (2002), the Connecticut Supreme Court sustained a town law that protected ridgelines in this broader context. The local law amended the zoning ordinance to exclude from the calculation for determining buildable lots all wetlands, watercourses, and land with a twenty-five percent slope or greater. The calculation was applicable only in residential districts and served to lower density in those districts by increasing the minimum lot size needed for single-family home construction. The plaintiffs' claims that the law lacked a rational basis and violated the uniformity requirement for zoning under Connecticut law were rejected by the court.

SELLON v. CITY OF MANITOU SPRINGS

Supreme Court of Colorado, En Banc, 1987.
745 P.2d 229.

KIRSHBAUM, JUSTICE.

* * *

In July of 1973, the City adopted a master plan for a parcel of property, referred to as "Crystal Hills," located adjacent to the City.

That plan provided that 194 home sites could be developed on the property. On September 1, 1981, the City annexed Crystal Hills. The landowners purchased the property in March 1982.

The City contains many areas characterized by hills of varying degrees of slope. Consequently, problems of erosion, drainage and access are of particular concern to property owners, residents and city planners. On May 4, 1982, after much debate and discussion, the City Council adopted the hillside ordinance in an effort to deal in a meaningful fashion with some of these concerns. The ordinance created a special hillside low density residential zone and established an equation for calculating the minimal lot sizes necessary for development of property placed in that zone.[5] When applied to steeply graded property, the equation requires in general that development plans be based on larger lot sizes than those required for properties not so steeply sloped. The equation also distinguishes between "platted" and "unplatted" land and requires larger lots for development of areas which are designated "unplatted" land at the time the property is zoned or rezoned hillside residential than in areas which are designated "platted" land.

On September 23, 1983, the City Council adopted a resolution placing Crystal Hills in a low density residential zone and authorizing the development of 108 residential units on the property. Many citizens disapproved of this decision, however, and the City Council decided to place the question of the rezoning of Crystal Hills before the voters of the City. In November of 1983, a majority of the City's voting electorate indicated approval for the rezoning of Crystal Hills as hillside low density residential property.

The City Council subsequently scheduled two public hearings to consider the question of the appropriate zoning for the Crystal Hills property. On November 18, 1983, the landowners were advised by City representatives that, based upon the hillside density equation, residential development of the Crystal Hills property would be limited to sixty units under hillside low density residential zoning.

Lengthy public hearings were held before the City Council on December 6, 1983, and January 3, 1984. Although one of the landowners attended the hearings and stated that he was opposed to the rezoning, the landowners offered no evidence at these hearings. At the conclusion of the January 1984 hearing, the City Council voted to rezone the Crystal Hills property as hillside low density residential.

5. That segment of the ordinance reads:

(3) Development Requirements

(a) Minimum Lot Size—Allowable lot size shall be based on the average percent of slope, defined as follows:

Average Percent of Slope shall mean the percent of slope as computed by the following formula—

$$S = \frac{100IL}{A}$$

Where S = average percent of slope
I = contour interval in feet
L = summation of length of all contour lines in feet
A = area in square feet of parcel being considered

The landowners appealed this decision to the El Paso County District Court. Following a two-day hearing, the district court affirmed the City Council's action.

The landowners assert that the hillside ordinance is insufficiently related to public health, safety and welfare objectives of the City and that its terms are impermissibly vague. They suggest that because of these alleged deficiencies the hillside ordinance violates the due process clauses of the United States and Colorado Constitutions. We disagree.

The principles applicable to a determination of whether a particular municipal legislative enactment violates constitutional due process standards are well settled. A presumption of validity attaches to zoning decisions of municipal zoning authorities. *Board of County Comm'rs v. Mountain Air Ranch*, 192 Colo. 364, 563 P.2d 341 (1977); *Wright v. City of Littleton*, 174 Colo. 318, 483 P.2d 953 (1971); *Baum v. City & County of Denver*, 147 Colo. 104, 363 P.2d 688 (1961). Thus, a party challenging a zoning ordinance on constitutional grounds assumes the burden of proving the asserted invalidity beyond a reasonable doubt. *Tri–State Generation & Transmission Co. v. City of Thornton*, 647 P.2d 670 (Colo.1982); *Holcomb v. City & County of Denver*, 199 Colo. 251, 606 P.2d 858 (1980); *Ford Leasing Dev. Co. v. Board of County Comm'rs*, 186 Colo. 418, 528 P.2d 237 (1974); *Baum v. City & County of Denver*, 147 Colo. 104, 363 P.2d 688.

For purposes of the United States Constitution, an ordinance containing provisions that bear a rational relationship to legitimate state concerns satisfies due process requirements. *Schad v. Borough of Mount Ephraim*, 452 U.S. 61, 101 S.Ct. 2176, 68 L.Ed.2d 671 (1981); *Village of Euclid v. Ambler Realty Co.*, 272 U.S. 365, 47 S.Ct. 114, 71 L.Ed. 303 (1926). The due process clause of article II, section 25, of Colorado's Constitution requires a reasonable relation between an ordinance and a valid interest, such as public health, safety, morals or general welfare. *Nopro Co. v. Town of Cherry Hills Village*, 180 Colo. 217, 504 P.2d 344 (1972); *Wright v. City of Littleton*, 174 Colo. 318, 483 P.2d 953. The hillside ordinance must be evaluated pursuant to these standards.

The record reflects that prior to the adoption of the hillside ordinance great attention had been directed by the City Council to problems that had developed after improvements were made to property containing relatively steep slopes. For example, the city manager testified that the development of single-family units on steeply graded plots of land continually forced the City to deal with erosion, drainage, maintenance and emergency access issues. The record also contains evidence that residents of various areas of the City historically had experienced significant difficulties with some or all of these problems. The adoption of the hillside ordinance reflected a considered effort by the City Council to deal with these very real problems. Viewed in light of these facts, the ordinance addresses significant issues directly affecting the health and welfare of the City's residents.

At the review hearing conducted by the district court the landowners introduced evidence to the effect that the hillside ordinance was not the best means available to address problems of erosion, drainage or emergency access associated with development of residential housing units in steep slope areas of the City. However, the question is not whether other solutions to a governmental problem are feasible or superior to the program actually adopted; the question is whether the decision made is itself reasonably and rationally related to the problem being addressed. *See Schad v. Borough of Mount Ephraim*, 452 U.S. 61, 101 S.Ct. 2176; *Nopro Co. v. Town of Cherry Hills Village*, 180 Colo. 217, 504 P.2d 344; *Wright v. City of Littleton*, 174 Colo. 318, 483 P.2d 953. In this case, it is abundantly clear that the provisions of the hillside ordinance are rationally and reasonably related to problems of erosion, drainage, maintenance and emergency access occurring on sloping terrain that affect the health and safety of the City's residents.

* * *

The landowners next contend that the hillside ordinance is confiscatory and therefore unconstitutional as applied to them because it, in effect, precludes the use of the Crystal Hills property for any reasonable purpose. It is true that a zoning ordinance that prohibits the use of property for any reasonable purpose will be deemed confiscatory and therefore violative of just compensation and due process protections afforded by Colorado's Constitution. *Nopro Co. v. Town of Cherry Hills Village*, 180 Colo. 217, 504 P.2d 344 (1972); *Bird v. City of Colo. Springs*, 176 Colo. 32, 489 P.2d 324 (1971); *Madis v. Higginson*, 164 Colo. 320, 434 P.2d 705 (1967). However, our decisions have consistently emphasized the principle that a landowner is not entitled to obtain maximum profits from the use of property, and that so long as the zoning ordinance leaves some reasonable use for the property, the ordinance does not violate state constitutional standards. *Nopro Co. v. Town of Cherry Hills Village*, 180 Colo.217, 504 P.2d 344; *see Bird v. City of Colo. Springs*, 176 Colo. 32, 489 P.2d 324; *Baum v. City & County of Denver*, 147 Colo. 104, 363 P.2d 688 (1961).

The evidence establishes that the hillside ordinance does not render the Crystal Hills property devoid of any reasonable use, and that the landowners may still build a minimum of sixty residential units on the land. They are not entitled to obtain maximum profits from the use of their land or to obtain the highest and best use for the property. *Nopro Co. v. Town of Cherry Hills Village*, 180 Colo. 217, 504 P.2d 344; *Wright v. City of Littleton*, 174 Colo. 318, 483 P.2d 953 (1971). The landowners failed to establish that as the result of the hillside ordinance they could not put their property to any reasonable use. They therefore failed to satisfy their burden of demonstrating beyond a reasonable doubt that the ordinance was confiscatory.

* * *

Finally, the landowners argue that the City Council's decision to rezone Crystal Hills was arbitrary, capricious and an abuse of discretion in violation of C.R.C.P. 106(a)(4). A trial court reviewing a quasi-judicial action pursuant to C.R.C.P. 106(a)(4) must uphold that decision unless there is no competent evidence in the record to support it. *E.g., Ross v. Fire & Police Pension Ass'n,* 713 P.2d 1304 (Colo.1986); *Corper v. City & County of Denver*, 191 Colo. 252, 552 P.2d 13 (1976). The record in this case reflects that the City Council adopted the hillside ordinance because of long-standing concern over problems of erosion, drainage, maintenance and emergency access affecting hilly property. The decision to place Crystal Hills in the zone established by the hillside ordinance was entirely consistent with prior actions of the City seeking to address these problems. The record also establishes that the sharply contrasting geographical configurations of Crystal Hills make it well-suited for the zoning requirements established in the hillside ordinance. The City Council's action represents a reasonable and responsible effort to reconcile the interests of property owners and residents in the context of the geographical realities of the City. It was not arbitrary and capricious.

For the foregoing reasons, the judgment of the district court is affirmed.

Notes

1. Does reducing allowed density of development, by itself, serve the public interest? How does it protect the environment to exclude wetlands, watercourses, and steep slopes from lot count calculations, for example? How are such calculations different from traditional wetlands laws that severely regulate what can be built in defined wetlands and their buffers? How much scientific justification of a land use regulation is needed to survive judicial scrutiny? In the Sellon case, the court cited evidence on the record that the city had difficulty with prior building on relatively steep slopes and the testimony of the city manager at trial. In Harris v. Zoning Com'n of the Town of New Milford, the court wrote that "our search of the record leads us to conclude that the zoning commission reasonably could have believed that conservation would be a corollary effect [of the net buildable lot calculation] * * *." Sellon further establishes that the regulator need not select the best solution but need only show that its solution "is itself reasonably and rationally related to the problem being addressed." What incentive do these judicial standards create to encourage regulators to use clear and convincing environmental science in drafting and supporting local environmental laws?

2. Another case involving restrictions on hillside development is City of San Marcos v. R.W. McDonald Development Corp., 700 S.W.2d 674 (Tex.App. 1985). The court assumed the validity of an ordinance which restricted development of land "located on hillsides or in areas with soil subject to erosion," but the decision turns on whether the developer made serious misrepresentations to the city (the city initially approved the developer's subdivision but sued when it learned of the misrepresentations). Also see Hensler v. City of Glendale, 8 Cal.4th 1, 32 Cal.Rptr.2d 244, 876 P.2d 1043 (1994), cert. denied 513 U.S. 1184, 115 S.Ct. 1176, 130 L.Ed.2d 1129 (1995),

where the court dismissed a developer's inverse condemnation action for failure to exhaust administrative remedies. The developer challenged a city ordinance that precluded the building of houses on ridgelines claiming that forty percent of his land was taken by the regulation. Similarly, in Lake Shore Estates, Inc. v. Denville Twp. Planning Bd., 127 N.J. 394, 605 A.2d 1073 (1992), the court upheld the retroactive application of a steep slope ordinance that frustrated a developer's subdivision plan. In Anello v. Zoning Bd. of Appeals of Dobbs Ferry, 89 N.Y.2d 535, 678 N.E.2d 870, 656 N.Y.S.2d 184 (1997), the court held that denial of a variance to build a single-family dwelling under the city's steep slope ordinance was not a taking because the owner acquired her property after the enactment of the ordinance; thus, she was not deprived of any property interest under the rationale of the Lucas case.

3. An explanation of the rationale and planning considerations for hillside development can be found in Robert B. Olshansky, Planning for Hillside Development, in Environment & Development (American Planning Ass'n, Sept./Oct. 1995).

4. In Pomona Pointe Assoc. v. Village of Pomona, 185 Misc.2d 131, 712 N.Y.S.2d 275 (N.Y.Sup.Ct.2000), the lower court upheld a local law which regulated the development of steep slopes to protect their environmental function. Local site plan regulations are authorized by New York state law to include standards that provide for proper parking, access, landscaping, location of buildings, protection of "adjacent land uses and physical features" and "any additional elements" specified by the local legislature. The court interpreted "any additional elements" broadly to include environmental considerations. The plaintiff owned two lots with slopes of varying steepness. The village's steep slope law required the issuance of a special permit for the disturbance of a "very steep" or "extremely steep slope" as defined in the law. The plaintiff challenged the law, arguing that it granted authority to the planning board in excess of the authority contained in the state site plan statute. The court found that consideration of steep slope criteria was within the authority delegated to the village pursuant to the site plan review statute. It held that the protection of "adjacent land uses and physical features" authorizes the adoption of regulations to protect steep slopes. Such provisions "are directly related to the possible impact that disturbance of very/extremely steep slopes could have on water runoff and the stable cohesive integrity of the soil, rocks, trees and vegetation on such slopes." The court thought that it was clear that site plan review could include consideration of natural resource protection, especially when adjacent resources may be adversely affected.

5. Pennsylvania courts have also upheld ordinances regulating development on steep slopes as a reasonable method to promote preservation of environmental areas, decrease landslides, and prevent erosion problems. See, e.g., Fisher v. Viola, 789 A.2d 782 (Pa.Cmwlth.2001).

6. The town of Castle Rock, Colorado, has adopted a ridgeline protection law that allows certain ridgelines and hilltops to be designated for protection of the visual environments they create. Development permits are then conditioned on keeping buildings and other structures out of sight.

Castle Rock, Co. Code ch. 17.14.060, No. 99–15 (2002). The regulation lists specific criteria:

> C. Mitigation of Impacts. Within * * * minor ridgeline areas of the district, all primary and accessory structures shall be required to comply with the following measures designated to mitigate the visual impact of the structure prior to occupancy, unless explicitly exempted elsewhere in this chapter.
>
> > 1. Colors. All occupied structures and accessory structures shall be constructed and maintained so that predominant exterior wall colors * * * and roof surfacing materials (a) repeat the colors most commonly in the land and vegetation around the building (earth tone), and (b) have a light reflective value of no more than forty percent.
> >
> > 2. Vegetation. The area around each primary structure and accessory structure shall include at least one tree of a species with a mature height of at least thirty-five feet for each 2500 square feet of a lot or parcel area * * *.

(3) Scenic Resources

As congestion of homes, traffic, and people has accompanied urban sprawl, a counter movement has begun focusing on one salient symptom: the disappearance of open space—the appearance that things are too crowded. Citizens and local voters notice and complain that their communities look different. They lobby for local laws that protect views and the visual environment. Local legislatures have responded by enacting laws that protect scenic resources and assets, including open views, country roads, panoramic landscapes, tree-lined streets, stone walls, and agricultural scenes. Local efforts to preserve scenic resources include the regulation of road construction and maintenance, land-clearing, architecture, and placement of utility lines and signage. Other requirements such as the maintenance of vegetative buffers, street trees, and other vegetation may be included to minimize the visual impact of development.

Municipalities may protect specific view corridors that have particular aesthetic or economic importance to the community. The town of Vail, Colorado, has adopted a View Corridors ordinance expressly because "[t]he protection and perpetuation of certain mountain views and other significant views from various pedestrian public ways" will "strengthen and preserve the Town's unique environmental heritage and attributes," and will "enhance the aesthetic and economic vitality and values of the Town." Focal points and prominent landmarks are protected which "contribute to the community's unique sense of place." (Ord. 18 (1992) § 1) In Landmark Land Co. v. City and County of Denver, 728 P.2d 1281 (Colo.1986), the Colorado Supreme Court upheld a similarly worded ordinance as being well within a city's police powers. Kern County, California, has implemented a Scenic Corridor Combining District "to designate areas which contain unique visual scenic resources as viewed from a major highway or freeway wherein the siting of off-site advertising signs needs to be reviewed on a case-by-case basis." [Ch. 19.74.010.] The district is intended "to safeguard the scenic qualities of the natural environment and the visual qualities of primary entrance-ways into the county." The district regulations are added to "the regulations of the base commercial or industrial zoning district with which the SC district is combined."

Scenic resources, of course, are part of the integrated mosaic of the landscape, and laws that protect them are beginning to respect these connections. The Upland Preservation Overlay district adopted by Brookfield, Wisconsin, is intended to preserve "all significant woodlands, wildlife habitat areas, areas of rough topography and related scenic areas." [Ch. 17.96.] In addition to maintaining "the natural beauty of the city," the overlay is intended to control erosion and sedimentation and to maintain water quality. The ordinance contains a deed restriction on subdivision plats prohibiting the erection of structures, the removal of vegetation, and any filling or excavating of land within the overlay, which runs with the land in perpetuity. [17.96.070.]

Local laws that protect scenic resources arise in other contexts, including the built environment. Albuquerque, New Mexico, has created a Historic Overlay Zone and an Urban Conservation Overlay Zone as a means of preserving areas that may have "high artistic value." Areas in the Historical Overlay are suitable for preservation for historical, architectural, or cultural reasons. Areas in the Urban Conservation Overlay have "distinctive characteristics that are worthy of conservation." [§ 14–16–2–28.] For both types of overlay, the ordinance requires that the city council identify the area's distinctive characteristics and general preservation guidelines. The following case arises in the context of preserving scenic assets in the context of an historic district as well as a coastal zone and demonstrates how scenic, historic, and coastal protection provisions are being built into the basic land use regulations and procedure of local governments.

SMITH v. ZONING BD. OF APPEALS OF TOWN OF GREENWICH

Supreme Court of Connecticut, 1993.
227 Conn. 71, 629 A.2d 1089.

KATZ, ASSOCIATE JUSTICE.

The dispositive issue in this appeal is whether the planning and zoning board of appeals for the town of Greenwich (board) is authorized, under the Greenwich town charter (charter) and the applicable subdivision regulations, to consider historical factors in determining whether to grant or deny an application to subdivide property located in a historic district. The defendants, the board, the Historical Society of the Town of Greenwich, Inc. (historical society), and Anita De Lesseps Keefe, a landowner within 100 feet of the property, appeal, upon our grant of certification, from the judgment of the Appellate Court. The Appellate Court concluded that the board had not been authorized to consider historical factors in reviewing a subdivision application and reversed the judgment of the trial court. *Smith v. Zoning Board of Appeals*, 29 Conn.App. 28, 35, 614 A.2d 464 (1992). We disagree with the Appellate Court and, accordingly, reverse the judgment.

The following relevant facts are undisputed. The plaintiffs, E. Don Smith and Eileen Smith, own property located at 35 Strickland Road in Greenwich (property). The property is situated in the Mill Pond Historic District (district), which was established under article 5 of the charter and General Statutes § 7–147b. The property is also in an R–7 zone classification, which encompasses single homes.

In January, 1987, the plaintiffs submitted a preliminary subdivision application to the planning and zoning commission of the town of Greenwich (commission), seeking to subdivide the property into three lots. After a hearing, the commission preliminarily approved the plaintiffs' application, subject to the resolution of fourteen issues prior to the submission of the final application. In particular, the commission required the plaintiffs to meet with the historic district commission "in order to determine an appropriate house location for lot 1." The commission further instructed that "[t]he preservation of significant trees shall be taken into consideration in determining house location, as well as conformity as nearby as possible to the existing setback/streetscape of house locations to the south."

Pursuant to the commission's requirement, the plaintiffs met with members of the historic district commission. Although, in the absence of a final, approved subdivision plan the historic district commission could not take any formal action concerning the appropriateness of the building on lot 1, the historic district commission did, nonetheless, express its opposition to the proposal.

The plaintiffs subsequently submitted a final subdivision application. On November 22, 1988, the commission denied the plaintiffs' final subdivision application because granting it would "permit construction of a house in the * * * significant open space, thereby disrupting the essential characteristic of the historic district."

The plaintiffs appealed from the decision of the commission to the board pursuant to § 103(a) of the charter. Pursuant to § 103(a), the board conducted a de novo review of the application and held a public hearing. The board found that the plaintiffs were seeking to subdivide the property into three lots. Lot 1 would contain the plaintiffs' residence; lot 2 would contain an existing barn; and lot 3, a presently unimproved area in front of the plaintiffs' residence, would contain a single family house. The proposed building on lot 3 is the focus of this dispute.

Following the public hearing, the board denied the plaintiffs' appeal. The board concluded that the proposed building on lot 3 would disrupt the "sweeping front lawn" and, therefore, would not be consistent with the district's historic streetscape. The board stated that "[t]he proposed subdivision did not meet the purposes of the Subdivision Regulations as provided in Section 6–260, thereof. It does not conform to the Town of Greenwich Plan of Development in that it does not meet the basic objectives of preservation of historic and architectural resources. Furthermore, it does not preserve the natural features of the landscape; namely, the historic streetscape." The board also concluded that the plaintiffs' application was subject to review under the Coastal Area Management Act (act), General Statutes § 22a–90 et seq. Applying the standards in the act, the board found that the subdivision proposal "would have an adverse impact on coastal resources because of the alteration of natural features of vistas."

The plaintiffs appealed from the decision of the board to the trial court pursuant to § 104 of the charter and General Statutes § 8–8(2)(b). Although the trial court disagreed with the applicability of one of the statutes, the act, on which the board had relied, the court concluded that other statutes, as well as the town's own land use regulations, supported the board's action. The trial court therefore dismissed the plaintiffs' appeal.

The trial court concluded that the board had the authority to consider the historic streetscape for three reasons: the provisions of the town's subdivision regulations, the statutory and town policy in favor of historic preservation and a restriction contained in the plaintiffs' deed. Section 6–260 provides that the purpose of the subdivision regulations is to "[f]urther the orderly development of the Town in accordance with the Town Plan of Development." Because the town plan has "as one of its 'Basic Objectives' the preservation of historic resources," the trial court concluded that the board acted within its authority in considering the historic streetscape. Additionally, § 6–266(a)(20) of the Greenwich Land Use Regulations specifically permits an evaluation of historical factors, noted in § 6–266(a)(19), in subdivisions located "within the coastal zone." Furthermore, the town's subdivision regulations are consistent with public policy favoring historic preservation that is contained in General Statutes § 7–147a et seq. and § 6–307 of the Greenwich Land Use Regulations. Finally, a restriction in the plaintiffs' deed states that " '[s]aid premises are conveyed subject to * * * [r]egulations imposed by reason of the fact that the premises are part of a historic district as established by the Town of Greenwich * * *.' "

The trial court affirmed the board's conclusion that the plaintiffs' subdivision proposal would impair the historic streetscape. The trial court reasoned that "[t]he Smiths' side of Strickland Road is characterized by homes on lots with sweeping front lawns. The plaintiffs plan to convert their front lawn into a building lot and construct thereon a house with the thirty feet by forty feet footprint, and setbacks of twenty-five feet from the front property line, twenty feet from the south property line, and fifteen feet from a line of trees. These exhibits show that construction of a house on the front lawn would drastically alter the streetscape, and support the Board's conclusion in that regard."

Finally, the trial court considered the plaintiffs' argument that "the denial of their plan constitutes a taking of property without due process of law." The court noted, however, that "[t]he Board rejected this claim, concluding that because other alternatives for development of the property exist, the plaintiffs were not deprived of their development rights. The defendant Board argues that [the] plaintiffs have failed to establish a diminution in the value of their property as a result of the decision, and further, only one proposal has been rejected, not all proposals."

Upon a grant of certification, the plaintiffs appealed to the Appellate Court, from the trial court's dismissal of their appeal. The Appellate Court reversed the judgment of the trial court, concluding that the board did not have the authority to consider historical factors in deciding whether to grant or deny a subdivision application because: "(1) the enabling statutes on subdivisions did not give the board the authority to include historical factors in its regulations; (2) the terms 'town plan of development,' 'historic factors' and 'historic streetscape' are not known and fixed standards required for subdivision regulations; (3) the Greenwich town charter forbids the board from denying a subdivision application based on the plan of development; and (4) it is the duty of the historic district commission, not the planning and zoning commission or the board of appeals, to decide whether a building should be erected in a historic district." *Smith v. Zoning Board of Appeals*, supra, 224 Conn. at 35, 617 A.2d 167. Having ourselves granted certification for the defendants to appeal, we now reverse the judgment of the Appellate Court.

In reviewing an appeal from an administrative agency, the trial court must determine whether " 'the agency has acted unreasonably, arbitrarily, illegally or in abuse of its discretion.' " *Board of Education v. State Employees Retirement Commission*, 210 Conn. 531, 541, 556 A.2d 572 (1989); *Frito-Lay, Inc. v. Planning & Zoning Commission*, 206 Conn. 554, 573, 538 A.2d 1039 (1988). " 'The trial court may not retry the case or substitute its judgment for that of the agency * * *.' " *Board of Education v. State Employees Retirement Commission*, supra, 210 Conn. at 540, 556 A.2d 572; *Burnham v. Planning & Zoning Commission*, 189 Conn. 261, 265, 455 A.2d 339 (1983). The principal issue in this case, however, presents "questions of law turning upon the interpretation of statutes." *Board of Education v. State Employees Retirement Commission*, supra. The defendants dispute the Appellate Court's conclusion that no statutory or regulatory authority existed allowing the commission to consider historical factors. "[T]he construction of a statute on an issue that has not previously been subjected to judicial scrutiny is a question of law on which an administrative ruling is not entitled to special deference." (Internal quotation marks omitted.) *Id.*

The defendants claim initially that the Appellate Court incorrectly concluded that the commission lacked the authority to promulgate subdivision regulations that provide for the consideration of historical or architectural factors. We agree with the defendants.

"It has been said that the whole field of subdivision regulation is peculiarly a creature of legislation. It is therefore imperative that before subdivision regulations may be made operative, the necessary statutory authorization of such regulation must exist * * *. In other words, in order to determine whether the regulation in question was within the authority of the commission to enact, we do not search for a statutory prohibition against such an enactment; rather, we must search for statutory authority for the enactment." (Internal quotation marks omitted.) *Finn v. Planning & Zoning Commission*, 156 Conn. 540, 545, 244 A.2d 391 (1968). In determining whether the board had the authority to deny subdivision applications for historical reasons, we must first determine whether the commission has the authority to enact subdivision regulations that provide for such consideration. The town of Greenwich exercises its zoning power by virtue of a special act. 26 Spec. Acts 325, No. 469 (1951). "This act established the [Greenwich Town Charter], which is the source of authority" to enact and enforce subdivision regulations. *Norwich v. Norwalk Wilbert Vault Co.*, 208 Conn. 1, 8, 544 A.2d 152 (1988); *O'Meara v. Norwich*, 167 Conn. 579, 581, 356 A.2d 906 (1975). "The charter serves as an enabling act, both creating power and prescribing the form in which it must be exercised * * *." (Internal quotation marks omitted.) *West Hartford Taxpayers Assn., Inc. v. Streeter*, 190 Conn. 736, 742, 462 A.2d 379 (1983). "Agents of a city, including commissions, have no source of authority beyond the charter. *Perretta v. New Britain*, 185 Conn. 88, 92, 440 A.2d 823 (1981)." (Internal quotation marks omitted.) *Norwich v. Norwalk Wilbert Vault Co.*, supra, 208 Conn. at 8–9, 544 A.2d 152.

The charter is the source of authority governing subdivisions, except if there is a clear legislative intent that the General Statutes control. *Pizzola v. Planning & Zoning Commission*, 167 Conn. 202, 206, 355 A.2d 21 (1974). The power of the planning and zoning commission to adopt subdivision regulations is limited by the terms of the statute or special act. *Caldrello v. Planning Board*, 193 Conn. 387, 391, 476 A.2d 1063 (1984); *Bishop v. Board of Zoning Appeals*, 133 Conn. 614, 619, 53 A.2d 659 (1947); see, e.g., *Reed v. Planning & Zoning Commission*, 208 Conn. 431, 544 A.2d 1213 (1988). "The ordinance must rest primarily upon the enabling act and must not go beyond the power delegated by it." *Bishop v. Board of Zoning Appeals*, supra.

Section 83 of the charter established the planning and zoning commission. In addition to other powers granted to the commission by the charter, § 83 also conferred upon the commission "the powers and duties conferred upon zoning commissions under the General Statutes." Section 101 of the charter sets forth those areas that the commission's subdivision regulations are meant to control or regulate. Section 101(d) provides that "[t]he regulations shall provide that the land to be subdivided shall be of such character that it can be used for building purposes without danger to health or the public safety, that proper provision shall be made for water, drainage and sewerage, and, in areas contiguous to brooks, rivers or other bodies of water subject to flooding, including tidal flooding, that provision shall be made for protective flood control measures and that the proposed streets are in harmony with existing or proposed principal thoroughfares shown in the Plan of Development as described in Section 94, especially in regard to safe intersections with such thoroughfares, and so arranged and of such width, as to provide an adequate and convenient system for present and prospective traffic needs." General Statutes § 8–25, the applicable section of the General Statutes, is substantially the same.

The plaintiffs argue that neither § 101 of the charter nor any other section of the charter addressing subdivisions specifically refers to historical factors. By contrast, there is specific language authorizing the commission to regulate and make provisions for such matters as water, drainage, sewage, flood control, street layout and grading, public utilities and the provision of parks and playgrounds. Greenwich Town Charter § 101(d), (e) and (g). Thus, the plaintiffs maintain that because the charter specially refers to several items that must be provided for in the regulations, and does not expressly include the consideration of historical factors, the commission lacks the authority to enact subdivision regulations that allow consideration of historical factors.

The defendants claim, on the contrary, that the commission's authority to promulgate regulations that consider historical factors arises from § 101(d) of the charter, which provides that subdivision "regulations shall provide that the land to be subdivided shall be of such character that it can be used for building purposes without danger to *health or the public safety* * * *." (Emphasis added.) The defendants argue that public health and safety includes protecting the environment, which, in turn, includes historic preservation. We agree with the defendants.

Although neither the charter nor the General Statutes provides a specific definition of "public health and safety" in the context of zoning regulations, other related statutes establish that environmental conservation is a legitimate concern within this broad regulatory rubric. The Environmental Protection Act (EPA); General Statutes § 22a–1 et seq.; includes the environment as a facet of public health and safety. Section 22a–1 provides in part that "the policy of the state of Connecticut is to conserve, improve and protect its * * * environment * * * in order to enhance the health, safety and welfare of the people of the state." (Emphasis added.) In addition, the Inland Wetlands and Watercourses Act; General Statutes § 22a–28 et seq.; provides that "[t]he preservation and protection of the wetlands and watercourses * * * is essential to the health, welfare and safety of the citizens of the state * * *." General Statutes § 22a–36; see *Mario v. Fairfield,* 217 Conn. 164, 168, 585 A.2d 87 (1991). These statutes illuminate the statutory phrase before us in this case because they address generally related subjects that the legislature may be presumed to have considered in like manner. *Link v. Shelton*, 186 Conn. 623, 627, 443 A.2d 902 (1982). In light of these principles, we find a relationship between protecting the public health and safety and protecting the environment. Accordingly, we conclude that public health and safety includes consideration of the "environment."

Although this court has not defined the contours of the term "environment," we may look again to the meaning given to this term in other statutory provisions. *Link v. Shelton*, supra. Once it is established that "public health and safety" includes consideration of environmental concerns, the environmental statutes make it clear that historical factors are a recognized element of environmental law. The EPA in General Statutes § 22a–1c includes a broad definition of actions that significantly affect the environment: "activities * * * proposed to be undertaken by state departments, institutions or agencies * * * which could have a major impact on the state's * * * *historic structures* * * *." (Emphasis added.) Additionally, General Statutes § 22a–19a states in part that the EPA "shall be applicable to the unreasonable destruction of historic structures and landmarks of the state, which shall be those properties (1) listed or under consideration for listing as individual units on the National Register of Historic Places (16 USC [§] 470a, as amended) or (2) which are a part of a district listed or under consideration for listing on said national register and which have been determined by the state historic preservation board to *contribute* to the *historic significance of such district*." (Emphasis added.) The EPA recognizes that the protection of many environmental concerns, such as air and water, is essentially the preservation of the resource that is being used. These regulations " 'guarantee that important land functions continue to operate while the land is being used, no matter what the use.' " T. Tondro, Connecticut Land Use Regulation 2d Ed.(1992), p. 263. Similarly, the protection of historical factors is a preservation of the function of the resource being used. *Id.*; see *Penn Central Transportation Co. v. New York City*, 438 U.S. 104, 108, 98 S.Ct. 2646, 2651, 57 L.Ed.2d 631 (1978) ("[h]istoric conservation is but one aspect of the much larger problem, *basically an environmental one*, of enhancing * * * the quality of life for people" [emphasis added; internal quotation marks omitted]). We note, as well, that we have interpreted the power to protect the "general welfare" to include the authority to consider historical factors. *Figarsky v. Historic District Commission*, 171 Conn. 198, 207–209, 368 A.2d 163 (1976).

Accordingly, we conclude that because the phrase "public health and safety" includes environmental factors, it includes historical factors. The commission, therefore, had the authority to promulgate subdivision regulations that take into account historical factors.

* * *

Our conclusion that the board incorrectly denied the plaintiffs' application on the basis of noncompliance with the town plan would ordinarily require that we affirm the Appellate Court's judgment. On appeal to the Appellate Court, as well as on appeal to this court, however, the defendants raised alternative grounds in their briefs upon which the trial court's decision may be affirmed. After review of the defendants' arguments, we conclude that the Appellate Court incorrectly dismissed one of these alternate grounds. "[T]his court is authorized to rely upon alternative grounds supported by the record to sustain a judgment * * *. 'The * * * judgment will be affirmed, though based on erroneous grounds, if the same result is required by law.' " Henderson v. Department of Motor Vehicles, 202 Conn. 453, 461, 521 A.2d 1040 (1987); *Ivey, Barnum & O'Mara v. Indian Harbor Properties, Inc.*, 190 Conn. 528, 532, 461 A.2d 1369 (1983); *A & H Corporation v. Bridgeport*, 180 Conn. 435, 443, 430 A.2d 25 (1980); *Johnny Cake, Inc. v. Zoning Board of Appeals,* 180 Conn. 296, 301, 429 A.2d 883 (1980); C. Tait, Connecticut Appellate Practice and Procedure (1991) § 7.14. We conclude that the trial court correctly concluded that the board was authorized, under the subdivision regulations, to consider historical factors when it acted on the application.

In construing regulations, the general rules of statutory construction apply. *Schwartz v. Planning & Zoning Commission*, 208 Conn. 146, 153, 543 A.2d 1339 (1988) (applying rules of statutory construction to interpretation of zoning regulations); see *Ghent v. Planning Commission*, 219 Conn. 511, 518–19, 594 A.2d 5 (1991); *Sonn v. Planning Commission*, 172 Conn. 156, 159–60, 374 A.2d 159 (1976). The commission is limited by the power conferred upon it by the subdivision regulations. See *Reed v. Planning & Zoning Commission*, 208 Conn. 431, 544 A.2d 1213 (1988) (planning commission cannot exercise a power that has been admittedly delegated to it, unless its own regulations give it the right to exercise that power). Section 6–266(a)[6] of the Greenwich Land Use Regulations sets forth the information that should be included in a preliminary subdivision application. "The preliminary layout shall be considered as a helpful guide in the preparation of a subdivision plan and should include the information set out in Section 6–266." Greenwich Land Use Regs. § 6–265. Subsection (a) of § 6–266 states that "[t]he

6. Section 6–266(a) of the Greenwich Land Use Regulations provides in pertinent part: 'The preliminary layout shall include as many of the following items of information as is practicable * * *.

"(19) For a subdivision of ten (10) lots or more or the subdivision of ten (10) or more acres, an environmental assessment by qualified environmental specialists shall be provided. The Commission may require said assessment for smaller subdivisions if deemed necessary. The assessment shall include an evaluation of the following:

"(a) Conformance with the Open Space Plan of Development

"(b) Significant wetlands

"(c) Steep Slopes

"(d) Stormwater Drainage

"(e) Soils capabilities

"(f) Vegetation including forested areas and the identification of trees over 10″ in caliper when not part of forested areas

"(g) Significant geological formations

"(h) Historical and archaeological factors

"(i) Animal habitats

"(j) Water availability and quality

"(k) Aquifer protection in accordance with the Statutes of the State of Connecticut

"(*l*) Other data which the Commission deems appropriate.

"The environmental assessment shall be subject to a review, after the receipt of recommendations of the Conservation Commission, by the Planning and Zoning Commission including the mitigation measures for minimizing environmental impact before the applicant proceeds to final plan."

preliminary layout shall include as many of the following items of information as is practicable." This general statement, set forth at the beginning of the regulation, indicates the commission's intent to require only the information that is pertinent to a particular subdivision application.

Section 6–266 (a)(19) permits the commission in its discretion to require an environmental assessment in the preliminary layout of subdivisions of fewer than ten lots or ten acres. Subsection (a)(19) lists twelve relevant considerations, including "[h]istorical and archaeological factors." Greenwich Land Use Regs. § 6–266(a)(19)(h). In this case, the commission requested an evaluation by the historic district commission of the historic implications of the subdivision application. It also requested an evaluation by the required experts of some of the other considerations listed in § 6–266(a)(19). It did not request that each and every one of these items be evaluated, presumably because it did not see such a need.

The plaintiffs argue that § 6–266 does not apply because the commission did not formally request an "environmental assessment." The consequence of the plaintiffs' argument is that, unless the commission formally requests each item of information by calling it an "environmental assessment," the commission cannot consider potentially relevant information. We decline to accept such a narrow construction of the regulation.

Regulations are to be construed as a whole. *Forest Construction Co. v. Planning & Zoning Commission*, 155 Conn. 669, 679, 236 A.2d 917 (1967). There is nothing in § 6–266(a) that specifically requires that the commission label its request for information an "environmental assessment." Rather, "environmental assessment" is a general label for the types of information that the commission is authorized to consider in its determination of subdivision applications. Further, the intent of the preliminary layout is to convey relevant information to the commission in order to facilitate the process. This intent is indicated by the overall description of what should be included in a layout in § 6–266(a), which states that the "preliminary layout shall include as many of the following items of information as is practicable."

The plaintiffs further argue that the commission did not consider a full environmental assessment as required by the language of § 6–266(a)(19), which states that "[t]he assessment *shall* include an evaluation of the following * * *." (Emphasis added.) The plaintiffs contend that this regulation makes it mandatory that each of the twelve factors listed be included in an assessment of the property to be subdivided. We disagree.

Although subsection (a)(19) of § 6–266 employs the word "shall," it does not make sense to require the commission to evaluate factors that are not relevant to a particular subdivision. Whether the word "shall" is mandatory or precatory depends upon its context. See, e.g., *Caron v. Inland Wetlands & Watercourses Commission*, 222 Conn. 269, 273, 610

A.2d 584 (1992). In construction of the words of a regulation, like those of a statute, common sense must be used. *Police Department v. State Board of Labor Relations*, 225 Conn. 297, 303, 622 A.2d 1005 (1993). The items listed to be considered include some specific items that will not be implicated in every subdivision application. For example, in addition to historical and archaeological factors, the list includes animal habitats, significant geological formations and aquifer protection. Greenwich Land Use Regs. § 6–266(a)(19)(g), (i) and (k). Not every subdivision application will require the consideration of each of these factors. It would be a waste of time, money and energy for the participants involved to be required to gather information that is not relevant to the subdivision application.

In addition, § 6–296(d) of the Greenwich Land Use Regulations explicitly permits the commission to require a redesign of a subdivision plan "in order to protect environmental or historic resources" if the environmental assessment indicates the need for a redesign. Thus, the regulations specifically anticipate a situation, like the one at hand, where historical preservation requires the redesign of subdivision plans.

We also must look to the overall intent of the applicable regulations in considering subdivision applications. *Forest Construction Co. v. Planning & Zoning Commission*, supra. "Regulations, like statutes, do not exist in a vacuum." *Bombero v. Planning & Zoning Commission*, 218 Conn. 737, 743, 591 A.2d 390 (1991). As noted above, § 6–266(a) requires the consideration of only that information that is necessary. Additionally, the purpose of the subdivision regulation is to "[f]urther the orderly development of the Town in accordance with the Town Plan of Development." Greenwich Land Use Regs. § 6–260(a)(1). Although, as noted above, the town plan cannot itself support the denial of a subdivision application, its provisions can serve as an interpretative guide to the meaning of properly enacted regulations. The plan has as one of its basic objectives the preservation of historic resources. The plan also provides that "Greenwich has a rich * * * historical heritage that should be protected for the benefit and enlightenment of future generations," and that "[c]onserving the Town's * * * historical resources is a notably effective land use tool for preserving the essential character and spirit of the community."

Accordingly, we conclude that § 6–266(a)(19)(h) expressly permits the commission to consider historical factors.

II

The defendants next claim that the Appellate Court incorrectly concluded that the terms "historical factors" and "historic streetscapes" do not comply with the established rules requiring regulations to be reasonably precise, adequate and sufficient. We agree with the defendants.

The standard for determining the adequacy of subdivision regulations is whether they " 'are as reasonably precise as the subject matter requires and are reasonably adequate and sufficient to guide the commission and to enable those affected to know their rights and obligations.' " *Nicoli v. Planning & Zoning Commission*, 171 Conn. 89, 93, 368 A.2d 24 (1976); *Forest Construction Co. v. Planning & Zoning Commission*, supra, 155 Conn. at 680, 236 A.2d 917. Although some standards may be general, the regulation must be " 'reasonably sufficient to identify the criteria to be evaluated in their enforcement in order to meet the many variables involved since it would be impossible to establish one standard which would adequately cover all future cases.' " *Nicoli v. Planning & Zoning Commission,* supra, 171 Conn. at 93, 368 A.2d 24.

In this case, the commission's subdivision regulations sufficiently apprised the plaintiffs that historical factors would be considered in evaluating their subdivision application. In evaluating the regulations, we must construe them "as a whole since particular words or sections of the regulations, considered separately, may be 'lacking in precision of meaning to afford a standard sufficient to sustain' them." *Forest Construction Co. v. Planning & Zoning Commission*, supra, 155 Conn. at 679, 236 A.2d 917. *Ghent v. Planning Commission*, supra, 219 Conn. at 517, 594 A.2d 5; *Sonn v. Planning Commission*, supra, 172 Conn. at 162, 374 A.2d 159. Although § 6–266(a)(19) does not specifically define the term historical factors, the general purpose of the regulations specifically references the town plan. Section 6–260(a)(1) states that "[t]he purposes of this Article shall be to (1) [f]urther the orderly development of the Town in accordance with the Town Plan of Development." This reference puts prospective subdivision applicants on notice that the town plan will help define the specific terms in the subdivision regulations.

The plan has as one of its basic objectives "[t]o preserve historic and architectural resources." In its further discussion of the preservation of historical resources, the plan specifically mentions historical "streetscapes and districts" as important aspects of Greenwich that the town wishes to preserve. In a subsequent section, the plan states that "[t]he following considerations should be the starting point for decisionmaking * * * [t]he goal is to sustain a climate where * * * historic streetscapes can be preserved." These specific references to streetscapes, the historical factor at issue in this case, define one aspect of "historical factors" and certainly apprised the plaintiffs that this would be a consideration in their subdivision application.

The consideration of historical factors does not occur in a vacuum. See *Bombero v. Planning & Zoning Commission*, supra. "It is unrealistic to demand detailed standards which are impracticable or impossible." *Forest Construction Co. v. Planning & Zoning Commission*, supra, 155 Conn. at 679, 236 A.2d 917. The term historic factors derives meaning from the physical environment of the historic district. See *A-S-P Associates v. Raleigh*, 298 N.C. 207, 223, 258 S.E.2d 444 (1979). In the context of a historic district, there are identifiable and sufficiently distinct historical standards by which the commission may be guided. These same characteristics also put property owners on notice of the types of historical factors that will be considered. "Although * * * discretion cannot be entirely eliminated because of the subjective nature of this process''; *Bellevue Shopping Center Associates v. Chase*, 574 A.2d 760, 764 (R.I.1990); the board is confined to the relevant historic period in its consideration of historical factors.

Accordingly, we conclude that the standards set forth in the regulations and the plan are reasonably precise and sufficient to guide the commission. Accord *Maher v. New Orleans*, 516 F.2d 1051, 1067 (5th Cir.1975), cert. denied, 426 U.S. 905, 96 S.Ct. 2225, 48 L.Ed.2d 830 (1976); *Bellevue Shopping Center Associates v. Chase*, supra, 574 A.2d at 764–65; see generally *Burnham v. Planning & Zoning Commission*, 189 Conn. 261, 263–64, 455 A.2d 339 (1983); *Figarsky v. Historic District Commission*, supra, 171 Conn. at 207–209, 368 A.2d 163 (implicitly endorsing the adequacy of ''historical factors'' to guide municipal agencies and applicants); see also *Carlson v. Fisher*, 18 Conn.App. 488, 506–507, 558 A.2d 1029 (1989) (referencing streetscape). The Appellate Court was, therefore, incorrect in concluding that the regulations did not support the action taken by the commission.

* * *

IV

The defendants next argue that the Appellate Court incorrectly concluded that the board's consideration of the subdivision regulations improperly encroached upon the applicable zoning regulations. The plaintiffs claim, to the contrary, that because it is undisputed that the application conformed with the zoning requirements of an R–7 zone, it could not be denied on the basis of nonconformance with subdivision regulations. *Smith v. Zoning Board of Appeals*, supra, 29 Conn.App. at 37, 614 A.2d 464. We agree with the defendants.

Citing *Cristofaro v. Burlington*, 217 Conn. 103, 107, 584 A.2d 1168 (1991), the Appellate Court concluded that the commission lacked the authority ''to include historical factors in its regulations'' because ''[s]ubdivision regulations cannot impose minimum lot size, shape, width and depth requirements greater than those required under the zoning regulations for the zone where the property is to be subdivided or deny approval of lots that meet all zoning requirements.'' *Smith v. Zoning Board of Appeals*, supra, 29 Conn.App. at 36, 614 A.2d 464. *Cristofaro*, however, is inapposite. In *Cristofaro*, the planning and zoning commission enacted a regulation that directly intruded on a subject that was exclusively a zoning matter. See *Avonside, Inc. v. Zoning & Planning Commission*, 153 Conn. 232, 238–39, 215 A.2d 409 (1965) (fees in subdivision regulations in excess of fees in zoning regulations invalid). A subdivision regulation may not conflict with applicable zoning regulations.

Although subdivision regulations and zoning regulations have separate functions, landowners must comply with the requirements of each applicable regulation. *Vose v. Planning & Zoning Commission*, 171 Conn. 480, 483, 370 A.2d 1026 (1976); see *Cristofaro v. Burlington*, supra, 217 Conn. at 106, 584 A.2d 1168; *Sheridan v. Planning Board*, 159 Conn. 1, 9, 266 A.2d 396 (1969). Only if the commission enacts subdivision regulations that exclusively concern zoning power, or if the subdivision regulations directly conflict with a zoning power, will the subdivision regulation be invalid. *Cristofaro v. Burlington*, supra, 217 Conn. at 107, 584 A.2d 1168; *Avonside, Inc. v. Zoning & Planning Commission*, supra.

In this case, the subdivision regulations neither encroach upon an area that is uniquely a zoning power, nor directly conflict with applicable zoning regulations. As we discussed above, § 101(d) of the charter permits the commission to enact regulations that consider historical factors. Although General Statutes § 8–2 authorized the zoning commission to enact zoning regulations that consider historical factors, the parties have not pointed to any zoning regulation that does so. The record therefore does not indicate any conflict between the pertinent subdivision regulations and any of the applicable zoning regulations.

Accordingly, the zoning regulations in this case do not prevent the board's review of historical factors in considering whether to grant or deny the plaintiffs' subdivision application. The Appellate Court was mistaken in relying on a conceived conflict of regulations as a ground for sustaining the plaintiffs' appeal.

* * *

The judgment of the Appellate Court is reversed and the case is remanded to that court with direction to affirm the trial court's judgment dismissing the plaintiffs' appeal.

Notes

1. Note how the scenic standards enforced in Smith arise in the course of the review of an application for the subdivision of land. One trend among communities interested in protecting environmental assets such as scenic views is to add standards to their traditional land use regulations, instead of adopting stand-alone regulations. Can you identify the local regulations and standards used in Smith that were used to deny the plaintiff's application? Were these standards contained in the zoning law, site plan regulations, or other local law?

2. In Wal–Mart Stores Inc. v. Planning Board of the Town of North Elba, 238 A.D.2d 93, 668 N.Y.S.2d 774 (1998), the board denied the big box retailer's application for a special permit and site plan approval for a large retail store. The Town's special permit regulations required that projects "not have a materially adverse impact on adjoining and nearby properties" and "will not result in a clearly adverse aesthetic impact." The Town, additionally, had adopted a Scenic Protection Overlay District to protect the view of nearby Whiteface Mountain that was visible to all incoming travelers on the main gateway entrance highway into the tourist community. New York local land use agencies have an obligation under state law to review the impact of their actions on the environment and the authority to impose conditions on their approvals to protect aesthetic resources. (Env. Cons.

Law. Art. 8.) The court sustained the denial finding that the record of the planning board's deliberation on the matter showed that "despite all efforts to screen the store and parking area from the road, their presence would nevertheless bring about noticeable change in the visual character of this cultural area."

3. The Smith and Wal–Mart cases raise the question of how local governments obtain their authority to regulate in the interest of the environment. Developers, applying for standard subdivision and site plan approvals, are sometimes baffled when they learn that aesthetic considerations can lead to a denial or significant alteration in their proposed projects. Trace the line of authority from the state legislature, to the local government, to the operative administrative board in these cases to understand the delegation of power that is found to sustain aesthetic regulations.

4. How broad is local authority to protect environmental assets? Does the Smith court hold that Connecticut localities can require that full environmental assessments be submitted with all major subdivision applications? If so, how does it come to that conclusion? For an interesting article discussing how far North Carolina courts will go in upholding local environmental laws, see David W. Owens, Local Government Authority to Implement Smart Growth Programs: Dillon's Rule, Legislative Reform, and the Current State of Affairs in North Carolina, 35 Wake Forest L. Rev. 671, 701 (2000) (quoting N.C. Gen. Stat. §§ 153A–340(a), 160A–381 (1999)).

5. The Town of Mount Pleasant, South Carolina, enacted a local law that requires an environmental impact review of individual development projects. South Carolina's legislature has not adopted a statute that authorizes state and local agencies to conduct environmental reviews of their actions. The impact assessment that developers must submit under this local law must address the negative effect their developments will have on marshes, creeks, rivers, plant and animal habitats, and buffer zones, and must describe the steps that will be taken to mitigate these effects and protect natural resources. The state Constitution provides that its provisions and all laws concerning local government shall be liberally construed in their favor and that any powers granted local government shall include those fairly implied and not prohibited by the Constitution. A state statute empowers localities to enact regulations regarding any subject that appears necessary and proper for the general welfare or for preserving health and good government. The land use enabling statute in South Carolina delegates local governments the authority to enact comprehensive plans, zoning, floating zones, and planned unit developments and provides that any other planning and zoning techniques may be used. Localities are authorized to consider the protection of ecologically sensitive areas through zoning. S.C. Const. Art. VIII, § 17; S.C. Ann. Code § 6–29–710.

6. In Swan v. Inhabitants of the Town of Norway, 1989 WL 1129562 (Me.1989), the Superior Court of Maine upheld a site plan ordinance containing standards that preserved landscapes and prevented "development that would have an undue adverse effect on the scenic or natural beauty of the area, aesthetics, historic sites, or rare and irreplaceable natural areas" as being a proper delegation of legislative authority to the planning board.

7. In Batchelder v. City of Seattle, 77 Wash.App. 154, 890 P.2d 25 (1995), the court approved a developer's plan to subdivide his waterfront parcel into four lots, rehabilitate an existing house, and build three new houses. A neighbor challenged the proposed plat on the ground that the plan would diminish his view. Seattle has a Shoreline Substantial Development Permit procedure. The court cited with approval a regulation promulgated to protect views of Portgage Bay; however, the court found that the impact of the proposed development on the neighbor's view was relatively minor; after construction, he would retain eighty percent of his view. The court remanded the case with instructions to reinstate the developer's permit.

8. In Ross v. City of Rolling Hills Estates, 192 Cal.App.3d 370, 238 Cal.Rptr. 561 (1987), parcel owners were prohibited from expanding their home because it violated the City's viewshed protection ordinance. The plaintiffs claimed that the language used was unconstitutionally vague, failed to provide adequate guidance to the planning commission, and contained unintelligible concepts. The ordinance referenced the "needless destruction and impairment of views and discouragement of the blockage and misuse of [hillside view lots]." The court found that this language was definite enough to pass the California standard for legislative precision. The language must be definite enough to provide a standard for those whose conduct is prescribed, as well as a standard by which administrative agencies can ascertain compliance. How definite is this language? How much guidance does it provide? If the courts create such low thresholds for the standards that local laws must contain, are there other reasons to strive for greater precision and persuasion in adopting innovative land use laws that restrict private land use? The regulated parties in the Ross case were local homeowners who applied to construct an addition to their current home.

9. To what degree can the police power be used to achieve such objectives? When will it be necessary to turn to public purchase programs to protect aesthetic resources? Can regulation and purchase programs be combined to achieve these goals and if so how? The discussion about how far localities should go—and what techniques they should use—in protecting views and open space is not new. William H. Whyte vigorously urged programs for the purchase of development easements. See Whyte, Open Space Action (Outdoor Recreation Review Commission Study Rep. 15, 1962). This approach was criticized by a Comment, Control of Urban Sprawl or Securing Open Space: Regulation by Condemnation or by Ordinance, 50 Calif.L.Rev. 483 (1962). Krasnowiecki & Paul, The Preservation of Open Space in Metropolitan Areas, 110 U.Pa.L.Rev. 179 (1961), urged a combined police power, public purchase program. In general see Jordahl, Conservation and Scenic Easements: An Experience Resume, 39 Land Econ. 343 (1963); Siegel, The Law of Open Space (N.Y. Regional Plan Ass'n, Inc., 1960); and Proceedings, Conservation Easements and Open Space Conference. (Wis. Dep't Resource Development, Dec. 13–14, 1961); 5 Williams, American Land Planning Law, Chap. 159 (1988). For an unusual perspective on the open space problem, see Platt, Feudal Origins of Open Space Law, 4 Land Use Controls Q. 27 (No. 4, 1970). Also see Williams, Scenic Protection as a Legitimate Goal of Public Regulation, 38 Wash.U.J.Urb. & Contemp.L. 3 (1990).

(4) Tree and Forest Preservation/Timber Preservation

Tree Preservation

Tree preservation ordinances typically establish a permit system under which tree removal is allowed, but only upon a showing of necessity and compliance with certain conditions, such as the replacement of some or all of the trees to be removed. Tree preservation ordinances may consider views, pruning, trimming, and setbacks from curbs, sidewalks, and street intersections. A number of states, including Georgia, Ga. Code Ann. § 12–2–8(h)(8) (2001); Hawaii, Haw. Rev. Stat. §§ 58–1 to 58–5 (2001); Maine, Me. Rev. Stat. § 38.439–A(5) (2001); and Maryland, Md. Code Ann., Nat. Res. I § 5–1603 (2000), have adopted statutes that either require or permit local governments to adopt tree preservation laws.

Some communities have adopted ordinances to protect native tree species, or "heritage trees," such as oak, sycamore, walnut, and eucalyptus. These ordinances require reports by professional arborists and practices to be followed to preserve such specimens from development activities, including additions to single-family homes. Steamboat Springs, Colorado, has adopted a Trees and Shrubs Ordinance. The purpose of this local law is to prescribe requirements "for the protection of plants, including * * * trees, shrubs, lawns, and all other landscaping located, standing, or growing within or upon city property, including * * * any city-owned street, alley, right-of-way, or other public place or city or mountain park, recreation area, or open space." Steamboat Springs, Colo., Code § 24–1 (2002).

The case below presents a different situation. The California city involved in this litigation enacted an ordinance allowing neighbors to apply for a permit compelling an owner to trim/remove trees grown in excess of a certain height that impair the neighbors' view.

ECHEVARRIETA v. CITY OF RANCHO PALOS VERDES

California Court of Appeal, Second District, 2001.
86 Cal.App.4th 472, 103 Cal.Rptr.2d 165.

HASTINGS, J.

Jon Echevarrieta (appellant) appeals from a judgment entered in favor of respondents the City of Rancho Palos Verdes (the City) and the City of Rancho Palos Verdes City Council (the City Council) after the trial court denied appellant's petition for writ of mandate. At issue is a "view protection" ordinance of the City. We affirm the trial court's judgment.

Voters in the City approved Proposition M on November 7, 1989. It was codified in section 17.02.040 of the Rancho Palos Verdes Municipal Code (hereinafter referred to as the Ordinance), and was most recently amended in January 1997.

In pertinent part, the Ordinance prohibits residents of the City from significantly impairing a view by permitting foliage to grow in excess of certain height limitations. If foliage in existence already exceeds those height limitations, the person whose view is impaired must first attempt to informally resolve the matter with the person who owns the foliage, and if that fails, may apply for a "view restoration permit." Hearings on the application for the permit are conducted by a view restoration Commission (VRC), a committee of seven members appointed by the City Council. The VRC may grant the permit only if certain specified findings are made. If the VRC orders any foliage trimmed or removed, or replacement foliage is ordered planted, the costs are to be borne by the permit applicant. Any interested party may appeal the VRC's decision to the City Council.

Since 1966, Norbert Keilbach has lived on Greve Drive in the City. His home faces south towards the Pacific Ocean and Catalina Island. Appellant lives on Ganado Drive, on a slope directly below Keilbach's home. Appellant has several trees which are near the border of his property and Keilbach's, which purportedly block Keilbach's view of the ocean and Catalina Island. Appellant purchased his property in 1964. The trees did not exist prior to the establishment of either Keilbach's or appellant's lots.

In February 1997, Keilbach filed an application with the City in order to compel appellant to trim trees that interfered with his view.

On May 1, 1997, a public hearing was held in connection with the view restoration application. Both appellant and Keilbach appeared. At the conclusion of the hearing, the VRC adopted Resolution No. 97–5, requiring that appellant remove the three pine trees, and to trim the tops of five other trees, at the expense of the applicant, Keilbach.

On May 16, 1997, appellant appealed the VRC's decision to the City Council. The City Council heard the appeal at its public meeting on July 1, 1997, and remanded the matter to the VRC for further consideration of the effect that trimming the trees would have on appellant's privacy.

The VRC held another public hearing on the application on October 2, 1997. At the conclusion of this hearing, the VRC ordered its staff to prepare for adoption at the next meeting a resolution requiring appellant to trim his trees.

On November 6, 1997, the VRC approved Resolution No. 97–22. This resolution required appellant to trim eight of his trees but also required Keilbach to plant a barrier of no more than 20 to 25 low-growing shrubs between his property and appellant's to mitigate appellant's privacy concerns.

Appellant appealed this decision to the City Council. On March 17, 1998, the City Council heard the appeal during its public meeting.

On April 7, 1998, the City Council adopted Resolution No. 98–21, affirming the VRC's approval of the view restoration permit application and requiring appellant to trim eight of his trees. Appellant then filed this lawsuit in superior court.

* * *

On appeal, appellant makes the following contentions: (1) the trial court erred in relying upon *Kucera v. Lizza*, supra, 59 Cal.App.4th 1141; (2) the ordinance violates the takings clause; (3) retroactive application of the ordinance deprives him of due process; (4) the ordinance is deceptive and uncertain; (5) as applied, the ordinance impermissibly expands the City's police power. We first address issues (1) and (5).

In *Kucera v. Lizza*, supra, 59 Cal.App.4th 1141, the Court of Appeal considered the validity of an ordinance of the Town of Tiburon similar to the ordinance presented here. The stated purpose of the Tiburon ordinance was to establish "the right of persons to preserve views or sunlight which existed at any time since they purchased or occupied a property from unreasonable obstruction by the growth of trees" and to establish a process to achieve restoration of views and sunlight. (Tiburon Mun. Code, former §§ 15–1.A & 15–1.B.) In accord with the provisions of the ordinance, the Kuceras petitioned for informal dispute resolution with respect to trees located on the downhill lot across the street, on property owned by Lizza. The Kuceras claimed the trees obstructed their views of the San Francisco Bay and the Marin County mainland. Lizza refused to participate in the process. The Kuceras filed a complaint in superior court seeking to compel restoration of their views and for abatement of a public nuisance. The trial court entered judgment in favor of Lizza concluding that the ordinance was unconstitutional and void because it was preempted by state law and was an arbitrary and unreasonable exercise of the police power.

The Court of Appeal reversed: "It is well settled that the state may legitimately exercise its police powers to advance aesthetic values * * *." The concept of the public welfare is broad and inclusive. The values it represents are spiritual as well as physical, aesthetic as well as monetary. "[Citations.] * * * [¶] * * * [¶] We hold the Tiburon ordinance is directed toward a valid police power goal—to preserve views and sunlight. Tiburon's choice of regulating obstructing trees and tree growth obviously bears a reasonable relationship to the achievement of those goals. [Citation.]" (59 Cal.App.4th at pp. 1148–1149.)

Here, appellant contends that the Ordinance does not state a valid purpose because it states only that "the peace, health, safety and welfare of the community will be served by the adoption of this section." We disagree.

The ballot measure which was approved by the voters states the purposes of the Ordinance as follows: "The hillsides of the City constitute a limited natural resource in their scenic value to all residents of and visitors to the City. The hillsides provide potential vista points and view lots. The City's General Plan recognizes these natural resources and calls for their protection. The public health, safety and welfare of the City require prevention of needless destruction and impairment of these limited vista points and view lots * * *. [¶] Specifically, this Ordinance: [¶] 1. Protects, enhances and perpetuates views available to property owners and visitors because of the unique topographical features of the Palos Verdes Peninsula. These views provide unique and irreplaceable assets to the City and its neighboring communities * * *. [¶] 2. Defines and protects finite visual resources by establishing limits which construction and plant growth can attain before encroaching onto a view. [¶] 3. Insures that the development of each parcel of land or additions to residences or structures occur in a manner which is harmonious and maintains neighborhood compatibility and the character of contiguous sub-community development as defined in the General Plan." These purposes were reprinted in the View Restoration Permit Guidelines and Procedures issued by the City.

Enacting the Ordinance for these purposes is a clearly a legitimate exercise of the city's traditional police power. (*Ehrlich v. City of Culver City* (1996) 12 Cal.4th 854, 886 [50 Cal.Rptr.2d 242, 911 P.2d 429]; *Kucera v. Lizza, supra*, 59 Cal.App.4th at p. 1149.) To the extent that the trial court cited *Kucera* for this proposition, it did not err.

* * *

The judgment of the superior court is affirmed.

VOGEL (C. S.), P. J., and EPSTEIN, J., concurred.

Notes

1. In the Echevarrietta case, the local law that was upheld required the property owner to trim eight tall trees on his property. Consider the nature of the regulation approved by the city's voters. What objectives did the voters have in mind when they approved the proposition limiting foliage growth through a view restoration permit? Do you think that topping or trimming tall trees is recommended by arborists who have the health and longevity of the trees in mind? Do large trees with abundant growth serve any positive purpose or do they just block views? What do your answers suggest regarding the narrowness of some local laws enacted to protect one of many possible environmental objectives?

2. In Wheat Ridge, Colorado, the city forester, upon thirty days notice, can enter private property in order to inspect trees and other plants in order "to determine if any destructive or communicable disease or other pestilence exists which is detrimental or endangers the good health and well-being of trees * * *." Wheat Ridge, Co. Code § 24–5 (2002).

3. Other cities require tree preservation plans. In the city of Carrollton, Texas, prior to construction or development of land, an owner must submit a tree preservation plan if one or more "protected trees" (one of thirty-eight listed trees, four inches or more in diameter and at least four feet in height) will be affected. If the land does not contain any protected trees, a registered surveyor, engineer, architect, or landscape architect must submit a letter verifying the absence of protected trees; where protected ones

exist, a permit must be obtained and the landowner must either avoid cutting them or replace them. City of Carrollton, Tex. Code ch.155 (2001).

4. In Hawaii a statute adopted in 1975, Hawaii Rev. Stat. § 58–1 et seq., commands each county to establish an arborist advisory committee to advise and recommend protective ordinances and review all actions deemed to endanger exceptional trees. Section 58–4 authorizes counties to enact protective regulations and to seek injunctions against removal or destruction of exceptional trees. Exceptional trees are defined as "a tree or stand or grove of trees with historic or cultural value, or which by reason of its age, variety, location, size, esthetic quality, or endemic status has been designated by the county committee as worthy of preservation."

Timber Preservation

The regulation of timber harvesting can help maintain an ecological balance while still meeting present and future demand for lumber and pulp. Some factors considered by local harvesting regulations include the successional role of species regeneration, the effects of competing vegetation, and potential damaging agents such as insects and pathogens. Construction of access roads, timber products processing centers, and other permanent structures in heavily forested areas are development activities that may be regulated by timber harvesting laws. The town of Pawling, New York, adopted a Timber Harvesting Law that regulates tree clearing and harvesting to prevent sedimentation and drainage problems. Pawling, NY Code §§ 45–2, 45–9 (1993). There are a variety of ways of limiting timber harvests in the public interest as the principal case demonstrates.

RANCHO LOBO v. DEVARGAS

United States Court of Appeals, Tenth Circuit, 2002.
303 F.3d 1195.

BRISCOE, CIRCUIT JUDGE.

Defendants, all members of the Board of Commissioners of the County of Rio Arriba, New Mexico (hereinafter "the County") appeal from a decision of the district court holding that the Rio Arriba County Timber Harvest Ordinance is invalid because it is preempted by the New Mexico Forest Conservation Act, N.M.S.A.1978 §§ 68–2–1 *et seq.*, and also holding that the ordinance's provisions for requiring an environmental assessment are invalid because they delegate unlimited power to the county planning and zoning commission. The County contends that the Timber Harvest Ordinance is not preempted by the Act, but instead asserts there is room for concurrent jurisdiction. The County further contends that the Timber Harvest Ordinance's provisions for environmental assessment do not improperly delegate unlimited power to the Planning and Zoning Commission. We reverse and remand.

I.

The facts in this case are undisputed. The New Mexico Forest Conservation Act establishes the State Forestry Division, which is authorized to enforce all laws, rules and regulations relating to all forested, cutover or brushlands within the state under the following circumstances:

A. prevention and suppression of fires;

B. logging and timber operations and practices;

C. trespass, waste and littering; and

D. conservation of commercial forest lands and products.

N.M.S.A 1978, § 68–2–14. The Division is authorized to make and enforce rules and regulations "for the prevention and suppression of forest or brush fires, and for the control of forest pests and for the application of commercial forest practices within the state." *Id.*, § 68–2–16. Section 68–2–16 also provides:

> Nothing in the Forest Conservation Act [citation omitted] shall prevent a landowner hereafter from converting forest vegetative types to nonforest vegetative types for such purposes as range, wildlife habitat, farming, surface mining or subdivision development; provided, however, any slash resulting from such conversion shall be treated in a manner that will minimize the spread of forest fires and the possibility of insect epidemic.

Pursuant to its authority under the Forest Conservation Act, the Division has promulgated a series of regulations concerning tree harvesting and forest regeneration. 19 NMAC 20.2. The objective of this series of regulations is to "require appropriate forest resource management in order to assist in the prevention and suppression of forest fires, the control of forest pests and to maintain and enhance the economic benefits of forests and forest resources to New Mexico." 19 NMAC 20.2.6. The regulations require a state harvest permit for the harvest of commercial forest species in an area of twenty-five acres or more, and require submission of the method of harvesting and the treatment of skid trails and slash, as well as a forest regeneration plan. 19 NMAC 20.2.8–20.2.10.

In response to a threat to its watershed caused by erosion from timber harvesting on private lands, the County in 1998 enacted the Timber Harvest Ordinance under its zoning authority and power to provide for the general welfare. The purpose of the ordinance is:

> to protect, maintain and restore fully functional forests and streams, rivers, watersheds and acequias while permitting the harvest of forest goods; to protect against immediate and long range threats to the quality of the Rio Arriba County's water; to preserve local customs, culture and traditions; to preserve the bosques from harm and exploitation; to protect landowners and the property value of timberlands; to encourage the location of compatible uses of land; to promote sustainable logging practices; to encourage logging operations within Rio Arriba County; and to protect the health, safety and welfare of the citizens of Rio Arriba County.

Timber Harvest Ordinance, Article II.

The Timber Harvest Ordinance requires those who wish to harvest timber to obtain a county permit in most instances. If a permit is required, the applicant must present a timber harvest plan detailing the action, including a plan to control erosion. *Id.*, Article VI(B)(4). In evaluating a plan, the county planning and zoning department considers: 1) the sustainability of timber production; 2) economic development and local employment; 3) water quality and availability; 4) soil protection; 5) logging roads and hauling; 6) harvest selection, techniques, old growth management and reforestation; 7) archeological, historic and cultural resources; 8) abatement of noise, dust, smoke and traffic; 9) hours of operation; 10) compatibility with adjacent land uses; and 11) the effect of existing harvests on the application. *Id.*, Article VI(C). In some cases where the planning and zoning department finds that the proposed harvest would create a significant environmental impact, the applicant may be required to prepare an environmental assessment. Id., Article VI(H), (I).

The Timber Harvest Ordinance requires compliance with measures that are recommended but left voluntary under the state scheme. Erosion control plans, logging roads, drainage systems, buffer zones to protect riparian areas, and regeneration plans must comply with the best management practices recommended in the New Mexico Guidelines. *Id.*, Article VI(B), (C).

In 1991, plaintiff Rancho Lobo acquired property in Rio Arriba County for the purpose of establishing a hunting preserve. In February of 2000, Rancho Lobo applied for and was granted a permit by the Forestry Division to harvest trees in order to "[r]elease understory trees," "[i]mprove residual tree health and growth," "[e]nhance wildlife habitat and utilization in the areas," "[p]romote the Englemann spruce as a stand component and/or aspen regeneration," and "[p]repare future prescribed burn areas by removing white fir and mistletoed Douglas fir from ponderosa pine/Douglas fir stand types and enhance their establishment." Aplt.App. at 85.

In March 2000, the County informed Rancho Lobo that it needed to apply for a county timber harvest permit under the Timber Harvest Ordinance. Rancho Lobo refused to seek a permit, and instead filed an action arguing that the ordinance was invalid because it conflicted with and was preempted by the Forest Conservation Act, that enforcement of the ordinance constituted a taking in violation of the Fifth and Fourteenth Amendments, and that the ordinance illegally deprived Rancho Lobo of its property.

Both parties filed motions for summary judgment on the issue of the validity of the ordinance. In its motion, Rancho Lobo alleged that the Timber Harvest Ordinance was invalid because it was preempted by the Forest Conservation Act and was not a proper use of the County's zoning authority. In ruling on the cross-motions, the district court first determined there was sufficient controlling New Mexico law for it to decide the validity of the ordinance without certifying the question to the New Mexico Supreme Court. The district court held that the Timber Harvest Ordinance conflicted with the Forest Conservation Act because the Act allows clear-cutting while the ordinance prohibits clear-cutting without a variance being obtained. The district court also held that the ordinance conflicted with the Forest Conservation Act because the ordinance required a more extensive and stricter permitting process.

On the issue of preemption, the district court found that the statutory language of the Forest Conservation Act providing that the Forestry Division is authorized to make and enforce rules and regulations, and enforce all laws, rules and regulations relating to forestry, logging and timber operations indicated an express preemption of the Timber Harvest Ordinance. The district court further found that although the ordinance was a valid exercise of zoning authority, its provision for requiring an environmental assessment was not a valid exercise of authority because it gave the county planning and zoning department "unlimited power" to determine who would be required to prepare an environmental assessment. Ultimately, the district court held that the entire Timber Harvest Ordinance was expressly preempted by the Forest Conservation Act, and was therefore invalid. As a result, the district court granted partial summary judgment in favor of Rancho Lobo. The district court certified the partial summary judgment as a final judgment pursuant to Fed.R.Civ.P. 54(b).

II.

* * *

The district court erred in determining the Forest Conservation Act preempts the Timber Harvest Ordinance.

III.

We now turn to the County's contention that the district court erred in finding that the provisions of the Timber Harvest Ordinance concerning the requirement of an environmental assessment are invalid because they give the county planning and zoning department unlimited power to decide who will be required to prepare an environmental assessment. The County contends that language stating that an assessment is necessary upon a finding that the proposed harvest would have a "significant effect on watercourses or acequia systems, county or private property, other natural or historic resources, or the public health, safety or welfare" is sufficient guidance to restrict the Department's discretion.

The Timber Harvest Ordinance provisions in question provide that:

> An applicant *may be* required to prepare an Environmental Assessment (EA) for a proposed harvest when the Planning and Zoning Department, upon review of the THP application, finds that the proposed harvest would cause a significant environmental impact. The department's findings shall be in writing and fully state the nature and significance of the environmental impact and the legal

and factual basis for the finding. Timber Harvest Ordinance, Article VI(I) (emphasis added.)

The ordinance further defines a significant environmental impact as "a significant effect on watercourses or acequia systems, county or private property, other natural or historic resources, or the public health, safety and welfare." *Id.*, Article VI(H.2). Similarly, another portion of the ordinance provides that, where the proposed harvest is part of a combined harvest plan:

> The Planning and Zoning Department may order an applicant to prepare an Environmental Assessment pursuant to this ordinance upon a finding that the proposed and existing harvests, when assessed together, would have significant effects on the environment, public and private property and infrastructure, and the public health safety and welfare. *Id.*, Article VI(C)(11) (emphasis added.)

The district court found that these provisions were invalid because use of the word "may" granted the planning and zoning department the "unlimited power to decide which persons will be ordered to prepare an Environmental Assessment."

It is true that, under New Mexico law, a legislative body "may not vest unbridled or arbitrary power in an administrative agency but must furnish a reasonably accurate standard to guide it." *City of Santa Fe v. Gamble-Skogmo, Inc.*, 73 N.M. 410, 389 P.2d 13, 18 (1964). However, such standards "need not be specific" and broad, general standards are permissible as long as they are capable of a reasonable application and are sufficient to limit and define the agencies' discretionary powers. *Id.*

In this case, the authority of the planning and zoning department to order an environmental assessment is limited by the requirement that such an assessment will be required only in cases where there is a significant environmental impact or where the "proposed and existing harvests, when assessed together, would have significant effects on the environment, public and private property and infrastructure, and the public health safety and welfare." While this may be a broad standard, it is not an impermissible one. The New Mexico Supreme Court has upheld a law with an equally broad standard. *See Parker v. Bd. of County Comm'rs*, 93 N.M. 641, 603 P.2d 1098, 1099–1100 (1979). In *Parker*, the court upheld a zoning regulation providing that the board of county commissioners "may" suspend or revoke approval of a plat if the applicant did not submit "sufficient information." The court noted that what constituted "sufficient information" was left to the board, but held that it was a valid broad general standard. *Id.* at 1100.

Similarly, the Timber Harvest Ordinance at issue in this case contains a valid general standard for the exercise of discretion. Contrary to the holding of the district court, the ordinance does not vest the planning and zoning board with the "unlimited power to decide which persons will be ordered to prepare an Environmental Assessment." Order at 8. Rather, the board may order an environmental assessment only when it finds that the planned timber harvest will have a "significant environmental impact" or where the "proposed and existing harvests, when assessed together, would have significant effects on the environment, public and private property and infrastructure, and the public health, safety and welfare." Timber Harvest Ordinance, Article VI(C)(11). This power is capable of review and is not arbitrary.

Rancho Lobo argues that complying with an order to prepare an environmental statement is expensive and burdensome. This argument has no bearing on whether the provision requiring an environmental assessment is a valid delegation of legislative authority. The district court erred when it concluded the Timber Harvest Ordinance provision that requires preparation of an environmental assessment was not properly promulgated under the county's zoning authority.

We REVERSE the district court's conclusion that the Timber Harvest Ordinance is preempted by the Forest Conservation Act. We also REVERSE the district court's conclusion that the ordinance's provision for requiring an environmental assessment constituted an invalid delegation of legislative authority. We REMAND for further proceedings. Appellee's motion to certify question of state law is DENIED.

(5) Fish and Wildlife Protection

Habitat destruction, which can be caused by land development, is the most crippling threat to biodiversity. Habitats provide the elements that species need to survive: temperature, water, soil, sunlight, food sources, places of refuge, and safe reproduction areas. The U.S. Fish and Wildlife Service has listed more than 1,200 species as endangered or threatened. Eighty-five percent of these listed species are threatened because of habitat degradation and loss. Timothy Beatley, Preserving Biodiversity: Challenges for Planners, APA Journal, vol. 66, No. 1 (Winter 2000).

Poorly planned development in critical wildlife areas creates harmful borders around isolated habitats, limits the number of islands of habitat that remain, and prevents migration of species from one suitable habitat to another. "Development fragments habitat by dividing it into smaller, spatially disjointed landscape units. A highly fragmented landscape is less likely to have large, intact habitat units. Furthermore, fragmentation isolates species and inhibits movement and reduces the probability of recolonization in the event that a species disappears from a given patch of habitat." Theobald, David, James Miller, and N. Thompson Hobbs, "Estimating the Cumulative Effects of Development on Wildlife Habitat," Landscape and Urban Planning 39 (1997): 25–36. Conversely, land use planning can ensure the preservation of areas of habitat, open up the borders around them, and provide migration corridors sensitive to the needs of vulnerable species. Factors that determine the effect of development on particular habitats include slope, proximity to water, and vegetative cover characteristics.

Washington State has been at the forefront of protecting fish and wildlife habitats. The state's Growth Management Act of 1990 implements what the Washington Department of Fish and Wildlife (WDFW) calls "a bottom-up approach to land use planning." It requires all counties, cities, and towns in the state to classify and designate resource lands and critical areas, including fish and wildlife habitats, and to adopt development regulations for them. The WDFW has created detailed checklists to assess the wildlife potential of urban areas and to aid local governments in reviewing the elements of their development regulations and comprehensive plans.

Classifications in the Critical Fish and Wildlife Habitat ordinance created by Cowlitz County, Washington, include species and habitats of local importance; commercial and recreation shellfish areas; kelp and eelgrass beds; herring and smelt spawning areas; and naturally occurring ponds under twenty acres and their submerged aquatic beds. The county has established performance standards and requires developers to secure permits before developing in critical habitat areas. Development projects must protect habitat and vegetated open space in contiguous blocks, in order to create a continuous system or corridor of open space and habitat areas. Native species must be used in any landscaping of disturbed, undeveloped, or buffer areas, and landscaping plans must emphasize heterogeneity and structural diversity of vegetation. Cowlitz County, Washington Sec. 15.08.110 Fish and Wildlife Habitat.

Colorado statutes provide local governments with the authority to adopt local environmental laws that protect wildlife habitat. Colo. Rev. Stat. §§ 29–20–101–107, 24–65–101–106 (2001). The purpose of the State's Local Government Land Use Control Enabling Act is to achieve orderly land development within the state that maintains a balance between the basic human needs of its changing population and "legitimate environmental concerns." Specifically, the Act empowers local governments

> to plan for and regulate the use of land by * * * [p]rotecting lands from activities which would cause immediate or foreseeable material danger to significant wildlife habitat and would endanger wildlife species * * * [and by] [o]therwise planning for and regulating the use of land so as to provide planned and orderly use of land and protection of the environment in a manner consistent with constitutional rights. Colo. Rev. Stat. §§ 29–20–104(1)(b), (h) (2001).

Pursuant to this authority, Summit County, Colorado, protects wildlife through a Wildlife Habitat Overlay District that "seeks to fully protect wildlife habitats * * * from the significant adverse affects of development." Summit County, Colo. Dev. Code § 4203.01 (2002). The ordinance requires that all proposals for development within the district include a special wildlife impact report that the State Division of Wildlife is to review and approve. Adding protective provisions to subdivision or site plan regulations, or adopting a separate local habitat protection law, can achieve habitat conservation for threatened species and help maintain biodiversity.

FLORIDA WILDLIFE FEDERATION v. COLLIER COUNTY

Florida District Court of Appeal, First District, 2002.
819 So.2d 200.

ERVIN, J.

The Florida Wildlife Federation and the Collier County Audubon Society, appellants, appeal from a final order of the Department of Community Affairs, appellee, which approved a recommended order from the Division of Administrative Hearings finding amendments to the Collier County comprehensive plan to be in compliance with state law. We affirm.

In 1997, appellee, Collier County, promulgated certain amendments to its comprehensive plan, but the Department of Community Affairs rejected those amendments as not in compliance with state law. Following an administrative challenge in which appellants intervened, the Governor and Cabinet, sitting as the Administration Commission, issued a final order directing the County to take specific remedial measures with regard to its plan, one of which was that the County designate certain specified areas within the county as Natural Resource Protection Areas (NRPAs). The principal purpose of this designation is to protect indigenous fauna and flora, especially the Florida panther, a highly endangered species. The final order provided further that the NRPAs "shall be refined as actual data and analysis is made available." The Commission finally directed that within the NRPAs "only agricultural and directly-related uses and one single family dwelling unit per parcel or lot created prior to June 22, 1999, shall be allowed."

Pursuant to the order, Collier County adopted certain interim amendments to its comprehensive plan, including amendments which designated as NRPAs those areas specifically identified in the Administration Commission's final order. The Department reviewed the amendments and determined that they were in compliance with state law. Appellants subsequently challenged that determination, and the matter proceeded to a formal hearing before the Division of Administrative Hearings.

In the recommended order which followed, the administrative law judge (ALJ) discussed in detail the mapping of the NRPAs. Appellants sought expansion of these areas, based upon telemetry data gathered regarding the movement of panthers and upon a 1994 report prepared by the Florida Fish and Wildlife Commission. In rejecting the argument that the NRPA boundaries were not sufficient to protect wildlife and were not based on a thorough assessment, the ALJ observed that "the 1999 Final Order [of the Administration Commission] contemplates that the Interim NRPAs are a necessary prelude to that very assessment." He added that appellants, in effect, had asked "the County to reach its conclusions as to the natural resource issues before it undertakes the

Assessment mandated by the Final Order * * * [and such a] request is impracticable.'' Appellants thereafter took exception to the ALJ's recommended conclusion that the agricultural usage of land was not subject to an intensity-of-use standard. The Department rejected this exception in its final order, which adopted the ALJ's findings of fact and conclusions of law.

On appeal, appellants argue, as they did before the Department, that the NRPAs, as designated in the interim amendments, do not comply with section 163.3177(6)(a), Florida Statutes (1999). More particularly, appellants maintain that this statute, case law, and the Department's rule require application of an ''intensity'' standard as to agricultural uses contained within the NRPAs. Appellants also claim that the record evidence does not establish, ''beyond fair debate,'' that the NRPA's boundaries do not require further expansion to protect the Florida panther, as the ALJ found and as the Department accepted in its final order.

Turning to the first issue, appellants rely primarily on the following emphasized language in section 163.3177(6), which provides, in pertinent part:

> (6) In addition to the requirements of subsections (1)–(5), the comprehensive plan *shall* include the following elements:
>
> > (a) *A future land use plan element designating proposed future general distribution, location, and extent of the uses of land* for residential uses, commercial uses, industry, agriculture, recreation, conservation, education, public buildings and grounds, other public facilities, and other categories of the public and private uses of land. The *future land use plan shall include standards to be followed in the control and distribution of population densities and building and structure intensities.* The proposed distribution, location, and extent of the various categories of land use shall be shown on a land use map or map series which shall be supplemented by goals, policies, and measurable objectives. *Each land use category shall be defined in terms of the types of uses included and specific standards for the density or intensity of use.*

(Emphasis added.)

Appellants observe that the above statute explicitly requires a designation of the ''extent of the uses of land for * * * agricultural * * * uses of land,'' and further that each land use, including agriculture, must be reviewed pursuant to ''standards for the density or intensity of use.'' Because of this language, they contend the approved interim NRPA amendments are not in compliance with the statutory directives because there is no standard within them regulating the intensity of an agricultural use.

Appellants also point out that the Department's own rule, Florida Administrative Code rule 9J–5.003(60), requires designation of an intensity standard, because this rule defines "intensity" as:

> [A]n objective measurement of the extent to which land may be developed *or used*, including the consumption or use of the space above, on or below ground; the measurement of the use of or demand on natural resources; and the measurement of the use of or demand on facilities and services.
>
> (Emphasis added.)

Appellants continue that the language in the rule clearly reflects that the use of the term "intensity" within the statute does not refer solely to buildings and structures, contrary to the Department's non-rule policy decision. Consequently, the Department's order violates not only the statute but its own rule in failing to apply an intensity-of-use standard to an agricultural land use category.

The Department of Community Affairs, Collier County and other appellees argue in response that the term "intensity" is applicable only to the presence of buildings and structures, as provided in subsection (a) of the statute. Moreover, because buildings and structures are incompatible with the agricultural use of land, there is no corresponding necessity for imposing an intensity standard on a land use designated agricultural within the NRPAs.

In that the legislature delegated to the Department the power to enforce section 163.3177, we note that we are required to be highly deferential to the agency's interpretation of such statute. As the supreme court recently reaffirmed in *Verizon Florida, Inc. v. Jacobs*, 810 So.2d 906 (Fla.2002), an "agency's interpretation of the statute it is charged with enforcing is entitled to great deference." *See also BellSouth Telecomms., Inc. v. Johnson*, 708 So.2d 594, 596 (Fla.1998). Moreover, a court will not depart from the contemporaneous construction of a statute by a state agency charged with its regulation unless the construction is "clearly erroneous." *PW Ventures, Inc. v. Nichols*, 533 So.2d 281, 283 (Fla.1988). *Accord Miles v. Fla. A & M Univ.*, 813 So.2d 242 (Fla. 1st DCA 2002).

The interpretation the Department has given section 163.3177(6)(a) is not clearly erroneous. Although certain isolated portions of the statute support appellants' argument that all land use categories must be subjected to an intensity-of-use standard, an established statutory maxim emphasizes that all parts of a statute should be given effect in order to achieve a harmonious whole. *See State v. Knight*, 98 Fla. 891, 124 So. 461 (1929). Not only do the provisions within section 163.3177(6)(a) undergird the Department's interpretation that an agricultural use of land is excluded from an intensity review, but other pertinent statutes do as well.

Section 163.3177 is included within the Local Government Comprehensive Planning and Land Development Regulation Act. A primary purpose of the Act is that it be carried out in conformity with and in furtherance of the Florida Environmental Land and Water Management Act of 1972, chapter 380, in order "to utilize and strengthen the existing role, processes, and powers of local governments in the establishment and implementation of comprehensive planning programs to guide and control future development." § 163.3161(2), Fla. Stat. (1999) (emphasis added). In implementing the legislative mandate, the Department, acting in its role as the state land planning agency, is required to review local governments' proposed plans for the purpose of determining whether they are in compliance with the Act. § 163.3184(8), Fla. Stat. (1999).

It is obvious, as the regulatory agency charged with enforcing the statutes, that the Department must conduct its review in accordance with the legislative mandate that a submitted plan comply with the Act's overarching concern that future development be subjected to objective standards of guidance and control. To that end, the appropriate land use elements of section 163.3177 are required to be set out in the local comprehensive plans.

* * *

Section 380.04, included within the provisions of the Florida Environmental Land and Water Management Act of 1972, was enacted to implement the stated purpose of the Act, which, similar to the goal of the Local Government Comprehensive Planning and Land Development Regulation Act, was designed to protect the natural resources of the state by, among other things, adequately planning for and guiding growth and development in the state § 380.021, Fla. Stat. (1999). This Act, which predated the Local Government Comprehensive Planning and Land Development Regulation Act by three years, was devised, as was the latter act, to provide for orderly developmental growth without endangering the state's finite natural resources. Under both acts, the Department, acting as the state land planning agency, is empowered to review a local government's developmental plans which may have an impact on the state's environment. Under chapter 380, part I, it has the responsibility of reviewing developments of regional impact, and under chapter 163, part II, of reviewing comprehensive plans.

The primary purpose of the review under both acts is to ensure that developmental uses comply with statutory standards for the conservation of the state's environment. It is obvious to us that if a land use can be excluded from review under chapter 380 because it does not meet the definition of a development, a use not involving development need not be reviewed for its intensity under chapter 163.

For the above reasons, the interpretation the Department placed on section 163.3177(6)(a) is not clearly erroneous. The interim amendments provide, consistent with the final order, that only agricultural and directly related uses, and one single family dwelling unit per parcel or lot, are permitted in NRPAs. Thus, the comprehensive plan, as amended, does provide a standard regarding the "extent of the uses of land," as required by section 163.3177(6)(a), and appellants have failed to show that the Department was obliged to require an intensity standard in order to certify the interim amendments in compliance with law.

* * *

As for the second issue raised on appeal, that the evidence does not support the finding that the approved NRPA boundaries were sufficient to protect the Florida panther, we also affirm. Appellants claim that such finding was erroneous because there was evidence that such wildlife frequented areas not included within the NRPAs' boundaries. Even if we were to accept this argument as established by the evidence, appellants have failed to demonstrate how such a fact makes the boundaries of the NRPAs erroneous. As the ALJ noted, the boundaries approved are only intended to be temporary, subject to additional adjustment as further studies indicate may be necessary.

AFFIRMED

Notes

1. The city of Tumwater, Washington, adopted a law that defines and protects wildlife habitat. Tumwater, Wash. Code §§ 16.32.050, 16.32.060, 16.32.090 (1991) ("Fish and Wildlife Protection"). The regulations require habitat protection plans and establish buffer zones to retain and protect adequate urban wildlife habitats. In Green River, Wyoming, the city designated conservation districts that require the protection of critical wildlife habitat. Where development occurs, adequate impact mitigation measures are required. Green River, Wy. Code § 7–1 (2002).

2. In Department of Community Affairs v. Moorman, 664 So.2d 930 (Fla.1995), the Florida court addressed the protection of the Florida Key deer. The court described the issue:

> This case involves the validity of a land-use ordinance enacted to protect an endangered species, the miniature Florida Key deer. The regulation affects Big Pine Key where the deer now are largely concentrated. Human development on the Key has put the deer perilously close to extinction, and their numbers are estimated to be only 350 to 400 animals. The minimum number needed to sustain a viable species is considered 100 to 250 animals. The animals are further endangered by human attempts to feed them, by pet dogs that may kill them, and by automobiles.
>
> The ordinance in question prohibits the erection of fencing in portions of Big Pine Key, where the respondents own property. It was enacted because, in a natural environment, Key deer must roam freely over slash pinelands and wetlands in search of food and water. This necessarily means the deer also must roam over some privately owned lands. 664 So.2d at 931–32.

The court upheld the revocation of the landowner's permit to erect a six-foot high, 400–foot long fence on his property, holding that the state's police power included protection of the environment and that "environmental degradation threatens not merely aesthetic concerns vital to the State's economy but also the health, welfare, and safety of substantial numbers of

Floridians.'' Residents of the Florida Keys are sharply divided over whether the species is really declining and whether further development of property on the Keys should be severely restricted. See Mireya Navarro, Striking a Balance Between Deer and Residents in the Florida Keys, N.Y. Times, Mar. 18, 1997, p. A 12.

3. In Southview Associates, Ltd. v. Bongartz, 980 F.2d 84 (2d Cir. 1992), a developer purchased an eighty-eight acre parcel of land near a ski resort in Vermont with the intent of developing seventy-eight vacation homes. The Vermont Conservation Commission found that the proposed development was situated within a 280–acre deeryard; *i.e.*, a winter habitat for white-tailed deer. This deeryard is the sole remaining, active deeryard within a 10.7 square mile area. The Commission denied the development permit and, on appeal to the state Environmental Board, the decision was affirmed on the ground that the development, if allowed to proceed, would "destroy and significantly imperil wildlife habitat.'' Even though white-tailed deer are not endangered (and the Endangered Species Act was not implicated in the case), the court held that the developer had not suffered a physical taking and that the question of a regulatory taking was not ripe for review.

(6) The Public Trust Doctrine

The public trust doctrine holds that certain natural resources are held by the sovereign in trust for the benefit of the people. The doctrine arose in Roman law, was incorporated into British common law, and has been adopted or abandoned to various degrees in the fifty states. Lands adjacent to or under oceans, tidally-influenced waters, and navigable surface water are purchased by private owners subject to the public's right to use the waters for navigation. Beachfront property is purchased subject to the public's right to use the beach to a point determined by the common law and statutes of coastal states. One of the earliest cases involving the public trust doctrine held that a person could not maintain a trespass action against another person when the properties trespassed on were under navigable rivers. Arnold v. Mundy, 6 N.J.L. 1 (1821). The New Jersey Supreme Court explained that "[n]avigable rivers, where the tide ebbs and flows, the ports, bays, coasts of the sea, including both the waters and the land under the waters, for the purposes of passing and repassing, navigation, fishing, fowling, sustenance, and all other uses of the water and its products, are common to all the people of New Jersey.'' Id.

Later, in Illinois Central Railroad Co. v. Illinois, 146 U.S. 387, 13 S.Ct. 110, 36 L.Ed. 1018 (1892), the United States Supreme Court held that although land submerged under Lake Michigan could be owned and used privately, the use could not conflict with the public's interest. Illinois Central Railroad Company purchased 1000 acres in fee simple of land submerged under Lake Michigan from the State of Illinois. The Court held that the land could not be transferred in fee simple free of public trust interests. The state was allowed to sell the land in small parcels with the public trust burden attached to such property, and could condition any future use of the land to benefit the public. In more recent cases, the Supreme Court has extended the public trust doctrine to apply to any land "subject to the ebb and flow of the tide." Phillips Petroleum Co. v. Mississippi, 484 U.S. 469, 108 S.Ct. 791, 98 L.Ed.2d 877 (1988).

The public trust doctrine is flexible and subject to interpretation by modern legislatures and courts. For example, in New Jersey, the public trust doctrine was applied beyond the high tide mark to the dry upland area, if a municipality owned this area. Neptune City v. Avon-By-The-Sea, 294 A.2d 47, 61 N.J. 296 (1972). The court stated that "[t]he public trust doctrine, like all common law principles, should not be considered fixed or static, but should be molded and extended to meet changing conditions and the needs of the public it was created to benefit." Id. at 54. New Jersey has since expanded the reach of the doctrine by removing the restriction that a municipality must own the upland area. See Matthews v. Bay Head Improvement Ass'n, 471 A.2d 355, 95 N.J. 306 (1984).

Public trust principles affect the jurisprudence of regulatory takings. A government regulation that limits development on land that may not be developed because of public trust rights does not effect a taking, even where the limitation constitutes a total deprivation of the right to develop the land; the land was subject to a common law limitation that is simply mirrored in the regulation. Purchasers of property are subject to the doctrine of caveat emptor (buyer beware); they are obliged to inspect their properties and take title to all defects and limitations that are discoverable. Where customary uses of the land arise under public trust concepts, the public's use of the land is as discoverable as the activities of an adjacent owner who owns an affirmative easement over the conveyed parcel. This duty to discover—to know the land and its inherent qualities—is relevant to the investment-backed expectations so important to determining whether a land use regulation is a regulatory taking. When a permit is issued by a land use agency subject to the public rights to use the land or to enjoy its benefits, courts will inquire whether and to what extent public rights in the land preexisted the plaintiff's purchase. If a permit condition requires the owner to allow the public on the land, such an invasive condition is not a regulatory taking if the public enjoys that same right under the common law of the state.

Developers who apply to develop submerged lands, tidal wetlands, freshwater wetlands, and associated upland areas have development rights that may be limited by the public trust doctrine of the state. These notions reinforce the reach and reasonableness of federal, state, and local tidal and freshwater wetland regulations and development permit conditions that protect the right of the community under the public trust doctrine.

ESPLANADE v. SEATTLE

United States Court of Appeals, Ninth Circuit, 2002.
307 F.3d 978.

B. FLETCHER, CIRCUIT JUDGE.

Plaintiff Esplanade Properties, LLC ("Esplanade") challenges the legality of the City of Seattle's ("the City's") denial of its application to develop shoreline property on Elliot Bay in Seattle, Washington. Esplanade contends that the City's action resulted in a complete deprivation of economic use of its property, constituting an inverse condemnation in violation of federal and state constitutional law, and violating both federal and state substantive due process. Specifically, plaintiff appeals three decisions of the district court which, *in toto*, resulted in the dismissal of its claims against the defendant, *to wit*, granting summary judgment to the defendant on plaintiff's takings claim, granting summary judgment to the defendant on plaintiff's federal substantive due process claim, and dismissing plaintiff's state substantive due process claim. We have jurisdiction under 28 U.S.C. § 1291 and we affirm.

In 1992, Esplanade began a long, and ultimately unsuccessful, process of attempting to secure permission to construct single-family residential housing on and over tidelands located below Magnolia bluff, near both a large city park and a large marina. The property is classified as first class tide-land, and is submerged completely for roughly half of the day, during which time it resembles a large sand bar.

Esplanade purchased the property for $40,000 in 1991, and quickly retained a development team to design and secure permits for nine waterfront homes, each to be constructed on platforms supported by pilings. In June of 1992, Esplanade applied for building permits, as well as various use permits, variance permits, and special use permits. None of these applications were ever approved.[7]

After reviewing Esplanade's permit applications, the City's Department of Construction and Land Use ("DCLU") identified three significant code compliance issues related to the proposed project: (1) the size of the proposed piers and docks, (2) the design of the causeway access to the houses, and (3) lack of parking on dry land. The City notified Esplanade of its concerns in a Correction Notice. Esplanade responded to the City's concerns, and sought three formal code interpretations from the DCLU, each relating to the issues raised by the City. Central to the ongoing dispute, the City was asked, *inter alia*, to interpret the code with respect to parking. According to the City's interpretation, parking built over water in a single-family zone was prohibited, despite the general requirement that single-family homes be constructed *with* on-site parking. Esplanade appealed this interpretation, which was eventually af-

7. Under Washington's Shoreline Management Act ("SMA"), RCW 90.58.010, enacted in 1971, localities are required to develop a set of regulations with respect to their shorelines. Before 1992, under the Seattle Shoreline Master Program ("SSMP"), developed pursuant to the dictates of the SMA, above-water residential construction was seemingly allowed where the lots had less than 30 feet of dry land. Though the Seattle City Council later amended that provision in the SSMP, instead allowing for such use only where a lot has at least 15 feet of dry land, Esplanade filed its building permit applications before this change took effect, thus vesting its application to the former provision. *West Main Assoc. v. City of Bellevue*, 106 Wash.2d 47, 720 P.2d 782, 786 (1986) ("A vested right merely establishes the ordinances to which a building permit and subsequent development must comply.").

firmed by the Washington Court of Appeals on the ground that residential housing was not a water-dependent or water-related use.

At the end of the appeals process, in November of 1997, Esplanade was informed by the City that it had 60 days to submit formal alterations to its proposed plan, in light of the DCLU's code interpretations, without which the application would be cancelled. Esplanade, instead of altering its parking proposal, simply applied for a variance. Because Esplanade failed to modify its plans with respect to each of the three design concerns raised by the City, on April 13, 1998, the City cancelled Esplanade's application, and later refused to reconsider its unappealable decision.

On June 5, 2000, Esplanade served a letter on the City threatening to make an inverse condemnation claim as a result of the cancellation of its application. Without a response from the City, Esplanade made good on its threat and filed the current action against the City on August 22, 2000.

In its complaint, Esplanade alleges, (1) "inverse condemnation [ ] in violation of the federal and state constitutional provisions prohibiting the taking of private property without just compensation," and (2) "violat[ion][of] plaintiff's right to substantive due process, in violation of the state and federal constitutions." Plaintiff seeks "monetary damages" under 42 U.S.C. § 1983 and RCW 64.40.020.

The district court granted the defendant's motion for partial summary judgment, dismissing Esplanade's federal substantive due process claim based upon our holding in *Armendariz v. Penman,* 75 F.3d 1311 (9th Cir.1996), that federal substantive due process claims are precluded where the alleged violation is addressed by explicit textual provisions of the Constitution, specifically, the Fifth Amendment's "Takings Clause."

The district court, in its Order, did not resolve Esplanade's state substantive due process claim, but requested further briefing from the parties on the question whether the matter should be certified for review by the Washington Supreme Court.

Having received supplemental briefing from the parties, the district court dismissed Esplanade's state substantive due process claim on the ground that Washington state courts had authoritatively held that the Washington Constitution provides no greater substantive due process protection than that afforded by the United States Constitution.

Subsequently, the district court granted the defendant's motion for summary judgment on Esplanade's remaining claim, to wit, the City's alleged taking of its property without just compensation, in violation of the Fifth Amendment. The court held that because Esplanade failed to establish that the City's action was the "proximate cause" of its alleged damages, and alternatively, because the "background principles" of Washington state law would have precluded the development, under *Lucas v. South Carolina Coastal Council*, 505 U.S. 1003, 112 S.Ct. 2886, 120 L.Ed.2d 798 (1992), the City was not liable to Esplanade.

Esplanade appealed, challenging each of the district court's three decisions.

* * *

Here, the district court found no taking of plaintiff's property for two reasons. First, the court found that the City's interpretation of the SSMP and its ultimate cancellation of Esplanade's development applications were not the proximate cause of Esplanade's alleged damages. Second, the court found that the background principles of Washington law, specifically the public trust doctrine, burdened plaintiff's property and precluded Esplanade from prevailing in a takings action against the City.

We agree with the district court that under both federal and state law a plaintiff must make a showing of causation between the government action and the alleged deprivation. *See Tahoe–Sierra* (9th Cir. 2000), 216 F.3d at 783 & n. 33 (discussing requirement that "plaintiff [in takings claim] must establish both causation-in-fact and proximate causation," and noting that while "true that there is little discussion of a 'causation' requirement in any of the case law involving regulatory takings," despite a passing reference to proximate cause in *Penn Central*, 438 U.S. at 124, 98 S.Ct. 2646, "this is due to nothing more than the fact that, in most regulatory takings cases, there is no doubt whatsoever about whether the government's action was the cause of the alleged taking."); *Ventures N.W. Ltd. P'ship v. State*, 81 Wash.App. 353, 914 P.2d 1180, 1187 (1996) ("An owner claiming loss of the economically viable use of property must show that the challenged government regulation proximately caused the loss of all such use.") (Citing *Guimont v. Clarke*, 121 Wash.2d 586, 854 P.2d 1 (1993), *cert. denied*, 510 U.S. 1176, 114 S.Ct. 1216, 127 L.Ed.2d 563 (1994); *Orion Corp. v. State*, 109 Wash.2d 621, 747 P.2d 1062 (1987), *cert. denied*, 486 U.S. 1022, 108 S.Ct. 1996, 100 L.Ed.2d 227 (1988)). However, because we find that the background principles of Washington state law would have precluded development of the proposed project, and therefore that plaintiff's claimed property right never existed, we do not address the question of causation.

As discussed above, a deprivation by the government of all beneficial uses of one's property results in a taking unless, inter alia, the "background principles" of state law already serve to deprive the property owner of such uses. *Lucas*, 505 U.S. at 1029, 112 S.Ct. 2886. In *Lucas*, subsequent to plaintiff's purchase of two residential lots of shoreline property, the state of South Carolina passed a statute having the "direct effect of barring petitioner from erecting any permanent structures on his two parcels," rendering them "valueless." 505 U.S. at 1007, 112 S.Ct. 2886. In response, the plaintiff sued, alleging that the government effected a complete deprivation of his property. The Court held that "[a]ny limitation so severe cannot be newly legislated or decreed (without compensation), but must inhere in the title itself, in the restrictions that background principles of the State's law of property and nuisance already place upon land ownership," and remanded for a determination of whether such "background principles" would have prevented the proposed use of plaintiff's property. *Id.*, 505 U.S. at 1029, 112 S.Ct. 2886.

In this case, the "restrictions that background principles" of Washington law place upon such ownership are found in the public trust doctrine. As the Washington Supreme Court recently explained, the "state's ownership of tidelands and shorelands is comprised of two distinct aspects—the *jus privatum* and the *jus publicum.*" *State v. Longshore*, 141 Wash.2d 414, 5 P.3d 1256, 1262 (2000). Relevant here, the "jus publicum, or public trust doctrine, is the right 'of navigation, together with its incidental rights of fishing, boating, swimming, water skiing, and other related recreational purposes generally regarded as corollary to the right of navigation and the use of public waters.' " Id. (quoting *Caminiti v. Boyle*, 107 Wash.2d 662, 732 P.2d 989, 994 (1987) (internal quotation marks and citation omitted)). The "doctrine reserves a public property interest, the jus publicum, in tidelands and the waters flowing over them, despite the sale of these lands into private ownership." *Weden v. San Juan County*, 135 Wash.2d 678, 958 P.2d 273, 283 (1998), (citing Ralph W. Johnson et al., *The Public Trust Doctrine and Coastal Zone Management in Washington State*, 67 Wash. L.Rev. 521, 524 (1992)). "The state can no more convey or give away this jus publicum interest than it can 'abdicate its police powers in the administration of government and the preservation of the peace.' " *Caminiti*, 732 P.2d at 994 (quoting *Illinois Cent. R.R. v. Illinois*, 146 U.S. 387, 453, 13 S.Ct. 110, 36 L.Ed. 1018 (1892)). Instead, the state may only divest itself of interests in the state's waters in a manner that does not substantially impair the public interest. *Id.* at 993–95.

It is beyond cavil that "a public trust doctrine has always existed in Washington." *Orion Corp.*, 747 P.2d at 1072 (citing *Caminiti*, 732 P.2d at 994). The doctrine is "partially encapsulated in the language of [Washington's] constitution which reserves state ownership in 'the beds and shores of all navigable waters in the state.' " *Rettkowski v. Dep't of Ecology*, 122 Wash.2d 219, 858 P.2d 232, 239 (1993) (quoting Wash. Const. art. 17, § 1). The doctrine is also reflected in Washington's Shoreline Management Act ("SMA"), adopted in 1971. RCW §§ 90.58.010–.930. Following a long history "favoring the sale of tidelands and shorelands," resulting in the privatization of approximately 60 percent of the tidelands and 30 percent of the shorelands originally owned by the state, *Caminiti*, 732 P.2d at 996, the Washington legislature found that the SMA was necessary because "unrestricted construction on the privately owned or public owned shorelines * * * is not in the best public interest." RCW 90.58.020.

The public trust doctrine, reflected in part in the SMA, unquestionably burdens Esplanade's property.

We agree with the district court that the Washington Supreme Court's decision in Orion controls the outcome of this case, and that Washington's public trust doctrine ran with the title to the tideland properties and alone precluded the shoreline residential development proposed by Esplanade.

In *Orion*, the plaintiff corporation, prior to the enactment of the SMA, purchased tideland property in Padilla Bay, the "most diverse, least disturbed, and most biologically productive of all major estuaries on Puget Sound." *Id.*, 747 P.2d at 1065. Orion Corp. proposed dredging and filling of the Bay to create a significant residential community. *Id.* In addressing plaintiff's challenge to subsequent local and state environmental regulations, which it alleged combined to completely deprive it of all economically viable use of its property, the court decided that the tidelands of the Bay were burdened by the public trust doctrine prior to the enactment of the SMA. *Id.* at 1072. At the time of Orion's purchase, "Orion could make no use of the tidelands which would substantially impair the [public] trust." *Id.* at 1073. Specifically, "Orion never had the right to dredge and fill its tidelands, either for a residential community or farmlands [s]ince a property right must exist before it can be taken, neither the SMA nor the SCSMMP effected a taking * * * " *Id.* (internal quotation marks and citation omitted).

We find that the development proposed by Esplanade would suffer the same fate under the public trust doctrine as the project proposed by Orion Corp.

* * *

Esplanade's contention that the proposed development *was* consistent with the SMA at the time his project vested in 1992 is similarly without merit. As the City concedes, at the time of the purchase, the SMA, theoretically, permitted single-family dwellings to be constructed on the property. As the district court noted, however, "[t]here are numerous limitations that the SMA places on developments of shorelines, even if those developments, like Esplanade's, are not categorically prohibited." (citing, *e.g.*, RCW 90.58.020(2)(requiring that shoreline developments "[p]reserve the natural character of the shoreline"), and RCW 90.58.020(4) (requiring that "[p]rojects protect the resources and ecology of the shoreline")). In this case, because Esplanade's tideland property is navigable for the purpose of public recreation (used for fishing and general recreation, including by Tribes), and located just 700 feet from Discovery Park, the development would have interfered with those uses, and thus would have been inconsistent with the public trust doctrine. Therefore, Esplanade's development plans never constituted a legally permissible use.

As the district court correctly noted, "Esplanade * * * took the risk," when it purchased this large tract of tidelands in 1991 for only $40,000, "that, despite extensive federal, state, and local regulations restricting shoreline development, it could nonetheless overcome those numerous hurdles to complete its project and realize a substantial return on its limited initial investment. Now, having failed * * *, it seeks indemnity from the City." The takings doctrine does not supply plaintiff with such a right to indemnification.

Esplanade's proposal to construct concrete pilings, driveways and houses in the navigable tidelands of Elliot Bay, an area regularly used by the public for various recreational and other activities, was inconsistent with the public trust that the State of Washington is obligated to protect.

For the reasons given, we affirm.

AFFIRMED.

Notes

1. In DeBeradinis v. Zoning Com'n of City of Norwalk, 228 Conn. 187, 635 A.2d 1220 (Conn. 1994), a landowner filed a coastal site plan in accordance with Gen. Statutes § 22a–94 to expand his existing recycling operation on an adjacent parcel of real estate that bordered the Norwalk river. The zoning commission approved plaintiff's coastal site plan, but imposed six conditions including a grant by plaintiff of an easement to provide public access along the river. Plaintiff appealed the commission's administrative decision to the Superior Court, which set aside approval of the site plan with conditions because of the statutory invalidity of one of the conditions. The commission had acted illegally by conditioning the approval of the plaintiff's application on the grant of a public access easement along the waterfront because this condition was not related to and did not mitigate the potential adverse impacts of the proposal. Having determined that the invalid condition was an "essential component" of the approval of the plaintiff's application, the court reversed the commission's decision, thereby voiding the approval of the plaintiff's application.

2. Other courts have also refused to expand the public trust doctrine to allow public access over private land. See Opinion of the Justices, 365 Mass. 681, 313 N.E.2d 561 (1974). This opinion invalidated a bill that declared that the 'reserved interests of the public' in coastal land included a public "on-foot free right-of-passage" along the shore of the coastline between the mean high water line and the extreme water line. The court stated that the Massachusetts Bay Colony Ordinance, specifically retains the public rights of fishing, fowling and navigation in privately owned coastal land and the public's "* * * right of passage over dry land at periods of low tide cannot be reasonably included as one of the traditional rights of navigation" 313 N.E.2d at 566. Also see Opinion of the Justices, 139 N.H. 82, 649 A.2d 604 (1994) (finding that a bill recognizing a public easement in "dry sand areas" between public trust areas and intersection of beach and high ground was unconstitutional taking).

3. The Public Trust doctrine provided some justification for the passage of certain federal environmental laws that delegate power to federal agencies to protect public property. Examples include the Wild Free–Roaming Horses and Burros Act, 16 U.S.C. §§ 1331–1340 (2000); the Federal Land Policy and Management Act, 43 U.S.C. §§ 1701–1784 (2000); the National Park Service Act, 16 U.S.C. §§ 1–460 (2000); the Comprehensive Environmental Response, Compensation and Liability Act, 42 U.S.C. §§ 9601–9657 (2000); the Wilderness Act, 16 U.S.C. §§ 1131–1136 (2000); and the Coastal Zone Management Act, 16 U.S.C. §§ 1457–1464 (2000).

4. A strong statement of the public trust doctrine is found in State ex rel. Thornton v. Hay, 254 Or. 584, 462 P.2d 671 (1969) which upheld the rights of the public to use beaches above the high tide line:

> The dry-sand area in Oregon has been enjoyed by the general public as a recreational adjunct of the wet-sand or foreshore area since the beginning of the state's political history. The first European settlers on these shores found the aboriginal inhabitants using the foreshore for clam-digging and the dry-sand area for their cooking fires. The newcomers continued these customs after statehood. Thus, from the time of the earliest settlement to the present day, the general public has assumed that the dry-sand area was a part of the public beach, and the public has used the dry-sand area for picnics, gathering wood, building warming fires, and generally as a headquarters from which to supervise children or to range out over the foreshore as the tides advance and recede. In the Cannon Beach vicinity, state and local officers have policed the dry sand, and municipal sanitary crews have attempted to keep the area reasonably free from man-made litter. 462 P.2d at 673.
>
> * * *
>
> Until very recently, no question concerning the right of the public to enjoy the dry-sand area appears to have been brought before the courts of this state. The public's assumption that the dry sand as well as the foreshore was "public property" had been reinforced by early judicial decisions. See Shively v. Bowlby, 152 U.S. 1, 14 S.Ct. 548, 38 L.Ed. 331 (1894), which affirmed Bowlby v. Shively, 22 Or. 410, 30 P. 154 (1892). These cases held that landowners claiming under federal patents owned seaward only to the "high-water" line, a line that was then assumed to be the vegetation line. Id., at 674.
>
> * * *
>
> Recently, however, the scarcity of oceanfront building sites has attracted substantial private investments in resort facilities. Resort owners like these defendants now desire to reserve for their paying guests the recreational advantages that accrue to the dry-sand portions of their deeded property. Consequently, in 1967, public debate and political activity resulted in legislative attempts to resolve conflicts between public and private interests in the dry-sand area * * *. Id., at 674.
>
> Because so much of our law is the product of legislation, we sometimes lose sight of the importance of custom as a source of law in our society. It seems particularly appropriate in the case at bar to look to an ancient and accepted custom in this state as the source of a rule of law. The rule in this case, based upon custom, is salutary in confirming a public right, and at the same time it takes from no man anything which he has had a legitimate reason to regard as exclusively his * * *. Id. at 678.

Chapter X

AESTHETIC HISTORIC AND CULTURAL INTEREST PRESERVATION

As we have seen in the previous chapters, zoning started out as a tool for segregating inconsistent land uses in the city and for regulating the height and size of structures and their placement on lots. As zoning became both acceptable and fashionable, the legal approval extended to zoning was seen as a convenient source of power to accomplish public objectives which had nothing to do with separating uses or regulating building bulk. In many respects the development was much like the expansion of federal regulation which took place in Congress in the twentieth century acting under the Commerce Clause of Article I of the Constitution. The zoning power was something of an empty vessel receptive to many land use regulations to accomplish multiple purposes. In this chapter, several different types of land use regulations are examined. Some of the cases deal with provisions in zoning ordinances, and many of the opinions talk in terms of zoning and the police power. However, the subject matter of the regulations is not, strictly speaking, consonant with the concept of zoning, and thus the editors feel that this material belongs in a separate chapter.

SECTION 1. AESTHETICS AND ARCHITECTURAL CONTROL

Until the mid 1950s courts would state almost routinely that aesthetic considerations in land use regulation, especially zoning, were not a sufficient basis for exercising the police power. This attitude was reflective of the notion that the law could not tolerate restrictions based on something as indefinable as aesthetic sense, as beauty, after all, lies in the eye of the beholder. However, when Justice Douglas wrote in 1954 in Berman v. Parker, 348 U.S. 26, 75 S.Ct. 98, 99 L.Ed. 27 that taking property for urban renewal was taking for a public use, and that aesthetic considerations formed a part of the valid public interest, state appellate courts began to reexamine the question of whether aesthetics were a legitimate basis for public regulation. Half a century later, the attitude of courts has shifted quite substantially on the issue. The main developments have come in two areas: Regulation of signs and billboards and regulation of the appearance of structures.

In considering the cases and materials in this chapter, a number of considerations must be taken into account. Among others, these include First Amendment concerns; how high aesthetic, environmental and related considerations rank on the scale of values in a particular jurisdiction; whether such concerns are or should be legitimately included within the police power without regard to whether tradition would exclude them unless joined with some other "legitimate" police power concern; and whether the judicial or statutory approval of such considerations would ultimately permit the aesthetic sensibilities of a few individuals to force others to conform to their particular ideas to the point of oppression.

A. FIRST AMENDMENT ISSUES RELATED TO REGULATION OF SIGNS AND BILLBOARDS

METROMEDIA, INC. v. CITY OF SAN DIEGO

Supreme Court of the United States, 1981.
453 U.S. 490, 101 S.Ct. 2882, 69 L.Ed.2d 800.

[The City of San Diego enacted an ordinance which, in effect banned all off-site billboards while allowing on-site advertising signs. The California Supreme Court upheld the ordinance, 26 Cal.3d 848, 610 P.2d 407 (1980), although the court also held that removal of some existing billboards after the expiration of an amortization period would require compensation under the Federal Highway Beautification Act.]

JUSTICE WHITE announced the judgment of the Court and delivered an opinion in which JUSTICE STEWART, JUSTICE MARSHALL and JUSTICE POWELL join.

This case involves the validity of an ordinance of the city of San Diego, Cal., imposing substantial prohibitions on the erection of outdoor advertising displays within the city.

* * *

Early cases in this Court sustaining regulation of and prohibitions aimed at billboards did not involve First Amendment considerations. See Packer Corporation v. Utah, 285 U.S. 105, 52 S.Ct. 273, 76 L.Ed. 643 (1932); St. Louis Poster Advertising Co. v. St. Louis, 249 U.S. 269, 39 S.Ct. 274, 63 L.Ed. 599 (1919); Cusack Co. v. City of Chicago, 242 U.S. 526, 37 S.Ct. 190, 61 L.Ed. 472 (1917). Since those decisions, we have not given plenary consideration to cases involving First Amendment challenges to statutes or ordinances limiting the use of billboards, preferring on several occasions summarily to affirm decisions sustaining state or local legislation directed at billboards.

Suffolk Outdoor Advertising Co. v. Hulse, 439 U.S. 808, 99 S.Ct. 66, 58 L.Ed.2d 101 (1978), involved a municipal ordinance that distinguished between off-site and on-site billboard advertising, prohibiting the former and permitting the latter. We summarily affirmed a judgment sustaining the ordinance, thereby rejecting the submission, repeated in this case, that prohibiting off-site commercial advertising violates the First Amendment. The definition of "billboard," however, was considerably narrower in *Suffolk* than it is here: "A sign which directs attention to a business, commodity, service, entertainment, or attraction sold, offered or existing elsewhere than upon the same lot where such sign is displayed." This definition did not sweep within its scope the broad range of noncommercial speech admittedly prohibited by the San Diego ordinance. Furthermore, the New York ordinance, unlike that in San Diego, contained a provision permitting the establishment of public information centers in which approved directional signs for businesses could be located. This Court has repeatedly stated that although summary dispositions are decisions on the merits, the decisions extend only to "the precise issues presented and necessarily decided by those actions." Mandel v. Bradley, 432 U.S. 173, 176, 97 S.Ct. 2238, 2240, 53 L.Ed.2d 199 (1977); see also Hicks v. Miranda, 422 U.S. 332, 345, n. 14, 95 S.Ct. 2281, 2290, 45 L.Ed.2d 223 (1975); Edelman v. Jordan, 415 U.S. 651, 671, 94 S.Ct. 1347, 1359, 39 L.Ed.2d 662 (1974). Insofar as the San Diego ordinance is challenged on the ground that it prohibits noncommercial speech, the *Suffolk* case does not directly support the decision below.

The Court has summarily disposed of appeals from state-court decisions upholding state restrictions on billboards on several other occasions. Markham Advertising Co. v. Washington, 393 U.S. 316, 89 S.Ct. 553, 21 L.Ed.2d 512 (1969), and Newman Signs, Inc. v. Hjelle, 440 U.S. 901, 99 S.Ct. 1205, 59 L.Ed.2d 449 (1979), both involved the facial validity of state billboard prohibitions that extended only to certain designated roadways or to areas zoned for certain uses. The statutes in both instances distinguished between on-site commercial billboards and off-site billboards within the protected areas. Our most recent summary action was Lotze v. Washington, 444 U.S. 921, 100 S.Ct. 257, 62 L.Ed.2d 177 (1979), which involved an "as applied" challenge to a Washington prohibition on off-site signs. In that case, appellants erected, on their own property, billboards expressing their political and social views. Although billboards conveying information relating to the commercial use of the property would have been permitted, appellants' billboards were prohibited, and the state courts ordered their removal. We affirmed a judgment rejecting the First Amendment challenge to the ordinance. * * *

Billboards are a well-established medium of communication, used to convey a broad range of different kinds of messages. As Justice Clark noted in his dissent below:

"The outdoor sign or symbol is a venerable medium for expressing political, social and commercial ideas. From the poster or 'broadside' to the billboard, outdoor signs have played a prominent role throughout American history, rallying support for political and social causes." 164 Cal.Rptr., at 533–534, 610 P.2d, at 430–431.

The record in this case indicates that besides the typical commercial uses, San Diego billboards have been used

"to publicize the 'City in motion' campaign of the City of San Diego, to communicate messages from candidates for municipal, state and national offices, including candidates for judicial office, to propose marriage, to seek employment, to encourage the use of seat belts, to denounce the United Nations, to seek support for Prisoners of War and Missing in Action, to promote the United Crusade and a variety of other charitable and socially-related endeavors and to provide directions to the traveling public."

But whatever its communicative function, the billboard remains a "large, immobile, and permanent structure which like other structures is subject to * * * regulation." 164 Cal.Rptr., at 522, 610 P.2d, at 419. Moreover, because it is designed to stand out and apart from its surroundings, the billboard creates a unique set of problems for land-use planning and development.

* * *

As construed by the California Supreme Court, the ordinance restricts the use of certain kinds of outdoor signs. That restriction is defined in two ways: first, by reference to the structural characteristics of the sign; second, by reference to the content, or message, of the sign. Thus, the regulation only applies to a "permanent structure constituting, or used for the display of, a commercial or other advertisement to the public." 164 Cal.Rptr., at 513, n. 2, 610 P.2d, at 410. Within that class, the only permitted signs are those (1) identifying the premises on which the sign is located, or its owner or occupant, or advertising the goods produced or services rendered on such property and (2) those within one of the specified exemptions to the general prohibition, such as temporary political campaign signs. To determine if any billboard is prohibited by the ordinance, one must determine how it is constructed, where it is located, and what message it carries.

Thus, under the ordinance (1) a sign advertising goods or services available on the property where the sign is located is allowed; (2) a sign on a building or other property advertising goods or services produced or offered elsewhere is barred; (3) noncommercial advertising, unless within one of the specific exceptions, is everywhere prohibited. The occupant of property may advertise his own goods or services; he may not advertise the goods or services of others, nor may he display most noncommercial messages.

* * *

* * * [I]n Central Hudson v. Public Service Comm'n, 447 U.S. 557, 100 S.Ct. 2343, 65 L.Ed.2d 341 (1980), we held that: "The Constitution * * * accords a lesser protection to commercial speech than to other constitutionally guaranteed expression. The protection available for a particular commercial expression turns on the nature both of the expression and of the governmental interests served by its regulation." Id., at 562–563, 100 S.Ct., at 2349–2350 (citation omitted). We then adopted a four-part test for determining the validity of government restrictions on commercial speech as distinguished from more fully protected speech. (1) The First Amendment protects commercial speech only if that speech concerns lawful activity and is not misleading. A restriction on otherwise protected commercial speech is valid only if it (2) seeks to implement a substantial governmental interest, (3) directly advances that interest, and (4) reaches no farther than necessary to accomplish the given objective. Id., at 563–566, 100 S.Ct., at 2350–2351.

Appellants agree that the proper approach to be taken in determining the validity of the restrictions on commercial speech is that which was articulated in *Central Hudson,* but assert that the San Diego ordinance fails that test. We do not agree.

There can be little controversy over the application of the first, second, and fourth criteria. There is no suggestion that the commercial advertising at issue here involves unlawful activity or is misleading. Nor can there be substantial doubt that the twin goals that the ordinance seeks to further—traffic safety and the appearance of the city—are substantial governmental goals. It is far too late to contend otherwise with respect to either traffic safety, Railway Express Agency, Inc. v. New York, 336 U.S. 106, 69 S.Ct. 463, 93 L.Ed. 533 (1949), or esthetics, see Penn Central Transportation Co. v. New York City, 438 U.S. 104, 98 S.Ct. 2646, 57 L.Ed.2d 631 (1978); Village of Belle Terre v. Boraas, 416 U.S. 1, 94 S.Ct. 1536, 39 L.Ed.2d 797 (1974); Berman v. Parker, 348 U.S. 26, 33, 75 S.Ct. 98, 102, 99 L.Ed. 27 (1954). Similarly, we reject appellants' claim that the ordinance is broader than necessary and, therefore, fails the fourth part of the *Central Hudson* test. If the city has a sufficient basis for believing that billboards are traffic hazards and are unattractive, then obviously the most direct and perhaps the only effective approach to solving the problems they create is to prohibit them. The city has gone no farther than necessary in seeking to meet its ends. Indeed, it has stopped short of fully accomplishing its ends: It has not prohibited all billboards, but allows on-site advertising and some other specifically exempted signs.

The more serious question, then, concerns the third of the *Central Hudson* criteria: Does the ordinance "directly advance" governmental interests in traffic safety and in the appearance of the city? It is asserted that the record is inadequate to show any connection between billboards and traffic safety. The California Supreme Court noted the meager record on this point but held "as a matter of law that an ordinance which eliminates billboards designed to be viewed from the streets and highways reasonably relates to traffic safety." 164 Cal.Rptr., at 515, 610

P.2d, at 412. Noting that "billboards are intended to, and undoubtedly do, divert a driver's attention from the roadway," ibid., and that whether the "distracting effect contributes to traffic accidents invokes an issue of continuing controversy," ibid., the California Supreme Court agreed with many other courts that a legislative judgment that billboards are traffic hazards is not manifestly unreasonable and should not be set aside. We likewise hesitate to disagree with the accumulated, commonsense judgments of local lawmakers and of the many reviewing courts that billboards are real and substantial hazards to traffic safety.[2] There is nothing here to suggest that these judgments are unreasonable. As we said in a different context, Railway Express Agency, Inc. v. People of New York, 336 U.S. 106, 109, 69 S.Ct. 463, 465, 93 L.Ed. 533 (1949):

> "We would be trespassing on one of the most intensely local and specialized of all municipal problems if we held that this regulation had no relation to the traffic problem of New York City. It is the judgment of the local authorities that it does have such a relation. And nothing has been advanced which shows that to be palpably false."

We reach a similar result with respect to the second asserted justification for the ordinance—advancement of the city's esthetic interests. It is not speculative to recognize that billboards by their very nature, wherever located and however constructed, can be perceived an "esthetic harm."[3] San Diego, like many other States and municipalities, has chosen to minimize the presence of such structures. Such esthetic judgments are necessarily subjective, defying objective evaluation, and for that reason must be carefully scrutinized to determine if they are only a public rationalization of an impermissible purpose. But there is no

2. See E.B. Elliott Advertising Co. v. Metropolitan Dade County, 425 F.2d 1141, 1152 (C.A.5 1970); Markham Advertising Co. v. Washington, 73 Wash.2d 405, 439 P.2d 248, 258 (1968); New York State Thruway Authority v. Ashley Motor Court, 10 N.Y.2d 151, 218 N.Y.S.2d 640, 642, 176 N.E.2d 566, 568 (1961); Ghaster Properties, Inc. v. Preston, 176 Ohio St. 425, 200 N.E.2d 328, 337 (1964); Newman Signs, Inc. v. Hjelle, 268 N.W.2d 741, 757 (N.D. 1978); Lubbock Poster Co. v. City of Lubbock, 569 S.W.2d 935, 939 (Tex.Civ.App. 1978); State v. Lotze, 92 Wash.2d 52, 593 P.2d 811, 814 (1979); Inhabitants, Town of Boothbay v. National Advertising Co., 347 A.2d 419, 422 (Me.1975); Stuckey's Stores, Inc. v. O'Cheskey, 93 N.M. 312, 600 P.2d 258, 267 (1979); In re Opinion of the Justices, 103 N.H. 268, 169 A.2d 762, 764 (1961); General Outdoor Advertising Co. v. Dept. of Public Works, 289 Mass. 149, 193 N.E. 799, 813–814 (1935). But see John Donnelly & Sons v. Campbell, 639 F.2d 6, 11 (C.A.1 1980); State ex rel. Dept. of Transportation v. Pile, 603 P.2d 337, 343 (Okla.1979); Metromedia, Inc. v. City of Des Plaines, 26 Ill.App.3d 942, 326 N.E.2d 59, 62 (1975).

3. See John Donnelly & Sons v. Campbell, supra, 639 F.2d at 11–12; E.B. Elliott Advertising Co. v. Metropolitan Dade County, supra, 425 F.2d at 1152; Newman Signs, Inc. v. Hjelle, supra, 268 N.W.2d at 757; Markham Advertising Co. v. Washington, supra, 439 P.2d at 259; Stuckey's Stores, Inc. v. O'Cheskey, supra, 600 P.2d at 267; Suffolk Outdoor Advertising Co. v. Hulse, 43 N.Y.2d 483, 402 N.Y.S.2d 368, 370, 373 N.E.2d 263, 265 (1977); John Donnelly & Sons, Inc. v. Outdoor Advertising Bd., 369 Mass. 206, 339 N.E.2d 709, 717 (1975); Cromwell v. Ferrier, 19 N.Y.2d 263, 279 N.Y.S.2d 22, 26, 225 N.E.2d 749, 753 (1967); State v. Diamond Motors, Inc., 50 Haw. 33, 429 P.2d 825, 827 (Haw.1967); United Advertising Corp. v. Metuchen, 42 N.J. 1, 198 A.2d 447, 449 (1964); In re Opinion of the Justices, supra, 169 A.2d at 764. But see State ex rel. Dept. of Transportation v. Pile, supra, 603 P.2d at 342; Sunad, Inc. v. Sarasota, 122 So.2d 611, 614–615 (Fla.1960).

claim in this case that San Diego has as an ulterior motive the suppression of speech, and the judgment involved here is not so unusual as to raise suspicions in itself.

It is nevertheless argued that the city denigrates its interest in traffic safety and beauty and defeats its own case by permitting on-site advertising and other specified signs. Appellants question whether the distinction between on-site and off-site advertising on the same property is justifiable in terms of either esthetics or traffic safety. The ordinance permits the occupant of property to use billboards located on that property to advertise goods and services offered at that location; identical billboards, equally distracting and unattractive, that advertise goods or services available elsewhere are prohibited even if permitting the latter would not multiply the number of billboards. Despite the apparent incongruity, this argument has been rejected, at least implicitly, in all of the cases sustaining the distinction between off-site and on-site commercial advertising. We agree with those cases and with our own decisions in Suffolk Outdoor Advertising Co. v. Hulse, 439 U.S. 808, 99 S.Ct. 66, 58 L.Ed.2d 101 (1978); Markham Advertising Co. v. Washington, 393 U.S. 316, 89 S.Ct. 553, 21 L.Ed.2d 512 (1969); Newman Signs, Inc. v. Hjelle, 440 U.S. 901, 99 S.Ct. 1205, 59 L.Ed.2d 449 (1979).

In the first place, whether on-site advertising is permitted or not, the prohibition of off-site advertising is directly related to the stated objectives of traffic safety and esthetics. This is not altered by the fact that the ordinance is under-inclusive because it permits on-site advertising. Second, the city may believe that off-site advertising, with its periodically changing content, presents a more acute problem than does on-site advertising. See *Railway Express,* supra, 336 U.S. at 110, 69 S.Ct. at 465. Third, San Diego has obviously chosen to value one kind of commercial speech—on-site advertising—more than another kind of commercial speech—off-site advertising. The ordinance reflects a decision by the city that the former interest, but not the latter, is stronger than the city's interests in traffic safety and esthetics. The city has decided that in a limited instance—on-site commercial advertising—its interests should yield. We do not reject that judgment. As we see it, the city could reasonably conclude that a commercial enterprise—as well as the interested public—has a stronger interest in identifying its place of business and advertising the products or services available there than it has in using or leasing its available space for the purpose of advertising commercial enterprises located elsewhere. See Railway Express v. New York, supra, 336 U.S., at 116, 69 S.Ct., at 468 (Jackson, J., concurring); Bradley v. Public Utilities Comm'n, 289 U.S. 92, 97, 53 S.Ct. 577, 579, 77 L.Ed. 1053 (1933). It does not follow from the fact that the city has concluded that some commercial interests outweigh its municipal interests in this context that it must give similar weight to all other commercial advertising. Thus, off-site commercial billboards may be prohibited while on-site commercial billboards are permitted.

The constitutional problem in this area requires resolution of the conflict between the city's land-use interests and the commercial interests of those seeking to purvey goods and services within the city. In light of the above analysis, we cannot conclude that the city has drawn an ordinance broader than is necessary to meet its interests, or that it fails directly to advance substantial government interests. In sum, insofar as it regulates commercial speech the San Diego ordinance meets the constitutional requirements of *Central Hudson,* supra.

It does not follow, however, that San Diego's general ban on signs carrying noncommercial advertising is also valid under the First and Fourteenth Amendments. The fact that the city may value commercial messages relating to on-site goods and services more than it values commercial communications relating to off-site goods and services does not justify prohibiting an occupant from displaying its own ideas or those of others.

As indicated above, our recent commercial speech cases have consistently accorded noncommercial speech a greater degree of protection than commercial speech. San Diego effectively inverts this judgment, by affording a greater degree of protection to commercial than to noncommercial speech. There is a broad exception for on-site commercial advertisements, but there is no similar exception for noncommercial speech. The use of on-site billboards to carry commercial messages related to the commercial use of the premises is freely permitted, but the use of otherwise identical billboards to carry noncommercial messages is generally prohibited. The city does not explain how or why noncommercial billboards located in places where commercial billboards are permitted would be more threatening to safe driving or would detract more from the beauty of the city. Insofar as the city tolerates billboards at all, it cannot choose to limit their content to commercial messages; the city may not conclude that the communication of commercial information concerning goods and services connected with a particular site is of greater value than the communication of noncommercial messages.

Furthermore, the ordinance contains exceptions that permit various kinds of noncommercial signs, whether on property where goods and services are offered or not, that would otherwise be within the general ban. A fixed sign may be used to identify any piece of property and its owner. Any piece of property may carry or display religious symbols, commemorative plaques of recognized historical societies and organizations, signs carrying news items or telling the time or temperature, signs erected in discharge of any governmental function, or temporary political campaign signs. No other noncommercial or ideological signs meeting the structural definition are permitted, regardless of their effect on traffic safety or esthetics.

Although the city may distinguish between the relative value of different categories of commercial speech, the city does not have the same range of choice in the area of noncommercial speech to evaluate the strength of, or distinguish between, various communicative interests. See Carey v. Brown, 447 U.S. 455, 462, 100 S.Ct. 2286, 2291, 65 L.Ed.2d 263 (1980); Police Department of Chicago v. Mosley, 408 U.S. 92, 96, 92

S.Ct. 2286, 2290, 33 L.Ed.2d 212 (1972). With respect to noncommercial speech, the city may not choose the appropriate subjects for public discourse: "To allow a government the choice of permissible subjects for public debate would be to allow that government control over the search for political truth." *Consolidated Edison Co.,* supra, 447 U.S., at 538, 100 S.Ct., at 2333. Because some noncommercial messages may be conveyed on billboards throughout the commercial and industrial zones, San Diego must similarly allow billboards conveying other noncommercial messages throughout those zones.[4]

Finally, we reject appellee's suggestion that the ordinance may be appropriately characterized as a reasonable "time, place and manner" restriction. The ordinance does not generally ban billboard advertising as an unacceptable "manner" of communicating information or ideas; rather, it permits various kinds of signs. Signs that are banned are banned everywhere and at all times. We have observed that time, place and manner restrictions are permissible if "they are justified without reference to the content of the regulated speech * * * serve a significant governmental interest, and * * * leave open ample alternative channels for communication of the information." Virginia Pharmacy Board v. Virginia Consumer Council, 425 U.S. 748, 771, 96 S.Ct. 1817, 1830, 48 L.Ed.2d 346 (1976). Here, it cannot be assumed that "alternative channels" are available, for the parties stipulated to just the opposite: "Many businesses, politicians and other persons rely upon outdoor advertising because other forms of advertising are insufficient, inappropriate and prohibitively expensive." A similar argument was made with respect to a prohibition on real estate "For Sale" signs in Linmark Associates, Inc. v. Willingboro, 431 U.S. 85, 97 S.Ct. 1614, 52 L.Ed.2d 155 (1977), and what we said there is equally applicable here:

> "Although in theory sellers remain free to employ a number of different alternatives, in practice [certain products are] not market-

4. Because a total prohibition of outdoor advertising is not before us, we do not indicate whether such a ban would be consistent with the First Amendment. But see Schad v. Borough of Mount Ephraim, 452 U.S. 61, 101 S.Ct. 2176, 68 L.Ed.2d 671, on the constitutional problems created by a total prohibition of a particular expressive forum, live entertainment in that case. Despite Justice Stevens' insistence to the contrary, post, at 1, 2, and 10, n. 14, we do not imply that the ordinance is unconstitutional because it "does not abridge enough speech."

Similarly, we need not reach any decision in this case as to the constitutionality of the federal Highway Beautification Act of 1965, Pub.L. 89–285, 79 Stat. 1028, 23 U.S.C.A. § 131. That Act, like the San Diego ordinance, permits on-site commercial billboards in areas in which it does not permit billboards with noncommercial messages. 23 U.S.C.A. § 131(c). However, unlike the San Diego ordinance, which prohibits billboards conveying noncommercial messages throughout the city, the federal law does not contain a total prohibition of such billboards in areas adjacent to the Interstate and primary highway systems. As far as the Federal Government is concerned, such billboards are permitted adjacent to the highways in areas zoned industrial or commercial under state law or in unzoned commercial or industrial areas. 23 U.S.C.A. § 131(d). Regulation of billboards in those areas is left primarily to the States. For this reason, the decision today does not determine the constitutionality of the federal statute. Whether, in fact, the distinction is constitutionally significant can only be determined on the basis of a record establishing the actual effect of the Act on billboards conveying noncommercial messages.

ed through leaflets, sound trucks, demonstrations, or the like. The options to which sellers realistically are relegated * * * involve more cost and less autonomy than * * * signs * * * are less likely to reach persons not deliberately seeking sales information * * * and may be less effective media for communicating the message that is conveyed by a * * * sign. * * * The alternatives, then, are far from satisfactory." 431 U.S., at 93, 97 S.Ct., at 1618.

It is apparent as well that the ordinance distinguishes in several ways between permissible and impermissible signs at a particular location by reference to their content.

* * *

Because the San Diego ordinance reaches too far into the realm of protected speech, we conclude that it is unconstitutional on its face. The judgment of the California Supreme Court is reversed and the case remanded to that court.

JUSTICE BRENNAN, with whom JUSTICE BLACKMUN joins, concurring in the judgment.

Believing that "a total prohibition of outdoor advertising is not before us," * * *, the plurality does not decide "whether such a ban would be consistent with the First Amendment." Instead, it concludes that San Diego may ban all billboards containing commercial speech messages without violating the First Amendment, thereby sending the signal to municipalities that bifurcated billboard regulations prohibiting commercial messages but allowing noncommercial messages would pass constitutional muster. * * * I write separately because I believe this case in effect presents the total ban question, and because I believe the plurality's bifurcated approach itself raises serious First Amendment problems and relies on a distinction between commercial and noncommercial speech unanticipated by our prior cases.

* * *

* * * In the case of billboards, I would hold that a city may totally ban them if it can show that a sufficiently substantial governmental interest is directly furthered by the total ban, and that any more narrowly drawn restriction, i.e., anything less than a total ban, would promote less well the achievement of that goal.

Applying that test to the instant case, I would invalidate the San Diego ordinance. The city has failed to provide adequate justification for its substantial restriction on protected activity. * * * First, although I have no quarrel with the substantiality of the city's interest in traffic safety, the city has failed to come forward with evidence demonstrating that billboards actually impair traffic safety in San Diego. Indeed, the Joint Stipulation of Facts is completely silent on this issue. Although the plurality hesitates "to disagree with the accumulated, common sense judgments of local lawmakers and of the many reviewing courts that billboards are real and substantial hazards to traffic safety," ante, at

2893, I would not be so quick to accept legal conclusions in other cases as an adequate substitute for evidence *in this case* that banning billboards directly furthers traffic safety. Moreover, the ordinance is not narrowly drawn to accomplish the traffic safety goal. Although it contains an exception for signs "not visible from any point on the boundary of the premises," App. to Juris. Statement 111a, billboards not visible from the street but nevertheless visible from the "boundary of the premises" are not exempted from the regulation's prohibition.

Second, I think that the city has failed to show that its asserted interest in aesthetics is sufficiently substantial in the commercial and industrial areas of San Diego. I do not doubt that "[i]t is within the power of the [city] to determine that the community should be beautiful," Berman v. Parker, 348 U.S. 26, 33, 75 S.Ct. 98, 102, 99 L.Ed. 27 (1954), but that power may not be exercised in contravention of the First Amendment. * * *

It is no doubt true that the appearance of certain areas of the city would be enhanced by the elimination of billboards, but "it is not immediately apparent as a matter of experience" that their elimination in all other areas as well would have more than a negligible impact on aesthetics. See John Donnelly & Sons v. Campbell, 639 F.2d 6, 23 (C.A.1 1980), petition for cert. filed (Mar. 19, 1981) (Pettine, J., concurring in the judgment.) The Joint Stipulation reveals that

> "[s]ome sections of the City of San Diego are scenic, some blighted, some containing strips of vehicle related commercial uses, some contain new and attractive office buildings, some functional industrial development and some areas contain older but useful commercial establishments." Joint Stipulation § 8, App. to Juris. Statement 121a.

A billboard is not *necessarily* inconsistent with oil storage tanks, blighted areas, or strip development. Of course, it is not for a court to impose its own notion of beauty on San Diego. But before deferring to a city's judgment, a court must be convinced that the city is seriously and comprehensively addressing aesthetic concerns with respect to its environment. Here, San Diego has failed to demonstrate a comprehensive coordinated effort in its commercial and industrial areas to address other obvious contributors to an unattractive environment. In this sense the ordinance is underinclusive. See Erznoznik v. City of Jacksonville, 422 U.S. 205, 214, 95 S.Ct. 2268, 2275, 45 L.Ed.2d 125 (1975). Of course, this is not to say that the city must address all aesthetic problems at the same time, or none at all. Indeed, from a planning point of view, attacking the problem incrementally and sequentially may represent the most sensible solution. On the other hand, if billboards alone are banned and no further steps are contemplated or likely, the commitment of the city to improving its physical environment is placed in doubt. By showing a comprehensive commitment to making its physical environment in commercial and industrial areas more attractive, and by allowing only narrowly tailored exceptions, if any, San Diego could demonstrate that its interest in creating an aesthetically pleasing environment is genuine and substantial. This is a requirement where, as here, there is an infringement of important constitutional consequence.

I have little doubt that some jurisdictions will easily carry the burden of proving the substantiality of their interest in aesthetics. For example, the parties acknowledge that a historical community such as Williamsburg, Va. should be able to prove that its interests in aesthetics and historical authenticity are sufficiently important that the First Amendment value attached to billboards must yield. And I would be surprised if the Federal Government had much trouble making the argument that billboards could be entirely banned in Yellowstone National Park, where their very existence would so obviously be inconsistent with the surrounding landscape. I express no view on whether San Diego or other large urban areas will be able to meet the burden. But San Diego failed to do so here, and for that reason I would strike down its ordinance.

* * *

[Dissenting opinions by CHIEF JUSTICE BURGER, JUSTICE REHNQUIST and JUSTICE STEVENS are omitted.]

MEMBERS OF THE CITY COUNCIL OF THE CITY OF LOS ANGELES et al. v. TAXPAYERS FOR VINCENT, et al.

Supreme Court of the United States, 1984.
466 U.S. 789, 104 S.Ct. 2118, 80 L.Ed.2d 772.

STEVENS, J.

Section 28.04 of the Los Angeles Municipal Code prohibits the posting of signs on public property. The question presented is whether that prohibition abridges appellees' freedom of speech within the meaning of the First Amendment. * * *

In March 1979, Roland Vincent was a candidate for election to the Los Angeles City Council. A group of his supporters known as Taxpayers for Vincent (Taxpayers) entered into a contract with a political sign service company known as Candidates' Outdoor Graphics Service (COGS) to fabricate and post signs with Vincent's name on them. COGS produced 15 by 44–inch cardboard signs and attached them to utility poles at various locations by draping them over crosswires which support the poles and stapling the cardboard together at the bottom. The signs' message was: "Roland Vincent–City Council."

Acting under the authority of § 28.04 of the Municipal Code, employees of the city's Bureau of Street Maintenance routinely removed all posters attached to utility poles and similar objects covered by the ordinance, including the COGS signs. * * *

On March 12, 1979, Taxpayers and COGS filed this action in the United States District Court for the Central District of California * * * for [sic] an injunction against enforcement of the ordinance as well as compensatory and punitive damages. * * *The District Court entered findings of fact, concluded that the ordinance was constitutional, and granted the City's motion.

* * *

The Court of Appeals did not question any of the District Court's findings of fact, but it * * * concluded that the City had not justified its total ban.

In its appeal to this Court the City challenges the Court of Appeals' holding that § 28.04 is unconstitutional on its face. Taxpayers and COGS defend that holding and also contend that the ordinance is unconstitutional as applied to their posting of political campaign signs on the crossarms of utility poles. There are two quite different ways in which a statute or ordinance may be considered invalid "on its face"- either because it is unconstitutional in every conceivable application, or because it seeks to prohibit such a broad range of protected conduct that it is unconstitutionally "overbroad." We shall analyze the "facial" challenges to the ordinance, and then address its specific application to appellees.

I

* * *

Taxpayers and COGS apparently would agree that the prohibition against posting signs on most of the publicly owned objects mentioned in the ordinance is perfectly reasonable. Thus, they do not dispute the City's power to proscribe the attachment of any handbill or sign to any sidewalk, crosswalk, curb, lamppost, hydrant, or lifesaving equipment. (citation omitted). Their position with respect to utility poles is not entirely clear, but they do contend that it is unconstitutional to prohibit the attachment of their cardboard signs to the horizontal crosswires supporting utility poles during a political campaign. They have, in short, failed to identify any significant difference between their claim that the ordinance is invalid on overbreadth grounds and their claim that it is unconstitutional when applied to their political signs. Specifically, Taxpayers and COGS have not attempted to demonstrate that the ordinance applies to any conduct more likely to be protected by the First Amendment than their own crosswires signs. Indeed, the record suggests that many of the signs posted in violation of the ordinance are posted in such a way that they may create safety or traffic problems that COGS has tried to avoid. Accordingly, on this record it appears that if the ordinance may be validly applied to COGS, it can be validly applied to most if not all of the signs of parties not before the Court. Appellees have simply failed to demonstrate a realistic danger that the ordinance will significantly compromise recognized First Amendment protections of individuals not before the Court. It would therefore be inappropriate in this case to entertain an overbreadth challenge to the ordinance.

Taxpayers and COGS do argue generally that the City's interest in eliminating visual blight is not sufficiently weighty to justify an abridgment of speech. If that were the only interest the ordinance advanced, then this argument would be analogous to the facial challenges involved in cases like Stromberg and Lovell. But as previously observed, appellees acknowledge that the ordinance serves safety interests in many of its applications, and hence do not argue that the ordinance can never be validly applied. Instead, appellees argue that they have placed their signs in locations where only the esthetic interest is implicated. In addition, they argue that they have developed an expertise in not "placing signs in offensive manners which will alienate its own clientele or their constituencies," (citation omitted) and emphasize the special value of free communication during political campaigns, see Metromedia, Inc. v. San Diego, 453 U.S. 490, 555, 101 S.Ct., at 2917 (1981) (STEVENS, J., dissenting in part); id., at 550, 101 S.Ct., at 2914 (REHNQUIST, J., dissenting). In light of these arguments, appellees' attack on the ordinance is basically a challenge to the ordinance as applied to their activities. We therefore limit our analysis of the constitutionality of the ordinance to the concrete case before us, and now turn to the arguments that it is invalid as applied to the expressive activity of Taxpayers and COGS. (citation omitted)

II

The ordinance prohibits appellees from communicating with the public in a certain manner, and presumably diminishes the total quantity of their communication in the City. (citation omitted). The application of the ordinance to appellees' expressive activities surely raises the question whether the ordinance abridges their "freedom of speech" within the meaning of the First Amendment, and appellees certainly have standing to challenge the application of the ordinance to their own expressive activities. "But to say the ordinance presents a First Amendment issue is not necessarily to say that it constitutes a First Amendment violation." Metromedia, Inc. v. San Diego, 453 U.S., at 561, 101 S.Ct., at 2920 (BURGER, C.J., dissenting). It has been clear since this Court's earliest decisions concerning the freedom of speech that the state may sometimes curtail speech when necessary to advance a significant and legitimate state interest. Schenck v. United States, 249 U.S. 47, 52, 39 S.Ct. 247, 249, 63 L.Ed. 470 (1919).

* * * [T]here are some purported interests-such as a desire to suppress support for a minority party or an unpopular cause, or to exclude the expression of certain points of view from the marketplace of ideas-that are so plainly illegitimate that they would immediately invalidate the rule. The general principle that has emerged from this line of cases is that the First Amendment forbids the government to regulate speech in ways that favor some viewpoints or ideas at the expense of others. * * *

That general rule has no application to this case. For there is not even a hint of bias or censorship in the City's enactment or enforcement of this ordinance. There is no claim that the ordinance was designed to suppress certain ideas that the City finds distasteful or that it has been applied to appellees because of the views that they express. The text of the ordinance is neutral-indeed it is silent-concerning any speaker's point of view, and the District Court's findings indicate that it has been applied to appellees and others in an evenhanded manner.

In United States v. O'Brien, 391 U.S. 367, 88 S.Ct. 1673, 20 L.Ed.2d 672 (1968), the Court set forth the appropriate framework for reviewing a viewpoint-neutral regulation of this kind:

> "[A] government regulation is sufficiently justified if it is within the constitutional power of the Government; if it furthers an important or substantial governmental interest; if the governmental interest is unrelated to the suppression of free expression; and if the incidental restriction on alleged First Amendment freedoms is no greater than is essential to the furtherance of that interest." Id., at 377, 88 S.Ct., at 1679.

It is well settled that the state may legitimately exercise its police powers to advance esthetic values. Thus, in Berman v. Parker, 348 U.S. 26, 32–33, 75 S.Ct. 98, 102–103, 99 L.Ed. 27 (1954), in referring to the power of the legislature to remove blighted housing, this Court observed that such housing may be "an ugly sore, a blight on the community which robs it of charm, which makes it a place from which men turn." Ibid. We concluded: "The concept of the public welfare is broad and inclusive. The values it represents are spiritual as well as physical, aesthetic as well as monetary." Id., at 33, 75 S.Ct., at 102 (citation omitted). * * *

In this case, taxpayers and COGS do not dispute that it is within the constitutional power of the City to attempt to improve its appearance, or that this interest is basically unrelated to the suppression of ideas. Therefore the critical inquiries are whether that interest is sufficiently substantial to justify the effect of the ordinance on appellees' expression, and whether that effect is no greater than necessary to accomplish the City's purpose.

III

In Kovacs v. Cooper, 336 U.S. 77, 69 S.Ct. 448, 93 L.Ed. 513 (1949), the Court rejected the notion that a city is powerless to protect its citizens from unwanted exposure to certain methods of expression which may legitimately be deemed a public nuisance. In upholding an ordinance that prohibited loud and raucous sound trucks, the Court held that the State had a substantial interest in protecting its citizens from unwelcome noise. (citation omitted) In Lehman v. City of Shaker Heights, 418 U.S. 298, 94 S.Ct. 2714, 41 L.Ed.2d 770 (1974), the Court upheld the city's prohibition of political advertising on its buses, stating that the city was entitled to protect unwilling viewers against intrusive advertising that may interfere with the city's goal of making its buses "rapid, convenient, pleasant, and inexpensive," id., at 302–303, 94 S.Ct., at 2717 (plurality opinion). See also id., at 307, 94 S.Ct., at 2719

(DOUGLAS, J., concurring in judgment); Erznoznik v. City of Jacksonville, 422 U.S., at 209, and n. 5, 95 S.Ct., at 2273 and n. 5. These cases indicate that the municipalities have a weighty, essentially esthetic interest in proscribing intrusive and unpleasant formats for expression.

Metromedia, Inc. v. San Diego, supra, dealt with San Diego's prohibition of certain forms of outdoor billboards. There the Court considered the city's interest in avoiding visual clutter, and seven Justices explicitly concluded that this interest was sufficient to justify a prohibition of Billboards. * * * Justice WHITE, writing for the plurality, expressly concluded that the city's esthetic interests were sufficiently substantial to provide an acceptable justification for a content-neutral prohibition against the use of billboards; San Diego's interest in its appearance was undoubtedly a substantial governmental goal. Id., at 507–508, 101 S.Ct., at 2892–2893. (citation omitted)

We reaffirm the conclusion of the majority in Metromedia. The problem addressed by this ordinance-the visual assault on the citizens of Los Angeles presented by an accumulation of signs posted on public property-constitutes a significant substantive evil within the City's power to prohibit. "[T]he city's interest in attempting to preserve [or improve] the quality of urban life is one that must be accorded high respect." Young v. American Mini Theatres, Inc., 427 U.S., at 71, 96 S.Ct., at 2453 (plurality opinion).

IV

We turn to the question whether the scope of the restriction on appellees' expressive activity is substantially broader than necessary to protect the City's interest in eliminating visual clutter. The incidental restriction on expression which results from the City's attempt to accomplish such a purpose is considered justified as a reasonable regulation of the time, place, or manner of expression if it is narrowly tailored to serve that interest. * * * The District Court found that the signs prohibited by the ordinance do constitute visual clutter and blight. By banning these signs, the City did no more than eliminate the exact source of the evil it sought to remedy (citation omitted). The plurality wrote in Metromedia: "It is not speculative to recognize that billboards by their very nature, wherever located and however constructed, can be perceived as an 'esthetic harm.' " 453 U.S., at 510, 101 S.Ct., at 2893–2894. The same is true of posted signs.

It is true that the esthetic interest in preventing the kind of litter that may result from the distribution of leaflets on the public streets and sidewalks cannot support a prophylactic prohibition against the citizen's exercise of that method of expressing his views. In Schneider v. State, 308 U.S. 147, 60 S.Ct. 146, 84 L.Ed. 155 (1939), the Court held that ordinances that absolutely prohibited handbilling on the streets were invalid. * * * Taxpayers contend that their interest in supporting Vincent's political campaign, which affords them a constitutional right to distribute brochures and leaflets on the public streets of Los Angeles, provides equal support for their asserted right to post temporary signs on objects adjacent to the streets and sidewalks. They argue that the mere fact that their temporary signs "add somewhat" to the city's visual clutter is entitled to no more weight than the temporary unsightliness of discarded handbills and the additional street-cleaning burden that were insufficient to justify the ordinances reviewed in Schneider.

The rationale of Schneider is inapposite in the context of the instant case. There, individual citizens were actively exercising their right to communicate directly with potential recipients of their message. The conduct continued only while the speakers or distributors remained on the scene. In this case, appellees posted dozens of temporary signs throughout an area where they would remain unattended until removed. As the Court expressly noted in Schneider, the First Amendment does not "deprive a municipality of power to enact regulations against throwing literature broadcast in the streets. Prohibition of such conduct would not abridge the constitutional liberty since such activity bears no necessary relationship to the freedom to speak, write, print or distribute information or opinion." 308 U.S., at 160–161, 60 S.Ct., at 150. In short, there is no constitutional impediment to "the punishment of those who actually throw papers on the streets." Id., at 162, 60 S.Ct., at 151. A distributor of leaflets has no right simply to scatter his pamphlets in the air-or to toss large quantities of paper from the window of a tall building or a low flying airplane. Characterizing such an activity as a separate means of communication does not diminish the State's power to condemn it as a public nuisance. The right recognized in Schneider is to tender the written material to the passerby who may reject it or accept it, and who thereafter may keep it, dispose of it properly, or incur the risk of punishment if he lets it fall to the ground. One who is rightfully on a street open to the public "carries with him there as elsewhere the constitutional right to express his views in an orderly fashion. This right extends to the communication of ideas by handbills and literature as well as by the spoken word." * * *

With respect to signs posted by appellees, however, it is the tangible medium of expressing the message that has the adverse impact on the appearance of the landscape. In Schneider, an antilittering statute could have addressed the substantive evil without prohibiting expressive activity, whereas application of the prophylactic rule actually employed gratuitously infringed upon the right of an individual to communicate directly with a willing listener. Here, the substantive evil-visual blight-is not merely a possible by-product of the activity, but is created by the medium of expression itself. In contrast to Schneider, therefore, the application of the ordinance in this case responds precisely to the substantive problem which legitimately concerns the City. The ordinance curtails no more speech than is necessary to accomplish its purpose.

V

The Court of Appeals accepted the argument that a prohibition against the use of unattractive signs cannot be justified on esthetic grounds if it fails to apply to all equally unattractive signs wherever they might be located. A comparable argument was categorically rejected in Metromedia. In that case it was argued that the city could not simultaneously permit billboards to be used for onsite advertising and also justify the prohibition against offsite advertising on esthetic grounds, since both types of advertising were equally unattractive. The Court held, however, that the city could reasonably conclude that the esthetic interest was outweighed by the countervailing interest in one kind of advertising even though it was not outweighed by the other. (citation omitted) So here, the validity of the esthetic interest in the elimination of signs on public property is not compromised by failing to extend the ban to private property. The private citizen's interest in controlling the use of his own property justifies the disparate treatment. Moreover, by not extending the ban to all locations, a significant opportunity to communicate by means of temporary signs is preserved, and private property owners' esthetic concerns will keep the posting of signs on their property within reasonable bounds. Even if some visual blight remains, a partial, content-neutral ban may nevertheless enhance the City's appearance.

Furthermore, there is no finding that in any area where appellees seek to place signs, there are already so many signs posted on adjacent private property that the elimination of appellees' signs would have an inconsequential effect on the esthetic values with which the City is concerned. There is simply no predicate in the findings of the District Court for the conclusion that the prohibition against the posting of appellees' signs fails to advance the City's esthetic interest.

VI

While the First Amendment does not guarantee the right to employ every conceivable method of communication at all times and in all places, Heffron v. International Society for Krishna Consciousness, Inc., 452 U.S., at 647, 101 S.Ct., at 2563–2564, a restriction on expressive activity may be invalid if the remaining modes of communication are inadequate. * * * The Los Angeles ordinance does not affect any individual's freedom to exercise the right to speak and to distribute literature in the same place where the posting of signs on public property is prohibited. (citation omitted) To the extent that the posting of signs on public property has advantages over these forms of expression, see, e.g., Talley v. California, 362 U.S. 60, 64–65, 80 S.Ct.536, 538–539, 4 L.Ed.2d 559 (1960), there is no reason to believe that these same advantages cannot be obtained through other means. To the contrary, the findings of the District Court indicate that there are ample alternative modes of communication in Los Angeles. Notwithstanding appellees' general assertions in their brief concerning the utility of political posters, nothing in the findings indicates that the posting of political posters on public property is a uniquely valuable or important mode of communication, or that appellees' ability to communicate effectively is threatened by ever-increasing restrictions on expression (citation omitted).

VII

Appellees suggest that the public property covered by the ordinance either is itself a "public forum" for First Amendment purposes, or at least should be treated in the same respect as the "public forum" in which the property is located. "Traditional public forum property occupies a special position in terms of First Amendment protection," United States v. Grace, 461 U.S., at 180, 103 S.Ct., at 1708, and appellees maintain that their sign-posting activities are entitled to this protection. * * *

Appellees' reliance on the public forum doctrine is misplaced. They fail to demonstrate the existence of a traditional right of access respecting such items as utility poles for purposes of their communication comparable to that recognized for public streets and parks, and it is clear that "the First Amendment does not guarantee access to government property simply because it is owned or controlled by the government." United States Postal Service v. Greenburgh Civic Assns., 453 U.S. 114, 129, 101 S.Ct. 2676, 2685, 69 L.Ed.2d 517 (1981). Rather, the "existence of a right of access to public property and the standard by which limitations upon such a right must be evaluated differ depending on the character of the property at issue." Perry Education Assn. v. Perry Local Educators' Assn., 460 U.S. 37, 44, 103 S.Ct. 948, 954, 74 L.Ed.2d 794 (1983).

Lampposts can of course be used as signposts, but the mere fact that government property can be used as a vehicle for communication does not mean that the Constitution requires such uses to be permitted. Cf. United States Postal Service v. Greenburgh Civic Assn., 453 U.S., at 131, 101 S.Ct. 2676, 2686, 69 L.Ed.2d 517 (citation omitted). Public property which is not by tradition or designation a forum for public communication may be reserved by the State "for its intended purposes, communicative or otherwise, as long as the regulation on speech is reasonable and not an effort to suppress expression merely because public officials oppose the speaker's view." Perry Education Assn. v. Perry Local Educators' Ass'n, 460 U.S., at 46, 103 S.Ct., at 955. Given our analysis of the legitimate interest served by the ordinance, its viewpoint neutrality, and the availability of alternative channels of communication, the ordinance is certainly constitutional as applied to appellees under this standard. (citation omitted)

VIII

Finally, Taxpayers and COGS argue that Los Angeles could have written an ordinance that would have had a less severe effect on expressive activity such as theirs, by permitting the posting of any kind of sign at any time on some types of public property, or by making a variety of other more specific exceptions to the ordinance: for signs carrying certain types of messages (such as political campaign signs), for signs posted during specific time periods (perhaps during political campaigns), for particular locations (perhaps for areas already cluttered by an excessive number of signs on adjacent private property), or for signs meeting design specifications (such as size or color). Plausible public policy arguments might well be made in support of any such exception, but it by no means follows that it is therefore constitutionally mandated, cf. Singer v. United States, 380 U.S. 24, 34–35, 85 S.Ct. 783, 789–790, 13 L.Ed.2d 630 (1965), nor is it clear that some of the suggested exceptions would even be constitutionally permissible. * * * To create an exception for appellees' political speech and not * * * other types of speech might create a risk of engaging in constitutionally forbidden content discrimination. * * * Moreover, the volume of permissible postings under such a mandated exemption might so limit the ordinance's effect as to defeat its aim of combating visual blight.

Any constitutionally mandated exception to the City's total prohibition against temporary signs on public property would necessarily rest on a judicial determination that the City's traffic control and safety interests had little or no applicability within the excepted category, and that the City's interests in esthetics are not sufficiently important to justify the prohibition in that category. But the findings of the District Court provide no basis for questioning the substantiality of the esthetic interest at stake, or for believing that a uniquely important form of communication has been abridged for the categories of expression engaged in by Taxpayers and COGS. Therefore, we accept the City's position that it may decide that the esthetic interest in avoiding "visual clutter" justifies a removal of signs creating or increasing that clutter. The findings of the District Court that COGS signs add to the problems addressed by the ordinance and, if permitted to remain, would encourage others to post additional signs, are sufficient to justify application of the ordinance to these appellees.

As recognized in Metromedia, if the city has a sufficient basis for believing that billboards are traffic hazards and are unattractive, "then obviously the most direct and perhaps the only effective approach to solving the problems they create is to prohibit them." 453 U.S., at 508, 101 S.Ct., at 2893. As is true of billboards, the esthetic interests that are implicated by temporary signs are presumptively at work in all parts of the city, including those where appellees posted their signs, and there is no basis in the record in this case upon which to rebut that presumption. These interests are both psychological and economic. The character of the environment affects the quality of life and the value of property in both residential and commercial areas. We hold that on this record these interests are sufficiently substantial to justify this content-neutral, impartially administered prohibition against the posting of appellees' temporary signs on public property and that such an application of the ordinance does not create an unacceptable threat to the "profound national commitment to the principle that debate on public issues should be uninhibited, robust, and wide-open." New York Times Co. v. Sullivan, 376 U.S. 254, 270, 84 S.Ct. 710, 720–721, 11 L.Ed.2d 686 (1964). (citation omitted)

The judgment of the Court of Appeals is reversed, and the case is remanded to that Court.

It is so ordered.

JUSTICE BRENNAN, with whom JUSTICE MARSHALL and JUSTICE BLACKMUN join, dissenting.

The plurality opinion in Metromedia, Inc. v. San Diego, 453 U.S. 490, 101 S.Ct. 2882, 69 L.Ed.2d 800 (1981), concluded that the City of San Diego could, consistently with the First Amendment, restrict the commercial use of billboards in order to "preserve and improve the appearance of the City." Id., at 493, 101 S.Ct., at 2885. Today, the Court sustains the constitutionality of Los Angeles' similarly motivated ban on the posting of political signs on public property. Because the Court's lenient approach towards the restriction of speech for reasons of aesthetics threatens seriously to undermine the protections of the First Amendment, I dissent.

The Court finds that the City's "interest [in eliminating visual clutter] is sufficiently substantial to justify the effect of the ordinance on appellees' expression" and that the effect of the ordinance on speech is "no greater than necessary to accomplish the City's purpose." * * * In my view, the City of Los Angeles has not shown that its interest in eliminating "visual clutter" justifies its restriction of appellees' ability to communicate with the local electorate.

I

* * * The posting of signs is, of course, a time-honored means of communicating a broad range of ideas and information, particularly in our cities and towns. At the same time, the unfettered proliferation of signs on public fixtures may offend the public's legitimate desire to preserve an orderly and aesthetically pleasing urban environment. In this case, as in Metromedia, we are called upon to adjudge the constitutionality under the First Amendment of a local government's response to this recurring dilemma-namely, the clash between the public's aesthetic interest in controlling the use of billboards, signs, handbills, and other similar means of communication, and the First Amendment interest of those who wish to use these media to express their views, or to learn the views of others, on matters of importance to the community. In deciding this First Amendment question, the critical importance of the posting of signs as a means of communication must not be overlooked. Use of this medium of communication is particularly valuable in part because it entails a relatively small expense in reaching a wide audience, allows flexibility in accommodating various formats, typographies, and graphics, and conveys its message in a manner that is easily read and understood by its reader or viewer. There may be alternative channels of communication, but the prevalence of a large number of signs in Los Angeles (citation omitted) is a strong indication that, for many speakers, those alternatives are far less satisfactory. Cf. Southeastern Promotions, Ltd. v. Conrad, 420 U.S. 546, 556, 95 S.Ct. 1239, 1245, 43 L.Ed.2d 448 (1975).

Nevertheless, the City of Los Angeles asserts that ample alternative avenues of communication are available. The City notes that, although the posting of signs on public property is prohibited, the posting of signs on private property and the distribution of handbills are not. Brief for Appellants 25–26. But there is no showing that either of these alternatives would serve appellees' needs nearly as well as would the posting of signs on public property. First, there is no proof that a sufficient number of private parties would allow the posting of signs on their property. Indeed, common sense suggests the contrary at least in some instances. A speaker with a message that is generally unpopular or simply unpopular among property owners is hardly likely to get his message across if forced to rely on this medium. It is difficult to believe, for example, that a group advocating an increase in the rate of a property tax would succeed in persuading private property owners to accept its signs.

Similarly, the adequacy of distributing handbills is dubious, despite certain advantages of handbills over signs. * * *

II

* * * The Court's first task is to determine whether the ordinance is aimed at suppressing the content of speech, and, if it is, whether a compelling state interest justifies the suppression. * * * If the restriction is content-neutral, the court's task is to determine (1) whether the governmental objective advanced by the restriction is substantial, and (2) whether the restriction imposed on speech is no greater than is essential to further that objective. Unless both conditions are met the restriction must be invalidated. See ante, at 2128, 2130–2132 (citation omitted).

My suggestion in Metromedia was that courts should exercise special care in addressing these questions when a purely aesthetic objective is asserted to justify a restriction of speech. Specifically, "before deferring to a city's judgment, a court must be convinced that the city is seriously and comprehensively addressing aesthetic concerns with respect to its environment." 453 U.S., at 531, 101 S.Ct., at 2905. I adhere to that view. Its correctness-premised largely on my concern that aesthetic interests are easy for a city to assert and difficult for a court to evaluate-is, for me, reaffirmed by this case.

The fundamental problem in this kind of case is that a purely aesthetic state interest offered to justify a restriction on speech-that is, a governmental objective justified solely in terms like "proscribing intrusive and unpleasant formats for expression," ante, at 2130 creates difficulties for a reviewing court in fulfilling its obligation to ensure that government regulation does not trespass upon protections secured by the First Amendment. The source of those difficulties is the unavoidable subjectivity of aesthetic judgments-the fact that "beauty is in the eye of the beholder." As a consequence of this subjectivity, laws defended on aesthetic grounds raise problems for judicial review that are not presented by laws defended on more objective grounds-such as national security, public health, or public safety (citation omitted). In practice, therefore, the inherent subjectivity of aesthetic judgments makes it all too easy for the government to fashion its justification for a law in a manner that impairs the ability of a reviewing court meaningfully to make the required inquiries. (citation omitted)

A

Initially, a reviewing court faces substantial difficulties determining whether the actual objective is related to the suppression of speech. The asserted interest in aesthetics may be only a facade for content-based suppression. Of course, all would agree that the improvement and preservation of the aesthetic environment are important governmental functions, and that some restrictions on speech may be necessary to carry out these functions. Metromedia, supra, at 530, 101 S.Ct., at 2904. But a governmental interest in aesthetics cannot be regarded as sufficiently compelling to justify a restriction of speech based on an assertion that the content of the speech is, in itself, aesthetically displeasing. Cohen v. California, 403 U.S.15, 91 S.Ct. 1780, 29 L.Ed.2d 284 (1971). Because aesthetic judgments are so subjective, however, it is too easy for government to enact restrictions on speech for just such illegitimate reasons and to evade effective judicial review by asserting that the restriction is aimed at some displeasing aspect of the speech that is not solely communicative-for example, its sound, its appearance, or its location. An objective standard for evaluating claimed aesthetic judgments is therefore essential; for without one, courts have no reliable means of assessing the genuineness of such claims.

For example, in evaluating the ordinance before us in this case, the City might be pursuing either of two objectives, motivated by two very different judgments. One objective might be the elimination of "visual clutter," attributable in whole or in part to signs posted on public property. The aesthetic judgment underlying this objective would be that the clutter created by these signs offends the community's desire for an orderly, visually pleasing environment. A second objective might simply be the elimination of the messages typically carried by the signs. (citation omitted) In that case, the aesthetic judgment would be that the signs' messages are themselves displeasing. The first objective is lawful, of course, but the second is not. Yet the City might easily mask the second objective by asserting the first and declaring that signs constitute visual clutter. In short, we must avoid unquestioned acceptance of the City's bare declaration of an aesthetic objective lest we fail in our duty to prevent unlawful trespasses upon First Amendment protections.

B

A total ban on an important medium of communication may be upheld only if the government proves that the ban (1) furthers a substantial government objective, and (2) constitutes the least speech-restrictive means of achieving that objective. Schad v. Mount Ephraim, 452 U.S. 61, 101 S.Ct. 2176, 68 L.Ed.2d 671 (1981). Here too, however, meaningful judicial application of these standards is seriously frustrated.

(1)

No one doubts the importance of a general governmental interest in aesthetics, but in order to justify a restriction of speech, the particular objective behind the restriction must be substantial. * * * Therefore, in order to uphold a restriction of speech imposed to further an aesthetic objective, a court must ascertain the substantiality of the specific objective pursued. Although courts ordinarily defer to the government's assertion that its objective is substantial, that assertion is not immune from critical examination. See, e.g., Schad v. Mount Ephraim, supra, 452 U.S., at 72–73, 101 S.Ct., at 2184–2185. This is particularly true when aesthetic objectives underlie the restrictions. * * *

(2)

Similarly, when a total ban is justified solely in terms of aesthetics, the means inquiry necessary to evaluate the constitutionality of the ban may be impeded by deliberate or unintended government manipulation. Governmental objectives that are purely aesthetic can usually be expressed in a virtually limitless variety of ways. Consequently, objectives can be tailored to fit whatever program the government devises to promote its general aesthetic interests. Once the government has identified a substantial aesthetic objective and has selected a preferred means of achieving its objective, it will be possible for the government to correct any mismatch between means and ends by redefining the ends to conform with the means.

In this case, for example, any of several objectives might be the City's actual substantial goal in banning temporary signs: (1) the elimination of all signs throughout the City, (2) the elimination of all signs in certain parts of the City, or (3) a reduction of the density of signs. Although a total ban on the posting of signs on public property would be the least restrictive means of achieving only the first objective, it would be a very effective means of achieving the other two as well. It is quite possible, therefore, that the City might select such a ban as the means by which to further its general interest in solving its sign problem, without explicitly considering which of the three specific objectives is really substantial. Then, having selected the total ban as its preferred means, the City would be strongly inclined to characterize the first objective as the substantial one. This might be done purposefully in order to conform the ban to the least-restrictive-means requirement, or it might be done inadvertently as a natural concomitant of considering means and ends together. But regardless of why it is done, a reviewing court will be confronted with a statement of substantiality the subjectivity of which makes it impossible to question on its face.

This possibility of interdependence between means and ends in the development of policies to promote aesthetics poses a major obstacle to judicial review of the availability of alternative means that are less restrictive of speech. * * *

The ease with which means can be equated with aesthetic ends only confirms the importance of close judicial scrutiny of the substantiality of such ends. See supra, at 2139–2140. In this case, for example, it is essential that the Court assess the City's ban on signs by evaluating whether the City has a substantial interest in eliminating the visual clutter caused by all posted signs throughout the City-as distinguished from an interest in banning signs in some areas or in preventing densely packed signs. If, in fact, either of the latter two objectives constitute the substantial interest underlying this ordinance, they could be achieved by means far less restrictive of speech than a total ban on signs, and the ban, therefore, would be invalid.

C

Regrettably, the Court's analysis is seriously inadequate. Because the Court has failed to develop a reliable means of gauging the nature or depth of the City's commitment to pursuing the goal of eradicating "visual clutter," it simply approves the ordinance with only the most cursory degree of judicial oversight. Without stopping to consider carefully whether this supposed commitment is genuine or substantial, the Court essentially defers to the City's aesthetic judgment and in so doing precludes serious assessment of the availability of alternative means.

* * *

III

* * *

In cases like this, where a total ban is imposed on a particularly valuable method of communication, a court should require the government to provide tangible proof of the legitimacy and substantiality of its aesthetic objective. Justifications for such restrictions articulated by the government should be critically examined to determine whether the government has committed itself to addressing the identified aesthetic problem.

* * *

Accordingly, in order for Los Angeles to succeed in defending its total ban on the posting of signs, the City would have to demonstrate that it is pursuing its goal of eliminating visual clutter in a serious and comprehensive manner. Most importantly, the City would have to show that it is pursuing its goal through programs other than its ban on signs, that at least some of those programs address the visual clutter problem through means that do not entail the restriction of speech, and that the programs parallel the ban in their stringency, geographical scope, and aesthetic focus. * * *

In light of the extreme stringency of Los Angeles' ban—barring all signs from being posted—and its wide geographical scope—covering the entire City—it might be difficult for Los Angeles to make the type of showing I have suggested. Cf. Metromedia, supra 453 U.S., at 533–534,

101 S.Ct., at 2905–2906. A more limited approach to the visual clutter problem, however, might well pass constitutional muster. I have no doubt that signs posted on public property in certain areas—including, perhaps, parts of Los Angeles—could contribute to the type of eyesore that a city would genuinely have a substantial interest in eliminating. These areas might include parts of the City that are particularly pristine, reserved for certain uses, designated to reflect certain themes, or so blighted that broad-gauged renovation is necessary. Presumably, in these types of areas, the City would also regulate the aesthetic environment in ways other than the banning of temporary signs. The City might zone such areas for a particular type of development or lack of development; it might actively create a particular type of environment; it might be especially vigilant in keeping the area clean; it might regulate the size and location of permanent signs; or it might reserve particular locations, such as kiosks, for the posting of temporary signs. Similarly, Los Angeles might be able to attack its visual clutter problem in more areas of the City by reducing the stringency of the ban, perhaps by regulating the density of temporary signs, and coupling that approach with additional measures designed to reduce other forms of visual clutter. There are a variety of ways that the aesthetic environment can be regulated, some restrictive of speech and others not, but it is only when aesthetic regulation is addressed in a comprehensive and focused manner that we can ensure that the goals pursued are substantial and that the manner in which they are pursued is no more restrictive of speech than is necessary.

In the absence of such a showing in this case, I believe that Los Angeles' total ban sweeps so broadly and trenches so completely on appellees' use of an important medium of political expression that it must be struck down as violative of the First Amendment. (citation omitted)

I therefore dissent.

Notes

1. Be sure to understand the consequences of labeling speech commercial or non-commercial. If speech is commercial, then regulations affecting it must only pass the Central Hudson test, as is explained in Metromedia. But when speech is non-commercial, restrictions are subject to greater scrutiny, and the tests used depend on such factors as whether the restriction is content-based, the type of forum involved, and whether the restriction is merely incidental. Despite the differing treatment of these categories of speech, distinguishing commercial from non-commercial speech is not always easy. Cincinnati v. Discovery Network, 507 U.S. 410, 113 S.Ct. 1505, 123 L.Ed.2d 99 (1993) involved an ordinance prohibiting newsracks that contained "commercial handbills" but permitting newsracks that held newspapers. The city justified its position, in part, on the basis that newspapers contained more valuable speech than the handbills. In a thoughtful explanation of the Court's treatment of commercial speech, Justice Stevens noted that "it is clear that much of the material in ordinary newspapers is

commercial speech and, conversely, that the editorial content in respondents' promotional publications is not what we have described as 'core' commercial speech. There is no doubt a "commonsense" basis for distinguishing between the two, but under both the city's code and our cases the difference is a matter of degree."

2. Do you agree with the principle announced in Metromedia that cities may rationally distinguish between off-site signs, totally prohibiting such signs, and on-site signs? Are not many on-site signs just as distracting and aesthetically offensive as off-site billboards? Similarly, is it appropriate for a city to rely on aesthetic interests to ban the posting of signs on public property but not on private property? Piecemeal sign regulations and prohibitions of off-site advertising have been upheld in numerous cases. See, Infinity Outdoor, Inc. v. City of New York, 165 F.Supp.2d 403 (E.D.N.Y. 2001); Marathon Outdoor, LLC v. Visconti, 107 F.Supp. 2d 355 (S.D.N.Y. 2000); and Long Island Bd. of Realtors, Inc. v. Incorporated Village of Massapequa Park, 277 F.3d 622 (2d Cir. 2002).

3. In Metromedia, the Court held that although it was permissible for the city to ban all off-site commercial signs, the ordinance was unconstitutional insofar as it permitted on-site commercial signs but did not allow on-site non-commercial signs. This distinction is a form of impermissible content discrimination, a subtle defect that often leads to sign regulations being deemed unconstitutional. The Court had an opportunity to clarify the implications of content discrimination several years later, in Boos v. Barry, 485 U.S. 312, 108 S.Ct. 1157, 99 L.Ed.2d 333 (1988). In that case, a Washington D.C. regulation prohibited the display of signs tending to bring a foreign government into "public odium" within 500 feet of that government's embassy. The government argued that the regulation was not content-based, since it did not draw distinctions among viewpoints. The Court disagreed:

> The display clause determines which viewpoint is acceptable in a neutral fashion by looking to the policies of foreign governments. While this prevents the display clause from being directly viewpoint-based, a label with potential First Amendment ramifications of its own, see, e. g., Members of City Council of Los Angeles v. Taxpayers for Vincent, 466 U.S. 789, 804 (1984); Schacht v. United States, 398 U.S. 58, 63 (1970), it does not render the statute content-neutral. Rather, we have held that a regulation that "does not favor either side of a political controversy" is nonetheless impermissible because the "First Amendment's hostility to content-based regulation extends . . . to prohibition of public discussion of an entire topic." Consolidated Edison Co. v. Public Service Comm'n, 447 U.S. 530, 537 (1980). Here the government has determined that an entire category of speech—signs or displays critical of foreign governments—is not to be permitted.
>
> * * *
>
> Applying these principles to the case at hand leads readily to the conclusion that the display clause is content-based. The clause is justified only by reference to the content of speech. Respondents and the United States do not point to the "secondary effects" of picket signs in front of embassies. They do not point to congestion, to interference with

ingress or egress, to visual clutter, or to the need to protect the security of embassies. Rather, they rely on the need to protect the dignity of foreign diplomatic personnel by shielding them from speech that is critical of their governments. This justification focuses only on the content of the speech and the direct impact that speech has on its listeners. The emotive impact of speech on its audience is not a "secondary effect." Because the display clause regulates speech due to its potential primary impact, we conclude it must be considered content-based.

In Village of Schaumberg v. Jeep Eagle Sales Corp., 285 Ill.App.3d 481, 221 Ill.Dec. 679, 676 N.E.2d 200 (1996) the court held that a local sign ordinance that prohibited display of more than three "corporate and official" flags at any one business violated the First Amendment because the ordinance did not limit the number of flags that could be displayed if they were other than "corporate and official." As the court explained, the regulations "facially discriminate between official and corporate flags and all others. Because the permissibility of a flag is dependent upon the nature of the message conveyed, the sign ordinance must be deemed content-based." See Barry P. McDonald, *Speech and Distrust: Rethinking the Content Approach to Protecting the Freedom of Expression*, 81 Notre Dame L.Rev. 1347 for a comprehensive discussion of content discrimination theories.

4. As noted in Taxpayers for Vincent, if a regulation is not content-based, but still has an incidental restrictive effect on speech, it may qualify as a permissible time, place, or manner regulation if it is narrowly tailored to serve a significant governmental interest and leaves open adequate alternative methods of communication. See also Ward v. Rock Against Racism, 491 U.S. 781, 109 S.Ct. 2746, 105 L.Ed.2d 661 (1989).

Within the area of sign regulation, restrictions on size, height, materials and placement are often upheld as time, place, and manner restrictions. For a case upholding regulation of *all* signs to a size of under four square feet, see People v. Goodman, 31 N.Y.2d 262, 338 N.Y.S.2d 97, 290 N.E.2d 139 (1972). See also Kroll v. Steere, 60 Conn.App. 376, 759 A.2d 541 (2000) (upholding size limits on a residential sign protesting the killing of a deer).

In Faustin v. City and & County of Denver, 423 F.3d 1192 (10th Cir.2005), the court held that Denver's unwritten policy of prohibiting the display of signs and banners on highway overpasses was a constitutional time, place, and manner regulation. Compare Brown v. California Dept. of Transportation, 321 F.3d 1217 (9th Cir.2003), where the court did not reach the time, place, or manner question because it found the state's unwritten policy of removing all signs and banners on highway overpasses, except American flags, to be content-based.

An unusual sign case is presented in Supersign of Boca Raton, Inc. v. City of Fort Lauderdale, 766 F.2d 1528 (11th Cir.1985), where the court upheld a local sign ordinance provision which prohibited advertising signs on watercraft and certain vehicles. Similarly, in Center for Bio-Ethical Reform v. Honolulu, 345 F.Supp.2d 1123, (2004) the court held that a ban on towing aerial banners over beaches was a valid time, place and manner restriction. San Diego is currently in the process of drafting a proposal to ban floating billboards towed behind boats. Diane Bell, *Boat towing billboards sputters into hot water*, San Diego Union–Tribune, July 24, 2007, at B–1.

Regulations restricting the use of illuminated signs have also tended to be upheld. See Schaffer v. Omaha, 197 Neb. 328, 248 N.W.2d 764 (1977) (portable electric signs); Hilton Head Island v. Fine Liquors, Ltd., 302 S.C. 550, 397 S.E.2d 662 (1990) (internally illuminated signs); Asselin v. Town of Conway, 137 N.H. 368, 628 A.2d 247 (1993) (internally illuminated signs); Wallace v. Brown County Area Plan Commission, 689 N.E.2d 491 (Ind.1998) (neon lighting prohibition); Eller Media Co. v. City of Tucson, 198 Ariz. 127, 7 P.3d 136 (2000) (billboard lighting restrictions). However, in Flying J Travel Plaza v. Commonwealth, Transportation Cabinet, 928 S.W.2d 344 (Ky.1996), a ban on flashing signs was invalidated because the local law made exceptions for time, date and weather signs. Digital billboards capable of transmitting video advertisements have recently become a subject of debate in many municipalities, as they are generally considered to present greater driving risks than conventional signs. Although very little case law currently exists concerning this format, it is likely that legislation limiting brightness and the frequency of changing messages will be upheld as content-neutral time, place, or manner restrictions. For more information on the problems associated with these signs, see Scenic America, *Billboards in the Digital Age: Unsafe (and Unsightly) at Any Speed*, available at http://www.scenic.org/pdfs/eb.pdf.

5. In Taxpayers for Vincent, the Court noted that even content-neutral speech restrictions may be invalid if alternative methods of communication are inadequate. Although Justice Brennan's dissent argued persuasively that Los Angeles' ban of temporary signs was one such type of regulation, it was not until City of Ladue v. Gilleo, 512 U.S. 43, 114 S.Ct. 2038, 129 L.Ed.2d 36 (1994) that the Court found a content-neutral sign regulation to be invalid on this ground. In that case, a homeowner challenged a zoning ordinance that prohibited her from hanging a sign the size of a piece of notebook paper in the window of her house:

> Although prohibitions foreclosing entire media may be completely free of content or viewpoint discrimination, the danger they pose to the freedom of speech is readily apparent—by eliminating a common means of speaking, such measures can suppress too much speech.
>
> Ladue contends, however, that its ordinance is a mere regulation of the "time, place, or manner" of speech because residents remain free to convey their desired messages by other means, such as hand-held signs, "letters, handbills, flyers, telephone calls, newspaper advertisements, bumper stickers, speeches, and neighborhood or community meetings." Brief for Petitioners 41. However, even regulations that do not foreclose an entire medium of expression, but merely shift the time, place, or manner of its use, must "leave open ample alternative channels for communication." Clark v. Community for Creative Non–Violence, 468 U.S. 288, 293, 104 S.Ct. 3065, 82 L.Ed.2d 221 (1984). In this case, we are not persuaded that adequate substitutes exist for the important medium of speech that Ladue has closed off.
>
> Displaying a sign from one's own residence often carries a message quite distinct from placing the same sign someplace else, or conveying

the same text or picture by other means. Precisely because of their location, such signs provide information about the identity of the "speaker.".... A sign advocating "Peace in the Gulf" in the front lawn of a retired general or decorated war veteran may provoke a different reaction than the same sign in a 10–year-old child's bedroom window or the same message on a bumper sticker of a passing automobile. An espousal of socialism may carry different implications when displayed on the grounds of a stately mansion than when pasted on a factory wall or an ambulatory sandwich board.

Residential signs are an unusually cheap and convenient form of communication. Especially for persons of modest means or limited mobility, a yard or window sign may have no practical substitute. Cf. Vincent, 466 U.S. at 812–813, n. 30; Anderson v. Celebrezze, 460 U.S. 780, 793–794 (1983); Martin v. City of Struthers, 319 U.S. at 146; Milk Wagon Drivers v. Meadowmoor Dairies, Inc., 312 U.S. 287, 293 (1941). Even for the affluent, the added costs in money or time of taking out a newspaper advertisement, handing out leaflets on the street, or standing in front of one's house with a hand-held sign may make the difference between participating and not participating in some public debate. n15 Furthermore, a person who puts up a sign at her residence often intends to reach neighbors, an audience that could not be reached nearly as well by other means.

A special respect for individual liberty in the home has long been part of our culture and our law, see, e. g., Payton v. New York, 445 U.S. 573, 596–597 and nn. 44–45 (1980); that principle has special resonance when the government seeks to constrain a person's ability to speak there. See Spence v. Washington, 418 U.S. 405, 406, 409, 411 (1974) (per curiam). Most Americans would be understandably dismayed, given that tradition, to learn that it was illegal to display from their window an 8–by 11–inch sign expressing their political views. Whereas the government's need to mediate among various competing uses, including expressive ones, for public streets and facilities is constant and unavoidable, see Cox v. New Hampshire, 312 U.S. 569, 574, 576 (1941); see also Widmar v. Vincent, 454 U.S. 263, 278 (1981) (Stevens, J., concurring in judgment), its need to regulate temperate speech from the home is surely much less pressing, see Spence, 418 U.S. at 409.

Our decision that Ladue's ban on almost all residential signs violates the First Amendment by no means leaves the City powerless to address the ills that may be associated with residential signs. It bears mentioning that individual residents themselves have strong incentives to keep their own property values up and to prevent "visual clutter" in their own yards and neighborhoods—incentives markedly different from those of persons who erect signs on others' land, in others' neighborhoods, or on public property. Residents' self-interest diminishes the danger of the "unlimited" proliferation of residential signs that concerns the City of Ladue. We are confident that more temperate measures could in large part satisfy Ladue's stated regulatory needs without harm to the First Amendment rights of its citizens. As currently framed, however, the ordinance abridges those rights.

6. Content-neutral sign regulations are also susceptible to vagueness challenges, although they are rarely successful. In a somewhat rare case, a court struck as unconstitutionally vague a city ordinance prohibiting signs or graphics with obscene words or illustrations.[1] The plaintiff was the owner of a pizza parlor whose sign depicted a reproduction of Leonardo da Vinci's famous anatomical illustration. Solomon v. City of Gainesville, 763 F.2d 1212 (11th Cir.1985). More typical is Nichols Media Group, LLC v. Town of Babylon, 365 F.Supp.2d 295 (E.D.N.Y.2005), where advertisers challenged an ordinance prohibiting "obscene" and "pornographic" billboards. The court noted that "[t]he Supreme Court has endeavored to define obscenity and pornography so that state statutes can conform to constitutional requirements regarding vagueness....A statute's use of the term 'obscenity' has been noted to inherently contain within it a reference to specifically defined conduct so that particular words need not be spelled out when this term is used."

7. Around Election Day every year, streets and lawns are filled with political signs. To what extent can and should government regulate political signs? Prior to Taxpayers for Vincent and City of Ladue v. Gilleo, ordinances which banned political signs in residential zones were struck down in Martin v. Wray, 473 F.Supp. 1131 (E.D.Wis.1979) and Farrell v. Township of Teaneck, 126 N.J.Super. 460, 315 A.2d 424 (1974). Also see two subsequent New Jersey cases, State v. J. & J. Painting, 167 N.J.Super. 384, 400 A.2d 1204 (1979) (holding that the commercial speech doctrine did not require that defendants be allowed to place temporary advertising signs on the lawns of houses they were in process of painting or roofing), and State v. Miller, 83 N.J. 402, 416 A.2d 821 (1980) (holding that free speech protected defendant's political expression in placing a large sign in his front yard welcoming prospective residents to "this flood hazard area"). City of Antioch v. Candidates' Outdoor Graphic Service, 557 F.Supp. 52 (N.D.Cal.1982), held that an ordinance which imposed a year-round ban on political signs except for sixty days prior to an election was unconstitutional because it was not the least drastic means of protecting visual amenities and aesthetics. In striking down a durational limit on political signs in Outdoor Systems, Inc. v. City of Merriam, Kan., 67 F.Supp.2d 1258 (D.Kan.1999), the Court said, "[n]early every court to address the issue has held that the government interest in aesthetics and safety is insufficient to justify a durational restriction on political signs in residential districts." See also, Sugarman v. Village of Chester, 192 F.Supp.2d 282 (S.D.N.Y.2002) (invalidating the sign regulations of more than nineteen separate municipalities in the county as they applied to political signs). Also, compare Taxpayers for Vincent with Klein v. Baise, 708 F.Supp. 863 (N.D.Ill.1989) (enjoining enforcement of a state law prohibiting advertising on bus shelters on behalf of a political candidate).

When applied to residential political signs, aesthetic interests have also been found insufficient to justify a permitting requirement that might delay a person from posting a sign for seventy-five days. As the Second Circuit explained: "Where, as here, a property owner wishes to take a public position on a pressing public issue, for example, or on the qualifications of a

1. Note that the ordinance was not content-based, even though it clearly discriminated against obscene speech, because such speech, when adequately defined, is not protected by the First Amendment.

candidate for public office in an imminent election, the time required to obtain approval may prevent him or her from doing so until after the public issue is settled or the election is over. Such belated approval is of little consolation...." Lusk v. Village of Cold Spring, 475 F.3d 480, 492 (2d Cir.2007).

8. Local sign ordinances also must contain sufficient criteria for the reviewing authority (e.g. the building inspector, planning director, etc.) to prevent an abuse of discretion. As explained in Lusk v. Village of Cold Spring, supra, "[a] government regulation that allows arbitrary application is inherently inconsistent with a valid time, place, and manner regulation because such discretion has the potential for becoming a means of suppressing a particular point of view. To curtail that risk, a law subjecting the exercise of First Amendment freedoms to the prior restraint on a license must contain narrow, objective, and definite standards to guide the licensing authority." In Lamar Advertising Co. v. City of Douglasville, Georgia, 254 F.Supp.2d 1321 (N.D.Ga.2003) the court said, "...City officials are to consider the value of the surrounding property, the environment of the surrounding property, the public good, and the purpose of the zoning ordinance before granting or denying a variance. Pursuant to *Lady J. Lingerie, [Inc. v. City of Jacksonville*, 176 F.3d 1358 (11th Cir.1999),] the breadth of these criteria provides the City unbridled discretion in granting and denying the right to post signs..." See also, North Olmstead Chamber of Commerce v. City of North Olmstead, 86 F.Supp.2d 755 (N.D.Ohio 2000); Lawson v. City of Kankakee, Ill., 81 F.Supp.2d 930 (C.D.Ill.2000); Young v. City of Roseville, 78 F.Supp.2d 970 (D.Minn.1999); and Young v. City of Roseville, 78 F. Supp. 2d 970 (D.Minn. 1999).

In addition to adequate criteria, sign regulations that require licensing must also ensure that decisions are made promptly. In Café Erotica of Florida, Inc. v. St. Johns County, 360 F.3d 1274 (11th Cir.2004) a thirty day approval period was deemed constitutional.

9. Some sign regulations have also been challenged as conflicting with federal statutes. In Lorillard Tobacco Co. v. Reilly, 533 U.S. 525, 121 S.Ct. 2404, 150 L.Ed.2d 532 (2001), the U. S. Supreme Court determined that the Federal Cigarette Labeling and Advertising Act does not restrict a State or locality's ability to enact generally applicable zoning restrictions that also regulate tobacco advertisements. The Court stated, "We have recognized that state interests in traffic safety and esthetics may justify zoning regulations for advertising. See Metromedia, Inc. v. San Diego, 453 U.S. 490, 507–508, 101 S.Ct. 2882, 69 L.Ed.2d 800 (1981). See also St. Louis Poster Advertising Co. v. St. Louis, 249 U.S. 269, 274, 39 S.Ct. 274, 63 L.Ed. 599 (1919); Thomas Cusack Co. v. Chicago, 242 U.S. 526, 529–531, 37 S.Ct. 190, 61 L.Ed. 472 (1917). Although Congress has taken into account the unique concerns about cigarette smoking and health in advertising, there is no indication that Congress intended to displace local community interests in general regulations of the location of billboards or large marquee advertising..." See also Center for Bio-Ethical Reform v. Honolulu, 345 F.Supp.2d 1123 (D.Haw.2004) (holding that Federal Aviation Administration regulations did not preempt Honolulu's ban on towing aerial signs over beaches).

B. AESTHETIC REGULATION OF SIGNS AND BILLBOARDS

Where sign regulations do not run afoul of the First Amendment, they are almost always justified, at least in part, on the governmental interest in preserving aesthetics. Yet, as Justice Brennan's dissent in Taxpayers for Vincent demonstrates, basing regulations on such subjective criteria may serve as a pretext. Indeed, the degree to which aesthetics should guide sign regulation has been dealt with extensively by the courts, especially in cases involving billboards and other forms of outdoor advertising. Opponents claim that billboards mar scenic landscapes, degrade community character and cause blight. Moreover, the campaign against billboards is supported by public opinion, as many people perceive billboards as providing little useful information. The following materials illustrate how these interests have shaped sign and billboard regulation.

STATE v. DIAMOND MOTORS, INC.

Supreme Court of Hawaii, 1967.
50 Hawaii 33, 429 P.2d 825.

LEVINSON, JUSTICE.

In 1957 the City and County of Honolulu enacted Ordinance No. 1557 which was codified, after the adoption in 1959 of the Charter of the City and County of Honolulu, as Article 26 (Signs Regulations) of Chapter 13 (Regulations Promoting General Welfare) of the Revised Ordinances of Honolulu 1961. The ordinance is comprehensive in nature and provides for the regulation and control of outdoor signs, the location, erection, maintenance and use of signs, and penalties for the violation thereof. It prohibits, among other things, the erection and the maintenance in industrial districts of ground signs exceeding 75 square feet in area or exceeding 16 feet in height from the ground.[1]

1. Findings and declarations contained in the ordinance include the following:

"(a) That the people of the City have a primary interest in controlling the erection, location and maintenance of outdoor signs in a manner designed to protect the public health, safety and morals and to promote the public welfare; and

"(b) That the rapid economic development of the City has resulted in a great increase in the number of businesses with a marked increase in the number and size of signs advertising such business activities; and

* * *

"(g) That the natural beauty of landscape, view and attractive surroundings of the Hawaiian Islands, including the City, constitutes an attraction for tourists and visitors; and

"(h) That a major source of income and revenue of the people of the City is derived from the tourist trade; and

"(i) That the indiscriminate erection and maintenance of large signs seriously detract from the enjoyment and pleasure of the natural scenic beauty of the City which in turn injuriously affect the tourist trade and thereby the economic wellbeing of the City; and

"(j) That it is necessary for the promotion and preservation of the public health, safety and welfare of the people of the City that the erection, construction, location, maintenance of signs be regulated and controlled. (Sec. 13–26.1 R.O. 1957)."

Permissible ground signs on any lot or parcel of land in industrial districts are limited by the ordinance to "One ground sign, lighted or unlighted, not exceeding 75 square feet in area, relating to businesses

Appellant Alexander is the owner of a ground sign 40 feet high and more than 75 square feet in area, which he installed in 1965 upon the premises of appellant Diamond Motors, Inc., located in an industrial district on the main highway between Honolulu International Airport and downtown Honolulu and the Waikiki beach area. As provided in the ordinance, the City's Building Superintendent gave written notice to appellants to correct the violation by appropriately reducing the area and height of the sign within 20 days. Appellants failed to make the corrections.

Each of the appellants was, thereafter, charged by an information filed August 25, 1965 with a violation of the ordinance and, upon a consolidated trial by jury, was found guilty as charged. * * *

Appellants assert: (1) that the ordinance, including its application to appellants, is based exclusively upon aesthetic considerations; (2) that legislation based exclusively upon aesthetic considerations is outside the scope of police powers and therefore invalid; and (3) that application of the ordinance to appellants constitutes a taking of private property without the payment of compensation in violation of the Fifth Amendment to the Constitution of the United States and Article I, Section 18 of the Constitution of the State of Hawaii.

Appellee disputes the first assertion and argues that the ordinance was enacted for a number of purposes, among which was the preservation of aesthetics as a means to the end of protecting and promoting the general welfare of the people of the City and County of Honolulu, particularly by protecting and promoting the tourist trade and thereby the economic well-being of the City and County of Honolulu.

Appellee's answering brief admittedly "does not extend to supporting the proposition that aesthetics alone is a proper objective for the exercise of the City's police power." Perhaps, the "weight of authority" in other jurisdictions persuaded the City to present the more traditional arguments because it felt that it was safer to do so. However, the brief of The Outdoor Circle as amicus curiae presents, as we think, a more modern and forthright position.

We accept beauty as a proper community objective, attainable through the use of the police power. We are mindful of the reasoning of most courts that have upheld the validity of ordinances regulating outdoor advertising and of the need felt by them to find some basis in economics, health, safety, or even morality. See Thomas Cusack Co. v. City of Chicago, 242 U.S. 526, 37 S.Ct. 190, 61 L.Ed. 472 (1917). We do not feel so constrained.

Hawaii's constitution provides:

> The State shall have power to conserve and develop its natural beauty, objects and places of historic or cultural interest, sightliness and physical good order, and for that purpose private property shall be subject to reasonable regulation. (Article VIII, Section 5.)

conducted on the premises, and not exceeding 16 feet in height from the ground."

Appellants argue that this constitutional provision has no application to this case because the offending sign is located in an industrial area. We do not agree. The natural beauty of the Hawaiian Islands is not confined to mountain areas and beaches. The term "sightliness and physical good order" does not refer only to junk yards, slaughter houses, sanitation, cleanliness, or incongruous business activities in residential areas as appellants argue.

* * *

Cromwell v. Ferrier, 19 N.Y.2d 263, 225 N.E.2d 749 (New York 1967) upheld the constitutionality of a town zoning ordinance which was a comprehensive and detailed plan for regulation of signs in the township. The court said:

> "* * * Advertising signs and billboards, if misplaced, often are egregious examples of ugliness, distraction, and deterioration. They are just as much subject to reasonable controls, including prohibition, as enterprises which emit offensive noises, odors, or debris. The eye is entitled to as much recognition as the other senses, but, of course, the offense to the eye must be substantial and be deemed to have material effect on the community or district pattern. * * *" (p. 755.)

Oregon City v. Hartke, 240 Or. 35, 400 P.2d 255, decided in 1965, in holding that an ordinance wholly excluding automobile wrecking yards from Oregon City was a valid exercise of the police power, said:

> "* * * there is a growing judicial recognition of the power of a city to impose zoning restrictions which can be justified solely upon the ground that they will tend to prevent or minimize discordant and unsightly surroundings. This change in attitude is a reflection of the refinement of our tastes and the growing appreciation of cultural values in a maturing society. The change may be ascribed more directly to the judicial expansion of the police power to include within the concept of 'general welfare' the enhancement of the citizen's cultural life." (pp. 46–47, 400 P.2d p. 261.)
>
> "We join in the view 'that aesthetic considerations alone may warrant an exercise of the police power.' " (p. 49, 400 P.2d p. 262.)

* * *

We hold that the application of the ordinance to appellants constituted a regulation for the public welfare under the City's police power in a legitimate field for legitimate aesthetic reasons and that it does not constitute a taking of private property without the payment of compensation. Cromwell v. Ferrier, supra, 19 N.Y.2d 263, 225 N.E.2d 749 (New York 1967).

The remaining question raised by appellants is whether the application of the ordinance to appellants is an arbitrary, discriminatory and unreasonable deprivation and denial of due process and equal protection in violation of the Fifth and Fourteenth Amendments to the Constitution of the United States and Article I, Section 4 of the Constitution of the State of Hawaii.

Appellants argue that "the arbitrary limitation of height and size of signs cannot be considered reasonably necessary and appropriate for the accomplishment of the aesthetic objective set forth in the * * * Ordinance, which seeks to eliminate the 'indiscriminate erection and maintenance of large signs which seriously detract from the enjoyment and pleasure of the natural scenic beauty' of the community."

The City has said through its legislative body that the limitations placed by the ordinance on height and size of signs are necessary. Classifications are obviously required. The burden is upon the appellants to show that the limitations and classifications are unreasonable. State v. Safeway Stores, Inc., 106 Mont. 182, 76 P.2d 81. The record does not so show. Appellants say that whether a classification violates the equal protection clause of the Fourteenth Amendment to the Constitution of the United States is a judicial question. It was incumbent on them in invoking the protection of the Fourteenth Amendment "to show with convincing clarity" that the ordinance created against them the discrimination of which they complain. Corporation Comm'n of Oklahoma v. Lowe, 281 U.S. 431, 50 S.Ct. 397, 74 L.Ed. 945. They have not done so.

* * *

The judgments are affirmed.

MAYOR AND CITY COUNCIL OF BALTIMORE v. MANO SWARTZ, INC.

Court of Appeals of Maryland, 1973.
268 Md. 79, 299 A.2d 828.

SINGLEY, JUDGE.

For the second time we have before us an attack on the validity of Ordinance No. 663 of the Mayor and City Council of Baltimore (the City), approved 1 November 1965, now Baltimore City Code Art. 1, § 39 (1966) (the Ordinance), which was designed to regulate signs in the central business district of Baltimore.

There was testimony that the City had been so successful in limiting the size and design of signs in agreements for the sale of sites in the Charles Center renewal area that a decision was made to endeavor to achieve uniformity in the whole of the downtown district.

In City of Baltimore v. Charles Center Parking, 259 Md. 595, 271 A.2d 144 (1970), we affirmed a decree of the Circuit Court of Baltimore City which had found arbitrary and discriminatory and violative of Article 23 of Maryland's Declaration of Rights and of the Fourteenth Amendment to the Constitution of the United States § 1(e)(4) of the Ordinance, which had made unlawful the painting of a sign on an exterior wall of a building. We concluded that this result was mandated by the fact that § 1(j) of the Ordinance permitted billboards and poster boards, subject to zoning regulations, in the same area where painted signs were prohibited, particularly since the City offered no testimony which would support a rational distinction between painted signs and billboards.

In that case, we addressed ourselves to a narrow issue—the validity of § 1(e)(4)—and expressed no opinion as regards the validity of the Ordinance as a whole. The assault mounted in this case is of wider scope.

On 30 October 1970, just before the expiration of the five-year moratorium contained in § 1(g) of the Ordinance, Mano Swartz, Inc., and nine other firms doing business in the central business district (Swartz) filed a bill of complaint in the Circuit Court of Baltimore City against the City and the City's Director of Construction and Building Inspection seeking to enjoin the enforcement of § 1(e)(1) which proscribes signs projecting more than 12 inches "from the primary surface of the building to which it is attached * * *" and § 1(e)(4) which prohibits roof top signs.

Filed with the bill of complaint was the text of the Ordinance: * * *

(a) A Commission on Signs is created. It shall have three members appointed as of January 1, 1966, under the provisions of Article IV, Section 6, of the City Charter. One of the three members shall represent the retail merchants in the area defined in this section. Another member shall represent the sign industry. The third member of the Commission shall be a representative of the public at large. * * *

(b) The Commission may retain technical advisors, amongst which shall be included an architect, a graphic artist and a sign designer.

* * *

(d) The Commission, after public notice and hearing may adopt and promulgate rules and regulations establishing standards and requirements for commercial signs, billboards, and other advertising structures and devices within the area described in this section. Any such rules and regulations shall be designed and intended to provide for beauty, attractiveness, esthetics, and symmetry in the commercial signs, billboards, and other advertising structures and devices, and to relieve conditions of gaudiness and drabness in certain portions of the defined area.

* * *

The Ordinance had as its sole purpose the achievement of an aesthetically pleasing result, and we have held this not to be a permissible use of the police power, Feldstein v. Kammauf, 209 Md. 479, 484–489, 121 A.2d 716 (1956); Goldman v. Crowther, 147 Md. 282, 302–309, 128 A. 50 (1925); Byrne v. Maryland Realty Co., 129 Md. 202, 211, 98 A. 547 (1916); see, 1 Anderson, American Law of Zoning § 7.21 at 520–21 (1968); 2 Metzenbaum, The Law of Zoning 1577–1578 (2d ed. 1955); 1 Rathkopf, The Law of Zoning and Planning 11–1 (3d ed. 1972); 16 Am.Jr.2d Constitutional Law § 292 at 569 (1964).

While aesthetic goals may legitimately serve as an additional legislative purpose, if health, morals or safety or other ends generally associated with the concept of public welfare are being served, * * * they cannot be the only purpose of regulation, Byrne v. Maryland Realty Co., supra, 129 Md. at 211, 98 A. 547.

The City might well have prevailed had the legislative intent been the elimination of signs or pennants which distracted motorists, Kenyon Peck, Inc. v. Kennedy, 210 Va. 60, 168 S.E.2d 117 (1969) or the promotion of highway safety, Stevens v. City of Salisbury, 240 Md. 556, 567–568, 214 A.2d 775 (1965); see E.B. Elliott Adv. Co. v. Metropolitan Dade County, 425 F.2d 1141 (5th Cir.1970), petition for cert. dismissed, 400 U.S. 805, 91 S.Ct. 12, 27 L.Ed.2d 35; Village of Larchmont v. Sutton, 30 Misc.2d 245, 217 N.Y.S.2d 929 (1961); *approved and followed in,* Village of Larchmont v. Levine, Sup., 225 N.Y.S.2d 452 (1961). The fact that another result might have been one which was aesthetically pleasing would not necessarily have imported an element of constitutional infirmity.

The effort to eliminate what was referred to in argument before us as "visual pollution" by controlling signs and billboards through the exercise of the zoning power has been slowly developing, General Outdoor Adv. Co. v. Indianapolis, 202 Ind. 85, 172 N.E. 309, 72 A.L.R. 453 (1930); Opinion of the Justices to the Senate, 333 Mass. 773, 128 N.E.2d 557, 561 (1955); People v. Sterling, 128 Misc. 650, 220 N.Y.S. 315 (1927); State ex rel. Saveland Park Holding Corp. v. Wieland, 269 Wis. 262, 69 N.W.2d 217, 222 (1955); 58 Am.Jur. Zoning § 30 at 959 (1948); 1 Anderson, American Law of Zoning, supra, § 7.21 at 520–23; 1 Rathkopf, Law of Zoning and Planning, supra, at 11–9, 11–22; 1 Yokely, Zoning Law and Practice § 2–4 at 28 (3d ed. 1965); Dukeminier, Zoning for Aesthetic Objectives: A Reappraisal, 20 Law & Contemp.Prob. 218 (1955); Masotti & Selfon, Aesthetic Zoning and the Police Power, supra, 46 J.Urban L. 773, 779–86; Note, 47 Cornell L.Rev. 647, 651–652 (1962); Annot., Aesthetic Objectives or Considerations as Affecting Validity of Zoning Ordinance, 21 A.L.R.3d 1222, 1225 (1968). The principal difficulty is that other forms of pollution, stench and noise and the like, can be measured by more nearly objective standards. If beauty, however, lies in the eyes of the beholder, so does the tawdry, the gaudy and the vulgar—and courts have traditionally taken a gingerly approach to legislation which circumscribes property rights by applying what amounts to subjective standards, which may well be those of an idiosyncratic group. See discussion in, General Outdoor Advertising Co. v. Department of Public Works, supra, 193 N.E. at 815–816; Cromwell v. Ferrier, 19 N.Y.2d 263, 279 N.Y.S.2d 22, 225 N.E.2d 749, 755, 21 A.L.R.3d 1212 (1967); Dukeminier, Zoning for Aesthetic Objectives: A Reappraisal, 20 Law & Contemp.Prob., supra, at 224–229 (1955); Michelman, Toward a Practical Standard for Aesthetic Regulation, 15 Prac.Law. 36 (1969); Norton, Police Power, Planning and Aesthetics, 7 Santa Clara Law. 171, 183–185 (1967); Note, Aesthetic Considerations in Land Use Planning, 35 Albany

L.Rev. 126, 131 (1970); Note, Zoning for Aesthetics—A Problem of Definition, 32 U.Cin.L.Rev. 367, 373 (1963).

We think Justice Cardozo had it about right when, speaking for the New York Court of Appeals in People v. Rubenfeld, 254 N.Y. 245, 172 N.E. 485, 486–487 (1930), he observed, by way of dicta:

> "The organs of smell and hearing, assailed by sounds and odors too pungent to be borne, have been ever favored of the law * * * more conspicuously, it seems, than sight, which perhaps is more inured to what is ugly or disfigured * * *. Even so, the test for all the senses, for sight as well as smell and hearing, has been the effect of the offensive practice upon the reasonable man or woman of average sensibilities * * *. One of the unsettled questions of the law is the extent to which the concept of nuisance may be enlarged by legislation so as to give protection to sensibilities that are merely cultural or aesthetic." [citations omitted]

Our predecessors recognized that this problem had long existed when in Byrne v. Maryland Realty Co., supra, 129 Md. at 211, 98 A. 547, they cited with approval the language of the Mississippi court which rejected an attempt through the exercise of the police power to exclude a market from a residential area in Quintini v. City of Bay St. Louis, 64 Miss. 483, 1 So. 625, 628 (1887):

> "The law can know no distinction between citizens because of the superior cultivation of the one over the other. It is with common humanity that courts and legislatures must deal; and that use of property which in all common sense and reason is not a nuisance to the average man cannot be prohibited because repugnant to some sentiment of a particular class."

Until now, only a minority of jurisdictions can be said to have validated regulatory schemes which were primarily or solely concerned with aesthetic considerations, Stone v. City of Maitland, 446 F.2d 83, 89 (5th Cir.1971); City of St. Paul v. Chicago, St. Paul, Minneapolis & Omaha Ry. Co., 413 F.2d 762, 767–768 (8th Cir.1969); Sunad, Inc. v. Sarasota, 122 So.2d 611, 614 (Fla.1960); State ex rel. Civello v. New Orleans, 154 La. 271, 97 So. 440, 444–445, 33 A.L.R. 260 (1923); Naegele Outdoor Adv. Co. v. Village of Minnetonka, 281 Minn. 492, 162 N.W.2d 206, 212 (1968); Cromwell v. Ferrier, supra, 225 N.E.2d at 753–755; People v. Stover, 12 N.Y.2d 462, 240 N.Y.S.2d 734, 191 N.E.2d 272, 274–276 (1963), appeal dismissed, 375 U.S. 42, 84 S.Ct. 147, 11 L.Ed.2d 107; United Advertising Corp. v. Metuchen, 42 N.J. 1, 198 A.2d 447, 449 (1964); Oregon City v. Hartke, 240 Or. 35, 400 P.2d 255, 262–263 (1965); State ex rel. Carter v. Harper, 182 Wis. 148, 196 N.W. 451, 454–456, 33 A.L.R. 269 (1923); 1 Anderson, American Law of Zoning, supra §§ 7.15, 7.22 at 508, 526 and cases cited therein; Annot., Aesthetic Objectives or Considerations as Affecting Validity of Zoning Ordinance, supra, 21 A.L.R.3d, § 4(a) at 1235 and cases cited therein.

* * *

We do not wish to be understood as saying that aesthetic considerations cannot play a proper role in the zoning process, because they do. It has long been recognized that the police power may rightly be exercised to preserve an area which is generally regarded by the public to be pleasing to the eye or historically or architecturally significant. * * *

In Footnote 88 to his article, Maryland Zoning—The Court and Its Critics, 27 Md.L.Rev. 39, 53 (1967), George W. Liebmann concludes, and we think quite rightly, that our case law and statutes have followed the approach urged by Ernst Freund, Standards of American Legislation 115–16 (1917):

> "[I]t is undesirable to force by law upon the community standards of taste which a representative legislative body may happen to approve of, and compulsion with that end in view would be justly resented as inconsistent with a traditional spirit of individualism. But it is a different question whether the state may not protect the works of nature or the achievements of art or the associations of history from being wilfully marred. In other words, emphasis should be laid upon the character of the place as having an established claim to consideration and upon the idea of disfigurement as distinguished from the falling short of some standard of beauty."

Because the purpose of the Ordinance was not the preservation or protection of something which was aesthetically pleasing, but rather was intended to achieve by regulation an aesthetically pleasing result, with no thought of enhancing the public welfare, we shall not disturb the result reached below.

Decree affirmed, costs to be paid by appellants.

Notes

1. A staggering amount of case law exists in the area of sign regulations. In the early years courts were sometimes quite inventive in conjuring up non-aesthetic reasons to justify regulation of billboards and other signs. See, e.g., St. Louis Gunning Advertisement Co. v. St. Louis, 235 Mo. 99, 137 S.W. 929 (1911), where the court said:

> In cases of fire they [signs] often cause their spread and constitute barriers against their extinction; and in cases of high wind, their temporary character, frail structure and broad surface render them liable to be blown down and to fall upon and injure those who may happen to be in their vicinity. The evidence shows and common observation teaches us that the ground in the rear thereof is being constantly used as privies and dumping ground for all kinds of waste * * * that behind [them] the lowest form of prostitution and other acts of immorality are frequently carried on, almost under public gaze; they offer shelter and concealment for the criminal while lying in wait for his victim * * *.

Courts have continued to recognize that aesthetic regulation is often interrelated with other non-aesthetic goals. As the First Circuit has explained, "[h]and in hand with aesthetics is tourism, one of Maine's important industries and a substantial economic resource.... It cannot be doubted that the legislature has the right to protect this industry, nor can we question...the direct connection between signs, scenery, and tourism." John Donnelly & Sons v. Campbell, 639 F.2d 6, 12 (1st Cir.1980). See also Center for Bio-Ethical Reform v. Honolulu, 345 F.Supp.2d 1123, 1134 (D.Haw.2004) (noting the importance of preserving aesthetics to the state's tourism industry). Such economic goals are commonly relied upon to support sign regulations, especially in those jurisdictions that have not recognized aesthetics as a sufficient independent basis for police power exercises. Just several years after the Mano Swartz case was decided, for example, the Maryland court distinguished Mano Swartz and upheld sign regulations in the Old Baltimore urban renewal district. In Donnelly Advertising Corp. v. City of Baltimore, 279 Md. 660, 370 A.2d 1127 (1977), the court explained that the billboard prohibition "was enacted for the purpose of removing slums and blight from the city.... These are not solely aesthetic grounds." Id. at 670. The court added that the regulation was also intended to preserve the character of the historically and architecturally significant area, a ground which was recognized as a sufficient basis for police power regulation in Mano Swartz. Also see Metromedia, Inc. v. Mayor and City Council of Baltimore, 538 F.Supp. 1183 (D.Md.1982) (holding the city's sign regulations to be constitutionally justified by the city's interests in traffic safety and aesthetics).

2. Outdoor advertisers have sometimes turned to the First Amendment overbreadth doctrine in order to challenge sign regulations on their face. By using this strategy, it is possible for a plaintiff to have an entire regulatory scheme invalidated due to the chilling effect it may have on others' speech, regardless of whether the plaintiff's own rights have been violated by the offensive aspects of the law. If a plaintiff is successful in having the regulations overturned, then outdoor advertisers will be free to construct billboards as they wish until a new regulation can be enacted. However, most courts have reacted to these suits by interposing standing requirements that billboard owners often cannot meet. In Prime Media, Inc. v. City of Brentwood, 485 F.3d 343 (6th Cir.2007), for example, the Sixth Circuit explained that "Prime Media's standing with regard to the size and height requirements does not magically carry over to allow it to litigate other independent provisions of the ordinance without a separate showing of an actual injury under those provisions." A similar result was reached in Tanner Advertising Group v. Fayette County, 451 F.3d 777 (11th Cir. 2006). In Advantage Media, L.L.C. v. City of Eden Prairie, 456 F.3d 793 (8th Cir. 2006), the plaintiff alleged that the sign code contained a number of constitutional infirmities, although most of those provisions were unrelated to the reasons for which its permit applications had been denied. In attempting to establish standing, Advantage relied on Metromedia to argue that the provisions of the sign code were not severable, and thus that its injury had been caused by the enforcement of the code in its entirety. The court dismissed this argument though, explaining that the regulation involved in Metromedia was made up of closely interrelated provisions whereas the sign code in issue was "a more comprehensive regulatory framework enacted piecemeal over a number of years, one in which universally applicable restrictions related to size and location can easily be severed from those which may necessitate more scrutiny."

3. Additional billboard cases worth consulting include National Advertising Co. v. City of Rolling Meadows, 789 F.2d 571 (7th Cir.1986); Naegele Outdoor Advertising, Inc. v. City of Durham, 844 F.2d 172 (4th Cir.1988); Rzadkowolski v. Village of Lake Orion, 845 F.2d 653 (6th Cir.1988); National Advertising Co. v. City of Orange, 861 F.2d 246 (9th Cir.1988); Ackerley Communications of Mass., Inc. v. City of Somerville, 878 F.2d 513 (1st Cir.1989); Major Media of Southeast, Inc. v. City of Raleigh, 621 F.Supp. 1446 (E.D.N.C.1985) cert. denied 479 U.S. 1102, 107 S.Ct. 1334, 94 L.Ed.2d 185 (1987); Jackson v. City Council of Charlottesville, Virginia, 659 F.Supp. 470 (W.D.Va.1987) affirmed in part 840 F.2d 10 (4th Cir.1988); National Advertising Co. v. Town of Babylon, 703 F.Supp. 228 (E.D.N.Y.1989) affirmed in part 900 F.2d 551 (2d Cir.1990).

A Note on the Federal Highway Beautification Act

On October 22, 1965, the Federal Highway Beautification Act (HBA) took effect, with President Lyndon B. Johnson stating that its goal was to "make sure that the America we see from these major highways is a beautiful America." The main provision of the HBA reduces federal transportation funding to states that do not adequately restrict the construction of billboards located within 660 feet of interstates and provide for the removal of nonconforming signs, although the Act gives authority to the states to control billboard growth along federal roads located in commercial, industrial and unzoned areas. See the Highway Beautification Act, 23 U.S.C. § 131. However, the HBA also contains a provision requiring just compensation to be paid to owners of billboards removed under the Act. Id. at § (g). While the HBA directs the federal government to provide 75% of the funds needed to pay such just compensation, another section of the HBA directs that "[n]o sign, display, or device shall be required to be removed under this section if the Federal share of just compensation to be paid upon removal of such sign, display, or device is not available to make such payment." Id. at § (n). For more detailed information about the 1965 law, see Roger A. Cunningham, *Billboard Control Under the Highway Beautification Act of 1965*, 71 Mich.L.R. 1296 (1973).

The 1978 amendments to the HBA are very specific in requiring compensation for removal of certain signs. To put the problem in perspective, as of Sept. 30, 1977, 463,724 billboards had been removed from along federal highways under the act, leaving 265,952. Compensation for the average billboard in 1978 was $1,500. The Federal Highway Administration estimated that about $40 million a year for ten years would be necessary to complete removal of all billboards along federal highways. Yet in 1978 Congress appropriated only $18 million for sign removal. See Charlton, The Billboard Act is Taking Effect, Ever So Slowly, N.Y. Times, Mar. 26, 1978, p. 18E. By 1984, federal funding for billboard removal had dropped to $2 million. Combined with the 75% federal funding requirement contained in the HBA, the failure to provide funding for billboard removal has taken the teeth out of the HBA; states may use their own funds to pay just compensation, but they do not lose any federal highway funds if they choose to allow nonconforming boards to remain in place. According to a 1997 study lead by Scenic America, there are now an estimated 73,000 billboards that do not conform with Highway Beautification Act standards and fewer than one percent of the remaining nonconforming billboards are removed annually. With an average growth of 5,000 to 15,000 billboards annually, further progress in billboard removal under the HBA is unlikely. See, http://www.scenic.org/billboards/hba/facts. Problems with the HBA are compounded by the fact that states have not consistently removed nonconforming billboards constructed after its enactment, even though the Act does not require just compensation to be paid for the removal of these signs. See Jacob Loshin, *Property on the Horizon: The Theory and Practice of Sign and Billboard Regulation*, 30 Environs Envtl. L. & Policy J. 101, 131–33 (2006).

Despite the shortfalls of the HBA, it allows states to adopt stricter billboard restrictions and Vermont, Maine, Hawaii and Alaska have taken the initiative to enact statewide billboard bans. Moreover, the HBA's just compensation requirement is not automatically applicable in cases where non-conforming signs within the scope of the HBA are removed pursuant to state or local laws. See Donnelly Advertising Corp. v. City of Baltimore, 279 Md. 660, 370 A.2d 1127 (1977), where the court applied state law and determined that no compensation was required for the billboards' removal because the owners had not been deprived of all beneficial uses of the property.

C. THE APPEARANCE OF STRUCTURES AND OTHER AESTHETIC REGULATIONS

STATE EX REL. STOYANOFF v. BERKELEY

Supreme Court of Missouri, Division No. 2, 1970.
458 S.W.2d 305.

PRITCHARD, COMMISSIONER.

Upon summary judgment the trial court issued a peremptory writ of mandamus to compel appellant to issue a residential building permit to respondents. The trial court's judgment is that the below-mentioned ordinances are violative of Section 10, Article I of the Constitution of Missouri, 1945, V.A.M.S., in that restrictions placed by the ordinances on the use of property deprive the owners of their property without due process of law. Relators' petition pleads that they applied to appellant Building Commissioner for a building permit to allow them to construct a single family residence in the City of Ladue, and that plans and specifications were submitted for the proposed residence, which was unusual in design, "but complied with all existing building and zoning regulations and ordinances of the City of Ladue, Missouri."

It is further pleaded that relators were refused a building permit for the construction of their proposed residence upon the ground that the permit was not approved by the Architectural Board of the City of Ladue. Ordinance 131, as amended by Ordinance 281 of that city, purports to set up an Architectural Board to approve plans and specifications for buildings and structures erected within the city and in a preamble to "conform to certain minimum architectural standards of appearance and conformity with surrounding structures, and that unsightly, grotesque and unsuitable structures, detrimental to the stability of value and the welfare of surrounding property, structures and residents, and to the general welfare and happiness of the community, be avoided, and that appropriate standards of beauty and conformity be fostered and encouraged." It is asserted in the petition that the ordinances are invalid, illegal and void, "are unconstitutional in that they are vague and provide no standard nor uniform rule by which to guide the architectural board," that the city acted in excess of statutory powers (§ 89.020, RSMo 1959, V.A.M.S.) in enacting the ordinances, which "attempt to allow respondent to impose aesthetic standards for buildings in the City of Ladue, and are in excess of the powers granted the City of Ladue by said statute."

Relators filed a motion for summary judgment and affidavits were filed in opposition thereto. Richard D. Shelton, Mayor of the City of Ladue, deponed that the facts in appellant's answer were true and correct, as here pertinent: that the City of Ladue constitutes one of the finer suburban residential areas of Metropolitan St. Louis, the homes therein are considerably more expensive than in cities of comparable size, being homes on lots from three fourths of an acre to three or more acres each; * * * It is then pleaded that relators' description of their proposed residence as " 'unusual in design' is the understatement of the year. It is in fact a monstrosity of grotesque design, which would seriously impair the value of property in the neighborhood."

The affidavit of Harold C. Simon, a developer of residential subdivisions in St. Louis County, is that he is familiar with relators' lot upon which they seek to build a house, and with the surrounding houses in the neighborhood; that the houses therein existent are virtually all two-story houses of conventional architectural design, such as Colonial, French Provincial or English; and that the house which relators propose to construct is of ultramodern design which would clash with and not be in conformity with any other house in the entire neighborhood. It is Mr. Simon's opinion that the design and appearance of relators' proposed residence would have a substantial adverse effect upon the market values of other residential property in the neighborhood, such average market value ranging from $60,000 to $85,000 each.

As a part of the affidavit of Russell H. Riley, consultant for the city planning and engineering firm of Harland Bartholomew & Associates, photographic exhibits of homes surrounding relators' lot were attached. * * * In substance Mr. Riley went on to say that the City of Ladue is one of the finer residential suburbs in the St. Louis area with a minimum of commercial or industrial usage. The development of residences in the city has been primarily by private subdivisions, usually with one main lane or drive leading therein (such as Lorenzo Road Subdivision which runs north off of Ladue Road in which relators' lot is located). The homes are considerably more expensive than average homes found in a city of comparable size. The ordinance which has been adopted by the City of Ladue is typical of those which have been adopted by a number of suburban cities in St. Louis County and in similar cities throughout the United States, the need therefor being based upon the protection of existing property values by preventing the construction of houses that are in complete conflict with the general type of houses in a given area. The intrusion into this neighborhood of relators' unusual, grotesque and nonconforming structure would have a substantial adverse effect on market values of other homes in the immediate area. According to Mr. Riley the standards of Ordinance 131, as amended by Ordinance 281, are usually and customarily applied in city planning work and are: "(1) whether the proposed house meets the customary architectural requirements in appearance and design for a house of the particular type which is proposed (whether it be Colonial, Tudor English, French Provincial, or Modern), (2) whether the proposed house is in general conformity with the style and design of surrounding structures, and (3) whether the proposed house lends itself to the proper architectural development of the City; and that in applying said standards the Architectural Board and its Chairman are to determine whether the proposed house will have an adverse affect on the stability of values in the surrounding area."

Photographic exhibits of relators' proposed residence were also attached to Mr. Riley's affidavit. They show the residence to be of a pyramid shape, with a flat top, and with triangular shaped windows or doors at one or more corners.

* * *

Section 89.020 provides: "For the purpose of promoting health, safety, morals or the general welfare of the community, the legislative body of all cities, towns, and villages is hereby empowered to regulate and restrict the height, number of stories, and size of buildings and other structures, the percentage of lot that may be occupied, the size of yards, courts, and other open spaces, the density of population, the preservation of features of historical significance, and the location and use of buildings, structures and land for trade, industry, residence or other purposes." Section 89.040 provides: "Such regulations shall be made in accordance with a comprehensive plan and designed to lessen congestion in the streets; to secure safety from fire, panic and other dangers; to promote health *and the general welfare;* to provide adequate light and air; to prevent the overcrowding of land; to avoid undue concentration of population; to preserve features of historical significance; to facilitate the adequate provision of transportation, water, sewerage, schools, parks, and other public requirements. *Such regulations shall be made with reasonable consideration, among other things, to the character of the district and its peculiar suitability for particular uses, and with a view to conserving the values of buildings and encouraging the most appropriate use of land throughout such municipality.*" (Italics added.)

Relators say that "Neither Sections 89.020 or 89.040 nor any other provision of Chapter 89 mentions or gives a city the authority to regulate architectural design and appearance. There exists no provision providing for an architectural board and no entity even remotely resembling such a board is mentioned under the enabling legislation." Relators conclude that the City of Ladue lacked any power to adopt Ordinance 131 as amended by Ordinance 281 "and its intrusion into this area is wholly unwarranted and without sanction in the law." As to this aspect of the appeal relators rely upon the 1961 decision of State ex rel. Magidson v. Henze, Mo.App., 342 S.W.2d 261. That case had the identical question presented. An Architectural Control Commission was set up by an ordinance of the City of University City. In its report to the Building Commissioner, the Architectural Control Commission disapproved the Magidson application for permits to build four houses. It was commented that the proposed houses did not provide for the minimum number of square feet, and "In considering the existing character of this neighborhood, the Commission is of the opinion that houses of the character proposed in these plans are not in harmony with and will not contribute to nor protect the general welfare of this neighborhood" (loc. cit. 264). The court held that § 89.020, RSMo1949, V.A.M.S., does not grant to the city the right to impose upon the landowner aesthetic standards for the buildings he chooses to erect.

As is clear from the affidavits and attached exhibits, the City of Ladue is an area composed principally of residences of the general types of Colonial, French Provincial and English Tudor. The city has a comprehensive plan of zoning to maintain the general character of buildings therein. The Magidson case, supra, did not consider the effect of § 89.040, supra, and the italicized portion relating to the character of the district, its suitability for particular uses, and the conservation of the values of buildings therein. These considerations, sanctioned by statute, are directly related to the general welfare of the community. That proposition has support in a number of cases cited by appellant. State ex rel. Carter v. Harper, Building Commissioner, 182 Wis. 148, 196 N.W. 451, 454, quotes Chicago B. & Q. Ry. Co. v. People of State of Illinois ex rel. Drainage Commissioners, 200 U.S. 561, 26 S.Ct. 341, 50 L.Ed. 596, 609, " 'We hold that the police power of a state embraces regulations designed to promote the public convenience or the general prosperity, as well as regulations designed to promote the public health, the public morals or the public safety.' " In Marrs v. City of Oxford (D.C.D.Kan.) 24 F.2d 541, 548, it was said, "The stabilizing of property values, and giving some assurance to the public that, if property is purchased in a residential district, its value as such will be preserved, is probably the most cogent reason back of zoning ordinances." See also People v. Calvar Corporation et al., Sup., 69 N.Y.S.2d 272, 279 (aff'd 286 N.Y. 419, 36 N.E.2d 644); Kovacs v. Cooper, Judge, 336 U.S. 77, 69 S.Ct. 448, 93 L.Ed. 513, 526; Wulfsohn v. Burden, 241 N.Y. 288, 150 N.E. 120, 122[3], 43 A.L.R. 651; and Price et al. v. Schwafel (Cal.), 92 Cal.App.2d 77, 206 P.2d 683, 685. The preamble to Ordinance 131, quoted above in part, demonstrates that its purpose is to conform to the dictates of § 89.040, with reference to preserving values of property by zoning procedure and restrictions on the use of property. This is an illustration of what was referred to in Deimeke v. State Highway Commission, Mo., 444 S.W.2d 480, 484, as a growing number of cases recognizing a change in the scope of the term "general welfare." In the Deimeke case on the same page it is said, "Property use which offends sensibilities and debases property values affects not only the adjoining property owners in that vicinity but the general public as well because when such property values are destroyed or seriously impaired, the tax base of the community is affected and the public suffers economically as a result."

Relators say further that Ordinances 131 and 281 are invalid and unconstitutional as being an unreasonable and arbitrary exercise of the police power. It is argued that a mere reading of these ordinances shows that they are based entirely on aesthetic factors in that the stated purpose of the Architectural Board is to maintain "conformity with surrounding structures" and to assure that structures "conform to certain minimum architectural standards of appearance." The argument ignores the further provisos in the ordinance: " * * * and that unsightly, grotesque and unsuitable structures, *detrimental to the stability of value and the welfare of surrounding property, structures, and residents,* and *to the general welfare and happiness of the community,* be avoided, and that appropriate standards of beauty and conformity be fostered and encouraged." (Italics added.) Relators' proposed residence does not descend to the " 'patently offensive character of vehicle graveyards in close proximity to such highways' " referred to in the Deimeke case, supra (444 S.W.2d 484). Nevertheless, the aesthetic factor to be taken into account by the Architectural Board is not to be considered alone. Along with that inherent factor is the effect that the proposed residence would have upon the property values in the area. In this time of burgeoning urban areas, congested with people and structures, it is certainly in keeping with the ultimate ideal of general welfare that the Architectural Board, in its function, preserve and protect existing areas in which structures of a general conformity of architecture have been erected. The area under consideration is clearly, from the record, a fashionable one. In State ex rel. Civello v. City of New Orleans, 154 La. 271, 97 So. 440, 444, the court said, "If by the term 'aesthetic considerations' is meant a regard merely for outward appearances, for good taste in the matter of the beauty of the neighborhood itself, we do not observe any substantial reason for saying that such a consideration is not a matter of general welfare. The beauty of a fashionable residence neighborhood in a city is for the comfort and happiness of the residents, and it sustains in a general way the value of property in the neighborhood." See also People v. Stover, 12 N.Y.2d 462, 240 N.Y.S.2d 734, 191 N.E.2d 272, 274[3]; State ex rel. Saveland Park Holding Corp. v. Wieland, 269 Wis. 262, 69 N.W.2d 217, 222; Reid v. Architectural Board of Review of the City of Cleveland Heights, 119 Ohio App. 67, 192 N.E.2d 74, 77; and Oregon City v. Hartke, 240 Or. 35, 400 P.2d 255, 261, for pronouncements of the principle that aesthetics is a factor to be considered in zoning matters.

* * * The denial by appellant of a building permit for relators' highly modernistic residence in this area where traditional Colonial, French Provincial and English Tudor styles of architecture are erected does not appear to be arbitrary and unreasonable when the basic

purpose to be served is that of the general welfare of persons in the entire community.

In addition to the above-stated purpose in the preamble to Ordinance 131, it establishes an Architectural Board of three members, all of whom must be architects. Meetings of the Board are to be open to the public, and every application for a building permit, except those not affecting the outward appearance of a building, shall be submitted to the Board along with plans, elevations, detail drawings and specifications, before being approved by the Building Commissioner. The Chairman of the Board shall examine the application to determine if it conforms to proper architectural standards in appearance and design and will be in general conformity with the style and design of surrounding structures and conducive to the proper architectural development of the city. If he so finds, he approves and returns the application to the Building Commissioner. If he does not find conformity, or has doubt, a full meeting of the Board is called, with notice of the time and place thereof given to the applicant. The Board shall disapprove the application if it determines the proposed structure will constitute an unsightly, grotesque or unsuitable structure in appearance, detrimental to the welfare of surrounding property or residents. If it cannot make that decision, the application shall be returned to the Building Commissioner either with or without suggestions or recommendations, and if that is done without disapproval, the Building Commissioner may issue the permit. If the Board's disapproval is given and the applicant refuses to comply with recommendations, the Building Commissioner shall refuse the permit. Thereafter provisions are made for an appeal to the Council of the city for review of the decision of the Architectural Board. Ordinance 281 amends Ordinance 131 only with respect to the application initially being submitted to and considered by all members of the Architectural Board.

Relators claim that the above provisions of the ordinance amount to an unconstitutional delegation of power by the city to the Architectural Board. It is argued that the Board cannot be given the power to determine what is unsightly and grotesque and that the standards, "whether the proposed structure will conform to proper architectural standards in appearance and design, and will be in general conformity with the style and design of surrounding structures and conducive to the proper architectural development of the City * * *" and "the Board shall disapprove the application if it determines that the proposed structure will constitute an unsightly, grotesque or unsuitable structure in appearance, detrimental to the welfare of surrounding property or residents * * *," are inadequate. * * * Ordinances 131 and 281 are sufficient in their general standards calling for a factual determination of the suitability of any proposed structure with reference to the character of the surrounding neighborhood and to the determination of any adverse effect on the general welfare and preservation of property values of the community. Like holdings were made involving Architectural Board ordinances in State ex rel. Saveland Park Holding Corp. v. Wieland, 269 Wis. 262, 69 N.W.2d 217, and Reid v. Architectural Board of Review of the City of Cleveland Heights, 119 Ohio App. 67, 192 N.E.2d 74, supra.

The judgment is reversed.

Notes

1. Like the cases dealing with the aesthetic regulation of signs, Stoyanoff alludes to the judicial hesitancy to recognize aesthetics alone as sufficient to sustain the police power. Should the issue be treated differently depending on whether a land use regulation prohibits certain types of structures, like billboards, or whether it seeks to achieve uniformity in the general appearance of structures? In both types of case, the trend of decisions today is in the frank recognition of the aesthetic justification as sufficient to support police power regulations. Many courts faced with the question have taken notice of Justice Douglas' comment in Berman v. Parker that:

> The concept of public welfare is broad and inclusive.... The values it represents are spiritual as well as physical, aesthetic as well as monetary. It is within the power of the Legislature to determine that the community should be beautiful as well as healthy, spacious as well as clean, well-balanced as well as carefully patrolled.

A recent survey of state court decisions illustrates the growing acceptance of aesthetics as a basis for the regulation of signs and architectural appearances. See Kenneth Pearlman, Elizabeth Linville, Andrea Phillips & Erin Prosser, *Beyond the Eye of the Beholder Once Again: A New Review of Aesthetic Regulation*, 38 Urb. Law 1119 (2006). In 2006, twenty-three states had recognized the authority to enact regulations based on aesthetics alone, as compared to sixteen in 1980. Id. at 1180–82. Moreover, the authors suggest that a significant number of the state courts that remain undecided on the issue are likely to accept aesthetics alone as a basis for such regulations. Id. at 1149–63.

2. Not all of the modern cases support the validity of architectural review. For example, in Anderson v. City of Issaquah, 70 Wash.App. 64, 851 P.2d 744 (1993), the City's "aesthetic zoning" ordinance was ruled unconstitutional for vagueness. The Building Design section of the City ordinance provided in part, "Monotony of design in single or multiple building projects shall be avoided. Efforts should be made to create an interesting project by use of complimentary details, functional orientation of buildings, parting and access provisions and relating the development to the site." The Court found that the commissioners had no objective guidelines to follow and that they "...enforced not a building design code but their own arbitrary concept of the provision of an unwritten 'statement'... This is the very epitome of discretionary, arbitrary enforcement of the law."

Board of Supervisors v. Rowe, 216 Va. 128, 216 S.E.2d 199 (1975) involved a parcel of land located between property owned by the Anheuser–Busch Company and the Colonial Williamsburg Foundation. When the parcel was rezoned as a "Business Tourist Entity District" in which permissible uses were limited to hotels, motels, service stations, gift shops and restaurants, the court invalidated the ordinance on the ground that it could not be supported by aesthetic justifications alone. As it explained, "[s]ome jurisdictions have adopted the rule upholding architectural design regulations when it appears that the purpose of the ordinance was to protect property values within the zone. State v. Berkeley, 458 S.W.2d 305 (Mo.1970); Reid v. Architectural Board of Review, 119 Ohio App. 67, 192 N.E.2d 74, 26 Ohio Op. 2d 178 (1963); Saveland Park Holding Corporation v. Wieland, 269 Wis. 262, 69 N.W.2d 217, *cert. denied,* 350 U.S. 841, 76 S.Ct. 81, 100 L.Ed. 750 (1955). We decline to follow this rule when, as here, it appears that the predominant purpose of the ordinance was to promote aesthetic values and the purpose recited in the ordinance to protect property values was merely an incidental goal."

On the point of whether aesthetic considerations affect the validity of zoning ordinances see the annotation in 21 A.L.R.3d 1222, and on architectural design regulations, see the annotation in 41 A.L.R.3d 1397.

3. Many municipalities have established architectural review boards. What should be the appropriate powers and duties of these boards? How should these boards work with respect to planning boards and zoning boards? In the case of Waterfront Estates Development, Inc. v. City of Palos Hills, 232 Ill.App.3d 367, 173 Ill.Dec. 667, 597 N.E.2d 641 (1992), the court found that the ordinance creating the city's appearance commission was an overbroad delegation of authority, and that the ordinance was unconstitutionally vague. The defendant unsuccessfully argued that the appearance commission only acted in an advisory capacity making recommendations to the city council. See also, Diller and Fisher Co., Inc. v. Architectural Review Board of Borough of Stone Harbour, 246 N.J.Super. 362, 587 A.2d 674 (1990) (holding that the local ordinance empowering the borough's architectural review board to examine, review, approve, or disapprove, because of location, quality, and appropriateness of design, applications for permits for signs in business and light industry districts was an improper arrogation of authority that was vested in borough's zoning board).

4. Should aesthetic regulations be treated differently when they are intended to preserve natural environments, as opposed to when they seek to promote uniformity of architectural design and appearance? Consider the following article, "Billboards, Glass Houses, and the Law," which appeared in the April, 1966, edition of Harper's Magazine, written by Richard F. Babcock, a member of the Illinois Bar:[13]

> Artistic creativeness is a function of the individual, and we social scientists, concerned with the place of grace in urban design, will have either to choose government by a Borgia or, if we insist upon a government of burghers, to declare design off-limits, for the politicians. The rub is that if we opt for the dictator we may get Dr. Goebbels rather than a Renaissance prince. So my choice, even at the cultural level, is to go for democracy but insist that design is not the function of government, except in the following limited area:
>
> First, we should be heartened by the evidence that a representative government is concerned enough to encourage the untried and the different in design and in any of the other arts. This is a different breed of cat from a command by government, municipal or federal, that design

13. Copyright © 1966, by Harper's Magazine, Inc. Reprinted from the April, 1966 issue of Harper's Magazine by permission of the author.

must conform to the established order. Nor do I regard as inconsistent with my thesis governmental efforts to preserve, by eminent domain or by regulation, those features of the man-made landscape that by any definition are landmarks of our heritage. And I do not regard as difficult the distinction that must be made between a thousand homogeneous suburbs and a Beacon Hill; a Galena, Illinois; portions of San Antonio; or the unique nineteenth-century square in Woodstock, Illinois. I am even ready to concede that from this exception it must logically follow that we must be prepared to preserve one or perhaps two postwar suburbs * * * which proves beyond question my devotion to logic if not to beauty!

Second, government cannot abdicate its duty to select which natural amenities shall be shielded from any scheme of man. (The only issue here is whether government must pay or can achieve the result by regulation.) The government, local and national, must play the dominant role in any debate over whether any construction shall be permitted along the Chicago lakefront; whether a hydroelectric project on the Hudson River should be constructed irrespective of the consequences to historic landmarks and natural beauty; whether the Allagash River in Maine or the Dinosaur Area or the Redwoods or the Dunes shall be preserved or sacrificed for the economic best interest of the country; and whether the public view of San Francisco Bay shall be spoiled.

Third, government can and should identify those circumstances where design in the private sector will have a demonstrable impact upon public services. Government must prescribe the perimeters of the choices allowed the designer in such cases. If, for example, one accepts the premise that building bulk and density do have an impact on the efficiency of public services such as streets, sanitation, and schools, then one can more readily accept regulation designed to protect these facilities that may limit freedom of choice by the designer.

Finally, the government should offer incentives to the builder to provide more open space than would otherwise be required. The Chicago zoning ordinance grants a bonus in the form of additional permitted floor area to the builder who will provide greater open space at ground level. Some suburban ordinances will permit a greater number of dwelling units per acre to the developer who clusters his houses, thereby creating more usable common open space. (Both are examples of what baseball vice presidents call the "natural trade." The developer gets increased gross revenues, the city gets additional open space.)

Beyond these limits I fear to go in the regulation of design.

PEOPLE v. STOVER

Court of Appeals of New York, 1963.
12 N.Y.2d 462, 240 N.Y.S.2d 734, 191 N.E.2d 272, appeal dismissed 375 U.S. 42, 84 S.Ct. 147, 11 L.Ed.2d 107 (1963).

FULD, JUDGE.

The defendants, Mr. and Mrs. Stover, residents of the City of Rye since 1940, live in a 2½–story 1–family dwelling, located in a pleasant and built-up residential district, on the corner of Rye Beach and Forest Avenues. A clothesline, filled with old clothes and rags, made its first appearance in the Stovers' front yard in 1956 as a form of "peaceful protest" against the high taxes imposed by the city. And, during each of the five succeeding years, the defendants added another clothesline to mark their continued displeasure with the taxes. In 1961, therefore, six lines, from which there hung tattered clothing, old uniforms, underwear, rags and scarecrows, were strung across the Stovers' yard—three from the porch across the front yard to trees along Forest Avenue and three from the porch across the side yard to trees along Rye Beach Avenue.

In August of 1961, the city enacted an ordinance prohibiting the erection and maintenance of clotheslines or other devices for hanging clothes or other fabrics in a front or side yard abutting a street (General Ordinances, § 4–3.7). However, the ordinance provides for the issuance of a permit for the use of such clotheslines if there is "a practical difficulty or unnecessary hardship in drying clothes elsewhere on the premises" and grants a right of appeal to the applicant if a permit is denied.[14]

Following enactment of the ordinance, Mrs. Stover, the record owner of the property, applied for a permit to maintain clotheslines in her yard. Her application was denied because, she was advised, she had sufficient other property available for hanging clothes and she was directed to remove the clotheslines which were in the yards abutting the streets. Although no appeal was taken from this determination and no permit ever issued, the clotheslines were not removed. Relying upon the ordinance, the city thereupon charged the defendants with violating its provisions. They were tried and convicted and their judgments of conviction have been affirmed by the County Court of Westchester County. Upon the trial the defendant Webster Stover disputed the sufficiency of the evidence to connect him with the erection or maintenance of the clotheslines but he does not do so here, urging instead that the ordinance, as it has been applied to him and his wife, is unconstitutional both as an interference with free speech and as a deprivation of property without due process.[15]

14. The full text of the ordinance reads in this way (General Ordinance, § 4–3.7):

"*Clothes lines.* No clothes lines, drying racks, poles or other similar devices for hanging clothes, rags or other fabrics shall be erected or maintained in a front yard or side yard abutting a street. If there is a practical difficulty or unnecessary hardship in drying clothes elsewhere on the premises, a permit shall be issued by the City Clerk permitting the use of said front or side yard for such purpose upon approval of and a finding by the Building Inspector that drying of clothes elsewhere on the premises would create a practical difficulty or unnecessary hardship. If a permit is denied, the applicant may appeal to the Board of Appeals of this city. The provisions of this section shall be applicable to existing conditions."

15. We merely note that the proof of Mr. Stover's participation is more than ample to support the conviction. He not only acknowledged, at a public hearing before the Rye City Council, that he had erected the lines as a protest against his taxes and was leaving them there "until he got some action on his assessment" but he alleged the same thing in a complaint in a declaratory judgment action which he and his wife had instituted against the city.

It is a fair inference that adoption of the ordinance before us was prompted by the conduct and action of the defendants but we deem it clear that, if the law would otherwise be held constitutional, it will not be stricken as discriminatory or invalid because of its motivation. Cf. Town of Hempstead v. Goldblatt, 9 N.Y.2d 101, 211 N.Y.S.2d 185, 172 N.E.2d 562, affirmed 369 U.S. 590, 82 S.Ct. 987, 8 L.Ed.2d 130. Our problem, therefore, is to determine whether the law violates First Amendment rights or otherwise exceeds the police power vested in a city on the ground that it was enacted without regard to considerations of public health, safety and welfare.

The People maintain that the prohibition against clotheslines in front and side yards was "intended to provide clear visibility at street corners and in driving out of driveways, and thus avoid and reduce accidents; to reduce distractions to motorists and pedestrians; and to provide greater opportunity for access in the event of fires". Although there may be considerable doubt whether there is a sufficiently reasonable relationship between clotheslines and traffic or fire safety to support an exercise of the police power, it is our opinion that the ordinance may be sustained as an attempt to preserve the residential appearance of the city and its property values by banning, insofar as practicable, unsightly clotheslines from yards abutting a public street. In other words, the statute, though based on what may be termed aesthetic considerations, proscribes conduct which offends sensibilities and tends to debase the community and reduce real estate values.

There are a number of early decisions, both in this State * * * and elsewhere * * *, which hold that aesthetic considerations are not alone sufficient to justify exercise of the police power. But since 1930 this court has taken pains repeatedly to declare that the issue is an open and "unsettled" one in New York. People v. Rubenfeld, 254 N.Y. 245, 248–249, 172 N.E. 485, 486–487; see, also, Perlmutter v. Greene, 259 N.Y. 327, 332, 182 N.E. 5, 6, 81 A.L.R. 1543; New York State Thruway Auth. v. Ashley Motor Ct., Inc., 10 N.Y.2d 151, 156–157, 218 N.Y.S.2d 640, 642–643, 176 N.E.2d 566, 568–569. In addition, we have actually recognized the governmental interest in preserving the appearance of the community by holding that, whether or not aesthetic considerations are in and of themselves sufficient to support an exercise of the police power, they may be taken into account by the legislative body in enacting laws which are also designed to promote health and safety. * * * "Aesthetic considerations", this court wrote in Dowsey v. Village of Kensington, 257 N.Y. 221, 230, 177 N.E. 427, 430, supra, "are, fortunately, not wholly without weight in a practical world."

Once it be conceded that aesthetics is a valid subject of legislative concern, the conclusion seems inescapable that reasonable legislation designed to promote that end is a valid and permissible exercise of the police power. If zoning restrictions "which implement a policy of neighborhood amenity" are to be stricken as invalid, it should be, one commentator has said, not because they seek to promote "aesthetic objectives" but solely because the restrictions constitute "unreasonable devices of implementing community policy." Dukeminier, Zoning for Aesthetic Objectives: A Reappraisal, 20 Law & Contemp.Prob. 218, 231. Consequently, whether such a statute or ordinance should be voided should depend upon whether the restriction was "an arbitrary and irrational method of achieving an attractive, efficiently functioning, prosperous community—and *not* upon whether the objectives were primarily aesthetic." Dukeminier, loc. cit. And, indeed, this view finds support in an ever-increasing number of cases from other jurisdictions which recognize that aesthetic considerations alone may warrant an exercise of the police power. * * *

Cases may undoubtedly arise, as we observed above, in which the legislative body goes too far in the name of aesthetics, cf. Matter of Mid–State Adv. Corp. v. Bond, 274 N.Y. 82, 8 N.E.2d 286; Dowsey v. Village of Kensington, 257 N.Y. 221, 177 N.E. 427, supra; Dukeminier, Zoning for Aesthetic Objectives: A Reappraisal, 20 Law & Contemp.Prob. 218, 231, but the present, quite clearly is not one of them. The ordinance before us is in large sense regulatory rather than prohibitory. It causes no undue hardship to any property owner, for it expressly provides for the issuance of a permit for clotheslines in front and side yards in cases where there is practical difficulty or unnecessary hardship in drying clothes elsewhere on the premises. Moreover, the ordinance imposes no arbitrary or capricious standard of beauty or conformity upon the community. It simply proscribes conduct which is unnecessarily offensive to the visual sensibilities of the average person. It is settled that conduct which is similarly offensive to the senses of hearing and smell may be a valid subject of regulation under the police power, see, e.g., People v. Rubenfeld, 254 N.Y. 245, 172 N.E. 485, supra, and we perceive no basis for a different result merely because the sense of sight is involved.

Nor is there any warrant or justification for a charge—which seems to have been abandoned on this appeal—that the ordinance is being enforced solely against the defendants or that there is a pattern of discrimination consciously being practiced against them. As the court below noted, the building superintendent testified, without contradiction, that all applications for permits were checked and investigated, that other applications for permits had been denied and that the defendants were the only persons who refused to remove clotheslines violative of the ordinance.

* * *

[The balance of the majority opinion, in which the court discusses the contention of the defendants that their freedom of speech had been denied them, is omitted. The court concluded that the prohibition against clotheslines had no necessary relationship to the dissemination of ideas or opinions.]

The judgment appealed from should be affirmed.

VAN VOORHIS, JUDGE (dissenting).

My concern in this case is not with limitation of free speech nor whether aesthetic considerations are enough in themselves to justify zoning regulations in prescribed instances, but with the extent to which a municipality can go in restricting the use of private property. The ordinance whose validity is now being upheld prohibits the erection and maintenance of clotheslines in a front or side yard abutting a street. Exceptions may be granted, and we were told upon the argument that 26 exceptions have been allowed in Rye, with the practical result that this ordinance is enforced against few others, if any, than the appellants. Even if that be held not to undermine the ordinance, it seems to me to exceed zoning powers for municipalities such as this to dictate to owners of houses and lots where they may put their clotheslines. The validity of ordinances may be tested in court according to whether the exercise of power delegated to the municipality is reasonable or arbitrary. People ex rel. City of Olean v. Western N.Y. & Pa. Traction Co., 214 N.Y. 526, 108 N.E. 847; Commissioners of Palisades Interstate Park v. Lent, 240 N.Y. 1, 147 N.E. 228. In the case last cited it was said that "What is reasonable is in large part tested by what is ordinary usage and common experience." 240 N.Y. p. 8, 147 N.E. p. 230. What has happened here is that these defendants conceived the unusual idea of hanging what the majority opinion describes as "tattered clothing, old uniforms, underwear, rags and scarecrows" across their yard as a form of protest against the amount of their taxes. The city, at the instance of other residents in the area, fought back by adopting this ordinance from the operation of which almost every other property owner applying for a permit has been excepted. Although the origin of this dispute is evidently political in nature, the validity of this ordinance is sought to be upheld entirely on the basis of aesthetic considerations, e.g., that the eye is offended by what hangs from these clotheslines. No cases have been cited from this or any other jurisdiction holding that a municipal corporation or political subdivision can direct house and lot owners where they shall hang their clothes. Aesthetic considerations, in a certain sense, underlie all zoning, usually in combination with other factors with which they are interwoven. Lot area, setback and height restrictions, for example, are based essentially on aesthetic factors. Occasionally public safety considerations are blended with aesthetics, such as the tendency of billboards to distract the attention of automobile drivers or of high hedges to block their view at street intersections. Aesthetic factors are given effect, in such cases, but have been limited to specific situations and not extended to anything which offends the taste of the neighbors or of the local legislature. One may assume, for example, that a clothesline ordinance would be invalid which permitted the hanging of white but not red blankets, or allowed shirts to be put out to dry after washing but not underwear. Probably, at least until the next step in zoning law, a municipality would be held unauthorized to direct house owners what colors their homes should be painted, or what kinds of trees or shrubbery they should be allowed to grow and where they should be planted. Nevertheless if they can be told where to hang their clothes in their yards, these items would be but a small step beyond the present holding, or to prescribe what architectural designs should be adopted so as to harmonize with the designs of the neighbors. To direct by ordinance that all buildings erected in a certain area should be one-story ranch houses would scarcely go beyond the present ruling as a question of power, or to lay down the law that they should be all of the same color, or of different colors, or that each should be of one or two or more color tones as might suit the aesthetic predilections of the city councillors or zoning boards of appeal.

This ordinance is unrelated to the public safety, health, morals or welfare except insofar as it compels conformity to what the neighbors like to look at. Zoning, important as it is within limits, is too rapidly becoming a legalized device to prevent property owners from doing whatever their neighbors dislike. Protection of minority rights is as essential to democracy as majority vote. In our age of conformity it is still not possible for all to be exactly alike, nor is it the instinct of our law to compel uniformity wherever diversity may offend the sensibilities of those who cast the largest numbers of votes in municipal elections. The right to be different has its place in this country. The United States has drawn strength from differences among its people in taste, experience, temperament, ideas, and ambitions as well as from differences in race, national or religious background. Even where the use of property is bizarre, unsuitable or obstreperous it is not to be curtailed in the absence of overriding reasons of public policy. The security and repose which come from protection of the right to be different in matter of aesthetics, taste, thought, expression and within limits in conduct are not to be cast aside without violating constitutional privileges and immunities. This is not merely a matter of legislative policy, at whatever level. In my view, this pertains to individual rights protected by the Constitution.

Aesthetic factors have always played an important part in zoning, as they have in the licensing of television and radio. Theatre and entertainment, as well as other forms of music, art, philosophy and literature are closely involved in aesthetics, which are not a veneer but are fundamental to the human mind and spirit. Nor are aesthetics confined to landscape gardening, tract development or architectural design. The avoidance by courts, sometimes seemingly to the point of evasion, of sustaining the constitutionality of zoning solely on aesthetic grounds has had its origin in a wholesome fear of allowing government to trespass through aesthetics on the human personality. In this instance, hanging tattered clothing, underwear, rags and scarecrows on a clothesline can scarcely be regarded as articulating a protest against excessive taxation, but to prohibit it by law upon the ground that it offends the aesthetic sensibilities of the neighbors or of the public officials of the municipality means—unless well defined and effectively enforced limits are placed upon this power to rule aesthetics by government—opening the door to the invasion by majority rule of a great deal of territory that belongs to the individual human being. It was once said of a famous lady of history that she had so much taste, and all of it so bad. Individual taste, good or bad, should ordinarily be let alone by government.

In authorizing the regulation of setback lines, yard areas, height of buildings and many permitted uses, the dominant factor has often been and should be aesthetic. But it is important not to allow general or unlimited power in government to regulate aesthetics in zoning or other departments of municipal administration. Extending aesthetic factors to the regulation of clotheslines suggests that zoning power, in the future, may extend to many other types of regulation also, since municipal boards and councils are being authorized in large degree to impose their ideas of aesthetics, and may be expected to do so on an expanding scale to placate the wishes of other property owners who constitute a large segment of the electorate. Unless clotheslines create traffic or health hazards, it seems to me that they should not be interfered with by law in suburban or rural areas. More important than this, however, does it seem that extensions of categories of local legislation for purely aesthetic purposes should be defined and limited, and, if they are to be enlarged, it should not be under reasoning which sets no ascertainable bounds to what can be done or attempted under this power.

The judgments of conviction of appellants should be reversed and the charges against them dismissed.

Notes

1. Is it correct that the Stovers' clothes line display was not an expression protected by the First Amendment? The Stovers certainly intended to express their political views through maintenance of the clothes lines, but the average passerby would have no way to ascertain this. Should the question of whether a display constitutes First Amendment expression be determined with reference to the speaker's point of view or by the interpretation of the reader or hearer? What if the Stovers had hung signs from the clothes lines indicating their purpose?

Courts have seldom addressed the issue of the regulation of artwork and other expressive displays placed on private property but visible to the public. In Historic District Commission v. Hall, 282 Conn. 672, 923 A.2d 726 (2007) the Supreme Court of Connecticut held that a six ton lawn sculpture was a "structure" and could therefore be regulated by the town's historic commission. And in Burke v. City of Charleston, 893 F.Supp. 589 (D.S.C.1995) the court found no constitutional violation in the City's refusal to grant a permit for a mural that was visible from the street in a historic district. See also, Galina Krasilovsky, *Note: A Sculpture is Worth a Thousand Words: The First Amendment Rights of Homeowners Publicly Displaying Art on Private Property*, 20 Colum. VLA J. L. & Arts 521 (1996); Russ Versteeg, *Iguanas, Toads and Toothbrushes: Land–Use Regulation of Art as Signage*, 25 Ga. L. Rev. 437 (1991) (describing displays of artwork placed on commercial property); and James Charles Smith, *The Law of Yards*, 33 Ecology L.Q. 203 (2006) (examining the issues of expressive architecture and yards and landscaping and weed ordinances).

2. For another case upholding aesthetic interests as a basis for land use regulations, see People v. Tolman, 110 Cal.App.3d Supp. 6, 168 Cal.Rptr. 328 (1980), where the court upheld an ordinance prohibiting parking of vehicles over three tons on residential streets. Moreover, just as in the area

of sign ordinances, aesthetic regulations controlling the appearance of property may be upheld when they also serve other non-aesthetic interests. In City of Smyrna v. Parks, 240 Ga. 699, 242 S.E.2d 73 (1978), the court upheld a prohibition against chain link fences in front yards, finding that, in addition to aesthetic objectives, the ordinance was a safety measure in that fire fighters would be able to enter premises more easily when faced with a wood fence. Also see Parking Association of Georgia, Inc. v. City of Atlanta, 264 Ga. 764, 450 S.E.2d 200 (1994), where an ordinance requiring parking lots with more than thirty spaces to have landscaped areas equal to or exceeding ten percent of their paved areas was upheld. Although the court noted that an ordinance may be valid even if designed only to improve aesthetics, it also noted that the parking lot ordinance furthered water run-off control and other environmental interests.

3. The theory of the Stover case does not necessarily mean that all aesthetic regulations are free from attack. In Sackson v. Zimmerman, 103 A.D.2d 843, 478 N.Y.S.2d 354 (1984) the court held that a purely aesthetic regulation must be supported by a showing that the offense to the eye has a substantial and material effect on the community. The court struck down application of a local ordinance which applied an inordinate setback on a property owner to preserve neighbors' views of nearby mansions which would be obstructed by the presence of a smaller house. Compare State v. Piemontese, 282 N.J.Super. 307, 659 A.2d 1385 (1995) where the court held that an ordinance requiring property owners to keep lawns, hedges and bushes from becoming "overgrown and unsightly" was vague and overly broad.

4. Discussions focusing on the aesthetic justifications for police power regulations are often accompanied by reasoning that considers the negative secondary effects of unsightly signs and structures, such as blight and falling property values. However, while many courts have come to accept aesthetics as a sufficient justification for legislative regulations, courts have been extremely reluctant to acknowledge any theory of "aesthetic nuisance" that would allow private actions to remove such signs and objects. Among the reasons for rejecting such claims, courts have most often suggested that "aesthetic nuisances" simply do not cause an unreasonable interference with others' uses of land. Another reason for denying the theory stems from the perception that visual disturbances can be avoided, whereas more common nuisances, such as unpleasant sounds and smells, cannot be ignored by simply turning one's eyes away. See Robie v. Lillis, 112 N.H. 492, 299 A.2d 155 (1972). Is it consistent to support regulations by reference to aesthetic qualities while denying private causes of actions based on the same types of problems associated with aesthetic regulations? Or is the difference appropriate given that the subjectivity of aesthetics is more likely to lead to abuses of discretion when wielded by individuals rather than by elected legislatures? For more information on aesthetic nuisance theories, see Robert D. Dodson, *Rethinking Private Nuisance Law: Recognizing Aesthetic Nuisances in the New Millennium*, 10 S.C. Envtl. L.J. 1 (2002).

SECTION 2. HISTORICAL LANDMARK AND CULTURAL PRESERVATION

A. FEDERAL GOVERNMENT'S ROLE IN HISTORICAL LANDMARK AND CULTURAL PRESERVATION

The following excerpt from a report of the Advisory Council on Historic Preservation describes the development of historic preservation law and regulation in the United States. The full report is available at http://www.achp.gov/book/sectionI.html#IA.

> Thirty years after passage of the National Historic Preservation Act of 1966 (NHPA), Federal law clearly reflects the Nation's commitment to preserving and protecting its wealth of historic resources. This was not always the case. Although Federal statutes containing preservation policies have existed since the turn of the 20th century, these laws typically were limited in scope and lacked effective means of enforcement.
>
> The earliest Federal preservation statute was the Antiquities Act of 1906, which authorized the President to set aside historic landmarks, structures, and objects located on lands controlled by the United States as national monuments. It required permits for archeological activities on Federal lands, and established criminal and civil penalties for violation of the act. The Historic Sites Act of 1935 was the second major piece of Federal historic preservation legislation. This act declared it national policy to preserve for public use historic sites, buildings, and objects of national significance and directed the Secretary of the Interior to conduct various programs with respect to historic preservation. Although these statutes were significant, they did not create a national awareness of the need for preservation or provide a means to incorporate preservation concerns into Federal agency programs.
>
> In 1964, the United States Conference of Mayors undertook a study of historic preservation in the United States. The resulting report, "With Heritage So Rich," revealed a growing public interest in preservation and the need for a unified approach to the protection of historic resources. This report influenced Congress to enact a strong new statute establishing a nationwide preservation policy: the National Historic Preservation Act of 1966.
>
> The National Historic Preservation Act was a watershed in preservation law, for it created a means by which the Nation's preservation goals could be achieved. Recognizing that increased knowledge and better administration of historic resources would improve the planning and execution of Federal undertakings and benefit economic growth and development nationwide, the act promoted the use of historic properties to meet the contemporary needs of society. It directed the Federal Government, in cooperation with State and local governments, Native Americans, and the public, to

take a leadership role in preservation. Since 1966, Congress has strengthened national preservation policy further by recognizing the importance of preserving historic aspects of the Nation's heritage in several other statutes, among them the National Environmental Policy Act and several transportation acts and by enacting statutes directed toward the protection and preservation of archeological resources. These laws require Federal agencies to consider historic resources in their planning and decisionmaking and, although they are not co-extensive with NHPA, often overlap with the provisions of NHPA.

The Executive Branch has expressed its support for preservation through several key Executive Orders. In 1971, for example, President Nixon signed Executive Order No. 11593, which instituted procedures Federal agencies must follow in their property management activities. In 1996, President Clinton signed another important Executive Order, this one setting forth the Administration's support for locating Federal offices and facilities in historic districts and properties in the Nation's inner cities: Executive Order No. 13006 directs Federal agencies to use and rehabilitate properties in such areas wherever feasible and reaffirms the commitment to Federal leadership in the preservation of historic properties set forth in NHPA thirty years before. Another 1996 Executive Order, No. 13007, expresses support for the protection of Native American sacred sites.

The National Historic Preservation Act and other preservation statutes, as well as the Executive Orders mentioned above, have clarified and refined the duties and responsibilities of Federal agencies with regard to the protection of America's cultural heritage. Federal compliance with these authorities, however, has not always been consistent, giving rise to a number of lawsuits brought primarily by citizens and preservation organizations. The resulting court opinions interpret and elucidate the historic preservation provisions of these laws.

* * *

Notes

1. One of the most important provisions of the NHPA is 16 U.S.C § 470f, commonly referred to as "section 106." The provision requires federal agencies to take into account the adverse effects that federal "undertakings" may have on properties included in or eligible for inclusion in the National Register before approving any federal expenditures. Federal agencies must allow sufficient time for the Advisory Council on Historic Preservation to comment on proposed projects, but they need not follow recommendations made by the committee and may proceed with projects that will adversely affect historic properties if they so choose. There is a limited exception to this rule when a proposed federal undertaking would directly and adversely affect a Nation Landmark property, in which cases the agency

must minimize possible adverse effects to that property. 16 U.S.C. § 470h–2(f).

The NHPA has often been criticized for its limited ability to ensure historic preservation. The act is essentially procedural in nature, and the courts accordingly give wide discretion to agency determinations so long as they comply with the NHPA's historic review requirements. In Coliseum Square Association v. Jackson, 465 F.3d 215 (5th Cir.2006), for example, the plaintiffs contended that the Department of Housing and Urban Development (HUD) had improperly relied on information provided to it by the National Park Service (NPS) in reaching its determination that the proposed project would not adversely affect any National Landmarks. Because HUD had relied on the NPS recommendation in good faith and the NPS had not withdrawn its statements, the court refused to find that the agency had acted arbitrarily or capriciously. See also Neighborhood Association of the Back Bay v. Federal Transit Administration, 463 F.3d 50 (1st Cir.2006), where the court extended deference to the agency's stance that it had conducted an independent historical analysis, even though it had relied on reports prepared by other entities. Additionally, the scope of the NHPA has often been drawn narrowly. Consider Lee v. Thornburgh, 877 F.2d 1053 (D.C.Cir.1989), a case in which several neighborhood community groups sought to block the construction of a prison on a property that had been nominated for inclusion in the National Register. Funding for the project, located in the District of Columbia, had been approved by Congress, and the parties conceded that the planning process for the prison did not comply with the NHPA. Yet, because Congress is not considered to be a "federal agency" under the NHPA, the court held that the statute was inapplicable. For a case finding a violation of the NHPA, see Morris County Trust for Historic Preservation v. Pierce, 714 F.2d 271 (3d Cir. 1983).

2. Other notable historic preservation laws include the Historical and Archeological Data Preservation Act of 1974, Pub. L. No. 93–291; the American Indian Religious Freedom Act of 1978, Pub. L. No. 95–341; the Archaeological Resources Protection Act of 1979, Pub. L. No. 96–95; the Abandoned Shipwreck Act of 1987, Pub. L. No. 100–298; the Native American Graves Protection and Repatriation Act of 1990, Pub. L. No. 101–610; and the American Battlefield Protection Act of 1996, Pub. L. No. 104–333. The Department of Transportation Act also requires the Secretary of Transportation to consider feasible alternatives to transportation projects that would negatively affect historic sites. See 49 U.S.C. § 303. Additionally, one of the goals of the the National Environmental Policy Act of (NEPA) is to "preserve important historic, cultural, and natural aspects of national heritage...." 42 U.S.C. § 4331 (b)(4). Accordingly, NEPA requires the federal government to take historical considerations into account when making decisions that may have adverse environmental effects.

B. THE ROLE OF STATE AND LOCAL GOVERNMENTS IN HISTORIC AND CULTURAL PRESERVATION

The 1966 Historic Preservation Act required, among other things, that each state establish a State Historic Preservation Office and that the governor of each state appoint an officer to oversee preservation activities.

State Historic Preservation Officers generally locate, record and nominate historic properties for inclusion in the National Register, create preservation ordinances and programs, provide funds for preservation projects and provide technical assistance to federal agencies, state and local governments and the private sector concerning restoration and other preservation activities. More information on state programs can be found in databases compiled by the National Conference of State Historic Preservation Officers, available at http://www.ncshpo.org, and through links provided by the National Conference of State Legislatures at http://www.ncsl.org/programs/arts/statehist_intro.htm.

More important to historic preservation programs are the commitments of local governments through the use of design regulations, historic districts and innovative zoning techniques to accomplish preservation goals. In 1997, the American Planning Association revised its policy on historic and cultural preservation. Calling upon planners to assume greater responsibility for historic preservation, the policy acknowledges the important role of local governments in planning for preservation and urges, "...the coordination of comprehensive planning programs and implementation tools (zoning, subdivision, and land development) with state preservation legislation (facade controls tax incentives, and other tools).... These programs should utilize a variety of tools which may include (but are not limited to): a) Transfer of development rights; b) Expansion of clustering and planned unit development to increase opportunities for landmarking, village preservation, and historic districts; and c) Preservation of village settlement patters as a desirable means to promote community character and diversity." See, http://www.planning.org/policyguides/historic.htm. Municipalities often create local historic preservation or review commissions. These commissions may be advisory in nature and they may issue necessary certifications to enable development and redevelopment projects to proceed.

(1) Historic Districts

OPINION OF THE JUSTICES TO THE SENATE

Supreme Judicial Court of Massachusetts, 1955.
333 Mass. 773, 128 N.E.2d 557.

On July 7, 1955, the Justices submitted the following answers to questions propounded to them by the Senate:

To the Honorable Senate of the Commonwealth of Massachusetts:

The Justices of the Supreme Judicial Court respectfully submit these answers to questions set forth in an order of the Senate dated June 14, 1955, and transmitted to us on June 21.

The questions relate to a proposed act known as House No. 775, now pending before the Senate, entitled "An Act establishing an historic districts commission for the town of Nantucket and defining its powers and duties, and establishing historic districts in the town of Nantucket."

The purpose of the act is stated to be to promote the general welfare of the inhabitants of the town "through the preservation and protection of historic buildings, places and districts of historic interest; through the development of an appropriate setting for these buildings, places and districts; and through the benefits resulting to the economy of Nantucket in developing and maintaining its vacation-travel industry through the promotion of these historic associations." § 1.

The act establishes a historic districts commission of five members, who shall be resident taxpayers of the town, to be appointed by the selectmen. § 2. It establishes by definite boundaries two districts in the town to be known as (1) Old and Historic Nantucket District, and (2) Old and Historic Siasconset District. § 3. It contains provisions applicable in those districts that "No building or structure shall hereafter be erected, reconstructed, altered or restored" until an application for a building permit "shall have been approved as to exterior architectural features which are subject to public view from a public street, way or place," and evidence of such approval shall be "a certificate of appropriateness" issued by the commission (§ 4); that no building or structure shall be raised (razed?) without a permit approved by the commission, which may be refused for any building or structure "the removal of which in the opinion of said commission would be detrimental to the public interest" of the town or the village of Siasconset (§ 5); that occupational or other signs exceeding two feet in length and six inches in width, or the erection or display of more than one such sign, irrespective of size, on any lot, building or structure must be approved and certified by the commission (§ 6); and that the commission may hold public or private hearings as it may deem advisable (§ 7). It shall be the function and duty of the commission "to pass upon the appropriateness of exterior architectural features of buildings and structures hereafter to be erected, reconstructed, altered or restored * * * wherever such exterior features are subject to public view from a public street or way" and also to pass upon the removal of buildings and the erection or display of signs according to §§ 5 and 6 (§ 8[a]). It is provided that the commission "in passing upon appropriateness of exterior architectural features in any case, shall keep in mind the purposes set forth" in § 1, and "shall consider among other things the general design, arrangement, texture, material and color of the building or structure in question, and the relation of such factors to similar features of buildings and structures in the immediate surroundings" (§ 8[b]). It is expressly provided that the commission shall not consider detailed designs, relative size of buildings, interior arrangement or building features not subject to public view, and shall make no recommendations or requirements except for the purpose of preventing developments obviously incongruous to the historic aspects of the surroundings and the Old and Historic Districts (§ 8[c]). Upon approval of plans the commission shall cause a certificate of appropriateness to be issued (§ 8[e]). There are provisions for a penalty for violations of the act and for appeal to the selectmen and ultimately to the Superior Court. §§ 9–11. Appeal to the Superior Court with "rights of appeal and exception as in other equity cases" is to be the final exclusive remedy. § 11. The provision for appeal to the court is in terms similar to those employed in statutes providing for appeal to the court from decisions of zoning boards of appeals, which in Pendergast v. Board of Appeals of Barnstable, 331 Mass. 555, 120 N.E.2d 916, were held to carry up questions of law. The act is to take effect upon acceptance by the voters of the town. § 14.

The act contains no provision for compensation as for property taken. The commission is to be "unpaid." § 2. But under § 7 it "may incur expenses necessary to the carrying on of its work within the amount of its annual appropriation."

* * *

If the proposed act is to be construed as a taking of the property of owners affected by it, manifestly it is unconstitutional, since no provision is made for compensation as required by art. 10 of the Declaration of Rights. On the other hand, there may be many regulations and restrictions upon the use of private property under the so called police power which do not amount to a taking of the property and which rest upon the general power to legislate for the public safety, health, morals, and welfare. We are of opinion that the proposed act is not a taking. There is no provision for a formal taking, and title will remain in the owner as will also the possession and usufruct for nearly all purposes, even though restricted in ways that conceivably may in occasional instances bear down heavily. See American Unitarian Association v. Commonwealth, 193 Mass. 470, 476–477, 79 N.E. 878.

The question then arises whether the proposed act can be supported without a taking and the paying of compensation as a police regulation in the interest of public safety, health, morals, or welfare. There are many regulations belonging in these categories too numerous and too familiar to require specific reference here. Those which in many respects most nearly resemble the proposed act are the zoning laws the constitutionality of which is in general thoroughly established. * * * Many zoning regulations are as severe in their operation upon landowners as any of the provisions of the proposed act would be likely to be.

But the zoning regulations are in general directly related to the public safety and health, and less directly to the public morals. The proposed act can hardly be said in any ordinary sense to relate to the public safety, health, or morals. Can it rest upon the less definite and more inclusive ground that it serves the public welfare? The term public welfare has never been and cannot be precisely defined. Sometimes it has been said to include public convenience, comfort, peace and order, prosperity, and similar concepts, but not to include "mere expediency." Opinion of the Justices, 234 Mass. 597, 603, 127 N.E. 525. And it has been held or stated that aesthetic considerations alone are not enough, but that they may be taken into account, if the primary objects of the regulation are sufficient to justify it. * * * There is reason to think that more weight might now be given to aesthetic considerations than was given to them a half century ago.

* * *

The definition of the purpose of the proposed act as set forth in § 1 is along these same lines and includes "the preservation and protection of historic buildings, places and districts of historic interest; through the development of an appropriate setting for these buildings, places and districts; and through the benefits resulting to the economy of Nantucket in developing and maintaining its vacation-travel industry through the promotion of these historic associations." In the case of City of New Bedford v. New Bedford, Woods Hole, Martha's Vineyard & Nantucket Steamship Authority, 330 Mass. 422, 114 N.E.2d 553, this court took judicial notice of the general characteristics of the island of Nantucket and of its great interest in the entertainment of summer visitors. We may also take judicial notice that Nantucket is one of the very old towns of the Commonwealth; that for perhaps a century it was a famous seat of the whaling industry and accumulated wealth and culture which made itself manifest in some fine examples of early American architecture; and that the sedate and quaint appearance of the old island town has to a large extent still remained unspoiled and in all probability constitutes a substantial part of the appeal which has enabled it to build up its summer vacation business to take the place of its former means of livelihood. In a general way much the same can be said of the village of Siasconset, which is a part of the town of Nantucket. There has been substantial recognition by the courts of the public interest in the preservation of historic buildings, places, and districts. Opinion of the Justices, 297 Mass. 567, 8 N.E.2d 753. General Outdoor Advertising Co., Inc. v. Department of Public Works, 289 Mass. 149, 187–189, 197–198, 200–201, 193 N.E. 799. United States v. Gettysburg Electric Railway, 160 U.S. 668, 16 S.Ct. 427, 40 L.Ed. 576. State v. Kemp, 124 Kan. 716, 261 P. 556. Flaccomio v. Mayor & City Council of Baltimore, 194 Md. 275, 71 A.2d 12. See art. 51 of the Amendments to the Constitution of this Commonwealth.

It is not difficult to imagine how the erection of a few wholly incongruous structures might destroy one of the principal assets of the town, and we assume that the boundaries of the districts are so drawn as to include only areas of special value to the public because of possession of those characteristics which it is the purpose of the act to preserve.

We think the requirements of the proposed act are not too indefinite or lacking in sufficient standards. The act does not require anything to be done to existing structures with the possible exception of signs (§ 6). With the same possible exception, it applies only to exterior architectural features subject to public view from a public place (§ 4). It does not apply to details of design or sizes of buildings or interior arrangement of building features not subject to public view, and requirements by the commission must be limited to the preventing of developments "obviously incongruous to the historic aspects of the surroundings" (§ 8[c]). This last provision is apparently intended to prevent decisions based upon peculiar individual tastes. All provisions must be interpreted with reference to the main purposes of the act. See § 8(b). In at least two very recent cases regulations based in part upon standards of architecture intended to comport with the established surroundings have been sustained. City of New Orleans v. Levy, 223 La. 14, 64 So.2d 798. State ex rel. Saveland Park Holding Corp. v. Wieland, 269 Wis. 262, 69 N.W.2d 217. See 64 U.S.Sts. at Large, p. 903, c. 984, relating to "Old Georgetown."

We are of opinion that in a general sense the proposed act would be an act for the promotion of the public welfare and would be constitutional, and we answer the questions on that basis. * * *

Notes

1. On the same day as the decision in the principal case, the justices rendered an opinion that a similar historic district to preserve Beacon Hill in Boston would be constitutional. See Opinion of the Justices to the Senate, 333 Mass. 783, 128 N.E.2d 563 (1955). The court stated:

> In addition to the facts appearing from the proposed act itself there are other facts of common knowledge in relation to Beacon Hill. The area was closely built up for the homes of persons of taste and culture in the architectural style of urban residences prevailing a century or more ago. There is general uniformity in design and structure. Although the area is not far from the business center of Boston, commercial development has proceeded in other directions, and the Beacon Hill section, with some exceptions, has remained to this day rather surprisingly free from inharmonious intrusions. Its general appearance is substantially what it was several generations ago. The Bulfinch front, so called, of the State House, completed before the year 1800, is at the highest point of the hill. The famous Boston Common is located on the side of Beacon Street opposite the southerly boundary of the proposed district. The area has contained the homes of many persons of distinction in the life of the State and Nation. That it is a locality of historic significance can hardly be doubted.
>
> The announced purpose of the act is to preserve this historic section for the educational, cultural, and economic advantage of the public. If the General Court believes that this object would be attained by the restrictions which the act would place upon the introduction into the district of inappropriate forms of construction that would destroy its unique value and associations, a court can hardly take the view that such legislative determination is so arbitrary or unreasonable that it cannot be comprehended within the public welfare.
>
> In our answers to recent questions of the Senate pertaining to proposed historic districts in Nantucket we have discussed at some length the constitutional aspects of restrictions upon the character of building in areas set apart as such districts, whether or not there is involved any element of aesthetic considerations, and we cited authorities revealed by our research into the subject. We beg to refer to what we there said without repeating it here. In that instance the districts of

historic interest intended to be preserved were in ancient villages that had survived into our day. In this instance it is an ancient section of the capital city of the Commonwealth. But the principles are the same. There are some other differences between the two proposed acts, but we think none is sufficient to render what we said in our discussion in the former instance inapplicable in this later instance.

2. In Gumley v. Board of Selectmen of Nantucket, 371 Mass. 718, 358 N.E.2d 1011 (1977), the court held that a decision of the Nantucket Historic District Commission denying a certificate of appropriateness to a developer was improper to the extent that it was based on incongruence with the open space aspect of Nantucket. The court said: "That decision did not relate to 'exterior architectural features.' It went beyond the statutory purpose of 'preventing developments obviously incongruous to the historic aspects of the surroundings' and the district. It therefore exceeded the authority of the commission * * *."

3. See also, City of Santa Fe v. Gamble–Skogmo, 73 N.M. 410, 389 P.2d 13 (1964), upholding zoning seeking to preserve "Old Santa Fe Style" architecture. Similar to the Santa Fe situation were the earlier efforts of New Orleans to preserve the distinctive character of the French Quarter. This effort was embodied in the "Vieux Carre Ordinance," enacted in 1936 pursuant to authorization contained in the state constitution for the purpose of exercising control over the architecture in the city's famous French Quarter. In City of New Orleans v. Pergament, 198 La. 852, 5 So.2d 129 (1941), the Supreme Court of Louisiana upheld the ordinance as a valid exercise of the city's police power, noting that the goal of the ordinance was not just "sentimental" but that it was also intended to preserve the commercial value of the Vieux Carre. The Fifth Circuit later reviewed the Vieux Carre ordinance and found it to be constitutional in Maher v. New Orleans, 516 F.2d 1051 (5th Cir.1975). The plaintiff, who had been seeking since 1963 to demolish his Victorian cottage and construct an apartment complex, argued that the ordinance violated due process because it did not contain objective criteria and was applied arbitrarily. The court dismissed these arguments, explaining that "[i]t may be difficult to capture the atmosphere of a region through a set of regulations. However, it would seem that old city plans and historic documents, as well as photographs and contemporary writings may provide an abundant and accurate compilation of data to guide the Commission." See also, City of New Orleans v. Levy, 223 La. 14, 64 So.2d 798 (1953); and City of New Orleans v. Impastato, 198 La. 206, 3 So.2d 559 (1941). Although the New Orleans cases were based on an ordinance adopted and a commission created pursuant to specific constitutional authority, they helped lay the groundwork for acceptance of the idea that municipalities (as in the Santa Fe case) could rely upon a general delegation of authority to sustain zoning for preservation purposes. In Williamsburg, Virginia, the zoning power was employed to protect a restored area, rather than to preserve an historic area in its existing state. See Agnor, Beauty Begins a Comeback: Aesthetic Considerations in Zoning, 11 J.Pub.L. 260, 274 (1962); and Note, Zoning: Aesthetics: The Chameleon of Zoning, 4 Tulsa L.J. 48, 56 (1967).

SOUTH OF SECOND ASSOCIATES v. GEORGETOWN

Supreme Court of Colorado, En Banc, 1978.
196 Colo. 89, 580 P.2d 807.

ERICKSON, JUSTICE.

Georgetown is a municipal corporation created by the Colorado territorial legislature in 1868. The town and surrounding area are rich in the culture and history of early Colorado. In 1966, the National Park Service of the U.S. Department of the Interior designated the Georgetown/Silver Plume area as a registered National Historic Landmark District.

On May 18, 1970, the Board of Selectmen of Georgetown enacted Ordinance No. 205. The ordinance amended Georgetown's existing zoning ordinance by creating a Historic Preservation District (District) and a seven-member Historic Preservation Commission (Commission). The District boundaries encompassed all real property within the municipal limits of Georgetown. * * *

South of Second Associates, one of the plaintiffs, owns approximately five acres of undeveloped real property in Georgetown located on Leavenworth Mountain south of the developed portion of the municipality. The property, at all times relevant to this proceeding, was zoned for multi-family use. On December 18, 1972, the plaintiffs submitted an application for a certificate of appropriateness to construct 57 townhouses which would occupy approximately 30% of their property on Leavenworth Mountain. The Commission reviewed the application and unanimously decided not to issue the requested certificate. The Georgetown Board of Selectmen voted four to two not to overrule the Commission's decision.

* * *

The pertinent provisions of Ordinance No. 205 provide:

"Section VII. 'HP—Historic Preservation District'

"A) GENERAL DESCRIPTION

This District is intended to promote the educational, cultural, economic, and general welfare of the public through the protection, enhancement, and use of structures and areas of historical and/or architectural significance. In order to maintain the character and beauty of such structures, and areas, restrictive requirements governing both the use of land and the erection, moving, demolition, reconstruction, restoration, or alteration of structures thereon are provided.

* * *

"B) DEFINITIONS FOR THE HISTORICAL PRESERVATION DISTRICT

* * *

4. Historical and/or Architectural Significance. That which has a special historical or aesthetic interest or value as part of the development, heritage, or cultural character of the city, region, state, or nation.

5. Area. Any land or buildings having notable character qualities of historical and/or architectural significance as determined by the Historical Preservation Commission. An area may include structures or other physical improvements on, above, or below the surface of the earth.

* * *

"C) ROLE OF HISTORICAL PRESERVATION COMMISSION

* * *

> "In determining the recommendation to be made concerning the issuance of a certificate of appropriateness, the Commission shall consider the following criteria:
>
> (1) The effect of the proposed change upon the general historical and/or architectural character of the structure or area."

* * *

The trial court concluded that the ordinances were unconstitutionally vague:

> "After reviewing the ordinances and after hearing the testimony of numerous witnesses concerned with their enforcement (each of whom seemed to have a different opinion as to the meaning of the term 'historical and architectural significance') the Court is convinced that the ordinances do not contain sufficient standards to advise ordinary and reasonable men as to the conduct which they attempt to proscribe or direct."

The trial court seems to have based its decision upon a finding that the "historical and/or architectural significance" language of the ordinance was vague. We find such language sufficiently definite, but hold the ordinances unconstitutionally vague in failing to delineate the differently classified areas within the District.

* * *

Courts in other jurisdictions have found similar enactments, although somewhat uncertain in the abstract, to be sufficiently definite in the context of actual application. In Town of Deering v. Tibbetts, 105 N.H. 481, 202 A.2d 232 (1964), the Court declared:

> "While determination of what is compatible with the 'atmosphere' of the town may on first impression be thought to be a matter of arbitrary and subjective judgment, under consideration it proves not to be. As stated in Anderson, 'Architectural Controls,' 12 Syracuse L.Rev. 26, 45, the language 'takes clear meaning from the observable character of the district to which it applies.' See also, 1 Rathkopf, The Law of Zoning and Planning (3d ed. 1969) 11–29."

Our conclusion that the "historical and/or architectural" language in the Georgetown ordinance is sufficiently definite reflects the consensus of those courts which have considered similar provisions designed to preserve historical areas through the enactment of reasonable regulations. Figarsky v. Historic District Commission of the City of Norwich, 171 Conn. 198, 368 A.2d 163 (1976); Trustees of Sailors' Snug Harbor v. Platt, 29 A.D.2d 376, 288 N.Y.S.2d 314 (1968); Town of Deering v. Tibbetts, supra; City of Santa Fe v. Gamble–Skogmo, Inc., 73 N.M. 410, 389 P.2d 13 (1964); Opinion of the Justices to the Senate, 333 Mass. 773, 128 N.E.2d 557 (1955); City of New Orleans v. Levy, 223 La. 14, 64 So.2d 798 (1953); See also 1 Rathkopf § 15.01, The Law of Zoning and Planning (4th ed.).

We conclude that the "historical and/or architectural character" language of the ordinance, when considered in conjunction with the objective factors contained in the ordinance, and in the context of the public purposes to be achieved, is sufficiently definite to pass constitutional muster. The ordinance contains sufficient standards to advise ordinary and reasonable men as to the type of construction permitted, permits reasonable application by the Commission, and limits the Commission's discretionary powers.

* * *

Georgetown's historical preservation ordinance designates all property within the municipal limits as a historical preservation district. Most municipalities which have established similar historical preservation districts, however, specifically delineate those areas which possess such a unique character as to be entitled to preservation. See Figarsky v. Historical District Commission of the City of Norwich, supra; Maher v. City of New Orleans, 516 F.2d 1051 (5th Cir.1975); Rebman v. City of Springfield, 111 Ill.App.2d 430, 250 N.E.2d 282 (1969); Opinion of the Justices to the Senate, supra; Opinion of the Justices to the Senate, 333 Mass. 783, 128 N.E.2d 563 (1955); see also section 24–65.1–201(1)(c), C.R.S.1973 (1977 Supp.).

Although the ordinance contains standards sufficient to give substance to the "historical and/or architectural character" language of the ordinance by reference to the area in which the proposed construction or structural alteration is to occur, nowhere in the ordinance is a delineation of the relevant areas to be found. The ordinances' definition of area * * * fails to set forth sufficient criteria to enable the potential applicant to reasonably ascertain in which area his property is situated.

The record indicates that the Commission members divide Georgetown into two or three distinct areas. Several members testified that Georgetown was divided into northern and southern areas. Still others, while agreeing that the northern and southern areas exist, felt that a transitional or buffer area exists between the two larger areas. The Commission's unpublished and indefinite delineation of the areas is legally insufficient.

We conclude that Ordinance Nos. 205 and 206 vested unreviewable discretion in the Commission. Under the ordinances a property owner cannot reasonably ascertain which architectural designs would entitle him to a certificate of appropriateness. Areas entitled to protection must be clearly delineated in the ordinance. The ordinances, therefore, are void for vagueness.

* * *

The judgment is affirmed.

Notes

1. After the decision in this case the plaintiffs were denied a building permit and sought a declaratory judgment that they were entitled to immediate issuance of a permit and damages for the delay in issuing a permit. The supreme court held that the plaintiffs were entitled to declaratory relief and remanded the case for a hearing on the damages issue. South of Second Associates v. Georgetown, 199 Colo. 394, 609 P.2d 125 (1980). In Unruh v. City of Asheville, 97 N.C.App. 287, 388 S.E.2d 235, rev. denied 326 N.C. 487, 391 S.E.2d 813 (1990) the court held that the city's historic district ordinance was invalid because the city did not follow the prescribed adoption procedures in the state enabling legislation.

2. Can historic districts be empowered to control development outside the district which might have a deleterious effect upon the district? In Rebman v. City of Springfield, 111 Ill.App.2d 430, 250 N.E.2d 282 (1969), the court upheld denial of a rezoning to permit a restaurant on a commercial street adjacent to a four block historic district containing one historical structure, the Abraham Lincoln home. Also see, Hall County Historical Soc., Inc. v. Georgia Dept. of Transp., 447 F.Supp. 741 (N.D.Ga.1978), where the county historical society sought to protect an established district from a highway widening project close to the district boundaries. After finding that the society had standing based on the allegation that several members resided in or owned property in the historical district, the court held that (1) the plaintiffs failed to meet their burden of proof that the defendants' decision not to file an environmental impact statement was unreasonable under the National Environmental Policy Act; (2) defendants had not violated Section 4(f) of the Transportation Act (23 U.S.C.A. § 138) mandating that the Secretary of Transportation not approve any project which requires the use of land from an historic site if there is a feasible alternative; (3) the Department of Transportation did violate the National Historic Preservation Act (16 U.S.C.A. § 470f) which requires the federal agency to take into account the effect of a project on historic sites, by merely "rubber stamping" the conclusions of the state highway department that the project would not affect the district. An injunction against completion of the project was granted. In Bellevue Shopping Center Associates v. Chase, 574 A.2d 760 (R.I.1990) the court upheld denial of a proposal to add a new building to an existing shopping center because the design of the building would seriously impair the historic or architectural value of the surrounding historic district. Compare these cases to Board of Supervisors v. Rowe, 216 Va. 128, 216 S.E.2d 199 (1975), where the court struck down architectural regulations imposed on a property located near historical landmarks.

3. In Globe Newspaper Co. v. Beacon Hill Architectural Comm'n, 100 F.3d 175 (1st Cir.1996) the Court held that the architectural commission for the Beacon Hill historic district did have power to regulate the placement of newsracks, and that the guidelines promulgated by the commission did not violate the First Amendment. Compare Lusk v. Village of Cold Spring, 475 F.3d 480 (2d Cir.2007). Although the court upheld the authority of the village to regulate the design characteristics of signs within the historic district, it found that the licensing scheme constituted an impermissible prior restraint on speech because it required prior administrative approval for the posting of noncommercial signs on residential properties.

(2) Preserving Landmark Structures

KENT COUNTY COUNCIL FOR HISTORIC PRESERVATION v. ROMNEY

United States District Court, Western District, Michigan, 1969.
304 F.Supp. 885.

THORNTON, DISTRICT JUDGE.

"This is a case of first impression insofar as the National Historic Sites Act of 1966, 16 U.S.C.A. § 470 et seq. is concerned, certainly in its application to the urban renewal process. Plaintiff is unaware of any reported decisions construing this Act. Potentially, it is a landmark case. For as it is true of the Act itself, the issue at hand is the capacity of the American people to prevent improvidence in matters relating to the conservation of our natural and manmade heritage."

Thus reads plaintiff's brief in support of its motions for preliminary injunction in the two cases before the Court (now consolidated for trial purposes). The defendants include George W. Romney, Secretary of the Department of Housing and Urban Development, the Mayor of the City of Grand Rapids and numerous City administration officials, and the Union Bank and Trust Company. The Court set down plaintiff's preliminary injunction motions for early hearing because of the imminence of the demolition (Old Grand Rapids City Hall), which plaintiff seeks to at least forestall, if not prevent entirely. Prior to the commencement of the hearing there were filed motions to dismiss by all defendants, lack of jurisdiction being a basis common to all. Also advanced are contentions of non-retroactivity of the applicable legislative enactments and lack of standing. The preliminary injunction hearing, therefore, was held in abeyance so as to give precedence to a hearing on and determination of the various motions to dismiss.

* * *

It should be clear from the above that the Old Grand Rapids City Hall is on a parcel which is only a small segment of a substantial renewal plan area, that the plan was adopted by the City on April 4, 1961 and that execution of the plan has been proceeding since that time. The Act which plaintiff seeks to take advantage of came into existence October 15, 1966. The section of said Act relied upon by plaintiff is as follows:

"16 U.S.C.A. § 470f. Effect of Federal undertakings upon property listed in the National Register; comment by Advisory Council on Historic Preservation.

"The head of any Federal agency having direct or indirect jurisdiction over a proposed Federal or federally assisted undertaking in any State and the head of any Federal department or independent agency having authority to license any undertaking shall, prior to the approval of the expenditure of any Federal funds on the undertaking or prior to the issuance of any license, as the case may be, take into account the effect of the undertaking on any district, site, building, structure, or object that is included in the National Register. The head of any such Federal agency shall afford the Advisory Council on Historic Preservation established under sections 470i–470m of this title a reasonable opportunity to comment with regard to such undertaking. Pub.L. 89–665, Title I, § 106, Oct. 15, 1966, 80 Stat. 917."

* * *

[W]e are concerned with a statute, 16 U.S.C.A. § 470f whose function is to provide the Advisory Council on Historic Preservation a reasonable opportunity to comment with regard to an undertaking and its effect on any district, site, building, structure or object that is included in the National Register, and further to provide that the undertaking conform to other requirements of the statute. The National Historic Preservation Act provides in part as follows:

"(a) The Secretary of the Interior is authorized—

"(1) to expand and maintain a national register of districts, sites, buildings, structures, and objects significant in American history, architecture, archeology, and culture, hereinafter referred to as the National Register, and to grant funds to States for the purpose of preparing comprehensive statewide historic surveys and plans, in accordance with criteria established by the Secretary, for the preservation, acquisition, and development of such properties;" 16 U.S.C.A. § 470a.

Thus we are concerned with a statute that has application to federal agencies, heads of federal departments or individual agencies and the Advisory Council on Historic Preservation, with the duties of each clearly spelled out. [The Advisory Council on Historic Preservation, composed of seventeen members (not to be confused with Kent County Council for Historic Preservation), is not a party to this suit, either as a plaintiff or a defendant.] We are concerned with inanimate objects such as districts, sites, buildings, structures, or objects that are included in the National Register, rather than with individuals, organizations or corporations. * * *

Plaintiff has failed to establish by proof, argument or citation that it has any interest that would give it the right to bring this action. Accordingly, it lacks standing to sue.

The motions to dismiss heretofore filed herein should be granted. The moving parties may submit orders in accordance with this Memorandum, for consideration by the Court, incorporating therein such proposed supplemental comments as they may find desirable.

Notes

1. Compare with the principal case, Edwards v. First Bank of Dundee, 393 F.Supp. 680 (N.D.Ill.1975), which allowed residents standing to challenge demolition of a building on the National Register on the theory that the structure was a bank and relocation of a bank is subject to approval by the Federal Deposit Insurance Corporation which has responsibilities under both the National Environmental Policy Act and the National Historical Preservation Act. (The court did not reach the merits.) Also see Hart v. Denver Urban Renewal Auth., 551 F.2d 1178 (10th Cir.1977).

2. Aluli v. Brown, 602 F.2d 876 (9th Cir.1979), and Romero–Barcelo v. Brown, 478 F.Supp. 646 (D.Puerto Rico 1979), modified 643 F.2d 835 (1st Cir.1981), both involve attempts to enjoin the United States Navy from using archaeologically and environmentally significant areas for bombing, shelling and other training operations. Although both courts found violations of NEPA and the National Historic Preservation Act, the district court in Barcelo refused to enjoin the Navy for reasons of national defense and the Ninth Circuit in Aluli reversed an injunction requiring the Navy to file annual environmental impact statements.

PENN CENTRAL TRANSP. CO. v. CITY OF NEW YORK

Court of Appeals of New York, 1977.
42 N.Y.2d 324, 397 N.Y.S.2d 914, 366 N.E.2d 1271, affirmed
438 U.S. 104, 98 S.Ct. 2646, 57 L.Ed.2d 631 (1978).

[The Supreme Court opinion in this case, which appears in Chapter V, deals primarily with the "taking" issue.]

BREITEL, CHIEF JUDGE.

In broad terms, the problem in this case is determining the scope of governmental power, within the Constitution, to preserve, without resorting to eminent domain, irreplaceable landmarks deemed to be of inestimable social or cultural significance. In controversy is the constitutionality of regulation which would prohibit appellants, owner and proposed developer of the air rights above Grand Central Terminal, from constructing an office building atop the terminal.

* * *

Plaintiffs, Penn Central Transportation Company and its affiliates, who have a fee interest in Grand Central Terminal, and UGP Properties, Inc., lessee of the development rights over the terminal, seek a declaration that the landmark preservation provisions of the Administrative Code of the City of New York, as applied to the terminal property, are unconstitutional. They also seek to enjoin defendants, the City of New

York and the City Landmarks Preservation Commission, from enforcing those provisions against the subject property. Trial Term granted the requested relief, but a divided Appellate Division reversed and granted judgment to defendants. Plaintiffs appeal.

The order of the Appellate Division should be affirmed. Although government regulation is invalid if it denies a property owner all reasonable return, there is no constitutional imperative that the return embrace all attributes, incidental influences, or contributing external factors derived from the social complex in which the property rests. So many of these attributes are not the result of private effort or investment but of opportunities for the utilization or exploitation which an organized society offers to any private enterprise, especially to a public utility, favored by government and the public. These, too, constitute a background of massive social and governmental investment in the organized community without which the private enterprise could neither exist nor prosper. It is enough, for the limited purposes of a landmarking statute, albeit it is also essential, that the privately created ingredient of property receive a reasonable return. It is that privately created and privately managed ingredient which is the property on which the reasonable return is to be based. All else is society's contribution by the sweat of its brow and the expenditure of its funds. To that extent society is also entitled to its due.

Moreover, in this case, the challenged regulation provides Penn Central with transferable above-the-surface development rights which, because they may be attached to specific parcels of property, some already owned by Penn Central or its affiliates, may be considered as part of the owner's return on the terminal property.

Thus, the regulation does not deprive plaintiffs of property without due process of law, and should be upheld as a valid exercise of the police power.

* * *

This is not a zoning case. In many ways, the restrictions imposed on the use of the property are similar to zoning restrictions, but the purposes are different, and in determining whether regulation is reasonable, the purposes behind the regulation assume considerable significance * * *. Zoning restrictions operate to advance a comprehensive community plan for the common good. Each property owner in the zone is both benefited and restricted from exploitation, presumably without discrimination, except for permitted continuing nonconforming uses. The restrictions may be designed to maintain the general character of the area, or to assure orderly development, objectives inuring to the benefit of all, which property owners acting individually would find difficult or impossible to achieve * * *.

Nor does this case involve landmark regulation of a historic district. Historic district regulation, like zoning regulation, may be designed to maintain the character, both economic and esthetic or cultural, of an area (see Maher v. City of New Orleans, 5 Cir., 516 F.2d 1051, esp. p. 1060, cert. den. 426 U.S. 905, 96 S.Ct. 2225, 48 L.Ed.2d 830; Opinion of the Justices to the Senate, 333 Mass. 773, 778–780, 128 N.E.2d 557). The difference, generally, is that zoning does this largely by regulating construction of new buildings, while historic district regulation concentrates instead on preventing alteration or demolition of existing structures. In each case, owners although burdened by the restrictions also benefit, to some extent, from the furtherance of a general community plan.

Nor does this case partake of the principles applicable to a taking in eminent domain. As noted earlier, there is no taking for which just compensation must be paid. And it is the concept of just compensation which is so integrally related to value based on return. Instead, landmark regulation is a limitation on exploitation of property, an attribute shared with the classifications of zoning and historic districting. Yet landmark regulation is different because the burden of limitation is borne by a single owner. He may or may not benefit from that limitation but his neighbors most likely will. In contrast both an owner and his neighbors benefit to some degree and in some manner from zoning and historic districting.

Restrictions on alteration of individual landmarks are not designed to further a general community plan. Landmark restrictions are designed to prevent alteration or demolition of a single piece of property. To this extent, such restrictions, resemble "discriminatory" zoning restrictions, properly condemned, affecting properties singled out in a zoning district for more restrictive or more liberal zoning limitations * * * There is, however, a significant difference. Discriminatory zoning is condemned because there is no acceptable reason for singling out one particular parcel for different and less favorable treatment. When landmark regulation is involved, there is such a reason: the cultural, architectural, historical, or social significance attached to the affected parcel. Even when regulation is designed to achieve such an acceptable purpose, however, the landowner must be allowed a reasonable return or equivalent private use of his property * * * That is, in the case of commercial property, the owner must be assured of a continued reasonable return on the property.

* * *

Grand Central Terminal is no ordinary landmark. It may be true that no property has economic value in the absence of the society around it, but how much more true it is of a railroad terminal, set amid a metropolitan population, and entirely dependent on a heavy traffic of travelers to make it an economically feasible operation. Without people Grand Central would never have been a successful railroad terminal, and without the terminal, a major transportation center, the proposed building site would be much less desirable for an office building.

Of course it may be argued that had Grand Central Terminal never been built, the area would not have developed as it has. Thus, the argument runs, construction of the terminal triggered growth of the area, and created much of the terminal property's current value. Indeed, the argument has some validity. But, in reality, it is of little moment which comes first, the terminal or the travelers. For it is the interaction of economic influences in the greatest megalopolis of the western hemisphere—the terminal initially drawing people to the area, and the society developing the area with shops, hotels, office buildings, and unmatched civil services—that has made the property so valuable. Neither factor alone accounts for the increase in the property's value; both, in tandem, have contributed to the increase.

* * *

To put the matter another way, the massive and indistinguishable public, governmental, and private contributions to a landmark like the Grand Central Terminal are inseparably joint, and for most of its existence, made both the terminal and the railroads of which it was an integral part, a great financial success for generations of stockholders and bondholders. Their investment has long been eliminated or impaired by the recent vicissitudes of the Penn Central complex. It is exceedingly difficult but imperative, nevertheless, to sort out the merged ingredients and to assess the rights and responsibilities of owner and society. A fair return is to be accorded the owner, but society is to receive its due for its share in the making of a once great railroad. The historical, cultural, and architectural resource that remains was neither created solely by the private owner nor solely by the society in which it was permitted to evolve.

* * *

The discussion thus far is in accord with the teachings of Lutheran Church In Amer. v. City of New York, 35 N.Y.2d 121, 359 N.Y.S.2d 7, 316 N.E.2d 305, supra. The Lutheran Church, owner of the landmark site, established, as plaintiffs here have not, that economic considerations did not permit maintenance of the landmark building in its existing form (id., p. 132, 359 N.Y.S.2d p. 16, 316 N.E.2d p. 312). Moreover, the Lutheran Church was a charitable institution which, over the years, did not and could not reap the same pecuniary benefits of massive governmental investment enjoyed by the railroads and Grand Central Terminal. Yet, the regulatory provisions prohibited replacement of the landmark building without any new ameliorative provisions, other than the pre-existing tax exemption to which it had always been entitled, to assure that the property remained capable of usefulness on a reasonable economic basis. The same problem was reached and discussed in Matter of Trustees of Sailors' Snug Harbor v. Platt, 29 A.D.2d 376, esp. p. 378, 288 N.Y.S.2d 314, 316. In recognizing the invalidity of the landmark regulation as applied to *Lutheran Church,* however, this court as had the court in the *Sailors' Snug Harbor* case, supra, declined to strike down the landmarks preservation provisions of the city administrative code * * *. In this case, by contrast, there has been no showing that the property, owned not by a charitable enterprise but by an entity existing to make a profit, is incapable in its economic context of producing a reasonable return, even if its development is limited.

Moreover, plaintiffs have not been wholly deprived of the development rights above the terminal. Those rights have been made transferable to other parcels of land in the vicinity, at least eight of them owned by Penn Central, including the sites of the Biltmore, Commodore, Barclay, and Roosevelt Hotels.

The many defects in New York City's program for development rights transfers have been detailed elsewhere (Costonis, The Chicago Plan: Incentive Zoning and the Preservation of Urban Landmarks, 85 Harv.L.Rev. 574, 585–589). The area to which transfer is permitted is severely limited, complex procedures are required to obtain a transfer permit, and the program, it has been said, has the unfortunate consequence of encouraging large, bulky buildings around landmarks which are dwarfed by comparison. But the possibility that a better program could have been devised does not preclude analysis and justification of the existing one in this particular application.

* * *

* * * Plaintiffs in this case have failed to meet that burden. In none of their analyses do they include the benefits provided to Penn Central's varied real estate holdings by the terminal's operation. These real, albeit indirect, benefits alone might suffice to provide Penn Central with a reasonable return. But there is more. The development rights above Grand Central Terminal have been made transferable, and could be transferred to several sites owned by Penn Central and suitable for office building construction. These substitute rights are valuable, and provide significant, perhaps "fair", compensation for the loss of rights above the terminal itself. Hence, no constitutional violation has been established.

In times of easy affluence, preservation of historic landmarks through use of the eminent domain power might be desirable, or even required. But when a less expensive alternative is available, especially when a city is in financial distress, it should not be forced to choose between witnessing the demolition of its glorious past and mortgaging its hopes for the future. The landmark preservation provisions of the Administrative Code represent an effort to take a middle way (Marcus, Mandatory Development Rights Transfer and the Taking Clause: The Case of Manhattan's Tudor City Parks, 24 Buff.L.Rev. 77, 78, 107–110). The statute needs improvement. In some cases it protects property owners inadequately * * *. But, in its generality and as applied to Grand Central Terminal, the statute does not deprive plaintiffs of due process of law.

* * *

Accordingly, the order of the Appellate Division should be affirmed, with costs.

Notes

1. As noted by Judge Breitel in the principal case, the court had, in 1974, found the landmarks ordinance unconstitutional as applied to the Lutheran Church in America insofar as the commission had refused a permit for demolition of the J.P. Morgan house owned by the church and used as its national headquarters. Judge Breitel was one of the two dissenters in the Lutheran Church case. Note that in Penn Central the court distinguished the Lutheran Church case by drawing a distinction between a charitable property owner which had not received the accumulated economic benefits enjoyed by commercial ventures through surrounding property development. Is that a sufficient distinction to demarcate a valid regulation from a taking? After the Supreme Court affirmed Penn Central, a New York Court upheld the landmark designation of a charitable corporation in a fact situation much like that in Lutheran Church. See Society for Ethical Culture v. Spatt, 68 A.D.2d 112, 416 N.Y.S.2d 246 (1979), affirmed 51 N.Y.2d 449, 434 N.Y.S.2d 932, 415 N.E.2d 922 (1980).

2. Some years after the Penn Central decision the developer of a building site a few blocks from Grand Central Terminal sought a permit for a seventy-four story office building utilizing TDRs from the railroad. Public opposition to the proposal was strong and the commission denied the TDR transfer on the ground that the developer's parcel was not adjacent to the landmarked terminal. In 383 Madison Associates v. City of New York, 193 A.D.2d 518, 598 N.Y.S.2d 180 (1993), appeal dismissed 82 N.Y.2d 748, 602 N.Y.S.2d 806, 622 N.E.2d 307, cert. denied 511 U.S. 1081, 114 S.Ct. 1830, 128 L.Ed.2d 459 (1994) the court sided in part with the commission, rejecting the commission's finding that the proposed building would have a disproportionate impact on the neighborhood, but upholding the finding that even though a pattern of common ownership once joined the parcel with the terminal, because of intervening sales of the parcel in question and also sales of intervening lots by Penn Central, the requisite "adjacency" was broken. The developer had argued that despite the sales of surface lots, underground tracks still connected the parcels.

3. The question of landmark designation for religious structures has been especially controversial. A controversy in New York City over granting air rights development permission to St. Bartholomew's Church on Park Avenue raged for several years with a number of celebrity residents taking sides. A federal district court upheld the landmark designation of the church and the denial of the permit in Rector, Wardens, and Members of the Vestry of St. Bartholomew's Church v. City of New York, 728 F.Supp. 958 (S.D.N.Y. 1989) affirmed 914 F.2d 348 (2d Cir.1990), cert. denied 499 U.S. 905, 111 S.Ct. 1103, 113 L.Ed.2d 214 (1991). In 1987 Chicago amended its landmark ordinance to give owners of religious property the right to veto landmarking of property used for religious worship.

4. The Religious Land Use and Institutionalized Persons Act of 2000 (RLUIPA) (discussed more fully in Chapter VI), may impact the ability of local governments to enforce historic preservation regulations on religious institutions. In Episcopal Student Foundation v. City of Ann Arbor, 341 F.Supp.2d 691 (E.D.Mich.2004), the city's historic commission denied the plaintiff's permit application to demolish its building in order to construct

larger facilities. The court upheld the historic commission's decision against the plaintiff's RLUIPA challenge because it found that it did not constitute a substantial burden on the plaintiff's religious exercise. See also, Noles, "Can Historic Preservation Coexist with Protections for Religious Land Uses?" 17 Nat. Resources & Env't 89 (Fall 2002).

5. A Pennsylvania court upheld landmark designation for the interior as well as the exterior of an art deco movie house in Sameric Corp. of Chestnut St., Inc. v. City of Philadelphia, 125 Pa.Cmwlth. 520, 558 A.2d 155 (1989). When the case got to the Pennsylvania Supreme Court, an opinion was rendered that rejected the landmark ordinance, United Artists Theater Circuit, Inc. v. City of Philadelphia, 528 Pa. 12, 595 A.2d 6 (1991). Shortly thereafter, and after much public criticism, the court granted a reargument in the case. After reargument, the court partially reversed itself and held that the designation of the theater as a historical landmark without the consent of the owners did not constitute a taking; however, the court also held that the Philadelphia ordinance did not authorize designation of the interior of the building as historical. 535 Pa. 370, 635 A.2d 612 (1993). Compare Teachers Insurance and Annuity Ass'n of America v. City of New York, 82 N.Y.2d 35, 603 N.Y.S.2d 399, 623 N.E.2d 526 (1993) (decided one month earlier than the Pennsylvania case) where the court held that designation of the Four Seasons Restaurant inside the Seagram Building as a landmark was within the powers of the Landmark Preservation Commission. The owners argued, without success, that the interior of a restaurant is not the same sort of public space as the interior of a railroad station, which is habitually and customarily open to the public at large, the standard prescribed by the ordinance.

FGL & L PROPERTY CORP. v. CITY OF RYE

Court of Appeals of New York, 1985.
66 N.Y.2d 111, 495 N.Y.S.2d 321, 485 N.E.2d 986.

MEYER, JUDGE.

* * *

Plaintiff is the owner in fee of a parcel of land situated in the City of Rye (City) of approximately 22 acres on which are located the Jay Mansion, built in 1838 by Peter Jay, son of John Jay, the first Chief Justice of the United States Supreme Court, and another building known as the Carriage House, built around 1912 in the Colonial Revival style. There is some dispute between the parties concerning the historic or landmark significance of the Carriage House, but for purposes of this opinion we assume that both buildings have such significance. * * *

* * * In June 1983, the City Council adopted Local Law No. 5–1983, which added a new section 197–13.2 to the City Code creating the Alansten Landmarks Preservation District (LPD–A). As the revised zoning map demonstrates, and defendants do not deny, the only property zoned LPD–A was plaintiff's 22 acres. Plaintiff then began the present action, which in seven causes of action sought an injunction against enforcement of the section, a declaration that it is invalid as ultra vires,

unconstitutional, site specific, spot zoning and not in accordance with a well-considered zoning plan, and money damages under 42 U.S.C.A. § 1983. * * *

The section as enacted declares that in order to provide for flexibility in the City's zoning "so that the significant historic buildings, the Jay Mansion and the Carriage House, and site features which characterize this site * * * are preserved for the future and that new construction be undertaken with care and consideration for these features and the environment", the new district is adopted. Subdivision B establishes standards for the new district, which include that "[t]he lot as approved shall have a minimum area of twenty-two (22) acres and shall be and remain in single ownership"; that "[t]he exterior of the Jay Mansion and Carriage House shall be rehabilitated and the interiors converted to residential use", for the Jay Mansion not to exceed three units and for the Carriage House not to exceed six; that there be a trapezoidal view way 90 feet in width at the rear of the Jay Mansion and 300 feet in width at the southerly property line; that the new dwelling units may not be occupied until the exteriors of the Jay Mansion and the Carriage House have been restored and the interiors converted to residential use and available for occupancy and that a bond be posted to assure such rehabilitation and conversion; and that the application for site plan approval be accompanied by, among other things, a draft condominium offering statement together with a draft of an easement and/or agreement for perpetual maintenance of the exteriors of the Jay Mansion and the Carriage House. Neither the statutes authorizing enactment of zoning provisions nor those dealing with historic landmarks empower the City Council to adopt a local law with such provisions, nor does anything in the Landmarks Preservation chapter of the City Code support its so doing.

* * *

Authority to enact section 197–13.2 of the Code of the City of Rye does not exist, therefore, unless it can be found in the historical preservation provisions contained in section 96–a and article 5–K of the General Municipal Law or the Landmarks Preservation provision of the Rye City Code (ch. 117).

Section 96–a of the General Municipal Law reads as follows: "In addition to any power or authority of a municipal corporation to regulate by planning or zoning laws and regulations or by local laws and regulations, the governing board or local legislative body of any county, city, town or village is empowered to provide by regulations, special conditions and restrictions for the protection, enhancement, perpetuation and use of places, districts, sites, buildings, structures, works of art, and other objects having a special character of special historical or aesthetic interest or value. Such regulations, special conditions and restrictions may include appropriate and reasonable control of the use or appearance of neighboring private property within public view, or both. In any such instance such measures, if adopted in the exercise of the police power, shall be reasonable and appropriate to the purpose, or if constituting a taking of private property shall provide for due compensation, which may include the limitation or remission of taxes." Article 5–K is broader in scope, covering historic preservation not only by regulation but by governmental acquisition as well. Section 119–bb(4) defines "historic preservation" to mean "for the purposes of this article and notwithstanding any other provision of law, the study, designation, protection, restoration, rehabilitation and use of buildings, structures, districts, areas, sites or objects significant in the history, architecture, archeology or culture of this state, its communities, or the nation." The operative provisions of the article are contained in section 119–dd, which is set forth in full in the margin.[17]

Of importance to the present issue is the fact that the regulation, special condition or restriction by which section 119–dd(1) authorizes control of private property is "for the protection, enhancement, perpetuation and use of places, districts, sites, buildings, structures". Nothing in the subdivision speaks to regulation of ownership. Noteworthy also is the fact that though section 119–bb(4) refers to "restoration" and "rehabilitation", those words are not to be found in section 119–dd(1), presumably because it was intended to permit a municipality acting under

17. The section, entitled "Local historic preservation programs," reads as follows:

"In addition to existing powers and authorities for local historic preservation programs including existing powers and authorities to regulate by planning or zoning laws and regulations or by local laws and regulations for preservation of historic landmarks and districts and use of techniques including transfer of development rights, the legislative body of any county, city, town or village is hereby empowered to:

"1. Provide by regulations, special conditions and restrictions for the protection, enhancement, perpetuation and use of places, districts, sites, buildings, structures, works of art and other objects having a special character or special historical, cultural or aesthetic interest or value. Such regulations, special conditions and restrictions may include appropriate and reasonable control of the use or appearance of neighboring private property within the public view, or both.

"2. Establish a landmark or historical preservation board of commission with such powers as are necessary to carry out all or any of the authority possessed by the municipality for a historic preservation program, as the local legislative body deems appropriate.

"3. After due notice and public hearing, by purchase, gift, grant, bequest, devise, lease or otherwise, acquire the fee or any lesser interest, development right, easement, covenant or other contractual right necessary to achieve the purposes of this article, to historical or cultural property within its jurisdiction. After acquisition of any such interest pursuant to this subdivision, the effect of the acquisition on the valuation placed on any remaining private interest in such property for purposes of real estate taxation shall be taken into account.

"4. Designate, purchase, restore, operate, lease and sell historic buildings or structures. Sales of such buildings and structures shall be upon such terms and conditions as the local legislative body deems appropriate to insure the maintenance of the historic quality of the buildings and structures, after public notice is appropriately given at least thirty days prior to the anticipated date of availability and shall be for fair and adequate consideration of such buildings and structures which in no event shall be less than the expenses incurred by the municipality with respect to such buildings and structures for acquisition, restoration, improvement and interest charges.

"5. Provide for transfer of development rights for purposes consistent with the purposes of this article."

section 119–dd(3) after acquisition of a fee or lesser interest to restore and rehabilitate historic buildings and sites, but not to permit the municipality to impose an obligation to restore or rehabilitate such buildings or sites as remain in private ownership. Here the Code sections creating the Alansten Landmarks Preservation District not only mandate that the entire 22–acre district remain in single ownership but also impose upon the developer the duty of rehabilitating the exteriors of the Jay Mansion and the Carriage House, proscribe the use of any new dwelling unit until that has been done, thus effectively requiring that the cost of rehabilitation be shared by owners in the district of units other than the Jay Mansion and the Carriage House, and by dictating condominium ownership of the entire district impose the cost of maintenance of the exteriors of the Mansion and the Carriage House upon owners of such units as well.

The right to impose reasonable controls on the use and appearance of neighboring private property within public view, given by General Municipal Law §§ 96–a and 119–dd(1), cannot be stretched to cover payment of restoration and maintenance costs, for such a construction, which would impose those costs upon every unit in the district, not just those "within public view," would render meaningless the limitation intended by those words which appear in both sections. Yet there is no question that such was the Council's intention, for its findings with respect to the final environmental impact statement flatly stated that "[o]nly under [condominium] ownership can the cost of maintaining the exteriors of the historic buildings be shared by all the homeowners", and that theme is repeatedly emphasized in the City's brief to this court. While that may be true, clearer authorization to enact such provisions than are contained in the General Municipal Law sections referred to is essential before section 197–13.2 can be upheld against the argument that it was beyond the City's power to enact.

Noteworthy also, in view of the requirement that the Mansion and Carriage House be completely restored before any other unit can be occupied is the absence from the General Municipal Law sections of authority to require restoration, as distinct from maintenance. Landmark and historic preservation laws normally prevent alteration or demolition of existing structures unless the owner can demonstrate hardship (*Penn Cent. Transp. Co. v. City of New York,* 42 N.Y.2d 324, 330, 397 N.Y.S.2d 914, 366 N.E.2d 1271, *affd.* 438 U.S. 104, 98 S.Ct. 2646, 57 L.Ed.2d 631), but if they place an undue and uncompensated burden on the individual owner they may be held unconstitutional (*Lutheran Church in Am. v. City of New York,* 35 N.Y.2d 121, 129, 359 N.Y.S.2d 7, 316 N.E.2d 305) because "it forces the owner to assume the cost of providing a benefit to the public without recoupment" (*French Investing Co. v. City of New York,* 39 N.Y.2d 587, 596, 385 N.Y.S.2d 5, 350 N.E.2d 381; *see,* Dunham, *A Legal and Economic Basis For City Planning,* 58 Colum.L.Rev. 650, 665). Here, society at large bears no part of the cost of restoration, it is rather to be borne initially by plaintiff and ultimately by the purchasers of dwelling units within the district. Yet the City's expert appraiser agreed that restoration costs of approximately $627,000 for the Jay Mansion and $588,000 for the Carriage House would be required.

We do not hold that the General Municipal Law sections could not be drafted to impose restoration costs on an owner without violating the Constitution, nor need we reach the question whether as applied to plaintiff's property section 197–13.2 is constitutional. We hold rather that in light of the well-recognized rule that statutes are to be construed so as to avoid constitutional issues if such a construction is fairly possible * * * the General Municipal Law sections under consideration as presently written should be construed not to authorize imposition of restoration costs solely upon plaintiff and purchasers from plaintiff or maintenance costs upon purchasers of properties other than those to be preserved.

* * *

For the foregoing reasons, the order of the Appellate Division declaring Rye City Code § 197–13.2 invalid is affirmed, with costs.

WACHTLER, C.J., and JASEN, SIMONS, KAYE, ALEXANDER AND TITONE, JJ., concur.

Order affirmed, with costs.

Notes

1. After the decision in this case the county board of legislators voted to take the property by eminent domain, and the developer entered into negotiations to sell the property to the county. Although the developer purchased the Jay house and land for $1.1 million in 1983, she set a price of $13.6 million on the property. The county had appraised the property at $6.9 million in 1989 and did not want to pay much more than the appraisal. The county also figured that the cost to rehabilitate the buildings would range from $2 million to $2.5 million and annual maintenance would run about $185,000. Today the Jay Mansion and its carriage house are managed as the Jay Heritage Center, described as "the focal point of the Boston Post Historic District."

2. The use of the police power to designate individual buildings as landmarks has proven to be much more controversial than the designation of areas as historic districts. One obvious reason for the disparate treatment is the view that creation of an historic district usually enhances the value of all the property in the district while the designation of a single building as a landmark usually imposes uncompensated burdens on the property owner. The validity of landmark ordinances has been questioned in several states. The Texas courts have used the constitutional principles of vagueness and unlawful delegation of legislative powers to strike down landmark designation efforts at both the state and local levels. See Texas Antiquities Committee v. Dallas County Community College Dist., 554 S.W.2d 924 (Tex.1977) and Southern Nat'l Bank of Houston v. City of Austin, 582 S.W.2d 229 (Tex.Civ.App.1979). Other cases showing some hostility to landmark preservation (although they do not involve particular ordinances) are Galich v.

Catholic Bishop of Chicago, 75 Ill.App.3d 538, 31 Ill.Dec. 370, 394 N.E.2d 572 (1979) and Hoboken Environment Committee, Inc. v. German Seaman's Mission of New York, 161 N.J.Super. 256, 391 A.2d 577 (1978). An intermediate appellate court upheld denial of a demolition permit for a church building in First Presbyterian Church of York v. City Council of City of York, 25 Pa.Cmwlth. 154, 360 A.2d 257 (1976), but a concurring opinion in the case made the following observation:

> * * * [T]he legislatures and courts are adding a new dimension which may do violence to constitutional private property rights, for now we hold that a private property owner must make his property available without compensation for public view. In effect, he must dedicate his property without compensation for public historical, aesthetic, educational, and museum purposes, which in reality are public uses. Under the provisions of the ordinance in question, the Church can permit the interior or rear portions of its property to rot or deteriorate in a burned condition in any manner it sees fit, but it can't touch that portion of its property viewable from the street without permission of the local governing body, which uses vague standards founded on aesthetics and historical values, two concepts upon which reasonable men can disagree. There are no state health or safety standards involved whatsoever, rather the standards are based solely upon the feelings or observations of people interested in protecting neighboring properties in the historical district in the name of public welfare. I am concerned that we have reached a constitutional precipice and that an advancement of even a fraction of an inch will result in excessive governmental encroachment upon private property rights.
>
> I want to make it clear that I agree with and applaud the scheme to protect, restore, and maintain places of historical value, but if the public wants to use, take, or apply a private property for that public purpose, then the public should pay for that laudatory purpose through constitutional means, e.g., eminent domain. In the past we have accomplished these purposes through parks and museums provided by public funds or the benevolence of private donors. Today we change that trend by our holding and instead provide for the establishment of public museums through restrictions on private property owners' rights. The very thought that the next step may be a governmental regulation that all buildings in York's historical district must be painted colonial blue is to me repugnant to the Constitution, and if anything like that should develop, perhaps that will be the place to draw the line.

Also see Lafayette Park Baptist Church v. Board of Adjustment of City of St. Louis, 599 S.W.2d 61 (Mo.App.1980), which involved a church seeking a demolition permit for a run-down structure it had purchased in order to expand parking facilities. Although the case deals with an historic district rather than a landmark designation, the opinion discusses the just compensation issue and the economics of preservation in a useful manner. Compare: Committee to Save the Bishop's House, Inc. v. Medical Center Hosp. of Vermont, Inc., 137 Vt. 142, 400 A.2d 1015 (1979). Another interesting case is Shubert Organization, Inc. v. Landmarks Preservation Comm'n of the City of New York, 166 A.D.2d 115, 570 N.Y.S.2d 504, appeal denied 79 N.Y.2d 751, 579 N.Y.S.2d 651, 587 N.E.2d 289, cert. denied 504 U.S. 946, 112 S.Ct.

2289, 119 L.Ed.2d 213 (1992). In this case the commission designated forty-five theaters in central Manhattan as landmarks. The plaintiffs challenged the designation on the ground that the mass designation had nothing to do with the individual architectural worth of the theater buildings but was, instead, a back-door effort to create a theater district and to preserve the industry rather than buildings. The court ruled in favor of the designations.

In Prentiss v. City of South Pasadena, 15 Cal.App.4th 85, 18 Cal.Rptr.2d 641 (1993) the court sided with a homeowner whose application for a permit to build an addition was denied because the city concluded the existing house was a "qualified historic structure" and that the city had discretion to require that alterations to the home be done in a manner best preserving the historical character of the architecture. The court agreed that the issuance of a building permit where the application showed compliance with all building codes was a ministerial act, negating any discretionary power to impose conditions on the permit.

Chapter XI

REVIEW BY THE PEOPLE, PARTIES, AND COURTS

SECTION 1. REVIEW BY THE PEOPLE—CONSENT, INITIATIVE AND REFERENDUM

A. INTRODUCTION

When parties are aggrieved by a land use decision, we normally think about their opportunity to seek redress from the courts. We readily understand that the land use decisions of public bodies are subject to judicial review. It is also possible for disgruntled neighbors, in some communities, to invoke consent requirements, for the public to subject legislative actions to popular referendum, and for the involved stakeholders to agree to mediate their disputes over land use decisions. Each of these forms of review is limited by the circumstances and the laws and practice of the state.

As we consider all of the options for reviewing the public body's decision, we are forced to review the nature of that decision, the characteristics of the decision-making entity, and the procedures that agencies follow. In this respect, our studies serve as a useful review of the preceding chapters. Whether the courts will review the legality of a land use decision will depend on whether the matter is ripe, the decision final, and the appeal timely. Were all administrative remedies pursued and exhausted? Was a variance requested? What standards do courts use in reviewing the actions of land use agencies? Does it matter if the decision is a legislative, quasi-judicial, or administrative one? Given the courts' standards of judicial review, am I likely to prevail if I chose the judicial route? Do state statutes provide me and my fellow citizens an opportunity to vote on the matter, that is, to reconsider it via referendum? Do the procedures of the decision-making board allow us and other affected parties to mediate the matter? Once litigation has been initiated, can we still settle the dispute through mediation or other alternative methods of dispute resolution? Will we be required to do so?

The practice varies from state to state with respect to all of these modes of review. Courts exhibit varying degrees of deference to regulatory decisions, legislatures adopt a range of direct democracy options (consent, petition, initiative, referendum, etc.), and administrative procedures and court rules allow for different ADR techniques to be used as a land use application proceeds from its conception, through board decision, to final review and determination.

B. CONSENT BY THE NEIGHBORS

At common law, landowners can bring a private nuisance action to enjoin an offensive use of neighboring land. What happens then, when the zoning ordinance allows, and an administrative body approves, the placement of a use offensive to the neighbors, such as a gasoline station or billboard, in a residential neighborhood? What if the local legislature subjects specified land uses to a requirement that a certain percent of the neighbors consent before those land uses can be approved as a specially permitted use by the planning commission, for example? Is the legislature simply recognizing the common law nuisance rights of neighbors or is it unlawfully delegating its legislative prerogatives to the public in violation of the due process rights of the landowner who is denied the right to build the gasoline station or billboard? Does the zoning enabling law of the state allow this type of delegation of discretionary decision-making?

VALKANET v. CITY OF CHICAGO

Supreme Court of Illinois, 1958.
13 Ill.2d 268, 148 N.E.2d 767.

[Plaintiffs asked for a declaratory judgment in the trial court that they were entitled to a license to operate a home for the aged in an apartment zone. The ordinance required consent by a majority of owners on both sides of the street for the block in which a home for the aged was to be located. Plaintiffs contended this requirement was invalid and did not obtain such consent. The trial court found the requirement void and the city appealed].

DAVIS, CHIEF JUSTICE.

* * * From the complaint and the record of the proceedings below, it appears that the plaintiffs' theory is that the ordinance is void in that it is an illegal delegation of legislative power to private individuals, a deprivation of property without due process of law, and a denial of equal protection of the law.

The defendant contends that the restriction imposed on operating such homes by section 136–6 is a reasonable and proper exercise of police power, and that the consent provision for waiver of the restriction is valid.

Unaided by brief and argument of plaintiffs, we have examined the state of the law concerning the validity of "frontage consent" provisions, and, like McQuillin, have found "a decided difference of judicial view and sometimes of jurisdictional consistency as to the validity of municipal legislation of this character, not entirely explainable by varying provisions of the ordinances or by differing statutory or charter grants of authority." (8 McQuillin, Municipal Corporations, 3rd ed., p. 348.) * * *

An analysis of * * * [our] decisions reveals that we have sustained frontage-consent provisions where the effect was to permit the waiver of a prohibition of a structure, business, trade or occupation properly subject to the police power, such as livery stables, saloons, garages and billboards. Spies v. Board of Appeals, 337 Ill. 507, 513, 169 N.E. 220. Yet we have consistently held that a municipality cannot deprive a citizen of a valuable property right under the guise of prohibiting or regulating some business or occupation which has no tendency to injure the public health or morals, or interfere with the general welfare. Spies v. Board of Appeals, 337 Ill. 507, 169 N.E. 220; People ex rel. Deitenbeck v. Village of Oak Park, 331 Ill. 406, 163 N.E. 445; People ex rel. Friend v. City of Chicago, 261 Ill. 16, 103 N.E. 609.

The prevailing view concerning such consent provisions is illustrated by two leading decisions of the United States Supreme Court. The first, Eubank v. City of Richmond, 226 U.S. 137, 33 S.Ct. 76, 57 L.Ed. 156, held invalid an ordinance allowing two thirds of the abutting property owners in the block to establish a set-back line, on the ground that such enactment was, in effect, legislative action by the property owners without the benefit of any standard for the exercise of such power, and therefore an improper delegation of a legislative function. Cf. Gorieb v. Fox, 274 U.S. 603, 47 S.Ct. 675, 71 L.Ed. 1228. The second decision, Thomas Cusack Co. v. City of Chicago, 242 U.S. 526, 37 S.Ct. 190, 61 L.Ed. 472, involved a billboard ordinance in language similar to the ordinance before us. It absolutely prohibited billboards in certain districts, but permitted the restriction to be modified with the consent of the persons most affected. The court, at Thomas Cusack Co. v. City of Chicago, 242 U.S. 526, 531, 37 S.Ct. 190, 61 L.Ed. 472, 476, in distinguishing the Eubank case, said:

> "The one ordinance permits two thirds of the lot owners to impose restrictions upon the other property in the block, while the other permits one-half of the lot owners to remove a restriction from the other property owners. This is not a delegation of legislative power, but is, as we have seen a familiar provision affecting the enforcement of laws and ordinances."

While the Cusack decision has been criticized, (University of Illinois 1954 Law Forum, 309, 311–312,) it has been generally followed. And, even though it is impossible to lay down a hard-and-fast rule, we conclude that if an ordinance permits a certain percentage of the property owners to impose or create a restriction upon their neighbors' property by the device of consent provisions, such limitation constitutes an invalid delegation of legislative power, but if the consent provision merely waives or modifies a lawful and reasonable legislative restriction or prohibition, it is within constitutional limitations. (2 Metzenbaum, Law of Zoning, 2d ed., p. 1067; 8 McQuillin, Municipal Corporations, 3rd ed., page 348, sec. 25.151; 1 Yokley, Zoning Law, p. 201, sec. 89; Anno: 21 A.L.R.2d 551 et seq.) It follows that the consent provisions of section 136–6 of the code are not an invalid delegation of legislative power. However, this does not determine that its proscription of homes for the aged is a reasonable exercise of the police power. The cases in which we have upheld prohibitions that might be waived by consent provisions have dealt with uses the location of which have a strong tendency to injure public health or morals or affect the general welfare, and have the general characteristics of a nuisance, such as saloons, Swift v. People ex rel. Ferris Wheel Co., 162 Ill. 534, 44 N.E. 528, junk shops, Smolensky v. City of Chicago, 282 Ill. 131, 118 N.E. 410, garages, People ex rel. Busching v. Ericsson, 263 Ill. 368, 105 N.E. 315, and billboards, Thomas Cusack Co. v. City of Chicago, 267 Ill. 344, 108 N.E. 340, affirmed in 242 U.S. 526, 37 S.Ct. 190, 61 L.Ed. 472. There is no showing in this record that homes for the aged are offensive to the health, morals and welfare of the community. The property in question is located in the "apartment house" use district which includes "boarding or lodging house, hotels, hospital home for dependents or nursing home." Defendant urges that such homes are properly subject to the police power, citing Father Basil's Lodge, Inc. v. City of Chicago, 393 Ill. 246, 65 N.E.2d 805 but in that case we merely held that a municipality had the power to regulate and license the establishment of homes for the aged for the purpose of protecting the health and safety of the occupants thereof. We refrained from passing upon the validity of the frontage-consent provisions of the ordinance, since we found such provisions to be severable and without application to the appellant.

The case most analogous to the facts here is State of Washington ex rel. Seattle Title Trust Co. v. Roberge, 278 U.S. 116, 49 S.Ct. 50, 73 L.Ed. 210. There an ordinance, similar to the one before us, prohibited erection of homes for the aged in a "first residence district" unless two thirds of the property owners within 400 feet of the proposed site gave their consent in writing. The court held this restriction violative of due process, State of Washington ex rel. Seattle Title Trust Co. v. Roberge, 278 U.S. 116, 121, 49 S.Ct. 50, 73 L.Ed. 210, 213, and stated: "Legislatures may not, under the guise of the police power, impose restrictions that are unnecessary and unreasonable upon the use of private property or the pursuit of useful activities. * * * The facts disclosed by the record make it clear that the exclusion of the new home from the first district is not indispensable to the general zoning plan. And there is no legislative determination that the proposed building and use would be inconsistent with public health, safety, morals or general welfare. The enactment itself plainly implies the contrary. The grant of permission for such building and use, although purporting to be subject to such consents, shows that the legislative body found that the construction and maintenance of the new home was in harmony with the public interest and with the general scope and plan of the zoning ordinance."

In its opinion the court also distinguished Thomas Cusack Co. v. City of Chicago, 242 U.S. 526, 37 S.Ct. 190, 61 L.Ed. 472, relied on by defendant, on the ground that the facts there were sufficient to warrant the conclusion that billboards were liable to endanger the safety and decency of the district involved and held that a home for the aged is clearly distinguishable "from such billboards or other uses which by reason of their nature are liable to be offensive." 278 U.S. 122, 49 S.Ct. 47, 73 L.Ed. 214.

Similar results have been reached in cases involving an "old ladies home," Women's Kansas City St. Andrew Society v. Kansas City, Mo., 58 F.2d 593, a church, State ex rel. Roman Catholic Bishop of Reno v. Hill, 59 Nev. 231, 90 P.2d 217, a retail store, Spies v. Board of Appeals, 337 Ill. 507, 169 N.E. 220, and a school, Concordia Collegiate Institute v. Miller, 301 N.Y. 189, 93 N.E.2d 632, 21 A.L.R.2d 544. Defendant has not cited, nor have we found, any case upholding the exclusion of homes for the aged from a use district similar to the one in question, either by application of frontage-consent provisions or otherwise. Defendant, however, urges that Shepard v. City of Seattle, 59 Wash. 363, 109 P. 1067, is analogous to the case at bar. We cannot agree. The court there upheld an ordinance which declared insane asylums to be a public nuisance, and provided for their abatement as such, subject to the written consent of any property owner within 200 feet. Such ordinance, which contained a legislative finding that the proposed use is a public nuisance, is clearly inapposite here. State of Washington ex rel. Seattle Title Trust Co. v. Roberge, 278 U.S. 116, 122, 73 L.Ed. 210, 214.

In the case at bar there is neither legislative finding that the proposed use is a public nuisance, or that it is apt to be such when operated in an apartment-house use district, nor satisfactory evidence tending to show that the maintenance of the home will work an injury, annoyance or inconvenience to any property owner. On the contrary, the general zoning plan of the city of Chicago declares a nursing home to be appropriate in an apartment-house-use district. The record fails to disclose a rational basis for subjecting homes for the aged to the requirement of frontage consents and is without evidence to support a conclusion that the proposed use has any different effect on the public health, welfare, safety and morals than the other permitted uses in the district.

Since we find no basis for the exercise of the police power in prohibiting the home for the aged in the apartment-house-use district, the ordinance as applied to this proposed use is an unconstitutional deprivation of property without due process of law. Spies v. Board of Appeals, 337 Ill. 507, 169 N.E. 220; State of Washington ex rel. Seattle Title Trust Co. v. Roberge, 278 U.S. 116, 49 S.Ct. 50, 73 L.Ed. 210. Accordingly, the judgment of the trial court is affirmed.

Judgment affirmed.

Notes

1. In Drovers Trust & Sav. Bank v. Chicago, 18 Ill.2d 476, 165 N.E.2d 314 (1960), a property owner and business person faced a neighbors' consent provision similar to the one found in *Valkanet*. The property owner wished to erect a gas station in a part of town zoned for commercial uses, and specifically permitting gas stations. However, a separate zoning ordinance prohibited the installation of storage tanks storing flammable liquids without a supportive neighbors' consent vote. This time, the Supreme Court of Illinois decided to do away with all such neighbors' consent laws: "Since *Valkanet* we have given the matter further study and feel that the subtle distinction between 'creating' and 'waiving' a restriction cannot be justified. Each constitutes an invalid delegation of legislative power where the ordinances, as here, leave the ultimate determination of whether the erection of the station would be detrimental to the public welfare in the discretion of individuals rather than the city."

2. In Cary v. City of Rapid City, 559 N.W.2d 891 (S.D.1997), the Supreme Court of South Dakota held that a protest statute was unconstitutional which allowed 40 percent of neighboring property owners to file a written protest that would completely bar the rezoning of property. The court noted that the statute allowed "a potentially small number of neighboring property owners to make the ultimate determination of the public's best interest."

3. In Town of Gardiner v. Stanley Orchards, Inc., 105 Misc.2d 460, 432 N.Y.S.2d 335 (1980), the court held invalid a provision in an ordinance which prohibited mobile homes unless all landowners within 500 feet consented in writing, and in Grendel's Den, Inc. v. Goodwin, 495 F.Supp. 761 (D.Mass. 1980), affirmed sub nom. Larkin v. Grendel's Den, 459 U.S. 116, 103 S.Ct. 505, 74 L.Ed.2d 297 (1982), the court struck down a state statute which provided that no premises within 500 feet of a church or school could receive a liquor license if the church or school filed a written objection. In both cases the courts discussed the problem of delegating legislative authority to private landowners. The latter case further discusses the Establishment Clause issue raised when a church, specifically, is given the authority to make land use decisions.

4. In Luger v. City of Burnsville, 295 N.W.2d 609 (Minn.1980), the court reversed a local decision to grant the property owner a variance "subject to letters of approval by all abutting property owners." The court indicated that a local zoning agency could not avoid the political implications of its decisions by such a transfer of power to the neighbors. Also, in Lakin v. City of Peoria, 129 Ill.App.3d 651, 84 Ill.Dec. 837, 472 N.E.2d 1233 (1984), the court held that requiring the applicant for a variance to obtain the consent of adjoining and abutting neighbors was an unconstitutional delegation of legislative authority.

5. New York's highest court struck down a village ordinance requiring the consent of 80 percent of the property owners in the neighborhood before a permit could be issued to an educational institution in a residential zoning district. The court held that the provision violated the Fourteenth Amendment of the Constitution of the United States because the neighbors could veto the as-of-right use by taking no action, unguided and unrestricted by

legislative standards. Had the use in question been a potential nuisance, however, the court might have found otherwise. It said: "In the case now before us, we are not dealing with billboards or garages or other offensive uses in connection with which consent provisions may be proper." Concordia Collegiate Institute v. Miller, 301 N.Y. 189, 93 N.E.2d 632 (1950).

C. THE INITIATIVE AND REFERENDUM PROCESS

Constitutions of the 50 states delegate the police power to state legislatures. The elected representatives of the people of the state are given the authority to adopt laws necessary to protect the public health, safety, welfare, and morals. Zoning enabling laws are enacted as one example of the exercise of this police power. In some states, the legislature has seen fit to give some of this legislative authority back to the people. At the local level, citizens may be authorized to enact land use regulations by initiative or to subject local legislative zoning decisions to review by referendum. Both initiative and referendum proceedings are begun by voter petitions which must follow the procedural and time prescriptions of state law.

The judicial questions that arise in this context are whether state law allows local citizens initiative or referendum rights and, when the answer is yes, whether the particular objective of the initiative or referendum is within the authority granted to citizens to act on by direct democratic means. A key inquiry here is often whether it matters that the decision subjected to popular vote is a legislative one, such as the adoption of a zoning law or amendment, or one that is administrative or quasi-judicial in nature, such as the issuance of a variance, special use permit, or zoning interpretation. The cases examine a range of nuts and bolts issues, as well, such as whether the petitions were properly drafted, submitted in a timely fashion, signed by a sufficient number of registered voters, and properly presented to the electorate.

CITY OF EASTLAKE v. FOREST CITY ENTERPRISES, INC.

Supreme Court of the United States, 1976.
426 U.S. 668, 96 S.Ct. 2358, 49 L.Ed.2d 132.

MR. CHIEF JUSTICE BURGER delivered the opinion of the Court.

The question in this case is whether a city charter provision requiring proposed land use changes to be ratified by 55% of the votes cast violates the due process rights of a landowner who applies for a zoning change.

The City of Eastlake, Ohio, a suburb of Cleveland, has a comprehensive zoning plan codified in a municipal ordinance. Respondent, a real estate developer, acquired an eight-acre parcel of real estate in Eastlake zoned for "light industrial" uses at the time of purchase.

In May 1971, respondent applied to the City Planning Commission for a zoning change to permit construction of a multifamily, high-rise apartment building. The Planning Commission recommended the proposed change to the City Council, which under Eastlake's procedures could either accept or reject the Planning Commission's recommendation. Meanwhile, by popular vote, the voters of Eastlake amended the city charter to require that any changes in land use agreed to by the Council be approved by a 55% vote in a referendum.[1] The City Council approved the Planning Commission's recommendation for reclassification of respondent's property to permit the proposed project. Respondent then applied to the Planning Commission for "parking and yard" approval for the proposed building. The Commission rejected the application, on the ground that the City Council's rezoning action had not yet been submitted to the voters for ratification.

Respondent then filed an action in state court, seeking a judgment declaring the charter provision invalid as an unconstitutional delegation of legislative power to the people. While the case was pending, the City Council's action was submitted to a referendum, but the proposed zoning change was not approved by the requisite 55% margin. Following the election, the Court of Common Pleas and the Ohio Court of Appeals sustained the charter provision.

The Ohio Supreme Court reversed. 41 Ohio St.2d 187, 324 N.E.2d 740 (1975). Concluding that enactment of zoning and rezoning provisions is a legislative function, the court held that a popular referendum requirement, lacking standards to guide the decision of the voters, permitted the police power to be exercised in a standardless, hence arbitrary and capricious manner. Relying on this Court's decisions in Washington ex rel. Seattle Title Trust Co. v. Roberge, 278 U.S. 116, 49 S.Ct. 50, 73 L.Ed. 210 (1928), Thomas Cusack Co. v. Chicago, 242 U.S. 526, 37 S.Ct. 190, 61 L.Ed. 472 (1917), and Eubank v. Richmond, 226 U.S. 137, 33 S.Ct. 76, 57 L.Ed. 156 (1912), but distinguishing James v. Valtierra, 402 U.S. 137, 91 S.Ct. 1331, 28 L.Ed.2d 678 (1971), the court concluded that the referendum provision constituted an unlawful delegation of legislative power.

We reverse.

The conclusion that Eastlake's procedure violates federal constitutional guarantees rests upon the proposition that a zoning referendum involves a delegation of legislative power. A referendum cannot, however, be characterized as a delegation of power. Under our constitutional

1. As adopted by the voters, Art. VIII, § 3, of the Eastlake City Charter provides in pertinent part:

> "That any change to the existing land uses or any change whatsoever to any ordinance * * * cannot be approved unless and until it shall have been submitted to the Planning Commission, for approval or disapproval. That in the event the city council should approve any of the preceding changes, or enactments, whether approved or disapproved by the Planning Commission it shall not be approved or passed by the declaration of an emergency, and it shall not be effective, but it shall be mandatory that the same be approved by a 55% favorable vote of all votes cast of the qualified electors of the City of Eastlake at the next regular municipal election, if one shall occur not less than sixty (60) or more than one hundred and twenty (120) days after its passage, otherwise at a special election falling on the generally established day of the primary election * * *."

assumptions, all power derives from the people, who can delegate it to representative instruments which they create. See, e.g., The Federalist No. 39 (J. Madison). In establishing legislative bodies, the people can reserve to themselves power to deal directly with matters which might otherwise be assigned to the legislature. Hunter v. Erickson, 393 U.S. 385, 392, 89 S.Ct. 557, 561, 21 L.Ed.2d 616 (1969).

The reservation of such power is the basis for the town meeting, a tradition which continues to this day in some States as both a practical and symbolic part of our democratic processes. The referendum, similarly, is a means for direct political participation, allowing the people the final decision, amounting to a veto power, over enactments of representative bodies. The practice is designed to "give citizens a voice on questions of public policy." James v. Valtierra, supra, 402 U.S., at 141, 91 S.Ct., at 1333.

In framing a state constitution, the people of Ohio specifically reserved the power of referendum to the people of each municipality within the State.

* * *

To be subject to Ohio's referendum procedure, the question must be one within the scope of legislative power. The Ohio Supreme Court expressly found that the City Council's action in rezoning respondent's eight acres from light industrial to high-density residential use was legislative in nature. Distinguishing between administrative and legislative acts, the court separated the power to zone or rezone, by passage or amendment of a zoning ordinance, from the power to grant relief from unnecessary hardship. The former function was found to be legislative in nature. * * *

The Ohio Supreme Court further concluded that the amendment to the city charter constituted a "delegation" of power violative of federal constitutional guarantees because the voters were given no standards to guide their decision. Under Eastlake's procedure, the Ohio Supreme Court reasoned, no mechanism existed, nor indeed could exist, to assure that the voters would act rationally in passing upon a proposed zoning change. This means that "appropriate legislative action [would] be made dependent upon the potentially arbitrary and unreasonable whims of the voting public." 41 Ohio St.2d, at 195, 324 N.E.2d, at 746. The potential for arbitrariness in the process, the court concluded, violated due process.

* * *

In basing its claim on federal due process requirements, respondent also invokes Euclid v. Ambler Realty Co., 272 U.S. 365, 47 S.Ct. 114, 71 L.Ed. 303 (1926), but it does not rely on the direct teaching of that case. Under *Euclid,* a property owner can challenge a zoning restriction if the measure is "clearly arbitrary and unreasonable, having no substantial relation to the public health, safety, morals, or general welfare." Id., at 395, 47 S.Ct., at 121. If the substantive result of the referendum is arbitrary and capricious, bearing no relation to the police power, then the fact that the voters of Eastlake wish it so would not save the restriction. * * *

But no challenge of the sort contemplated in Euclid v. Ambler Realty is before us. The Ohio Supreme Court did not hold, and respondent does not argue, that the present zoning classification under Eastlake's comprehensive ordinance violates the principles established in Euclid v. Ambler Realty. If respondent considers the referendum result itself to be unreasonable, the zoning restriction is open to challenge in state court, where the scope of the state remedy available to respondent would be determined as a matter of state law, as well as under Fourteenth Amendment standards. That being so, nothing more is required by the Constitution.

Nothing in our cases is inconsistent with this conclusion. Two decisions of this Court were relied on by the Ohio Supreme Court in invalidating Eastlake's procedure. The thread common to both decisions is the delegation of legislative power, originally given by the people to a legislative body, and in turn delegated by the legislature to a *narrow segment* of the community, not to the people at large. In Eubank v. Richmond, 226 U.S. 137, 33 S.Ct. 76, 57 L.Ed. 156 (1912), the Court invalidated a city ordinance which conferred the power to establish building setback lines upon the owners of two-thirds of the property abutting any street. Similarly, in Washington ex rel. Seattle Title Trust Co. v. Roberge, 278 U.S. 116, 49 S.Ct. 50, 73 L.Ed. 210 (1928), the Court struck down an ordinance which permitted the establishment of philanthropic homes for the aged in residential areas, but only upon the written consent of the owners of two-thirds of the property within 400 feet of the proposed facility.[2]

Neither *Eubank* nor *Roberge* involved a referendum procedure such as we have in this case; the standardless delegation of power to a limited group of property owners condemned by the Court in *Eubank* and *Roberge* is not to be equated with decisionmaking by the people through the referendum process. The Court of Appeals for the Ninth Circuit put it this way:

> "A referendum, however, is far more than an expression of ambiguously founded neighborhood preference. It is the city itself

2. The Ohio Supreme Court also considered this Court's decision in Thomas Cusack Co. v. Chicago, 242 U.S. 526, 37 S.Ct. 190, 61 L.Ed. 472 (1917). In contrast to *Eubank* and *Roberge,* the *Cusack* Court *upheld* a neighborhood consent provision which permitted property owners to waive a municipal restriction prohibiting the construction of billboards. This Court in *Cusack* distinguished *Eubank* in the following way:

> "[The ordinance in *Eubank*] left the establishment of the building line untouched until the lot owners should act and then * * * gave to it the effect of law. The ordinance in the case at bar absolutely prohibits the erection of any billboards * * * but permits this prohibition to be modified with the consent of the persons who are to be most affected by such modification." 242 U.S., at 531, 37 S.Ct. at 192.

Since the property owners could simply waive an otherwise applicable legislative limitation, the Court in *Cusack* determined that the provision did not delegate legislative power at all. Ibid.

legislating through its voters—an exercise by the voters of their traditional right through direct legislation to override the views of their elected representatives as to what serves the public interest." Southern Alameda Spanish Speaking Organization v. Union City, California, 424 F.2d 291, 294 (1970).

Our decision in James v. Valtierra, upholding California's mandatory referendum requirement, confirms this view. Mr. Justice Black, speaking for the Court in that case, said:

> This procedure ensures that *all the people* of a community will have a voice in a decision which may lead to large expenditures of local governmental funds for increased public services * * *. 402 U.S., at 143, 91 S.Ct., at 1334 (emphasis added).

Mr. Justice Black went on to say that a referendum procedure, such as the one at issue here, is a classic demonstration of "devotion to democracy * * *." Id., at 141. As a basic instrument of democratic government, the referendum process does not, in itself, violate the Due Process Clause of the Fourteenth Amendment when applied to a rezoning ordinance.[3] Since the rezoning decision in this case was properly reserved to the people of Eastlake under the Ohio Constitution, the Ohio Supreme Court erred in holding invalid, on federal constitutional grounds, the charter amendment permitting the voters to decide whether the zoned use of respondent's property could be altered.

The judgment of the Ohio Supreme Court is reversed, and the case is remanded for further proceedings not inconsistent with this opinion.

Reversed and remanded.

[A dissenting opinion by MR. JUSTICE POWELL is omitted.]

MR. JUSTICE STEVENS, with whom MR. JUSTICE BRENNAN joins, dissenting.

* * *

A zoning code is unlike other legislation affecting the use of property. The deprivation caused by a zoning code is customarily qualified by recognizing the property owner's right to apply for an amendment or variance to accommodate his individual needs. The expectancy that particular changes consistent with the basic zoning plan will be allowed frequently and on their merits is a normal incident of property ownership. When the governing body offers the owner the opportunity to seek such a change—whether that opportunity is denominated a privilege or a

3. The fears expressed in dissent rest on the proposition that the procedure at issue here is "fundamentally unfair" to landowners; this fails to take into account the mechanisms for relief potentially available to property owners whose desired land use changes are rejected by the voters. First, if hardship is occasioned by zoning restrictions, *administrative* relief is potentially available. Indeed, the very purpose of "variances" allowed by zoning officials is to avoid "practical difficulties and unnecessary hardship." 8 E. McQuillan, Municipal Corporations § 25.159, p. 511 (3d ed. 1965). As we noted, *supra,* at 677, remedies remain available under the Ohio Supreme Court's holding and provide a means to challenge unreasonable or arbitrary action. Euclid v. Ambler Realty Co., 272 U.S. 365, 47 S.Ct. 114, 71 L.Ed. 303 (1926).

right—it is affording protection to the owner's interest in making legitimate use of his property.

The fact that an individual owner (like any other petitioner or plaintiff) may not have a legal right to the relief he seeks does not mean that he has no right to fair procedure in the consideration of the merits of his application. The fact that codes regularly provide a procedure for granting individual exceptions or changes, the fact that such changes are granted in individual cases with great frequency, and the fact that the particular code in the record before us contemplates that changes consistent with the basic plan will be allowed, all support my opinion that the opportunity to apply for an amendment is an aspect of property ownership protected by the Due Process Clause of the Fourteenth Amendment.

* * *

Although this Court has decided only a handful of zoning cases, literally thousands of zoning disputes have been resolved by state courts. Those courts have repeatedly identified the obvious difference between the adoption of a comprehensive citywide plan by legislative action and the decision of particular issues involving specific uses of specific parcels. In the former situation there is generally great deference to the judgment of the legislature; in the latter situation state courts have not hesitated to correct manifest injustice.

* * *

Specialists in the practice of zoning law are unhappily familiar with the potential for abuse which exists when inadequate procedural safeguards apply to the dispensation of special grants. The power to deny arbitrarily may give rise to the power to exact intolerable conditions.[4] The insistence on fair procedure in this area of the law falls squarely within the purpose of the Due Process Clause of the Fourteenth Amendment.

* * *

As the Justices of the Ohio Supreme Court recognized, we are concerned with the fairness of a provision for determining the right to make a particular use of a particular parcel of land. In such cases, the state courts have frequently described the capricious character of a

4. One expert on zoning matters has made the following comment:

"The freedom from accountability of the municipal governing body may be tolerable in those cases where the legislature is engaged in legislating but it makes no sense where the legislature is dispensing or refusing to dispense special grants. When the local legislature acts to pass general laws applicable generally it is performing its traditional role and it is entitled to be free from those strictures we place upon an agency that is charged with granting or denying special privileges to particular persons. When the municipal legislature crosses over into the role of hearing and passing on individual petitions in adversary proceedings it should be required to meet the same procedural standards we expect from a traditional administrative agency." R. Babcock, The Zoning Game 158 (1966). Compare this comment with the practice of another "zoning man." See United States v. Staszcuk, 517 F.2d 53, 56 (C.A.7 1975).

decision supported by majority sentiment rather than reference to articulable standards. Moreover, they have limited statutory referendum procedures to apply only to approvals of comprehensive zoning ordinances as opposed to amendments affecting specific parcels. This conclusion has been supported by characterizing particular amendments as "administrative" and revision of an entire plan as "legislative."

In this case the Ohio Supreme Court characterized the Council's approval of respondent's proposal as "legislative." I think many state courts would have characterized it as "administrative." The courts thus may well differ in their selection of the label to apply to this action, but I find substantial agreement among state tribunals on the proposition that requiring a citywide referendum for approval of a particular proposal like this is manifestly unreasonable. Surely that is my view.

* * *

I have no doubt about the validity of the initiative or the referendum as an appropriate method of deciding questions of community policy. I think it is equally clear that the popular vote is not an acceptable method of adjudicating the rights of individual litigants. The problem presented by this case is unique, because it may involve a three-sided controversy, in which there is at least potential conflict between the rights of the property owner and the rights of his neighbors, and also potential conflict with the public interest in preserving the city's basic zoning plan. If the latter aspect of the controversy were predominant, the referendum would be an acceptable procedure. On the other hand, when the record indicates without contradiction that there is no threat to the general public interest in preserving the city's plan—as it does in this case, since respondent's proposal was approved by both the Planning Commission and the City Council and there has been no allegation that the use of this eight-acre parcel for apartments rather than light industry would adversely affect the community or raise any policy issue of citywide concern—I think the case should be treated as one in which it is essential that the private property owner be given a fair opportunity to have his claim determined on its merits.

As Justice Stern points out in his concurring opinion, it would be absurd to use a referendum to decide whether a gasoline station could be operated on a particular corner in the city of Cleveland. The case before us is not that clear because we are told that there are only 20,000 people in the city of Eastlake. Conceivably, an eight-acre development could be sufficiently dramatic to arouse the legitimate interest of the entire community; it is also conceivable that most of the voters would be indifferent and uninformed about the wisdom of building apartments rather than a warehouse or factory on these eight acres. The record is silent on which of these alternatives is the more probable. Since the ordinance places a manifestly unreasonable obstacle in the path of every property owner seeking any zoning change, since it provides no standards or procedures for exempting particular parcels or claims from the referendum requirement, and since the record contains no justification for the use of the procedure in this case, I am persuaded that we should respect the state judiciary's appraisal of the fundamental fairness of this decisionmaking process in his case.

I therefore conclude that the Ohio Supreme Court correctly held that Art. VIII, § 3, of the Eastlake charter violates the Due Process Clause of the Fourteenth Amendment, and that its judgment should be affirmed.

Notes

1. On remand, the Ohio Supreme Court found no state constitutional issues in the case and dismissed the proceedings. Forest City Enterprises v. City of Eastlake, 48 Ohio St.2d 47, 356 N.E.2d 499 (1976). In Jurkiewicz v. Butler County Bd. of Elections, 85 Ohio App.3d 503, 620 N.E.2d 146 (1993), the court held that a change of zoning to planned unit development was a legislative act and thus subject to referendum.

2. The U.S. Supreme Court reinforced Eastlake in City of Cuyahoga Falls v. Buckeye Community Hope Foundation, 538 U.S. 188, 123 S.Ct. 1389, 155 L.Ed.2d 349 (2003). The city planning commission approved a site plan application for a multifamily, low-income housing complex, finding that the development was permitted under the zoning law of the city. The city council, by ordinance, approved the project, which was vigorously opposed by local citizens. After the council's approval, a group of citizens filed a formal petition with the city requesting that the ordinance be repealed or submitted to a popular vote. This had the effect, under Ohio law, of staying the approval and the non-profit developer was denied its application for a building permit. The approval was submitted to a local referendum that then passed. The Ohio Supreme Court held the referendum unconstitutional because the state constitution allows only legislative acts, not administrative acts, to be subject to referendums. The Supreme Court, in an opinion written by Justice O'Connor, reversed stating:

> As a matter of federal constitutional law, we have rejected the distinction that respondents ask us to draw, and that the Ohio Supreme Court drew as a matter of state law, between legislative and administrative referendums. In *Eastlake v. Forest City Enterprises, Inc.,* 426 U.S., at 672, 675, 96 S.Ct. 2358, we made clear that because all power stems from the people, "[a] referendum cannot * * * be characterized as a delegation of power," unlawful unless accompanied by "discernible standards." The people retain the power to govern through referendum " 'with respect to any matter, legislative or administrative, within the realm of local affairs.' " *Id.,* at 674, n. 9,. Cf. *James v. Valtierra,* 402 U.S., at 137, 91 S.Ct. 1331. Though the "substantive result" of a referendum may be invalid if it is "arbitrary and capricious," *Eastlake v. Forest City Enterprises, supra,* at 676, respondents do not challenge the referendum itself. The subjection of the site-plan ordinance to the City's referendum process, regardless of whether that ordinance reflected an administrative or legislative decision, did not constitute *per se* arbitrary government conduct in violation of due process.

In Land Use Law & Zoning Dig., July 2003 pp. 3–14 six commentators reflect on the Buckeye decision, under the general title, "The Tyranny of the Majority." Most of the commentaries are critical of the decision.

3. In James v. Valtierra, 402 U.S. 137, 91 S.Ct. 1331, 28 L.Ed.2d 678 (1971), relied on in the principal case, the Court upheld a California constitutional provision which provided that no low-rent public housing project could be developed unless approved by referendum in the community. The California Supreme Court held, in DeVita v. County of Napa, 9 Cal.4th 763, 38 Cal.Rptr.2d 699, 889 P.2d 1019 (1995), that voters could amend a comprehensive plan by use of the initiative and could, in that amended plan, provide that any land use designations enacted by initiative can only be changed during the following 30 years by majority vote of the county electorate. The purpose and effect of the amended plan was to keep land designated as agricultural or open space in those categories for 30 years, unless voters agreed to change.

4. By holding that the federal constitution does not inhibit mandatory referenda in zoning cases, the Court is essentially leaving the issue to state law and state court determination. Some state courts have held that a zoning amendment is not subject to referendum because a zoning amendment is quasi-judicial or administrative in nature and is not a legislative act. See Leonard v. City of Bothell, 87 Wash.2d 847, 557 P.2d 1306 (1976). Also see Copple v. Lincoln, 210 Neb. 504, 315 N.W.2d 628 (1982) which overruled Kelley v. John, 162 Neb. 319, 75 N.W.2d 713 (1956) and deemed rezoning a legislative act, subject to referendum. Compare Arnel Development Co. v. City of Costa Mesa, 28 Cal.3d 511, 169 Cal.Rptr. 904, 620 P.2d 565 (1980), where the court held that the enactment or amendment of a zoning ordinance is a legislative act even if it affects only a small area or a few landowners and is subject to the initiative and referendum provisions of the state constitution. On remand, the Court of Appeals found the initiative arbitrary and discriminatory as it was directed at one developer. 126 Cal. App.3d 330, 178 Cal.Rptr. 723 (1981).

A majority of states find rezonings to be legislative. See State ex rel. Hickman v. City Council of Kirksville, 690 S.W.2d 799 (Mo.App.1985); Florida Land Co. v. City of Winter Springs, 427 So.2d 170 (Fla.1983); Wright v. City of Lakewood, 43 Colo.App. 480, 608 P.2d 361 (1979), cf. Margolis v. District Ct., County of Arapahoe, 638 P.2d 297 (Colo.1981); Schanz v. City of Billings, 182 Mont. 328, 597 P.2d 67 (1979) ("A rezoning ordinance, like a zoning ordinance is a legislative enactment"), Greens at Fort Missoula, LLC v. City of Missoula, 271 Mont. 398, 897 P.2d 1078 (1995) (rezoning ordinance subject to referendum); Albright v. City of Portage, 188 Mich.App. 342, 470 N.W.2d 657 (1991); R. G. Moore Building Corp. v. Committee for the Repeal of Ordinance R(C)–88–13, 239 Va. 484, 391 S.E.2d 587 (1990); Garvin v. Ninth Judicial District, 118 Nev. 749, 59 P.3d 1180 (2002) (sustaining the use of initiative for zoning amendments, and holding that a sustainable growth initiative measure was legislation, and not an administrative act). In Kirschenman v. Hutchinson County Board of Commissioners, 656 N.W.2d 330 (S.D.2003), the Supreme Court of South Dakota held that a conditional use permit allowing a hog confinement facility was a legislative rather than administrative act and thus subject to referendum. The court found that the lack of objective criteria for granting the permit in the county ordinance made the board's actions discretionary.

5. The application of initiative and referendum mechanisms to local land use decisions is offensive to some. After all, the law provides for the adoption of a comprehensive plan with citizen participation, the adoption of conforming zoning following public hearings, and public involvement in most site specific land use decisions. In 1991, the Urban, State and Local Government Law Section of the American Bar Association approved a recommendation to the ABA House of Delegates regarding the problem reflected in the City of Eastlake situation. Part A of the recommendation was that the ABA recommend: "That all state legislatures adopt legislation prohibiting the use of the initiative/referendum in 'site specific' zoning cases." Part B urged state legislatures in states with initiative and referendum provisions to adopt legislation prohibiting general land-use policy proposals from being submitted for initiative or referendum unless the proposal conforms with the comprehensive plan or amends such plan. For an explanation of the reasons for the proposals see 14 Urban, State and Local Law Newsletter, No. 3, Spring 1991 (American Bar Association). Apparently, at the House of Delegates meeting, August 12–13, 1991, the section report (No. 111) on site-specific zoning referenda and initiatives (Part A) was withdrawn by the proponents. ABA, Summary of Action of the House of Delegates, 1991 Annual Meeting. Why do you suppose Part A was withdrawn? What are the pros and cons of the use of referenda to review land use decisions?

6. A distinction is frequently made between use of the initiative to adopt a zoning ordinance and the use of a referendum to subject a zoning decision to the electorate for approval or rejection. Many courts have held that an initiated zoning ordinance is improper because of conflict with the state zoning enabling legislation which usually requires notice and hearing prior to adoption of a zoning ordinance. However, in Oregon, a 1974 case holding the initiative process inapplicable to zoning, Tatum v. Clackamas County, 19 Or.App. 770, 529 P.2d 393 (1974), was overruled in Allison v. Washington County, 24 Or.App. 571, 548 P.2d 188 (1976). Ohio has long held that zoning ordinances or amendments are subject to initiative. Drockton v. Board of Elections, 16 Ohio Misc. 211, 240 N.E.2d 896 (1968). Also see Queen Creek Land & Cattle Corp. v. Yavapai County Bd. of Supervisors, 108 Ariz. 449, 501 P.2d 391 (1972), discussing initiative as a right under the state constitution.

Hawaii allows referenda on zoning ordinances: County of Kauai v. Pacific Standard Life Insurance, 65 Hawaii 318, 653 P.2d 766 (1982). However, the state Supreme Court has held that zoning by initiative is inconsistent with comprehensive planning: Kaiser Hawaii Kai Development Co. v. City and County of Honolulu, 70 Hawaii 480, 777 P.2d 244 (1989). New Jersey's Municipal Land Use Act prohibits zoning by initiative and referendum. N.J.S.A. 40:55D–62. A non-binding referendum to determine public sentiment about a proposed zoning amendment is permitted. See Great Atlantic & Pacific Tea Co. v. Borough of Point Pleasant, 137 N.J. 136, 644 A.2d 598 (1994). In I'On, L.L.C. v. Town of Mt. Pleasant, 338 S.C. 406, 526 S.E.2d 716 (2000), the South Carolina Supreme Court quoted the New Jersey Supreme Court: "Zoning ordinances touch people where they live. Sensitive to the intense public interest in local land use development, the

Legislature has developed an orderly structure for public participation in the process. That process also contemplates the rational development of land use, free from undue political influence." The South Carolina court held that, under the state's detailed comprehensive planning and enabling legislation, the state legislature "has not condoned—and we should not approve—a process by which voters could circumvent this deliberative process by deciding zoning matters in an initiative and referendum process."

SECTION 2. MEDIATION

A. AN INTRODUCTION TO LAND USE MEDIATION

As early as 1886, the New York Legislature recognized the importance of mediation in resolving conflicts in collective bargaining disputes. In this context, mediation was conceived not as an alternative to litigation but as a means of preventing labor strikes and the societal disruptions they cause. By 1925, mediation was being used in New York City in court-related conciliation programs as a cost-effective means of resolving cases through conciliation rather than adjudication.

In this early period, the lesson of mediation was that consensus-based compromise was an effective method of producing mutually satisfying results to critical disputes in society and to particular quarrels among individuals. By the 1970s, the field of alternative dispute resolution had emerged, sparked by the interest of jurists in caseload management. In 1982, Chief Justice Burger warned that we had "reached a period where our system of justice may literally break down before the end of the century..." He called for a "fresh, hard look" at alternative methods of dispute resolution.

At the time the Chief Justice spoke, community-based mediation programs were emerging as a productive method of resolving disputes among community members who had to live with one another in shared environments. More recently, mediation has been embraced by corporation counsel in large companies as a method of achieving settlement based on sound business practices rather than strict legal standards. Today, federal and state agencies are experimenting with mediation as a method of developing consensus on pending regulations and of resolving disputes that arise in the administrative process of issuing development and environmental permits. Mediation is beginning to be used at the local level in a variety of land use and environmental contexts.

The first significant land use dispute employing alternative dispute resolution took place in Washington State in 1974. In order to settle a dispute over the proposed location of a flood control dam on the Snoqualmie River, two mediators facilitated a discussion among opposing parties. Environmental advocates opposed the project's proponents because of their concern over the survival of the river's ecosystem; farmers were concerned about proposed reductions in water for irrigation; and citizens worried about the potential for uncontrolled suburban sprawl. Although the dam was never constructed, many of the land use recommendations that were agreed to among the parties were implemented, and a coordinating council formed by the stakeholders continued operating for 10 years.

As it has evolved, mediation has been defined in a variety of ways and has developed a range of applications and approaches about which there is vigorous debate. It has remained vibrant, however, as a voluntary, consensus-based conflict prevention and resolution strategy. It is a non-predictive method that leaves the outcomes to its participants. In essence, it is a negotiation-assisting process that works when the contestants believe that settlement is a better alternative than protracted hostility or the winner-take-all results of litigation.

The Consensus Building Institute (CBI) and the Lincoln Institute of Land Policy undertook a study in 1999 of mediated land use disputes based on interviews with participants in 100 cases in which a professional neutral assisted in the resolution of a land use dispute. This study indicated that 85 percent of participants had a positive view of assisted negotiation. Additionally, of respondents who participated in cases that were settled, 92 percent believed that their own interests were well served by the settlement and 86 percent believed that all parties' interests were served by the agreement reached.

(1) Land Use Approvals as Negotiations

When a landowner submits an application for a development permit to a local land use agency, an extended process of negotiation is initiated. The parties to this negotiation are the owner, the members of the local administrative agency with approval authority, other involved public agencies, and those affected by the proposed project: neighbors, taxpayers, and citizens of the community. Unlike commercial and personal negotiations, this process is not viewed by most of its participants as a negotiation, in the traditional sense. Local zoning ordinances give the landowner property rights that must be respected. State and local statutes prescribe standards and procedures that the agency members must follow. Affected neighbors and citizens receive notice of their right to attend and speak at one or more public hearings. This process is not organized, in most localities, as a structured negotiation in which the parties meet face-to-face, follow a self-determined process of decision-making, and arrive at a mutually acceptable agreement based on facts gathered in the process and compromise on all sides.

The local development approval process often costs the applicant significant sums of money, involves only indirect contacts among interested parties, and provides little opportunity to develop creative, win-win solutions. For most significant development proposals, the process is lengthy, inflexible, and frustrating. The outcomes are unpredictable and relationships among those involved are more often damaged than strengthened. Nonetheless, during the awkward journey of a development proposal through the local approval process, critical interests of many stakeholders in the matter are expressed, heard, considered, and disposed of by a decision rendered by a voluntary board of local citizens. This is, in the classic sense, a negotiation that resolves, if not satisfies, each participant's interests. When it is seen as such, methods of making it more productive, satisfying, and efficient seem obvious.

Although mediation is described as a dispute *resolution* technique, it is also an effective means of *avoiding* disputes in the land use area. Often, when a developer seeks approval of a project from a local board, the public may not become involved in the process until the public hearing stage. By this time, the developer may have invested substantial time, money, and energy in the proposal and have become highly invested in it. Due to this investment, the developer may resist suggested changes, more so than if those suggestions had been made earlier. Public hearings and public comment periods, which occur in the later stages of project review, often result in requests to modify the proposal significantly.

Mediation may be employed to bring the interested parties together much earlier in the process, so that a project's design accommodates the concerns of as many of the interested parties as possible. Introduced at this point, mediation influences the developer's application, resulting in early amendments to plans based on the results achieved in mediation. Disputes that arise later in the land use approval process may be resolved through mediation as well. When the local government allows the parties to mediate these differences as and when they occur, they are provided with an opportunity to explore a variety of ways of realizing the objectives of all interested parties.

(2) Mediators and Facilitators

Mediation is properly understood as negotiation assisted by a third party who is usually a neutral. Professional mediators can be called in when the parties to a dispute recognize that they have a dispute, understand the importance of mediated resolution, and can agree upon, and have the resources to pay, a neutral mediator. Where these conditions do not exist, someone involved in the local matter may come forward and attempt to structure a process that results in a facilitated decision, using the techniques of the experienced mediator. The alternative to traditional mediation or structured facilitation is for the parties to proceed at arms length through the local decision-making process and to risk litigation by those not satisfied by it.

Facilitators and mediators are process experts who carefully structure multi-party negotiations. They are skilled in effective negotiation and decision-making processes. They help by bringing involved parties together, building trust, clearly establishing the interests of those involved, serving as intermediaries, seeing that options to the resolution of the matter are generated, and working toward a settlement that is acceptable to all parties.

Mediated proceedings are usually informal and flexible, allow the parties to structure the decision-making process itself, and result in consensus-based settlements that are not binding on the participants or public bodies. When the agreement is based on the consensus of all affected parties, supported by credible facts, and consistent with regulatory standards, it can be highly influential in determining the administrative review body's decision on a development proposal.

(3) Broader Applications

Mediation has been used in recent years as a method of building consensus regarding public policies and formulating land use plans and regulations. In this context, mediation techniques assist parties with disparate interests to participate in a productive public decision-making process. In the land use field, this can involve developing a comprehensive land use plan, recognizing the scope of an environmental impact study of a proposed project, determining how to rezone a community, a landscape, or a neighborhood, and coming to agreement regarding specific development proposals advanced by a land developer during the permit issuance process.

Illustrations of this use of mediation methods include the Negotiated Rulemaking Act (5 USC § 581), the Administrative Dispute Resolution Act (Pub. L. No. 101–552), and the U.S. Department of Labor's Negotiated Rulemaking Handbook (1992) at the federal level. Several state legislatures have adopted statutes establishing negotiated rulemaking processes. (Fla. Stat. § 120.54; Neb. Rev. Stat. §§ 84–919.01 et seq.; Idaho Code §§ 67–5206(3)(c), 67–5220; 1993 Or. Laws 647; Mont. Code Ann. § 2–5–101; Tex. Govt. Code ch. 2008).

B. KEY STEPS IN THE MEDIATION PROCESS

(This section is included with permission from Lawrence Susskind and Alexis Gensberg, *The Important Role of Consensus Building in Planning for Smart Growth* (Jan. 28, 2002).)

The consensus-building process by which such agreements can be negotiated has five basic steps. The first is called ***convening***. A sponsoring or convening body (usually a governmental agency) must initiate a discussion about whether or not to have a consensus building dialogue. This is best done by commissioning a mediator or some other "professional neutral" to talk privately with the obvious stakeholders to see if they have sufficient reason to support such an effort. Such consultations usually lead to the preparation of a draft conflict assessment (a written report) mapping the views and interests of all the relevant stakeholders. The stakeholders must be interviewed individually, but not for attribution. A summary of their interests (and the points of agreement and disagreement among them) will help to clarify whether it is worth trying to bring them all together in an extended (public) dialogue. In addition, if there appears to be sufficient interest in initiating a dialogue, the conflict assessment can then be used to generate a work plan, timetable, operating ground rules, budget, and an outline of the data or technical material that needs to be gathered. A conflict assessment also contains the neutral's suggestion regarding the categories of stakeholders that ought to be represented in the dialogue, as well as an indication of which groups or individuals might actually be invited (by the convenor) to participate. The neutral may also be called upon to caucus the various categories of stakeholders to help them choose their spokespeople. Finally, during Pre–Negotiations, the mediator may be asked to develop joint fact finding proposals, identify potential technical consultants or advisors to the full group, assist in fund raising, and even help to train the participants in negotiation techniques.

The tasks of the mediator stretch from the behind-the-scenes "Pre–Negotiation" work crucial to launching a consensus-building process, through the facilitation of face-to-face interaction when the parties finally come to the table, to the "Post–Negotiation" dynamics of helping to implement whatever agreement is reached. Only someone with the requisite skill, experience, and credibility can "add value" in such politically-charged circumstances.

The second step in the consensus-building process is ***clarifying responsibilities***. Assuming the parties decide to proceed, it will be necessary to select a facilitator or mediator as well as a recorder. The responsibilities of each of these "helpers" is usually spelled out in a contract between the neutral providing such services and the participants in the process. Face-to-face dialogue in a consensus building process usually takes place in a public forum. Thus, rules must be set regarding the participation (if any) of observers. The ground rules spelling out the role of each stakeholder representative must also be initialed by the participants and often by their organizational leadership. Technical consultants, selected to assist with any joint fact-finding, work for the group as a whole and are coordinated by the facilitator or the mediator.

The third step in the process involves ***deliberating***. This can be a daunting challenge for groups that involve 25 or more participants. It falls to the facilitator or mediator to ensure that each face-to-face session is professionally managed. An agenda (approved by all participants) must be prepared prior to each meeting. Often sub-committees of participants (assisted by external experts agreed to by everyone involved) prepare reports on specific issues laying out options or arguments for the full group to consider. Deliberations are most effective when the "invention" of options or packages spelling out possible ways of meeting the conflicting interests of the stakeholders are explored independently of any final decisions. Ultimately, what has come to be known as "a single text procedure" can be used to synthesize the views expressed during the "inventing" phase of deliberations as the parties seek to reach agreement on suggested actions. A single text procedure usually takes advantage of the neutral party who can introduce a working draft of an agreement for parties to discuss and revise.

When the parties are face-to-face, during the deliberation and decision-making phases of the consensus-building process, the mediator is expected to manage the brainstorming process, coordinate the drafting of options, and generate a single text that offers a draft written agreement that the group can work to enhance. Often, a mediator meets privately with each party to identify and test possible trades or "packages." A mediator can even help the participants present proposed agreements to their respective constituencies, ensuring that all representatives have been in touch with the groups or individuals they are supposed to represent. Finally, during this phase of the consensus-building process, a mediator may serve as a point of contact with the media or approach outsiders on behalf of the group, seeking assistance of various kinds.

The fourth step in a consensus building-process, ***deciding***, is handled quite differently from what most people are used to in public policy-making settings. The goals are to (1) maximize joint gains, not merely to find a minimally acceptable (i.e., lowest common denominator) agreement; (2) formulate a set of suggestions that can be adopted by consensus, rather than to vote on something that pleases only a majority; and (3) pursue a process of conversation that clarifies the reasons that people want or don't want to support a particular proposal, so that group problem-solving becomes easier. Consensus does not necessarily mean unanimity, but it does mean overwhelming agreement in response to the question, "Who can live with this?" In a consensus-building dialogue, participants are responsible not only for presenting their own views but for suggesting ways of meeting the interests of others as well.

The final step involves a focus on ***implementing agreements***. The product of most consensus-building efforts in the growth management field is a proposal that must still be approved by elected or appointed agencies or officials. It is not appropriate to substitute ad hoc decision-making for the formal (and accountable) judgment of duly appointed boards or officials. Yet, since officials are the ones serving as convenors of the consensus-building process, their staff often participate in the process and the mediator or facilitator routinely keeps the officials updated about the group's progress. The final product of the group is a proposal that is often sent to officials via the mediator or facilitator. Decision-makers are almost always eager to know what they could recommend that would satisfy all the stakeholders involved and to learn what the product of informed discussion and debate (as opposed to the emotion-laden outbursts at a traditional public hearing) might be.

The implementation phase of a consensus-building process involves finding ways of linking the informal agreement to the formal mechanisms of decision-making. For example, a negotiated agreement may still have to be acted upon by an administrative agency. A mediator may be asked to approach the relevant elected or appointed officials on behalf of the group (even if those agencies were represented at the staff level at the table). Mediators are often "written into" agreements to serve as monitors of on-going efforts at implementation or given a mandate to reassemble the participants if some aspect of the agreement goes awry.

C. MEDIATION STATUTES

Mediation may be used to address land use disputes regardless of whether there is specific legislative authorization. However, the existence of legislative authority serves several purposes. Among other things, statutory provisions provide guidance and encouragement for the appropriate use of mediation; offer a suggested framework and time frame; and inform the public of the right to request mediation. Laws authorizing or prescribing mediation can exist at either the local, state, or federal level.

Land use mediation of various types is authorized by statute in about two dozen states. Mediation may be authorized for very specific issues such as regional impact development projects, border disputes between local governments, or decisions on land use applications. The point at which mediation is encouraged or required varies under these laws from early in the development approval process until after a project decision is made and litigation has been initiated. At least twelve states[5] offer some type of mediation or dispute resolution services to assist parties mediate in the land use context. Some state mediation statutes use the word mediation but describe a process that it is not completely voluntary so is more akin to arbitration. About half of the statutes are directed to the resolution of a specific type of issue, an example being reuse of a military base.[6] Fourteen states authorize mediation for regional planning disputes.[7] These statutes define procedures for the adoption of plans such as a comprehensive plan, or a plan for growth management or for water quality. These statutes require notice to and authorize intervention by a neighboring government before a plan is adopted.

A number of states have statutes that recognize and define a mediation procedure for land use disputes between a private individual and a government body.[8] These procedures are voluntary and arise in the context of the application for a land use permit. The greatest distinction among the statutes that authorize mediation of land use applications is the point at which mediation is authorized. In Maine and Florida, mediation is authorized after a final decision on the application is rendered, and in California, Connecticut, and Oregon mediation is not expressly authorized until after a court action has been filed. Idaho, Pennsylvania, and Hawaii,[9] provide for mediation once an application for a land use proposal is submitted for approval; that is, before a final decision is rendered on the application. Under these proceedings, involved and affected parties have the opportunity to influence modifications to a project before it is approved by the governing authority.

5. CO, DE, GA, ME, MN, NJ, NY, OR, PA, UT, VT, WA.

6. Cal. Gov't Code § 65050.

7. CA, CO, DE, FL, GA, HI, MN, NJ, OK, OR, PA, TN, VT, WA.

8. CA, CT, FL, ID, ME, OR, PA. Utah and Virginia have dispute resolution procedures but are not included in the count because Utah's statute is purely for takings claims, and Virginia's statute was only adopted in 2002 legislation and so far there are no codified statutes that utilize such process.

9. Hawaii's statute is unique. It is listed as a regional planning statute because it applies specifically to applications for geothermal development, and not to development proposals in general. Hawaii's statute differs from the other regional planning statutes in that it allows a private person to participate in the mediation as a party. The Hawaii statute authorizes a mediation proceeding on a particular issue raised at a public hearing in the context of a geothermal development proposal.

Most of these statutes address several basic mediation issues:[10]

- How does a mediation proceeding affect the applicable time limits?
- Who qualifies to participate?
- What rules of evidence apply to the mediation proceedings?
- How are the costs allocated?

In California, Connecticut, and Oregon, the law provides for mediation only after a court action is filed. A notice of mediation stays the appeal. In Florida and Maine, mediation tolls the time for seeking judicial review. The toll period is 165 days in Florida and the parties may extend the toll, while in Maine the maximum toll is 120 days. The deadlines regarding decisions on pending applications are tolled in Idaho and Pennsylvania. In Pennsylvania, the time limits are suspended as agreed by the parties, including the land use approval body.

Each of these statutes stipulates that representations and evidence obtained through the mediation proceedings are not admissible in subsequent litigation. Where a state or local agency is involved in an official way, open meetings laws may be triggered; in these proceedings statements made are not confidential and are admissible in litigation. In Oregon, the parties can overrule the default provision and agree that the proceedings are admissible. The statutes vary as to the admissibility of the final report of the mediator. In Connecticut and Maine, the final report can become part of the court's record. In Florida, the Special Master's report is a public record, and likewise in Pennsylvania the final written report is admissible.

Pennsylvania's statute is an example of a brief yet complete land use mediation statute.

PENNSYLVANIA STATUTES
TITLE 53. MUNICIPAL AND QUASI–MUNICIPAL CORPORATIONS
PART I. GENERAL MUNICIPAL LAW
CHAPTER 30. PLANNING AND DEVELOPMENT
ARTICLE IX. ZONING HEARING BOARD AND OTHER ADMINISTRATIVE PROCEEDINGS

53 P.S. § 10908.1 (2002)

§ 10908.1. Mediation option

(a) Parties to proceedings authorized in this article and Article X–A may utilize mediation as an aid in completing such proceedings. In proceedings before the zoning hearing board, in no case shall the zoning hearing board initiate mediation or participate as a mediating party. Mediation shall supplement, not replace, those procedures in this article and Article X–A once they have been formally initiated. Nothing in this section shall be interpreted as expanding or limiting municipal police powers or as modifying any principles of substantive law.

10. The California statute does not mention cost allocation.

(b) Participation in mediation shall be wholly voluntary. The appropriateness of mediation shall be determined by the particulars of each case and the willingness of the parties to negotiate. Any municipality offering the mediation option shall assure that, in each case, the mediating parties, assisted by the mediator as appropriate, develop terms and conditions for:

(1) Funding mediation.

(2) Selecting a mediator who, at a minimum, shall have a working knowledge of municipal zoning and subdivision procedures and demonstrated skills in mediation.

(3) Completing mediation, including time limits for such completion.

(4) Suspending time limits otherwise authorized in this act, provided there is written consent by the mediating parties, and by an applicant or municipal decision making body if either is not a party to the mediation.

(5) Identifying all parties and affording them the opportunity to participate.

(6) Subject to legal restraints, determining whether some or all of the mediation sessions shall be open or closed to the public.

(7) Assuring that mediated solutions are in writing and signed by the parties, and become subject to review and approval by the appropriate decision making body pursuant to the authorized procedures set forth in the other sections of this act.

(c) No offers or statements made in the mediation sessions, excluding the final written mediated agreement, shall be admissible as evidence in any subsequent judicial or administrative proceedings.

The following California case illustrates how mediation provisions can be insinuated into the local land use decision-making and dispute resolution process by local law.

KUCERA v. LIZZA

Court of Appeal, First District, Division 2, California, 1997.
59 Cal.App.4th 1141, 69 Cal.Rptr.2d 582.

LAMBDEN, ASSOCIATE JUSTICE.

We consider the validity of an ordinance of the Town of Tiburon which preserves views and sunlight against unreasonable obstruction by tree growth. Gilbert and Heidi Kucera, owners of an apartment building, used the ordinance to attempt resolution of a dispute with neighboring apartment building owner Tiberio Lizza over eight Monterey Pines which had grown to obstruct their view. Reaching no resolution through less formal procedures dictated by the ordinance, they brought this superior court action against Lizza, also under the ordinance, to compel restoration of their views.

The case presented the trial court with issues of whether the obstruction was unreasonable under the ordinance and, more fundamentally, whether the ordinance was invalid. In a bifurcated trial on stipulated facts, the court gave judgment for Lizza on the latter ground. It held the ordinance unconstitutional and "void as (1) preempted by state law governing the creation of servitudes and land burdens, and (2) an arbitrary and unreasonable exercise of police power.

* * *

The ordinance, entitled "View and Sunlight Obstruction from Trees," comprises chapter 15 of the Tiburon Municipal Code. Its purpose is to establish "the right of persons to preserve views or sunlight which existed at any time since they purchased or occupied a property from unreasonable obstruction by the growth of trees" (§ 15–1.A.) and "a process" to seek "restoration" of views and sunlight (§ 15–1B).

* * *

The ordinance grants persons "the right to preserve and seek restoration of views or sunlight which existed at any time since they purchased or occupied a property, when such views or sunlight are from the primary living area or active use area and have subsequently been unreasonably obstructed by the growth of trees." (§ 15–3.) Concomitantly, "No person shall plant, maintain, or permit to grow any tree which unreasonably obstructs the view from, or sunlight reaching, the primary living area or active use area of any other parcel of property" within the town (§ 15–4(a)). Prescribed procedures must be followed to establish rights under the ordinance, but private parties also retain their "right to seek remedial action for imminent danger" caused by trees. (§ 15–3.)

The ordinance defines pertinent [criteria] for determining what constitutes an "unreasonable obstruction" [and guidance for appropriate] "Restorative Action" to resolve a tree dispute (§ 15–2). [T]he ordinance favors "aggressive action" for "Undesirable Trees": "By reason of their tall height at maturity, rapid growth, dense foliage, shallow root structure, flammability, break ability, or invasiveness, certain types of trees have been deemed 'undesirable' by the Town, including Blue Gum Eucalyptus, Coast Redwood, Monterey Pine, Monterey Cypress trees, or any other tree which generally grows more than 3 feet per year in height and is capable of reaching a height of over 35 feet at maturity. When considering restorative action for 'undesirable' trees, aggressive action is preferred." (§ 15–8.)

The ordinance imposes a progression of informal and alternative dispute resolution before resort to litigation. "Initial Reconciliation" calls for written notice to and personal discussions with the tree owner plus community association assistance, the aim being a mutually agreeable solution. Failing in that, the party must propose voluntary mediation, which is informal and cannot yield binding orders under the ordinance. (§ 15–9.) Should mediation fail or be declined by the tree owner, the party must present the owner with a written claim containing specified evidence and proposed restorative action (§ 15–10) and offer voluntary, binding arbitration. The aim is a written report by the agreed arbitrator containing findings on unreasonable obstruction and restorative action. (§ 15–11.) Costs of mediation and arbitration are shared equally unless the participants agree otherwise or empower the mediator or arbitrator to allocate costs. Costs of restorative action are set by mutual agreement, mediation or arbitration, as the case may be. (§ 15–13.)

Should the owner decline binding arbitration, "then civil action may be pursued by the Complaining Party for resolution of the view or sunlight obstruction dispute under the rights and provisions of this Chapter." (§ 15–12) Copies of "the lawsuit" and any order or settlement are filed with the town attorney (§ 15–12), and costs of litigation and restorative action are determined by the court or by settlement (§ 15–13).

According to the stipulated facts, Lizza purchased his property in 1978 and the Kuceras theirs in 1990. Lizza's is across the street and downhill from the Kuceras', and trees on his property have grown, since the Kuceras purchased their property, to obstruct their views of San Francisco Bay and the Marin County mainland from primary living or active use areas. The ordinance was passed in December 1991. The Kuceras initiated the ordinance's informal dispute resolution process in June 1992 and have satisfied all of its procedures. Lizza refused to participate in mediation (or, evidently, arbitration). He had no use or building or other land entitlement applications pending in Tiburon.

* * *

The [trial court found the ordinance invalid and] gave judgment for Lizza. [After finding the locality could validly regulate views and sunlight using the means employed, the appellate court reversed. The validity of the mediation provisions was not challenged or discussed.]

Notes

1. Mediation can be encouraged and enabled by the local government through the creation of local land use mediation laws such as the Tiburon ordinance. In most states, there is no general state law that expressly permits or preempts the adoption of a local land use mediation law of this type. There are, however, general state laws that require local land use agencies to follow specific procedures and respect discrete timetables when an application for a land use approval is filed. A local mediation law modifies these timetables to accommodate effective mediation of the interests implicated by the proposal. For example, in New York, state statutes allow local governments to alter, or supersede, these procedures and the time requirements contained in state law or, with the consent of the parties, to suspend the deadlines involved in a specific land use proceeding.

2. Unlike Tiburon's view and sunlight protection ordinance, which *requires* the party seeking relief to propose mediation, most land use ordinances involving mediation encourage mediation as a *voluntary* tech-

nique for resolving land use disputes. For example, in Bainbridge Island, Washington, the Municipal Code provides that "[l]and use mediation is an optional, voluntary method for the resolution of contested land use applications and code enforcement." What are the advantages and disadvantages of requiring mediation versus incorporating mediation as an alternative option for resolving land use disputes? Are there certain situations where one method would be preferable to the other?

3. In City of New London v. University of Connecticut, 1994 WL 65316, 11 Conn. L. Rptr. 133, Sup. Conn. Super., (Feb. 24, 1994), the defendants sought to establish an HIV research project in New London, which had the third highest per capita AIDS rate in the state. When defendants met and discussed the project with members of New London's planning and zoning commission they were informed that under the present zoning regulations the research facility was prohibited. Shortly thereafter the city obtained a temporary injunction against the defendants. In dissolving the temporary injunction and ordering the parties to prepare the case for the trial, the court noted that "it is both wasteful and doubly unfortunate for two governmental bodies to litigate this issue of great public significance; rather, the court urges them to earnestly pursue a resolution of this matter by way of negotiation and mediation."

D. MEDIATION BEFORE A LAND USE APPLICATION IS MADE

Mediation too soon or too late in the maturation of a dispute is problematic. Early in the land use development process, for example, the parties affected by a proposed development may not be identified or may not realize the nature of their affected interest. They are less likely, however, to have developed the distrust that plagues attempts to mediate disputes late in the process after the parties have developed rigid positions and a palpable dislike for one another. In the case that follows, the county land use authority successfully secured the participation of critical players and developed some consensus regarding a very dramatic development project even before an official application was made.

SANTA MARGARITA AREA RESIDENTS v. SAN LUIS OBISPO COUNTY BOARD OF SUPERVISORS

Court of Appeal, Second District, Division 6, California, 2000.
84 Cal.App.4th 221, 100 Cal.Rptr.2d 740.

PERREN, J.

* * *

The Santa Margarita Ranch (Ranch) consists of approximately 13,-800 acres of real property in San Luis Obispo County. The owner of the Ranch, Santa Margarita Limited, has long desired to develop the Ranch. Santa Margarita Area Advisory Council, a community organization, has opposed the development. After Santa Margarita Limited sued the County to facilitate development by increasing the number of legal parcels in the Ranch, Santa Margarita Limited, the County, and representatives of the Santa Margarita Area Advisory Council agreed to mediate their differences over long-range development of the Ranch. The mediation achieved a consensus among most of the participants, including representatives from the Santa Margarita Area Advisory Council. A mediation report reflecting the consensus recommended approval of a project which would include 550 housing units and non-residential improvements in an 1,800 acre area, devote at least 8,400 acres to permanent open space easements, and place a minimum of 3,600 acres under 40–year Williamson Act contracts for preservation of agricultural land.[11] The report also recommended use of a development agreement to guarantee that the 550 residential units would be "subject to applicable laws and regulations."

Shortly after the mediation, the County began preparing a development agreement with Santa Margarita Limited for the specific planning of a project which would include the improvements and other land uses specified in the mediation report and which also designated a golf course, guest lodge, equestrian center, bikeways, and parklands as non-residential improvements (Project). At the same time, the County amended part of its general plan, the Salinas River Area Plan, to describe the Project and establish certain criteria for its ultimate implementation.

After lengthy negotiations and a public hearing, the County enacted an ordinance authorizing it to enter into the development agreement (Agreement). The next day, the chairperson of the County's Board of Supervisors signed the Agreement.

In general, the Agreement freezes zoning on the Project property in return for the developer's commitment to submit a specific plan for construction in compliance with County land use requirements. Contingencies and further approvals remain, but the Agreement commits the County and Santa Margarita Limited to the Project, including its public improvements and amenities.

Specifically, the Agreement provides that Santa Margarita Limited will file a comprehensive application for approval of the Project, including a specific plan, a vesting tentative map, and an environmental impact report. The specific plan must incorporate the standards set forth in the Salinas River Area Plan. The application must state that Santa Margarita Limited will commit itself to develop the Project in its entirety and to engage in all necessary environmental review. The Agreement also provides that Santa Margarita Limited will dedicate land for a public swimming pool, sewer treatment plant, and cemetery expansion.

In return for these commitments, the County agrees to process, review, and approve or disapprove the specific plan, and to apply its current zoning and other land use regulations to the plan without

11. The Williamson Act, section 51200 et seq., permits local governments to enter into contracts limiting the use of land to agricultural purposes in return for preferential tax treatment. (*Kelsey v. Colwell* (1973) 30 Cal.App.3d 590, 592, 106 Cal. Rptr. 420.)

change for up to five years during the review and approval period.[12] The Agreement is entered into under the authority of the Development Agreement Statute and satisfies its technical requirements.

The Agreement does not give Santa Margarita Limited a right to construct the Project or impose upon it an obligation to do so. Rather, the Agreement contemplates a second development agreement pertaining to the actual construction of the Project, and requires that the County and Santa Margarita Limited "will make a good faith effort to negotiate a Subsequent Development Agreement that shall, if agreed upon, provide [Santa Margarita Limited] with a vested right to the benefits and burdens of the Project." It provides that the parties "ultimately seek to secure ... an enforceable arrangement" allowing construction, but neither party "obligates itself to benefit or burden the Project Site with the above-described Project until such time as a Final EIR is certified, the Specific Plan application is favorably acted upon by the County, [and] the Subsequent Development Agreement ... becomes binding on the parties...."

The development agreement statute permits a city or county to "enter into a development agreement" with any property owner "for the development of the property." (§ 65865, subd. (a).) In essence, the statute allows a city or county to freeze zoning and other land use regulation applicable to specified property to guarantee that a developer will not be affected by changes in the standards for government approval during the period of development. (*City of West Hollywood v. Beverly Towers, Inc.* (1991) 52 Cal.3d 1184, 1193, fn. 6, 278 Cal.Rptr. 375, 805 P.2d 329; *Citizens for Responsible Government v. City of Albany* (1997) 56 Cal.App.4th 1199, 1213, 66 Cal.Rptr.2d 102.) In the words of the statute, "[u]nless otherwise provided by the development agreement, rules, regulations, and official policies governing permitted uses of the land, governing density, and governing design, improvement, and construction standards and specifications, applicable to development of the property subject to a development agreement, shall be those rules, regulations, and official policies in force at the time of execution of the agreement." (§ 65866.)

The statute declares that "lack of certainty in the approval of development projects can result in a waste of resources, escalate the cost of housing and other development to the consumer, and discourage investment in and commitment to comprehensive planning which would make maximum efficient utilization of resources at the least economic cost to the public." (§ 65864, subd. (a).) The statute reflects the Legislature's conclusion that giving "[a]ssurance to the applicant for a development project that upon approval of the project, the applicant may proceed with the project in accordance with existing policies, rules and regulations, and subject to conditions of approval, will strengthen the public planning process, encourage private participation in comprehen-

12. The Agreement provides for a five-year term with a two-year extension in the event of litigation concerning the Agreement. Although this lawsuit may trigger the two-year extension, we will refer to the Agreement as having a five-year term.

sive planning, and reduce the economic costs of development." (§ 65864, subd. (b).)

Particulars of the statute include requirements that a development agreement may be approved only after a public hearing (§ 65867) and must be consistent with the general plan and any specific plan (§ 65867.5), a provision permitting annual review by the governmental entity and termination for noncompliance (§ 65865.1), and a statement that the agreement is subject to referendum (§ 65867.5). The statute also specifies certain provisions which may or must be included in a development agreement. (§ 65865.2.)

Appellants contend that the Agreement is invalid under the statute because the statute permits a development agreement only after a project has been approved for actual construction. Appellants claim that, without a fully-designed and approved project, the Agreement is essentially a unilateral County agreement to freeze zoning without obtaining any public benefits in return.

Appellants interpret the statute and the Agreement too narrowly. The statute is best served through a liberal construction which encompasses agreements that substantially comply with its specific terms and conditions and achieve its essential objectives. (*National Parks & Conservation Assn. v. County of Riverside* (1996) 42 Cal.App.4th 1505, 1522, 50 Cal.Rptr.2d 339.) To interpret the statute and Agreement in any other manner would unduly restrict the County from working with a private landowner to plan and develop facilities which support public needs.

Moreover, the statement of legislative purpose in section 65864 encourages the creation of rights and obligations early in a project in order to promote public and private participation during planning, especially when the scope of a project requires a lengthy process of obtaining regulatory approvals. The statute recognizes that comprehensive planning is important in controlling the economic and environmental costs of development. It should be construed to allow development agreements as soon as the government and developer are required to make significant financial and personnel commitments to a project.

The Agreement conforms to this construction of the statute. Because it focuses on the planning stage of the Project, the Agreement meets, rather than evades, the purpose of the statute. The Agreement maximizes the public's role in the final development and control over the inclusion of public facilities and benefits in the project. It also permits the County to monitor the planning of the Project to effectively assure compliance with existing County land use regulations.

Additionally, environmental review is advanced by considering environmental issues at the earliest feasible time. (*Fullerton Joint Union High School Dist. v. State Bd. of Education* (1982) 32 Cal.3d 779, 797, 187 Cal.Rptr. 398, 654 P.2d 168.) The Agreement makes environmental review an integral part of the planning process, thus avoiding the sort of "*post hoc* rationalizations to support action already taken" which might occur if environmental review were deferred until later. (See *Laurel Heights Improvement Assn. v. Regents of University of California* (1988) 47 Cal.3d 376, 394, 253 Cal.Rptr. 426, 764 P.2d 278.)

While further agreement and discretionary approvals are necessary, every approval or denial permitted by the Agreement is designed to advance the project in accordance with the standards for Ranch development adopted by the County in the Salinas River Area Plan. As shown by the record, the County and the participants in the mediation which preceded the Agreement intend the Agreement to play a critical role in facilitating the completion of a large-scale real estate development. There is nothing in the Development Agreement Statute inconsistent with this type of development agreement.

Finally, the Agreement was approved by an ordinance duly enacted by the County Board of Supervisors and we defer to that body in matters pertaining to the merits, usefulness and public advantages of the Agreement. One of the purposes of development agreements is to obtain benefits for the public, and the record shows that the County believed that an agreement was required as an incentive to the developer to engage in the comprehensive planning desired by the County, and also as an incentive to expand the public facilities and benefits included in the Project.

The Agreement also represents the resolution of a protracted dispute and balances the interests of all concerned parties. Santa Margarita Limited sought a more comprehensive agreement but, according to a planning commission staff report, the County decided to "lock-in" the Salinas River Area Plan standards while deferring construction approval. The record reveals that the County's decision resulted from careful assessment of the importance of the Ranch to the region.

The record also reveals that the Agreement resulted from a mediation by parties interested in the future of the Ranch. The mediation did not result in unanimity but produced an agreement among most participants, including representatives of the public. As such, the mediation and Agreement reflect an inclusive and open governmental process.

As well as arguing that the Agreement does too little to satisfy the statute, appellants argue that it does too much to avoid constitutional infirmity. Appellants contend that the freeze on Ranch zoning before a project that is ready for construction constitutes the contracting away of the County's zoning authority and, therefore, a surrender of the right to exercise its police power in the future. We disagree. If anything, case law concerning a municipality's "surrender" of its regulatory authority supports the conclusion that the Agreement, as well as the development agreement statute, satisfy all constitutional mandates concerning a city or county's exercise of its regulatory authority.

It is established that a city or county may not contract away its right to exercise police power in the future (*Avco Community Developers, Inc. v. South Coast Regional Com., supra,* 17 Cal.3d at p. 800, 132 Cal.Rptr. 386, 553 P.2d 546) and that the power to enact, modify, and amend zoning and other land use regulations constitutes a part of a county's police power. (*Alameda County Land Use Assn. v. City of Hayward* (1995) 38 Cal.App.4th 1716, 1724, 45 Cal.Rptr.2d 752.) Therefore, the development agreement statute must be construed in a manner that does not permit the County to surrender its police power in the name of planning efficiency. (See *Conway v. Pasadena Humane Society* (1996) 45 Cal.App.4th 163, 177, 52 Cal.Rptr.2d 777.)

The Agreement in this case presents no such constitutional infirmity. Land use regulation is an established function of local government and the County has authority to enter into contracts to carry out this function. (§ 23004, subd. (c); *Carruth v. City of Madera* (1965) 233 Cal.App.2d 688, 695, 43 Cal.Rptr. 855; see also *Professional Engineers v. Department of Transportation* (1993) 13 Cal.App.4th 585, 591–592, 16 Cal.Rptr.2d 599.) A contract which "appears to have been fair, just, and reasonable at the time of its execution, and prompted by the necessities of the situation or in its nature advantageous to the municipality at the time it was entered into, is neither void nor voidable merely because some of its executory features may extend beyond the terms of office of the members" of the legislative body which entered into the contract. (*Denio v. City of Huntington Beach* (1943) 22 Cal.2d 580, 590, 140 P.2d 392; *Carruth, supra,* at p. 695, 43 Cal.Rptr. 855.)

A governmental entity does not contract away its police power unless the contract amounts to the "surrender" or "abnegation" of a proper governmental function. (*Morrison Homes Corp. v. City of Pleasanton* (1976) 58 Cal.App.3d 724, 734, 130 Cal.Rptr. 196.) The zoning freeze in the Agreement is not such a surrender or abnegation. The Project must be developed in accordance with the County's general plan (§ 65867.5), and the Agreement does not permit construction until the County has approved detailed building plans. The Agreement retains the County's discretionary authority in the future and, in any event, the zoning freeze is for five years. It is not of unlimited duration.

Seventy-five years ago, the Supreme Court stated that the "police power, as such, is not confined within the narrow circumspection of precedents, resting upon past conditions which do not cover and control present-day conditions obviously calling for revised regulations to promote the health, safety, morals, or general welfare of the public. That is to say, as a commonwealth develops politically, economically, and socially, the police power likewise develops, within reason, to meet the changed and changing conditions." (*Miller v. Board of Public Works* (1925) 195 Cal. 477, 484, 234 P. 381.) If anything, the court's statement in *Miller* resonates more clearly today than when it was first made, and provides a framework for the analysis of this case. Here, the development agreement statute and the constitutional mandate requiring the County to retain its regulatory power intersect to permit the contemporary approach to land use regulation reflected in the Agreement.

It is true that local government may not surrender its regulatory power through ad hoc commitments. It may, however, act in partnership with private enterprise, as authorized by the development agreement statute and the Agreement. The Agreement addresses recurring land use issues without limiting the County's regulatory discretion. Through the Agreement, the County tailors the exercise of its legislative power to the complex issues involved in regulating a major real estate project in the public interest. By requiring expeditious Project planning and preserving future options, the Agreement enhances the County's power to regulate land use to achieve its Salinas River Area Plan and other land use goals.

The judgment is affirmed. Costs on appeal are awarded to Santa Margarita Limited.

Notes

1. In the principal case, the court noted that the California statute encourages the creation of rights and obligations early in a project to promote public and private participation during planning. This, it says, maximizes the public's role at the earliest feasible time. The court refers to benefits to the public that result and notes that the interests involved are balanced in the process. The court also noted that although the mediation did not result in unanimity on all issues, it did produce an agreement among the participants, including representatives of the public. As such, it concluded, the mediation reflects an inclusive and open governmental process. Despite this enthusiastic endorsement, can you think of any down side to an agreement of this type made so early in the planning process?

2. Section 65864 of California's Development Agreement Statute states: "The Legislature finds and declares that: (a) The lack of certainty in the approval of development projects can result in a waste of resources, escalate the cost of housing and other development to the consumer, and discourage investment in and commitment to comprehensive planning which would make maximum efficient utilization of resources at the least economic cost to the public." In what way do negotiated discussions between land use approval officials and developers contribute to the reduction of wasted costs and resources?

E. MEDIATION DURING THE DEVELOPMENT APPROVAL PROCESS

MERSON v. McNALLY

Court of Appeals of New York, 1997.
90 N.Y.2d 742, 665 N.Y.S.2d 605, 688 N.E.2d 479.

SMITH, JUDGE.

We hold that, under certain circumstances, a negative declaration may be issued under the State Environmental Quality Review Act (SEQRA) even where the project—a Type I action—has been modified during the initial review process to accommodate environmental concerns of the lead agency and other interested parties.

In the first case, *Matter of Merson v. McNally*, we conclude that the modifications made to the project in response to environmental concerns raised during the Planning Board's review, were a legitimate product of the process and did not implicitly convert the ultimate determination of nonsignificance into an improperly conditioned negative declaration. Thus, the order of the Appellate Division annulling the negative declaration should be reversed. Since that decision was relied upon by the Appellate Division to dismiss the project developer's petition in the second action, *Matter of Philipstown Indus. Park v. Town Bd.*, a reversal is also appropriate in that case. Each case must be remitted to the Appellate Division for a determination of issues raised but not decided on the appeal to that Court.

The cases before us represent two parts of one long story for which the relevant facts will be summarized herein. Philipstown Industrial Park, Inc. (PIP) is the owner of over 80 acres of real property located within an industrial zoning district in the Town of Philipstown, Putnam County, New York. PIP's development plans for the land included soil mining and reclamation on the southern portion of the parcel.

Prior to PIP's purchase of the land in 1987, the property had been extensively mined but had not been relandscaped. Under its proposal, about 9.8 acres would again be subject to surface mining which would consist of "sizing" gravel by sifting the material through a portable screen. Another area of about 7.5 acres would not be mined but would be regraded and reclaimed and a third area would be subject to various activities necessary to the operation of the mine. The mining project would result in an expansion of the pond located on the parcel which PIP claims would "yield environmental benefits and recreational opportunities."

PIP applied to the Department of Environmental Conservation (DEC) for a "mined land reclamation permit" pursuant to New York's Mined Land Reclamation Law (MLRL; ECL 23–2701—23–2727). PIP also applied to the Planning Board for a temporary Town Special Use Mining Permit pursuant to the Town Mining Law.

The Planning Board first determined that the mining project qualified as a Type I action under SEQRA because it "involve[d] the physical alteration of 10 acres" (6 NYCRR 617.12[b][6][i]). PIP then submitted a draft of a full Environmental Assessment Form (EAF) pursuant to the SEQRA regulations. During the review process, the Planning Board identified several "potentially large" environmental impacts from the proposed project. In response to concerns raised by the interested agencies, the Planning Board and community members during public meetings and hearings, PIP continually revised portions of its project plans. All of the modifications were discussed and considered by the Planning Board during these open meetings. The entire project proposal was reduced to a single bound volume (which included a completed EAF) and was finally submitted on May 4, 1993.

On May 18, 1993, the Planning Board received an opinion from the DEC that a determination of nonsignificance in the form of a negative declaration would be appropriate for the mining project. Two days later, on May 20, 1993, the Planning Board issued a negative declaration by unanimous vote. The Planning Board also granted the temporary special use permit (subject to the final approval of the Town Board) upon its finding that "the applicant has met or exceeded the performance standards outlined" in the Town Zoning Law. Soon afterward, a group of community residents filed a CPLR article 78 petition in Supreme Court seeking to annul the negative declaration of the Planning Board and PIP intervened.

Supreme Court dismissed the proceeding and concluded that the determination of the Planning Board was not improperly issued. In so holding, the court found that "the environmental assessment form adequately identified areas of environmental impact." The court stated that it would "defer to the planning board's discretion as to the * * * issuance of a negative declaration under SEQRA."

The Appellate Division reversed and annulled the negative declaration. The Court held (227 A.D.2d 487, 490, 643 N.Y.S.2d 129):

> "Inherent in the Planning Board's determination was a recognition of significant environmental impacts posed by the intervenor's project * * *. It is evident that the numerous measures proposed by the intervenor in mitigation of these impacts were conditional prerequisites for the issuance of the negative declaration * * *. Under these circumstances, we conclude that the Planning Board's negative declaration was the functional equivalent of a conditioned negative declaration" (citations omitted).

"SEQRA's fundamental policy is to inject environmental considerations directly into governmental decision making" (*Matter of Coca–Cola Bottling Co. v. Board of Estimate*, 72 N.Y.2d 674, 679, 536 N.Y.S.2d 33, 532 N.E.2d 1261). This policy is effectuated, in part, through strict compliance with the review procedures outlined in the environmental laws and regulations (see, *Matter of King v. Saratoga County Bd. of Supervisors*, 89 N.Y.2d 341, 347–348, 653 N.Y.S.2d 233, 675 N.E.2d 1185). A SEQRA review process conducted through closed bilateral negotiations between an agency and a developer would bypass, if not eliminate, the comprehensive, open weighing of environmentally compatible alternatives both to the proposed action and to any suggested mitigation measures.

However, we disagree with the Appellate Division's holding to the extent it can be read to bar *any* significant modification during the review process as a conditioned negative declaration. Instead, we adopt an analysis which allows for consideration of the legitimate maturation of a development project in accordance with the goals of environmental regulation. In exercising our judicial review function concerning the process at issue, we conclude that the determination of nonsignificance made by the lead agency was not improper.

The Regulatory Process Under SEQRA

Under the procedures set forth in the DEC regulations, when a developer first submits a proposal for a particular project, it is determined whether the project qualifies as a Type I, Type II or an unlisted action for purposes of SEQRA review (6 NYCRR 617.5[a][4]). For Type I actions, the developer must submit a full EAF which "must be used to determine the significance of such actions" (6 NYCRR 617.5[b]).[13]

The very purpose of an EAF is to assist an agency "in determining the environmental significance or nonsignificance of actions" (6 NYCRR 617.2 [m]). As the form itself states, "[t]he full EAF is intended to provide a method whereby applicants and agencies can be assured that the determination process has been orderly, comprehensive in nature, yet flexible enough to allow introduction of information to fit a project or action" (6 NYCRR 617.20, appendix A). Part 2 of the EAF allows the lead agency to identify "the range of possible impacts" and "whether an impact can be mitigated or reduced" (6 NYCRR 617.20, appendix A). As stated on the required form, "[i]dentifying that an impact will be potentially large * * * does not mean that it is also necessarily significant. Any large impact must be evaluated in Part 3 to determine significance. Identifying an impact in column 2 simply asks that it be looked at further." This highlights the functional difference between an EAF and an Environmental Impact Statement (EIS). While an EAF is used to determine significance or nonsignificance, the purpose of an EIS is to examine the identified potentially significant environmental impacts which may result from a project (*Matter of Coca–Cola Bottling Co. v. Board of Estimate*, 72 N.Y.2d, at 680, 536 N.Y.S.2d 33, 532 N.E.2d 1261).[14]

To arrive at its determination of significance, the lead agency must identify "the relevant areas of environmental concern" and take a "hard look" at them (*Matter of Chemical Specialties Mfrs. Assn. v. Jorling*, 85 N.Y.2d 382, 397, 626 N.Y.S.2d 1, 649 N.E.2d 1145; see also, *Matter of Kahn v. Pasnik*, 90 N.Y.2d 569, 664 N.Y.S.2d 584, 687 N.E.2d 402 [decided today]). The agency must set forth a reasoned elaboration for its determination (*see, Matter of WEOK Broadcasting Corp. v. Planning Bd.*, 79 N.Y.2d 373, 381, 583 N.Y.S.2d 170, 592 N.E.2d 778; *Matter of Coca–Cola Bottling Co. v. Board of Estimate*, 72 N.Y.2d, at 680, 536 N.Y.S.2d 33, 532 N.E.2d 1261). As we have stated, "[w]here an agency fails to take the requisite hard look and make a reasoned elaboration, or its determination is affected by an error of law, or its decision was not rational, or is arbitrary and capricious or not supported by substantial evidence, the agency's determination may be annulled" (*Matter of*

13. The agency may waive the requirement of an EAF if a draft EIS is submitted instead (6 NYCRR 617.6[a][4]).

14. As stated in the current regulations, "[a]n EIS provides a means for agencies, project sponsors and the public to systematically consider significant adverse environmental impacts, alternatives and mitigation" (6 NYCRR 617.2[n]). If the lead agency determines "that the action may include the potential for at least one significant environmental effect" (6 NYCRR 617.6[g][1][i]), the agency must issue a positive declaration (6 NYCRR 617.2[cc]; Matter of Coca–Cola Bottling Co. v. Board of Estimate, 72 N.Y.2d, at 680, 536 N.Y.S.2d 33, 532 N.E.2d 1261). However, when the agency determines that "the implementation of the action as proposed will not result in any significant environmental effects," the agency may issue an unqualified negative declaration (see, 6 NYCRR 617.2 [y]).

WEOK Broadcasting Corp. v. Planning Bd., 79 N.Y.2d, at 383, 583 N.Y.S.2d 170, 592 N.E.2d 778). However, we have also cautioned that "[w]hile judicial review must be meaningful, the courts may not substitute their judgment for that of the agency for it is not their role to 'weigh the desirability of any action or [to] choose among alternatives'" (*Akpan v. Koch*, 75 N.Y.2d 561, 570, 555 N.Y.S.2d 16, 554 N.E.2d 53, quoting *Matter of Jackson v. New York State Urban Dev. Corp.*, 67 N.Y.2d 400, 416, 503 N.Y.S.2d 298, 494 N.E.2d 429).

Although the parties presently contest issues such as whether the agency took a "hard look," the Appellate Division resolved these cases solely on the ground that modifications made to the project were an improper circumvention of the procedural requirements under the environmental regulations. Thus, that is the threshold critical issue that we must address.

THE IMPACT OF MODIFICATIONS ON THE SEQRA PROCESS

The dilemma is this—how to permit an evolving process for identification of environmental concerns and initiatives to meet those concerns yet, on the other hand, to guard against an avoidance of the EIS process through private bilateral negotiations between a developer and a lead agency when a project may have potentially significant environmental impacts which need full and open consideration.

To deal with this dilemma, we start with the definition of a conditioned negative declaration, permitted only in unlisted actions:

> "a negative declaration issued by a lead agency for an unlisted action, involving an applicant, in which the action as *initially proposed may result in one or more significant adverse environmental effects; however, mitigation measures identified and required by the lead agency* * * * will modify the proposed action so that no significant environmental impacts will result" (6 NYCRR 617.2[h]).

Applying this definition in the context of a Type I action, we prescribe a twofold inquiry to examine whether a negative declaration has been impermissibly conditioned: (1) whether the project, as initially proposed, might result in the identification of one or more "significant adverse environmental effects"; and (2) whether the proposed mitigating measures incorporated into part 3 of the EAF were "identified and required by the lead agency" as a condition precedent to the issuance of the negative declaration.

On the first point, if all areas of concern involve a minimal risk to the environment, no further inquiry is necessary and modifications in these areas would not impermissibly condition or invalidate an otherwise proper negative declaration. However, where the lead agency has identified potentially significant impacts (*see,Chinese Staff & Workers Assn. v. City of New York*, 68 N.Y.2d 359, 364–365, 509 N.Y.S.2d 499, 502 N.E.2d 176), or where the record supports the inference that the identified impacts would have to be considered potentially significant (*see, Inland Vale Farm Co. v. Stergianopoulos*, 104 A.D.2d 395, 397, 478 N.Y.S.2d

926, affd. 65 N.Y.2d 718, 492 N.Y.S.2d 7, 481 N.E.2d 547), or where the identified impacts fall within typically environmentally sensitive areas or locations, the second prong of the test must be examined.

At the second phase of analysis, a court must examine whether the proposed mitigating measures, incorporated as part of an open and deliberative process, negated the project's potential adverse effects. Under such circumstances, the proposal, as revised, could still result in a determination of nonsignificance and the issuance of a valid negative declaration. In this regard, mitigating measures could be viewed as part of the "give and take" of the application process, and would be less of a concern than those revisions or mitigation measures made after final submission of the EAF.

However, a lead agency clearly may not issue a negative declaration on the basis of conditions contained in the declaration itself. Nor could the lead agency achieve the same end by other means, such as supporting the negative declaration with a statement that conditions would be imposed only on an underlying special use permit to reduce environmental impacts; extracting concessions from the developer as necessary prerequisites to the issuance of the negative declaration (*Matter of Shawangunk Mtn. Envtl. Assn. v. Planning Bd.*, 157 A.D.2d 273, 277, 557 N.Y.S.2d 495); or requiring specific mitigation measures, and then approving a proposal that has been revised in compliance with the mandate of the lead agency.

The environmental review process was not meant to be a bilateral negotiation between a developer and lead agency but, rather, an open process that also involves other interested agencies and the public. Thus, there would ordinarily be no inherent problem in revising or modifying project plans to address concerns raised during the environmental review, particularly concerns raised by other agencies.

However, mitigating measures will not obviate the need for an EIS unless they clearly negate the continued potentiality of the adverse effects of the proposed action. Otherwise, the EIS process would be necessary to review the adequacy of the mitigating measures, and any environmentally compatible alternatives to the suggested mitigations. The lead agency's determination of the sufficiency of the proposed mitigation measures would of course be subject to a judicial examination of whether the lead agency took the requisite hard look (*see, e.g., Matter of Kahn v. Pasnik*, 90 N.Y.2d 569, 664 N.Y.S.2d 584, 687 N.E.2d 402, *supra* [decided today]); the more numerous and significant the environmental impacts identified at the outset, the greater possibility that mitigation measures would not suffice, and an EIS would be required.

Here, the Planning Board, in reviewing part 2 of the EAF identified a number of impacts as "potentially large." For example, the Town's planning consultant articulated his concern with "ambient noise level and access to a mining operation through a subdivision." Indeed, the consultant specifically stated that "the Board must consider the noise issue more in depth as it has been shown to be one of the most complex and important matters in connection with the application" bearing on SEQRA review.

Nevertheless, the agency's general concerns relating to noise levels were alleviated through the review process by the actions of, and open discussions with, the developer. In response to such concerns, PIP explained that it had taken several surveys and readings of the ambient noise in the area of the mining operation and, as a result of its analysis, PIP concluded that "an ambient noise level within the guidelines of the [local] zoning law will be maintainable by the mining operation." Additionally, in this regard, the agency suggested that Saturday hours and operations be limited only to the sale of materials and the developer agreed.

A similar open and deliberative process surrounded the concerns raised by the increased traffic stemming from the project. The Board suggested that the developer "consider" a separate access road and the mining plan was amended in response to such comments. PIP pursued a temporary access route onto Route 9 and other measures to lessen the traffic on residential streets.

Thus, the modifications here were not conditions unilaterally imposed by the lead agency, but essentially were adjustments incorporated by the project sponsor to mitigate the concerns identified by the public and the reviewing agencies, with only minor variations requested by the lead agency during the review process. Of distinguishing dispositive import here is that the modifications were examined openly and with input from all parties involved. This process comports with the overriding purposes of SEQRA.

The revisions thus came about as part of the review process and were submitted and publicly evaluated prior to the issuance of the negative declaration. Moreover, the lead agency properly sought the views of other interested agencies before making a final determination regarding significance. In fact, the DEC issued its recommendation of nonsignificance based upon the final revised project plans in accordance with the regulations (*see,* 6 NYCRR 617.3 [e]). These considerations combine to support the conclusion that the negative declaration in this case was not improperly conditioned.

This case illustrates the practical reality that a project, especially a large undertaking such as a Type I action, usually undergoes modifications from its initial specifications. Modifications made to a project during the review process should not necessarily be characterized as impermissible "conditions." Indeed, the SEQRA regulations themselves help to show that the purpose of identifying "potentially large" environmental impacts in the midst of the EAF process is to allow a developer the opportunity to address those potential impacts in the project proposal.

In sum, the mere circumstance that modifications may have been made to a proposal is an insufficient basis to nullify a negative declaration otherwise properly issued. What is dispositive is the character and source of the identified modifications. The SEQRA process here was conducted openly and deliberatively. Moreover, the agency's elaboration of the basis for its determination of nonsignificance is reasonable. Accordingly, in each case, the order of the Appellate Division should be reversed, with costs, and the matter remitted to the Appellate Division for further proceedings in accordance with this opinion.

Notes

1. Does the Merson case really involve a mediation? Who is the mediator? Need there be a mediator? Perhaps the sessions were simply skillfully conducted negotiations facilitated by a planning board chair who understood, intuitively or through training, the skills needed for effective dispute resolution. Note how, apparently, the interested parties were involved in an open and deliberative process organized by the review board. The court made clear that the process was not a bilateral negotiation, but part of the "give and take" of the review process. Modifications in the proposal, it said, were not unilaterally imposed, but were adjustments incorporated by the applicant to mitigate concerns identified by the public and the involved public agencies. What went wrong? Who sued? Why?

2. If, during the give and take of a mediation, the applicant agrees to modify the proposal to meet the interest of a party involved in the negotiations, is this the same as the review board imposing a condition on a project as part of the approval process? See In the Matter of Waste Management of New York v. Doherty, 267 A.D.2d 464, 700 N.Y.S.2d 494 (1999): As stated by the Court of Appeals in Merson v. McNally, "modifications made to a project during the review process should not necessarily be characterized as impermissible 'conditions,' * * * the mere circumstance that modifications may have been made to a proposal is an insufficient basis to nullify a negative declaration otherwise properly issued."

3. Do you think the court struck the right balance between providing all parties with a meaningful role in the environmental review and allowing flexibility in the project review stage? Note that New York has no statute authorizing or encouraging mediation of disputes over local land use applications. Neither did the town of Philipstown. How is it that the planning board (lead agency) had the authority to conduct a mediation of the interests of concern to the parties involved in the application? The state regulations prescribing the rules for local environmental review allow all applicable time frames to be waived upon the consent of the parties. Do you think that taking time to conduct a mediation of the issues in such a case is a good reason for an applicant to agree to waive deadlines in the review process? What are the pros and cons?

4. Do interested parties have reason to complain that mediation sessions of the type held in the Merson case are not adequate to guarantee their full and effective participation? See In the Matter of Tarrytown v. Planning Board of Village of Sleepy Hollow, 292 A.D.2d 617, 741 N.Y.S.2d 44 (2002): "Where a developer works with the lead agency and other reviewing agencies in public and, as a result of open consultation, incorporates changes in the project which mitigate the potential environmental impacts, a negative declaration may be appropriate–provided that such declaration is not the

product of closed-door negotiations or of the developer's compliance with conditions unilaterally imposed by the lead agency."

MEDEIROS v. HAWAII COUNTY PLANNING COMMISSION

Intermediate Court of Appeals of Hawaii, 1990.
8 Haw.App. 183, 797 P.2d 59.

HEEN, JUDGE.

Appellants Delan Perry, Jennifer Perry (the Perrys), and Nelson Ho (collectively Appellants) appeal from Appellee Hawaii County Planning Commission's (Commission) August 15, 1989 approval of a geothermal resource permit (the permit) authorizing Appellees Hawaii Natural Energy Institute and the Research Corporation of the University of Hawaii (Applicants) to drill four exploratory geothermal wells in the East Rift Zone of the Puna District on the Island of Hawaii. We affirm.

I.

The general procedures for considering geothermal resource permit applications by the counties are established by HRS [Hawaii Revised Statutes] § 205–5.1(e) and (f) which read as follows:

> (e) If geothermal development activities are proposed within agricultural, rural, or urban districts and such proposed activities are not permitted uses pursuant to county general plan and zoning ordinances, then after receipt of a properly filed and completed application, including all required supporting data, the appropriate county authority shall conduct a public hearing. Upon appropriate request for mediation from any party who submitted comment at the public hearing, the county authority shall appoint a mediator within five days. The county authority shall require the parties to participate in mediation. The mediator shall not be an employee of any county agency or its staff. The mediation period shall not extend beyond thirty days after mediation started, except by order of the county authority. Mediation shall be confined to the issues raised at the public hearing by the party requesting mediation. The mediator will submit a written recommendation to the county authority, based upon any mediation agreement reached between the parties for consideration by the county authority in its final decision. If there is no mediation agreement, the county authority may have a second public hearing to receive additional comment related to the mediation issues. Within ten days after the second public hearing, the county authority may receive additional written comment on the issues raised at the second public hearing from any party.
>
> The county authority shall consider the comments raised at the second hearing before rendering its final decision. The county authority shall then determine whether a geothermal resource permit shall be granted to authorize the geothermal development activities described in the application. The appropriate county authority shall

grant a geothermal resource permit if it finds that applicant has demonstrated that:

(1) The desired uses would not have unreasonable adverse health, environmental, or socio-economic effects on residents or surrounding property;

(2) The desired uses would not unreasonably burden public agencies to provide roads and streets, sewers, water, drainage, school improvements, and police and fire protection; and

(3) That there are reasonable measures available to mitigate the unreasonable adverse effects or burdens referred to above.

Unless there is a mutual agreement to extend, a decision shall be made on the application by the appropriate county authority within six months of the date a complete application was filed; provided that the time limit may be extended by agreement between the applicant and the appropriate county authority.

(f) Requests for mediation shall be received by the board or county authority within five days after the close of the initial public hearing. Within five days thereafter, the board or county authority shall appoint a mediator. Any person submitting an appropriate request for mediation shall be notified by the board or county authority of the date, time, and place of the mediation conference by depositing such notice in the mail to the return address stated on the request for mediation. The notice shall be mailed no later than ten days before the start of the mediation conference. The conference shall be held on the island where the public hearing is held.

An authority's decision on a geothermal resource permit application pursuant to a public hearing or hearings is appealable directly to the supreme court for review in accordance with the provisions of HRS § 91–14(b) and (g) (1985). However, the decision is not subject to a contested case hearing. HRS § 205–5.1(g).[15]

III.

On January 31, 1989, Applicants applied to the Commission for permission to drill four Scientific Observation Holes (Holes), numbered 1 through 4, in the Subzone established by the Board within the Kilauea East Rift Zone. According to the application, each Hole will be approxi-

15. HRS § 205–5.1(g) (Supp.1989) provides:

(g) Any decision made by an appropriate county authority or the board pursuant to a public hearing or hearings under this section may be appealed directly on the record to the supreme court for final decision and shall not be subject to a contested case hearing. Sections 91–14(b) and (g) shall govern the appeal, notwithstanding the lack of a contested case hearing on the matter. The appropriate county authority or the board shall provide a court reporter to produce a transcript of the proceedings at all public hearings under this section for purposes of an appeal.

mately four inches in diameter and 4,000 feet deep, and will be located on approximately one quarter acre of land.

The public hearing began on April 11, 1989. At the public hearing a member of the staff of the Hawaii County Planning Department (Planning Department) recommended approval of the application with a number of conditions. Twenty-nine people, including Appellants, also spoke. All speakers, except the Planning Department's staff member, were limited to three minutes, and only Commission members were allowed to question any of the speakers. Mr. Harry Kim, Director of Civil Defense for Hawaii County, spoke and requested mediation. At the close of the proceedings, the Commission voted to continue the hearing at a later date.

When the hearing resumed on May 9, 1989, forty-five people spoke, including the Perrys. The speakers were limited to five minutes each and, again, the audience was not allowed to question any of the speakers. At the close of the hearing the Commission's chairman announced that all parties who wanted mediation should submit written requests within five days. Numerous persons, including the Perrys, requested mediation.

On May 19, 1989, the Commission appointed Dee Dee Letts (Letts), Assistant Director of the Program on Alternative Dispute Resolution of the State Judiciary, as mediator. Subsequently, Letts was joined by Dr. Kem Lowry of the University of Hawaii and Richard Spiegel of the West Hawaii Mediation Service as "co-mediators." The first mediation meeting was held on June 7, 1989, and the last on July 6. On July 10, 1989, the president of the Kapoho Community Association (Association) wrote a letter to the Commission pointing out that, during mediation, Applicants revealed there will be hydrogen sulfide emission from the wells, contrary to their statement in the application. The Association requested a contested case hearing. On July 13, 1989, the mediators submitted their final report, outlining the items of agreement and disagreement among the participants.

On August 15, 1989, the Commission approved the permit and Appellants appealed.

IV.

Appellants wage a four-pronged attack on the permit. First, they argue that HRS § 205–5.1(g)'s provision that the authority's decision "shall not be subject to a contested case hearing" violates their constitutional right to due process of law under Article I, § 5 of the Hawaii State Constitution. Second, they assert that the procedures employed by the Commission violated their due process rights. We find no merit in Appellants' arguments.

A.

HRS § 205–5.1 was enacted in 1983. Act 296, § 3, 1983 Haw.Sess. Laws 636, 637–38. In 1984, the statute was amended to provide for contested case hearings on applications submitted under the statute. Act

151, § 2, 1984 Haw.Sess.Laws 278, 280. In 1987, the legislature deleted the provisions for contested case hearings and substituted public hearings and a mediation process. Act 378, § 1, 1987 Haw.Sess.Laws 1198, 1200–01. The purpose of the change was "to provide for a simpler procedure to consider and act on permits for geothermal development before state and county agencies." Sen. Stand. Comm. Rep. No. 1118, in 1987 Senate Journal, at 1387.

Appellants argue that "[t]he ability to cross examine witnesses and the preservation of arguments for the reviewing body to assess are key to the most basic citizen rights as included in the Hawaii State Constitution Bill of Rights[.]" They contend that a contested case hearing is essential to the preservation of those rights.

Applicants argue that Appellants' interests are aesthetic and environmental and are not "property" in the context of due process. However, the record shows that the Perrys own and farm property abutting the land covered by the permit. It is at least arguable that the Perrys' use of their property might be so severely curtailed by Applicants' geothermal activities as to constitute a deprivation of property. In any event, we need not decide whether or not Appellants have a protectible property interest. This is for the reason that, even if Appellants do have a protectible property interest, HRS § 205–5.1 satisfies due process requirements.

A contested case hearing is not essential to the guarantee of due process. The legislature has inherent power to establish the procedure for a particular type of case. *See Marcello v. Bonds,* 349 U.S. 302, 75 S.Ct. 757, 99 L.Ed. 1107, *reh'g denied,* 350 U.S. 856, 76 S.Ct. 38, 100 L.Ed. 761 (1955).

In *Marcello,* the Court recognized that Congress often had good reasons for requiring different procedures for resolving different types of disputes because of the nature and context of the decisions to be made. Congress is free to establish different decision-making procedures for different agencies and different types of decisions as long as the procedures it establishes do not fall below the minimum procedures required by due process. Since *Marcello,* the Court determines the adequacy of the procedures used by an agency through independent analysis of the requirements of statutes and of the Constitution.

R. Pierce, S. Shapiro & P. Verkuil, *Administrative Law and Process* § 6.4, at 281 (1985).

Due process is not a fixed concept requiring a specific procedural course in every situation. "[D]ue process is flexible and calls for such procedural protections as the particular situation demands." *Morrissey v. Brewer,* 408 U.S. 471, 481, 92 S.Ct. 2593, 2600, 33 L.Ed.2d 484, 494 (1972). The full rights of due process present in a court of law, including presentation of witnesses and cross-examination, do not automatically attach to a quasi-judicial hearing. *See Goss v. Lopez,* 419 U.S. 565, 95 S.Ct. 729, 42 L.Ed.2d 725 (1975); *Arnett v. Kennedy,* 416 U.S. 134, 94 S.Ct. 1633, 40 L.Ed.2d 15 (1974). The basic elements of procedural due process of law require notice and an opportunity to be heard at a meaningful time and in a meaningful manner before governmental deprivation of a significant property interest. *Mathews v. Eldridge,* 424 U.S. 319, 333, 96 S.Ct. 893, 902, 47 L.Ed.2d 18, 32 (1976); *North Georgia Finishing, Inc. v. Di–Chem, Inc.,* 419 U.S. 601, 605–606, 95 S.Ct. 719, 722, 42 L.Ed.2d 751, 756–57 (1975).

Determination of the specific procedures required to satisfy due process requires a balancing of several factors: (1) the private interest which will be affected; (2) the risk of an erroneous deprivation of such interest through the procedures actually used, and the probable value, if any, of additional or alternative procedural safeguards; and (3) the governmental interest, including the burden that additional procedural safeguards would entail. *Mathews v. Eldridge,* 424 U.S. at 335, 96 S.Ct. at 903, 47 L.Ed.2d at 33; *Silver v. Castle Memorial Hosp.,* 53 Haw. [475,] 484, 497 P.2d [564,] 571 [1972]. *Sandy Beach Defense Fund v. City Council,* 70 Haw. 361, 378, 773 P.2d 250, 261 (1989).

Considering the factors set forth in *Sandy Beach,* we find that, even assuming Appellants have a property interest requiring protection under the due process clause, the procedures established by the statute are sufficient to protect Appellants' property from erroneous deprivation.

The state government is keenly interested in exploring and developing geothermal energy as a cheaper alternative to oil as a source of electrical energy for the general populace. The legislature has decided that geothermal energy development is so important that it should not be delayed by protracted contested case hearings. However, mindful of the potential adverse impact of geothermal energy development on the surrounding properties, the legislature has required the appropriate authority to provide notice, an opportunity to be heard, and a record of the proceedings for appellate review.

The public hearing, together with the mediation process, was viewed by the legislature as a reasonable alternative to the contested case. Indeed, since it allows the interested parties the opportunity to meet with the developers on a one-to-one basis and to attempt to resolve their differences, mediation may, as a practical matter, provide the residents and property owners with greater impact on the decision than a contested case. The fact that the differences between the Applicants and the affected property owners may not always be resolved in favor of the property owners does not mean that the process fails to pass constitutional muster. The constitution guarantees the right to be heard, not the right to have one's views adopted. Neither does the constitution establish the contested case as the only forum for ensuring a property owner's right to be heard. *See Sandy Beach, supra.*

Here, Appellants were afforded a hearing and an opportunity to present testimony and evidence. They have not convinced us that a contested case hearing would have given them any further protection, and we have no doubt that it would have considerably burdened the process.

In the final analysis, a geothermal permit proceeding is essentially a zoning matter. Historically, and universally, such matters have been decided after notice and a public hearing. We are not aware of any precedent for holding that the constitution requires a contested case hearing on a zoning change application.

Appellants further argue that, even if the statute meets due process requirements, the procedures actually employed by the Commission did not provide them with the opportunity to be heard in a meaningful manner:

Appellants assert the following as constitutional error:

(1) time limitations were imposed on the testimony at the public hearing;

(2) public comments on the procedures employed by the Commission were not accepted;

(3) the request for a second hearing was denied;

(4) the parties had no voice in selecting the mediator; and

(5) strict time constraints were imposed on the mediation process.

We find that the complained of Commission actions did not violate Appellants' due process rights.

The participants at the public hearing were allowed to speak and present written evidence. It was not unreasonable to limit the speaking time, since testimony at such large public hearings tends to be repetitious. *See In re Haw. Elec. Light Co.,* 67 Haw. 425, 690 P.2d 274 (1984).

Since the Commission's procedures were lawful, we do not think it was error to disallow public comment on them.

A second hearing was not necessary. Appellants argue that Applicants' revelation during the mediation process that the Holes would emit hydrogen sulfide gas should have prompted the Commission to hold a second hearing. However, one of the conditions of the permit is that, prior to the start of any drilling, Applicants will submit and get the Planning Department's approval for an air monitoring plan, which must be operational in all phases of the project. The condition is obviously meant by the Commission to address the issue of gaseous emissions, and a second hearing was not necessary.

The time constraints in the mediation process were in accord with the dictates of HRS § 205–5.1(e). However, Appellants argue that, although they were required to share the cost of mediation, they were not given a voice in the selection of the mediators. We do not believe it is essential to due process that Appellants participate in naming the mediator or mediators. Appellants' due process rights are protected so long as the selection process and the chosen mediator are unbiased. Appellants do not claim the mediators were biased or prejudiced and do not claim to have been prejudiced by the Commission's selection.

Affirmed.

Notes

1. In Pele v. Puna Geothermal, 8 Haw.App. 203, 797 P.2d 69 (1990), the appellants argued that HRS 205–5.1 violated their due process rights under the Fourteenth Amendment of the United States Constitution and Article I, Section 5 of the Hawaii State Constitution. The court disagreed, reaffirmed the Medeiros decision, and further concluded that for all the same reasons enumerated in Medeiros, HRS § 205–5.1 satisfies the due process requirements of the United States Constitution.

2. Reflect again on the value of mediation of land use disputes. In Medeiros, the court enthusiastically endorsed mediation with these words: "[S]ince it allows the interested parties the opportunity to meet with the developers on a one-to one basis and to attempt to resolve their differences, mediation may, as a practical matter, provide the residents and property owners with greater impact on the decision than a contested case." The concurring opinion by Justice Bryson in Fasano v. Washington County, Bd. of County Comm'rs, 264 Or. 574, 507 P.2d 23 (1973), is also instructive: "The basic facts in this case exemplify the prohibitive cost and extended uncertainty to a homeowner when a government body decides to change or modify a zoning ordinance or comprehensive plan * * * No average homeowner or small business enterprise can afford a judicial process such as described above nor can the judicial system cope with or endure such a process in achieving justice. The number of controversies is ascending."

3. The Medieros case involves a state mediation statute related to a very specific topic: applications for geothermal resource permits. Other state mediation statutes that limit themselves to specific contexts include:

Housing:

a. Mass General Law Chap. 40B—Mass. Office of Dispute Resolution established mediation program to resolve disputes arising under state anti-snob zoning act.

b. RI Gen Laws § 45–34—Mediation before state housing appeal board renders decision.

c. NJ—Under New Jersey Fair Housing Act, local governments are required to adopt housing plans, may choose to participate in mediation.

Growth Management/Regional Planning:

a. New Jersey State Planning Act—"cross-acceptance" process—§ 52:18A–202.

b. The Washington State Growth Management Act—36.70A.190.

c. Vermont Growth Management Act—VT Stat. Ann. T. 24 § 4305(b).

Comprehensive Plans:

a. Florida—F.S.A. § 163.3184.

b. Colorado—C.R.S. § 24–32–3209 (mandatory mediation between local governments).

c. Delaware—Del.C. § 9103.

d. Minnesota—M.S.A. § 572A.01.

e. Oregon—O.R.S. § 197.633 (periodic review of comprehensive plans).

f. Tennessee—T.C.A. § 6–58–104 (comprehensive growth plans).

Other Contexts:

a. Hazardous Waste/Radiation Cleanup Statutes: CA, NJ, PN, WA, WV, WI

b. Annexation: GA, ND, TX. See also Higdon v. City of Senoia, 273 Ga. 83, 538 S.E.2d 39 (2000).

c. Coastal zone management (HI), natural gas pipelines (ME), watershed plans(MN), Hudson River Greenway(NY), Farmland tax assessment (NJ).

d. North Carolina (§ 7A–38.3) encourages the mediation of farmland nuisance disputes any time during the dispute, but requires that "prior to bringing a civil action involving a farm nuisance dispute, a farm resident or any other party shall initiate mediation pursuant to this section."

F. MEDIATION AFTER THE DEVELOPMENT APPROVAL PROCESS

SCOTT v. POLK COUNTY

District Court of Appeal of Florida, Second District, 2001.
793 So.2d 85.

THREADGILL, ACTING CHIEF JUDGE.

* * *

In March 1999, the Polk County Board of County Commissioners denied a Planned Unit Development (PUD) application submitted by Scott for the LKP property. The proposed PUD sought to convert the waterfront portion of the LKP's property into a marina and resort.

After the PUD application was denied [in April], pursuant to section 70.51(4), Florida Statutes (1999), [Scott] filed a letter with the county board, seeking alternative, nonjudicial review of the board's order by a special master, who, as provided by the statute, would be duly chosen by both Scott and the county board. Eight days later, Scott filed this lawsuit against Polk County, alleging that, with regard to his PUD application, his substantive due process rights were violated by unlawful, ex parte communications between county personnel and the South Florida Water Management District, which had a prospective interest in the LKP property. Scott claimed that those ex parte communications were improperly considered and were instrumental in the county board's denial of the subject PUD application. On October 19, 1999, Scott filed an amended complaint, alleging more specific due process violation claims against the county, pursuant to 42 U.S.C. § 1983 (1999). All efforts by the county to dismiss Scott's lawsuit were denied by the trial court.

On November 22, 1999, the special master filed a "Mediator's Report" in Scott's civil lawsuit, indicating that a proper section 70.51 special master proceeding had been conducted but had culminated in an impasse. The report went on to indicate that the special master was prepared to continue either "upon agreement of the parties or further direction of [the trial] court."

On February 10, 2000, the county filed—in the civil lawsuit—an amended motion to dismiss, abate, or stay the special master proceedings. After a hearing, the trial court entered an order, dismissing the special master proceedings. The trial court found that the special master proceedings were intended only as an alternative to judicial proceedings—of any kind, presumably—and that, once judicial proceedings were instituted, the right to a special master proceeding was waived.

On review, Scott, in essence, contends that the trial court departed from the essential requirements of the law in dismissing the special master proceedings, because it was without jurisdiction to do so. We agree.

The instant judicial action involves a § 1983 due process claim, which, in the context of a zoning case, may be viewed as an action independent and distinct from the judicial review process relating to the approval or denial of a zoning request. *See Jennings v. Dade County*, 589 So.2d 1337 (Fla. 3d DCA 1991) (holding that an original judicial action for declaratory and injunctive relief regarding due process violations in a quasi-judicial zoning proceeding before a county board can be maintained apart from the judicial review process of the board's actual zoning decision). On the other hand, the section 70.51 special master proceeding at issue herein is an alternative dispute resolution process instituted to resolve challenges to the actual merit of a zoning decision, in lieu of judicial review. This court reaches no conclusion as to whether, pursuant to *Jennings*, section 70.51 special master proceedings may be maintained simultaneously with a § 1983 judicial proceeding arising from the process employed by a governmental entity in evaluating a zoning request. We do conclude, however, that the trial court in this instance was without the legal authority to dismiss the special master proceeding. The statute provides for optional review by a special master of final zoning decisions issued by governmental entities. The option may be exercised before judicial review of a zoning decision is sought. § 70.51(10)(a). If the option is exercised, the time for filing a judicial challenge to a final zoning decision is tolled "until the special master's recommendation is acted upon by the local government." *Id.* The property owner's election to file for judicial review of a final zoning order prior to initiating a nonjudicial proceeding under the statute waives any right to a special master proceeding. *Id.* Judicial review of a final zoning order is obtained by certiorari in the circuit court and then, if necessary, by certiorari in the district court. *See ABG Real Estate Dev. Co. of Fla., Inc. v. St. Johns County*, 608 So.2d 59, 61–62 (Fla. 5th DCA 1992). In this instance, judicial review of the subject zoning order has not been initiated.

The plain language of section 70.51 indicates that the alternative proceedings contemplated by that section are informal and nonjudicial and are controlled strictly by the special master and the parties. No provision within section 70.51 confers jurisdiction on any court of law or otherwise authorizes judicial intervention or involvement in a special master proceeding, because judicial review of a zoning decision is an entirely separate formal process that may be initiated. *See* § 70.51(10)(a)-(b); *see also* ABG, 608 So.2d at 61–62. The trial court in this instance was therefore without the authority to intervene in the special master proceedings or to otherwise dismiss them. It thus departed from the essential requirements of the law in doing so.

Based on the foregoing, common law certiorari is granted. The trial court's order is quashed, and this cause is remanded for further proceedings consistent with this opinion.

Notes

1. In Maine's Land Use Mediation Statute (5 M.R.S.A. § 3341), as in Florida's Land Use Mediation Statute (F.S.A. § 70.51), the application for mediation tolls the time to seek judicial review.

2. Unlike the Pennsylvania, Hawaii, and Idaho land use mediation statutes mentioned above, which encourage mediation during the permit approval process, the Florida mediation statute applicable in the principal case permits mediation only after a final decision on a permit approval has occurred. See also California (Cal. Gov. Code §§ 66030–66037), Connecticut (C.G.S.A. § 8–8), Oregon (O.R.S. § 197.860), and Maine (5 M.R.S.A. § 3341). In Brand v. Town of Brunswick, 2000 WL 33675557 (unreported), the defendant filed a motion to dismiss the plaintiff's application for land use mediation under statute 5 M.R.S.A. § 3341. The plaintiff had violated a zoning ordinance by cutting down trees on her property and appealed that violation. However, prior to her application for land use mediation, the plaintiff had not requested any permit, variance, or special exception. The court found that the case was not ripe for mediation pursuant to § 3341.

G. MEDIATION AND LAWYERING

WILMINGTON HOSPITALITY v. NEW CASTLE COUNTY

Court of Chancery of Delaware, New Castle County, 2001.
788 A.2d 536.

LAMB, VICE CHANCELLOR

Plaintiff Wilmington Hospitality ("WH") moved to enforce a settlement agreement that it claims to have reached with plaintiff-in-intervention Republic Bank ("RB")—but not with the defendant, New Castle County ("County")—during the course of voluntary mediation. * * * I find that the mediation was subject to Court of Chancery Rule 174 and that the terms of that rule and the public policy underlying it require denial of WH's application. I also conclude that WH has failed to show that WH ever agreed to settle without the active agreement of the County. Thus, the motion to enforce a settlement that does not include the County must be denied.

This * * * [case] arise[s] out of the refusal of the County to issue a certificate of occupancy ("CO") and other necessary permits and licenses for the Wilmington Radisson Hotel to open for business. The County initially refused the CO when its inspectors discovered that the square footage of the hotel, as built, greatly exceeded the limits set in the record plan for the development. RB was allowed to intervene in the action to better protect its collateral interest in the property. On October 20 and November 3, 2000, I heard WH's applications for temporary and preliminary injunctive relief. * * * I denied the relief sought because WH failed to satisfy the standards for obtaining mandatory equitable relief.

At the time of the second hearing, there appeared to be two obstacles to opening the hotel. First, there were a number of health and safety issues that needed to be addressed and resolved before any CO could issue. These issues were more or less technical in nature and, while difficult to resolve in the context of a litigation, could be worked through by a well-designed and implemented program of mediation undertaken in good faith. Second, from a legal perspective, the continued financial and managerial involvement of the principals of WH in the project posed an obstacle to the ultimate ability of WH or RB to obtain the relief needed to open the hotel.

For these reasons, I suggested to the parties that they engage in a two-part mediation effort: one part aimed at eliminating (or at least minimizing) the health and safety issues, and the other at finding a solution to end WH's principals' continued involvement in the project. I suggested that Retired Resident Judge Bifferato serve as mediator. The parties agreed and met with Judge Bifferato on November 3, 2000. In connection with the mediation, I also scheduled trial.

As the mediation progressed, it became apparent that the arrangement to remove the WH principals from the deal, although dependent on the County's agreement to issue a CO, mostly involved a negotiation between WH and RB, who pursued those discussions with Judge Bifferato. The County's involvement in this aspect of the discussions was largely limited to reacting to structures proposed by the others and identifying conditions to its agreement to issue the CO and cooperate in opening the hotel in full.

Although not spelled out in detail in the record before me on this motion, I understand that the other aspect of the mediation made progress in addressing and narrowing the health and safety issues that stood in the way of issuing a CO. In particular, I understand that, assuming a satisfactory resolution of the other aspect of the mediation, the County was prepared to issue a temporary CO for a 102,000 square foot operation and to work cooperatively with a new owner to secure the permits necessary to open all 158,000 square feet of the building.

On November 27, 2000, the day before the scheduled trial, I met with counsel for all parties, at the request of RB's counsel. * * * [C]ounsel for both RB and WH indicated that their clients had reached an agreement in principle to resolve the financial and managerial aspect of the mediation and that, with a single exception, there was an overall agreement with the County. That exception related to the County's demand for the inclusion of a restrictive deed covenant relating to the involvement, directly or indirectly, of WH's principals and their affiliates and relatives in future ownership of the hotel. * * *

In what now appears to have been a gambit to force the County to come to terms on its deed restriction demand, counsel for RB and WH expressed a willingness to settle the issues between them without the County's agreement. * * *

RB's counsel quickly made clear, however, that it did not propose to move forward without the County's agreement. Instead, it proposed to delay the trial and to continue the mediation process with Judge Bifferato over the County's deed restriction demands. * * * I put the trial off without date and directed that the parties present a formal written settlement agreement on December 6, 2000.

Thereafter, counsel for RB prepared a draft three-party settlement agreement and circulated it to WH, but not the County. WH, through its counsel, objected to its terms and made a counter-proposal that was not acceptable to RB. Eventually, discussions broke down between RB and WH, leading to RB's decision to substitute new counsel. On December 6, 2000, the parties informed the court of the lack of progress. WH thereafter filed a motion to enforce the terms of a claimed two-party agreement to settle between it and RB.

WH contends that the terms of this settlement can be gleaned from a series of letters counsel for RB and WH exchanged between November 17 and 21, 2000. These letters were written in connection with the mediation and reflect the parties' efforts to reach a mediated settlement. WH also relies on several affidavits, including an affidavit of its counsel discussing at length the substance of the mediation.

[The court first finds that Court of Chancery Rule 174 ("Voluntary mediation in the Court of Chancery") governs the mediation at issue.] * * * [T]wo subparts of [Rule 174] are of particular importance. Subpart (g) provides that, if the parties to the mediation reach an agreement, "their agreement shall be reduced to writing and signed by the parties and the mediator. The agreement shall set forth the terms of the resolution of the issues and the future responsibility of each party." Subpart (d) provides that any "communication made in or in connection with the mediation that relates to the controversy being mediated, whether made to the mediator or a party, . . . is confidential" and is "not subject to disclosure in *any judicial or administrative proceeding*" (emphasis added). The only exceptions to this rule of confidentiality are where all the mediation parties agree in writing to waive confidentiality, or where the material was not prepared specifically for mediation and is otherwise subject to discovery. RB and the County argue that, taken together, these provisions preclude (i) WH's motion to enforce a mediated settlement not reduced to writing and signed by the parties and the mediator, and (ii) WH's introduction into the record and reliance on any communications between the parties to the mediation made in connection with it. * * *

WH [counters] that the confidentiality provisions of the rule only apply to communications made at a mediation conference and that the four letters it relies on as evidencing the terms of the settlement were exchanged outside the context of a specific mediation conference. This argument misreads the rule. The portion of Rule 174(d) WH relies on provides for the confidential treatment of communications made to *any person* "if made at a mediation conference." WH ignores the far broader confidential treatment accorded by the same subpart of the rule to communications to *the mediator or a party* "made *in or in connection with* the mediation that relates to the controversy being mediated." (Emphasis added.) This broader treatment plainly and unambiguously covers the series of letters WH relies on to prove the terms of the alleged settlement agreement. Those letters contain communications to parties to the mediation, were sent in connection with the mediation, and relate to the controversy being mediated. * * *

Confidentiality of all communications between the parties or among them and the mediator serves the important public policy of promoting a broad discussion of potential resolutions to the matters being mediated. Without the expectation of confidentiality, parties would hesitate to propose compromise solutions out of the concern that they would later be prejudiced by their disclosure. I have already concluded that the series of letters on which WH seeks to rely are entitled to confidential treatment in accordance with subpart (d) of the rule and, thus, "are not subject to disclosure in any judicial . . . proceeding." For these reasons, I cannot rely on them to discover the terms of the settlement WH says it reached with RB [and WH's motion to enforce must be denied.]

Relatedly, it is consistent with the purpose of Rule 174 to interpret subpart (g) thereof as requiring that any settlement between the parties to the mediation be reduced to writing and signed by them and the mediator as a condition to its enforceability. As this proceeding itself well illustrates, it is reasonable to expect that such a bright-line rule is the best way to protect the confidentiality of the mediation when disputes arise over the terms of a putative settlement. Where, as here, there is *no* written settlement signed by *anyone,* it is impossible for the parties to litigate over the terms of the putative agreement without breaching the confidentiality of the mediation process in a substantial way. Indeed, WH argues that the terms of the settlement can be gleaned from a series of four letters each prepared and sent in connection with the mediation. [I recognize that a dispute could arise about the enforceability of a settlement memorialized in writing and signed by fewer than all the parties and do not decide the questions raised by that scenario. *See, e.g. Few v. Hammack Enterprises, Inc.,* 511 S E.2d 665 (N.C. Ct. App. 1999). ("Mediated Settlement Agreement" prepared by mediator and, subsequently signed by plaintiff, could be enforced against non-signing defendant without invading privileged confidentiality of mediation).] * * *

I also conclude that the motion should be denied because the County is not a party to WH's putative agreement with RB. Yet, the object of the litigation and the mediation—opening the Wilmington Radisson Hotel—could not be accomplished by a settlement that did not include the County. While it is possible that WH and RB could have agreed to resolve some issues arising out of their lending relationship that were not even part of a litigation at the time, they could not have agreed to a settlement of this case without the participation of the County. * * *

For the reasons stated above, I deny plaintiff's motion for enforcement of settlement. I also conclude that all confidential mediation material that has been made part of the record in this proceeding and all other documents that reveal or discuss confidential information relating to the mediation should be sealed. Counsel for Republic Bank are to submit an order within 5 days of the date of this opinion.

Notes

1. The cases discuss agreements that are the result of mediations. Once an agreement has been reached, what is the role of the mediator in drafting the agreement? What is the role of counsel for the disputants? How does a mediation agreement differ, if at all, from an ordinary contract? What terms should a mediation agreement contain? How clearly must the mediation agreement, or contract, be drafted to guide the parties in the post-mediation phase? What happens if the mediation agreement isn't complete, clear, or comprehensive?

2. The case describes a breakdown in the mediation when the parties attempted to commit the agreement to paper. What practices within the mediation process could have helped avoid an impasse at this point?

3. In West Beach Marina, Ltd. v. Erdeljac, 94 S.W.3d 248 (Tex.App. 2002), one of the issues adjudicated was whether a mediation agreement was sufficiently detailed to be enforceable. The case involved a dispute that arose when West Beach Marina applied for a permit to build a marina which neighbors contended would interfere with their easement across the property. Following a lengthy mediation, the parties authorized their attorneys to prepare and sign an agreement. West Beach then repudiated the agreement. Although the agreement did not refer to or settle certain aspects of the dispute, the court found that it was definite enough to be enforceable. The agreement demonstrated that the parties intended to be bound by it and contained sufficient terms to bind the parties to the representations it contained. Compare Haghighi v. Russian–American Broadcasting Co., 577 N.W.2d 927 (Minn. 1998) (under the requirements of the Minnesota Civil Mediation Act, a handwritten agreement prepared by the parties' attorneys at the close of a mediation session was unenforceable where the document

failed to state that the agreement was binding); Schwartz v. Adamson, 1999 WL 170676 (Minn.App.1999, unpublished) (an oral agreement reached in a mediation session was unenforceable where a written agreement prepared by the mediator a day after the mediation was never signed by the parties and failed to state that the agreement was binding); Environmental Abatement, Inc. v. Astrum R.E. Corp., 27 S.W.3d 530 (Tenn.Ct.App.2000) (where a contractor was allowed to withdraw consent to a mediated agreement that was not made on the record or in open court, as defined by the rules of the state Supreme Court).

4. Plum Creek Timber Co., L.P. v. Hillman, 95 Wash.App. 1061 (1999) (settlement agreements are considered to be contracts and their construction is governed by contract law); Brown v. Brown, 2002 WL 1343222 (Tex.App. 2002, not designated for publication) (a mediated settlement reserving mineral rights held enforceable as a binding contract under general contract law).

5. The American Bar Association's Model Rules of Professional Conduct contain interesting language regarding the lawyer's duty to advise clients regarding mediation and ADR. Model Rule 1.4(b) states: "A lawyer shall explain a matter to the extent reasonably necessary to permit the client to make informed decisions regarding the representation." Model Rule 1.2(a) states: "A lawyer shall abide by a client's decisions concerning the objectives of representation * * * and shall consult with the client as to the means by which they are to be pursued." The language of the Model Rules does not clearly require lawyers to allow clients to decide whether and how to pursue ADR. The Comment to Model Rule 2.1 states: "[W]hen a matter is likely to involve litigation it may be necessary * * * to inform the client of forms of dispute resolution that might constitute reasonable alternatives to litigation." State rules adopted by Arkansas, Colorado, Georgia, Hawaii, and Ohio encourage discussing ADR with clients; rules in Massachusetts, Michigan, Pennsylvania, and Virginia require lawyers to inform clients of ADR options. See Robert F. Cochran, Jr., Educating Clients on ADR Alternatives, Los Angeles Lawyer, October, 2002, and Professional Rules and ADR: Control of Alternative Dispute Resolution Under the ABA Ethics 2000 Committee Proposal and Other Professional Responsibility Standards, 28 Fordham Urb. L. J. 895 (2001).

SECTION 3. REVIEW BY THE COURTS

A. INTRODUCTION

We have been studying judicial review from the outset. Every land use case raises important questions about the role of the courts, and the posture and attitude of the courts shed light on the land use decision-making process. The Standard Zoning Enabling Act established rules that govern judicial review of the decisions of zoning and planning boards. These bodies typically conduct hearings and keep a record of their proceedings. This record can be certified to a court issuing a writ of certiorari. Once again, statutes in each state define the matter and redress from administrative and quasi-judicial land use decisions varies according to the state law definitions. The definition of an aggrieved party, the statute of limitations for bringing an action, and the administrative remedies available prior to court review are built into most state land use enabling statutes. What happens, however, when the aggrieved party challenges a legislative decision, such as a rezoning of a parcel? The rights of individuals to challenge the legislative decisions of governments are governed by a different body of law, and other writs, statutes of limitation, standards of review, and remedies may apply.

In this section we encounter a variety of judicial review issues: standing, ripeness, finality, exhaustion, standards of review, burdens of proof, res judicata, and remedies, among other matters.

FRITTS v. CITY OF ASHLAND

Court of Appeals of Kentucky, 1961.
348 S.W.2d 712.

CULLEN, COMMISSIONER.

The Board of Commissioners of the City of Ashland rezoned from R–2 Residential to I–1 Light Industrial a tract of four acres which was in single ownership. A group of neighboring property owners brought action attacking the rezoning ordinance on the ground that it was arbitrary, capricious and unreasonable. The circuit court entered judgment upholding the ordinance and the plaintiffs have appealed.

Ashland adopted a comprehensive zoning ordinance in 1955, following a study with the assistance of state experts that began in 1951. The city bounds on the Ohio River on the northeast and extends to the south and west. The area along the river was zoned for industrial and commercial uses. Aside from this area only two other districts were zoned for light industry, one in the northwest quarter of the city and the other near the west boundary. The rest of the city was zoned residential, except for appropriately located small commercial districts and for necessary educational, institutional and recreational areas. The tract here in question, which is called the Wilson tract, is located near the geographical center of the city in a neighborhood that is residential in character. The tract is two blocks from a grade school accommodating 350 children and three blocks from the presently being constructed senior high school which will have an enrollment of some 1200 students. The nearest industrially zoned property is one and one-half miles away.

* * *

The Wilson tract was rezoned in September 1960. It is clear from the record that the zoning change was made because the owners of a garment factory, which had outgrown its existing location in the city, desired to build a new factory on the Wilson tract, and threatened to leave the city unless this tract was made available. There is no pretense that the zoning change was a step in any coordinated plan for establishment of industrial districts.

The contention of the appellants is, of course, that this is a case of spot zoning.

There was no evidence of any change in the neighborhood since the enactment of the original zoning ordinance in 1955, nor was there proof that the Wilson tract was by its situation distinguishable in character from the surrounding or adjoining property. Therefore, under the decision in Byrn v. Beechwood Village, Ky., 253 S.W.2d 395, the zoning change on its face was arbitrary, capricious and unreasonable, and the burden was on the city authorities to justify the change.

The city authorities have attempted to justify their action on two grounds. One is that the "general welfare" of the city will be promoted by reason of employment being provided for some 400 citizens in the relocated garment factory. The other is that zoning in Ashland was still in a formative state and therefore the city should be entitled to great latitude in modifying the original plan.

The argument with respect to the first ground points up a common fallacy that seems to exist in the minds of zoning agencies. It is that the particular use that a particular owner says he intends to make of a particular tract of land is a controlling factor. Here the Wilson tract was rezoned because the Wilsons said they intended to convey it to the owners of the garment factory who said they intended to build a new garment factory there. However, the ordinance did not rezone the tract for use by the Ashland Crafts Garment Factory but for any appropriate light industry use. There was no guaranty that either the Wilsons or the garment factory people would not change their minds, resulting in the tract being occupied by some light industry that would not have the appealing features of the proposed garment factory. * * * The point is that in establishing a light industry zone the only proper consideration is whether in the light of a comprehensive, coordinated zoning plan the particular area should be set aside for general light industry uses. See Pierson Trapp Co. v. Peak, Ky., 340 S.W.2d 456.

Regardless of the foregoing considerations, the general welfare argument is not sound. The providing of employment opportunities is merely one element of general welfare as that term relates to the zoning field. Sociological factors, protection of property values, traffic and safety considerations, preservation of health, providing adequate light and air, all enter into the question of general welfare. See KRS 100.066, 100.520. If the appellees' argument were carried to its logical conclusion the mere fact that employment would be provided through a particular use of land would overcome all other factors, and a boiler factory could be put in the middle of a beautiful residential neighborhood.

The appellees argue that it is essential to the welfare of the city that the garment factory be retained, and that there are not suitable light industry sites in the city other than the Wilson tract. Our answer to that is that if the lack of suitable industrial sites is due to the restrictions of the present zoning ordinance a study and survey of the situation should be made, suitable areas for industrial development selected, and changes made in the zoning ordinance in accordance with systematic planning. On the other hand, if lack of suitable sites is due to other factors no real solution to the long range problem is reached by momentarily satisfying one particular industry.

The proposition that zoning in Ashland is in the formative state is based upon a statement in the report of the consultants who prepared the 1959 *master plan,* to the effect that the work on the master plan was of limited scope and therefore should be considered subject to modification when additional studies were made, and that the "Land Use Plan" and the "Major Street Plan" were designated as "preliminary". As hereinbefore mentioned, the master plan relates only to *public facilities,* such as streets, sewers, parks, public utilities, airports, etc., and does not establish private use restrictions or districts. Accordingly, the fact that the master plan may have been in a formative state does not mean that the zoning ordinance establishing private use restrictions and districts was in any way preliminary or conditional. Furthermore, even if the zoning ordinance should be considered in a formative state it would not follow that modifications could be made without regard to any coordinated plan.

The circuit court found as a fact that the zoning change was "in accord with an orderly plan of zoning development." The evidence does not support that finding but on the contrary shows that the change was made solely to meet a particular exigency.

The circuit court further found that there was no evidence to show that the plaintiffs or other property owners would be injured by the rezoning, and that there was substantial proof that the neighborhood would be improved. However, as pointed out in Byrn v. Beechwood Village, Ky., 253 S.W.2d 395, Shemwell v. Speck, Ky., 265 S.W.2d 468, and Pierson Trapp Co. v. Peak, Ky., 340 S.W.2d 456, the effect of a zoning change on the value of neighboring property is only one factor to be considered, and the purpose of zoning is not to protect the value of the property of particular individuals but rather to promote the welfare of the community as a whole. The entire community is damaged by haphazard zoning because it causes insecurity of property values throughout the city. So the mere fact that the particular complaining parties may not suffer a decrease in the value of their property will not redeem a zoning change that is not related to proper zoning objects.

In our opinion we have here a clear case of spot zoning and the ordinance making the zoning change must be held invalid.

We feel impelled to express briefly our view of the proper theory of zoning as relates to the making of changes in an original comprehensive ordinance. We think the theory is that after the enactment of the original ordinance there should be a continuous or periodic study of the development of property uses, the nature of population trends, and the commercial and industrial growth, both actual and prospective. On the basis of such study, changes may be made intelligently, systematically, and according to a coordinated plan designed to promote zoning objectives. An examination of the multitude of zoning cases that have reached this court leads us to the conclusion that the common practice of zoning agencies, after the adoption of an original ordinance, is simply to wait until some property owner finds an opportunity to acquire a financial advantage by devoting his property to a use other than that for which it is zoned, and then struggle with the question of whether some excuse can be found for complying with his request for a rezoning. The result has been that in most of the rezoning cases reaching the courts there actually has been spot zoning and the courts have upheld or invalidated the change according to how flagrant the violation of true zoning principles has been. It is to be hoped that in the future zoning authorities will give recognition to the fact that an essential feature of zoning is *planning.*

The judgment is reversed, with directions to enter judgment holding the rezoning ordinance invalid.

Notes

1. Does the local legislative body, the Board of Commissioners in the principal case, have the legal authority to adopt a zoning amendment that does not conform with the comprehensive plan? If not, its action is *ultra vires*, beyond the city's legal authority. Is it a legitimate function for the judiciary to review whether municipal corporations act within their authority? What does this case tell us about the importance of having a comprehensive plan and using it as the predicate for subsequent legislative zoning decisions?

2. When a court considers the remedy available in a land use case, does it matter what type of body made the decision being reviewed? When will a court, for example, issue a writ of mandamus ordering a legislature to rezone a parcel? In Landgrave v. Watson, 593 S.W.2d 875 (Ky.App.1979), the local legislative authority refused to rezone property for use as a liquor store in an area where the factual setting prevented any realistic development for residential purposes. The trial court ordered the rezoning and the court of appeals reversed, stating: "The scope of the circuit court's inquiry in reviewing the action of a legislative body in a zoning case is limited. It can decide if the agency acted in excess of granted powers and if it afforded procedural due process to all parties * * *. Further, a de novo trial is impermissible." What does the court mean when it says a trial de novo is impermissible? Did the legislative body create a record of the facts it gathered on which its decision is based? Why should a court refrain from conducting a trial to discover and reassess the facts chosen by the legislative body to guide its discretion in deciding whether and how to act? Must a local legislature entertain any property owner's petition to rezone land or can it simply refuse to act as a method of ratifying its current comprehensive plan and zoning scheme? Also see State ex rel. Barber & Sons Tobacco Co., Inc. v. Jackson County, 869 S.W.2d 113 (Mo.App.1993), where the court affirmed the refusal to rezone a 12–acre parcel from residential to a zoning classification to permit construction of a concrete batch mixing plant despite the fact that the property was in the middle of a rock quarry, adjacent to an asphalt plant and rock crusher, and was used to store crushed rock and by-products.

3. Is the decision of the local legislature to rezone a parcel a legislative one or an administrative or quasi-judicial one? Do you think that a court will act differently, using different standards of review, if it is reviewing a legislative rather than an administrative or quasi-judicial decision? One difficulty prominent in zoning cases is the uncertainty about whether to classify zoning decisions as legislative in character, which would dictate a narrow scope of review (arbitrary, irrational), or administrative or quasi-judicial, which would give the court more flexibility in considering the "reasonableness" of the zoning decision. Complicating the problem even more is the evident penchant of some courts to engage in what might be called "judicial zoning."

Consider the following expressions of judicial opinion:

a. City of Phoenix v. Beall, 22 Ariz.App. 141, 524 P.2d 1314 (1974):

The plaintiffs concede that the enactment of an overall zoning ordinance is legislative action. They contend that the City Council, in enacting or declining to enact a zoning amendment of the type which the plaintiffs request, is acting more nearly in a judicial than in a legislative capacity. This contention appears to relate to the quantum of proof necessary for a court decision overturning the refusal to rezone. We do not agree. The United States Supreme Court in Village of Belle Terre v. Boraas, 416 U.S. 1, 94 S.Ct. 1536, 39 L.Ed.2d 797 (1974), stated:

* * * But every line drawn by a legislature leaves some out that might well have been included. That exercise of discretion, however, is a legislative not a judicial function. [Footnote omitted.] 416 U.S. at 7, 94 S.Ct. at 1540, 39 L.Ed.2d at 803, 804.

The Arizona Legislature in empowering cities to zone specifies that zoning and zoning changes be "by ordinance." The Arizona cases recognize that zoning is legislative and that there is a presumption of the validity of zoning enactments. * * * Zoning will be upheld unless it is clearly arbitrary and unreasonable and without a substantial relation to public health, safety, morals or general welfare. * * *

If the evidence is fairly debatable the zoning or failure to change the zoning as requested will be upheld in the appellate courts. * * *

The test to be used by the trial court is that zoning will be upheld unless it is clearly arbitrary and unreasonable and without substantial relation to public health, safety, morals or general welfare. Zoning ordinances are presumed valid, and where the reasonableness of the ordinance is fairly debatable, the trial court must uphold its validity.

What is the applicable standard to be used by the appellate court in reviewing the trial court's decision to upset the zoning ordinance which in effect finds that the presumption of validity of zoning has been overcome? In one case, City of Phoenix v. Burke, 9 Ariz.App. 395, 452 P.2d 722 (1969), a case not presented to our Supreme Court for review, the majority of the Court used the usual standards of review in civil actions, namely, that the trial court will be upheld if there is evidence in support of its judgment. We hold that the test applied in Burke is not the law in Arizona. * * * The ruling of a trial court which upsets zoning will be upheld only if the zoning is clearly arbitrary and unreasonable and without substantial relation to the public health, safety, morals or general welfare. Furthermore, if in a review of the record, the appellate court finds that it is fairly debatable as to whether the zoning is clearly arbitrary and unreasonable and without a substantial relation to the above factors, then the zoning or the failure to amend the zoning will be upheld and the trial court will be reversed. The fact that the property would be more valuable if zoned for a different use is not controlling.

b. Carter v. Adams, 928 S.W.2d 39 (Tenn.App.1996):

[Landowners sought a zoning change from A–1, Agriculture, Light Industry to M–2, Heavy Industry to operate a demolition landfill; the planning commission denied the request, but the county commission rezoned the land. The lower court held the zoning change to be unreasonable and arbitrary.] On appeal:

Zoning bodies are legislative in nature and the scope of judicial review for their actions is restricted. * * * Over time, the standards of "fairly debatable," "rational basis," and "arbitrary and capricious" have come to hold the same meaning * * *. Whichever term is applied, the level of scrutiny required of the court is to "refrain from substituting its judgment for that of a local governmental body * * * If any possible reason exists justifying the action, it will be upheld." [Citation omitted.]

c. MacDonald v. Board of County Comm'rs, 238 Md. 549, 210 A.2d 325 (1965) (dissenting opinion):

The majority states, in effect, that rezoning can only be sustained when there is "strong evidence of mistake" in the original zoning or where there is "a substantial change in conditions" in the neighborhood. This "mistake-change in conditions" rule came into the Maryland law by way of dicta of our predecessors and in a rather oblique way. The "change in conditions" concept seems to be first stated, without any supporting authority, in Northwest Merchants Terminal v. O'Rourke, 191 Md. 171, 60 A.2d 743 (1948). It was repeated in a restricted form in Cassel v. Mayor and City Council of Baltimore, 195 Md. 348, 358, 73 A.2d 486, 488 (1950). This *dictum* was then expanded by additional *dicta* in Kracke v. Weinberg, 197 Md. 339, 79 A.2d 387, 391 (1951) which added "mistake in original zoning" to a "change in the character of the neighborhood"—and so the Maryland Rule of "mistake-change in conditions" was born. It was entirely judicially conceived and delivered. It had no legislative assistance. It has had a rapid and, to my mind, unhealthy growth in the Maryland law. The formulae have become talismanic phrases now applied with Draconian severity to the rezoning efforts of the local legislative bodies, with unfortunate results. In my opinion, the time to re-examine the entire doctrine and its premises is long overdue. As it is entirely "judge-made," a change in, or broadening of, the doctrine would operate only prospectively and would in no way impair vested rights, inasmuch as it is not a rule of property. Under these circumstances, the doctrine of *stare decisis* is not a substantial obstacle in effecting a much-needed change. If my Brethren are reluctant to overrule or modify the "mistake-change" doctrine, I suggest with great respect, that the Legislative Council and ultimately the General Assembly give serious thought to a change by appropriate legislation.

In Buckel v. Board of County Commissioners, 80 Md.App. 305, 562 A.2d 1297 (1989), cert. denied 318 Md. 96, 566 A.2d 1112 (1989), the court, applying the same principles decried by the dissenter in the MacDonald case, held that a small increase in population, construction of a shopping center, and neighborhood rezonings did not constitute a substantial change. The planning staff and the board had both approved the rezoning of land zoned agricultural for the construction of a motel and the neighbors were the appellants.

NEUZIL v. CITY OF IOWA CITY

Supreme Court of Iowa, 1990.
451 N.W.2d 159.

LAVORATO, JUSTICE.

In this law action, the district court concluded a zoning amendment that downzoned undeveloped property was valid. The property owners appealed. We transferred the case to the court of appeals, which reversed. Because we think the district court was right, we vacate the decision of the court of appeals and affirm the judgment of the district court.

I. BACKGROUND FACTS AND PROCEEDINGS.

The Neuzil family owns an eight and one-half acre tract of land (tract) southwest of the University of Iowa Hospitals and Clinics in Iowa City. They have owned the tract since 1941. Mrs. Ella Neuzil and a son Gregory occupy houses on the tract. There also is a rental house there, but the remainder of the tract is undeveloped.

* * *

In 1962 Iowa City adopted a comprehensive zoning plan known as the Bartholomew Plan. Under the plan the tract was zoned R–3A. The R–3A zoning allowed multifamily dwellings and permitted up to forty-four units per acre.

In 1972 the tract was rezoned from R–3A to R–3. The R–3 zoning also allowed multifamily dwellings but limited the number of units per acre to fourteen.

In 1978 Iowa City adopted a new comprehensive plan. * * *

There was no new zoning concerning the tract pursuant to the 1978 Comprehensive Plan. However, this plan recommended that the tract be limited to residential development at a density of eight to sixteen dwellings per acre.

In 1983 Iowa City updated its comprehensive zoning plan. The tract was then zoned RM–12, a zoning that had the same limitations as the R–3 zoning. For all practical purposes the tract was under the same use restrictions as it was in 1972.

In 1985 after many requests from area residents, the tract was again downzoned, this time to RS–8. RS–8 zoning is for single-family or duplex dwellings and permits only eight units per acre.

The Neuzil family has consistently objected to the downzoning. Each time the family claimed that the proposed zoning would decrease the value of the tract. The family, however, had agreed not to sell or begin developing the tract for commercial purposes while Ella was still alive.

In the 1960s and 1970s much of the area surrounding the tract was highly developed. The tract borders University Heights on the north and west side. In fact, the only access to the tract is through streets from University Heights although the tract is in Iowa City. The land abutting the tract in University Heights is single-family residential. The land to the east and south of the tract consists of single-family dwellings. A ravine runs east and west on the tract and drains into Melrose Lake, which is on the land immediately east of the tract. The land * * * immediately east of the tract was also downzoned to RS–8 in 1985. But its owners did apply for, and received, a variance to permit multifamily occupancy.

Because the tract was undeveloped, the neighbors often used it for recreational purposes. In fact, residents in the area tried unsuccessfully to get University Heights and Iowa City to purchase the tract for a neighborhood park.

Shortly after the 1983 zoning ordinance was adopted, owners of the Smith land were making plans to develop their land as permitted under the then existing zoning ordinance. Residents from University Heights and Iowa City who lived close to the tract organized the Melrose Lake Association.

Because the association did not want more multifamily housing in the area, it petitioned the Iowa City Planning Commission to downzone the tract, as well as the Smith land to RS–8. When the commission refused, the association petitioned the city council of Iowa City to downzone the tract.

The city council held two public hearings on the petition in March and April 1985. Proponents and opponents of the proposed downzoning were heard. On June 4, 1985, the council voted to downzone the tract to RS–8.

The city council drafted its findings and reasons for approving the downzoning after the Neuzils filed the present lawsuit. The district court, however, found that the council had indeed relied on these reasons in downzoning the tract. These reasons included the following: 1. The Neuzil tract contains 8.5 acres of land, with direct access only into streets through residential neighborhoods. 2. The Neuzil tract is surrounded on three sides by single-family residential neighborhoods, those on the north and west being located in the Town of University Heights. On June 4, 1985, the property to the east of the Neuzil tract was also rezoned to RS–8. 3. The streets in the single-family neighborhood abutting the Neuzil tract were not designed to handle heavy amounts of traffic, and the other streets in the area are already heavily traveled. 4. Development of the Neuzil tract at the maximum density permitted in the RM–12 zone would allow construction of approximately 126 additional dwelling units raising the potential for generating approximately 1550 motor vehicle trips daily. 5. The allowable density on the Neuzil tract will reduce the potential increase to traffic congestion on the streets in the immediate area. 6. The area is shown on the City's Comprehensive Plan as being developed at 8 to 16 dwellings per acre, and the RS–8 zoning is consistent with that Plan. 7. Multifamily development of the tract, at the density permitted in the RM–12 zone, would have a negative impact on the value of property surrounding the tract. Development of the density permitted in the RS–8 zone should help maintain the value of neighboring properties. 8. The Neuzil tract contains a pond and two large, partially wooded ravines, and the property immediately to the east of the Neuzil tract contains Melrose Lake, an environmentally sensitive and important feature of the area. 9. Storm water runoff occasionally causes Melrose Lake to overflow, floods areas downstream, and contributes to pollution of the lake. 10. Development at a lower density will reduce the magnitude of the increase in Melrose Lake drainage, flooding and pollution problems, but will still permit development which is sensitive to the fragile environment.

Following the 1985 rezoning, the Neuzils brought this suit against Iowa City, seeking a declaratory judgment and damages. They wanted the 1985 downzoning declared void as unreasonable. They also sought damages based on claims of tortious interference with business opportunities, an unconstitutional taking without just compensation, and inverse condemnation. The suit was filed at law and tried to the court. On the day of trial, the Neuzils withdrew their inverse condemnation claim.

The district court found that the 1985 downzoning amendment was reasonable and that the Neuzils had not proven their claims of tortious interference or civil rights violation. The Neuzils appealed, raising one issue: Was the 1985 downzoning amendment valid under the circumstances?

The court of appeals, using a de novo review, reversed. We granted the city's petition for further review, and the case is now before us.

* * *

III. Validity of the 1985 Amendment Downzoning the Tract.

Zoning is an exercise of the police powers delegated by the State to municipalities. Iowa Code § 414.1 (1985). A zoning ordinance, including any amendments to it, carries a strong presumption of validity. This means that if the ordinance is facially valid and the reasonableness of the ordinance is fairly debatable, it must be allowed to stand. Anderson v. City of Cedar Rapids, 168 N.W.2d 739, 742 (Iowa 1969). Stated another way,

> [t]he validity of an ordinance is said to be fairly debatable when for any reason it is open to dispute or controversy on grounds that make sense or point to a logical deduction that in no way involves its constitutional validity, and validity is fairly debatable where reasonable minds may differ, or where the evidence provides a basis for a fair difference of opinion as to the constitutionality of the ordinance or its application to particular property. 1 Anderson, American Law of Zoning 3d, § 3.20, at 137 (1986) (citations omitted).

So "if there is some basis for the ordinance . . . and there is room for two opinions, the challenged ordinance is valid." Id.

An ordinance is valid if it has any real, substantial relation to the public health, comfort, safety, and welfare, including the maintenance of property values. Anderson v. City of Cedar Rapids, 168 N.W.2d at 742; Iowa Code § 414.1. In applying this test, the court's prime consideration is the ordinance's general purpose and not the hardship of an individual case. Id.

Even though a challenged zoning ordinance adversely affects a property interest or prohibits the most beneficial use of the property, a court should not, for that reason alone, strike it down. Stone v. City of Wilton, 331 N.W.2d 398, 402 (Iowa 1983). This rule applies to the original zoning ordinance and amendments to it because we recognize that zoning is not static. Id. at 403.

Iowa law requires municipalities to pass all zoning ordinances in accordance with a comprehensive plan. Iowa Code § 414.3. Among other things, such ordinances should be designed to encourage efficient urban development patterns; to lessen congestion in the streets; to service the public from fire, flood, panic, and other dangers; to promote health and the general welfare; to provide adequate light and air; to prevent the overcrowding of land; and to avoid undue concentration of population. Id. In passing such ordinances a municipality is required by law to give reasonable consideration . . . to the character of the [area in question] and the peculiar suitability of [the area] for particular uses, and with a view to conserving the value of buildings and encouraging the most appropriate use of land throughout [the] city. Id.

A change in conditions sometimes calls for a change in plans. For this reason, a property owner has no vested right to continuity of zoning of the general area in which the owner resides. Likewise, the owners of property adjacent to a district which is restricted to a particular use have no vested right in the continuation of that use when the public interest dictates otherwise. Anderson, § 4.26, at 286.

A municipality's power to amend zoning ordinances does have some restrictions. Generally, the municipality may not "amend a comprehensive zoning law to remove or impose more or less onerous restrictions upon a small tract or lot similar in character and use to the surrounding property." Hermann v. City of Des Moines, 250 Iowa 1281, 1286–87, 97 N.W.2d 893, 896 (1959). A zoning amendment reflecting such a discrepancy in similarly-situated property is discriminatory. Id. This type of regulation is called spot zoning and should be upheld only if there are "substantial and reasonable grounds or basis" for the discriminatory treatment. Id. 97 N.W.2d at 897.

Nor may the municipality downzone property to the point that the property cannot be improved with any development that would be economically feasible. Kempf v. City of Iowa City, 402 N.W.2d 393, 400 (Iowa 1987). In these circumstances the downzoning amounts to an unconstitutional taking. Id. at 400–01. Such a result is another way of saying that the ordinance, as applied to the particular property, is unreasonable.

The Neuzils did not contend in the district court that the 1985 downzoning amendment constituted spot zoning. Although the Neuzils did claim the amendment constituted inverse condemnation, they withdrew that claim on the day of trial.

In the district court the Neuzils tried the case on the theory that the 1985 rezoning amendment was unreasonable, arbitrary, and capricious. In support of their theory the Neuzils urged a number of reasons why the amendment was unreasonable. We restrict our review to that theory and to those reasons.

The district court noted that for the Neuzils to prevail the court would have to adopt the Maryland rule on rezoning. The district court properly refused to do so, recognizing that it was bound to follow our pronouncements on the subject.

Under the Maryland rule once land is zoned it can only be rezoned to correct an original error or because of a change in circumstances. Northwest Merchants Terminal v. O'Rourke, 191 Md. 171, 189–193, 60 A.2d 743, 752–53 (1948). Undergirding the rule is the presumption of reasonableness as to the original ordinance. Id. Moreover, if the question of correctness or change is fairly debatable, the court will not substitute its judgment for that of the zoning authority. Wakefield v. Kraft, 202 Md. 136, 147, 96 A.2d 27, 29 (1953). Such an approach gives the original zoning regulation a greater presumption of correctness than the amendment.

After surveying cases concerning the Maryland rule, one writer observed that the greatest drawback in using the rule is that it completely thwarts the efforts of legislative or zoning authorities in the absence of satisfaction of [the "mistake or change" rule]; there are many circumstances where change is desirable, but impossible, due to the rule. H. Goldman, Zoning Change: Flexibility v. Stability, 26 Md.L.Rev. 48, 51 (1966) [hereinafter Goldman]. The facts in one Maryland case illustrate exactly what the writer means. See MacDonald v. Board of County Comm'rs for Prince George's County, 238 Md. 549, 210 A.2d 325 (1965). In MacDonald the property in question was zoned single family residential but had never been developed. As such there could be no showing of a change in condition. The developers wanted to build high-rise apartments on the land. The zoning board decided this might be a better use for the land, but no one had been able to prove the original zoning was erroneous when passed. As the writer concluded, [t]he reason for the change [in MacDonald] was evident—ideas had changed. A more modern jurisdiction would have allowed the change had the proponents shown the amendment to be reasonable and not arbitrary or capricious; the Maryland court, not able to satisfy the "mistake or change" test, had no choice but to strike down the amendment, no matter how reasonable and desirable it appeared to be. Goldman at 52.

In contrast our rule on amending zoning ordinances is considered more liberal and flexible. Under our approach we give the original zoning ordinance no greater presumption of validity than the amendment. The same standards used to justify original zoning are used in determining the propriety of amendatory ordinances. Id. at 53–54. We expressed our view on this point in Keller v. City of Council Bluffs, 246 Iowa 202, 207–08, 66 N.W.2d 113, 116–17 (1954):

> We are of the opinion the governing body of a municipality may amend its zoning ordinances anytime it deems circumstances and conditions warrant such actions, and such an amendment is valid if the procedural requirements of the statute are followed and it is not unreasonable or capricious nor inconsistent with the spirit and design of the zoning statute. The burden is upon the plaintiffs attacking the amendment to establish that the acts of the council were arbitrary, unreasonable, unjust and out of keeping with the spirit of the zoning statute. See also Iowa Code § 414.5 (municipality "may from time to time ... amend, supplement, change, modify, or repeal" zoning ordinances).

This liberality and flexibility expressed in Keller is consistent with the rule that in legislative matters a municipality may not bind its successors. Hanna v. Rathje, 171 N.W.2d 876, 880 (Iowa 1969). Such a rule is necessary because city council members are "trustees for the public." Id. So the determination of when the public's interest requires a change in zoning must be within the discretion of the municipality. Anderson, § 4.27 at 291. Because of this discretion, courts reviewing zoning amendments should not substitute their judgment as to the wisdom or propriety of the municipality's action when the reasonableness of the amendments is fairly debatable. Anderson v. City of Cedar Rapids, 168 N.W.2d at 742.

Here we need to review the written reasons the city gave for enacting the 1985 amendment that downzoned the tract. Only after such a review can we determine whether circumstances and conditions warranted the downzoning.

The district court found that the city had relied on the written reasons in downzoning the tract, that the reasons were proper ones to consider, and that the reasons were "debatably reasonable." The court concluded it could not, therefore, strike down the amendatory ordinance. For reasons that follow, we think there is substantial evidence to support the district court's findings.

The Neuzils cite their own reasons why the 1985 downzoning amendment is unreasonable, arbitrary, and capricious. They include the following: 1. The tract has proximity to the largest employer—The University of Iowa Hospitals and Clinics—in Johnson County, which is within walking distance. 2. City utilities are available. 3. The size of the tract will permit large-scale development and preserve open space. 4. Housing on this tract will help reduce the need for private automobile transportation. The city bus service is one block away. 5. Public schools are in the vicinity. 6. There are three access streets to the tract. 7. The tract is adjacent to other multifamily dwellings. 8. The area has been zoned for multifamily use since 1962. 9. Prior to the 1985 rezoning, there were no changes in the area or environment since the adoption of the most recent Iowa City Zoning Ordinance. All these reasons are arguments for developing the tract with multifamily units. However, balanced against Neuzils' reasons are the city's reasons for downzoning the tract. All the city's reasons are statutorily recognized. Moreover, there is substantial evidence to support each one.

While the tract was originally zoned for multifamily dwellings, the actual development of the surrounding area is mostly single-family and duplex dwellings. So the challenged amendment seeks to place the tract in conformity with other land in the same area. See Iowa Code § 414.3 (municipality is required to give reasonable consideration to the character of the area).

The city found that the prior zoning—RM–12—would increase the traffic flow in the area past its current accommodation. According to the city's thinking, the downzoning would reduce the potential for such burdensome traffic increases. Traffic considerations are reasonable grounds, under the city's police power, for amending zoning ordinances. See Iowa Code § 414.3 (zoning ordinances should be designed to lessen congestion in the streets).

Additionally, the city found that downzoning would help maintain the current property values in the area—a consideration that bears a substantial relationship to the public's health, safety, welfare and comfort. * * * Finally, the city considered the environmental impact of the current zoning. Consideration included both aesthetic impact and flood-pollution consequences of the prior RM–12 zoning. These two considerations take into account the safety and security of the area as well as the general public's comfort and welfare. * * *

One fact that bears on our analysis is that the 1978 Comprehensive Plan contemplated limiting development of the tract at eight to sixteen dwellings per acre. As the city recognized in its written reasons, the 1985 downzoning amendment is consistent with what the city had been contemplating since 1978. So the Neuzils should not have been surprised that what was contemplated in 1978 occurred in 1985. What the city did in 1985 was in keeping with the spirit of the 1978 Comprehensive Plan.

What immediately becomes apparent from our analysis is that there is a difference of opinion between the Neuzils and the city. Differing opinions are the crux of the "fairly debatable" rule—"if there is some basis for the ordinance ... and there is room for two opinions, the challenged ordinance is valid." Anderson, § 3.20, at 138.

The Neuzils' reasons boil down to this: the 1985 downzoning amendment prohibited the most beneficial use of the tract. As we said, this is not enough to brand a zoning ordinance as unreasonable, capricious or discriminatory. Stone v. City of Wilton, 331 N.W.2d at 402. The Neuzils offered no proof, as the plaintiffs did in Kempf, that the tract could not be improved with any development that would be economically feasible. See Kempf v. City of Iowa City, 402 N.W.2d at 400.

IV. Disposition.

The Neuzils' burden on appeal is a heavy one: to establish, as a matter of law, that the 1985 downzoning amendment was unreasonable, capricious or discriminatory. We think they failed to do so. Under the facts as found by the district court, we are convinced that the city acted within its authorized police power in downzoning the tract in 1985.

Accordingly, we vacate the decision of the court of appeals and affirm the judgment of the district court.

DECISION OF COURT OF APPEALS VACATED; DISTRICT COURT JUDGMENT AFFIRMED.

All justices concur except Schultz, J., who dissents.

Schultz, Justice (dissenting).

The fundamental justification for amending a zoning ordinance is a change in conditions making the amendment reasonably necessary to protect the public interest. 8 E. McQuillin, The Law of Municipal Corporations § 25.67b, at 170 (3d rev. ed. 1976). Here, the trial court found that there was no significant change in the general location from the 1983–84 zoning ordinance to the 1985 downzoning. Under the facts of this case, I would conclude that the action of the city council was unreasonable and should be declared invalid.

From the time this property was annexed by the city in 1956 until 1985, the city has never zoned the property in a manner that would prevent the construction of multifamily residences. In 1962 the city commissioned a comprehensive zoning plan which affected the property but allowed multifamily dwellings. In the 1960s and 1970s the surrounding property was highly developed. In 1978 the property was rezoned and a new comprehensive plan adopted. Following extensive studies a new ordinance was adopted in 1983. Because of a defect it was readopted during the spring of 1985. While the property was downzoned during this period, multi-resident dwellings were still allowed.

At the insistence of a group of neighbors and over the recommendation of its planning and zoning commission, the city council, four months after its latest ordinance, rezoned the property to a type of district which disallows multi-dwelling construction. Neighbors also use the land for recreational purposes, and their representatives had previously attempted to have the same undeveloped property made into a city park.

Because of its location near the stadium and the hospital, this property is best used as multifamily dwellings. The object of zoning is to put property to its best use.

I am aware that zoning is not static and existing ordinances are subject to reasonable revision as the need appears and that ordinances may be amended any time circumstances and conditions warrant such action. * * *

What was the reason for the ordinance amendment? After this action was filed, the city set forth the purported reasons for the rezoning. Traffic, pollution and congestion are not new to the area and were present both four months and two years earlier when the city studied this tract. This rezoning procedure was instituted by neighbors and not by the city or its planning staff. The obvious reason for the rezoning was neighborhood pressure. While I do not challenge or condemn the political process, I do not believe that the city council acted reasonably under the circumstances. It ignored the best use of the property and the interest of the general public in having housing convenient to Iowa City's largest employer. It bowed to a group who has enjoyed the use of this property and wishes to dictate its further use at the owners' expense. Without a careful restudy of the property in the area, the council had no legitimate reason to make changes.

I would reverse the trial court.

Notes

1. Neuzil is similar to many cases presented in the casebook. In this section, it permits the student to consider several aspects of the role of the courts in land use decision-making. What standard of review of the legislature's decision did the court use? Does that standard reflect a posture of deference on the part of the court to the legislative determination? If there is a fair difference of opinion about how a site should be zoned in one community in the state, which body—the local legislature or the state court—should decide which view prevails? Why? What remedies did the landowner petition the court to apply? Did it ask the court to rezone the property to a particular use or to declare that the allowed use was unreasonable under the circumstances? What would the effect be if a court determined that a rezoning decision was unreasonable? Who, then, would decide the use to which the land could be put?

2. Did the court in the principal case actually characterize the rezoning decision as a legislative one? Did the court treat it as one? Upon which party, the city or the landowner, did the court impose the burden of proof? Why?

FASANO v. BOARD OF COUNTY COMM'RS OF WASHINGTON COUNTY

Supreme Court of Oregon, In Banc, 1973.
264 Or. 574, 507 P.2d 23.

HOWELL, JUSTICE. The plaintiffs, homeowners in Washington county, unsuccessfully opposed a zone change before the Board of County Commissioners of Washington County. Plaintiffs applied for and received a writ of review of the action of the commissioners allowing the change. The trial court found in favor of plaintiffs, disallowed the zone change, and reversed the commissioners' order. The Court of Appeals affirmed, 489 P.2d 693 (1971), and this court granted review.

The defendants are the Board of County Commissioners and A.G.S. Development Company. A.G.S., the owner of 32 acres which had been zoned R–7 (Single Family Residential), applied for a zone change to P–R (Planned Residential), which allows for the construction of a mobile home park. The change failed to receive a majority vote of the Planning Commission. The Board of County Commissioners approved the change and found, among other matters, that the change allows for "increased densities and different types of housing to meet the needs of urbanization over that allowed by the existing zoning."

The trial court, relying on its interpretation of Roseta v. County of Washington, 254 Or. 161, 458 P.2d 405, 40 A.L.R.3d 364 (1969), reversed the order of the commissioners because the commissioners had not shown any change in the character of the neighborhood which would justify the rezoning. The Court of Appeals affirmed for the same reason, but added the additional ground that the defendants failed to show that the change was consistent with the comprehensive plan for Washington county.

According to the briefs, the comprehensive plan of development for Washington county was adopted in 1959 and included classifications in the county for residential, neighborhood commercial, retail commercial, general commercial, industrial park and light industry, general and heavy industry, and agricultural areas.

The land in question, which was designated "residential" by the comprehensive plan, was zoned R–7, Single Family Residential.

Subsequent to the time the comprehensive plan was adopted, Washington county established a Planned Residential (P–R) zoning classification in 1963. The P–R classification was adopted by ordinance and provided that a planned residential unit development could be established and should include open space for utilities, access, and recreation; should not be less than 10 acres in size; and should be located in or adjacent to a residential zone. The P–R zone adopted by the 1963 ordinance is of the type known as a "floating zone," so-called because the ordinance creates a zone classification authorized for future use but not placed on the zoning map until its use at a particular location is approved by the governing body. The R–7 classification for the 32 acres continued until April 1970 when the classification was changed to P–R to permit the defendant A.G.S. to construct the mobile home park on the 32 acres involved.

The defendants argue that (1) the action of the county commissioners approving the change is presumptively valid, requiring plaintiffs to show that the commissioners acted arbitrarily in approving the zone change; (2) it was not necessary to show a change of conditions in the area before a zone change could be accomplished; and (3) the change from R–7 to P–R was in accordance with the Washington county comprehensive plan.

We granted review in this case to consider the questions—by what standards does a county commission exercise its authority in zoning matters; who has the burden of meeting those standards when a request for change of zone is made; and what is the scope of court review of such actions?

Any meaningful decision as to the proper scope of judicial review of a zoning decision must start with a characterization of the nature of that decision. The majority of jurisdictions state that a zoning ordinance is a legislative act and is thereby entitled to presumptive validity. This court made such a characterization of zoning decisions in Smith v. County of Washington, 241 Or. 380, 406 P.2d 545 (1965):

> "Inasmuch as ORS 215.110 specifically grants to the governing board of the county the power to amend zoning ordinances, a challenged amendment is a legislative act and is clothed with a presumption in its favor. Jehovah's Witnesses v. Mullen et al., 214 Or. 281, 292, 330 P.2d 5, 74 A.L.R.2d 347 (1958), appeal dismissed and cert. denied, 359 U.S. 436, 79 S.Ct. 940, 3 L.Ed.2d 932 (1959)." 241 Or. at 383, 406 P.2d at 547.

However, in *Smith* an exception to the presumption was found and the zoning held invalid. Furthermore, the case cited by the *Smith* court, Jehovah's Witnesses v. Mullen et al., supra, at least at one point viewed the contested zoning in that case as an administrative as opposed to legislative act.

At this juncture we feel we would be ignoring reality to rigidly view all zoning decisions by local governing bodies as legislative acts to be accorded a full presumption of validity and shielded from less than constitutional scrutiny by the theory of separation of powers. Local and small decision groups are simply not the equivalent in all respects of state and national legislatures. There is a growing judicial recognition of this fact of life:

> "It is not a part of the legislative function to grant permits, make special exceptions, or decide particular cases. Such activities are not legislative but administrative, quasi-judicial, or judicial in character. To place them in the hands of legislative bodies, whose acts as such are not judicially reviewable, is to open the door completely to arbitrary government." Ward v. Village of Skokie, 26 Ill.2d 415, 186 N.E.2d 529, 533 (1962) (Klingbiel, J., specially concurring).

The Supreme Court of Washington, in reviewing a rezoning decision, recently stated:

> "Whatever descriptive characterization may be otherwise attached to the role or function of the planning commission in zoning procedures, e.g., advisory, recommendatory, investigatory, administrative or legislative, it is manifest * * * that it is a public agency, * * * a principle [sic] and statutory duty of which is to conduct public hearings in specified planning and zoning matters, enter findings of fact—often on the basis of disputed facts—and make recommendations with reasons assigned thereto. Certainly, in its role as a hearing and fact-finding tribunal, the planning commission's function more nearly than not partakes of the nature of an administrative, quasi-judicial proceeding, * * *." Chrobuck v. Snohomish County, 78 Wash.2d 858, 480 P.2d 489, 495–496 (1971).

Ordinances laying down general policies without regard to a specific piece of property are usually an exercise of legislative authority, are subject to limited review, and may only be attacked upon constitutional grounds for an arbitrary abuse of authority. On the other hand, a determination whether the permissible use of a specific piece of property should be changed is usually an exercise of judicial authority and its propriety is subject to an altogether different test. An illustration of an exercise of legislative authority is the passage of the ordinance by the Washington County Commission in 1963 which provided for the formation of a planned residential classification to be located in or adjacent to any residential zone. An exercise of judicial authority is the county commissioners' determination in this particular matter to change the classification of A.G.S. Development Company's specific piece of property. The distinction is stated, as follows, in Comment, Zoning Amendments—The Product of Judicial or Quasi-Judicial Action, 33 Ohio St.L.J. 130 (1972):

> "* * * Basically, this test involves the determination of whether action produces a general rule or policy which is applicable to an open class of individuals, interest, or situations, or whether it entails the application of a general rule or policy to specific individuals, interests, or situations. If the former determination is satisfied, there is legislative action; if the latter determination is satisfied, the action is judicial." 33 Ohio St.L.J. at 137.

We reject the proposition that judicial review of the county commissioners' determination to change the zoning of the particular property in question is limited to a determination whether the change was arbitrary and capricious.

In order to establish a standard of review, it is necessary to delineate certain basic principles relating to land use regulation.

* * *

In Oregon the county planning commission is required by ORS 215.050 to adopt a comprehensive plan for the use of some or all of the land in the county. Under ORS 215.110(1), after the comprehensive plan has been adopted, the planning commission recommends to the governing body of the county the ordinances necessary to "carry out" the comprehensive plan. The purpose of the zoning ordinances, both under our statute and the general law of land use regulation, is to "carry out" or implement the comprehensive plan. 1 Anderson, American Law of Zoning, § 1.12 (1968). Although we are aware of the analytical distinction between zoning and planning, it is clear that under our statutes the plan adopted by the planning commission and the zoning ordinances enacted by the county governing body are closely related; both are intended to be parts of a single integrated procedure for land use control. The plan embodies policy determinations and guiding principles; the zoning ordinances provide the detailed means of giving effect to those principles.

* * *

We believe that the state legislature has conditioned the county's power to zone upon the prerequisite that the zoning attempt to further the general welfare of the community through consciousness, in a prospective sense, of the factors mentioned above. In other words, except as noted later in this opinion, it must be proved that the change is in conformance with the comprehensive plan.

In proving that the change is in conformance with the comprehensive plan in this case, the proof at a minimum, should show (1) there is a public need for a change of the kind in question, and (2) that the need will be best served by changing the classification of the particular piece of property in question as compared with other available property.

* * *

Because the action of the commission in this instance is an exercise of judicial authority, the burden of proof should be placed, as is usual in judicial proceedings, upon the one seeking change. The more drastic the change, the greater will be the burden of showing that it is in conformance with the comprehensive plan as implemented by the ordinance, that there is a public need for the kind of change in question, and that the need is best met by the proposal under consideration. As the degree of change increases, the burden of showing that the potential impact upon the area in question was carefully considered and weighed will also increase. If other areas have previously been designated for the particular type of development, it must be shown why it is necessary to introduce it into an area not previously contemplated and why the property owners there should bear the burden of the departure.[16]

Although we have said in *Roseta* that zoning changes may be justified without a showing of a mistake in the original plan or ordi-

16. For example, if an area is designated by the plan as generally appropriate for residential development, the plan may also indicate that some high-density residential development within the area is to be anticipated, without specifying the exact location at which that development is to take place. The comprehensive plan might provide that

nance, or of changes in the physical characteristics of an affected area, any of these factors which are present in a particular case would, of course, be relevant. Their importance would depend upon the nature of the precise change under consideration.

By treating the exercise of authority by the commission in this case as the exercise of judicial rather than of legislative authority and thus enlarging the scope of review on appeal, and by placing the burden of the above level of proof upon the one seeking change, we may lay the court open to criticism by legal scholars who think it desirable that planning authorities be vested with the ability to adjust more freely to changed conditions. However, having weighed the dangers of making desirable change more difficult against the dangers of the almost irresistible pressures that can be asserted by private economic interests on local government, we believe that the latter dangers are more to be feared.

What we have said above is necessarily general, as the approach we adopt contains no absolute standards or mechanical tests. We believe, however, that it is adequate to provide meaningful guidance for local governments making zoning decisions and for trial courts called upon to review them. With future cases in mind, it is appropriate to add some brief remarks on questions of procedure. Parties at the hearing before the county governing body are entitled to an opportunity to be heard, to an opportunity to present and rebut evidence, to a tribunal which is impartial in the matter—i.e., having had no prehearing or ex parte contacts concerning the question at issue—and to a record made and adequate findings executed. Comment, Zoning Amendments—The Product of Judicial or Quasi–Judicial Action, 33 Ohio St.L.J. 130–143 (1972).

* * *

its goal for residential development is to assure that residential areas are healthful, pleasant and safe places in which to live. The plan might also list the following policies which, among others, are to be pursued in achieving that goal:

1. High-density residential areas should be located close to the urban core area.

2. Residential neighborhoods should be protected from any land use activity involving an excessive level of noise, pollution or traffic volume.

3. High trip-generating multiple family units should have ready access to arterial or collector streets.

4. A variety of living areas and housing types should be provided appropriate to the needs of the special and general groups they are to serve.

5. Residential development at urban densities should be within planned sewer and water service areas and where other utilities can be adequately provided.

Under such a hypothetical plan, property originally zoned for single family dwellings might later be rezoned for duplexes, for garden apartments, or for high-rise apartment buildings. Each of these changes could be shown to be consistent with the plan. Although in addition we would require a showing that the county governing body found a bona fide need for a zone change in order to accommodate new high-density development which at least balanced the disruption shown by the challengers, that requirement would be met in most instances by a record which disclosed that the governing body had considered the facts relevant to this question and exercised its judgment in good faith. However, these changes, while all could be shown to be consistent with the plan, could be expected to have differing impacts on the surrounding area, depending on the nature of that area. As the potential impact on the area in question increases, so will the necessity to show a justification.

As there has not been an adequate showing that the change was in accord with the plan, or that the factors listed in ORS 215.055 were given proper consideration, the judgment is affirmed.

BRYSON, JUSTICE (specially concurring).

The basic facts in this case exemplify the prohibitive cost and extended uncertainty to a homeowner when a governmental body decides to change or modify a zoning ordinance or comprehensive plan affecting such owner's real property.

This controversy has proceeded through the following steps:

1. The respondent opposed the zone change before the Washington County Planning Department and Planning Commission.

2. The County Commission, after a hearing, allowed the change.

3. The trial court reversed (disallowed the change).

4. The Court of Appeals affirmed the trial court.

5. We ordered reargument and additional briefs.

6. This court affirmed.

The principal respondent in this case, Fasano, happens to be an attorney at law, and his residence is near the proposed mobile home park of the petitioner A.G.S. No average homeowner or small business enterprise can afford a judicial process such as described above nor can a judicial system cope with or endure such a process in achieving justice. The number of such controversies is ascending.

In this case the majority opinion, in which I concur, adopts some sound rules to enable county and municipal planning commissions and governing bodies, as well as trial courts, to reach finality in decision. However, the procedure is no panacea and it is still burdensome.

It is solely within the domain of the legislative branch of government to devise a new and simplified statutory procedure to expedite finality of decision.

Notes

1. The Fasano doctrine was re-examined in a subsequent case and applied to a rezoning of a 600–acre tract for multifamily housing, Neuberger v. City of Portland, 37 Or.App. 13, 586 P.2d 351 (1978). On appeal, the Oregon Supreme Court modified the court of appeals' decision, but adhered to the application of Fasano to the rezoning in issue, and devoted considerable attention to the question of which land use decisions might be legislative in nature and which would be treated as quasi-judicial. Neuberger v. City of Portland, 288 Or. 155, 603 P.2d 771 (1979), rehearing denied 288 Or. 585, 607 P.2d 722 (1980). The court stated:

> * * * [O]ur land use decisions indicate that when a particular action by a local government is directed at a relatively small number of identifiable persons, and when that action also involves the application

> of existing policy to a specific factual setting, the requirement of quasi-judicial procedures has been implied from the governing law.
>
> Although both of these factors are frequently present in the cases in which we have held or assumed that quasi-judicial functions were exercised, each is * * * a separate indicator of the possible need for adjudicatory procedures. The reasons, moreover, are different in each instance.
>
> When specific facts must be determined in order that pre-existing criteria may be applied, procedures similar to those used in adjudications are important in order to assure that factual determinations will be made correctly. When the requirement of such procedures is implied because a relatively small number of persons is directly affected, even though the decision-maker is not entirely bound by pre-existing criteria but is empowered to exercise broad discretion the law may require a formal hearing procedure. * * *
>
> A third consideration * * * is whether the process is bound to result in a decision. Although that factor is rarely discussed in the cases because in many contexts its presence is readily apparent, it was not so obvious in * * * the recent case of Henthorn v. Grand Prairie School Dist., 287 Or. 683, 601 P.2d 1243 (1979). In *Henthorn* the determination that the school board was required to make a decision on the basis of information produced at a hearing required by statute was important to our conclusion that the proceedings were quasi-judicial and, therefore subject to judicial review under the writ of review.

2. The Fasano court imposed the burden of proof on the legislative body, the Board of County Commissioners. Why? What precisely is the Board required to prove? Consider the following statement of the Fasano majority: "Because the action of the commission in this instance is an exercise of judicial authority, the burden of proof should be placed, as is usual in judicial proceedings, upon the one seeking change. The more drastic the change, the greater will be the burden of showing that it is in conformance with the comprehensive plan as implemented by the ordinance, that there is a public need for the kind of change in question, and that the need is best met by tho proposal under consideration."

3. In Cooper v. Board of County Comm'rs of Ada County, 101 Idaho 407, 614 P.2d 947 (1980), the court held that a decision to not rezone 99 acres from low density residential (one unit per acre) to a density which would permit two to three units per acre, was a quasi-judicial decision, entitling the property owner to procedural due process, which, on the facts, the court found had been denied. The Cooper court's reasoning was affirmed and followed 20 years later in Idaho Historic Pres. Council v. City Council of Boise, 134 Idaho 651, 8 P.3d 646 (2000), a case involving a city council's decision to issue a certificate allowing for the demolition of an historic site. The court in this case reiterated the Cooper court's test to distinguish legislative from quasi-judicial action:

> Basically, this test involves the determination of whether action produces a general rule or policy which is applicable to an open class of individuals, interest (sic), or situations, or whether it entails the application of a general rule or policy to specific individuals, interests, or

> situations. If the former determination is satisfied, there is legislative action; if the latter determination is satisfied, the action is judicial.

Also see Golden v. City of Overland Park, 224 Kan. 591, 584 P.2d 130 (1978), where the city denied approval to a rezoning request from an office designation to permit a small shopping center, and the court also found the decision to be quasi-judicial and, on the facts, unreasonable. Similar to the Idaho cases above, the Golden decision was also affirmed and followed nearly 20 years later by the court in McPherson Landfill v. Board of County Comm'rs, 274 Kan. 303, 49 P.3d 522 (2002). The McPherson court summarized the Golden determination as follows:

> ... [T]his court has decided that where the focus of zoning authority shifts from the entire city or county to one specific tract of land for which a zoning change is urged, the function of the zoning authority becomes more quasi-judicial in nature than legislative. In such quasi-judicial proceedings, it is incumbent upon the authority to comply with the requirements of due process in its proceedings. Thus, the proceedings must be fair, open, and impartial. A denial of due process renders the resulting decision void.

4. The Supreme Court of Florida moved in the direction of Fasano and overruled some earlier cases in Board of County Comm'rs of Brevard County v. Snyder, 627 So.2d 469 (Fla.1993). In this case, the owner of a half-acre parcel located in a district zoned for single-family use applied for a rezoning to multifamily, intending to build four to six units. The planning director indicated he approved of the rezoning as it was consistent with the comprehensive plan, but several citizens were opposed because of a potential increase in traffic and the rezoning was denied. The court held that although earlier cases had applied the fairly debatable rule in rezonings as well as initial zoning efforts, rezoning actions which have an impact on a limited number of persons where the decision can be viewed as policy application rather than policy setting, should be viewed as quasi-judicial. The court delineated the following procedure:

> Upon consideration, we hold that a landowner seeking to rezone property has the burden of proving that the proposal is consistent with the comprehensive plan and complies with all procedural requirements of the zoning ordinance. At this point, the burden shifts to the governmental board to demonstrate that maintaining the existing zoning classification with respect to the property accomplishes a legitimate public purpose. In effect the landowners' traditional remedies will be subsumed within this rule, and the board will now have the burden of showing that the refusal to rezone the property is not arbitrary, discriminatory, or unreasonable. If the board carries its burden, the application should be denied.

5. Compare this case with the above cases, South Gwinnett Venture v. Pruitt, 491 F.2d 5 (5th Cir.1974), where the entire court, sitting en banc, overturned a panel decision and held "that local zoning is a quasi-legislative procedure, not subject to federal judicial consideration in the absence of arbitrary action. Moreover, we see no viable distinction between zoning board functions involved in the adoption of a comprehensive zoning plan and those exercised in reclassification of a piece of property under an existing

plan * * *." This was in line with Higginbotham v. Barrett, 473 F.2d 745 (5th Cir.1973), in which the same court had stated that "the law is settled that the zoning of property, including the preparation of comprehensive land plans, involves the exercise of judgment which is legislative in character and is subject to judicial control only if arbitrary and without rational basis." The majority of the panel in the earlier version of South Gwinnett Venture v. Pruitt, 482 F.2d 389 (5th Cir.1973), certiorari denied 416 U.S. 901, 94 S.Ct. 1625, 40 L.Ed.2d 119 (1974), attempted to distinguish the legislative action of adopting a comprehensive zoning plan from "the adjudicative decision inherent in tract rezoning"—the latter situation deemed to require adherence to minimal standards of due process.

NOVA HORIZON, INC. v. CITY COUNCIL OF THE CITY OF RENO

Supreme Court of Nevada, 1989.
105 Nev. 92, 769 P.2d 721.

Per Curiam

Appellants are developers who planned to build a hotel/convention center (the Project) on land next to the Bally Grand in Reno. Prior to submitting an application for necessary approvals, appellants purchased the land in question. The plot consists of 2.9 acres, bordered on three sides by the Bally Grand. On August 29, 1984, appellants submitted to the Reno Planning Commission an application requesting:

1. a change of zoning, M–1 to C–3;
2. a Special Use Permit; and
3. acceptance of a tentative subdivision map,

to construct a twenty-eight story, 804–room hotel and casino. At that time, the property owned by appellants was zoned M–1 as defined and limited in Section 18.06.270 of the Reno Municipal Code. M–1 zoning allows commercial development but imposes height restrictions of sixty-five feet, which would not accommodate appellants' project as planned. Additionally, M–1 does not allow any residential use and the proposed project was planned to include the sale of 312 units on a time-share basis.

On November 7, 1984, the Reno Planning Commission, by a vote of four to three, recommended to the City Council that it approve the three separate requests. Appellants' application came before respondents on December 10, 1984. At that time, a public hearing was held wherein appellants presented their case and the community was given the opportunity to respond. After the conclusion of testimony, the City Council unanimously voted to deny all of appellants' requests.

* * *

We note, preliminarily, that the district court properly subjected the City's action to a substantial evidence standard of review. This court, in addressing the propriety of a district court ruling reversing a zone change approval by the appropriate governmental body, declared:

> Respondents recognize the general rule that a court is not empowered to substitute its judgment for that of a zoning board, in this case the board of county commissioners, when the board's action is supported by substantial evidence.
>
> * * *
>
> The lower court had before it the same evidence as the board. Its function was not to conduct a trial de novo, but only to ascertain as a matter of law if there was any substantial evidence before the board which would sustain the board's action. The function of this court at this time is the same as that of the lower court. [Citation omitted.]
>
> * * *
>
> Under the police power, zoning is a matter within sound legislative action and such legislative action must be upheld if the facts do not show that the bounds of that discretion have been exceeded.

McKenzie v. Shelly, 77 Nev. 237, 240–242, 362 P.2d 268, 269–70 (1961). In *Shelly,* we reversed the district court since the presumptive validity of the board's action was supported by substantial evidence and there was no showing that the board abused its discretion.

Numerous cases support the premise that zoning boards may not unreasonably or arbitrarily deprive property owners of legitimate, advantageous land uses. For example, the Supreme Court of Virginia affirmed a trial court decision holding an unduly restrictive zoning classification void. *Town of Vienna Council v. Kohler,* 218 Va. 966, 244 S.E.2d 542 (1978). The *Kohler* court concluded that "a denial of a rezoning request will not be sustained if under all the facts of the particular case, the denial is unreasonable, or is discriminatory, or is without substantial relationship to the public health, safety, morals and general welfare." *Id.* 244 S.E.2d at 548. *See also,* e.g., *Raabe v. City of Walker,* 383 Mich. 165, 174 N.W.2d 789 (1970) (invalidating rezoning of small enclave in midst of residential area to accommodate an industrial park); *City of Conway v. Housing Authority,* 266 Ark. 404, 584 S.W.2d 10 (1979) (City of Conway directed to rezone property, as the denial of the rezoning request was arbitrary and inconsistent with surrounding zoning); *Lowe v. City of Missoula,* 165 Mont. 38, 525 P.2d 551 (1974) (restrictive zoning impressed on landowner's property was so lacking in fact information as to constitute an abuse of discretion; rezoning held to be invalid). In the latter case, the Montana Supreme Court, quoting from an earlier case, stated:

> Under the guise of protecting the public or advancing its interest, the state may not unduly interfere with private business or prohibit lawful occupations, or impose unreasonable or unnecessary restrictions upon them. Any law or regulation which imposes unjust

> limitations upon the full use and enjoyment of property, or destroys property value or use, deprives the owner of property rights.

In the instant case, the requested change in zoning was in conformity with the long-range development plans adopted by the City of Reno. The zone change was requested at the suggestion of the Reno City Planning staff and is consistent with the zoning of the surrounding property. Moreover, it appears that appellants may have invested substantial sums of money (allegedly over $1,200,000.00) in land acquisition and project development costs in anticipation of the City's approval of their application.

At the public hearing in which appellants' application was considered, only one person presented opposition to the project and his objections were basically rebuffed by members of the Reno City Council. Nevertheless, the Council unanimously denied approval to what was described as an architecturally "superior" project on the specified grounds that approval would violate a campaign promise against locating new casinos outside the "downtown area" and a similar pledge to diversification that would pay higher employee wages.

In determining whether the action of the Council concerning the zone change was without substantial evidentiary support and, consequently, an abuse of discretion, it is essential to first consider the effect of the City's master plan, as amended, and land use/transportation guide on the Council's latitude in zoning matters.

Chapter 278 of the Nevada Revised Statutes governs many aspects of planning and zoning. It not only provides for the formation and compensation of planning commissions and the adoption of master plans, it also provides for zoning in accordance with an adopted master plan. NRS 278.250(2) provides, in pertinent part: "2. The zoning regulations shall be adopted in accordance with the master plan for land use * * *." (Emphasis supplied.) This suggests that municipal entities must adopt zoning regulations that are in substantial agreement with the master plan, including a land-use guide if one is also adopted by the city council. Other jurisdictions have construed their statutes as requiring strict conformity between master plans and zoning ordinances, even to the point of requiring changes in zoning after a modification in a master plan. *See Baker v. City of Milwaukie,* 271 Or. 500, 533 P.2d 772 (1975); *Fasano v. Board of County Comm'rs,* 264 Or. 574, 507 P.2d 23 (1973). While such a strict view of the invariable application of a master plan on zoning matters may lend a high degree of predictability to prospective land uses and facilitate usage planning by land owners, we do not perceive the legislative intent to be so confining and inflexible. We therefore choose to view a master plan as a standard that commands deference and a presumption of applicability, rather than a legislative straightjacket from which no leave may be taken. In pertinent part, the Montana Supreme Court analyzed the issue as follows:

> To require strict compliance with the master plan would result in a master plan so unworkable that it would have to be constantly

> changed to comply with the realities. The master plan is, after all, a plan. On the other hand, to require no compliance at all would defeat the whole idea of planning. Why have a plan if the local government units are free to ignore it at any time? The statutes are clear enough to send the message that in reaching zoning decisions, the local governmental unit should at least substantially comply with the comprehensive plan (or master plan).

Little v. Board of County Comm'rs, 631 P.2d 1282, 1293 (Mont.1981).

Having determined that master plans are to be accorded substantial compliance under Nevada's statutory scheme, and recognizing anew the general reluctance to judicially intervene in zoning determinations absent clear necessity, *Board of Comm'rs v. Dayton Dev. Co.,* 91 Nev. 71, 530 P.2d 1187 (1975), we turn now to the issue of respondents' zoning action in the instant case. It is clear on the record that no evidentiary basis exists for the Council's denial of appellants' zone change request. It is equally clear that no deference, let alone a presumptive applicability, was accorded Reno's master plan by the Council. In one instance, an expression of deference to a campaign promise was the stated basis for what was tantamount to a disregard for the master plan. The other expression offered as a specific basis for rejecting appellants' application was a pledge, presumably to constituents, to seek diversification in favor of higher employee wages. The latter point was equally untenable as a basis for zoning denial. Moreover, as noted above, the surrounding properties enjoyed the same zoning sought by appellants and no evidence, let alone reasoning, was presented to justify a denial of appellants' request for rezoning. We therefore are compelled to reverse the district court on this point.

We are not constrained to grant similar relief concerning appellants' request for a special use permit and acceptance of a tentative subdivision map. While the record provides no existing or prospective basis for denying the zone change, we are loathe to direct authorization for a project that may or may not be deserving of the Council's approval. The Council simply did not effectively address the effect of the impact of such a substantial project on the City of Reno. While it may be argued with considerable cogency from the record that appellants justified an approval of their entire application, and that it is unfair to subject them to further proceedings, we nevertheless conclude that it would be unwise and inappropriate for this court to accommodate an approval by forfeiture.

If appellants remain interested in the construction of their project, we will assume that, upon rehearing, the Council will exercise its judgment fairly and in accordance with the merits as reflected by the evidence and deliberations of record.

We realize that our ruling may appear to be inconsistent with our opinion in *City Council, Reno v. Travelers Hotel,* 100 Nev. 436, 683 P.2d 960 (1984), where we affirmed the issuance of a peremptory writ of mandamus requiring approval of a special use permit for a hotel-casino.

In that case, however, rezoning was not an issue and the Council was able to focus directly on the project itself. Here, the only specified basis for rejecting appellants' application was essentially the project's location outside the downtown area, a reason which, if implemented, would constitute an inappropriate *de facto* amendment to the City's master plan and land use/transportation guide. We are simply unable to discern from the record that the Council adequately focused its attention on the merits of the project and its total impact on the community. Considerations of public health, safety and welfare demand both such a focused attention and the exercise of a fair and enlightened discretion by the Council based upon substantial evidence.

The judgment of the district court is reversed insofar as the zone change is concerned, and remanded with instructions to issue a peremptory writ of mandamus requiring respondents to grant appellants' application for zone change. The district court shall also modify its judgment to the extent of requiring respondents, upon application by appellants, to entertain anew the merits of appellants' application for special use permit and acceptance of tentative subdivision map, all in accordance with this opinion.

Notes

1. Compare this case with the Nevada decision, Tate v. Miles, 503 A.2d 187 (Del.1986). In the latter case, the planning commission held a hearing on a rezoning application and recommended approval to the county council; the council held a public hearing and subsequently enacted a rezoning ordinance with no findings or statement of reasons, merely stating that change was in accord with the comprehensive plan and promoted public welfare. The trial court gave the neighbors a summary judgment and the supreme court affirmed, stating that although under Delaware law rezoning is a legislative act, it "resembles" a judicial determination because a zoning decision must be supported by a record sufficient to withstand judicial challenge. With no reasons for the change in the record, a court has no means to review the decision. The court held that a rezoning decision must be accompanied by findings and a statement of the reasons for the rezoning.

2. In addition to the question of the standard of review when rezoning is viewed as a quasi-judicial rather than a legislative act, other consequences may flow from the characterization of rezoning decisions. For example, in a judicial challenge to a city's decision not to rezone, may the plaintiff-property owner compel members of the city legislative body to testify as to their reasons or motivations for voting to deny the petition? In Wait v. City of Scottsdale, 127 Ariz. 107, 618 P.2d 601 (1980), the court held that the denial of a rezoning petition was a legislative act and that the motives of council members in denying the petition and the reasons they considered were beyond the scope of judicial inquiry. Similarly, in Sheffield Development Co. v. City of Troy, 99 Mich.App. 527, 298 N.W.2d 23 (1980), the court held that because rezoning was a legislative act, council members could not be compelled to answer questions regarding their motives in denying the rezoning application. The court did state that the motives of legislators could be examined when the complaint alleges fraud, personal interest, or corrup-

tion. In Pythagorean, Inc. v. Grand Rapids Twp., 253 Mich.App. 525, 656 N.W.2d 212 (2002), the court extended this protection from inquiry to planning commission members who make recommendations, as a board, to the town board concerning rezoning proposals. The court stated:

> [W]e fail to see how the motivation of members of a planning commission with respect to a zoning question can have any relevance.... Plaintiff has simply come forward with no argument by which we could conclude that the motivation or thought processes of the planning commission members in making their recommendation to the board might be relevant or might reasonably be calculated to lead to the discovery of any relevant evidence. See MCR 2.302(B)(1). Further, we note that the planning commission members are volunteers who willingly give of their time and efforts for the good of the community. Justice requires that they be protected from the annoyance and undue burden and expense of deposition discovery that has no relevance to the issues involved in plaintiff's complaint. See MCR 2.302(C).

3. The particular method of reviewing zoning decisions varies from state to state. Some enabling acts and some zoning ordinances prescribe the method of seeking review. Where statutes or ordinances are silent, injunction suits and certiorari are quite common. See, e.g., Platte Woods United Methodist Church v. City of Platte Woods, 935 S.W.2d 735 (Mo.App.1996). In recent years attorneys have sometimes sought to utilize the federal courts to review zoning decisions, relying on civil rights legislation or other, more novel, theories of federal jurisdiction.

a. Bodor v. East Coventry Twp., 325 F.Supp. 1102 (E.D.Pa.1971). Plaintiff sued to restrain the township officials from preventing him from establishing a 70–foot-by–12–foot mobile home as a permanent residence on a four-acre tract of land. "Plaintiffs' complaint raises the substantial constitutional issues of due process of law and equal protection under the law in that in order for Plaintiffs to avail themselves of the administrative remedies provided in the township's zoning ordinance and building code ordinance, Plaintiffs would allegedly have to pay a $750.00 filing fee. * * * Plaintiffs have alleged facts which, if proved, establish a concerted effort by the Board of Supervisors of East Coventry Township to preclude the review of their Zoning and Building Code Ordinances through the establishment of a prohibitive filing fee. Such an allegation sets forth a claim upon which relief can be granted."

b. City of Miami v. Woolin, 387 F.2d 893 (5th Cir.1968). The city ordinances prohibited erection of gasoline filling stations within 350 yards of a church, hospital, or school, and within 750 feet of another filling station. The court held that the equal protection clause of the Fourteenth Amendment rendered the ordinance unconstitutional and upheld a permanent injunction. Cf. Stone v. Maitland, 446 F.2d 83 (5th Cir.1971), in which a city zoning ordinance imposed a 350 yard separation requirement upon a gas station and another gas station or a place of public assembly. This time, the court found the ordinance constitutional, stating that the city presented an adequate rational purpose: protection of community aesthetics. If too many stations were packed into a small area, some would inevitably fail due to the competition, become abandoned, and subsequently constitute an eyesore.

c. Minshew v. Smith, 380 F.Supp. 918 (N.D.Miss.1974). Plaintiffs, homeowners and adjacent property owners, sued the owner of a motel and several city officials for compensatory and punitive damages on a theory that the defendants conspired to achieve an illegal amendment of the zoning ordinance to allow the motel to expand into the adjacent residential zone. The court found for the plaintiffs and ordered compensatory damages (the motel had already been built), but refused to award punitive damages.

d. DeFalco v. Dirie, 923 F.Supp. 473 (S.D.N.Y.1996). Real estate developers sued town officials and others for extortion under RICO (Racketeer Influenced and Corrupt Organizations), 18 U.S.C.A. § 1962 (c). The court held that the plaintiffs stated a cause of action based on municipal employees' activities in extorting money in return for necessary permits. The court also held that a municipality could be considered as an "enterprise" for purposes of bringing a RICO claim. Also see Manor Healthcare Corp. v. Lomelo, 929 F.2d 633 (11th Cir.1991), a suit against the mayor and president of the city council under § 1983 alleging that the defendants extorted $30,000 from a nursing home in a rezoning matter. The court held that the city was properly dismissed as a party because the city neither adopted nor ratified the mayor's bribery and extortion.

4. Use of § 1983 to review zoning decisions has grown more popular since the Supreme Court ruled that cities are subject to suit under that provision in Monell v. Department of Social Services of the City of New York, 436 U.S. 658, 98 S.Ct. 2018, 56 L.Ed.2d 611 (1978). However, § 1983 suits may have limitations. First, the complaint must allege deprivation of a constitutional right, which can be difficult for the disappointed property owner denied a rezoning; many federal courts have held that a zoning permit is not a property right. Second, the local legislators may have immunity. See T & M Homes, Inc. v. Township of Mansfield, 162 N.J.Super. 497, 393 A.2d 613 (1978); Gorman Towers, Inc. v. Bogoslavsky, 626 F.2d 607 (8th Cir. 1980); Creative Environments, Inc. v. Estabrook, 491 F.Supp. 547 (D.Mass. 1980); Robinson v. City of Raytown, 606 S.W.2d 460 (Mo.App.1980); Haskell v. Washington Township, 864 F.2d 1266 (6th Cir.1988). However, in Dunmore v. City of Natchez, 703 F.Supp. 31 (S.D.Miss.1988), the court held that to the extent city officials were acting in a legislative capacity in denying a variance they were immune from personal liability, but to the extent that they may have participated in a conspiracy to deny a black female applicant a variance because of her race, they had no immunity.

5. Students should be aware that zoning disputes sometimes turn on the interpretation of words in the ordinance. For example, many zoning ordinances prohibit the keeping of "livestock" in residential districts. Persons who keep exotic pets often find themselves embroiled in a dispute over the issue of whether their pet is "livestock." See, e.g., Barnes v. City of Anderson, 642 N.E.2d 1004 (Ind.App.1994), where the court considered if "Sassy" the Vietnamese pot-bellied pig was a household pet or "livestock." Sometimes the ordinance uses the term "wild animal" thus placing pet lions, tigers, and bears in jeopardy when neighbors complain. Another example is Saurer v. Board of Zoning Appeals, 629 N.E.2d 893 (Ind.App.1994), where the court held that rusty trailers, building trusses, semi-trailers, hog roasters and tables kept outdoors in a rural area did not constitute "junk" under a zoning ordinance defining a junkyard as a lot for the storage or sale of junk,

scrap metal, scrap vehicles, or scrap machinery. The court said that junk, like pornography, is difficult to define but that "we know them when we see them." Just because the items are unpleasant to view does not make them junk, and courts are not arbiters of aesthetics and good taste.

6. Courts often strictly interpret the language of land use regulations, resolving ambiguities in favor of landowners, because such regulations are said to be "in derogation of common law property rights." How does this general rule of interpretation square with the presumption of validity that courts afford the regulations themselves? Can you determine the difference between presuming that a land use law is valid and restrictively interpreting its meaning as applied?

B. RIPENESS AND FINALITY

The question of whether an action by an aggrieved party is ripe for adjudication requires an understanding of how land use boards make decisions. Ripeness often arises as a question when a developer's proposed project has been denied by a planning board or commission. It can also arise when the local legislature rezones property and the affected property owners object. Unless and until the affected property owners have submitted proposals in good faith and been denied or limited in their development plans, how are courts to determine whether and to what extent they have been damaged? It is not sufficient to submit, for example, a grandiose development proposal, obtain a denial, and then challenge the regulations as a regulatory taking. In the ordinary context, land use agencies have a high degree of discretion to soften the strictures of the regulations they administer. It remains the law that the landowner must submit applications that give the agency the opportunity to decide and explain the reach of a challenged regulation.

This was the question presented in Williamson County Regional Planning Commission v. Hamilton Bank of Johnson City, 473 U.S. 172, 105 S.Ct. 3108, 87 L.Ed.2d 126 (1985). The city rezoned the plaintiff's land, which had already been approved for development by the local planning commission. Under the rezoning, the approved, but unbuilt, project no longer complied with local law. The plaintiff claimed that this rezoning action, by itself, constituted a regulatory taking because it limited the number of homes that could be built and caused a net loss of $1 million. The Supreme Court determined that the case was not ripe and would not be until the plaintiff obtained a final decision from the zoning authority under the new law. The court held a takings claim cannot be properly decided until the aggrieved party has "obtained a final decision regarding how it will be allowed to develop its property." Because courts in takings actions look at the economic impact and the reasonable investment-backed expectations of the affected party, "[t]hose factors simply cannot be evaluated until the administrative agency has arrived at a final, definite position regarding how it will apply the regulations at issue to the particular land in question."

The plaintiff in Williamson County made the argument that it was not required to exhaust its administrative remedies. In response, the

Court explained the difference between exhaustion of remedies and ripeness:

> The question of whether administrative remedies must be exhausted is conceptually distinct, however, from the question whether an administrative action must be final before it is judicially reviewable. While the policies underlying the two concepts often overlap, the finality requirement is concerned with whether the initial decision-maker has arrived at a definitive position on the issue that inflicts an actual, concrete injury; the exhaustion requirement generally refers to administrative and judicial procedures by which an injured party may seek review of an adverse decision and obtain a remedy if the decision is found to be unlawful or otherwise inappropriate.

Chapter XII

EMERGING ISSUES IN LAND USE LAW

By the end of your course in land use law, and by the time you are reading this concluding chapter, you are probably more aware now than ever before just how much land use planning and land use controls influence community development all around us. From the very beginning of deciding what uses are most appropriate for which parcels of land, to creating opportunities to accommodate and even to encouraging the availability of desired community amenities for things including affordable housing, open space and recreation areas, to the availability of public transportation and environmental protection, local governments have a tremendous amount of legal authority to positively impact everyday quality of life by creating sustainable communities.

Land use law is an evolving field that both influences, and is influenced by, cutting edge societal issues. For example, in the context of the recent devastation in New Orleans and the Mississippi Delta caused by Hurricane Katrina, a number of land use issues have emerged front and center in the debate including: what uses should be allowed to be developed in hurricane prone and flood prone areas; if rebuilding in certain areas is not allowed, would this amount to a taking requiring compensation; and what types of land use controls are appropriate to protect the public health, safety and welfare in these areas. The regulation of land use in the area of disaster mitigation is receiving growing attention given other recent challenges from wild fires in the West and Southeast, and from earthquakes and other natural disasters that impact public safety. In addition, land use regulation is being used to facilitate the use of alternative energy sources, such as the siting of wind farms. Land use regulations are also being employed to promote green development, and as a technique to address critical climate change challenges. With technological advances in the field including geographic information systems, lawyers, planners and citizens now have ready access through state-of-the-art technology to current and accurate data to best inform decisionmaking. All of these issues are addressed in this chapter which focuses on the application of land use law to emerging issues.

SECTION 1. CLIMATE CHANGE

The following excerpts from "The Lawyers Confront Hot Air" by Lora Lucero, Esq., AICP, appears in the July/August 2007 issue of the Zoning and Planning Law Report:

* * *

Why should government lawyers be interested in global warming from a professional perspective—over and above the impacts everyone should be concerned about? First, state and local government lawyers are going to be asked to draft and implement a whole host of new land use, environmental, transportation and utility regulations which respond to climate change, and then enforce and defend such measures. Second, global warming litigation is coming into its own as a field which requires an understanding of law, policy and science. As an example, in April 2007, California's Attorney General sued San Bernardino County for failing to address the effects of global warming in its environmental impact report prepared for its general plan update. (citation omitted) The county anticipates increasing its population by 25% by 2030, but did not analyze the effects of this increase on greenhouse gas emissions or how it proposed to reduce GHG emissions.

Justin R. Pidot from the Georgetown Environmental Law & Policy Institute describes a variety of global warming litigation in the following categories—(1) Clean Air Act litigation, (2) NEPA litigation, (3) Nuisance litigation, (4) Preemption litigation, and other types of lawsuits related to global warming. (citation omitted) Tim Dowling, General Counsel of the Community Rights Counsel, would add Freedom of Information Act (FOIA) cases to the list which seek to require the government to generate or share information related to global warming. (citation omitted) Global warming litigation is being compared to the tobacco litigation of the 1990s (citation omitted)—perhaps the ultimate public interest litigation of the 21st century. Keep track of these global warming cases at http://warminglaw.typepad.com/—a website maintained by the Community Rights Counsel. * * *

* * * There can be little disagreement that global warming (citation omitted) is real and occurring on a scale that warrants serious attention and action. The IPCC's two reports in the spring of 2007 were the last nails in the coffin containing the common myths that have plagued intelligent debate for many years, including: (1) climate changes are cyclical and this recent warming is just part of random fluctuations, (2) humans cannot possibly have an effect on the vast environment, (3) the sun is the cause of warming, and we can't possibly control the sun, (4) global warming scientists are just alarmists looking to scare everyone to

get funding for their projects, and (5) we can't say for sure whether CO_2 causes global warming. (citation omitted)

* * *

The science behind global warming is finally making its way into the mainstream press and the public consciousness, due in no small measure to two authors—Elizabeth Kolbert and Tim Flannery. Kolbert is a staff writer for the New Yorker, a self-described climate journalist. (citation omitted) With the publication last year of Field Notes from a Catastrophe—Man, Nature, and Climate Change, she has become this generation's Rachel Carson. (citation omitted) Kolbert is a non-scientist who has spent a lot of time with scientists in many different parts of the world, watching and learning how global warming works and how its effects are impacting the natural world. She has a gift for making the jargon of climatologists accessible to the general public. Unlike Kolbert, Tim Flannery is a scientist. His book, The Weather Makers—How Man is Changing the Climate and What It Means for Life on Earth, is a huge wake-up call for action now. Flannery writes:

> Some time this century, the day will arrive when the human influence on the climate will overwhelm all natural factors. Then, the insurance industry and the courts will no longer be able to talk of acts of God, because even the most unreasonable of us could have foreseen the consequences. Instead, the judiciary will be faced with apportioning guilt and responsibility for human actions resulting from the new climate. And that, I think, will change everything. (citation omitted)

Most discussions about global warming typically include three graphs, all remarkably similar—population growth, rising temperatures, and increasing levels of CO_2.

* * * More than six billion people call Planet Earth home today, but two thousand years ago, at the dawn of the first millennium [0 A.D.], the world's population was only 300 million. The first billion people didn't arrive on the scene until about 1800 A.D.; the second billion quickly followed in a mere 127 years and from there the race was on. In the next 33 years (1960), the third billion; in 14 years (1974), the fourth billion; the fifth billion in the next 13 years (1987); and by the turn of the Century, the Earth is now laboring under a human population of just over six billion! (citation omitted) We could be stretching to nine billion people by 2050. (citation omitted)

The CO_2 connection to global warming is not a new phenomenon. A Swedish chemist, Svante Arrhenius, is credited with making the first measurements of the impact of carbon dioxide on the Earth's greenhouse effect in 1897. (citation omitted) No one was concerned about global warming back then, but the measurements have been rising steadily. Dr. Keeling was the first to measure CO_2 on a continuous basis since 1958 at a station on top of Mauna Loa in Hawaii. (citation omitted) The resulting graph, known as the Keeling Curve, shows the continuous increase in CO_2 emissions. Since 1860, global CO_2 emissions have increased by 1000%. (citation omitted)

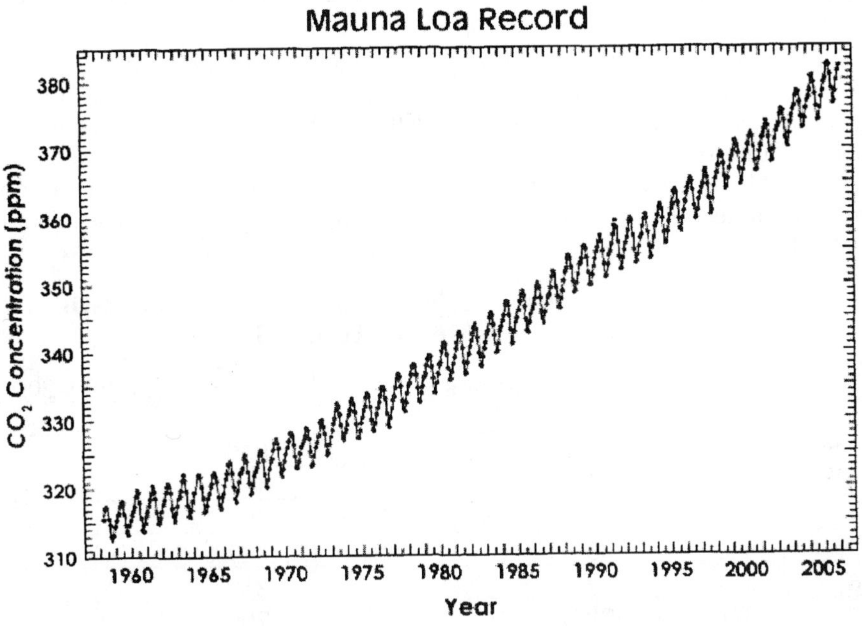

From 1750 to 2000, CO_2 increased from 280 parts per million (ppm) to 368 ppm. A report released by the U.K. government in October 2006, commonly referred to as the Stern Report, stated the number is now about 430 ppm. (citation omitted)

> According to the report, even if the annual flow of emissions did not increase beyond current rates, the level would reach 550 ppm by 2050; current rates of development could lead to a 550 ppm level as early as 2035. The report went on to say that stabilizing at or below a 550 ppm level would require global emissions to be around 25% below current levels by 2050. That level would lead to severe adverse environmental impacts. To stabilize at 450 ppm and thereby make the adverse effects less severe, global emissions would need to peak in the next 10 years and then fall at more than 5% per year, reaching 70% below current levels by 2050. (citation omitted)

Temperatures have risen dramatically as well. Eleven of the last twelve years (1995–2006) rank among the 12 warmest years since 1850. (citation omitted) The IPCC Third Assessment concluded: "There is new and stronger evidence that most of the observed warming over the last 50 years is attributable to human activities." (citation omitted) With a moderate pace of greenhouse gas accumulation in the atmosphere, the IPCC predicts the average temperature by the end of this century could match temperatures we haven't seen in 125,000 years! (citation omitted)

The top five GHG emitting countries in 2000 were the United States (20.6% of the world total GHG emissions); China (14.7%); European Union (14.0%); Russia (5.7%), and India (5.6%). (citation omitted) China is expected to overtake the U.S. by 2010.

Ten states account for half of all U.S. carbon dioxide emissions from fossil fuel combustion. Both Texas and Florida saw a huge increase between 1990 and 2001, which the Editor of the new book from ABA, Global Climate Change and U.S. Law, concludes is attributable to a substantial increase in vehicle travel due to population growth in those two states as well as the sprawling development patterns. (citation omitted)

Carbon Dioxide Emissions from Fossil Fuel Combustion, 2001[1] Million Metric Tons (MMT)

Rank	State	CO_2 Emissions (MMT)	% Change, 1990–2001
1	TX	668.5	178%
2	CA	368.7	85%
3	PA	258.0	4%
4	OH	249.5	20%
5	FL	235.6	347%
6	IL	224.7	21%
7	IN	223.8	79%
8	NY	207.6	–0.2%
9	MI	189.1	46%
10	LA	183.0	128%

The most recent report from the IPCC released this spring concludes that (1) humans are having a profound impact on the CO_2 levels, (2) global warming is unequivocal, (3) the warming of the last half century is unusual in at least the previous 1500 years, and (4) even if CO_2 emissions are stabilized to 2000 levels, temperatures are going to continue to rise. (citation omitted) * * *

* * *

The state and local response to global warming has been gaining momentum and visibility in the past year or two. Most of the methods to control greenhouse gas emissions generally fall into three categories: energy efficiency and conservation, energy sources, and carbon sequestration. (citation omitted) The first involves such measures as more stringent vehicle fuel economy standards, and "changing land use patterns to reduce vehicle miles traveled by passenger vehicles and to increase trips by mass transit, bicycles and walking." (citation omitted) Energy efficiency also includes "green buildings" and more efficient home appliances and office equipment. The second category—energy

1. U.S. PIRG Education Fund, The Carbon Boom: National and State Trends in Global Warming Pollution Since 1960 (June 2006), Appx. A, B, cited in Global Climate Change and U.S. Law, Michael B. Gerrard, Ed., ABA, April 2007.

sources—is focusing on finding alternatives to oil and gas, such as wind, solar and biomass. The third category—carbon sequestration—involves finding ways to either biologically sequester carbon using the natural function of plants to take up carbon dioxide through photosynthesis or finding ways to capture and store carbon before it is emitted into the atmosphere. (citation omitted)

Federal Initiatives

110th Congress Responds to Global Warming—Dozens of energy and climate bills have been introduced, including the Zero–Emissions Building Act of 2007 (S.1059 introduced by Senator Clinton) which directs federal agencies to require all new federal buildings or major renovations of existing buildings to reduce carbon dioxide emissions by 50 percent compared to a 2003 baseline. The emissions reduction level would increase in future years until federal buildings become "zero-emissions" buildings by 2030. Sens. McCain (R–AZ) and Lieberman (D–CT) have introduced the Climate Stewardship and Innovation Act of 2007 (S.280), a new and improved version of the bill they offered in 2003 and 2005, to establish a National Greenhouse Gas Database to collect, verify, and analyze information on greenhouse gas emissions. It establishes a program for market-driven reduction of GHGs through the use of tradeable allowances. Sens. Jeff Bingaman (D–N.M.) and Pete Domenici (R–N.M.) have introduced the Energy Efficiency Promotion Act (S.1115), aimed at reducing the use of fossil fuels by improving efficiency of vehicles, buildings, home appliances, and industrial equipment. Sens. Barbara Boxer (D–Calif.) and Dianne Feinstein (D–Calif.) have introduced the Marine Vessel Emissions Reduction Act of 2007 * * * which directs the EPA to reduce the significant pollution emitted by ocean-going vessels at America's ports. Sen. Feinstein re-introduced the Ten-in-Ten Fuel Economy Act (S.357) which would raise the fuel economy standard for passenger cars from 25 to 35 mpg over the next 10 years, and—for the first time—would require improvements in fuel efficiency for medium and heavy-duty trucks.

President Bush Issues Greenhouse Gas Executive Order—In response to the Supreme Court's ruling on April 2 in *Massachusetts v. EPA*, President Bush announced his executive order calling for cooperation among federal agencies to find a way to begin regulating vehicle emissions by the time he leaves office based on his "twenty in Ten" goal—cutting U.S. gasoline consumption by 20 percent over the next 10 years.

State Initiatives

Environmental Defense reports that more than 300 global warming bills have been filed in 40 states, and more than 400 mayors have committed to reducing GHG emissions in their cities.

The State Response to Climate Change: 50 State Survey—Pace Law School Center for Environmental Legal Studies completed a comprehensive survey of state legislation, rules and executive orders that specifically address climate change as of the end of March 2006. The survey is contained in a new book from the American Bar Association released

April 2007 entitled GLOBAL CLIMATE CHANGE AND U.S. LAW, edited by Michael B. Gerrard. The 50–state survey is available at http://www.abanet.org/abapubs/globalclimate/stateupdate4–30–07.pdf. The survey found that nearly all 50 states have adopted some climate change measures, a number of regional initiatives are occurring, and "a growing number of states are adopting renewable portfolio standards and many states are poised to adopt California's greenhouse gas emissions standards for motor vehicles."

Regional Greenhouse Gas Initiative (RGGI)—New York Governor George Pataki kicked off this initiative in 2003, which includes ten states in the Northeast (Conn., Del., Md., Mass., Me., N.H., N.J., N.Y., R.I. and Vt.) who have joined together to reduce GHG emissions from utilities. Mandatory emission reduction targets will take effect on January 1, 2009. The RGGI is developing a cap and trade program similar to the European Union's Emissions Trading System. http://www.rggi.org/.

The Climate Registry—Thirty-one states, representing 70 percent of the country's population, announced a multi-state and tribe collaboration aimed at developing and managing a common greenhouse gas emissions reporting system. http://www.theclimateregistry.org/.

California's AB 32—The Global Warming Solutions Act of 2006—introduced by Assembly Speaker Fabian Nunez (D–Los Angeles) and signed by Governor Schwarzenegger, codifies the state's goal of requiring the state's global warming emissions be reduced to 1990 levels by 2020 through an enforceable statewide cap on global warming emissions that will be phased in starting in 2012. Since California is the world's 12th largest source of CO_2, the impacts of this cap will be significant and establish a model for other states to follow. AB 32 requires the California Air Resources Board (CARB) to develop regulations and market mechanisms to reach the state's goals. CARB is also required to convene an Environmental Justice Advisory Committee and an Economic and Technology Advancement Advisory Committee.

* * *

Local Initiatives

Neal Peirce notes that "cities may cover less than 1 percent of the earth's surface, but they generate 80 percent of the globe's heat-trapping greenhouse gases. Cities can take quicker, more inventive steps to curb emissions than cumbersome or politically encumbered national bureaucracies." (citation omitted)

Berkeley voters pass Measure G—Measure G establishes a goal of 80% reduction in GHG emissions by 2050 and advises the Mayor to work with the community to develop a plan for council adoption which sets a ten year emissions reduction target and identifies actions for the city and its residents to take to achieve both the ten year target and the ultimate goal of 80% reduction in emissions. The city has one of the most comprehensive efforts to address climate change. http://www.cityofberkeley.info/sustainable/. In addition to converting city vehicles and buildings to meet conservation goals, the city is requiring landlords to give their tenants free passes for the transit and considering adopting an assessment district that would pay for installation of solar panels and then tack the costs on to the property tax bills over the course of 30 years.

New York's PlaNYC—Mayor Michael Bloomberg proposes to reduce GHG emissions by 30 percent by 2030 rather than the currently projected 25 percent increase by using many different measures: congestion pricing; energy rehabbing of existing buildings; roadways landscaped and 1 million trees planted; "green" building standards required of all new buildings; all of the city's power plants and contaminated brownfields will be cleaned up which will help create new areas for 250,000 additional housing units, among other ideas. In May, the Mayor announced that the Taxi and Limousine Commission will implement new emissions and mileage standards for yellow taxicabs that will lead to a fully hybrid fleet by 2012. The new standards will be phased in over a four-year period and will reduce the carbon emissions of New York City's taxicab and for-hire vehicle fleet by 50% during the next decade, and will also save individual operators an average of $10,000 a year in fuel costs. http://www.nyc.gov/html/planyc2030/html/home/home.shtml.

U.S. Mayors Climate Protection Agreement—After the Kyoto Protocol Agreement took effect in February 2005 without the support of the U.S., Seattle Mayor Greg Nickels issued a challenge to his fellow U.S. Mayors to address climate change locally. http://www.seattle.gov/mayor/climate/. The U.S. Mayors Climate Protection Agreement was passed unanimously in June 2005. http://www.seattle.gov/mayor/climate/PDF/Resolution_FinalLanguage_06–13–05.pdf. As of May 23, 2007, 522 mayors representing over 65 million Americans have accepted the challenge to meet or exceed Kyoto Protocol targets for reducing global warming pollution. Climate Action Handbook was prepared by ICLEI—Local Governments for Sustainability in partnership with the City of Seattle and the U.S. Conference of Mayors. It includes actions & tools, as well as best practices & resources for addressing climate change at the local level. http://www.iclei.org/documents/USA/documents/CCP/Climate_Action_Handbook–0906.pdf.

Salt Lake City Green—Mayor Rocky Anderson has initiated a comprehensive community-wide program that ties climate change, air quality, pollution and human health together. http://www.slcgreen.com/. Specific actions include lighting efficiency retrofits, wind power purchases, LED traffic signal upgrades, alternative fuel use, cogeneration, and methane capture. Salt Lake City's goal is to reduce GHG emissions by 3% per year for the next 10 years, with a long-term goal of reducing emissions 70% by 2040. The City's Action Plan http://www.slcgreen.com/CAP/default.htm provides a detail [sic] list of actions and initiatives the city has undertaken and will pursue to meet its goal.

* * *

Private Initiatives

Chicago Climate Exchange—"Chicago Climate Exchange (CCX) is the world's first and North America's only legally binding rules-based greenhouse gas emissions allowance trading system, as well as the world's only global system for emissions trading based on all six greenhouse gases. CCX members are leaders in greenhouse gas management and represent all sectors of the global economy, as well as public sector innovators. Reductions achieved through CCX are the only reductions in North America being achieved through a legally binding compliance regime, providing independent third party verification provided by NASD and price transparency." (citation omitted)

Global Banking Initiative—President Bill Clinton has garnered commitments from five major global banking institutions to lend city government and landlords somewhere in the range of $5 billion in energy efficiency loans to replace heating, cooling, and lighting systems, to seal and upgrade windows, and to install sensors to make lighting and air conditioning more efficient. The savings in energy costs will pay back the initial investments. (citation omitted)

U.S. Climate Action Partnership—A group of businesses and environmental organizations have come together to press the federal government to enact strong legislation to require significant reductions in greenhouse gas emissions. * * * They issued a 16–page report "A Call for Action," (citation omitted) which includes their recommendations: (1) Establish a cap and trade system that places specified limits on GHG emissions; (2) Establish short and mid-term GHG emission targets; (3) Establish a national inventory and registry by legislation no later than the end of 2008; (4) Establish a federal technology research, development and demonstration and deployment program; (5) "Congress should encourage the Administration to engage in international negotiations with the aim of establishing commitments by all major emitting countries. The post–2021 global framework should establish international GHG markets, assist vulnerable populations in adopting to climate impacts, and boost support for climate-friendly technology in developing countries." (citation omitted)

* * *

The 2030 Challenge—Initiated by an architect in Santa Fe, N.M. who asserts that buildings are the major source of demand for energy and materials that produce by-product greenhouse gases. Ed Mazria, AIA [American Institute of Architects], wants his fellow architects and others in the building community to adopt the following targets: "All new buildings, developments and major renovations shall be designed to meet a fossil fuel, GHG-emitting, energy consumption performance standard of 50% of the regional (or country) average for that building type. At a minimum, an equal amount of existing building area shall be renovated annually to meet a fossil fuel, GHG-emitting, energy consumption performance standard of 50% of the regional (or country) average for that building type. The fossil fuel reduction standard for all new buildings shall be increased to: 60% in 2010, 70% in 2015, 80% in 2020, 90% in

2025. Carbon-neutral in 2030 (using no fossil fuel GHG emitting energy to operate). These targets may be accomplished by implementing innovative sustainable design strategies, generating on-site renewable power and/or purchasing (20% maximum) renewable energy and/or certified renewable energy credits. (citation omitted)

MASSACHUSETTS v. ENVIRONMENTAL PROTECTION AGENCY

Supreme Court of the United States, 2007.
___ U.S. ___, 127 S.Ct. 1438, 167 L.Ed.2d 248.

JUSTICE STEVENS delivered the opinion of the Court.

A well-documented rise in global temperatures has coincided with a significant increase in the concentration of carbon dioxide in the atmosphere. Respected scientists believe the two trends are related. For when carbon dioxide is released into the atmosphere, it acts like the ceiling of a greenhouse, trapping solar energy and retarding the escape of reflected heat. It is therefore a species—the most important species—of a "greenhouse gas."

Calling global warming "the most pressing environmental challenge of our time," (citation omitted) a group of States, (citation omitted) local governments, (citation omitted) and private organizations, (citation omitted) alleged in a petition for certiorari that the Environmental Protection Agency (EPA) has abdicated its responsibility under the Clean Air Act to regulate the emissions of four greenhouse gases, including carbon dioxide. Specifically, petitioners asked us to answer two questions concerning the meaning of § 202(a)(1) of the Act: whether EPA has the statutory authority to regulate greenhouse gas emissions from new motor vehicles; and if so, whether its stated reasons for refusing to do so are consistent with the statute.

In response, EPA, supported by 10 intervening States (citation omitted) and six trade associations,(citation omitted) correctly argued that we may not address those two questions unless at least one petitioner has standing to invoke our jurisdiction under Article III of the Constitution. Notwithstanding the serious character of that jurisdictional argument and the absence of any conflicting decisions construing § 202(a)(1),the unusual importance of the underlying issue persuaded us to grant the writ. 126 S.Ct. 2960, 165 L.Ed.2d 949 (2006).

I

Section 202(a)(1) of the Clean Air Act, as added by Pub.L. 89–272, § 101(8), 79 Stat. 992, and as amended by, inter alia, 84 Stat. 1690 and 91stat. 791, 42 U.S.C. § 7521(a)(1), provides:

> "The [EPA] Administrator shall by regulation prescribe (and from time to time revise) in accordance with the provisions of this section, standards applicable to the emission of any air pollutant from any class or classes of new motor vehicles or new motor vehicle engines,

which in his judgment cause, or contribute to, air pollution which may reasonably be anticipated to endanger public health or welfare. . . ." (citation omitted)

The Act defines "air pollutant" to include "any air pollution agent or combination of such agents, including any physical, chemical, biological, radioactive ... substance or matter which is emitted into or otherwise enters the ambient air." § 7602(g). "Welfare" is also defined broadly: among other things, it includes "effects on ... weather ... and climate." § 7602(h).

When Congress enacted these provisions, the study of climate change was in its infancy. (citation omitted) In 1959, shortly after the U.S. Weather Bureau began monitoring atmospheric carbon dioxide levels, an observatory in Mauna Loa, Hawaii, recorded a mean level of 316 parts per million. This was well above the highest carbon dioxide concentration-no more than 300 parts per million-revealed in the 420,000–year-old ice-core record. (citation omitted) By the time Congress drafted § 202(a)(1) in 1970, carbon dioxide levels had reached 325 parts per million. (citation omitted)

In the late 1970's, the Federal Government began devoting serious attention to the possibility that carbon dioxide emissions associated with human activity could provoke climate change. In 1978, Congress enacted the National Climate Program Act, 92 Stat. 601, which required the President to establish a program to "assist the Nation and the world to understand and respond to natural and man-induced climate processes and their implications," id., § 3. President Carter, in turn, asked the National Research Council, the working arm of the National Academy of Sciences, to investigate the subject. The Council's response was unequivocal: "If carbon dioxide continues to increase, the study group finds no reason to doubt that climate changes will result and no reason to believe that these changes will be negligible. . . . A wait-and-see policy may mean waiting until it is too late." (citation omitted)

Congress next addressed the issue in 1987, when it enacted the Global Climate Protection Act, Title XI of Pub.L. 100–204, 101 Stat. 1407, note following 15 U.S.C. § 2901. Finding that "manmade pollution—the release of carbon dioxide, chlorofluorocarbons, methane, and other trace gases into the atmosphere—may be producing a long-term and substantial increase in the average temperature on Earth," § 1102(1), 101 Stat. 1408, Congress directed EPA to propose to Congress a "coordinated national policy on global climate change," § 1103(b), and ordered the Secretary of State to work "through the channels of multilateral diplomacy" and coordinate diplomatic efforts to combat global warming, § 1103(c). Congress emphasized that "ongoing pollution and deforestation may be contributing now to an irreversible process" and that "[n]ecessary actions must be identified and implemented in time to protect the climate." § 1102(4).

Meanwhile, the scientific understanding of climate change progressed. In 1990, the Intergovernmental Panel on Climate Change (IPCC), a multinational scientific body organized under the auspices of the United Nations, published its first comprehensive report on the topic. Drawing on expert opinions from across the globe, the IPCC concluded that "emissions resulting from human activities are substantially increasing the atmospheric concentrations of ... greenhouse gases [which] will enhance the greenhouse effect, resulting on average in an additional warming of the Earth's surface." (citation omitted)

Responding to the IPCC report, the United Nations convened the "Earth Summit" in 1992 in Rio de Janeiro. The first President Bush attended and signed the United Nations Framework Convention on Climate Change (UNFCCC), a nonbinding agreement among 154 nations to reduce atmospheric concentrations of carbon dioxide and other greenhouse gases for the purpose of "prevent[ing] dangerous anthropogenic [i.e., human-induced] interference with the [Earth's] climate system." (citation omitted) S. Treaty Doc. No. 102–38, Art. 2, p.5 (1992). The Senate unanimously ratified the treaty.

Some five years later-after the IPCC issued a second comprehensive report in 1995 concluding that "[t]he balance of evidence suggests there is a discernible human influence on global climate" (citation omitted)—the UNFCCC signatories met in Kyoto, Japan, and adopted a protocol that assigned mandatory targets for industrialized nations to reduce greenhouse gas emissions. Because those targets did not apply to developing and heavily polluting nations such as China and India, the Senate unanimously passed a resolution expressing its sense that the United States should not enter into the Kyoto Protocol. See S. Res. 98, 105th Cong., 1st Sess. (July 25, 1997) (as passed). President Clinton did not submit the protocol to the Senate for ratification.

II

On October 20, 1999, a group of 19 private organizations (citation omitted) filed a rulemaking petition asking EPA to regulate "greenhouse gas emissions from new motor vehicles under § 202 of the Clean Air Act." App. 5. Petitioners maintained that 1998 was the "warmest year on record"; that carbon dioxide, methane, nitrous oxide, and hydrofluorocarbons are "heat trapping greenhouse gases"; that greenhouse gas emissions have significantly accelerated climate change; and that the IPCC's 1995 report warned that "carbon dioxide remains the most important contributor to [man-made] forcing of climate change." Id., at 13 (internal quotation marks omitted). The petition further alleged that climate change will have serious adverse effects on human health and the environment. Id., at 22–35. As to EPA's statutory authority, the petition observed that the agency itself had already confirmed that it had the power to regulate carbon dioxide. See id., at 18, n. 21. In 1998, Jonathan Z.Cannon, then EPA's General Counsel, prepared a legal opinion concluding that "CO(2) emissions are within the scope of EPA's authority to regulate," even as he recognized that EPA had so far declined to exercise that authority. Id., at 54 (memorandum to Carol M. Browner, Administrator (Apr. 10, 1998) (hereinafter Cannon memorandum)). Cannon's successor, Gary S. Guzy, reiterated that opinion before a congressional Committee just two weeks before the rulemaking petition was filed. See id., at 61.

Fifteen months after the petition's submission, EPA requested public comment on "all the issues raised in [the] petition," adding a "particular" request for comments on "any scientific, technical, legal, economic or other aspect of these issues that may be relevant to EPA's consideration of this petition." 66 Fed.Reg. 7486, 7487 (2001). EPA received more than 50,000 comments over the next five months. See 68 Fed.Reg. 52924 (2003).

Before the close of the comment period, the White House sought "assistance in identifying the areas in the science of climate change where there are the greatest certainties and uncertainties" from the National Research Council, asking for a response "as soon as possible." App. 213. The result was a 2001 report titled Climate Change: An Analysis of Some Key Questions (NRC Report), which, drawing heavily on the 1995 IPCC report, concluded that "[g]reenhouse gases are accumulating in Earth's atmosphere as a result of human activities, causing surface air temperatures and subsurface ocean temperatures to rise. Temperatures are, in fact, rising." NRC Report 1.

On September 8, 2003, EPA entered an order denying the rulemaking petition. 68 Fed.Reg. 52922. The agency gave two reasons for its decision: (1) that contrary to the opinions of its former general counsels, the Clean Air Act does not authorize EPA to issue mandatory regulations to address global climate change, see id., at 52925–52929; and (2) that even if the agency had the authority to set greenhouse gas emission standards, it would be unwise to do so at this time, id., at 52929–52931.

In concluding that it lacked statutory authority over greenhouse gases, EPA observed that Congress "was well aware of the global climate change issue when it last comprehensively amended the [Clean Air Act] in 1990," yet it declined to adopt a proposed amendment establishing binding emissions limitations. Id., at 52926. Congress instead chose to authorize further investigation into climate change. Ibid. (citing §§ 103(g) and 602(e)of the Clean Air Act Amendments of 1990, 104 Stat. 2652, 2703, 42 U.S.C. §§ 7403(g)(1) and 7671a(e)). EPA further reasoned that Congress' "specially tailored solutions to global atmospheric issues," 68 Fed.Reg. 52926—in particular, its 1990 enactment of a comprehensive scheme to regulate pollutants that depleted the ozone layer, see Title VI, 104 Stat. 2649, 42 U.S.C. §§ 7671–7671q—counseled against reading the general authorization of § 202(a)(1) to confer regulatory authority over greenhouse gases.

* * *

EPA reasoned that climate change had its own "political history": Congress designed the original Clean Air Act to address local air pollutants rather than a substance that "is fairly consistent in its concentration throughout the world's atmosphere," 68 Fed.Reg. 52927 (emphasis added); declined in 1990 to enact proposed amendments to force EPA to set carbon dioxide emission standards for motor vehicles, ibid. (citing H.R. 5966, 101st Cong., 2d Sess. (1990)); and addressed global climate change in other legislation, 68 Fed.Reg. 52927. Because of this political history, and because imposing emission limitations on greenhouse gases would have even greater economic and political repercussions than regulating tobacco, EPA was persuaded that it lacked the power to do so. Id., at 52928. In essence, EPA concluded that climate change was so important that unless Congress spoke with exacting specificity, it could not have meant the agency to address it.

Having reached that conclusion, EPA believed it followed that greenhouse gases cannot be "air pollutants" within the meaning of the Act. See ibid. ("It follows from this conclusion, that [greenhouse gases], as such, are not air pollutants under the [Clean Air Act's] regulatory provisions . . ."). The agency bolstered this conclusion by explaining that if carbon dioxide were an air pollutant, the only feasible method of reducing tailpipe emissions would be to improve fuel economy. But because Congress has already created detailed mandatory fuel economy standards subject to Department of Transportation (DOT) administration, the agency concluded that EPA regulation would either conflict with those standards or be superfluous. Id., at 52929.

Even assuming that it had authority over greenhouse gases, EPA explained in detail why it would refuse to exercise that authority. The agency began by recognizing that the concentration of greenhouse gases has dramatically increased as a result of human activities, and acknowledged the attendant increase in global surface air temperatures. Id., at 52930. EPA nevertheless gave controlling importance to the NRC Report's statement that a causal link between the two " 'cannot be unequivocally established.' " Ibid. quoting NRC Report 17). Given that residual uncertainty, EPA concluded that regulating greenhouse gas emissions would be unwise.68 Fed.Reg. 52930.

The agency furthermore characterized any EPA regulation of motor-vehicle emissions as a "piecemeal approach" to climate change, id., at 52931, and stated that such regulation would conflict with the President's "comprehensive approach" to the problem, id., at 52932. That approach involves additional support for technological innovation, the creation of nonregulatory programs to encourage voluntary private-sector reductions in greenhouse gas emissions, and further research on climate change—not actual regulation. Id., at 52932–52933. According to EPA, unilateral EPA regulation of motor-vehicle greenhouse gas emissions might also hamper the President's ability to persuade key developing countries to reduce greenhouse gas emissions. Id., at 52931.

III

Petitioners, now joined by intervenor States and local governments, sought review of EPA's order in the United States Court of Appeals for the District of Columbia Circuit. Although each of the three judges on the panel wrote a separate opinion, two judges agreed "that the EPA Administrator properly exercised his discretion under § 202(a)(1) in denying the petition for rule making." 415 F.3d 50, 58 (2005). The court therefore denied the petition for review.

* * *

IV

Article III of the Constitution limits federal-court jurisdiction to "Cases" and "Controversies." Those two words confine "the business of federal courts to questions presented in an adversary context and in a form historically viewed as capable of resolution through the judicial process." Flast v. Cohen, 392 U.S. 83, 95, 88 S.Ct. 1942, 20 L.Ed.2d 947 (1968). It is therefore familiar learning that no justiciable "controversy" exists when parties seek adjudication of a political question, Luther v. Borden, 7 How. 1, 12 L.Ed. 581 (1849), when they ask for an advisory opinion, Hayburn's Case, 2 Dall. 409, 1 L.Ed. 436 (1792), see also Clinton v. Jones, 520 U.S. 681, 700, n. 33, 117 S.Ct. 1636, 137 L.Ed.2d 945 (1997), or when the question sought to be adjudicated has been mooted by subsequent developments, California v. San Pablo & Tulare R. Co., 149 U.S. 308, 13 S.Ct. 876, 37 L.Ed. 747 (1893). This case suffers from none of these defects.

The parties' dispute turns on the proper construction of a congressional statute, a question eminently suitable to resolution in federal court. Congress has moreover authorized this type of challenge to EPA action. See 42 U.S.C. § 7607(b)(1). That authorization is of critical importance to the standing inquiry: "Congress has the power to define injuries and articulate chains of causation that will give rise to a case or controversy where none existed before." Lujan, 504 U.S., at 580, 112 S.Ct. 2130 (KENNEDY, J., concurring in part and concurring in judgment). "In exercising this power, however, Congress must at the very least identify the injury it seeks to vindicate and relate the injury to the class of persons entitled to bring suit." Ibid. We will not, therefore, "entertain citizen suits to vindicate the public's nonconcrete interest in the proper administration of the laws." Id., at 581, 112 S.Ct. 2130.

EPA maintains that because greenhouse gas emissions inflict widespread harm, the doctrine of standing presents an insuperable jurisdictional obstacle. We do not agree. At bottom, "the gist of the question of standing" is whether petitioners have "such a personal stake in the outcome of the controversy as to assure that concrete adverseness which sharpens the presentation of issues upon which the court so largely depends for illumination." Baker v. Carr, 369 U.S. 186, 204, 82 S.Ct. 691, 7 L.Ed.2d 663 (1962). As Justice KENNEDY explained in his Lujan concurrence: "While it does not matter how many persons have been injured by the challenged action, the party bringing suit must show that the action injures him in a concrete and personal way. This requirement is not just an empty formality. It preserves the vitality of the adversarial process by assuring both that the parties before the court have an actual, as opposed to professed, stake in the outcome, and that the legal questions presented . . . will be resolved, not in the rarified atmosphere of a debating society, but in a concrete factual context conducive to a realistic appreciation of the consequences of judicial action." 504 U.S., at 581, 112 S.Ct. 2130 (internal quotation marks omitted).

To ensure the proper adversarial presentation, Lujan holds that a litigant must demonstrate that it has suffered a concrete and particularized injury that is either actual or imminent, that the injury is fairly traceable to the defendant, and that it is likely that a favorable decision will redress that injury. See id., at 560–561, 112 S.Ct. 2130. However, a litigant to whom Congress has "accorded a procedural right to protect his concrete interests," id., at 572, n. 7, 112 S.Ct. 2130—here, the right to challenge agency action unlawfully withheld, § 7607(b)(1)—"can assert that right without meeting all the normal standards for redressability and immediacy," ibid. When a litigant is vested with a procedural right, that litigant has standing if there is some possibility that the requested relief will prompt the injury-causing party to reconsider the decision that allegedly harmed the litigant. Ibid.; see also Sugar Cane Growers Cooperative of Fla. v. Veneman, 289 F.3d 89, 94–95 (C.A.D.C. 2002) ("A [litigant] who alleges a deprivation of a procedural protection to which he is entitled never has to prove that if he had received the procedure the substantive result would have been altered. All that is necessary is to show that the procedural step was connected to the substantive result").

Only one of the petitioners needs to have standing to permit us to consider the petition for review. See Rumsfeld v. Forum for Academic and Institutional Rights, Inc., 547 U.S. 47, 52, n. 2, 126 S.Ct. 1297, 164 L.Ed.2d 156 (2006). We stress here, as did Judge Tatel below, the special position and interest of Massachusetts. It is of considerable relevance that the party seeking review here is a sovereign State and not, as it was in Lujan, a private individual.

Well before the creation of the modern administrative state, we recognized that States are not normal litigants for the purposes of invoking federal jurisdiction. As Justice Holmes explained in Georgia v. Tennessee Copper Co., 206 U.S. 230, 237, 27 S.Ct. 618, 51 L.Ed. 1038 (1907), a case in which Georgia sought to protect its citizens from air pollution originating outside its borders:

> "The case has been argued largely as if it were one between two private parties; but it is not. The very elements that would be relied upon in a suit between fellow-citizens as a ground for equitable relief are wanting here. The State owns very little of the territory alleged to be affected, and the damage to it capable of estimate in money, possibly, at least, is small. This is a suit by a State for an injury to it in its capacity of quasi-sovereign. In that capacity the State has an interest independent of and behind the titles of its citizens, in all the earth and air within its domain. It has the last

word as to whether its mountains shall be stripped of their forests and its inhabitants shall breathe pure air."

Just as Georgia's "independent interest ... in all the earth and air within its domain" supported federal jurisdiction a century ago, so too does Massachusetts' well-founded desire to preserve its sovereign territory today. Cf. Alden v. Maine, 527 U.S. 706, 715, 119 S.Ct. 2240, 144 L.Ed.2d 636 (1999) (observing that in the federal system, the States "are not relegated to the role of mere provinces or political corporations, but retain the dignity, though not the full authority, of sovereignty"). That Massachusetts does in fact own a great deal of the "territory alleged to be affected" only reinforces the conclusion that its stake in the outcome of this case is sufficiently concrete to warrant the exercise of federal judicial power.

When a State enters the Union, it surrenders certain sovereign prerogatives. Massachusetts cannot invade Rhode Island to force reductions in greenhouse gas emissions, it cannot negotiate an emissions treaty with China or India, and in some circumstances the exercise of its police powers to reduce in-state motor-vehicle emissions might well be pre-empted. See Alfred L. Snapp & Son, Inc. v. Puerto Rico ex rel. Barez, 458 U.S. 592, 607, 102 S.Ct. 3260, 73 L.Ed.2d 995 (1982) ("One helpful indication in determining whether an alleged injury to the health and welfare of its citizens suffices to give the State standing to sue parens patriae is whether the injury is one that the State, if it could, would likely attempt to address through its sovereign lawmaking powers").

These sovereign prerogatives are now lodged in the Federal Government, and Congress has ordered EPA to protect Massachusetts (among others) by prescribing standards applicable to the "emission of any air pollutant from any class or classes of new motor vehicle engines, which in [the Administrator's] judgment cause, or contribute to, air pollution which may reasonably be anticipated to endanger public health or welfare." 42 U.S.C. § 7521(a)(1). Congress has moreover recognized a concomitant procedural right to challenge the rejection of its rulemaking petition as arbitrary and capricious. § 7607(b)(1). Given that procedural right and Massachusetts' stake in protecting its quasi-sovereign interests, the Commonwealth is entitled to special solicitude in our standing analysis. (citation omitted)

With that in mind, it is clear that petitioners' submissions as they pertain to Massachusetts have satisfied the most demanding standards of the adversarial process. EPA's steadfast refusal to regulate greenhouse gas emissions presents a risk of harm to Massachusetts that is both "actual" and "imminent." Lujan, 504 U.S., at 560, 112 S.Ct. 2130 (internal quotation marks omitted). There is, moreover, a "substantial likelihood that the judicial relief requested" will prompt EPA to take steps to reduce that risk. Duke Power Co. v. Carolina Environmental Study Group, Inc., 438 U.S. 59, 79, 98 S.Ct. 2620, 57 L.Ed.2d 595 (1978).

The Injury

The harms associated with climate change are serious and well recognized. Indeed, the NRC Report itself—which EPA regards as an "objective and independent assessment of the relevant science," 68 Fed.Reg. 52930—identifies a number of environmental changes that have already inflicted significant harms, including "the global retreat of mountain glaciers, reduction in snow-cover extent, the earlier spring melting of rivers and lakes, [and] the accelerated rate of rise of sea levels during the 20th century relative to the past few thousand years...." NRC Report 16.

Petitioners allege that this only hints at the environmental damage yet to come. According to the climate scientist Michael MacCracken, "qualified scientific experts involved in climate change research" have reached a "strong consensus" that global warming threatens (among other things) a precipitate rise in sea levels by the end of the century, MacCracken Decl. para. 15, Stdg.App. 207, "severe and irreversible changes to natural ecosystems," id., para. 5(d), at 209, a "significant reduction in water storage in winter snowpack in mountainous regions with direct and important economic consequences," ibid., and an increase in the spread of disease, id., para. 28, at 218–219. He also observes that rising ocean temperatures may contribute to the ferocity of hurricanes. Id., paragraphs 23–25, at 216–217. (citation omitted)

That these climate-change risks are "widely shared" does not minimize Massachusetts' interest in the outcome of this litigation. See Federal Election Comm'n v. Akins, 524 U.S. 11, 24, 118 S.Ct. 1777, 141 L.Ed.2d 10(1998) ("[W]here a harm is concrete, though widely shared, the Court has found 'injury in fact' "). According to petitioners' unchallenged affidavits, global sea levels rose somewhere between 10 and 20 centimeters over the 20th century as a result of global warming. MacCracken Decl. para. 5(c), Stdg.App. 208. These rising seas have already begun to swallow Massachusetts' coastal land. Id., at 196 (declaration of Paul H. Kirshen para. 5), 216 (MacCracken Decl. para. 23). Because the Commonwealth "owns a substantial portion of the state's coastal property," id., at 171 (declaration of Karst R. Hoogeboom para. 4), (citation omitted) it has alleged a particularized injury in its capacity as a landowner. The severity of that injury will only increase over the course of the next century: If sea levels continue to rise as predicted, one Massachusetts official believes that a significant fraction of coastal property will be "either permanently lost through inundation or temporarily lost through periodic storm surge and flooding events." Id., para. 6, at 172. (citation omitted) Remediation costs alone, petitioners allege, could run well into the hundreds of millions of dollars. Id., para. 7, at 172; see also Kirshen Decl. para. 12, at 198. (citation omitted)

Causation

EPA does not dispute the existence of a causal connection between man-made greenhouse gas emissions and global warming. At a minimum, therefore, EPA's refusal to regulate such emissions "contributes" to Massachusetts' injuries.

EPA nevertheless maintains that its decision not to regulate greenhouse gas emissions from new motor vehicles contributes so insignificantly to petitioners' injuries that the agency cannot be haled into federal court to answer for them. For the same reason, EPA does not believe that any realistic possibility exists that the relief petitioners seek would mitigate global climate change and remedy their injuries. That is especially so because predicted increases in greenhouse gas emissions from developing nations, particularly China and India, are likely to offset any marginal domestic decrease.

But EPA overstates its case. Its argument rests on the erroneous assumption that a small incremental step, because it is incremental, can never be attacked in a federal judicial forum. Yet accepting that premise would doom most challenges to regulatory action. Agencies, like legislatures, do not generally resolve massive problems in one fell regulatory swoop. See Williamson v. Lee Optical of Okla., Inc., 348 U.S. 483, 489, 75 S.Ct. 461, 99 L.Ed. 563 (1955) ("[A] reform may take one step at a time, addressing itself to the phase of the problem which seems most acute to the legislative mind"). They instead whittle away at them over time, refining their preferred approach as circumstances change and as they develop a more-nuanced understanding of how best to proceed. Cf. SEC v. Chenery Corp., 332 U.S. 194, 202, 67 S.Ct. 1575, 91 L.Ed. 1995 (1947) ("Some principles must await their own development, while others must be adjusted to meet particular, unforeseeable situations"). That a first step might be tentative does not by itself support the notion that federal courts lack jurisdiction to determine whether that step conforms to law.

And reducing domestic automobile emissions is hardly a tentative step. Even leaving aside the other greenhouse gases, the United States transportation sector emits an enormous quantity of carbon dioxide into the atmosphere-according to the MacCracken affidavit, more than 1.7 billion metric tons in 1999 alone. Para. 30, Stdg.App. 219. That accounts for more than 6% of worldwide carbon dioxide emissions. Id., at 232 (Oppenheimer Decl. para. 3); see also MacCracken Decl. para. 31,at 220. To put this in perspective: Considering just emissions from the transportation sector, which represent less than one-third of this country's total carbon dioxide emissions, the United States would still rank as the third-largest emitter of carbon dioxide in the world, outpaced only by the European Union and China.(citation omitted) Judged by any standard, U.S. motor-vehicle emissions make a meaningful contribution to greenhouse gas concentrations and hence, according to petitioners, to global warming.

The Remedy

While it may be true that regulating motor-vehicle emissions will not by itself reverse global warming, it by no means follows that we lack jurisdiction to decide whether EPA has a duty to take steps to slow or reduce it. See also Larson v. Valente, 456 U.S. 228, 244, n. 15, 102 S.Ct. 1673, 72 L.Ed.2d 33 (1982) ("[A] plaintiff satisfies the redressability requirement when he shows that a favorable decision will relieve a discrete injury to himself. He need not show that a favorable decision will relieve his every injury"). Because of the enormity of the potential consequences associated with man-made climate change, the fact that the effectiveness of a remedy might be delayed during the (relatively short) time it takes for a new motor-vehicle fleet to replace an older one is essentially irrelevant. (citation omitted) Nor is it dispositive that developing countries such as China and India are poised to increase greenhouse gas emissions substantially over the next century: A reduction in domestic emissions would slow the pace of global emissions increases, no matter what happens elsewhere.

We moreover attach considerable significance to EPA's "agree[ment] with the President that 'we must address the issue of global climate change,'" 68 Fed.Reg. 52929 (quoting remarks announcing Clear Skies and Global Climate Initiatives, 2002 Public Papers of George W. Bush, Vol. 1, Feb. 14, p. 227 (2004)), and to EPA's ardent support for various voluntary emission-reduction programs, 68 Fed.Reg. 52932. As Judge Tatel observed in dissent below, "EPA would presumably not bother with such efforts if it thought emissions reductions would have no discernable impact on future global warming." 415 F.3d, at 66.

In sum—at least according to petitioners' uncontested affidavits—the rise in sea levels associated with global warming has already harmed and will continue to harm Massachusetts. The risk of catastrophic harm, though remote, is nevertheless real. That risk would be reduced to some extent if petitioners received the relief they seek. We therefore hold that petitioners have standing to challenge the EPA's denial of their rulemaking petition. (citation omitted)

V

The scope of our review of the merits of the statutory issues is narrow. As we have repeated time and again, an agency has broad discretion to choose how best to marshal its limited resources and personnel to carry out its delegated responsibilities. See Chevron U.S.A. Inc. v. Natural Resources Defense Council, Inc., 467 U.S. 837, 842–845, 104 S.Ct. 2778, 81 L.Ed.2d 694 (1984). That discretion is at its height when the agency decides not to bring an enforcement action. Therefore, in Heckler v. Chaney, 470 U.S. 821,105 S.Ct. 1649, 84 L.Ed.2d 714 (1985), we held that an agency's refusal to initiate enforcement proceedings is not ordinarily subject to judicial review. Some debate remains, however, as to the rigor with which we review an agency's denial of a petition for rulemaking.

There are key differences between a denial of a petition for rulemaking and an agency's decision not to initiate an enforcement action. See American Horse Protection Assn., Inc. v. Lyng, 812 F.2d 1, 3–4 (C.A.D.C.

1987). In contrast to nonenforcement decisions, agency refusals to initiate rulemaking "are less frequent, more apt to involve legal as opposed to factual analysis, and subject to special formalities, including a public explanation." Id., at 4; see also 5 U.S.C. § 555(e). They moreover arise out of denials of petitions for rulemaking which (at least in the circumstances here) the affected party had an undoubted procedural right to file in the first instance. Refusals to promulgate rules are thus susceptible to judicial review, though such review is "extremely limited" and "highly deferential." National Customs Brokers & Forwarders Assn. of America, Inc. v. United States, 883 F.2d 93, 96 (C.A.D.C.1989).

EPA concluded in its denial of the petition for rulemaking that it lacked authority under 42 U.S.C. § 7521(a)(1) to regulate new vehicle emissions because carbon dioxide is not an "air pollutant" as that term is defined in § 7602. In the alternative, it concluded that even if it possessed authority, it would decline to do so because regulation would conflict with other administration priorities. As discussed earlier, the Clean Air Act expressly permits review of such an action. § 7607(b)(1). We therefore "may reverse any such action found to be ... arbitrary,capricious, an abuse of discretion, or otherwise not in accordance with law." § 7607(d)(9).

VI

On the merits, the first question is whether § 202(a)(1) of the Clean Air Act authorizes EPA to regulate greenhouse gas emissions from new motor vehicles in the event that it forms a "judgment" that such emissions contribute to climate change. We have little trouble concluding that it does. In relevant part, § 202(a)(1) provides that EPA "shall by regulation prescribe ... standards applicable to the emission of any air pollutant from any class or classes of new motor vehicles or new motor vehicle engines, which in [the Administrator's] judgment cause, or contribute to, air pollution which may reasonably be anticipated to endanger public health or welfare." 42 U.S.C. § 7521(a)(1). Because EPA believes that Congress did not intend it to regulate substances that contribute to climate change, the agency maintains that carbon dioxide is not an "air pollutant" within the meaning of the provision.

The statutory text forecloses EPA's reading. The Clean Air Act's sweeping definition of "air pollutant" includes "any air pollution agent or combination of such agents, including any physical, chemical ... substance or matter which is emitted into or otherwise enters the ambient air...." § 7602(g) (emphasis added). On its face, the definition embraces all airborne compounds of whatever stripe, and underscores that intent through the repeated use of the word "any." (citation omitted) Carbon dioxide, methane, nitrous oxide, and hydrofluorocarbons are without a doubt "physical [and] chemical ... substance[s] which [are] emitted into ... the ambient air." The statute is unambiguous. (citation omitted)

Rather than relying on statutory text, EPA invokes postenactment congressional actions and deliberations it views as tantamount to a congressional command to refrain from regulating greenhouse gas emissions. Even if such postenactment legislative history could shed light on the meaning of an otherwise-unambiguous statute, EPA never identifies any action remotely suggesting that Congress meant to curtail its power to treat greenhouse gases as air pollutants. That subsequent Congresses have eschewed enacting binding emissions limitations to combat global warming tells us nothing about what Congress meant when it amended § 202(a)(1) in 1970 and 1977. (citation omitted) And unlike EPA, we have no difficulty reconciling Congress' various efforts to promote interagency collaboration and research to better understand climate change (citation omitted) with the agency's pre-existing mandate to regulate "any air pollutant" that may endanger the public welfare. See 42 U.S.C. § 7601(a)(1). Collaboration and research do not conflict with any thoughtful regulatory effort; they complement it. (citation omitted)

* * *

There is no reason, much less a compelling reason, to accept EPA's invitation to read ambiguity into a clear statute.

EPA finally argues that it cannot regulate carbon dioxide emissions from motor vehicles because doing so would require it to tighten mileage standards, a job (according to EPA) that Congress has assigned to DOT. See 68 Fed.Reg. 52929. But that DOT sets mileage standards in no way licenses EPA to shirk its environmental responsibilities. EPA has been charged with protecting the public's "health" and "welfare," 42 U.S.C. § 7521(a)(1), a statutory obligation wholly independent of DOT's mandate to promote energy efficiency. See Energy Policy and Conservation Act, § 2(5), 89 Stat. 874, 42 U.S.C. § 6201(5). The two obligations may overlap, but there is no reason to think the two agencies cannot both administer their obligations and yet avoid inconsistency.

While the Congresses that drafted § 202(a)(1) might not have appreciated the possibility that burning fossil fuels could lead to global warming, they did understand that without regulatory flexibility, changing circumstances and scientific developments would soon render the Clean Air Act obsolete. The broad language of § 202(a)(1) reflects an intentional effort to confer the flexibility necessary to forestall such obsolescence. See Pennsylvania Dept. of Corrections v. Yeskey, 524 U.S. 206, 212, 118 S.Ct.1952, 141 L.Ed.2d 215 (1998). ("[T]he fact that a statute can be applied in situations not expressly anticipated by Congress does not demonstrate ambiguity. It demonstrates breadth" (internal quotation marks omitted)). Because greenhouse gases fit well within the Clean Air Act's capacious definition of "air pollutant," we hold that EPA has the statutory authority to regulate the emission of such gases from new motor vehicles.

VII

The alternative basis for EPA's decision—that even if it does have statutory authority to regulate greenhouse gases, it would be unwise to do so at this time—rests on reasoning divorced from the statutory text. While the statute does condition the exercise of EPA's authority on its formation of a "judgment," 42 U.S.C. § 7521(a)(1), that judgment must relate to whether an air pollutant "cause[s], or contribute[s] to, air pollution which may reasonably be anticipated to endanger public health or welfare," ibid. Put another way, the use of the word "judgment" is not a roving license to ignore the statutory text. It is but a direction to exercise discretion within defined statutory limits.

If EPA makes a finding of endangerment, the Clean Air Act requires the agency to regulate emissions of the deleterious pollutant from new motor vehicles. Ibid. (stating that "[EPA] shall by regulation prescribe . . . standards applicable to the emission of any air pollutant from any class of new motor vehicles"). EPA no doubt has significant latitude as to the manner, timing, content, and coordination of its regulations with those of other agencies. But once EPA has responded to a petition for rulemaking, its reasons for action or inaction must conform to the authorizing statute. Under the clear terms of the Clean Air Act, EPA can avoid taking further action only if it determines that greenhouse gases do not contribute to climate change or if it provides some reasonable explanation as to why it cannot or will not exercise its discretion to determine whether they do. Ibid. To the extent that this constrains agency discretion to pursue other priorities of the Administrator or the President, this is the congressional design.

EPA has refused to comply with this clear statutory command. Instead, it has offered a laundry list of reasons not to regulate. For example, EPA said that a number of voluntary executive branch programs already provide an effective response to the threat of global warming, 68 Fed.Reg. 52932, that regulating greenhouse gases might impair the President's ability to negotiate with "key developing nations" to reduce emissions, id., at 52931, and that curtailing motor-vehicle emissions would reflect "an inefficient, piecemeal approach to address the climate change issue," ibid.

Although we have neither the expertise nor the authority to evaluate these policy judgments, it is evident they have nothing to do with whether greenhouse gas emissions contribute to climate change. Still less do they amount to a reasoned justification for declining to form a scientific judgment. In particular, while the President has broad authority in foreign affairs, that authority does not extend to the refusal to execute domestic laws. In the Global Climate Protection Act of 1987, Congress authorized the State Department—not EPA—to formulate United States foreign policy with reference to environmental matters relating to climate. See § 1103(c), 101 Stat. 1409. EPA has made no showing that it issued the ruling in question here after consultation with the State Department. Congress did direct EPA to consult with other agencies in the formulation of its policies and rules, but the State Department is absent from that list. § 1103(b).

Nor can EPA avoid its statutory obligation by noting the uncertainty surrounding various features of climate change and concluding that it would therefore be better not to regulate at this time. See 68 Fed.Reg. 52930–52931. If the scientific uncertainty is so profound that it precludes EPA from making a reasoned judgment as to whether greenhouse gases contribute to global warming, EPA must say so. That EPA would prefer not to regulate greenhouse gases because of some residual uncertainty—which, contrary to Justice SCALIA's apparent belief, post, at 1466–1468, is in fact all that it said, see 68 Fed.Reg. 52929 ("We do not believe . . . that it would be either effective or appropriate for EPA to establish [greenhouse gas] standards for motor vehicles at this time" emphasis added))—is irrelevant. The statutory question is whether sufficient information exists to make an endangerment finding.

In short, EPA has offered no reasoned explanation for its refusal to decide whether greenhouse gases cause or contribute to climate change. Its action was therefore "arbitrary, capricious, . . . or otherwise not in accordance with law." 42 U.S.C. § 7607(d)(9)(A). We need not and do not reach the question whether on remand EPA must make an endangerment finding, or whether policy concerns can inform EPA's actions in the event that it makes such a finding. Cf. Chevron U.S.A. Inc. v. Natural Resources Defense Council, Inc., 467 U.S. 837, 843–844, 104 S.Ct. 2778, 81 L.Ed.2d 694 (1984). We hold only that EPA must ground its reasons for action or inaction in the statute.

VIII

The judgment of the Court of Appeals is reversed, and the case is remanded for further proceedings consistent with this opinion.

It is so ordered.

CHIEF JUSTICE ROBERTS, with whom JUSTICE SCALIA, JUSTICE THOMAS, and JUSTICE ALITO join, dissenting. [Dissenting opinion omitted]

JUSTICE SCALIA, with whom THE CHIEF JUSTICE, JUSTICE THOMAS, and JUSTICE ALITO join, dissenting. [Dissenting opinion omitted]

Notes

1. Copies of the briefs submitted in the Massachusetts v. EPA case, as well as a transcript of the oral argument are available at http://www.warminglaw.com. While this case is perhaps more appropriately categorized as an environmental and administrative law matter, the beginning of the opinion is highly instructive in how it lays out the accepted climate change science. Understanding the scientific and political dimensions of what appears to be the beginning of a watershed of litigation on global warming is important. With the growing interest of states and non-governmental advocacy organizations in taking steps to slow climate change, it is appropriate for practitioners in the land use planning and zoning fields to examine the opportunities presented in this discipline to address this pressing challenge. Lora Lucero's article at the start of this Section offers some insights into actions that state and local governments are beginning to take.

2. In *Zoning and Climate Change*, published in the New York Law Journal in April 2007, John Nolon and Jessica A. Bacher make the following observations:

> How we travel from home to work, shop, and recreate is dictated by land use laws that establish population densities and that either separate or mix retail, office, and residential development. When density is increased for both residential and commercial uses, the distance between origin and destination is shorter and walking, bicycling, and mass transit services are more feasible. In order for increased densities to be tolerated, attractive building, landscape, and streetscape design must be employed. Studies have shown that increased population density decreases automobile ownership and the number of vehicle miles traveled. "[D]oubling the population density of a community could reduce per-family driving by as much as 20 to 30 percent." (citation omitted) "[O]ne study found that at high density, levels of 10,000 to 50,000 people per square mile, half of all trips were not by automobile, and walking and bicycling increased significantly." (citation omitted) Minimum population densities are also required to support mass transit. Four to eight housing units per acre are necessary to support a transit system at a minimum level and more than 15 units per acre support frequent service. Increased commercial density also increases transit ridership.
>
> * * *
>
> What emerging suburban communities do to adjust their land use regulations is a critical component of accommodating the nation's projected increase of 100 million people by the year 2043 in a climate-friendly fashion. Land use patterns in suburban New York Metropolitan communities have generated automobile dependence, commutes by car to work that greatly exceed 23 miles, home sizes in excess of the 2,400 square foot national average, and households whose members routinely make from seven to 15 separate trips a day to destinations they can only reach by car.

3. The Climate, Community & Biodiversity Alliance (CCB) announced that standards certifying land-use projects that reduce global warming while helping communities and conserving biodiversity were launched at the 2005 Carbon Expo in Cologne Germany. See, http://www.climate-standards.org/news/news_may2005_launch.html. The organization explained that, "The CCB standards are primarily designed for projects that mitigate climate change. Land-use projects, also called land use, land-use change and forestry projects in climate circles (abbreviated to LULUCF) can reduce or prevent emissions by managing land in specific ways. Conserving threatened ecosystems, reforestation, agro-forestry, and bioenergy projects that grow wood for energy are examples of LULUCF activities that help lower atmospheric greenhouse gases." Similar to the manner in which buildings may be LEED certified, to earn approval under the CCB Standards, projects must satisfy fifteen required criteria to demonstrate compelling net benefits for fighting climate change, conserving biodiversity, and improving socio-economic conditions for local communities.

A. GREEN DEVELOPMENT AND ENERGY EFFICIENCY

"Green development" means that as real estate is developed, it occurs in a manner that integrates social and environmental goals with financial considerations. More and more municipalities are adopting "green building codes" and they are beginning to integrate these building and design concepts with local planning and zoning provisions. Loans, grants and tax benefits for energy efficient building projects are also available, and a number of states and municipalities have enacted green building requirements for the construction of public buildings. Most of these incentive programs are based on the U.S. Green Building Council's Leadership in Energy and Environmental Design (LEED) rating system. LEED guidelines are available for new commercial construction and major renovation projects, existing building operations and maintenance, schools and retail buildings, commercial interiors, and core and shell (*i.e.* building structures) development. Pilot programs have also been created for residential construction and neighborhood development, and guidelines are being formulated for healthcare and laboratory facilities. The LEED guidelines employ a rating system, whereby points are awarded for various energy efficient building elements such as site selection, access to alternative transportation, stormwater design, water efficient landscaping, on-site renewable energy, and use of recycled building materials. For detailed information about the LEED standards, see http://www.usgbc.org/. To locate state green building programs and incentives, see http://www.dsireusa.org. Also see Christopher P. Perzan, *Environmental Protection: What You Should Know About Green Building*, 20 CBA Record 38 (2006), and for information on green development codes and ordinances, see http://www.smartcommunities.ncat.org/greendev/codes.shtml, maintained by the Smart Communities Network.

While the "green building" phenomenon has tended to focus on energy efficient design and the use of energy efficient and recycled products during building construction, the notion of "green development" is shifting into the land use arena. In describing the relationship between the green building movement and local land use, the U.S.Green Building Council explains that "Development and construction projects are often destructive to local ecology. For example, stormwater runoff from developed areas can impact water quality in receiving waters, hinder navigation and recreation, and disrupt aquatic life. Site clearing and earth moving during construction often results in significant erosion problems because adequate environmental protection strategies are not employed. In addition, development activities may encroach on productive agricultural land areas and open space." See, http://www.greenbuildings.com.

In September 2004, two Yale professors published "The LAND Code: Guidelines for Sustainable Land Development" as a "research-based guide to ecologically sound land development intended for architects, engineers, developers, city officials, and interested individuals." See, http://environment.yale.edu/962/the_land_code/. The Code is organized into the following main subject areas: water quality and hydrology, air pollution and micrometeorology, plant ecology and population/community ecology, on-site energy and transportation, environmental engineering, industrial ecology, legal strategies for municipalities and developers, and approaches to green development—saving time and money. Focusing on the legal strategies, the LAND Code attempts to guide local lawmakers who desire to change zoning codes/laws to encourage more environmentally responsible land use and it includes strategies for developers who, in the absence of local regulations, desire to protect the environment through conservation subdivisions and green design. The Code begins by recommending that localities conduct an audit of current conditions and then conduct a build-out analysis to determine what the municipality would look like if all the land were to be developed as currently zoned. After making any necessary revisions to the comprehensive land use plan, the Code recommends a series of zoning strategies to make land use regulations more environmentally friendly including the use of: incentive zoning, performance zoning, overlay zoning, cluster development, and planned unit development. Other recommendations and strategies include: requiring environmental impact statements for all development projects; adopting individual ordinances to protect natural resources; using floating zones to promote particular land uses; allowing for transfer of development rights; offering incentives for developers to undertake natural development projects within the municipality (*e.g.*, by developing a "fast-tracking" program for the permitting process); building personal relationships between developers and the community; and engaging in public education on this issue. See, http://www.governmentlaw.org/files/green_development.pdf.

B. RENEWABLE ENERGY

BURCH v. NEDPOWER MOUNT STORM, LLC

Supreme Court of Appeals of West Virginia, 2007.
647 S.E.2d 879.

MAYNARD, J.

The appellants appeal the April 7, 2006, order of the Circuit Court of Grant County that dismissed their nuisance claim in which they sought an injunction against the appellees, NedPower Mount Storm, LLC and Shell WindEnergy, Inc., to enjoin the appellees from constructing a wind power electric generating facility in close proximity to the appellants' property. For the reasons that follow, we reverse the circuit court and remand for proceedings consistent with this opinion.

I.

FACTS

By final order dated April 2, 2003, the Public Service Commission ("the PSC") granted NedPower Mount Storm LLC, an appellee herein, a certificate of convenience and necessity (citation omitted) to construct and operate a wind power electric generating facility along the Allegheny

Front in Grant County. (citation omitted) NedPower has entered into a contract with appellee Shell WindEnergy, Inc., to sell the entire facility to Shell upon its completion. It is contemplated that the wind power facility will be located on a site approximately 14 miles long with an average width of one-half mile. (citation omitted) The facility is to include up to 200 wind turbines. Each turbine is to be mounted on a steel tower approximately 15 feet in diameter and 210 to 450 feet in height, and have three blades of approximately 115 feet.

The appellants are seven homeowners who live from about one-half mile to two miles from the projected wind turbines. (citation omitted) On November 23, 2005, the appellants filed a complaint in the Circuit Court of Grant County seeking to permanently enjoin NedPower and Shell WindEnergy, Inc., from constructing and operating the wind power facility on the basis that it would create a private nuisance. Specifically, the appellants asserted that they will be negatively impacted by noise from the wind turbines; the turbines will create a "flicker" or "strobe" effect when the sun is near the horizon; the turbines will pose a significant danger from broken blades, ice throws, and collapsing towers; and the wind power facility will cause a reduction in the appellants' property values.

The appellees subsequently filed a joint motion for judgment on the pleadings in which they essentially argued that a circuit court has no jurisdiction to enjoin, as a prospective private nuisance, projects authorized by the PSC, and that a private party cannot collaterally attack a final order of the PSC by means of bringing an injunction action in circuit court.

By order of April 7, 2006, the circuit court granted the appellees' motion for judgment on the pleadings and dismissed the appellants' action with prejudice. The circuit court based its ruling on the following grounds: it has no jurisdiction to enjoin the construction of a project that was approved by the PSC; most of the assertions made by the appellants concern activities that constitute a public rather than a private nuisance; a prospective injunction is not a proper remedy in this case because the wind facility is not a nuisance per se and does not constitute an impending or imminent danger of certain effect; and the PSC's approval of the facility collaterally estops the appellants from challenging it in circuit court.

The appellants now appeal the circuit court's order. * * *

III.

Discussion

The appellants raise two assignments of error in this appeal. The first assignment is that the circuit court erred in finding that the siting certificate granted by the PSC to the appellees for the construction of the wind power facility immunizes the appellees from liability under the common law doctrine of nuisance. Second, the appellants allege error in the circuit court's finding that the appellants failed to prove various allegations in their complaint, notwithstanding that on a motion for judgment on the pleadings the well-pled facts of the complaint must be taken as true.

As noted above, in its April 7, 2006, order, the circuit court dismissed the appellants' nuisance claim for an injunction on several independent grounds. This Court will now proceed to consider each of these separate grounds.

1. Jurisdiction

The circuit court first found that because the Legislature granted the PSC the power to decide the siting of electric generating facilities that are designated under federal law as exempt wholesale generators, the circuit court lacks jurisdiction to enjoin the construction and operation of these facilities under our law of nuisance. (citation omitted)

We begin our discussion with the recognition that our common law has always provided a remedy for a nuisance. This Court has explained that

> "nuisance is a flexible area of the law that is adaptable to a wide variety of factual situations." Sharon Steel Corp. v. City of Fairmont, 175 W.Va. 479, 483, 334 S.E.2d 616, 621 (1985). In fact, "[i]t has been said that the term 'nuisance' is incapable of an exact and exhaustive definition which will fit all cases, because the controlling facts are seldom alike, and each case stands on its own footing." Harless v. Workman, 145 W.Va. 266, 273–74, 114 S.E.2d 548, 552 (1960). Nonetheless, "the term ['nuisance'] is generally 'applied to that class of wrongs which arises from the unreasonable, unwarrantable or unlawful use by a person of his own property and produces such material annoyance, inconvenience, discomfort, or hurt that the law will presume a consequent damage.' " Harless, 145 W.Va. at 274, 114 S.E.2d at 552 (citation omitted). Stated another way, "nuisance is the unreasonable, unusual, or unnatural use of one's property so that it substantially impairs the right of another to peacefully enjoy his or her property." 58 Am.Jur.2d Nuisances § 2 (2002).

Booker v. Foose, 216 W.Va. 727, 730, 613 S.E.2d 94, 97 (2005). In the past, we described a nuisance as

> anything which annoys or disturbs the free use of one's property, or which renders its ordinary use or physical occupation uncomfortable. A nuisance is anything which interferes with the rights of a citizen, either in person, property, the enjoyment of his property, or his comfort. A condition is a nuisance when it clearly appears that enjoyment of property is materially lessened, and physical comfort of persons in their homes is materially interfered with thereby.

Martin v. Williams, 141 W.Va. 595, 610–611, 93 S.E.2d 835, 844 (1956) (citations omitted). More recently, we held that "[a] private nuisance is a substantial and unreasonable interference with the private use and enjoyment of another's land." Syllabus Point 1, Hendricks v. Stalnaker, 181 W.Va. 31, 380 S.E.2d 198 (1989). The test to determine unreasonableness has been stated by this Court as follows: "An interference with the private use and enjoyment of another's land is unreasonable when the gravity of the harm outweighs the social value of the activity alleged to cause the harm." Syllabus Point 2, Hendricks, supra. With regard to remedying a nuisance, it has long been understood that "[j]urisdiction in equity to abate nuisances is undoubted and of universal recognition." State v. Ehrlick, 65 W.Va. 700, 705, 64 S.E. 935, 937 (1909).

* * *

Our examination of the express language of the * * * statutes reveals no specific language indicating the Legislature's intent to disregard or abrogate the common law doctrine of nuisance as it applies to electric generating facilities designated as exempt wholesale generators. * * * [W]e * * * read the * * * statutes in context with the common law. Therefore, this Court will presume that the Legislature left intact the circuit court's jurisdiction in equity over electric generating facilities like the one at issue.

* * *

2. *Private Nuisance Claim for a Prospective Injunction*

In addition to finding that it had no jurisdiction to hear the appellants' nuisance claim for an injunction, the circuit court ruled that the appellants failed to set forth sufficient facts in their complaint alleging a private nuisance that would support the granting of a prospective injunction against the appellees. Specifically, the circuit court found that even if the appellants alleged injuries for which remedies are available in nuisance, these alleged injuries do not support a prospective injunction because the injuries are speculative and contingent.

Our reading of the appellants' complaint indicates that the appellants allege, as private nuisances, that the wind turbines will cause constant noise when the wind is blowing and an increase in noise as the wind velocity increases; the turbines will create an eyesore as a result of the turbines' "flicker" or "strobe" effect when the sun is near the horizon; and proximity of the appellants' property to the turbines will result in a diminution in the appellants' property values. We will now determine the legal effect of each of these allegations under our settled law of nuisance.

First, the appellants allege that the noise from the turbines will constitute a nuisance. This Court has held that "[n]oise alone may create a nuisance, depending on time, locality and degree." Syllabus Point 1, Ritz v. Woman's Club of Charleston, 114 W.Va. 675, 173 S.E. 564 (1934). We have further held that "[w]here an unusual and recurring noise is introduced in a residential district, and the noise prevents sleep or otherwise disturbs materially the rest and comfort of the residents, the noise may be inhibited by a court of equity." Syllabus

Point 2, Ritz, supra. See also Snyder v. Cabell, 29 W.Va. 48, 1 S.E. 241 (1886) (affirming injunction against skating rink's operation where it was found that noise from the rink materially interfered with the comfort and enjoyment of nearby residents.). These holdings are grounded on a principle that is essential to a civil society which is that "every person ... has the right not to be disturbed in his house; he has the right to rest and quiet and not to be materially disturbed in his rest and enjoyment of home by loud noises." Snyder, 29 W.Va. at 62, 1 S.E. at 251. Thus, we find that the appellants' allegation of noise is cognizable under our law as an abatable nuisance.

Second, the appellants allege that a "flicker" or "strobe" effect from the turbines will create an eyesore. Traditionally "courts of equity have hesitated to exercise authority in the abatement of nuisances where the subject matter is objected to by the complainants merely because it is offensive to the sight." Parkersburg Builders Material Co. v. Barrack, 118 W.Va. 608, 610, 191 S.E. 368, 369 (1937). This Court has explained in further detail that

> [e]quity should act only where there is presented a situation which is offensive to the view of average persons of the community. And, even where there is a situation which the average person would deem offensive to the sight, such fact alone will not justify interference by a court of equity. The surroundings must be considered. Unsightly things are not to be banned solely on that account. Many of them are necessary in carrying on the proper activities of organized society. But such things should be properly placed, and not so located as to be unduly offensive to neighbors or to the public.

Barrack, 118 W.Va. at 613, 191 S.E. at 371. When an unsightly activity is not properly placed, when it is unduly offensive to its neighbors, and when it is accompanied by other interferences to the use and enjoyment of another's property, this Court has shown a willingness to abate the activity as a nuisance. For example, in Syllabus Point 3 of Mahoney v. Walter, 157 W.Va. 882, 205 S.E.2d 692 (1974), it was held:

> The establishment of an automobile salvage yard with its incident noise, unsightliness, hazards from the presence of flammable materials, open vehicles, rodents and insects, and resultant depreciation of adjoining residential property values in an area which, though unrestricted and containing some commercial businesses, is primarily residential, together with the interference with the use, comfort and enjoyment of the surrounding properties caused by its operation, may be a nuisance and may be abated by a court of competent jurisdiction.

We hold, therefore, that while unsightliness alone rarely justifies interference by a circuit court applying equitable principles, an unsightly activity may be abated when it occurs in a residential area and is accompanied by other nuisances.

Third, the appellants allege that construction of the wind turbines will cause a reduction in their property values. With regard to the legal effect of mere diminution in the value of property, this Court has explained:

> Upon the question of reduction in value of the plaintiffs' properties, as the result of the establishment of the used car lot nearby, we find this statement in Wood on Nuisances, 3rd Edition, § 640: "Mere diminution of the value of the property, in consequence of the use to which adjoining premises are devoted, unaccompanied with other ill-results, is damnum absque injuria." Also in 66 C.J.S., Nuisances, § 19, P. 771, it is stated that: "However, a use of property which does not create a nuisance cannot be enjoined or a lawful structure abated merely because it renders neighboring property less valuable."

Martin, 141 W.Va. at 609–610, 93 S.E.2d at 843–844. However, the appellants in this case do not rely merely upon diminution of property values to support their nuisance claim, but also noise and unsightliness. According to Syllabus Point 1 of Martin, supra, the establishment of what is commonly known as a "used car lot" with its incident noise, light, unsightliness and resultant depreciation of adjoining residential property values in an area which, though unrestricted and without the corporate limits of a town or city, was across a highway from zoned residential property lying within the corporate limits, and which area had previously been exclusively residential on both sides of the highway for a distance of approximately one-fourth of a mile, and which "used car lot" greatly interferes with the use, comfort and enjoyment of such surrounding residential properties, constitutes a nuisance in fact, and may be abated by a court of equity.

See also Mahoney, supra (holding that automobile salvage yard with noise, unsightliness, flammable materials hazards, rodents and insects, and resultant depreciation of adjoining residential property values may be a nuisance and may be abated). We hold, therefore, that an activity that diminishes the value of nearby property and also creates interferences to the use and enjoyment of the nearby property may be abated by a circuit court applying equitable principles. In addition, the landowners may seek compensation for any diminution in the value of their property caused by the nuisance.

Finally, the remedy sought by the appellants is an injunction against the construction and operation of the wind power facility. It is a general rule that when the thing complained of is not a nuisance per se, but may or may not become so, according to circumstances, and the injury apprehended is eventual or contingent, equity will not interfere; the presumption being that a person entering into a legitimate business will conduct it in a proper way, so that it will not constitute a nuisance. Syllabus Point 2, Chambers v. Cramer, 49 W.Va. 395, 38 S.E. 691 (1901). We have recognized that a lawful business or a business authorized to be conducted by the government cannot constitute a nuisance per se. In the early case of McGregor v. Camden, 47 W.Va. 193, 196, 34 S.E. 936, 937 (1899), this Court succinctly stated that "[a] lawful business cannot be a nuisance per se, but from its surrounding places and circumstances, or the manner in which it is conducted it may become a nuisance." (Citation omitted). See also, Martin, 141 W.Va. at 599, 93 S.E.2d at 838 ("The operation of a used car lot is a lawful business, and, as a general rule, it cannot be a nuisance per se"); Frye v. McCrory Corp., 144 W.Va. 123, 129, 107 S.E.2d 378, 382 (1959), quoting 66 C.J.S., Nuisances, Section 9 ("The lawful and proper use of property or conduct of business does not ordinarily create an actionable nuisance, and is never a 'nuisance per se' in the strict sense of that term."). (citation omitted) Further, according to Syllabus Point 6 of Watson v. Fairmont & S. Ry. Co., 49 W.Va. 528, 39 S.E. 193 (1901).

When a person or corporation is authorized by the legislature by an express statute to do an act, or by the council of a city or town to which the power to authorize it has been delegated by a legislative act, such person or corporation cannot be regarded as committing a nuisance in the execution of such act nor proceeded against merely upon the theory that it is a nuisance, either at law or in equity. See also, Syllabus Point 1, Frye, supra ("The maintaining of a vault under a public sidewalk of a municipality, by authority of law, does not constitute a nuisance per se."). Therefore, when we apply these holdings to the instant facts, we must conclude that, as a lawful business which has been granted a siting certificate by the PSC, the appellees' wind power facility cannot be considered a nuisance per se.

However, the fact that the appellees' electric generating facility does not constitute a nuisance per se a does not mean that it cannot be abated as a nuisance. * * *

* * * [W]e conclude that the allegations are legally sufficient to state a claim to prospectively enjoin a nuisance. Stated differently, it does not definitively appear to us that the appellants can prove no set of facts in support of their claim. The appellants have alleged certain injury to the use and enjoyment of their properties as a result of constant loud noise from the wind turbines, the turbines' unsightliness, and reduction in the appellants' property values. If the appellants are able to adduce sufficient evidence to prove these allegations beyond all ground of fair questioning, abatement would be appropriate. Therefore, we find that the circuit court erred in ruling that the appellants failed to assert any facts of a private nuisance that would support a prospective injunction.

* * *

III.

CONCLUSION

In conclusion, having found no basis in law for the circuit court's ruling that dismissed on the pleadings the appellants' nuisance claim for an injunction, we reverse the April 7, 2006, order of the Circuit Court of Grant County, and we remand this case to the circuit court for proceedings consistent with this opinion.

Reversed and remanded.

JUSTICE BENJAMIN dissents and reserves the right to file a dissenting opinion.

Notes

1. In an earlier wind turbine case the Supreme Court of North Dakota rejected the plaintiff's claim that her neighbor's wind generator constituted a private nuisance because she had not shown that it unreasonably interfered with the use of her property. Rassier v. Houim, 488 N.W.2d 635 (1992). Here the defendant was operating his wind turbine for two years before the plaintiff positioned his mobile home forty feet from the turbine. The Court determined that the plaintiff "came to the nuisance." But see, Rose v. Chaikin, 187 N.J.Super. 210, 453 A.2d 1378 (1982), where the defendant placed a turbine (that was operating above the town's noise ordinance level) ten feet from his neighbor's property line. Is it a good idea to use nuisance law to prevent the construction and operation of wind turbines? Should public policy support and encourage the siting of wind turbines wherever they can generate electricity? What types of considerations are important? In Prah v. Maretti, 108 Wis.2d 223, 321 N.W.2d 182 (1982), the plaintiff sought an injunction against the construction of a building on a neighboring parcel that would block the sunlight needed to fuel the plaintiff's solar energy system. The Supreme Court of Wisconsin held that the complaint stated a cause of action for a common law private nuisance and reversed the lower court's grant of summary judgment.

In order to better resolve these types of disputes, some states have enacted wind and solar easement laws that specify the means through which such easements may be created, transferred and extinguished. A few states have even created rights to sunlight for energy production purposes or have enacted laws prohibiting private covenants that restrict property owners from using solar or wind power. In Garden Lakes Community Association v. Madigan, 204 Ariz. 238, 62 P.3d 983 (2003), an Arizona court held that a statute prohibiting private restrictions interfering with the use of solar energy devices barred certain architectural guidelines issued by a homeowners' association. Although the association argued that alternative designs for the devices existed that would comply with the aesthetic guidelines, the court held that it was proper to take the increased cost of these alternatives into account in determining whether the guidelines "effectively prohibit[ed]" the defendant homeowners from installing solar energy systems.

2. Green energy may be taking on a new appreciation given the rapid rise in energy costs following Hurricane Katrina in August 2005. Utilizing wind power as a renewable energy source has become a popular and, at times, a controversial topic, as the nation looks towards supplementing its oil consumption with alternative sources of energy. This nationwide interest has resulted in a boon for the wind power industry resulting in over six billion dollars invested and a 500% increase in the amount of generating capacity from 1997–2003. As interest in wind power grows, the technology supporting this energy option has evolved to the point where a modern 1.5 megawatt (MW) turbine can supply over 400 homes with power for a year, and newer 2–3 MW turbines are becoming available with 5 MW models

currently in testing. Municipalities across the country have adopted wind energy ordinances to specifically allow for wind farms, subject to various types of local land use controls. See, Patricia E. Salkin and Michael Donohue, *Planning and Zoning for Wind Power in New York*, New York Zoning and Planning Law Report, vol. 6 no. 2 (September/October 2005).

3. Wind power and other forms of alternative energy play an indispensable role in reducing GHG emissions, but they are not always the most economical or practical choice for energy production. At the federal level, appropriations for the Renewable Energy Production Incentive, which offers financial incentives for the production and sale of renewable energy, have been authorized until 2026. See 42 U.S.C. § 13317. State incentives are by far more extensive. In addition to loans, grants and tax incentives, twenty-four states have adopted renewable energy portfolio standards, which require electric utilities to produce a minimum percentage of renewable energy. Four other states have voluntary renewable energy production goals. See U.S. Department of Energy, http://www.eere.energy.gov/states/maps/renewable_portfolio_states.cfm#chart. Several states also require certain utilities to give customers the choice of buying power produced through renewable methods. The Database of State Incentives for Renewables and Efficiency, available at http://www.dsireusa.org, provides comprehensive information concerning these and other state and local renewable energy programs.

4. In April 2004, the American Planning Association (APA) adopted a Policy Guide on Energy, noting that to create sustainable communities, the country must not only increase energy conservation but must also increase renewable energy production. The APA urges planners to "work with utility providers to plan for the land-use and infrastructure requirements of renewable energy production such that they only minimally impact the environment." See, http://www.planning.org/policyguides/energy.htm.

5. The largest type of wind turbine is the offshore model. These structures tower at 260 feet with turbine lengths around 100 feet long. What makes this type of wind farm relevant to land use law is the absence of any land use regulations. While comprehensive laws exist for underwater natural gas extraction (including a system for leasing the submerged land), there are no laws governing offshore wind farms. Currently the United States does not have an offshore wind farm/turbine. However, litigation in the northeast is attempting to establish such a facility in the waters of the Nantucket Sound. A company is attempting to place wind turbines in the federal waters off the coast of Massachusetts (where the Nantucket Sound is located) and supply power back to the state. The company's request to erect a measuring station at sea to monitor wind and ocean conditions touched off a series of legal debates. In Alliance to Protect Nantucket Sound v. U.S. Dep't of the Army, 288 F.Supp.2d 64 (D.Mass.2003) and Ten Taxpayers Citizen Group v. Cape Wind Associates, 373 F.3d 183 (1st Cir.2004), the courts gave the go-ahead to construct the data measuring station. However, both courts noted that the ability to establish one measuring station is separate from the ability to install 130 turbines.

6. The visual impacts of wind turbines may be also the focus of community concern. For a wind turbine to be effective, it must be placed

above trees, buildings, and other obstacles that will disturb the wind flow. These requirements often restrict wind development to rural or remote areas. Several factors go into the aesthetic impact of a wind farm: lighting, coloring and signage are obvious ones, but spacing can also be a factor. The size of the turbines must also be considered, as smaller turbines can be placed closer together and have blades that spin faster, while large turbines have slower rotors and must be placed further apart, but are visible from a greater distance. The distance between turbines is determined based upon the distance needed for the wind to replenish. While turbines may need to be constructed at certain heights, zoning ordinances can provide maximum allowable height limitations to ensure that the turbines are not any higher than necessary. Through a local site plan review law, municipalities can effectively examine the proposed layout of the wind project including spacing, how the wind turbine array is set against the landscape, buffering, and other visual impacts. For information concerning aesthetic opposition to wind turbines, see Avi Brisman, *The Aesthetics of Wind Energy Systems*, 13 N.Y.U. Envtl. L.J. 1 (2005).

C. DISASTER MITIGATION

Following Hurricane Katrina, municipal officials and land use planners renewed interest in the use of planning and zoning tools and techniques to effectively mitigate the devastating results of natural disasters. Building codes, land use policies, zoning and subdivision regulations, comprehensive plans, site plan review, floodplain management plans, buffers, steep slope ordinances, open space plans, stormwater management plans, transportation plans, and conservation and natural resource protection policies are some of the techniques that can be employed. The American Planning Association's 2002 Growing Smart Legislative Guidebook (hereinafter "APA Guidebook") explains: "States and communities across the country are slowly, but increasingly, realizing that simply responding to natural disasters, without addressing ways to minimize their potential effect, is no longer an adequate role for government. Striving to prevent unnecessary damage from natural disasters through proactive planning that characterizes the hazard, assesses the community's vulnerability, and designs appropriate land-use policies and building code requirements is a more effective and fiscally sound approach to achieving public safety goals related to natural hazards."

Examples of development regulations that may be employed as effective disaster mitigation techniques include: limitations on how property may be developed in flood-zones; setbacks from fault lines, steep slopes and coastal erosion areas (as well as shorelines and other areas prone to natural disasters); and overlay zones that introduce additional requirements pertaining to sensitive environmental areas such as wetlands, dunes and hillsides. The APA Guidebook recommends the use of overlay districts as a natural hazard mitigation technique, and advises communities to include "procedures and criteria for the designation of ... natural hazard area overlay districts" when drafting ordinances for areas that are prone to natural hazards. Furthermore, the APA encourages local governments to develop a list of uses and activities that should be prohibited in the overlay zone, therefore allowing the local government to implement its mitigation strategies in a manner that is specifically tailored to address the effects of natural hazards that pose the biggest threat to their community. Overlay zones can be created for many different purposes. In addition to offering protection from flooding, overlay zones can be used to mitigate damage from potential disasters in watersheds, tidal basins, hillsides and other sensitive environmental areas.

Subdivision regulations can prohibit the subdivision of land in areas located within mapped floodplains, applicants may be required in fire-prone areas to include appropriate facilities to suppress wildfires as a condition of subdivision approval, and applicants may be required to avoid construction that results in encroachment upon watercourses and water bodies; avoid filling or excavation of, or encroachment on, wetlands, floodplains and other lands subject to flooding; and they may be directed to avoid removal of desirable vegetation. Local governments can use the site plan review process to examine the proposed development in relation to other on-site conditions, such as fault lines, steep slopes, shorelines, or other areas that are prone to natural disasters, and make decisions to grant or deny permits and/or add conditions to approvals based on the objectives of the local hazard mitigation plan.

Performance zoning can also be employed as part of a subdivision or site plan review to aid in disaster mitigation. For example, vegetation requirements such as tree ordinances can help to minimize flooding by preventing removal and destruction or by requiring replacement. In areas that are prone to wildfires, local governments can help to mitigate the impact of fires on homes by requiring buffer areas that eliminate natural fuels around residences such as requiring a clearing of small trees, fallen leaves, branches, pine needles and the like, around an appropriate perimeter of a home.

The following excerpt from "Losing Ground: A Nation on the Edge," edited by John R. Nolon and Daniel B. Rodriguez, explores some of the current federal and state issues relating to disaster management:

II. The Local Role in Development Disaster–Resilient Communities

Another question * * * is how to integrate land use decisionmaking—a role generally assigned to local governments under our federal system—with disaster mitigation planning: a function assumed largely by the federal and state governments. Most state legislatures have delegated local governments (counties, cities, towns, and villages) the principal legal authority to determine what type of development may be built within their jurisdiction, including disaster-prone areas. This authority is found in state constitutions, planning enabling acts, zoning enabling acts, home-rule authority, and additional state laws that permit localities to protect health and safety, to preserve the local physical environment, and to mitigate disaster damage.

Using this authority, local governments can create disaster-resilient communities that have increased capacity to adapt to the effects of natural disasters, resulting in less property damage, environmental impact and loss of life. (citation omitted) .

* * *

It should be immediately apparent that local governments can use this same legal authority to develop the adaptive capacity to conduct land use planning that builds centers and neighborhoods, increases their tax base, provides for needed transportation and other infrastructure, establishes affordable housing and jobs, prevents stormwater runoff, protects coastal environment, preserves wetlands and habitats, and accomplishes a host of other land use objectives that promote state and federal interest.

Hurricanes Katrina and Rita demonstrate the critical importance of having a response and recovery plan that fully engages the municipal role and coordinates federal, state, and local responsibilities and resources. Developing disaster-resilient communities and rebuilding after a disaster strikes requires both local competency and intergovernmental coordination regarding community and land use planning. There is evidence of a shift in governmental policy toward the vertical integration of federal, state, and local government action in order to most effectively and comprehensively address land development in disaster-prone areas as well as a host of other economic development and environmental problems.

III. A Sea Change in Federal Policy: The Disaster Mitigation Act (DMA) of 2000

In the rancorous debate that followed Hurricane Katrina, there may be hope—a breath of fresh air blown in following the gale force winds. In focusing attention on disaster mitigation, the nation's numerous recent disasters call for a review of federal policy on the matter. As it happens, the U.S. Congress recently took stock of the nation's disaster response, recovery, and mitigation efforts and created a more coordinated approach to planning at all levels of government, one which assigns roles to each. Under the DMA, (citation omitted) a framework of federal, state, and local cooperation is evident that could be a blueprint for an integrated Federalist approach to a host of land use and environmental problems.

The DMA articulates national legislative objectives that provide an opportunity to enhance local mitigation planning implementation and to coordinate land use planning and regulation to promote disaster mitigation. The Act provides that in order to qualify for federal hazard mitigation grants, state and local governments must "develop and submit for approval to the President a mitigation plan that outlines processes for identifying the natural hazards, risks and vulnerabilities of the area under the jurisdiction of the government." (citation omitted)

* * *

These regulations describe an intelligently interwoven system of mitigation planning and implementation. According to anecdotal information from those who prepared the first round of state and local disaster mitigation plans submitted to FEMA, however, there is little emphasis in them on the use of effective local land use strategies to create disaster-resilient, or adaptive, communities. The reasons for this are, at best, speculative, but include the fact that disaster mitigation planning encompasses a large number of critical issues including education, response, recovery and the lack of clear understanding of the considerable authority that local governments have in order to use land use authority to properly shape an strengthen community development in the interested of disaster resiliency.

* * *

V. Building on a Firm Foundation: Local Land Use Law and Disaster Preparation and Mitigation

Local land use authority is the foundation of the planning that determines how communities and natural resources are developed and preserved, and how disaster-resilient communities are created. With respect to floodplain and watershed management, natural resource preservation, suburban smart growth, and urban revitalization, federal and state planners must engage the local land use decision-making process to be effective in achieving critical objectives. This can happen in the field of disaster mitigation planning. In the state of Washington, for example, its comprehensive land use planning programs serve as a critical predicate for the state's disaster mitigation plan under the DMA and as the method for integrating local land use and disaster planning with that of the state. (citation omitted)

In most states, it is understood that municipalities have no inherent powers, but can exercise only that authority expressly granted or necessarily implied from, or incident to, the powers expressly granted. (citation omitted) In all 50 states, of course, localities have been authorized to control the private use of land under state zoning enabling acts and statutes that empower them to review and approve land subdivision and site development. These traditional local land use laws can be used to create disaster-resilient communities as a key objective of a community's land use regime. The arguments in support of this proposition are several. First, the zoning enabling act adopted in most states makes it clear that one of its purposes is to encourage "the most appropriate use of land throughout the municipality." (citation omitted) Laws that lessen the prospect of damage from natural disasters certainly encourage the most appropriate use of land. Further, the statutes delegating power to localities to adopt subdivision and site plan regulation make it clear that standards may be included in such regulations that prevent and control the impacts of storms and other calamities. (citation omitted)

* * *

Note

For more information about the DMA and its implementing regulations, see http://www.fema.gov/plan/mitplanning/DMA.shtm. In addition to the state hazard mitigation plans, more than 8,000 municipalities have approved hazard mitigation plans. The impact of these planning efforts may be substantial; a recent congressionally mandated study conducted by the Multihazard Mitigation Council concluded that for every dollar spent on planning for disasters, approximately four dollars in societal costs will be saved. The cost-benefit ratio was determined to be even higher for investments in wind and flood projects. Additionally, the Multihazard Mitigation Council's recommendations affirmed the need to improve linkages between local planning efforts and federal funding projects. See http://www,nibs.org/MMC/mmcactiv5.html.

D. GEOGRAPHIC INFORMATION SYSTEMS

The advent of computerized mapping and the global positioning systems (GPS) has resulted in a powerful tool for land use practitioners, Geographic Information Systems, or GIS for short. Information from a GIS database can take the form of charts, graphs, tables and spreadsheets in ways that could not be viewed and analyzed through the use of traditional maps. These charts and graphs provide information to help solve geographic challenges, or problems involving spatially related information. For example, a municipality can now overlay soil data on a traditional map and a zoning map to identify areas that may not be well suited to particular development. Currently, forty-two states have laws relating to GIS, the majority of which establish a statewide system or clearinghouse for the exchange of GIS data between governmental entities.

The most important part of a geographic information system is the data it relies upon. Information that is out of date or inaccurate can have a significant impact on the reliability of the end product. For example, a pond or river that was plotted using GPS after the spring thaw might not represent the same pond or river in late August. Land use lawyers need to be familiar with GIS technology so that, where appropriate, they may find expert witnesses in GIS for trials to enable important GIS data to be admitted into evidence.

GIS information can be a persuasive tool in court. The U.S. Marine Corps was successfully able to show a lack of alternatives for placement of military housing in Surfrider Foundation v. Dalton 989 F.Supp. 1309 (S.D.Cal.1998). It relied, in part, on GIS maps that illustrated topographic, land use and natural resource restraints. Having the GIS "map" admitted in court can fall under one of several hearsay exemptions depending on how the information is used (e.g., computer generated records, business records, or public records).

The use of GIS and computerized mapping by municipalities is becoming routine. These maps not only represent a benefit to the municipal employees and boards by eliminating the need to pour through non-electronic maps, but access to the system through freedom of information laws may also help the community at large. For example, a corporation wishing to build around pre-existing gas/electric lines that may already be mapped on a municipal GIS database could save thousands of dollars and months of time in locating the ideal building site if the municipal data is accessible to the private developer. GIS data will also contribute to the information available to environmental justice advocates and will empower communities to address disparate impacts of land use decisionmaking. Recent litigation has focused on whether municipally owned GIS datasets are considered "records" and are therefore obtainable by the public under state Freedom on Information Laws. Municipalities are at times reluctant to turn over GIS databases to the public (and private sector) due to the fact that there has been a significant public investment in developing the GIS system. A recent Connecticut case, excerpted below, demonstrates this tension.

The use of GIS will undoubtedly continue to increase and an emerging body of statutory and caselaw will define the parameters of the use of this important land use technology.

DIRECTOR, DEPARTMENT OF INFORMATION TECHNOLOGY OF THE TOWN OF GREENWICH v. FREEDOM OF INFORMATION COMMISSION

Supreme Court of Connecticut, 2005.
274 Conn. 179, 874 A.2d 785.

VERTEFEUILLE, J.

The plaintiff, the director of the department of information technology of the town of Greenwich (town), appeals from the trial court's judgment dismissing his administrative appeal from a final decision of the named defendant, the freedom of information commission (commission). In its decision, the commission ordered the plaintiff to provide the complainant, Stephen Whitaker, (citation omitted) with copies of certain computerized data from the town's geographic information system (GIS). We affirm the judgment of the trial court.

* * * In December, 2001, Whitaker submitted a written request to the town's board of estimate and taxation, asking for a copy of all GIS data concerning orthophotography, arc info coverages, structured query language server databases, and all documentation created to support and define coverages for the arc info data set. (citation omitted) His request was forwarded to the plaintiff, who subsequently denied Whitaker's request, claiming that the data was exempt from disclosure under the Freedom of Information Act (act), General Statutes § 1–200 et seq. Specifically, the plaintiff claimed that the data requested by Whitaker was exempt from disclosure pursuant to General Statutes § 1–210(b)(5)(A), (citation omitted) which provides an exemption from disclosure for trade secrets, and § 1–210(b)(20), (citation omitted) which exempts from disclosure information that would compromise the security of an information technology system. Whitaker subsequently filed a complaint with the commission, claiming that the plaintiff refused to

provide him with a copy of the town's computerized GIS records that he requested. The commission held a hearing in January, 2002, at which it found that the information requested by Whitaker was not exempt because it did not constitute either a trade secret within the meaning of § 1–210(b)(5)(A), or the type of information that would pose a threat to the security of the town's information technology system within the meaning of § 1–210(b)(20). Accordingly, the commission issued a final decision in November, 2002, in which it ordered the plaintiff to disclose the requested records, excluding only medical information and social security numbers, should any appear in the requested data.

The plaintiff subsequently appealed from the commission's decision to the trial court, which concluded, after a hearing, that the plaintiff had failed to substantiate his claim that the requested records were exempt from disclosure. Specifically, the trial court found that the plaintiff had failed to provide any specific evidence that would demonstrate that disclosure of the requested data would compromise the security or integrity of the town's information technology system. Further, the trial court found that the records did not constitute trade secrets within the meaning of § 1–210(b)(5)(A), because the requested data was merely a computerized compilation of the town's records that otherwise could be obtained by requesting the information piecemeal from various individual town departments. The trial court therefore dismissed the plaintiff's appeal. The plaintiff appealed from the trial court's judgment to the Appellate Court, and we thereafter transferred the appeal to this court pursuant to General Statutes § 51–199(c) and Practice Book § 65–1.

On appeal, the plaintiff claims that the trial court improperly determined that the commission was correct in concluding that the data requested by Whitaker was not exempt pursuant to § 1–210(b)(5)(A), (19) and (20). The plaintiff first argues that No. 02–133, § 1, of the 2002 Public Acts (P.A. 02–133) (citation omitted) amended § 1–210(b)(19) (citation omitted) to broaden the public safety exemption such that the data requested by Whitaker were exempt from disclosure, and the legislative history surrounding the enactment of the public act demonstrates that it was intended to address exactly this type of case. (citation omitted) Thus, the plaintiff claims that the commission improperly failed to apply the expanded exemption in this case. The plaintiff further claims that, although the act does not expressly require a balancing of the government's and the public's interests, the trial court failed to weigh appropriately the public's interest in disclosure against the town's public safety interest, and that the trial court improperly required the plaintiff to present statistical data showing a correlation between the disclosure of GIS data and a threat of criminal or terrorist activity. The plaintiff also contends that the requested GIS data satisfies the requirements of the trade secret exemption to the act in § 1–210(b)(5)(A), because the data constitutes a compilation that derives intrinsic economic value by not being readily ascertainable by those wishing to obtain economic value from its use. Finally, the plaintiff claims that the disclosure of the requested GIS data would compromise the integrity of the town's information technology system, possibly exposing it to computer hackers, which in turn would create a security risk for the town.

The commission counters that the policy of the act favors free access to government records, and, although the commission's final decision and the trial court's memorandum of decision did not discuss at length P.A. 02–133, § 1, both the commission and the trial court considered the public act in analyzing the existence of any threat to public safety posed by the disclosure of the requested data. Further, the commission claims that the trial court correctly balanced any possible safety risk against the public's right to access the requested data, and the trial court did not require statistical data correlating criminal and terrorist activity with disclosure, but, rather, merely observed that such correlation data would have been a method by which the plaintiff could have met his burden of showing the existence of a safety risk. The commission also argues that the right to information under P.A. 02–133, § 1, includes the right to access the data in the same computerized form that the government agency itself uses. In addition, the commission claims that disclosure of the requested GIS data will not reveal any exempt trade secrets in violation of § 1–210(b)(5)(A), because the plaintiff is not engaged in a trade and is not protecting secrets of such a trade. The commission further argues that there is no evidence that the disclosure of the GIS data presents a security threat to the town's information technology system within the meaning of § 1–210(b)(20). We agree with the commission, and, accordingly, we affirm the judgment of the trial court.

* * *

* * * "[a] The appropriate standard of judicial review, therefore, is whether the commission's factual determinations are reasonably supported by substantial evidence in the record taken as a whole." Rocque v. Freedom of Information Commission, 255 Conn. 651, 659–60, 774 A.2d 957 (2001).

I

We begin by addressing whether the trial court improperly failed to consider the applicability of P.A. 02–133, § 1, to the records sought by Whitaker. The plaintiff claims that the trial court did not apply § 1–210(b)(19) as amended by P.A. 02–133, § 1, and it improperly failed to remand the matter to the commission to determine whether the requested records were exempt under the public act. The commission counters that the trial court properly considered the applicability of P.A. 02–133, § 1. We agree with the commission. In setting forth the standard of review applicable to the commission's decision, the trial court explicitly referenced § 1–210(b)(19), as amended, and it analyzed whether the requested GIS data were exempt due to public safety concerns. The trial court decision thereby implicated § 1–210(b)(19) and (20), both of which subdivisions provide exemptions from disclosure under certain circumstances when public safety is at risk. Accordingly, contrary to the plaintiff's claim, the trial court did consider the amended version of § 1–210(b)(19). (citation omitted)

Section 1–210(b)(19) sets forth the procedure through which a state or municipal agency may pursue an exemption from disclosure under the act when there are reasonable grounds to believe that disclosure would pose a safety risk to any person or government-owned facility. When there are reasonable grounds to believe disclosure may pose a risk to public safety, "[s]uch reasonable grounds shall be determined ... with respect to records concerning any executive branch agency of the state or any municipal, district or regional agency, by the Commissioner of Public Works, after consultation with the chief executive officer of the agency...." General Statutes § 1–210(b)(19)(A). In the present case, the plaintiff specifically argues that he was not afforded the opportunity to have the requested GIS data reviewed by the commissioner of public works in order to ascertain whether its disclosure would pose a safety risk within the meaning of § 1–210(b)(19) as amended. The plaintiff claims that the trial court was remiss in not remanding the matter to the commission so that the commissioner of public works could conduct such a review. We disagree.

Although § 1–210(b)(19) does not specifically provide which party is to seek a public safety determination by the commissioner of public works, we conclude that the plaintiff bore the burden of seeking such a determination. It is axiomatic that the burden of proving the applicability of any exemption in the act rests with the party claiming the exemption. See Ottochian v. Freedom of Information Commission, supra, 221 Conn. at 398, 604 A.2d 351. Here, that is the plaintiff. It follows that the plaintiff, therefore, was obligated to seek a public safety determination from the commissioner of public works in support of his claim that the GIS records were exempt from disclosure. Moreover, we note that the floor debate in the legislature regarding the passage of P.A. 02–133, § 1, described the law as providing that municipalities, certain state agencies, public service companies, telecommunication companies and water utilities may apply for permission to keep sensitive documents from the public 45 H.R. Proc., Pt. 15, 2002 Sess., pp. 4580–81. The use of the word "apply" makes clear the legislative intent that the party claiming a public safety exemption must seek the determination from the commissioner. The plaintiff never sought the required consultation with the commissioner of public works. Nor did he at any time request that the trial court remand the case so that the public works commissioner could make a public safety determination. Accordingly, we conclude that the plaintiff's first claim on appeal is unavailing.

II

We turn next to the plaintiff's assertion that the trial court improperly failed to balance the town's interest in public safety with the public's right to disclosure under the act, and that the trial court improperly required the plaintiff to present statistical data correlating criminal or terrorist activity with the disclosure of GIS data. The commission responds that the trial court did balance appropriately the town's interest in public safety with the public's right to accessible information, and that the trial court did not "require" the plaintiff to produce statistical data. We conclude that the trial court was not required to undertake any balancing to resolve the public safety exemption and that the trial court did not require that the plaintiff submit statistical data.

The following additional facts are relevant to the resolution of this issue. At the hearing before the commission, Peter J. Robbins, the town's chief of police, testified generally about his concerns regarding the potential threat to the safety of the town's residents if the requested GIS data were to be disclosed. Robbins testified that, "[b]ecause of [the town's] affluence [it is] frequently targeted for criminal activity. . . ." He further testified that the town's proximity to the Merritt Parkway, Interstate 95, and the waterfront made the town an inviting target for professional thieves. When asked how the disclosure of the GIS data would assist in such criminal activities, Robbins responded, "that type of information can certainly have a severe impact on the community," and that he thought that "it also can provide some serious risk for homeowners because that access ... would provide overhead views of structures, the footprints of those structures, fence lines, the topography, in some cases it may, depending on when those photos were taken from the air, could reveal some security measures that individual homeowners have put in place." Robbins further testified that the GIS data might be used to carry out identity theft or disturb the privacy of public figures who live in the town, or it could be used to interfere with the safety and security of town residents or to allow someone to compromise the police radio system and communications network.

In assessing whether this testimony was sufficient to establish the existence of a legitimate public safety risk, the trial court observed that "[t]here is no nexus between [Robbins'] opinion and the ultimate conclusion. More importantly, [the] plaintiff fails to provide through [Robbins'] testimony any specific statistical data that correlates criminal activity or potential terrorist type activity with disclosure of GIS data. Additionally, no specific evidence was provided to demonstrate how disclosure of the requested data would compromise the security or integrity of the GIS."

As we noted previously, "[t]he burden of proving the applicability of an exception [to disclosure under the act] rests upon the party claiming it." (Internal quotation marks omitted.) Ottochian v. Freedom of Information Commission, supra, 221 Conn. at 398, 604 A.2d 351. In particular, "[t]his burden requires the claimant of the exemption to provide more than conclusory language, generalized allegations or mere arguments of counsel. Rather, a sufficiently detailed record must reflect the reasons why an exemption applies to the materials requested." New Haven v. Freedom of Information Commission, 205 Conn. 767, 776, 535 A.2d 1297 (1988). With regard to weighing the interests of a party claiming an exemption against the public's interest in disclosure, this court has stated that "within the language itself of the [act], the legislature has [already balanced] the public's right to know and the private needs for confidentiality.... Therefore, neither the [commission] nor the courts are required to engage in a separate balancing procedure beyond the limits of the statute." (Citation omitted; internal quotation marks omitted.) Chairman, Criminal Justice Commission v. Freedom of Information Commission, supra, 217 Conn. at 200–201, 585 A.2d 96.

The exemptions provided in § 1–210(b) of the act incorporate the judgment of the legislature with regard to balancing the public interest in disclosure of records with the need for confidentiality. As the passage of P.A. 02–133, § 1, demonstrates, the legislature adjusts the balance between the right to know and the need for confidentiality as circumstances change. The text of § 1–210(b)(19), as amended, does not require the courts to conduct any balancing in order to determine the applicability of that exemption. The silence on this issue is in contrast to exemptions where such a balancing explicitly is required, such as, for example, § 1–210(b)(1). We find no merit to the plaintiff's unsupported claim that the trial court's judgment should be reversed for the court's failure to undertake a balancing of public interest disclosure against necessary confidentiality when the statute providing the exemption does not require such a balancing.

We further conclude, contrary to the plaintiff's contention, that the trial court did not require specific statistical data correlating criminal and terrorist activity with the disclosure of GIS data. The trial court stated that it did not find convincing the generalized testimony by Robbins as the plaintiff's sole evidence to support his argument that the release of the GIS data would pose a legitimate public safety concern. Such generalized claims of a possible safety risk do not satisfy the plaintiff's burden of proving the applicability of an exemption from disclosure under the act. See New Haven v. Freedom of Information Commission, supra, 205 Conn. at 776, 535 A.2d 1297. In explaining why it was not convinced by Robbins' testimony at the commission hearing, the trial court stated that the town did not present any evidence through the police chief to establish a nexus between his opinion and the conclusion that the release of the data would pose a safety risk. In doing so, the trial court merely suggested that one way of demonstrating the safety risk would have been through the use of statistical data correlating criminal or terrorist activity with the disclosure of GIS data. The trial court similarly suggested that the plaintiff could have provided evidence demonstrating how the disclosure of GIS data would compromise the security or integrity of GIS. Nowhere in its opinion, however, did the trial court require the plaintiff to provide such statistical data to prove a correlation between criminal or terrorist activity and the disclosure of GIS data. Accordingly, the trial court did not improperly impose an inappropriate burden on the plaintiff.

III

Finally, we address the issue of whether the trial court properly found that the plaintiff failed to meet his burden of proof to show that the requested GIS data were exempt under the act because disclosure would either reveal a trade secret within the meaning of § 1–

210(b)(5)(A), or pose a threat to the security of the town's information technology system within the meaning of § 1–210(b)(20). The plaintiff contends that the requested documents fall within the definition of a trade secret under the act because the GIS database derives its economic value from not being available to members of the public, such as Whitaker, who may use the information for their own economic gain. The plaintiff further claims that the requested information falls within the § 1–210(b)(20) security exemption under the act because its disclosure would pose a security risk to the town's information technology system. The commission counters that neither exemption applies to the records sought in this case. We agree with the commission.

As we have noted previously, the party claiming an exemption from disclosure under the act has the burden of proving its applicability, and in order to meet that burden, the party claiming the exemption must provide more than general or conclusory statements in support of its contention. See Chairman, Criminal Justice Commission v. Freedom of Information Commission, supra, 217 Conn. at 196, 585 A.2d 96; New Haven v. Freedom of Information Commission, supra, 205 Conn. at 776, 535 A.2d 1297.

To qualify for an exemption within the meaning of § 1–210(b)(5)(A), the requested records must constitute a trade secret within the meaning of the act, which is defined as "information, including formulas, patterns, compilations, programs, devices, methods, techniques, processes, drawings, cost data, or customer lists that (i) derive independent economic value, actual or potential, from not being generally known to, and not being readily ascertainable by proper means by, other persons who can obtain economic value from their disclosure or use, and (ii) are the subject of efforts that are reasonable under the circumstances to maintain secrecy...." In order to qualify for a trade secret exemption under § 1–210(b)(5)(A), "[a] substantial element of secrecy must exist, to the extent that there would be difficulty in acquiring the information except by the use of improper means." (Internal quotation marks omitted.) Dept. of Public Utilities v. Freedom of Information Commission, 55 Conn.App. 527, 532, 739 A.2d 328 (1999). The requested GIS data in the present case, however, is readily available to the public, and, accordingly, it does not fall within the plain language of § 1–210(b)(5)(A) as a trade secret. As the trial court noted, the GIS database is an electronic compilation of the records of many of the town's departments. Members of the public seeking the GIS data could obtain separate portions of the data from various town departments, where that data is available for disclosure. The requested GIS database simply is a convenient compilation of information that is already available to the public. The records therefore fail to meet the threshold test for trade secrets, that the information is not generally ascertainable by others.

We turn now to the plaintiff's claim that the trial court improperly found that the plaintiff did not meet his burden of proof that the records were exempt under § 1–210(b)(20). That subsection provides an exemption to disclosure for "[r]ecords of standards, procedures, processes, software and codes, not otherwise available to the public, the disclosure of which would compromise the security or integrity of an information technology system...." General Statutes § 1–210(b)(20). The trial court found that the plaintiff did not meet his burden in attempting to show that the requested disclosure would compromise the security of the town's entire information technology system. As the trial court noted, the plaintiff did not present any specific evidence to demonstrate how the disclosure of the requested GIS data would compromise the overall security of the town's information technology system. The plaintiff testified that he was concerned about the vulnerability of the town's network to a security breach should the network become available to the public. In support of this concern, the plaintiff stated that computer firewalls are not foolproof, and that the firewalls of "[m]any high security agencies" had been breached. The plaintiff, however, did not provide specific examples of such security breaches, or evidence that any such breaches had been caused by the disclosure of GIS data.

We agree with the trial court that the plaintiff failed to meet his burden to show that the security or integrity of the town's information technology system would be compromised by disclosure of the GIS data. Accordingly, the evidence presented in this case was insufficient to establish that the requested GIS data were exempt from public disclosure under the act.

The judgment is affirmed.

Note

Through their Growing Smart Legislative Guidebook, the American Planning Association has recognized the importance of GIS as a land use planning tool that enables governments to more quickly and better portray, communicate, and analyze existing and potential environmental conditions from a visual perspective, fostering greater understanding of complex environmental issues. Noting that the general public availability of GIS data enables the public and advocacy organizations to be better informed and more effectively involved in the governing process, in 2002 as part of its growing smart effort, the APA recommended a model state statute for GIS that, among other things, calls upon states to establish statewide GIS clearinghouses and geographic information advisory boards, and to address data sensitivity issues so that information is available to the public while protecting needed confidentiality. Prior to the tragedy on September 11, 2001, the debate over the accessibility of GIS data was focused on an argument by some governments that the data should not be subject to Freedom of Information Laws primarily because the government had a concern that the data collected at public expense would be put to private commercial use without adequate compensation back to the government. However, as the Greenwich case demonstrates, since the terrorist attack, governments are reluctant to share certain GIS data on the grounds of homeland security concerns. Do these governmental concerns outweigh the public's interest in having access to GIS information? Should land use lawyers, planners and the general public have access to all government GIS data related to specific projects or initiatives? See, Patricia E. Salkin, *GIS in an Age of Homeland Security: Accessing [Public] Information to Ensure a Sustainable Environment*, 30 Wm & Mary Envtl L. Rev. 55 (2005).

†